W9-CNB-857

Rereading America

Cultural Contexts for
Critical Thinking and Writing

Top CASH For BOOKS-Anytime

BOOKSTORE

"Yours For Lower Costs
of Higher Education"

Rereading America

Cultural Contexts for
Critical Thinking and Writing

Fifth Edition

Edited by

Gary Colombo
LOS ANGELES CITY COLLEGE

Robert Cullen
SAN JOSE STATE UNIVERSITY

Bonnie Lisle
UNIVERSITY OF CALIFORNIA, LOS ANGELES

Bedford/St. Martin's   Boston • New York

For Bedford/St. Martin's

Developmental Editor: John Sullivan
Production Editor: Lori Chong Roncka
Production Supervisors: Cheryl Mamaril, Sarah Zwiebach
Marketing Manager: Brian Wheel
Editorial Assistants: Katherine Gilbert, Kristen Harvey, Caroline Thompson
Production Assistant: Thomas P. Crehan
Copyeditor: Sarah Richards Doerries
Cover Design: Trudi Gershenov
Cover Art: Flag by Nancy Kozikowski
Composition: Pine Tree Composition, Inc.
Printing and Binding: Haddon Craftsmen, Inc., an R.R. Donnelley & Sons
   Company

President: Charles H. Christensen
Editorial Director: Joan E. Feinberg
Editor in Chief: Karen S. Henry
Director of Marketing: Karen Melton
Director of Editing, Design, and Production: Marcia Cohen
Managing Editor: Elizabeth M. Schaaf

Library of Congress Control Number: 00–106438

Copyright © 2001 by Bedford/St. Martin's

All rights reserved. No part of this book may be reproduced, stored in a retrieval system, or transmitted in any form or by any means, electronic, mechanical, photocopying, recordng, or otherwise, except as may be expressly permitted by the applicable copyright statutes or in writing by the Publisher.

Manufactured in the United States of America.

6 5 4 3 2 1
f e d c b a

For information, write: Bedford/St. Martin's, 75 Arlington Street, Boston, MA
02116 (617-399-4000)

ISBN: 0–312–24917–9

Acknowledgments and copyrights appear at the back of the book on pages 852–60, which constitute an extension of the copyright page. It is a violation of the law to reproduce these selections by any means whatsoever without the written permission of the copyright holder.

Preface for Instructors

About *Rereading America*

Designed for first-year writing and critical thinking courses, *Rereading America* anthologizes a diverse set of readings focused on the myths that dominate U.S. culture. This central theme brings together thought-provoking selections on a broad range of topics—family, education, success, gender roles, race, and the frontier—topics that raise controversial issues meaningful to college students of all backgrounds. We've drawn these readings from many sources, both within the academy and outside of it; the selections are both multicultural and cross-curricular and thus represent an unusual variety of voices, styles, and subjects.

The readings in this anthology speak directly to students' experiences and concerns. Every college student has had some brush with prejudice, and most have something to say about education, the family, or the gender stereotypes they see in films and on television. The issues raised here help students link their personal experiences with broader cultural perspectives and lead them to analyze, or "read," the cultural forces that have shaped and continue to shape their lives. By linking the personal and the cultural, students begin to recognize that they are not academic outsiders—they too have knowledge, assumptions, and intellectual frameworks that give them authority in academic culture. Connecting personal knowledge and academic discourse helps students see that they are able to think, speak, and write academically and that they don't have to absorb passively what the "experts" say.

Features of the Fifth Edition

A Cultural Approach to Critical Thinking   Like its predecessors, the fifth edition of *Rereading America* is committed to the premise that learning to think critically means learning to identify and see beyond dominant cultural myths—collective and often unconsciously held beliefs that influence our thinking, reading, and writing. Instead of treating cultural diversity as just another topic to be studied or "appreciated," *Rereading America* encourages students to grapple with the real differences in perspective that arise in a pluralistic society like ours. This method helps students to break through conventional assumptions and patterns of thought that hinder fresh critical responses and inhibit dialogue. It helps them recognize that even the most apparently "natural" fact or obvious idea results from a process of social construction. And it helps them to develop the intellectual independence essential to critical thinking, reading, and writing.

Classic and Conservative Perspectives   To provide students with the historical context they often need, each chapter in this edition of *Rereading America* begins with a "classic" expression of the myth under examination. Approaching the myth of success, for example, by way of Horatio Alger's *Ragged Dick* — or the myth of racial superiority by way of Thomas Jefferson's infamous diatribe against "race mixing" — gives students a better sense of the myth's origins and impact. We've also included at least one contemporary conservative revision of the myth in each chapter, so you'll find in this edition more readings by cultural critics who stand to the right of center, writers like Christina Hoff Sommers, Shelby Steele, Lynne V. Cheney, and Ken Hamblin.

New Issues   This edition of *Rereading America* dedicates a new chapter to exploring one of the most important themes in our national mythography — the myth of the American frontier. The story of westward expansion and settlement fueled the American myth of limitless individual opportunity. It also convinced us of our "exceptionalism." For generations the myth of the frontier has told us that we as a nation are both freer and somehow better than the Old World of Europe. In "Westward Ho!: The Myth of Frontier Freedom," we invite students to examine the ideology of frontier America through a series of historical and contemporary selections on the meaning of the American West. Readings by classic and contemporary authors like Frederick Jackson Turner, N. Scott Momaday, Wallace Stegner, Linda Hogan, Patricia Nelson Limerick, and Louise Erdrich challenge students to consider the role that frontier thinking has played in shaping American identities and attitudes and to evaluate the continuing impact of the myth of the West on their lives. This new chapter also gives students the opportunity to address issues that are bound to elicit strong reactions — issues like censorship in the new "Wild West" of the Internet, the origins of "gun culture" in the United States, and the impact of consumerism on American attitudes toward nature. As the setting for some of our most revealing national fantasies about what it means to be an American, the notion of the frontier provides a logical conclusion to the examination of cultural myths contained in *Rereading America*.

Timely New Readings   To keep *Rereading America* up to date, we've worked hard to bring you the best new voices speaking on issues of race, gender, class, family, and education. As in past editions, we've retained old favorites like Malcolm X, Richard Rodriguez, Shelby Steele, Jamaica Kincaid, Paula Gunn Allen, Toni Cade Bambara, Gary Soto, Bebe Moore Campbell, Judith Ortiz Cofer, and Mike Rose. But you'll also find a host of new selections by such authors as Claude M. Steele, Deborah Tannen,

Kyoko Mori, James Fallows, Sharon Olds, Susan Faludi, Joan Morgan, Eric Liu, Sherman Alexie, Jean Kilbourne, Veronica Chambers, and Jennifer Price. And like earlier versions, this edition of *Rereading America* includes a healthy mix of personal and academic writing, representing a wide variety of genres, styles, and rhetorical strategies.

New Visual Portfolios In addition to the frontispieces and cartoons that have been standard features in past editions, we've included a Visual Portfolio of myth-related images in every chapter of this edition of *Rereading America*. These collections of photographs, advertisements, and reproductions of famous paintings invite students to examine how visual "texts" are constructed and how, like written texts, they are susceptible to multiple readings and rereadings. Each portfolio is accompanied by a series of questions that encourage critical analysis and connect portfolio images to ideas and themes in chapter reading selections. As in earlier editions, the visual frontispieces that open each chapter are integrated into the prereading assignments found in the chapter introductions. The cartoons, offered as a bit of comic relief and as opportunities for visual thinking, are paired with appropriate readings thoughout the text.

Focus on Media We've continued the practice of including one or more selections focusing on the media in each chapter of *Rereading America*. This distribution of media pieces throughout the book allows you to discuss media representations in the context of the specific myths your class addresses. In the first chapter, you'll find an examination of the impact of the "Military-Nintendo Complex" on American families. Chapter Four offers several analyses of gender issues in the media, from the essays by Jean Kilbourne and Jackson Katz on images of women and men in advertising to Susan Faludi's disturbing report on teen masculinity and the culture of celebrity to Joan Morgan's examination of black feminism and hip-hop culture. "Created Equal: The Myth of the Melting Pot" introduces the notion of media-created "virtual integration," and the new chapter on the frontier offers a history of the mutual development of popular media and the myth of the Old West. Recognizing the growing importance of computers in American life, we've also included Henry Jenkins's manifesto for educational reform in the "digital age" and Stephanie Brail's warning about the high price of freedom on the Internet.

Focus on Struggle and Resistance Most multicultural readers approach diversity in one of two ways: either they adopt a pluralist approach and conceive of American society as a kind of salad bowl of cultures, or, in response to recent worries about the lack of "objectivity" in the new multicultural curriculum, they take what might be called the "talk show" approach and present American culture as a series of pro-and-con debates on a number of social issues. The fifth edition of *Rereading America,* like its predecessors, follows neither of these approaches. Pluralist readers, we feel, make a promise that's impossible to keep: no single text, and no single course, can do justice to the many complex cultures that inhabit the United States. Thus, the materials selected for *Rereading America* aren't meant to offer a taste of what "family" means for Native Americans, or the flavor of gender relations among recent immigrants. Instead, we've included selections like Melvin Dixon's "Aunt Ida Pieces a Quilt" or Harlon Dalton's "Horatio Alger," because they offer us fresh critical perspectives on the common myths that shape our ideas, values, and beliefs. Rather than seeing this anthology as a mosaic or kaleidoscope of cultural fragments that combine to form a beautiful picture, it's more accurate to think of *Rereading America* as a handbook that helps students explore the ways that the dominant culture shapes their ideas, values, and beliefs.

This notion of cultural dominance is studiously avoided in most recent multicultural anthologies. "Salad bowl" readers generally sidestep the issue of cultural dynamics: intent on celebrating America's cultural diversity, they offer a relatively static picture of a nation fragmented into a kind of cultural archipelago. "Talk show" readers admit the idea of conflict, but they distort the reality of cultural dynamics by presenting cultural conflicts as a matter of rational—and equally balanced—debate. All of the materials anthologized in *Rereading America* address the cultural struggles that animate American society—the tensions that result from the expectations established by our dominant cultural myths and the diverse realities that these myths often contradict.

Ultimately, *Rereading America* is about resistance. In this new edition we continue to include readings that offer positive alternatives to the dilemmas of cultural conflict—from Henry Jenkins's call for the empowerment of children through the institution of a critical literacy curriculum in American schools to the teens who are rewriting the myth of the melting pot in Lynell George's "Gray Boys, Funky Aztecs, and Honorary Homegirls." To make this commitment to resistance as visible as possible, we've tried to conclude every chapter of this new edition with a suite of readings offering creative and, we hope, empowering examples of Americans who work together to redefine our national myths.

Extensive Apparatus   *Rereading America* offers a wealth of features to help students hone their analytic abilities and to aid instructors as they plan class discussions, critical thinking activities, and writing assignments. These include:

- A *Comprehensive Introductory Essay*   The book begins with a comprehensive essay, "Thinking Critically, Challenging Cultural Myths," that introduces students to the relationships between thinking, cultural diversity, and the notion of dominant cultural myths, and shows how such myths can influence their academic performance. We've also included a section devoted to active reading, which offers suggestions for prereading, prewriting, note taking, text marking, and keeping a reading journal. A new section helps students work with the many new visual images that have been added to the book.

- *Detailed Chapter Introductions*   An introductory essay at the beginning of each chapter offers students a thorough overview of each cultural myth, placing it in historical context, raising some of the chapter's central questions, and orienting students to the chapter's internal structure.

- *Prereading Activities*   Following each chapter introduction you'll find prereading activities designed to encourage students to reflect on what they already know about the cultural myth in question. Often connected to the images that open every chapter, these prereading activities help students to engage the topic even before they begin to read.

- *Questions to Stimulate Critical Thinking*   Three groups of questions following each selection encourage students to consider the reading carefully in several contexts: "Engaging the Text" focuses on close reading of the selection itself; "Exploring Connections" puts the selection into dialogue with other selections throughout the book; "Extending the Critical Context" invites students to connect the ideas they read about here with sources of knowledge outside the anthology, including library research, personal experience, interviews, ethnographic-style observations, and so forth. As in past editions, we've included a number of questions linking readings with contemporary television shows and feature films for instructors who want to address the interplay of cultural myths and the mass media.

- *An Extensive Instructor's Manual*   Resources for Teaching REREADING AMERICA provides detailed advice about ways to make the most of both the readings and the questions; it also offers further ideas for discussion, class activities, and writing assignments, as well as practical hints and suggestions that we've garnered from our own classroom experiences.

- *Online Resources*   The TopLinks Web site for *Rereading America* contains annotated research links. For more information, visit www.bedfordstmartins.com to explore this site and other helpful electronic resources for both students and instructors.

Acknowledgments

Critical thinking is always a collaborative activity, and the kind of critical thinking involved in the creation of an anthology like *Rereading America* represents collegial collaboration at its very best. Since publication of the last edition, we've heard from instructors across the country who have generously offered suggestions for new classroom activities and comments for further refinements and improvements. Among the many instructors who shared their insights with us as we reworked this edition, we'd particularly like to thank the following: Etta C. Abrahams, Michigan State University; Richard L. Arthur, Miami University of Ohio; Scott E. Ash, Nassau Community College; Michael Augsperger, University of Iowa; Larry Cain, Chabot College; Rosann M. Cook, Purdue University at Calumet; Mary Jean Corbett, Miami University of Ohio; Stephen Curley, Texas A&M University at Galveston; Ann M. DeDad, Gannon University; Florence Emch, California State University, Los Angeles; Juan F. Flores, Del Mar College; Nancy Gonchar, The College of New Rochelle; Tara Hart, Howard Community College; Sue Ellen Holbrook, Southern Connecticut State University; Stephen Horvath, Howard Community College; Irwin J. Koplik, Hofstra University; Michael Lewis, University of Iowa; Linda Maitland, University of Houston; Doug Merrell, University of Washington; Robert Murray, St. Thomas Aquinas College; Kathleen O'Brien, Boston University; Renee Ruderman, The Metropolitan State College of Denver; Karen Ryan-Engel, Gannon University; Amy Sileven, Southern Illinois University at Carbondale; Jane E. Simonsen, University of Iowa; Juliet Sloger, University of Rochester; Ken Smith, Indiana University, South Bend; Judith A. Stainbrook, Gannon University; Douglas Steward, University of Kansas.

For their help with the fourth edition of *Rereading America*, we'd particularly like to thank the following: Dan Armstrong, Lane Community College; H. Inness Asher, University of Louisiana, Lafayette; Margot Gayle Backis, St. John Fisher College; Marlow Belschner, Southern Illinois University; Nancy Botkin, University of Indiana, South Bend; Carol Brown, South Puget Sound Community College; William Carroll, Norfolk State University; Dolores Crim, Purdue University, Hammond; Linda L. Danielson, Lane Community College; Emily Detiner, Miami University; Kathy Doherty, Bentley College; Melinda M. Fiala, University of Missouri, Kansas City; Sara Gogol, Portland Community College; Joyce Huff, George Washington University; Kim Lang, Shippensburg University; Uvieja Leighton, The Union Institute; Elizabeth L. Lewis, Vermilion Community College; Jennifer Lowood, Vista Community College; Brij Lurine, University of New Mexico; Eunice M. Madison, Purdue University, Calumet; Kenneth K. Martin, Community College of Philadelphia; James McWard, University of Kansas; Kevin A. Moberg, University of North Dakota; John G. Morris, Cameron University; Craig J. Nauman, University of Wisconsin, Madison; Bruce Ouderkirk, University of Nebraska, Lincoln; E. Suzanne Owens, Lorain County Community College; Elizabeth Paulson, California State University; Amy Sapowith, University of California, Los Angeles; Jurgen Schlunk, West Virginia University; Tony Slagle, The Ohio State University; Penny L. Smith, Gannon University; Sharon Snyder, Purdue University, Calumet; Deborah Tenneg, Yale University; Ruthe Thompson, University of Arizona; Lorraine Threadgill, Community College of Philadelphia; Steve Turnwall, Los Medanos College; Riley Vann, West Virginia University; Nancy Wallace, Temple University; Ellen Weinauer, University of Southern Mississippi; Claudia L. Whitling, South Puget Sound Community College; Judy Wilkinson, Skyline College; Mark Wollarges, Vanderbilt University; Phyllis Zrzuay, Franklin Pierce College.

We are also grateful to the following people for responding to a questionnaire for previous editions: Katya Amato, Portland State University; Jeanne Anderson, University of Louisville; Julie Drew Anderson, University of South Florida; Sharon K. Anthony, Portland Community College; Rodney Ash, Western State College of Colorado; David Axelson, Western State College of Colorado; Valerie Babb, Georgetown University; Flavia Bacarella, Herbert H. Lehman College; Michael A. Balas, Nassau Community College; Gwen Barday, East Carolina University; Jim Baril, Western State College of Colorado; Richard Barney, University of Oklahoma; Jeannette Batz, Saint Louis University; Les Belikian, Los Angeles City College; Patricia Ann Bender, Rutgers University, Newark; Jon Bentley, Albuquerque Technical Vocational Institute; Sara Blake, El Camino College; Jean L. Blanning, Michigan Technological University; Maurice Blauf, Hutchins School of Liberal Studies; Joseph Bodziock, Clarion University; Will Bohnaker, Portland State University; Susan R. Bowers, Susquehanna University; Laura Brady, George Mason University; Eugenia M. Bragen, Baruch College; Byron Caminero-Santangelo, Saddleback College; Julianna de Magalhaes Castro, Highline Community College; Cheryl Christiansen, California State University, Stanislaus; Ann Christie, Goucher College; Stuart Christie, University of California, Santa Cruz; Renny Christopher, Cabrillo College; Gloria Collins, San Jose State University; Richard Conway, Lamar Community College; Harry James Cook, Dundalk Community College; Richard Courage, Westchester Community College; Cynthia Cox, Belmont University; Dulce M. Cruz, Indiana University; Wendy J. Cutler, Hocking Technical College; Patricia A. Daskivich, Los Angeles Harbor College; Anthony Dawahare, Loyola University, Chicago; Thomas Dean, Cardinal Stritch College; Elise Donovan, Union County College; Miriam Dow, George Washington University; Douglass T. Doyle, University of South Florida; Diana Dreyer, Slippery Rock University; Michele Driscoll, San Francisco State University; Cynthia Dubielak, Hocking Technical College; M. H. Dunlop, Iowa State University; Steve Dunn, Western State College of Colorado; Mary DuPree, University of Idaho; Harriet Dwinell, American University; K. C. Eapen, Clark Atlanta University; Iain J. W. Ellis, Bowling Green State University; Sharon Emmons, University of Portland; G. Euridge, Ohio State University; Rand Floren, Santa Rosa Junior College; Marie Foley, Santa Barbara City College; Barry Fruchter, Nassau Community College; Sandy Fugate, Western Michigan University; Arra M. Garab, Northern Illinois University; Peter Gardner, Berklee College of Music; Mary R. Georges, University of California, Los Angeles; Paul Gery, Western State College of Colorado; Michele Glazer, Portland Community College–Sylvania; William Gleason, University of California, Los Angeles; Sara Gogal, Portland Community College; Krystyna Golkowska,

Ithaca College; Jim Gorman; Andrea Greenbaum, University of South Florida; Ervene Gulley, Bloomsburg University; James C. Hall, University of Iowa; Craig Hancock, State University of New York, Albany; Jan Hayhurst, Community College of Pittsburgh; G. Held, Queens College; Jay W. Helman, Western State College of Colorado; Penny L. Hirsch, Northwestern University; Roseanne L. Hoefel, Iowa State University; Carol Hovanec, Ramapo College; Allison A. Hutira, Youngstown State University; John M. Jakaitis, Indiana State University; Jeannette J. Jeneault, Syracuse University; Robert T. Kelley, Urstnus College; Kathleen Kelly, Northeastern University; Kathleen Kiehl, Cabrillo College; Frances E. Kino, Iona College, Yonkers Campus; Blanche Jamson, Southeastern Oklahoma State University; Ron Johnson, Skyline College; Elizabeth Mary Kirchen, University of Michigan, Dearborn; Judith Kirscht, University of California, Santa Barbara; Jeffrey A. Kisner, Waynesburg College; Phil Klingsmith, Western State College of Colorado; Philip A. Korth, Michigan State University; S. J. Kotz, Virginia Polytechnic Institute and State University; Joann Krieg, Hofstra University; Catherine W. Kroll, Sonoma State American Language Institute; Jim Krusoe, Santa Monica College; Frank La Ferriere, Los Angeles City College; Susan Latta, Purdue University; Sheila A. Lebo, University of California, Los Angeles; D. Lebofsky, Temple University; Mitzi Lewellen, Normandale Community College; Lis Leyson, Fullerton College; Joseph Like, Beloit College; Don Lipman, Los Angeles City College; Solange Lira, Boston University; L. Loeffel, Syracuse University; Paul Loukides, Albion College; Bernadette Flynn Low, Dundalk Community College; Paul Lowdenslager, Western State College of Colorado; Susan G. Luck, Lorain County Community College; Janet Madden-Simpson, El Camino College; Annette March, Cabrillo College; Kathleen Marley, Fairleigh Dickinson University; Lorraine Mercer, Portland State University; Clifford Marks, University of Wyoming; Peggy Marron, University of Wyoming; David Martinez, University of California, Los Angeles; Laura McCall, Western State College of Colorado; K. Ann McCarthy, Shoreline Community College; Richard McGowan, St. Joseph's College; Grace McLaughlin, Portland Community College; Ann A. Merrill, Emory University; Dale Metcalfe, University of California, Davis; Charles Miller, Western State College of Colorado; Carol Porterfield Milowski, Bemidji State University; Ann Mine, Oregon State University; Kathy Molloy, Santa Barbara City College; Candace Montoya, University of Oregon; Amy Mooney, South Puget Sound Community College; Fred Moss, University of Wisconsin–Waukesha; Merlyn E. Mowrey, Central Michigan University; Denise Muller, San Jose State University; William Murphy, University of Maine, Machias; Susan Nance, Bowling Green State University; Patricia M. Naulty, Canisius College; Scott R. Nelson, Louisiana State University; Robert Newman, State University of New York at Buffalo; Thu Nguyen, Irvine Valley College; Todd T. Nilson, University of Kentucky; Fran O'Connor, Nassau Community College; Sarah-Hope Parmeter, University of California, Santa Cruz; Sandra Patterson, Western State College of Colorado; Marsha Penti, Michigan Technological University; Erik Peterson, University of Minnesota; Linda Peterson, Salt Lake Community College; Michele Peterson, Santa Barbara City College; Madeleine Picciotto, Oglethorpe University; Kirsten Pierce, Villanova University; Dan Pinti, Ohio State University; Fritz H. Pointer, Contra Costa College; Paige S. Price, University of Oregon; Teresa M. Redd, Howard University; Thomas C. Renzi, State University College at Buffalo; Geri Rhodes, Albuquerque Technical Vocational Institute; Walter G. Rice, Dundalk Community College; Bruce Richardson, University of Wyoming; Randall Rightmire, Los Angeles Southwest College; Jeffrey Ritchie, Northern Kentucky University; Patricia Roberts, Allentown College of St. Francis de Sales; Marjorie Roemer, University of Cincinnati; Bonnie Ross, Los Angeles Valley College; Renee Ruderman, Metropolitan State College, Denver; Lillian Ruiz-Powell, Miracosta College; Geoffrey J. Sadock, Bergen Community College; Mollie Sandock, Valparaiso University; Bryan Scanlon, Western Michigan University; Wayne Scheer, Atlanta Metro College; Linda Scholer, College of San Mateo; Jurgen E. Schlunk, West Virginia University; Esther L. Schwartz, Allegheny County Community College; David Seitz, University of Illinois, Chicago; Jennifer A. Senft, University of California, Los Angeles; Ann Shapiro, State University of New York, Farmingdale; Nancy Shaw, Ursinus College; Eric Shibuya, University of Oklahoma; Jeanette Shumaker, San Diego State University; Michele Moragne e Silva, St. Edward's University; Rashna B. Singh, Holyoke Community College; Craig Sirles, De Paul University; Bill Siverly, Portland Community College; Antony Sloan, Bowling Green State University; Susan Belasco Smith, Allegheny College; Cynthia Solem, Cabrillo College; Andrew M. Stauffer, University of Virginia; Joseph Steinbach, Purdue University; Skai Stelzer, University of Toledo; Susan Sterr, Santa Monica College; Mark Stiger, Western State College of Colorado; Ann Marie Stock, Hamline University; John B. Stoker, Kent State University; Ann Stolls, University of Illinois, Chicago; Brendan D. Strasser, Bowling Green State University; David Strong, Indiana University; Miriam Stuarts, Loyola University; Bonnie Surfus, University of South Florida; Karen Thomas, University of California, Los Angeles; Alice L. Trupe, Community College of Allegheny County; Eileen Turaff, Cleveland State University; Ruth Ann Thompson, Fordham University; Mark Todd, Western State College of Colorado; Michael Uebel, University of Virginia; James Varn, Morris College; Keith Walters, Ohio State University; Robert R. Watson, Grand Valley State University; Nola J. Wegman, Valparaiso University; Edwin Weihe, Seattle University; R. L. Welker, University of Virginia; Douglas Wixson, University of Missouri; Janice M. Wolff, Saginaw Valley State University; Brent Yaciw, University of South Florida; Nancy Young, Bentley, Curry, and Regis Colleges; and Naomi F. Zucker, University of Rhode Island.

As always, we'd also like to thank all the kind folks at Bedford/ St. Martin's, who do their best to make the effort of producing a book like this a genuine pleasure. Our publishers, Charles Christensen and Joan Feinberg, deserve special praise for the support they've shown us over the years and for the wise counsel they've offered in the occasional hour of need. Our editor, John Sullivan, has been a true partner in the development of this edition and has again demonstrated the kind of style and grace we've come to expect from him as the consummate professional. We also want to thank Lori Roncka, who served as production editor on this edition; Sarah Doerries, who expertly copyedited the manuscript; Donna Dennison, who produced our new cover; Eva Pettersson, for clearing text permissions; Susan Doheny, for researching and tracking down art; Kelly Caufield, who helped with research; and editorial assistants Katherine Gilbert, Kristen Harvey, and Caroline Thompson, who helped out with many of the hundreds of details that go into a project such as this. Finally, we'd like to acknowledge Elena Barcia, Liz Silver, and Roy Weitz, who, after these many years, have mastered the art of ignoring us completely while we put our shoulders to the task of revision one more time.

Contents

1

Harmony at Home:
The Myth of the Model Family   17

2

Learning Power:
The Myth of Education and Empowerment 134

"Ads don't directly cause violence, of course. But the violent images contribute to the state of terror . . . a climate in which there is widespread and increasing violence."

"The appeal of violent behavior for men, including its rewards, is coded into mainstream advertising in numerous ways: from violent male icons . . . overtly threatening consumers to buy products to ads that exploit men's feelings of not being big, strong, or violent enough. . . ."

"G.I. Joes have morphed over the last three decades into muscle-bound hunks that can harm the self-esteem of boys, according to a new study."

". . . American women enjoy many aspects of 'la différence.' Many want things that gender feminists are trying to free them from, be it conventional marriages and families, or fashions and makeup that sometimes render them 'sex objects.'"

"At the simplest level, looking or behaving like the stereotypical gay man or lesbian is reason enough to provoke a homophobic assault."

"I needed to figure out if there was any Christian support somewhere that said I could reconcile my love for Jean and my love for my faith."

"Tirelessly they repeated the details of a Spur Posse 'game' that had riveted the media. It was a sex-for-points intramural contest in which each time you had sex with a girl, which they called 'hooking up,' you racked up a point. You had to achieve penetration and you could only get one point per girl."

"The seemingly impenetrable wall of sexism in rap music is really the complex mask African-Americans often wear both to hide and express the pain."

5

Created Equal:
The Myth of the Melting Pot   534

"I advance it therefore, as a suspicion only, that the blacks...are inferior to the whites in the endowments both of body and mind."

"O, let America be America again—
The land that never has been yet—
And yet must be—the land where every man is free."

"Prejudice is a complex phenomenon, and it is most likely the product of more than one causal agent."

"A Klansman and a militant black woman, co-chairmen of the school committee. It was impossible. How could I work with her?"

"I think the racial struggle in America has always been primarily a struggle for innocence....Both races instinctively understand that to lose innocence is to lose power."

6

Westward Ho!
The Myth of Frontier Freedom   676

Rereading America

Cultural Contexts for
Critical Thinking and Writing

Thinking Critically, Challenging Cultural Myths

Becoming a College Student

Beginning college can be a disconcerting experience. It may be the first time you've lived away from home and had to deal with the stresses and pleasures of independence. There's increased academic competition, increased temptation, and a whole new set of peer pressures. In the dorms you may find yourself among people whose backgrounds make them seem foreign and unapproachable. If you commute, you may be struggling against a feeling of isolation that you've never faced before. And then there are increased expectations. For an introductory history class you may read as many books as you covered in a year of high school coursework. In anthropology, you might be asked to conduct ethnographic research — when you've barely heard of an ethnography before, much less written one. In English you may tackle more formal analytic writing in a single semester than you've ever done in your life.

College typically imposes fewer rules than high school, but also gives you less guidance and makes greater demands — demands that affect the quality as well as the quantity of your work. By your first midterm exam, you may suspect that your previous academic experience is irrelevant, that nothing you've done in school has prepared you to think, read, or write in the ways your professors expect. Your sociology instructor says she doesn't care whether you can remember all the examples in the textbook as long as you can apply the theoretical concepts to real situations. In your composition class, the perfect five-paragraph essay you turn in for your first assignment is dismissed as "superficial, mechanical, and dull." Meanwhile, the lecturer in your political science or psychology course is rejecting ideas about country, religion, family, and self that have always been a part of your deepest beliefs. How can you cope with these new expectations and challenges?

There is no simple solution, no infallible five-step method that works for everyone. As you meet the personal challenges of college, you'll grow as a human being. You'll begin to look critically at your old habits, beliefs, and values, to see them in relation to the new world you're entering. You may have to re-examine your relationships to family, friends, neighborhood, and heritage. You'll have to sort out your strengths from your weaknesses and make tough choices about who you are and who you want to become. Your academic work demands the same process of serious self-examination. To excel in college work you need to grow intellectually — to become a critical thinker.

What Is Critical Thinking?

What do instructors mean when they tell you to think critically? Most would say that it involves asking questions rather than memorizing information. Instead of simply collecting the "facts," a critical thinker probes them, looking for underlying assumptions and ideas. Instead of focusing on dates and events in history or symptoms in psychology, she probes for motives, causes — an explanation of how these things came to be. A critical thinker cultivates the ability to imagine and value points of view different from her own — then strengthens, refines, enlarges, or reshapes her ideas in light of those other perspectives. She is at once open and skeptical: receptive to new ideas yet careful to test them against previous experience and knowledge. In short, a critical thinker is an active learner, someone with the ability to shape, not merely absorb, knowledge.

All this is difficult to put into practice, because it requires getting outside your own skin and seeing the world from multiple perspectives. To see why critical thinking doesn't come naturally, take another look at the cover of this book. Many would scan the title, *Rereading America*, take in the surface meaning — to reconsider America — and go on to page one. There isn't much to question here; it just "makes sense." But what happens with the student who brings a different perspective? For example, a student from El Salvador might justly complain that the title reflects an ethnocentric view of what it means to be an American. After all, since America encompasses all the countries of North, South, and Central America, he lived in "America" long before arriving in the United States. When this student reads the title, then, he actually does *reread* it; he reads it once in the "commonsense" way but also from the perspective of someone who has lived in a country dominated by U.S. intervention and interests. This double vision or double perspective frees him to look beyond the "obvious" meaning of the book and to question its assumptions.

Of course, you don't have to be bicultural to become a proficient critical thinker. You can develop a genuine sensitivity to alternative perspectives even if you've never lived outside your hometown. But to do so you need to recognize that there are no "obvious meanings." The automatic equation that the native-born student makes between "America" and the United States seems to make sense only because our culture has traditionally endorsed the idea that the United States *is* America and, by implication, that other countries in this hemisphere are somehow inferior — not the genuine article. We tend to accept this equation and its unfortunate implications because we are products of our culture.

The Power of Cultural Myths

Culture shapes the way we think; it tells us what "makes sense." It holds people together by providing us with a shared set of customs, values, ideas, and beliefs, as well as a common language. We live enmeshed in this cultural web: it influences the way we relate to others, the way we look, our tastes, our habits; it enters our dreams and desires. But as culture binds us together it also selectively blinds us. As we grow up, we accept ways of looking at the world, ways of thinking and being that might best be characterized as cultural frames of reference or cultural myths. These myths help us understand our place in the world — our place as prescribed by our culture. They define our relationships to friends and lovers, to the past and future, to nature, to power, and to nation. Becoming a critical thinker means learning how to look beyond these cultural myths and the assumptions embedded in them.

You may associate the word "myth" primarily with the myths of the ancient Greeks. The legends of gods and heroes like Athena, Zeus, and Oedipus embodied the central ideals and values of Greek civilization — notions like civic responsibility, the primacy of male authority, and humility before the gods. The stories were "true" not in a literal sense but as reflections of important cultural beliefs. These myths assured the Greeks of the nobility of their origins; they provided models for the roles that Greeks would play in their public and private lives; they justified inequities in Greek society; they helped the Greeks understand human life and destiny in terms that "made sense" within the framework of that culture.

Our cultural myths do much the same. Take, for example, the American dream of success. Since the first European colonists came to the "New World" some four centuries ago, America has been synonymous with the idea of individual opportunity. For generations, immigrants have been lured across the ocean to make their fortunes in a land where the streets were said to be paved with gold. Of course, we don't always agree on what success means or how it should be measured. Some calculate the meaning of success in terms of multi-digit salaries or the acreage of their country estates. Others discover success in the attainment of a dream — whether it's graduating from college, achieving excellence on the playing field, or winning new rights and opportunities for less-fortunate fellow citizens. For some Americans, the dream of success is the very foundation of everything that's right about life in the United States. For others, the American dream is a cultural mirage that keeps workers happy in low-paying jobs while their bosses pocket the profits of an unfair system. But whether you embrace or reject the dream of success, you can't escape its influence. As Americans, we are steeped in a culture that prizes individual achievement; growing up in the United States, we are told again and again by parents, teachers, advertisers, Hollywood writers, politicians, and opinion makers that we, too, can achieve our dream — that we, too, can "Just Do It" if we try. You might aspire to become an Internet tycoon, or you might rebel and opt for a simple life, but you can't ignore the impact of the myth. We each define success in our own way, but, ultimately, the myth of success defines who we are and what we think, feel, and believe.

Cultural myths gain such enormous power over us by insinuating themselves into our thinking before we're aware of them. Most are learned at a deep, even unconscious level. Gender roles are a good example. As children we get gender role models from our families, our schools, our churches, and other important institutions. We see them acted out in the relationships between family members or portrayed on television, in the movies, or in song lyrics. Before long, the culturally determined roles we see for women and men appear to us as "self-evident": it seems "natural" for a man to be strong, responsible, competitive, and heterosexual, just as it may seem "unnatural" for a man to shun competitive activity or to take a romantic interest in other men. Our most dominant cultural myths shape the way we perceive the world and blind us to alternative ways of seeing and being. When something violates the expectations that such myths create, it may even be called unnatural, immoral, or perverse.

Cultural Myths as Obstacles to Critical Thinking

Cultural myths can have more subtle effects as well. In academic work they can reduce the complexity of our reading and thinking. A few years ago, for example, a professor at Los Angeles City College noted that he and his students couldn't agree in their interpretations of the following poem by Theodore Roethke:

> My Papa's Waltz
>
> The whiskey on your breath
> Could make a small boy dizzy;
> But I hung on like death:
> Such waltzing was not easy.
>
> We romped until the pans
> Slid from the kitchen shelf;
> My mother's countenance
> Could not unfrown itself.
>
> The hand that held my wrist
> Was battered on one knuckle;
> At every step you missed
> My right ear scraped a buckle.
>
> You beat time on my head
> With a palm caked hard by dirt,
> Then waltzed me off to bed
> Still clinging to your shirt.

The instructor read this poem as a clear expression of a child's love for his blue-collar father, a rough-and-tumble man who had worked hard all his life ("a palm caked hard by dirt"), who was not above taking a drink of whiskey to ease his mind, but who also found the time to "waltz" his son off to bed. The students didn't see this at all. They saw the poem as a story about an abusive father and heavy drinker. They seemed unwilling to look beyond the father's roughness and the whiskey on his breath, equating these with drunken violence. Although the poem does suggest an element of fear mingled with the boy's excitement ("I hung on like death"), the class ignored its complexity — the mixture of fear, love, and boisterous fun that colors the son's memory of his father. It's possible that some students might overlook the positive traits in the father in this poem because they have suffered child abuse themselves. But this couldn't be true for all the students in the class. The difference between these interpretations lies, instead, in the influence of cultural myths. After all, in a culture now dominated by images of the family that emphasize "positive" parenting, middle-class values, and sensitive fathers, it's no wonder that students refused to see this father sympathetically. Our culture simply doesn't associate good, loving families with drinking or with even the suggestion of physical roughness.

Years of acculturation — the process of internalizing cultural values — leave us with a set of rigid categories for "good" and "bad" parents, narrow conceptions of how parents should look, talk, and behave toward their children. These cultural categories work like mental pigeonholes: they help us sort out and evaluate our experiences rapidly, almost before we're consciously aware of them. They give us a helpful shorthand for interpreting the world; after all, we can't stop to ponder every new situation we meet as if it were a puzzle or a philosophical problem. But while cultural categories help us make practical decisions in everyday life, they also impose their inherent rigidity on our thinking and thus limit our ability to understand the complexity of our experience. They reduce the world to dichotomies — simplified either/or choices: either women or men, either heterosexuals or homosexuals, either nature or culture, either animal or human, either "alien" or American, either them or us.

Rigid cultural beliefs can present serious obstacles to success for first-year college students. In a psychology class, for example, students' cultural myths may so color their thinking that they find it nearly impossible to comprehend Freud's ideas about infant sexuality. Ingrained assumptions about childhood innocence and sexual guilt may make it impossible for them to see children as sexual beings — a concept absolutely basic to an understanding of the history of psychoanalytic theory. Yet college-level critical inquiry thrives on exactly this kind of revision of common sense: academics prize the unusual, the subtle, the ambiguous, the complex — and expect students to appreciate them as well. Good critical thinkers in all academic disciplines welcome the opportunity to challenge conventional ways of seeing the world; they seem to take delight in questioning everything that appears clear and self-evident.

Questioning: The Basis of Critical Thinking

By questioning the myths that dominate our culture, we can begin to resist the limits they impose on our vision. In fact, they invite such questioning. Often our personal experience fails to fit the images the myths project: a young woman's ambition to be a test pilot may clash with the ideal of femininity our culture promotes; a Cambodian immigrant who has suffered from racism in the United States may question our professed commitment to equality; a student in the vocational track may not see education as the road to success that we assume it is; and few of our families these days fit the mythic model of husband, wife, two kids, a dog, and a house in the suburbs.

Moreover, because cultural myths serve such large and varied needs, they're not always coherent or consistent. Powerful contradictory myths co-exist in our society and our own minds. For example, while the myth of "the melting pot" celebrates equality, the myth of individual success pushes us to strive for inequality — to "get ahead" of everyone else. Likewise, our attitudes toward education are deeply paradoxical: on one level Americans tend to see schooling as a valuable experience that unites us in a common culture and helps us bring out the best in ourselves; yet at the same time we suspect that formal classroom instruction stifles creativity and chokes off natural intelligence and enthusiasm. These contradictions infuse our history, literature, and popular culture; they're so much a part of our thinking that we tend to take them for granted, unaware of their inconsistencies.

Learning to recognize contradictions lies at the very heart of critical thinking, for intellectual conflict inevitably generates questions. Can both (or all) perspectives be true? What evidence do I have for the validity of each? Is there some way to reconcile them? Are there still other alternatives? Questions like these represent the beginning of serious academic analysis. They stimulate the reflection, discussion, and research that are the essence of good scholarship. Thus, whether we find contradictions between myth and lived experience, or between opposing myths, the wealth of powerful, conflicting material generated by our cultural mythology offers a particularly rich context for critical inquiry.

The Structure of *Rereading America*

We've designed this book to help you develop the habits of mind you'll need to become a critical thinker — someone who recognizes the way that cultural myths shape thinking and can move beyond them to evaluate issues from multiple perspectives. Each of the book's six chapters addresses one of the dominant myths of American culture. We begin with the myth that's literally closest to home — the myth of the model family. In "Harmony at

Home" we look at the impact that the idea of the nuclear family has had on generations of Americans, including those who don't fit comfortably within its limitations. We also present some serious challenges to this time-honored definition of American family life. Next we turn to a topic that every student should have a lot to say about — the myth of educational empowerment. "Learning Power" gives you the chance to reflect on how the "hidden curriculum" of schooling has shaped your own attitudes toward learning. We begin our exploration of American cultural myths by focusing on home and education because most students find it easy to make personal connections with these topics and because they both involve institutions — families and schools — that are surrounded by a rich legacy of cultural stories and myths. These two introductory chapters are followed by consideration of what is perhaps the most famous of all American myths, the American Dream. Chapter Three, "Money and Success," addresses the idea of unlimited personal opportunity that brought millions of immigrants to our shores and set the story of America in motion. It invites you to weigh some of the human costs of the dream and to reconsider your own definition of a successful life.

The second half of the book focuses on three cultural myths that offer greater intellectual and emotional challenges, in part because they are so intertwined with every American's personal identity and because they touch on highly charged social issues. "True Women and Real Men" considers the socially constructed categories of gender — the traditional roles that enforce differences between women and men. This chapter also explores the perspectives of Americans who defy conventional gender boundaries. The book's fifth chapter, "Created Equal," examines two myths that have powerfully shaped racial and ethnic relations in the United States: the myth of the melting pot, which celebrates cultural homogenization, and the myth of racial and ethnic superiority, which promotes separateness and inequality. This chapter probes the nature of prejudice, explores the ways that prejudicial attitudes are created, and examines ethnic identities within a race-divided society. Each of these two chapters questions how our culture divides and defines our world, how it artificially channels our experience into oppositions like black and white, male and female, straight and gay. The book concludes by addressing an important source of much of America's cultural mythology — the myth of the frontier. In "Westward Ho!: The Myth of Frontier Freedom" we examine how the idea of the West — with its vast, apparently open and unsettled expanses — affected American thinking about our national destiny and shaped our attitudes about opportunity, individualism, heroism, gender, and the natural world. This final chapter invites you to consider how the myth of the frontier continues to influence American attitudes and values more than a hundred years after the frontier itself ceased to exist as a historical reality in Amercan life.

The Selections

Our identities — who we are and how we relate to others — are deeply entangled with the cultural values we have internalized since infancy. Cultural myths become so closely identified with our personal beliefs that rereading them actually means rereading ourselves, rethinking the way we see the world. Questioning long-held assumptions can be an exhilarating experience, but it can be distressing too. Thus, you may find certain selections in *Rereading America* difficult, controversial, or even downright offensive. They are meant to challenge you and to provoke classroom debate. But as you discuss the ideas you encounter in this book, remind yourself that your classmates may bring with them very different, and equally profound, beliefs. Keep an open mind, listen carefully, and treat other perspectives with the same respect you'd expect other people to show for your own. It's by encountering new ideas and engaging with others in open dialogue that we learn to grow.

Because *Rereading America* explores cultural myths that shape our thinking, it doesn't focus on the kind of well-defined public issues you might expect to find in a traditional composition anthology. You won't be reading arguments for and against affirmative action, bilingual education, or the death penalty here. Although we do include conservative as well as liberal — and even radical — perspectives, we've deliberately avoided the traditional pro-and-con approach because we want you to aim deeper than that; we want you to focus on the subtle cultural beliefs that underlie, and frequently determine, the debates that are waged on public issues. We've also steered clear of the "issues approach" because we feel it reinforces simplistic either/or thinking. Polarizing American culture into a series of debates doesn't encourage you to examine your own beliefs or explore how they've been shaped by the cultures you're part of. To begin to appreciate the influence of your own cultural myths, you need new perspectives: you need to stand outside the ideological machinery that makes American culture run to begin to appreciate its power. That's why we've included many strongly dissenting views: there are works by community activists, gay-rights activists, socialists, libertarians, and more. You may find that their views confirm your own experience of what it means to be an American, or you may find that you bitterly disagree with them. We only hope that you will use the materials here to gain some insight into the values and beliefs that shape our thinking and our national identity. This book is meant to complicate the mental categories that our cultural myths have established for us. Our intention is not to present a new "truth" to replace the old but to expand the range of ideas you bring to all your reading and writing in college. We believe that learning to see and value other perspectives will enable you to think more critically — to question, for yourself, the truth of any statement.

You may also note that several selections in *Rereading America* challenge the way you think writing is supposed to look or sound. You won't find many "classic" essays in this book, the finely crafted reflective essays on general topics that are often held up as models of "good writing." It's not that we reject this type of essay in principle. It's just that most writers who stand outside mainstream culture seem to have little use for it.

Our selections, instead, come from a wide variety of sources: professional books and journals from many disciplines, popular magazines, college textbooks, autobiographies, oral histories, and literary works. We've included this variety partly for the very practical reason that you're likely to encounter texts like these in your college coursework. But we also see textual diversity, like ethnic and political diversity, as a way to multiply perspectives and stimulate critical analysis. For example, an academic article like Jean Anyon's study of social class and school curriculum might give you a new way of understanding Mike Rose's personal narrative about his classroom experiences. On the other hand, you may find that some of the teachers Rose encounters don't neatly fit Anyon's theoretical model. Do such discrepancies mean that Anyon's argument is invalid? That her analysis needs to be modified to account for these teachers? That the teachers are simply exceptions to the rule? You'll probably want to consider your own classroom experience as you wrestle with such questions. Throughout the book, we've chosen readings that "talk to each other" in this way and that draw on the cultural knowledge you bring with you. These readings invite you to join the conversation; we hope they raise difficult questions, prompt lively discussion, and stimulate critical inquiry.

The Power of Dialogue

Good thinking, like good writing and good reading, is an intensely social activity. Thinking, reading, and writing are all forms of relationship — when you read, you enter into dialogue with an author about the subject at hand; when you write, you address an imaginary reader, testing your ideas against probable responses, reservations, and arguments. Thus, you can't become an accomplished writer simply by declaring your right to speak or by criticizing as an act of principle: real authority comes when you enter into the discipline of an active exchange of opinions and interpretations. Critical thinking, then, is always a matter of dialogue and debate — discovering relationships between apparently unrelated ideas, finding parallels between your own experiences and the ideas you read about, exploring points of agreement and conflict between yourself and other people.

We've designed the readings and questions in this text to encourage you to make just these kinds of connections. You'll notice, for example, that we often ask you to divide into small groups to discuss readings, and we frequently suggest that you take part in projects that require you to collaborate with your classmates. We're convinced that the only way you can learn critical reading, thinking, and writing is by actively engaging others in an intellectual exchange. So we've built into the text many opportunities for listening, discussion, and debate.

The questions that follow each selection should guide you in critical thinking. Like the readings, they're intended to get you started, not to set limits; we strongly recommend that you also devise your own questions and pursue them either individually or in study groups. We've divided our questions into three categories. Here's what to expect from each:

- Those labeled "Engaging the Text" focus on the individual selection they follow. They're designed to highlight important issues in the reading, to help you begin questioning and evaluating what you've read, and sometimes to remind you to consider the author's choices of language, evidence, structure, and style.

- The questions labeled "Exploring Connections" will lead you from the selection you've just finished to one or more other readings in this book. It's hard to make sparks fly from just one stone; if you think hard about these connecting questions, though, you'll see some real collisions of ideas and perspectives, not just polite and predictable "differences of opinion."

- The final questions for each reading, "Extending the Critical Context," invite you to extend your thinking beyond the book — to your family, your community, your college, the media, or the more traditional research environment of the library. The emphasis here is on creating new knowledge by applying ideas from this book to the world around you and by testing these ideas in your world.

Active Reading

You've undoubtedly read many textbooks, but it's unlikely that you've had to deal with the kind of analytic, argumentative, and scholarly writing you'll find in college and in *Rereading America*. These different writing styles require a different approach to reading as well. In high school you probably read to "take in" information, often for the sole purpose of reproducing it later on a test. In college you'll also be expected to recognize larger issues, such as the author's theoretical slant, her goals and methods, her assumptions, and her relationship to other writers and researchers. These expectations can be especially difficult in the first two years of college, when you take introductory courses that survey large, complex fields of knowledge. With all these demands on your attention, you'll need to read actively to keep your bearings. Think of active reading as a conversation between you and the text: instead of listening passively as the writer talks, respond to what she says with questions and comments of your own. Here are some specific techniques you can practice to become a more active reader.

Prereading and Prewriting

It's best with most college reading to "preread" the text. In prereading, you briefly look over whatever information you have on the author and the selection itself. Reading chapter introductions and headnotes like those provided in this book can save you time and effort by giving you information about the author's background and concerns, the subject or thesis of the selection, and its place in the chapter as a whole. Also take a look at the title and at any headings or subheadings in the piece. These will give you further clues about an article's general scope and organization. Next, quickly skim the entire selection, paying a bit more attention to the first few paragraphs and the conclusion. Now you should have a pretty good sense of the author's position — what she's trying to say in this piece of writing.

At this point you may do one of several things before you settle down to in-depth reading. You may want to jot down in a few lines what you think the author is doing. Or you may want to make a list of questions you can ask about this topic based on your prereading. Or you may want to freewrite a page or so on the subject. Informally writing out your own ideas will prepare you for more in-depth reading by recalling what you already know about the topic.

We emphasize writing about what you've read because reading and writing are complementary activities: being an avid reader will help you as a writer by familiarizing you with a wide range of ideas and styles to draw on; likewise, writing about what you've read will give you a deeper understanding of your reading. In fact, the more actively you "process" or reshape what you've read, the better you'll comprehend and remember it. So you'll learn more effectively by marking a text as you read than by simply reading; taking notes as you read is even more effective than marking, and writing about the material for your own purposes (putting it in your own words and connecting it with what you already know) is better still.

Marking the Text and Taking Notes

After prereading and prewriting, you're ready to begin critical reading in earnest. As you read, be sure to highlight ideas and phrases that strike you as especially significant — those that seem to capture the gist of a particular paragraph or section, or those that relate directly to the author's purpose or argument. While prereading can help you identify central ideas, you may find that you need to reread difficult sections or flip back and skim an earlier passage if you feel yourself getting lost. Many students think of themselves as poor readers if they can't whip through an article at high speed without pausing. However, the best readers read recursively — that is, they shuttle back and forth, browsing, skimming, and rereading as necessary, depending on their interest, their familiarity with the subject, and the difficulty of the material. This shuttling actually parallels what goes on in your mind when you read actively, as you alternately recall prior knowledge or experience and predict or look for clues about where the writer is going next.

Keep a record of your mental shuttling by writing comments in the margins as you read. It's often useful to gloss the contents of each paragraph or section, to summarize it in a word or two written alongside the text. This note will serve as a reminder or key to the section when you return to it for further thinking, discussion, or writing. You may also want to note passages that puzzled you. Or you may want to write down personal reactions or questions stimulated by the reading. Take time to ponder why you felt confused or annoyed or affirmed by a particular passage. Let yourself wonder "out loud" in the margins as you read.

The following section illustrates one student's notes on a few stanzas of Inés Hernández-Ávila's "Para Teresa" (p. 207). In this example, you can see that the reader puts glosses or summary comments to the left of the poem and questions or personal responses to the right. You should experiment and create your own system of note taking, one that works best for the way you read. Just remember that your main goals in taking notes are to help you understand the author's overall position, to deepen and refine your responses to the selection, and to create a permanent record of those responses.

Para Teresa[1]

INÉS HERNÁNDEZ-ÁVILA

This poem explores and attempts to resolve an old conflict between its speaker and her schoolmate, two Chicanas at "Alamo which-had-to-be-its-name" Elementary School who have radically different ideas about what education means and does. Inés Hernández-Ávila (b. 1947) is an associate professor of Native American studies at the University of California, Davis. This poem appeared in her collection Con Razón, Corazón *(1987).*

Writes ⌈ A tí-Teresa —————————— *Why in Spanish?*
to │ Te dedico las palabras estás ⟋
Teresa ⌊ que (explotan) de mi corazón[2] —— *Why do her words explode?*
⌈ That day during lunch hour
│ at <u>Alamo which-had-to-be-its-name</u>　*!Why?*

---

[1] *Para Teresa:* For Teresa. [All notes are the author's.]

[2] *A ... corazón:* To you, Teresa, I dedicate these words that explode from my heart.

The day of their confrontation

> Elementary   — *Feels close to T. (?)*
> my <u>dear raza</u>
> That day in the bathroom
> Door guarded
> Myself cornered
> I was accused by you, Teresa
> Tú y las demás de tus amigas
> Pachucas todas
> Eran Uds. cinco.[3]

T.'s accusation

> Me gritaban que porque me creía tan grande[4]
> What was I trying to do, you growled
> <u>Show you up?</u>
> Make the teachers like me, pet me,   *Teachers must be*
> Tell me what a credit (to my people) I was?   *white / Anglo.*
> I was <u>playing right into their hands</u>, you challenged
> And you would have none of it.
> I was to stop.

Speaker is a "good student."

Keeping a Reading Journal

You may also want (or be required) to keep a reading journal in response to the selections you cover in *Rereading America*. In such a journal you'd keep all the freewriting that you do either before or after reading. Some students find it helpful to keep a double-entry journal, writing initial responses on the left side of the page and adding later reflections and reconsiderations on the right. You may want to use your journal as a place to explore personal reactions to your reading. You can do this by writing out imaginary dialogues — between two writers who address the same subject, between yourself and the writer of the selection, or between two parts of yourself. You can use the journal as a place to rewrite passages from a poem or essay in your own voice and from your own point of view. You can write letters to an author you particularly like or dislike or to a character in a story or poem. You might even draw a cartoon that comments on one of the reading selections.

Many students don't write as well as they could because they're afraid to take risks. They may have been repeatedly penalized for breaking "rules" of grammar or essay form; their main concern in writing becomes avoiding trouble rather than exploring ideas or experimenting with style. But without risk and experimentation, there's little possibility of growth. One of the benefits of journal writing is that it gives you a place to experiment with ideas, free from worries about "correctness." Here are two examples of student journal entries, in response to "Para Teresa" (we reprint the entries as they were written):

---

[3]*Tú . . . cinco:* You and the rest of your friends, all Pachucas, there were five of you.
[4]*Me . . . grande:* You were screaming at me, asking me why I thought I was so hot.

Entry 1: Internal Dialogue

ME 1: I agree with Inés Hernández-Ávila's speaker. Her actions were justifiable in a way that if you can't fight 'em, join 'em. After all, Teresa is just making the situation worse for her because not only is she sabotaging the teacher-student relationship, she's also destroying her chance for a good education.

ME 2: Hey, Teresa's action was justifiable. Why else would the speaker admit at the end of the poem that what Teresa did was fine thus she respects Teresa more?

ME 1: The reason the speaker respected Teresa was because she (Teresa) was still keeping her culture alive, although through different means. It wasn't her action that the speaker respected, it was the representation of it.

ME 2: The reason I think Teresa acted the way she did was because she felt she had something to prove to society. She wanted to show that no one could push her people around; that her people were tough.

Entry 2: Personal Response

"Con cố gắng học gioi, cho Bá Má,
Rõi sau nây dời sống cua con sẽ thõai mái lắm."[5]
What if I don't want to?
What if I can't?
Sometimes I feel my parents don't understand what
I'm going through.
To them, education is money.
And money is success.
They don't see beyond that.
Sometimes I want to fail my classes purposely to
See their reaction, but that is too cruel.
They have taught me to value education.
Education makes you a person, makes you somebody, they say.
I agree.
They are proud I am going to UCLA.
They brag to their friends, our Vietnamese community, people
I don't even know.
They believe in me, but I doubt myself. . . .

You'll notice that neither of these students talks directly about "Para Teresa" as a poem. Instead, each uses it as a point of departure for her own reflections on ethnicity, identity, and education. Although we've included a number of literary works in *Rereading America,* we don't expect you to do literary analysis. We want you to use these pieces to stimulate your own thinking about the cultural myths they address. So don't feel you have to

---

[5]*"Con . . . lắm":* "Daughter, study hard (for us, your Mom and Dad), so your future will be bright and easy."

discuss imagery in Inés Hernández-Ávila's "Para Teresa" or characterization in Toni Cade Bambara's "The Lesson" in order to understand and appreciate them.

Working with Visual Images

The myths we examine in *Rereading America* make their presence felt not only in the world of print — essays, stories, poems, memoirs — but in every aspect of our culture. Consider, for example, the myth of "the American family." If you want to design a minivan, a restaurant, a cineplex, a park, a synagogue, a personal computer, or a tax code, you had better have some idea of what families are like and how they behave. Most important, you need a good grasp of what Americans *believe* about families, about the mythology of the American family. The Visual Portfolio in each chapter, while it maintains our focus on myths, also carries you beyond the medium of print and thus lets you practice your analytical skills in a different arena.

Although we are all surrounded by visual stimuli, we don't always think critically about what we see. Perhaps we are numbed by constant exposure to a barrage of images on TV, in magazines and newspapers, in video games and films. In any case, here are a few tips on how to get the most out of the images we have collected for this book. Take the time to look at the images carefully; first impressions are important, but many of the photographs contain details that might not strike you immediately. Once you have noted the immediate impact of an image, try focusing on separate elements such as background, foreground, facial expressions, and body language. Read any text that appears in the photograph, even if it's on a T-shirt or a belt buckle. Remember that many photographs are carefully *constructed,* no matter how "natural" they may look. In a photo for a magazine advertisement, for example, everything is meticulously chosen and arranged: certain actors or models are cast for their roles; they wear makeup; their clothes are really costumes; the location or setting of the ad is designed to reinforce its message; lighting is artificial; and someone is trying to sell you something.

Also be sure to consider the visual images contextually, not in isolation. How does each resemble or differ from its neighbors in the portfolio? How does it reinforce or challenge cultural beliefs or stereotypes? Put another way, how can it be understood in the context of the myths examined in *Rereading America?* Each portfolio is accompanied by a few questions to help you begin this type of analysis. You can also build a broader context for our visual images by collecting your own, then working in small groups to create a portfolio or collage.

Finally, remember that both readings and visual images are just starting points for discussion. You have access to a wealth of other perspectives and ideas among your family, friends, classmates; in your college library; in your personal experience; and in your imagination. We urge you to consult them all as you grapple with the perspectives you encounter in this text.

1

Harmony at Home
The Myth of the Model Family

The Donna Reed Show.

What would an American political campaign be without wholesome photographs of the candidates kissing babies and posing with their loving families? Politicians understand the cultural power of these symbols; they appreciate the family as one of our most sacred American institutions. The vision of the ideal nuclear family — Dad, Mom, a couple of kids, maybe a dog, and a spacious suburban home — is a cliché but also a potent myth, a dream that millions of Americans work to fulfill. The image is so compelling that it's easy to forget what a short time it's been around, especially compared with the long history of the family itself.

In fact, what we call the "traditional" family, headed by a breadwinner-father and a housewife-mother, has existed for little more than two hundred years, and the suburbs only came into being in the 1950s. But the family as a social institution was legally recognized in Western culture at least as far back as the Code of Hammurabi, created in ancient Mesopotamia some four thousand years ago. To appreciate how profoundly concepts of family life have changed, consider the absolute power of the Mesopotamian father, the patriarch: the law allowed him to use any of his dependents, including his wife, as collateral for loans or even to sell family members outright to pay his debts.

Although patriarchal authority was less absolute in Puritan America, fathers remained the undisputed heads of families. Seventeenth-century Connecticut, Massachusetts, and New Hampshire enacted laws condemning rebellious children to severe punishment and, in extreme cases, to death. In the early years of the American colonies, as in Western culture stretching back to Hammurabi's time, unquestioned authority within the family served as both the model for and the basis of state authority. Just as family members owed complete obedience to the father, so all citizens owed unquestioned loyalty to the king and his legal representatives. In his influential volume *Democracy in America* (1835), French aristocrat Alexis de Tocqueville describes the relationship between the traditional European family and the old political order:

> Among aristocratic nations, social institutions recognize, in truth, no one in the family but the father; children are received by society at his hands; society governs him, he governs them. Thus, the parent not only has a natural right, but acquires a political right to command them; he is the author and the support of his family; but he is also its constituted ruler.

By the mid-eighteenth century, however, new ideas about individual freedom and democracy were stirring the colonies. And by the time Tocqueville visited the United States in 1831, they had evidently worked a revolution in the family as well as in the nation's political structure: he observes, "When the condition of society becomes democratic, and men adopt as their general principle that it is good and lawful to judge of all things for one's self, . . . the power which the opinions of a father exercise over those of his sons diminishes, as well as his legal power." To Tocqueville, this shift away from strict patriarchal rule signaled a change in the emotional climate of families: "as manners and laws become more democratic, the relation of father and son becomes more intimate and more affectionate; rules and authority are less talked of, confidence and tenderness are oftentimes increased, and it would seem that the natural bond is drawn closer." In his view, the American family heralded a new era in human relations. Freed from the rigid hierarchy of the past, parents and children could meet as near equals, joined by "filial love and fraternal affection."

This vision of the democratic family — a harmonious association of parents and children united by love and trust — has mesmerized popular culture in the United States. From the nineteenth century to the present, popular novels, magazines, music, and advertising images have glorified the comforts of loving domesticity. In recent years, we've probably absorbed our strongest impressions of the ideal family from television situation comedies. In the 1950s we had the Andersons on *Father Knows Best,* the Stones on *The Donna Reed Show,* and the real-life Nelson family on *The Adventures of Ozzie & Harriet.* Over the next three decades, the model stretched to include single parents, second marriages, and interracial adoptions on *My Three Sons, The Brady Bunch,* and *Diff'rent Strokes,* but the underlying ideal of wise, loving parents and harmonious, happy families remained unchanged. But today, America has begun to worry about the health of its families: even the families on TV no longer reflect the domestic tranquility of the Anderson clan. America is becoming increasingly ambivalent about the future of family life, and perhaps with good reason. The myth of the family scarcely reflects the complexities of modern American life. High divorce rates, the rise of the single-parent household, the impact of remarriage, and a growing frankness about domestic violence are transforming the way we see family life; many families must also contend with the stresses of urban life and economic hardship. Such pressures on and within the family can be particularly devastating to young people, as the high suicide rate for teens grimly attests. In our world it's no longer clear whether the family is a blessing to be cherished or an ordeal to be survived.

This chapter examines the myth of the model family and explores alternative visions of family life. It opens with three paintings by Norman Rockwell that express the meaning of "family values" circa 1950, an era some consider the heyday of American family life. The next four readings challenge the ideal of the harmonious nuclear family. First, E. J. Graff uses historical information to sweep away common misconceptions about the traditional family and to recommend more flexible and realistic models, including, for example, gay marriage. In "Looking for Work," Gary Soto recalls his boyhood desire to live the myth and recounts his humorously futile attempts to transform his working-class Chicano family into a facsimile of the Cleavers on *Leave It to Beaver.* Anndee Hochman's painful memoir about her parents' response to her coming out as a lesbian invites you to consider the chilling idea that behind family unity lurks the demand for utter conformity. Stephanie Coontz then takes a close look at the 1950s family, explaining its lasting appeal to some Americans but also documenting its dark side.

The essay that follows, by conservative commentator Danielle Crittenden, defends traditional family values, suggesting that their decline accounts for many of the problems she sees in society. Next you'll find a Visual Portfolio that offers you the chance to practice your hand at interpreting images. The images provided in this collection suggest some of the complex ways the contemporary American family intersects with issues of gender, race, and media. In "The Military-Nintendo Complex," the chapter's media selection, John Naisbitt warns that many parents are blithely ignoring an insidious threat to their children — computer games that teach violent behavior.

The chapter concludes with four readings that explore alternative family structures and show families functioning well under trying circumstances. In "An Indian Story," Roger Jack paints a warm, magical portrait of the bond between a Native American boy and his caretaker aunt. Bebe Moore Campbell's "Envy" is a fascinating personal account of growing up father-hungry in a female-dominated African American family. In "Black Women and Motherhood," Patricia Hill Collins presents another perspective on the many roles played by black mothers and offers a model of the extended family that defies the narrow definitions of the Eurocentric family myth. Finally, Melvin Dixon's poem "Aunt Ida Pieces a Quilt" celebrates a woman who rises above prejudice to commemorate a nephew lost to AIDS. These closing selections affirm the continuing power of families as sources of acceptance, love, and support.

Sources

Gerda Lerner, *The Creation of Patriarchy*. New York: Oxford University Press, 1986.

Steven Mintz and Susan Kellogg, *Domestic Revolutions: A Social History of American Family Life*. New York: Free Press, 1988.

Alexis de Tocqueville, *Democracy in America*. 1835; New York: Vintage Books, 1990.

BEFORE READING

- Spend ten minutes or so jotting down every word, phrase, or image you associate with the idea of "family." Write as freely as possible, without censoring your thoughts or worrying about grammatical correctness. Working in small groups, compare lists and try to categorize your responses. What assumptions about families do they reveal?

- Draw a visual representation of your family. This could take the form of a graph, chart, diagram, map, cartoon, symbolic picture, or literal portrait. Don't worry if you're not a skillful artist: the main point is to convey an idea, and even stick figures can speak eloquently. When you're finished, write a journal entry about your drawing. Was it easier to depict some feelings or ideas visually than it would have been to describe them in words? Did you find some things about your family difficult or impossible to convey visually? Does your drawing "say" anything that surprises you?

- Do a brief freewrite about the television family — from *The Donna Reed Show* — pictured on the title page of this chapter (p. 17). What can you tell about their relationship? What does this image suggest to you about the ideals and realities of American family life?

A Family Tree, Freedom from Want, and *Freedom from Fear*

NORMAN ROCKWELL

The first "reading" for this book consists of three paintings by Norman Rockwell (1894–1978), one of America's most prolific and popular artists. Together they capture what the idea of family meant to the nation half a century ago, a time some consider the golden age of American family life. A Family Tree *(1959) is an oil painting that, like hundreds of Rockwell's images, became cover art for* The Saturday Evening Post. Freedom from Want *and* Freedom from Fear *are part of Rockwell's* Four Freedoms *series (1943). Their appearance in the* Post, *along with* Freedom of Speech *and* Freedom of Worship, *generated millions of requests for reprints.*

A Family Tree, by Norman Rockwell.

Freedom from Want, by Norman Rockwell.

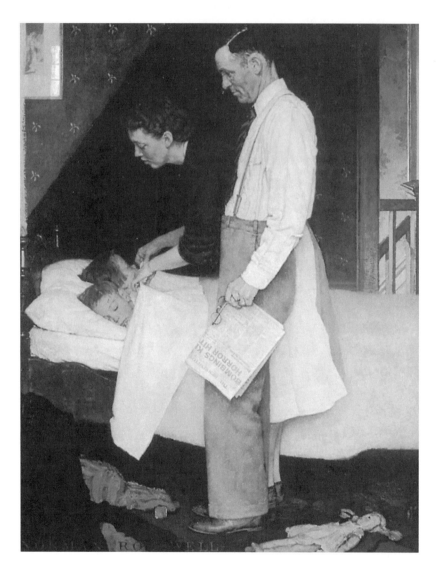

Freedom from Fear, by Norman Rockwell.

ENGAGING THE TEXT

1. What is the usual purpose of family trees? Why do you think they are important to many Americans? How significant is a family tree to you or others in your family?

2. Discuss the details of *A Family Tree* and their significance. For example, identify each figure and explain what it contributes to Rockwell's composite picture of America.

3. How does Rockwell's painting differ from your image of a typical family tree? What is its basic message? How accurate do you consider its portrayal of the American family?

4. What is the appeal of *Freedom from Want?* What ideas about family does it assume or promote? What's your own reaction to Rockwell's image? Support your answers with reference to details of the painting.

5. In *Freedom from Fear*, why did Rockwell choose this moment to paint? What can you guess about the relationships within the family? What about its relationship to the rest of the world?

EXPLORING CONNECTIONS

6. Compare Rockwell's paintings to the frontispiece photo for this chapter (p. 17). How does Rockwell's vision of family life differ from that depicted by the photo?

EXTENDING THE CRITICAL CONTEXT

7. Research your family tree and make your own drawing of it. How does it compare to the family tree Rockwell has created? Write a journal entry or short essay about your family tree.

8. Rockwell's family tree appeared in 1959. Draw an updated version for today.

9. What might pictures entitled *Freedom from Want* and *Freedom from Fear* look like if they were painted today? Describe in detail a scene or image to fit each of these titles; if possible, draw, paint, or photograph your image.

What Makes a Family?
E. J. GRAFF

The question posed by E. J. Graff — "What makes a family?" — sounds simple enough, but it's surprisingly hard to answer. The very notion of what constitutes a family has changed dramatically throughout history; the "traditional" 1950s television image of a nuclear family, for example, actually promoted a relatively new conception of family life, one that bore little resemblance to the living arrangements of most Americans. Whatever you think a family is or should be, Graff is likely to challenge and complicate your thinking. As she gives a historical overview of how the family has been defined in Western culture, she also demonstrates how definitions of "family" are crucial to a society's understanding of work, authority, gender, money, social class, and law. Graff (b. 1958) is a journalist whose work has appeared in the New York Times, Ms., *and* Out; *this selection is from her recent book, which poses another excellent question:* What Is Marriage For? *(1999).*

One of the first and most urgent questions that faces any society is: How can we best ensure that children will grow up into a successful adulthood? The contemporary intuition that a child must be raised by his "natural" parents is one about which many feel quite passionately. It's therefore exceedingly disconcerting to discover how recently we got sealed off into the "family" we now call traditional, the one whose goal is to provide a safe and secure nest for the tender young. Of course, the idea that a child belongs to its parents is ancient — but the key phrase in that sentence is belongs *to*, not belongs *with*. In many eras, while plenty of parents raised their own children, they also felt free to ship them off with impunity, from infancy through adolescence.

Most historians warn readers that to grasp "family" history you must first abandon the idea that you already know what "family" means. "Family" seems to be a word invented by Humpty Dumpty, who told Alice that "a word means what I say it should mean, neither more nor less: the question is, which is to be master, that is all." Historians always remind us of the word's etymology. Our "family" is related to its root in the Roman *"familia"* just about as closely as a Chevy Suburban is related to an elephant- and camel-drawn caravan. Sure, both of them move — but who's inside, and what are they doing in there?

Inside the Roman *familia* was everyone in the household: legitimate children, adopted adults, secretaries and other dependents, slaves of various ages. "The Romans rarely used it to mean family in the sense of kin," writes Roman family historian Suzanne Dixon.[1] What counted, rather, was ownership. The words for children, slaves, and servants were so often interchanged that historians can't always tell how many of which lived under one roof. And for good reason. The patriarch's rule was complete: he could educate, beat, sell, give, indenture, marry off, endow, or kill any one of them, almost at will.[2]

He could, of course, care for his *familia* as well. Romans lived with their slaves and servants so closely that it "in some ways resembled kinship, even if the slaves were always in the position of poor relations," explains Dixon.[3] Masters might inscribe the tombstones of especially beloved slaves in grieving words that mourned someone expected to care for the masters during old age; ex-slaves might write similar gravestone encomiums to former masters. (Did slaves really feel affection for their masters, or were they hoping to keep those ex-masters' children as patrons? Probably both — although at this distance, it's hard to read between the epitaphs' lines.) Dixon cites one hard-fought custody battle between a freed slave and her former owners over who would keep the ex-slave's daughter Patronia Iusta, a custody battle as vicious as that over Baby M.[4] The masters "clearly wanted to treat [Patronia] as a daughter and were prepared to insist on her servile birth as a means of keeping her from her mother."[5] Could it be that the daughter was biologically the patriarch's?

Maybe — or maybe not. Romans didn't consider birth the only way to acquire offspring. Just as they felt free to expose (in other words, kill) any child they didn't need, they also felt free to adopt — adults, that is. Adoption's goal was not to nurture a child but to install an heir to carry on the house, a goal better served by adults — and so nearly all adoptions were of grown men (yes, men). Adoptees were usually nephews or grandsons or cousins, sometimes adopted through a will. As one historian explains, "A citizen of Rome did not 'have' a child; he 'took' a child. . . . The Romans made no fetish of natural kinship."[6] Choice, not biology, made a *familia*.

Since so much of the Romans' attitude toward human life seems foreign, perhaps it's not strange to discover their families feel foreign as well (except by comparing them with Southern plantation owners who might sentimentalize their extended enslaved "family"). What *is* strange is

[1]"*The Romans rarely used it to mean family*": Dixon, 2. [All notes are the author's, except 4, 13, 14, 23–26, 33, and 35.]

[2]The Roman patriarch's legal authority to kill his family members was used mostly for newborns; there were social limits on his right to kill his family's adults, although the symbolic threat could be usefully wielded. Dixon, 36, and Susan Treggiari, personal communication.

[3]"*in some ways resembled kinship*": Dixon, 114.

[4]*Baby M:* The child in a nationally publicized legal case in which a surrogate mother fought the biological father for legal custody.

[5]"*clearly wanted to treat [Patronia] as a daughter*": Dixon, 113.

[6]"*A citizen of Rome did not 'have' a child*": Veyne, "The Roman Empire," in Ariès and Duby, vol. 1, 9.

discovering that the Romans' idea that "family" meant everyone under one roof, biologically related or not, lasted until the eighteenth century's end.[7]

Historians and anthropologists frankly throw up their hands and admit they can't define "family" in a way that works universally. "Before the eighteenth century no European language had a term for the mother-father-children group,"[8] one pair of historians writes, mainly because that grouping — although widespread — wasn't important enough to need its own word. A 1287 Bologna statute defined "family" to include a father, mother, brothers, sisters, and daughters-in-law (sons brought home their wives), but Italy was an exception. For Northern and Western Europe, the extended family is a myth. New-marrieds almost always launched their own households — if their parents signed over the farm, the contract often included a clause insisting that the old folks must be built their own separate dwelling — and socialized as much or more with neighbors and work partners as with kin. Rather, the European family, like the Roman, included people we'd consider legal strangers: they were grouped together in that word "family" not by blood but by whether they lived under one roof. "Most households included non-kin inmates, sojourners, boarders or lodgers occupying rooms vacated by children or kin, as well as indentured apprentices and resident servants, employed either for domestic work about the house or as an additional resident labour force for the field or shop," writes historian Lawrence Stone of the British between 1500 and 1800. "This composite group was confusingly known as a 'family.'"[9] A baker might have a family of a dozen or fifteen, including four journeymen, two apprentices, two maidservants, and three or four bio-children, all of whom worked, lived, and ate under his roof, at his table, and by his rules. A baronet might have a family of thirty-seven, including seven daughters and twenty-eight servants. Or was that ten daughters and twenty-five servants? Historians grind their teeth as they try to figure out from church, census, and tax records which "menservants" and "maids" were children, stepchildren, or nephews and which were hired labor. Children, apprentices, servants — all were under the master's rule. In other words, until very recently, not love, not biology, but labor made a family.

Sometimes, of course, that family's labor was less than voluntary. As Africans crossed the ocean into slavery, they often created "uncle-" and

---

[7]For fuller discussions of the frustrating plasticity of "the family" (and therefore the impossibility of defining it and studying it as a single phenomenon), see, for instance, Dixon, Ch. 1; Gies and Gies, introduction; Burguière and Lebrun, "The One Hundred and One Families of Europe," in Burguière et al., vol. 2, 1–39; Cherlin, 85–87; Stone, FSM, 37–66; Laslett, Oosterveen, and Smith, introduction; and de La Roncière, "Tuscan Notables on the Eve of the Renaissance," in Ariès and Duby, vol. 2, 157–170.

[8]"Before the eighteenth century no European language": Gies and Gies, 4.

[9]"Most households included non-kin": Stone, FSM, 28. For illuminating glimpses of demographic and family historians straining to determine which "servants" were or were not biological children, see, for instance, Laslett, Oosterveen, and Smith, and Rotberg and Rabb.

"aunthood" amongst shipmates. Those new-hatched kinship links were taken so seriously that they were taught to the children — and even, as much as possible, to the masters — by insisting that a particular woman or man be respected as "Aunt" or "Uncle," with all the attendant obligations.

While it might seem strange to see hired or enslaved or indentured labor called "family" — not just patronizing but actually meaningless — it makes more sense when you remember that children, whether bio- or borrowed, were laborers. By age four, a child might be minding the infants; by age six he or she was herding geese, fishing, gathering firewood, drawing water, doing laundry, sieving flour, carrying goods to market, and so on. That might be at home — or it might not. Depending on era and region, a late medieval or early modern British or French or Swiss middle- or upper-class man indentured or "fostered out" his children — at age six or eight or ten or, at the very latest, twelve — as servants or apprentices in other families. Just as regularly, he took relatives' or friends' or neighbors' children to be servants or apprentices or pages in his own. Aristocrats, shopkeepers, artisans, lawyers, butchers, blacksmiths: everyone did it, however rich or poor. The custom seems to have hung on longer in Britain than on the Continent. One sixteenth-century Italian traveler wrote,

> The want of affection in the English is strongly manifested towards their children . . . at the age of seven or nine years at the utmost, they put them out, both males and females, to hard service in the houses of other people . . . and few are born who are exempted from this fate, for everyone, however rich he may be, sends away his children in to the houses of others, whilst he, in return, receives those of strangers into his own. And on enquiring the reason for the severity, they answered that they did it in order that their children might learn better manners.[10]

No good father wanted to see his child morally warped by his own, or his wife's, over-tender affections.

But children didn't leave their parents only at seven or eight; they often *started* life with "strangers." Until the eighteenth century, in a startling number of Western societies, regions, and eras, infants and toddlers — except those of the extremely poor — were sent off to wetnurses miles away on a farm or hidden in the manor's back halls, despite (or because of?) the fact that wetnursed children died at a much higher rate. Among Tuscan pre-Renaissance householders, for instance, three out of four children spent their first months away from their families — more than half until they were eighteen months old.[11] Not always, not everywhere, but often enough that, for centuries, the Catholic Church inveighed vehemently

10

---

[10]"*The want of affection*": Hanawalt, 157.
[11]Tuscan wetnursing statistics given in de La Roncière, in Ariès and Duby, vol. 2, 220.

against wetnursing — to the point of commissioning Madonna-and-child paintings as propaganda, one historian believes.[12]

In other words, a child might well live with her own parents only from age two to age nine, making Mom and Dad just one stop in her peripatetic[13] family life. And why not? In some ways, which "family" you lived with didn't matter, since you were always under someone's authority: you had no local social or political power until you ruled a household yourself. That throws new light on the word "patronizing": whether your patron or *pater*, the master was equally able to rule and condescend to you. The difference between servitude for an upper-class youngster and servitude for everyone else: the young male aristocrat knew someday he'd be in command. In the baker's or tanner's or husbandman's[14] "family," sons, daughters, apprentices, maidservants, and journeymen might someday hope to be master or mistress themselves — but only if they made enough money to marry and found a "family" themselves. What's different in our own time: today's young people feel free to marry *before* they've finished their apprenticeships and saved a down payment on a house, whether via medical school or working a UPS route. We get sex and companionship comparatively young; but (except for that blip downward in the 1950s, when making a living was startlingly easy) most of us who believe that our futures can be prosperous wait until we're financially settled before we start making babies.

But the household merry-go-round was not as orderly as those descriptions imply. Often, children spilled into a new family because they lost their own. Even if you and your brother were the two out of three children who lived to adulthood, you probably didn't get there with two parents — either because of desertion, plague, famine, flu, fever, childbirth, or accident. "Less than half of the children who reached adulthood did so while both their parents were alive," explains Lawrence Stone.[15] Marriages lasted, on average, seventeen to twenty-two years, depending on region and century — which is how long my own parents' marriage lasted (a pretty good run when you realize they raced down the aisle at barely twenty-one and twenty-four during the 1950s marriage madness, each a significant five years younger than Europe's historic norms).

Although I was nineteen and off in college when my parents split, my baby sister was only six — and therefore grew up in a stepfamily, making her upbringing more "traditional" than mine. Since Roman aristocrats divorced at will and children always stayed with their fathers — who some-

---

[12]The Catholic Church commissioned "pictures of the Madonna suckling the Child, a representation that must have stood as a perpetual reproach to those mothers, not only from the richer households, who had their children breast-fed by others, a practice that the Church had tried to stop as far back as the eighth century. . . .": Goody, 154.

[13]*peripatetic:* Traveling about, itinerant.

[14]*husbandman:* Farmer.

[15]*"Less than half of the children"*: Stone, *FSM*, 50.

times sent the kids home to be raised by granddad — most Roman upper-class children grew up alongside step- and half-sibs and cousins, in addition to semi-acknowledged half-sibs born to their father's masters/slaves. At the end of the seventeenth century, 50 percent of all French children had lived with a stepparent at some time in their lives.[16] Roughly a quarter of all British premodern families included stepchildren or, at the very least, orphaned or abandoned nephews and nieces.[17] That's quite a bit more than the 11.3 percent of American children who lived in stepfamilies in 1990.[18] Remarriage was often the time to "foster out" or indenture the first marriage's children, in contracts binding for roughly seven years. Some children did spend their entire early lives with one biological mother and one biological father — but that was not as common as it is today.

Today's families, historians note over and over, are vastly more stable than their predecessors, however defined. To put it another way, children today spend twice as many years with their bio-families than they did in the past. One historian suggests it's no wonder far more murders happen within the family today (only 8 percent of fourteenth-century Britain's homicides were between family members, while today's proportions are 53 percent in Britain and 30 percent in the United States).[19] You have to feel pretty strongly to kill someone — and perhaps the earlier versions of the family weren't confined tightly enough to cause our era's nuclear explosions.

In 1996, *Christianity Today* called Gary Bauer, president of the Family   15
Research Council, a "defender of the two-parent family and other radical ideas." The "radical" tag, surely intended as an ironic comment on today's morals, turns out to be historically accurate. In fact, the nuclear family has so recently become the standard household unit that U.S. demographers can't accurately track it before 1940.[20] Bauer and his ideological kin want the definition of "family" to remain static at the recently minted sense of "people related by blood, marriage, or adoption." But why should the rest of us pay attention to his prescription? The adaptable human young have throughout history managed to grow into successful adulthood under the tutelage of wetnurses, tutors, godparents, stepparents, nannies, uncles, neighbors, masters, lords — whichever version the ever-vanishing family

[16]Seventeenth-century French stepchildren: Burguière and Lebrun, in Burguière et al., vol. 2, 59.

[17]British premodern children in stepfamilies: Stone, *FSM,* 46–50.

[18]U.S. Bureau of the Census, 1992, "Marriage, Divorce, and Remarriage in the 1990s," quoted in D. Popenoe, 127.

[19]Fourteenth-century and contemporary British family homicide rates: Hanawalt, 208, and Stone, *FSM,* 77.

[20]Limited demographic history for the nuclear family: Howard V. Hayghe, Division of Labor Force Statistics, "Family members in the work force," *Monthly Labor Review,* March 1990, 14–19. Presumably demographers' change to using the nuclear family as a census standard came as sprawling rural families became fewer, and as fewer urban families kept servants or boarders.

happens to take in a given lifetime, region, and class. We might, however, want to be wary of the tightly confined stationwagon version, which did leave an awful lot of people carsick (or rather, depressed, addicted, eating-disordered) before many women and children burst out of it, gasping for air.

Despite this century's uprush in family stability, the 1930s, 1940s, and 1950s — like our own time — saw a flood of writing about the family's imminent death. As one pair of historians recently wrote about Scandinavia, which today has (as it has had historically) the highest rate of cohabitation and unmarried births. "The irony remains, however, that during the whole period of the 'death throes of the family,' the family continued to prosper. Although we can nowadays establish that the intellectuals were wrong, they were no less anxious about the . . . fall in the birth rate, relaxed divorce laws and premarital sexual relations, etc. What they forgot, however, is that the family is not a thing but a network of human relations, which survive even when their forms change."[21]

What Do We Do About Those Little Bastards?[22]

Among the many places we can see change in family forms is in the changing meaning of the word "bastard." Keeping parents tied to their children — and ensuring that people made only babies that they could and would feed, clothe, and rear responsibly — has always been one of society's key interests in "the family." And so, since marriage was the one and only way to be a fully functioning economic unit, societies urgently worked to confine parenthood within marriage — or to put it more clearly, if you were going to have a baby, you had to marry first. From Murphy Brown to Heather's two mommies to Madonna,[23] this mandate has notoriously collapsed — giving rise to a great deal of political hand-wringing. Not surprisingly, during today's boom in independent motherhood, we may use "bastard" as a bad word meaning an especially bad person — but we no longer use it to mean someone stuck permanently in an outcast (or rather, undercaste) status because of his parents' premarital sex. When and why did that stop being so sternly enforced? What has made possible today's unrepentant and unpunished surge in mom-only childrearing? Have we fallen from a moral order in which virginal brides-in-white patiently awaited their wombs' owners to a moral chaos in which loose women employ their wombs with dangerous recklessness — or have economic changes altered mother-

---

[21]*"The irony remains, however"*: Gaunt and Nyström, in Burguière et al., vol. 2, 486–487.

[22]Much of the bastardy discussion is based on Laslett et al., *Bastardy.*

[23]*Murphy Brown . . . to Madonna:* Each of these became a symbol in the national debate over "family values." In the TV sitcom *Murphy Brown,* the title character chooses to raise her child without the biological father. *Heather Has Two Mommies* is a children's book by Lesléa Newman in which a young girl lives with her two lesbian mothers. Pop superstar Madonna's single-motherhood was a hot topic in the 1990s.

and fatherhood, making the two parents far more equivalent? In other words, inside the book's title question[24] lurks yet another one: what is "legitimacy" for?

Bastardy really did once bar you from your class or caste, from the property and status and possibilities you'd have had if your parents had married. And yet European history teems with a lot more bastards — and a lot more brides preggers[25] at the altar — than most of us would suspect. Or does it? How do you know which child's a bastard and which one's legitimate — or to put it differently, who counts as married? The answer depends on who's counting, and why. Different groups answered that question differently, based on their own worries — worries unrelated to today's psychological concerns about children needing to know their two biological parents.

For ruling classes, the worry was: Can that baby claim my property or power? Almost everyone else was asking: Who's gonna pay for that baby? Among Greek citizens, that first question was a stern one. They wanted to be absolutely sure each new citizen was properly conceived, that he had two citizen-grandfathers who fully approved of sending property and status his way, that no concubine's bastard claimed political or inheritance rights. This concern, shared by the British aristocracy, was put with admirable clarity by Samuel Johnson:[26] "Consider of what importance to society the chastity of women is. Upon that all the property in the world depends. We hang a thief for stealing a sheep, but the unchastity of woman transfers sheep, and farm, and all from the right owner."[27] Besides worrying about wives or daughters who foolishly believed their bodies to be their own, a British aristocrat wanted protection in case some kitchen maid insisted that his philandering (or rapist) son must marry her and legitimate their baby. British jurist William Blackstone wrote that to allow children to be legitimized by their parents' later marriage "is plainly a great discouragement to the matrimonial state; to which one main inducement is usually not only the desire of having *children,* but also of procreating lawful heirs."[28] Clearly that's what the British aristocracy thought marriage was for. As a result, in British law a bastard was *fillius nullius,* literally, the child of no one. No one was obliged to care for her: she could not legally demand food, clothing, housing, or inheritance. In practice, that wasn't much different from the Greeks and Romans, who "exposed" or abandoned any child they didn't want. Across medieval and early modern Europe, from 68 to 91 percent of infants sent to foundling hospitals died before they reached age six — and foundlings'

---

[24]*the book's title question:* Graff's book is titled *What Is Marriage For?*

[25]*preggers:* Pregnant (slang).

[26]*Samuel Johnson:* British author (1709–1784) who created the first comprehensive English dictionary.

[27]*"Consider of what importance to society":* Johnson, quoted in Laslett et al., *Bastardy,* 214.

[28]*"is plainly a great discouragement":* Blackstone, quoted in Laslett, Grossberg, 198.

death rates actually went *up* in the eighteenth century. And even if the bastards managed to make it to adulthood, their parents had guaranteed them a harder life than usual for a child from their class: Premodern aristocracies wouldn't or couldn't pass them a full inheritance, while German guilds refused membership to any child who could not prove "honest birth."

Fillius nullius, of course, meant the most to aristocratic men who   20
wanted to protect their property from the consequences of their brothelgoing. Everyone else worried more that the child would, in their language, "fall to the parish." Except for the period when the early Protestants were actively policing souls (whipping fornicators or putting them in the stocks, even if the fallen pair was engaged), medieval and early modern European societies worried less about preventing sin than about controlling costs. Priests trying to convert the Irish complained that mothers didn't think an unmarried daughter's pregnancy was as bad as, say, theft. The French and Germans had a category called "mantle children" — children who were made legitimate by being held under a mantle during their mother's subsequent wedding (not necessarily to the biological father).

Of course, individual interests were always at stake in deciding who was a bastard and who was legitimate. One fourteenth-century English peasant tried to bastardize his older brother "because he was born before the marriage was solemnized at the church porch, but after the plighting of troth privately between them. Robert, the elder brother, says it is the custom on the lord's land in these parts for the elder brother, born after trothplight, to be heir."[29] The peasant jury agreed with Robert — endorsing the idea that a working couple's bodies were their own. Had the brothers been an aristocrat's sons, Robert would have been out on his ear. In just the same way, the Anglican Church was more interested in a child's and her mother's souls than in inheritance rights — and so decreed that a child was legitimate so long as her mother married, no matter when (or, for that matter, whom). Since the child was then considered legit ecclesiastically but illegit civilly, her condition was called "special bastardy." Robert's parents certainly behaved as many of my friends have: living together and having kids before bothering to make things formal. Unlike today's pundits, the peasant jury was *not* shocked; they saw it as customary. The local Church was more concerned that the mother get married to someone, anyone, using her children's legitimacy as a kind of carrot to urge her into wedlock, than it was with punishing their slippage.

So were your parents acceptably coupled or illegally fornicating? Once again, the answer depended on who you asked.

And so who can be surprised that Robert's semibastard status was shared by a great many people? In late-sixteenth-century England, for instance, one out of three first babies was conceived before — not after — the wedding. That dropped to one out of six in the late seventeenth

---

[29]*"because he was born before the marriage"*: Hanawalt, 72.

century, when Puritans were strictly enforcing marriage's boundaries, but bounced back up to one in three at the nineteenth century's end.[30] In post-colonial North America, the number of women whose first children were born soon after marriage was one in three in 1800; this percentage dipped slightly in the Victorian era and spiked back up to one in four by 1910.[31]

What can such numbers mean? In large part, it means that "marriage" was a less formal concept in the past than today. Scandinavians especially disliked the idea that any institution, church or state, had to authorize or bless a pairing, and so often didn't hold the wedding until after the child was born — making the wedding a celebration not just of the pairing but of their fruitfulness. (In other words, Scandinavians' current unmarried birthrates — roughly one out of two, the highest in the developed world — are the result *not* of recent social policies but of stubbornly private traditions.)[32] Meanwhile, in most communities the gap between first pledge and final vows — between betrothal and wedding — was a kind of marriage twilight in which the couple was neither exactly married nor exactly single. The engaged pair might well live together under one roof: In early medieval Jewish families, for instance, the prospective groom moved in with his promised bride's family while he got his financial footing, while in many Italian city-states, the bride-to-be was sent to grow up in her future husband's household — at age five, or eight, or ten. Even the northern medieval peasants, the young people who, after saving up a marriage "portion," were finally ready to pick themselves a spouse, often did so via some hanky-panky; they might even wait to see if they were fertile before they got formal. In other words, today's apparently startling habit of getting married only after you're pregnant, or even with your children gathered round, is actually quite traditional. What's more, all these "bridal pregnancies" (as social historians delicately phrase it), trothplight babies, and mantle children reveal that marriage has never been a simple either/or question. Rather, marriage's boundaries are blurry. And exactly what counts as marriage, when, changes according to whose interests are at stake.

So how many children were born entirely outside wedlock — or to put   25
it differently, how many were real bastards? To figure that out from the demographic records, historians have to figure out how to define a marriage — which they wrestle with for pages upon pages. One key social historian, Peter Laslett, throws up his hands and concludes that whatever the local community counted as a "regular union" was — although by that measure, you'd have to include my heterosexual friends who've lived together for sixteen years and are treated as coupled by employers, banks, hospitals,

[30]Statistics on pregnant English brides from Laslett, in Laslett et al., *Bastardy,* 23.

[31]Figures for postcolonial American pregnancies before marriage from Wells, in Laslett et al., *Bastardy,* 353.

[32]Scandinavian "out of wedlock" birthrates from Laslett et al., *Bastardy,* 56, 329, 330; and Gaunt and Nyström, "The Scandinavian Model," in Burguière et al., vol. 2, 488.

friends, and family (although not insurers or tax law). Across the ocean, Americans hated to bastardize a child (partly for democratic reasons, rejecting the aristocratic British insistence on primogeniture[33] and lineage), and so colonial judges and state legislators temporarily invented "common law marriage" — a form that was widely accepted during the nineteenth century and then outlawed by most states in the twentieth; it exists today in only thirteen states. "If two parties, living together, speak of each other as husband and wife, this public acknowledgment is all that is requisite to constitute their relation in the eyes of the law a perfectly valid marriage," one nineteenth-century legal commentator explained to his audience, *"yet children born from such a union and legitimate in New York, are counted as bastards by every nation of Europe."*[34] Bastardy — in other words, marriage — lies in the eyes (or nation, or class) of the beholder.

For the same reason that most European communities and authorities were willing to legitimate a child *post hoc* — because once the mother married there was a husband helping to feed and house that child — most early modern European law codes made it almost impossible for a husband to bastardize his wife's child. Even if you gave birth three years after your husband had left on a long sea voyage, even if when he finally got back your village held a *charivari* (parading you both on donkeys while jeering and flinging mudballs and maybe covering you with honey to attract stinging insects) to shame you for being a whore and him for being a cuckold — even then, in local law, your husband was your child's father. Period. Somebody had to support that baby, and that somebody was your Mr. — unless he exercised his traditional veto by disappearing.

So what? Why should societies care about children born outside marriage at all? Why not just let women have babies whenever they want? Why pressure men into marriage?

Every historian, anthropologist, or sociologist who writes about bastards mentions anthropologist Bronislaw Malinowski's "principle of legitimacy": the idea that each child must have a "sociological father" — not necessarily the genetic dad — willing to be "guardian and protector, the male link between the child and the rest of the community." In some societies that man is the maternal uncle. In some, it can be a dead man, as when early Hebrew societies charged men with marrying a brother's childless widow and begetting and rearing a child who carries the brother's name. (Onan's famous sin[35] came when he pulled back from this obligatory duty.) In one well-known New Testament family, that man was Joseph, through whom Mary's miraculously conceived son claims descent from King David (or has it claimed for him by his followers). In most modern law codes, it's still the mother's

[33]*primogeniture:* System of inheritance in which the eldest son inherits.

[34]*"If two parties, living together":* (italics in original) Laslett et al., 11.

[35]*Onan's famous sin:* See chapter 38 of Genesis in the Bible. Today, "Onanism" refers both to masturbation and to withdrawal in sexual intercourse before ejaculation.

husband, even if (as in one famous U.S. case, *Michael H v. Gerald D*)[36] everyone knows the child was conceived during an adulterous affair, or even if the child was made with the help of a doctor and an anonymous stranger's sperm. According to Malinowski, by punishing anyone who doesn't follow the rule of il/legitimacy, a society ensures it won't have too many mouths to feed.

From this point of view, what is marriage for? Discouraging overbreeding — first, by insisting that each child be assigned to a working wallet, and second, by punishing children not so assigned via abandonment, disdain, and poverty.

This makes sense when your income and status — whether a landed   30
barony or guild membership or tenant plot — must be inherited from some man, because men, and only men, control all resources, financial, social, and political. Or to put it in terms that Samuel Johnson and William Blackstone would understand: if children matter to men because men want and need heirs, then fathers matter to children because children need property and status. Legitimacy is less urgent when each person forges his or her own future from his or her own efforts — whether that's in our frontier past or our capitalist present.

So what happens when a woman can make her own living, passing on property, skills, and status? Shouldn't, then, a mother be able to assign another woman as her child's sociological "father"? To put it simply: if a dead man, or an uncle, or an absent cuckold, or a holy ghost, or a sperm-bank-supplemented husband can be a sociological "father," why can't I?

Selected Bibliography

Ariès, Philippe, and Georges Duby, eds. *A History of Private Life.* Volumes 1–4. Trans. Arthur Goldhammer. Cambridge, MA: Belknap Press of Harvard University Press, 1987–1991.

Boswell, John. *The Kindness of Strangers: The Abandonment of Children in Western Europe from Late Antiquity to the Renaissance.* London: Penguin, 1989.

Burguière, André, Christiane Klapisch-Zuber, Martine Segalen, and Françoise Zonabend, eds. *A History of the Family.* Volumes 1 and 2. Trans. Sarah Hanbury Tenison, Rosemary Morris, and Andrew Wilson. Cambridge, MA: Belknap Press of Harvard University Press, 1996.

Cherlin, Andrew J. *Marriage, Divorce, Remarriage: Social Trends in the United States.* Rev. ed. Cambridge, MA: Harvard University Press, 1992.

Dixon, Suzanne. *The Roman Family: Ancient Society and History.* Baltimore: Johns Hopkins University Press, 1992.

[36]In the *Michael H v. Gerald D* case, "the state invoked the existence of a marriage to actually *sever* the link between procreation and child-rearing." Brief filed by Robinson, Murray, and Bonauto, for the Supreme Court of the State of Vermont, *Baker v. Vermont,* Spring 1998, 28 and 32.

Gies, Frances, and Joseph Gies. *Marriage and the Family in the Middle Ages.* New York: Harper and Row, 1987.

Goody, Jack. *The Development of the Family and Marriage in Europe.* Cambridge, England: Cambridge University Press, 1983.

Grossberg, Michael. *Governing the Hearth: Law and the Family in Nineteenth-Century America.* Chapel Hill: University of North Carolina Press, 1985.

Hanawalt, Barbara A. *The Ties That Bound: Peasant Families in Medieval England.* New York and Oxford: Oxford University Press, 1986.

Laslett, Peter, Karla Oosterveen, and Richard M. Smith, eds. *Bastardy and Its Comparative History: Studies in the History of Illegitimacy and Marital Nonconformism in Britain, France, Germany, Sweden, North America, Jamaica, and Japan.* Cambridge, MA: Harvard University Press, 1980.

Popenoe, David. *Life Without Father: Compelling New Evidence That Fatherhood and Marriage Are Indispensable for the Good of Children and Society.* New York: Martin Kessler Books, 1996.

Rotberg, Robert I., and Theodore K. Rabb, eds. *Marriage and Fertility: Studies in Interdisciplinary History.* Princeton, NJ: Princeton University Press, 1980.

Stone, Lawrence. *The Family, Sex and Marriage in England, 1500–1800.* Abridged ed. New York: Harper and Row, 1979.

ENGAGING THE TEXT

1. What were some of the key characteristics of the Roman *familia*? Why does Graff want her contemporary audience to understand the *familia*?

2. List the important points Graff makes about European families after the decline of Rome and up to the present. How much of this information is new to you? Does it change your perception of the meaning of "family"? If so, how?

3. Why does Graff's analysis detail how the concept of family in previous centuries differed so greatly from most of our contemporary ideas? What goals does she appear to have beyond those of historical accuracy?

4. What does it mean to say a family is "not a thing but a network of human relations, which survive even when their forms change" (para. 16)? Explain why this definition — quoted from Gaunt and Nyström — is important to Graff's analysis, and explain why you agree or disagree with it.

5. Explain the role of "bastards" in Graff's discussion of what makes a family.

6. Carefully examine the last few paragraphs of this reading selection. What is a "sociological father"? What argument is Graff making at the end of this excerpt from her book, and how valid do you think it is?

EXPLORING CONNECTIONS

7. How might Graff critique the images of family contained in the paintings by Norman Rockwell (pp. 22–24)? Draw an image that captures one or more of the ideas Graff wants to communicate about families.

8. Whether it shows the history of an actual family or a schematized version as in Rockwell's painting (p. 22), a family tree is a metaphor or an analogy. (Whatever they may be, families are not literally trees.) With Graff's arguments in mind, discuss how well the idea of a tree can represent what you know about families. Are there ways in which the tree image or metaphor might be misleading or inaccurate? What other analogies or metaphors can you suggest for depicting family histories?

EXTENDING THE CRITICAL CONTEXT

9. "Illegitimate child" is generally considered a more polite term than "bastard." Discuss the meaning of "bastard," "illegitimate child," "love child," and any similar terms you can think of. What problems, if any, do you see with these terms?

10. Based on this reading selection, how would you expect Graff to answer the question of her book's title — What is marriage for? You can of course check the accuracy of your predictions by consulting the book itself.

11. Write an outline for a children's book set in ancient Rome that takes into account what Graff tells us about the Roman *familia*. Quickly sketch some of the illustrations for this book.

Looking for Work

GARY SOTO

"Looking for Work" is the narrative of a nine-year-old Mexican American boy who wants his family to imitate the "perfect families" he sees on TV. Much of the humor in this essay comes from the author's perspective as an adult looking back at his childhood self, but Soto also respects the child's point of view. In the marvelous details of this midsummer day, Soto captures the interplay of seductive myth and complex reality. Gary Soto (b. 1952) grew up "on the industrial side of Fresno, right smack against a junkyard and the junkyard's cross-eyed German shepherd." Having discovered poetry almost by chance in a city college library, he has now published several volumes of his own, including Junior College *(1997). He has also published essays, prose memoirs, novels for young readers, including* Buried Onions *(1997), and a book of short stories titled* Baseball in April and Other Stories *(1991). "Looking for Work" appeared in* Living Up the Street: Narrative Recollections *(1985). His latest book is* The Effects of Knut Hamsun on a Fresno Boy *(2000).*

One July, while killing ants on the kitchen sink with a rolled newspaper, I had a nine-year-old's vision of wealth that would save us from ourselves. For weeks I had drunk Kool-Aid and watched morning reruns of *Father Knows Best,* whose family was so uncomplicated in its routine that I very much wanted to imitate it. The first step was to get my brother and sister to wear shoes at dinner.

"Come on, Rick — come on, Deb," I whined. But Rick mimicked me and the same day that I asked him to wear shoes he came to the dinner table in only his swim trunks. My mother didn't notice, nor did my sister, as we sat to eat our beans and tortillas in the stifling heat of our kitchen. We all gleamed like cellophane, wiping the sweat from our brows with the backs of our hands as we talked about the day: Frankie our neighbor was beat up by Faustino; the swimming pool at the playground would be closed for a day because the pump was broken.

Such was our life. So that morning, while doing-in the train of ants which arrived each day, I decided to become wealthy, and right away! After downing a bowl of cereal, I took a rake from the garage and started up the block to look for work.

We lived on an ordinary block of mostly working class people: ware-housemen, egg candlers,[1] welders, mechanics, and a union plumber. And there were many retired people who kept their lawns green and the gutters uncluttered of the chewing gum wrappers we dropped as we rode by on our bikes. They bent down to gather our litter, muttering at our evilness.

At the corner house I rapped the screen door and a very large woman   5
in a muu-muu answered. She sized me up and then asked what I could do.

"Rake leaves," I answered smiling.

"It's summer, and there ain't no leaves," she countered. Her face was pinched with lines; fat jiggled under her chin. She pointed to the lawn, then the flower bed, and said: "You see any leaves there — or there?" I followed her pointing arm, stupidly. But she had a job for me and that was to get her a Coke at the liquor store. She gave me twenty cents, and after ditching my rake in a bush, off I ran. I returned with an unbagged Pepsi, for which she thanked me and gave me a nickel from her apron.

I skipped off her porch, fetched my rake, and crossed the street to the next block where Mrs. Moore, mother of Earl the retarded man, let me weed a flower bed. She handed me a trowel and for a good part of the morning my fingers dipped into the moist dirt, ripping up runners of Bermuda grass. Worms surfaced in my search for deep roots, and I cut them in halves, tossing them to Mrs. Moore's cat who pawed them playfully as they dried in the sun. I made out Earl whose face was pressed to the back window of the house, and although he was calling to me I couldn't understand what he was trying to say. Embarrassed, I worked without looking up, but I imagined his contorted mouth and the ring of keys attached to his belt — keys that jingled with each

---

[1]*egg candler:* One who inspects eggs by holding them up to a light.

palsied step. He scared me and I worked quickly to finish the flower bed. When I did finish Mrs. Moore gave me a quarter and two peaches from her tree, which I washed there but ate in the alley behind my house.

I was sucking on the second one, a bit of juice staining the front of my T-shirt, when Little John, my best friend, came walking down the alley with a baseball bat over his shoulder, knocking over trash cans as he made his way toward me.

Little John and I went to St. John's Catholic School, where we sat   10 among the "stupids." Miss Marino, our teacher, alternated the rows of good students with the bad, hoping that by sitting side-by-side with the bright students the stupids might become more intelligent, as though intelligence were contagious. But we didn't progress as she had hoped. She grew frustrated when one day, while dismissing class for recess, Little John couldn't get up because his arms were stuck in the slats of the chair's backrest. She scolded us with a shaking finger when we knocked over the globe, denting the already troubled Africa. She muttered curses when Leroy White, a real stupid but a great softball player with the gift to hit to all fields, openly chewed his host[2] when he made his First Communion; his hands swung at his sides as he returned to the pew looking around with a big smile.

Little John asked what I was doing, and I told him that I was taking a break from work, as I sat comfortably among high weeds. He wanted to join me, but I reminded him that the last time he'd gone door-to-door asking for work his mother had whipped him. I was with him when his mother, a New Jersey Italian who could rise up in anger one moment and love the next, told me in a polite but matter-of-fact voice that I had to leave because she was going to beat her son. She gave me a homemade popsicle, ushered me to the door, and said that I could see Little John the next day. But it was sooner than that. I went around to his bedroom window to suck my popsicle and watch Little John dodge his mother's blows, a few hitting their mark but many whirring air.

It was midday when Little John and I converged in the alley, the sun blazing in the high nineties, and he suggested that we go to Roosevelt High School to swim. He needed five cents to make fifteen, the cost of admission, and I lent him a nickel. We ran home for my bike and when my sister found out that we were going swimming, she started to cry because she didn't have the fifteen cents but only an empty Coke bottle. I waved for her to come and three of us mounted the bike — Debra on the cross bar, Little John on the handle bars and holding the Coke bottle which we would cash for a nickel and make up the difference that would allow all of us to get in, and me pumping up the crooked streets, dodging cars and pot holes. We spent the day swimming under the afternoon sun, so that when we got home our mom asked us what was darker, the floor or us? She feigned a

---

[2]*his host:* The wafer that represents, in the Catholic sacrament of Communion, the bread of the Last Supper and the body of Christ.

stern posture, her hands on her hips and her mouth puckered. We played along. Looking down, Debbie and I said in unison, "Us."

That evening at dinner we all sat down in our bathing suits to eat our beans, laughing and chewing loudly. Our mom was in a good mood, so I took a risk and asked her if sometime we could have turtle soup. A few days before I had watched a television program in which a Polynesian tribe killed a large turtle, gutted it, and then stewed it over an open fire. The turtle, basted in a sugary sauce, looked delicious as I ate an afternoon bowl of cereal, but my sister, who was watching the program with a glass of Kool-Aid between her knees, said, "Caca."

My mother looked at me in bewilderment. "Boy, are you a crazy Mexican. Where did you get the idea that people eat turtles?"

"On television," I said, explaining the program. Then I took it a step   15
further. "Mom, do you think we could get dressed up for dinner one of these days? David King does."

"Ay, Dios," my mother laughed. She started collecting the dinner plates, but my brother wouldn't let go of his. He was still drawing a picture in the bean sauce. Giggling, he said it was me, but I didn't want to listen because I wanted an answer from Mom. This was the summer when I spent the mornings in front of the television that showed the comfortable lives of white kids. There were no beatings, no rifts in the family. They wore bright clothes; toys tumbled from their closets. They hopped into bed with kisses and woke to glasses of fresh orange juice, and to a father sitting before his morning coffee while the mother buttered his toast. They hurried through the day making friends and gobs of money, returning home to a warmly lit living room, and then dinner. *Leave It to Beaver* was the program I re-played in my mind:

"May I have the mashed potatoes?" asks Beaver with a smile.

"Sure, Beav," replies Wally as he taps the corners of his mouth with a starched napkin.

The father looks on in his suit. The mother, decked out in earrings and a pearl necklace, cuts into her steak and blushes. Their conversation is politely clipped.

"Swell," says Beaver, his cheeks puffed with food.   20

Our own talk at dinner was loud with belly laughs and marked by our pointing forks at one another. The subjects were commonplace.

"Gary, let's go to the ditch tomorrow," my brother suggests. He explains that he has made a life preserver out of four empty detergent bottles strung together with twine and that he will make me one if I can find more bottles. "No way are we going to drown."

"Yeah, then we could have a dirt clod fight," I reply, so happy to be alive.

Whereas the Beaver's family enjoyed dessert in dishes at the table, our mom sent us outside, and more often than not I went into the alley to peek over the neighbor's fences and spy out fruit, apricots or peaches.

I had asked my mom and again she laughed that I was a crazy *chavalo*[3]   25
as she stood in front of the sink, her arms rising and falling with suds, face
glistening from the heat. She sent me outside where my brother and sister
were sitting in the shade that the fence threw out like a blanket. They were
talking about me when I plopped down next to them. They looked at one
another and then Debbie, my eight-year-old sister, started in.

"What's this crap about getting dressed up?"

She had entered her *profanity* stage. A year later she would give up
such words and slip into her Catholic uniform, and into squealing on my
brother and me when we "cussed this" and "cussed that."

I tried to convince them that if we improved the way we looked we
might get along better in life. White people would like us more. They might
invite us to places, like their homes or front yards. They might not hate us
so much.

My sister called me a "craphead," and got up to leave with a stalk of
grass dangling from her mouth. "They'll never like us."

My brother's mood lightened as he talked about the ditch — the white   30
water, the broken pieces of glass, and the rusted car fenders that awaited
our knees. There would be toads, and rocks to smash them.

David King, the only person we knew who resembled the middle class,
called from over the fence. David was Catholic, of Armenian and French
descent, and his closet was filled with toys. A bear-shaped cookie jar, like
the ones on television, sat on the kitchen counter. His mother was remarkably kind while she put up with the racket we made on the street. Evenings,
she often watered the front yard and it must have upset her to see us — my
brother and I and others — jump from trees laughing, the unkillable kids of
the very poor, who got up unshaken, brushed off, and climbed into another
one to try again.

David called again. Rick got up and slapped grass from his pants. When
I asked if I could come along he said no. David said no. They were two
years older so their affairs were different from mine. They greeted one another with foul names and took off down the alley to look for trouble.

I went inside the house, turned on the television, and was about to sit
down with a glass of Kool-Aid when Mom shooed me outside.

"It's still light," she said. "Later you'll bug me to let you stay out longer.
So go on."

I downed my Kool-Aid and went outside to the front yard. No one was   35
around. The day had cooled and a breeze rustled the trees. Mr. Jackson, the
plumber, was watering his lawn and when he saw me he turned away to
wash off his front steps. There was more than an hour of light left, so I took
advantage of it and decided to look for work. I felt suddenly alive as I
skipped down the block in search of an overgrown flower bed and the dime
that would end the day right.

[3]*chavalo:* Kid.

ENGAGING THE TEXT

1. Why is the narrator attracted to the kind of family life depicted on TV? What, if anything, does he think is wrong with his life? Why do his desires apparently have so little impact on his family?

2. Why does the narrator first go looking for work? How has the meaning of work changed by the end of the story, when he goes out again "in search of an overgrown flower bed and the dime that would end the day right"? Explain.

3. As Soto looks back on his nine-year-old self, he has a different perspective on things than he had as a child. How would you characterize the mature Soto's thoughts about his childhood family life? (Was it "a good family"? What was wrong with Soto's thinking as a nine-year-old?) Back up your remarks with specific references to the narrative.

4. Review the story to find each mention of food or drink. Explain the role these references play.

5. Review the cast of "supporting characters" in this narrative — the mother, sister, brother, friends, and neighbors. What does each contribute to the story and in particular to the meaning of family within the story?

EXPLORING CONNECTIONS

6. Read Bebe Moore Campbell's "Envy" (p. 98) or Roger Jack's "An Indian Story" (p. 89) and compare Soto's family to one of the families portrayed in these selections. In particular, consider gender roles, the household atmosphere, and the expectations placed on children and parents.

7. Compare and contrast the relationship of school and family in this narrative to that described by Mike Rose (p. 162), Richard Rodriguez (p. 194), or Inés Hernández-Ávila (p. 207).

8. Like Soto's story, the cartoon on page 55 attests to the power of the media to shape our ideas about family. Write a journal entry describing the media family that most accurately reflects your image of family life. Discuss these entries, and the impact of media on your image of the family, with your classmates.

EXTENDING THE CRITICAL CONTEXT

9. Write a journal entry about a time when you wished your family were somehow different. What caused your dissatisfaction? What did you want your family to be like? Was your dissatisfaction ever resolved?

10. "Looking for Work" is essentially the story of a single day. Write a narrative of one day when you were eight or nine or ten; use details as Soto does to give the events of the day broader significance.

Growing Pains: Beyond "One Big Happy Family"

ANNDEE HOCHMAN

This narrative shows how life in what looks like "one big happy family" can be a lot more complicated when viewed from the inside. Hochman writes evocatively about her childhood and about how her emerging lesbian identity tested the boundaries of family love. Hochman (b. 1962) has worked as a reporter for the Washington Post, *a VISTA volunteer, a counselor for homeless teenagers, and a creative writing teacher. She is author of* Anatomies: A Novella and Stories *(2000) and* Everyday Acts and Small Subversions: Women Reinventing Family, Community, and Home *(1994), in which "Growing Pains" appeared.*

I remember waking up to the smell of salt.

Each August when I was little, my parents loaded the car with Bermuda shorts and groceries, beach towels and Scrabble board, and drove to the New Jersey shore. My great-uncle Bernie Ochman had bought a $16,000 bay-front house there in the mid-1950s; he imagined it as a sort of free-wheeling compound, where all the aunts, grandparents, and cousins of my mother's large extended family could gather each summer.

Bernie died before my parents were married, but my mother carried out his vision with her usual zest. She made sure the taxes on the house were paid quarterly, the water valve was turned on each May, and there were enough hamburgers for everyone on Memorial Day and the Fourth of July.

In August, my parents worked feverishly for two weeks, then packed up and headed to the shore for what my father used to call, with some sarcasm, "a little peace and quiet." We left at night to avoid traffic on the Atlantic City Expressway. I always fell asleep in the car and always woke up as we came over the bay bridge, where the smell of salt, moist and thick, would touch me like a mitten dipped in the ocean.

"Are we there yet?" I'd mumble from the back seat.   5

"Almost," my mom would say, and my dad would turn left, then left again, and park the car as close as he could to the big white house.

I loved the shore house because it was so different from home. The front steps tilted a little. Gray paint flaked off the window frames. Two daybeds in the living room were draped with pea green spreads, and the loveseats wore crunchy plastic slipcovers. The picket fence was red.

Even the architecture broke rules. The front room had been added as an afterthought, a low-budget job. The carpenters never removed what had once been the house's front window, now ridiculous in the wall between the front room and the kitchen. I used to sit on the stairs, tapping on the kitchen window and making faces until my mother or my grandmother or Aunt Sadie looked up from the dishes and waved at me. Then I would collapse in giggles.

Upstairs, there was no hall, no doors on the bedrooms. In fact, the bedrooms were not really separate rooms at all, just thin-walled divisions of the upper floor. The front stairs climbed right into the middle of Aunt Charlotte and Uncle Freddie's room; you could stand on the top step and almost tickle Uncle Freddie's feet.

Walk through that bedroom, and the next one, and the next, and you arrived at the bathroom, which had its own quirks — a white claw-foot tub, a hasty shower rigged up with red rubber tubing, and two doors. When I was older, I would check the sliding locks on both doors several times before I dared to unpeel my damp, sandy bathing suit.

Aunt Sadie and Uncle Izzy slept in the larger of the two rear bedrooms, in twin beds pushed together to make one. The very back room was long and narrow, like a single-lane swimming pool, with windows that let in wet salty air off the bay. My grandparents — Bubie and Pop-pop — slept here.

My mother loves to tell the story of my father's first visit to this family compound, during their courtship. He recoiled at the upstairs setup; a private motel room, with a door that locked, was more what he had in mind. My mother informed him firmly that she was a package deal; if he loved her, he would learn to love her family — the father who smoked terrible cigars, the sister who rolled her hair in Kotex sanitary pads, the mother who stewed bruised peaches in the hot, tiny kitchen. And he could start loving them here, in their peculiar summer habitat.

I thought the house was wonderful. The connecting rooms reminded me of a maze, the sort of place where surprises could hunch in old dressers, under beds. Later I realized how the physical space shaped our time there, dissolving the barriers that, in most houses, separate adults from children, private from communal space, eating from work. At the shore, my friends and I played jacks in the middle of the living room, hide and seek in the freestanding metal closets. When people got hungry, they helped themselves from one of the three refrigerators. If I wanted to be alone, I opened a book.

There was one last room upstairs, an odd sixth bedroom lodged in the center of the house. It was the only bedroom with a door, and it belonged to my parents. When I was younger, I assumed they took that room out of generosity. It was small and dark and hot, and you had to grope for the light switch behind a high wooden headboard. It was also the only room in the house in which two people could have a private talk, or take a nap, without somebody else clomping through on her way to the bathroom.

Much later, the summer I was twenty-two, I finally grasped the full sig-   15
nificance of that room and made love with Jon Feldstein in it one June
weekend when the family wasn't there. "Do you want to have sex?" he had
asked, without expectation in his voice, as if it were a foregone conclusion.
Later he said, "Well, you know, it gets better with practice."

I did not practice with Jon Feldstein again. In fact, I didn't practice
with anyone until more than two years later. By then, I had fallen into a
deep and surprising infatuation with one of my closest friends, driven my
Datsun cross-country alone, and settled in Portland.

Early in the summer of 1987, I flew back east to tell my parents I was in
love with a woman and believed I was destined to be in love with women
throughout the foreseeable future. It was Memorial Day weekend, the time
we traditionally turned on the water valve and began to inhabit the house at
the shore. My mother and I drove there in her blue Honda.

"I think that's how it's going to be for me. With women, I mean," I told
her.

"Well, your father thought so," she said finally. "He thought so back in
November. I told him that was ridiculous, that you'd always had
boyfriends."

She said a lot of other things after that, about not having grandchildren   20
and what a hard path I'd chosen and how she and my father weren't going
to be around forever and had hoped to see me taken care of. I concentrated
on driving and on the way blood was beating in my ankles, my thumbs, my
neck, my ears. I wanted to go to sleep and not wake up until I smelled salt.
When we came close to the bay, my mother asked me to pull into a parking
lot so she could cry for a while. "I'm sorry," I said, but it didn't seem to help.

At the house, I walked around, touching things, while my mother told
my father that he was right, I *was* having an affair with a woman. I wanted
to eat something, anything, off the familiar mismatched dishes, play
Scrabble until the stars came out, stand on the back porch and watch boats
slip under the bridge, tap on the kitchen window until someone waved at
me. Instead I went into the bathroom and locked both doors.

About midnight, while I lay sleepless in Aunt Sadie and Uncle Izzy's
room, my mother came in and crawled into the other twin bed. "I feel so
empty," she said. "I feel empty inside. . . . I don't feel any joy anymore. I feel
like the family is breaking apart. I remember how the family was when
Uncle Bernie was alive, how this house was. . . ." And her voice, already
thin, cracked like a bowl dropped on a tile floor — a splintering and then silence where something used to be.

2 A.M. 3 A.M. Everyone had trooped off to bed in pairs — cousins Joni
and Gerry, cousins Debbie and Ralph. Except for my grandfather, who had
always stayed up late to watch television and stayed up even later since my
grandmother died three years before. Finally he switched off the set, and
the house went dark and quiet.

"Don't you feel it's unnatural?" my mother asked. "Don't you feel it's just wrong, that it's weird?"

How can you ask me about being weird in this house, I wanted to shout. This house, with its bedrooms barging into each other and its mismatched dishes, its double-doored bathroom and its red picket fence. When I used to complain that our family wasn't like other families, you laughed and said, "Well, we may not be normal, but we have a lot of fun."

I didn't say these things. I only thought them. And it wasn't until much later, until very recently, that I began to understand why my mother could tolerate the quirks in that house. The madcap shell at the shore housed a solid, predictable center. Relatives came and went in pairs. Someday, presumably, I would join the procession; one of my children would tap on the kitchen window and giggle when I waved. The house might be a little cracked, but the family was predictable, enduring.

I understand why you are so upset, I could tell my mother now. The world has gone crazy and all the walls are too thin and your mother is dead and your sister divorced and your daughter loves women and everything is coming unglued and nothing turns out the way we plan.

4 A.M. 5 A.M. My mother stayed in my room all night, talking and weeping. Toward morning, as boats began to slosh in the bay, I fell into an exhausted, tear-stained sleep. When I woke up at noon, we ate tuna subs and drove back to Philadelphia.

The New Jersey beach house was never just a summertime shelter. It housed my family's favorite image of itself at our expansive best — gathered around the huge dining room table, traipsing through the bedrooms, one big happy family. Just like all the television shows I watched and worshipped.

It is no accident that this particular image clung. The picture of such charmed and cheerful families took hold in the decade preceding my birth, a bit of postwar propaganda that paid homage to the supposedly idyllic families of Victorian times. Mass-marketed by television, the Cleaver clan and others were burned into our minds by millions of cathode-ray tubes.

The feminist movement challenged that postwar myth as women began to examine the contents inside the "happy family" cliché. Feminists of the late 1960s and 1970s urged their sisters to live authentic lives and to begin them at home. They insisted that personal choices had political import — that is, the daily, minute interactions of our lives *mattered*, not just for each of us alone, but potentially for everyone, for the world. "When a woman tells the truth," Adrienne Rich wrote, "she is creating the possibility for more truth around her."

Women pointed out that families maintained the illusion of happiness only by denying important facts — about adoptions, abortions, illness and illegitimate births, divorces and deaths. Some families devoted their lives to maintaining the secret of a son's homosexuality, a grandmother's alcoholism, a father's violent rage. Melancholy and despair split family members not only from outsiders but from each other; certain topics, one understood, were simply not discussed.

In consciousness-raising groups, women discovered the exhilaration of telling each other unvarnished stories of their bodies, relationships, and families. Back at home, in their kitchens and living rooms, they began to apply these feminist ideals: that *how* people talked meant as much as the conclusions they reached; that the only way to solve problems was to actively engage them; that keeping secrets cost too much.

It was feminism, in part, that prompted me to tell my own family a difficult truth, one I was sure would cause misunderstanding and pain. I was frightened to disturb the jovial peace that was a source of such family pride; at the same time, I could not visit that unpretentious house and pretend I was someone else. I wanted to be known, and seen, in the ways I had come to know and see myself.

I did it because I chose truth over tranquility. Because I had come to   35
believe that real families fight and resist, sob and explode, apologize and forgive. Beneath the fiction of happiness lies the raw, important tissue of human relationships.

And I did it because I had watched other women live without lying. For some, that meant no longer passing as heterosexual. For others, it meant acknowledging they did not want partners or children. Some urged their biological relatives and chosen kin to talk about subjects long considered taboo. Their example made my own convictions more fierce. Their bravery buoyed me.

"It's hard. We argue and struggle," Selma Miriam of the Bloodroot restaurant collective told me, with a glance around the room at her "cronies."

"You know each other's weaknesses," said Betsey Beaven, another Bloodroot member. "Love requires a lot of cultivation. It can be tenuous. You have to work on it all the time. It's very difficult at times, but so rewarding when you get through to the other side."

I remember my friend Susan's assessment, at the end of a long discussion about what separates family from friends. "Family," she said, "are the people I've struggled through things with."

Again, always, the personal becomes political. Women striving daily to   40
make plain the good and the bad of their lives also contribute to a larger change, the breakdown of fictions that divide us from each other — white from black, lesbian from straight, old from young. Women who refuse to act out lies at home can turn the same honest scrutiny outside, demanding truth in their work, their education, their politics.

Maybe happiness, I have come to think, is a limiting proposition, a flat summary of human emotion in the same way a sitcom is a flat summary of real life. "Happy families" don't account for the ways people are knit by sorrow, the way bonds grow stronger through anger and grief.

This is it, I tell myself now; this mess is as real as it gets. I try to cherish flux — the mercurial moods, the feelings that flood and recede, the infinite chaos in which families become families.

Two days after I came out to my parents at the beach house, I returned to Portland, with my bicycle packed in a United Airlines baggage carrier and my grandmother's cameo ring on the pinky finger of my left hand. I'd found the ring in a jewelry box in my bedroom. It was delicate, a filigree setting with a small oblong cameo, the ivory-faced women profiled on a peach background.

The thin silver band barely eased over the knuckle on my pinky — lesbians' traditional ring-bearing finger. Wearing it, I felt marked, as though I were bringing contraband across the border in broad daylight, all my conflicting allegiances exposed.

My head ached. Would my relatives still love me if I failed to do my part by marrying and enlarging the family with children? Could I ever bring a woman lover to the shore? Where would we sleep?   45

How would I reconcile my relatives with the various families I developed as a writer, a Jew, a lesbian, a social worker, an East Coast expatriate in the Northwest? How far could everyone stretch without snapping, refusing wholeness, flying apart like shrapnel?

I stumbled off the plane at midnight into a solid hug from Marian, a coworker at the social service agency where I counseled street youth. At work that week, I walked numbly through my routine. On Friday, while cleaning up the drop-in center after the last round of kids, I looked at my left hand. Where the cameo of my grandmother's ring had been, a little rectangle of skin showed through the filigree window. In the agency's dim basement, I leaned against a paneled wall and sobbed.

All the rest of that summer my parents and I exchanged letters, envelopes full of anger and accusation, concern and caution, guilt and grief. I had been such a good child, cheerful, diligent, and brainy — good citizen awards in ninth grade, acceptance to Yale, an internship, then a job, at the *Washington Post*. It was bad enough that I had left the *Post* after two years, moved 3,000 miles away and begun to work with homeless teenagers. Now this! Where had I gotten such subversive ideas?

Perhaps in a certain south Jersey beach house, in a maze of doorless rooms.

From the West Coast, I glanced anxiously over my shoulder: Were my   50
relatives still there, with their shopping and their sweaters, their softening faces and their stiff resistance to change? If I returned, would I be swallowed up? If I stayed, would I be left adrift? Is that the brittle choice that, ultimately, forms the boundary line of every family: Be like us, or be alone?

I took off the empty ring and put it in a drawer. I spent that summer prowling my past, looking for signposts to help navigate the present. I heard voices, comforting and cautionary, joyous and pained, voices that chased in endless loops through my head.

"You can do anything you set your mind to."
"Don't leave."
"The world is full of interesting people and places."
"This family is the only safe spot on earth."
"Follow your dreams."
"Stay put."
I listened, and remembered, and wrote things down.

55

ENGAGING THE TEXT

1. How do you explain the title of this piece? What tone does it set, and what message does it convey?

2. Throughout this essay, Hochman uses the shore house as a symbol of her family. Review her descriptions of the house and discuss in some detail what made the house special to her. To what extent is it an apt symbol for her family life?

3. Why does the revelation that Hochman is in love with a woman so disturb her family? How — and how well — do the author and her family deal with this situation?

4. What is Hochman's notion of "family"? Aside from the issue of homosexuality, does it differ from "mainstream" or "traditional" views, and if so, how?

5. Why did Hochman include the description of her brief "affair" with Jon Feldstein? How do you interpret this incident?

EXPLORING CONNECTIONS

6. In the previous selection (p. 39), Gary Soto is frustrated because his parents won't or can't meet his expectations of what ideal parents should be. Brainstorm a list of qualities that both Soto and Hochman seem to expect in their ideal parents. Are these qualities what any child might desire in a parent? What other qualities would you add to this list?

7. Write a conversation among Richard Rodriguez (p. 194), Kathleen Boatwright (p. 500), and Anndee Hochman on the costs of conformity to and rebellion against family traditions and values.

EXTENDING THE CRITICAL CONTEXT

8. At the end of Hochman's essay she offers a brief sample of past family voices that continue to haunt her (para. 51). Make your own list of voices from your family's past. What do these voices tell you? What do they say about your family's beliefs, values, and attitudes?

9. Hochman's essay challenges us to consider the chilling idea that families demand that sons and daughters "be like us, or be alone" (para. 50). To what extent do you agree that families are held together by conformity?

10. Think back to a particular time or place in your childhood that seemed as special or meaningful to you as her summer house seemed to Hochman. Try to describe this time or place in as much detail as possible, and then explain how it shaped your own view of family life.

11. Watch *The Wedding Banquet,* and compare the actions and reactions of the parents and children in this film with those of Hochman and her parents. What underlying values and assumptions about family unity do these responses suggest?

What We Really Miss About the 1950s

STEPHANIE COONTZ

Popular myth has it that the 1950s were the ideal decade for the American family. In this example of academic writing at its best, Stephanie Coontz provides a clear, well-documented, and insightful analysis of what was really going on and suggests that our nostalgia for the 1950s could mislead us today. Stephanie Coontz teaches history and family studies at The Evergreen State College in Olympia, Washington. An award-winning writer and nationally recognized expert on the family, she has published her work in books, popular magazines, and academic journals; she has also testified before a House Select Committee on families and appeared in several television documentaries. This selection is from her book, The Way We Really Are: Coming to Terms with America's Changing Families *(1997).*

In a 1996 poll by the Knight-Ridder news agency, more Americans chose the 1950s than any other single decade as the best time for children to grow up.[1] And despite the research I've done on the underside of 1950s families, I don't think it's crazy for people to feel nostalgic about the period. For one thing, it's easy to see why people might look back fondly to a decade when real wages grew more in any single year than in the entire ten years of the 1980s combined, a time when the average 30-year-old man could buy a median-priced home on only 15–18 percent of his salary.[2]

---

[1]Steven Thomma, "Nostalgia for '50s Surfaces," *Philadelphia Inquirer,* Feb. 4, 1996. [All notes are the author's.]

[2]Frank Levy, *Dollars and Dreams: The Changing American Income Distribution* (New York: Russell Sage, 1987), p. 6; Frank Levy, "Incomes and Income Inequality," in Reynolds Farley, ed., *State of the Union: America in the 1990s,* vol. 1 (New York: Russell Sage, 1995), pp. 1–57; Richard May and Kathryn Porter, "Poverty and Income Trends, 1994," Washington, D.C.: Center on Budget and Policy Priorities, March 1996; Rob Nelson and Jon Cowan, "Buster Power," *USA Weekend,* October 14–16, 1994, p. 10.

But it's more than just a financial issue. When I talk with modern parents, even ones who grew up in unhappy families, they associate the 1950s with a yearning they feel for a time when there were fewer complicated choices for kids or parents to grapple with, when there was more predictability in how people formed and maintained families, and when there was a coherent "moral order" in their community to serve as a reference point for family norms. Even people who found that moral order grossly unfair or repressive often say that its presence provided them with something concrete to push against.

I can sympathize entirely. One of my most empowering moments occurred the summer I turned 12, when my mother marched down to the library with me to confront a librarian who'd curtly refused to let me check out a book that was "not appropriate" for my age. "Don't you *ever* tell my daughter what she can and can't read," fumed my mom. "She's a mature young lady and she can make her own choices." In recent years I've often thought back to the gratitude I felt toward my mother for that act of trust in me. I wish I had some way of earning similar points from my own son. But much as I've always respected his values, I certainly wouldn't have walked into my local video store when he was 12 and demanded that he be allowed to check out absolutely anything he wanted!

Still, I have no illusions that I'd actually like to go back to the 1950s, and neither do most people who express such occasional nostalgia. For example, although the 1950s got more votes than any other decade in the Knight-Ridder poll, it did not win an outright majority: 38 percent of respondents picked the 1950s; 27 percent picked the 1960s or the 1970s. Voters between the ages of 50 and 64 were most likely to choose the 1950s, the decade in which they themselves came of age, as the best time for kids; voters under 30 were more likely to choose the 1970s. African Americans differed over whether the 1960s, 1970s, or 1980s were best, but all age groups of blacks agreed that later decades were definitely preferable to the 1950s.

Nostalgia for the 1950s is real and deserves to be taken seriously, 5 but it usually shouldn't be taken literally. Even people who *do* pick the 1950s as the best decade generally end up saying, once they start discussing their feelings in depth, that it's not the family arrangements in and of themselves that they want to revive. They don't miss the way women used to be treated, they sure wouldn't want to live with most of the fathers they knew in their neighborhoods, and "come to think of it" — I don't know how many times I've recorded these exact words — "I communicate with my kids *much* better than my parents or grandparents did." When Judith Wallerstein recently interviewed 100 spouses in "happy" marriages, she found that only five "wanted a marriage like their parents'." The husbands "consciously rejected the role models provided by their fathers. The women said they could never be happy living as their mothers did."[3]

People today understandably feel that their lives are out of balance, but they yearn for something totally *new* — a more equal distribution of work, family, and community time for both men and women, children and adults. If the 1990s are lopsided in one direction, the 1950s were equally lopsided in the opposite direction.

What most people really feel nostalgic about has little to do with the internal structure of 1950s families. It is the belief that the 1950s provided a more family-friendly economic and social environment, an easier climate in which to keep kids on the straight and narrow, and above all, a greater feeling of hope for a family's long-term future, especially for its young. The contrast between the perceived hopefulness of the fifties and our own misgivings about the future is key to contemporary nostalgia for the period. Greater optimism *did* exist then, even among many individuals and groups who were in terrible circumstances. But if we are to take people's sense of loss seriously, rather than merely to capitalize on it for a hidden political agenda, we need to develop a historical perspective on where that hope came from.

Part of it came from families comparing their prospects in the 1950s to their unstable, often grindingly uncomfortable pasts, especially the two horrible decades just before. In the 1920s, after two centuries of child labor and income insecurity, and for the first time in American history, a bare majority of children had come to live in a family with a male breadwinner, a female homemaker, and a chance at a high school education. Yet no sooner did the ideals associated with such a family begin to blossom than they were buried by the stock market crash of 1929 and the Great Depression of the 1930s. During the 1930s domestic violence soared; divorce rates fell, but informal separations jumped; fertility plummeted. Murder rates were higher in 1933 than they were in the 1980s. Families were uprooted or torn apart. Thousands of young people left home to seek work, often riding the rails across the country.[4]

World War II brought the beginning of economic recovery, and people's renewed interest in forming families resulted in a marriage and childbearing boom, but stability was still beyond most people's grasp. Postwar communities were rocked by racial tensions, labor strife, and a right-wing backlash against the radical union movement of the 1930s. Many women resented being fired from wartime jobs they had grown to enjoy.

---

[3]Judith Wallerstein and Sandra Blakeslee, *The Good Marriage: How and Why Love Lasts* (Boston: Houghton Mifflin, 1995), p. 15.

[4]Donald Hernandez, *America's Children: Resources from Family, Government and the Economy* (New York: Russell Sage, 1993), pp. 99, 102; James Morone, "The Corrosive Politics of Virtue," *American Prospect* 26 (May–June 1996), p. 37; "Study Finds U.S. No. 1 in Violence," *Olympian*, November 13, 1992. See also Stephen Mintz and Susan Kellogg, *Domestic Revolutions: A Social History of American Family Life* (New York: The Free Press, 1988).

ROGER REALIZES A CHERISHED CHILDHOOD MEMORY IS ACTUALLY A SCENE FROM AN OLD MOVIE.

Veterans often came home to find that they had to elbow their way back into their families, with wives and children resisting their attempts to re-assert domestic authority. In one recent study of fathers who returned from the war, four times as many reported painful, even traumatic, reunions as remembered happy ones.[5]

[5]William Tuttle, Jr., *"Daddy's Gone to War": The Second World War in the Lives of America's Children* (New York: Oxford University Press, 1993).

By 1946 one in every three marriages was ending in divorce. Even   10
couples who stayed together went through rough times, as an acute housing
shortage forced families to double up with relatives or friends. Tempers
frayed and generational relations grew strained. "No home is big enough to
house two families, particularly two of different generations, with opposite
theories on child training," warned a 1948 film on the problems of modern
marriage.[6]

So after the widespread domestic strife, family disruptions, and violence of the 1930s and the instability of the World War II period, people
were ready to try something new. The postwar economic boom gave them
the chance. The 1950s was the first time that a majority of Americans could
even *dream* of creating a secure oasis in their immediate nuclear families.
There they could focus their emotional and financial investments, reduce
obligations to others that might keep them from seizing their own chance at
a new start, and escape the interference of an older generation of neighbors
or relatives who tried to tell them how to run their lives and raise their kids.
Oral histories of the postwar period resound with the theme of escaping
from in-laws, maiden aunts, older parents, even needy siblings.

The private family also provided a refuge from the anxieties of the new
nuclear age and the cold war, as well as a place to get away from the political witch-hunts led by Senator Joe McCarthy and his allies. When having
the wrong friends at the wrong time or belonging to any "suspicious" organization could ruin your career and reputation, it was safer to pull out of
groups you might have joined earlier and to focus on your family. On a
more positive note, the nuclear family was where people could try to satisfy
their long-pent-up desires for a more stable marriage, a decent home, and
the chance to really enjoy their children.

The 1950s Family Experiment

The key to understanding the successes, failures, and comparatively
short life of 1950s family forms and values is to understand the period as
one of *experimentation* with the possibilities of a new kind of family, not as
the expression of some longstanding tradition. At the end of the 1940s, the
divorce rate, which had been rising steadily since the 1890s, dropped
sharply; the age of marriage fell to a 100-year low; and the birth rate soared.
Women who had worked during the Depression or World War II quit their
jobs as soon as they became pregnant, which meant quite a few women
were specializing in child raising; fewer women remained childless during
the 1950s than in any decade since the late nineteenth century. The timing
and spacing of childbearing became far more compressed, so that young
mothers were likely to have two or more children in diapers at once, with no
older sibling to help in their care. At the same time, again for the first time

[6]"Marriage and Divorce," *March of Time*, film series 14 (1948).

in 100 years, the educational gap between young middle-class women and men increased, while job segregation for working men and women seems to have peaked. These demographic changes increased the dependence of women on marriage, in contrast to gradual trends in the opposite direction since the early twentieth century.[7]

The result was that family life and gender roles became much more predictable, orderly, and settled in the 1950s than they were either twenty years earlier or would be twenty years later. Only slightly more than one in four marriages ended in divorce during the 1950s. Very few young people spent any extended period of time in a nonfamily setting: They moved from their parents' family into their own family, after just a brief experience with independent living, and they started having children soon after marriage. Whereas two-thirds of women aged 20 to 24 were not yet married in 1990, only 28 percent of women this age were still single in 1960.[8]

Ninety percent of all the households in the country were families in the 1950s, in comparison with only 71 percent by 1990. Eighty-six percent of all children lived in two-parent homes in 1950, as opposed to just 72 percent in 1990. And the percentage living with both biological parents — rather than, say, a parent and stepparent — was dramatically higher than it had been at the turn of the century or is today: seventy percent in 1950, compared with only 50 percent in 1990. Nearly 60 percent of kids — an all-time high — were born into male breadwinner–female homemaker families; only a minority of the rest had mothers who worked in the paid labor force.[9]

15

If the organization and uniformity of family life in the 1950s were new, so were the values, especially the emphasis on putting all one's emotional and financial eggs in the small basket of the immediate nuclear family. Right up through the 1940s, ties of work, friendship, neighborhood, ethnicity, extended kin, and voluntary organizations were as important a source of identity for most Americans, and sometimes a *more* important source of obligation, than marriage and the nuclear family. All this changed in the

[7]Arlene Skolnick and Stacey Rosencrantz, "The New Crusade for the Old Family," *American Prospect*, Summer 1994, p. 65; Hernandez, *America's Children*, pp. 128–32; Andrew Cherlin, "Changing Family and Household: Contemporary Lessons from Historical Research," *Annual Review of Sociology* 9 (1983), pp. 54–58; Sam Roberts, *Who We Are: A Portrait of America Based on the Latest Census* (New York: Times Books, 1995), p. 45.

[8]Levy, "Incomes and Income Inequality," p. 20; Arthur Norton and Louisa Miller, *Marriage, Divorce, and Remarriage in the 1990s*, Current Population Reports Series P23–180 (Washington, D.C.: Bureau of the Census, October 1992); Roberts, *Who We Are* (1995 ed.), pp. 50–53.

[9]Dennis Hogan and Daniel Lichter, "Children and Youth: Living Arrangements and Welfare," in Farley, ed., *State of the Union*, vol. 2, p. 99; Richard Gelles, *Contemporary Families: A Sociological View* (Thousand Oaks, Calif.: Sage, 1995), p. 115; Hernandez, *America's Children*, p. 102. The fact that only a small percentage of children had mothers in the paid labor force, though a full 40 percent did not live in male breadwinner–female homemaker families, was because some children had mothers who worked, unpaid, in farms or family businesses, or fathers who were unemployed, or the children were not living with both parents.

postwar era. The spread of suburbs and automobiles, combined with the destruction of older ethnic neighborhoods in many cities, led to the decline of the neighborhood social club. Young couples moved away from parents and kin, cutting ties with traditional extrafamilial networks that might compete for their attention. A critical factor in this trend was the emergence of a group of family sociologists and marriage counselors who followed Talcott Parsons in claiming that the nuclear family, built on a sharp division of labor between husband and wife, was the cornerstone of modern society.

The new family experts tended to advocate views such as those first raised in a 1946 book, *Their Mothers' Sons*, by psychiatrist Edward Strecker. Strecker and his followers argued that American boys were infantilized and emasculated by women who were old-fashioned "moms" instead of modern "mothers." One sign that you might be that dreaded "mom," Strecker warned women, was if you felt you should take your aging parents into your own home, rather than putting them in "a good institution . . . where they will receive adequate care and comfort." Modern "mothers" placed their parents in nursing homes and poured all their energies into their nuclear family. They were discouraged from diluting their wifely and maternal commitments by maintaining "competing" interests in friends, jobs, or extended family networks, yet they were also supposed to cheerfully grant early independence to their (male) children — an emotional double bind that may explain why so many women who took this advice to heart ended up abusing alcohol or tranquilizers over the course of the decade.[10]

The call for young couples to break from their parents and youthful friends was a consistent theme in 1950s popular culture. In *Marty,* one of the most highly praised TV plays and movies of the 1950s, the hero almost loses his chance at love by listening to the carping of his mother and aunt and letting himself be influenced by old friends who resent the time he spends with his new girlfriend. In the end, he turns his back on mother, aunt, and friends to get his new marriage and a little business of his own off to a good start. Other movies, novels, and popular psychology tracts portrayed the dreadful things that happened when women became more interested in careers than marriage or men resisted domestic conformity.

Yet many people felt guilty about moving away from older parents and relatives; "modern mothers" worried that fostering independence in their kids could lead to defiance or even juvenile delinquency (the recurring nightmare of the age); there was considerable confusion about how men and women could maintain clear breadwinner-homemaker distinctions in a period of expanding education, job openings, and consumer aspirations. People clamored for advice. They got it from the new family education specialists and marriage counselors, from columns in women's magazines, from government pamphlets, and above all from television. While 1950s TV

---

[10]Edward Strecker, *Their Mothers' Sons: The Psychiatrist Examines an American Problem* (Philadelphia: J. B. Lippincott, 1946), p. 209.

melodramas warned against letting anything dilute the commitment to getting married and having kids, the new family sitcoms gave people nightly lessons on how to make their marriage or rapidly expanding family work — or, in the case of *I Love Lucy,* probably the most popular show of the era, how *not* to make their marriage and family work. Lucy and Ricky gave weekly comic reminders of how much trouble a woman could get into by wanting a career or hatching some hare-brained scheme behind her husband's back.

At the time, everyone knew that shows such as *Donna Reed, Ozzie and*   20
Harriet, Leave It to Beaver, and *Father Knows Best* were not the way families really were. People didn't watch those shows to see their own lives reflected back at them. They watched them to see how families were *supposed* to live — and also to get a little reassurance that they were headed in the right direction. The sitcoms were simultaneously advertisements, etiquette manuals, and how-to lessons for a new way of organizing marriage and child raising. I have studied the scripts of these shows for years, since I often use them in my classes on family history, but it wasn't until I became a parent that I felt their extraordinary pull. The secret of their appeal, I suddenly realized, was that they offered 1950s viewers, wracked with the same feelings of parental inadequacy as was I, the promise that there were easy answers and surefire techniques for raising kids.

Ever since, I have found it useful to think of the sitcoms as the 1950s equivalent of today's beer ads. As most people know, beer ads are consciously aimed at men who *aren't* as strong and sexy as the models in the commercials, guys who are uneasily aware of the gap between the ideal masculine pursuits and their own achievements. The promise is that if the viewers on the couch will just drink brand X, they too will be able to run 10 miles without gasping for breath. Their bodies will firm up, their complexions will clear up, and maybe the Swedish bikini team will come over and hang out at their place.

Similarly, the 1950s sitcoms were aimed at young couples who had married in haste, women who had tasted new freedoms during World War II and given up their jobs with regret, veterans whose children resented their attempts to reassert paternal authority, and individuals disturbed by the changing racial and ethnic mix of postwar America. The message was clear: Buy these ranch houses, Hotpoint appliances, and child-raising ideals; relate to your spouse like this; get a new car to wash with your kids on Sunday afternoons; organize your dinners like that — and you too can escape from the conflicts of race, class, and political witch-hunts into harmonious families where father knows best, mothers are never bored or irritated, and teenagers rush to the dinner table each night, eager to get their latest dose of parental wisdom.

Many families found it possible to put together a good imitation of this way of living during the 1950s and 1960s. Couples were often able to construct marriages that were much more harmonious than those in which they had grown up, and to devote far more time to their children. Even when marriages were deeply unhappy, as many were, the new stability, economic security, and educational advantages parents were able to offer their kids counted for a lot in people's assessment of their life satisfaction. And in some matters, ignorance could be bliss: The lack of media coverage of problems such as abuse or incest was terribly hard on the casualties, but it protected more fortunate families from knowledge and fear of many social ills.[11]

There was tremendous hostility to people who could be defined as "others": Jews, African Americans, Puerto Ricans, the poor, gays or lesbians, and "the red menace." Yet on a day-to-day basis, the civility that prevailed in homogeneous neighborhoods allowed people to ignore larger patterns of racial and political repression. Racial clashes were ever-present in the 1950s, sometimes escalating into full-scale antiblack riots, but individual homicide rates fell to almost half the levels of the 1930s. As nuclear families moved into the suburbs, they retreated from social activism but entered voluntary relationships with people who had children the same age; they became involved in PTAs together, joined bridge clubs, went bowling. There does seem to have been a stronger sense of neighborly commonalities than many of us feel today. Even though this local community was often the product of exclusion or repression, it sometimes looks attractive to modern Americans whose commutes are getting longer and whose family or work patterns give them little in common with their neighbors.[12]

The optimism that allowed many families to rise above their internal difficulties and to put limits on their individualistic values during the 1950s came from the sense that America was on a dramatically different trajectory than it had been in the past, an upward and expansionary path that had already taken people to better places than they had ever seen before and would certainly take their children even further. This confidence that almost everyone could look forward to a better future stands in sharp contrast

25

---

[11]For discussion of the discontents, and often searing misery, that were considered normal in a "good-enough" marriage in the 1950s and 1960s, see Lillian Rubin, *Worlds of Pain: Life in the Working-Class Family* (New York: Basic Books, 1976); Mirra Komarovsky, *Blue Collar Marriage* (New Haven, Conn.: Vintage, 1962); Elaine Tyler May, *Homeward Bound: American Families in the Cold War Era* (New York: Basic Books, 1988).

[12]See Robert Putnam, "The Strange Disappearance of Civic America," *American Prospect,* Winter 1996. For a glowing if somewhat lopsided picture of 1950s community solidarities, see Alan Ehrenhalt, *The Lost City: Discovering the Forgotten Virtues of Community in the Chicago of the 1950s* (New York: Basic Books, 1995). For a chilling account of communities uniting against perceived outsiders, in the same city, see Arnold Hirsch, *Making the Second Ghetto: Race and Housing in Chicago, 1940–1960* (Cambridge, Mass.: Harvard University Press, 1983). On homicide rates, see "Study Finds United States No. 1 in Violence," *Olympian,* November 13, 1992; *New York Times,* November 13, 1992, p. A9; and Douglas Lee Eckberg, "Estimates of Early Twentieth-Century U.S. Homicide Rates: An Econometric Forecasting Approach," *Demography* 32 (1995), p. 14. On lengthening commutes, see "It's Taking Longer to Get to Work," *Olympian,* December 6, 1995.

to how most contemporary Americans feel, and it explains why a period in which many people were much worse off than today sometimes still looks like a better period for families than our own.

Throughout the 1950s, poverty was higher than it is today, but it was less concentrated in pockets of blight existing side-by-side with extremes of wealth, and, unlike today, it was falling rather than rising. At the end of the 1930s, almost two-thirds of the population had incomes below the poverty standards of the day, while only one in eight had a middle-class income (defined as two to five times the poverty line). By 1960, a majority of the population had climbed into the middle-income range.[13]

Unmarried people were hardly sexually abstinent in the 1950s, but the age of first intercourse was somewhat higher than it is now, and despite a tripling of nonmarital birth rates between 1940 and 1958, more than 70 percent of nonmarital pregnancies led to weddings before the child was born. Teenage birth rates were almost twice as high in 1957 as in the 1990s, but most teen births were to married couples, and the effect of teen pregnancy in reducing further schooling for young people did not hurt their life prospects the way it does today. High school graduation rates were lower in the 1950s than they are today, and minority students had far worse test scores, but there were jobs for people who dropped out of high school or graduated without good reading skills — jobs that actually had a future. People entering the job market in the 1950s had no way of knowing that they would be the last generation to have a good shot at reaching middle-class status without the benefit of postsecondary schooling.

Millions of men from impoverished, rural, unemployed, or poorly educated family backgrounds found steady jobs in the steel, auto, appliance, construction, and shipping industries. Lower-middle-class men went further on in college during the 1950s than they would have been able to expect in earlier decades, enabling them to make the transition to secure white-collar work. The experience of shared sacrifices in the Depression and war, reinforced by a New Deal–inspired belief in the ability of government to make life better, gave people a sense of hope for the future. Confidence in government, business, education, and other institutions was on the rise. This general optimism affected people's experience and assessment of family life. It is no wonder modern Americans yearn for a similar sense of hope.

But before we sign on to any attempts to turn the family clock back to the 1950s we should note that the family successes and community

---

[13]The figures in this and the following paragraph come from Levy, "Incomes and Income Inequality," pp. 1–57; May and Porter, "Poverty and Income Trends, 1994"; Reynolds Farley, *The New American Reality: Who We Are, How We Got Here, Where We Are Going* (New York: Russell Sage, 1996), pp. 83–85; Gelles, *Contemporary Families*, p. 115; David Grissmer, Sheila Nataraj Kirby, Mark Bender, and Stephanie Williamson, *Student Achievement and the Changing American Family*, Rand Institute on Education and Training (Santa Monica, Calif: Rand, 1994), p. 106.

solidarities of the 1950s rested on a totally different set of political and economic conditions than we have today. Contrary to widespread belief, the 1950s was not an age of laissez-faire government and free market competition. A major cause of the social mobility of young families in the 1950s was that federal assistance programs were much more generous and widespread than they are today.

In the most ambitious and successful affirmative action program ever 30 adopted in America, 40 percent of young men were eligible for veterans' benefits, and these benefits were far more extensive than those available to Vietnam-era vets. Financed in part by a federal income tax on the rich that went up to 87 percent and a corporate tax rate of 52 percent, such benefits provided quite a jump start for a generation of young families. The GI bill paid most tuition costs for vets who attended college, doubling the percentage of college students from prewar levels. At the other end of the life span, Social Security began to build up a significant safety net for the elderly, formerly the poorest segment of the population. Starting in 1950, the federal government regularly mandated raises in the minimum wage to keep pace with inflation. The minimum wage may have been only $1.40 as late as 1968, but a person who worked for that amount full-time, year-round, earned 118 percent of the poverty figure for a family of three. By 1995, a full-time minimum-wage worker could earn only 72 percent of the poverty level.[14]

An important source of the economic expansion of the 1950s was that public works spending at all levels of government comprised nearly 20 percent of total expenditures in 1950, as compared to less than 7 percent in 1984. Between 1950 and 1960, nonmilitary, nonresidential public construction rose by 58 percent. Construction expenditures for new schools (in dollar amounts adjusted for inflation) rose by 72 percent; funding on sewers and waterworks rose by 46 percent. Government paid 90 percent of the costs of building the new Interstate Highway System. These programs opened up suburbia to growing numbers of middle-class Americans and created secure, well-paying jobs for blue-collar workers.[15]

Government also reorganized home financing, underwriting low down payments and long-term mortgages that had been rejected as bad business

---

[14]William Chafe, *The Unfinished Journey: America Since World War II* (New York: Oxford University Press, 1986), pp. 113, 143; Marc Linder, "Eisenhower-Era Marxist-Confiscatory Taxation: Requiem for the Rhetoric of Rate Reduction for the Rich," *Tulane Law Review* 70 (1996), p. 917; Barry Bluestone and Teresa Ghilarducci, "Rewarding Work: Feasible Antipoverty Policy," *American Prospect* 28 (1996), p. 42; Theda Skocpol, "Delivering for Young Families," *American Prospect* 28 (1996), p. 67.

[15]Joel Tarr, "The Evolution of the Urban Infrastructure in the Nineteenth and Twentieth Centuries," in Royce Hanson, ed., *Perspectives on Urban Infrastructure* (Washington, D.C.: National Academy Press, 1984); Mark Aldrich, *A History of Public Works Investment in the United States,* report prepared by the CPNSAD Research Corporation for the U.S. Department of Commerce, April 1980.

by private industry. To do this, government put public assets behind housing lending programs, created two new national financial institutions to facilitate home loans, allowed veterans to put down payments as low as a dollar on a house, and offered tax breaks to people who bought homes. The National Education Defense Act funded the socioeconomic mobility of thousands of young men who trained themselves for well-paying jobs in such fields as engineering.[16]

Unlike contemporary welfare programs, government investment in 1950s families was not just for immediate subsistence but encouraged long-term asset development, rewarding people for increasing their investment in homes and education. Thus it was far less likely that such families or individuals would ever fall back to where they started, even after a string of bad luck. Subsidies for higher education were greater the longer people stayed in school and the more expensive the school they selected. Mortgage deductions got bigger as people traded up to better houses.[17]

These social and political support systems magnified the impact of the postwar economic boom. "In the years between 1947 and 1973," reports economist Robert Kuttner, "the median paycheck more than doubled, and the bottom 20 percent enjoyed the greatest gains." High rates of unionization meant that blue-collar workers were making much more financial progress than most of their counterparts today. In 1952, when eager home buyers flocked to the opening of Levittown, Pennsylvania, the largest planned community yet constructed, "it took a factory worker one day to earn enough money to pay the closing costs on a new Levittown house, then selling for $10,000." By 1991, such a home was selling for $100,000 or more, and it took a factory worker *eighteen weeks* to earn enough money for just the closing costs.[18]

The legacy of the union struggle of the 1930s and 1940s, combined with government support for raising people's living standards, set limits on corporations that have disappeared in recent decades. Corporations paid 23 percent of federal income taxes in the 1950s, as compared to just 9.2 percent in 1991. Big companies earned higher profit margins than smaller firms, partly due to their dominance of the market, partly to America's postwar economic advantage. They chose (or were forced) to share these extra earnings, which economists call "rents," with employees. Economists at the Brookings Institution and Harvard University estimate that 70 percent of

35

[16]For more information on this government financing, see Kenneth Jackson, *Crabgrass Frontier: The Suburbanization of the United States* (New York: Oxford University Press, 1985); and *The Way We Never Were*, chapter 4.

[17]John Cook and Laura Sherman, "Economic Security Among America's Poor: The Impact of State Welfare Waivers on Asset Accumulation," Center on Hunger, Poverty, and Nutrition Policy, Tufts University, May 1996.

[18]Robert Kuttner, "The Incredible Shrinking American Paycheck," *Washington Post National Weekly Edition,* November 6–12, 1995, p. 23; Donald Bartlett and James Steele, *America: What Went Wrong?* (Kansas City: Andrews McMeel, 1992), p. 20.

such corporate rents were passed on to workers at all levels of the firm, benefiting secretaries and janitors as well as CEOs. Corporations routinely retained workers even in slack periods, as a way of ensuring workplace stability. Although they often received more generous tax breaks from communities than they gave back in investment, at least they kept their plants and employment offices in the same place. AT&T, for example, received much of the technology it used to finance its postwar expansion from publicly funded communications research conducted as part of the war effort, and, as current AT&T Chairman Robert Allen puts it, there "used to be a lifelong commitment on the employee's part and on our part." Today, however, he admits, "the contract doesn't exist anymore."[19]

Television trivia experts still argue over exactly what the fathers in many 1950s sitcoms did for a living. Whatever it was, though, they obviously didn't have to worry about downsizing. If most married people stayed in long-term relationships during the 1950s, so did most corporations, sticking with the communities they grew up in and the employees they originally hired. Corporations were not constantly relocating in search of cheap labor during the 1950s; unlike today, increases in worker productivity usually led to increases in wages. The number of workers covered by corporate pension plans and health benefits increased steadily. So did limits on the work week. There is good reason that people look back to the 1950s as a less hurried age: The average American was working a shorter workday in the 1950s than his or her counterpart today, when a quarter of the workforce puts in 49 or more hours a week.[20]

So politicians are practicing quite a double standard when they tell us to return to the family forms of the 1950s while they do nothing to restore the job programs and family subsidies of that era, the limits on corporate relocation and financial wheeling-dealing, the much higher share of taxes paid by corporations then, the availability of union jobs for noncollege youth, and the subsidies for higher education such as the National Defense Education Act loans. Furthermore, they're not telling the whole story when they claim that the 1950s was the most prosperous time for families and the most secure decade for children. Instead, playing to our understandable nostalgia for a time when things seemed to be getting better, not worse, they engage

---

[19]Richard Barnet, "Lords of the Global Economy," *Nation,* December 19, 1994, p. 756; Clay Chandler, "U.S. Corporations: Good Citizens or Bad?" *Washington Post National Weekly Edition,* May 20–26, 1996, p. 16; Steven Pearlstein, "No More Mr. Nice Guy: Corporate America Has Done an About-Face in How It Pays and Treats Employees," *Washington Post National Weekly Edition,* December 18–24, 1995, p. 10; Robert Kuttner, "Ducking Class Warfare," *Washington Post National Weekly Edition,* March 11–17, 1996, p. 5; Henry Allen, "Ha! So Much for Loyalty," *Washington Post National Weekly Edition,* March 4–10, 1996, p. 11.

[20]Ehrenhalt, *The Lost City,* pp. 11–12; Jeremy Rifken, *The End of Work: The Decline of the Global Labor Force and the Dawn of the Post-Market Era* (New York: G. P. Putnam's Sons, 1995), pp. 169, 170, 231; Juliet Schorr, *The Overworked American: The Unexpected Decline of Leisure* (New York: Basic Books, 1991).

in a tricky chronological shell game with their figures, diverting our attention from two important points. First, many individuals, families, and groups were excluded from the economic prosperity, family optimism, and social civility of the 1950s. Second, the all-time high point of child well-being and family economic security came not during the 1950s but *at the end of the 1960s*.

We now know that 1950s family culture was not only nontraditional; it was also not idyllic. In important ways, the stability of family and community life during the 1950s rested on pervasive discrimination against women, gays, political dissidents, non-Christians, and racial or ethnic minorities, as well as on a systematic cover-up of the underside of many families. Families that were harmonious and fair of their own free will may have been able to function more easily in the fifties, but few alternatives existed for members of discordant or oppressive families. Victims of child abuse, incest, alcoholism, spousal rape, and wife battering had no recourse, no place to go, until well into the 1960s.[21]

At the end of the 1950s, despite ten years of economic growth, 27.3 percent of the nation's children were poor, including those in white "underclass" communities such as Appalachia. Almost 50 percent of married-couple African-American families were impoverished — a figure far higher than today. It's no wonder African Americans are not likely to pick the 1950s as a golden age, even in comparison with the setbacks they experienced in the 1980s. When blacks moved north to find jobs in the postwar urban manufacturing boom they met vicious harassment and violence, first to prevent them from moving out of the central cities, then to exclude them from public space such as parks or beaches.

In Philadelphia, for example, the City of Brotherly Love, there were   40
more than 200 racial incidents over housing in the first six months of 1955 alone. The Federal Housing Authority, such a boon to white working-class families, refused to insure homes in all-black or in racially mixed neighborhoods. Two-thirds of the city dwellers evicted by the urban renewal projects of the decade were African Americans and Latinos; government did almost nothing to help such displaced families find substitute housing.[22]

Women were unable to take out loans or even credit cards in their own names. They were excluded from juries in many states. A lack of options outside marriage led some women to remain in desperately unhappy unions that were often not in the best interests of their children or themselves. Even women in happy marriages often felt humiliated by the constant

[21]For documentation that these problems existed, see chapter 2 of *The Way We Never Were.*

[22]The poverty figures come from census data collected in *The State of America's Children Yearbook, 1996* (Washington, D.C.: Children's Defense Fund, 1996), p. 77. See also Hirsch, *Making the Second Ghetto;* Raymond Mohl, "Making the Second Ghetto in Metropolitan Miami, 1940–1960," *Journal of Urban History* 25 (1995), p. 396; Micaela di Leonardo, "Boys on the Hood," *Nation,* August 17–24, 1992, p. 180; Jackson, *Crabgrass Frontier,* pp. 226–227.

messages they received that their whole lives had to revolve around a man. "You are not ready when he calls — miss one turn," was a rule in the Barbie game marketed to 1950s girls; "he criticizes your hairdo — go to the beauty shop." Episodes of *Father Knows Best* advised young women: "The worst thing you can do is to try to beat a man at his own game. You just beat the women at theirs." One character on the show told women to always ask themselves, "Are you after a job or a man? You can't have both."[23]

The Fifties Experiment Comes to an End

The social stability of the 1950s, then, was a response to the stick of racism, sexism, and repression as well as to the carrot of economic opportunity and government aid. Because social protest mounted in the 1960s and unsettling challenges were posed to the gender roles and sexual mores of the previous decade, many people forget that families continued to make gains throughout the 1960s and into the first few years of the 1970s. By 1969, child poverty was down to 14 percent, its lowest level ever; it hovered just above that marker until 1975, when it began its steady climb up to contemporary figures (22 percent in 1993; 21.2 percent in 1994). The high point of health and nutrition for poor children was reached in the early 1970s.[24]

So commentators are being misleading when they claim that the 1950s was the golden age of American families. They are disregarding the number of people who were excluded during that decade and ignoring the socioeconomic gains that continued to be made through the 1960s. But they are quite right to note that the improvements of the 1950s and 1960s came to an end at some point in the 1970s (though not for the elderly, who continued to make progress).

Ironically, it was the children of those stable, enduring, supposedly idyllic 1950s families, the recipients of so much maternal time and attention, that pioneered the sharp break with their parents' family forms and gender roles in the 1970s. This was not because they were led astray by some youthful Murphy Brown in her student rebel days or inadvertently spoiled by parents who read too many of Dr. Spock's child-raising manuals.

Partly, the departure from 1950s family arrangements was a logical extension of trends and beliefs pioneered in the 1950s, or of inherent contradictions in those patterns. For example, early and close-spaced childbearing freed more wives up to join the labor force, and married women began to flock to work. By 1960, more than 40 percent of women over the age of 16 held a job, and working mothers were the fastest growing component of the

[23]Susan Douglas, *Where the Girls Are: Growing Up Female with the Mass Media* (New York: Times Books, 1994), pp. 25, 37.

[24]*The State of America's Children Yearbook, 1966,* p. 77; May and Porter, "Poverty and Income Trends: 1994," p. 23; Sara McLanahan et al., *Losing Ground: A Critique,* University of Wisconsin Institute for Research on Poverty, Special Report No. 38, 1985.

labor force. The educational aspirations and opportunities that opened up for kids of the baby boom could not be confined to males, and many tight-knit, male-breadwinner, nuclear families in the 1950s instilled in their daughters the ambition to be something other than a homemaker.[25]

Another part of the transformation was a shift in values. Most people would probably agree that some changes in values were urgently needed: the extension of civil rights to racial minorities and to women; a rejection of property rights in children by parents and in women by husbands; a reaction against the political intolerance and the wasteful materialism of 1950s culture. Other changes in values remain more controversial: opposition to American intervention abroad; repudiation of the traditional sexual double standard; rebellion against what many young people saw as the hypocrisy of parents who preached sexual morality but ignored social immorality such as racism and militarism.

Still other developments, such as the growth of me-first individualism, are widely regarded as problematic by people on all points along the political spectrum. It's worth noting, though, that the origins of antisocial individualism and self-indulgent consumerism lay at least as much in the family values of the 1950s as in the youth rebellion of the 1960s. The marketing experts who never allowed the kids in *Ozzie and Harriet* sitcoms to be shown drinking milk, for fear of offending soft-drink companies that might sponsor the show in syndication, were ultimately the same people who slightly later invested billions of dollars to channel sexual rebelliousness and a depoliticized individualism into mainstream culture.

There were big cultural changes brewing by the beginning of the 1970s, and tremendous upheavals in social, sexual, and family values. And yes, there were sometimes reckless or simply laughable excesses in some of the early experiments with new gender roles, family forms, and personal expression. But the excesses of 1950s gender roles and family forms were every bit as repellent and stupid as the excesses of the sixties: Just watch a dating etiquette film of the time period, or recall that therapists of the day often told victims of incest that they were merely having unconscious oedipal fantasies.

Ultimately, though, changes in values were not what brought the 1950s family experiment to an end. The postwar family compacts between husbands and wives, parents and children, young and old, were based on the postwar social compact between government, corporations, and workers. While there was some discontent with those family bargains among women and youth, the old relations did not really start to unravel until people began to face the erosion of the corporate wage bargain and government broke its

---

[25]For studies of how both middle-class and working-class women in the 1950s quickly departed from, or never quite accepted, the predominant image of women, see Joanne Meyerowitz, ed., *Not June Cleaver: Women and Gender in Postwar America, 1945–1960* (Philadelphia: Temple University Press, 1994).

tacit societal bargain that it would continue to invest in jobs and education
for the younger generation.

In the 1970s, new economic trends began to clash with all the social ex-   50
pectations that 1950s families had instilled in their children. That clash, not
the willful abandonment of responsibility and commitment, has been the
primary cause of both family rearrangements and the growing social
problems that are usually attributed to such family changes, but in fact have
separate origins.

ENGAGING THE TEXT

1. According to Coontz, what do we really miss about the 1950s? In addition,
   what *don't* we miss?

2. In Coontz's view, what was the role of the government in making the 1950s
   in America what they were? What part did broader historical forces or
   other circumstances play?

3. Although she concentrates on the 1950s, Coontz also describes the other
   decades from the 1920s to the present. Use her information to create a
   brief chart naming the key characteristics of each decade. Then consider
   your own family history and see how well it fits the pattern Coontz outlines.
   Discuss the results with classmates or write a journal entry reflecting on
   what you learn.

EXPLORING CONNECTIONS

4. Review "Looking for Work," by Gary Soto (p. 39) and "Growing Pains" by
   Anndee Hochman (p. 45). How do these narratives evoke nostalgia for a
   simpler, better era for families? Do they reveal any of the problems with
   the 1950s that Coontz describes?

5. Compare Norman Rockwell's enormously popular portrayals of family life
   (pp. 22–24) with the account provided by Coontz. Do you think she would
   call Rockwell's paintings "nostalgic"? What do we mean by this word?

EXTENDING THE CRITICAL CONTEXT

6. Coontz suggests that an uninformed nostalgia for the 1950s could promote
   harmful political agendas today. (See, for example, paras. 7 and 37.) What
   evidence, if any, do you see in contemporary media that nostalgia for the
   1950s is on the rise? Do you agree with Coontz that such nostalgia can be
   dangerous? Why or why not?

7. Watch an episode of a 1950s sitcom (if possible, videotape it) such as *Father Knows Best, The Donna Reed Show, Leave It to Beaver,* or *I Love
   Lucy.* Analyze the extent to which it reveals both positive and negative aspects of the 1950s that Coontz discusses (for example, an authoritarian father figure, limited roles for wives, economic prosperity, or a sense of a secure community).

About Marriage

Danielle Crittenden

When the modern feminist movement was getting under way in the 1960s and 1970s, many feminist leaders scorned the nuclear family as an institution that bound women to oppressive gender roles. Freeing women, in this analysis, meant rejecting or redefining the family. Danielle Crittenden objects to such views in this selection from What Our Mothers Didn't Tell Us: Why Happiness Eludes the Modern Woman *(1999). Crittenden argues that feminism, which has challenged traditional views of marriage and family, has actually hurt many women by cheapening wedding vows, discounting the value of women's traditional roles within the family, and making it easy for husbands to abandon their duties. From Crittenden's vantage point, stereotypical 1950s suburban marriages — ones feminists consider restrictive and sexist — look "peaceful and affluent." Crittenden (b. 1963) is the founder of the* Women's Quarterly, *published in Washington, D.C.*

Despite having suffered through the highest divorce rate in the nation's history, despite the casualness with which people are often accused of seeking divorce, nearly three quarters of Americans persist in believing that "marriage is a lifelong commitment that should not be broken except under extreme circumstances." If this is true, then we have to seriously reexamine our opinions toward the so-called traditional marriage that we rejected in favor of the more egalitarian but less enduring modern one.

The many feminist critics of marriage insist that traditional marriage is incompatible with modern women's lives: that very few women would be willing to return to marriages in which the wives confine themselves largely to home and family while their husbands go to work. These critics damn any attempt to salvage, or reexamine, traditional marriage as a pointless exercise in nostalgia — when not an actively subversive attempt to "turn back the clock" on women's achievements outside the home. Indeed, feminists mistrust marriage so profoundly that their response to the harm done to women by divorce has been to urge women to avoid it entirely, and they resent all efforts to preserve it. Like disciples of Le Corbusier[1] surveying a row of Victorian houses, they think there is nothing wrong with marriage that could not be solved by bulldozers and dynamite. As Barbara Ehrenreich wrote in *Time*, "Yes, divorce is bad — but so is the institution that generates it: marriage." Ideally, such critics believe, relationships should be formed and dissolved at whim, and there should be no assigned roles for

---

[1]*Le Corbusier:* Swiss architect Charles Edouard Jenneret (1887–1965).

either sex. There are thinkers, too, like Barbara Dafoe Whitehead, who recognize the harsh consequences of divorce upon women and children but who are equally reluctant to see any return to the division of labor according to sex. As she notes in the conclusion of her 1997 book, *The Divorce Culture,* "If men and women are to *find a way to share the tasks of parenthood in marriage,* that way can come about only through a change of heart and mind, a new consciousness about the meaning of commitment itself . . ." [italics mine].

Yet this quest for perfect parity in marriage will never liberate women from our duties and cravings as mothers. What it can do — what it has done for nearly half the men in America — is provide an excuse for shirking the duties of fatherhood. If men are told they are not needed to support their wives and children, if they are made to understand that their role as father is interchangeable with the mother's — or, for that matter, with the baby-sitter's, or the day-care worker's — what compelling reason do men have to remain with their families? To open sticky jar lids and move heavy furniture? Hardly an incentive for lifelong commitment or inspiration for enduring romance. What the feminist vision of marriage amounts to is that every marriage should resemble a gay marriage, without husbands or wives or fathers or mothers. Instead, both "partners" or "spouses" should occupy the same roles within and outside the home. And all of this may sound fine, even attractive, in a science fiction sort of way, and it will last precisely as long as the romantic attraction between the two partners lasts. But what happens then? The female partner doesn't really *need* her male partner in this unisex utopia: She has her job and her day-care center and (for a while, anyway) a succession of available lovers. Nor does the male partner really *need* his female partner. He can get take-out Chinese food and (for rather longer) girlfriends and the new line of Hallmark divorced-dad cards to send to his offspring. All but the happiest marriages are held together for *reasons:* because husbands and wives seek different, supportive roles within marriage, because they rely upon each other for different things. And marriages are held together even more by *opinion* — the opinion of society that marriage is good and laudable, that separation is a calamity and a failure, and by the opinion of the husband and wife themselves that only the gravest incompatibility can justify divorce. But we have, step by step, weakened these reasons and discarded these opinions.

There is nothing now left to bind a man to his wife and children — or a wife to her husband — but the very tenuous bonds of affection and sexual attraction. If a man is decent and loves his wife and would never abandon her, well, lucky her — she's found, by today's standards, a rare gem. But what if his sense of duty and obligation is not so strong? What if he's feeling resentful or trapped or bored or sexually listless or financially overburdened? His children might be passing through some sullen and unrewarding phase, his house might be constantly messy, his wallet may feel as if it is being consumed daily by piranhas, and his wife may be cranky and tired all

"So, are you still with the same parents?"

the time because of the pressure *she's* facing. What holds him there? Certainly not the cost of divorce — he'll be able to escape that. He will not face banishment from his church (if he goes to church), or ostracism by his friends, or disapproving looks from his neighbors, or, if he acts civilized about it, even a harsh word from his in-laws. It's not the Dark Ages, after all, he might tell himself. And then there's that smart, attractive, and, above all, *unencumbered* young woman down the hall from his office. Hey, it could be great — for *him.* He might feel guilty for a while, sure, particularly those first few weekends when the kids come around looking all mopey-eyed, but guilt is easily the most short-lived emotion, especially when the society around you tells you that you are foolish for putting up with what doesn't make you happy. For what doesn't feel right for you. For what threatens your identity as an individual. For what, above all, doesn't seem *fair.*

So how *should* women today approach marriage?

5

For all the scorn that has been leveled against the marriages of the 1950s, those of us who are too young to have experienced them can only read about them with a kind of awe and — dare I say it? — wistfulness. Compared to today's frantic two-career households, the suburban married life that was deemed so stifling and unfulfilling a generation ago seems blissfully peaceful and affluent. The loyal, responsible, hardworking dads of that era, long ridiculed as insensitive drones, look like pure catnip to women fed up with the inconstant, immature men of our time.

Yet the feminists are probably right in believing that very few women — and very few men — could envision themselves returning to the starkly defined roles of the past. And that's not only because these roles feel, to a modern sensibility, thwarting and unfair. It's also because it would actually make no sense today for a woman to surrender her ambitions in order to run her home and raise her children. The reason it makes no sense, however, has less to do with women's attainment of sexual equality than it does with the fact that we live in an age when we can even consider lives unhampered by our biology. Until relatively recently, no woman — unless she was very poor — would wish to face working outside the home on top of everything else. True, ironing clothes with a red-hot piece of metal and cooking meals over a wood stove was not a very attractive destiny. But coal-mining in an unventilated shaft, or pulling wheat from the ground, or riveting girders thirty storeys up was, if anything, even worse. It's no accident that the most forceful and successful push for women in the workforce occurred at the same historical moment that the birth-control pill became available, childbirth was at last safe, antibiotics and healthier diets increased the average life span, and technological advance produced hundreds of thousands of jobs that could be described as pleasant or interesting, let alone "fulfilling." Today, no woman has to be "trapped" at home and confined to her role as mother — even if, in fact, she's traditionally minded and *does* decide to take five, ten, or even twenty years out of the workforce. Not only will she emerge from the experience a more youthful and fit person than her grandmother was, with many years of life ahead of her, but the advent of personal computers and the increasing flexibility of our economy are creating jobs she will be able to do from her living room or on a part-time basis when her children start school.

Perhaps we can't have — or don't want — the marriages of the past, but that doesn't mean that the basic centuries-old principles upon which marriage was founded have ceased to apply. As Tolstoy[2] reminds us, "If the purpose of marriage is the family, the person who wishes to have several wives or husbands may perhaps receive a great deal of pleasure, but in that case will not have a family." The different roles we assume as mothers and fathers, the different deals we wish to cut with each other in order to sustain these roles — these have persisted through thirty years of social revolution and beyond. What has not persisted is the society that recognized the mutual sacrifices husbands and wives make for each other, that understood marriage as an arrangement of give-and-take rather than quid pro quo.[3] A woman who had been happily married for fifty-two years told a *Washington Post* reporter that when she was wed, at twenty-one, "Divorce was not an option. You know, in those days, you couldn't say cancer out loud, you said

---

[2]*Tolstoy:* Leo Tolstoy (1828–1910), Russian novelist, author of *War and Peace*.
[3]*quid pro quo:* Latin phrase meaning "one thing in return for another." The phrase often has a negative connotation, as it does here, implying selfish and amoral bartering.

the 'Big C.' Divorce was the same thing, you said the 'Big D,' you would never discuss it. It was a disgrace in the family. When you got married, we never said, 'Well, if it doesn't work out we could always end it.' People got married and that was that. After more than a half-century of marriage, I can also tell you that it is important to realize early on that no one person can give you everything that you want or need."

Unfortunately, there is no contemporary model for a marriage in which our modern belief in sexual equality could be reconciled with the inherent differences of our sexual natures. This is why, I suppose, women are so fearful about "going back": The only alternative to the obsessively egalitarian marriage of today that they can imagine is the rejected inegalitarian one of the past. They enter into their marriages clinging to their newfound identities and newly gained territories as tenaciously as break-away republics cling to theirs, fearful of surrendering a scrap of their independence lest the old country move in and take over again.

But it may be that in order for modern women to have the marriages   10 we want, we will have to stop being so preoccupied about our identities, and instead develop an appreciation for the mutual, if differing, contributions we make to marriage as men and women. Maybe what we should expect from our marriages is not so much an equality in kind but an equality in spirit. We want our husbands to love and respect us, to see us as their equal in all aspects of the mind and soul, but that doesn't mean we have to do exactly the same things in our day-to-day lives or to occupy identical roles. We must also understand that family has never been about the promotion of rights but about the surrender of them — by *both* the man and the woman. A wife and husband give up their sexual freedom, their financial freedom, their right to "pursue happiness" entirely on their own terms the moment they leave the altar. No matter what may come of their marriage, they have tied their identities — and fates — together. Through the act of having children, they seal them. And this is what a woman today who takes her husband's name acknowledges with that symbolic act. She is hardly declaring herself his chattel. She is asserting, rather, that she and her husband have formed a new family, distinct from all their previous ties, both permanent and total in its commitment. It may seem arbitrary that they take the man's name instead of making up a new one or hyphenating both names like English nobles. But that is our custom, and it is by now a harmless one. (Matrilineal societies do exist, but this doesn't mean they necessarily have a superior record in the treatment-of-women department — ask the Spanish.) The husband's name, in any case, ceases to refer to just him and now reflects the combined personality of the family itself, like a newly merged corporation.

Alas, by withholding ourselves, or pieces of ourselves, instead of giving to our marriages wholeheartedly, we can't expect our husbands to do so, either. After all, it's not as if postponing marriage and going into it with our eyes more wide-open has made marriage any more stable than it was when men and women went into it practically blind. A young man I know told me that he'd "at last" moved in with his girlfriend of a few years. "We're more serious now," he said proudly. And I thought, No you're not. For marriage, as the married know, is about more than signing a lease, splitting bills, sharing chores, and professing a vague sort of long-term commitment; it's about more than being home in the evenings or spending weekends together or deciding what color to paint the walls; it's about more, even, than happiness and contentment and compatibility. It is about life and death, blood and sacrifice, about this generation and the next, and one's connection to eternity.

It is not nostalgic to wonder why this very obvious truth now seems to escape us; why so many men don't understand that it's wrong to walk out on their children and wives — or why so many women feel so nervous, so insecure, and so frightened about "losing themselves" the moment they marry. What is strange is that for so long we could be persuaded otherwise, that we could grow up mistrusting and steeling ourselves against so essential a human condition as love.

ENGAGING THE TEXT

1. This reading selection begins with Crittenden's claim that "nearly three quarters of Americans persist in believing that 'marriage is a lifelong commitment that should not be broken except under extreme circumstances.'" Explain why you do or do not share this belief yourself.

2. Discuss what grounds, if any, you believe a person should need to divorce her or his spouse. Don't worry about current law; focus instead on how you think things *should* work.

3. What is the feminist view of marriage, according to Crittenden, and what does she think is wrong with this view?

4. Summarize how Crittenden thinks women should approach marriage, then discuss the merits of this philosophy.

5. Crittenden refers to "the inherent differences of our sexual natures" (para. 9). What do you think she means by this phrase, and to what extent do you believe in such differences?

6. What is symbolized, according to Crittenden, by a wife taking her husband's name? What is your own view of this traditional custom?

EXPLORING CONNECTIONS

7. Near the end of this reading selection, Crittenden lists what marriage is and is not about (para. 11). Compare her view to E. J. Graff's in "What Makes a Family?" (p. 26). Whose ideas do you find more persuasive, and why?

8. Compare Crittenden's description of the 1950s family to that of Stephanie Coontz (p. 52). For example, how do they differ in emphasis? Are they ever

flatly contradictory? Which description of family life in the 1950s do you find more sensible, plausible, or compelling?

EXTENDING THE CRITICAL CONTEXT

9. Think of a current TV show — soap opera, sitcom, or drama — in which marriage figures prominently. Examine how marriage is portrayed in this show, supporting your analysis with specific examples from several episodes. To extend the assignment, pool your response with those of other students to see if TV seems to reflect a cultural consensus about what marriage is or should be.

10. Watch the film *American Beauty* and discuss how its portrayal of family life confirms or complicates Crittenden's argument for a return to traditional family values.

11. Create a questionnaire designed to probe current student ideas about marriage; focus on ideas you consider most interesting, controversial, or important. Respondents should be anonymous, but they should probably indicate their gender. If possible, give the questionnaire to another class taught by your instructor, then tabulate and analyze the results.

Visual Portfolio

READING IMAGES OF AMERICAN FAMILIES

HDTV. It's A Joy.

Simply from Samsung. For the digital generation. High-Definition Television. The ultimate viewing experience from the world leader in extrasensory reception. Picture and sound so clear, you won't believe your eyes and ears. Samsung's Tantus HDTV is the finest high-definition (1080i resolution), 55" widescreen (16:9 display design), fully-integrated system you can buy. Samsung circuitry transforms your regular television signal into absolute clarity. And the 45-watt Dolby Digital* system makes it sound-sational. A dreamlike experience: reality will never seem the same. Tantus HDTV. The beginning of a new era in home entertainment. For more information on Samsung's full line of digital televisions, call 1 800 SAMSUNG or visit our web site at www.samsungdigital.com

SAMSUNG
DIGITAL

Visual Portfolio
READING IMAGES OF AMERICAN FAMILIES

1. One of Samsung's objectives with this photograph (p. 76) is to grab your attention with a dramatic and unusual image: you have presumably never seen a 55-inch TV atop a baby carriage. But why does the company choose, of all things in the world, a baby carriage? Analyze Samsung's strategy and explain what the image and the strategy imply about the American family. Also discuss the caption, "HDTV. It's A Joy." Finally, compare this advertisement to the Tom Tomorrow cartoon on page 84.

2. What is the emotional impact of the photograph of a woman bathing her child in a washtub in the kitchen? What do you feel when you see this image, and why? Why does the photographer consider this moment worthy of our attention?

3. This photograph of Thomas Jefferson's descendants is clearly posed. Explain in detail why you think photographer Erica Burger constructed the image as she did.

4. The photograph on page 78 encompasses more than 250 years of American history, from Thomas Jefferson's birth in 1743 to 1999. What parts of American history can you link to specific details in the photo? What does the photo say to you about the next century of American history?

5. First, describe your initial reaction to the photograph of the lesbian brides; for example, did it surprise you or work against your expectations? Next, tell the story of this picture: discuss what's happening and find out if your classmates "read" the photo in the same way you do. Explain the significance of as many details in the image as possible — for example, gowns, facial expression, setting, and background. This photograph was published with the caption, "Love and Marriage"; explain why you think it is or is not a good title for the image.

6. Compare any of these contemporary images to one or more of the Norman Rockwell paintings that opened this chapter (pp. 22–24). What questions does this comparison raise?

The Military-Nintendo Complex

JOHN NAISBITT WITH NANA NAISBITT AND DOUGLAS PHILLIPS

Are today's youth being raised by television and violent video games as much as by their parents? Do children need to be protected from computers rather than baby-sat by them? Is there a plausible link between the Columbine High School massacre and computer games? The answer to all these questions may be "Yes," according to this reading selection, which indicts popular video games as a powerful contributor to violent and even murderous behavior. John Naisbitt (b. 1929) believes that most parents are paying altogether too little attention to this violent medium of "entertainment," with potentially disastrous consequences. From his perspective, TV and video games can sometimes even become substitute "evil" parents. Naisbitt, a former executive with IBM and Kodak, is author of Megatrends *(1982, 1984),* Global Paradox *(1994), and other works; this selection is abridged from a longer chapter in his recent book,* High Tech / High Touch: Technology and Our Search for Meaning *(1999).*

In America, children are being drafted into war at about the age of seven. The Military-Industrial Complex that President Eisenhower warned against is becoming a Military-Nintendo Complex, with insidious consequences for our children and our society. American military actions resemble high-tech electronic games while on our own soil we are witnessing another war: The soldiers are children, the battlegrounds their schools, and their engagements resemble the same violent electronic games that train our military and "entertain" our children.

"Doom will become reality!" wrote one of the two Littleton terrorists before the Columbine High School killings began. Those two student killers won a place in history (for the moment) on April 20, 1999, by committing the worst school massacre in American history: They killed twelve fellow classmates, one teacher, themselves, and wounded twenty-three others in a five-hour siege. "What they did wasn't about anger or hate," said their friend Brooks Brown. "It was about them living in the moment, like they were inside a video game."

The two teenage boys were immersed in America's culture of violence delivered through television, films, the Internet, stereo systems, and electronic games such as Doom, which they played for hours daily, including a personalized version of the game that one of the boys had modified to match the corridors of his high school, Columbine. "You're one of earth's crack soldiers, hard-bitten, tough, and heavily armed," describes the instruction manual of Doom, which has sold about 2.7 million copies. "When the alien invasion struck Mars, you were the first on the scene. By killing, killing, and killing, you've won." The boys had linked their home computers so they could play first-person-shooter "death matches" against each other while sitting alone in their own rooms.

Retired Lieutenant Colonel David Grossman, an expert at desensitizing soldiers to increase their killing efficiency and author of *On Killing: The Psychological Cost of Learning to Kill in War and Society,* says, "Violent video games hardwire young people for shooting at humans. The entertainment industry conditions the young in exactly the same way the military does. Civilian society apes the training and conditioning techniques of the military at its peril." The two students mimicked the game Doom in the Littleton high school massacre. *Time* magazine's diagram of the boys' arsenal of weapons and pipe bombs they used that day looked as if it were copied from the Doom manual.

America is entrenched in a culture of violence. Our reputation in the world as a violent culture is based on crime statistics, but far more prevalent — and damaging — is the steady stream of violence on our screens: film, television, Internet, and electronic games. And many electronic games, which grant the player the privilege of pulling the trigger, are *relentlessly* violent, militaristic, and graphic. Living in a Technologically Intoxicated Zone, we are not troubled by the violence on our screens, yet we are perplexed by the violence committed by our young.   5

A 1998 advertisement in *Next Generation,* a magazine marketed to children, promoted an electronic game called Vigilance (rated Teen 13+). The ad encouraged the player to "put your violent nature to good use." Mimicking schoolyard tragedies, the ad pictured a boy's legs from the knees down, in tennis shoes and jeans, the barrel of a shotgun at his side and two dead classmates at his feet. The tag-line read: "You Should Fit Right In."

Left alone in their homes, their bedrooms, in arcades, playing games that we brush off as harmless sport or watching violent shows we insist are not real, many American children are left unprotected in the electronic war zone. Ninety-eight percent of American homes have at least one television set. Movie attendance is at an all-time high. Films are projected on screens in multiplexes that exercise little control over which movies children actually view, and electronic games have been incorporated into the daily routines of 65 percent of all U.S. households, 85 percent of those with male children. Video games are the most dangerous medium of the electronic war zone.

Stephen Kline, a Simon Fraser University communications professor, director of the Media Analysis Lab, and a researcher of electronic games and children, found that few parents understand the nature of these games. "I don't think people are fully aware of either the scope of the industry or the impact video games are having on our kids. Parents don't monitor it.

They see it simply as a kind of benign pastime. They have no sense of the scale or the avidity with which their children play the games or the way it disrupts their lives." . . .

Packaged Emotions

The technology of electronic games is addictive. "Every species is born with the ability to monitor their environment for danger and as soon as they identify danger they stay riveted to it," says Lieutenant Colonel David Grossman, who also is a former professor of psychology at West Point. "They cannot look away from it. That's the addiction. Children, until they are five, six, or seven years of age, cannot tell the difference between fantasy and reality, so when they see someone shot, stabbed, brutalized, or degraded on the screen, for them it is real."

The electronic game industry, which includes interactive games on the TV, Internet, computer, and in arcades, pours money into making electronic games real but consistently denies any impact its games might have on children, insisting that they can distinguish between what is real and fantasy.

"The computer is far more powerful than television," says Jane Healy, educational psychologist and author of three books on media's impact on children. And although nearly all media violence studies to date focus on television programming, Healy warns that computers are more insidious. "The computer is even more engaging. When children are watching television they are frequently playing or doing something else, but computer software is designed to rivet their attention." Unlike television, where the audience passively absorbs the images, in electronic games children inflict the violence themselves.

Professor Stephen Kline worries about what children are learning through playing electronic games: "Play is paradoxical: It subsumes both a connection to reality and imagination by definition. Video game violence is not real violence, but it is an intense simulation of personal conflict. We should think about whether that is something worth encouraging our children to do on a regular basis with high degrees of engagement."

The influence of violent media is both psychological and physical. Kline calls electronic games packaged emotions: "Here we have a form of entertainment that is producing high levels of emotional stress and intensity — the same heart rate acceleration that people experience in either a stressful job or while doing a strenuous physical exercise. This will increasingly be documented."

Kline's research has found that one in four children who plays electronic games is addicted. "They constantly refer to this experience of not being able to put it down, not being able to quit in the middle of the game," he said. "The whole structure is an emotional roller coaster which configures itself not unlike other addictive activities."

10

On the other hand, Arthur Pober, executive director of Entertainment
Software Rating Board (ESRB), champions the positive benefits of video
games: "Electronic games are a social medium, a social vehicle to talk with
other kids." Professor Kline's study found the opposite to be true. Playing
video and computer games isolates children rather than providing them opportunities for socialization. Children typically play electronic games by
themselves in their own rooms, his study found. "I have looked at the
changes of play culture as kids' lives become colonized by technology," says
Kline. "They are being drawn into their bedrooms and playing packaged
emotion machines."

While Pober suggests that "there are a lot of tremendous positive things
that these games do in many ways, whether it is increasing thinking skills,

15

motor coordination, and just sheer enjoyment," Professor Kline thinks otherwise. "I am always asked, 'Surely video games teach eye-hand coordination, right?' My response to this is, yes. For $2,500 you can buy the latest computer that delivers eye-hand coordination. On the other hand, for $1 you can go get them a ball. Put them in the backyard and have a good time with them too. You know, this idea that computers teach eye-hand coordination is such an idiot argument."

Computer simulation trains and conditions our young more like soldiers killing and less like children playing catch. . . .

Serious War Games

. . . In the mid-1980s, according to [General H. Norman] Schwarzkopf, the military turned to computer simulation [for training soldiers]. "We had these wonderful breakthroughs in computer technology and simulation and everything became computerized," Schwarzkopf told us. "An entire war was fought on the computers. We had our intelligence personnel playing the enemy because they were the ones who knew the enemy's tactics. I commanded 350,000 to 500,000 troops in Corps exercises against the enemy — against scenarios we actually expected to fight. Plus there were a bunch of type-A people who did not plan to lose. We were able to exercise the entire spectrum of the organization."

General Schwarzkopf said that the professionalism in the military was greatly enhanced by simulation training. "The great deal of success we enjoyed in the Gulf War, as compared to the lack of success we had in Vietnam, was a direct result of this entire change in the mentality of the armed forces.

"In World War I there were dogfights," recalled Schwarzkopf. "Everybody flew around on everybody's tail shooting each other down with machine guns." By the time of the Gulf War, most pilots sat in an airplane with a display screen. Schwarzkopf's description indicates how American military actions resemble high-tech electronic games: "You can't see the enemy from where you are, but the display screen tells you he is there. You pop off a missile. That missile goes out there and knocks out the enemy. There is a total disassociation from what used to be air combat. Today pilots have what they call a pickle. With one hand they are manipulating this pickle and shooting off missiles. It's pure manual dexterity. If you watch my son play his computer games, he's got his joystick and he's fighting the damnedest war you ever saw. I personally can't do it! I didn't grow up in the computer age. I get on the computer and I look away, and I'm dead."

This disassociated warfare wouldn't have been possible without electronic game training, yet not everyone is as enthusiastic about simulation training as Schwarzkopf. In the colloquial language of a decorated Gulf War army lieutenant, J. T. Terranova, who spent months on the front lines, "Simulation don't mean dick. Put a guy in simulation — he's not suffering.

20

Field training is the only thing that separates the men from the boys. Living in the dirt makes you aggressive. A soldier's got to be out in the cold, deprived of sleep and food. Technology has made a weaker solider." When it comes to infantrymen, the general agrees. "The infantrymen's battle is eyeball to eyeball. Simulation only goes so far."

The two Littleton boys also trained "eyeball to eyeball" for the attack by playing paintball, a derivative of Laser Tag. At Wal-Mart, any kid sixteen or older can purchase paintball guns priced from $34 to $99. If accompanied by a parent, a child of any age can purchase paintball guns, which are in display cases next to real rifles, shotguns, and handguns and are hard to distinguish. It turns out that paintball, the next best thing to shooting real people with real bullets, is a growth industry. An Arkansas-based manufacturer of paintball equipment, Brass Eagle, is the second-fastest-growing company in the world, according to *Business Week*. . . .

Electronic Parenting

Parental response to media violence varies: giving children limitless viewing rights, banishing television from the home, teaching children critical media literacy skills, or monitoring a child's media involvement with hypervigilance.

Victor Strasburger, pediatrician and author of the American Association of Pediatrics' study on media violence, alerts parents to "a third electronic parent [the television set] in the household," which he argues "can teach children good things or bad things." How much control the "real" parents exert over what comes into the home determines what the child will learn electronically. Strasburger reminds parents that they would not invite strangers into their home and give them free access to talk to their children. The television, he believes, can be just that: an intrusive stranger.

If the television is the third parent, then the computer may be the fourth. Psychologist Jane Healy, who has authored three books on children and computers, warns against relying on the computer to parent your child. "We are all busy," she says. "I have been a working mom forever. It is wonderful to believe that there is a parental substitute when you are tired and really don't have the patience after a long day to sit down with a three-year-old, or a ten-year-old, or a fifteen-year-old. It is so tempting to believe that the computer is doing more than you can do (which parents actually believe) and that belief has been encouraged in the computer ads. It is really annoying to find out that the thing that is best for your children is still your time and attention. And the computer may actually be doing your child harm."

Although advertisements have created a belief that computers are educational, and therefore desirable, Healy advocates keeping children away from computers until they are seven; other experts push that number up as far as ten or eleven.

"In this country, we as a culture — and I put myself in this category too — we are desperately eager to believe that something we have purchased can make things better," said Healy. "As a clinician, I truly believe that I am already seeing children who would have been well within the range of normal, whose responses are already distorted by having computers pushed on them since they were about eighteen months old." . . .

All of the adolescent assailants in the spate of school killings between 1997 and 1999 were deeply engrossed in media violence. The fourteen-year-old student killer in Moses Lake, Washington, who was reportedly addicted to violent electronic games, imitated a particular killing pose of Mickey, the star of his favorite movie, *Natural Born Killers* (the most imitated murder film in history). The student killer in Pearl, Mississippi, was obsessed with Marilyn Manson (the "gothic" rock star) and violent electronic games. The boy from Springfield who opened fire on his classmates delved regularly into violent Internet sites and violent films. And as was widely reported, the two Littleton boys were absorbed in the nihilistic music of a German rock band, violent Internet sites, violent electronic games, and watched *Natural Born Killers* repeatedly.

When children are all but invisible to their parents, the consequences are devastating and dehumanizing. A mother of one of the many boys who killed his classmates in 1998 said that she never even "thought" about her child. Her child felt invisible, and he figured out a way to be seen. This deadly combination of desensitization to violence, a loss of compassion for human life, a paranoia that the world is a bad place, and the desire to be a celebrity creates the need to be seen as important, good-hero or bad-hero. And technology is only too willingly used as the conduit for incendiary information.

American children are shooting each other, but they are also sending out signals of their ensuing crimes. And the hundreds of children who mimicked the Littleton boys in the days following the massacre (without the massive carnage) were signaling that they are stuck in an adult-sanctioned electronic war zone, and they want out. If we think of this copycat violence by children as a cry for help rather than another opportunity to lay blame, we might begin to reverse America's culture of violence. If we begin to understand that what is on our screens is real, we will no longer send our children into an electronic war zone daily and expect them to remain unaffected and unscathed.

30

ENGAGING THE TEXT

1. Naisbitt links the Columbine High School shootings to computer games like Doom. What evidence does he present in this excerpt to support this assertion? Discuss the plausibility and strength of his argument. Support your reasoning with a description of your own or friends' experiences with violent video games. Do you agree with Naisbitt that computer games can

desensitize people to violence or even provoke them to violence? Do you think games like Doom can be addictive?

2. Why does Naisbitt believe that video games are the most dangerous of the violent media to which children and teens are exposed? Explain why you agree or disagree with his assessment.

3. Think about your own or your friends' parents. Are they clueless or savvy about violent computer games? What attempts, if any, have you seen on the part of parents to curb their children's exposure to violent media, and with what results? Have you ever seen parents use media as baby-sitters? What realistic advice would you give parents about video games?

Exploring Connections

4. To what extent do violent games appeal to males rather than females? Are you aware of any games that seem gender-biased in some way — for example, by endorsing violence against women, by portraying women as helpless, or by portraying women as grotesquely masculinized? To help answer this question, you may wish to consult one or more of these readings:

> Holly Devor, "Becoming Members of Society: Learning the Social Meanings of Gender" (p. 414)
>
> Stephanie Brail, "The Price of Admission: Harassment and Free Speech in the Wild Wild West" (p. 777)
>
> Jean Kilbourne, "'Two Ways a Woman Can Get Hurt': Advertising and Violence" (p. 444)
>
> *New York Times,* "The Evolution of G.I. Joe, 1964–1998" (p. 476)

5. Discuss how the day Gary Soto describes in "Looking for Work" (p. 39) might be different if he'd had computer games when growing up.

6. What points is Tom Tomorrow making in the cartoon on page 84? What connections can you make between the cartoon and Naisbitt's' analysis of video games? Sketch a cartoon based on one or more of Naisbitt's claims about video games.

Extending the Critical Context

7. Observe someone playing a video game. Describe what happens in the game and assess the extent to which the game incorporates violence. Interview one or more avid game players. How important are the violent aspects of the game to the players? Do they think the games have any significant impact on their personalities or behavior?

An Indian Story

ROGER JACK

This narrative concerns growing up away from one's father in one of the Indian cultures of the Pacific Northwest. It's also an intimate view of a nonnuclear family; the author is interested in the family not as a static set of defined relationships but as a social network that adapts to the ever-changing circumstances and needs of its members. Roger Jack's work has been published in several journals and anthologies, including Spawning the Medicine River, Earth Power Coming, *and* The Clouds Threw This Light. *"An Indian Story" appeared in* Dancing on the Rim of the World: An Anthology of Contemporary Northwest Native American Writing *(1990), edited by Andrea Lerner.*

Aunt Greta was always a slow person. Grandpa used to say she was like an old lady out of the old days who never hurried herself for anything, no matter what. She was only forty-five, heavyset, dark-complexioned, and very knowledgeable of the old ways, which made her seem even older. Most of the time she wore her hair straight up or in a ponytail that hung below her beltline. At home she wore pants and big, baggy shirts, but at ritual gatherings she wore her light blue calico dress, beaded moccasins, hair braided and clasped with beaded barrettes. Sometimes she wore a scarf on her head like ladies older than she. She said we emulate those we love and care for. I liked seeing her dressed for ceremonials. Even more, I liked seeing her stand before crowds of tribal members and guests translating the old language to the new for our elders, or speaking on behalf of the younger people who had no understanding of the Indian language. It made me proud to be her nephew and her son.

My mom died when I was little. Dad took care of me as best he could after that. He worked hard and earned good money as an accountant at the agency. But about a year after Mom died he married a half-breed Indian and this made me feel very uncomfortable. Besides, she had a child of her own who was white. We fought a lot — me and Jeffrey Pine — and then I'd get into trouble because I was older and was supposed to know better than to misbehave.

I ran away from home one day when everyone was gone — actually, I walked to Aunt Greta's and asked if I could move in with her since I had already spent so much time with her anyway. Then after I had gone to bed that night, Dad came looking for me and Aunt Greta told him what I had told her about my wanting to move in with her. He said it would be all right for a while, then we would decide what to do about it later. That was a long time ago. Now I am out of high school and going to college. Meanwhile, Jeffrey Pine is a high-school dropout and living with the folks.

Aunt Greta was married a long time ago. She married a guy named Mathew who made her very happy. They never had children, but when persistent people asked either of them what was wrong, they would simply reply they were working on it. Then Mathew died during their fifth year of marriage. No children. No legacy. After that Aunt Greta took care of Grandpa, who had moved in with them earlier when Grandma died. Grandpa wasn't too old, but sometimes he acted like it. I guess it came from that long, drawn-out transition from horse riding and breeding out in the wild country to reservation life in buggies, dirt roads, and cars. He walked slowly everywhere he went; he and Aunt Greta complemented each other that way.

Eventually, Aunt Greta became interested in tribal politics and threatened to run for tribal council, so Grandpa changed her Indian name from Little Girl Heart to Old Woman Walking, which he had called Grandma when she was alive. Aunt Greta didn't mind. In fact, she was proud of her new name. Little Girl Heart was her baby name, she said. When Grandpa died a couple of years later she was all alone. She decided tribal politics wasn't for her but began teaching Indian culture and language classes. That's when I walked into her life like a newborn Mathew or Grandpa or the baby she never had. She had so much love and knowledge to share, which she passed on to me naturally and freely; she received wages for teaching others. But that was gesticulation, she said.

My home and academic life improved a lot after I had moved in with Aunt Greta. Dad and his wife had a baby boy, and then a girl, but I didn't see too much of them. It was like we were strangers living a quarter mile from one another. Aunt Greta and I went on vacations together from the time I graduated from the eighth grade. We were trailblazers, she said, because our ancestors never traveled very far from the homeland.

The first year we went to Maryhill, Washington, which is about a ten-hour drive from our reservation home in Park City, and saw the imitation Stonehenge Monument. We arrived there late in the evening because we had to stop off in every other town along the road to eat, whether or not we were hungry, because that was Aunt Greta's way and Grandma's and all the other old ladies of the tribe. You have to eat to survive, they would say. It was almost dark when we arrived at the park. We saw the huge outlines of the massive hewn stones placed in a circular position and towering well over our heads. We stood small and in awe of their magnificence, especially seeing darkness fall upon us. Stars grew brighter and we saw them more keenly as time passed. Then they started falling, dropping out of the sky to meet us where we stood. I could see the power of Aunt Greta protruding through her eyes; if I had power I wouldn't have to explore, physically, the sensation I imagined her feeling. She said nothing for a long time. Then, barely audible, she murmured something like, "I have no teepee. I need no cover. This moment has been waiting for me here all this time." She paused. Then, "I wasn't sure what I would find here, but I'm glad we came. I was going to say something goofy like 'we should have brought the teepee and we could call upon Coyote to come and knock over these poles so we could drape our canvas over the skeleton and camp!' But I won't. I'm just glad we came here."

"Oh no, you aren't flipping out on me, are you?" I ribbed her. She always said good Indians remember two things: their humor and their history. These are the elements that dictate our culture and our survival in this crazy world. If these are somehow destroyed or forgotten, we would be doomed to extinction. Our power gone. And she had the biggest, silliest grin on her face. She said, "I want to camp right here!" and I knew she was serious.

We camped in the car, in the parking lot, that night. But neither of us slept until nearly daybreak. She told me Coyote stories and Indian stories and asked me what I planned to do with my life. "I want to be like you," I told her. Then she reminded me that I had a Dad to think about, too, and that maybe I should think about taking up his trade. I thought about a lot of stories I had heard about boys following in their father's footsteps — good or bad — and I told Aunt Greta that I wasn't too sure about living on the reservation and working at the agency all my life. Then I tried to sleep, keeping in mind everything we had talked about. I was young, but my Indian memory was good and strong.

On our way home from Maryhill we stopped off at Coyote's Sweat-house down by Soap Lake. I crawled inside the small cavernous stone structure and Aunt Greta said to make a wish for something good. She tossed a coin inside before we left the site. Then we drove through miles of desert country and basalt cliffs and canyons, but we knew we were getting closer to home when the pine trees starting weeding out the sagebrush, and the mountains overrode the flatland.

Our annual treks after that brought us to the Olympic Peninsula on the coast and the Redwood Forest in northern California; Yellowstone National Park in Wyoming and Glacier Park in Montana; and the Crazy Horse / Mount Rushmore Monuments in South Dakota. We were careful in coordinating our trips with pow-wows too. Then we talked about going all the way to Washington, D.C., and New York City to see the sights and how the other half lived, but we never did.

After high-school graduation we went to Calgary for a pow-wow and I got into trouble for drinking and fighting with some local Indians I had met. They talked me into it. The fight occurred when a girlfriend of one of the guys started acting very friendly toward me. Her boyfriend got jealous and started pushing me around and calling me names; only after I defended myself did the others join in the fight. Three of us were thrown into the tribe's makeshift jail. Aunt Greta was not happy when she came to pay my bail. As a matter of fact, I had never seen her angry before. Our neighbors at the campground thought it was funny that I had been arrested and thrown into jail and treated the incident as an everyday occurrence. I sat in the car imagining my own untimely death. I was so sick.

After dropping the ear poles, I watched Aunt Greta take down the rest of the teepee with the same meticulousness with which we had set it up. She went around the radius of the teepee removing wooden stakes from the ground that held fast the teepee's body to the earth. Then she stood on a folding chair to reach the pins that held the face of the teepee together. She folded the teepee into halves as it hung, still, on the center pole. She folded it again and again until it grew clumsy and uneven, then she motioned for me to come and drop the pole so she could untie the fastener that made the teepee our home. Meanwhile, I had to drop all skeletal poles from the sky and all that remained were a few holes in the ground and flattened patches of grass that said we had been there. I stood looking over the crowd. Lots of people had come from throughout Canada and the northern states for the pow-wow. Hundreds of people sat watching the war dance. Other people watched the stick-games and card games. But what caught my attention were the obvious drunks in the crowd. I was "one of them" now.

Aunt Greta didn't talk much while we drove home. It was a long, lonely drive. We stopped only twice to eat cold, tasteless meals. Once in Canada and once stateside. When we finally got home, Aunt Greta said, "Good night," and went to bed. It was only eight o'clock in the evening. I felt a heavy calling to go talk to Dad about what had happened. So I did.

He was alone when I arrived at his house. As usual I walked through the front door without knocking, but immediately heard him call out, "Son?"   15

"Yeah," I said as I went to sit on a couch facing him. "How did you know it was me?"

He smiled, said hello, and told me a father is always tuned in to his son. Then he sensed my hesitation to speak and asked, "What's wrong?"

"I got drunk in Calgary." My voice cracked. "I got into a fight and thrown in jail too. Aunt Greta had to bail me out. Now she's mad at me. She hasn't said much since we packed to come home."

"Did you tell her you were sorry for screwing up?" Dad asked.

"Yeah. I tried to tell her. But she clammed up on me."   20

"I wouldn't worry about it," Dad said. "This was bound to happen sooner or later. You really feel guilty when you take that first drink and get caught doing it. Hell, when I got drunk the first time, my Mom and Dad took turns preaching to me about the evils of drinking, fornication, and loose living. It didn't stop me though. I was one of those smart asses who had to have his own way. What you have to do is come up with some sort of reparation. Something that will get you back on Greta's good side."

"I guess that's what got to me. She didn't holler or preach to me. All the while I was driving I could feel her staring at me." My voice strengthened, "But she wouldn't say anything."

"Well, Son. You have to try to imagine what's going through her mind too. As much as I love you, you have been Greta's boy since you were knee-high to a grasshopper. She has done nothing but try to provide all the love and proper caring that she can for you. Maybe she thinks she has done something wrong in your upbringing. She probably feels more guilty about what happened than you. Maybe she hasn't said anything because she isn't handling this very well either." Dad became a little less serious before adding, "Of course, Greta's been around the block a time or two herself."

Stunned, I asked, "What do you mean?"

"Son, as much as Greta's life has changed, there are some of us who re-   25 member her younger days. She liked drinking, partying, and loud music along with war dancing, stick-games, and pow-wows. She got along wherever she went looking for a good time. She was one of the few who could do that. The rest of us either took to drinking all the time, or we hit the pow-wow circuit all straight-faced and sober, never mixing up the two. Another good thing about Greta was that when she found her mate and decided to settle down, she did it right. After she married Mathew she quit running around." Dad smiled, "Of course, Mathew may have had some influence on her behavior, since he worked for the alcohol program."

"I wonder why she never remarried?" I asked.

"Some women just don't," Dad said authoritatively. "But she never had a shortage of men to take care of. She had your Grandpa — and YOU!" We laughed. Then he continued, "Greta could have had her pick of any man on the reservation. A lot of men chased after her before she married, and a lot of them chased after her after Mathew died. But she never had time for them."

"I wonder if she would have gotten married again if I hadn't moved in on her?"

"That's a question only Greta can answer. You know, she may work in tribal programs and college programs, but if she had to give it all up for one reason in the world, it would be you." Dad became intent, "You are her bloodline. You know that? Otherwise I wouldn't have let you stay with her all these years. The way her family believes is that two sisters coming from the same mother and father are the same. Especially blood. After your Mother died and you asked to go and live with your Aunt, that was all right. As a matter of fact, according to her way, we were supposed to have gotten married after our period of mourning was over."

"You — married to Aunt Greta!" I half-bellowed and again we laughed.   30

"Yeah. We could have made a hell of a family, don't you think?" Dad tried steadying his mood. "But, you know, maybe Greta's afraid of losing you too. Maybe she's afraid that you're entering manhood and that you'll be leaving her. Like when you go away to college. You are still going to college, aren't you?"

"Yeah. But I never thought of it as leaving her. I thought it more like going out and doing what's expected of me. Ain't I supposed to strike out on my own one day?"

"Yeah. Your leaving your family and friends behind may be expected, but like I said, 'you are everything to Greta,' and maybe she has other plans for you." Dad looked down to the floor and I caught a glimpse of graying streaks of hair on top of his head. Then he asked me which college I planned on attending.

"One in Spokane," I answered. "I ain't decided which one yet."

Then we talked about other things and before we knew it his missus 35 and the kids were home. Junior was nine, Anna Lee eight; they had gone to the last day of the tribe's celebration and carnival in Nespelem, which was what Aunt Greta and I had gone to Calgary to get away from for once. I sat quietly and wondered what Aunt Greta must have felt for my wrongdoing. The kids got louder as they told Dad about their carnival rides and games and prizes they had won. They shared their goodies with him and he looked to be having a good time eating popcorn and cotton candy.

I remembered a time when Mom and Dad brought me to the carnival. Grandpa and Grandma were with us. Mom and Dad stuck me on a big, black merry-go-round horse with flaming red nostrils and fiery eyes. Its long, dangling tongue hung out of its mouth. I didn't really want to ride that horse, but I felt I had to because Grandpa kept telling Mom and Dad that I belonged on a real horse and not some wooden thing. I didn't like the horse, when it hit certain angles it jolted and scared me even more. Mom and Dad offered me another ride on it, but I refused.

"Want some cotton candy?" Junior brought me back to reality. "We had fun going on the rides and trying to win some prizes. Here, you can have this one." He handed me one of his prizes. And, "Are you gonna stay with us tonight?"

I didn't realize it was after eleven o'clock.

"You can sleep in my bed," Junior offered.

"Yeah. Maybe I will, Little Brother." Junior smiled. I bade everyone 40 good night and went to his room and pulled back his top blanket revealing his Star Wars sheets. I chuckled at the sight of them before lying down and trying to sleep on them. This would be my first time sleeping away from Aunt Greta in a long time. I still felt tired from my drinking and the long drive home, but I was glad to have talked to Dad. I smiled in thinking that he said he loved me, because Indian men hardly ever verbalize their emotions. I went to sleep thinking how alone Aunt Greta must have felt after I had left home and promised myself to return there as early as I could.

I ate breakfast with the family before leaving. Dad told me one last thing that he and Aunt Greta had talked about sometime before. "You know, she talked about giving you an Indian name. She asked me if you had one and I said 'no.' She talked about it and I thought maybe she would go ahead and do it too, but her way of doing this is: boys are named for their father's side and girls are named for their mother's. Maybe she's still waiting for me to give you a name. I don't know."

"I remember when Grandpa named her, but I never thought of having a name myself. What was the name?" I asked.

"I don't remember. Something about stars."

Aunt Greta was sitting at the kitchen table drinking coffee and listening to an Elvis album when I got home. Elvis always made her lonesome for the old days or it cheered her up when she felt down. I didn't know what to say, but showed her the toy totem pole Junior had given me.

"That's cute," she said. "So you spent the night at the carnival?" 45

"No. Junior gave it to me," I explained. "I camped at Dad's."

"Are you hungry?" she was about to get up from the table.

"No. I've eaten." I saw a stack of pancakes on the stove. I hesitated another moment before asking, "What's with Elvis?"

"He's dead!" she said and smiled, because that's what I usually said to her. "Oh well, I just needed a little cheering up, I guess."

I remember hearing a story about Aunt Greta that happened a long time 50 ago. She was a teenager when the Elvis craze hit the reservation. Back then hardly any families had television sets, so they couldn't see Elvis. But when his songs hit the airwaves on the radio the girls went crazy. The guys went kind of crazy too — but they were pissed off crazy. A guy can't be that good looking and talented too, they claimed. They were jealous of Elvis. Elvis had a concert in Seattle and my Mom and Aunt Greta and a couple other girls went to it. Legend said that Elvis kissed Aunt Greta on the cheek during his performance and she took to heart the old "ain't never going to wash that cheek again" promissory and never washed her cheek for a long time and it got chapped and cracked until Grandpa and Grandma finally had to order her to go to the clinic to get some medicine to clean up her face. She hated them for a while, still swearing Elvis would be her number one man forever.

"How's your Dad?"

"He's all right. The kids were at the carnival when I got to his house, so we had a nice, long visit." I paused momentarily before adding, "And he told me some stories about you too."

"Oh?" she acted concerned even though her crow's feet showed.

"Yeah. He said you were quite a fox when you were young. And he said you probably could have had any man you wanted before you married Uncle Mathew, and you could have had any man after Uncle Mathew died. So, how come you never snagged yourself another husband?"

Aunt Greta sat quietly for a moment. I could see her slumping into the 55 old way of doing things which said you thought things through before saying them. "I suppose I could have had my pick of the litter. It's just that after my old man died I didn't want anyone else. He was so good to me that I didn't think I could find any better. Besides, I had you and Grandpa to care for, didn't I? Have I ever complained about that?"

"Yeah," I persisted, "but haven't you ever thought about what might have happened if you had gotten married again? You might have done like Dad and started a whole new family. Babies, even!"

Aunt Greta was truly embarrassed. "Will you get away from here with talk like that. I don't need babies. Probably won't be long now and you'll be bringing them home for me to take care of anyhow."

Now I was embarrassed. We got along great after that initial conversation. It was like we had never gone to Calgary and I had never gotten on to her wrong side at all. We were like kids rediscovering what it was worth to have a real good friend go away for a while and then come back. To be appreciative of each other, I imagined Aunt Greta might have said.

Our trip to Calgary happened in July. August and September found me dumbfounded as to what to do with myself college-wise. I felt grateful that Indian parents don't throw out their offspring when they reach a certain age. Aunt Greta said it was too late for fall term and that I should rest my brain for a while and think about going to college after Christmas. So I explored different schools in the area and talked to people who had gone to them. Meanwhile, some of my friends were going to Haskell Indian Junior College in Kansas. Aunt Greta frowned upon my going there. She said it was too far away from home, people die of malaria there, and if you're not drunk, you're just crazy. So I stuck with the Spokane plan.

That fall Aunt Greta was invited to attend a language seminar in Port-   60
land. She taught Indian language classes when asked to. So we decided to take a side trip to our old campsite at Stonehenge. This time we arrived early in the morning and it was foggy and drizzling rain. The sight of the stones didn't provide the feeling we had experienced earlier. To us, the sight seemed to be just a bunch of rocks standing, overlooking the Columbia River, a lot of sagebrush, and two state highways. It didn't offer us feelings of mysticism and power anymore. Unhappy with the mood, Aunt Greta said we might as well leave; her words hung heavy on the air.

We stayed in Portland for a week and then made it a special point to leave late in the afternoon so we could stop by Stonehenge again at dusk. So with careful planning we arrived with just enough light to take a couple pictures and then darkness began settling in. We sat in the car eating baloney sandwiches and potato chips and drinking pop because we were tired of restaurant food and we didn't want people staring at us when we ate. That's where we were when an early evening star fell. Aunt Greta's mouth fell open, potato chip crumbs clung to the sides of her mouth. "This is it!" she squealed in English, Indian, and English again. "Get out of the car, Son," and she half pushed me out the door. "Go and stand in the middle of the circle and pray for something good to happen to you." I ran out and stood waiting and wondering what was supposed to happen. I knew better than to doubt Aunt Greta's wishes or superstitions. Then the moment came to pass.

"Did you feel it?" she asked as she led me back to the car.

"I don't know," I told her because I didn't think anything had happened.

"I guess it just takes some people a little longer to realize," she said.

I never quite understood what was supposed to have happened that day.   65
A couple months later I was packing up to move to Spokane. I decided to go into the accounting business, like Dad. Aunt Greta quizzed me hourly before I was to leave whether I was all right and if I would be all right in the city.

"Yeah, yeah," I heard myself repeating. So by the time I really was to leave she clued me in on her new philosophy: it wasn't that I was leaving her, it was just that she wouldn't be around to take care of me much anymore. She told me, "Good Indians stick together," and that I should search out our people who were already there, but not forget those who were still at home.

After I arrived in Spokane and settled down I went home all too frequently to actually experience what Aunt Greta and everyone told me. Then my studies got so intense that I didn't think I could travel home as much anymore. So I stayed in Spokane a lot more than before. Finally it got so I didn't worry as much about the folks at home. I would be out walking in the evening and know someone's presence was with me. I never bothered telephoning Dad at his office at the agency; and I never knew where or when Aunt Greta worked. She might have been at the agency or school. Then one day Dad telephoned me at school. After asking how I was doing, he told me why he was calling. "Your Aunt Greta is sick. The doctors don't know what's wrong with her yet. They just told me to advise her family of the possibility that it could be serious." I only half heard what he was saying, "Son, are you there?"

"Yeah."

"Did you hear me? Did you hear what I said?"

"Yeah. I don't think you have to worry about Aunt Greta though. She'll be all right. Like the old timers used to say, 'she might go away for a while, but she'll be back,'" and I hung up the telephone unalarmed.

ENGAGING THE TEXT

1. Give specific examples of how the narrator's extended family or kinship structure works to solve family problems. What problems does it seem to create or make worse?

2. What key choices does the narrator make in this story? How are these choices influenced by family members or family considerations?

3. Is the family portrayed here matriarchal, patriarchal, egalitarian, or something else? Explain. To what extent is parenting influenced by gender roles?

4. What events narrated in this story might threaten the survival of a nuclear family? How well does the extended family manage these crises?

5. How strong an influence does the narrator's father have on him? How can you explain the father's influence given how rarely the two see each other?

6. How do you interpret the narrator's reaction when he hears about Aunt Greta's failing health? What is implied in the story's closing lines?

EXPLORING CONNECTIONS

7. Earlier in this chapter, E. J. Graff described European and American families in eras and locations ranging from ancient Rome to contemporary

America. Review "What Makes a Family?" (p. 26) to see which of Graff's
ideas seem applicable to Roger Jack's world.

8. Read Patricia Hill Collins's "Black Women and Motherhood" (p. 112). To
what extent does Aunt Greta fulfill the roles of "othermother" and "community othermother" as defined by Collins? In what ways does her parenting depart from the African American models Collins describes?

EXTENDING THE CRITICAL CONTEXT

9. This story celebrates the power of stories to connect people and to shape or
affirm one's identity. Throughout, the narrator relates family stories about
his father and his aunt that give him a clearer sense of himself and his relationship to those he loves. In a journal entry or essay, relate one or two
family stories that are important to you and explain how they help you define who you are.

Envy

BEBE MOORE CAMPBELL

*What would make a schoolgirl who is afraid to chew gum in class
threaten to stab her teacher? In this narrative, at least, it's not grammar
drills or sentence diagrams — it's anger, frustration, and envy caused by an
absentee father. Like Gary Soto's "Looking for Work" (p. 39), this personal
recollection of childhood combines the authenticity of actual experience with
the artistry of expert storytelling. Bebe Moore Campbell (b. 1950) has published articles in many national newspapers and magazines, including* The
New York Times Magazine, Ebony, Working Mother, Ms., *and the* Los Angeles Times. *She is also a recipient of the NAACP Image Award for outstanding literary work. Her books include* Your Blues Ain't Like Mine
(1992); Brothers and Sisters *(1995); and* Sweet Summer: Growing Up With
and Without My Dad *(1989), from which this selection is taken. Her latest
book is called* Singing in the Comeback Choir *(1998).*

The red bricks of 2239 North 16th Street melded into the uniformity of
look-alike doors, windows, and brownstone-steps. From the outside our
rowhouse looked the same as any other. When I was a toddler, the similarity
was unsettling. The family story was that my mother and I were out walking
on the street one day when panic rumbled through me. "Where's our
house? Where's our house?" I cried, grabbing my mother's hand.

My mother walked me to our house, pointed to the numbers painted next to the door. "Twenty-two thirty-nine," she said, slapping the wall. "This is our house."

Much later I learned that the real difference was inside.

In my house there was no morning stubble, no long johns or Fruit of the Loom on the clothesline, no baritone hollering for keys that were sitting on the table. There was no beer in the refrigerator, no ball game on TV, no loud cussing. After dark the snores that emanated from the bedrooms were subtle, ladylike, little moans really.

Growing up, I could have died from overexposure to femininity.   5
Women ruled at 2239. A grandmother, a mother, occasionally an aunt, grown-up girlfriends from at least two generations, all the time rubbing up against me, fixing my food, running my bathwater, telling me to sit still and be good in those grown-up, girly-girl voices. Chanel and Prince Matchabelli wafting through the bedrooms. Bubble bath and Jergens came from the bathroom, scents unbroken by aftershave, macho beer breath, a good he-man funk. I remember a house full of 'do rags and rollers, the soft, sweet allure of Dixie peach and bergamot;[1] brown-skinned queens wearing pastel housecoats and worn-out size six-and-a-half flip-flops that slapped softly against the wood as the royal women climbed the stairs at night carrying their paperbacks to bed.

The outside world offered no retreat. School was taught by stern, old-maid white women with age spots and merciless gray eyes; ballet lessons, piano lessons, Sunday school, and choir were all led by colored sisters with a hands-on-their-hips attitude who cajoled and screeched in distaff[2] tongues.

And what did they want from me, these Bosoms? Achievement! This desire had nothing to do with the pittance they collected from the Philadelphia Board of Education or the few dollars my mother paid them. Pushing little colored girls forward was in their blood. They made it clear: a life of white picket fences and teas was for other girls to aspire to. I was to *do* something. And if I didn't climb willingly up their ladder, they'd drag me to the top. Rap my knuckles hard for not practicing. Make me lift my leg until I wanted to die. Stay after school and write "I will listen to the teacher" five hundred times. They were not playing. "Obey them," my mother commanded.

When I entered 2B — the Philadelphia school system divided grades into A and B — in September 1957, I sensed immediately that Miss Bradley was not a woman to be challenged. She looked like one of those evil old spinsters Shirley Temple[3] was always getting shipped off to live with; she was kind of hefty, but so tightly corseted that if she happened to grab you or

---

[1]*bergamot:* A citrus tree with a fragrant fruit.

[2]*distaff:* Female, maternal.

[3]*Shirley Temple:* Famous child actor (b. 1928); later, Shirley Temple Black, U.S. ambassador.

if you fell against her during recess, it felt as if you were bouncing into a steel wall. In reality she was a sweet lady who was probably a good five years past her retirement age when I wound up in her class. Miss Bradley remained at Logan for one reason and one reason only: she was dedicated. She wanted her students to learn! learn! learn! Miss Bradley was halfway sick, hacking and coughing her lungs out through every lesson, spitting the phlegm into fluffy white tissues from the box on her desk, but she was *never* absent. Each day at three o'clock she kissed each one of her "little pupils" on the cheek, sending a faint scent of Emeraude home with us. Her rules for teaching children seemed to be: love them; discipline them; reward them; and make sure they are clean.

Every morning she ran a hygiene check on the entire class. She marched down the aisle like a stormtrooper, rummaging through the ears of hapless students, checking for embedded wax. She looked under our fingernails for dirt. Too bad on you if she found any. Once she made David, a stringy-haired white boy who thought Elvis Presley was a living deity and who was the most notorious booger-eater in the entire school, go to the nurse's office to have the dirt cleaned from under his fingernails. Everybody knew that what was under David's fingernails was most likely dried-up boogies and not dirt, but nobody said anything.

If she was death on dirt and earwax, Miss Bradley's specialty was head-   10
lice patrol. Down the aisles she stomped in her black Enna Jettick shoes,[4] stopping at each student to part strands of blond, brown, or dark hair, looking for cooties. Miss Bradley would flip through plaits, curls, kinks — the woman was relentless. I always passed inspection. Nana put enough Nu Nile in my hair to suffocate any living creature that had the nerve to come tipping up on my scalp. Nu Nile was the official cootie killer. I was clean, wax-free, bug-free, and smart. The folder inside my desk contained a stack of spelling and arithmetic papers with A's emblazoned across the top, gold stars in the corner. Miss Bradley always called on me. She sent me to run errands for her too. I was her pet.

When Mrs. Clark, my piano teacher and my mother's good friend, told my mother that Logan Elementary School was accepting children who didn't live in the neighborhood, my mother immediately enrolled Michael and later me. "It's not crowded and it's mixed," she told a nodding, smiling Nana. The fact that Logan was integrated was the main reason Michael and I were sent there. Nana and Mommy, like most upwardly mobile colored women, believed that to have the same education as a white child was the first step up the rocky road to success. This viewpoint was buttressed by the fact that George Washington Carver, my neighborhood school, was severely overcrowded. Logan was just barely integrated, with only a handful of black kids thrown in with hordes of square-jawed, pale-eyed second-generation Ukrainians whose immigrant parents and grandparents populated the

[4]*Enna Jettick shoes:* Brand name of "sensible" women's shoes.

neighborhood near the school. There were a few dark-haired Jews and aristocratic-looking WASPs too. My first day in kindergarten it was Nana who enthusiastically grabbed Michael's and my hands, pulling us away from North Philly's stacked-up rowhouses, from the hucksters whose wagons bounced down the streets with trucks full of ripe fruits and vegetables, from the street-corner singers and jitterbugs who filled my block with all-day doo-wahs. It was Nana who resolutely walked me past the early-morning hordes of colored kids heading two blocks away to Carver Elementary School, Nana who pulled me by the hand and led me in another direction.

We went underground at the Susquehanna and Dauphin subway station, leaving behind the unremitting asphalt and bricks and the bits of paper strewn in the streets above us. We emerged at Logan station, where sunlight, brilliant red and pink roses and yellow chrysanthemums, and neatly clipped lawns and clean streets startled me. There were robins and blue jays flying overhead. The only birds in my neighborhood were sparrows and pigeons. Delivering me at the schoolyard, Nana firmly cupped my chin with her hand as she bent down to instruct me. "Your mother's sending you up here to learn, so you do everything your teacher tells you to, okay?" To Michael she turned and said, "You're not up here to be a monkey on a stick." Then to both of us: "Don't talk. Listen. Act like you've got some home training. You've got as much brains as anybody up here. Do you know that? All right now. Make Nana proud of you."

A month after I returned from Pasquotank County,[5] I sat in Miss Bradley's classroom on a rainy Monday watching her write spelling words on the blackboard. The harsh sccurr, sccurr of Miss Bradley's chalk and the tinny sound the rain made against the window took my mind to faraway places. I couldn't get as far away as I wanted. Wallace, the bane of the whole class, had only moments earlier laid the most gigunda fart in history, one in a never-ending series, and the air was just clearing. His farts were silent wonders. Not a hint, not the slightest sound. You could be in the middle of a sentence and then wham! bam! Mystery Funk would knock you down.

Two seats ahead of me was Leonard, a lean colored boy from West Philly who always wore suits and ties to school, waving his hand like a crazy man. A showoff if ever there was one.

I was bored that day. I looked around at the walls. Miss Bradley had   15
decorated the room with pictures of the ABCs in cursive. Portraits of the presidents were hanging in a row on one wall above the blackboard. On the bulletin board there was a display of the Russian satellite, *Sputnik I*, and the American satellite, *Explorer I*. Miss Bradley was satellite-crazy. She thought it was just wonderful that America was in the "space race" and she constantly filled our heads with space fantasies. "Boys and girls," she told us,

---

[5]*Pasquotank County:* County in North Carolina where Campbell's father lived; she visited him there every summer.

"one day man will walk on the moon." In the far corner on another bulletin board there was a Thanksgiving scene of turkeys and pilgrims. And stuck in the corner was a picture of Sacajawea.[6] Sacajawea, Indian Woman Guide. I preferred looking at Sacajawea over satellites any day.

Thinking about the bubble gum that lay in my pocket, I decided to sneak a piece, even though gum chewing was strictly forbidden. I rarely broke the rules. Could anyone hear the loud drumming of my heart, I wondered, as I slid my hand into my skirt pocket and felt for the Double Bubble? I peeked cautiously to either side of me. Then I managed to unwrap it without even rustling the paper; I drew my hands to my lips, coughed, and popped the gum in my mouth. Ahhh! Miss Bradley's back was to the class. I chomped down hard on the Double Bubble. Miss Bradley turned around. I quickly packed the gum under my tongue. My hands were folded on top of my desk. "Who can give me a sentence for 'birthday'?" Leonard just about went nuts. Miss Bradley ignored him, which she did a lot. "Sandra," Miss Bradley called.

A petite white girl rose obediently. I liked Sandra. She had shared her crayons with me once when I left mine at home. I remember her drawing: a white house with smoke coming out of the chimney, a little girl with yellow hair like hers, a mommy, a daddy, a little boy, and a dog standing in front of the house in a yard full of flowers. Her voice was crystal clear when she spoke. There were smiles in that voice. She said, "My father made me a beautiful dollhouse for my birthday."

The lump under my tongue was suddenly a stone and when I swallowed, the taste was bitter. I coughed into a piece of tablet paper, spit out the bubble gum, and crumpled up the wad and pushed it inside my desk. The center of my chest was burning. I breathed deeply and slowly. Sandra sat down as demurely as a princess. She crossed her ankles. Her words came back to me in a rush. "Muuuy fatha made me a bee-yoo-tee-ful dollhouse." Miss Bradley said, "Very good," and moved on to the next word. Around me hands were waving, waving. Pick me! Pick me! Behind me I could hear David softly crooning, "You ain't nothin' but a hound dog, cryin' all the time." Sometimes he would stick his head inside his desk, sing Elvis songs, and pick his boogies at the same time. Somebody was jabbing pins in my chest. Ping! Ping! Ping! I wanted to holler, "Yowee! Stop!" as loud as I could, but I pressed my lips together hard.

"Now who can give me a sentence?" Miss Bradley asked. I put my head down on my desk and when Miss Bradley asked me what was wrong I told her that I didn't feel well and that I didn't want to be chosen. When Leonard collected the homework, I shoved mine at him so hard all the papers he was carrying fell on the floor.

---

[6]*Sacajawea:* A Shoshone Indian woman (1786–1812), captured and sold to a white man; she became the famous guide of the 1804 Lewis and Clark expedition.

Bile was still clogging my throat when Miss Bradley sent me into the   20
cloakroom to get my lunchbox. The rule was, only one student in the cloakroom at a time. When the second one came in, the first one had to leave. I
was still rummaging around in my bookbag when I saw Sandra.

"Miss Bradley said for you to come out," she said. She was smiling. That
dollhouse girl was always smiling. I glared at her.

"Leave when I get ready to," I said, my words full of venom.

Sandra's eyes darted around in confusion. "Miss Bradley said . . ." she
began again, still trying to smile as if she expected somebody to crown her
Miss America or something and come take her picture any minute.

In my head a dam broke. Terrible waters rushed out. "I don't care
about any Miss Bradley. If she messes with me I'll, I'll . . . I'll take my
butcher knife and stab her until she bleeds." What I lacked in props I made
up for in drama. My balled-up hand swung menacingly in the air. I aimed
the invisible dagger toward Sandra. Her Miss America smile faded instantly.
Her eyes grew round and frightened as she blinked rapidly. "Think I won't,
huh? Huh?" I whispered, enjoying my meanness, liking the scared look on
Sandra's face. Scaredy cat! Scaredy cat! Muuuy fatha made me a bee-yoo-
tee-full dollhouse. "What do you think about that?" I added viciously, looking into her eyes to see the total effect of my daring words.

But Sandra wasn't looking at me. Upon closer inspection, I realized that   25
she was looking *over* me with sudden relief in her face. I turned to see what
was so interesting, and my chin jammed smack into the Emeraude-scented
iron bosom of Miss Bradley. Even as my mind scrambled for an excuse, I
knew I was lost.

Miss Bradley had a look of horror on her face. For a minute she didn't
say anything, just stood there looking as though someone had slapped her
across the face. Sandra didn't say anything. I didn't move. Finally, "Would
you mind repeating what you just said, Bebe."

"I didn't say anything, Miss Bradley." I could feel my dress sticking to
my body.

"Sandra, what did Bebe say?"

Sandra was crying softly, little delicate tears streaming down her face.
For just a second she paused, giving a tiny shudder. I rubbed my ear vigorously, thinking, "Oh, please . . ."

"She said, she said, if you bothered with her she would cut you with her   30
knife."

"Unh unh, Miss Bradley, I didn't say that. I didn't. I didn't say anything
like that."

Miss Bradley's gray eyes penetrated mine. She locked me into her gaze
until I looked down at the floor. Then she looked at Sandra.

"Bebe, you and I had better go see the principal."

The floor blurred. The principal!! Jennie G., the students called her
with awe and fear. As Miss Bradley wrapped her thick knuckles around my
forearm and dutifully steered me from the cloakroom and out the classroom

door, I completely lost what little cool I had left. I began to cry, a jerky, hic-cuping, snot-filled cry for mercy. "I didn't say it. I didn't say it," I moaned.

Miss Bradley was nonplussed. Dedication and duty overruled compas-   35
sion. Always. "Too late for that now," she said grimly.

Jennie G.'s office was small, neat, and dim. The principal was dwarfed by the large brown desk she sat behind, and when she stood up she wasn't much bigger than I. But she was big enough to make me tremble as I stood in front of her, listening to Miss Bradley recount the sordid details of my downfall. Jennie G. was one of those pale, pale vein-showing white women. She had a vocabulary of about six horrible phrases, designed to send chills of despair down the spine of any young transgressor. Phrases like "We'll just see about that" or "come with me, young lady," spoken ominously. Her face was impassive as she listened to Miss Bradley. I'd been told that she had a six-foot paddle in her office used solely to beat young transgressors. Sup-pose she tried to beat me? My heart gave a lurch. I tugged rapidly at my ears. I longed to suck my thumb.

"Well, Bebe, I think we'll have to call your mother."

My mother! I wanted the floor to swallow me up and take me whole. My mother! As Jennie G. dialed the number, I envisioned my mother's face, clouded with disappointment and shame. I started crying again as I listened to the principal telling my mother what had happened. They talked for a pretty long time. When she hung up, ole Jennie G. flipped through some paper on her desk before looking at me sternly.

"You go back to class and watch your mouth, young lady."

As I was closing the door to her office I heard her say to Miss Bradley,   40
"What can you expect?"

"Ooooh, you're gonna get it girl," is how Michael greeted me after school.
Logan's colored world was small, and news of my demise had blazed its way through hallways and classrooms, via the brown-skinned grapevine. Every-one from North Philly, West Philly, and Germantown knew about my crime. The subway ride home was depressing. My fellow commuters kept coming up to me and asking, "Are you gonna get in trouble?" Did they think my mother would give me a reward or something? I stared at the floor for most of the ride, looking up only when the train came to a stop and the doors hissed open. Logan. Wyoming. Hunting Park. Each station drew me closer to my doom, whatever that was going to be. "What can you expect?" I mulled over those words. What did she mean? My mother rarely spanked, although Nana would give Michael or me, usually Michael, a whack across the butt from time to time. My mother's social-worker instincts were too strong for such undigni-fied displays; Doris believed in talking things out, which was sometimes worse than a thousand beatings. As the train drew closer to Susquehanna and Dauphin I thought of how much I hated for my mother to be disappointed in me. And now she would be. "What can you expect?"

Of me? Didn't Jennie G. know that I was riding a subway halfway across town as opposed to walking around the corner to Carver Elementary

School, for a reason: the same reason I was dragged away from Saturday cartoons and pulled from museum to museum, to Judimar School of Dance for ballet (art class for Michael), to Mrs. Clark for piano. The Bosoms wanted me to Be Somebody, to be the second generation to live out my life as far away from a mop and scrub brush and Miss Ann's floors as possible.

My mother had won a full scholarship to the University of Pennsylvania. The story of that miracle was a treasured family heirloom. Sometimes Nana told the tale and sometimes my mother described how the old Jewish counselor at William Penn High School approached her and asked why a girl with straight E's (for "excellent") was taking the commercial course. My mother replied that Nana couldn't afford to send her to college, that she planned to become a secretary. "Sweetheart, you switch to academic," the woman told her. "You'll get to college." When her graduation day approached, the counselor pulled her aside. "I have two scholarships for you. One to Cheyney State Teacher's College and the other to the University of Pennsylvania." Cheyney was a small black school outside of Philadelphia. My mother chose Penn. I had been born to a family of hopeful women. One miracle had already taken place. They expected more. And now I'd thrown away my chance. Michael, who was seated next to me on the subway and whose generosity of spirit had lasted a record five subway stops, poked me in my arm. "Bebe," he told me gleefully, "your ass is grass."

Nana took one look at my guilty face, scowled at me, and sucked her teeth until they whistled. My mother had called her and told her what happened and now she was possessed by a legion of demons. I had barely entered the room when she exploded. "Don't. Come. In. Here. Crying," Nana said, her voice booming, her lips quivering and puffy with anger. When Nana talked in staccato language she was beyond pissed off. Waaaay beyond. "What. Could. Possess. You. To. Say. Such. A. Thing? Embarrassingyourmotherlikethatinfrontof *those people!*" Before I could answer she started singing some Dinah Washington[7] song, real loud. Volume all the way up. With every word she sang I sank deeper and deeper into gloom.

Later that evening, when my mother got home and Aunt Ruth, 45 Michael's mother, came to visit, the three women lectured me in unison. The room was full of flying feathers. Three hens clucking away at me, their breasts heaving with emotion. Cluck! Cluck! Cluck! How could I have said such a thing? What on earth was I thinking about? Cluck! Cluck! Cluck! A knife, such a *colored* weapon.

"But I didn't do anything," I wailed, the tears that had been trickling all day now falling in full force.

"Umph, umph, umph," Nana said, and started singing. Billie Holiday[8] this time.

---

[7]*Dinah Washington:* Blues singer, born Ruth Jones (1924–1963).
[8]*Billie Holiday:* Celebrated jazz singer (1915–1959).

"You call threatening somebody with a knife nothing?" Aunt Ruth asked. Ruth was Nana's middle girl. She was the family beauty, as pretty as Dorothy Dandridge[9] or Lena Horne.[10] Now her coral lips were curled up in disdain and her Maybelline eyebrows were raised in judgment against me. "They expect us to act like animals and you have to go and say that. My God."

Animals. Oh. Oh. Oh.

My mother glared at her sister, but I looked at Aunt Ruth in momen-   50
tary wonder and appreciation. Now I understood. The unspoken rule that I had sensed all my life was that a colored child had to be on her best behavior whenever she visited the white world. Otherwise, whatever opportunity was being presented would be snatched away. I had broken the rule. I had committed the unpardonable sin of embarrassing my family in front of *them.* Sensing my remorse and shame, Mommy led me out of the kitchen. We sat down on the living room sofa; my mother took my hand, "Bebe, I want you to go to your room and think about what you've done. I don't understand your behavior. It was very hard for me to get you in Logan." She drew a breath. I drew a breath and looked into the eyes of a social worker. "I'm extremely disappointed in you."

I didn't go straight to my room. Instead I sneaked into Michael's room, which overlooked Mole Street, the tiny, one-sided alley of narrow rowhouses that faced the backyards of 16th Street. Michael and I usually played on the "back street." Alone in Michael's room with the window open, I could hear Mr. Watson, our neighbor, hollering at one of his kids. Why had I said what I said? What had possessed me? Then I remembered. "Muuuy fatha made me a bee-yoo-tee-ful dollhouse for muuuuy birthday." Something pinched me inside my chest when I heard those words. Pain oozed from my heart like a tube of toothpaste bursting open, going every whichaway. Blue-eyes kept yapping away with her golden hair and her goofy little smile. Who cared what her fatha did? Who cared? I couldn't help it. When she came into the cloakroom I got mad all over again. When I said I had a knife, she looked just like Grandma Mary's chickens. Scared. And my chest stopped hurting. Just stopped.

Mr. Watson's baritone voice was a seismic rumble echoing with the threat of upheaval, violence. His words floated over Mole Street and into the bedroom window. Whoever was in trouble over there was really gonna get it. None of this "go to your room" stuff. None of this corny "I'm disappointed in you" stuff. Mr. Watson was getting ready to beat somebody's ass.

Adam's. He was the youngest and one of my playmates. I could tell by his pleading voice. "Please, Daddy. I won't do it anymore, Daddy. I'm sorry, Daddy."

---

[9]*Dorothy Dandridge:* Glamorous film star (1923–1965).
[10]*Lena Horne:* Singer, actor (b. 1917); first black woman vocalist to be featured with a white band.

Michael came into the room. "What are you doing?" he whispered.

"Shhh. Adam's getting a whipping."   55

"You better go to your room before Aunt Doris comes upstairs."

"Shhhh."

My playmate's misery took my mind off my own. His father's exotic yelling hypnotized me. From downstairs I could hear the hens, still clucking away. Michael and I sat quietly, not making a sound. Mr. Watson's voice sounded so foreign coming into our house. For a moment I pretended that his anger was emanating from Michael's bedroom, and I remembered how only last year he got mad and ran after all of us kids — Jackie, Jane, and Adam, his own three, and me. His face was covered with shaving cream and he held a razor in one hand and a thick leather belt in the other. I don't recall what we had done, but I remember him chasing us and yelling ferociously, "This belt's got your name on it too, Miss Bebe!" And I recall that I was thrilled when the leather grazed my hiney with the vengeance of a father's wrath.

My mind drifted back a few years. The memory was vague and fuzzy. When I was four or five I was playing on Mole Street when my ten-year-old neighbor, a boy named Buddy, asked me to come inside his yard. He was sitting on an old soda crate. "Come closer," he told me. "Wanna play doctor?"

"Uh huh."   60

"You can examine me."

I told my mother, prattling on about the "game" I had played. She sat me down on her bed. "Did he touch your private parts?"

"Nope." Why was Mommy's face so serious?

"Did you touch his?"

"I touched his zipper." Had I done something wrong?   65

Nana went into hysterics, singing and screeching like a wild woman. "Mother, just calm down," Mommy told her.

Mommy was cool, every inch the social worker; she took my hand and we walked down the street to Buddy's house. He was in his yard making a scooter out of the crate. "Buddy," my mother said softly. When he saw the two of us, he dropped his hammer. "Buddy, I want to talk with you."

My mother questioned him. Calmly put the fear of God in him. Warned him of penalties for a repeat performance. And that was that. Not quite. Weeks, maybe months later, my father came to visit me, one of his pop-in, no-real-occasion visits. My mother, my father, and I were sitting in his car and she told him about my playing doctor. His leg shot out in wild, uncontrollable spasms. His face became contorted and he started yelling. Nana's screeching paled in contrast. This was rage that my mother and Nana could not even begin to muster. And it was in my honor. This energy was for my avengement, my protection. Or should have been. But the sound of his fury frightened me. I remember angling away from my father, this man who was yelling like an animal in pain. I leaned toward my mother, and she put one arm around me and with her other hand tried to pat my father's shoulder, only he snatched [it] away. He leaned forward and started reaching for his chair.[11] "I may not be able to walk, goddammit, but I can tear that little son of a bitch's ass up."

My mother kept talking very softly, saying, "No, no, no. It's all right. He's just a kid. I took care of it. It's okay." I leaned away from my father's anger, his determination. He frightened me. But the rage was fascinating too. And after a while, when my father was shouting only a little, I moved closer to him. I wanted to see the natural progression of his hot words. If he snatched his wheelchair out of the backseat and rolled up to Buddy's house, what would he do? What should he do in my honor? My mother calmed my father. His shouting subsided. I was relieved. I was disappointed.

"Hey" — I suddenly heard Michael's persistent voice — "ain't you glad   70
Mr. Watson ain't your father?" I felt Michael's hands, shaking my shoulder. "Ain't you?"

I didn't answer. I was thinking about Miss Bradley, Jennie G., Aunt Ruth, Nana, and Mommy. All these women with power over me. I could hear Mrs. Watson telling her husband that enough was enough and then the baritone telling her he knew when to stop and Adam letting out another feeble little yelp. "Muuuy fatha made me a bee-yoo-tee-ful dollhouse." Maybe my mother would write my daddy and tell him how bad I had been. Maybe he would get so mad he would get into his car and drive all the way to Philly just to whip my behind. Or tell me he was disappointed in me. Either one.

The Bosoms decided to forgive me. My mother woke me up with a kiss and a snuggle and then a crisp, "All right, Bebe. It's a brand-new day. Forget about yesterday." When I went to get a bowl of cereal that morning, my Aunt Ruth was sitting in the kitchen drinking coffee and reading the newspaper. She had spent the night. "Did you comb your hair?" she asked me.

I nodded.

"That's not what I call combed. Go get me the comb and brush."

She combed out my hair and braided it all over again. This time there   75
were no wispy little ends sticking out. "Now you look nice," she said. "Now you look like a pretty girl, and when you go to school today, act like a pretty girl. All right?"

I nodded.

Last night Nana had hissed at me between her teeth. "If you want to behave like a little *heathen,* if you want go up there acting like a, a . . . *monkey on a stick* . . . well, thenyoucangotoschoolrightaroundthecornerand I'llwalkyoubackhomeandI'llcomeandgetyouforlunchnowyou*behave*yourself!" But today she was sanguine, even jovial, as she fixed my lunch. She kissed me when I left for school.

---

[11]*his chair:* Campbell's father had lost the use of his legs in an automobile accident.

On my way out the door my mother handed me two elegant letters, one to Miss Bradley and the other to Jennie G., assuring them that I had an overactive imagination, that I had no access to butcher knives or weapons of any kind, that she had spoken to me at length about my unfortunate outburst, and that henceforth my behavior would be exemplary. These letters were written on her very best personalized stationery. The paper was light pink and had "D.C.M." in embossed letters across the top. Doris C. knew lots of big words and she had used every single one of them in those letters. I knew that all of her *i*'s were dotted and all of her *t*'s were crossed. I knew the letters were extremely dignified. My mother was very big on personal dignity. Anyone who messed with her dignity was in serious trouble.

I was only five when an unfortunate teller at her bank called her by her first name loud enough for the other customers to hear. My mother's body stiffened when she heard, "Doris, oh Doris," coming from a girl almost young enough to be her child.

"Are you talking to *me*, dear?" Her English was so clipped, her words so   80 razor sharp she could have taken one, stabbed the teller, and drawn blood. The girl nodded, her speckled green eyes wide and gaping, aware that something was going on, not quite sure what, and speechless because she was no match at all for this imperious little brown-skinned woman. "The people in *my* office all call me *Mrs. Moore.*"

And she grabbed me by the hand and we swept out of the bank. Me and Bette Davis.[12] Me and Claudia McNeil.[13] People stepped aside to let us pass.

So I knew my mother's letters not only would impress Miss Bradley and Jennie G. but also would go a long way toward redeeming me. After Miss Bradley read the note she told me I have a very nice mother and let me know that if I was willing to be exemplary she would let bygones be bygones and I could get back into her good graces. She was, after all, a dedicated teacher. And I had learned my lesson.

My mother wrote my father about the knife incident. I waited anxiously to hear from him. Would he suddenly appear? I searched the street in front of the school every afternoon. At home I jumped up nervously whenever I heard a horn beep. Finally, a letter from my dad arrived — one page of southpaw scribble.

> Dear Bebe,
> Your mother told me what happened in school about the knife. That wasn't a good thing to say. I think maybe you were joking. Remember, a lot of times white people don't understand how colored people joke, so you have to be careful what you say around them. Be a good girl.
> Lots of love,
Daddy.

---

[12]*Bette Davis:* Actor (1908–1989) known for her portrayals of strong, beautiful, intelligent women.

[13]*Claudia McNeil:* Emmy-winning actor (1917–1993).

The crumpled letter hit the edge of the wastepaper basket in my mother's room and landed in front of her bureau. I picked it up and slammed it into the basket, hitting my hand in the process. I flung myself across the bed, buried my face into my pillow, and howled with pain, rage, and sadness. "It's not fair," I wailed. Ole Blondie had her dollhouse-making daddy whenever she wanted him. "Muuuy fatha . . ." Jackie, Jane, and Adam had their wild, ass-whipping daddy. All they had to do was walk outside their house, look under a car, and there he was, tinkering away. Ole ugly grease-monkey man. Why couldn't I have my daddy all the time too? I didn't want a letter signed "Lots of love," I wanted my father to come and yell at me for acting like a monkey on a stick. I wanted him to come and beat my butt or shake his finger in my face, or tell me that what I did wasn't so bad after all. Anything, I just wanted him to come.

ENGAGING THE TEXT

1. Why does Sandra's sentence in Miss Bradley's class so upset Bebe?

2. The family in "Envy" is clearly matriarchal: "Women ruled at 2239" (para. 5). What positive and negative effects did this matriarchal family have on the author when she was a child?

3. How did the matriarchs groom young Bebe for success? What lessons were taught in this family? Do you think the women's methods of raising the child were the best possible?

4. What does the young Bebe think she is missing with her father's absence? What might he provide that the women do not? Do you think the mature author sees the situation much differently than she did as a child?

5. What traditionally male roles do the women in Bebe's family play? How well do you think they perform these roles?

EXPLORING CONNECTIONS

6. Compare Campbell's family life with Roger Jack's in "An Indian Story" (p. 89). In what ways and for what reasons does each depart from the structure of the Western European nuclear family?

7. Compare the mother-daughter relationships portrayed in this story and in Anndee Hochman's "Growing Pains" (p. 45). How do you account for any differences you see?

8. Referring to the cartoon on page 111 and to the narrative by Bebe Moore Campbell (p. 98), discuss the meaning of the phrase "a close family." For example, is a "close family" synonymous with a "good family" or a "happy family"? What impact do you think modern technologies, such as phones, TVs, and computers, have on the closeness of American families?

EXTENDING THE CRITICAL CONTEXT

9. If you have ever felt the lack of a father, mother, sister, brother, or grandparent in your family, write a journal entry or narrative memoir exploring your memories and emotions.

10. At the end of *Sweet Summer*, Campbell decides that, while she saw her father only during the summer, her extended family, including uncles, boarders, and family friends, had provided her with plenty of healthy male influences. Read the rest of the book and report to the class on Campbell's portrayal of her relationship with her immediate and extended family.

Black Women and Motherhood
PATRICIA HILL COLLINS

For decades many American sociologists failed to understand African American families because their assumption that Western European families were "normal" made any different families seem flawed or deficient. Even today, politicians and religious leaders sometimes criticize family relationships and parenting styles that fall outside the norm of the nuclear family. This essay by Patricia Hill Collins, focusing on women within the black family, offers a close look at the positive roles that black women have played in American family and community life. Collins (b. 1948) is a professor of sociology and African American studies at the University of Cincinnati. This selection is taken from her award-winning book Black Feminist Thought: Knowledge, Consciousness, and the Politics of Empowerment *(1991).*

The institution of Black motherhood consists of a series of constantly renegotiated relationships that African-American women experience with one another, with Black children, with the larger African-American community, and with self. These relationships occur in specific locations such as the individual households that make up African-American extended family networks, as well as in Black community institutions (Martin and Martin 1978; Sudarkasa 1981b). Moreover, just as Black women's work and family experiences varied during the transition from slavery to the post–World War II political economy, how Black women define, value, and shape Black motherhood as an institution shows comparable diversity.

Black motherhood as an institution is both dynamic and dialectical.[1] An ongoing tension exists between efforts to mold the institution of Black motherhood to benefit systems of race, gender, and class oppression and efforts by African-American women to define and value our own experiences with motherhood. The controlling images of the mammy, the matriarch, and the welfare mother and the practices they justify are designed to oppress. In contrast, motherhood can serve as a site where Black women express and learn the power of self-definition, the importance of valuing and respecting ourselves, the necessity of self-reliance and independence, and a belief in Black women's empowerment. This tension leads to a continuum of responses. Some women view motherhood as a truly burdensome condition that stifles their creativity, exploits their labor, and makes them

---

[1]*dialectical:* Based on opposition or tension between competing "truths" or viewpoints. An example follows in Collins's text: the stereotype of the black "mammy" versus the image of a self-reliant, independent mother.

partners in their own oppression. Others see motherhood as providing a base for self-actualization, status in the Black community, and a catalyst for social activism. These alleged contradictions can exist side by side in African-American communities and families and even within individual women.

Embedded in these changing relationships are [a number of] enduring themes that characterize a Black woman's standpoint on Black motherhood. For any given historical moment, the particular form that Black women's relationships with one another, children, community, and self actually take depends on how this dialectical relationship between the severity of oppression facing African-American women and our actions in resisting that oppression is expressed.

Bloodmothers, Othermothers, and Women-Centered Networks

In African-American communities, fluid and changing boundaries often distinguish biological mothers from other women who care for children. Biological mothers, or bloodmothers, are expected to care for their children. But African and African-American communities have also recognized that vesting one person with full responsibility for mothering a child may not be wise or possible. As a result, othermothers — women who assist bloodmothers by sharing mothering responsibilities — traditionally have been central to the institution of Black motherhood (Troester 1984).

The centrality of women in African-American extended families reflects both a continuation of West African cultural values and functional adaptations to race and gender oppression (Tanner 1974; Stack 1974; Aschenbrenner 1975; Martin and Martin 1978; Sudarkasa 1981b; Reagon 1987). This centrality is not characterized by the absence of husbands and fathers. Men may be physically present and/or have well-defined and culturally significant roles in the extended family and the kin unit may be woman-centered. Bebe Moore Campbell's (1989) parents separated when she was small. Even though she spent the school year in the North Philadelphia household maintained by her grandmother and mother, Campbell's father assumed an important role in her life. "My father took care of me," Campbell remembers. "Our separation didn't stunt me or condemn me to a lesser humanity. His absence never made me a fatherless child. I'm not fatherless now" (271). In woman-centered kin units such as Campbell's — whether a mother-child household unit, a married couple household, or a larger unit extending over several households — the centrality of mothers is not predicated on male powerlessness (Tanner 1974, 133).

Organized, resilient, women-centered networks of bloodmothers and othermothers are key in understanding this centrality. Grandmothers, sisters, aunts, or cousins act as othermothers by taking on child-care responsibilities for one another's children. When needed, temporary child-care arrangements can turn into long-term care or informal adoption (Stack 1974; Gutman 1976). Despite strong cultural norms encouraging women to become biological mothers, women who choose not to do so often receive recognition and status from othermother relationships that they establish with Black children.

In African-American communities these women-centered networks of community-based child care often extend beyond the boundaries of biologically related individuals and include "fictive kin" (Stack 1974). Civil rights activist Ella Baker describes how informal adoption by othermothers functioned in the rural southern community of her childhood:

> My aunt who had thirteen children of her own raised three more. She had become a midwife, and a child was born who was covered with sores. Nobody was particularly wanting the child, so she took the child and raised him . . . and another mother decided she didn't want to be bothered with two children. So my aunt took one and raised him . . . they were part of the family. (Cantarow 1980, 59)

Even when relationships are not between kin or fictive kin, African-American community norms traditionally were such that neighbors cared for one another's children. Sara Brooks, a southern domestic worker, describes the importance that the community-based child care a neighbor offered her daughter had for her: "She kept Vivian and she didn't charge me nothin' either. You see, people used to look after each other, but now it's not that way. I reckon it's because we all was poor, and I guess they put theirself in the place of the person that they was helpin'" (Simonsen 1986, 181). Brooks's experiences demonstrate how the African-American cultural value placed on cooperative child care traditionally found institutional support in the adverse conditions under which so many Black women mothered.

Othermothers are key not only in supporting children but also in helping bloodmothers who, for whatever reason, lack the preparation or desire for motherhood. In confronting racial oppression, maintaining community-based child care and respecting othermothers who assume child-care responsibilities serve a critical function in African-American communities. Children orphaned by sale or death of their parents under slavery, children conceived through rape, children of young mothers, children born into extreme poverty or to alcoholic or drug-addicted mothers, or children who for other reasons cannot remain with their bloodmothers have all been supported by othermothers, who, like Ella Baker's aunt, take in additional children even when they have enough of their own.

Young women are often carefully groomed at an early age to become othermothers. As a ten-year-old, civil rights activist Ella Baker learned to be an othermother by caring for the children of a widowed neighbor: "Mama would say, 'You must take the clothes to Mr. Powell's house, and give so-and-so a bath.' The children were running wild. . . . The kids . . . would take off across the field. We'd chase them down, and bring them back, and put 'em in the tub, and wash 'em off, and change clothes, and carry the dirty ones home, and wash them. Those kind of things were routine" (Cantarow 1980, 59).

Many Black men also value community-based child care but exercise these values to a lesser extent. Young Black men are taught how to care for children (Young 1970; Lewis 1975). During slavery, for example, Black children under age ten experienced little division of labor. They were dressed alike and performed similar tasks. If the activities of work and play are any indication of the degree of gender role differentiation that existed among slave children, "then young girls probably grew up minimizing the difference between the sexes while learning far more about the differences between the races" (D. White 1985, 94). Differences among Black men and women in attitudes toward children may have more to do with male labor force patterns. As Ella Baker observes, "my father took care of people too, but . . . my father had to work" (Cantarow 1980, 60).

Historically, community-based child care and the relationships among bloodmothers and othermothers in women-centered networks have taken diverse institutional forms. In some polygynous West African societies, the children of the same father but different mothers referred to one another as brothers and sisters. While a strong bond existed between the biological mother and her child — one so strong that, among the Ashanti for example, "to show disrespect towards one's mother is tantamount to sacrilege" (Fortes 1950, 263) — children could be disciplined by any of their other "mothers." Cross-culturally, the high status given to othermothers and the cooperative nature of child-care arrangements among bloodmothers and othermothers in Caribbean and other Black societies gives credence to the importance that people of African descent place on mothering (Clarke 1966; Shimkin et al. 1978; Sudarkasa 1981a, 1981b).

Although the political economy of slavery brought profound changes to enslaved Africans, cultural values concerning the importance of motherhood and the value of cooperative approaches to child care continued. While older women served as nurses and midwives, their most common occupation was caring for the children of parents who worked (D. White 1985). Informal adoption of orphaned children reinforced the importance of social motherhood in African-American communities (Gutman 1976).

The relationship between bloodmothers and othermothers survived the transition from a slave economy to postemancipation southern rural agriculture. Children in southern rural communities were not solely the responsibility of their biological mothers. Aunts, grandmothers, and others who had time to supervise children served as othermothers (Young 1970; Dougherty 1978). The significant status women enjoyed in family networks and in African-American communities continued to be linked to their bloodmother and othermother activities.

The entire community structure of bloodmothers and othermothers is   15
under assault in many inner-city neighborhoods, where the very fabric of
African-American community life is being eroded by illegal drugs. But even
in the most troubled communities, remnants of the othermother tradition
endure. Bebe Moore Campbell's 1950s North Philadelphia neighborhood
underwent some startling changes when crack cocaine flooded the streets in
the 1980s. Increases in birth defects, child abuse, and parental neglect left
many children without care. But some residents, such as Miss Nee, continue the othermother tradition. After raising her younger brothers and sisters and five children of her own, Miss Nee cares for three additional children whose families fell apart. Moreover, on any given night Miss Nee's
house may be filled by up to a dozen children because she has a reputation
for never turning away a needy child ("Children of the Underclass" 1989).

Traditionally, community-based child care certainly has been functional
for African-American communities and for Black women. Black feminist
theorist bell hooks suggests that the relationships among bloodmothers and
othermothers may have greater theoretical importance than currently
recognized:

> This form of parenting is revolutionary in this society because it takes
> place in opposition to the ideas that parents, especially mothers,
> should be the only childrearers.... This kind of shared responsibility
> for child care can happen in small community settings where people
> know and trust one another. It cannot happen in those settings if par-
> ents regard children as their "property," their possession. (1984, 144)

The resiliency of women-centered family networks illustrates how traditional cultural values — namely, the African origins of community-based
child care — can help people cope with and resist oppression. By continuing community-based child care, African-American women challenge one
fundamental assumption underlying the capitalist system itself: that children are "private property" and can be disposed of as such. Notions of property, child care, and gender differences in parenting styles are embedded in
the institutional arrangements of any given political economy. Under the
property model stemming from capitalist patriarchal families, parents may
not literally assert that their children are pieces of property, but their parenting may reflect assumptions analogous to those they make in connection
with property (J. Smith 1983). For example, the exclusive parental "right" to
discipline children as parents see fit, even if discipline borders on abuse,
parallels the widespread assumption that property owners may dispose of
their property without consulting members of the larger community. By
seeing the larger community as responsible for children and by giving
othermothers and other nonparents "rights" in child rearing, African-
Americans challenge prevailing property relations. It is in this sense that
traditional bloodmother/othermother relationships in women-centered networks are "revolutionary."

Mothers, Daughters, and Socialization for Survival

Black mothers of daughters face a troubling dilemma. On one hand, to ensure their daughters' physical survival, mothers must teach them to fit into systems of oppression. For example, as a young girl Black activist Ann Moody questioned why she was paid so little for the domestic work she began at age nine, why Black women domestics were sexually harassed by their white male employers, why no one would explain the activities of the National Association for the Advancement of Colored People to her, and why whites had so much more than Blacks. But her mother refused to answer her questions and actually chastised her for questioning the system and stepping out of her "place" (Moody 1968). Like Ann Moody, Black daughters learn to expect to work, to strive for an education so they can support themselves, and to anticipate carrying heavy responsibilities in their families and communities because these skills are essential to their own survival and those for whom they will eventually be responsible (Ladner 1972; Joseph 1981). New Yorker Michele Wallace recounts: "I can't remember when I first learned that my family expected me to work, to be able to take care of myself when I grew up. . . . It had been drilled into me that the best and only sure support was self-support" (1978, 89–90). Mothers also know that if their daughters uncritically accept the limited opportunities offered Black women, they become willing participants in their own subordination. Mothers may have ensured their daughters' physical survival, but at the high cost of their emotional destruction.

On the other hand, Black daughters with strong self-definitions and self-valuations who offer serious challenges to oppressive situations may not physically survive. When Ann Moody became active in the early 1960s in sit-ins and voter registration activities, her mother first begged her not to participate and then told her not to come home because she feared the whites in Moody's hometown would kill her. Despite the dangers, mothers routinely encourage Black daughters to develop skills to confront oppressive conditions. Learning that they will work and that education is a vehicle for advancement can also be seen as ways of enhancing positive self-definitions and self-valuations in Black girls. Emotional strength is essential, but not at the cost of physical survival.

Historian Elsa Barkley Brown captures this delicate balance Black mothers negotiate by pointing out that her mother's behavior demonstrated the "need to teach me to live my life one way and, at the same time, to provide all the tools I would need to live it quite differently" (1989, 929). Black daughters must learn how to survive in interlocking structures of race, class, and gender oppression while rejecting and transcending those same structures. In order to develop these skills in their daughters, mothers demonstrate varying combinations of behaviors devoted to ensuring their daughters' survival — such as providing them with basic necessities and protecting them in dangerous environments — to helping their daughters go further than mothers themselves were allowed to go.

This special vision of Black mothers may grow from the nature of work women have done to ensure Black children's survival. These work experiences have provided Black women with a unique angle of vision, a particular perspective on the world to be passed on to Black daughters. African and African-American women have long integrated economic self-reliance with mothering. In contrast to the cult of true womanhood,[2] in which work is defined as being in opposition to and incompatible with motherhood, work for Black women has been an important and valued dimension of Afrocentric definitions of Black motherhood. Sara Brooks describes the powerful connections that economic self-reliance and mothering had in her childhood: "When I was about nine I was nursin' my sister Sally — I'm about seven or eight years older than Sally. And when I would put her to sleep, instead of me goin' somewhere and sit down and play, I'd get my little old hoe and get out there and work right in the field around the house" (in Simonsen 1986, 86).

Mothers who are domestic workers or who work in proximity to whites may experience a unique relationship with the dominant group. For example, African-American women domestics are exposed to all the intimate details of the lives of their white employers. Working for whites offers domestic workers a view from the inside and exposes them to ideas and resources that might aid in their children's upward mobility. In some cases domestic workers form close, long-lasting relationships with their employers. But domestic workers also encounter some of the harshest exploitation confronting women of color. The work is low paid, has few benefits, and exposes women to the threat and reality of sexual harassment. Black domestics could see the dangers awaiting their daughters.

Willi Coleman's mother used a Saturday-night hair-combing ritual to impart a Black women's standpoint on domestic work to her daughters:

> Except for special occasions mama came home from work early on Saturdays. She spent six days a week mopping, waxing, and dusting other women's houses and keeping out of reach of other women's husbands. Saturday nights were reserved for "taking care of them girls" hair and the telling of stories. Some of which included a recitation of what she had endured and how she had triumphed over "folks that were lower than dirt" and "no-good snakes in the grass." She combed, patted, twisted, and talked, saying things which would have embarrassed or shamed her at other times. (Coleman 1987, 34)

Bonnie Thornton Dill's (1980) study of the child-rearing goals of domestic workers illustrates how African-American women see their work as both

---

[2]*cult of true womanhood:* The nineteenth-century ideal of women as saintly, even angelic, beings — passive and innocent creatures who should be sheltered from the rough world of men.

contributing to their children's survival and instilling values that will encourage their children to reject their proscribed "place" as Blacks and strive for more. Providing a better chance for their children was a dominant theme among Black women. Domestic workers described themselves as "struggling to give their children the skills and training they did not have; and as praying that opportunities which had not been open to them would be open to their children" (110). But the women also realized that while they wanted to communicate the value of their work as part of the ethics of caring and personal accountability, the work itself was undesirable. Bebe Moore Campbell's (1989) grandmother and college-educated mother stressed the importance of education. Campbell remembers, "[they] wanted me to Be Somebody, to be the second generation to live out my life as far away from a mop and scrub brush and Miss Ann's floors as possible" (83).

Understanding this goal of balancing the need for the physical survival of their daughters with the vision of encouraging them to transcend the boundaries confronting them explains many apparent contradictions in Black mother-daughter relationships. Black mothers are often described as strong disciplinarians and overly protective; yet these same women manage to raise daughters who are self-reliant and assertive. To explain this apparent contradiction, Gloria Wade-Gayles suggests that Black mothers:

> do not socialize their daughters to be "passive" or "irrational." Quite the contrary, they socialize their daughters to be independent, strong, and self-confident. Black mothers are suffocatingly protective and domineering precisely because they are determined to mold their daughters into whole and self-actualizing persons in a society that devalues Black women. (1984, 12)

African-American mothers place a strong emphasis on protection, either by trying to shield their daughters as long as possible from the penalties attached to their race, class, and gender status or by teaching them skills of independence and self-reliance so that they will be able to protect themselves. Consider the following verse from a traditional blues song:

> I ain't good lookin' and ain't got waist-long hair
> I say I ain't good lookin' and I ain't got waist-long hair
> But my mama gave me something that'll take me anywhere.
> (Washington 1984, 144)

Unlike white women, symbolized by "good looks" and "waist-long hair," Black women have been denied male protection. Under such conditions it becomes essential that Black mothers teach their daughters skills that will "take them anywhere."

Black women's autobiographies and fiction can be read as texts revealing the multiple ways that African-American mothers aim to shield their daughters from the demands of being Black women in oppressive conditions. Michele Wallace describes her growing understanding of how her mother viewed raising Black daughters in Harlem: "My mother has since explained to me that since it was obvious her attempt to protect me was going to prove a failure, she was determined to make me realize that as a black girl in white America I was going to find it an uphill climb to keep myself together" (1978, 98). In discussing the mother-daughter relationship in Paule Marshall's *Brown Girl, Brownstones,* Rosalie Troester catalogues the ways mothers have aimed to protect their daughters and the impact this may have on relationships themselves:

> Black mothers, particularly those with strong ties to their community, sometimes build high banks around their young daughters, isolating them from the dangers of the larger world until they are old and strong enough to function as autonomous women. Often these dikes are religious, but sometimes they are built with education, family, or the restrictions of a close-knit and homogeneous community. . . . This isolation causes the currents between Black mothers and daughters to run deep and the relationship to be fraught with an emotional intensity often missing from the lives of women with more freedom. (1984, 13)

Michele Wallace's mother built banks around her headstrong adolescent daughter by institutionalizing her in a Catholic home for troubled girls. Wallace went willingly, believing "I thought at the time that I would rather live in hell than be with my mother" (1978, 98). But years later Wallace's evaluation of her mother's decision changed: "Now that I know my mother better, I know that her sense of powerlessness made it all the more essential to her that she take radical action" (98).

African-American mothers try to protect their daughters from the dangers that lie ahead by offering them a sense of their own unique self-worth. Many contemporary Black women writers report the experience of being singled out, of being given a sense of specialness at an early age which encouraged them to develop their talents. My own mother marched me to the public library at age five, helped me get my first library card, and told me that I could do anything if I learned how to read. In discussing the works of Paule Marshall, Dorothy West, and Alice Walker, Mary Helen Washington observes that all three writers make special claims about the roles their mothers played in the development of their creativity: "The bond with their mothers is such a fundamental and powerful source that the term 'mothering the mind' might have been coined specifically to define their experiences as writers" (1984, 144).

Black women's efforts to provide a physical and psychic base for their children can affect mothering styles and the emotional intensity of Black mother-daughter relationships. As Gloria Wade-Gayles points out, "mothers in Black Women's fiction are strong and devoted . . . they are rarely affectionate" (1984, 10). For example, in Toni Morrison's *Sula* (1974), Eva Peace's husband ran off, leaving her with three small children and no money. Despite her feelings, "the demands of feeding her three children were so acute she had to postpone her anger for two years until she had both the time and energy for it" (32). Later in the novel Eva's daughter Hannah asks, "Mamma, did you ever love us?" (67). Eva angrily replies, "What you talkin' bout did I love you girl I stayed alive for you" (69). For far too many Black mothers, the demands of providing for children in inter-locking systems of oppression are sometimes so demanding that they have neither the time nor the patience for affection. And yet most Black daugh-ters love and admire their mothers and are convinced that their mothers truly love them (Joseph 1981).

Black daughters raised by mothers grappling with hostile environments have to come to terms with their feelings about the difference between the idealized versions of maternal love extant in popular culture and the strict and often troubled mothers in their lives. For a daughter, growing up means developing a better understanding that even though she may desire more affection and greater freedom, her mother's physical care and protec-tion are acts of maternal love. Ann Moody describes her growing awareness of the cost her mother paid as a domestic worker who was a single mother of three. Watching her mother sleep after the birth of another child, Moody remembers:

> For a long time I stood there looking at her. I didn't want to wake her up. I wanted to enjoy and preserve that calm, peaceful look on her face, I wanted to think she would always be that happy. . . . Adline and Junior were too young to feel the things I felt and know the things I knew about Mama. They couldn't remember when she and Daddy separated. They had never heard her cry at night as I had or worked and helped as I had done when we were starving. (1968, 57)

Moody initially sees her mother as a strict disciplinarian, a woman who tries to protect her daughter by withholding information. But as Moody matures and better understands the oppression in her community, her ideas change. On one occasion Moody left school early the day after a Black family had been brutally murdered by local whites. Moody's description of her mother's reaction reflects her deepening understanding: "When I walked in the house Mama didn't even ask me why I came home. She just looked at me. And for the first time I realized she understood what was going on within me or was trying to anyway" (1968, 136).

Another example of a daughter's efforts to understand her mother is of-fered in Renita Weems's account of coming to grips with maternal deser-tion. In the following passage Weems struggles with the difference between the stereotypical image of the superstrong Black mother and her own alco-holic mother's decision to leave her children: "My mother loved us. I must believe that. She worked all day in a department store bakery to buy shoes and school tablets, came home to curse out neighbors who wrongly accused her children of any impropriety (which in an apartment complex usually meant stealing), and kept her house cleaner than most sober women" (1984,

26). Weems concludes that her mother loved her because she provided for her to the best of her ability.

Othermothers often help to defuse the emotional intensity of relation- 30 ships between bloodmothers and their daughters. In recounting how she dealt with the intensity of her relationship with her mother, Weems describes the women teachers, neighbors, friends, and othermothers she turned to — women who, she observes, "did not have the onus of providing for me, and so had the luxury of talking to me" (1984, 27). Cheryl West's household included her brother, her lesbian mother, and Jan, her mother's lover. Jan became an othermother to West: "Yellow-colored, rotund and short in stature, Jan was like a second mother. . . . Jan braided my hair in the morning, mother worked two jobs and tucked me in at night. Loving, gentle, and fastidious in the domestic arena, Jan could be a rigid disciplinarian. . . . To the outside world . . . she was my 'aunt' who happened to live with us. But she was much more involved and nurturing than any of my 'real' aunts" (1987, 43).

June Jordan offers an eloquent analysis of one daughter's realization of the high personal cost African-American women can pay in providing an economic and emotional foundation for their children. In the following passage Jordan offers a powerful testament of how she came to see that her mother's work was an act of love:

> As a child I noticed the sadness of my mother as she sat alone in the kitchen at night. . . . Her woman's work never won permanent victories of any kind. It never enlarged the universe of her imagination or her power to influence what happened beyond the front door of our house. Her woman's work never tickled her to laugh or shout or dance. But she did raise me to respect her way of offering love and to believe that hard work is often the irreducible factor for survival, not something to avoid. Her woman's work produced a reliable home base where I could pursue the privileges of books and music. Her woman's work invented the potential for a completely different kind of work for us, the next generation of Black women: huge, rewarding hard work demanded by the huge, new ambitions that her perfect confidence in us engendered. (1985, 105)

Community Othermothers and Political Activism

Black women's experiences as othermothers provide a foundation for Black women's political activism. Nurturing children in Black extended family networks stimulates a more generalized ethic of caring and personal accountability among African-American women who often feel accountable to all the Black community's children.

This notion of Black women as community othermothers for all Black children traditionally allowed African-American women to treat biologically unrelated children as if they were members of their own families. For example, sociologist Karen Fields describes how her grandmother, Mamie Garvin Fields, draws on her power as a community othermother when dealing with unfamiliar children: "She will say to a child on the street who looks up to no good, picking out a name at random, 'Aren't you Miz Pinckney's boy?' in that same reproving tone. If the reply is, 'No, *ma'am,* my mother is Miz Gadsden,' whatever threat there was dissipates" (Fields and Fields 1983, xvii).

The use of family language in referring to members of the African-American community also illustrates this dimension of Black motherhood. In the following passage, Mamie Garvin Fields describes how she became active in surveying substandard housing conditions among African-Americans in Charleston. Note her explanation of why she uses family language:

> I was one of the volunteers they got to make a survey of the places where we were paying extortious rents for indescribable property. I said "we," although it wasn't Bob and me. We had our own home, and so did many of the Federated Women. Yet we still felt like it really was "we" living in those terrible places, and it was up to us to do something about them. (Fields and Fields 1983, 195)

Black women frequently describe Black children using family language. In recounting her increasingly successful efforts to teach a boy who had given other teachers problems, my daughter's kindergarten teacher stated, "You know how it can be — the majority of children in the learning disabled classes are *our children.* I know he didn't belong there, so I volunteered to take him." In their statements both women use family language to describe the ties that bind them as Black women to their responsibilities as members of an African-American community/family.

In explaining why the South Carolina Federation of Colored Women's   35 Clubs founded a home for girls, Ms. Fields observes, "We all could see that we had a responsibility for those girls: they were the daughters of our community coming up" (Fields and Fields 1983, 197). Ms. Fields's activities as a community othermother on behalf of the "daughters" of her community represent an established tradition among educated Black women. Serving as othermothers to women in the Black community has a long history. A study of 108 of the first generation of Black club women found that three-quarters were married, three-quarters worked outside the home, but only one-fourth had children (Giddings 1984). These women emphasized self-report for Black women, whether married or not, and realized that self-sufficient community othermothers were important. "Not all women are intended for mothers," declares an 1894 edition of the *Woman's Era.* "Some of us have not the temperament for family life.... Clubs will make women think seriously of their future lives, and not make girls think their only alternative is to marry" (Giddings 1984, 108).

Black women writers also explore this theme of the African-American community othermother who nurtures the Black community. One of the earliest examples is found in Frances Ellen Watkins Harper's 1892 novel *Iola Leroy*. By rejecting an opportunity to marry a prestigious physician and dissociate herself from the Black community, nearly white Iola, the main character, chooses instead to serve the African-American community. Similarly, in Alice Walker's *Meridian* (1976), the main character rejects the controlling image of the "happy slave," the self-sacrificing Black mother, and chooses to become a community othermother. Giving up her biological child to the care of an othermother, Meridian gets an education, works in the civil rights movement, and eventually takes on responsibility for the children of a small southern town. She engages in a "quest that will take her beyond the society's narrow meaning of the word *mother* as a physical state and expand its meaning to those who create, nurture, and save life in social and psychological as well as physical terms" (Christian 1985, 242).

Sociologist Cheryl Gilkes (1980, 1982, 1983) suggests that community othermother relationships can be key in stimulating Black women's decisions to become community activists. Gilkes asserts that many of the Black women community activists in her study became involved in community organizing in response to the needs of their own children and of those in their communities. The following comment is typical of how many of the Black women in Gilkes's study relate to Black children: "There were a lot of summer programs springing up for kids, but they were exclusive . . . and I found that most of *our kids* were excluded" (1980, 219). For many women what began as the daily expression of their obligations as community othermothers, as was the case for the kindergarten teacher, developed into full-fledged actions as community leaders.

This community othermother tradition also explains the "mothering the mind" relationships that can develop between Black women teachers and their Black women students. Unlike the traditional mentoring so widely reported in educational literature, this relationship goes far beyond that of providing students with either technical skills or a network of academic and professional contacts. Bell hooks shares the special vision that teachers who see our work in community othermother terms can pass on to our students: "I understood from the teachers in those segregated schools that the work of any teacher committed to the full self-realization of students was necessarily and fundamentally radical, that ideas were not neutral, that to teach in a way that liberates, that expands consciousness, that awakens, is to challenge domination at its very core" (1989, 50). Like the mother-daughter relationship, this "mothering the mind" among Black women seeks to move toward the mutuality of a shared sisterhood that binds African-American women as community othermothers.

Community othermothers have made important contributions in building a different type of community in often hostile political and economic surroundings (Reagon 1987). Community othermothers' actions demonstrate a clear rejection of separateness and individual interest as the basis of either community organization or individual self-actualization. Instead, the connectedness with others and common interest expressed by community othermothers models a very different value system, one whereby Afrocentric feminist ethics of caring and personal accountability move communities forward.

Motherhood as a Symbol of Power

Motherhood — whether bloodmother, othermother, or community   40
othermother — can be invoked by African-American communities as a symbol of power. Much of Black women's status in African-American communities stems not only from actions as mothers in Black family networks but from contributions as community othermothers.

Black women's involvement in fostering African-American community development forms the basis for community-based power. This is the type of power many African-Americans have in mind when they describe the "strong Black women" they see around them in traditional African-American communities. Community othermothers work on behalf of the Black community by expressing ethics of caring and personal accountability which embrace conceptions of transformative power and mutuality (Kuykendall 1983). Such power is transformative in that Black women's relationships with children and other vulnerable community members are not intended to dominate or control. Rather, their purpose is to bring people along, to — in the words of late-nineteenth-century Black feminists — "uplift the race" so that vulnerable members of the community will be able to attain the self-reliance and independence essential for resistance.

When older African-American women invoke their power as community othermothers, the results can be quite striking. Karen Fields recounts a telling incident:

> One night . . . as Grandmother sat crocheting alone at about two in the morning, a young man walked into the living room carrying the portable TV from upstairs. She said, "Who are you looking for *this* time of night?" As Grandmother [described] the incident to me over the phone, I could hear a tone of voice that I know well. It said, "Nice boys don't do that." So I imagine the burglar heard his own mother or grandmother at that moment. He joined in the familial game just created: "Well, he told me that I could borrow it." "*Who* told you?" "John." "Um um, no *John* lives here. You got the wrong house." (Fields and Fields, 1983, xvi)

After this dialogue, the teenager turned around, went back upstairs, and returned the television.

In local African-American communities, community othermothers become identified as powerful figures through furthering the community's well-being. Sociologist Charles Johnson (1934/1979) describes the behavior

MORE NONTRADITIONAL FAMILY UNITS

Guy, Chair, Three-Way Lamp

A Woman, Her Daughter, Forty-four
My Little Ponies

The Troy Triplets and Their
Personal Trainer

Two Guys, Two Gals, Two Phones,
a Fax, and a Blender

R. Chast

Drawing by R. Chast © 1992, The New Yorker Magazine, Inc.

of an elderly Black woman at a church service in rural 1930s Alabama. Even though she was not on the program, the woman stood up to speak. The master of ceremonies rang for her to sit down, but she refused to do so claiming, "I am the mother of this church, and I will say what I please" (172). The master of ceremonies offered the following explanation to the congregation as to why he let the woman continue: "Brothers, I know you all honor Sister Moore. Course our time is short but she has acted as a mother to me. . . . Any time old folks get up I give way to them" (173).

References

Aschenbrenner, Joyce. 1975. *Lifelines, Black Families in Chicago.* Prospect Heights, IL: Waveland Press.

Brown, Elsa Barkley. 1989. "African-American Women's Quilting: A Framework for Conceptualizing and Teaching African-American Women's History." *Signs* 14 (4): 921–29.

Campbell, Bebe Moore. 1989. *Sweet Summer: Growing Up With and Without My Dad.* New York: Putnam.

Cantarow, Ellen. 1980. *Moving the Mountain: Women Working for Social Change.* Old Westbury, NY: Feminist Press.

Christian, Barbara. 1985. *Black Feminist Criticism, Perspectives on Black Women Writers.* New York: Pergamon.

Clarke, Edith. 1966. *My Mother Who Fathered Me.* 2d ed. London: Allen and Unwin.

Coleman, Willi. 1987. "Closets and Keepsakes." *Sage: A Scholarly Journal on Black Women* 4 (2): 34–35.

Dill, Bonnie Thornton. 1980. "'The Means to Put My Children Through': Child-Rearing Goals and Strategies among Black Female Domestic Servants." In *The Black Woman,* edited by La Frances Rodgers-Rose, 107–23. Beverly Hills, CA: Sage.

Dougherty, Molly C. 1978. *Becoming a Woman in Rural Black Culture.* New York: Holt, Rinehart and Winston.

Fields, Mamie Garvin, and Karen Fields. 1983. *Lemon Swamp and Other Places: A Carolina Memoir.* New York: Free Press.

Fortes, Meyer. 1950. "Kinship and Marriage among the Ashanti." In *African Systems of Kinship and Marriage,* edited by A. R. Radcliffe-Brown and Daryll Forde, 252–84. New York: Oxford University Press.

Giddings, Paula. 1984. *When and Where I Enter . . . The Impact of Black Women on Race and Sex in America.* New York: William Morrow.

Gilkes, Cheryl Townsend. 1980. "'Holding Back the Ocean with a Broom': Black Women and Community Work." In *The Black Woman,* edited by La Frances Rodgers-Rose, 217–32. Beverly Hills, CA: Sage.

———. 1982. "Successful Rebellious Professionals: The Black Woman's Professional Identity and Community Commitment." *Psychology of Women Quarterly* 6 (3): 289–311.

———. 1983. "Going Up for the Oppressed: The Career Mobility of Black Women Community Workers." *Journal of Social Issues* 39 (3): 1115–39.

Gutman, Herbert. 1976. *The Black Family in Slavery and Freedom, 1750–1925.* New York: Random House.

hooks, bell. 1984. *From Margin to Center.* Boston: South End Press.

———. 1989. *Talking Back: Thinking Feminist, Thinking Black.* Boston: South End Press.

Johnson, Charles S. [1934] 1979. *Shadow of the Plantation.* Chicago: University of Chicago Press.

Jordan, June. 1985. *On Call.* Boston: South End Press.

Joseph, Gloria. 1981. "Black Mothers and Daughters: Their Roles and Functions in American Society." In *Common Differences,* edited by Gloria Joseph and Jill Lewis, 75–126. Garden City, NY: Anchor.

Kuykendall, Eleanor H. 1983. "Toward an Ethic of Nurturance: Luce Irigaray on Mothering and Power." In *Motherhood: Essays in Feminist Theory,* edited by Joyce Treblicot, 263–74. Totowa, NJ: Rowman & Allanheld.

Ladner, Joyce. 1972. *Tomorrow's Tomorrow.* Garden City, NJ: Doubleday.

Lewis, Diane K. 1975. "The Black Family: Socialization and Sex Roles." *Phylon* 36 (3): 221–37.

Martin, Elmer, and Joanne Mitchell Martin. 1978. *The Black Extended Family.* Chicago: University of Chicago Press.

Moody, Ann. 1968. *Coming of Age in Mississippi.* New York: Dell.

Morrison, Toni. 1974. *Sula.* New York: Random House.

Reagon, Bernice Johnson. 1987. "African Diaspora Women: The Making of Cultural Workers." In *Women in Africa and the African Diaspora,* edited by Rosalyn Terborg-Penn, Sharon Harley, and Andrea Benton Rushing, 167–80. Washington, DC: Howard University Press.

Shimkin, Demitri B., Edith M. Shimkin, and Dennis A. Frate, eds. 1978. *The Extended Family in Black Societies.* Chicago: Aldine.

Simonsen, Thordis, ed. 1986. *You May Plow Here: The Narrative of Sara Brooks.* New York: Touchstone.

Smith, Janet Farrell. 1983. "Parenting as Property." In *Mothering: Essays in Feminist Theory,* edited by Joyce Treblicot, 199–212. Totowa, NJ: Rowman & Allanheld.

Stack, Carol D. 1974. *All Our Kin: Strategies for Survival in a Black Community.* New York: Harper & Row.

Sudarkasa, Niara. 1981a. "Female Employment and Family Organization in West Africa." In *The Black Woman Cross-Culturally,* edited by Filomina Chioma Steady, 49–64. Cambridge, MA: Schenkman.

———. 1981b. "Interpreting the African Heritage in Afro-American Family Organization." In *Black Families,* edited by Harriette Pipes McAdoo, 37–53. Beverly Hills, CA: Sage.

Tanner, Nancy. 1974. "Matrifocality in Indonesia and Africa and among Black Americans." In *Woman, Culture, and Society,* edited by Michelle Z. Rosaldo and Louise Lamphere, 129–56. Stanford: Stanford University Press.

Troester, Rosalie Riegle. 1984. "Turbulence and Tenderness: Mothers, Daughters, and 'Othermothers' in Paule Marshall's *Brown Girl, Brownstones.*" *Sage: A Scholarly Journal on Black Women* 1 (2): 13–16.

Wade-Gayles, Gloria. 1984. "The Truths of Our Mothers' Lives: Mother-Daughter Relationships in Black Women's Fiction." *Sage: A Scholarly Journal on Black Women* 1 (2): 8–12.

Walker, Alice. 1976. *Meridian.* New York: Pocket Books.

Wallace, Michele. 1978. *Black Macho and the Myth of the Superwoman.* New York: Dial Press.

Washington, Mary Helen. 1984. "I Sign My Mother's Name: Alice Walker, Dorothy West and Paule Marshall." In *Mothering the Mind: Twelve Studies of Writers and Their Silent Partners,* edited by Ruth Perry and Martine Watson Broronley, 143–63. New York: Holmes & Meier.

Weems, Renita. 1984. "'Hush. Mama's Gotta Go Bye Bye': A Personal Narrative." *Sage: A Scholarly Journal on Black Women* 1 (2): 25–28.

West, Cheryl. 1987. "Lesbian Daughter." *Sage: A Scholarly Journal on Black Women* 4 (2): 42–44.

White, Deborah Gray. 1985. *Ar'n't I a Woman? Female Slaves in the Plantation South.* New York: W. W. Norton.

Young, Virginia Heyer. 1970. "Family and Childhood in a Southern Negro Community." *American Anthropologist* 72 (32): 269–88.

ENGAGING THE TEXT

1. In what ways do the African American families described by Collins differ from traditional Eurocentric views of family structure?

2. Define "othermother" and "fictive kin." Why are these roles important to the African American family? Can you think of similar roles in families that are not African American?

3. What explanations does Collins give for the centrality of women in extended African American families?

4. Explain what Collins means by "socialization for survival" (para. 17) and define the dilemma it presents to black mothers. Do you think this dilemma still exists?

5. Explain the connections Collins sees between African American family life and political struggle.

EXPLORING CONNECTIONS

6. Apply Collins's terms and ideas to Bebe Moore Campbell's "Envy" (p. 98). To what extent does Collins's analysis help explain Campbell's narrative? Does it change your understanding of "Envy"?

7. Read Toni Cade Bambara's "The Lesson" (p. 394) and discuss how Collins's description of community othermothers might illuminate Miss Moore's attitude toward Sylvia and her friends.

8. What interests and values does Roz Chast suggest lie at the heart of the "nontraditional family units" that she depicts in the cartoon on page 126? How do these differ from the interests and values that unite the alternative families described by Collins?

EXTENDING THE CRITICAL CONTEXT

9. Survey several depictions of African American family life on recent TV shows. To what extent do the mothers on these shows display the attitudes, values, and behaviors that Collins describes? What images of black motherhood does TV create?

10. Watch the film *Soul Food* and explore the roles that African American women are given in this film. To what extent do their portrayals confirm or

complicate Collins's analysis of the roles typically played by African American women?

11. Write a paper exploring the dynamics of a particular family relationship (for example, father-son, sisters) within some group in American society *other than* African American. Following Collins's example, you may wish to include anecdotal support as well as published research. In any case, try to identify the definitive characteristics or patterns of the chosen relationship. How does this relationship connect to the family, the community, or one's sense of self?

Aunt Ida Pieces a Quilt

MELVIN DIXON

This is an extraordinary poem about AIDS, love, and family life. Its author, Melvin Dixon (b. 1950), received his Ph.D. from Brown University; in addition to teaching English at Queens College in New York, he published poetry, literary criticism, translations, and two novels. "Aunt Ida" appeared in Brother to Brother: New Writings by Black Gay Men *(1991). Dixon died of complications from AIDS in 1992.*

> You are right, but your patch isn't big enough.
> — JESSE JACKSON

> *When a cure is found and the last panel is*
> *sewn into place, the Quilt will be displayed*
> *in a permanent home as a national monument*
> *to the individual, irreplaceable people lost to AIDS —*
> *and the people who knew and loved them most.*
> — CLEVE JONES, *founder, The NAMES Project*

They brought me some of his clothes. The hospital gown,
those too-tight dungarees, his blue choir robe
with the gold sash. How that boy could sing!
His favorite color in a necktie. A Sunday shirt.
What I'm gonna do with all this stuff?   5
I can remember Junie without this business.
My niece Francine say they quilting all over the country.
So many good boys like her boy, gone.

At my age I ain't studying no needle and thread.
My eyes ain't so good now and my fingers lock in a fist,   10

they so eaten up with arthritis. This old back
don't take kindly to bending over a frame no more.
Francine say ain't I a mess carrying on like this.
I could make two quilts the time I spend running my mouth.

Just cut his name out the cloths, stitch something nice   15
about him. Something to bring him back. You can do it,
Francine say. Best sewing our family ever had.
Quilting ain't that easy, I say. Never was easy.
Y'all got to help me remember him good.

Most of my quilts was made down South. My mama   20
And my mama's mama taught me. Popped me on the tail
if I missed a stitch or threw the pattern out of line.
I did "Bright Star" and "Lonesome Square" and "Rally Round,"
what many folks don't bother with nowadays. Then Elmo and me
married and came North where the cold in Connecticut   25
cuts you like a knife. We was warm, though.
We had sackcloth and calico and cotton, 100% pure.
What they got now but polyester rayon. Factory made.

Let me tell you something. In all my quilts there's a secret
nobody knows. Every last one of them got my name Ida   30
stitched on the back side in red thread.
That's where Junie got his flair. Don't let nobody fool you.
When he got the Youth Choir standing up and singing
the whole church would rock. He'd throw up his hands
from them wide blue sleeves and the church would hush   35
right down to the funeral parlor fans whisking the air.
He'd toss his head back and holler and we'd all cry holy.

And nevermind his too-tight dungarees.
I caught him switching down the street one Saturday night,
and I seen him more than once. I said, Junie,   40
you ain't got to let the world know all your business.
Who cared where he went when he wanted to have fun.
He'd be singing his heart out come Sunday morning.

When Francine say she gonna hang this quilt in the church
I like to fall out. A quilt ain't no showpiece,   45
it's to keep you warm. Francine say it can do both.
Now I ain't so old-fashioned I can't change,
but I made Francine come over and bring her daughter
Belinda. We cut and tacked his name, *JUNIE.*
Just plain and simple, "*JUNIE, our boy.*"   50
Cut the *J* in blue, the *U* in gold. *N* in dungarees
just as tight as you please. The *I* from the hospital gown

and the white shirt he wore First Sunday. Belinda
put the necktie in *E* in the cross stitch I showed her.

Wouldn't you know we got to talking about Junie.   55
We could smell him in the cloth.
Underarm. Afro Sheen pomade.[1] Gravy stains.
I forgot all about my arthritis.
When Francine left me to finish up, I swear
I heard Junie giggling right along with me   60
as I stitched Ida on the back side in red thread.

Francine say she gonna send this quilt to Washington
like folks doing from all 'cross the country,
so many good people gone. Babies, mothers, fathers
and boys like our Junie. Francine say   65
they gonna piece this quilt to another one,
another name and another patch
all in a larger quilt getting larger and larger.

Maybe we all like that, patches waiting to be pieced.
Well, I don't know about Washington.   70
We need Junie here with us. And Maxine,
she cousin May's husband's sister's people,
she having a baby and here comes winter already.
The cold cutting like knives. Now where did I put that needle?

ENGAGING THE TEXT

1. Identify all of the characters and their relationships in the poem. Then retell the story of the poem in your own words.

2. Discuss the movement of Aunt Ida's mind and her emotions as we move from stanza to stanza. What happens to Aunt Ida in the poem? What is the dominant feeling at the end of the poem?

3. Junie's clothes take on symbolic weight in the quilt and, of course, in the poem as well. What do the hospital gown, the dungarees, the choir robe, and the white shirt and necktie represent?

4. What is Aunt Ida about to make at the end of the poem, and what is its significance?

EXPLORING CONNECTIONS

5. Discuss the actions of the women in this poem in light of Patricia Hill Collins's discussion of African American families (p. 112). To what extent do the authors share similar beliefs about black families?

---

[1]*Afro Sheen pomade:* Hair-care product for African Americans.

6. How might Melvin Dixon (p. 130) and Roger Jack (p. 89) respond to Anndee Hochman's suggestion (p. 45) that belonging to a family requires complete conformity? Which vision of family membership seems the most realistic to you?

EXTENDING THE CRITICAL CONTEXT

7. Write a screenplay or dramatic script to "translate" the story of "Aunt Ida Pieces a Quilt" into dramatic form. Time permitting, organize a group to read or perform the piece for the class.
8. Through this chapter, families have been portrayed through a variety of metaphors: they have appeared as a nuclear unit, a house with many connecting rooms, a network of relationships, and a quilt with many parts. What are the implications of each of these metaphors? How do they affect our view of family? What other metaphors might capture your vision of American family life?
9. Watch the documentary *Common Threads: Stories from the Quilt* and write a poem based on the life of one of the people profiled in this film.

2

Learning Power

The Myth of Education and Empowerment

Skeptical Student, photo by Charles Agel.

Broke out of Chester gaol,[1] last night, one James Rockett, a very short well set fellow, pretends to be a schoolmaster, of a fair complexion, and smooth fac'd; Had on when he went away, a light colored camblet coat, a blue cloth jacket, without sleeves, a check shirt, a pair of old dy'd leather breaches, gray worsted stockings, a pair of half worn pumps, and an almost new beaver hat; his hair is cut off, and wears a cap; he is a great taker of snuff, and very apt to get drunk; he has with him two certificates, one from some inhabitants in Burlington county, Jersey, which he will no doubt produce as a pass. Who ever takes up and secures said Rockett in any gaol, shall have two Pistoles reward, paid by October 27, 1756. — SAMUEL SMITH, Gaoler

— Advertisement for a "runaway schoolmaster"
Pennsylvania Gazette, November 25, 1756

Americans have always had mixed feelings about schooling. Today, most Americans tend to see education as something intrinsically valuable or important. After all, education is the engine that drives the American Dream. The chance to learn, better oneself, and gain the skills that pay off in upward mobility has sustained the hope of millions of Americans. As a nation we look up to figures like Abraham Lincoln and Frederick Douglass, who learned to see beyond poverty and slavery by learning to read. Education tells us that the American Dream can work for everyone. It reassures us that we are, in fact, "created equal" and that the path to achievement lies through individual effort and hard work, not blind luck or birth.

But as the advertisement quoted above suggests, American attitudes toward teachers and teaching haven't always been overwhelmingly positive. The Puritans who established the Massachusetts Bay Colony viewed education with respectful skepticism. Schooling in Puritan society was a force for spiritual rather than worldly advancement. Lessons were designed to reinforce moral and religious training and to teach children to read the Bible for themselves. Education was important to the Puritan "Divines" because it was a source of order, control, and discipline. But when education aimed at more worldly goals or was undertaken for self-improvement, it was seen as a menacing, sinful luxury. Little wonder, then, that the Puritans often viewed teaching as something less than an ennobling profession. In fact, teachers in the early colonies were commonly treated as menial employees by the families and communities they served. The following list of the "Duties of a Schoolmaster" gives you some idea of the status of American educators in the year 1661:

1. Act as court-messenger
2. Serve summonses
3. Conduct certain ceremonial church services

[1]*gaol:* Jail.

4. Lead Sunday choir
5. Ring bell for public worship
6. Dig graves
7. Take charge of school
8. Perform other occasional duties

Colonial American teachers were frequently indentured servants who had sold themselves for five to ten years, often for the price of passage to the New World. Once here, they drilled their masters' children in spiritual exercises until they earned their freedom — or escaped.

The reputation of education in America began to improve with the onset of the Revolutionary War. Following the overthrow of British rule, leaders sought to create a spirit of nationalism that would unify the former colonies. Differences were to be set aside, for, as George Washington pointed out, "the more homogeneous our citizens can be made . . . the greater will be our prospect of permanent union." The goal of schooling became the creation of uniformly loyal, patriotic Americans. In the words of Benjamin Rush, one of the signers of the Declaration of Independence, "Our schools of learning, by producing one general and uniform system of education, will render the mass of people more homogeneous and thereby fit them more easily for uniform and peaceable government."

Thomas Jefferson saw school as a training ground for citizenship and democratic leadership. Recognizing that an illiterate and ill-informed population would be unable to assume the responsibilities of self-government, Jefferson laid out a comprehensive plan in 1781 for public education in the state of Virginia. According to Jefferson's blueprint, all children would be eligible for three years of free public instruction. Of those who could not afford further schooling, one promising "genius" from each school was to be "raked from the rubbish" and given six more years of free education. At the end of that time, ten boys would be selected to attend college at public expense. Jeffersonian Virginia may have been the first place in the United States where education so clearly offered the penniless boy a path to self-improvement. However, this path was open to very few, and Jefferson, like Washington and Rush, was more concerned with benefiting the state than serving the individual student: "We hope to avail the state of those talents which nature has sown as liberally among the poor as the rich, but which perish without use, if not sought for and cultivated." For leaders of the American Revolution, education was seen as a tool for nation-building, not personal development.

Perhaps that's why Native American leaders remained lukewarm to the idea of formal education despite its growing popularity with their colonial neighbors. When, according to Ben Franklin's report, the government of Virginia offered to provide six American Indian youths with the best college education it could afford in 1744, the tribal leaders of the Six Nations politely declined, pointing out that our ideas of this kind of education happen not to be the same with yours. We have had some experience of it; several of our young people were formerly brought up at the colleges of the northern provinces; they were instructed in all your sciences; but when they came back to us, they were bad runners; ignorant of every means of living in the woods; unable to bear either cold or hunger; knew neither how to build a cabin, take a deer, or kill an enemy; spoke our language imperfectly; were therefore neither fit for hunters, warriors, or counselors: they were totally good for nothing.

It's not surprising that these tribal leaders saw American education as useless. Education works to socialize young people — to teach them the values, beliefs, and skills central to their society; the same schooling that prepared students for life in Anglo-American culture made them singularly unfit for tribal life. As people who stood outside the dominant society, Native Americans were quick to realize education's potential as a tool for enforcing cultural conformity. But despite their resistance, by the 1880s the U.S. government had established special "Indian schools" dedicated to assimilating Indian children into Anglo-American culture and destroying tribal knowledge and tribal ways.

In the nineteenth century two great historical forces — industrialization and immigration — combined to exert even greater pressure for the "homogenization" of young Americans. Massive immigration from Ireland and Eastern and Central Europe led to fears that "non-native" peoples would undermine the cultural identity of the United States. Many saw school as the first line of defense against this perceived threat, a place where the children of "foreigners" could become Americanized. In a meeting of educators in 1836, one college professor stated the problem as bluntly as possible:

> Let us now be reminded, that unless we educate our immigrants, they will be our ruin. It is no longer a mere question of benevolence, of duty, or of enlightened self-interest, but the intellectual and religious training of our foreign population has become essential to our own safety; we are prompted to it by the instinct of self-preservation.

Industrialization gave rise to another kind of uniformity in nineteenth-century public education. Factory work didn't require the kind of educational preparation needed to transform a child into a craftsman or merchant. So, for the first time in American history, school systems began to categorize students into different educational "tracks" that offered qualitatively different kinds of education to different groups. Some — typically students from well-to-do homes — were prepared for professional and managerial positions. But most were consigned to education for life "on the line." Increasing demand for factory workers put a premium on young people who were obedient and able to work in large groups according to fixed schedules. As a result, leading educators in 1874 proposed a system of schooling that would meet the needs of the "modern industrial community" by stressing "punctuality, regularity, attention, and silence, as habits necessary through life." History complicates the myth of education as a source of personal empowerment. School can bind as effectively as it can liberate; it can enforce conformity and limit life chances as well as foster individual talent.

But history also supplies examples of education serving the idealistic goals of democracy, equality, and self-improvement. Nineteenth-century educator and reformer Horace Mann worked to expand educational opportunity to all Americans. Mann believed that genuine democratic self-government would become a reality only if every citizen were sufficiently educated to make reasoned judgments about even the thorniest public issues. "Education," according to Mann, "must prepare our citizens to become municipal officers, intelligent jurors, honest witnesses, legislators, or competent judges of legislation — in fine, to fill all the manifold relations of life." In Mann's conception, the "common school," offering educational opportunity to anyone with the will to learn, would make good on the central promise of American democracy; it would become "the great equalizer of the conditions of men."

At the turn of the century, philosopher and educational theorist John Dewey made even greater claims for educational empowerment. A fierce opponent of the kind of "tracking" associated with industrial education, Dewey proposed that schools should strive to produce thinking citizens rather than obedient workers. As members of a democracy, all men and women, according to Dewey, are entitled to an education that helps them make the best of their natural talents and enables them to participate as fully as possible in the life of their community: "only by being true to the full growth of the individuals who make it up, can society by any chance be true to itself." Most of our current myths of education echo the optimism of Mann and Dewey. Guided by these two men's ideas, most Americans still believe that education leads to self-improvement and can help us empower ourselves — and perhaps even transform our society.

Does education empower us? Or does it stifle personal growth by squeezing us into prefabricated cultural molds? This chapter takes a critical look at American education: what it can do and how it shapes or enhances our identities. The first four readings provide a starting point for exploring the myth of educational empowerment. We begin with a classic statement of the goals of American education — Horace Mann's 1848 "Report of the Massachusetts Board of Education." Mann's optimistic view of education as a means of social mobility in a democratic state provides a clear statement of the myth of personal empowerment through education. For a counterpoint, we turn to a veteran teacher, John Taylor Gatto, and his searing analysis of the debilitating "hidden curriculem" of American schooling. In "I Just Wanna Be Average," Mike Rose provides a moving personal account of the dream of educational success and pays tribute to an inner-city teacher who never loses sight of what can be achieved in a classroom. An excerpt from Jean Anyon's "Social Class and the Hidden Curriculum of Work" rounds off the section by suggesting that schools virtually program students for success or failure according to their socioeconomic status.

Following these initial readings, the chapter's Visual Portfolio presents three paintings by Norman Rockwell that reflect some of America's most hallowed cultural memories of the classroom experience. The reproductions include *The Spirit of Education, The Graduate,* and Rockwell's famous civil-rights-movement portrait of Ruby Bridges as she was escorted to the schoolhouse door. They offer you the chance to consider the place of education in America's cultural mythology and to imagine how a contemporary artist might update the story of educational success for the twenty-first century.

The next group of readings offers a closer look at the tensions experienced by so-called nontraditional students as they struggle with the complexities — and prejudices — of a deeply traditional educational system. The section begins with a classic autobiographical selection by Richard Rodriguez, which raises questions about the ambivalent role schooling plays in the lives of many Americans who come from families new to the world of higher education. In her dramatic narrative poem "Para Teresa," Inés Hernández-Ávila asks whether academic achievement demands cultural conformity or whether it can become a form of protest against oppression and racism. Claude M. Steele's "Thin Ice: 'Stereotype Threat' and Black College Students" presents research suggesting that the academic performance of many minority college students is limited by persistent negative cultural stereotypes and not, as some have argued, by genetics or inherited intelligence. "Learning to Read" closes the section with the moving story of Malcom X's spiritual and political rebirth through his self-made and highly untraditional education in prison.

The three selections that follow extend this examination of the nature of American education by focusing more directly on the experiences of college women. Deborah Tannen's "The Roots of Debate in Education and the Hope of Dialogue" explores the patriarchal roots of the "agonistic" culture of American higher education and suggests that this combative intellectual style works against the interests of female students. Kyoko Mori's "School" offers a cross-cultural counterpoint to Tannen. In this personal essay, Mori compares her positive experience as a student of English and creative writing in an American college with the more authoritarian education she received in Japanese schools. "Politics in the Schoolroom" by former Reagan appointee Lynne V. Cheney offers a conservative rebuttal to feminist and multicultural critiques of American educational practices. The final selection of the chapter takes up the issue of electronic media and their relation to education. In "Empowering Children in the Digital Age: Towards a Radical Media Pedagogy" Henry Jenkins presents his case for a program of critical media education and for open, uncensored Internet access for all American children.

Sources

John Hardin Best and Robert T. Sidwell, eds., *The American Legacy of Learning: Readings in the History of Education*. Philadelphia: J. B. Lippincott Co., 1966.

Sol Cohen, ed., *Education in the United States: A Documentary History*, 5 vols. New York: Random House, 1974.

John Dewey, "The School and Society" (1899) and "My Pedagogic Creed" (1897). In *John Dewey on Education*. New York: Modern Library, 1964.

Benjamin Franklin, "Remarks Concerning the Savages of North America." In *The Works of Dr. Benjamin Franklin*. Hartford: S. Andrus and Son, 1849.

Thomas Jefferson, *Notes on the State of Virginia*. Chapel Hill: University of North Carolina Press, 1955.

Lorraine Smith Pangle and Thomas L. Pangle, *The Learning of Liberty: The Educational Ideas of the American Founders*. Lawrence: University Press of Kansas, 1993.

Leonard Pitt, *We Americans*, vol. 2, 3rd ed. Dubuque: Kendall/Hunt, 1987.

Edward Stevens and George H. Wood, *Justice, Ideology, and Education: An Introduction to the Social Foundations of Education*. New York: Random House, 1987.

Elizabeth Vallance, "Hiding the Hidden Curriculum: An Interpretation of the Language of Justification in Nineteenth-Century Educational Reform." *Curriculum Theory Network,* vol. 4. no. 1 (1973–74), pp. 5–21.

Robert B. Westbrook, "Public Schooling and American Democracy." In *Democracy, Education, and the Schools,* Roger Soder, ed. San Francisco: Jossey-Bass Publishers, 1996.

BEFORE READING

- Freewrite for fifteen or twenty minutes about your best and worst educational experiences. Then, working in groups, compare notes to see if you can find recurring themes or ideas in what you've written. What aspects of school seem to stand out most clearly in your memories? Do the best experiences have anything in common? How about the worst? What aspects of your school experience didn't show up in the freewriting?

- Work in small groups to draw a collective picture that expresses your experience of high school or college. Don't worry about your drawing skill — just load the page with imagery, feelings, and ideas. Then show your work to other class members and let them try to interpret it.

- Write a journal entry from the point of view of the girl pictured on the title page of this chapter (p. 134). Try to capture the thoughts that are going through her head. What has her day in school been like? What is she looking forward to? What is she dreading? Share your entries with your classmates and discuss your responses.

From *Report of the Massachusetts Board of Education, 1848*

HORACE MANN

If you check a list of schools in your home state, you'll probably discover at least a few dedicated to the memory of Horace Mann. We memorialize Mann today in school systems across the country because he may have done more than any other American to codify the myth of empowerment through education. Born on a farm in Franklin, Massachusetts, in 1796, Mann raised himself out of rural poverty to a position of national eminence through hard work and study. His first personal educational experiences, however, were far from pleasurable: the ill-trained and often brutal schoolmasters he first encountered in rural Massachusetts made rote memorization and the power of the rod the focus of their educational approach. After graduating from Brown University in 1819, Mann pursued a career in law and politics and eventually served as president of the Massachusetts State Senate. Discouraged by the condition of the state's public schools, Mann abandoned his political career to become secretary of the Massachusetts Board of Education in 1837. Mann's vision of "the common school," the centerpiece of his approach to democratic education, grew out of research he conducted on the Prussian school system during his tour of Europe in 1843. Presented originally as an address to the Massachusetts State Legislature, the report of 1848 has had a lasting impact on the goals and content of American education.

Without undervaluing any other human agency, it may be safely affirmed that the common school, improved and energized as it can easily be, may become the most effective and benignant of all the forces of civilization. Two reasons sustain this position. In the first place, there is a universality in its operation, which can be affirmed of no other institution whatever. If administered in the spirit of justice and conciliation, all the rising generation may be brought within the circle of its reformatory and elevating influences. And, in the second place, the materials upon which it operates are so pliant and ductile as to be susceptible of assuming a greater variety of forms than any other earthly work of the Creator. The inflexibility and ruggedness of the oak, when compared with the lithe sapling or the tender germ, are but feeble emblems to typify the docility of childhood when contrasted with the obduracy and intractableness of man. It is these inherent advantages of the common school, which, in our own State, have produced results so striking, from a system so imperfect, and an administration so feeble. In teaching the blind and the deaf and dumb, in kindling the latent spark of intelligence that lurks in an idiot's mind, and in the more holy work of reforming abandoned and outcast children, education has proved what it can do by glorious experiments. These wonders it has done in its infancy, and with the lights of a limited experience; but when its faculties shall be fully developed, when it shall be trained to wield its mighty energies for the protection of society against the giant vices which now invade and torment it, — against intemperance, avarice, war, slavery, bigotry, the woes of want, and the wickedness of waste, — then there will not be a height to which these enemies of the race can escape which it will not scale, nor a Titan among them all whom it will not slay.

I proceed, then, in endeavoring to show how the true business of the schoolroom connects itself, and becomes identical, with the great interests of society. The former is the infant, immature state of those interests; the latter their developed, adult state. As "the child is father to the man," so may the training of the schoolroom expand into the institutions and fortunes of the State.

Physical Education

In the worldy prosperity of mankind, health and strength are indispensable ingredients. . . .

Leaving out, then, for the present purpose, all consideration of the pains of sickness and the anguish of bereavement, the momentous truth still remains, that sickness and premature death are positive evils for the statesman and political economist to cope with. The earth, as a hospital for the diseased, would soon wear out the love of life; and, if but the half of mankind were sick, famine, from non-production, would speedily threaten the whole.

Now, modern science has made nothing more certain than that both good and ill health are the direct result of causes mainly within our own control. In other words, the health of the race is dependent upon the conduct of the race. The health of the individual is determined primarily by his parents, secondarily by himself. The vigorous growth of the body, its strength and its activity, its powers of endurance, and its length of life, on the one hand; and dwarfishness, sluggishness, infirmity, and premature death on the other, — are all the subjects of unchangeable laws. These laws are ordained of God; but the knowledge of them is left to our diligence, and the observance of them to our free agency. . . .

My general conclusion, then, under this head, is, that it is the duty of all the governing minds in society — whether in office or out of it — to diffuse a knowledge of these beautiful and beneficent laws of health and life throughout the length and breadth of the State; to popularize them; to make them, in the first place, the common acquisition of all, and, through education and custom, the common inheritance of all, so that the healthful

5

habits naturally growing out of their observance shall be inbred in the people, exemplified in the personal regimen of each individual, incorporated into the economy of every household, observable in all private dwellings, and in all public edifices, especially in those buildings which are erected by capitalists for the residence of their work-people, or for renting to the poorer classes; obeyed, by supplying cities with pure water; by providing public baths, public walks, and public squares; by rural cemeteries; by the drainage and sewerage of populous towns, and by whatever else may promote the general salubrity of the atmosphere: in fine, by a religious observance of all those sanitary regulations with which modern science has blessed the world.

For this thorough diffusion of sanitary intelligence, the common school is the only agency. It is, however, an adequate agency. . . .

Intellectual Education as a Means of Removing Poverty, and Securing Abundance

. . . According to the European theory, men are divided into classes, — some to toil and earn, others to seize and enjoy. According to the Massachusetts theory, all are to have an equal chance for earning, and equal security in the enjoyment of what they earn. The latter tends to equality of condition; the former, to the grossest inequalities. . . .

But is it not true that Massachusetts, in some respects, instead of adhering more and more closely to her own theory, is becoming emulous of the baneful examples of Europe? The distance between the two extremes of society is lengthening, instead of being abridged. With every generation, fortunes increase on the one hand, and some new privation is added to poverty on the other. We are verging towards those extremes of opulence and of penury, each of which unhumanizes the human mind. A perpetual struggle for the bare necessaries of life, without the ability to obtain them, makes men wolfish. Avarice, on the other hand, sees, in all the victims of misery around it, not objects for pity and succor, but only crude materials to be worked up into more money.

I suppose it to be the universal sentiment of all those who mingle any 10 ingredient of benevolence with their notions on political economy, that vast and overshadowing private fortunes are among the greatest dangers to which the happiness of the people in a republic can be subjected. Such fortunes would create a feudalism of a new kind, but one more oppressive and unrelenting than that of the middle ages. The feudal lords in England and on the Continent never held their retainers in a more abject condition of servitude than the great majority of foreign manufacturers and capitalists hold their operatives and laborers at the present day. The means employed are different; but the similarity in results is striking. What force did then, money does now. The villein of the middle ages had no spot of earth on which he could live, unless one were granted to him by his lord. The operative or laborer of the present day has no employment, and therefore no bread, unless the capitalist will accept his services. The vassal had no shelter but such as his master provided for him. Not one in five thousand of English operatives or farm-laborers is able to build or own even a hovel; and therefore they must accept such shelter as capital offers them. The baron prescribed his own terms to his retainers: those terms were peremptory, and the serf must submit or perish. The British manufacturer or farmer pre-scribes the rate of wages he will give to his work-people; he reduces these wages under whatever pretext he pleases; and they, too, have no alternative but submission or starvation. In some respects, indeed, the condition of the modern dependant is more forlorn than that of the corresponding serf class in former times. Some attributes of the patriarchal relation did spring up between the lord and his lieges to soften the harsh relations subsisting be-tween them. Hence came some oversight of the condition of children, some relief in sickness, some protection and support in the decrepitude of age. But only in instances comparatively few have kindly offices smoothed the rugged relation between British capital and British labor. The children of the work-people are abandoned to their fate; and notwithstanding the priva-tions they suffer, and the dangers they threaten, no power in the realm has yet been able to secure them an education; and when the adult laborer is prostrated by sickness, or eventually worn out by toil and age, the poor-house, which has all along been his destination, becomes his destiny. . . .

Now, surely nothing but universal education can counterwork this ten-dency to the domination of capital and servility of labor. If one class pos-sesses all the wealth and the education, while the residue of society is igno-rant and poor, it matters not by what name the relation between them may be called: the latter, in fact and in truth, will be the servile dependants and subjects of the former. But, if education be equably diffused, it will draw property after it by the strongest of all attractions, for such a thing never did happen, and never can happen, as that an intelligent and practical body of men should be permanently poor. Property and labor in different classes are essentially antagonistic; but property and labor in the same class are es-sentially fraternal. The people of Massachusetts have, in some degree, appreciated the truth, that the unexampled prosperity of the State — its comfort, its competence, its general intelligence and virtue — is attributable to the education, more or less perfect, which all its people have received: but are they sensible of a fact equally important; namely, that it is to this same education that two-thirds of the people are indebted for not being to-day the vassals of as severe a tyranny, in the form of capital, as the lower classes of Europe are bound to in the form of brute force?

Education, then, beyond all other devices of human origin, is the great equalizer of the conditions of men, — the balance-wheel of the social ma-chinery. I do not here mean that it so elevates the moral nature as to make men disdain and abhor the oppression of their fellow-men. This idea per-tains to another of its attributes. But I mean that it gives each man the independence and the means by which he can resist the selfishness of other men. It does better than to disarm the poor of their hostility towards the rich: it prevents being poor. Agrarianism is the revenge of poverty against wealth. The wanton destruction of the property of others — the burning of hay-ricks and corn-ricks, the demolition of machinery because it supersedes hand-labor, the sprinkling of vitriol on rich dresses — is only agrarianism run mad. Education prevents both the revenge and the madness. On the other hand, a fellow-feeling for one's class or caste is the common instinct of hearts not wholly sunk in selfish regards for person or for family. The spread of education, by enlarging the cultivated class or caste, will open a wider area over which the social feelings will expand; and, if this education should be universal and complete, it would do more than all things else to obliterate factitious distinctions in society. . . .

For the creation of wealth, then, — for the existence of a wealthy people and a wealthy nation, — intelligence is the grand condition. The number of improvers will increase as the intellectual constituency, if I may call it, increases. In former times, and in most parts of the world even at the present day, not one man in a million has ever had such a development of mind as made it possible for him to become a contributor to art or science. Let this development precede, and contributions, numberless, and of inestimable value, will be sure to follow. That political economy, therefore, which busies itself about capital and labor, supply and demand, interest and rents, favorable and unfavorable balances of trade, but leaves out of account the element of a widespread mental development, is nought but stupendous folly. The greatest of all the arts in political economy is to change a consumer into a producer; and the next greatest is to increase the producer's producing power, — an end to be directly attained by increasing his intelligence. For mere delving, an ignorant man is but little better than a swine, whom he so much resembles in his appetites, and surpasses in his powers of mischief. . . .

Political Education

The necessity of general intelligence, — that is, of education (for I use the terms as substantially synonymous, because general intelligence can never exist without general education, and general education will be sure to produce general intelligence), — the necessity of general intelligence under a republican form of government, like most other very important truths, has become a very trite one. It is so trite, indeed, as to have lost much of its force by its familiarity. Almost all the champions of education seize upon this argument first of all, because it is so simple as to be understood by the ignorant, and so strong as to convince the sceptical. Nothing would be easier than to follow in the train of so many writers, and to demonstrate by logic, by history, and by the nature of the case, that a republican form of government, without intelligence in the people, must be, on a vast scale, what a madhouse, without superintendent or keepers, would be on a small one, — the despotism of a few succeeded by universal anarchy, and anarchy by despotism, with no change but from bad to worse. . . .

However elevated the moral character of a constituency may be, how- 15
ever well informed in matters of general science or history, yet they must, if citizens of a republic, understand something of the true nature and functions of the government under which they live. That any one, who is to participate in the government of a country when he becomes a man, should receive no instruction respecting the nature and functions of the government he is afterwards to administer, is a political solecism. In all nations, hardly excepting the most rude and barbarous, the future sovereign receives some training which is supposed to fit him for the exercise of the powers and duties of his anticipated station. Where, by force of law, the government devolves upon the heir while yet in a state of legal infancy, some regency, or other substitute, is appointed to act in his stead until his arrival at mature age; and, in the mean time, he is subjected to such a course of study and discipline as will tend to prepare him, according to the political theory of the time and the place, to assume the reins of authority at the appointed age. If in England, or in the most enlightened European monarchies, it would be a proof of restored barbarism to permit the future sovereign to grow up without any knowledge of his duties, — and who can doubt that it would be such a proof? — then, surely, it would be not less a proof of restored or of never-removed barbarism amongst us to empower any individual to use the elective franchise without preparing him for so momentous a trust. Hence the Constitution of the United States, and of our own State, should be made a study in our public schools. The partition of the powers of government into the three co-ordinate branches, — legislative, judicial, and executive — with the duties appropriately devolving upon each; the mode of electing or of appointing all officers, with the reasons on which it was founded; and, especially, the duty of every citizen, in a government of laws, to appeal to the courts for redress in all cases of alleged wrong, instead of undertaking to vindicate his own rights by his own arm; and, in a government where the people are the acknowledged sources of power, the duty of changing laws and rulers by an appeal to the ballot, and not by rebellion, — should be taught to all the children until they are fully understood.

Had the obligations of the future citizen been sedulously inculcated upon all the children of this Republic, would the patriot have had to mourn over so many instances where the voter, not being able to accomplish his purpose by voting, has proceeded to accomplish it by violence; where, agreeing with his fellow-citizens to use the machinery of the ballot, he makes a tacit reservation, that, if that machinery does not move according to his pleasure, he will wrest or break it? If the responsibleness and value of the elective franchise were duly appreciated, the day of our state and national elections would be among the most solemn and religious days in the calendar. Men would approach them, not only with preparation and solicitude, but with the sobriety and solemnity with which discreet and religious-minded men meet the great crises of life. No man would throw away his vote through caprice or wanton-ness, any more than he would throw away his estate, or sell his family into bondage. No man would cast his vote through malice or revenge, any more than a good surgeon would amputate a limb, or a good navigator sail through perilous straits, under the same criminal passions.

But perhaps it will be objected, that the Constitution is subject to dif-ferent readings, or that the policy of different administrations has become the subject of party strife; and, therefore, if any thing of constitutional or political law is introduced into our schools, there is danger that teachers will be chosen on account of their affinities to this or that political party, or that teachers will feign affinities which they do not feel in order that they may be chosen; and so each schoolroom will at length become a miniature political club-room, exploding with political resolves, or flaming out with political ad-dresses, prepared by beardless boys in scarcely legible hand-writing and in worse grammar.

With the most limited exercise of discretion, all apprehensions of this kind are wholly groundless. There are different readings of the Constitu-tion, it is true; and there are partisan topics which agitate the country from side to side: but the controverted points, compared with those about which there is no dispute, do not bear the proportion of one to a hundred. And, what is more, no man is qualified, or can be qualified, to discuss the dis-putable questions, unless previously and thoroughly versed in those ques-tions about which there is no dispute. In the terms and principles common to all, and recognized by all, is to be found the only common medium of language and of idea by which the parties can become intelligible to each other; and there, too, is the only common ground whence the arguments of the disputants can be drawn. . . .

. . . Thus may all the children of the Commonwealth receive instruction in all the great essentials of political knowledge, — in those elementary ideas without which they will never be able to investigate more recondite and debatable questions; thus will the only practicable method be adopted for discovering new truths, and for discarding, instead of perpetuating, old errors; and thus, too, will that pernicious race of intolerant zealots, whose whole faith may be summed up in two articles, — that they themselves are always infallibly right, and that all dissenters are certainly wrong, — be ex-tinguished, — extinguished, not by violence, nor by proscription, but by the more copious inflowing of the light of truth.

Moral Education

Moral education is a primal necessity of social existence. The unre-strained passions of men are not only homicidal, but suicidal; and a commu-nity without a conscience would soon extinguish itself. Even with a natural conscience, how often has evil triumphed over good! From the beginning of time, wrong has followed right, as the shadow the substance. . . .

But to all doubters, disbelievers, or despairers in human progress, it may still be said, there is one experiment which has never yet been tried. It is an experiment, which, even before its inception, offers the highest authority for its ultimate success. Its formula is intelligible to all; and it is as legible as though written in starry letters on an azure sky. It is expressed in these few and simple words: *"Train up a child in the way he should go; and, when he is old, he will not depart from it."* This declaration is positive. If the conditions are complied with, it makes no provision for a failure. Though pertaining to morals, yet, if the terms of the direction are observed, there is no more reason to doubt the result than there would be in an optical or a chemical experiment.

But this experiment has never yet been tried. Education has never yet been brought to bear with one-hundredth part of its potential force upon the natures of children, and, through them, upon the character of men and of the race. In all the attempts to reform mankind which have hitherto been made, whether by changing the frame of government, by aggravating or softening the severity of the penal code, or by substituting a government-created for a God-created religion, — in all these attempts, the infantile and youthful mind, its amenability to influences, and the enduring and self-operating character of the influences it receives, have been almost wholly unrecognized. Here, then, is a new agency, whose powers are but just beginning to be understood, and whose mighty energies hitherto have been but feebly invoked; and yet, from our experience, limited and imperfect as it is, we do know, that, far beyond any other earthly instrumentality, it is comprehensive and decisive. . . .

. . . So far as human instrumentalities are concerned, we have abundant means for surrounding every child in the State with preservative and moral influences as extensive and as efficient as those under which the present industrious, worthy, and virtuous members of the community were reared. And as to all those things in regard to which we are directly dependent upon the divine favor, have we not the promise, explicit and unconditional, that the men SHALL NOT depart from the way in which they should go, if the children are trained up in it? It has been overlooked that this promise is not restricted to parents, but seems to be addressed indiscriminately to all, whether parents, communities, states, or mankind. . . .

Religious Education

But it will be said that this grand result in practical morals is a consummation of blessedness that can never be attained without religion, and that no community will ever be religious without a religious education. Both these propositions I regard as eternal and immutable truths. Devoid of religious principles and religious affections, the race can never fall so low but that it may sink still lower; animated and sanctified by them, it can never rise so high but that it may ascend still higher. And is it not at least as presumptuous to expect that mankind will attain to the knowledge of truth, without being instructed in truth, and without that general expansion and development of faculty which will enable them to recognize and comprehend truth in any other department of human interest as in the department of religion? . . .

. . . That our public schools are not theological seminaries, is admitted. That they are debarred by law from inculcating the peculiar and distinctive doctrines of any one religious denomination amongst us, is claimed; and that they are also prohibited from ever teaching that what they do teach is the whole of religion, or all that is essential to religion or to salvation, is equally certain. But our system earnestly inculcates all Christian morals; it founds its morals on the basis of religion; it welcomes the religion of the Bible; and, in receiving the Bible, it allows it to do what it is allowed to do in no other system, — *to speak for itself.* But here it stops, not because it claims to have compassed all truth, but because it disclaims to act as an umpire between hostile religious opinions.

The very terms "public school" and "common school" bear upon their face that they are schools which the children of the entire community may attend. Every man not on the pauper-list is taxed for their support; but he is not taxed to support them as special religious institutions: if he were, it would satisfy at once the largest definition of a religious establishment. But he is taxed to support them as a *preventive* means against dishonesty, against fraud, and against violence, on the same principle that he is taxed to support criminal courts as a *punitive* means against the same offences. He is taxed to support schools, on the same principle that he is taxed to support paupers, — because a child without education is poorer and more wretched than a man without bread. He is taxed to support schools, on the same principle that he would be taxed to defend the nation against foreign invasion, or against rapine committed by a foreign foe, — because the general prevalence of ignorance, superstition, and vice, will breed Goth and Vandal at home more fatal to the public well-being than any Goth or Vandal from abroad. And, finally, he is taxed to support schools, because they are the most effective means of developing and training those powers and faculties in a child, by which, when he becomes a man, he may understand what his highest interests and his highest duties are, and may be in fact, and not in name only, a free agent. The elements of a political education are not bestowed upon any school child for the purpose of making him vote with this or that political party when he becomes of age, but for the purpose of enabling him to choose for himself with which party he will vote. So the religious education which a child receives at school is not imparted to him for the purpose of making him join this or that denomination when he arrives at years of discretion, but for the purpose of enabling him to judge for himself, according to the dictates of his own reason and conscience, what his religious obligations are, and whither they lead. . . .

Such, then, in a religious point of view, is the Massachusetts system of common schools. Reverently it recognizes and affirms the sovereign rights of the Creator, sedulously and sacredly it guards the religious rights of the creature; while it seeks to remove all hinderances, and to supply all furtherances, to a filial and paternal communion between man and his Maker. In a social and political sense, it is a *free* school-system. It knows no distinction of rich and poor, of bond and free, or between those, who, in the imperfect light of this world, are seeking, through different avenues, to reach the gate of heaven. Without money and without price, it throws open its doors, and spreads the table of its bounty, for all the children of the State. Like the sun, it shines not only upon the good, but upon the evil, that they may become good; and, like the rain, its blessings descend not only upon the just, but upon the unjust, that their injustice may depart from them, and be known no more.

ENGAGING THE TEXT

1. What is Mann's view of the powers of education? What does he see as education's role in society? To what extent would you agree that education successfully carries out these functions today?

2. What does Mann mean by "sanitary intelligence" (para. 7)? Why did he feel that the development of this kind of intelligence was such an important aspect of schooling? In what ways has your own education stressed the development of sanitary intelligence? How valuable was this nonacademic instruction?

3. How does Mann view the role of education in relation to wealth and poverty? How do you think such views would be received today if advocated by a school-board candidate or contender for the presidency? In your estimation, how effective has education been in addressing economic differences in American society?

4. Mann suggests that education plays a special role in preparing citizens to become active participants in a republican form of government. In what ways has your education prepared you to participate in democratic decision making? How effective has this preparation been? What could be done to improve the way that schools currently prepare students for their role as citizens?

5. What, according to Mann, is the proper relationship of public education to issues of morality and religion? What specific moral or ethical principles should public schools attempt to teach?

EXPLORING CONNECTIONS

6. Reread E. J. Graff's "What Makes a Family?" (p. 26) and explore how the structure of American families during the mid-1800s might have shaped some of Mann's views on the nonacademic functions of public schooling. How should the realities of contemporary American family life be addressed — or compensated for — in public schools today?

7. Read "Class in America: Myths and Realities" by Gregory Mantsios (p. 318), "The Invisible Poor" by James Fallows (p. 356), "Stephen Cruz"

IF ALL THE "EDUCATION REFORMS" HAPPENED AT ONCE,

by Studs Terkel (p. 335), and "Race at the End of History" by Ronald Takaki (p. 383) and write an essay in which you discuss how class differences in American society complicate the educational program outlined by Mann.

8. Review the cartoon "If All the 'Education Reforms' Happened at Once," which appears at the top of this page. As a class, debate whether or not American education is trying to do too much today.

EXTENDING THE CRITICAL CONTEXT

9. Research recent court decisions and legislative initiatives on the issue of prayer in school. How do prevailing views of the separation of church and state compare with the ideas presented in Mann's assessment of the goals

of public education in 1848? Then, as a class, debate the proper role of moral and religious instruction in public education.

10. Working in small groups, draft a list of what you think the proper goals of public education in a democracy should be. Exchange these lists, then compare and discuss your results. How does your class's view of the powers of education differ from that offered by Mann?

The Seven-Lesson Schoolteacher

JOHN TAYLOR GATTO

There's no doubt that America's schools are meant to benefit the students they serve; they're intended to transmit a body of knowledge — a curriculum — that equips students with all the ideas, skills, and attitudes necessary to help them lead happy and productive lives. But even the best intentions can go awry; as John Taylor Gatto argues in this selection, education in the United States may harbor a "hidden curriculum" — an unwritten, unacknowledged set of lessons about self and society that schooling inflicts on every student from kindergarten to graduate school. An award-winning educator and ardent Libertarian, Gatto suggests that what school does best is to inculcate seven such unconscious and debilitating lessons. Gatto has taught in New York City public schools for more than two decades. In 1990 he was named New York City Teacher of the Year. This selection comes from Dumbing Us Down: The Hidden Curriculum of Compulsory Schooling *(1992). His most recent book is* A Different Kind of Teacher: Reflections on the Bitter Lessons of American Schooling *(2000).*

I

Call me Mr. Gatto, please. Twenty-six years ago, having nothing better to do with myself at the time, I tried my hand at schoolteaching. The license I have certifies that I am an instructor of English language and English literature, but that isn't what I do at all. I don't teach English, I teach school — and I win awards doing it.

Teaching means different things in different places, but seven lessons are universally taught from Harlem to Hollywood Hills. They constitute a national curriculum you pay for in more ways than you can imagine, so you might as well know what it is. You are at liberty, of course, to regard these lessons any way you like, but believe me when I say I intend no irony in this presentation. These are the things I teach, these are the things you pay me to teach. Make of them what you will.

1. Confusion

A lady named Kathy wrote this to me from Dubois, Indiana, the other day:

> What big ideas are important to little kids? Well, the biggest idea I think they need is that what they are learning isn't idiosyncratic — that there is some system to it all and it's not just raining down on them as they helplessly absorb. That's the task, to understand, to make coherent.

Kathy has it wrong. *The first lesson I teach is confusion. Everything* I teach is out of context. I teach the un-relating of everything. I teach disconnections. I teach too much: the orbiting of planets, the law of large numbers, slavery, adjectives, architectural drawing, dance, gymnasium, choral singing, assemblies, surprise guests, fire drills, computer languages, parents' nights, staff-development days, pull-out programs, guidance with strangers my students may never see again, standardized tests, age-segregation unlike anything seen in the outside world. . . . What do any of these things have to do with each other?

Even in the best schools a close examination of curriculum and its sequences turns up a lack of coherence, full of internal contradictions. Fortunately the children have no words to define the panic and anger they feel *at constant violations of natural order and sequence* fobbed off on them as quality in education. The logic of the school-mind is that it is better to leave school with a tool kit of superficial jargon derived from economics, sociology, natural science, and so on, than with one genuine enthusiasm. But quality in education entails learning about something in depth. Confusion is thrust upon kids by too many strange adults, each working alone with only the thinnest relationship with each other, pretending, for the most part, to an expertise they do not possess.

Meaning, not disconnected facts, is what sane human beings seek, and education is a set of codes for processing raw data into meaning. Behind the patchwork quilt of school sequences and the school obsession with facts and theories, the age-old human search for meaning lies well concealed. This is harder to see in elementary school where the hierarchy of school experience seems to make better sense because the good-natured simple relationship between "let's do this" and "let's do that" is just assumed to mean something and the clientele has not yet consciously discerned how little substance is behind the play and pretense.

Think of the great natural sequences — like learning to walk and learning to talk; the progression of light from sunrise to sunset; the ancient procedures of a farmer, a smithy, or a shoemaker; or the preparation of a Thanksgiving feast — all of the parts are in perfect harmony with each

5

other, each action justifies itself and illuminates the past and the future. School sequences aren't like that, not inside a single class and not among the total menu of daily classes. School sequences are crazy. There is no particular reason for any of them, nothing that bears close scrutiny. Few teachers would dare to teach the tools whereby dogmas of a school or a teacher could be criticized, since everything must be accepted. School subjects are learned, if they *can* be learned, like children learn the catechism or memorize the Thirty-nine Articles of Anglicanism.

I teach the un-relating of everything, an infinite fragmentation the opposite of cohesion; what I do is more related to television programming than to making a scheme of order. In a world where home is only a ghost, because both parents work, or because of too many moves or too many job changes or too much ambition, or because something else has left everybody too confused to maintain a family relation, I teach you how to accept confusion as your destiny. That's the first lesson I teach.

2. Class Position

The second lesson I teach is class position. I teach that students must stay in the class where they belong. I don't know who decides my kids belong there but that's not my business. The children are numbered so that if any get away they can be returned to the right class. Over the years the variety of ways children are numbered by schools has increased dramatically, until it is hard to see the human beings plainly under the weight of numbers they carry. Numbering children is a big and very profitable undertaking, though what the strategy is designed to accomplish is elusive. I don't even know why parents would, without a fight, allow it to be done to their kids.

In any case, that's not my business. My job is to make them like being   10
locked together with children who bear numbers like their own. Or at the least to endure it like good sports. If I do my job well, the kids can't even *imagine* themselves somewhere else, because I've shown them how to envy and fear the better classes and how to have contempt for the dumb classes. Under this efficient discipline the class mostly polices itself into good marching order. That's the real lesson of any rigged competition like school. You come to know your place.

In spite of the overall class blueprint, which assumes that ninety-nine percent of the kids are in their class to stay, I nevertheless make a public effort to exhort children to higher levels of test success, hinting at eventual transfer from the lower class as a reward. I frequently insinuate the day will come when an employer will hire them on the basis of test scores and grades, even though my own experience is that employers are rightly indifferent to such things. I never lie outright, but I've come to see that truth and schoolteaching are, at bottom, incompatible, just as Socrates said thousands of years ago. The lesson of numbered classes is that everyone has a proper place in the pyramid and there is no way out of your class except by number magic. Failing that, you must stay where you are put.

3. Indifference

The third lesson I teach is indifference. I teach children not to care too much about anything, even though they want to make it appear that they do. How I do this is very subtle. I do it by demanding that they become totally involved in my lessons, jumping up and down in their seats with anticipation, competing vigorously with each other for my favor. It's heartwarming when they do that; it impresses everyone, even me. When I'm at my best I plan lessons very carefully in order to produce this show of enthusiasm. But when the bell rings I insist they drop whatever it is we have been doing and proceed quickly to the next work station. They must turn on and off like a light switch. Nothing important is ever finished in my class nor in any class I know of. Students never have a complete experience except on the installment plan.

Indeed, the lesson of bells is that no work is worth finishing, so why care too deeply about anything? Years of bells will condition all but the strongest to a world that can no longer offer important work to do. Bells are the secret logic of schooltime; their logic is inexorable. Bells destroy the past and future, rendering every interval the same as any other, as the abstraction of a map renders every living mountain and river the same, even though they are not. Bells inoculate each undertaking with indifference.

4. Emotional Dependency

The fourth lesson I teach is emotional dependency. By stars and red checks, smiles and frowns, prizes, honors, and disgraces, I teach kids to surrender their will to the predestinated chain of command. Rights may be granted or withheld by any authority without appeal, because rights do not exist inside a school — not even the right of free speech, as the Supreme Court has ruled — unless school authorities say they do. As a schoolteacher, I intervene in many personal decisions, issuing a pass for those I deem legitimate, or initiating a disciplinary confrontation for behavior that threatens my control. Individuality is constantly trying to assert itself among children and teenagers, so my judgments come thick and fast. Individuality is a contradiction of class theory, a curse to all systems of classification.

Here are some common ways it shows up: children sneak away for a private moment in the toilet on the pretext of moving their bowels, or they steal a private instant in the hallway on the grounds they need water. I know they don't, but I allow them to "deceive" me because this conditions them to depend on my favors. Sometimes free will appears right in front of me in pockets of children angry, depressed, or unhappy about things outside my ken; rights in such matters cannot be recognized by schoolteachers, only privileges that can be withdrawn, hostages to good behavior.

15

5. Intellectual Dependency

The fifth lesson I teach is intellectual dependency. Good students wait for a teacher to tell them what to do. It is the most important lesson, that we must wait for other people, better trained than ourselves, to make the meanings of our lives. The expert makes all the important choices; only I, the teacher, can determine what my kids must study, or rather, only the people who pay me can make those decisions, which I then enforce. If I'm told that evolution is a fact instead of a theory, I transmit that as ordered, punishing deviants who resist what I have been told to tell them to think. This power to control what children will think lets me separate successful students from failures very easily.

Successful children do the thinking I assign them with a minimum of resistance and a decent show of enthusiasm. Of the millions of things of value to study, I decide what few we have time for, or actually it is decided by my faceless employers. The choices are theirs, why should I argue? Curiosity has no important place in my work, only conformity.

Bad kids fight this, of course, even though they lack the concepts to know what they are fighting, struggling to make decisions for themselves about what they will learn and when they will learn it. How can we allow that and survive as schoolteachers? Fortunately there are tested procedures to break the will of those who resist; it is more difficult, naturally, if the kids have respectable parents who come to their aid, but that happens less and less in spite of the bad reputation of schools. No middle-class parents I have ever met actually believe that *their* kid's school is one of the bad ones. Not one single parent in twenty-six years of teaching. That's amazing, and probably the best testimony to what happens to families when mother and father have been well-schooled themselves, learning the seven lessons.

Good people wait for an expert to tell them what to do. It is hardly an exaggeration to say that our entire economy depends upon this lesson being learned. Think of what might fall apart if children weren't trained to be dependent: the social services could hardly survive; they would vanish, I think, into the recent historical limbo out of which they arose. Counselors and therapists would look on in horror as the supply of psychic invalids vanished. Commercial entertainment of all sorts, including television, would wither as people learned again how to make their own fun. Restaurants, the prepared-food industry, and a whole host of other assorted food services would be drastically down-sized if people returned to making their own meals rather than depending on strangers to plant, pick, chop, and cook for them. Much of modern law, medicine, and engineering would go too, the clothing business and schoolteaching as well, unless a guaranteed supply of helpless people continued to pour out of our schools each year.

Don't be too quick to vote for radical school reform if you want to continue getting a paycheck. We've built a way of life that depends on people doing what they are told because they don't know how to tell *themselves* what to do. It's one of the biggest lessons I teach.

6. Provisional Self-Esteem

The sixth lesson I teach is provisional self-esteem. If you've ever tried to wrestle into line kids whose parents have convinced them to believe they'll be loved in spite of anything, you know how impossible it is to make self-confident spirits conform. Our world wouldn't survive a flood of confident people very long, so I teach that a kid's self-respect should depend on expert opinion. My kids are constantly evaluated and judged.

A monthly report, impressive in its provision, is sent into a student's home to elicit approval or mark exactly, down to a single percentage point, how dissatisfied with the child a parent should be. The ecology of "good" schooling depends on perpetuating dissatisfaction, just as the commercial economy depends on the same fertilizer. Although some people might be surprised how little time or reflection goes into making up these mathematical records, the cumulative weight of these objective-seeming documents establishes a profile that compels children to arrive at certain decisions about themselves and their futures based on the casual judgment of strangers. Self-evaluation, the staple of every major philosophical system that ever appeared on the planet, is never considered a factor. The lesson of report cards, grades, and tests is that children should not trust themselves or their parents but should instead rely on the evaluation of certified officials. People need to be told what they are worth.

7. One Can't Hide

The seventh lesson I teach is that one can't hide. I teach students they are always watched, that each is under constant surveillance by myself and my colleagues. There are no private spaces for children, there is no private time. Class change lasts exactly three hundred seconds to keep promiscuous fraternization at low levels. Students are encouraged to tattle on each other or even to tattle on their own parents. Of course, I encourage parents to file reports about their own child's waywardness too. A family trained to snitch on itself isn't likely to conceal any dangerous secrets.

I assign a type of extended schooling called "homework," so that the effect of surveillance, if not that surveillance itself, travels into private households, where students might otherwise use free time to learn something unauthorized from a father or mother, by exploration, or by apprenticing to some wise person in the neighborhood. Disloyalty to the idea of schooling is a devil always ready to find work for idle hands.

The meaning of constant surveillance and denial of privacy is that no   25
one can be trusted, that privacy is not legitimate. Surveillance is an ancient imperative, espoused by certain influential thinkers, a central prescription set down in *The Republic*, in *The City of God*, in the *Institutes of the Christian Religion*, in *New Atlantis*, in *Leviathan*,[1] and in a host of other places. All these childless men who wrote these books discovered the same thing: children must be closely watched if you want to keep a society under tight central control. Children will follow a private drummer if you can't get them into a uniformed marching band.

---

[1]*The Republic*, in *The City of God* . . . *Leviathan:* Famous political and philosophical writings by authors like Plato, St. Augustine, and Thomas Hobbes.

II

It is the great triumph of compulsory government monopoly mass-schooling that among even the best of my fellow teachers, and among even the best of my students' parents, only a small number can imagine a different way to do things. "The kids have to know how to read and write, don't they?" "They have to know how to add and subtract, don't they?" "They have to learn to follow orders if they ever expect to keep a job."

Only a few lifetimes ago things were very different in the United States. Originality and variety were common currency; our freedom from regimentation made us the miracle of the world; social-class boundaries were relatively easy to cross; our citizenry was marvelously confident, inventive, and able to do much for themselves independently, and to think for themselves. We were something special, we Americans, all by ourselves, without government sticking its nose into and measuring every aspect of our lives, without institutions and social agencies telling us how to think and feel. We were something special, as individuals, as Americans.

But we've had a society essentially under central control in the United States since just before the Civil War, and such a society requires compulsory schooling, government monopoly schooling, to maintain itself. Before this development schooling wasn't very important anywhere. We had it, but not too much of it, and only as much as an individual *wanted*. People learned to read, write, and do arithmetic just fine anyway; there are some studies that suggest literacy at the time of the American Revolution, at least for non-slaves on the Eastern seaboard, was close to total. Thomas Paine's *Common Sense*[2] sold 600,000 copies to a population of 3,000,000, 20 percent of whom were slaves, and 50 percent indentured servants.

Were the colonists geniuses? No, the truth is that reading, writing, and arithmetic only take about one hundred hours to transmit as long as the audience is eager and willing to learn. The trick is to wait until someone asks and then move fast while the mood is on. Millions of people teach themselves these things, it really isn't very hard. Pick up a fifth-grade math or rhetoric textbook from 1850 and you'll see that the texts were pitched then on what would today be considered college level. The continuing cry for "basic skills" practice is a smoke screen behind which schools preempt the time of children for twelve years and teach them the seven lessons I've just described to you.

The society that has come increasingly under central control since just   30
before the Civil War shows itself in the lives we lead, the clothes we wear, the food we eat, and the green highway signs we drive by from coast to coast, all of which are the products of this control. So too, I think, are the epidemics of drugs, suicide, divorce, violence, cruelty, and hardening of class into caste in

---

[2]*Common Sense:* Paine's fifty-page pamphlet, published January 10, 1776, was recognized as the war-cry of the American revolutionary movement.

the United States products of the dehumanization of our lives, the lessening of individual, family, and community importance, a diminishment that proceeds from central control. The character of large compulsory institutions is inevitable; they want more and more until there isn't any more to give. School takes our children away from any possibility of an active role in community life — in fact it destroys communities by relegating the training of children to the hands of certified experts — and by doing so it ensures our children cannot grow up fully human. Aristotle taught that without a fully active role in community life one could not hope to become a healthy human being. Surely he was right. Look around you the next time you are near a school or an old people's reservation if you wish a demonstration.

School as it was built is an essential support system for a model of social engineering that condemns most people to be subordinate stones in a pyramid that narrows as it ascends to a terminal of control. School is an artifice that makes such a pyramidical social order seem inevitable, although such a premise is a fundamental betrayal of the American Revolution. From Colonial days through the period of the Republic we had no schools to speak of — read Benjamin Franklin's *Autobiography* for an example of a man who had no time to waste in school — and yet the promise of democracy was beginning to be realized. We turned our backs on this promise by bringing to life the ancient pharaonic dream of Egypt: compulsory subordination for all. That was the secret Plato reluctantly transmitted in *The Republic* when Glaucon and Adeimantus extort from Socrates the plan for total state control of human life, a plan necessary to maintain a society where some people take more than their share. "I will show you," says Socrates, "how to bring about such a feverish city, but you will not like what I am going to say." And so the blueprint of the seven-lesson school was first sketched.

The current debate about whether we should have a national curriculum is phony. We already have a national curriculum locked up in the seven lessons I have just outlined. Such a curriculum produces physical, moral, and intellectual paralysis, and no curriculum of content will be sufficient to reverse its hideous effects. What is currently under discussion in our national hysteria about failing academic performance misses the point. Schools teach exactly what they are intended to teach and they do it well: how to be a good Egyptian and remain in your place in the pyramid.

Engaging the Text

1. Working in groups, try to summarize each of the seven lessons that Gatto claims are taught as part of the hidden curriculum in all American schools. To what extent does the collective experience of your group support or challenge Gatto's claims?

2. Working together in small groups, construct an imaginary profile of the kind of student that Gatto's seven-lesson teacher would be likely to

produce. How accurately does this portrait describe most high school graduates intellectually, socially, and emotionally?

3. Freewrite for a page or two about a particular teacher you had who didn't fit Gatto's description of the seven-lesson teacher. What set this teacher apart or made her stand out for you? To what extent did she teach any or all of the lessons outlined by Gatto?

4. What does Gatto mean when he says that "truth and schoolteaching are, at bottom, incompatible" (para. 11)? Given his concerns about the impact of public education, why do you think Gatto continues to teach?

From *School Is Hell* © 1987 Matt Groening. All rights reserved. Reprinted by permission of Pantheon Books, a division of Random House Publishers, Inc., New York.

From *Love Is Hell* © 1986 Matt Groening. All rights reserved. Reprinted by permission of Pantheon Books, a division of Random House Publishers, Inc., New York.

EXPLORING CONNECTIONS

5. How might Gatto assess the vision of education presented in the excerpt from Horace Mann's report of 1848 (p. 141)? How might you account for the gulf between Gatto's views of the function of education and those forwarded by Mann?

6. Compare the "lessons" taught in the Matt Groening cartoons (pictured here and on p. 160) with those described by Gatto. To what extent is Gatto's indictment of education simply a matter of perspective?

7. Look ahead to Jean Anyon's excerpt from *Social Class and the Hidden Curriculum of Work* (p. 174) and compare Anyon's analysis of the hidden agenda of American education with that described by Gatto. Which of

Gatto's seven lessons might be explained by differences of social class? Which, if any, seem unrelated to issues of status or class position?

EXTENDING THE CRITICAL CONTEXT

8. Evaluate the hidden curriculum of the college courses you've taken or are currently enrolled in. To what extent do they reinforce or counter the lessons that Gatto describes?

9. Working in groups, brainstorm a design for a school that would make it *impossible* to teach the hidden curriculum that Gatto describes. How would classes be structured in such a school? What roles would teachers and students play? What would students study? How would they be graded?

"I Just Wanna Be Average"

MIKE ROSE

Mike Rose is anything but average: he has published poetry, scholarly research, a textbook, and two widely praised books on education in America. A professor in the School of Education at UCLA, Rose has won awards from the National Academy of Education, the National Council of Teachers of English, and the John Simon Guggenheim Memorial Foundation. Below you'll read the story of how this highly successful teacher and writer started high school in the "vocational education" track, learning dead-end skills from teachers who were often underprepared or incompetent. Rose shows that students whom the system has written off can have tremendous unrealized potential, and his critique of the school system specifies several reasons for the "failure" of students who go through high school belligerent, fearful, stoned, frustrated, or just plain bored. This selection comes from Lives on the Boundary *(1989), Rose's exploration of America's educationally underprivileged. His most recent book,* Possible Lives *(1996), offers a nationwide tour of creative classrooms and innovative educational programs. Rose is currently researching a new book on the thinking patterns of blue-collar workers.*

It took two buses to get to Our Lady of Mercy. The first started deep in South Los Angeles and caught me at midpoint. The second drifted through neighborhoods with trees, parks, big lawns, and lots of flowers. The rides were long but were livened up by a group of South L.A. veterans whose parents also thought that Hope had set up shop in the west end of the county. There was Christy Biggars, who, at sixteen, was dealing and was, according to rumor, a pimp as well. There were Bill Cobb and Johnny Gonzales, grease-pencil artists extraordinaire, who left Nembutal-enhanced[1] swirls of "Cobb" and "Johnny" on the corrugated walls of the bus. And then there was Tyrrell Wilson. Tyrrell was the coolest kid I knew. He ran the dozens[2] like a metric halfback, laid down a rap that outrhymed and outpointed Cobb, whose rap was good but not great — the curse of a moderately soulful kid trapped in white skin. But it was Cobb who would sneak a radio onto the bus, and thus underwrote his patter with Little Richard, Fats Domino, Chuck Berry, the Coasters, and Ernie K. Doe's[3] mother-in-law, an awful woman who was "sent from down below." And so it was that Christy and Cobb and Johnny G. and Tyrrell and I and assorted others picked up along the way passed our days in the back of the bus, a funny mix brought together by geography and parental desire.

Entrance to school brings with it forms and releases and assessments. Mercy relied on a series of tests, mostly the Stanford-Binet,[4] for placement, and somehow the results of my tests got confused with those of another student named Rose. The other Rose apparently didn't do very well, for I was placed in the vocational track, a euphemism for the bottom level. Neither I nor my parents realized what this meant. We had no sense that Business Math, Typing, and English–Level D were dead ends. The current spate of reports on the schools criticizes parents for not involving themselves in the education of their children. But how would someone like Tommy Rose, with his two years of Italian schooling, know what to ask? And what sort of pressure could an exhausted waitress apply? The error went undetected, and I remained in the vocational track for two years. What a place.

My homeroom was supervised by Brother Dill, a troubled and unstable man who also taught freshman English. When his class drifted away from him, which was often, his voice would rise in paranoid accusations, and occasionally he would lose control and shake or smack us. I hadn't been there two months when one of his brisk, face-turning slaps had my glasses sliding down the aisle. Physical education was also pretty harsh. Our teacher was a stubby ex-lineman who had played old-time pro ball in the Midwest. He routinely had us grabbing our ankles to receive his stinging paddle across our butts. He did that, he said, to make men of us. "Rose," he bellowed on our first encounter; me standing geeky in line in my baggy shorts. "'Rose'? What the hell kind of name is that?"

---

[1]*Nembutal:* Trade name for pentobarbital, a sedative drug.

[2]*the dozens:* A verbal game of African origin in which competitors try to top each other's insults.

[3]*Little Richard, Fats Domino, Chuck Berry, the Coasters, and Ernie K. Doe:* Popular black musicians of the 1950s.

[4]*Stanford-Binet:* An IQ test.

"Italian, sir," I squeaked.

"Italian! Ho. Rose, do you know the sound a bag of shit makes when it   5
hits the wall?"

"No, sir."

"Wop!"[5]

Sophomore English was taught by Mr. Mitropetros. He was a large, be-jeweled man who managed the parking lot at the Shrine Auditorium. He would crow and preen and list for us the stars he'd brushed against. We'd ask questions and glance knowingly and snicker, and all that fueled the poor guy to brag some more. Parking cars was his night job. He had little training in English, so his lesson plan for his day work had us reading the district's required text, *Julius Caesar,* aloud for the semester. We'd finished the play way before the twenty weeks was up, so he'd have us switch parts again and again and start again: Dave Snyder, the fastest guy at Mercy, muscling through Caesar to the breathless squeals of Calpurnia, as interpreted by Steve Fusco, a surfer who owned the school's most envied paneled wagon. Week ten and Dave and Steve would take on new roles, as would we all, and render a water-logged Cassius and a Brutus that are beyond my powers of description.

Spanish I — taken in the second year — fell into the hands of a new recruit. Mr. Montez was a tiny man, slight, five foot six at the most, soft-spoken and delicate. Spanish was a particularly rowdy class, and Mr. Montez was as prepared for it as a doily maker at a hammer throw. He would tap his pencil to a room in which Steve Fusco was propelling spitballs from his heavy lips, in which Mike Dweetz was taunting Billy Hawk, a half-Indian, half-Spanish, reed-thin, quietly explosive boy. The vocational track at Our Lady of Mercy mixed kids traveling in from South L.A. with South Bay surfers and a few Slavs and Chicanos from the harbors of San Pedro. This was a dangerous miscellany: surfers and hodads[6] and South-Central blacks all ablaze to the metronomic tapping of Hector Montez's pencil.

One day Billy lost it. Out of the corner of my eye I saw him strike out   10
with his right arm and catch Dweetz across the neck. Quick as a spasm, Dweetz was out of his seat, scattering desks, cracking Billy on the side of the head, right behind the eye. Snyder and Fusco and others broke it up, but the room felt hot and close and naked. Mr. Montez's tenuous authority was finally ripped to shreds, and I think everyone felt a little strange about that. The charade was over, and when it came down to it, I don't think any of the kids really wanted it to end this way. They had pushed and pushed and bullied their way into a freedom that both scared and embarrassed them.

Students will float to the mark you set. I and the others in the vocational classes were bobbing in pretty shallow water. Vocational education

[5]*Wop:* Derogatory term for Italian.
[6]*hodads:* Nonsurfers.

has aimed at increasing the economic opportunities of students who do not do well in our schools. Some serious programs succeed in doing that, and through exceptional teachers — like Mr. Gross in *Horace's Compromise*[7] — students learn to develop hypotheses and troubleshoot, reason through a problem, and communicate effectively — the true job skills. The vocational track, however, is most often a place for those who are just not making it, a dumping ground for the disaffected. There were a few teachers who worked hard at education; young Brother Slattery, for example, combined a stern voice with weekly quizzes to try to pass along to us a skeletal outline of world history. But mostly the teachers had no idea of how to engage the imaginations of us kids who were scuttling along at the bottom of the pond.

And the teachers would have needed some inventiveness, for none of us was groomed for the classroom. It wasn't just that I didn't know things — didn't know how to simplify algebraic fractions, couldn't identify different kinds of clauses, bungled Spanish translations — but that I had developed various faulty and inadequate ways of doing algebra and making sense of Spanish. Worse yet, the years of defensive tuning out in elementary school had given me a way to escape quickly while seeming at least half alert. During my time in Voc. Ed., I developed further into a mediocre student and a somnambulant problem solver, and that affected the subjects I did have the wherewithal to handle: I detested Shakespeare; I got bored with history. My attention flitted here and there. I fooled around in class and read my books indifferently — the intellectual equivalent of playing with your food. I did what I had to do to get by, and I did it with half a mind.

But I did learn things about people and eventually came into my own socially. I liked the guys in Voc. Ed. Growing up where I did, I understood and admired physical prowess, and there was an abundance of muscle here. There was Dave Snyder, a sprinter and halfback of true quality. Dave's ability and his quick wit gave him a natural appeal, and he was welcome in any clique, though he always kept a little independent. He enjoyed acting the fool and could care less about studies, but he possessed a certain maturity and never caused the faculty much trouble. It was a testament to his independence that he included me among his friends — I eventually went out for track, but I was no jock. Owing to the Latin alphabet and a dearth of *R*s and *S*s, Snyder sat behind Rose, and we started exchanging one-liners and became friends.

There was Ted Richard, a much-touted Little League pitcher. He was chunky and had a baby face and came to Our Lady of Mercy as a seasoned street fighter. Ted was quick to laugh and he had a loud, jolly laugh, but when he got angry he'd smile a little smile, the kind that simply raises the corner of the mouth a quarter of an inch. For those who knew, it was an eerie signal. Those who didn't found themselves in big trouble, for Ted was very quick. He loved to carry on what we would come to call philosophical

---

[7]*Horace's Compromise:* A book on American education by Theodore Sizer.

discussions: What is courage? Does God exist? He also loved words, enjoyed picking up big ones like *salubrious* and *equivocal* and using them in our conversations — laughing at himself as the word hit a chuckhole rolling off his tongue. Ted didn't do all that well in school — baseball and parties and testing the courage he'd speculated about took up his time. His textbooks were *Argosy* and *Field and Stream,* whatever newspapers he'd find on the bus stop — from the *Daily Worker* to pornography — conversations with uncles or hobos or businessmen he'd meet in a coffee shop, *The Old Man and the Sea.* With hindsight, I can see that Ted was developing into one of those rough-hewn intellectuals whose sources are a mix of the learned and the apocryphal, whose discussions are both assured and sad.

And then there was Ken Harvey. Ken was good-looking in a puffy way 15 and had a full and oily ducktail and was a car enthusiast . . . a hodad. One day in religion class, he said the sentence that turned out to be one of the most memorable of the hundreds of thousands I heard in those Voc. Ed. years. We were talking about the parable of the talents, about achievement, working hard, doing the best you can do, blah-blah-blah, when the teacher called on the restive Ken Harvey for an opinion. Ken thought about it, but just for a second, and said (with studied, minimal affect), "I just wanna be average." That woke me up. Average? Who wants to be average? Then the athletes chimed in with the clichés that make you want to laryngectomize them, and the exchange became a platitudinous melee. At the time, I thought Ken's assertion was stupid, and I wrote him off. But his sentence has stayed with me all these years, and I think I am finally coming to understand it.

Ken Harvey was gasping for air. School can be a tremendously disorienting place. No matter how bad the school, you're going to encounter notions that don't fit with the assumptions and beliefs that you grew up with — maybe you'll hear these dissonant notions from teachers, maybe from the other students, and maybe you'll read them. You'll also be thrown in with all kinds of kids from all kinds of backgrounds, and that can be unsettling — this is especially true in places of rich ethnic and linguistic mix, like the L.A. basin. You'll see a handful of students far excel you in courses that sound exotic and that are only in the curriculum of the elite: French, physics, trigonometry. And all this is happening while you're trying to shape an identity, your body is changing, and your emotions are running wild. If you're a working-class kid in the vocational track, the options you'll have to deal with this will be constrained in certain ways: you're defined by your school as "slow"; you're placed in a curriculum that isn't designed to liberate you but to occupy you, or, if you're lucky, train you, though the training is for work the society does not esteem; other students are picking up the cues from your school and your curriculum and interacting with you in particular ways. If you're a kid like Ted Richard, you turn your back on all this and let your mind roam where it may. But youngsters like Ted are rare. What Ken and so many others do is protect themselves from such suffocating madness by taking on with a vengeance the identity implied in the vocational track.

Reject the confusion and frustration by openly defining yourself as the Common Joe. Champion the average. Rely on your own good sense. Fuck this bullshit. Bullshit, of course, is everything you — and the others — fear is beyond you: books, essays, tests, academic scrambling, complexity, scientific reasoning, philosophical inquiry.

The tragedy is that you have to twist the knife in your own gray matter to make this defense work. You'll have to shut down, have to reject intellectual stimuli or diffuse them with sarcasm, have to cultivate stupidity, have to convert boredom from a malady into a way of confronting the world. Keep your vocabulary simple, act stoned when you're not or act more stoned than you are, flaunt ignorance, materialize your dreams. It is a powerful and effective defense — it neutralizes the insult and the frustration of being a vocational kid and, when perfected, it drives teachers up the wall, a delightful secondary effect. But like all strong magic, it exacts a price.

My own deliverance from the Voc. Ed. world began with sophomore biology. Every student, college prep to vocational, had to take biology, and unlike the other courses, the same person taught all sections. When teaching the vocational group, Brother Clint probably slowed down a bit or omitted a little of the fundamental biochemistry, but he used the same book and more or less the same syllabus across the board. If one class got tough, he could get tougher. He was young and powerful and very handsome, and looks and physical strength were high currency. No one gave him any trouble.

I was pretty bad at the dissecting table, but the lectures and the textbook were interesting: plastic overlays that, with each turned page, peeled away skin, then veins and muscle, then organs, down to the very bones that Brother Clint, pointer in hand, would tap out on our hanging skeleton. Dave Snyder was in big trouble, for the study of life — versus the living of it — was sticking in his craw. We worked out a code for our multiple-choice exams. He'd poke me in the back: once for the answer under *A*, twice for *B*, and so on; and when he'd hit the right one, I'd look up to the ceiling as though I were lost in thought. Poke: cytoplasm. Poke, poke: methane. Poke, poke, poke: William Harvey. Poke, poke, poke, poke: islets of Langerhans. This didn't work out perfectly, but Dave passed the course, and I mastered the dreamy look of a guy on a record jacket. And something else happened. Brother Clint puzzled over this Voc. Ed. kid who was racking up 98s and 99s on his tests. He checked the school's records and discovered the error. He recommended that I begin my junior year in the College Prep program. According to all I've read since, such a shift, as one report put it, is virtually impossible. Kids at that level rarely cross tracks. The telling thing is how chancy both my placement into and exit from Voc. Ed. was; neither I nor my parents had anything to do with it. I lived in one world during spring semester, and when I came back to school in the fall, I was living in another.

Switching to College Prep was a mixed blessing. I was an erratic student. I was undisciplined. And I hadn't caught onto the rules of the game: 20

why work hard in a class that didn't grab my fancy? I was also hopelessly behind in math. Chemistry was hard; toying with my chemistry set years before hadn't prepared me for the chemist's equations. Fortunately, the priest who taught both chemistry and second-year algebra was also the school's athletic director. Membership on the track team covered me; I knew I wouldn't get lower than a C. U.S. history was taught pretty well, and I did okay. But civics was taken over by a football coach who had trouble reading the textbook aloud — and reading aloud was the centerpiece of his pedagogy. College Prep at Mercy was certainly an improvement over the vocational program — at least it carried some status — but the social science curriculum was weak, and the mathematics and physical sciences were simply beyond me. I had a miserable quantitative background and ended up copying some assignments and finessing the rest as best I could. Let me try to explain how it feels to see again and again material you should once have learned but didn't.

You are given a problem. It requires you to simplify algebraic fractions or to multiply expressions containing square roots. You know this is pretty basic material because you've seen it for years. Once a teacher took some time with you, and you learned how to carry out these operations. Simple versions, anyway. But that was a year or two or more in the past, and these are more complex versions, and now you're not sure. And this, you keep telling yourself, is ninth- or even eighth-grade stuff.

Next it's a word problem. This is also old hat. The basic elements are as familiar as story characters: trains speeding so many miles per hour or shadows of buildings angling so many degrees. Maybe you know enough, have sat through enough explanations, to be able to begin setting up the problem: "If one train is going this fast . . ." or "This shadow is really one line of a triangle . . ." Then: "Let's see . . ." "How did Jones do this?" "Hmmmm." "No." "No, that won't work." Your attention wavers. You wonder about other things: a football game, a dance, that cute new checker at the market. You try to focus on the problem again. You scribble on paper for a while, but the tension wins out and your attention flits elsewhere. You crumple the paper and begin daydreaming to ease the frustration.

The particulars will vary, but in essence this is what a number of students go through, especially those in so-called remedial classes. They open their textbooks and see once again the familiar and impenetrable formulas and diagrams and terms that have stumped them for years. There is no excitement here. *No* excitement. Regardless of what the teacher says, this is not a new challenge. There is, rather, embarrassment and frustration and, not surprisingly, some anger in being reminded once again of long-standing inadequacies. No wonder so many students finally attribute their difficulties to something inborn, organic: "That part of my brain just doesn't work." Given the troubling histories many of these students have, it's miraculous that any of them can lift the shroud of hopelessness sufficiently to make deliverance from these classes possible.

Through this entire period, my father's health was deteriorating with cruel momentum. His arteriosclerosis progressed to the point where a simple nick on his shin wouldn't heal. Eventually it ulcerated and widened. Lou Minton would come by daily to change the dressing. We tried renting an oscillating bed — which we placed in the front room — to force blood through the constricted arteries in my father's legs. The bed hummed through the night, moving in place to ward off the inevitable. The ulcer continued to spread, and the doctors finally had to amputate. My grandfather had lost his leg in a stockyard accident. Now my father too was crippled. His convalescence was slow but steady, and the doctors placed him in the Santa Monica Rehabilitation Center, a sun-bleached building that opened out onto the warm spray of the Pacific. The place gave him some strength and some color and some training in walking with an artificial leg. He did pretty well for a year or so until he slipped and broke his hip. He was confined to a wheelchair after that, and the confinement contributed to the diminishing of his body and spirit.

I am holding a picture of him. He is sitting in his wheelchair and smiling   25
at the camera. The smile appears forced, unsteady, seems to quaver, though it is frozen in silver nitrate. He is in his mid-sixties and looks eighty. Late in my junior year, he had a stroke and never came out of the resulting coma. After that, I would see him only in dreams, and to this day that is how I join him. Sometimes the dreams are sad and grisly and primal: my father lying in a bed soaked with his suppuration,[8] holding me, rocking me. But sometimes the dreams bring him back to me healthy: him talking to me on an empty street, or buying some pictures to decorate our old house, or transformed somehow into someone strong and adept with tools and the physical.

Jack MacFarland couldn't have come into my life at a better time. My father was dead, and I had logged up too many years of scholastic indifference. Mr. MacFarland had a master's degree from Columbia and decided, at twenty-six, to find a little school and teach his heart out. He never took any credentialing courses, couldn't bear to, he said, so he had to find employment in a private system. He ended up at Our Lady of Mercy teaching five sections of senior English. He was a beatnik who was born too late. His teeth were stained, he tucked his sorry tie in between the third and fourth buttons of his shirt, and his pants were chronically wrinkled. At first, we couldn't believe this guy, thought he slept in his car. But within no time, he had us so startled with work that we didn't much worry about where he slept or if he slept at all. We wrote three or four essays a month. We read a book every two to three weeks, starting with the *Iliad* and ending up with Hemingway. He gave us a quiz on the reading every other day. He brought a prep school curriculum to Mercy High.

MacFarland's lectures were crafted, and as he delivered them he would pace the room jiggling a piece of chalk in his cupped hand, using it to

---

[8]*suppuration:* Discharge from wounds.

scribble on the board the names of all the writers and philosophers and plays and novels he was weaving into his discussion. He asked questions often, raised everything from Zeno's paradox to the repeated last line of Frost's "Stopping by Woods on a Snowy Evening." He slowly and carefully built up our knowledge of Western intellectual history — with facts, with connections, with speculations. We learned about Greek philosophy, about Dante, the Elizabethan world view, the Age of Reason, existentialism. He analyzed poems with us, had us reading sections from John Ciardi's *How Does a Poem Mean?*, making a potentially difficult book accessible with his own explanations. We gave oral reports on poems Ciardi didn't cover. We imitated the styles of Conrad, Hemingway, and *Time* magazine. We wrote and talked, wrote and talked. The man immersed us in language.

Even MacFarland's barbs were literary. If Jim Fitzsimmons, hung over and irritable, tried to smart-ass him, he'd rejoin with a flourish that would spark the indomitable Skip Madison — who'd lost his front teeth in a hapless tackle — to flick his tongue through the gap and opine, "good chop," drawing out the single "o" in stinging indictment. Jack MacFarland, this tobacco-stained intellectual, brandished linguistic weapons of a kind I hadn't encountered before. Here was this *egghead,* for God's sake, keeping some pretty difficult people in line. And from what I heard, Mike Dweetz and Steve Fusco and all the notorious Voc. Ed. crowd settled down as well when MacFarland took the podium. Though a lot of guys groused in the schoolyard, it just seemed that giving trouble to this particular teacher was a silly thing to do. Tomfoolery, not to mention assault, had no place in the world he was trying to create for us, and instinctively everyone knew that. If nothing else, we all recognized MacFarland's considerable intelligence and respected the hours he put into his work. It came to this: the troublemaker would look foolish rather than daring. Even Jim Fitzsimmons was reading *On the Road* and turning his incipient alcoholism to literary ends.

There were some lives that were already beyond Jack MacFarland's ministrations, but mine was not. I started reading again as I hadn't since elementary school. I would go into our gloomy little bedroom or sit at the dinner table while, on the television, Danny McShane was paralyzing Mr. Moto with the atomic drop, and work slowly back through *Heart of Darkness,* trying to catch the words in Conrad's sentences. I certainly was not MacFarland's best student; most of the other guys in College Prep, even my fellow slackers, had better backgrounds than I did. But I worked very hard, for MacFarland had hooked me. He tapped my old interest in reading and creating stories. He gave me a way to feel special by using my mind. And he provided a role model that wasn't shaped on physical prowess alone, and something inside me that I wasn't quite aware of responded to that. Jack MacFarland established a literacy club, to borrow a phrase of Frank Smith's, and invited me — invited all of us — to join.

There's been a good deal of research and speculation suggesting that 30 the acknowledgment of school performance with extrinsic rewards — smiling faces, stars, numbers, grades — diminishes the intrinsic satisfaction children experience by engaging in reading or writing or problem solving. While it's certainly true that we've created an educational system that encourages our best and brightest to become cynical grade collectors and, in general, have developed an obsession with evaluation and assessment, I must tell you that venal though it may have been, I loved getting good grades from MacFarland. I now know how subjective grades can be, but then they came tucked in the back of essays like bits of scientific data, some sort of spectroscopic readout that said, objectively and publicly, that I had made something of value. I suppose I'd been mediocre for too long and enjoyed a public redefinition. And I suppose the workings of my mind, such as they were, had been private for too long. My linguistic play moved into the world; . . . these papers with their circled, red B-pluses and A-minuses linked my mind to something outside it. I carried them around like a club emblem.

One day in the December of my senior year, Mr. MacFarland asked me where I was going to go to college. I hadn't thought much about it. Many of the students I teach today spent their last year in high school with a physics text in one hand and the Stanford catalog in the other, but I wasn't even aware of what "entrance requirements" were. My folks would say that they wanted me to go to college and be a doctor, but I don't know how seriously I ever took that; it seemed a sweet thing to say, a bit of supportive family chatter, like telling a gangly daughter she's graceful. The reality of higher education wasn't in my scheme of things: no one in the family had gone to college; only two of my uncles had completed high school. I figured I'd get a night job and go to the local junior college because I knew that Snyder and Company were going there to play ball. But I hadn't even prepared for that. When I finally said, "I don't know," MacFarland looked down at me — I was seated in his office — and said, "Listen, you can write."

My grades stank. I had A's in biology and a handful of B's in a few English and social science classes. All the rest were C's — or worse. MacFarland said I would do well in his class and laid down the law about doing well in the others. Still, the record for my first three years wouldn't have been acceptable to any four-year school. To nobody's surprise, I was turned down flat by USC and UCLA. But Jack MacFarland was on the case. He had received his bachelor's degree from Loyola University, so he made calls to old professors and talked to somebody in admissions and wrote me a strong letter. Loyola finally accepted me as a probationary student. I would be on trial for the first year, and if I did okay, I would be granted regular status. MacFarland also intervened to get me a loan, for I could never have afforded a private college without it. Four more years of religion classes and four more years of boys at one school, girls at another. But at least I was going to college. Amazing.

In my last semester of high school, I elected a special English course fashioned by Mr. MacFarland, and it was through this elective that there arose at Mercy a fledgling literati. Art Mitz, the editor of the school newspaper and a very smart guy, was the kingpin. He was joined by me and by Mark Dever, a quiet boy who wrote beautifully and who would die before he was forty. MacFarland occasionally invited us to his apartment, and those visits became the high point of our apprenticeship: we'd clamp on our training wheels and drive to his salon.

He lived in a cramped and cluttered place near the airport, tucked away in the kind of building that architectural critic Reyner Banham calls a *dingbat*. Books were all over: stacked, piled, tossed, and crated, underlined and dog eared, well worn and new. Cigarette ashes crusted with coffee in saucers or spilling over the sides of motel ashtrays. The little bedroom had, along two of its walls, bricks and boards loaded with notes, magazines, and oversized books. The kitchen joined the living room, and there was a stack of German newspapers under the sink. I had never seen anything like it: a great flophouse of language furnished by City Lights and Café le Metro. I read every title. I flipped through paperbacks and scanned jackets and memorized names: Gogol, *Finnegans Wake,* Djuna Barnes, Jackson Pollock, *A Coney Island of the Mind,* F. O. Matthiessen's *American Renaissance,* all sorts of Freud, *Troubled Sleep,* Man Ray, *The Education of Henry Adams,* Richard Wright, *Film as Art,* William Butler Yeats, Marguerite Duras, *Redburn, A Season in Hell, Kapital.* On the cover of Alain-Fournier's *The Wanderer* was an Edward Gorey drawing of a young man on a road winding into dark trees. By the hotplate sat a strange Kafka novel called *Amerika,* in which an adolescent hero crosses the Atlantic to find the Nature Theater of Oklahoma. Art and Mark would be talking about a movie or the school newspaper, and I would be consuming my English teacher's library. It was heady stuff. I felt like a Pop Warner[9] athlete on steroids.

Art, Mark, and I would buy stogies and triangulate from MacFarland's apartment to the Cinema, which now shows X-rated films but was then L.A.'s premier art theater, and then to the musty Cherokee Bookstore in Hollywood to hobnob with beatnik homosexuals — smoking, drinking bourbon and coffee, and trying out awkward phrases we'd gleaned from our mentor's bookshelves. I was happy and precocious and a little scared as well, for Hollywood Boulevard was thick with a kind of decadence that was foreign to the South Side. After the Cherokee, we would head back to the security of MacFarland's apartment, slaphappy with hipness.

Let me be the first to admit that there was a good deal of adolescent passion in this embrace of the avant-garde: self-absorption, sexually charged pedantry, an elevation of the odd and abandoned. Still it was a time during which I absorbed an awful lot of information: long lists of titles, images from expressionist paintings, new wave shibboleths,[10] snippets of philosophy, and names that read like Steve Fusco's misspellings — Goethe, Nietzsche,

35

---

[9]*Pop Warner:* A nationwide youth athletics organization.
[10]*new wave shibboleths:* Trendy phrases or jargon.

Kierkegaard. Now this is hardly the stuff of deep understanding. But it was an introduction, a phrase book, a Baedeker[11] to a vocabulary of ideas, and it felt good at the time to know all these words. With hindsight I realize how layered and important that knowledge was.

It enabled me to do things in the world. I could browse bohemian bookstores in far-off, mysterious Hollywood; I could go to the Cinema and see events through the lenses of European directors; and, most of all, I could share an evening, talk that talk, with Jack MacFarland, the man I most admired at the time. Knowledge was becoming a bonding agent. Within a year or two, the persona of the disaffected hipster would prove too cynical, too alienated to last. But for a time it was new and exciting: it provided a critical perspective on society, and it allowed me to act as though I were living beyond the limiting boundaries of South Vermont.[12]

ENGAGING THE TEXT

1. Describe Rose's life in Voc. Ed. What were his teachers like? Have you ever had experience with teachers like these?

2. What did Voc. Ed. do to Rose and his fellow students? How did it affect them intellectually, emotionally, and socially? Why was it subsequently so hard for Rose to catch up in math?

3. Why is high school so disorienting to students like Ken Harvey? How does he cope with it? What other strategies do students use to cope with the pressures and judgments they encounter in school?

4. What does Jack MacFarland offer Rose that finally helps him learn? Do you think it was inevitable that someone with Rose's intelligence would eventually succeed?

EXPLORING CONNECTIONS

5. To what extent do Rose's experiences challenge or confirm John Taylor Gatto's critique of public education in "The Seven-Lesson Schoolteacher" (p. 152)?

6. Draw a Groening-style cartoon (see pp. 160–61) or comic strip of Rose in the vocational track, or of Rose before and after his liberation from Voc. Ed.

7. Read Gregory Mantsios's "Class in America: Myths and Realities" (p. 318) and write an imaginary dialogue between Rose and Mantsios about why some students, like Rose, seem to be able to break through social class barriers and others, like Dave Snyder, Ted Richard, and Ken Harvey, do not.

EXTENDING THE CRITICAL CONTEXT

8. Rose explains that high school can be a "tremendously disorienting place" (para. 16). What, if anything, do you find disorienting about college? What

---

[11]*Baedeker:* Travel guide.
[12]*South Vermont:* A street in an economically depressed area of Los Angeles.

steps can students at your school take to lessen feelings of disorientation? What could the college do to help them?

9. Review one or more of Rose's descriptions of his high school classmates; then write a description of one of your own high school classmates, trying to capture in a nutshell how that person coped or failed to cope with the educational system.

10. Watch on videotape any one of the many films that have been made in the last ten years about charismatic teachers (for example, *Dangerous Minds, Renaissance Man, Stand and Deliver,* or *Dead Poets Society*) and compare Hollywood's depiction of a dynamic teacher to Rose's portrayal of Jack MacFarland. What do such charismatic teachers offer their students personally and intellectually? Do you see any disadvantages to classes taught by teachers like these?

From *Social Class and the Hidden Curriculum of Work*

JEAN ANYON

It's no surprise that schools in wealthy communities are better than those in poor communities, or that they better prepare their students for desirable jobs. It may be shocking, however, to learn how vast the differences in schools are — not so much in resources as in teaching methods and philosophies of education. Jean Anyon observed five elementary schools over the course of a full school year and concluded that fifth graders of different economic backgrounds are already being prepared to occupy particular rungs on the social ladder. In a sense, some whole schools are on the vocational education track, while others are geared to produce future doctors, lawyers, and business leaders. Anyon's main audience is professional educators, so you may find her style and vocabulary challenging, but, once you've read her descriptions of specific classroom activities, the more analytic parts of the essay should prove easier to understand. Anyon is chairperson of the Department of Education at Rutgers University, Newark. Her most recent book is Ghetto Schooling: A Political Economy of Urban Educational Reform *(1997). This essay first appeared in the* Journal of Education *in 1980.*

Scholars in political economy and the sociology of knowledge have recently argued that public schools in complex industrial societies like our own make available different types of educational experience and curriculum knowledge to students in different social classes. Bowles and Gintis[1] for example, have argued that students in different social-class backgrounds are rewarded for classroom behaviors that correspond to personality traits allegedly rewarded in the different occupational strata — the working classes for docility and obedience, the managerial classes for initiative and personal assertiveness. Basil Bernstein, Pierre Bourdieu, and Michael W. Apple,[2] focusing on school knowledge, have argued that knowledge and skills leading to social power and regard (medical, legal, managerial) are made available to the advantaged social groups but are withheld from the working classes, to whom a more "practical" curriculum is offered (manual skills, clerical knowledge). While there has been considerable argumentation of these points regarding education in England, France, and North America, there has been little or no attempt to investigate these ideas empirically in elementary or secondary schools and classrooms in this country.[3]

This article offers tentative empirical support (and qualification) of the above arguments by providing illustrative examples of differences in student *work* in classrooms in contrasting social-class communities. The examples were gathered as part of an ethnographical[4] study of curricular, pedagogical, and pupil evaluation practices in five elementary schools. The article attempts a theoretical contribution as well and assesses student work in the light of a theoretical approach to social-class analysis. . . . It will be suggested that there is a "hidden curriculum" in schoolwork that has profound implications for the theory — and consequence — of everyday activity in education. . . .

The Sample of Schools

. . . The social-class designation of each of the five schools will be identified, and the income, occupation, and other relevant available social characteristics of the students and their parents will be described. The first three schools are in a medium-sized city district in northern New Jersey, and the other two are in a nearby New Jersey suburb.

The first two schools I will call *working-class schools*. Most of the parents have blue-collar jobs. Less than a third of the fathers are skilled, while

---

[1]S. Bowles and H. Gintis, *Schooling in Capitalist America: Educational Reform and the Contradictions of Economic Life* (New York: Basic Books, 1976). [All notes are the author's except 4 and 11.]

[2]B. Bernstein, *Class, Codes and Control,* Vol. 3. *Towards a Theory of Educational Transmission,* 2d ed. (London: Routledge & Kegan Paul, 1977); P. Bourdieu and J. Passeron, *Reproduction in Education, Society and Culture* (Beverly Hills, Calif.: Sage, 1977); M. W. Apple, *Ideology and Curriculum* (Boston: Routledge & Kegan Paul, 1979).

[3]But see, in a related vein, M. W. Apple and N. King, "What Do Schools Teach?" *Curriculum Inquiry* 6 (1977): 341–58; R. C. Rist, *The Urban School: A Factory for Failure* (Cambridge, Mass.: MIT Press, 1973).

[4]*ethnographical:* Based on an anthropological study of cultures or subcultures — the "cultures" in this case being the five schools observed.

the majority are in unskilled or semiskilled jobs. During the period of the study (1978–1979), approximately 15 percent of the fathers were unemployed. The large majority (85 percent) of the families are white. The following occupations are typical: platform, storeroom, and stockroom workers; foundrymen, pipe welders, and boilermakers; semiskilled and unskilled assemblyline operatives; gas station attendants, auto mechanics, maintenance workers, and security guards. Less than 30 percent of the women work, some part-time and some full-time, on assembly lines, in storerooms and stockrooms, as waitresses, barmaids, or sales clerks. Of the fifth-grade parents, none of the wives of the skilled workers had jobs. Approximately 15 percent of the families in each school are at or below the federal "poverty" level;[5] most of the rest of the family incomes are at or below $12,000, except some of the skilled workers whose incomes are higher. The incomes of the majority of the families in these two schools (at or below $12,000) are typical of 38.6 percent of the families in the United States.[6]

The third school is called the *middle-class school,* although because of   5
neighborhood residence patterns, the population is a mixture of several social classes. The parents' occupations can be divided into three groups: a small group of blue-collar "rich," who are skilled, well-paid workers such as printers, carpenters, plumbers, and construction workers. The second group is composed of parents in working-class and middle-class white-collar jobs: women in office jobs, technicians, supervisors in industry, and parents employed by the city (such as firemen, policemen, and several of the school's teachers). The third group is composed of occupations such as personnel directors in local firms, accountants, "middle management," and a few small capitalists (owners of shops in the area). The children of several local doctors attend this school. Most family incomes are between $13,000 and $25,000, with a few higher. This income range is typical of 38.9 percent of the families in the United States.[7]

The fourth school has a parent population that is at the upper income level of the upper middle class and is predominantly professional. This school will be called the *affluent professional school.* Typical jobs are: cardiologist, interior designer, corporate lawyer or engineer, executive in advertising or television. There are some families who are not as affluent as the majority (the family of the superintendent of the district's schools, and the one or two families in which the fathers are skilled workers). In addition, a few of the families are more affluent than the majority and can be classified in the capitalist class (a partner in a prestigious Wall Street stock brokerage

[5]The U.S. Bureau of the Census defines *poverty* for a nonfarm family of four as a yearly income of $6,191 a year or less. U.S. Bureau of the Census, *Statistical Abstract of the United States: 1978* (Washington, D.C.: U.S. Government Printing Office, 1978), 465, table 754.

[6]U.S. Bureau of the Census, "Money Income in 1977 of Families and Persons in the United States," *Current Population Reports* Series P-60, no. 118 (Washington, D.C.: U.S. Government Printing Office, 1979), p. 2, table A.

[7]Ibid.

firm). Approximately 90 percent of the children in this school are white. Most family incomes are between $40,000 and $80,000. This income span represents approximately 7 percent of the families in the United States.[8]

In the fifth school the majority of the families belong to the capitalist class. This school will be called the *executive elite school* because most of the fathers are top executives (for example, presidents and vice-presidents) in major United States–based multinational corporations — for example, AT&T, RCA, Citibank, American Express, U.S. Steel. A sizable group of fathers are top executives in financial firms on Wall Street. There are also a number of fathers who list their occupations as "general counsel" to a particular corporation, and these corporations are also among the large multinationals. Many of the mothers do volunteer work in the Junior League, Junior Fortnightly, or other service groups; some are intricately involved in town politics; and some are themselves in well-paid occupations. There are no minority children in the school. Almost all the family incomes are over $100,000, with some in the $500,000 range. The incomes in this school represent less than 1 percent of the families in the United States.[9]

Since each of the five schools is only one instance of elementary education in a particular social-class context, I will not generalize beyond the sample. However, the examples of schoolwork which follow will suggest characteristics of education in each social setting that appear to have theoretical and social significance and to be worth investigation in a larger number of schools. . . .

The Working-Class Schools

In the two working-class schools, work is following the steps of a procedure. The procedure is usually mechanical, involving rote behavior and very little decision making or choice. The teachers rarely explain why the work is being assigned, how it might connect to other assignments, or what the idea is that lies behind the procedure or gives it coherence and perhaps meaning or significance. Available textbooks are not always used, and the teachers often prepare their own dittos or put work examples on the board. Most of the rules regarding work are designations of what the children are to do; the rules are steps to follow. These steps are told to the children by the teachers and are often written on the board. The children are usually told to copy the steps as notes. These notes are to be studied. Work is often evaluated not according to whether it is right or wrong but according to whether the children followed the right steps.

[8]This figure is an estimate. According to the Bureau of the Census, only 2.6 percent of families in the United States have money income of $50,000 or over. U.S. Bureau of the Census, *Current Population Reports* Series P-60. For figures on income at these higher levels, see J. D. Smith and S. Franklin, "The Concentration of Personal Wealth, 1922–1969," *American Economic Review* 64 (1974): 162–67.

[9]Smith and Franklin, "The Concentration of Personal Wealth."

The following examples illustrate these points. In math, when two-digit   10
division was introduced, the teacher in one school gave a four-minute lecture on what the terms are called (which number is the divisor, dividend,
quotient, and remainder). The children were told to copy these names in
their notebooks. Then the teacher told them the steps to follow to do the
problems, saying, "This is how you do them." The teacher listed the steps
on the board, and they appeared several days later as a chart hung in the
middle of the front wall: "Divide, Multiply, Subtract, Bring Down." The
children often did examples of two-digit division. When the teacher went
over the examples with them, he told them what the procedure was for each
problem, rarely asking them to conceptualize or explain it themselves:
"Three into twenty-two is seven; do your subtraction and one is left over."
During the week that two-digit division was introduced (or at any other
time), the investigator did not observe any discussion of the idea of grouping involved in division, any use of manipulables, or any attempt to relate
two-digit division to any other mathematical process. Nor was there any attempt to relate the steps to an actual or possible thought process of the children. The observer did not hear the terms *dividend, quotient,* and so on,
used again. The math teacher in the other working-class school followed
similar procedures regarding two-digit division and at one point her class
seemed confused. She said, "You're confusing yourselves. You're tensing
up. Remember, when you do this, it's the same steps over and over again —
and that's the way division always is." Several weeks later, after a test, a
group of her children "still didn't get it," and she made no attempt to explain the concept of dividing things into groups or to give them manipulables for their own investigation. Rather, she went over the steps with them
again and told them that they "needed more practice."

In other areas of math, work is also carrying out often unexplained fragmented procedures. For example, one of the teachers led the children
through a series of steps to make a 1-inch grid on their paper *without* telling
them that they were making a 1-inch grid or that it would be used to study
scale. She said, "Take your ruler. Put it across the top. Make a mark at every
number. Then move your ruler down to the bottom. No, put it across the
bottom. Now make a mark on top of every number. Now draw a line
from . . ." At this point a girl said that she had a faster way to do it and the
teacher said, "No, you don't; you don't even know what I'm making yet. Do
it this way or it's wrong." After they had made the lines up and down and
across, the teacher told them she wanted them to make a figure by connecting some dots and to measure that, using the scale of 1 inch equals 1 mile.
Then they were to cut it out. She said, "Don't cut it until I check it."

In both working-class schools, work in language arts is mechanics of
punctuation (commas, periods, question marks, exclamation points), capital-
ization, and the four kinds of sentences. One teacher explained to me,
"Simple punctuation is all they'll ever use." Regarding punctuation, either a
teacher or a ditto stated the rules for where, for example, to put commas. The

investigator heard no classroom discussion of the aural context of punctuation (which, of course, is what gives each mark its meaning). Nor did the investigator hear any statement or inference that placing a punctuation mark could be a decision-making process, depending, for example, on one's intended meaning. Rather, the children were told to follow the rules. Language arts did not involve creative writing. There were several writing assignments throughout the year, but in each instance the children were given a ditto, and they wrote answers to questions on the sheet. For example, they wrote their "autobiography" by answering such questions as "Where were you born?" "What is your favorite animal?" on a sheet entitled "All About Me."

In one of the working-class schools, the class had a science period several times a week. On the three occasions observed, the children were not called upon to set up experiments or to give explanations for facts or concepts. Rather, on each occasion the teacher told them in his own words what the book said. The children copied the teacher's sentences from the board. Each day that preceded the day they were to do a science experiment, the teacher told them to copy the directions from the book for the procedure they would carry out the next day and to study the list at home that night. The day after each experiment, the teacher went over what they had "found" (they did the experiments as a class, and each was actually a class demonstration led by the teacher). Then the teacher wrote what they "found" on the board, and the children copied that in their notebooks. Once or twice a year there are science projects. The project is chosen and assigned by the teacher from a box of 3-by-5-inch cards. On the card the teacher has written the question to be answered, the books to use, and how much to write. Explaining the cards to the observer, the teacher said, "It tells them exactly what to do, or they couldn't do it."

Social studies in the working-class schools is also largely mechanical, rote work that was given little explanation or connection to larger contexts. In one school, for example, although there was a book available, social studies work was to copy the teacher's notes from the board. Several times a week for a period of several months the children copied these notes. The fifth grades in the district were to study United States history. The teacher used a booklet she had purchased called "The Fabulous Fifty States." Each day she put information from the booklet in outline form on the board and the children copied it. The type of information did not vary: the name of the state, its abbreviation, state capital, nickname of the state, its main products, main business, and a "Fabulous Fact" ("Idaho grew twenty-seven billion potatoes in one year. That's enough potatoes for each man, woman, and . . ."). As the children finished copying the sentences, the teacher erased them and wrote more. Children would occasionally go to the front to pull down the wall map in order to locate the states they were copying, and the teacher did not dissuade them. But the observer never saw her refer to the map; nor did the observer ever hear her make other than perfunctory remarks concerning the information the children were copying. Occasionally the children colored in a ditto and cut it out to make a stand-up figure (representing, for example, a man roping a cow in the Southwest). These were referred to by the teacher as their social studies "projects."

Rote behavior was often called for in classroom work. When going over math and language arts skills sheets, for example, as the teacher asked for the answer to each problem, he fired the questions rapidly, staccato, and the scene reminded the observer of a sergeant drilling recruits: above all, the questions demanded that you stay at attention: "The next one? What do I put here? . . . Here? Give us the next." Or "How many commas in this sentence? Where do I put them . . . The next one?" 15

. The four fifth-grade teachers observed in the working-class schools attempted to control classroom time and space by making decisions without consulting the children and without explaining the basis for their decisions. The teacher's control thus often seemed capricious. Teachers, for instance, very often ignored the bells to switch classes — deciding among themselves to keep the children after the period was officially over to continue with the work or for disciplinary reasons or so they (the teachers) could stand in the hall and talk. There were no clocks in the rooms in either school, and the children often asked, "What period is this?" "When do we go to gym?" The children had no access to materials. These were handed out by teachers and closely guarded. Things in the room "belonged" to the teacher: "Bob, bring me my garbage can." The teachers continually gave the children orders. Only three times did the investigator hear a teacher in either working-class school preface a directive with an unsarcastic "please," or "let's," or "would you." Instead, the teachers said, "Shut up," "Shut your mouth," "Open your books," "Throw your gum away — if you want to rot your teeth, do it on your own time." Teachers made every effort to control the movement of the children, and often shouted, "Why are you out of your seat??!!" If the children got permission to leave the room, they had to take a written pass with the date and time. . . .

Middle-Class School

In the middle-class school, work is getting the right answer. If one accumulates enough right answers, one gets a good grade. One must follow the directions in order to get the right answers, but the directions often call for some figuring, some choice, some decision making. For example, the children must often figure out by themselves what the directions ask them to do and how to get the answer: what do you do first, second, and perhaps third? Answers are usually found in books or by listening to the teacher. Answers are usually words, sentences, numbers, or facts and dates; one writes them on paper, and one should be neat. Answers must be given in the right order, and one cannot make them up.

The following activities are illustrative. Math involves some choice: one may do two-digit division the long way or the short way, and there are some math problems that can be done "in your head." When the teacher explains how to do two-digit division, there is recognition that a cognitive process is involved; she gives you several ways and says, "I want to make sure you understand what you're doing — so you get it right"; and, when they go over the homework, she asks the *children* to tell how they did the problem and what answer they got.

In social studies the daily work is to read the assigned pages in the textbook and to answer the teacher's questions. The questions are almost always designed to check on whether the students have read the assignment and understood it: who did so-and-so; what happened after that; when did it happen, where, and sometimes, why did it happen? The answers are in the book and in one's understanding of the book; the teacher's hints when one doesn't know the answers are to "read it again" or to look at the picture or at the rest of the paragraph. One is to search for the answer in the "context," in what is given.

Language arts is "simple grammar, what they need for everyday life." 20 The language arts teacher says, "They should learn to speak properly, to write business letters and thank-you letters, and to understand what nouns and verbs and simple subjects are." Here, as well, actual work is to choose the right answers, to understand what is given. The teacher often says, "Please read the next sentence and then I'll question you about it." One teacher said in some exasperation to a boy who was fooling around in class, "If you don't know the answers to the questions I ask, then you can't stay in this *class!* [pause] You *never* know the answers to the questions I ask, and it's not fair to me — and certainly not to you!"

Most lessons are based on the textbook. This does not involve a critical perspective on what is given there. For example, a critical perspective in social studies is perceived as dangerous by these teachers because it may lead to controversial topics; the parents might complain. The children, however, are often curious, especially in social studies. Their questions are tolerated and usually answered perfunctorily. But after a few minutes the teacher will say, "All right, we're not going any farther. Please open your social studies workbook." While the teachers spend a lot of time explaining and expanding on what the textbooks say, there is little attempt to analyze how or why things happen, or to give thought to how pieces of a culture, or, say, a system of numbers or elements of a language fit together or can be analyzed. What has happened in the past and what exists now may not be equitable or fair, but (shrug) that is the way things are and one does not confront such matters in school. For example, in social studies after a child is called on to read a passage about the pilgrims, the teacher summarizes the paragraph and then says, "So you can see how strict they were about everything." A child asks, "Why?" "Well, because they felt that if you weren't busy you'd get into trouble." Another child asks, "Is it true that they burned women at the stake?" The teacher says, "Yes, if a woman did anything strange, they hanged them. [*sic*] What would a woman do, do you think, to make them burn them? [*sic*] See if you can come up with better answers than my other [social studies] class." Several children offer suggestions, to which the teacher nods but does not comment. Then she says, "Okay, good," and calls on the next child to read.

Work tasks do not usually request creativity. Serious attention is rarely given in school work on *how* the children develop or express their own feelings and ideas, either linguistically or in graphic form. On the occasions when creativity or self-expression is requested, it is peripheral to the main activity or it is "enrichment" or "for fun." During a lesson on what similes are, for example, the teacher explains what they are, puts several on the board, gives some other examples herself, and then asks the children if they can "make some up." She calls on three children who give similes, two of which are actually in the book they have open before them. The teacher does not comment on this and then asks several others to choose similes from the list of phrases in the book. Several do so correctly, and she says, "Oh good! You're picking them out! See how good we are?" Their homework is to pick out the rest of the similes from the list.

Creativity is not often requested in social studies and science projects, either. Social studies projects, for example, are given with directions to "find information on your topic" and write it up. The children are not supposed to copy but to "put it in your own words." Although a number of the projects subsequently went beyond the teacher's direction to find information and had quite expressive covers and inside illustrations, the teacher's evaluative comments had to do with the amount of information, whether they had "copied," and if their work was neat.

The style of control of the three fifth-grade teachers observed in this school varied from somewhat easygoing to strict, but in contrast to the working-class schools, the teachers' decisions were usually based on external rules and regulations — for example, on criteria that were known or available to the children. Thus, the teachers always honor the bells for changing classes, and they usually evaluate children's work by what is in the textbooks and answer booklets.

There is little excitement in schoolwork for the children, and the assignments are perceived as having little to do with their interests and feelings. As one child said, what you do is "store facts up in your head like cold storage — until you need it later for a test or your job." Thus, doing well is important because there are thought to be *other*, likely rewards: a good job or college.[10]

Affluent Professional School

In the affluent professional school, work is creative activity carried out independently. The students are continually asked to express and apply ideas and concepts. Work involves individual thought and expressiveness,

[10]A dominant feeling, expressed directly and indirectly by teachers in this school, was boredom with their work. They did, however, in contrast to the working-class schools, almost always carry out lessons during class times.

expansion and illustration of ideas, and choice of appropriate method and material. (The class is not considered an open classroom, and the principal explained that because of the large number of discipline problems in the fifth grade this year they did not departmentalize. The teacher who agreed to take part in the study said she is "more structured" this year than she usually is.) The products of work in this class are often written stories, editorials and essays, or representations of ideas in mural, graph, or craft form. The products of work should not be like everybody else's and should show individuality. They should exhibit good design, and (this is important) they must also fit empirical reality. Moreover, one's work should attempt to interpret or "make sense" of reality. The relatively few rules to be followed regarding work are usually criteria for, or limits on, individual activity. One's product is usually evaluated for the quality of its expression and for the appropriateness of its conception to the task. In many cases, one's own satisfaction with the product is an important criterion for its evaluation. When right answers are called for, as in commercial materials like SRA (Science Research Associates) and math, it is important that the children decide on an answer as a result of thinking about the idea involved in what they're being asked to do. Teacher's hints are to "think about it some more."

The following activities are illustrative. The class takes home a sheet requesting each child's parents to fill in the number of cars they have, the number of television sets, refrigerators, games, or rooms in the house, and so on. Each child is to figure the average number of a type of possession owned by the fifth grade. Each child must compile the "data" from all the sheets. A calculator is available in the classroom to do the mechanics of finding the average. Some children decide to send sheets to the fourth-grade families for comparison. Their work should be "verified" by a classmate before it is handed in.

Each child and his or her family has made a geoboard. The teacher asks the class to get their geoboards from the side cabinet, to take a handful of rubber bands, and then to listen to what she would like them to do. She says, "I would like you to design a figure and then find the perimeter and area. When you have it, check with your neighbor. After you've done that, please transfer it to graph paper and tomorrow I'll ask you to make up a question about it for someone. When you hand it in, please let me know whose it is and who verified it. Then I have something else for you to do that's really fun. [pause] Find the average number of chocolate chips in three cookies. I'll give you three cookies, and you'll have to *eat* your way through, I'm afraid!" Then she goes around the room and gives help, suggestions, praise, and admonitions that they are getting noisy. They work sitting, or standing up at their desks, at benches in the back, or on the floor. A child hands the teacher his paper and she comments, "I'm not accepting this paper. Do a better design." To another child she says, "That's fantastic! But you'll never find the area. Why don't you draw a figure inside [the big one] and subtract to get the area?"

The school district requires the fifth grade to study ancient civilization (in particular, Egypt, Athens, and Sumer). In this classroom, the emphasis is on illustrating and re-creating the culture of the people of ancient times. The following are typical activities: the children made an 8mm film on Egypt, which one of the parents edited. A girl in the class wrote the script, and the class acted it out. They put the sound on themselves. They read stories of those days. They wrote essays and stories depicting the lives of the people and the societal and occupational divisions. They chose from a list of projects, all of which involved graphic representations of ideas: for example, "Make a mural depicting the division of labor in Egyptian society."

Each child wrote and exchanged a letter in hieroglyphics with a fifth 30 grader in another class, and they also exchanged stories they wrote in cuneiform. They made a scroll and singed the edges so it looked authentic. They each chose an occupation and made an Egyptian plaque representing that occupation, simulating the appropriate Egyptian design. They carved their design on a cylinder of wax, pressed the wax into clay, and then baked the clay. Although one girl did not choose an occupation but carved instead a series of gods and slaves, the teacher said, "That's all right, Amber, it's beautiful." As they were working the teacher said, "Don't cut into your clay until you're satisfied with your design."

Social studies also involves almost daily presentation by the children of some event from the news. The teacher's questions ask the children to expand what they say, to give more details, and to be more specific. Occasionally she adds some remarks to help them see connections between events.

The emphasis on expressing and illustrating ideas in social studies is accompanied in language arts by an emphasis on creative writing. Each child wrote a rebus story for a first grader whom they had interviewed to see what kind of story the child liked best. They wrote editorials on pending decisions by the school board and radio plays, some of which were read over the school intercom from the office and one of which was performed in the auditorium. There is no language arts textbook because, the teacher said, "The principal wants us to be creative." There is not much grammar, but there is punctuation. One morning when the observer arrived, the class was doing a punctuation ditto. The teacher later apologized for using the ditto. "It's just for review," she said. "I don't teach punctuation that way. We use their language." The ditto had three unambiguous rules for where to put commas in a sentence. As the teacher was going around to help the children with the ditto, she repeated several times, "Where you put commas depends on how you say the sentence; it depends on the situation and what you want to say." Several weeks later the observer saw another punctuation activity. The teacher had printed a five-paragraph story on an oak tag and then cut it into phrases. She read the whole story to the class from the book, then passed out the phrases. The group had to decide how the phrases could best be put together again. (They arranged the phrases on the floor.) The point was not to replicate the story, although that was not irrelevant, but to "decide what you think the best way is." Punctuation marks on cardboard pieces were then handed out, and the children discussed and then decided what mark was best at each place they thought one was needed. At the end of each paragraph the teacher asked, "Are you satisfied with the way the paragraphs are now? Read it to yourself and see how it sounds." Then she read the original story again, and they compared the two.

Describing her goals in science to the investigator, the teacher said, "We use ESS (Elementary Science Study). It's very good because it gives a hands-on experience — so they can make *sense* out of it. It doesn't matter whether it [what they find] is right or wrong. I bring them together and there's value in discussing their ideas."

The products of work in this class are often highly valued by the children and the teacher. In fact, this was the only school in which the investigator was not allowed to take original pieces of the children's work for her files. If the work was small enough, however, and was on paper, the investigator could duplicate it on the copying machine in the office.

The teacher's attempt to control the class involves constant negotiation.   35
She does not give direct orders unless she is angry because the children have been too noisy. Normally, she tries to get them to foresee the consequences of their actions and to decide accordingly. For example, lining them up to go see a play written by the sixth graders, she says, "I presume you're lined up by someone with whom you want to sit. I hope you're lined up by someone you won't get in trouble with." . . .

One of the few rules governing the children's movement is that no more than three children may be out of the room at once. There is a school rule that anyone can go to the library at any time to get a book. In the fifth grade I observed, they sign their name on the chalkboard and leave. There are no passes. Finally, the children have a fair amount of officially sanctioned say over what happens in the class. For example, they often negotiate what work is to be done. If the teacher wants to move on to the next subject, but the children say they are not ready, they want to work on their present projects some more, she very often lets them do it.

Executive Elite School

In the executive elite school, work is developing one's analytical intellectual powers. Children are continually asked to reason through a problem, to produce intellectual products that are both logically sound and of top academic quality. A primary goal of thought is to conceptualize rules by which elements may fit together in systems and then to apply these rules in solving a problem. Schoolwork helps one to achieve, to excel, to prepare for life.

The following are illustrative. The math teacher teaches area and perimeter by having the children derive formulas for each. First she helps them, through discussion at the board, to arrive at $A = W \times L$ as a formula (not *the* formula) for area. After discussing several, she says, "Can anyone make up a formula for perimeter? Can you figure that out yourselves? [pause] Knowing what we know, can we think of a formula?" She works out three children's suggestions at the board, saying to two, "Yes, that's a good one," and then asks the class if they can think of any more. No one volunteers. To prod them, she says, "If you use rules and good reasoning, you get many ways. Chris, can you think up a formula?"

She discusses two-digit division with the children as a decision-making process. Presenting a new type of problem to them, she asks, "What's the *first* decision you'd make if presented with this kind of example? What is the first thing you'd *think?* Craig?" Craig says, "To find my first partial quotient." She responds, "Yes, that would be your first decision. How would you do that?" Craig explains, and then the teacher says, "OK, we'll see how that works for you." The class tries his way. Subsequently, she comments on the merits and shortcomings of several other children's decisions. Later, she tells the investigator that her goals in math are to develop their reasoning and mathematical thinking and that, unfortunately, "there's no *time* for manipulables."

While right answers are important in math, they are not "given" by the   40 book or by the teacher but may be challenged by the children. Going over some problems in late September the teacher says, "Raise your hand if you do not agree." A child says, "I don't agree with sixty-four." The teacher responds, "OK, there's a question about sixty-four. [to class] Please check it. Owen, they're disagreeing with you. Kristen, they're checking yours." The teacher emphasized this repeatedly during September and October with statements like "Don't be afraid to say you disagree. In the last [math] class, somebody disagreed, and they were right. Before you disagree, check yours, and if you still think we're wrong, then we'll check it out." By Thanksgiving, the children did not often speak in terms of right and wrong math problems but of whether they agreed with the answer that had been given.

There are complicated math mimeos with many word problems. Whenever they go over the examples, they discuss how each child has set up the problem. The children must explain it precisely. On one occasion the teacher said, "I'm more — just as interested in *how* you set up the problem as in what answer you find. If you set up a problem in a good way, the answer is *easy* to find."

Social studies work is most often reading and discussion of concepts and independent research. There are only occasional artistic, expressive, or illustrative projects. Ancient Athens and Sumer are, rather, societies to analyze. The following questions are typical of those that guide the children's independent research. "What mistakes did Pericles make after the war?" "What mistakes did the citizens of Athens make?" "What are the elements of a civilization?" "How did Greece build an economic empire?" "Compare the way Athens chose its leaders with the way we choose ours." Occasionally the children are asked to make up sample questions for their social studies tests. On an occasion when the investigator was present, the social studies teacher rejected a child's question by saying, "That's just fact. If I asked you that question on a test, you'd complain it was just memory! Good questions ask for concepts."

In social studies — but also in reading, science, and health — the teachers initiate classroom discussions of current social issues and problems. These discussions occurred on every one of the investigator's visits, and a teacher told me, "These children's opinions are important — it's important that they learn to reason things through." The classroom discussions always struck the observer as quite realistic and analytical, dealing with concrete social issues like the following: "Why do workers strike?" "Is that right or wrong?" "Why do we have inflation, and what can be done to stop it?" "Why do companies put chemicals in food when the natural ingredients are available?" and so on. Usually the children did not have to be prodded to give their opinions. In fact, their statements and the interchanges between them struck the observer as quite sophisticated conceptually and verbally, and well-informed. Occasionally the teachers would prod with statements such as, "Even if you don't know [the answers], if you think logically about it, you can figure it out." And "I'm asking you [these] questions to help you think this through."

Language arts emphasizes language as a complex system, one that should be mastered. The children are asked to diagram sentences of complex grammatical construction, to memorize irregular verb conjugations (he lay, he has lain, and so on . . .), and to use the proper participles, conjunctions, and interjections in their speech. The teacher (the same one who teaches social studies) told them, "It is not enough to get these right on tests; you must use what you learn [in grammar classes] in your written and oral work. I will grade you on that."

Most writing assignments are either research reports and essays for social studies or experiment analyses and write-ups for science. There is only an occasional story or other "creative writing" assignment. On the occasion observed by the investigator (the writing of a Halloween story), the points the teacher stressed in preparing the children to write involved the structural aspects of a story rather than the expression of feelings or other ideas. The teacher showed them a filmstrip, "The Seven Parts of a Story," and lectured them on plot development, mood setting, character development, consistency, and the use of a logical or appropriate ending. The stories they subsequently wrote were, in fact, well-structured, but many were also personal and expressive. The teacher's evaluative comments, however, did not refer to the expressiveness or artistry but were all directed toward whether they had "developed" the story well.

Language arts work also involved a large amount of practice in presentation of the self and in managing situations where the child was expected to be in charge. For example, there was a series of assignments in which each child had to be a "student teacher." The child had to plan a lesson in grammar, outlining, punctuation, or other language arts topic and explain the concept to the class. Each child was to prepare a worksheet or game and a homework assignment as well. After each presentation, the teacher and other children gave a critical appraisal of the "student teacher's" performance. Their criteria were: whether the student spoke clearly, whether the lesson was interesting, whether the student made any mistakes, and whether he or she kept control of the class. On an occasion when a child did not maintain control, the teacher said, "When you're up there, you have authority and you have to use it. I'll back you up." . . .

The executive elite school is the only school where bells do not demarcate the periods of time. The two fifth-grade teachers were very strict about changing classes on schedule, however, as specific plans for each session had been made. The teachers attempted to keep tight control over the children during lessons, and the children were sometimes flippant, boisterous, and occasionally rude. However, the children may be brought into line by reminding them that "It is up to you," "You must control yourself," "You are responsible for your work," you must "set your own priorities." One teacher told a child, "You are the only driver of your car — and only you can regulate your speed." A new teacher complained to the observer that she had thought "these children" would have more control.

While strict attention to the lesson at hand is required, the teachers make relatively little attempt to regulate the movement of the children at other times. For example, except for the kindergartners the children in this school do not have to wait for the bell to ring in the morning; they may go to their classroom when they arrive at school. Fifth graders often came early to read, to finish work, or to catch up. After the first two months of school, the fifth-grade teachers did not line the children up to change classes or to go to gym, and so on, but, when the children were ready and quiet, they were told they could go — sometimes without the teachers.

In the classroom, the children could get materials when they needed them and took what they needed from closets and from the teacher's desk. They were in charge of the office at lunchtime. During class they did not have to sign out or ask permission to leave the room; they just got up and left. Because of the pressure to get work done, however, they did not leave the room very often. The teachers were very polite to the children, and the investigator heard no sarcasm, no nasty remarks, and few direct orders. The teachers never called the children "honey" or "dear" but always called them by name. The teachers were expected to be available before school, after school, and for part of their lunchtime to provide extra help if needed. . . .

The foregoing analysis of differences in schoolwork in contrasting   50
social-class contexts suggests the following conclusion: the "hidden curriculum" of schoolwork is tacit preparation for relating to the process of production in a particular way. Differing curricular, pedagogical, and pupil evaluation practices emphasize different cognitive and behavioral skills in each social setting and thus contribute to the development in the children of cer-

tain potential relationships to physical and symbolic capital,[11] to authority, and to the process of work. School experience, in the sample of schools discussed here, differed qualitatively by social class. These differences may not only contribute to the development in the children in each social class of certain types of economically significant relationships and not others but would thereby help to *reproduce* this system of relations in society. In the contribution to the reproduction of unequal social relations lies a theoretical meaning and social consequence of classroom practice.

The identification of different emphases in classrooms in a sample of contrasting social-class contexts implies that further research should be conducted in a large number of schools to investigate the types of work tasks and interactions in each to see if they differ in the ways discussed here and to see if similar potential relationships are uncovered. Such research could have as a product the further elucidation of complex but not readily apparent connections between everyday activity in schools and classrooms and the unequal structure of economic relationships in which we work and live.

ENGAGING THE TEXT

1. Examine the ways any single subject is taught in the four types of schools Anyon describes. What differences in teaching methods and in the student-teacher relationship do they reflect? What other differences do you note in the schools? What schools in your geographic region would closely approximate the working-class, middle-class, affluent professional, and executive elite schools of her article?

2. What attitudes toward knowledge and work are the four types of schools teaching their students? What kinds of jobs are students being prepared to do? Do you see any evidence that the schools in your community are producing particular kinds of workers?

3. What is the "hidden curriculum" of Anyon's title? How is this curriculum taught, and what social, cultural, or political purposes does it serve?

EXPLORING CONNECTIONS

4. Contrast Anyon's depiction of the "hidden curriculum" of American education with that proposed by John Taylor Gatto (p. 152). How common would you expect the "Seven-Lesson Schoolteacher" to be in each of the four types of schools Anyon mentions?

5. Draw a Groening-like (see pp. 160–61) cartoon or comic strip about a classroom situation in a working-class, middle-class, professional, or elite school (but do not identify the type of school explicitly). Pool all the

[11]*physical and symbolic capital:* Elsewhere Anyon defines *capital* as "property that is used to produce profit, interest, or rent"; she defines *symbolic capital* as the knowledge and skills that "may yield social and cultural power."

cartoons from the class. In small groups, sort the comics according to the type of school they represent.

6. Analyze the teaching styles that Mike Rose encounters at Our Lady of Mercy (p. 162). Which of Anyon's categories would they fit best? Do Rose's experiences at his high school tend to confirm or complicate Anyon's analysis?

EXTENDING THE CRITICAL CONTEXT

7. Should all schools be run like professional or elite schools? What would be the advantages of making these schools models for all social classes? Do you see any possible disadvantages?

8. Choose a common elementary school task or skill that Anyon does not mention. Outline four ways it might be taught in the four types of schools.

Visual Portfolio

READING IMAGES OF EDUCATION AND EMPOWERMENT

The Spirit of Education (1934), by Norman Rockwell.

The Graduate (1959), by Norman Rockwell.

The Problem We All Live With (1964), by Norman Rockwell.

Visual Portfolio

READING IMAGES OF EDUCATION AND EMPOWERMENT

1. What is happening in "The Spirit of Education"? What is Norman Rockwell saying about the situation — and about education — through the attitudes of the boy and the seated woman?

2. What meaning can you find in the elements that make up the boy's costume? What significance is there in the book, the torch, the laurel crown, the toga and sandals? What are these symbols supposed to suggest about education? If you were to costume someone to represent education today, how would you do it?

3. In "The Graduate," why has Rockwell chosen to place his subject in front of a newspaper? To what extent are the headlines of the paper relevant? What is Rockwell suggesting through the young man's posture and attitude?

4. Plan an updated version of the portrait on page 192, featuring a twenty-first-century graduate and a more contemporary background.

5. What is the setting of "The Problem We All Live With"? What event does it commemorate? How do you interpret the painting's title?

6. What does Rockwell suggest about the relationship of education, society, power, and violence through the visual details included in this painting? What significance do you see, for example, in the absence of the men's faces, the position of their hands and arms, the rhythm of their strides, the smallness of the girl, her attitude, the materials she carries, and so forth?

The Achievement of Desire

RICHARD RODRIGUEZ

Hunger of Memory, *the autobiography of Richard Rodriguez and the source of the following selection, set off a storm of controversy in the Chicano community when it appeared in 1981. Some hailed it as an uncompromising portrayal of the difficulties of growing up between two cultures; others condemned it because it seemed to blame Mexican Americans for the difficulties they encountered assimilating into mainstream American society. Rodriguez was born in 1944 into an immigrant family outside San Francisco. Though he was unable to speak English when he entered school, his educational career can only be described as brilliant: undergraduate work at Stanford University, graduate study at Berkeley and Columbia, a Fulbright fellowship to study English literature in London, a subsequent grant from the National Endowment for the Humanities. In this selection, Rod-riguez analyzes the motives that led him to abandon his study of Renais-sance literature and return to live with his parents. He is currently an asso-ciate editor with the Pacific News Service in San Francisco, an essayist for the* Newshour with Jim Lehrer, *and a contributing editor for* Harper's *magazine and for the Opinion section of the* Los Angeles Times. *His other books include* Mexico's Children *(1991) and* Days of Obligation: An Argu-ment with My Mexican Father *(1993), which was nominated for the Pulitzer Prize in nonfiction.*

I stand in the ghetto classroom — "the guest speaker" — attempting to lecture on the mystery of the sounds of our words to rows of diffident stu-dents. "Don't you hear it? Listen! The music of our words. '*Sumer is i-cumen in.*[1] . . .' And songs on the car radio. We need Aretha Franklin's voice to fill plain words with music — her life." In the face of their empty stares, I try to create an enthusiasm. But the girls in the back row turn to watch some boy passing outside. There are flutters of smiles, waves. And someone's mouth elongates heavy, silent words through the barrier of glass. Silent words — the lips straining to shape each voiceless syllable: "*Meet meee late errr.*" By the door, the instructor smiles at me, apparently hoping that I will be able to spark some enthusiasm in the class. But only one student seems to be listening. A girl, maybe fourteen. In this gray room her eyes shine with am-bition. She keeps nodding and nodding at all that I say; she even takes notes. And each time I ask a question, she jerks up and down in her desk like a mar-ionette, while her hand waves over the bowed heads of her classmates. It is myself (as a boy) I see as she faces me now (a man in my thirties).

The boy who first entered a classroom barely able to speak English, twenty years later concluded his studies in the stately quiet of the reading room in the British Museum. Thus with one sentence I can summarize my academic career. It will be harder to summarize what sort of life connects the boy to the man.

With every award, each graduation from one level of education to the next, people I'd meet would congratulate me. Their refrain always the same: "Your parents must be very proud." Sometimes then they'd ask me how I managed it — my "success." (How?) After a while, I had several quick answers to give in reply. I'd admit, for one thing, that I went to an excellent grammar school. (My earliest teachers, the nuns, made my success their ambition.) And my brother and both my sisters were very good students. (They often brought home the shiny school trophies I came to want.) And my mother and father always encouraged me. (At every graduation they were behind the stunning flash of the camera when I turned to look at the crowd.)

---

[1]*Sumer is i-cumen in:* Opening line of a Middle English poem ("Summer has come").

As important as these factors were, however, they account inadequately for my academic advance. Nor do they suggest what an odd success I managed. For although I was a very good student, I was also a very bad student. I was a "scholarship boy," a certain kind of scholarship boy. Always successful, I was always unconfident. Exhilarated by my progress. Sad. I became the prized student — anxious and eager to learn. Too eager, too anxious — an imitative and unoriginal pupil. My brother and two sisters enjoyed the advantages I did, and they grew to be as successful as I, but none of them ever seemed so anxious about their schooling. A second-grade student, I was the one who came home and corrected the "simple" grammatical mistakes of our parents. ("Two negatives make a positive.") Proudly I announced — to my family's startled silence — that a teacher had said I was losing all trace of a Spanish accent. I was oddly annoyed when I was unable to get parental help with a homework assignment. The night my father tried to help me with an arithmetic exercise, he kept reading the instructions, each time more deliberately, until I pried the textbook out of his hands, saying, "I'll try to figure it out some more by myself."

When I reached the third grade, I outgrew such behavior. I became   5
more tactful, careful to keep separate the two very different worlds of my day. But then, with ever-increasing intensity, I devoted myself to my studies. I became bookish, puzzling to all my family. Ambition set me apart. When my brother saw me struggling home with stacks of library books, he would laugh, shouting: "Hey, Four Eyes!" My father opened a closet one day and was startled to find me inside, reading a novel. My mother would find me reading when I was supposed to be asleep or helping around the house or playing outside. In a voice angry or worried or just curious, she'd ask: "What do you see in your books?" It became the family's joke. When I was called and wouldn't reply, someone would say I must be hiding under my bed with a book.

(How did I manage my success?)

What I am about to say to you has taken me more than twenty years to admit: *A primary reason for my success in the classroom was that I couldn't forget that schooling was changing me and separating me from the life I enjoyed before becoming a student.* That simple realization! For years I never spoke to anyone about it. Never mentioned a thing to my family or my teachers or classmates. From a very early age, I understood enough, just enough about my classroom experiences to keep what I knew repressed, hidden beneath layers of embarrassment. Not until my last months as a graduate student, nearly thirty years old, was it possible for me to think much about the reasons for my academic success. Only then. At the end of my schooling, I needed to determine how far I had moved from my past. The adult finally confronted, and now must publicly say, what the child shuddered from knowing and could never admit to himself or to those many faces that smiled at his every success. ("Your parents must be very proud. . . .")

At the end, in the British Museum (too distracted to finish my dissertation) for weeks I read, speed-read, books by modern educational theorists, only to find infrequent and slight mention of students like me. (Much more is written about the more typical case, the lower-class student who barely is helped by his schooling.) Then one day, leafing through Richard Hoggart's *The Uses of Literacy,* I found, in his description of the scholarship boy, myself. For the first time I realized that there were other students like me, and so I was able to frame the meaning of my academic success, its consequent price — the loss.

Hoggart's description is distinguished, at least initially, by deep understanding. What he grasps very well is that the scholarship boy must move between environments, his home and the classroom, which are at cultural extremes, opposed. With his family, the boy has the intense pleasure of intimacy, the family's consolation in feeling public alienation. Lavish emotions texture home life. *Then,* at school, the instruction bids him to trust lonely reason primarily. Immediate needs set the pace of his parents' lives. From his mother and father the boy learns to trust spontaneity and nonrational ways of knowing. *Then,* at school, there is mental calm. Teachers emphasize the value of a reflectiveness that opens a space between thinking and immediate action.

Years of schooling must pass before the boy will be able to sketch the cultural differences in his day as abstractly as this. But he senses those differences early. Perhaps as early as the night he brings home an assignment from school and finds the house too noisy for study.

> He has to be more and more alone, if he is going to "get on." He will have, probably unconsciously, to oppose the ethos[2] of the hearth, the intense gregariousness of the working-class family group. Since everything centres upon the living-room, there is unlikely to be a room of his own; the bedrooms are cold and inhospitable, and to warm them or the front room, if there is one, would not only be expensive, but would require an imaginative leap — out of the tradition — which most families are not capable of making. There is a corner of the living-room table. On the other side Mother is ironing, the wireless is on, someone is singing a snatch of song or Father says intermittently whatever comes into his head. The boy has to cut himself off mentally, so as to do his homework, as well as he can.[3]

The next day, the lesson is as apparent at school. There are even rows of desks. Discussion is ordered. The boy must rehearse his thoughts and raise his hand before speaking out in a loud voice to an audience of classmates. And there is time enough, and silence, to think about ideas (big ideas) never considered at home by his parents.

Not for the working-class child alone is adjustment to the classroom difficult. Good schooling requires that any student alter early childhood

10

---

[2]*ethos:* The fundamental spirit or character of a thing.
[3]All quotations are from Richard Hoggart, *The Uses of Literacy* (London: Chatto and Windus, 1957), Chapter 10. [Author's note]

habits. But the working-class child is usually least prepared for the change. And, unlike many middle-class children, he goes home and sees in his parents a way of life not only different but starkly opposed to that of the classroom. (He enters the house and hears his parents talking in ways his teachers discourage.)

Without extraordinary determination and the great assistance of others — at home and at school — there is little chance for success. Typically most working-class children are barely changed by the classroom. The exception succeeds. The relative few become scholarship students. Of these, Richard Hoggart estimates, most manage a fairly graceful transition. Somehow they learn to live in the two very different worlds of their day. There are some others, however, those Hoggart pejoratively terms "scholarship boys," for whom success comes with special anxiety. Scholarship boy: good student, troubled son. The child is "moderately endowed," intellectually mediocre, Hoggart supposes — though it may be more pertinent to note the special qualities of temperament in the child. High-strung child. Brooding. Sensitive. Haunted by the knowledge that one *chooses* to become a student. (Education is not an inevitable or natural step in growing up.) Here is a child who cannot forget that his academic success distances him from a life he loved, even from his own memory of himself.

Initially, he wavers, balances allegiance. ("The boy is himself [until he reaches, say, the upper forms[4]] very much of *both* the worlds of home and school. He is enormously obedient to the dictates of the world of school, but emotionally still strongly wants to continue as part of the family circle.") Gradually, necessarily, the balance is lost. The boy needs to spend more and more time studying, each night enclosing himself in the silence permitted and required by intense concentration. He takes his first step toward academic success, away from his family.

From the very first days, through the years following, it will be with his parents — the figures of lost authority, the persons toward whom he feels deepest love — that the change will be most powerfully measured. A separation will unravel between them. Advancing in his studies, the boy notices that his mother and father have not changed as much as he. Rather, when he sees them, they often remind him of the person he once was and the life he earlier shared with them. He realizes what some Romantics[5] also know when they praise the working class for the capacity for human closeness, qualities of passion and spontaneity, that the rest of us experience in like measure only in the earliest part of our youth. For the Romantic, this doesn't make working-class life childish. Working-class life challenges precisely because it is an *adult* way of life.

15

[4]*upper forms:* Upper grades or classes in British secondary schools.
[5]*Romantics:* Adherents of the principles of romanticism — a literary and philosophical movement that emphasized the imagination, freedom, nature, the return to a simple life, and the ordinary individual.

The scholarship boy reaches a different conclusion. He cannot afford to admire his parents. (How could he and still pursue such a contrary life?) He permits himself embarrassment at their lack of education. And to evade nostalgia for the life he has lost, he concentrates on the benefits education will bestow upon him. He becomes especially ambitious. Without the support of old certainties and consolations, almost mechanically, he assumes the procedures and doctrines of the classroom. The kind of allegiance the young student might have given his mother and father only days earlier, he transfers to the teacher, the new figure of authority. "[The scholarship boy] tends to make a father-figure of his form-master,"[6] Hoggart observes.

But Hoggart's calm prose only makes me recall the urgency with which I came to idolize my grammar school teachers. I began by imitating their accents, using their diction, trusting their every direction. The very first facts they dispensed, I grasped with awe. Any book they told me to read, I read — then waited for them to tell me which books I enjoyed. Their every casual opinion I came to adopt and to trumpet when I returned home. I stayed after school "to help" — to get my teacher's undivided attention. It was the nun's encouragement that mattered most to me. (She understood exactly what — my parents never seemed to appraise so well — all my achievements entailed.) Memory gently caressed each word of praise bestowed in the classroom so that compliments teachers paid me years ago come quickly to mind even today.

The enthusiasm I felt in second-grade classes I flaunted before both my parents. The docile, obedient student came home a shrill and precocious son who insisted on correcting and teaching his parents with the remark: "My teacher told us. . . ."

I intended to hurt my mother and father. I was still angry at them for having encouraged me toward classroom English. But gradually this anger was exhausted, replaced by guilt as school grew more and more attractive to me. I grew increasingly successful, a talkative student. My hand was raised in the classroom; I yearned to answer any question. At home, life was less noisy than it had been. (I spoke to classmates and teachers more often each day than to family members.) Quiet at home, I sat with my papers for hours each night. I never forgot that schooling had irretrievably changed my family's life. That knowledge, however, did not weaken ambition. Instead, it strengthened resolve. Those times I remembered the loss of my past with regret, I quickly reminded myself of all the things my teachers could give me. (They could make me an educated man.) I tightened my grip on pencil and books. I evaded nostalgia. Tried hard to forget. But one does not forget by trying to forget. One only remembers. I remembered too well that education had changed my family's life. I would not have become a scholarship boy had I not so often remembered.

---

[6]*form-master:* A teacher in a British secondary school.

Once she was sure that her children knew English, my mother would   20
tell us, "You should keep up your Spanish." Voices playfully groaned in response. "*¡Pochos!*"[7] my mother would tease. I listened silently.

After a while, I grew more calm at home. I developed tact. A fourth-
grade student, I was no longer the show-off in front of my parents. I became a conventionally dutiful son, politely affectionate, cheerful enough,
even — for reasons beyond choosing — my father's favorite. And much
about my family life was easy then, comfortable, happy in the rhythm of our
living together: hearing my father getting ready for work; eating the breakfast my mother had made me; looking up from a novel to hear my brother
or one of my sisters playing with friends in the backyard; in winter, coming
upon the house all lighted up after dark.

But withheld from my mother and father was any mention of what
most mattered to me: the extraordinary experience of first-learning. Late
afternoon: in the midst of preparing dinner, my mother would come up
behind me while I was trying to read. Her head just over mine, her breath
warmly scented with food. "What are you reading?" Or, "Tell me about your
new courses." I would barely respond, "Just the usual things, nothing
special." (A half smile, then silence. Her head moving back in the silence.
Silence! Instead of the flood of intimate sounds that had once flowed
smoothly between us, there was this silence.) After dinner, I would rush
to a bedroom with papers and books. As often as possible, I resisted
parental pleas to "save lights" by coming to the kitchen to work. I kept
so much, so often, to myself. Sad. Enthusiastic. Troubled by the excitement of coming upon new ideas. Eager. Fascinated by the promising texture of a brand-new book. I hoarded the pleasures of learning.
Alone for hours. Enthralled. Nervous. I rarely looked away from my
books — or back on my memories. Nights when relatives visited and
the front rooms were warmed by Spanish sounds, I slipped quietly out of
the house.

It mattered that education was changing me. It never ceased to matter.
My brother and sisters would giggle at our mother's mispronounced words.
They'd correct her gently. My mother laughed girlishly one night, trying not
to pronounce *sheep* as *ship*. From a distance I listened sullenly. From that
distance, pretending not to notice on another occasion, I saw my father
looking at the title pages of my library books. That was the scene on my
mind when I walked home with a fourth-grade companion and heard him
say that his parents read to him every night. (A strange-sounding book —
Winnie the Pooh.) Immediately, I wanted to know, "What is it like?" My
companion, however, thought I wanted to know about the plot of the book.
Another day, my mother surprised me by asking for a "nice" book to read.
"Something not too hard you think I might like." Carefully I chose one,

---

[7]*Pocho:* A derogatory Spanish word for a Mexican American who has adopted the attitudes, values, and lifestyle of Anglo culture.

Willa Cather's[8] *My Antonia.* But when, several weeks later, I happened to see it next to her bed unread except for the first few pages, I was furious and suddenly wanted to cry. I grabbed up the book and took it back to my room and placed it in its place, alphabetically on my shelf.

"Your parents must be very proud of you." People began to say that to me about the time I was in sixth grade. To answer affirmatively, I'd smile. Shyly I'd smile, never betraying my sense of the irony: I was not proud of my mother and father. I was embarrassed by their lack of education. It was not that I ever thought they were stupid, though stupidly I took for granted their enormous native intelligence. Simply, what mattered to me was that they were not like my teachers.

But, "Why didn't you tell us about the award?" my mother demanded, her frown weakened by pride. At the grammar school ceremony several weeks after, her eyes were brighter than the trophy I'd won. Pushing back the hair from my forehead, she whispered that I had "shown" the *gringos.*[9] A few minutes later, I heard my father speak to my teacher and felt ashamed of his labored, accented words. Then guilty for the shame. I felt such contrary feelings. (There is no simple roadmap through the heart of the scholarship boy.) My teacher was so soft-spoken and her words were edged sharp and clean. I admired her until it seemed to me that she spoke too carefully. Sensing that she was condescending to them, I became nervous. Resentful. Protective. I tried to move my parents away. "You both must be very proud of Richard," the nun said. They responded quickly. (They were proud.) "We are proud of all our children." Then this afterthought: "They sure didn't get their brains from us." They all laughed. I smiled.

In fourth grade I embarked upon a grandiose reading program. "Give me the names of important books," I would say to startled teachers. They soon found out that I had in mind "adult books." I ignored their suggestion of anything I suspected was written for children. (Not until I was in college, as a result, did I read *Huckleberry Finn* or *Alice's Adventures in Wonderland.*) Instead, I read *The Scarlet Letter* and Franklin's *Autobiography.* And whatever I read I read for extra credit. Each time I finished a book, I reported the achievement to a teacher and basked in the praise my effort earned. Despite my best efforts, however, there seemed to be more and more books I needed to read. At the library I would literally tremble as I came upon whole shelves of books I hadn't read. So I read and I read and I read: *Great Expectations;* all the short stories of Kipling; *The Babe Ruth Story;* the entire first volume of the *Encyclopaedia Britannica* (A–ANSTEY); the *Iliad; Moby Dick; Gone with the Wind; The Good Earth; Ramona; Forever Amber; The Lives of the Saints; Crime and Punishment; The Pearl. . . .*

[8]*Willa Cather:* American novelist (1876–1947).
[9]*gringos:* Anglos.

Librarians who initially frowned when I checked out the maximum ten books at a time started saving books they thought I might like. Teachers would say to the rest of the class, "I only wish the rest of you took reading as seriously as Richard obviously does."

But at home I would hear my mother wondering, "What do you see in your books?" (Was reading a hobby like her knitting? Was so much reading even healthy for a boy? Was it the sign of "brains"? Or was it just a convenient excuse for not helping around the house on Saturday mornings?) Always, "What do you see . . . ?"

What *did* I see in my books? I had the idea that they were crucial for my academic success, though I couldn't have said exactly how or why. In the sixth grade I simply concluded that what gave a book its value was some major idea or theme it contained. If that core essence could be mined and memorized, I would become learned like my teachers. I decided to record in a notebook the themes of the books that I read. After reading *Robinson Crusoe,* I wrote that its theme was "the value of learning to live by oneself." When I completed *Wuthering Heights,* I noted the danger of "letting emotions get out of control." Rereading these brief moralistic appraisals usually left me disheartened. I couldn't believe that they were really the source of reading's value. But for many more years, they constituted the only means I had of describing to myself the educational value of books.

I entered high school having read hundreds of books. My habit of reading made me a confident speaker and writer of English. Reading also enabled me to sense something of the shape, the major concerns, of Western thought. (I was able to say something about Dante[10] and Descartes[11] and Engels[12] and James Baldwin[13] in my high school term papers.) In these various ways, books brought me academic success as I hoped that they would. But I was not a good reader. Merely bookish, I lacked a point of view when I read. Rather, I read in order to acquire a point of view. I vacuumed books for epigrams, scraps of information, ideas, themes — anything to fill the hollow within me and make me feel educated. When one of my teachers suggested to his drowsy tenth-grade English class that a person could not have a "complicated idea" until he had read at least two thousand books, I heard the remark without detecting either its irony or its very complicated truth. I merely determined to compile a list of all the books I had ever read. Harsh with myself, I included only once a title I might have read several times. (How, after all, could one read a book more than once?) And I included only those books over a hundred pages in length. (Could anything shorter be a book?)

---

[10]*Dante:* Dante Alighieri, Italian poet (1265–1321); author of the *Divine Comedy.*

[11]*Descartes:* René Descartes, French philosopher and mathematician (1596–1650).

[12]*Engels:* Friedrich Engels, German socialist (1820–1895); coauthor with Karl Marx of the *Communist Manifesto* in 1848.

[13]*James Baldwin:* American novelist and essayist (1924–1987).

There was yet another high school list I compiled. One day I came   30
across a newspaper article about the retirement of an English professor at a
nearby state college. The article was accompanied by a list of the "hundred
most important books of Western Civilization." "More than anything else in
my life," the professor told the reporter with finality, "these books have
made me all that I am." That was the kind of remark I couldn't ignore. I
clipped out the list and kept it for the several months it took me to read all
of the titles. Most books, of course, I barely understood. While reading
Plato's *Republic,* for instance, I needed to keep looking at the book jacket
comments to remind myself what the text was about. Nevertheless, with the
special patience and superstition of a scholarship boy, I looked at every
word of the text. And by the time I reached the last word, relieved, I convinced myself that I had read *The Republic.* In a ceremony of great pride, I
solemnly crossed Plato off my list.

... The scholarship boy does not straddle, cannot reconcile, the two
great opposing cultures of his life. His success is unromantic and plain. He
sits in the classroom and offers those sitting beside him no calming reassurance about their own lives. He sits in the seminar room — a man with
brown skin, the son of working-class Mexican immigrant parents. (Addressing the professor at the head of the table, his voice catches with nervous-
ness.) There is no trace of his parents' accent in his speech. Instead he ap-
proximates the accents of teachers and classmates. Coming from *him* those
sounds seem suddenly odd. Odd too is the effect produced when *he* uses
academic jargon — bubbles at the tip of his tongue: "*Topos* . . . negative capability . . . vegetation imagery in Shakespearean comedy."[14] He lifts an
opinion from Coleridge, takes something else from Frye or Empson or
Leavis.[15] He even repeats exactly his professor's earlier comment. All his
ideas are clearly borrowed. He seems to have no thought of his own. He
chatters while his listeners smile — their look one of disdain.

When he is older and thus when so little of the person he was survives,
the scholarship boy makes only too apparent his profound lack of *self-
confidence.* This is the conventional assessment that even Richard Hoggart
repeats:

> [The scholarship boy] tends to over-stress the importance of examina-
> tions, of the piling-up of knowledge and of received opinions. He dis-
> covers a technique of apparent learning, of the acquiring of facts
> rather than of the handling and use of facts. He learns how to receive a
> purely literate education, one using only a small part of the personality
> and challenging only a limited area of his being. He begins to see life
> as a ladder, as a permanent examination with some praise and some
> further exhortation at each stage. He becomes an expert imbiber and

[14]*topos . . . negative capability . . . :* Technical terms associated with the study of literary
criticism.
[15]*Coleridge . . . Frye . . . Empson . . . Leavis:* Important literary critics.

dolerout; his competence will vary, but will rarely be accompanied by genuine enthusiasms. He rarely feels the reality of knowledge, of other men's thoughts and imaginings, on his own pulses. . . . He has something of the blinkered pony about him. . . .

But this is criticism more accurate than fair. The scholarship boy is a very bad student. He is the great mimic; a collector of thoughts, not a thinker; the very last person in class who ever feels obliged to have an opinion of his own. In large part, however, the reason he is such a bad student is because he realizes more often and more acutely than most other students — than Hoggart himself — that education requires radical self-reformation. As a very young boy, regarding his parents, as he struggles with an early homework assignment, he knows this too well. That is why he lacks self-assurance. He does not forget that the classroom is responsible for re-making him. He relies on his teacher, depends on all that he hears in the classroom and reads in his books. He becomes in every obvious way the worst student, a dummy mouthing the opinions of others. But he would not be so bad — nor would he become so successful, a *scholarship* boy — if he did not accurately perceive that the best synonym for primary "education" is "imitation."

Like me, Hoggart's imagined scholarship boy spends most of his years in the classroom afraid to long for his past. Only at the very end of his schooling does the boy-man become nostalgic. In this sudden change of heart, Richard Hoggart notes:

> He longs for the membership he lost, "he pines for some Nameless Eden where he never was." The nostalgia is the stronger and the more ambiguous because he is really "in quest of his own absconded self yet scared to find it." He both wants to go back and yet thinks he has gone beyond his class, feels himself weighted with knowledge of his own and their situation, which hereafter forbids him the simpler pleasures of his father and mother. . . .

According to Hoggart, the scholarship boy grows nostalgic because he 35 remains the uncertain scholar, bright enough to have moved from his past, yet unable to feel easy, a part of a community of academics.

This analysis, however, only partially suggests what happened to me in my last years as a graduate student. When I traveled to London to write a dissertation on English Renaissance literature, I was finally confident of membership in a "community of scholars." But the pleasure that confidence gave me faded rapidly. After only two or three months in the reading room of the British Museum, it became clear that I had joined a lonely community. Around me each day were dour faces eclipsed by large piles of books. There were the regulars, like the old couple who arrived every morning, each holding a loop of the shopping bag which contained all their notes. And there was the historian who chattered madly to herself. ("Oh dear! Oh!

Now, what's this? What? Oh, my!") There were also the faces of young men and women worn by long study. And everywhere eyes turned away the moment our glance accidentally met. Some persons I sat beside day after day, yet we passed silently at the end of the day, strangers. Still, we were united by a common respect for the written word and for scholarship. We did form a union, though one in which we remained distant from one another.

More profound and unsettling was the bond I recognized with those writers whose books I consulted. Whenever I opened a text that hadn't been used for years, I realized that my special interests and skills united me to a mere handful of academics. We formed an exclusive — eccentric! — society, separated from others who would never care or be able to share our concerns. (The pages I turned were stiff like layers of dead skin.) I began to wonder: Who, beside my dissertation director and a few faculty members, would ever read what I wrote? and: Was my dissertation much more than an act of social withdrawal? These questions went unanswered in the silence of the Museum reading room. They remained to trouble me after I'd leave the library each afternoon and feel myself shy — unsteady, speaking simple sentences at the grocer's or the butcher's on my way back to my bed-sitter.[16]

Meanwhile my file cards accumulated. A professional, I knew exactly how to search a book for pertinent information. I could quickly assess and summarize the usability of the many books I consulted. But whenever I started to write, I knew too much (and not enough) to be able to write anything but sentences that were overly cautious, timid, strained brittle under the heavy weight of footnotes and qualifications. I seemed unable to dare a passionate statement. I felt drawn by professionalism to the edge of sterility, capable of no more than pedantic, lifeless, unassailable prose.

Then nostalgia began.

After years spent unwilling to admit its attractions, I gestured nostalgically toward the past. I yearned for that time when I had not been so alone. I became impatient with books. I wanted experience more immediate. I feared the library's silence. I silently scorned the gray, timid faces around me. I grew to hate the growing pages of my dissertation on genre[17] and Renaissance literature. (In my mind I heard relatives laughing as they tried to make sense of its title.) I wanted something — I couldn't say exactly what. I told myself that I wanted a more passionate life. And a life less thoughtful. And above all, I wanted to be less alone. One day I heard some Spanish academics whispering back and forth to each other, and their sounds seemed ghostly voices recalling my life. Yearning became preoccupation then. Boyhood memories beckoned, flooded my mind. (Laughing intimate voices. Bounding up the front steps of the porch. A sudden embrace inside the door.)

40

---

[16]*bed-sitter:* A one-room apartment.

[17]*genre:* A class or category of artistic work; e.g., the genre of poetry.

For weeks after, I turned to books by educational experts. I needed to learn how far I had moved from my past — to determine how fast I would be able to recover something of it once again. But I found little. Only a chapter in a book by Richard Hoggart . . . I left the reading room and the circle of faces.

I came home. After the year in England, I spent three summer months living with my mother and father, relieved by how easy it was to be home. It no longer seemed very important to me that we had little to say. I felt easy sitting and eating and walking with them. I watched them, nevertheless, looking for evidence of those elastic, sturdy strands that bind generations in a web of inheritance. I thought as I watched my mother one night: of course a friend had been right when she told me that I gestured and laughed just like my mother. Another time I saw for myself: my father's eyes were much like my own, constantly watchful.

But after the early relief, this return, came suspicion, nagging until I realized that I had not neatly sidestepped the impact of schooling. My desire to do so was precisely the measure of how much I remained an academic. *Negatively* (for that is how this idea first occurred to me): my need to think so much and so abstractly about my parents and our relationship was in itself an indication of my long education. My father and mother did not pass their time thinking about the cultural meanings of their experience. It was I who described their daily lives with airy ideas. And yet, *positively:* the ability to consider experience so abstractly allowed me to shape into desire what would otherwise have remained indefinite, meaningless longing in the British Museum. If, because of my schooling, I had grown culturally separated from my parents, my education finally had given me ways of speaking and caring about that fact.

My best teachers in college and graduate school, years before, had tried to prepare me for this conclusion, I think, when they discussed texts of aristocratic pastoral literature. Faithfully, I wrote down all that they said. I memorized it: "The praise of the unlettered by the highly educated is one of the primary themes of 'elitist' literature." But, "the importance of the praise given the unsolitary, richly passionate and spontaneous life is that it simultaneously reflects the value of a reflective life." I heard it all. But there was no way for any of it to mean very much to me. I was a scholarship boy at the time, busily laddering my way up the rungs of education. To pass an examination, I copied down exactly what my teachers told me. It would require many more years of schooling (an inevitable miseducation) in which I came to trust the silence of reading and the habit of abstracting from immediate experience — moving away from a life of closeness and immediacy I remembered with my parents, growing older — before I turned unafraid to desire the past, and thereby achieved what had eluded me for so long — the end of education.

ENGAGING THE TEXT

1. How does education affect Rodriguez's relationship to his family, his past, and his culture? Do you agree with him that education requires "radical self-reformation" (para. 33)?

2. What is a "scholarship boy"? Why does Rodriguez consider himself a bad student despite his academic success?

3. What happens to Rodriguez in London? Why does he ultimately abandon his studies there?

4. What drives Rodriguez to succeed? What does education represent to him? To his father and mother?

5. What is Rodriguez's final assessment of what he has gained and lost through his education? Do you agree with his analysis?

EXPLORING CONNECTIONS

6. Compare Rodriguez's attitude toward education and success with that of Mike Rose (p. 162) in "I Just Wanna Be Average."

7. To what extent do Rodriguez's experiences as a "scholarship boy" confirm or complicate Jean Anyon's analysis (p. 174) of the relationship between social class, education, and success?

8. Read "Stephen Cruz" (p. 335) and compare his attitudes toward education and success with those of Rodriguez.

EXTENDING THE CRITICAL CONTEXT

9. What are your personal motives for academic success? How do they compare with those of Rodriguez?

10. Today many college students find that they're following in the footsteps of family members — not breaking ground as Rodriguez did. What special difficulties do such second- or third-generation college students face?

Para Teresa[1]

INÉS HERNÁNDEZ-ÁVILA

This poem explores and attempts to resolve an old conflict between its speaker and her schoolmate, two Chicanas at "Alamo which-had-to-be-its-name" Elementary School who have radically different ideas about what education means and does. Inés Hernández-Ávila (b. 1947) is an associate

---

[1]*Para Teresa:* For Teresa. [All notes are the author's.]

professor of Native American studies at the University of California, Davis.
This poem appeared in her collection Con Razón, Corazón *(1987).*

A tí-Teresa
Te dedico las palabras estás
que explotan de mi corazón[2]

That day during lunch hour
at Alamo which-had-to-be-its-name   5
Elementary
my dear raza
That day in the bathroom
Door guarded
Myself cornered   10
I was accused by you, Teresa
Tú y las demás de tus amigas
Pachucas todas
Eran Uds. cinco.[3]

Me gritaban que porque me creía tan grande[4]   15
What was I trying to do, you growled
Show you up?
Make the teachers like me, pet me,
Tell me what a credit to my people I was?
I was playing right into their hands, you challenged   20
And you would have none of it.
I was to stop.

I was to be like you
I was to play your game of deadly defiance
Arrogance, refusal to submit.   25
The game in which the winner takes nothing
Asks for nothing
Never lets his weaknesses show.

But I didn't understand.
My fear salted with confusion   30
Charged me to explain to you
I did nothing *for the teachers.*
I studied for my parents and for my grandparents
Who cut out honor roll lists

---

[2] *A ... corazón:* To you, Teresa, I dedicate these words that explode from my heart.
[3] *Tu ... cinco:* You and the rest of your friends, all Pachucas, there were five of you.
[4] *Me ... grande:* You were screaming at me, asking me why I thought I was so hot.

Whenever their nietos'[5] names appeared   35
For my shy mother who mastered her terror
to demand her place in mother's clubs
For my carpenter-father who helped me patiently with my math.
For my abuelos que me regalaron lápices en la Navidad[6]
And for myself.   40

Porque reconocí en aquel entonces
una verdad tremenda
que me hizo a mi un rebelde
Aunque tú no te habías dadocuenta[7]
We were not inferior   45
You and I, y las demás de tus amigas
Y los demás de nuestra gente[8]
I knew it the way I knew I was alive
We were good, honorable, brave
Genuine, loyal, strong   50
And smart.
Mine was a deadly game of defiance, also.
My contest was to prove
beyond any doubt
that we were not only equal but superior to them.   55
That was why I studied.
If I could do it, we all could.

You let me go then.
Your friends unblocked the way
I who-did-not-know-how-to-fight   60
was not made to engage with you-who-grew-up-fighting
Tu y yo,[9] Teresa
We went in different directions
Pero fuimos juntas.[10]
                                                                              65
In sixth grade we did not understand
Uds. with the teased, dyed-black-but-reddening hair,
Full petticoats, red lipsticks
and sweaters with the sleeves
pushed up

---

[5] *nietos':* Grandchildren's.

[6] *abuelos . . . Navidad:* Grandparents who gave me gifts of pencils at Christmas.

[7] *Porque . . . dadocuenta:* Because I recognized a great truth then that made me a rebel, even though you didn't realize it.

[8] *Y . . . gente:* And the rest of your friends / And the rest of our people.

[9] *Tu y yo:* You and I.

[10] *Pero fuimos juntas:* But we were together.

Y yo conformándome con lo que deseaba mi mamá[11]   70
Certainly never allowed to dye, to tease, to paint myself
I did not accept your way of anger,
Your judgements
You did not accept mine.

But now in 1975, when I am twenty-eight   75
Teresa
I remember you.
Y sabes —
Te comprendo,
Es más, te respeto.   80
Y si me permites,
Te nombro — "hermana."[12]

ENGAGING THE TEXT

1. The speaker says that she didn't understand Teresa at the time of the incident she describes. What didn't she understand, and why? How have her views of Teresa and of herself changed since then? What seems to have brought about this change?

2. What attitudes toward school and the majority culture do Teresa and the speaker represent? What about the speaker's family? In what way are both girls playing a game of "deadly defiance"? What arguments can you make for each form of rebellion?

3. Why do you think Hernández-Ávila wrote this poem in both Spanish and English? What does doing so say about the speaker's life? About her change of attitude toward Teresa?

EXPLORING CONNECTIONS

4. Compare the speaker's attitude toward school and family with those of Richard Rodriguez (p. 194). What motivates each of them? What tensions do they feel?

5. Write a dialogue between the speaker of this poem, who wants to excel, and Ken Harvey, the boy whom Mike Rose said just wanted to be average (p. 162). Explore the uncertainties, pressures, and desires that these students felt. In what ways are these two apparently contrasting students actually similar?

EXTENDING THE CRITICAL CONTEXT

6. Was there a person or group you disliked, feared, or fought with in elementary school? Has your understanding of your adversary or of your own motives changed since then? If so, what brought about this change?

---

[11] *Y…mamá:* And I conforming to my mother's wishes.

[12] *Y sabes…"hermana":* And do you know what, I understand you. Even more, I respect you. And, if you permit me, I name you my sister.

Thin Ice: "Stereotype Threat" and Black College Students

CLAUDE M. STEELE

In 1994 Richard Herrnstein and Charles Murray rocked the world of higher education by publishing The Bell Curve: Intelligence and Class Structure in American Life. *In this highly controversial book, the authors argued that differences in performance on standardized tests are due primarily to genetics and not to differences of opportunity or cultural background. Minority groups, the authors claimed, score lower on aptitude tests and have lower GPAs in college than their white counterparts because of inherited intelligence and not because of historical factors like racism or unequal access to educational resources. This selection by noted African American psychologist Claude M. Steele suggests that even the best minority students may encounter academic difficulties in American colleges, not because of genetics but because of persistent negative stereotypes — stereotypes that books like* The Bell Curve *perpetuate. According to Steele, differences in minority student performance can be eliminated if colleges take positive steps to minimize these subtle forms of discrimination. Steele is a professor and chair of the Department of Psychology at Stanford University.*

The buildings had hardly changed in the thirty years since I'd been there. "There" was a small liberal-arts school quite near the college that I attended. In my student days I had visited it many times to see friends. This time I was there to give a speech about how racial and gender stereotypes, floating and abstract though they might seem, can affect concrete things like grades, test scores, and academic identity. My talk was received warmly, and the next morning I met with a small group of African-American students. I have done this on many campuses. But this time, perhaps cued by the familiarity of the place, I had an experience of déjà vu. The students expressed a litany of complaints that could have come straight from the mouths of the black friends I had visited there thirty years earlier: the curriculum was too white, they heard too little black music, they were ignored in class, and too often they felt slighted by faculty members and other students. Despite the school's recruitment efforts, they were a small minority. The core of their social life was their own group. To relieve the dysphoria, they went home a lot on weekends.

I found myself giving them the same advice my father gave me when I was in college: lighten up on the politics, get the best education you can, and move on. But then I surprised myself by saying, "To do this you have to learn from people who part of yourself tells you are difficult to trust."

Over the past four decades African-American college students have been more in the spotlight than any other American students. This is because they aren't just college students; they are a cutting edge in America's effort to integrate itself in the thirty-five years since the passage of the Civil Rights Act. These students have borne much of the burden for our national experiment in racial integration. And to a significant degree the success of the experiment will be determined by their success.

Nonetheless, throughout the 1990s the national college-dropout rate for African-Americans has been 20 to 25 percent higher than that for whites. Among those who finish college, the grade-point average of black students is two-thirds of a grade below that of whites.

A recent study by William Bowen and Derek Bok, reported in their 5 book *The Shape of the River*, brings some happy news: despite this underachievement in college, black students who attend the most selective schools in the country go on to do just as well in postgraduate programs and professional attainment as other students from those schools. This is a telling fact in support of affirmative action, since only these schools use affirmative action in admissions. Still, the underperformance of black undergraduates is an unsettling problem, one that may alter or hamper career development, especially among blacks not attending the most selective schools.

Attempts to explain the problem can sound like a debate about whether America is a good society, at least by the standard of racial fairness, and maybe even about whether racial integration is possible. It is an uncomfortably finger-pointing debate. Does the problem stem from something about black students themselves, such as poor motivation, a distracting peer culture, lack of family values, or — the unsettling suggestion of *The Bell Curve* — genes? Or does it stem from the conditions of blacks' lives: social and economic deprivation, a society that views blacks through the lens of diminishing stereotypes and low expectations, too much coddling, or too much neglect?

In recent years this debate has acquired a finer focus: the fate of middle-class black students. Americans have come to view the disadvantages associated with being black as disadvantages primarily of social and economic resources and opportunity. This assumption is often taken to imply that if you are black and come from a socioeconomically middle-class home, you no longer suffer a significant disadvantage of race. "Why should the son of a black physician be given an advantage in college admission over the son of a white delivery-truck driver?" This is a standard question in the controversy over affirmative action. And the assumption behind it is that surely in today's society the disadvantages of race are overcome when lower socioeconomic status is overcome.

But virtually all aspects of underperformance — lower standardized-test scores, lower college grades, lower graduation rates — persist among students from the African-American middle class. This situation forces on us an uncomfortable recognition: that beyond class, something racial is depressing the academic performance of these students.

Some time ago I and two colleagues, Joshua Aronson and Steven Spencer, tried to see the world from the standpoint of these students, concerning ourselves less with features of theirs that might explain their troubles than with features of the world they see. A story I was told recently depicts some of these. The storyteller was worried about his friend, a normally energetic black student who had broken up with his longtime girlfriend and had since learned that she, a Hispanic, was now dating a white student. This hit him hard. Not long after hearing about his girlfriend, he sat through an hour's discussion of *The Bell Curve*[1] in his psychology class, during which the possible genetic inferiority of his race was openly considered. Then he overheard students at lunch arguing that affirmative action allowed in too many underqualified blacks. By his own account, this young man had experienced very little of what he thought of as racial discrimination on campus. Still, these were features of his world. Could they have a bearing on his academic life?

My colleagues and I have called such features "stereotype threat"— the   10
threat of being viewed through the lens of a negative stereotype, or the fear of doing something that would inadvertently confirm that stereotype. Everyone experiences stereotype threat. We are all members of some group about which negative stereotypes exist, from white males and Methodists to women and the elderly. And in a situation where one of those stereotypes applies — a man talking to women about pay equity, for example, or an aging faculty member trying to remember a number sequence in the middle of a lecture — we know that we may be judged by it.

Like the young man in the story, we can feel mistrustful and apprehensive in such situations. For him, as for African-American students generally, negative stereotypes apply in many situations, even personal ones. Why was that old roommate unfriendly to him? Did that young white woman who has been so nice to him in class not return his phone call because she's afraid he'll ask her for a date? Is it because of his race or something else about him? He cannot know the answers, but neither can his rational self fully dismiss the questions. Together they raise a deeper question: Will his race be a boundary to his experience, to his emotions, to his relationships?

With time he may weary of the extra vigilance these situations require and of what the psychologists Jennifer Crocker and Brenda Major have called the "attributional ambiguity" of being on the receiving end of negative stereotypes. To reduce this stress he may learn to care less about the situations and activities that bring it about — to realign his self-regard so that it no longer depends on how he does in the situation. We have called this psychic adjustment "disidentification." Pain is lessened by ceasing to identify with the part of life in which the pain occurs. This withdrawal of

---

[1]*The Bell Curve:* See headnote (p. 211).

psychic investment may be supported by other members of the stereotype-threatened group — even to the point of its becoming a group norm. But not caring can mean not being motivated. And this can have real costs. When stereotype threat affects school life, disidentification is a high price to pay for psychic comfort. Still, it is a price that groups contending with powerful negative stereotypes about their abilities — women in advanced math, African-Americans in all academic areas — may too often pay.

Stereotype Threat Versus Self-Fulfilling Prophecy

Another question arises: Do the effects of stereotype threat come entirely from the fear of being stereotyped, or do they come from something internal to black students — self-doubt, for example?

Beginning with George Herbert Mead's[2] idea of the "looking-glass self," social psychology has assumed that one's self-image derives in large part from how one is viewed by others — family, school, and the broader society. When those views are negative, people may internalize them, resulting in lower self-esteem — or self-hatred, as it has been called. This theory was first applied to the experience of Jews, by Sigmund Freud and Bruno Bettelheim, but it was also soon applied to the experience of African-Americans, by Gordon Allport, Frantz Fanon, Kenneth Clark, and others.[3] According to the theory, black students internalize negative stereotypes as performance anxiety and low expectations for achievement, which they then fulfill. The "self-fulfilling prophecy" has become a commonplace about these students. Stereotype threat, however, is something different, something external: the situational threat of being negatively stereotyped. Which of these two processes, then, caused the results of our experiments?

Joshua Aronson, Michael Lustina, Kelli Keough, Joseph Brown, Catherine Good, and I devised a way to find out. Suppose we told white male students who were strong in math that a difficult math test they were about to take was one on which Asians generally did better than whites. White males should not have a sense of group inferiority about math, since no societal stereotype alleges such an inferiority. Yet this comment would put them under a form of stereotype threat: any faltering on the test could cause them to be seen negatively from the standpoint of the positive stereotype about Asians and math ability. If stereotype threat alone — in the absence of any internalized self-doubt — was capable of disrupting test performance, then white males taking the test after this comment should perform less well than white males taking the test without hearing the comment. That is just what happened. Stereotype threat impaired intellectual functioning in a group unlikely to have any sense of group inferiority.

15

---

[2]*George Herbert Mead:* Noted early-twentieth-century American philosopher (1863–1931).

[3]*Sigmund Freud . . . Kenneth Clark:* Famous psychologists and social critics.

In science, as in the rest of life, few things are definitive. But these results are pretty good evidence that stereotype threat's impairment of standardized-test performance does not depend on cueing a pre-existing anxiety. Steven Spencer, Diane Quinn, and I have shown how stereotype threat depresses the performance of accomplished female math students on a difficult math test, and how that performance improves dramatically when the threat is lifted. Jean-Claude Croizet, working in France with a stereotype that links poor verbal skills with lower-class status, found analogous results: lower-class college students performed less well than upper-class college students under the threat of a stereotype-based judgment, but performed as well when the threat was removed.

Is everyone equally threatened and disrupted by a stereotype? One might expect, for example, that it would affect the weakest students most. But in all our research the most achievement-oriented students, who were also the most skilled, motivated, and confident, were the most impaired by stereotype threat. This fact had been under our noses all along — in our data and even in our theory. A person has to care about a domain in order to be disturbed by the prospect of being stereotyped in it. That is the whole idea of disidentification — protecting against stereotype threat by ceasing to care about the domain in which the stereotype applies. Our earlier experiments had selected black students who identified with verbal skills and women who identified with math. But when we tested participants who identified less with these domains, what had been under our noses hit us in the face. None of them showed any effect of stereotype threat whatsoever.

These weakly identified students did not perform well on the test: once they discovered its difficulty, they stopped trying very hard and got a low score. But their performance did not differ depending on whether they felt they were at risk of being judged stereotypically.

Why Strong Students Are Stereotype-Threatened

This finding, I believe, tells us two important things. The first is that the poorer college performance of black students may have another source in addition to the one — lack of good preparation and, perhaps, of identification with school achievement — that is commonly understood. This additional source — the threat of being negatively stereotyped in the environment — has not been well understood. The distinction has important policy implications: different kinds of students may require different pedagogies of improvement.

The second thing is poignant: what exposes students to the pressure of   20
stereotype threat is not weaker academic identity and skills but stronger academic identity and skills. They may have long seen themselves as good students — better than most. But led into the domain by their strengths, they pay an extra tax on their investment — vigilant worry that their future will be compromised by society's perception and treatment of their group.

This tax has a long tradition in the black community. The Jackie Robinson story[4] is a central narrative of black life, literature, and journalism. *Ebony* magazine has run a page for fifty years featuring people who have broken down one or another racial barrier. Surely the academic vanguard among black college students today knows this tradition — and knows, therefore, that the thing to do, as my father told me, is to buckle down, pay whatever tax is required, and disprove the damn stereotype.

That, however, seems to be precisely what these students are trying to do. In some of our experiments we administered the test of ability by computer, so that we could see how long participants spent looking at different parts of the test questions. Black students taking the test under stereotype threat seemed to be trying too hard rather than not hard enough. They reread the questions, reread the multiple choices, rechecked their answers, more than when they were not under stereotype threat. The threat made them inefficient on a test that, like most standardized tests, is set up so that thinking long often means thinking wrong, especially on difficult items like the ones we used.

Philip Uri Treisman, an innovator in math workshops for minority students who is based at the University of Texas, saw something similar in his black calculus students at the University of California at Berkeley: they worked long hours alone but they worked inefficiently — for example, checking and rechecking their calculations against the correct answers at the back of the book, rather than focusing on the concepts involved. Of course, trying extra hard helps with some school tasks. But under stereotype threat this effort may be misdirected. Achievement at the frontier of one's skills may be furthered more by a relaxed, open concentration than by a strong desire to disprove a stereotype by not making mistakes.

Sadly, the effort that accompanies stereotype threat exacts an additional price. Led by James Blascovich, of the University of California at Santa Barbara, we found that the blood pressure of black students performing a difficult cognitive task under stereotype threat was elevated compared with that of black students not under stereotype threat or white students in either situation.

In the old song about the "steel-drivin' man," John Henry races the new   25
steam-driven drill to see who can dig a hole faster. When the race is over, John Henry has prevailed by digging the deeper hole — only to drop dead. The social psychologist Sherman James uses the term "John Henryism" to describe a psychological syndrome that he found to be associated with hypertension in several samples of North Carolina blacks: holding too rigidly to the faith that discrimination and disadvantage can be overcome with hard work and persistence. Certainly this is the right attitude. But taken to extremes, it can backfire. A deterioration of performance under stereotype

---

[4]*The Jackie Robinson story:* In 1947, Jackie Robinson (1919–1972) was the first African American baseball player to join a white major-league team.

threat by the skilled, confident black students in our experiments may be rooted in John Henryism.

This last point can be disheartening. Our research, however, offers an interesting suggestion about what can be done to overcome stereotype threat and its detrimental effects. The success of black students may depend less on expectations and motivation — things that are thought to drive academic performance — than on trust that stereotypes about their group will not have a limiting effect in their school world.

How to Reduce Stereotype Threat

Putting this idea to the test, Joseph Brown and I asked, How can the usual detrimental effect of stereotype threat on the standardized-test performance of these students be reduced? By strengthening students' expectations and confidence, or by strengthening their trust that they are not at risk of being judged on the basis of stereotypes? In the ensuing experiment we strengthened or weakened participants' confidence in their verbal skills, by arranging for them to have either an impressive success or an impressive failure on a test of verbal skills, just before they took the same difficult verbal test we had used in our earlier research. When the second test was presented as a test of ability, the boosting or weakening of confidence in their verbal skills had no effect on performance: black participants performed less well than equally skilled white participants. What does this say about the commonsense idea that black students' academic problems are rooted in lack of self-confidence?

What did raise the level of black students' performance to that of equally qualified whites was reducing stereotype threat — in this case by explicitly presenting the test as racially fair. When this was done, blacks performed at the same high level as whites even if their self-confidence had been weakened by a prior failure.

These results suggest something that I think has not been made clear elsewhere: when strong black students sit down to take a difficult standardized test, the extra apprehension they feel in comparison with whites is less about their own ability than it is about having to perform on a test and in a situation that may be primed to treat them stereotypically. We discovered the extent of this apprehension when we tried to develop procedures that would make our black participants see the test as "race-fair." It wasn't easy. African-Americans have endured so much bad press about test scores for so long that, in our experience, they are instinctively wary about the tests' fairness. We were able to convince them that our test was race-fair only when we implied that the research generating the test had been done by blacks. When they felt trust, they performed well regardless of whether we had weakened their self-confidence beforehand. And when they didn't feel trust, no amount of bolstering of self-confidence helped.

Policies for helping black students rest in significant part on assump- 30
tions about their psychology. As noted, they are typically assumed to lack
confidence, which spawns a policy of confidence-building. This may be useful for students at the academic rearguard of the group. But the psychology
of the academic vanguard appears different — underperformance appears
to be rooted less in self-doubt than in social mistrust.

Education policy relevant to non-Asian minorities might fruitfully shift
its focus forward fostering racial trust in the schooling situation — at least
among students who come to school with good skills and high expectations.
But how should this be done? Without particulars this conclusion can fade
into banality, suggesting, as Alan Ryan has wryly put it in *Liberal Anxieties
and Liberal Education,* that these students "will hardly be able to work at all
unless everyone else exercises the utmost sensitivity to [their] anxieties."
Sensitivity is nice, but it is an awful lot to expect, and even then, would it instill trust?

That is exactly what Geoffrey Cohen, Lee Rosa, and I wondered as we
took up the question of how a teacher or a mentor could give critical feedback across the "racial divide" and have that feedback be trusted. We reasoned that an answer to this question might yield insights about how to instill trust more broadly in the schooling environment. Cohen's hunch was
that niceness alone wouldn't be enough. But the first question had to be
whether there was in fact a racial divide between teachers and students, especially in the elite college environment in which we worked.

We set up a simple experiment. Cohen asked black and white Stanford
students one at a time to write essays about their favorite teachers, for possible publication in a journal on teaching. They were asked to return several
days later for feedback on their essays. Before each student left the first
writing session, Cohen put a Polaroid snapshot of the student on top of his
or her essay. His ostensible purpose was to publish the picture if the essay
was published. His real purpose was to let the essay writers know that the
evaluator of their writing would be aware of their race. When they returned
days later, they were given constructive but critical feedback. We looked at
whether different ways of giving this feedback engendered different degrees of trust in it.

We found that neither straight feedback nor feedback preceded by the
"niceness" of a cushioning statement ("There were many good things about
your essay") was trusted by black students. They saw these criticisms as
probably biased, and they were less motivated than white students to improve their essays. White students took the criticism at face value — even as
an indication of interest in them. Black students, however, faced a different
meaning: the "ambiguating" possibility that the criticism was motivated by
negative stereotypes about their group as much as by the work itself. Herein
lies the power of race to make one's world insecure — quite apart from
whatever actual discrimination one may experience.

But this experiment also revealed a way to be critical across the racial 35
divide: tell the students that you are using high standards (this signals that
the criticism reflects standards rather than race), and that your reading of
their essays leads you to believe that they can meet those standards (this signals that you do not view them stereotypically). This shouldn't be faked.
High standards, at least in a relative sense, should be an inherent part of
teaching, and critical feedback should be given in the belief that the recipient can reach those standards. These things go without saying for many students. But they have to be made explicit for students under stereotype
threat. The good news of this study is that when they *are* made explicit, the
students trust and respond to criticism. Black students who got this kind of
feedback saw it as unbiased and were motivated to take their essays home
and work on them even though this was not a class for credit. They were
more motivated than any other group of students in the study — as if this
combination of high standards and assurance was like water on parched
land, a much needed but seldom received balm.

Reassessing the Test-Score Gap

There is, of course, another explanation for why black college students
haven't fared well on predominantly white campuses: they aren't prepared
for the competition. This has become an assumption of those who oppose
affirmative action in college admissions. Racial preference, the argument
goes, brings black students onto campuses where they simply aren't prepared to compete.

The fact most often cited in support of the underpreparation explanation is the lower SAT scores of black students, which sometimes average
200 points below those of other students on the same campus. The test-
score gap has become shorthand for black students' achievement problems.
But the gap must be assessed cautiously.

First, black students have better skills than the gap suggests. Most of
the gap exists because the proportion of blacks with very high SAT scores is
smaller than the corresponding proportions of whites and Asians. Thus
when each group's scores are averaged, the black average will be lower than
the white and Asian averages. This would be true even if the same admissions cut-off score were used for each group — even if, for example, affirmative action were eliminated entirely. Why a smaller proportion of blacks
have very high scores is, of course, a complex question with multiple answers, involving, among other things, the effects of race on educational access and experience as well as the processes dwelt on in this article. The
point, though, is that blacks' test-score deficits are taken as a sign of underpreparation, whereas in fact virtually all black students on a given campus
have tested skills within the same range as the tested skills of other students
on the campus.

In any case, the skills and preparation measured by these tests also turn out not to be good determinants of college success. As the makers of the SAT themselves tell us, although this test is among the best of its kind, it measures only about 18 percent of the skills that influence first-year grades, and even less of what influences subsequent grades, graduation rates, and professional success.

Indulge a basketball analogy that my colleagues Jay Rosner and Lee Ross   40
and I have developed. Suppose that you were obliged to select a basketball team on the basis of how many of ten free throws a player makes. You'd regret having to select players on the basis of a single criterion. You'd know that free-throw shooting involves only a few of the skills that go into basketball — and, worse, you'd know that you'd never pick a Shaquille O'Neal.[5]

You'd also wonder how to interpret a player's score. If he made ten out of ten or zero out of ten, you'd be fairly confident about making a judgment. But what about the kid who makes five, six, or seven? Middling scores like these could be influenced by many things other than underlying potential for free-throw shooting or basketball playing. How much practice was involved? Was the kid having a good or a bad day? Roughly the same is true, I suggest, for standardized-test scores. Are they inflated by middle-class advantages such as prep courses, private schools, and tours of European cathedrals? Are they deflated by race-linked experiences such as social segregation and being consistently assigned to the lower tracks in school?

In sum, black college students are not as underprepared in academic skills as their group score deficit is taken to suggest. The deficit can appear large, but it is not likely to be the sole cause of the troubles they have once they get on campus.

Showing the insufficiency of one cause, of course, does not prove the sufficiency of another. My colleagues and I believed that our laboratory experiments had brought to light an overlooked cause of poor college performance among non-Asian minorities: the threat to social trust brought about by the stereotypes of the larger society. But to know the real-life importance of this threat would require testing *in situ*, in the buzz of everyday life.

To this end Steven Spencer, Richard Nisbett, Kent Harber, Mary Hummel, and I undertook a program aimed at incoming first-year students at the University of Michigan. Like virtually all other institutions of higher learning, Michigan had evidence of black students' underachievement. Our mission was clear: to see if we could improve their achievement by focusing on their transition into college life.

We also wanted to see how little we could get away with — that is, to   45
develop a program that would succeed broadly without special efforts. The

[5]*Shaquille O'Neal:* Outstanding center (b. 1972) on the Los Angeles Lakers basketball team.

program (which started in 1991 and is ongoing) created a racially integrated "living and learning" community in a 250-student wing of a large dormitory. It focused students on academic work (through weekly "challenge" workshops), provided an outlet for discussing the personal side of college life (through weekly rap sessions), and affirmed the students' abilities (through, for example, reminding them that their admission was a vote of confidence). The program lasted just one semester, although most students remained in the dormitory wing for the rest of their first year.

Still, it worked: it gave black students a significant academic jump start. Those in the program (about 15 percent of the entering class) got better first-year grades than black students outside the program, even after controlling for differences between these groups in the skills with which they entered college. Equally important, the program greatly reduced underperformance: black students in the program got first-year grades almost as high as those of white students in the general Michigan population who entered with comparable test scores. This result signaled the achievement of an academic climate nearly as favorable to black students as to white students. And it was achieved through a concert of simple things that enabled black students to feel racially secure.

One tactic that worked surprisingly well was the weekly rap sessions — black and white students talking to one another in an informal dormitory setting, over pizza, about the personal side of their new lives in college. Participation in these sessions reduced students' feelings of stereotype threat and improved grades. Why? Perhaps when members of one racial group hear members of another racial group express the same concerns they have, the concerns seem less racial. Students may also learn that racial and gender stereotypes are either less at play than they might have feared or don't reflect the worst-feared prejudicial intent. Talking at a personal level across group lines can thus build trust in the larger campus community. The racial segregation besetting most college campuses can block this experience, allowing mistrust to build where cross-group communication would discourage it.

Our research bears a practical message: even though the stereotypes held by the larger society may be difficult to change, it is possible to create niches in which negative stereotypes are not felt to apply. In specific classrooms, within specific programs, even in the climate of entire schools, it is possible to weaken a group's sense of being threatened by negative stereotypes, to allow its members a trust that would otherwise be difficult to sustain. Thus when schools try to decide how important black-white test-score gaps are in determining the fate of black students on their campuses, they should keep something in mind: for the greatest portion of black students — those with strong academic identities — the degree of racial trust they feel in their campus life, rather than a few ticks on a standardized test, may be the key to their success.

ENGAGING THE TEXT

1. According to Steele, how does stereotype threat affect minority students in terms of their performance on standardized tests and their attitudes toward education? Why does Steele reject arguments that black students perform less successfully than other groups because of poor preparation?

2. What difference does Steele see between the impact of stereotype threat and the effect of "self-fulfilling prophecies" of minority-student failure? Why is this distinction important to his argument?

3. What is "John Henryism" and how is it involved with the phenomenon of stereotype threat? To what extent do you think these problems affect members of other groups, such as Asian Americans, Latinos, women, and gays?

4. In Steele's view, what can instructors do to minimize stereotype threat in testing situations or when critiquing student work? What can colleges do to discourage it throughout the campus community? How effective do you think these approaches would be in practice? Why?

EXPLORING CONNECTIONS

5. To what extent might the concept of stereotype threat be used to account for the difficulties encountered by Mike Rose in "I Just Wanna Be Average" (p. 162) and Richard Rodriguez in "The Achievement of Desire" (p. 194)?

6. How might Malcolm X (p. 223) respond to Steele's claim that black students need to be able to trust their teachers in order to cope with stereotype threat?

7. Read the experiences of Colin Powell (p. 305), Stephen Cruz (p. 335), and Cora Tucker (p. 340). What do these differing perspectives on success suggest about the impact of John Henryism?

EXTENDING THE CRITICAL CONTEXT

8. Working in groups, draft a list of actions students, teachers, and administrators might engage in to build trust across racial boundaries and minimize stereotype threat on your college campus.

9. Steele describes two styles of instructor comments in response to student papers: one that attempts to cushion criticism with a few gentle introductory remarks of praise, and a second that offers more direct criticism in the name of high standards. In small groups, discuss the kinds of responses you've received from instructors on past writing assignments. Is there any one style you've found to be particularly helpful? Do male and female students or students from different ethnic or economic backgrounds tend to prefer one style of response over another?

10. Form your class into small "application review committees" to determine standards for granting admission to your college. What criteria would you

use, in addition to or in place of standardized test scores, in making admission decisions? Why?

11. Some critics of *Rereading America* might argue that essays like Steele's actually increase the likelihood of stereotype threat by focusing on the academic performance of different student groups. To what extent do you agree that discussing issues like stereotypes and stereotype threat may place additional pressures on minority students in their college classes? Would it be better to avoid such topics? Why or why not?

Learning to Read

MALCOLM X

Born Malcolm Little on May 19, 1925, Malcolm X was one of the most articulate and powerful leaders of black America during the 1960s. A street hustler convicted of robbery in 1946, he spent seven years in prison, where he educated himself and became a disciple of Elijah Muhammad, founder of the Nation of Islam. In the days of the civil rights movement, Malcolm X emerged as the leading spokesman for black separatism, a philosophy that urged black Americans to cut political, social, and economic ties with the white community. After a pilgrimage to Mecca, the capital of the Muslim world, in 1964, he became an orthodox Muslim, adopted the Muslim name El Hajj Malik El-Shabazz, and distanced himself from the teachings of the black Muslims. He was assassinated in 1965. In the following excerpt from his autobiography (1965), coauthored with Alex Haley and published the year of his death, Malcolm X describes his self-education.

It was because of my letters that I happened to stumble upon starting to acquire some kind of a homemade education.

I became increasingly frustrated at not being able to express what I wanted to convey in letters that I wrote, especially those to Mr. Elijah Muhammad.[1] In the street, I had been the most articulate hustler out there — I had commanded attention when I said something. But now, trying to write simple English, I not only wasn't articulate, I wasn't even functional. How would I sound writing in slang, the way I would *say* it, something such as, "Look, daddy, let me pull your coat about a cat, Elijah Muhammad —"

---

[1]*Elijah Muhammad:* American clergyman (1897–1975); leader of the Nation of Islam, 1935–1975.

Many who today hear me somewhere in person, or on television, or those who read something I've said, will think I went to school far beyond the eighth grade. This impression is due entirely to my prison studies.

It had really begun back in the Charlestown Prison, when Bimbi[2] first made me feel envy of his stock of knowledge. Bimbi had always taken charge of any conversations he was in, and I had tried to emulate him. But every book I picked up had few sentences which didn't contain anywhere from one to nearly all of the words that might as well have been in Chinese. When I just skipped those words, of course, I really ended up with little idea of what the book said. So I had come to the Norfolk Prison Colony still going through only book-reading motions. Pretty soon, I would have quit even these motions, unless I had received the motivation that I did.

I saw that the best thing I could do was get hold of a dictionary — to   5
study, to learn some words. I was lucky enough to reason also that I should try to improve my penmanship. It was sad. I couldn't even write in a straight line. It was both ideas together that moved me to request a dictionary along with some tablets and pencils from the Norfolk Prison Colony school.

I spent two days just riffling uncertainly through the dictionary's pages. I'd never realized so many words existed! I didn't know *which* words I needed to learn. Finally, just to start some kind of action, I began copying.

In my slow, painstaking, ragged handwriting, I copied into my tablet everything printed on that first page, down to the punctuation marks.

I believe it took me a day. Then, aloud, I read back, to myself, everything I'd written on the tablet. Over and over, aloud, to myself, I read my own handwriting.

I woke up the next morning, thinking about those words — immensely proud to realize that not only had I written so much at one time, but I'd written words that I never knew were in the world. Moreover, with a little effort, I also could remember what many of these words meant. I reviewed the words whose meanings I didn't remember. Funny thing, from the dictionary first page right now, that "aardvark" springs to my mind. The dictionary had a picture of it, a long-tailed, long-eared, burrowing African mammal, which lives off termites caught by sticking out its tongue as an anteater does for ants.

I was so fascinated that I went on — I copied the dictionary's next page.   10
And the same experience came when I studied that. With every succeeding page, I also learned of people and places and events from history. Actually the dictionary is like a miniature encyclopedia. Finally the dictionary's A section had filled a whole tablet — and I went on into the B's. That was the way I started copying what eventually became the entire dictionary. It went a lot faster after so much practice helped me to pick up handwriting speed. Between what I wrote in my tablet, and writing letters, during the rest of my time in prison I would guess I wrote a million words.

[2]*Bimbi:* A fellow inmate whose encyclopedic learning and verbal facility greatly impressed Malcolm X.

I suppose it was inevitable that as my word-base broadened, I could for the first time pick up a book and read and now begin to understand what the book was saying. Anyone who has read a great deal can imagine the new world that opened. Let me tell you something: from then until I left that prison, in every free moment I had, if I was not reading in the library, I was reading on my bunk. You couldn't have gotten me out of books with a wedge. Between Mr. Muhammad's teachings, my correspondence, my visitors, . . . and my reading of books, months passed without my even thinking about being imprisoned. In fact, up to then, I never had been so truly free in my life.

The Norfolk Prison Colony's library was in the school building. A variety of classes was taught there by instructors who came from such places as Harvard and Boston universities. The weekly debates between inmate teams were also held in the school building. You would be astonished to know how worked up convict debaters and audiences would get over subjects like "Should Babies Be Fed Milk?"

Available on the prison library's shelves were books on just about every general subject. Much of the big private collection that Parkhurst[3] had willed to the prison was still in crates and boxes in the back of the library — thousands of old books. Some of them looked ancient: covers faded, old-time parchment-looking binding. Parkhurst . . . seemed to have been principally interested in history and religion. He had the money and the special interest to have a lot of books that you wouldn't have in a general circulation. Any college library would have been lucky to get that collection.

As you can imagine, especially in a prison where there was heavy emphasis on rehabilitation, an inmate was smiled upon if he demonstrated an unusually intense interest in books. There was a sizable number of well-read inmates, especially the popular debaters. Some were said by many to be practically walking encyclopedias. They were almost celebrities. No university would ask any student to devour literature as I did when this new world opened to me, of being able to read and *understand.*

I read more in my room than in the library itself. An inmate who was   15
known to read a lot could check out more than the permitted maximum number of books. I preferred reading in the total isolation of my own room.

When I had progressed to really serious reading, every night at about ten P.M. I would be outraged with the "lights out." It always seemed to catch me right in the middle of something engrossing.

Fortunately, right outside my door was a corridor light that cast a glow into my room. The glow was enough to read by, once my eyes adjusted to it. So when "lights out" came, I would sit on the floor where I could continue reading in that glow.

At one-hour intervals at night guards paced past every room. Each time I heard the approaching footsteps, I jumped into bed and feigned sleep.

---

[3]*Parkhurst:* Charles Henry Parkhurst (1842–1933); American clergyman, reformer, and president of the Society for the Prevention of Crime.

And as soon as the guard passed, I got back out of bed onto the floor area of that light-glow, where I would read for another fifty-eight minutes until the guard approached again. That went on until three or four every morning. Three or four hours of sleep a night was enough for me. Often in the years in the streets I had slept less than that.

The teachings of Mr. Muhammad stressed how history had been "whitened" — when white men had written history books, the black man simply had been left out. Mr. Muhammad couldn't have said anything that would have struck me much harder. I had never forgotten how when my class, me and all of those whites, had studied seventh-grade United States history back in Mason, the history of the Negro had been covered in one paragraph, and the teacher had gotten a big laugh with his joke, "Negroes' feet are so big that when they walk, they leave a hole in the ground."

This is one reason why Mr. Muhammad's teachings spread so swiftly all 20 over the United States, among *all* Negroes, whether or not they became followers of Mr. Muhammad. The teachings ring true — to every Negro. You can hardly show me a black adult in America — or a white one, for that matter — who knows from the history books anything like the truth about the black man's role. In my own case, once I heard of the "glorious history of the black man," I took special pains to hunt in the library for books that would inform me on details about black history.

I can remember accurately the very first set of books that really impressed me. I have since bought that set of books and I have it at home for my children to read as they grow up. It's called *Wonders of the World*. It's full of pictures of archeological finds, statues that depict, usually, non-European people.

I found books like Will Durant's[4] *Story of Civilization*. I read H. G. Wells'[5] *Outline of History*. *Souls of Black Folk* by W. E. B. Du Bois[6] gave me a glimpse into the black people's history before they came to this country. Carter G. Woodson's[7] *Negro History* opened my eyes about black empires before the black slave was brought to the United States, and the early Negro struggles for freedom.

J. A. Rogers'[8] three volumes of *Sex and Race* told about race-mixing before Christ's time; and Aesop being a black man who told fables; about Egypt's Pharaohs; about the great Coptic Christian Empire;[9] about

---

[4]*Will Durant:* American author and historian (1885–1981).

[5]*H. G. Wells:* English novelist and historian (1866–1946).

[6]*W. E. B. Du Bois:* William Edward Burghardt Du Bois, distinguished black scholar, author, and activist (1868–1963). Du Bois was the first director of the NAACP and was an important figure in the Harlem Renaissance; his best-known book is *Souls of Black Folk.*

[7]*Carter G. Woodson:* Distinguished African American historian (1875–1950); considered the father of black history.

[8]*J. A. Rogers:* African American historian and journalist (1883–1965).

[9]*Coptic Christian Empire:* The domain of the Coptic Church, a native Egyptian Christian church that retains elements of its African origins.

Ethiopia, the earth's oldest continuous black civilization, as China is the oldest continuous civilization.

Mr. Muhammad's teaching about how the white man had been created led me to *Findings in Genetics,* by Gregor Mendel.[10] (The dictionary's G section was where I had learned what "genetics" meant.) I really studied this book by the Austrian monk. Reading it over and over, especially certain sections, helped me to understand that if you started with a black man, a white man could be produced; but starting with a white man, you never could produce a black man — because the white chromosome is recessive. And since no one disputes that there was but one Original Man, the conclusion is clear.

During the last year or so, in the *New York Times,* Arnold Toynbee[11]   25 used the word "bleached" in describing the white man. His words were: "White (i.e., bleached) human beings of North European origin...." Toynbee also referred to the European geographic area as only a peninsula of Asia. He said there was no such thing as Europe. And if you look at the globe, you will see for yourself that America is only an extension of Asia. (But at the same time Toynbee is among those who have helped to bleach history. He has written that Africa was the only continent that produced no history. He won't write that again. Every day now, the truth is coming to light.)

I never will forget how shocked I was when I began reading about slavery's total horror. It made such an impact upon me that it later became one of my favorite subjects when I became a minister of Mr. Muhammad's. The world's most monstrous crime, the sin and the blood on the white man's hands, are almost impossible to believe. Books like the one by Frederick Olmsted[12] opened my eyes to the horrors suffered when the slave was landed in the United States. The European woman, Fanny Kemble,[13] who had married a Southern white slaveowner, described how human beings were degraded. Of course I read *Uncle Tom's Cabin.*[14] In fact, I believe that's the only novel I have ever read since I started serious reading.

Parkhurst's collection also contained some bound pamphlets of the Abolitionist[15] Anti-Slavery Society of New England. I read descriptions of atrocities, saw those illustrations of black slave women tied up and flogged with whips; of black mothers watching their babies being dragged off, never to be seen by their mothers again; of dogs after slaves, and of the fugitive

---

[10]*Gregor Mendel:* Austrian monk, botanist, and pioneer in genetic research (1822–1884).

[11]*Arnold Toynbee:* English historian (1889–1975).

[12]*Frederick Olmsted:* Frederick Law Olmsted (1822–1903), American landscape architect, city planner, and opponent of slavery.

[13]*Fanny Kemble:* Frances Anne Kemble, English actress and author (1809–1893); best known for her autobiographical *Journal of a Residence on a Georgia Plantation,* published in 1863 to win support in Britain for the abolitionist cause.

[14]*Uncle Tom's Cabin:* Harriet Beecher Stowe's 1852 antislavery novel.

[15]*Abolitionist:* Advocating the prohibition of slavery.

slave catchers, evil white men with whips and clubs and chains and guns. I read about the slave preacher Nat Turner, who put the fear of God into the white slavemaster. Nat Turner wasn't going around preaching pie-in-the-sky and "non-violent" freedom for the black man. There in Virginia one night in 1831, Nat and seven other slaves started out at his master's home and through the night they went from one plantation "big house" to the next, killing, until by the next morning 57 white people were dead and Nat had about 70 slaves following him. White people, terrified for their lives, fled from their homes, locked themselves up in public buildings, hid in the woods, and some even left the state. A small army of soldiers took two months to catch and hang Nat Turner. Somewhere I have read where Nat Turner's example is said to have inspired John Brown[16] to invade Virginia and attack Harpers Ferry nearly thirty years later, with thirteen white men and five Negroes.

I read Herodotus,[17] "the father of History," or, rather, I read about him. And I read the histories of various nations, which opened my eyes gradually, then wider and wider, to how the whole world's white men had indeed acted like devils, pillaging and raping and bleeding and draining the whole world's non-white people. I remember, for instance, books such as Will Durant's *The Story of Oriental Civilization,* and Mahatma Gandhi's[18] accounts of the struggle to drive the British out of India.

Book after book showed me how the white man had brought upon the world's black, brown, red, and yellow peoples every variety of the suffering of exploitation. I saw how since the sixteenth century, the so-called "Christian trader" white man began to ply the seas in his lust for Asian and African empires, and plunder, and power. I read, I saw, how the white man never has gone among the non-white peoples bearing the Cross in the true manner and spirit of Christ's teachings — meek, humble, and Christlike.

I perceived, as I read, how the collective white man had been actually   30 nothing but a piratical opportunist who used Faustian machinations[19] to make his own Christianity his initial wedge in criminal conquests. First, always "religiously," he branded "heathen" and "pagan" labels upon ancient non-white cultures and civilizations. The stage thus set, he then turned upon his non-white victims his weapons of war.

I read how, entering India — half a *billion* deeply religious brown people — the British white man, by 1759, through promises, trickery, and manipulations, controlled much of India through Great Britain's East India Company. The parasitical British administration kept tentacling out to half

---

[16]*John Brown:* American abolitionist (1800–1859); leader of an attack on Harpers Ferry, West Virginia, in 1859.

[17]*Herodotus:* Early Greek historian (484?–425? B.C.).

[18]*Mahatma Gandhi:* Hindu religious leader, social reformer, and advocate of nonviolence (1869–1948).

[19]*Faustian machinations:* Evil plots or schemes. Faust was a legendary character who sold his soul to the devil for knowledge and power.

of the sub-continent. In 1857, some of the desperate people of India finally mutinied — and, excepting the African slave trade, nowhere has history recorded any more unnecessary bestial and ruthless human carnage than the British suppression of the non-white Indian people.

Over 115 million African blacks — close to the 1930's population of the United States — were murdered or enslaved during the slave trade. And I read how when the slave market was glutted, the cannibalistic white powers of Europe next carved up, as their colonies, the richest areas of the black continent. And Europe's chancelleries for the next century played a chess game of naked exploitation and power from Cape Horn to Cairo.

Ten guards and the warden couldn't have torn me out of those books. Not even Elijah Muhammad could have been more eloquent than those books were in providing indisputable proof that the collective white man had acted like a devil in virtually every contact he had with the world's collective non-white man. I listen today to the radio, and watch television, and read the headlines about the collective white man's fear and tension concerning China. When the white man professes ignorance about why the Chinese hate him so, my mind can't help flashing back to what I read, there in prison, about how the blood forebears of this same white man raped China at a time when China was trusting and helpless. Those original white "Christian traders" sent into China millions of pounds of opium. By 1839, so many of the Chinese were addicts that China's desperate government destroyed twenty thousand chests of opium. The first Opium War[20] was promptly declared by the white man. Imagine! Declaring *war* upon someone who objects to being narcotized! The Chinese were severely beaten, with Chinese-invented gunpowder.

The Treaty of Nanking made China pay the British white man for the destroyed opium; forced open China's major ports to British trade; forced China to abandon Hong Kong; fixed China's import tariffs so low that cheap British articles soon flooded in, maiming China's industrial development.

After a second Opium War, the Tientsin Treaties legalized the ravaging   35 opium trade, legalized a British-French-American control of China's customs. China tried delaying that Treaty's ratification; Peking was looted and burned.

"Kill the foreign white devils!" was the 1901 Chinese war cry in the Boxer Rebellion.[21] Losing again, this time the Chinese were driven from Peking's choicest areas. The vicious, arrogant white man put up the famous signs, "Chinese and dogs not allowed."

Red China after World War II closed its doors to the Western white world. Massive Chinese agricultural, scientific, and industrial efforts are

[20]*Opium War:* 1839–1842 war between Britain and China that ended with China's cession of Hong Kong to British rule.

[21]*Boxer Rebellion:* The 1898–1900 uprising by members of a secret Chinese society who opposed foreign influence in Chinese affairs.

described in a book that *Life* magazine recently published. Some observers inside Red China have reported that the world never has known such a hate-white campaign as is now going on in this non-white country where, present birth-rates continuing, in fifty more years Chinese will be half the earth's population. And it seems that some Chinese chickens will soon come home to roost, with China's recent successful nuclear tests.

Let us face reality. We can see in the United Nations a new world order being shaped, along color lines — an alliance among the non-white nations. America's U.N. Ambassador Adlai Stevenson[22] complained not long ago that in the United Nations "a skin game"[23] was being played. He was right. He was facing reality. A "skin game" *is* being played. But Ambassador Stevenson sounded like Jesse James accusing the marshal of carrying a gun. Because who in the world's history ever has played a worse "skin game" than the white man?

Mr. Muhammad, to whom I was writing daily, had no idea of what a new world had opened up to me through my efforts to document his teachings in books.

When I discovered philosophy, I tried to touch all the landmarks of   40
philosophical development. Gradually, I read most of the old philosophers, Occidental and Oriental. The Oriental philosophers were the ones I came to prefer; finally, my impression was that most Occidental philosophy had largely been borrowed from the Oriental thinkers. Socrates, for instance, traveled in Egypt. Some sources even say that Socrates was initiated into some of the Egyptian mysteries. Obviously Socrates got some of his wisdom among the East's wise men.

I have often reflected upon the new vistas that reading opened to me. I knew right there in prison that reading had changed forever the course of my life. As I see it today, the ability to read awoke inside me some long dormant craving to be mentally alive. I certainly wasn't seeking any degree, the way a college confers a status symbol upon its students. My homemade education gave me, with every additional book that I read, a little bit more sensitivity to the deafness, dumbness, and blindness that was afflicting the black race in America. Not long ago, an English writer telephoned me from London, asking questions. One was, "What's your alma mater?" I told him, "Books." You will never catch me with a free fifteen minutes in which I'm not studying something I feel might be able to help the black man.

Yesterday I spoke in London, and both ways on the plane across the Atlantic I was studying a document about how the United Nations proposes to insure the human rights of the oppressed minorities of the world. The American black man is the world's most shameful case of minority oppres-

[22]*Adlai Stevenson:* American politician (1900–1965); Democratic candidate for the presidency in 1952 and 1956.

[23]*skin game:* A dishonest or fraudulent scheme, business operation, or trick, with the added reference in this instance to skin color.

sion. What makes the black man think of himself as only an internal United States issue is just a catch-phrase, two words, "civil rights." How is the black man going to get "civil rights" before first he wins his *human* rights? If the American black man will start thinking about his *human* rights, and then start thinking of himself as part of one of the world's great peoples, he will see he has a case for the United Nations.

I can't think of a better case! Four hundred years of black blood and sweat invested here in America, and the white man still has the black man begging for what every immigrant fresh off the ship can take for granted the minute he walks down the gangplank.

But I'm digressing. I told the Englishman that my alma mater was books, a good library. Every time I catch a plane, I have with me a book that I want to read — and that's a lot of books these days. If I weren't out here every day battling the white man, I could spend the rest of my life reading, just satisfying my curiosity — because you can hardly mention anything I'm not curious about. I don't think anybody ever got more out of going to prison than I did. In fact, prison enabled me to study far more intensively than I would have if my life had gone differently and I had attended some college. I imagine that one of the biggest troubles with colleges is there are too many distractions, too much panty-raiding, fraternities, and boola-boola and all of that. Where else but in a prison could I have attacked my ignorance by being able to study intensely sometimes as much as fifteen hours a day?

ENGAGING THE TEXT

1. What motivated Malcolm X to educate himself?
2. What kind of knowledge did Malcolm X gain by learning to read? How did this knowledge free or empower him?
3. Would it be possible for public schools to empower students in the way that Malcolm X's self-education empowered him? If so, how? If not, why not?
4. Some readers are offended by the strength of Malcolm X's accusations and by his grouping of all members of a given race into "collectives." Given the history of racial injustice he recounts here, do you feel he is justified in taking such a position?

EXPLORING CONNECTIONS

5. Compare and contrast Malcolm X's views on the meaning and purpose of education — or on the value and nature of reading — with those of Richard Rodriguez (p. 194). How can you account for the differences in their attitudes?
6. Imagine that John Taylor Gatto (p. 152), Mike Rose (p. 162), Richard Rodriguez (p. 194), and Malcolm X have been appointed to redesign American education. Working in groups, role-play a meeting in which the

THE BOONDOCKS   **by AARON MCGRUDER**

committee attempts to reach consensus on its recommendations. Report to the class the results of the committee's deliberations and discuss them.

7. Given his experience of self-education, how might Malcolm X respond to Claude M. Steele's concerns (p. 211) about the impact of stereotype threat and John Henryism on the best minority students today?

8. What does the *Boondocks* cartoon on this page suggest about the possibility of teaching and learning "revolutionary" ideas within the setting of a public school system?

EXTENDING THE CRITICAL CONTEXT

9. Survey some typical elementary or secondary school textbooks to test the currency of Malcolm X's charge that the educational establishment presents a "whitened" view of America. What view of America is presently being projected in public school history and social science texts?

10. Go to the library and read one page of the dictionary chosen at random. Study the meanings of any unfamiliar words and follow up on the information on your page by consulting encyclopedias, books, or articles. Let yourself be guided by chance and by your interests. After you've tried this experiment, discuss in class the benefits and drawbacks of an unsystematic self-education like Malcolm X's.

The Roots of Debate in Education and the Hope of Dialogue

Deborah Tannen

From the perspective of the twenty-first century, it's hard to imagine a time when women were excluded from institutions of higher education. Although many American colleges began admitting women in significant numbers little more than a century ago, female students now outnumber males on almost every co-educational campus in the nation. But as Deborah Tannen reminds us, the history of higher education stretches back far earlier than the founding of the United States. The college as an institution grew up in the male-dominated cultures of ancient Greece and medieval Europe and continues to this day to value an "agonistic," or conflict-based, mode of intellectual inquiry that, in Tannen's view, undermines the performance of many female students. A professor of linguistics at Georgetown University and a regular guest and commentator on television news shows like 20/20 and The McNeil/Lehrer News Hour, *Tannen has authored sixteen books on issues of interpersonal and crossgender communication. Her publications include* That's Not What I Meant: How Conversational Style Makes or Breaks Relationships *(1986),* You Just Don't Understand: Women and Men in Conversation *(1990), and the source of this selection,* The Argument Culture: Stopping America's War of Words *(1999).*

The teacher sits at the head of the classroom, feeling pleased with herself and her class. The students are engaged in a heated debate. The very noise level reassures the teacher that the students are participating, taking responsibility for their own learning. Education is going on. The class is a success.

But look again, cautions Patricia Rosof, a high school history teacher who admits to having experienced that wave of satisfaction with herself and the job she is doing. On closer inspection, you notice that only a few students are participating in the debate; the majority of the class is sitting silently, maybe attentive but perhaps either indifferent or actively turned off. And the students who are arguing are not addressing the subtleties, nuances, or complexities of the points they are making or disputing. They do not have that luxury because they want to win the argument — so they must go for the most gross and dramatic statements they can muster. They will not concede an opponent's point, even if they can see its validity, because that would weaken their position. Anyone tempted to synthesize the varying views would not dare to do so because it would look like a "cop-out," an inability to take a stand.

One reason so many teachers use the debate format to promote student involvement is that it is relatively easy to set up and the rewards are quick and obvious: the decibel level of noise, the excitement of those who are taking part. Showing students how to integrate ideas and explore subtleties and complexities is much harder. And the rewards are quieter — but more lasting.

Our schools and universities, our ways of doing science and approaching knowledge, are deeply agonistic. We all pass through our country's educational system, and it is there that the seeds of our adversarial culture are planted. Seeing how these seeds develop, and where they came from, is a key to understanding the argument culture and a necessary foundation for determining what changes we would like to make.

Roots of the Adversarial
Approach to Knowledge

The argument culture, with its tendency to approach issues as a polarized debate, and the culture of critique, with its inclination to regard criticism and attack as the best if not the only type of rigorous thinking, are deeply rooted in Western tradition, going back to the ancient Greeks.[1] This point is made by Walter Ong, a Jesuit professor at Saint Louis University, in his book *Fighting for Life.* Ong credits the ancient Greeks with a fascination with adversativeness in language and thought.[2] He also connects the adver-

5

---

[1] This does not mean it goes back in an unbroken chain. David Noble, in *A World Without Women,* claims that Aristotle was all but lost to the West during the early Christian era and was rediscovered in the medieval era, when universities were first established. This is significant for his observation that many early Christian monasteries welcomed both women and men who could equally aspire to an androgynous ideal, in contrast to the Middle Ages, when the female was stigmatized, unmarried women were consigned to convents, priests were required to be celibate, and women were excluded from spiritual authority. [All notes are the author's, except 6, 15, 18, 20, and 21.]

[2] There is a fascinating parallel in the evolution of the early Christian Church and the Southern Baptist Church: Noble shows that the early Christian Church regarded women as equally beloved of Jesus and equally capable of devoting their lives to religious study, so women comprised a majority of early converts to Christianity, some of them leaving their husbands — or bringing their husbands along — to join monastic communities. It was later, leading up to the medieval period, that the clerical movement gained ascendancy in part by systematically separating women, confining them in either marriage or convents, stigmatizing them, and barring them from positions of power within the church. Christine Leigh Heyrman, in *Southern Cross: The Beginnings of the Bible Belt,* shows that a similar trajectory characterized the Southern Baptist movement. At first, young Baptist and Methodist preachers (in the 1740s to 1830s) preached that both women and blacks were equally God's children, deserving of spiritual authority — with the result that the majority of converts were women and slaves. To counteract this distressing demography, the message was changed: antislavery rhetoric faded, and women's roles were narrowed to domesticity and subservience. With these shifts, the evangelical movement swept the South. At the same time, Heyrman shows, military imagery took over: The ideal man of God was transformed from a "willing martyr" to a "formidable fighter" led by "warrior preachers."

sarial tradition of educational institutions to their all-male character. To attend the earliest universities, in the Middle Ages, young men were torn
from their families and deposited in cloistered environments where corpo-
ral, even brutal, punishment was rampant. Their suffering drove them to
bond with each other in opposition to their keepers — the teachers who
were their symbolic enemies. Similar in many ways to puberty rites in traditional cultures, this secret society to which young men were confined also
had a private language, Latin, in which students read about military exploits. Knowledge was gleaned through public oral disputation and tested
by combative oral performance, which carried with it the risk of public humiliation. Students at these institutions were trained not to discover the
truth but to argue either side of an argument — in other words, to debate.
Ong points out that the Latin term for school, *ludus,* also referred to play or
games, but it derived from the military sense of the word — training exercises for war.

If debate seems self-evidently the appropriate or even the only path to
insight and knowledge, says Ong, consider the Chinese approach. Disputation was rejected in ancient China as "incompatible with the decorum and
harmony cultivated by the true sage."[3] During the Classical periods in both
China and India, according to Robert T. Oliver, the preferred mode of
rhetoric was exposition rather than argument. The aim was to "enlighten an
inquirer," not to "overwhelm an opponent." And the preferred style
reflected "the earnestness of investigation" rather than "the fervor of conviction." In contrast to Aristotle's trust of logic and mistrust of emotion, in
ancient Asia intuitive insight was considered the superior means of perceiv-
ing truth. Asian rhetoric was devoted not to devising logical arguments but
to explicating widely accepted propositions. Furthermore, the search for abstract truth that we assume is the goal of philosophy, while taken for
granted in the West, was not found in the East, where philosophy was concerned with observation and experience.

If Aristotelian philosophy, with its emphasis on formal logic, was based
on the assumption that truth is gained by opposition, Chinese philosophy
offers an alternative view. With its emphasis on harmony, says anthropologist Linda Young, Chinese philosophy sees a diverse universe in precarious
balance that is maintained by talk. This translates into methods of investigation that focus more on integrating ideas and exploring relations among
them than on opposing ideas and fighting over them.

Onward, Christian Soldiers

The military-like culture of early universities is also described by historian David Noble, who describes how young men attending medieval universities were like marauding soldiers: The students — all seminarians —

---

[3]Ong, *Fighting for Life,* p. 122. Ong's source, on which I also rely, is Oliver, *Communication and Culture in Ancient India and China.* My own quotations from Oliver are from p. 259.

roamed the streets bearing arms, assaulting women, and generally creating mayhem. Noble traces the history of Western science and of universities to joint origins in the Christian Church. The scientific revolution, he shows, was created by religious devotees setting up monastery-like institutions devoted to learning. Early universities were seminaries, and early scientists were either clergy or devoutly religious individuals who led monk-like lives. (Until as recently as 1888, fellows at Oxford were expected to be unmarried.)

That Western science is rooted in the Christian Church helps explain why our approach to knowledge tends to be conceived as a metaphorical battle: The Christian Church, Noble shows, has origins and early forms rooted in the military. Many early monks had actually been soldiers before becoming monks.[4] Not only were obedience and strict military-like discipline required, but monks saw themselves as serving "in God's knighthood," warriors in a battle against evil. In later centuries, the Crusades brought actual warrior-monks.

The history of science in the Church holds the key to understanding   10
our tradition of regarding the search for truth as an enterprise of oral disputation in which positions are propounded, defended, and attacked without regard to the debater's personal conviction. It is a notion of truth as objective, best captured by formal logic, that Ong traces to Aristotle. Aristotle regarded logic as the only trustworthy means for human judgment; emotions get in the way: "The man who is to judge would not have his judgment warped by speakers arousing him to anger, jealousy, or compassion. One might as well make a carpenter's tool crooked before using it as a measure."[5]

This assumption explains why Plato wanted to ban poets from education in his ideal community. As a lover of poetry, I can still recall my surprise and distress on reading this in *The Republic*[6] when I was in high school. Not until much later did I understand what it was all about.[7] Poets in ancient Greece were wandering bards who traveled from place to place performing oral poetry that persuaded audiences by moving them emotionally. They were like what we think of as demagogues: people with a danger-

---

[4]Pachomius, for example, "the father of communal monasticism . . . and organizer of the first monastic community, had been a soldier under Constantine" and modeled his community on the military, emphasizing order, efficiency, and military obedience. Cassian, a fourth-century proselytizer, "'likened the monk's discipline to that of the soldier,' and Chrysostom, another great champion of the movement, 'sternly reminded the monks that Christ had armed them to be soldiers in a noble fight'" (Noble, *A World Without Women*, p. 54).

[5]Aristotle, quoted in Oliver, *Communication and Culture in Ancient India and China*, p. 259.

[6]*The Republic:* Plato's utopian vision of the ideal state.

[7]I came to understand the different meaning of "poet" in Classical Greece from reading Ong and also *Preface to Plato* by Eric Havelock. These insights informed many articles I wrote about oral and literate tradition in Western culture, including "Oral and Literate Strategies in Spoken and Written Narratives" and "The Oral/Literate Continuum in Discourse."

ous power to persuade others by getting them all worked up. Ong likens this to our discomfort with advertising in schools, which we see as places where children should learn to think logically, not be influenced by "teachers" with ulterior motives who use unfair persuasive tactics.

Sharing Time: Early Training in School

A commitment to formal logic as the truest form of intellectual pursuit remains with us today. Our glorification of opposition as the path to truth is related to the development of formal logic, which encourages thinkers to regard truth seeking as a step-by-step alternation of claims and counterclaims.[8] Truth, in this schema, is an abstract notion that tends to be taken out of context. This formal approach to learning is taught in our schools, often indirectly.

Educational researcher James Wertsch shows that schools place great emphasis on formal representation of knowledge. The common elementary school practice of "sharing time" (or, as it used to be called, "show-and-tell") is a prime arena for such training. Wertsch gives the example of a kindergarten pupil named Danny who took a piece of lava to class.[9] Danny told his classmates, "My mom went to the volcano and got it." When the teacher asked what he wanted to tell about it, he said, "I've always been taking care of it." This placed the rock at the center of his feelings and his family: the rock's connection to his mother, who gave it to him, and the attention and care he has lavished on it. The teacher reframed the children's interest in the rock as informational: "Is it rough or smooth?" "Is it heavy or light?" She also suggested they look up "volcano" and "lava" in the dictionary. This is not to imply that the teacher harmed the child; she built on his personal attachment to the rock to teach him a new way of thinking about it. But the example shows the focus of education on formal rather than relational knowledge — information about the rock that has meaning out of context, rather than information tied to the context: Who got the rock for him? How did she get it? What is his relation to it?

Here's another example of how a teacher uses sharing time to train children to speak and think formally. Sarah Michaels spent time watching and tape-recording in a first-grade classroom. During sharing time, a little girl named Mindy held up two candles and told her classmates, "When I was in day camp we made these candles. And I tried it with different colors with both of them but one just came out, this one just came out blue and I don't know what this color is." The teacher responded, "That's neat-o. Tell the kids how you do it from the very start. Pretend we don't know a thing about candles. OK, what did you do first? What did you use?" She

---

[8]Moulton, "A Paradigm of Philosophy"; Ong, *Fighting for Life.*
[9]The example of Danny and the lava: Wertsch, *Voices of the Mind*, pp. 113–14.

continued to prompt: "What makes it have a shape?" and "Who knows what the string is for?" By encouraging Mindy to give information in a sequential manner, even if it might not seem the most important to her and if the children might already know some of it, the teacher was training her to talk in a focused, explicit way.

The tendency to value formal, objective knowledge over relational, intuitive knowledge grows out of our notion of education as training for debate. It is a legacy of the agonistic heritage. There are many other traces as well. Many Ph.D. programs still require public "defenses" of dissertations or dissertation proposals, and oral performance of knowledge in comprehensive exams. Throughout our educational system, the most pervasive inheritance is the conviction that issues have two sides, that knowledge is best gained through debate, that ideas should be presented orally to an audience that does its best to poke holes and find weaknesses, and that to get recognition, one has to "stake out a position" in opposition to another.

Integrating Women in the Classroom Army

If Ong is right, the adversarial character of our educational institutions is inseparable from their all-male heritage. I wondered whether teaching techniques still tend to be adversarial today and whether, if they are, this may hold a clue to a dilemma that has received much recent attention: that girls often receive less attention and speak up less in class.[10] One term I taught a large lecture class of 140 students and decided to take advantage of this army (as it were) of researchers to answer these questions. Becoming observers in their own classrooms, my students found plenty of support for Ong's ideas.

I asked the students to note how relatively adversarial the teaching methods were in their other classes and how the students responded. Gabrielle DeRouen-Hawkins's description of a theology class was typical:

> The class is in the format of lecture with class discussion and participation. There are thirteen boys and eleven girls in the class.[11] In a fifty-minute class:
>
> Number of times a male student spoke: 8
> Number of times a female student spoke: 3
> . . . In our readings, theologians present their theories surrounding G–D, life, spirituality, and sacredness. As the professor (a male) outlined the main ideas about the readings, he posed questions like "And what is the fault with / Smith's / basis that the sacred is individualistic?" The only hands that went up were male. Not one female <u>dared</u> challenge or refute an author's writings. The only questions that

---

[10]See David and Myra Sadker, *Failing at Fairness.*

[11]Although my colleagues and I make efforts to refer to our students — all over the age of eighteen — as "women" and "men" and some students in my classes do the same, the majority refer to each other and themselves as "girls" and "boys" or "girls" and "guys."

15

the females asked (and all female comments were questions) involved a problem they had with the content of the reading. The males, on the other hand, openly questioned, criticized, and refuted the readings on five separate occasions. The three other times that males spoke involved them saying something like: "/ Smith / is very vague in her theory of XX. Can you explain it further?" They were openly argumentative.

This description raises a number of fascinating issues. First, it gives concrete evidence that at least college classrooms proceed on the assumption that the educational process should be adversarial: The teacher invited students to criticize the reading. (Theology, a required course at Georgetown, was a subject where my students most often found adversarial methods — interestingly, given the background I laid out earlier.) Again, there is nothing inherently wrong with using such methods. Clearly, they are very effective in many ways. However, among the potential liabilities is the risk that women students may be less likely to take part in classroom discussions that are framed as arguments between opposing sides — that is, debate — or as attacks on the authors — that is, critique. (The vast majority of students' observations revealed that men tended to speak more than women in their classes — which is not to say that individual women did not speak more than individual men.)

Gabrielle commented that since class participation counted for 10 percent of students' grades, it might not be fair to women students that the agonistic style is more congenial to men. Not only might women's grades suffer because they speak up less, but they might be evaluated as less intelligent or prepared because when they did speak, they asked questions rather than challenging the readings.

I was intrigued by the student's comment "/Smith/ is very vague in her theory of XX. Can you explain it further?" It could have been phrased "I didn't understand the author's theory. Can you explain it to me?" By beginning "The author is vague in her theory," the questioner blamed the author for his failure to understand. A student who asks a question in class risks appearing ignorant. Prefacing the question this way was an excellent way to minimize that risk.

In her description of this class, Gabrielle wrote that not a single woman "<u>dared</u> challenge or refute" an author. She herself underlined the word "dared." But in reading this I wondered whether "dared" was necessarily the right word. It implies that the women in the class wished to challenge the author but did not have the courage. It is possible that not a single woman *cared* to challenge the author. Criticizing or challenging might not be something that appealed to them or seemed worth their efforts. Going back to the childhoods of boys and girls, it seems possible that the boys had had more experiences, from the time they were small, that encouraged them to challenge and argue with authority figures than the girls had.

This is not to say that classrooms are more congenial to boys than girls in every way. Especially in the lowest grades, the requirement that children sit quietly in their seats seems clearly to be easier for girls to fulfill than boys, since many girls frequently sit fairly quietly for long periods of time when they play, while most boys' idea of play involves at least running around, if not also jumping and roughhousing. And researchers have pointed out that some of the extra attention boys receive is aimed at controlling such physical exuberance. The adversarial aspect of educational traditions is just one small piece of the pie, but it seems to reflect boys' experiences and predilections more than girls'.

A colleague commented that he had always taken for granted that the best way to deal with students' comments is to challenge them; he took it to be self-evident that this technique sharpens their minds and helps them develop debating skills. But he noticed that women were relatively silent in his classes. He decided to try beginning discussion with relatively open questions and letting comments go unchallenged. He found, to his amazement and satisfaction, that more women began to speak up in class.

Clearly, women can learn to perform in adversarial ways. Anyone who doubts this need only attend an academic conference in the field of women's studies or feminist studies — or read Duke University professor Jane Tompkins's essay showing how a conference in these fields can be like a Western shoot-out. My point is rather about the roots of the tradition and the tendency of the style to appeal initially to more men than women in the Western cultural context. Ong and Noble show that the adversarial culture of Western science and its exclusion of women were part and parcel of the same historical roots — not that individual women may not learn to practice and enjoy agonistic debate or that individual men may not recoil from it. There are many people, women as well as men, who assume a discussion must be contentious to be interesting. Author Mary Catherine Bateson recalls that when her mother, the anthropologist Margaret Mead, said, "I had an argument with" someone, it was a positive comment. "An argument," to her, meant a spirited intellectual interchange, not a rancorous conflict. The same assumption emerged in an obituary for Diana Trilling, called "one of the very last of the great midcentury New York intellectuals."[12] She and her friends had tried to live what they called "a life of significant contention"— the contention apparently enhancing rather than undercutting the significance.

Learning by Fighting

Although there are patterns that tend to typify women and men in a given culture, there is an even greater range among members of widely divergent cultural backgrounds. In addition to observing adversarial encoun-   25

---

[12]Jonathan Alter, "The End of the Journey," *Newsweek*, Nov. 4, 1996, p. 61. Trilling died at the age of ninety-one.

ters in their current classrooms, many students recalled having spent a junior year in Germany or France and commented that American classrooms seemed very placid compared to what they had experienced abroad. One student, Zach Tyler, described his impressions this way:

> I have very vivid memories of my junior year of high school, which I spent in Germany as an exchange student. The classroom was very debate-oriented and agonistic. One particular instance I remember well was in physics class, when a very confrontational friend of mine had a heated debate with the teacher about solving a problem. My friend ran to the board and scribbled out how he would have solved the problem, completely different from the teacher's, which also gave my friend the right answer and made the teacher wrong.
>
> STUDENT: "You see! This is how it should be, and you are wrong!"
> TEACHER: "No! No! No! You are absolutely wrong in every respect! Just look at how you did this!" (He goes over my friend's solution and shows that it does not work.) "Your solution has no base, as I just showed you!"
> STUDENT: "You can't prove that. Mine works just as well!"
> TEACHER: "My God, if the world were full of technical idiots like yourself! Look again!" (And he clearly shows how my friend's approach was wrong, after which my friend shut up.)

In Zach's opinion, the teacher encouraged this type of argument. The student learned he was wrong, but he got practice in arguing his point of view.

This incident occurred in high school. But European classrooms can be adversarial even at the elementary school level, according to another student, Megan Smyth, who reported on a videotape she saw in her French class:

> Today in French class we watched an excerpt of a classroom scene of fifth-graders. One at a time, each student was asked to stand up and recite a poem that they were supposed to have memorized. The teacher screamed at the students if they forgot a line or if they didn't speak with enough emotion. They were reprimanded and asked to repeat the task until they did it perfectly and passed the "oral test."

There is probably little question about how Americans would view this way of teaching, but the students put it into words:

> After watching this scene, my French teacher asked the class what our opinion was. The various responses included: French schools are very strict, the professor was "mean" and didn't have respect for the students, and there's too much emphasis on memorization, which is pointless.

If teaching methods can be more openly adversarial in European than American elementary and high schools, academic debate can be more openly adversarial there as well. For example, Alice Kaplan, a professor of

French at Duke University, describes a colloquium on the French writer Céline that she attended in Paris:

> After the first speech, people started yelling at each other. "Are you suggesting that Céline was fascist!" "You call that evidence!" "I will not accept ignorance in the place of argument!" I was scared.[13]

These examples dramatize that many individuals can thrive in an adversarial atmosphere. And those who learn to participate effectively in any verbal game eventually enjoy it, if nothing else than for the pleasure of exercising that learned skill. It is important to keep these examples in mind in order to avoid the impression that adversarial tactics are always destructive. Clearly, such tactics sometimes admirably serve the purpose of intellectual inquiry. In addition to individual predilection, cultural learning plays a role in whether or not someone enjoys the game played this way.

Graduate School as Boot Camp

Although the invective Kaplan heard at a scholarly meeting in Paris is more extreme than what is typical at American conferences, the assumption that challenge and attack are the best modes of scholarly inquiry is pervasive in American scholarly communities as well. Graduate education is a training ground not only for teaching but also for scientific research. Many graduate programs are geared to training young scholars in rigorous thinking, defined as the ability to launch and field verbal attacks.

Communications researchers Karen Tracy and Sheryl Baratz tapped into some of the ethics that lead to this atmosphere in a study of weekly symposia attended by faculty and graduate students at a major research university. When they asked participants about the purpose of the symposia, they were told it was to "trade ideas" and "learn things." But it didn't take too much discussion to uncover the participants' deeper concern: to be seen as intellectually competent. And here's the rub: to be seen as competent, a student had to ask "tough and challenging questions."

One faculty member commented, when asked about who participated actively in a symposium,

> Among the graduate students, the people I think about are Jess, Tim, uh let's see, Felicia will ask a question but it'll be a nice little supportive question.[14]

"A nice little supportive question" diminished the value of Felicia's participation and her intelligence — the sort of judgment a student would wish to avoid. Just as with White House correspondents, there is value placed on

---

[13]Kaplan, *French Lessons*, p. 119.
[14]Tracy and Baratz, "Intellectual Discussion in the Academy as Situated Discourse," p. 309.

asking "tough questions." Those who want to impress their peers and supe-riors (as most, if not all, do) are motivated to ask the sorts of questions that gain approval.

Valuing attack as a sign of respect is part of the argument culture of academia — our conception of intellectual interchange as a metaphorical battle. As one colleague put it, "In order to play with the big boys, you have to be willing to get into the ring and wrestle with them." Yet many graduate students (and quite a few established scholars) remain ambivalent about this ethic, especially when they are on the receiving rather than the distrib-ution end. Sociolinguist Winnie Or tape-recorded a symposium at which a graduate student presented her fledgling research to other students and graduate faculty. The student later told Or that she left the symposium feel-ing that a truck had rolled over her. She did not say she regretted having taken part; she felt she had received valuable feedback. But she also men-tioned that she had not looked at her research project once since the sym-posium several weeks before. This is telling. Shouldn't an opportunity to discuss your research with peers and experts fire you up and send you back to the isolation of research renewed and reinspired? Isn't something awry if it leaves you not wanting to face your research project at all? 30

This young scholar persevered, but others drop out of graduate school, in some cases because they are turned off by the atmosphere of critique. One woman who wrote to me said she had been encouraged to enroll in graduate school by her college professors, but she lasted only one year in a major midwest university's doctoral program in art history. This is how she described her experience and her decision not to continue.

> Grad school was the nightmare I never knew existed. . . . Into the den of wolves I go, like a lamb to slaughter. . . . When, at the end of my first year (masters) I was offered a job as a curator for a private collec-tion, I jumped at the chance. I wasn't cut out for academia — better try the "real world."

Reading this I thought, is it that she was not cut out for academia, or is it that academia as it was practiced in that university is not cut out for people like her. It is cut out for those who enjoy, or can tolerate, a contentious en-vironment.

(These examples remind us again of the gender dynamic. The graduate student who left academia for museum work was a woman. The student who asked a "nice little supportive question" instead of a "tough, challeng-ing one" was a woman. More than one commentator has wondered aloud if part of the reason women drop out of science courses and degree programs is their discomfort with the agonistic culture of Western science. And Lani Guinier[15] has recently shown that discomfort with the agonistic procedures

---

[15]*Lani Guinier:* Legal scholar (b. 1950) whose 1993 nomination to the Supreme Court was defeated in Congress.

of law school is partly responsible for women's lower grade point averages in law school, since the women arrive at law school with records as strong as the men's.)

The Culture of Critique: Attack in the Academy

The standard way of writing an academic paper is to position your work in opposition to someone else's, which you prove wrong. This creates a *need* to make others wrong, which is quite a different matter from reading something with an open mind and discovering that you disagree with it. Students are taught that they must disprove others' arguments in order to be original, make a contribution, and demonstrate their intellectual ability. When there is a *need* to make others wrong, the temptation is great to oversimplify at best, and at worst to distort or even misrepresent others' positions, the better to refute them — to search for the most foolish statement in a generally reasonable treatise, seize upon the weakest examples, ignore facts that support your opponent's views, and focus only on those that support yours. Straw men spring up like scarecrows in a cornfield.

Sometimes it seems as if there is a maxim driving academic discourse that counsels, "If you can't find something bad to say, don't say anything." As a result, any work that gets a lot of attention is immediately opposed. There is an advantage to this approach: Weaknesses are exposed, and that is surely good. But another result is that it is difficult for those outside the field (or even inside) to know what is "true." Like two expert witnesses hired by opposing attorneys, academics can seem to be canceling each other out. In the words of policy analysts David Greenberg and Philip Robins:

> The process of scientific inquiry almost ensures that competing sets of results will be obtained.... Once the first set of findings are published, other researchers eager to make a name for themselves must come up with different approaches and results to get their studies published.[16]

How are outsiders (or insiders, for that matter) to know which "side" to believe? As a result, it is extremely difficult for research to influence public policy.

A leading researcher in psychology commented that he knew of two young colleagues who had achieved tenure by writing articles attacking him. One of them told him, in confidence, that he actually agreed with him, but of course he could not get tenure by writing articles simply supporting someone else's work; he had to stake out a position in opposition. Attacking an established scholar has particular appeal because it demonstrates originality and independence of thought without requiring true innovation. After

35

---

[16]Greenberg and Robins, "The Changing Role of Social Experiments in Policy Analysis," p. 350.

all, the domain of inquiry and the terms of debate have already been established. The critic has only to say, like the child who wants to pick a fight, "Is not!" Younger or less prominent scholars can achieve a level of attention otherwise denied or eluding them by stepping into the ring with someone who has already attracted the spotlight.

The young psychologist who confessed his motives to the established one was unusual, I suspect, only in his self-awareness and willingness to articulate it. More commonly, younger scholars, or less prominent ones, convince themselves that they are fighting for truth, that they are among the few who see that the emperor has no clothes. In the essay mentioned earlier, Jane Tompkins describes how a young scholar-critic can work herself into a passionate conviction that she is morally obligated to attack, because she is fighting on the side of good against the side of evil. Like the reluctant hero in the film *High Noon,* she feels she has no choice but to strap on her holster and shoot. Tompkins recalls that her own career was launched by an essay that

> began with a frontal assault on another woman scholar. When I wrote it I felt the way the hero does in a Western. Not only had this critic argued *a, b,* and *c,* she had held *x, y,* and *z!* It was a clear case of outrageous provocation.[17]

Because her attack was aimed at someone with an established career ("She was famous and I was not. She was teaching at a prestigious university and I was not. She had published a major book and I had not."), it was a "David and Goliath situation" that made her feel she was "justified in hitting her with everything I had." (This is analogous to what William Safire[18] describes as his philosophy in the sphere of political journalism: "Kick 'em when they're up.")[19]

The claim of objectivity is belied by Tompkins's account of the spirit in which attack is often launched: the many motivations, other than the search for truth, that drive a critic to pick a fight with another scholar. Objectivity would entail a disinterested evaluation of all claims. But there is nothing disinterested about it when scholars set out with the need to make others wrong and transform them not only into opponents but into villains.

In academia, as in other walks of life, anonymity breeds contempt. Some of the nastiest rhetoric shows up in "blind" reviews — of articles submitted to journals or book proposals submitted to publishers. "Peer review" is the cornerstone of academic life. When someone submits an article to a journal, a book to a publisher, or a proposal to a funding institution, the

---

[17]These and other quotes from Tompkins appear in her essay "Fighting Words," pp. 588–89.

[18]*William Safire:* Political commentator (b. 1929).

[19]Safire is quoted in Howard Kurtz, "Safire Made No Secret of Dislike for Inman," *The Washington Post,* Jan. 19, 1994, p. A6.

work is sent to established scholars for evaluation. To enable reviewers to be honest, they remain anonymous. But anonymous reviewers often take a tone of derision such as people tend to use only when talking about someone who is not there — after all, the evaluation is not addressed to the author. But authors typically receive copies of the evaluations, especially if their work is rejected. This can be particularly destructive to young scholars just starting out. For example, one sociolinguist wrote her dissertation in a firmly established tradition: She tape-recorded conversations at the company where she worked part-time. Experts in our field believe it is best to examine conversations in which the researcher is a natural participant, because when strangers appear asking to tape-record, people get nervous and may change their behavior. The publisher sent the manuscript to a reviewer who was used to different research methods. In rejecting the proposal, she referred to the young scholar "using the audiotaped detritus from an old job." Ouch. What could justify the sneering term "detritus"? What is added by appending "old" to "job," other than hurting the author? Like Heathcliff,[20] the target hears only the negative and — like Heathcliff —may respond by fleeing the field altogether.

One reason the argument culture is so widespread is that arguing is so   40 easy to do. Lynne Hewitt, Judith Duchan, and Erwin Segal came up with a fascinating finding: Speakers with language disabilities who had trouble taking part in other types of verbal interaction were able to participate in arguments. Observing adults with mental retardation who lived in a group home, the researchers found that the residents often engaged in verbal conflicts as a means of prolonging interaction. It was a form of sociability. Most surprising, this was equally true of two residents who had severe language and comprehension disorders yet were able to take part in the verbal disputes, because arguments have a predictable structure.

Academics, too, know that it is easy to ask challenging questions without listening, reading, or thinking very carefully. Critics can always complain about research methods, sample size, and what has been left out. To study anything, a researcher must isolate a piece of the subject and narrow the scope of vision in order to focus. An entire tree cannot be placed under a microscope; a tiny bit has to be separated to be examined closely. This gives critics the handle of a weapon with which to strike an easy blow: They can point out all the bits that were not studied. Like family members or partners in a close relationship, anyone looking for things to pick on will have no trouble finding them.

All of this is not to imply that scholars should not criticize each other or disagree. In the words of poet William Blake,[21] "Without contraries is no

---

[20]*Heathcliff:* The male protagonist of Emily Brontë's nineteenth-century novel *Wuthering Heights.* He overreacts when he hears the novel's heroine criticize him.

[21]*William Blake:* English Romantic poet (1757–1827).

progression."[22] The point is to distinguish constructive ways of doing so from nonconstructive ones. Criticizing a colleague on empirical grounds is the beginning of a discussion; if researchers come up with different findings, they can engage in a dialogue: What is it about their methods, data, or means of analysis that explains the different results? In some cases, those who set out to disprove another's claims end up proving them instead — something that is highly unlikely to happen in fields that deal in argumentation alone.

A stunning example in which opponents attempting to disprove a heretical claim ended up proving it involves the cause and treatment of ulcers. It is now widely known and accepted that ulcers are caused by bacteria in the stomach and can be cured by massive doses of antibiotics. For years, however, the cure and treatment of ulcers remained elusive, as all the experts agreed that ulcers were the classic psychogenic illness caused by stress. The stomach, experts further agreed, was a sterile environment: No bacteria could live there. So pathologists did not look for bacteria in the stomachs of ailing or deceased patients, and those who came across them simply ignored them, in effect not seeing what was before their eyes because they did not believe it could be there. When Dr. Barry Marshall, an Australian resident in internal medicine, presented evidence that ulcers are caused by bacteria, no one believed him. His findings were ultimately confirmed by researchers intent on proving him wrong.[23]

The case of ulcers shows that setting out to prove others wrong can be constructive — when it is driven by genuine differences and when it motivates others to undertake new research. But if seeking to prove others wrong becomes a habit, an end in itself, the sole line of inquiry, the results can be far less rewarding.

Believing as Thinking

"The doubting game" is the name English professor Peter Elbow gives   45
to what educators are trained to do. In playing the doubting game, you approach others' work by looking for what's wrong, much as the press corps follows the president hoping to catch him stumble or an attorney pores over an opposing witness's deposition looking for inconsistencies that can be challenged on the stand. It is an attorney's job to discredit opposing witnesses, but is it a scholar's job to approach colleagues like an opposing attorney?

Elbow recommends learning to approach new ideas, and ideas different from your own, in a different spirit — what he calls a "believing game." This does not mean accepting everything anyone says or writes in an

---

[22]I've borrowed the William Blake quote from Peter Elbow, who used it to open his book *Embracing Contraries.*

[23]Terence Monmaney, "Marshall's Hunch," *The New Yorker,* Sept. 20, 1993, pp. 64–72.

unthinking way. That would be just as superficial as rejecting everything without thinking deeply about it. The believing game is still a game. It simply asks you to give it a whirl: Read *as if* you believed, and see where it takes you. Then you can go back and ask whether you want to accept or reject elements in the argument or the whole argument or idea. Elbow is not recommending that we stop doubting altogether. He is telling us to stop doubting exclusively. We need a systematic and respected way to detect and expose strengths, just as we have a systematic and respected way of detecting faults.

Americans need little encouragement to play the doubting game because we regard it as synonymous with intellectual inquiry, a sign of intelligence. In Elbow's words, "We tend to assume that the ability to criticize a claim we disagree with counts as more serious intellectual work than the ability to enter into it and temporarily assent."[24] It is the believing game that needs to be encouraged and recognized as an equally serious intellectual pursuit.

Although criticizing is surely part of critical thinking, it is not synonymous with it. Again, limiting critical response to critique means not doing the other kinds of critical thinking that could be helpful: looking for new insights, new perspectives, new ways of thinking, new knowledge. Critiquing relieves you of the responsibility of doing integrative thinking. It also has the advantage of making the critics feel smart, smarter than the ill-fated author whose work is being picked apart like carrion. But it has the disadvantage of making them less likely to learn from the author's work.

The Socratic Method — or Is It?

Another scholar who questions the usefulness of opposition as the sole path to truth is philosopher Janice Moulton. Philosophy, she shows, equates logical reasoning with the Adversary Paradigm, a matter of making claims and then trying to find, and argue against, counterexamples to that claim. The result is a debate between adversaries trying to defend their ideas against counterexamples and to come up with counterexamples that refute the opponent's ideas. In this paradigm, the best way to evaluate someone's work is to "subject it to the strongest or most extreme opposition."[25]

But if you parry individual points — a negative and defensive enter-   50
prise — you never step back and actively imagine a world in which a different system of ideas could be true — a positive act. And you never ask how larger systems of thought relate to each other. According to Moulton, our devotion to the Adversary Paradigm has led us to misinterpret the type of argumentation that Socrates favored: We think of the Socratic method as

[24]Elbow, *Embracing Contraries*, p. 258.
[25]Moulton, "A Paradigm of Philosophy," p. 153.

systematically leading an opponent into admitting error. This is primarily a way of showing up an adversary as wrong. Moulton shows that the original Socratic method — the *elenchus* — was designed to convince others, to shake them out of their habitual mode of thought and lead them to new insight. Our version of the Socratic method — an adversarial public debate — is unlikely to result in opponents changing their minds. Someone who loses a debate usually attributes that loss to poor performance or to an adversary's unfair tactics. . . .

Getting Beyond Dualism

At the heart of the argument culture is our habit of seeing issues and ideas as absolute and irreconcilable principles continually at war. To move beyond this static and limiting view, we can remember the Chinese approach to yin and yang. They are two principles, yes, but they are conceived not as irreconcilable polar opposites but as elements that coexist and should be brought into balance as much as possible. As sociolinguist Suzanne Wong Scollon notes, "Yin is always present in and changing into yang and vice versa."[26] How can we translate this abstract idea into daily practice?

To overcome our bias toward dualism, we can make special efforts not to think in twos. Mary Catherine Bateson, an author and anthropologist who teaches at George Mason University, makes a point of having her class compare *three* cultures, not two. If students compare two cultures, she finds, they are inclined to polarize them, to think of the two as opposite to each other. But if they compare three cultures, they are more likely to think about each on its own terms.[27]

As a goal, we could all try to catch ourselves when we talk about "both sides" of an issue — and talk instead about "all sides." And people in any field can try to resist the temptation to pick on details when they see a chance to score a point. If the detail really does not speak to the main issue, bite your tongue. Draw back and consider the whole picture. After asking, "Where is this wrong?" make an effort to ask, "What is right about this?"— not necessarily *instead,* but *in addition.* . . .

Perhaps, too, it is time to question our glorification of debate as the best, if not the only, means of inquiry. The debate format leads us to regard those doing different kinds of research as belonging to warring camps. There is something very appealing about conceptualizing differing approaches in this way, because dichotomies appeal to our sense of how knowledge should be organized.

Well, what's wrong with that?   55

What's wrong is that it obscures aspects of disparate work that overlap and can enlighten each other.

[26]Suzanne Wong Scollon, personal communication.
[27]Mary Catherine Bateson, personal communication.

What's wrong is that it obscures the complexity of research. Fitting ideas into a particular camp requires you to oversimplify them. Again, disinformation and distortion can result. Less knowledge is gained, not more. And time spent attacking an opponent or defending against attacks is not spent doing something else — like original research.

What's wrong is that it implies that only one framework can apply, when in most cases many can. As a colleague put it, "Most theories are wrong not in what they assert but in what they deny."[28] Clinging to the elephant's leg, they loudly proclaim that the person describing the elephant's tail is wrong. This is not going to help them — or their readers — understand an elephant. Again, there are parallels in personal relationships. I recall a man who had just returned from a weekend human-development seminar. Full of enthusiasm, he explained the main lesson he had learned: "I don't have to make others wrong to prove that I'm right." He experienced this revelation as a liberation; it relieved him of the burden of trying to prove others wrong.

If you limit your view of a problem to choosing between two sides, you inevitably reject much that is true, and you narrow your field of vision to the limits of those two sides, making it unlikely you'll pull back, widen your field of vision, and discover the paradigm shift that will permit truly new understanding.

In moving away from a narrow view of debate, we need not give up conflict and criticism altogether. Quite the contrary, we can develop more varied — and more constructive — ways of expressing opposition and negotiating disagreement.

We need to use our imaginations and ingenuity to find different ways to seek truth and gain knowledge, and add them to our arsenal — or, should I say, to the ingredients for our stew. It will take creativity to find ways to blunt the most dangerous blades of the argument culture. It's a challenge we must undertake, because our public and private lives are at stake.

References

Bateson, Mary Catherine. *With a Daughter's Eye: A Memoir of Margaret Mead and Gregory Bateson* (New York: William Morrow, 1984).

Elbow, Peter. *Embracing Contraries: Explorations in Learning and Teaching* (New York and Oxford: Oxford University Press, 1986).

Greenberg, David H., and Philip K. Robins. "The Changing Role of Social Experiments in Policy Analysis." *Journal of Policy Analysis and Management* 5:2 (1986), pp. 340–62.

Guinier, Lani, Michelle Fine, and Jane Balin, with Ann Bartow and Deborah Lee Stachel. "Becoming Gentlemen: Women's Experiences at One Ivy League Law School." 143 *University of Pennsylvania Law Review* (Nov. 1994), pp. 1–110.

[28]I got this from A. L. Becker, who got it from Kenneth Pike, who got it from . . .

Havelock, Eric A. *Preface to Plato* (Cambridge, Mass.: Belknap Press, Harvard University Press, 1963).

Hewitt, Lynne E., Judith F. Duchan, and Erwin M. Segal. "Structure and Function of Verbal Conflicts Among Adults with Mental Retardation." *Discourse Processes* 16(4) (1993), pp. 525–43.

Heyrman, Christine Leigh. *Southern Cross: The Beginnings of the Bible Belt* (New York: Knopf, 1997).

Kaplan, Alice. *French Lessons: A Memoir* (Chicago: University of Chicago Press, 1993).

Kurtz, Howard. *Hot Air: All Talk, All the Time* (New York: Times Books, 1996).

Michaels, Sarah. "'Sharing Time': Children's Narrative Styles and Differential Access to Literacy." *Language in Society* 10:3 (1981), pp. 423–42.

Moulton, Janice. "A Paradigm of Philosophy: The Adversary Method." In *Discovering Reality*, Sandra Harding and Merrill B. Hintikka, eds. (Dordrecht, Holland: Reidel, 1983), pp. 149–64.

Noble, David. *A World Without Women: The Christian Clerical Culture of Western Science* (New York and Oxford: Oxford University Press, 1992).

Oliver, Robert T. *Communication and Culture in Ancient India and China* (Syracuse, N.Y.: Syracuse University Press, 1971).

Ong, Walter J. *Fighting for Life: Contest, Sexuality, and Consciousness* (Ithaca, N.Y.: Cornell University Press, 1981).

Or, Winnie Wing Fung. "Agonism in Academic Discussion." Paper presented at the 96th Annual Meeting of the American Anthropological Association, Nov. 19–23, 1997, Washington, D.C.

Rosof, Patricia J. F. "Beyond Rhetoric." *The History Teacher* 26(4) (1993), pp. 493–97.

Sadker, Myra, and David Sadker. *Failing at Fairness: How America's Schools Cheat Girls* (New York: Scribner's, 1994).

Tompkins, Jane. "Fighting Words: Unlearning to Write the Critical Essay." *Georgia Review* 42 (1988), pp. 585–90.

Tracy, Karen, and Sheryl Baratz. "Intellectual Discussion in the Academy as Situated Discourse." *Communication Monographs* 60 (1993), pp. 300–20.

Wertsch, James V. *Voices of the Mind: A Sociocultural Approach to Mediated Action* (Cambridge, Mass.: Harvard University Press, 1991).

Young, Linda W. L. *Crosstalk and Culture in Sino-American Communication* (Cambridge, England: Cambridge University Press, 1994).

ENGAGING THE TEXT

1. How, according to Tannen, do today's classrooms reflect their origin in Greek philosophy and the Christian universities of the medieval era? What

relationship does Tannen see between the thinking of the early Christian Church and Western science?

2. Explain the distinction that Tannen makes between "formal, objective knowledge" and "relational, intuitive knowledge" (paras. 12–15). How, according to Tannen, do these different understandings of knowledge affect the experiences of male and female students in contemporary college classrooms?

3. What is the "culture of critique" that, in Tannen's view, dominates higher education? To what extent does your experience of schooling support the claim that critical, or Socratic, thinking is taught within an "Adversary Paradigm" in American colleges? Do you agree that "the argument culture" has become so widespread in our society because arguing is "easy to do"?

4. What's wrong, according to Tannen, with the argumentative, or "agonistic," intellectual culture of higher education? How does Tannen suggest we move beyond it? Does Tannen herself move beyond an argumentative approach to critical thinking in this analysis of higher education?

EXPLORING CONNECTIONS

5. Compare Tannen's evaluation of the culture of schooling with that offered by John Taylor Gatto in "The Seven-Lesson Schoolteacher" (p. 152). Which of these views of education and its impact on students most nearly agrees with the experiences you've had in school? How might you account for the differences in Tannen's and Gatto's views of the culture of education?

6. In examining the educational cultures of schools serving students from differing social classes, Jean Anyon (p. 174) describes a "hidden curriculum" that reinforces social class position. Compare Anyon's notion of a hidden curriculum with the one revealed by Tannen in her analysis of education's culture of argument.

7. Explain the *Doonesbury* cartoon on this page in terms of Tannen's discussion of the male-centeredness of American education.

Doonesbury

BY GARRY TRUDEAU

Doonesbury © G. B. Trudeau. Reprinted with permission of Universal Press Syndicate. All rights reserved.

EXTENDING THE CRITICAL CONTEXT

8. Replicate the informal research Tannen assigns her students by observing
    how frequently adversarial teaching methods are employed in the other
    classes you are taking. In your observations, describe the type of conflict in-
    volved as well as the way that students respond to it. Do your conclusions
    support or challenge Tannen's analysis of the culture of higher education?

9. In recent years, there has been growing interest in returning to same-sex
    schooling at all educational levels. Working in groups, debate the advan-
    tages and disadvantages of same-sex schools.

10. Read "Girls Rule" by Christina Hoff Sommers in the May 2000 issue of the
    Atlantic Monthly magazine, an article that disputes the claim that the cul-
    ture of American classrooms encourages educational inequality. Report to
    the class on Sommers's objections to the position that schools and teachers
    tend to favor boys over girls. To what extent do you think that teachers and
    teaching styles generally favor either male or female students in American
    schools?

School

KYOKO MORI

*Because we are a nation of immigrants, many Americans enter school
with experiences of education in other cultures. This is particularly true of
recent immigrants who enter college to learn English and prepare themselves for new careers in the United States. Award-winning novelist Kyoko
Mori began her educational career in Japanese schools but left Japan in her
twenties to study writing in English, her adopted language. In this selection
from* Polite Lies: On Being a Woman Caught Between Cultures *(1997),
Mori reflects on the differences of content and style between Japanese and
American approaches to education and offers some eye-opening observations on the powers and limitations of both. She is an instructor of creative
writing at St. Norbert's College in De Pere, Wisconsin. Her novel* Shizuko's
Daughter *(1995) was a* Publishers Weekly *Book of the Year. In addition to
several other novels for young adults, she is the author of* The Dream of
Water: A Memoir *(1996).*

During our senior year at college, some of my classmates said they
could hardly wait to graduate, to join "the real world." They couldn't concentrate on classes, knowing that they would soon be out of school forever. I

didn't feel the same way at all. School seemed as "real" to me as "the out-side world" — only more interesting.

I still don't trust the distinction often made between school and "the real world," which implies that there is something insubstantial or artificial about school. The business meetings I attended in Milwaukee as an inter-preter confirmed my suspicion that arcane and "academic" discussions don't happen only at colleges. The directors of two small companies, one Japan-ese and the other American, once had a twenty-minute debate about whether the plastic cover of a particular camera lens should be "pumpkin yellow" or "the yellow of raincoats." What each man meant by these terms was unclear to the other and had to be redefined many times over. This is the conversation I recall now when I attend academic conferences and can-not understand what is being said about a book I have read more than once.

School and "the real world" both have their absurd moments, but school is where people go when they are not satisfied with their "real world" lives and want a change. Many Americans in their thirties and forties go back to college to get trained for a different line of work or to pursue a life-long interest they couldn't afford to study earlier. Until they are in need of such second chances, most Americans take colleges for granted because they are always there — almost any adult can get into some college at any age.

Being able to go back to school is a particularly American opportunity. My Japanese friends will never be able to do the same. In Japan, school does not give anyone a second chance. Many of my Japanese friends are married women with money who already have college degrees. But none of them can go back to college to earn a second degree in art, education, or so-cial work, as their American counterparts may do.

Recently, a few Japanese colleges have started accepting applications   5 from adults who have been out of school for years, but these colleges are ex-ceptions. The only way most people can get into a college in Japan is to take and pass the entrance examination for that particular college immediately after graduating from high school. The number of exams a student can sit for in a given year is limited, since many schools give their exams on the same day.

A student who does not get into any college will have to wait a year, at-tending a cram school. There is a word for a student in this situation — *ronin* (floating person). In feudal times, the word referred to samurai whose clan had been dissolved. Feudal *ronin* had to roam around until they could find a new master to serve. To be a modern *ronin* is scarcely better: while their friends move on to colleges or jobs, *ronin* must float around for a year without any allegiance. In Japan, anyone who doesn't belong to the right group at the right time feels like a failure. If a *ronin* can't get into a college after a year at a cram school, he or she usually gives up and settles for a low-paying job rather than spending another year floating around.

In the States, young people who don't feel ready for college can work for a few years and then apply when they feel more motivated or mature.

Young Japanese people don't have the same chance. For older adults to go back to school to have a second chance — at a job or an artistic career or personal fulfillment — is practically impossible.

The very accessibility of schools in America adds to the perception that they are not real or substantial enough. Many Americans who criticize their own school system for being "too easy" idealize the Japanese school system because they are drawn to its tough image. The details Americans cite as the merits of the Japanese system actually reflect their ideal of the mythical "real world" where people must work hard — long hours, the emphasis on discipline and basic skills, the tough competition among peers. These people admire the Japanese school system because they see it as a samurai version of their own fantasies about the American work ethic.

My education at a traditional Japanese grade school was nothing so glorious. Day-to-day life at a Japanese public school was harsh but also boring. Until I transferred to a private school in seventh grade, I didn't learn anything that I couldn't have learned at home by reading and memorizing the same books with my mother's help.

Recently when I was in Japan, I was asked why I did not write my novels in Japanese, why I did not at least translate my own work. The question surprised me at first. The people who asked knew that for twelve years I have lived in a small Wisconsin town where I have few opportunities to speak Japanese. No one can write novels in a language she has not spoken every day for more than a decade. But there is another reason I could not possibly have written my novels or poems in Japanese: I was never taught to write in what was my native language. My public education in Japan prepared me to make the correct letters to spell out the correct sounds, but that is not the same as teaching me how to write.

When I started the first grade at six, I had not been taught to read at home — at least not in a formal way. Because my mother read to me all the time, I had memorized my favorite books and could read along with her. Sometimes, when my mother and I were standing on the street corner waiting for a taxi, I noticed that I could read the license plates of the cars passing by. I would read the plates and she would nod and smile because I was right, but no big fuss was made about my being able to read. Most of the other kids starting school with me were the same way: we sort of knew how to read because of our mothers, but we hadn't been formally trained.

In first grade, we were taught the fifty phonetic signs that make up the Japanese alphabet, a dozen simple pictorial characters, and the basic numbers. By the end of the year, everyone in our class could read our textbooks and write simple messages to our family and friends in our sprawling, uneven handwriting. People who admire the Japanese education system are partially right. Japanese schools *are* very good at teaching skills like basic writing — which can only be learned through memorization and repeated practice.

Once we learned the alphabet and some pictorial characters, my classmates and I wrote compositions about our families, our vacations, our friends. Occasionally, our teachers had us write stories and poems as well. In summer, we were given notebooks in which we had to keep "picture diaries": on the upper, blank half we drew pictures, and on the lower, lined half we wrote sentences about what we did every day. These assignments gave us a lot of practice at writing.

When we got to the upper grades, though, our assignments changed. We no longer wrote stories or poems; our compositions weren't about our personal experiences or feelings. Almost every writing assignment was a book report or a summary of our reading. We had to follow a very strict formula, organizing our thoughts under predetermined headings like "plot," "characters," "setting," "themes," "what we learned from the book." If we didn't follow the format, we got poor grades.

The grades didn't always make sense. Luckily, I did well most of the time, but I wasn't sure what I did right aside from adhering to the format. The only suggestions I got were circled corrections where I had used the wrong pictorial characters or general remarks about my bad penmanship.   15

A few of my friends didn't do so well, but they were never given suggestions for improvement. They would simply get low grades and comments like "Your writing needs improvement," "You didn't really follow the directions for the assignment," or "I can see you tried some but you still have a long way to go." Often, our teachers openly scolded pupils. In front of the whole class, my friends were told to "pay better attention" and to "try harder." It didn't matter that most of them were serious and well-behaved students, not lazy and inattentive troublemakers; they were already trying hard, trying to pay attention.

No matter what the subject, our teachers never gave us very clear advice about how to do better. When I couldn't understand long division or fractions and decimals in math, I felt bad at first. On the timed tests we had every day, I could finish only half the problems before the teacher's stopwatch beeped, telling us to put down our pencils. The results were put up on the wall, and my name was always near the bottom. I was told to "try harder," but none of my teachers spent extra time with me to go over what I was doing wrong. Since I wasn't given a real chance to improve, I decided after a while that I didn't really care how I did.

Over and over again, our Japanese education offered this sort of harsh judgment combined with vague exhortation. In every subject, kids who didn't do well were made to feel ashamed and yet given no chance to improve. The humiliation was especially obvious in physical education classes. At our grade school we were expected to learn to swim in the same way we were expected to learn to write: by sheer repetition and "trying harder." We were left to swim around on our own, but the pool hours weren't just for fun. Each of us had to wear a cloth swim-cap with the symbol that indicated our skill level. Students who couldn't swim at all were singled out by the big red circle sewn on top of their caps. "Red mark, red mark, you'll sink like a big hammer," some of the other kids taunted, and the teachers did nothing to stop them. I was glad that I already knew how to swim by the time I started school.

For those of us who could swim, there were monthly tests to determine how far we could go without stopping. For every five or ten meters we could swim, our mothers sewed red or black lines on the side of our caps. Those who could swim fifty meters in the crawl, sidestroke, or breaststroke got the best marks on their caps: five all-black lines. In fifth grade, when I passed the test for fifty meters, my teachers praised me for having "tried so hard," even though I was able to do so well only because my mother had taught me to swim in the river near her parents' home. Unlike my teachers, my mother enjoyed giving specific instructions. She drew diagrams on paper to show me what my arms and legs should be doing for crawl and sidestroke. Then she made me lie down on the sand on the river bank to practice the arm and leg movements. Once I was in the water, she stood on the bank shouting out instructions like "Stretch your arms all the way," "Turn your head sideways." When my form was wrong, she showed me by imitating me — exaggerating my awkward movements and making me laugh. "I don't look like *that*," I protested, but I knew exactly what I needed to improve.

I did not learn how to write in Japanese because even at the private   20
school I attended after seventh grade, Japanese language classes were taught by older men who had studied classical Japanese literature or Chinese poetry at the national universities before the war. They were the most conservative and traditional of all our teachers. In their classes, we read the works of famous authors and wrote essays to answer questions like "What is the theme?" "When does the main character realize the importance of morality?" "What important Buddhist philosophy is expressed in this passage?" All the writing we did for our extracurricular activities — for skits or school newspapers and magazines — was supervised by younger teachers who did not teach Japanese.

During those same years, we learned how to write in English. Our English teachers were young Japanese women who had studied in the States or England, and American women from small Midwestern towns who had just graduated from college. In their classes, we wrote essays about our families, friends, hobbies, future dreams — personal subjects we had not written about at school since third grade. We were given plenty of instruction about the specifics of writing: word choice, description, style. Our essays came back with comments both about our writing and about the thoughts we had expressed. I looked forward to writing essays and reading my teachers' comments. By the time I was a high school senior, I wanted to be a writer, and English was the only language I could write in.

To study writing, I had to go to an American college. Creative writing was not — and still is not — offered at Japanese colleges, in English or in Japanese. I don't know how Japanese writers learn to write, since most of them, as children, must have had the same kind of education I had. There are no schools or writers' conferences where a person can study creative writing as an adult. I have never heard of people getting together to form a writing group or workshop.

Writing is not something that comes naturally to the chosen few. Most American writers of my generation didn't just learn to write on their own. Without the classes we took in creative writing and modern literature, we wouldn't have known what to read, how to read it, how to pay attention to form and content. We needed to be shown how to write good dialogue, smooth transitions, pared-down but vivid character descriptions. These things didn't come naturally. It would have taken us thirty years to learn, on our own, the same skills we learned in eight years of college and graduate school. My friends at graduate school came from average Midwestern homes; they were not children of famous writers. School gave us a chance we would never have had otherwise. In America, we are proof that the romantic notion of the natural writer is a myth. In Japan, where no formal training is offered in writing, the myth may be a sad reality that prevents many people from becoming writers.

My stepmother used the traditional method of harsh judgment even though she was not a teacher. When Michiko came to live with my family, I was twelve and already knew how to cook and bake simple foods like omelettes and chocolate chip cookies and how to clean up the kitchen. But my attempts to help Michiko always ended in disaster. She complained endlessly about how I had not been taught to do things the "proper way." Everything I did, from drying the dishes to sweeping the floor, was wrong. "I can't believe that you don't know how to do this," she would scold in her shrill voice, and yet she never showed me exactly what the "proper way" was. When I asked, "What do you mean? What am I doing wrong?" she would scream, "If I have to tell you, then it's no good. I can't show you something you should already know." I was supposed to watch her silently and learn on my own through observation, but she made me too nervous to concentrate. I had no idea what I was supposed to be looking for. If I gave up and asked, "Do you mean the way I am holding the broom or are you saying that I should start over there instead of here?" she would stomp out of the kitchen without a word.

I know that Michiko's silent and judgmental manner was a manifesta- 25 tion of her meanspiritedness, but she didn't invent the method. The tradition of not giving specific instruction comes from Zen. In traditional Zen philosophy, satori, or enlightenment, is considered to be beyond human description. Since no one can describe satori or ways to attain it, the teacher-monk asks his disciples a series of koans — questions meant to puzzle and disturb rather than to provide answers. The whole purpose of the koan is to break down the disciples' reliance on their own intellect by humiliating them. At its worst, the teaching technique amounts to intellectual or spiritual hazing. The disciples are supposed to hit bottom and suffer terrible despair before they can open their eyes to satori and experience beauty and peace that is beyond logic or description.

To my American friends who took up Zen in college, this style of teaching seemed liberating because of its apparent emphasis on a larger and unexplainable truth instead of minute and trivial details. After years of American education, my friends were tired of specific instruction. All the rules they had to learn about writing good paragraphs or improving their tennis swings struck them as fussy and superficial. Zen taught them that everything they had learned in their Western education was an illusion that needed to be shattered. The very destructiveness and uncertainty of enlightenment sounded uplifting.

But in the Zen-style teaching actually practiced in Japan, students are not liberated from minute details. The details are everything. A beginning calligraphy student writes the same letters over and over, trying to make her brush strokes look exactly like her master's. If she puts one dot five millimeters too far to the right, her work is considered flawed. The master does not point out her mistake. "No, not right yet," he grunts. "Do it over." Until the student can see for herself that her dot is in the wrong place, she will have to keep copying the same letters — she has not reached "enlightenment."

In America, students are often drilled on the details of grammar or form and yet are forgiven for the minor mistakes they make in their writing. Their teacher might say, "You have a couple of awkward sentences and punctuation mistakes here, but your paper is excellent overall. Your ideas are good and you write with a wonderful voice." Hearing comments like these, my friends concluded that their teachers were being inconsistent. If the minor details weren't important in the end, why did the teachers spend so much time on them?

The paradox about the two styles of teaching is that neither emphasizes what it considers to be truly important. In calligraphy and other traditional arts derived from Zen, following the correct form is everything — there is no possibility that you can make a few minor mistakes and still "get" the spirit or the essence of the "truth" — and yet instruction consists of vague exhortation about "following the right balance" and "working hard." In America, where teachers actually value the overall spirit of the work, they spend most of their time talking about details.

This paradox reflects a common ground all teachers share. No matter what and how we teach, we believe that what we value the most is beyond our meager ability to describe. We are struck dumb with admiration at the things we value, so we try to teach the secondary things that we think are

30

easier to talk about. Like most American writing teachers, I value the over-all spirit or genuine voice in my students' work and yet nag them about the smaller details of technique like trimming their lines or writing better dialogue. Mine is a Western approach — the same method of instruction is apparent even in the Bible, which gives God a name that cannot be spoken, while offering book after book detailing the laws about how to build a temple or what foods should not be eaten together.

My Japanese teachers, who thought that detail was everything, must have felt that precision was so important that it could not be described: only the truly enlightened can be in perfect harmony with the correct form. In the meantime, they must have reasoned, they could at least talk about the value of hard work, something everyone can easily understand. The contradiction we share points to the difficulty of teaching anything: trying to pass on knowledge that seems so clear to ourselves to people who don't have that knowledge. When my stepmother complained, "How can I teach you something you should already know?" she was expressing in its meanest form the universal frustration of teachers.

In spite of our shared frustration, though, I have a hard time forgiving some of my former teachers in Japan because they never seemed humbled by the near impossibility of their task. Many of my teachers felt entitled to be both strict and arbitrary — strict about their own authority and the rules of the system and yet so arbitrary and lax about helping us.

In Japan, whether you are in school or at your private karate, judo, or *ikebana*[1] lesson, you can never question the authority of the teacher, whom you address simply as "sensei," literally, "one whose life comes first." Unless there are multiple teachers who need to be distinguished from one another, you do not even use their family names, much less first names (which you most likely do not know). The teacher is like the biblical God, whom you cannot name.

Students are not expected to question the competence of their teachers or the usefulness of their assignments, any more than Zen disciples can rebel against their master and his koans. Japanese students who study at American universities are amazed that at the end of the semester most universities ask their students to evaluate their teachers. Even though students in Japan complain to each other about their teachers, they would never think of writing an evaluation or filing official grievances.

In the teaching of many traditional Japanese art forms, the teacher's authority is backed up by a complex hierarchy called *ie* that controls instruction. Even the choice of this word, since it means both "house" and "family origin," reflects high expectations of allegiance. What is described in English as a "school" (such as a school of writing or painting) is actually a "family" in Japanese. Each *ie* is structured like a family hierarchy: at the top is

35

---

[1] *ikebana:* The Japanese art of flower arranging.

the head teacher, called *iemoto* (source of the house), and under him are various assistant teachers who, in turn, take their own assistants. All these teachers are licensed by the *ie*. A beginner in *ikebana* or Japanese dance will study with a minor assistant teacher for a few years and then move on to a more advanced teacher. There are various levels of competence awarded along the way, but every advancement must be approved by the *ie*.

The system makes it impossible for a student to challenge any teacher's decision, since the teacher can invoke the authority of the whole clanlike hierarchy. Teachers can make any arbitrary decision so long as it can be backed up by the *ie*. When my cousin Kazumi studied *ikebana,* she was disillusioned by the unfair judgments her teachers made every year about who should be allowed to advance to the next level of competence. There were no tests or lists of tasks and qualities that determined the advancements. Who advanced and who didn't seemed entirely up to the teachers' whims. People who were related to any of the teachers rose through the ranks much faster than those who weren't.

Whether or not they won an advancement to the next level, all the students were required to attend the annual certificate ceremony in their best kimonos. The year of the Kobe earthquake Kazumi received a letter from her *ie* advising students to rent a good kimono to attend the annual ceremony if theirs had been destroyed in the earthquake.

"I had been disillusioned with *ikebana* for some time anyway," Kazumi told me, "but the letter was the last straw. I couldn't believe that the teachers thought this was a time for people to be worrying about their kimonos. Even though the letter said that we didn't necessarily have to have a nice kimono if our family had suffered such a great damage that we had no money, the tone was very condescending — and it was obvious that they were really saying that we should rent one no matter what the cost. They didn't write and say, 'We are so sorry about the earthquake. We would be so happy if you could still come to the annual ceremony in spite of the damage many of you must have suffered, and of course, you can wear whatever you would like.' "

She switched to Dutch-style flower arrangement even though it, too, has a nationwide association that oversees its teaching and licensing. Like *ikebana*, Dutch flower arrangement has different levels of teachers and different levels of competence, but Kazumi sees a big difference between the two. To advance from one [level] to the next in the Dutch style, people take tests in which each person is given a bucket of flowers to make into a table arrangement, a small bouquet, and a corsage; a group of judges scores the results. Everybody has the same amount of time, the same number of arrangements to complete, similar flowers in the bucket, and the same group of judges. Evaluation isn't arbitrary the way it was for *ikebana*. In the lessons she took — mostly from Dutch teachers — plenty of specific instruction was given about colors, textures, shapes, and the flowers themselves. Her teachers looked at her work and gave her suggestions — something none of her *ikebana* teachers ever did.

•   •   •

Until I talked to Kazumi, I was hoping that even though my Japanese   40
friends could not go back to school in their thirties and forties, they might
be able to take private lessons or receive training through volunteer work in
order to pursue some of their interests. Even in small towns like Green Bay,
many people my age can learn new skills, pursue their hobbies, or work for
causes they believe in without enrolling in school.

My Japanese friends do not have similar chances to learn something new
or feel useful. There are very few volunteer organizations in Japan for nature
conservation, crisis intervention, helping children, or working with families
who are poor or homeless. The few soup kitchens one might find in big Japanese cities are operated by international organizations like the Salvation Army.
People who work at them are mostly foreigners. A nice Japanese housewife is
not expected to do volunteer work for strangers. "If she has time to help
people she doesn't even know," her relatives would grumble, "why doesn't
she do more to help her own kids study? Why doesn't she run for an office in
the P.T.A. at their school?" Most middle-class Japanese people seem to think
that poor people deserve to be poor — it's their own fault or the fault of their
families and relatives. Nobody should expect help from total strangers. As for
conserving nature, that is the job of biologists. My friends have a hard time
justifying their passion for gardening to their husbands and in-laws. If they
were to spend their afternoons taking care of injured wildlife or clearing
marshes of trash instead of cleaning their houses and preparing special meals
for their children, their families would probably disown them.

Nice housewives like my friends can take private lessons only if they
can be justified as genteel means of cultivating fine, feminine tastes — like
ikebana, tea, koto and samisen music — but these are the traditional Japanese arts with the strict *ie* structure. Joining the *ie* would involve my friends
in another burdensome system of duties and obligations, something they already experience in every facet of their lives.

In so many ways, Japan is a place of no second chances. Many of my
friends are in very unhappy marriages. They write to me about the shouting
and shoving matches they have with their husbands, about the night they
tried to run away, only to have the husband chase them down the street,
catch them, and drag them home. Unable to run away, my friends lock
themselves up in the guest room or sleep in their daughters' rooms to avoid
sleeping with their husbands. For most American women, leaving a bad
marriage like theirs would be nothing but happiness. My friends stay because divorce still carries a big stigma in Japan. If they leave their husbands,
they may never be able to see their children again. Certainly, they will not
be able to marry again and try another chance at marriage. Nobody marries
a divorced middle-aged woman in Japan.

Life in Japan is like an unending stint at a school where you have to
keep taking tests — giving your answers under pressure without help or

guidance, knowing that you will get no second chance if you make a mistake. Japanese people have to make many of the big decisions of their lives — whom to marry, what company to join — without detailed information, since it is rude to ask direct questions even at *omiai* meetings[2] and job interviews. They have no choice but to trust authority and do their best, just as they were supposed to do in school. If their job or marriage turns out to be a disappointment, they will be given the same vague exhortations they heard from their teachers: keep trying, work hard, pay attention.

There is nothing intrinsically wrong with trying harder. Sometimes   45
when I see my former students in Green Bay seeming to flounder — waiting on tables or working clerical jobs they hate, the whole time talking about their big plans to "go back to school" soon — I think maybe a little Japanese perseverance might not hurt them. I know that for them or for anyone else, going back to school does not guarantee a job or happiness. Within school, too, when my students complain that everything we read in a modern American literature class is depressing or that I simply do not "like" their work (when every poem they wrote in the class is a love poem in couplets), I long for a little Japanese respect for authority. Some of my students would be better off if they trusted me a little rather than questioning my decisions at every turn. Still, I would rather have students who question too much than those who assume that I know best and don't owe them any explanations. No one should have power that is unjustified and unjustifiable, regardless of how convenient or efficient it may seem for the smooth running of the classroom, the educational system, or the country.

The problem with the Japanese system, ultimately, is that individual freedom — to question the teacher, to disagree — is sacrificed for the supposed convenience and protection of the whole group. The system works well for people who feel no desire to rebel. The Japanese *ie* system my cousin complained about does ensure that anyone who perseveres in a given art form will have some recognition; periodically, every student is asked to take part in public exhibitions or concerts. Most Japanese students have public-performance opportunities many of my American friends — artists and musicians — don't.

But for me — as well as for my cousin — the price is too high. The security comes with too many obligations. The *ie* system asks that you trust your teachers who have not earned or deserved your trust. What you are required to have is blind faith in the *ie:* like the church or the mosque, the *ie* is an institution that is designed to inspire total obedience to its rules. In Japan, if you reject your chance to enjoy the security that comes from joining the right group such as an *ie*, an elite school, a good company, or a respectable family, you will have to leave the country or live in it as an outcast. Life in Japan resembles the harshest interpretation of a religious faith: the Koran or the sword, either you are with Christ or against him, either you join the sheltering umbrella of Japanese security or you have nothing. In

---

[2]*omiai meetings:* Meetings with a matchmaker to set up an arranged marriage.

school and elsewhere, people are rewarded for obeying the rules diligently, never for taking a chance and being different, or for asking good questions.

But words like *security* and *uncertainty* are misleading. Because Dutch-style flower arrangement is not as popular as *ikebana* and the association does not provide the same kind of protection that a traditional *ie* gives its teachers, my cousin is struggling to get enough students for the classes she offers. She has quit her clerical job, which she did not like, and committed herself to the life of a flower-arrangement teacher. She isn't going to get a second chance at being a clerk or going back to *ikebana*. My cousin's life is uncertain and inse-cure. But daily, as she arranges her own flowers and watches her students cut-ting and arranging theirs, she is certain of other things. She knows when she is making a good arrangement and when she is not. In Dutch-style arrange-ments, my cousin has learned what colors and shapes look pleasing; she has a firm sense of what she considers beautiful. She also knows that she will tell her students exactly what she thinks about their work rather than keeping her criticism to herself or being vague. Kazumi feels a certainty about truth, beauty, honesty. That is the only certainty worth choosing.

ENGAGING THE TEXT

1. Why, according to Mori, do many Americans feel that the work they do in college is not directly related to "the real world"? Why do many Americans also feel that Japanese schools, by contrast, are worthy of admiration? To what extent do you agree that the world of American higher education is "unreal" and that Japanese schools appear to be more connected to prevail-ing social or economic realities?

2. What are the limitations of the Japanese educational system according to Mori? What is her view of the American educational system? To what ex-tent have your experiences in American schools confirmed or challenged Mori's conclusions?

3. What does Mori find "paradoxical" about the styles of both the Japanese and American educational systems? How does she explain this paradox? Do you generally agree that American educators value "the overall spirit" of a student's work and spend more time in class offering advice about how to improve details and technique?

EXPLORING CONNECTIONS

4. Compare Mori's view of American education with those of John Taylor Gatto (p. 152) and Deborah Tannen (p. 233). Which of these perspectives agrees most nearly with your own experiences in American schools?

5. Compare Mori's experience of learning English with that of Richard Rodriguez (p. 194). How would you account for the differences in their at-titudes toward the English language?

6. How might Claude M. Steele (p. 211) evaluate the kinds of comments Mori finds to be typical of American writing teachers?

EXTENDING THE CRITICAL CONTEXT

7. Write a brief description of the style of the writing instruction you received in school. How does it compare with Mori's experience of learning Japanese and English in Japan? How well prepared has the instruction you received left you? What, if anything, do you wish your teachers had done differently?

8. If you have ever studied in another country, write a paper in which you compare the educational style of that nation with the style of education you have encountered since attending school or college in the United States. How does your crosscultural educational experience compare with that of Mori?

Politics in the Schoolroom

LYNNE V. CHENEY

The last few decades have witnessed a sea change in American education. Forty years ago the typical American college classroom was filled with mostly white male students listening to a white male instructor lecturing about the achievements of — you guessed it — their white male predecessors. But after the civil rights movement, American education began to open its doors, not only to a new, more ethnically and racially diverse group of students, but to the ideas, experiences, and perspectives they brought with them. The presence of growing numbers of minority, low-income, and female students at all instructional levels has challenged America's educators to rethink and revise their pedagogy and the content of their classrooms. Not all cultural commentators, however, are invigorated by these changes. Some, like former Reagan appointee Lynne V. Cheney, see classroom innovations that feature multicultural or feminist perspectives as an unnecessary diversion from more important academic concerns. The following selection, excerpted from Cheney's Telling the Truth: Why Our Culture and Our Country Have Stopped Making Sense — and What We Can Do About It *(1995), presents a conservative critique of what Cheney sees as the recent politicization of our nation's classrooms. Cheney chaired the National Endowment for the Humanities from 1986 to 1993. She is currently a Senior Fellow at the American Enterprise Institute.*

> Ignorance is strength.
> — One of the mottoes of the Party in GEORGE ORWELL, *1984*

- A Massachusetts educator warns teachers about using *The Story of Babar* because it "extols the virtues of a European, middle-class lifestyle and disparages the animals and people who have remained in the jungle."[1]

- A teacher of "radical math literacy" warns against bombarding students with "oppressive procapitalist ideology." Among the practical applications of mathematics that she says should be avoided is totaling a grocery bill since such an exercise "carries the nonneutral message that paying for food is natural."[2]

- The author of a textbook for future teachers urges skepticism for the idea that the people now known as American Indians came to this hemisphere across the Bering land bridge. Indian myths do not tell this story, she writes. Moreover, she observes, the scientific account has nothing "except logic" to recommend it. A committee of parents and teachers in Berkeley, California, subsequently offers this argument as reason for rejecting a fourth-grade history text.[3]

Disparate as these examples seem, the people in them have a common goal. They want to be sure that American schools show no favor to — and, indeed, positively downgrade — ideas and practices associated with the United States and its Western heritage, including, in the last instance, the Enlightenment legacy of scientific thought. While such efforts can seem foolish and extreme (someone really wants to ban *Babar*?), it would be a mistake to overlook the trend they represent: the growing tendency for politics to drive the education of the young in this country, very often at the expense of truth.

A teacher in New Jersey describes at length her way of teaching fourth-graders that Columbus wasn't a hero who "discovered" America, but a "greedy" man and a "murderer" who "stole" it. In order to help them understand why they have been taught lies about 1492, she has the children in her class imagine that every year the principal of their school speaks of Columbus as a man to be respected. Meanwhile, the fourth-graders are further to imagine, the principal regularly leads an army of the school's strongest students on raids of neighboring schools where they confiscate valuable materials and round up prisoners to be the principal's servants. By asking the fourth-graders "to explain the connection between the principal's spirited promotion of the Columbus myth and the invasions of neighboring schools," the teacher claims to help her students understand how the posi-

---

[1] Patricia G. Ramsey, *Teaching and Learning in a Diverse World: Multicultural Education for Young Children* (New York: Teachers College Press, 1987), 73. [All notes are the author's, except 9 and 31.]

[2] Marilyn Frankenstein, "A Different Third R: Radical Math," *Politics of Education: Essays from* Radical Teacher, Susan Gushee O'Malley, Robert C. Rosen, and Leonard Vogt, eds. (Albany: State University of New York Press, 1990), 220.

[3] Christine I. Bennett, *Comprehensive Multicultural Education: Theory and Practice* (Boston: Allyn and Bacon, 1990), 287; Eugenie C. Scott, "The Social Context of Pseudoscience," *The Natural History of Paradigms*, J. H. Langdon and M. E. McGann, eds. (Indianapolis: University of Indiana Press, 1993), 350.

tive Columbus myth is used by their government "to forestall any critical questioning of U.S. imperialistic foreign policy today." As the teacher explains it:

> Widespread belief in the myth makes it easy for U.S. officials to get away with invading Vietnam, Grenada, Panama, and so on. Those books (containing the myth) teach children that any nation with sufficient military power has the right to invade other lands. In particular, they reinforce blind patriotism and the belief that the United States has a moral imperative to control the "New World Order."[4]

Although this teacher is particularly expansive about the views she presents in the classroom, she is hardly unique in conveying to those she teaches that the events leading up to their country's founding should be regarded with loathing. At a multicultural conference in California, a teacher offers her colleagues an example of how to deal with students who want to be positive instead of negative about Columbus and study him as an exemplar of the Age of Exploration. When faced with this in her own classroom, says the teacher, she simply told the student, "That would be like a Jew celebrating Hitler because he had a dream."[5]

Fourth-graders in Chapel Hill, North Carolina, have had to use the following words in a fill-in-the-blank test about Columbus: *conquer, genocide, holocaust, subjugate, annihilate,* and *propaganda.*[6] A seventh-grader in Minnesota recounted for me her difficulties with a writing assignment about Columbus:

> The history teacher wanted us to write a story for first-graders, wanted us to tell the story over the way it was supposed to be. We were supposed to write a negative story on the bad things Columbus did.

The seventh-grader went on to explain that she didn't follow instructions: "I didn't think we should go out and tell first-graders he was so awful." As a result, she got what she called "a really bad grade." She wrote the story again, "half and half " this time, and thus managed to get by.[7]

We should not, of course, retreat into the old myths, should not hide from students that Columbus and other European explorers were often brutal. But there was also brutality in indigenous cultures — as well as much to be admired. And much to praise about Europeans as well, who did, after all, bring with them the foundations for our legal, educational, and

5

---

[4]Maria Sweeney, "Columbus, A Hero? Rethinking Columbus in an Elementary Classroom," *Radical Teacher* (Fall 1993), 25–29.

[5]Quoted in Robert Holland, "Re-education, the Multicultural Way," *Richmond Times-Dispatch* (21 February 1993), F7.

[6]"Spelling Test 3" given in October 1992 to a fourth-grade gifted and talented class in the Chapel Hill–Carrboro, North Carolina, school district.

[7]Conversation with author, 27 May 1993.

political institutions. But instead of being encouraged to search for a complicated truth, students are increasingly presented with oversimple versions of the American past that focus on the negative.

Sandra Stotsky, a researcher at Harvard University, reviewed teaching materials being used in the Brookline, Massachusetts, high school and concluded in 1991 that there was "one major theme" running through the course outlines and examinations for social studies: "the systematic denigration of America's Western heritage." A ninth-grade exam on ancient history, for example, asked students to identify the "Hellenic epic which established egotistical individualism as heroic." Almost all the questions on Greece and Rome, according to Stotsky, emphasized negative aspects, while "all items about ancient China . . . were worded positively or drew attention only to China's positive features, such as 'Chinese belief in pacifism and relativism.' Not a word, for example, about the existence of slavery in ancient China and the thousands of slaves who built, and died building, the Great Wall." Similarly, Stotsky observed:

> Students . . . learn about racism as an American and European phenomenon only. Even though Islamic and African history are extensively covered in the curriculum . . . students learn only about the trans-Atlantic slave trade and nothing about the slave trade conducted by African kings or Arab traders for centuries preceding and following the trans-Atlantic slave trade.[8]

The National History Standards[9] developed at the University of California at Los Angeles and released in the fall of 1994 are the most egregious example to date of encouraging students to take a benign view of — or totally overlook — the failings of other cultures while being hypercritical of the one in which they live. Published in two volumes — one for U.S. history and one for world history — and intended for schools across the nation, the standards suggest that students consider the architecture, labor systems, and agriculture of the Aztecs — but not their practice of human sacrifice. The gathering of wealth, presented as an admirable activity when an African king, Mansa Musa, undertakes it, is presented as cause for outrage when it occurs in the American context. One suggested student activity is to "conduct a trial of John D. Rockefeller on the following charge: 'The plaintiff [sic] had knowingly and willfully participated in unethical and amoral business practices designed to undermine traditions of fair and open competition for personal and private aggrandizement in direct violation of the common welfare.'"[10]

---

[8]Sandra Stotsky, "Multicultural Education in the Brookline Public Schools: The Deconstruction of an Academic Curriculum," *Network News & Views* (October 1991), 30, 32.

[9]*The National History Standards:* After heated public debate, the curriculum standards discussed here were not adopted by the state of California.

[10]Charlotte Crabtree and Gary B. Nash, *National Standards for United States History: Exploring the American Experience, Grades 5–12* (Los Angeles: National Center for History in the Schools, University of California at Los Angeles, 1994), 48, 44, 139.

Although the standards for U.S. history neglect to mention that George Washington was our first president or that James Madison was the father of the Constitution, they do manage to include a great deal about the Ku Klux Klan (which appears seventeen times in the document), Senator Joe Mc-Carthy and McCarthyism (cited nineteen times), and the Great Depression (cited twenty-five times). The U.S. standards also pay little attention to scientific and technological achievement. Among the figures *not* discussed are Alexander Graham Bell, the Wright Brothers, Thomas Edison, Albert Einstein, Jonas Salk, and Neil Armstrong (or any astronaut). The exquisite consciousness of race and gender that characterizes the standards may have contributed to the omission of this group (its members are all white males), but it is also the case that science and technology are now held in extremely low regard in certain parts of the academy. Feminists argue that science represents destructive male thinking. Why not call Newton's *Principia* Newton's "rape manual"? asks one.[11] Both feminists and environmentalists argue that because of the high value that science places on objectivity and rationality, it is now in deep and deserved crisis — information that tends to come as a surprise to practicing scientists.[12] Did the authors of the U.S. standards decide that in the case of a field so disdained by so many of their colleagues, the less said the better? Whatever the motive, to overlook American accomplishment in science and technology is to omit some of our most dazzling achievements.

The World History Standards do mention Edison and Einstein; and while there is heavy emphasis on the role that technological advancement has had in increasing the brutality of war, there is also some recognition that science has played a role in improving quality of life — though it is usually coupled with a reminder that not everyone has benefited equally. Students are asked, for example, to assess "why scientific, technological, and medical advances have improved living standards for many but have failed to eradicate hunger, poverty, and epidemic disease."[13]

In the World History Standards, the fact that women generally had dif-   10
ferent roles from men in the ancient world is seen simply as a matter of gender "differentiation" — until it happens in Athens, the birthplace of Western civilization. Then it becomes a matter of "restrictions on the rights and freedoms of women." Just as sexism is first introduced in the context of Greek civilization, so, too, is ethnocentrism — as though in previous

[11]Sandra Harding, *The Science Question in Feminism* (Ithaca: Cornell University Press, 1986), 113.

[12]Andrew Ross, *Strange Weather: Culture, Science, and Technology in the Age of Limits* (London: Verso, 1991), 11; Paul R. Gross and Norman Levitt, *Higher Superstition: The Academic Left and Its Quarrels with Science* (Baltimore: Johns Hopkins University Press, 1994), 235.

[13]Charlotte Crabtree and Gary B. Nash, *National Standards for World History: Exploring Paths to the Present, Grades 5–12* (Los Angeles: National Center for History in the Schools, University of California at Los Angeles, 1994), 274.

cultures in Asia and Africa, people had never considered their ethnic group superior.[14] Nowhere is it mentioned that it was, in fact, in Western civilization that the unjust treatment of women and minorities was first condemned and curiosity about other cultures first encouraged.

In one of the sillier sections of the World History Standards — and one of the most quintessentially politically correct — students are asked to read a book about Michelangelo, not in order to discuss art, but so that they can "discuss social oppression and conflict in Europe during the Renaissance." In what may be the most irresponsible section of the World History Standards, fifth- and sixth-graders are asked to read a book about a Japanese girl of their age who died a painful death as a result of radiation from the atomic weapon dropped on Hiroshima in 1945.[15] No mention is made of why American leaders decided to use atomic weapons, about the casualties they believed an invasion of Japan would have entailed, for example. No mention is made of death and suffering caused by the Japanese. The rape of Nanking is not discussed, nor is Pearl Harbor, nor the Bataan death march. What fifth- and sixth-graders would be likely to conclude is that their country was guilty of a horrible — and completely unjustified — act of cruelty against innocents.

In the World History Standards, as in those for the United States, the Cold War is presented as a deadly competition between two equally culpable superpowers, each bent on world domination. Ignored is the most salient fact: that the struggle was between the communist totalitarianism of the Soviet Union, on the one hand, and the freedom offered by the United States, on the other. One might almost conclude from reading the standards that it would have made very little difference in terms of human freedom how the Cold War ended.[16]

It is sometimes said that the negative slant to what we are teaching now is overreaction to a too positive slant in the past, and it is true that in the past we sometimes presented celebratory history in our schools. But this explanation is of no help to students who were not around when prideful, positive stories were told, and who, day after day, are presented a drearily distorted picture of the society in which they live. Nor is this explanation complete. For those intent on political and social transformation, a bleak version of history is better than a balanced one. The grimmer the picture, the more heavily underscored is the need for the reforms they have in mind. . . .

One of the ways in which schools have changed — and for the better — is in recognizing the contributions that women have made and will continue

---

[14]Ibid., 52, 79.

[15]Ibid., 177, 268.

[16]Ibid., 270–71; Crabtree and Nash, *National Standards for United States History,* 214–15.

to make to our society. But a 1992 study sponsored by the American Association of University Women (AAUW) claimed that education reformers have ignored girls, left them on the sidelines. Entitled *How Schools Shortchange Girls*, the report concluded that schools were biased in favor of boys, though, in fact, research in this area — including research cited in the AAUW report itself — is hardly clear on this point.[17] As education historian Diane Ravitch has pointed out, when one compares the educational record of females to males, it is very hard to find evidence that girls are victims of gender bias:

> While boys get higher scores in mathematics and science, girls get higher scores in reading and writing. Boys in eighth grade are 50 percent likelier than girls to be held back a grade, and boys in high school constitute 68 percent of the "special education" population.[18]

Research done shortly after the release of the AAUW report was especially devastating to its conclusions. A 1993 survey showed that female college freshmen — recent products, most of them, of American elementary and secondary schools — have higher aspirations than male college freshmen: 27.3 percent of the women declared their intention to pursue medical, law, or doctoral degrees; 25.8 percent of male freshmen had the same ambitions. Numbers for 1994 showed an even higher percentage for women — 28.1 — and a slightly lower one for men — 25.6. These numbers represent an enormous turnaround from a quarter century ago when three times as many male as female freshmen said they intended to pursue advanced degrees.[19]

The AAUW report found textbooks to be discriminatory, a claim that   15 was repeated uncritically in many news stories about the report. But as anyone who has looked at textbooks recently is aware, they have undergone enormous change. In order to make this point, I frequently cite for audiences a study showing that 83.8 percent of seventeen-year-olds know who Harriet Tubman is — more than know that George Washington was the commander of the American army during the Revolutionary War.[20] When I use this example, the over-thirty-five-year-olds in the audience almost always look disconcerted because they haven't the least idea of who Tubman — so familiar to seventeen-year-olds — was. Their puzzlement is testimony to how much textbooks — and, as a result, school curricula — have changed.

[17]*How Schools Shortchange Girls* (Washington, D.C.: American Association of University Women, 1992).

[18]Diane Ravitch, "What Gender Bias?" *Washington Post* (21 November 1993), C7.

[19]Alexander W. Astin, William S. Korn, and Ellyne R. Riggs, *The American Freshman: National Norms for Fall 1993* (Los Angeles: Higher Education Research Institute, December 1993), 2; Alexander W. Astin et al., *The American Freshman: National Norms for Fall 1994* (Los Angeles: Higher Education Research Institute, December 1994), 48, 32.

[20]See Diane Ravitch and Chester E. Finn, Jr., *What Do Our 17-Year-Olds Know?* (New York: Harper & Row, 1987), 263.

A group of researchers at Smith College in Massachusetts analyzed three leading high school American history textbooks and found that they not only include women, but show a pro-female bias. Wrote Robert Lerner, Althea K. Nagai, and Stanley Rothman:

> Of [the figures] they do evaluate, textbooks portray 99 percent of the women positively. Only one female character is portrayed both positively and negatively; no woman is depicted in a negative light. When textbooks rate men, they also portray them positively, but only 71 percent of the time. By contrast 14 percent of the men rated mixed portrayals, while 14 percent are portrayed negatively.

The researchers also noted a pro-feminist bias. The National Organization for Woman (NOW) and the Equal Rights Amendment (ERA), for example, both received uncritical, favorable coverage. Opposition to groups like NOW and legal measures like ERA was uniformly ignored.[21]

A study of elementary school textbooks published in 1986 found:

> Not one of the many families described in these books features a homemaker — that is, referred to a woman principally dedicated to acting as a wife and mother — as a model. . . . There are countless references to mothers and other women working outside of the home in occupations such as medicine, transportation, and politics. There is not one citation indicating that the occupation of a mother or housewife represents an important job, one with integrity, one that provides real satisfactions.[22]

In light of the results of this research — indeed, in light of what any parent who opens up a recently published textbook will see for him- or herself — it is astonishing that the president of the AAUW, Jackie DeFazio, in defending her organization's report, would write, "Textbooks rarely include references to the achievements of women, and when women are included, they are generally in sex-stereotyped roles."[23] Not even the report she was defending made that claim. Its primary concern, in fact, was almost the opposite: that the women in textbooks tended to be famous; that is, they had suc-

---

[21]Robert Lerner, Althea K. Nagai, and Stanley Rothman, "Filler Feminism in High School History," *Academic Questions* (Winter 1991–1992), 31, 36–37.

[22]Paul C. Vitz, *Censorship: Evidence of Bias in Our Children's Textbooks* (Ann Arbor, Mich.: Servant Books, 1986), 38. An indignant mother in the Wallingford-Swarthmore school district of Philadelphia pointed out to me the way this theme carried over into exercises sixth-graders were asked to do in the school district in which she lived. A handout given to her son declared "the traditional nuclear family" to be a relic of the past and deservedly so since it "depended on the wife subordinating many of her individual interests to those of her husband and children." The handout further asked sixth-graders to assess who in their families was responsible for such tasks as grocery shopping, preparing meals, making major expenditures, and disciplining children. On the basis of the answers, each sixth-grader was to decide whether his or her family was "egalitarian or traditional" — and report the results to the school.

[23]Jackie DeFazio, letter to the editor, *Washington Post* (25 December 1993), A21.

ceeded by supposedly male standards, rather than being representative of "women's perspectives and cultures."[24]

In 1993, the AAUW issued a second report, this one on sexual harassment. According to *Hostile Hallways,* 81 percent of students had experienced sexual harassment in school. Some of the instances of harassment cited were quite serious: 11 percent said they had been "forced to do something sexual at school other than kissing." But others were much less so. Two-thirds said they had been harassed by "sexual comments, jokes, gestures, or looks."[25] One of the commentators to point out how expansive is the AAUW definition of sexual harassment was Albert Shanker, president of the American Federation of Teachers, who wrote:

> *Hostile Hallways* defines sexual harassment so broadly that it can be anything from being raped on the stairs to "unwelcome" words or gestures from someone you don't find attractive. . . . And the glance/ gesture/remark kind of harassment is by far the most frequently reported.

Observing that an all-inclusive definition of sexual harassment trivializes the harm done to students who suffer serious abuse, Shanker asked, "What possible benefit is it to anyone to define sexual harassment so broadly that it includes most of the kids in a school — a girl who doesn't like the way a guy looked at her as well as one who suffered several broken bones when she was attacked?"[26]

The political point of the AAUW's research became clear when a "gender equity" bill was introduced in the Congress in 1993. In 1994, many provisions of this bill were enacted into law as part of the Elementary and Secondary Education Act. Millions of dollars of federal funds were thus dedicated to the purpose of making schools more congenial places for girls — despite statistics showing that males, in fact, have at least as much if not more difficulty than females at succeeding in school.

The research efforts of the AAUW illustrate well a point made by   20 Cynthia Crossen in her book *Tainted Truth* about how postmodern thinking has affected the research enterprise. "Researchers have almost given up on the quaint notion that there is any such thing as 'fact' or 'objectivity,'" Crossen writes.[27] Instead, the point has become to amass data in order to support an agenda, in the case of the AAUW, an agenda that is moving sharply left, aligning it with organizations like the National Women's Studies Association. Vivien Ng, who as president of the NWSA expounded at

[24]*How Schools Shortchange Girls,* 62.

[25]*Hostile Hallways: The AAUW Survey on Sexual Harassment in America's Schools* (Washington, D.C.: American Association of University Women, 1993), 7, 10, 8.

[26]Albert Shanker, "Lewd or Rude?" *New Republic* (23–30 August 1993), Advertisement.

[27]Cynthia Crossen, *Tainted Truth: The Manipulation of Fact in America* (New York: Simon & Schuster, 1994), 17.

that group's 1993 convention on her love for "political work, both inside the classroom and outside it,"[28] is a member of the AAUW foundation that funded *Hostile Hallways*. The other AAUW study, *How Schools Short-change Girls*, was written in part by Peggy McIntosh, associate director of Wellesley College's Center for Research on Women, who has gained a certain measure of fame lecturing to parents and teachers across the country about how schools must stress the "lateral" thinking typical of women and minorities and deemphasize the "vertical" thinking that white males exhibit. Lateral thinking, as McIntosh defines it, aims "not to win, but to be in a decent relationship with the universe." Vertical thinking, on the other hand, is what makes "our young white males dangerous to themselves and the rest of us — especially in a nuclear age."[29]

One of the worst ideas that vertical thinking produces, according to McIntosh, is the notion of excellence. It holds "in thrall," she explains, those who think of life in terms of advancement upward.[30] Many feminists — and other political activists as well — maintain that we should do away with the idea of excellence not only on the grounds that it is oppressive but because it is an illusion. Although they usually assert this point rather than explain it, their view seems to be that since complete objectivity is impossible, any judgment about excellence is completely subjective and meaningless. That this line of thought sets up a false dichotomy (complete objectivity and complete subjectivity are not the only choices; varying degrees of each are possible) and makes all valuations thoroughly arbitrary (including those that feminists would substitute) does nothing to slow down the attack. In her book *Ed School Follies*, educator Rita Kramer tells about listening to one of the most popular professors at Columbia University's Teacher College, one of the most prestigious institutions of teacher education in the country, condemn "norms of success, effectiveness, [and] efficiency"; assert that "we have to do something about our preoccupation with rewards and competition in this country"; and declare "relativism"[31] to be "a *good* thing." "There are no 'objective standards,'" the professor tells her students, "there is no such thing as 'objective norms.'"[32]

Inspired particularly by Harvard psychologist Carol Gilligan's *In a Different Voice*, as well as by *Women's Ways of Knowing*, a collaboratively writ-

[28]Vivien Ng (Washington, D.C.: Presentation to National Women's Studies Association Annual Conference, 20 June 1993).

[29]McIntosh quoted in Robert Costrell, "The Mother of All Curriculums," *Brookline Citizen* (15 March 1991), 7.

[30]Ibid.

[31]*relativism:* The notion, frequently associated with feminist or multicultural approaches to education, that all values, beliefs, ideas, and so forth are culturally constructed and thus "true" only within a specific social, historical, or cultural context, the opposite of "absolutism" or "fundamentalism."

[32]Rita Kramer, *Ed School Follies: The Miseducation of America's Teachers* (New York: Free Press, 1991), 28–29.

ten book, many feminists have declared excellence and objectivity to be male constructs, part of a male sphere where abstract principles, intellect, rationality, and logical thinking are valued.[33] The research on which these books depend is idiosyncratic and limited. *In a Different Voice* is based on three small studies, including one of twenty-nine women considering having an abortion; *Women's Ways of Knowing* reaches its conclusions on the basis of 135 open-ended interviews. The authors of these books do not claim to offer conclusive evidence (indeed, attempting to amass the data needed to do so would, by their lights, be a decidedly masculine undertaking). But despite this and despite the fact that the theories they offer portray women in stereotypical ways that previous generations of feminists would have found highly offensive, *In a Different Voice* and *Women's Ways of Knowing* have become widely influential. Among many professional educators, the conventional wisdom is that for female students, caring, sharing, and connectedness are what matter; that for them, feelings, emotions, and intuition provide natural ways of proceeding. Schools, which have traditionally undervalued these ways of knowing, must — so the thinking goes — now bring them to the fore.

One of the first steps in achieving this transformation is to do away with situations that create hierarchies, thus elevating some at the expense of others. Grades do this, of course, and one of the trends of our time at all levels of education has been to do away with meaningful grading:

- According to research reported by Randy Moore, editor of the *American Biology Teacher,* high school teachers gave twice as many C's as A's in 1966. By 1978, the ratio had changed dramatically, with the number of A's given exceeding the number of C's. By 1990, 20 percent of entering college students reported an A average for their entire high school career.[34]
- According to a survey conducted by the Higher Education Research Institute at the University of California at Los Angeles, in the fall of 1994, 28.1 percent of college freshmen reported average high school grades of A- or higher.[35]

The same phenomenon has occurred in higher education. At Stanford, over 70 percent of undergraduates get A's and B's; at Princeton, the number is 80 percent.[36] According to Harvard instructor William Cole, the "gentle-

[33]Carol Gilligan, *In a Different Voice: Psychological Theory and Women's Development* (Cambridge: Harvard University Press, 1982); Mary Field Belenky et al., *Women's Ways of Knowing: The Development of Self, Voice, and Mind* (New York: Basic Books, 1986).

[34]Randy Moore, "Grades and Self-Esteem," *American Biology Teacher* (October 1993), 388.

[35]Astin et al., *The American Freshman* (1994), 13.

[36]Suzanne Alexander, "Trophy Transcript Hunters Are Finding Professors Have Become an Easy Mark," *Wall Street Journal* (27 April 1993), B1; Committee on Academic Appraisal and Achievement, "A Study of Grading Practices at Stanford University: Faculty Attitudes, Student Concerns, and Proposed Changes to Grading Policy" (Stanford, Calif.: Stanford University, April 1994), figure 3.

man's C" has been replaced at his school by the "'gentleperson's B,' and A- is gaining ground fast, especially in the humanities."[37]

Grade inflation is certainly not the accomplishment of feminists alone, but they have contributed mightily to the notion that the world in general and schools in particular have for too long been run according to standards that have no justification except to advance the interests of white males. "Relativism is the key word today," explains Harvard's Cole. "There's a general conception in the literary-academic world that holding things to high standards — like logic, argument, having an interesting thesis — is patriarchal, Eurocentric and conservative."[38] So out of fashion has meaningful grading become that the *New York Times* declared Stanford University's 1994 decision to reinstitute the grade of F "an event of seismic proportions."[39]

One also senses the radical egalitarianism espoused by many feminists 25 in the movement to do away with other kinds of competition in the schools. In a section of *How Schools Shortchange Girls* that Peggy McIntosh helped write, current events and civics curricula are condemned for their tendency to focus on "controversy and conflict." Debate clubs are said to be harmful since they take for granted an "adversarial, win/lose orientation."[40] Other examples of this kind of thinking abound:

- According to an article in the *New York Times,* physical education is no longer what it used to be: "[In] the new P.E. . . . competition is out and cooperation is in." In every part of the country, schoolchildren are dancing and jumping rope, activities that do not involve competition, instead of playing games like dodgeball, from which a winner emerges.[41]

- A mother in Michigan reports to Ann Landers that her child's school no longer has spelling bees because they are regarded as unfair to children who are not good spellers.[42]

- The president of the Independent Schools Association of the Central States reports that the Illinois Junior Academy of Science prohibited a small independent school in Downers Grove, Illinois, from competing in the 1995 State Science Fair. The Downers Grove

---

[37]William Cole, "By Rewarding Mediocrity We Discourage Excellence," *Chronicle of Higher Education* (6 January 1993), B1.

[38]Quoted in John Leo, "A for Effort. Or for Showing Up," *U.S. News & World Report* (18 October 1993), 22.

[39]"Making the Grades," *New York Times* (5 June 1994), Sec. 4, p. 16.

[40]*How Schools Shortchange Girls,* 66.

[41]Melinda Henneberger, "New Gym Class: No More Choosing Up Sides," *New York Times* (16 May 1993), A1.

[42]Ann Landers, "Part of Me Will Always Be Missing," *Chicago Tribune* (17 January 1994), Tempo section, 3.

school, which makes a point of encouraging excellence, puts other schools at too much of a disadvantage, an Academy of Science official said: "We want to spread the wealth around."[43]

- Meanwhile, the executive director of the Maryland Coalition for Inclusive Education argues that honor rolls should be abolished. They rely on "objective" cutoff points, he complains, and reinforce "some of the least attractive aspects of our culture."[44]

Meritocracy in general has come under assault in the schools. A few years ago in the *Harvard Educational Review,* there appeared an article that has become something of a classic in the annals of educational egalitarianism. Entitled *"Tootle:* A Parable of Schooling and Destiny," the article warned about the lesson implicit in the Little Golden Book story *Tootle.* The story is about a talented young train who, after going through a period in which he breaks the first rule of trainhood and repeatedly jumps the tracks in order to wander through the meadows, learns that success, in the words of the *Harvard Educational Review* article, comes from "deferred gratification, hard work, and an achievement orientation." While one might think these good lessons to teach children, they are, according to the *Harvard Educational Review* article, part of the repressive "masculine world of technology [and] competition" to which Tootle's "sensitive, emotional, and relational qualities . . . must give way."[45]

Although this heavyhanded analysis of a simple story reads like a parody, it has been taken quite seriously. In her book *Ed School Follies,* Rita Kramer reports on a class for future teachers at Eastern Michigan University in which the professor assigns the *Harvard Educational Review* article. An older woman in the class is skeptical about the analysis it offers. "What would a six-year-old get out of [the story of Tootle]?" she asks. "I read it to my kid. 'Work hard in school' — isn't that what we all want?"

The teacher pounces on her question. "What does that sound like? Anyone?"

A young woman named Amy — the star of the class, according to Kramer — knows exactly what mistaken notion the older student is advancing: "Meritocracy! And if it doesn't work, if you don't succeed, you think, What's wrong with me?"[46]

---

[43]Quoted in Patrick F. Bassett, "The Academy of (Lesser) Science," *Education Week* (3 August 1994), 51.

[44]Mark A. Mlawer, " 'My Kid Beat Up Your Honor Student,' " *Education Week* (13 July 1994), 39.

[45]Nicholas C. Burbules, *"Tootle:* A Parable of Schooling and Destiny," *Harvard Educational Review* (August 1986), 253, 250.

[46]Quoted in Kramer, *Ed School Follies,* 95.

ENGAGING THE TEXT

1. Working in small groups, discuss the threat that Cheney sees in multicultural approaches to education. To what extent does your own experience in American classrooms support or complicate Cheney's claim that multiculturalism presents "a drearily distorted picture of [American] society" (para. 13)? Do you agree that non-Western cultures are typically glorified in American classrooms today at the expense of American and European achievements?

2. Write a journal entry on your own experience in science classes. How accurate are Cheney's claims that American education "overlooks" the achievements of U.S. scientists and that students are taught to view science as an example of "destructive male thinking" (para. 8)?

3. Drawing on your own experiences, debate whether American schools and textbooks are overly influenced by a pro-female or feminist bias. To what extent has concern for promoting "female" behavioral and thinking styles been responsible for undermining the idea of excellence or the desire to compete and achieve in America's schools?

EXPLORING CONNECTIONS

4. Contrast Cheney's interpretation of the position of women in education with that presented by Deborah Tannen (p. 233). Which of these analyses strikes you as more accurate? What specific aspects of each argument seem particularly persuasive or particularly weak?

5. Write an imaginary letter of response to Cheney from Mike Rose (p. 162), Richard Rodriguez (p. 194), Inés Hernández-Ávila (p. 207), or Malcolm X (p. 223). How might they react to her assessment of multicultural education and its impact on American students?

6. How might John Taylor Gatto (p. 152) or Jean Anyon (p. 174) respond to the idea that "politics" has only recently entered American classrooms through the inclusion of multicultural and feminist perspectives?

EXTENDING THE CRITICAL CONTEXT

7. Working in small groups, research the way women and women's achievements are portrayed in a number of recent secondary school textbooks. Based on your findings, what conclusions can you reach about gender bias in textbooks?

8. Design a brief survey to test several of Cheney's claims (for example, her assertion that Americans know more about Harriet Tubman than George Washington or that Christopher Columbus is portrayed in American schoolrooms as a greedy murderer). Then administer your survey to a number of people who come from different age groups. To what extent do their responses sustain Cheney's depiction of what's happening in America's classrooms?

"Please don't give him any ideas."

Empowering Children in the Digital Age: Towards a Radical Media Pedagogy

HENRY JENKINS

An unsuspecting ten-year-old surfing the Net for information about the Presidency might logically run a search for the "White House," but if she did, she could easily find herself logging on to the home page of one of the Web's busiest purveyors of pornography. Do children need to be protected from the free speech of adults on the Internet? What role should our schools play in preparing children to cope with a world dominated by the mass media? Self-described radical teacher Henry Jenkins thinks that media studies shouldn't merely be included in the curriculum — it should be the heart and soul of American education. Jenkins is director of Comparative Media Studies at the Massachusetts Institute of Technology. His ideas about media literacy originally appeared in Radical Teacher 50 *(1998).*

The glowing light casts sinister shadows across his face. He looks at us with entranced eyes from the cover of the July 3, 1995, *Time* magazine (Elmer-Dewitt). His hands clutch the computer keyboard with anticipation. This blond-haired, blue-eyed, white-skinned, and male child was presented to us as the "victim" of an "epidemic" of "cyberporn." His parents felt powerless to protect him from the corrupting influence of new media. *Time* made him the embodiment of "childhood innocence," his purity to be preserved "at all costs." As one letter writer acknowledged, "if we lose our kids to cyberporn, free speech won't matter" (*Time,* July 24, 1995).

Time's cover story, reporting the results of a Carnegie Mellon study of Internet content, added new fuel to Senator James Exon's attempts to pass what became the Communications Decency Act, a cornerstone of the conservative "family values" agenda. The Carnegie Mellon study turned out to be an undergraduate term paper of dubious methodology and unreliable results; the Rimm "report" was published in a prestigious academic journal without peer review under political pressure from antiporn activists (including Andrea Dworkin[1]) and there attracted national media coverage. Carnegie Mellon University distanced itself from the study. *Time* publicly retracted its story. But, the ghostly visage of the child did not go away, haunting the many congressmen and senators who voted to pass the Communications Decency Act.

The Communications Decency Act is a particularly noxious bit of legislation empowering the state to prosecute anyone who digitally distributes "indecent" materials; one provision of the act specifically prohibits online discussion of birth control or abortion, adopting language originally introduced by Anthony Comstock in his campaign against Margaret Sanger.[2] The act was signed into law by Bill Clinton last spring and currently faces numerous court challenges. If sustained, it threatens the Net's potential as a tool for democratic participation, grass-roots activism, and public outreach. At a time when growing numbers of gay, lesbian, and bisexual teenagers are committing suicide (Sedgwick, 1993) and when local, state, and national governments are restricting teachers' abilities to respond to this crisis, the Net has offered many queer youths a lifeline — a safe space to communicate anonymously with each other, to seek out relevant information, and to develop the secure knowledge that they are not alone. The Communications Decency Act could subject such frank sexual conversation to severe penalties. Such restrictions are only one of many ways in which the act will silence children and youths, isolating them from each other and from information they need to function (Cherny and Weise, 1996).

Our goals . . . should be to find ways to expand, rather than cut off, access to the Net. Many [teachers] are struggling to overcome economic bar-

[1]*Andrea Dworkin:* Feminist activist and critic (b. 1946).

[2]*Anthony Comstock . . . Margaret Sanger:* Comstock (1844–1915) was an early crusader for restricting the circulation of contraceptives and information on the sexual rights of women; Sanger (1883–1966) was his contemporary and a proponent of birth control.

riers and declining literacy rates which block poor and inner-city children from participating in the new "online" communities. The "electronic republic," many believe, will be the locus of political power in the coming decade, further exaggerating the gap between the haves and the have-nots within our society (Grossman, 1995). We need to struggle now to insure full enfranchisement for all of America's citizens by building computer stations at community centers and public libraries, a far wiser solution than Newt Gingrich's flippant "Let Them Eat Chips" plan to provide tax deductions for the poor to buy laptops for their children.

At the same time, we should be using our influence to question the commercialization and commodification of cyberspace. For decades, the left has complained about the centralization of mass communications in the hands of a smaller and smaller number of multinational corporations. Now that we have a profoundly decentralized communications system which allows no one agency (corporate or state) to function as a gatekeeper, appeals to "childhood innocence" are being mobilized to build public support for shutting down that open channel.

Many radicals have their own concerns about the openness of this communication, worried that the militias, the skinheads, and other "hate" groups are using the Net to captivate our children. The seductiveness of a rhetoric of "childhood innocence" is that it can articulate the fears of the left and the right. We all want to protect our children. Yet, in giving public support to the myth of "childhood innocence," we find ourselves incapable of responding adequately when the right uses this same argument to reject progressive classroom materials (notably multicultural and queer positive) or to fire gay and lesbian educators. After all, the right is quick to remind us, "innocent" children must be protected *at all costs!*

The myth of "childhood innocence" "empties" children of any thoughts of their own, stripping them of their own political agency and social agendas so that they may become vehicles for adult needs, desires, and politics (Kincaid, 1992). The "innocent" child is an increasingly dangerous abstraction when it starts to substitute in our thinking for actual children or when it helps justify efforts to restrict real children's minds and to regulate their bodies. The myth of "childhood innocence," which sees children only as potential victims of the adult world or as beneficiaries of paternalistic protection, opposes pedagogies that empower children as active agents in the educational process. We cannot teach children how to engage in critical thought by denying them access to challenging information or provocative images.

Adopting this position, Jon Katz (1996) has argued for children's "cyber-rights," claiming that kids' access to the Net technology and other forms of popular culture is central to their political participation within American society. As he puts it, such media literacy "may mean the difference between economic well-being and economic hardship." The Net, Katz argues, promises children unfettered participation in public discourse, for better or for worse, and meaningful access to information (including ideas which grown-ups on either the right or the left would prefer they didn't confront).

If we, as politically committed teachers and parents, want to meaningfully participate in this new struggle for children's political rights, we must first divest ourselves of our clinging myths about "childhood innocence" and the passivity of children's media consumption. Instead, we need a more sophisticated model for thinking about the interactions between children and popular culture. What I hope to do in this essay is to outline the growing body of research into children's culture and its potential pedagogical and political implications. I will end with a call for a new kind of radical media education based on the assumption that children are active participants within popular culture rather than passive victims. We need to help our children become more critically reflective about the media they use and the popular culture they embrace, yet we can only achieve this by recognizing and respecting their existing investments, skills, and knowledge as media users. In the end, our goals must be not to protect our children but to empower them.

Part One: The Hidden Political Baggage of Childhood Innocence

For more than a century, the dominant paradigm of media reform and education has described our relationships to popular culture through metaphors of addiction, intoxication, seduction, or mind control. In the early 1900s, reformers focused on joke books and comic strips as the root cause of children's "lawlessness" and disrespect for authority. Comics were blamed for "overstimulating" children's nervous systems, causing potential health and psychological damage, resulting in nightmares and violent tendencies. Despite differences between media, their institutional status, consumption practices, content, or the larger political climate, most of these arguments surface in contemporary campaigns against video games or television programs (West, 1988). The culture industry has been consistently represented as an evil seducer and merciless exploiter of children. Television, "the plug-in drug," is often depicted as an inherently dangerous and pacifying technology, competing with rather than contributing to education and family life (Winn, 1987). The reform literature (Mander, 1978; Postman, 1985; Minnow, 1995) spends a great deal of time worrying about the potential effects of media upon children's impressionable minds yet far less time thinking about what pleasures or desires motivate media consumption or what uses children make of media content. The Communications Decency Act and the V-chip are simply the latest versions of a longstanding campaign for the abolishment of media or the refusal to participate within popular culture: "Just say No to Nintendo!"

As with most other reform movements, such campaigns depend on the construction of "victims" who are powerless to shape their own fate and incapable of speaking in their own defense. Children have been the ultimate "victim" in whose name a broad range of political struggles, progressive and reactionary, have been waged. Within reform rhetoric, childhood is presented as timeless, outside history and culture. At the same time, childhood must always be represented as under threat, on the verge of irreparable harm, as when writers like Neil Postman (1982) warn of the impending "disappearance of childhood." In fact, there has been no point in the twentieth century when childhood was not seen as being under threat from one manifestation or another of mass culture (comic strips, joke books, pulp fiction, radio, comic books, rock music, television, video games, etc.), and no time in which it was not possible to look back upon the previous decade as a simpler, purer, more wholesome time to be a child. History offers a different picture of American childhood, with many of these "good old days" being characterized by child labor, poverty, racial inequality, sexual inequality, etc., which prevented most of America's children from enjoying the "wholesome" lifestyles so fondly recalled by reformers.

The "demonization" of media displaces serious public examination of the material conditions that more concretely impact upon children's lives. The same week that Congress voted to end federal guarantees of financial assistance to poor children, the same week that Republicans were advocating ending educational rights for the children of illegal aliens, the headlines of many newspapers featured Bob Dole's[3] critiques of violence in Hollywood films and Bill Clinton's White House conference with the producers of children's television. Dole and Clinton wanted to show us their "concern" for kids. Here, the goal is to displace the "special interests" of the underclass into "generic" problems "shared" with the middle class.

As Jacqueline Rose (1984) notes, the innocent child is a universalized child, existing outside of the contradictions and pressures of gender, sexuality, race, and class. In the postwar period, the most persistent image of the child is that of a tow-haired boy in a striped shirt, with his whiteness, his suburban middle-classness, and his boyness read as standing for all children. (The child on the cover of *Time* was a modern reincarnation of this figure.) The "whiteness" of our dominant image of the innocent child should cause us to pause. What this myth does is normalize white suburban middle-class experience as the ideal against which other forms of family life get judged, often giving rise to racist and classist charges against "inappropriate" parents and "unsupervised" children (Nandy, 1987). Often, reformers march into battle not to protect their own (mostly middle-class) children, who are assumed to have a proper upbringing, but to protect the children of the underclass, who are assumed to not know how best to look

---

[3]*Bob Dole:* Robert Dole (b. 1923), former U.S. senator and Republican candidate for the presidency in 1996.

after their interests or, implicitly, to protect middle-class kids from contaminating contact with the "unwashed."

Although reform rhetoric often universalizes its concept of childhood innocence, it originates in a specific historical context. While aspects of a concept of childhood innocence can be traced back to Rousseau and Locke[4] (Kline, 1993; Aries, 1962), recent historians argue that its modern manifestation arose in response to the shift from an agrarian and craft-based economy toward an industrialized economy (Zelizer, 1985). No longer a source of productive labor within domestic production, the child became an economic liability for the poor or a means of conspicuous consumption for middle-class families. A new sentimentality now sees children's value in emotional terms, pointing to children as the hope for the future and the vehicle of social transformation. The declining infant mortality allowed parents to make greater emotional investments in individual children. As many childhood diseases were defeated, medical concerns gave way to psychological ones, resulting in an increased pathologization of mass culture as a potential source of trauma or as a negative influence on children's moral development.

At the same time, this sentimental conception of childhood played an important role in defining gender relations (Spigel, 1993). On the one hand, the sentimentalization of the child justified women's domestication, ennobling motherhood as women's divine destiny. On the other hand, early feminist thinkers evoked this responsibility to protect the child to justify their increased political activity in the public sphere. Today, increased attacks on media violence and the use of television as "an electronic babysitter" still put tremendous pressure on working mothers to return to the home.

Governed by myths of childhood innocence, much contemporary media education emphasizes media's dangers and not its potentials, treating children as "videots" (to use a term preferred by my son's sixth-grade teacher) incapable of making their own meaningful judgments about the media. Such an approach closes the schoolhouse gates to the ideas and images children most value (i.e., those they acquire living and interacting with popular culture). A knee-jerk dismissal of popular culture at school teaches youngsters that what they learn in the rest of their lives has no value in the classroom (Hodge and Tripp, 1986). Of course, at the same time, children are learning that what they learn in the classroom has no relevance to what happens once the school bell rings.

Radical media education should start by mobilizing what students already know about and through the media, helping them refine their interpretive skills and challenging them to think through the race, gender, and class implications of conventional narratives. We need to respect children's

---

[4]*Rousseau and Locke:* Jean-Jacques Rousseau (1712–1778) and John Locke (1632–1704) were philosophers who speculated about the nature of children and their relationship to society.

own tastes and cultural choices. This does not mean we are required to remain silent about the misogyny, racism, class bias, homophobia, and other ideologies which run through contemporary children's culture. Quite the contrary, we should help our children to recognize the incompleteness of commercial representations and to fill those gaps with their own creative output. We should train students to talk back to the media, rather than try to isolate them from it. This does not mean we should remain silent about the control corporate capitalism has gained over communication. Rather, we should teach children at an early age to recognize the commercial motives behind the production and circulation of popular culture and to identify their own interests as distinct from those of media producers.

Part Two: Children as Active Media Consumers

Media reformers often tell us to return to the "timeless children's classics" as substitutes for degraded kidvid. If we look there, we can, actually, learn something. With that end, I propose taking a fresh look at L. M. Montgomery's *Anne of Green Gables* (1908), a book that offers a more dynamic picture of children at play with their culture than is found in most reform literature, a book that preserves a strong sense of children's social agency. Anne has been learning at school the tales of King Arthur and the Lily Maid, so she gets the idea of enacting the story with her playmates. "They had analyzed and parsed it and torn it to pieces in general until it was a wonder there was any meaning at all left in it for them, but at last the fair lily maid and Lancelot and Guinevere and King Arthur had become very real people to them." Anne proceeds to distribute roles and gather the necessary props, a black shawl borrowed from one girl's mother and an abandoned raft upon which Elaine could float. One girl raises an objection: "Do you suppose it's really right to act like this? Mrs. Lynde says that all playacting is abominably wicked." And Anne quickly responds, "Ruby, you shouldn't talk about Mrs. Lynde. It spoils the effect because this is hundreds of years before Mrs. Lynde was born." Anne's story is consistent with historical accounts of children's play during the nineteenth century (Formanek-Brunnel, 1993). Anne's story also illustrates many conclusions being drawn by media ethnographers who have looked at contemporary children's cultural consumption. I offer Anne's story less as a countermyth to the prevailing ideology of childhood innocence than as a composite picture illustrating what we have learned about children as readers and creative participants in popular culture, recognizing that a key part of what we have learned is that no one child can be seen as "typical" of American childhood.

First, the social context(s) within which children encounter popular narratives matter. In Montgomery's novel, it is important that the children learned the Arthurian legends in school, and that, as Montgomery stressed, the characters maintained vitality and relevance despite rather heavy-handed instruction. It also matters that there is such an extraordinary gap between Camelot and the rural Canada of Green Gables, and that the children must draw on their imagination to negotiate that gap. This story suggests the need to be attentive to the different social contexts where children encounter popular stories and to how such cultural materials feed into their other social interactions. (Children don't watch television in the same way in research labs as they do at their friend's house, and a new focus on social contexts of viewing makes us suspicious of the findings of empirical researchers, who are often closely aligned with media reform organizations.) It should also matter that children bring to popular culture the resources and restrictions imposed upon them through their varied class, race, gender, and other cultural backgrounds which shape the meanings they make from media materials and how those meanings feed back into their lives. Most research on media consumption — both traditional empirical research and the new ethnographic studies — has centered on white suburban children; we need more studies which examine the role that racial and class differences play in shaping children's interactions with mass culture.

And that brings us to the second point. Anne's relationship to the text is [20] imaginative and transforming. She translates what she reads into other kinds of activities. Shelby Anne Wolf and Shirley Brice Heath (1992) offer a similar picture in their detailed study of two young girls as readers. Wolf and Heath offer numerous examples of how children actively appropriate the contents and concepts of a favorite story, using it as a basis for home theatrics, artworks, and creative writing, a resource for making jokes or explaining their own real-world situations, and a tool for understanding other stories. Ethnographic accounts of children's media consumption or play consistently record similar creative reworking of television content, be it my account of kindergartners puzzling over Pee-Wee Herman's[5] ambiguous status as adult/child to make sense of their shift from the home to more institutionalized school environments (Jenkins, 1993), or Erica Rand's analysis (1995) of how young girls' play with Barbies allows them to rewrite and rethink dominant social narratives about gender and sexuality (see also Thorne, 1993; Palmer, 1986). Raised in an environment pervaded by pop cultural icons, children become adept at "playing" with those materials, exploring hidden possibilities and inverting their meanings. Teachers often look upon all play and conversation surrounding television content as evidence of the media's colonization of children's minds; rather, we should examine how media content gets transformed (or fails to be transformed) through its incorporation into children's cultures on the playground and in the housing projects.

Third, for Anne, reading is a social act rather than an isolated one. Her reading pleasures form the basis of her interactions with her friends. And the same is clearly the case for contemporary children. Competency in tele-

---

[5]*Pee-Wee Herman:* Pseudonym of actor Paul Rubens, star of the popular 1980s children's show *Pee-Wee's Playhouse.*

vision content facilitates participation within peer culture. Children do not simply watch television in silence, they talk about it. Through the television-related talk, the program's meanings become their meanings. They imagine and share stories which go against generic constraints or norms of propriety on television. Children at an early age know how to distinguish fiction from reality and commercials from programs, responding to advertising pitches with a healthy degree of skepticism — if not always, at least some of the time. Nobody is totally outside dominant ideology, but by the same token, none of us lives totally under its sway. The day-to-day struggle against and within ideology is as much a reality for our children as it is for us.

Fourth, Anne's play with the text occurs outside adult supervision and in direct defiance of it. Anne rejected the notion that adult rules have any place in the realm of her imagination, and part of her pleasure was undoubtedly bound up in the desire to take classroom materials and make them part of her own culture — on her own terms. E. Arthur Rotundo (1993) examines nineteenth-century "boy culture" as a space away from maternal supervision and domestic constraints, while Miriam Formanek-Brunnel (1993) finds girls' dollplay during this same period as actively resisting maternal guidance toward "true womanhood." Modern children's cultures often define themselves in opposition to parental restraint, inverting adult values or transgressing our taste hierarchies (James, 1995). Children may need an unpoliced arena of popular culture if they are going to develop autonomy from their parents and learn to think for themselves.

If traditional media, such as television, comic books, and films, can spark this kind of creative and social interaction, the potentials of new media technologies are even greater. The term "interactivity" has quickly been co-opted by marketeers for their own commercial ends. Its widespread appeal speaks to a popular desire for media we can actively reshape to reflect our own life experiences, desires, and agendas. Children are seizing the imaginative and participatory potential of the digital realm to play with their social identities (Turkle, 1995). On line, children form communities and alliances extending beyond physical restrictions on their mobility. In many parts of the country, projects link black and white children of various class backgrounds so that they can communicate about their lives. For the first time, children have access to a means of mass communication not firmly policed by adult gatekeepers, where their age (often unknown to those reading their words) is not a barrier to being taken seriously.

Part Three: Transforming Turtles into Freedom Fighters

What I hope has emerged from this discussion is a more complex account of children's media consumption as active and reactive rather than passive and addictive, as significant and meaningful to children rather than trivial and meaningless, as social rather than isolated, and as already linked to children's emerging political identities. This more complex and nuanced account of children as media consumers does not make the issue of media content disappear. Far from it. It matters which stories form the basis of children's imaginative life. If we are going to frame a meaningful political response to media content, we need to tap into children's dynamic, creative, parodic, and sometimes resistant impulses, to incite them to play with the materials of their culture and reshape them to better reflect the diversity of their lives.

Media education needs to be integrated into the schooling process 25 from kindergarten through college, not as an occasional "special treat" activity, a break from the real business of learning, but as a set of knowledges and skills central to all of the subjects we teach. Media education needs to be taught as part of what it means to write and communicate in the modern era; as a basic citizenship skill; as part of the consumer-oriented math; as central to our understanding of contemporary expression, including art and storytelling; and as a fundamental aspect of race, gender, sexuality, and class studies. Such teaching should encourage students to think independently and critically about the pleasures and politics of media consumption, to reflect on what stories get told and what stories don't get told through commercial entertainment, and to begin to imagine how those media materials can be used in a more principled and democratic fashion. Children at an early age can articulate the differences between representation and reality; media education should help them to understand more fully why those differences matter.

Young video-game players need to be asked why Princess Toadstool is always being rescued by the Mario Brothers and then encouraged to make up stories where the reverse occurs or where the princess and the brothers work together. Young fans need to ask why the black sidekicks are always the first to die or why there are so few working-class characters on television. They need to be encouraged to create a better children's culture, one that includes room for all of them to participate, and one that enables them to speak out against the injustices and inequalities they see around them. Television's version of the American family is extraordinarily narrow, not conforming well to the lives of many of our students. As classroom teachers, we can draw on the contrast between media images and lived experiences to open up discussion and to generate creative reworkings of television content.

As recent studies of media fan cultures suggest, many adults find writing original stories about media characters and situations a useful way of asking questions about gender roles and of proposing alternative understandings of masculinity and femininity (Jenkins, 1992; Bacon-Smith, 1992; Penley, 1991). We need to be helping children to develop these same skills of critical rewriting and cultural appropriation. Such approaches do not "destroy the pleasure" of participating in popular culture; rather, they open up a range of alternative pleasures which confront racism, homophobia, and misogyny on different terms. Stories based on media content can be circulated, shared, and exchanged with other communities of children of different class or racial backgrounds via the Internet. Exchanging stories about popular fictional characters and situations can allow children to compare notes about their lives, their politics, and their fantasies. Here, we can tap into the powerful marketing of popular culture to provide a "common framework" of shared cultural reference points to facilitate communication across other kinds of cultural difference.

Many of the core myths of popular culture have their roots in movements of popular resistance (Zipes, 1979; Zipes, 1991). We need to restore those more "radicalizing" elements to contemporary superhero stories so that the Ninja Turtles,[6] like Robin Hood before them, will fight to build a better world rather than simply defend property rights. Such instruction should not consist of forcing our own stories and interests onto children's imaginative play. Rather, instructors should recognize and foster the radical potential of children's own fantasy lives and build on those fantasies, by providing additional stories and historical background. At the same time, our students come from diverse ethnic backgrounds and can draw on alternative cultural traditions that may further enrich our attempts to rewrite and re-contextualize popular narratives. Children's play is not always progressive; often, it can be brutally reactionary. However, children use their play to explore the social structures that surround them; sites of play represent places where students are questioning the nature of reality. If we want to participate meaningfully in that playful resistance, we need to give them new models for thinking about the world.

As children grow older, we need to encourage their participation within the Net community, using it as an arena to teach them about social justice, democracy, and mutual respect, helping them find their own voice and express their own thoughts. A new breed of media-savvy activists and educators are designing models for children's communities on the Net and developing techniques for collaborative teaching and learning that take advantage of the educational potentials of the Web (Clai, 1996).

The Net is no utopia. As we move on line, we are going to confront   30
there, in slightly different forms, all of the problems that block meaningful communication in the "Real World." Old issues about "Black English" are forcefully raised as oral-based urban cultures confront the challenges posed by this text-based genre and get "flamed" for their "poor communication." For many, written language has been used as a weapon to hold them in place — the language of the workplace and the schoolroom. For many, written English has not been a natural means of communicating among social equals. No technical fix is going to open the online realm to oral-based communication. We need to discuss with our students the social

---

[6]*Ninja Turtles:* Turtle superheros made popular in comic books and feature films in the late 1980s and early 1990s.

consequences of bringing together oral-based and written-based cultures. Women face sexual harassment on line that deters many from fully participating in this world and need to know basic "survival skills" for holding their own in such hostile contexts.

Arguments for children's "cyber-rights" depend upon teaching children how to use the media responsibly, how to use language in a constructive rather than hurtful way, how to critically judge the content of messages they receive and how to protect themselves against unwanted attention from strangers (Katz, 1996). When they are comfortable with the technology, children often do their best writing in the digital realm, developing there a self-confidence and a personal expression that rarely surface in class papers; educators must help students value the writing they do on line as part of what it means to be socially committed communicators.

Such education can best occur in a climate of collaboration rather than conflict, one where children are respected as already skilled and knowledgeable media users, and one where they are encouraged to see themselves as participants in the creation of a new and more democratic popular culture through creative reworking and appropriation. The stakes are too high for us to fall back onto the simplifying mythology of childhood innocence. Cyberspace is the new public sphere; we must be doing our part to empower children for full participation there. What they do not need from us as educators is a knee-jerk dismissal of popular culture as debased or contaminated. "Just say no to Nintendo!" is every bit as simplistic a response to the modern media age as "just say no to drugs" is to the social conditions which give rise to drug abuse and despair. What they need from us are the critical tools that can allow them to fight back and reclaim room for themselves in the discursive space opened up by the new media.

Note

This essay is dedicated to Louis Kampf upon his retirement from the Literature faculty at MIT in recognition of his inspiration to my work and his lifelong commitment to teaching students to critically and creatively engage with popular culture.

References

Aries, Phillipe (1962). *Centuries of Childhood: A Social History of Family Life*. New York: Vintage.

Cherny, Lynn, and Elizabeth Reba Weise, eds. (1996). *Wired Women: Gender and New Realities in Cyberspace*. Seattle: Seal Press.

Elmer-Dewitt, Philip (1995). "On a Screen Near You: Cyberporn." *Time*, 2 July 1995: 38–45.

Formanek-Brunnel, Miriam (1993). *Made to Play House: Dolls and the Commercialization of American Girlhood, 1830–1930*. New Haven: Yale University Press.

Grossman, Lawrence K. (1995). *The Electronic Republic: Reshaping Democracy in the Information Age.* New York: Viking.

Hodge, Robert, and David Tripp (1986). *Children and Television.* Stanford, CA: Stanford University Press.

James, Alison (1996). *Childhood Conceptions.* New York: Columbia University Press.

Jenkins, Henry. "Going Bonkers!: Children, Play, and Pee-Wee." In Constance Penley and Sharon Willis, eds. *Male Trouble.* Minneapolis: University of Minnesota Press.

Katz, Jon (1996). "The Rights of Kids in the Digital Age." *Wired.* July 1996: 120ff.

Kincaid, James R. (1992). *Child-loving: The Erotic Child and Victorian Culture.* New York: Routledge.

Kinder, Marsha (1991). *Playing with Power in the Movies, TV, and Videogames.* Berkeley: University of California Press.

Kline, Stephen (1993). *Out of the Garden: Toys and Children's Culture in the Age of TV Marketing.* London: Verso.

Levy, Steven (1995). "No Place For Kids?: A Parent's Guide to Sex on the Net." *Newsweek.* 3 July 1995: 47–51.

Mander, Jerry (1978). *Four Arguments for the Elimination of Television.* New York: Morrow.

Minnow, Newton (1995). *Abandoned in the Wasteland.* New York: Hill and Wang.

Montgomery, J. M. (1902). *Anne of Green Gables.* New York: Random House.

Nandy, Ashis (1987). "Reconstructing Childhood: A Critique of the Ideology of Adulthood." In *Traditions, Tyranny, and Utopias: Essays in the Politics of Awareness.* Delhi: Oxford University Press.

Palmer, Patricia (1986). *The Lively Audience: A Study of Children Around the TV Set.* Sydney: Allen and Unwyn.

Postman, Neil (1982). *The Disappearance of Childhood.* New York: Delacorte.

Postman, Neil (1985). *Amusing Ourselves to Death.* New York: Viking.

Rand, Erica (1995). *Barbie's Queer Accessories.* Durham: Duke University Press.

Rose, Jacqueline (1984). *The Case of Peter Pan: The Impossibility of Children's Fiction.* London: Macmillan.

Rotundo, E. Anthony (1993). *American Manhood: Transformations in Masculinity from the Revolution to the Modern Era.* New York: Basic.

Sedgwick, Eve. "How to Bring Your Kids Up Gay." In Michael Warner, ed. *Fear of a Queer Planet: Queer Politics and Social Theory.* Minneapolis: University of Minnesota Press.

Seiter, Ellen (1993). *Sold Separately: Parents and Children in Consumer Culture.* Berkeley: University of California Press.

Spigel, Lynn (1993). "Seducing the Innocent: Childhood and Television in Postwar America." In William S. Solomon and Robert W. McChesney, eds. *Ruthless Criticism: New Perspectives in U.S. Communications History*. Minneapolis: University of Minnesota Press.

Thorne, Barrie (1993). *Gender Play: Girls and Boys in School*. New Brunswick, NJ: Rutgers University Press.

Turkle, Sherry (1995). *Life on the Screen: Identity in the Age of the Internet*. New York: Simon and Schuster.

West, Mark I. (1988). *Children, Culture, and Controversy*. Hamden, CT: Archon.

Winn, Marie (1987). *Unplugging the Plug-In Drug*. New York: Penguin.

Wolf, Shelby Anne, and Shirley Brice Heath (1992). *The Braid of Literature: Children's Worlds of Reading*. Cambridge, MA: Harvard University Press.

Zelizer, Viviana A. (1985). *Pricing the Priceless Child: The Changing Social Value of Children*. Princeton, NJ: Princeton University Press.

Zipes, Jack (1979). *Breaking the Magic Spell: Radical Theories of Folk and Fairy Tales*. Austin: University of Texas Press.

Zipes, Jack (1986). *Don't Bet on the Prince: Contemporary Feminist Fairy Tales in North America and England*. New York: Methuen.

ENGAGING THE TEXT

1. Briefly summarize the history of "childhood innocence" that Jenkins offers as part of his criticism of the concept. Why does he claim that the idea of childhood innocence is a "dangerous abstraction"?

2. What alternative image of the child does Jenkins offer in relation to mass media? How does this model of the child contrast with the image of childhood innocence that, Jenkins claims, dominates the discourse of media critics? Why does he prefer this alternative image of children?

3. What would Jenkins's "radical" approach to media education offer students? Why does he see it as preferable to media censorship?

4. While Jenkins acknowledges that children at play can often be "brutally reactionary" (para. 28), he clearly assumes that children also generally have the ability to think clearly and critically about media programming. To what extent do you think his proposed approach to media education is based on an accurate assessment of children and their abilities?

EXPLORING CONNECTIONS

5. Reread the history of the American family offered in E. J. Graff's "What Makes a Family?" (p. 26). What does Graff's overview of family life suggest about the notion of "childhood innocence"?

6. To what extent does the youthful narrator of Gary Soto's "Looking for Work" (p. 39) actively critique or reshape the stories of family life he en-

counters on TV? Is he an active participant in his relationship with mass media or a passive victim? How actively do most children "talk back" to the representations they encounter in the media?

7. Would Stephanie Brail, author of "The Price of Admission: Harassment and Free Speech in the Wild Wild West" (p. 777), be likely to support or oppose Jenkins's call for a fully accessible Internet for all children?

8. How might Jenkins respond to the concerned mother in the cartoon by William Haefeli that precedes this selection (p. 279)?

EXTENDING THE CRITICAL CONTEXT

9. Working in groups, analyze the content of a few popular television shows or video games to determine how women, children, the elderly, and members of ethnic groups or other minority groups are portrayed. What dangers, if any, do you see in prolonged exposure to such images for children?

10. Locate and visit some Internet "virtual community" Web sites designed specifically for or by children. Do you agree with Jenkins's assertion that children must learn to negotiate the Net in all its complexity in order to become responsible citizens in the future? Why?

3

Money and Success

The Myth of Individual Opportunity

Affluence, photo by Steven Weinrebe.

Mighty strange things are happening in the world of money these days. Housing prices in Santa Clara County, California—also known as Silicon Valley—jumped 45 percent in a single year, to $578,000 for the average single-family home. Dot-com millionaires and millionaire wannabes drive $60,000 BMW all-terrain vehicles to upscale grocery stores, where for $18 a pound they can buy ostrich meat. The wealthiest Americans make or lose millions as stock markets rise or fall, and anyone with Internet access can bid in an online auction for items ranging from impressionist paintings to the raft on which Elián Gonzáles supposedly fled Cuba.

Of course the so-called new economy, like the old one, has left many Americans in a familiar place—on the outside looking in. There are upwards of two million poor people in New York City alone, and a worker earning the minimum wage would have to work four thousand years to match the annual income of a top executive. In affluent Silicon Valley, some people with full-time jobs have to sleep in their cars; less fortunate folks take long nightly bus rides through this land of riches in order to stay warm, safe, and dry. Across the country, cities and towns built on manufacturing, textiles, logging, mining, family farming, and other traditional economies are living through hard times indeed. Given the disparity between rich and poor Americans, it's perhaps appropriate that the presidential portraits on paper money are now being placed off-center, as if the country itself has fallen out of balance.

There may be a new economy for the new millenium, but it's absolutely consistent with a mythology of individual success that reaches back centuries. The dream of individual opportunity has been at home in America since Europeans discovered a "new world" in the Western Hemisphere. Early immigrants like Hector St. Jean de Crèvecoeur extolled the freedom and opportunity to be found in this new land. His glowing descriptions of a classless society where anyone could attain success through honesty and hard work fired the imaginations of many European readers: in *Letters from an American Farmer* (1782) he wrote, "We are all animated with the spirit of an industry which is unfettered and unrestrained, because each person works for himself....We have no princes, for whom we toil, starve, and bleed: we are the most perfect society now existing in the world." The promise of a land where "the rewards of [a man's] industry follow with equal steps the progress of his labor" drew poor immigrants from Europe and fueled national expansion into the western territories.

Our national mythology abounds with illustrations of the American success story. There's Benjamin Franklin, the very model of the self-educated, self-made man, who rose from modest origins to become a renowned scientist, philosopher, and statesman. In the nineteenth century, Horatio Alger, a writer of pulp fiction for young boys—fiction that you will get to sample below—became America's best-selling author with rags-to-riches tales like *Struggling Upward* (1886) and *Bound to Rise* (1873). The notion of success haunts us: we spend millions every year reading about the rich and famous, learning how to "make a fortune in real estate with no money down," and "dressing for success." The myth of success has even invaded our personal relationships: today it's as important to be "successful" in marriage or parenthood as it is to come out on top in business.

But dreams easily turn into nightmares. Every American who hopes to "make it" also knows the fear of failure, because the myth of success inevitably implies comparison between the haves and the have-nots, the achievers and the drones, the stars and the anonymous crowd. Under pressure of the myth, we become engrossed in status symbols: we try to live in the "right" neighborhoods, wear the "right" clothes, eat the "right" foods. These emblems of distinction assure us and others that we are different, that we stand out from the crowd. It is one of the great paradoxes of our culture that we believe passionately in the fundamental equality of all yet strive as hard as we can to separate ourselves from our fellow citizens.

Steeped in a Puritan theology that vigorously preached the individual's responsibility to the larger community, colonial America balanced the drive for individual gain with concern for the common good. To Franklin, the way to wealth lay in practicing the virtues of honesty, hard work, and thrift: "Without industry and frugality nothing will do, and with them every thing. He that gets all he can honestly, and saves all he gets . . . will certainly become RICH" ("Advice to a Young Tradesman," 1748). And Alger's heroes were as concerned with moral rectitude as they were with financial gain: a benefactor advises Ragged Dick, "If you'll try to be somebody, and grow up into a respectable member of society, you will. You may not become rich, — it isn't everybody that becomes rich, you know, — but you can obtain a good position and be respected." But in the twentieth century the mood of the myth changed. Contemporary guides to success, like Robert Ringer's enormously popular *Looking Out for Number One* (1977), urge readers to "forget foundationless traditions, forget the 'moral' standards others may have tried to cram down your throat . . . and, most important, think of yourself— Number One. . . . You and you alone will be responsible for your success or failure." The myth of success may have been responsible for making the United States what it is today, but it also seems to be pulling us apart. Can we exist as a living community if our greatest value can be summed up by the slogan "Me first"?

The chapter begins with two readings that define the myth of success; indeed, these readings celebrate and promote the myth unambiguously. First, an excerpt from Horatio Alger's *Ragged Dick* serves as a classic expression of the American Dream: a young man moves from rags to riches thanks to his individual effort. The myth is updated—and extended to African Americans—with the selection from Rose Blue and Corinne Naden's *Colin Powell: Straight to the Top*, a biography of the black military leader written for young readers.

The rosy picture painted in these opening pieces is complicated by subsequent readings. Harlon Dalton's "Horatio Alger" examines the myth that Alger made popular and finds it not just misleading but "socially destructive." "Class in America," by Gregory Mantsios, points to the overwhelming importance of social class in the United States; what we may want to believe about upward mobility and equal opportunity is everywhere contradicted by Mantsios's stark portrayal of a social and economic system that serves the powerful and wealthy.

The next two readings offer personal responses to the American Dream. The oral history of Stephen Cruz, a successful Mexican American engineer, reveals a man pursuing the Dream but gradually becoming disillusioned with it. The Dream is radically redefined in Anne Witte Garland's "Good Noise: Cora Tucker," which presents the story of an African American activist who measures success in terms of lives saved instead of dollars spent. The Visual Portfolio captures many of the themes that have been introduced—dreams of success, fear of failure, the reality of social class.

After the portfolio comes "The Invisible Poor" by James Fallows, an essay exploring the possibility that we are doing more to hide poverty—to make the poor invisible—than actually to reduce poverty. The poem "From Seven Floors Up," by Sharon Olds, examines a similar idea, namely the distance between affluence and homelessness. Dana Gioia's poem "Money" demonstrates the importance of money in our daily lives by highlighting our obsession with the language of cold, hard cash.

The chapter's final three readings all deal with race and success, but they are remarkably different otherwise. "The Black Avenger," by conservative talk show host Ken Hamblin, downplays the importance of race and celebrates the vitality of the American Dream, specifically its openness to black Americans willing to seize their opportunities. In contrast, Ronald Takaki's "Race at the End of History," as its title indicates, sees race as a fundamental component of myths of success; Takaki challenges the media-created stereotype of the successful Asian American, the "model minority." The chapter closes with Toni Cade Bambara's "The Lesson," a lively story that dramatizes economic inequality by presenting it through the eyes of a group of kids from Harlem who venture uptown to see how the rich live and spend.

Sources

Peter Baida, *Poor Richard's Legacy: American Business Values from Benjamin Franklin to Donald Trump.* New York: William Morrow, 1990.

J. Hector St. Jean de Crèvecoeur, *Letters from an American Farmer.* New York: Dolphin Books, 1961. First published in London, 1782.

David A. Kaplan, *The Silicon Boys and Their Valley of Dreams.* New York: William Morrow, 1999.

Sue McAllister, "Housing Prices Surge." *San Jose Mercury News,* 26 May 2000, A1.

Evelyn Nieves, "Many in Silicon Valley Cannot Afford Housing, Even at $50,000 a Year." *New York Times*, 20 February 2000, 16 (N), A20 (L), Col. 1.

Joelle Tessler, "EBay Is Feeling Growing Pains." *San Jose Mercury News*, 26 May 2000, A1.

BEFORE READING

- Working alone or in groups, make a list of people who best represent your idea of success. (You may want to consider public and political figures, leaders in government, entertainment, sports, education, or other fields.) List the specific qualities or accomplishments that make these people successful. Compare notes with your classmates, then freewrite about the meaning of success: What does it mean to you? To the class as a whole?

- Keep your list and your definition. As you work through this chapter, reread and reflect on what you've written, comparing your ideas with those of the authors included here.

- Write a journal entry that captures the thoughts of the man pictured in the photo at the beginning of this chapter (p. 294). What feelings or attitudes can you read in his expression, his dress, and his body language? How do you think he got where he is today?

From *Ragged Dick*

HORATIO ALGER

The choice of Horatio Alger to exemplify the myth of individual opportunity is almost automatic. Alger's rags-to-riches stories have become synonymous with the notion that anyone can succeed—even to generations of Americans who have never read one of the books that were best-sellers a century ago. The excerpt below is typical of Alger's work in that it focuses on a young man's progress from a poor background toward "fame and fortune." Alger (1832–1899) published over a hundred such stories; most observers agree that their popularity depended less on their literary accomplishments than on the promises they made about opportunity in America and the rewards of hard work.

Dick now began to look about for a position in a store or counting-room. Until he should obtain one he determined to devote half the day to blacking boots, not being willing to break in upon his small capital. He found that he could earn enough in half a day to pay all his necessary expenses, including the entire rent of the room. Fosdick desired to pay his half; but Dick steadily refused, insisting upon paying so much as compensation for his friend's services as instructor.

It should be added that Dick's peculiar way of speaking and use of slang terms had been somewhat modified by his education and his intimacy with Henry Fosdick. Still he continued to indulge in them to some extent, especially when he felt like joking, and it was natural to Dick to joke, as my readers have probably found out by this time. Still his manners were considerably improved, so that he was more likely to obtain a situation than when first introduced to our notice.

Just now, however, business was very dull, and merchants, instead of hiring new assistants, were disposed to part with those already in their employ. After making several ineffectual applications, Dick began to think he should be obliged to stick to his profession until the next season. But about this time something occurred which considerably improved his chances of preferment.

This is the way it happened.

As Dick, with a balance of more than a hundred dollars in the savings bank, might fairly consider himself a young man of property, he thought himself justified in occasionally taking a half holiday from business, and going on an excursion. On Wednesday afternoon Henry Fosdick was sent by his employer on an errand to that part of Brooklyn near Greenwood Cemetery. Dick hastily dressed himself in his best, and determined to accompany him.

The two boys walked down to the South Ferry, and, paying their two cents each, entered the ferry-boat. They remained at the stern, and stood by the railing, watching the great city, with its crowded wharves, receding from view. Beside them was a gentleman with two children,—a girl of eight and a little boy of six. The children were talking gayly to their father. While he was pointing out some object of interest to the little girl, the boy managed to creep, unobserved, beneath the chain that extends across the boat, for the protection of passengers, and, stepping incautiously to the edge of the boat, fell over into the foaming water.

At the child's scream, the father looked up, and, with a cry of horror, sprang to the edge of the boat. He would have plunged in, but, being unable to swim, would only have endangered his own life, without being able to save his child.

"My child!" he exclaimed in anguish,—"who will save my child? A thousand—ten thousand dollars to any one who will save him!"

There chanced to be but few passengers on board at the time, and nearly all these were either in the cabins or standing forward. Among the few who saw the child fall was our hero.

shows his kindness & compassion (handwritten margin note)

Now Dick was an expert swimmer. It was an accomplishment which he 10
had possessed for years, and he no sooner saw the boy fall than he resolved
to rescue him. His determination was formed before he heard the liberal
offer made by the boy's father. Indeed, I must do Dick the justice to say
that, in the excitement of the moment, he did not hear it at all, nor would it
have stimulated the alacrity with which he sprang to the rescue of the little
boy.

Little Johnny had already risen once, and gone under for the second
time, when our hero plunged in. He was obliged to strike out for the boy,
and this took time. He reached him none too soon. Just as he was sinking
for the third and last time, he caught him by the jacket. Dick was stout and
strong, but Johnny clung to him so tightly, that it was with great difficulty he
was able to sustain himself.

"Put your arms round my neck," said Dick.

The little boy mechanically obeyed, and clung with a grasp strengthened by his terror. In this position Dick could bear his weight better. But
the ferry-boat was receding fast. It was quite impossible to reach it. The father, his face pale with terror and anguish, and his hands clasped in sus-
pense, saw the brave boy's struggles, and prayed with agonizing fervor that
he might be successful. But it is probable, for they were now midway of the
river, that both Dick and the little boy whom he had bravely undertaken to
rescue would have been drowned, had not a row-boat been fortunately
near. The two men who were in it witnessed the accident, and hastened to
the rescue of our hero.

"Keep up a little longer," they shouted, bending to their oars, "and we
will save you."

Dick heard the shout, and it put fresh strength into him. He battled 15
manfully with the treacherous sea, his eyes fixed longingly upon the approaching boat.

"Hold on tight, little boy," he said. "There's a boat coming."

The little boy did not see the boat. His eyes were closed to shut out the
fearful water, but he clung the closer to his young preserver. Six long,
steady strokes, and the boat dashed along side. Strong hands seized Dick
and his youthful burden, and drew them into the boat, both dripping with
water.

"God be thanked!" exclaimed the father, as from the steamer he saw
the child's rescue. "That brave boy shall be rewarded, if I sacrifice my whole
fortune to compass it."

"You've had a pretty narrow escape, young chap," said one of the boat-
men to Dick. "It was a pretty tough job you undertook."

"Yes," said Dick. "That's what I thought when I was in the water. If it 20
hadn't been for you, I don't know what would have 'come of us."

"Anyhow you're a plucky boy, or you wouldn't have dared to jump into
the water after this little chap. It was a risky thing to do."

move compass

"I'm used to the water," said Dick, modestly. "I didn't stop to think of the danger, but I wasn't going to see that little fellow drown without tryin' to save him."

The boat at once headed for the ferry wharf on the Brooklyn side. The captain of the ferry-boat, seeing the rescue, did not think it necessary to stop his boat, but kept on his way. The whole occurrence took place in less time than I have occupied in telling it.

The father was waiting on the wharf to receive his little boy, with what feeling of gratitude and joy can be easily understood. With a burst of happy tears he clasped him to his arms. Dick was about to withdraw modestly, but the gentleman perceived the movement, and, putting down the child, came forward, and, clasping his hand, said with emotion, "My brave boy, I owe you a debt I can never repay. But for your timely service I should now be plunged into an anguish which I cannot think of without a shudder."

Our hero was ready enough to speak on most occasions, but always felt   25
awkward when he was praised.

"It wasn't any trouble," he said, modestly. "I can swim like a top."

"But not many boys would have risked their lives for a stranger," said the gentleman. "But," he added with a sudden thought, as his glance rested on Dick's dripping garments, "both you and my little boy will take cold in wet clothes. Fortunately I have a friend living close at hand, at whose house you will have an opportunity of taking off your clothes, and having them dried."

humble Dick protested that he never took cold; but Fosdick, who had now joined them, and who, it is needless to say, had been greatly alarmed at Dick's danger, joined in urging compliance with the gentleman's proposal, and in the end our hero had to yield. His new friend secured a hack, the driver of which agreed for extra recompense to receive the dripping boys into his carriage, and they were whirled rapidly to a pleasant house in a side street, where matters were quickly explained, and both boys were put to bed.

"I aint used to goin' to bed quite so early," thought Dick. "This is the queerest excursion I ever took."

Like most active boys Dick did not enjoy the prospect of spending half   30
a day in bed; but his confinement did not last as long as he anticipated.

In about an hour the door of his chamber was opened, and a servant appeared, bringing a new and handsome suit of clothes throughout.

"You are to put on these," said the servant to Dick; "but you needn't get up till you feel like it."

"Whose clothes are they?" asked Dick.

"They are yours."

"Mine! Where did they come from?"   35

"Mr. Rockwell sent out and bought them for you. They are the same size as your wet ones."

"Is he here now?"

"No. He bought another suit for the little boy, and has gone back to New York. Here's a note he asked me to give you."

Dick opened the paper, and read as follows, —

"Please accept this outfit of clothes as the first instalment of a debt   40 which I can never repay. I have asked to have your wet suit dried, when you can reclaim it. Will you oblige me by calling to-morrow at my counting room, No. —, Pearl Street.

> "Your friend,
> "JAMES ROCKWELL."

When Dick was dressed in his new suit, he surveyed his figure with pardonable complacency. It was the best he had ever worn, and fitted him as well as if it had been made expressly for him.

"He's done the handsome thing," said Dick to himself; "but there wasn't no 'casion for his givin' me these clothes. My lucky stars are shinin' pretty bright now. Jumpin' into the water pays better than shinin' boots; but I don't think I'd like to try it more'n once a week."

About eleven o'clock the next morning Dick repaired to Mr. Rockwell's counting-room on Pearl Street. He found himself in front of a large and handsome warehouse. The counting-room was on the lower floor. Our hero entered, and found Mr. Rockwell sitting at a desk. No sooner did that gentleman see him than he arose, and, advancing, shook Dick by the hand in the most friendly manner.

"My young friend," he said, "you have done me so great a service that I wish to be of some service to you in return. Tell me about yourself, and what plans or wishes you have formed for the future."

Dick frankly related his past history, and told Mr. Rockwell of his de-   45 sire to get into a store or counting-room, and of the failure of all his applications thus far. The merchant listened attentively to Dick's statement, and, when he had finished, placed a sheet of paper before him, and, handing him a pen, said, "Will you write your name on this piece of paper?"

Dick wrote, in a free, bold hand, the name Richard Hunter. He had very much improved his penmanship, as has already been mentioned, and now had no cause to be ashamed of it.

Mr. Rockwell surveyed it approvingly.

"How would you like to enter my counting-room as clerk, Richard?" he asked.

Dick was about to say "Bully," when he recollected himself, and answered, "Very much."

"I suppose you know something of arithmetic, do you not?"   50

"Yes, sir."

"Then you may consider yourself engaged at a salary of ten dollars a week. You may come next Monday morning."

"Ten dollars!" repeated Dick, thinking he must have misunderstood.

"Yes; will that be sufficient?"

"It's more than I can earn," said Dick, honestly.   55

"Perhaps it is at first," said Mr. Rockwell, smiling; "but I am willing to pay you that. I will besides advance you as fast as your progress will justify it."

Dick was so elated that he hardly restrained himself from some demonstration which would have astonished the merchant; but he exercised self-control, and only said, "I'll try to serve you so faithfully, sir, that you won't repent having taken me into your service."

"And I think you will succeed," said Mr. Rockwell, encouragingly. "I will not detain you any longer, for I have some important business to attend to. I shall expect to see you on Monday morning."

Dick left the counting-room, hardly knowing whether he stood on his head or his heels, so overjoyed was he at the sudden change in his fortunes. Ten dollars a week was to him a fortune, and three times as much as he had expected to obtain at first. Indeed he would have been glad, only the day before, to get a place at three dollars a week. He reflected that with the stock of clothes which he had now on hand, he could save up at least half of it, and even then live better than he had been accustomed to do; so that his little fund in the savings bank, instead of being diminished, would be steadily increasing. Then he was to be advanced if he deserved it. It was indeed a bright prospect for a boy who, only a year before, could neither read nor write, and depended for a night's lodging upon the chance hospitality of an alley-way or old wagon. Dick's great ambition to "grow up 'spectable" seemed likely to be accomplished after all.

"I wish Fosdick was as well off as I am," he thought generously. But he   60 determined to help his less fortunate friend, and assist him up the ladder as he advanced himself.

When Dick entered his room on Mott Street, he discovered that some one else had been there before him, and two articles of wearing apparel had disappeared.

"By gracious!" he exclaimed; "somebody's stole my Washington coat and Napoleon pants. Maybe it's an agent of Barnum's, who expects to make a fortun' by exhibitin' the valooable wardrobe of a gentleman of fashion."

Dick did not shed many tears over his loss, as, in his present circumstances, he never expected to have any further use for the well-worn garments. It may be stated that he afterwards saw them adorning the figure of Micky Maguire; but whether that estimable young man stole them himself, he never ascertained. As to the loss, Dick was rather pleased that it had occurred. It seemed to cut him off from the old vagabond life which he hoped never to resume. Henceforward he meant to press onward, and rise as high as possible.

Although it was yet only noon, Dick did not go out again with his brush. He felt that it was time to retire from business. He would leave his share of

the public patronage to other boys less fortunate than himself. That evening
Dick and Fosdick had a long conversation. Fosdick rejoiced heartily in his
friend's success, and on his side had the pleasant news to communicate that
his pay had been advanced to six dollars a week.

"I think we can afford to leave Mott Street now," he continued. "This 65
house isn't as neat as it might be, and I should like to live in a nicer quarter
of the city."

"All right," said Dick. "We'll hunt up a new room tomorrow. I shall
have plenty of time, having retired from business. I'll try to get my reg'lar
customers to take Johnny Nolan in my place. That boy hasn't any enterprise. He needs somebody to look out for him."

"You might give him your box and brush, too, Dick."

"No," said Dick; "I'll give him some new ones, but mine I want to keep,
to remind me of the hard times I've had, when I was an ignorant boot-black,
and never expected to be anything better."

"When, in short, you were 'Ragged Dick.' You must drop that name,
and think of yourself now as" —

"Richard Hunter, Esq.," said our hero, smiling. 70

"A young gentleman on the way to fame and fortune," added Fosdick.

Engaging the Text

1. List the values, characteristics, and actions that help Ragged Dick succeed.
   How valuable do you consider these today? How important is virtue compared to good luck — in the story and in your own experience?

2. Skim the Alger selection to find as many mentions of money as you can.
   How frequent are they? What seem to be Alger's ideas about money,
   wealth, salaries, and other financial issues?

3. By the time we reach the end of this story, quite a few things have changed
   from the time Dick "was an ignorant boot-black, and never expected to be
   anything better" (para. 68). Working in small groups, list as many changes
   as you can. What seems to be Alger's attitude toward them?

4. Why is Alger careful to note that Dick does not hear Mr. Rockwell's offer
   of $10,000 to whoever would save Little Johnny? Is Dick being short-
   changed by getting a job and clothes but not a $10,000 reward?

Exploring Connections

5. Look ahead to "Horatio Alger" by Harlon Dalton (p. 311). Does Dalton's
   analysis of the Alger myth change your understanding of this excerpt? Explain. What elements in this story might Dalton cite to support his claims?

6. Read "Looking for Work" by Gary Soto (p. 39). Compare and contrast
   Alger's ideas about work, money, and aspiration to those found in Soto's
   narrative.

EXTENDING THE CRITICAL CONTEXT

7. Dick considers himself a "young man of property" when he has $100 in the bank. Talk to classmates and see if you can reach any consensus about what it would take today to be a "young man or woman of property." Similarly, see if you can agree on what a good starting salary would be for a recent college graduate, or on what levels of wealth and income define the poor, the middle class, and the upper class in the United States today. Write a note summarizing your conclusions and keep it for reference as you read the rest of this chapter.

8. If you did the first "Before Reading" assignment on page 298, compare and contrast the qualities that made the people on your list successful with the qualities Alger gives to Ragged Dick.

From *Colin Powell: Straight to the Top*

ROSE BLUE AND CORINNE J. NADEN

Nowadays America's appetite for mythic heroes is fed by fact more than fiction. News shows and magazines profile "stars" who have achieved remarkable success in almost every field. But the stars that burn brightest are those, like General Colin Powell, who embody the rags-to-riches story of success. This selection comes from a book for young readers that reduces the full-length biographies of Powell to their mythic essence. Powell, who rose from humble roots to become the top-ranking U.S. military officer, has often been called the modern embodiment of the American Dream, a kind of real-life Horatio Alger hero. Most important, Powell's success is often cited as a validation of the Dream for African Americans. Working both independently and as collaborators, Rose Blue (b. 1931) and Corinne J. Naden (b. 1930) have published many books for children and young adults; this excerpt comes from one of their several coauthored biographies of famous Americans.

On August 2, 1990, Iraq invaded and conquered Kuwait. The news shocked the world. Kuwait is on the Persian Gulf, sandwiched between Iraq to the north and west and Saudi Arabia to the south. This is part of the troubled area called the Middle East.

Oil-rich Kuwait is a tiny desert land that is only a little larger than the state of Connecticut. Overpowered by Iraq, Kuwait asked the United Nations (UN) for help. Saudi Arabia, afraid of being invaded next, also turned to the world organization. The United Nations said Iraq was wrong. To protect Saudi Arabia, President George Bush sent U.S. troops there. This was the start of Operation Desert Shield. The U.S. forces were soon joined by troops from Britain, France, Egypt, and other UN members.

During the next few months, many countries urged Iraq to leave Kuwait. Iraq's leader, Saddam Hussein, refused. Finally, the United Nations ordered Iraq to get out of Kuwait by January 15, 1991. War was threatened.

January 15 came and went. Iraq did not budge. One day later, on January 16, Operation Desert Shield turned into Operation Desert Storm. The United States and its allies went to war against Iraq. U.S. Secretary of Defense Richard Cheney told the nation, "The liberation of Kuwait has begun."

The war became known as the Persian Gulf War. The allied forces   5
numbered more than half a million. Most were U.S. troops. They faced an even larger Iraqi army. The Americans were fighting a war in a desert thousands of miles from home.

Even before the first shot was fired, President Bush counted on the help of his top military adviser, the chairman of the Joint Chiefs of Staff (JCS). The JCS includes the top people in all the branches of the U.S. military. The chairman that President Bush counted on was a four-star general in the U.S. Army. His name is Colin Luther Powell.

As chairman of the JCS, Colin Powell was the highest-ranking military officer in the United States and the world's most powerful soldier. He was fifty-two years old when he took over as chairman on October 1, 1989. That made him the youngest chairman ever. He was also the first black American to have this job.

Colin Luther Powell is an impressive person. He stands six feet, one inch tall and weighs two hundred pounds. His dark, close-cropped hair is graying. It is said (although probably not to his face) that he has "teddy bear" good looks. His husky frame is held straight. He *looks* like a general.

Powell is every inch the military professional. He is quiet, serious, and businesslike. His manner is polished and even-tempered. He also has a sense of humor, and he can talk to civilians and military people with the same ease.

Powell was born into a poor black immigrant family. How did he rise to   10
become the country's top military man? There was no magic shortcut. Powell once said, "People keep asking the secret of my success. There isn't any secret. I work hard and spend long hours. It's as simple as that." He advised young people, "There is no substitute for hard work and study. Nothing comes easy."

Things were not easy for young Colin Powell. He was born in Harlem in New York City on April 5, 1937. Many blacks and other minorities live in

Harlem. It is part of the borough of Manhattan. New York City, the nation's largest city, has four other boroughs—Brooklyn, Queens, Staten Island, and the Bronx. When Colin was still a young child, his family moved to the South Bronx. He grew up in a four-bedroom apartment on Kelly Street.

The South Bronx was, and still is, a poor neighborhood. Colin's mother and father came to America in the 1920s from the island of Jamaica in the Caribbean. Both parents worked in the garment district of New York City. Maud, Colin's mother, was a seamstress. Luther, his father, was a shipping clerk.

Colin Powell grew up to be a serious, strong military leader. But tears can still cloud his eyes when he speaks of his mother and father. They both died in the 1980s. "As I grow older," he has said, "I have greater and greater affection for my parents."

Maud and Luther Powell were serious people with a dream. They wanted a better life for Colin and his sister, Marilyn, who is five and a half years older than Colin. For the Powells, education was the key to a better life. Colin's mother graduated from high school; his father did not. If Maud Powell got annoyed at her husband, she would remind him just *who* had the high school diploma.

The Powells taught their children that success comes with hard work. "You must set a goal and do your job well," they said.

A reporter once suggested that Colin Powell got to the top because his parents taught him values. The general had this reply: "Kids don't pick up training because parents sit around and talk to them about values. Children watch their parents *live* values. Youngsters don't care what you say, but they watch what you do."

The future general grew up in a warm, loving, hardworking family. His sister, Marilyn, remembers that when the family first moved to the South Bronx, there were few children his age in the neighborhood. So Colin went everywhere with her. "He was a tagalong brother," she says. She recalls that he was "really a pretty average boy," but he always "had a sense of direction." She was not surprised by his later success, only by the "greatness of it." Today Marilyn Powell Berns is married and is a teacher in Santa Ana, California.

The neighborhood around Kelly Street included people of many kinds. There were blacks and Puerto Ricans, and there was a large Jewish population. As Colin grew older, he played stickball on the streets with friends. He served as an altar boy at St. Margaret's Episcopal Church. And, of course, he went to school—first to the neighborhood elementary school, and then to Morris High School nearby. After school, he worked at a furniture store in his neighborhood. He learned a little of the Yiddish language from the store's Jewish owners. "I had a great childhood," he later recalled.

Colin was not an honor student. He admits that at school he sometimes "horsed around." His sister laughingly says that he was a "late bloomer." A late bloomer is someone who succeeds in school or at a career at an older age than most other people do. Colin Powell gives hope to all late bloomers who are C students. That was his grade average during high school and college.

Powell went to City College of New York (CCNY) in 1954. The school   20 is now part of City University of New York (CUNY). He had no career in mind, but City College was free to New York students. He worked part-time after classes.

In his second semester of college, Powell joined the Reserve Officers Training Corps (ROTC). This program trains college students to become officers in the army. Powell's group was known as the Pershing Rifles. He later said that he joined because he liked the uniform. Actually, the military had always impressed him. He was a young boy during World War II and a teenager during the Korean War.

According to an old saying, some people "find a home in the army." In other words, sometimes a person is just right for military life. Colin Powell and the army seemed just right together. This C student got straight As in his ROTC classes in all four years of college. When his group took summer training at Fort Bragg, North Carolina, he was named "outstanding cadet."

Powell earned a degree in geology (the study of the history of the earth, especially through rocks) from CCNY in 1958. He graduated at the top of his ROTC group. He was a Pershing Rifles company commander, a cadet colonel (ROTC's highest rank), and a "distinguished military graduate." The late bloomer was blooming.

One of Powell's ROTC classmates at CCNY was Mitchell Strear, who later became a school principal in New York City. Strear recalls: "Even back then Colin drew attention when he entered a room. At the age of eighteen, his bearing, manner, and presence were special. You just knew he would become a leader. The infantry has a motto: 'Follow me.' Colin's manner of acceptance of responsibility and leadership all said 'Follow me.'"

Powell decided to follow the army. On June 9, 1958, he became a sec-   25 ond lieutenant. He earned sixty dollars a week. His parents encouraged him. They felt that, like most young men at the time, he would have been drafted into the military anyway. The Powells thought that their son would serve a tour of duty, then come home and get a "real job." Instead, he went into the army to stay. He had "found a home." To him, a career in the military was "an honorable profession and a contribution to society."

But success in the military was not certain for Powell. In his profession, the most successful people have usually come from "the Point"—the U.S. Military Academy at West Point, New York. Many famous American generals were West Pointers. They include President Dwight D. Eisenhower and General Douglas MacArthur, who fought in World War II, and Robert E. Lee and Ulysses S. Grant, both generals in the Civil War.

General Colin Powell did not go to West Point. Yet he did make it to the top in the army. He once said: "Although I had to compete in my military schooling with West Pointers . . . my CCNY foundation was so solid, I never regretted going anywhere but to City."

Lieutenant Powell was sent to training school at Fort Benning, Georgia. At that time, blacks and whites were segregated—kept apart by law—in many places. In the South, blacks were required to attend separate schools, which were generally not as good as the schools for whites. Blacks ate at segregated restaurants, sat in separate seats on buses and in movie theaters, and drank from separate water fountains.

Late in the 1950s, that was beginning to change. Blacks all over the country were beginning to demand, and win, civil rights—the basic rights of all citizens. But many whites still wanted the races to be kept separate. Thus, when Colin Powell went to Fort Benning at the age of twenty-one, he felt the shock of racism for the first time.

"On Kelly Street in the South Bronx, everybody was a minority," Powell later said. "I didn't know what a 'majority' was." But he realized his status soon enough. When he stopped at a restaurant in Columbus, Georgia, the waitress refused to serve him a hamburger unless he went around to the back door.

Even after he became the army's top man, Powell never forgot how much blacks had suffered. He became a student of black history and an admirer of Martin Luther King, Jr., who led the civil rights struggle in the 1950s and 1960s. Powell has advised young black Americans: "Don't let your blackness, your minority status, be a problem to you. Let it be a problem to somebody else. . . . Beat them at it. Prove they're wrong. If you work hard, do the best you can, take advantage of every opportunity that's put in front of you, success will come your way."

In his own career, Powell has done just that. "In the army," he once said, "I never felt I was looked down on by my white colleagues. I've been given the opportunity to compete fair and square with them." It helped, he added, that he "came along at a time of change, a time of growth in civil rights."

Today, blacks make up about 12 percent of the U.S. population but about 30 percent of the U.S. Army. Why? The main reason is opportunity. Segregation is against the law, but blacks still face many barriers to success. The military offers a chance for education and advancement. It also offers less racism than probably any other career.

Black Americans have fought with honor in all of America's wars. But the military has not always treated them so honorably. Blacks fought in the American Revolution, but many were slaves. During the War of 1812 against the British, blacks fought in the Battle of New Orleans. But General Andrew Jackson had to argue with the government before they were paid.

Black troops fought in the Civil War, in World War I, and in World War II. They served bravely and well. But they were segregated—in separate fighting units, separate officers' clubs, and separate jobs. Men who cooked or served food to officers, for instance, were nearly always black.

In 1948, after World War II, President Harry S Truman signed Executive Order 9981. It *officially* ended segregation in the armed forces. The problem didn't go away overnight. There was still racism. But today there is no segregation in any of the U.S. armed services.

Besides Colin Powell, a number of blacks have had outstanding military careers. During World War II, Benjamin O. Davis, Sr., became the first black general in the U.S. Army. Benjamin O. Davis, Jr., his son, became a lieutenant general in the U.S. Air Force and the highest-ranking black in the military in 1965. At West Point in 1932, his classmates had refused to talk to him because of his race.

Black women have also succeeded in the military. Such people have made Colin Powell's path easier. "We should be grateful," he once said, "for what all these men and women have done before. We cannot let the torch drop."

Shows that no matter how poor or your skin color you can succeed in life - not just the military

ENGAGING THE TEXT

1. Why do people point to Powell as the embodiment of the American Dream?

2. Asked about the secret of his success, Powell said, "There isn't any secret. I work hard and spend long hours. It's as simple as that" (para. 10). Is it that simple? Explain.

3. Aside from the biographical facts about Powell, what are the primary messages about success, hard work, and race embedded in this text? To what extent do you agree or disagree with them?

4. What features of this text mark it as having been written specifically for young readers?

EXPLORING CONNECTIONS

5. Compare Powell to Ragged Dick (p. 298). How can these two rather different figures both embody the same myth? Has the myth changed in any way between Dick's time and ours?

6. Look ahead at the cartoon by Aaron McGruder on page 315. What ideas and attitudes about success are expressed in the cartoon, and how do they compare and contrast with the myth of success as embodied by Colin Powell and Ragged Dick (p. 298)?

EXTENDING THE CRITICAL CONTEXT

7. The brief account of the Persian Gulf War given above cannot, of course, explore the full complexity of that historical event. What are some of the Persian Gulf War issues that don't show up in this account for young readers? Also discuss other issues or events the authors simplify for their audience.

8. Find one or more of the full-length biographies of Powell in your college or
    community library. Read the "adult" version of some of the events men-
    tioned above, such as Powell's schooling, his role in the Persian Gulf War,
    his experience with segregation, and so forth. Report to the class what you
    find, making special note of how accurately the biography for young read-
    ers reflects the fuller accounts you read.

Horatio Alger

HARLON L. DALTON

*The two preceding selections dramatize the American Dream coming
true: the success stories of the fictional Ragged Dick and the real-life Colin
Powell exemplify the myth of individual success in America, as both men
rise above poverty to reach their goals. This piece by Harlon L. Dalton questions that myth, calling it not only false, but worse — "socially destructive."
Using Alger as his prime example, Dalton systematically explains how the
rags-to-riches myth can conceal important social realities like race and class.
Dalton is a professor at Yale Law School and author of* Racial Healing: Confronting the Fear Between Blacks and Whites *(1995), from which this selection is taken.*

Ah, Horatio Alger, whose name more than any other is associated with
the classic American hero. A writer of mediocre fiction, Alger had a formula
for commercial success that was simple and straightforward: his lead characters, young boys born into poverty, invariably managed to transcend their
station in life by dint of hard work, persistence, initiative, and daring.[1] Nice
story line. There is just one problem — it is a myth. Not just in the sense
that it is fictional, but more fundamentally because the lesson Alger conveys
is a false one. To be sure, many myths are perfectly benign, and more than a
few are salutary, but on balance Alger's myth is socially destructive.

The Horatio Alger myth conveys three basic messages: (1) each of us is
judged solely on her or his own merits; (2) we each have a fair opportunity
to develop those merits; and (3) ultimately, merit will out. Each of them is,
to be charitable, problematic. The first message is a variant on the rugged

---

[1]Edwin P. Hoyt, *Horatio's Boys: The Life and Works of Horatio Alger, Jr.* (Radnor,
Penn.: Chilton Book Company, 1974). [All notes are Dalton's.]

individualism ethos. . . . In this form, it suggests that success in life has nothing to do with pedigree, race, class background, gender, national origin, sexual orientation—in short, with anything beyond our individual control. Those variables may exist, but they play no appreciable role in how our actions are appraised.

This simply flies in the face of reality. There are doubtless circumstances—the hiring of a letter carrier in a large metropolitan post office, for example—where none of this may matter, but that is the exception rather than the rule. Black folk certainly know what it is like to be favored, disfavored, scrutinized, and ignored all on the basis of our race. Sometimes we are judged on a different scale altogether. Stephen Carter has written movingly about what he calls "the best black syndrome," the tendency of White folk to judge successful Black people only in relation to each other rather than against all comers. Thus, when Carter earned the second-highest score in his high school on the National Merit Scholarship qualifying test, he was readily recognized as "the best Black" around, but somehow not seen as one of the best students, period.[2]

Although I would like to think that things are much different now, I know better. Not long ago a student sought my advice regarding how to deal with the fact that a liberal colleague of mine (and of Stephen Carter's) had written a judicial clerkship recommendation for her in which he described her as the best Black student to have ever taken his class. Apparently the letter caused a mild stir among current law clerks in several courthouses, one of whom saw fit to inform the student. "What was the professor [whom she declined to name] thinking of?" she wondered aloud. "What does his comment mean? What is a judge supposed to make of it? 'If for some reason you think you have to hire one of them, then she's the way to go'? I could understand if he said I was one of the top ten students or even the top thousand, but what does the 'best Black' mean?"

Black folk also know what it is like to be underestimated because of the color of their skin. For example, those of us who communicate in standard English are often praised unduly for how well we speak. This is, I might add, an experience all too familiar to Asian-Americans, including those born and bred in the U.S.A. And we know what it is like to be feared, pitied, admired, and scorned on account of our race, before we even have a chance to say boo! We, in turn, view White people through the prism of our own race-based expectations. I honestly am surprised every time I see a White man who can play basketball above the rim, just as Puerto Ricans and Cubans tend to be surprised to discover "Americans" who salsa truly well. All of which is to say that the notion that every individual is judged solely on personal merit, without regard for sociological wrapping, is mythical at best.

5

---

[2]Stephen L. Carter, *Reflections of an Affirmative Action Baby* (New York: Basic Books, 1991), 47–49.

The second message conveyed by Horatio Alger is that we all have a shot at reaching our true potential. To be fair, neither Alger nor the myth he underwrote suggests that we start out equal. Nor does the myth necessarily require that we be given an equal opportunity to succeed. Rather, Alger's point is that each of us has the power to create our own opportunities. That turns out to be a difficult proposition to completely disprove, for no matter what evidence is offered up to show that a particular group of people have not fared well, it can always be argued that they did not try hard enough, or that they spent too much time wallowing in their predicament and not enough figuring out how to rise above it. Besides, there are always up-by-the-bootstraps examples to point to, like Colin Powell, whose name has so frequently been linked with that of Horatio Alger's that he must think they are related.[3] Nevertheless, it is by now generally agreed that there is a large category of Americans—some have called it the underclass—for whom upward mobility is practically impossible without massive changes in the structure of the economy and in the location of public resources.

As for the notion that merit will out, it assumes not only a commitment to merit-based decision making but also the existence of standards for measuring merit that do not unfairly favor one individual over another. Such standards, of course, must come from somewhere. They must be decided upon by somebody. And that somebody is rarely without a point of view. Ask a devotee of West Coast basketball what skills you should look for in recruiting talent and near the top of his list will be the ability to "get out on the break," to "be creative in the open court," and "to finish the play." On the other hand, ask someone who prefers East Coast basketball and her list will rank highly the ability "to d-up [play defense]," "to board [rebound]," and "to maintain focus and intensity."

Or, to take another example, what makes a great Supreme Court justice? Brains to spare? Common sense? Proper judicial temperament? Political savvy? Extensive lawyering experience? A well-developed ability to abstract? Vision? Well-honed rhetorical skills? A reverence for our rich legal heritage? The capacity to adapt to changing times? Even if one is tempted to say "all of the above," how should these (or any other set of characteristics) be ranked? Measured? Evaluated?

---

[3]Sandy Grady, "Will He or Won't He?: Win or Lose, Presidential Pursuit by Colin Powell Would Do America a Necessary Service," *Kansas City Star,* 24 April 1995; Thomas B. Edsall, "For Powell, Timing Could be Crucial: As Gulf War Hero Hints at 1996 Bid, Associates Look into Details," *Washington Post,* 6 April 1995; J. F. O. McAllister, "The Candidate of Dreams," *Time,* 13 March 1995; Deroy Murdock, "Colin Powell: Many Things to Many People," *Washington Times,* 16 January 1995; Doug Fischer, "U.S. Politics: War Hero Well-Placed to Become First Black President," *Ottawa Citizen,* 8 October 1994; "General Nice Guy: Profile Colin Powell," *Sunday Telegraph,* 25 September 1994; Otto Kreisher, "As a Civilian, Powell's Options are Enviable," *San Diego Union-Tribune,* 26 September 1993.

[margin handwritten note: good pt. — whom you ask]

The answers depend in part on whom you ask. Practicing lawyers, for example, are probably likely to rank extensive lawyering experience more highly than, say, brains. They are also likely to pay close attention to judicial temperament, which for them means whether the prospective justice would be inclined to treat them with respect during a court appearance. Sitting judges are also likely to rank judicial temperament highly, meaning whether the prospective justice would be a good colleague. In choosing among the other characteristics, they might each favor the ones that they happen to possess in abundance. Politicians might well see more merit in political savvy than would, say, academics, who could be expected to favor brains, the ability to abstract, and perhaps rhetorical skills.

All of these relevant actors might be honestly trying to come up with   10 appropriate standards for measuring merit, but they would arrive at markedly different results. And any given result would screen out people who would succeed under another, equally plausible set of standards. Thus, if there is a genuine commitment to merit-based decision making it is possible that merit will out, but only for those who have the right kind of merit.

Which brings us to the prior question: is merit all we care about in deciding who gets what share of life's goodies? Clearly not. Does anyone, for example, honestly believe that any Supreme Court justice in recent memory was nominated solely on the basis of merit (however defined)? Any President? Any member of Congress? Does anyone believe that America's health-care resources are distributed solely on merit? That tax breaks are distributed solely on merit? That baseball club owners are selected solely on merit?

As I suggested earlier, the mere fact that a myth is based on false premises or conveys a false image of the world does not necessarily make it undesirable. Indeed, I place great stock in the idea that some illusions are, or at least can be, positive. As social psychologist Shelley Taylor has observed, "[normal] people who are confronted with the normal rebuffs of everyday life seem to construe their experience [so] as to develop and maintain an exaggeratedly positive view of their own attributes, an unrealistic optimism about the future, and a distorted faith in their ability to control what goes on around them."[4] Taylor's research suggests that, up to a point, such self-aggrandizement actually improves one's chances of worldly success.[5]

This may well explain the deep appeal of the Horatio Alger myth. True or not, it can help to pull people in the direction they want to go. After all, in order to succeed in life, especially when the odds are stacked against you, it is often necessary to first convince yourself that there is a reason to get up in the morning. So what is my beef? Where is the harm?

---

[4]Shelley E. Taylor, *Positive Illusions: Creative Self-Deception and the Healthy Mind* (New York: Basic Books, 1989), xi.

[5]Ibid., xi, 7, 228–46.

THE BOONDOCKS   by **AARON MCGRUDER**

In a nutshell, my objection to the Alger myth is that it serves to maintain the racial pecking order. It does so by mentally bypassing the role of race in American society. And it does so by fostering beliefs that themselves serve to trivialize, if not erase, the social meaning of race. The Alger myth encourages people to blink at the many barriers to racial equality (historical, structural, and institutional) that litter the social landscape. Yes, slavery was built on the notion that Africans were property and not persons; yes, even after that "peculiar institution" collapsed, it continued to shape the life prospects of those who previously were enslaved; yes, the enforced illiteracy and cultural disruption of slavery, together with the collapse of Reconstruction, virtually assured that the vast majority of "freedmen" and "freedwomen" would not be successfully integrated into society; yes, Jim Crow laws, segregation, and a separate and unequal social reality severely undermined the prospects for Black achievement; yes, these and other features of our national life created a racial caste system that persists to this day; yes, the short-lived civil rights era of the 1950s and 1960s was undone by a broad and sustained White backlash; yes, the majority of Black people in America are mired in poverty; yes, economic mobility is not what it used to be, given the decline in our manufacturing and industrial base; yes, the siting of the illicit drug industry in our inner cities has had pernicious effects on Black and Latino neighborhoods; yes, yes, yes, BUT (drumroll) "all it takes to make it in America is initiative, hard work, persistence, and pluck." After all, just look at Colin Powell!

There is a fundamental tension between the promise of opportunity enshrined in the Alger myth and the realities of a racial caste system. The main point of such a system is to promote and maintain inequality. The main point of the Alger myth is to proclaim that everyone can rise above her station in life. Despite this tension, it is possible for the myth to coexist with social reality. To quote Shelley Taylor once again: 15

> [T]he normal human mind is oriented toward mental health and . . . at every turn it construes events in a manner that promotes benign fictions about the self, the world, and the future. The mind is, with some significant exceptions, intrinsically adaptive, oriented toward overcoming

rather than succumbing to the adverse events of life. . . . At one level, it constructs beneficent interpretations of threatening events that raise self-esteem and promote motivation; yet at another level, it recognizes the threat or challenge that is posed by these events.[6]

Not surprisingly, then, there are lots of Black folk who subscribe to the Alger myth and at the same time understand it to be deeply false. They live with the dissonance between myth and reality because both are helpful and healthful in dealing with "the adverse events of life." Many Whites, however, have a strong interest in resolving the dissonance in favor of the myth. Far from needing to be on guard against racial "threat[s] or challenge[s]," they would just as soon put the ugliness of racism out of mind. For them, the Horatio Alger myth provides them the opportunity to do just that.[7]

Quite apart from the general way in which the myth works to submerge the social realities of race, each of the messages it projects is also incompatible with the idea of race-based advantage or disadvantage. If, as the myth suggests, we are judged solely on our individual merits, then caste has little practical meaning. If we all can acquire the tools needed to reach our full potential, then how important can the disadvantage of race be? If merit will eventually carry the day, then shouldn't we be directing our energies toward encouraging Black initiative and follow-through rather than worrying about questions of power and privilege?

By interring the myth of Horatio Alger, or at least forcing it to coexist with social reality, we can accomplish two important goals. First, we can give the lie to the idea that Black people can simply lift themselves up by their own bootstraps. With that pesky idea out of the way, it is easier to see why White folk need to take joint ownership of the nation's race problem. Second, the realization that hard work and individual merit, while certainly critical, are not guarantors of success should lead at least some White people to reflect on whether their own achievements have been helped along by their preferred social position.

Finally, quite apart from race, it is in our national interest to give the Horatio Alger myth a rest, for it broadcasts a fourth message no less false than the first three—that we live in a land of unlimited potential. Although that belief may have served us well in the past, we live today in an era of diminished possibilities. We need to make a series of hard choices, followed by yet more hard choices regarding how to live with the promise of less. Confronting that reality is made that much harder by a mythology that assures us we can have it all.

what exactly
is that myth

[6]Ibid., xi.

[7]Robert T. Carter, et al., "White Racial Identity Development and Work Values," *Journal of Vocational Behavior, Special Issue: Racial Identity and Vocational Behavior* 44, no. 2 (April 1994): 185–97.

ENGAGING THE TEXT

1. The first message communicated by the Alger myth, according to Dalton, is that "each of us is judged solely on her or his own merits" (para. 2). What does this message mean to Dalton, and why does he object to it? How does he make his case against it, and what kind of evidence does he provide? Explain why you agree or disagree with his claim that this first message "simply flies in the face of reality" (para. 3).

2. Dalton says it is "generally agreed," but do *you* agree that "there is a large category of Americans . . . for whom upward mobility is practically impossible" (para. 6)? Why or why not?

3. How persuasive do you find Dalton's claims that American society is far from operating as a strictly merit-based system?

4. Why does Dalton believe that the Alger myth is destructive? Do you think the power of the American Dream to inspire or motivate people is outweighed by the negative effects Dalton cites, or vice versa? Write a journal entry explaining your position.

EXPLORING CONNECTIONS

5. Test Dalton's claims against the actual excerpt from Horatio Alger's *Ragged Dick* (p. 298). For example, does the novel seem to match the formula Dalton summarizes in his first paragraph? Similarly, can you find in the novel any examples of the three messages Dalton identifies in his second paragraph? On balance, does the excerpt from Alger seem to promote ideas that you consider socially destructive? Why or why not?

6. How well does Colin Powell's story (p. 305) fit the Alger formula as defined in Dalton's first paragraph?

7. How would Dalton explain the humor of the *Boondocks* cartoon on page 315?

EXTENDING THE CRITICAL CONTEXT

8. Pick a few contemporary cultural heroes like Powell, Tiger Woods, and Oprah Winfrey. Conduct a minipoll about what their success means to race relations in the United States. Do the responses you get support Dalton's contention that such heroes encourage people "to blink at the many barriers to racial equality" (para. 14)?

9. Dalton argues that the Alger myth should be buried, or, to use his word, "interred." Supposing for the moment that you agree, how could that be accomplished? How is a cultural myth challenged, revised, or robbed of its mythic power?

Class in America: Myths and Realities
GREGORY MANTSIOS

Which of these gifts might a high school graduate in your family receive — a corsage, a savings bond, or a BMW? The answer indicates your social class, a key factor in American lives that many of us conspire to ignore. The selection below, however, makes it hard to deny class distinctions and their nearly universal influence on our lives. The essay's title aptly describes its method: the author outlines four widely held beliefs about class in the United States and then systematically refutes them with statistical evidence. Even if your eyes are already open to the existence of classes in the United States, some of the numbers Mantsios cites are likely to surprise you. Mantsios is director of worker education at Queens College of the City University of New York. He recently edited A New Labor Movement for the New Century *(1998). The essay reprinted below appeared in* Race, Class, and Gender in the United States: An Integrated Study, *edited by Paula S. Rothenberg (1998).*

People in the United States don't like to talk about class. Or so it would seem. We don't speak about class privileges, or class oppression, or the class nature of society. These terms are not part of our everyday vocabulary, and in most circles they are associated with the language of the rhetorical fringe. Unlike people in most other parts of the world, we shrink from using words that classify along economic lines or that point to class distinctions: phrases like "working class," "upper class," and "ruling class" are rarely uttered by Americans.

For the most part, avoidance of class-laden vocabulary crosses class boundaries. There are few among the poor who speak of themselves as lower class; instead they refer to their race, ethnic group, or geographic location. Workers are more likely to identify with their employer, industry, or occupational group than with other workers, or with the working class.[1]

The author wishes to thank Vincent Serravallo for his assistance in updating this article. [All notes, except 15, are Mantsios's.]

[1]See Jay Maclead, *Ain't No Makin' It: Aspirations and Attainment in a Lower-Income Neighborhood,* Boulder, CO, Westview Press, 1995; Benjamin DeMott, *The Imperial Middle,* New York, William Morrow, 1990; Ira Katznelson, *City Trenches: Urban Politics and Patterning of Class in the United States.* New York, Pantheon Books, 1981; Charles W. Tucker, "A Comparative Analysis of Subjective Social Class: 1945–1963," *Social Forces,* no. 46, June 1968, pp. 508–514; Robert Nisbet, "The Decline and Fall of Social Class," *Pacific Sociological Review,* vol. 2, Spring 1959, pp. 11–17; and Oscar Glantz, "Class Consciousness and Political Solidarity," *American Sociological Review,* vol. 23, August 1958, pp. 375–382.

Neither are those at the other end of the economic spectrum likely to use the word "class." In her study of thirty-eight wealthy and socially prominent women, Susan Ostander asked participants if they considered themselves members of the upper class. One participant responded, "I hate to use the word 'class.' We are responsible, fortunate people, old families, the people who have something." Another said, "I hate [the term] 'upper class.' It is so non–upper class to use it. I just call it 'all of us,' those who are wellborn."[2]

It is not that Americans, rich or poor, aren't keenly aware of class differences — those quoted above obviously are; it is that class is not in the domain of public discourse. Class is not discussed or debated in public because class identity has been stripped from popular culture. The institutions that shape mass culture and define the parameters of public debate have avoided class issues. In politics, in primary and secondary education, and in the mass media, formulating issues in terms of class is unacceptable, perhaps even un-American.

There are, however, two notable exceptions to this phenomenon. First,   5
it is acceptable in the United States to talk about "the middle class." Interestingly enough, such references appear to be acceptable precisely because they mute class differences. References to the middle class by politicians, for example, are designed to encompass and attract the broadest possible constituency. Not only do references to the middle class gloss over differences, these references also avoid any suggestion of conflict or exploitation.

This leads us to the second exception to the class-avoidance phenomenon. We are, on occasion, presented with glimpses of the upper class and the lower class (the language used is "the wealthy" and "the poor"). In the media, these presentations are designed to satisfy some real or imagined voyeuristic need of "the ordinary person." As curiosities, the ground-level view of street life and the inside look at the rich and the famous serve as unique models, one to avoid and one to aspire to. In either case, the two models are presented without causal relation to each other: one is not rich because the other is poor. Similarly, when social commentators or liberal politicians draw attention to the plight of the poor, they do so in a manner that obscures the class structure and denies class exploitation. Wealth and poverty are viewed as one of several natural and inevitable states of being: differences are only differences. One may even say differences are the American way, a reflection of American social diversity.

We are left with one of two possibilities: either talking about class and recognizing class distinctions are not relevant to U.S. society, or we

---

[2]Susan Ostander, "Upper-Class Women: Class Consciousness as Conduct and Meaning," in G. William Domhoff, *Power Structure Research,* Beverly Hills, CA, Sage Productions, 1980, pp. 78–79. Also see Stephen Birmingham, *America's Secret Aristocracy,* Boston, Little Brown, 1987.

mistakenly hold a set of beliefs that obscure the reality of class differences and their impact on people's lives.

Let us look at four common, albeit contradictory, beliefs about the United States.

Myth 1:   The United States is fundamentally a classless society. Class distinctions are largely irrelevant today, and whatever differences do exist in economic standing are, for the most part, insignificant. Rich or poor, we are all equal in the eyes of the law, and such basic needs as health care and education are provided to all regardless of economic standing.

Myth 2:   We are, essentially, a middle-class nation. Despite some variations in economic status, most Americans have achieved relative affluence in what is widely recognized as a consumer society.

Myth 3:   We are all getting richer. The American public as a whole is steadily moving up the economic ladder, and each generation propels itself to greater economic well-being. Despite some fluctuations, the U.S. position in the global economy has brought previously unknown prosperity to most, if not all, North Americans.

Myth 4:   Everyone has an equal chance to succeed. Success in the United States requires no more than hard work, sacrifice, and perseverance: "In America, anyone can become a millionaire; it's just a matter of being in the right place at the right time."

In trying to assess the legitimacy of these beliefs, we want to ask several important questions. Are there significant class differences among Americans? If these differences do exist, are they getting bigger or smaller, and do these differences have a significant impact on the way we live? Finally, does everyone in the United States really have an equal opportunity to succeed?

The Economic Spectrum

We will begin by looking at differences. An examination of available data reveals that variations in economic well-being are in fact immense. Consider the following:

- The wealthiest 20 percent of the American population holds 85 percent of the total household wealth in the country. That is, they own nearly seven-eighths of all the consumer durables (such as houses, cars, and stereos) and financial assets (such as stocks, bonds, property, and savings accounts).[3]

- Approximately 100,000 Americans or 0.1 percent of the adult working population earn more than $1 million *annually*, with many of these in-

---

[3]Edward Wolff, in Lawrence Mishel and Jared Bernstein, *The State of Working America*, Armonk, NY, M.E. Sharpe, 1994, p. 245.

dividuals earning over $10 million and some earning over $100 million annually. It would take the average American, earning $34,000 per year, more than 65 *lifetimes* to earn $100 million.[4]

Affluence and prosperity are clearly alive and well in certain segments   15
of the U.S. population. However, this abundance is in contrast to the poverty and despair that are also prevalent in the United States. At the other end of the spectrum:

- A total of 14 percent of the American population—that is, one of every seven—live below the government's official poverty line (calculated in 1996 at $7,992 for an individual and $16,029 for a family of four).[5] These poor include a significant number of homeless people—approximately 3 million Americans.

- More than a quarter of all the children in the United States under the age of six live in poverty.[6]

The contrast between rich and poor is sharp, and with nearly one-third of the American population living at one extreme or the other, it is difficult to argue that we live in a classless society. The income gap between rich and poor in the United States (measured as the percentage of total income held by the wealthiest 20 percent of the population versus the poorest 20 percent) is approximately 9 to 1, one of the highest ratios in the industrialized world. The ratio in Japan, by contrast, is 4 to 1.[7]

Reality 1:   There are enormous differences in the economic status of American citizens. A sizeable proportion of the U.S. population occupies opposite ends of the economic spectrum. And it cannot be said that the majority of the American population fares very well. In the middle range of the economic spectrum:

- Fifty percent of the American population holds less than 3.5 percent of the nation's wealth.[8]

- While the real income of the top 1 percent of U.S. families skyrocketed by 78 percent during the economic growth period leading up to the 1990s, the income of the middle fifth of the population actually declined by 5.3 percent. This led one prominent economist to describe

---

[4]Jean-Paul Dubois, "Living on Different Planets," *World Press Review,* July 1996, p. 43.

[5]"Preliminary Estimates of Poverty Thresholds in 1996," Washington, DC, Department of Commerce, Bureau of Census, 1996.

[6]Mishel and Bernstein, *The State of Working America,* p. 8.

[7]Derived from U.S. Department of Commerce, "Current Population Reports: Consumer Income: 1992," Washington, DC, 1993; and World Bank, "World Development Report: 1992," Washington, DC, International Bank for Reconstruction and Development, 1992.

[8]See U.S. Bureau of the Census, "Current Population Reports," series P60, no. 146, 1989; and Steven Rose, *The American Profile Poster,* New York, Pantheon Books, 1986, p. 31.

economic growth as a "spectator sport for the majority of American families."[9]

The level of inequality is sometimes difficult to comprehend fully with dollar figures and percentages. To help his students visualize the distribution of income, the well-known economist Paul Samuelson asked them to picture an income pyramid made of children's blocks, with each layer of blocks representing $1,000. If we were to construct Samuelson's pyramid today, the peak of the pyramid would be much higher than the Eiffel Tower, yet almost all of us would be within six feet of the ground.[10] In other words, the distribution of income is heavily skewed; a small minority of families take the lion's share of national income, and the remaining income is distributed among the vast majority of middle-income and low-income families. Keep in mind that Samuelson's pyramid represents the distribution of income, not wealth. The distribution of wealth is skewed even further.

Realty 2:   The middle class in the United States holds a very small share of the nation's wealth.

Lottery millionaires and celebrity salaries notwithstanding, evidence suggests that the level of inequality in the United States is growing. Statistically, it is getting harder to "make it big" and more difficult to even stay in the middle-income level. Census data show the gap between the rich and the poor to be the widest since the government began collecting information in 1947. Furthermore, the percentage of households earning at a middle-income level (the middle quintile) has been falling steadily since 1968.[11] Most of those who disappeared from the middle-income level moved downward, not upward. And economic polarization is expected to increase over the next several decades.[12]

Reality 3:   The middle class is shrinking in size, and most of those leaving the ranks of the middle class are falling to a lower economic standing.

American Life-Styles

At last count, nearly 40 million Americans across the nation lived in unrelenting poverty. Yet, as political scientist Michael Harrington once commented, "America has the best dressed poverty the world has ever known."[13] Clothing disguises much of the poverty in the United States, and

---

[9]Paul Krugman, quoting Alan Blinder, in "Disparity and Despair," *U.S. News and World Report*, March 23, 1992, p. 54.

[10]Paul Samuelson, *Economics*, 10th ed., New York, McGraw Hill, 1976, p. 84.

[11]"Money Income of Households, Families, and Persons in the United States: 1992," U.S. Department of Commerce, "Current Population Reports: Consumer Income" series P60–184, Washington, DC, 1993, p. B6.

[12]Paul Blumberg, *Inequality in an Age of Decline*, New York, Oxford University Press, 1980.

[13]Michael Harrington, *The Other America*, New York, Macmillan, 1962, pp. 12–13.

this may explain, in part, its middle-class image. With increased mass marketing of "designer" clothing and with shifts in the nation's economy from blue-collar (and often better-paying) manufacturing jobs to white-collar and pink-collar jobs in the service sector, it is becoming increasingly difficult to distinguish class differences based on appearance.[14]

Beneath the surface, there is another reality. Let us look at some "typical" and not-so-typical life-styles.

American Profile No. 1

Name:	Harold S. Browning
Father:	manufacturer, industrialist
Mother:	prominent social figure in the community
Principal child-rearer:	governess
Primary education:	an exclusive private school in Manhattan's Upper East Side *Note:* a small, well-respected primary school where teachers and administrators have a reputation for nurturing student creativity and for providing the finest educational preparation *Ambition:* "to become President"
Supplemental tutoring:	tutors in French and mathematics
Summer camp:	sleep-away camp in northern Connecticut *Note:* camp provides instruction in the creative arts, athletics, and the natural sciences
Secondary education:	a prestigious preparatory school in Westchester County *Note:* classmates included the sons of ambassadors, doctors, attorneys, television personalities, and well-known business leaders *After-school activities:* private riding lessons *Ambition:* "to take over my father's business" *High-school graduation gift:* BMW
Family activities:	theater, recitals, museums, summer vacations in Europe, occasional winter trips to the Caribbean *Note:* as members and donors of the local art museum, the Brownings and their children attend private receptions and exhibit openings at the invitation of the museum director

---

[14]Stuart Ewen and Elizabeth Ewen, *Channels of Desire: Mass Images and the Shaping of American Consciousness,* New York, McGraw-Hill, 1982.

Higher education:	an Ivy League liberal arts college in Massachusetts
	Major: economics and political science
	After-class activities: debating club, college newspaper, swim team
	Ambition: "to become a leader in business"
First full-time job (age 23):	assistant manager of operations, Browning Tool and Die, Inc. (family enterprise)
Subsequent employment:	*3 years* — executive assistant to the president, Browning Tool and Die
	Responsibilities included: purchasing (materials and equipment), personnel, and distribution networks
	4 years — advertising manager, Lackheed Manufacturing (home appliances)
	3 years — director of marketing and sales, Comerex, Inc. (business machines)
Present employment (age 38):	executive vice president, SmithBond and Co. (digital instruments)
	Typical daily activities: review financial reports and computer printouts, dictate memoranda, lunch with clients, initiate conference calls, meet with assistants, plan business trips, meet with associates
	Transportation to and from work: chauffeured company limousine
	Annual salary: $315,000
	Ambition: "to become chief executive officer of the firm, or one like it, within the next five to ten years"
Present residence:	eighteenth-floor condominium in Manhattan's Upper West Side, eleven rooms, including five spacious bedrooms and terrace overlooking river
	Interior: professionally designed and accented with elegant furnishings, valuable antiques, and expensive artwork
	Note: building management provides doorman and elevator attendant; family employs au pair[15] for children and maid for other domestic chores

---

[15]*au pair:* A young woman from another country who works for a family, typically caring for children in exchange for room and board.

Second residence: farm in northwestern Connecticut, used for weekend retreats and for horse breeding (investment/hobby)
Note: to maintain the farm and cater to their needs when they are there, the Brownings employ a part-time maid, groundskeeper, and horse breeder

Harold Browning was born into a world of nurses, maids, and governesses. His world today is one of airplanes and limousines, five-star restaurants, and luxurious living accommodations. The life-style of Harold Browning is in sharp contrast to that of Bob Farrell.

American Profile No. 2

Name:	Bob Farrell
Father:	machinist
Mother:	retail clerk
Principal child-rearer:	mother and sitter
Primary education:	a medium-sized public school in Queens, New York *Note:* characterized by large class size, outmoded physical facilities, and an educational philosophy emphasizing basic skills and student discipline *Ambition:* "to become president"
Supplemental tutoring:	none
Summer camp:	YMCA day camp *Note:* emphasis on team sports, arts and crafts
Secondary education:	large regional high school in Queens *Note:* classmates included the sons and daughters of carpenters, postal clerks, teachers, nurses, shopkeepers, mechanics, bus drivers, police officers, salespersons *After-school activities:* basketball and handball in school park

	Ambition: "to make it through college" *High-school graduation gift:* $500 savings bond
Family activities:	family gatherings around television set, bowling, an occasional trip to the movie theater, summer Sundays at the public beach
Higher education:	a two-year community college with a technical orientation *Major:* electrical technology *After-school activities:* employed as a part-time bagger in local supermarket *Ambition:* "to become an electrical engineer"
First full-time job (age 19):	service-station attendant *Note:* continued to take college classes in the evening
Subsequent employment:	mail clerk at large insurance firm; manager trainee, large retail chain
Present employment (age 38):	assistant sales manager, building supply firm *Typical daily activities:* demonstrate products, write up product orders, handle customer complaints, check inventory *Transportation to and from work:* city subway *Annual salary:* $32,000 *Ambition:* "to open up my own business" *Additional income:* $6,100 in commissions from evening and weekend work as salesman in local men's clothing store
Present residence:	the Farrells own their own home in a working-class neighborhood in Queens

Bob Farrell and Harold Browning live very differently: the life-style of one is privileged; the other is not so privileged. The differences are class differences, and these differences have a profound impact on the way the men live. They are differences between playing a game of handball in the park and taking riding lessons at a private stable; watching a movie on television and going to the theater; taking the subway to work and being driven in a limousine. More important, the difference in class determines where they live, who their friends are, how well they are educated, what they do for a living, and what they expect from life. 25

Yet, as dissimilar as their life-styles are, Harold Browning and Bob Farrell have some things in common. They live in the same city, they work long hours, and they are highly motivated. More important, they are both white males.

Let us look at someone else who works long and hard and is highly motivated. This person, however, is black and female.

American Profile No. 3

Name:	Cheryl Mitchell
Father:	janitor
Mother:	waitress
Principal child-rearer:	grandmother
Primary education:	large public school in Ocean Hill–Brownsville, Brooklyn, New York *Note:* rote teaching of basic skills and emphasis on conveying the importance of good attendance, good manners, and good work habits; school patrolled by security guards *Ambition:* "to be a teacher"
Supplemental tutoring:	none
Summer camp:	none
Secondary education:	large public school in Ocean Hill–Brownsville *Note:* classmates included sons and daughters of hairdressers, groundskeepers, painters, dressmakers, dishwashers, domestics *After-school activities:* domestic chores, part-time employment as babysitter and housekeeper *Ambition:* "to be a social worker" *High-school graduation gift:* corsage
Family activities:	church-sponsored socials
Higher education:	one semester of local community college *Note:* dropped out of school for financial reasons
First full-time job (age 17):	counter clerk, local bakery
Subsequent employment:	file clerk with temporary service agency; supermarket checker
Present employment (age 38):	nurse's aide at a municipal hospital *Typical daily activities:* make up hospital beds, clean out bedpans, weigh patients and assist them to the bathroom, take temperature

readings, pass out and collect food trays, feed
patients who need help, bathe patients, and
change dressings
Annual salary: $16,000
Ambition: "to get out of the ghetto"

Present residence: three-room apartment in the South Bronx;
needs painting, has poor ventilation, is in a
high-crime area
Note: Cheryl Mitchell lives with her two children and her elderly mother

When we look at Cheryl Mitchell, Bob Farrell, and Harold Browning,
we see life-styles that are very different. We are not looking, however, at
economic extremes. Cheryl Mitchell's income as a nurse's aid puts her
above the government's official poverty line. Below her on the income pyramid are 40 million poverty-stricken Americans. Far from being poor, Bob
Farrell's annual income as an assistant sales manager puts him in the fifty-
first percentile of the income distribution. More than 50 percent of the U.S.
population earns less than Bob Farrell. And while Harold Browning's income puts him in a high-income bracket, he stands only a fraction of the
way up Samuelson's income pyramid. Well above him are the 17,000 individuals whose annual salary exceeds $1 million. Yet Harold Browning
spends more money on his horses than Cheryl Mitchell earns in a year.

Reality 4:   Even ignoring the extreme poles of the economic spectrum, we find enormous class differences in the life-styles among the haves,
the have-nots, and the have-littles.

Class affects more than life-style and material well-being. It has a sig-   30
nificant impact on physical and mental well-being as well.

Researchers have found an inverse relationship between social class
and health. Lower-class standing is correlated with higher rates of infant
mortality, eye and ear disease, arthritis, physical disability, diabetes, nutritional deficiency, respiratory disease, mental illness, and heart disease.[16] In
all areas of health, poor people do not share the same life chances as those
in the social class above them. Furthermore, lower-class standing is corre-

[16]Vincente Navarro, "Class, Race, and Health Care in the United States," in Bersh
Berberoglu, *Critical Perspectives in Sociology,* 2nd ed., Dubuque, IA, Kendall/Hunt, 1993,
pp. 148–156; Melvin Krasner, *Poverty and Health in New York City,* United Hospital Fund of
New York, 1989. See also U.S. Dept. of Health and Human Services, *Health Status of Minorities
and Low Income Groups,* 1985; and Dan Hughes, Kay Johnson, Sara Rosenbaum, Elizabeth
Butler, Janet Simons, *The Health of America's Children,* Children's Defense Fund, 1988.

lated with a lower quality of treatment for illness and disease. The results of poor health and poor treatment are borne out in the life expectancy rates within each class. Researchers have found that the higher one's class standing, the higher one's life expectancy. Conversely, they have also found that within each age group, the lower one's class standing, the higher the death rate; in some age groups, the figures are as much as two and three times as high.[17]

Reality 5:   From cradle to grave, class standing has a significant impact on our chances for survival.

The lower one's class standing, the more difficult it is to secure appropriate housing, the more time is spent on the routine tasks of everyday life, the greater is the percentage of income that goes to pay for food and other basic necessities, and the greater is the likelihood of crime victimization.[18] Class can predict chances for both survival and success.

Class and Educational Attainment

School performance (grades and test scores) and educational attainment (level of schooling completed) also correlate strongly with economic class. Furthermore, despite some efforts to make testing more fair and schooling more accessible, current data suggest that the level of inequity is staying the same or getting worse.

In his study for the Carnegie Council on Children [in the 1970s], Richard de Lone examined the test scores of over half a million students who took the College Board exams (SATs). His findings were consistent with earlier studies that showed a relationship between class and scores on standardized tests; his conclusion: "the higher the student's social status, the higher the probability that he or she will get higher grades."[19] Fifteen years after the release of the Carnegie report, College Board surveys reveal data that are no different: test scores still correlate strongly with family income.

A little more than twenty years ago, researcher William Sewell showed a positive correlation between class and overall educational achievement. In comparing the top quartile (25 percent) of his sample to the bottom quartile, he found that students from upper-class families were twice as likely to obtain training beyond high school and four times as likely to attain a postgraduate degree. Sewell concluded: "Socioeconomic background . . .

35

[17]Kenneth Neubeck and Davita Glassberg, *Sociology: A Critical Approach,* New York, McGraw Hill, 1996, pp. 436–438; Aaron Antonovsky, "Social Class, Life Expectancy, and Overall Mortality," in *The Impact of Social Class,* New York, Thomas Crowell, 1972, pp. 467–491. See also Harriet Duleep, "Measuring the Effect of Income on Adult Mortality Using Longitudinal Administrative Record Data," *Journal of Human Resources,* vol. 21, no. 2, Spring 1986.

[18]Dennis W. Roncek, "Dangerous Places: Crime and Residential Environment," *Social Forces,* vol. 60, no. 1, September 1981, pp. 74–96.

[19]Richard De Lone, *Small Futures,* New York, Harcourt Brace Jovanovich, 1978, pp. 14–19.

Table 1 Average Combined Scores by Income
(400 to 1600 scale)

FAMILY INCOME		MEDIAN SCORE
More than	$100,000	1129
$80,000 to	$100,000	1085
$70,000 to	$80,000	1064
$60,000 to	$70,000	1049
$50,000 to	$60,000	1034
$40,000 to	$50,000	1016
$30,000 to	$40,000	992
$20,000 to	$30,000	964
$10,000 to	$20,000	920
less than	$10,000	873

Based on the test results of 898,596 SAT takers.
Source: Derived from the College Entrance Examination
Board and Educational Testing Service, "1996 College-
Bound Seniors: A Profile of SAT Test Takers" (Princeton,
NJ: 1993), p. 7.

operates independently of academic ability at every stage in the process of educational attainment."[20]

Today, the pattern persists. There are, however, two significant changes. On the one hand, the odds of getting into college have improved for the bottom quartile of the population, although they still remain relatively low compared to the top. On the other hand, the chances of completing a college degree have deteriorated markedly for the bottom quartile. Researchers estimate the chances of completing a four-year college degree (by age twenty-four) to be nineteen times as great for the top 25 percent of the population as it is for the bottom 25 percent. "Those from the bottom quartile of family income … are faring worse than they have at any time in the twenty-three years of published Current Population Survey data."[21]

Reality 6:   Class standing has a significant impact on chances for educational attainment.

Class standing, and consequently life chances, are largely determined at birth. Although examples of individuals who have gone from rags to riches abound in the mass media, statistics on class mobility show these leaps to be extremely rare. In fact, dramatic advances in class standing are relatively few. One study showed that fewer than one in five men surpass the economic status of their fathers.[22] For those whose annual income is in six fig-

[20]William H. Sewell, "Inequality of Opportunity for Higher Education," *American Sociological Review,* vol. 36, no. 5, 1971, pp. 793–809.

[21]The Mortenson Report on Public Policy Analysis of Opportunity for Postsecondary Education, "Postsecondary Education Opportunity," Iowa City, September 1993, no. 16.

[22]De Lone, *Small Futures,* pp. 14–19.

do not agree!

ures, economic success is due in large part to the wealth and privileges be-stowed on them at birth. Over 66 percent of the consumer units with in-comes of $100,000 or more have some inherited assets. Of these units, over 86 percent reported that inheritances constituted a substantial portion of their total assets.[23]

Economist Howard Wachtel likens inheritance to a series of Monopoly   40
games in which the winner of the first game refuses to relinquish his or her cash and commercial property for the second game. "After all," argues the winner, "I accumulated my wealth and income by my own wits." With such an arrangement, it is not difficult to predict the outcome of subsequent games.[24]

Reality 7:   All Americans do not have an equal opportunity to succeed. *don't agree* Inheritance laws ensure a greater likelihood of success for the offspring of the wealthy.

Spheres of Power and Oppression

When we look at society and try to determine what it is that keeps most people down—what holds them back from realizing their potential as healthy, creative, productive individuals—we find institutionally oppressive forces that are largely beyond individual control. Class domination is one of these forces. People do not choose to be poor or working class; instead, they *b-s.* are limited and confined by the opportunities afforded or denied them by a social and economic system. The class structure in the United States is a function of its economic system—capitalism, a system that is based on pri-vate rather than public ownership and control of commercial enterprises, and on the class division between those who own and control and those who do not. Under capitalism, these enterprises are governed by the need to produce a profit for the owners, rather than to fulfill collective needs.

Racial and gender domination are other such forces that hold people down. Although there are significant differences in the way capitalism, racism, and sexism affect our lives, there are also a multitude of parallels. And although race, class, and gender act independently of each other, they are at the same time very much interrelated.

On the one hand, issues of race and gender oppression cut across class lines. Women experience the effects of sexism whether they are well-paid professionals or poorly paid clerks. As women, they face discrimination and male domination as well as catcalls and stereotyping. Similarly, a black man faces racial oppression, is subjected to racial slurs, and is denied opportuni-ties because of his color. Regardless of their class standing, women and members of minority races are confronted with oppressive forces precisely because of their gender, color, or both.

[23]Howard Tuchman, *Economics of the Rich,* New York, Random House, 1973, p. 15.
[24]Howard Wachtel, *Labor and the Economy,* Orlando, FL, Academic Press, 1984, pp. 161–162.

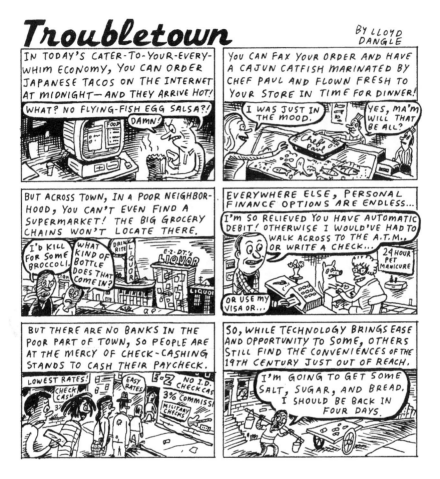

On the other hand, class oppression permeates other spheres of power and oppression, so that the oppression experienced by women and minorities is also differentiated along class lines. Although women and minorities find themselves in subordinate positions vis-à-vis white men, the particular issues they confront may be quite different depending on their position in the class structure. Inequalities in the class structure distinguish social functions and individual power, and these distinctions carry over to race and gender categories.

Power is incremental, and class privileges can accrue to individual women and to individual members of a racial minority. At the same time, class-oppressed men, whether they are white or black, have privileges afforded them as men in a sexist society. Similarly, class-oppressed whites, whether they are men or women, have privileges afforded them as whites in a racist society. Spheres of power and oppression divide us deeply in our society, and the schisms between us are often difficult to bridge.

Table 2   Chances of Being Poor in America

WHITE MALE/ FEMALE	WHITE FEMALE HEAD°	HISPANIC MALE/ FEMALE	HISPANIC FEMALE HEAD°	BLACK MALE/ FEMALE	BLACK FEMALE HEAD°
1 in 11	1 in 4	1 in 3	1 in 2	1 in 3	1 in 2

°Persons in families with female householder, no husband present.
Source: Derived from "Poverty 1995" (Washington, DC: U.S. Census Bureau, 1996), p. 1.

[handwritten margin note: makes people feel bad who upper c(lass)]

Whereas power is incremental, oppression is cumulative, and those who are poor, black, and female have all the forces of classism, racism, and sexism bearing down on them. This cumulative oppression is what is meant by the double and triple jeopardy of women and minorities.

Furthermore, oppression in one sphere is related to the likelihood of oppression in another. If you are black and female, for example, you are much more likely to be poor or working class than you would be as a white male. Census figures show that the incidence of poverty varies greatly by race and gender.

In other words, being female and being nonwhite are attributes in our society that increase the chances of poverty and of lower-class standing.

Reality 8:   Racism and sexism compound the effects of classism in society.   50

ENGAGING THE TEXT

1. Reexamine the four myths Mantsios identifies (paras. 9–12). What does Mantsios say is wrong about each myth, and what evidence does he provide to critique each? How persuasive do you find his evidence and reasoning?

2. Early in the essay, Mantsios refers to exploitation and oppression. Does the essay make a case that the wealthy are exploiting the poor, or does it simply assume this? To what extent do you agree with Mantsios's position?

3. Work out a rough budget for a family of four with an annual income of $16,000. Be sure to include costs for food, clothing, housing, transportation, healthcare, and other unavoidable expenses. Do you think this is a reasonable "poverty line," or is it too high or too low?

4. Imagine that you are Harold S. Browning, Bob Farrell, or Cheryl Mitchell. Write an entry for this person's journal after a tough day on the job. Compare and contrast your entry with those written by other students.

5. Mantsios clearly sees our class system as oppressive, but in this essay he does not address solutions to the problems he cites. What changes do you imagine Mantsios would like to see? What changes, if any, would you recommend?

EXPLORING CONNECTIONS

6. Working in small groups, discuss which class each of the following would belong to and how this class affiliation would shape the life chances of each:

> Gary Soto in "Looking for Work" (p. 39)
> Anndee Hochman in "Growing Pains" (p. 45)
> the narrator of "An Indian Story" (p. 89)
> Stephen Cruz (p. 335)
> Miss Moore in "The Lesson" (p. 394)
> Cora Tucker (p. 340)
> C. P. Ellis (p. 562)
> Mike Rose (p. 162)
> Richard Rodriguez (p. 194)

7. Although Mantsios does not focus on the Horatio Alger myth as does Harlon Dalton (p. 311), both authors concern themselves with seeing beyond myths of success to underlying realities. Compare the ways these two writers challenge the American mythology of success. Do the two readings complement one another, or do you see fundamental disagreements between the two authors? Whose approach do you find more persuasive, insightful, or informative, and why?

8. Compare this essay by Mantsios to "The Invisible Poor" by James Fallows (p. 356). What similarities or differences do you see in the ways they understand and write about social class, wealth, and poverty?

EXTENDING THE CRITICAL CONTEXT

9. Mantsios points out that "inheritance laws assure a greater likelihood of success for the offspring of the wealthy" (para. 41). Explain why you think this is or is not a serious problem. Keeping in mind the difference between wealth and income, discuss how society might attempt to remedy this problem and what policies you would endorse.

10. Skim through several recent issues of a financial magazine like *Forbes* or *Money*. Who is the audience for these publications? What kind of advice is offered, what kinds of products and services are advertised, and what levels of income and investment are discussed?

11. Study the employment pages of a major newspaper in your area. Roughly what percentage of the openings would you consider upper class, middle class, and lower class? On what basis do you make your distinctions? What do the available jobs suggest about the current levels of affluence in your area?

12. The data Mantsios offers are now at least five years old. Do you imagine the statistics today would be more or less dramatic than those he cites? Research one or more of the measures he uses and report to the class the most current information you can find.

Stephen Cruz

Studs Terkel

The speaker of the following oral history is Stephen Cruz, a man who at first glance seems to be living the American Dream of success and upward mobility. He is never content, however, and he comes to question his own values and the meaning of success in the world of corporate America. Studs Terkel (b. 1912) is probably the best-known practitioner of oral history in the United States. He has compiled several books by interviewing dozens of widely varying people—ordinary people for the most part—about important subjects like work, social class, race, and the Great Depression. The edited versions of these interviews are often surprisingly powerful crystallizations of American social history: Terkel's subjects give voice to the frustrations and hopes of whole generations of Americans. Terkel won a Pulitzer Prize in 1985 for "The Good War": An Oral History of World War II. *This selection first appeared in his* American Dreams: Lost and Found *(1980).*

He is thirty-nine.

"The family came in stages from Mexico. Your grandparents usually came first, did a little work, found little roots, put together a few bucks, and brought the family in, one at a time. Those were the days when controls at the border didn't exist as they do now."

You just tried very hard to be whatever it is the system wanted of you. I was a good student and, as small as I was, a pretty good athlete. I was well liked, I thought. We were fairly affluent, but we lived down where all the trashy whites were. It was the only housing we could get. As kids, we never understood why. We did everything right. We didn't have those Mexican accents, we were never on welfare. Dad wouldn't be on welfare to save his soul. He woulda died first. He worked during the Depression. He carries that pride with him, even today.

Of the five children, I'm the only one who really got into the business world. We learned quickly that you have to look for opportunities and add things up very quickly. I was in liberal arts, but as soon as Sputnik[1] went up, well, golly, hell, we knew where the bucks were. I went right over to the registrar's office and signed up for engineering. I got my degree in '62. If you had a master's in business as well, they were just paying all kinds of bucks. So that's what I did. Sure enough, the market was super. I had fourteen job offers. I could have had a hundred if I wanted to look around.

---

[1]*Sputnik:* Satellite launched by the Soviet Union in 1957; this launch signaled the beginning of the "space race" between the United States and the USSR.

I never once associated these offers with my being a minority. I was   5
aware of the Civil Rights Act of 1964, but I was still self-confident enough
to feel they wanted me because of my abilities. Looking back, the reason I
got more offers than the other guys was because of the government edict.
And I thought it was because I was so goddamned brilliant. (Laughs.) In
1962, I didn't get as many offers as those who were less qualified. You have
a tendency to blame the job market. You just don't want to face the issue of
discrimination.

I went to work with Procter & Gamble. After about two years, they told
me I was one of the best supervisors they ever had and they were gonna
promote me. Okay, I went into personnel. Again, I thought it was because I
was such a brilliant guy. Now I started getting wise to the ways of the American Dream. My office was glass-enclosed, while all the other offices were
enclosed so you couldn't see into them. I was the visible man.

They made sure I interviewed most of the people that came in. I just
didn't really think there was anything wrong until we got a new plant manager, a southerner. I received instructions from him on how I should interview blacks. Just check and see if they smell, okay? That was the beginning
of my training program. I started asking: Why weren't we hiring more minorities? I realized I was the only one in a management position.

I guess as a Mexican I was more acceptable because I wasn't really black.
I was a good compromise. I was visibly good. I hired a black secretary, which
was *verboten*. When I came back from my vacation, she was gone. My boss
fired her while I was away. I asked why and never got a good reason.

Until then, I never questioned the American Dream. I was convinced if
you worked hard, you could make it. I never considered myself different.
That was the trouble. We had been discriminated against a lot, but I never
associated it with society. I considered it an individual matter. Bad people,
my mother used to say. In '68 I began to question.

I was doing fine. My very first year out of college, I was making twelve   10
thousand dollars. I left Procter & Gamble because I really saw no opportunity. They were content to leave me visible, but my thoughts were not really
solicited. I may have overreacted a bit, with the plant manager's attitude,
but I felt there's no way a Mexican could get ahead here.

I went to work for Blue Cross. It's 1969. The Great Society[2] is in full
swing. Those who never thought of being minorities before are being
turned on. Consciousness raising is going on. Black programs are popping
up in universities. Cultural identity and all that. But what about the one
issue in this country: economics? There were very few management jobs for
minorities, especially blacks.

The stereotypes popped up again. If you're Oriental, you're real good in
mathematics. If you're Mexican, you're a happy guy to have around, pleas-

---

[2]*The Great Society:* President Lyndon B. Johnson's term for the American society he
hoped to establish through social reforms, including an antipoverty program.

ant but emotional. Mexicans are either sleeping or laughing all the time. Life is just one big happy kind of event. *Mañana*. Good to have as part of the management team, as long as you weren't allowed to make decisions.

I was thinking there were two possibilities why minorities were not making it in business. One was deep, ingrained racism. But there was still the possibility that they were simply a bunch of bad managers who just couldn't cut it. You see, until now I believed everything I was taught about the dream: the American businessman is omnipotent and fair. If we could show these turkeys there's money to be made in hiring minorities, these businessmen—good managers, good decision makers—would respond. I naively thought American businessmen gave a damn about society, that given a choice they would do the right thing. I had that faith.

I was hungry for learning about decision-making criteria. I was still too far away from top management to see exactly how they were working. I needed to learn more. Hey, just learn more and you'll make it. That part of the dream hadn't left me yet. I was still clinging to the notion of work your ass off, learn more than anybody else, and you'll get in that sphere.

During my fifth year at Blue Cross, I discovered another flaw in the American Dream. Minorities are as bad to other minorities as whites are to minorities. The strongest weapon the white manager had is the old divide and conquer routine. My mistake was thinking we were all at the same level of consciousness.

I had attempted to bring together some blacks with the other minorities. There weren't too many of them anyway. The Orientals never really got involved. The blacks misunderstood what I was presenting, perhaps I said it badly. They were on the cultural kick: a manager should be crucified for saying "Negro" instead of "black." I said as long as the Negro or the black gets the job, it doesn't mean a damn what he's called. We got into a huge hassle. Management, of course, merely smiled. The whole struggle fell flat on its face. It crumpled from divisiveness. So I learned another lesson. People have their own agenda. It doesn't matter what group you're with, there is a tendency to put the other guy down regardless.

The American Dream began to look so damn complicated, I began to think: Hell, if I wanted, I could just back away and reap the harvest myself. By this time, I'm up to twenty-five thousand dollars a year. It's beginning to look good, and a lot of people are beginning to look good. And they're saying: "Hey, the American Dream, you got it. Why don't you lay off?" I wasn't falling in line.

My bosses were telling me I had all the "ingredients" for top management. All that was required was to "get to know our business." This term comes up all the time. If I could just warn all minorities and women whenever you hear "get to know our business," they're really saying "fall in line." Stay within that fence, and glory can be yours. I left Blue Cross disillusioned. They offered me a director's job at thirty thousand dollars before I quit.

All I had to do was behave myself. I had the "ingredients" of being a good Chicano, the equivalent of the good nigger. I was smart. I could articulate well. People didn't know by my speech patterns that I was of Mexican heritage. Some tell me I don't look Mexican, that I have a certain amount of Italian, Lebanese, or who knows. (Laughs.)

One could easily say: "Hey, what's your bitch? The American Dream 20
has treated you beautifully. So just knock it off and quit this crap you're spreading around." It was a real problem. Every time I turned around, America seemed to be treating me very well.

Hell, I even thought of dropping out, the hell with it. Maybe get a job in a factory. But what happened? Offers kept coming in. I just said to myself: God, isn't this silly? You might as well take the bucks and continue looking for the answer. So I did that. But each time I took the money, the conflict in me got more intense, not less.

Wow, I'm up to thirty-five thousand a year. This is a savings and loan business. I have faith in the executive director. He was the kind of guy I was looking for in top management: understanding, humane, also looking for the formula. Until he was up for consideration as executive v.p. of the entire organization. All of a sudden everything changed. It wasn't until I saw this guy flip-flop that I realized how powerful vested interests are. Suddenly he's saying: "Don't rock the boat. Keep a low profile. Get in line." Another disappointment.

Subsequently, I went to work for a consulting firm. I said to myself: Okay, I've got to get close to the executive mind. I need to know how they work. Wow, a consulting firm.

Consulting firms are saving a lot of American businessmen. They're doing it in ways that defy the whole notion of capitalism. They're not allowing these businesses to fail. Lockheed was successful in getting U.S. funding guarantees because of the efforts of consulting firms working on their behalf, helping them look better. In this kind of work, you don't find minorities. You've got to be a proven success in business before you get there.

The American Dream, I see now, is governed not by education, oppor- 25
tunity, and hard work, but by power and fear. The higher up in the organization you go, the more you have to lose. The dream is *not losing*. This is the notion pervading America today: don't lose.

When I left the consulting business, I was making fifty thousand dollars a year. My last performance appraisal was: you can go a long way in this business, you can be a partner, but you gotta know our business. It came up again. At this point, I was incapable of being disillusioned any more. How easy it is to be swallowed up by the same set of values that governs the top guy. I was becoming that way. I was becoming concerned about losing that fifty grand or so a year. So I asked other minorities who had it made. I'd go up and ask 'em: "Look, do you owe anything to others?" The answer was: "We owe nothing to anybody." They drew from the civil rights movement but felt no debt. They've quickly forgotten how it happened. It's like I was when I first got out of college. Hey, it's really me, I'm great. I'm great. I'm as angry with these guys as I am with the top guys.

Right now, it's confused. I've had fifteen years in the business world as "a success." Many Anglos would be envious of my progress. Fifty thousand dollars a year puts you in the one or two top percent of all Americans. Plus my wife making another thirty thousand. We had lots of money. When I gave it up, my cohorts looked at me not just as strange, but as something of a traitor. "You're screwing it up for all of us. You're part of our union, we're the elite, we should govern. What the hell are you doing?" So now I'm looked at suspiciously by my peer group as well.

I'm teaching at the University of Wisconsin at Platteville. It's nice. My colleagues tell me what's on their minds. I got a farm next-door to Platteville. With farm prices being what they are (laughs), it's a losing proposition. But with university work and what money we've saved, we're gonna be all right.

The American Dream is getting more elusive. The dream is being governed by a few people's notion of what the dream is. Sometimes I feel it's a small group of financiers that gets together once a year and decides all the world's issues.

It's getting so big. The small-business venture is not there any more.   30
Business has become too big to influence. It can't be changed internally. A counterpower is needed.

ENGAGING THE TEXT

1. As Cruz moves up the economic ladder, he experiences growing conflict that keeps him from being content and proud of his accomplishments. To what do you attribute his discontent? Is his "solution" one that you would recommend?

2. Cruz says that the real force in America is the dream of "not losing" (para. 25). What does he mean by this? Do you agree?

3. What, according to Stephen Cruz, is wrong with the American Dream? Write an essay in which you first define and then either defend or critique his position.

4. Imagine the remainder of Stephen Cruz's life. Write a few paragraphs continuing his story. Read these aloud and discuss.

EXPLORING CONNECTIONS

5. Compare Stephen Cruz to Ragged Dick (p. 298) and Colin Powell (p. 305) in terms of the American Dream and individual success. How similar are Cruz's circumstances, goals, beliefs, and values to those examples of the Dream come true? What distinguishes him from those figures?

6. Compare Stephen Cruz to Richard Rodriguez (p. 194), Gary Soto (p. 39), and Mike Rose (p. 162) in terms of their attitudes toward education and success.

EXTENDING THE CRITICAL CONTEXT

7. According to Cruz, in 1969 few management positions were open to members of minority groups. Working in small groups, go to the library and look up current statistics on minorities in business (for example, the number of large minority-owned companies; the number of minority chief executives among major corporations; the distribution of minorities among top management, middle management, supervisory, and clerical positions). Compare notes with classmates and discuss.

Good Noise: Cora Tucker
ANNE WITTE GARLAND

When most people think about the American Dream, they don't visualize a factory job and a cluttered house right next to the railroad tracks. As you read this selection about community activist Cora Tucker, however, think about the connection of her life to core American values like democracy, progress, and individual rights. Author Anne Witte Garland is a freelance writer covering environmental, public health, consumer, and women's issues. This selection comes from her 1988 book Women Activists: Challenging the Abuse of Power.

Cora Tucker's house is so close to the railroad tracks that at night when trains thunder by, the beds shake. The house and furniture are modest, and in the kitchen there's a lingering smell of the lard Cora cooks with. There are traces of Virginia red clay on the kitchen floor, and piled up on the bedroom floor are cardboard boxes overflowing with newspaper clippings and other papers.

Cora admits she doesn't like housekeeping anymore. The plaques and photographs hanging in the kitchen and living room attest to what she does enjoy; alongside religious pictures and photos of her children and grandchildren, there are several citizenship awards, certificates acknowledging her work in civil rights, and photos of her—a pretty, smiling black woman—with various politicians. One framed picture in the kitchen was handmade for Cora by some of the inmates in a nearby prison, whom Cora has visited and helped. In it, Old English letters made of foil spell out, "God grant me the serenity to accept the things I cannot change, the courage to change the things I can, and wisdom to know the difference." Cora has plenty of all three virtues, although "serene" probably isn't the first adjective a stranger would pin on her. But then, there isn't much that Cora would say she can't change, either.

Cora Tucker is something of an institution in Halifax County, Virginia, a rural county bordering North Carolina. In more than a dozen years, she has missed only a handful of the county board of supervisors' monthly meetings. Her name appears in the letters columns of the two daily newspapers several times a week—either signed onto her own letter or, almost as often, vilified in someone else's. She seems to know and be known by every black person on the street, in the post offices, and in stores and restaurants. And she is known by white and black people alike as having taken on many of the local, white-controlled institutions. Her main concern is simply fighting for the underdog, which she does in many ways—from social work–like visits to the elderly and invalids, to legal fights against racial discrimination, registering people to vote, and lobbying on issues like health care and the environment.

Cora was born in 1941 ten miles from where she lives now, near the Halifax county seat, in the small town of South Boston. Her father was a school teacher and later a railway porter. He died when Cora was three, and her mother and the nine children became sharecroppers on white men's farms. It was as a sharecropper, Cora says, that she learned how to do community organizing. She started by trying to help other sharecroppers to get things like better heating and food stamps. "I didn't call it 'organizing,' then," she says. "I just called it 'being concerned.' When you do sharecropping, you move around a lot. So I got to know everybody in the county, and to know what people's problems were.

"Sharecropping is the worst form of drudgery; it's slavery really. You 5 work on a man's farm, supposedly for half the profit on the crops you grow. That's what the contract says. But you pay for all the stuff that goes into the crop—seeds, fertilizer, and all. You get free housing, but most sharecroppers' housing is dilapidated and cold. It isn't insulated—it's just shacks, really. Sharecroppers are poor. I know of a family of twelve who grew fifteen acres of tobacco, and at the end of the year, they had earned just fifty dollars. And I know sharecroppers who needed food and applied for food stamps, but couldn't get them because they supposedly made too much money; the boss went to the food stamp office, and said they made such and such, so they couldn't qualify."

Cora went to work very young, planting and plowing with the others in the family. Her mother taught her to cook when she was six; Cora remembers having to stand on a crate to reach the kitchen counter. She was a curious and intelligent child who loved school and was unhappy when she had to stay out of school to clean house for the white woman on the farm where they lived.

Cora always adored her mother. Bertha Plenty Moesley was a "chief stringer"—a step in tobacco processing that involves picking the green tobacco leaves from the plants one at a time, and stringing them together three leaves to a stick, so that they can be hung to dry and cure. "My mama worked hard," Cora says. "She would plow and do all the things the men did. She was independent; she raised her children alone for eighteen years. When I was little, I felt so bad that she had to work that hard just so we could survive. There was welfare out there—all kinds of help, if only somebody had told her how to go about getting it. She had very little education, and didn't know to go down to the welfare office for help. As I got older, I was upset by that and made up my mind, when I was about eight or nine years old, that if I ever got grown, I'd make sure that everybody knew how to get everything there was to get. And I really meant it. I learned early how to get things done, and I learned it would take initiative to get what I wanted."

By the time Cora learned about welfare, her mother wouldn't take advantage of it. She was proud, and she told the children to have self-respect. "We didn't have anything else," Cora's mother says. "The kids had only themselves to be proud of." Cora took the advice to heart. There's a story she tells about growing up that has found a permanent place in community-organizing lore. In her high school, which was segregated at the time (Halifax County schools didn't integrate until 1969, under court order), Cora entered an essay contest on the topic of "what America means to me." She was taken by surprise when her bitter essay about growing up black in the South won a statewide award. But on awards night she was in for another surprise. The winners were to have their essays read, and then shake hands with the Virginia governor. Cora's mother was in the audience beaming, along with Cora's friends and teachers. But when her essay was read, Cora didn't recognize it—it had been rewritten, and the less critical sentiments weren't hers at all. She refused to greet the governor. "I disappointed everyone— my mother even cried."

The only person who supported her that night, she says, was a high school literature teacher, whom she credits as an important influence on her. "He spent a lot of time with me, encouraging me. Every time an issue came up that I felt strongly about, he'd have me write about it—letters to the editor that never got printed. He told me, 'Nobody can make you a second-class citizen but you. You should be involved in what's going on around you.'"

Instead, at seventeen she dropped out of high school to get married. As she describes it, the next several years were consumed with housekeeping and having children—six of them in rapid succession. She and her husband adopted a seventh. At first, Cora says, she threw herself enthusiastically into her new role. "I just wanted to be married. My father-in-law used to tease me about making myself so busy just being married. He'd say, 'You ain't going to keep this up for long.' But I'd say yes I would. Every morning, I put clean sheets on our beds—washed and ironed them. I ironed every diaper. I read all the housekeeping magazines; my house was immaculate. But I was beginning to find myself so bored, even then. My husband was farming then, sharecropping, and he'd get up early; I'd get up too, and feed him and the kids, and then do the cleaning. But when you clean every day, there just isn't that much to do, so I'd be finished by ten in the morning! I joined a book club, so that I would get a book every month—but I would get bored in between. I would read the book in two days—I tried to savor it, but I couldn't make it last any longer. Then, when the kids started growing up and going to school, that would occupy me a little more. I'd feed them, then take them to school, and come back and clean and then start making lunch. But just as soon as my baby started school, I went out and got a job."

Halifax County has several textile and garment factories, and Cora went to work as a seamstress for one of the largest, a knit sportswear manufacturer. It was a fairly new operation, and the mostly women employees were expected to do everything, from lifting fabric bolts weighing forty or fifty pounds each, to sitting at sewing machines for eight hour stretches. There was no union; the county boasts in promotional material that less than 5 percent of the county's workforce is unionized. "Every time I used to talk to the girls there, my boss thought I was trying to get a union started. And I sure thought there *should* be a union; there were lots of health hazards, and people were always getting hurt. People got back injuries, two people even had heart attacks in the factory, because of the working conditions. I once got a woman to come down from Baltimore to talk about forming a union, but people got frightened because the bosses warned us that if there was any union activity, we'd lose our jobs."

Cora worked at the factory for seven years. The first thing she did with the money she was earning was to buy land for a house. "We had lived in places where we were so cold," she says. "We'd have no windows, and no wood. My dream was always to grow up and build me a house—my own house, out of brick. My husband never really wanted one; he was just as happy moving around. But after I had the babies and went to work at the factory, I told him I was going to build me a house. So the first year I worked, I saved a thousand dollars. The next year I saved another thousand, and then borrowed some from the company, to buy some land. Then I started saving again, for the house. But when I went to the FHA, they said I couldn't get a house without my husband's permission. At first, he said he wasn't going to have anything to do with it, so I said I'd buy a trailer instead. When he found out, he figured I might just as well put the money into a house, so he signed the papers. We built the house; it was the first time any of us had been inside a new house. I was crazy about it; we could sit down and say exactly where we wanted things. And while I was working, I bought every stick of furniture in it."

In 1976 Cora hurt her back and had to leave her job. Over the next few years she underwent surgery several times—first for her back, and then for cancer (for which she has had to have periodic treatments ever since). In the meantime, she had become active in the community. In the 1960s, she had participated in organizations like the National Association for the Advancement of Colored People, and another group called the Assemblies, but they moved too slowly for her tastes. ("They weren't really interested in taking on the power structure," she complains.) She had also organized her own letter-writing campaign in support of the federal Voting Rights Act to make it easier for blacks to vote. She had gone around to local churches, speaking to people and encouraging them to write to their representatives in Washington. She also took advantage of knowing women who ran beauty parlors—she provided the paper and pens, so that women could write letters while they sat under the hair dryers. "People would say to me, 'What good will it do?' But I think politicians have to be responsive if enough pressure can be brought to bear on them. You can complain, I can complain, but that's just two people. A politician needs to get piles of letters saying vote for this bill, because if you don't, you won't be in office much longer!" Cora was responsible for generating about five hundred letters supporting the voting law.

She takes voting very seriously. In 1977, she campaigned for a populist candidate for Virginia governor. She was undergoing cancer treatments at the time, but they made her tired, so she stopped the treatments in order to register people to vote. She had taught herself to drive, and personally rode around the county from house to house, filling her car with everyone there who was of voting age, driving them to the court house to register, and then home again. She's credited with having registered over one thousand people this way, and on election day, she personally drove many of them to the polling place.

While Cora was growing up, her mother's house was always filled with people—besides her own family, several cousins lived with them, and aunts and uncles who had moved up north and came back to visit would stay with Cora's mother. Cora's own house was the same way—always filled with neighborhood teenagers, white and black. Cora became a confidante for the young people, and she encouraged them to read about black history, and to be concerned about the community. One of the things that upset the teenagers was the fate of a county recreation center. Halifax had no recreation facilities, and the county had applied for money from the federal Department of Housing and Urban Development (HUD) to build a center. When HUD awarded the county $500,000, however, the county turned it down because, as Cora puts it, there were "too many strings attached"—meaning it would have to be integrated. At home because of her back trouble and cancer, Cora took it on herself to help steer the teenagers' anger toward research into community problems. "When I heard about the recreation center, I went to the county board meeting and raised hell," she says. "But they went ahead and did what they wanted anyway. What I realized then was that if I had had all those kids come with me to the meeting, there would have been some changes. You need warm bodies—persons present and accounted for—if you want to get things done."

In 1975, Cora founded her own organization, Citizens for a Better America. CBA's first project was a study of black spending and employment patterns in the county. The study was based on a survey of three hundred people; it took two years to complete, with Cora's teenage friends doing much of the legwork. The findings painted a clear picture of inequality. Blacks made up nearly half the county population, and according to the survey, spent a disproportionate share of their salaries on food, cars, and furniture. But, as the study pointed out, there were very few black employees at the grocery stores where the money was spent, not a single black salesperson in the furniture stores, and no black salesperson at the auto dealerships. Blacks weren't represented at all on newspaper or radio station staffs.

Cora saw to it that the survey results were published in the local newspaper. The next step was to act on the results. The survey had uncovered problems with hiring practices and promotions of blacks in the school system, so Cora complained to the school board. After waiting in vain for the board to respond, CBA filed a complaint with what was then the federal Department of Health, Education, and Welfare. An HEW investigation confirmed the problems, and the agency threatened to cut off federal education funds to the county if the discrimination wasn't corrected. The county promised that the next principals it hired would be black.

CBA then took on other aspects of the county government. The survey had found that of all the county employees, only 7 percent were black—chiefly custodial workers or workers hired with federal Comprehensive Employment Training Administration (CETA) funds. Only one black person in the county government made over $20,000 a year. When the county refused to negotiate with Cora's organization about their hiring practices, CBA filed a complaint with the federal revenue sharing program. A Virginia state senator was successful in getting a federal investigation into the complaint stalled, but Cora went over his head, to the congressional Black Caucus and Maryland's black congressman, Parren Mitchell. Mitchell contacted Senator Edward Kennedy's office, which pressed to have the investigation completed. The findings confirmed CBA's, and the county was told to improve its hiring practices or stand to lose federal revenues.

CBA also initiated a boycott of local businesses that didn't hire minorities—Cora avoided the term "boycott," and instead called the action the "Spend Your Money Wisely Campaign." Leaflets were distributed listing the stores that hired black employees, and urging people, "Where Blacks are not HIRED, Blacks should not buy!"

Cora was developing a reputation. She started having frequent contact with the congressional Black Caucus, and would be called occasionally to testify in Washington on welfare issues. "They don't usually get people like me to testify; they get all these 'experts' instead. But every once in a while, it's good for them to hear from someone who isn't a professional, whose English isn't good, and who talks from a grassroots level."

It wasn't just in Washington that her reputation was growing, but back home, too. "I have a lot of enemies," she says. "There are derogatory things in the papers about me all the time. And the county government doesn't like me, because I keep going to all those board meetings and raising hell about what they do. When I go sometimes, they say, 'Yes, what do you want now, Ms. Tucker?' But I don't care what they think—I just tell them what I want. So a lot of the white power structure don't really like me. They think I'm a troublemaker, but I'm not really. I just believe what I believe in. Then there are black people too, who think that I want too much too soon. But when you think about it, black people have been in America 360-some years, so when is the time ever going to be right? The time doesn't *get* right; you make it right. So I'm not offended by what anybody says about me."

Sometimes the problem isn't just what people say; it's what they do. Cora has had many experiences with harassment. At first it was phone calls, from people threatening to burn her house down or telling her to "go back to Africa." Once she wrote a letter to the editor saying, "This is an open letter to all the people who call me and ask, what do you niggers want now? and hang up before I can tell them. . . .

"Blacks and poor people want to share in the economic progress of Halifax County, and when we get our children educated and motivated we would like them to come back to Halifax County and do something other than push mops and brooms. And a few of us would like our grandchildren to grow up near us, and if our children decide to make their home elsewhere it will be due to choice and not an economic necessity."

The harassment has taken other forms as well. Cora was followed and run off the highway one night, and had all four tires slashed one day when her car was parked in town. Once she was in the post office and a man recognized her, walked over, and spit on her; another time a car with out-of-state license plates pulled up next to her car as if to ask directions, and the man spat into her face. She came home from a meeting one night to find that someone had broken into her home and drenched her bed with gasoline. But Cora views the abuses with amazing equanimity: "If you stop doing things because somebody says something bad about you or does something to you," she says, "then you'll never get *anything* done."

25

And she wasn't making only enemies; she was also gaining a following. One woman, who now works in the local legal aid office where Cora stops in frequently to get answers to legal questions, tells how she first met Cora. The woman had been born in Halifax, but had moved to New Jersey when she was a young girl. The civil rights movement progressed, and when the woman was finished with school, she moved back to Virginia, thinking that things there would be much better than they *had* been for blacks. But she found that any progress had been superficial only. When she started looking for work, she discovered that there were no blacks in responsible positions. She wore her hair in an Afro, and in hindsight thinks that it cost her jobs: at one point, it seemed she would be offered a position with the county, but when the man who was to be her boss saw her, he didn't give her the job. Another prospective employer turned her down with the flat statement that he didn't want any union people around.

She became disillusioned, and was shocked at the complacency around her. About that time, she saw Cora Tucker's name in the paper. She was impressed, and started asking around about Cora. Not too long afterwards, she went to a community action program meeting, and noticed that Cora was scheduled to speak. "I was excited. I thought, finally, I'm going to meet a black person who's alive!" But she was initially disappointed. "I had pictured her as a towering woman—a fiery, eloquent speaker, like Barbara Jordan. Instead, there she was, short, and not that articulate."

But she quickly got drawn to Cora's strengths. "Cora wouldn't be happy at home, doing housekeeping," she says. "She's just not cut out for that. She's cut out for doing exactly what she's doing—getting out and raising hell about issues that affect people. She keeps pushing. When I get burned, I back off. But when Cora gets burned, she just blows out the fire and goes on."

Even people who don't like Cora give her credit: "I'm not a Cora Tucker fan," says one South Boston resident. "But I admit that she might just be the most informed person on political issues in this county." People credit Cora with having stamina and with inspiring others. An old friend of hers who runs a corner grocery says, "She keeps people fired up; she won't let us get lazy. It's because of her that I even watch the news!" One woman who was in school with Cora and now works for the county government says, "She was always making noise at school. We knew she'd grow up noisy. But it's *good* noise. When Cora talks, she knows what she's talking about."

And although Cora thinks she'll never be much of a public speaker, others disagree. One man who has worked with Cora for several years described a dinner ceremony sponsored by a human rights coalition in Richmond. "They had asked Cora to come and be a featured speaker. The woman who spoke before her gave this very polished speech. And then Cora got up, and gave her very unpolished speech. But it was moving to everyone in the room, because it was so much from the heart. It was the contrast of day and night between her and the previous speaker. What she had to say was so honest and down to earth, that people were very touched by it. And that's just the way she is."

Cora is very religious. "I believe in God, and in the providence of prayer. I go to church regularly." The churches in her area are still segregated; she attends the Crystal Hill Baptist Church, which, she points out with a chuckle, is brick-colored, while the white congregation down the

30

road painted their brick church white. In an essay called "Halifax County and Blacks," under a subtitle "Things Blacks Must Do To Succeed," Cora once wrote, "First, blacks must go to church. The church is the backbone of black progress." Every summer for several years Cora has organized a "Citizenship Day of Prayer" on the lawn of the county courthouse in South Boston, which attracts hundreds of people who probably wouldn't gather if the event were called a rally. At the event a list of grievances is always read off—including complaints about such things as how people are treated by the welfare system, unfair employment practices, or disproportionate suspensions of black pupils in the schools.

Problems like that—and what to do about them—are raised regularly at Citizens for a Better America meetings, held the fourth Friday of each month at a local funeral home. CBA has several hundred members, and with help from friends, Cora publishes a monthly one-page newsletter, which she decorates with American flag stickers and short religious sayings. The newsletter is a hodgepodge of useful information, including notices of food stamp law changes, regular updates on what the Virginia General Assembly is considering, board of supervisors' actions, community news, and news about other subjects that Cora is currently concerned with. One issue might have an essay on education, something on federal budget cutbacks and poor people, and a paragraph on the dangers of uranium mining. In 1986, when the federal government was considering southern Virginia, including part of Halifax County, as a possible site for a high-level nuclear waste dump, Cora and CBA fought back, using a section of the federal law requiring that the siting consideration take Indians and other minorities into account. Among other things, CBA found that blacks owned more farmland in Halifax County than in any other county in the country, and that historically, the first black-owned businesses and land in the country were on the site that would be affected by the nuclear waste dump.

Cora learns facts quickly; she can attend a meeting on the problems of family farmers one day, and the next, go to another meeting and be able to reel off facts and figures about farm foreclosures, the cost of fertilizers, trends in agribusiness, and the harmful effect of various pesticides. She reads constantly—newspapers, books, anything on an issue that interests her. "I save newspaper clippings—especially statements from politicians. That way, five years from now when they say, 'I'm definitely against that,' I can go back and say, 'But on such and such a date, you said *this*.'"

Cora stays extremely busy. Several years ago, she went back and got her graduate equivalency diploma, and took some courses at the community college. She thought she might want her degree: "I used to think I wanted to be a social worker. But I changed my mind, because you can't do as much inside the system as you can on the outside. There are so many people who become social workers, and then sit there with their hands tied. What people really need is somebody on the outside who's going to go and raise hell for them about laws and regulations."

Besides CBA gatherings, meetings of the county board of supervisors, and her usual rounds to the legal aid office and the county office building, Cora still visits elderly people, helps women without cars to do their shopping, reads and explains people's mail about food stamps and social security to them, and answers frequent letters. She takes every letter seriously. One, for instance, addressed simply to "Cora Tucker, Halifax, Virginia," read, "Dear Mrs. Tucker, Please don't let the county send us to be experimented on. We heard that they are going to take people on welfare to be experimented on." Cora remembered that there had been separate articles in the newspaper recently, on the "workfare" program to employ welfare recipients, and on a county decision to allow dogs from the animal pound to be used for medical experiments. Cora concluded that the person who wrote the letter had gotten the two issues confused—but she wasn't satisfied until she had called the county administrator and had gotten him to pledge to do a better job of explaining the issues publicly.

Cora's work goes far beyond Halifax. CBA itself has chapters in several 35 other places, including one started in Baltimore by one of Cora's sisters. In addition, when a new coalition group, Virginia Action, was started in the state in 1980, Cora was on the founding committee and was elected its first president. She also became active on the board of its national affiliate, Citizen Action. And in 1981, on top of everything else she was doing, this woman who as a girl had refused to shake the governor's hand was talked into running as a write-in protest candidate for governor by several black groups. She didn't get many votes, but her campaign was covered in the press, and she thinks that she raised issues about black people's concerns that otherwise would have been ignored.

Cora hasn't received much support in her work from her family, except from her mother. She and her husband are estranged, and her children haven't taken an active interest in Cora's work. Cora visits her mother often, in an old house several miles away that has woodburning stoves for heat, religious pictures in the downstairs room, and, hanging in the stairway, a plastic placemat depicting Martin Luther King's tomb. Cora's mother is clearly proud of her; she emphasizes what a smart girl Cora was, and is, and how courageous.

Others agree. As a man who works with Cora at Virginia Action puts it, "All of the issues Cora has taken on—like voting rights and employment discrimination—had been problems in Halifax County for decades. But nobody was willing to fight. And the reason was that it's very, very hard to be somebody going against the mainstream in a small rural community. It's a hell of a lot easier to play the role of the gadfly when you live in an urban environment, where you have your own community of friends, and you don't have to worry about the world. In a small rural community, your community *is* your world. And it's hard to fight the people you have to face every single day. Cora's able to do it because she's got guts. There's just nothing else to it but courage. In a small community those people writing nasty letters to the editor about you are people you're going to run into at the grocery, or whose kids go to school with yours. In addition, being black in a southern rural community, and being a woman, make it that much harder. She hasn't even had the active support of a large part of the black community—they feel threatened by her; she's stolen a lot of their fire. And she's always fighting back as opposed to the blacks who always cooperate with the white power structure. She just reached a point where she decided that slow-moving efforts weren't enough for the things that needed doing—things that were clear in her mind. She recognized the dangers that would be involved, but went ahead because she knew she was right."

ENGAGING THE TEXT

1. How might Cora Tucker define success? To what extent has she achieved it?

2. What motivates Cora Tucker? How do you explain her courage and commitment? Can you think of any ways to encourage more people to emulate some of her virtues?

3. What has her experience taught Cora Tucker about "organizing"? What are her strategies for getting things done?

4. Do you think people in small towns or rural communities are better able than urban dwellers to influence political decisions that affect them? Why or why not?

EXPLORING CONNECTIONS

5. Review the stories of Ragged Dick (p. 298) and Colin Powell (p. 305) to refresh in your mind those definitive, archetypal versions of the American Dream. What, if anything, does Cora Tucker have in common with Dick and Powell? How does she differ? What, if anything, will keep Cora Tucker from becoming a mythic figure in our culture?

6. In "Class in America: Myths and Realities" (p. 318), Gregory Mantsios writes, "When we look at society and try to determine what it is that keeps most people down—what holds them back from realizing their full potential as healthy, creative, productive individuals—we find institutionally oppressive forces that are largely beyond individual control." How do you think Cora Tucker might respond to this statement? Does her story challenge this or other claims by Mantsios?

EXTENDING THE CRITICAL CONTEXT

7. Research grass-roots organizations like Citizens for a Better America in your community. Choose one and attend a meeting and interview members of the organization. Report to the class on its goals, strategies, accomplishments, and current objectives and challenges.

8. In May 2000, the American Association of Retired Persons (AARP) released "Money and the American Family," a report based on nationwide interviews. The report contains several interesting findings—for example, that 11 percent of Americans are "wealth-averse" and, like Cora Tucker, don't particularly crave money. Consult the AARP report and summarize what you find for the class. If you have Internet access, visit the AARP Web site at www.aarp.org or the *Reading America* site: www.bedfordstmartins.com/ra.

Visual Portfolio

READING IMAGES OF INDIVIDUAL OPPORTUNITY

Visual Portfolio

READING IMAGES OF INDIVIDUAL OPPORTUNITY

1. Explain the appeal of the Simmons mattress ad. Consider in particular the different ways the idea of money is being used to sell mattresses. Also discuss such details of the photograph as its overhead perspective, the woman's posture and facial expression, and the amount of money actually pictured.

2. What's happening in the photograph of the bank meeting? Discuss such elements of the photo as the setting, the bankers' clothes, their facial expressions, and the framed portraits on the wall. What does this image tell you about money and success?

3. How does the urban scene with the TV fit into a portfolio of images about money and success? What ideas and emotions does it trigger in you? Explain the prominence of the broken TV: Why is a portion of the image framed by a TV rather than by one of countless alternatives (picture frame, doorway, window, etc.)?

4. In the photograph of a man repairing novelty items during vocational training, what else is going on? What is the man thinking? What is his relationship to his work, to the toys, and to his coworker? What do you make of the slogan on his T-shirt, "Freedom by any means necessary"?

5. Working in small groups, take a close look at the design of whatever coins and paper money you have handy. What information is being conveyed in their words and images?

The Invisible Poor

JAMES FALLOWS

Evidence abounds to support the old saying that the rich are getting richer and the poor are getting poorer. In this essay, James Fallows looks beyond that cliché and sees a changed relationship between rich Americans and poor; he endeavors to explain how and why we have made the poor among us "invisible." Fallows (b. 1949) is national correspondent for the Atlantic Monthly *and author of several books, including* Looking at the Sun: The Rise of the New East Asian Economic and Political System *(1995) and* National Defense *(1981, recipient of the National Book Award). His most recent book is* Breaking the News: How the Media Undermine American Democracy *(1997).*

The way a rich nation thinks about its poor will always be convoluted. The richer people become in general, the easier it theoretically becomes for them to share with people who are left out. But the richer people become, the less they naturally stay in touch with the realities of life on the bottom, and the more they naturally prefer to be excited about their own prospects rather than concerned about someone else's.

All aspects of the convolution now affect our politics and culture, in a form with no exact precedent. The last time the United States self-consciously thought of itself as rich, in the early 1960s, discussions of how the wealth should be shared were under way even before real prosperity arrived. Welfare programs, with all their subsequent mixed effects, were expanded. But so were Social Security benefits, which along with Medicare converted the over-sixty-five age group from the poorest to the richest cohort of Americans within a generation. Before that, America's last significant wave of individual fortune-building, the original Gilded Age,[1] a century ago, touched off decades' worth of struggles over the distribution and domestication of that wealth: union battles, antitrust laws, muckraking exposés, the rapid growth of public education, laws establishing minimum wages and maximum hours and even the income tax.

Before, whenever we had wealth, we started discussing poverty. Why not now? Why is the current politics of wealth and poverty seemingly about wealth alone? Eight years ago, when Bill Clinton first ran for president, the Dow Jones average was under 3,500, yearly federal budget deficits were projected at hundreds of billions of dollars forever and beyond, and no one talked about the "permanent boom" or the "new economy." Yet in that more straitened time, Clinton made much of the importance of "not leaving a single person behind." It is possible that similar "compassionate" rhetoric might yet play a part in the general election.[2]

But it is striking how much less talk there is about the poor than there was eight years ago, when the country was economically uncertain, or in previous eras, when the country felt flush. Even last summer, when Clinton spent several days on a remarkable, Bobby Kennedy–like pilgrimage through impoverished areas from Indian reservations in South Dakota to ghetto neighborhoods in East St. Louis, the administration decided to refer to the effort not as a poverty tour but as a "new-markets initiative."

What is happening is partly a logical, policy-driven reaction. Poverty   5 really is lower than it has been in decades, especially for minority groups. The most attractive solution to it—a growing economy—is being applied. The people who have been totally left out of this boom often have medical, mental or other problems for which no one has an immediate solution. "The

[1]*Gilded Age:* Roughly 1875–1900, a period known for shallow glitz masking political and social corruption.
[2]*general election:* Fallows was looking forward from May 2000 to the November elections, including the presidential election.

In the Shadow of Wealth (Brooklyn) Angelica Rosete with her one-year-old daughter, Angie: "I moved from Mexico to New York six years ago, and got a job working for a sewing company. I don't have anything against rich people, but people who own factories or businesses, they treat the poor people really badly. They think, 'Oh, they're Mexican, they'll work for nothing.' I moved down to Atlanta to look for a better job to make more money and live better. I got a job cleaning offices, but it's just for a little while until I get enough money so I can go back home. You have to move wherever the work is, because you have to work to support these kids."
(Photograph by Taryn Simon.)

In the Shadow of Wealth (Manhattan)   Julio E. Santiago, next to the F.D.R. Drive: "They call me Willie. I've lived here for three years. I used to come out here with other people from the neighborhood and drink a lot of beer, and this place was burned up, and people used it as a crack and coke area, a place to shoot up. I picked up five hundred needles, burned them and buried the refuse under the ground. The Parks Department appreciated that because it's right next to a park. Little by little I cleaned it up. They never told me to leave, and they gave me plastic bags to cover my tent. Two cops come around to check on me to make sure I'm all right. I grew up in the neighborhood, I panhandle here, and people know me. I see people doing much better. Even the homeless are doing much better. People are more generous now. I used to get a lot of change, now I get more bills. When people have more, they give more. I go out every morning at 5 A.M. to a brokerage house on 46th and Park. Bear Stearns. You know it? I've been panhandling there for the last five years. These guys make millions of dollars in bonuses and they treat me good. Every morning between 5 A.M. and 8 A.M., I make $30 to $40. It helps me for breakfast, and for food for my cat. I spend $9 to $10 every day on the lottery. I'd rather spend it on this than on drugs. Like everyone else, I want to get a better life. I got a feeling one of these days I might hit. And if I hit, I would take a whole tenement building in Spanish Harlem and get some homeless people and hire them to fix it up, give them homes and get them back in the working system. People have helped me out all my life, and I want to return the favor."
(Photograph by Taryn Simon.)

economy has sucked in anyone who has any preparation, any ability to cope with modern life," says Franklin D. Raines, the former director of the Office of Management and Budget who is now head of Fannie Mae.[3] When he and other people who specialize in the issue talk about solutions, they talk analytically and long-term: education, development of work skills, shifts in the labor market, adjustments in welfare reform.

But I think there is another force that has made this a rich era with barely visible poor people. It is the unusual social and imaginative separation between prosperous America and those still left out. This is not the embattled distance of the *Bonfire of the Vanities*[4] period, with its gated communities and atmosphere of urban armed camps. It's more like simple invisibility, because of increasing geographic, occupational, and social barriers that block one group from the other's view. Prosperous America does not seem hostile to the poor, and often responds generously when reminded. But our poor are like people in Madagascar. We feel bad for them, but they live someplace else.

I recently worked for several months on a temporary project inside a large software company. During the business day I mixed with people who were generally younger and invariably richer than I was. I liked nearly all of them and soon adjusted to the view from the bottom of their economic ladder. I envied some of the things their money let them do or buy, but I rationalized that I was happy with the life I normally lived. Although I've wound up with more money than I ever expected when going into journalism, these surroundings allowed me to congratulate myself on the Gandhi-like antimaterialism I had displayed in making my career choice.

Because I had a long commute I often stayed late to wait out the traffic. Around 9 P.M. I'd hear a knock on the office door. A woman in her sixties, wearing a stiff-fabric vest with the logo of an office-cleaning company, stepped into the room to empty my wastebasket and collect Mountain Dew cans from the recycling bin. She would say something I could barely understand, and I would nod back. It seemed that she was Russian. She walked as if her feet hurt. She did not have the bounce of the people I saw during the day. She kept making her rounds until about midnight.

Eventually I started leaving the office to go home as soon as I heard her a few doors down. I was willing to read articles about the travails of the working poor or the adjustment problems of older, unskilled immigrants. I just didn't want to watch her limp.

The computer-financial complex, with strongholds in Silicon Valley,   10
San Francisco, and Seattle, and connections to New York, Boston, Austin, and elsewhere, has been both principal source and spiritual symbol of this

---

[3]*Fannie Mae:* The Federal National Mortgage Association, a government-sponsored organization that buys mortgages from lenders and repackages them for investors.

[4]*The Bonfire of the Vanities:* Tom Wolfe's 1987 satirical novel on money, greed, lust, and power in 1980s New York.

era of wealth. Relatively few Americans actually work in the "information technology" business, ranging from chips to computers to the Internet. But it has created the billion-dollar fortunes of recent years, and it has buoyed the stock market and therefore the wealth of mutual-fund America in general. Economists are now ready to concede that by cutting costs and raising productivity in "normal" businesses, from automaking to medical care, information technology has allowed the economy to keep growing without inflation, which in turn has lowered unemployment rates and created work for people who had not found jobs before.

Tech wealth has the same disproportionate, commanding-heights effect on today's culture as Wall Street's takeover-and-junk-bond complex had fifteen years ago, and as the biotech-financial complex presumably will fifteen years from now—and as the mass-production economy had at the start of the twentieth century, and as the boom in cars, highways, and real estate subdivision had after World War II. Therefore it is disproportionately significant that for reasons of geography, personal background, and working style the tech wealthy have very little sense that they live in the same country as anyone who is poor. The new millionaires are not a representative sample of the rest of the country, but they are a leading indicator.

The routes to tech wealth are more varied than they may look from outside this fevered economy. From Allentown or Cleveland it may seem as if twenty-year-olds in Silicon Valley simply drive up to a venture-capital office and drive out with a carful of money. In fact, that's only one of the business models. Tens of thousands of people have become millionaires through what has been, at least for the decade, the most predictable path to wealth in U.S. history: they have signed on with Microsoft; earned their stock options; and assumed that by the time the options vested four and a half years later, they'd be worth a million dollars or more. The simplest way to figure out how much a Microsoft employee is worth is knowing when he joined the company, and therefore how many rounds of options-granting and stock-splitting he has been through.

This route to wealth presumably can't last forever, since it has depended on Microsoft's stock value doubling on average every fifteen months through the 1990s. Yet while it has lasted it has not only created three of the five largest fortunes in the world (Bill Gates, Paul Allen, and Steve Ballmer[5]), and several more in the billions, but has also allowed people to start thinking, quite early in life, about what they will do when they become rich. "A surprisingly small number of people expect to stay with the company in the long run," says Eric Fox, twenty-seven, a software developer who came to Microsoft straight out of Yale six years ago (and who says he has no plans to leave). "The standard thing is to say that you expect to be here two more years, or five more years"— or until you hit "the number,"

---

[5]*Bill Gates, Paul Allen, and Steve Ballmer:* Gates and Allen founded Microsoft; Ballmer became its president.

the amount of wealth people have in mind as allowing them to quit. It is apparently not a matter of the work being unendurable, or even unpleasant, that causes so many Microsoft employees to talk about the time when they will leave; it is the near certainty of their having enough money, soon, to allow them to decide what they would "really" like to do. I have heard widely varying estimates of what "the number" typically is. A man in his twenties said $1 million, and a man in his forties said $15 million.

The highly publicized wealth of Internet start-up companies has been less predictable than Microsoft's, and more like that of the Klondike era. Everyone is trudging up the mountain together, like the prospectors going over Chilcoot Pass in *White Fang*,[6] and some of them end up frozen and broke while others are stumbling across lumps of gold. In an upcoming book called *The Leap*, Tom Ashbrook, who quit a job as deputy managing editor of the *Boston Globe* when he turned forty to start a Net company, describes his night sweats as he wondered if he'd have to sell the family house, take on loan-shark debt and by implication drive his wife away in order keep his experiment going. (At the last minute he found nearly $25 million in venture capital, and now has more than one hundred employees.) "This is not trickle down—it's all or nothing, you get it or you don't," says one woman who lives and works in Silicon Valley, and whose husband is a prominent technology C.E.O. "You make your first million, then five, then ten, and the numbers just get crazy. They're almost unbelievable. I remember being told about five years ago, if you don't have $25 million you're not a player—now that number sounds very small. If you have $250 million, well, you need to be a billionaire. The ripple effect of this on a society is large and alarming. It's like looking at the robber barons,[7] but thousands of them."

There are other routes to wealth too—for instance, being a venture 15 capitalist who places bets on ten new companies, assuming that if even one succeeds the returns will be immense. These cultures and subeconomies of course are full of individuals with (nearly) as wide a range of philosophies and goals and outlooks as the rest of the world. But they have several things in common that mark the era and, I believe, have a spillover effect on the rest of American life.

For one: money doesn't matter, at least not in the normal way. Estimates vary of when this effect kicks in, as you stop evaluating extra assets in terms of the leisure, possessions, choices, or other things you can buy and

[6]*White Fang:* The 1905 novel by Jack London (1876–1916) and companion book to his runaway best-seller, *The Call of the Wild* (1903); *White Fang* tells the story of a half-wolf dog during the Klondike gold rush of 1897–98.

[7]*robber barons:* The most successful American businessmen of the late nineteenth and early twentieth centuries — for example, Andrew Carnegie, John D. Rockefeller, J. P. Morgan, and Cornelius Vanderbilt — who amassed huge fortunes in steel, oil, banking, and railroads, respectively. "Robber barons" implies unfettered capitalism and unscrupulous business practices.

instead think of them mainly as markers of how you stand relative to others at the top. One young software developer, new on the job, said that he thought $200,000 a year would be the level at which no conceivable choice could be constrained. A venture capitalist has jokingly introduced the concept of the Fundamental Economic Unit, or F.E.U. This is the amount of money you will spend without thinking about it, because taking the time to shop around would just not be worthwhile. For a commuter the F.E.U. might be $3.50 for a fancy espresso whose raw ingredients cost twenty-five cents. I have heard discussions among software millionaires about an F.E.U. of half a million dollars, for a home bought on a whim.

The founder of an Internet company says that every dollar earned up to $300 million is positive, but beyond that point, since it mainly becomes a gauge for comparison with others, it increasingly reminds you that others have more—like coming in fifth in the Miss America contest. Rob Glaser, who is the founder of RealNetworks, an Internet audio company, and whose personal holdings are now valued at more than $2 billion, says, "For many of the people who have had the good fortune to achieve extreme wealth, it may now be a scorecard, or one of the things that sort of motivates them and helps them keep track, but it is more of an introduced phenomenon than an inherent one." That is, people who came into the business in the 1980s thought it would be interesting, and found that it made them rich. For many new arrivals, he says, sheer wealth is the draw.

A world where money is a marker and all comparisons are directed upward makes it hard to understand people for whom a million dollars would be a fortune, or those for whom $10,000 would be the difference between affording college or not, not to mention those for whom $246 is a full week's earnings, before tax, at the minimum wage. The titans of earlier eras were forced into an awareness that there was a proletariat. Andrew Carnegie and J. P. Morgan had to consider at least the existence of a working class willing to strike over a dollar's difference in weekly pay. The financial-engineering wave of the 1980s also gave leveraged-buyout artists the same uneasy exposure to working America that bomber pilots have to the civilians below, since reorganizing a company often meant liquidating jobs. With the tech economy the connection is faint. "If you were manufacturing cars, you had no choice but to deal with a large blue-collar work force of comparatively uneducated people," says Charles Ferguson, a writer and consultant who founded a software company and sold it to Microsoft for well over $100 million. "If you are a Net entrepreneur, you don't have to give a damn."

A young man who had worked exclusively at one software company told me, "Speaking for myself, I really don't know people who aren't comfortable." He pointed out that no matter what country his workmates came from, they all had surprisingly comparable professional-class upbringings. "I've dealt with very few people whose position is different from mine." That is why, he said, when he saved up enough money he wanted to quit and teach high school.

"Because of the intensity of the work, you tend to operate in a cocoon,"   20
says Glaser of RealNetworks. Like other Americans, but even more so,
people in fast-growing tech companies work long hours, are on the phone or
in their cars when not working, largely socialize with those they know from
work and are so desperate to make time for their spouses, children, and
friends that they feel they have very little left over for anyone else. "Inside
that cocoon you tend to be oblivious to the role the surrounding ecostruc-
ture plays in your success. From inside the cocoon you see only the cocoon.
It is unfortunate but understandable that people who have achieved these
results have an insular view of why they have achieved it—and why others
haven't."

The tech establishment has solved, in a fashion, a problem that vexes
the rest of America—and therefore thinks about it in a way that seems to
prefigure a larger shift. The hallway traffic in any major technology firm is
more racially varied than in other institutions in the country. (It is also overwhelmingly male.) But the very numerous black and brown faces belong
overwhelmingly to immigrants, notably from India, rather than to members
of American minority groups. The percentage of African-Americans and
Latinos in professional positions in booming tech businesses is extremely
low, nearing zero at many firms. "Where I grew up in Missouri, I never met
a Jewish person," says Reed Koch, forty, a manager at Microsoft. "Then I
went off to college"— Reed College, in Oregon —"and the culture was 40
percent Jewish. Suddenly I was exposed to something that was part of the
national culture, but until then I'd had absolutely no awareness of." He
drew the analogy to the racial situation in the rich tech world. "If you go ten
years and extremely rarely in your daily life ever encounter an American
black person, I think they disappear from your awareness."

People in the tech world inhabit what they know to be a basically post-
racial meritocracy. I would sit at a lunch table in the software firm with an
ethnic Chinese from Malaysia on one side of me, a Pole on the other side, a
man from Colombia across the table, and a man born in India but reared in
America next to him. This seems, to those inside it, the way the rest of the
world should work, and makes the entrenched racial problems of black-and-
white America seem like some Balkan rivalry one is grateful to know is on
the other side of the world.

As the wealth has piled up and the original tech pioneers have aged,
more of them have started to think about philanthropy. But the ones who
proceed from the assumption that the new elite has something to "give
back" turn out to be revealing exceptions to the general rule of emotional
detachment. Almost all of them have some distinctive factors in their background that seem to have motivated them to feel tied to a culture many of
their colleagues ignore.

Rob Glaser, who founded his Glaser Family Foundation nearly seven
years ago, was reared by liberal activists in Yonkers, N.Y. Eric Benhamou,
chairman and C.E.O. of 3Com, who has been involved in various civic ef-

forts, was born in Algeria, reared in France, and then came to the United States. Patty Stonesifer, a onetime Microsoft executive who now directs the world's largest pool of charitable assets, the Bill and Melinda Gates Foundation, grew up in a family of Dorothy Day–style Catholic activists.[8] Reed Koch began giving money early for care of disabled and retarded children. When he was growing up, as a Quaker, he spent summers working on a farm that cared for such children.

And then there is Paul Brainerd, fifty-two, a tall, lean, Lincolnesque figure, with gangly limbs and a little beard. He started his working life as a journalist, but was eventually inducted into a computer-industry Hall of Fame for inventing "desktop publishing," through the PageMaker program of his company, Aldus. This program allowed personal-computer users to combine pictures, fancy layouts, and text to create newsletters or journals without going to a commercial printer. Its success brought Brainerd well over $100 million when he sold the company—a third of which he promptly plunged into his Brainerd Family Foundation, concentrating on environmental causes. He is now chairman of Social Venture Partners, an effort to coordinate giving by other recently wealthy people.

Brainerd grew up in Medford, a small town in southern Oregon where his parents ran a camera shop and most other people depended on either the lumber industry or the pear orchards. "You could really see it in a town like that, all the direct connections," he says. "Whenever interest rates went up, the mills would close, and the unemployment rate would go to 20 percent. Three or four hundred people had individual charge accounts at my parents' store, and when they were laid off they couldn't pay. My parents would take out a $10,000 loan to buy their inventory for Christmas, and they would sit down and tell us: if the season went well, we could take a vacation, and if not, we'd stay home as they paid off the loan. I feel fortunate to have had that experience to see all the bits and pieces that make up a community and how it works."

It sounds like Jimmy Stewart in *It's a Wonderful Life*, but what Brainerd describes was something widespread in America about a generation ago: the ability to imagine large groups of people laid off for reasons beyond their control, an instinctive understanding of how the effects could ripple through a community, the idea that there was a community at all. The living memory of the Depression was the main vessel for this message. I grew up in the prospering '60s but amid constant reminders that my mother's family was ruined during the Depression, and that my father's felt blessed because my grandfather held onto his job. "You take a place like Microsoft, it's made of people who grew up not feeling part of their surrounding culture wherever it was, in America or France or India," says Reed Koch of Microsoft. "They're closer to each other than to anyone else."

[8]*Dorothy Day–style Catholic activists:* Dorothy Day (1897–1980) was a journalist and co-founder of the Catholic Workers, a social-reform organization.

The one political issue that deeply embroils the tech world is environmental protection. In part this is because the tech zone overlies some of America's most gorgeous scenery, from Puget Sound to the San Francisco Bay area to the central Texas hill country. But it is also because the most vivid link between the tech elite and the larger community is through the natural environment. A software engineer with $2 million in stock options can't really imagine being laid off. He can imagine ill-planned urban growth ruining a forest where he likes to hike.

What about the rest of America, denied the billion-dollar fortunes but riding comfortably in technology's lee through a decade of full employment and growing 401(k)s? We're different from the tech elite, as long as we operate in the realm where money is still real rather than symbolic. Perhaps the very reality of money explains one journalistic oddity: I found it far easier to get people worth $100 million to talk about their wealth than the typical lawyer, consultant, or recently promoted corporate manager. Professional models can talk with detachment about their beauty, because it's an established, independent entity—like fortunes for the newly wealthy, and unlike economic standing for most of us.

Compared with the software elite, the professional-class American   30
finds it easier to imagine financial ruin. Compared with technology employees, people who work in almost any other industry are brought into closer day-by-day contact with the ongoing tangles of black-white racial issues. And compared with the C.E.O.s who start high-tech companies and the clever programmers and designers they employ, Americans of comparable intellectual power outside the industry spend more time thinking about public policy issues (which would not be hard, since the standard tech official spends almost none). But there is a great similarity between the view from the top and the view from the next few tiers: the increasing haziness and "Oh, yes, now that you remind me" nature of the view of the poor.

In part this is a matter of simple party politics. "During the Reagan years, at least you had an opposition party to draw attention to poverty," says Arianna Huffington, the syndicated columnist. "Because there has been a Democrat in the White House who is supposed to care about their issue, a lot of people on the Left have lost their voices."

Jamie S. Gorelick, vice chairman of Fannie Mae, notes an encouraging rise in volunteer social service but says, "I have a pessimistic view, we're not talking about poverty as much as we should be and we don't have the degree of public effort that we should have."

And Bill Shore, executive director of Share Our Strength, which works to fight hunger and poverty, echoes those thoughts: "In a perverse way prosperity hides poverty," he says. "During a recession or hard economic times, you'll read lots of stories about people out of work or homeless people. During a boom it seems unimaginable even if it's going on. Society at large is so

consumed with how wealthy it is becoming that it leaves little mind share for anything else."

To an even larger extent, it reflects either the fatigue or the maturation of thinking about policy. "Since so many people have been absorbed in the work force, the ones that haven't are relatively worse off," says Frank Raines of Fannie Mae. "A lot of the people who are not 'in' yet are having trouble dealing with society. You've got people in very rural areas, Indian reservations, central cities, who have almost no contact with the mainstream society. They don't know what the rules of the game are, how you interview, how you go about seeking a job, what you do if you're late. There's a huge socialization need to bring people into contact with the rest of the world."

Steven Rattner, a former deputy chairman at Lazard Frères and a   35
prominent supporter of Al Gore, says: "The people I talk with—well, I guess I wish they thought and talked about it more than they do." But like most other people thinking and talking about the issue, he suggests that the only available remedies are indirect and long-term. "The one thing I'm sure of is that the way to solve the problem is not by taxes. First you understand the problem, which is a shift in the demand for labor. There have been huge increases in the demand for skilled labor, so wages have gone up, and falling demand for unskilled labor, so wages have gone down. Once you agree that that's the main problem, then the solution becomes fairly obvious: you have to train people to compete for better jobs, which will also reduce the supply of unskilled workers and force up wages at McDonald's."

And there is also the distance caused by politics in the deepest sense. "There is a historical puzzle to work out," says Michael Sandel, a professor of government at Harvard. "Today's accumulation of enormous wealth is unparalleled since the last Gilded Age. But the Gilded Age of a century ago brought in its wake a wave of progressive reform and public investment— in parks, libraries, schools, and municipal projects. Today's gilded age, by contrast, hasn't generated any comparable resolve to ease the effects of inequality by strengthening public institutions."

Underneath all the incidental explanations, Sandel says, lay a shift in the conception of what a "nation" was and what might hold a national community together. "If you look back to the Progressive Era,"[9] he says, all of those public undertakings were consciously part of *nation* building. "Teddy Roosevelt spoke of a new nationalism. Government undertook to regulate big business and the effects of great wealth, in the name of the national interest. There were appeals to a sense of national community, and to the mutual responsibilities of citizens of the nation, that don't seem so readily available today."

And the root of the difference may be, he suggests, that the first Gilded Age attended the growth of a national industrial base and economy, whereas today's second wave largely reflects the emergence of a global economy with global markets. Its beneficiaries pay less attention to national borders when it comes to exploring markets, and seeking finance, and recruiting workers—and feeling connection to other "citizens." "There is something very abstract and distant about the dependencies of the new

---

[9]*Progressive Era:* The late nineteenth and early twentieth centuries, characterized by reform movements in working conditions, politics, and other areas of social life — in many ways a reaction to the Gilded Age.

economy," he says. "This may have something to do with the difficulty of summoning Americans to a sense of national community now."

And there may be a simpler explanation too. National problems are one thing when considered abstractly — "poverty," "inequality," "racism," problems stated as if they were debate topics. They can be altogether different when connected with human beings — real or fictional. Tom Joad.[10] Rosa Parks.[11] The little girls blown up in a Birmingham church in 1963. The faces and families that Robert Kennedy discovered in Appalachia in the 1960s and that Michael Harrington, Robert Coles, and others of the era depicted in print.

These days, "the poor" are like "the Rwandans,"[12] a problem without a   40
name or face. I never knew the name of the Russian woman on the cleaning crew. I didn't want to ask.

ENGAGING THE TEXT

1. Fallows says that rich Americans today are less in touch with "the realities of life on the bottom" (para. 1) than in previous eras. What evidence does he provide to support this claim, and how persuasive do you find it?

2. Fallows points out that big business a century ago, unlike many companies today, had to consider the possibility of strikes if workers were pressed too far. Do you agree that high-tech companies can essentially ignore blue-collar workers? What forces, if any, counterbalance the economic power of companies like Microsoft, Intel, and Cisco?

3. Fallows includes in his article a personal story about a cleaning woman. What do you think he is trying to accomplish by telling this story, and how well do you think he succeeds? How do the photos and short profiles accompanying the article extend, complicate, or comment on the text?

4. Fallows reports that Microsoft employees sometimes discuss "the number"— an amount of money that would let them leave the company and do whatever they want (para. 13). What would "the number" be for you? Is a desire for that level of wealth a significant factor in your life? Explain.

5. What is your "Fundamental Economic Unit" (para. 16) — the amount of money you would spend without thinking about it? Compare your answer to those of classmates and to estimated F.E.U.s for family, friends, and employers.

[10]*Tom Joad:* Major character in the Pulitzer Prize–winning novel *The Grapes of Wrath* (1939) by John Steinbeck (1902–1968), about the westward migration of a dispossessed Dust Bowl family.

[11]*Rosa Parks:* African American woman who refused to give up her bus seat to a white passenger on December 1, 1955; her act, which sparked a Montgomery, Alabama, bus boycott, is often considered the dawn of the civil rights movement.

[12]*"the Rwandans":* In the small Central African country of Rwanda, a tribal conflict between Hutus and Tutsis reached genocidal proportions in 1994, with some 800,000 people killed.

EXPLORING CONNECTIONS

6. Compare Fallows's ideas about wealth with the ideas about work, success, and money in the Horatio Alger myth as illustrated in *Ragged Dick* (p. 298) and critiqued in "Horatio Alger" (p. 311).

7. Both Fallows and Gregory Mantsios (p. 318) are much concerned with poverty coexisting beside immense wealth. Compare the ways they explain the problem of American poverty, whom (or what) they blame for the problem, and what measures they might endorse to reduce the gap between rich and poor.

8. Imagine a continuation of Stephen Cruz's story (p. 335) in which he gives up his teaching job and returns to the business world, perhaps at Microsoft or a venture-capital firm that funds Internet start-up companies. How does the contemporary business world Fallows describes differ from the one Cruz lived in from the 1960s to the 1970s? How would you expect Cruz to react to the business environment today?

EXTENDING THE CRITICAL CONTEXT

9. Write a letter to Fallows about "The Invisible Poor," from the perspective of "the Russian woman," one of the people profiled in the photos, or another member of the cleaning crew Fallows says he preferred not to know too much about.

10. What does it mean to be "invisible"? Write a journal entry about a job or social situation in which you felt "invisible." How did you respond? What, if anything, might you have done differently if you'd had the opportunity?

11. In this era of global corporations, workers are sometimes "invisible" because they live thousands of miles away in distant countries. Visit the Web site of one or more of the following organizations to research how these groups are trying to make the lives and working conditions of such employees "visible" to U.S. citizens:

> Sweatshop Watch at www.sweatshopwatch.org
> International Forum on Globalization at www.ifg.org
> Public Citizen Global Trade Watch at www.tradewatch.org
> Global Policy Forum at www.globalpolicy.org/index
> Global Exchange at www.globalexchange.org/economy
> OneWorld at www.oneworld.net/guides/globalisation
> Ralph Nader on globalization at www.pbs.org/globalization/nader.html

From Seven Floors Up

Sharon Olds

Like the preceding essay by James Fallows, this poem asks you to think hard about poverty versus affluence—to resist letting the poor among us become "invisible." Sharon Olds (b. 1942) is author of several books of poetry, including Satan Says *(1980),* The Dead and the Living *(1983, winner of the National Book Critics Circle Award),* The Gold Cell *(1987),* The Father *(1992), and* Blood, Tin, Straw *(1999). Olds was honored as poet laureate of New York State for 1998–2000; she teaches at New York University.*

He is pushing a shopping cart up the ramp
out of the park.[1] He owns, in the world,
only what he has there—no sink, no water,
no heat. When we had come out of the wilderness,
after the week in the desert, in tents,   5
and on the river, by canoe, and when I had my own
motel-room, I cried for humble dreading
joy in the shower, I kneeled and put
my arms around the cold, clean
toilet. From up here, his profile looks   10
like Che Guevara's,[2] in the last picture,
the stitches like marks on a butcher's chart.
Suddenly I see that I have thought that it could not
happen to me, homelessness
—like death, by definition it would not happen.   15
And he shoulders his earth, his wheeled hovel,
north, the wind at his back—November,
the trees coming bare in earnest. November,
month of my easy birth.

Engaging the Text

1. Why do you think Olds chose the title "From Seven Floors Up"? Why is this detail important enough to become the poem's title?

2. Take a few moments to visualize each image in the poem. Identify those you consider most powerful or interesting.

3. What is the dominant feeling about homelessness expressed in this poem? Does it express any of your own feelings about poverty? Explain.

[1]*up the ramp/out of the park:* This suggests Central Park in New York City.
[2]*Che Guevara:* Ernesto Guevara, Argentina-born Cuban revolutionary (1928–1967).

4. What does the speaker mean when she says that hers was an "easy birth"? The speaker seems to think she could become homeless; how likely does this seem to you?

5. Do you think homelessness could ever happen to you? Explain why or why not.

EXPLORING CONNECTIONS

6. Compare the situation described in this poem with the story James Fallows tells about not wanting to know about the cleaning woman in "The Invisible Poor" (p. 356). Be sure to analyze both the settings and the writers' reactions.

7. Compare this poem with the one by Dana Gioia that follows. Think about the tone of each poem, about each poem's speaker or voice, and about the ways each poem tries to appeal to you.

EXTENDING THE CRITICAL CONTEXT

8. Write a brief poem from the point of view of the homeless man, imagining him looking seven stories up and seeing someone gazing down at him.

Money

DANA GIOIA

Money and poetry are strange bedfellows: we rarely think of them together. Dana Gioia (b. 1950) is well suited to couple them, however; he did graduate study in both comparative literature and business administration, and even when he worked as a product manager for Kool-Aid, he set aside two hours a day for reading and writing poetry. Gioia's books include Daily Horoscope *(1986) and* The Gods of Winter: Poems *(1991). In this poem, published in* Forbes, *he invites us to think about the ways we talk about money.*

> Money is a kind of poetry.
> —WALLACE STEVENS

Money, the long green,
cash, stash, rhino, jack
or just plain dough.

Chock it up, fork it over,
shell it out. Watch it   5
burn holes through pockets.

To be made of it! To have it
to burn! Greenbacks, double eagles,
megabucks and Ginnie Maes.

It greases the palm, feathers a nest,
holds heads above water,
makes both ends meet.

Money breeds money.
Gathering interest, compounding daily.
Always in circulation

Money. You don't know where it's been,
but you put it where your mouth is.
And it talks.

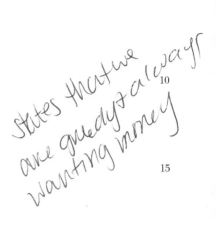

10

15

ENGAGING THE TEXT

1. Which words and phrases in the poem are familiar to you, which unfamiliar? Work with classmates to clarify the meanings of as many words and phrases as possible. As you do so, try to associate each word or phrase with one or more particular settings where it might be used (for example, banks, casinos, Wall Street, drug deals) and with any particular ideas about money it expresses.

2. What is the dominant attitude about money expressed in the poem? To what extent do you share this attitude?

3. The brevity of the last line and its placement at the poem's conclusion give it special emphasis. Why do you think Gioia ends his poem this way?

EXPLORING CONNECTIONS

4. Compare this poem with the one by Sharon Olds that precedes it (p. 371). Think about the tone of each poem, about each poem's speaker or voice, and about the ways each poem tries to appeal to you.

EXTENDING THE CRITICAL CONTEXT

5. An ordinary dictionary may not help you much with understanding synonyms for money like "rhino" and "jack." How might you find out more about the meanings of these words, and perhaps about their derivation or history? In other words, what resources beyond your dictionary are available to you for learning about language? Consult some of these resources and see what you can find out.

6. Gioia constructs his poem by using many words and phrases either meaning "money" or associated with money. Write your own poem using the same strategy, but with a different main topic—food, music, friendship, TV, or a topic of your choice. A dictionary of quotations and a thesaurus might help you.

The Black Avenger

KEN HAMBLIN

If radio talk show hosts are paid to be controversial, Ken Hamblin earns his money. He refers to young black women who bear children out of wedlock as "brood mares"; most of their children were sired, he writes, by "black thugs." Hamblin's main theme is the vitality of the American Dream and, in particular, his belief that black Americans should embrace that dream, quit whining about white racism, forget affirmative action, and make successes of themselves in the best country on earth. "The Black Avenger" touches on many of Hamblin's most provocative ideas. It is excerpted from his book Pick a Better Country: An Unassuming Colored Guy Speaks His Mind about America *(1996). Hamblin has himself lived a version of the American Dream. Raised in a poor area of Brooklyn by West Indian immigrant parents, his work in varied media fields (photojournalism, cinematography, TV production, newspapers, talk radio) has led to national recognition and an audience of over two million for* The Ken Hamblin Show. *In 1999 he published* Plain Talk and Common Sense from the Black Avenger.

Broad brushstrokes have been used over the last couple of years to paint a simplistic picture of the serious grievances emanating from middle America.

This picture painted and broadcast by the mainstream media is far different from the complex white backlash that I see and fear, however. The mainstream media have reduced nearly every political and social phenomenon I have written about in this book to a simple sound bite and a three-word headline: "Angry White Men."

The premise is that the black race and the white race are moving farther and farther apart because these angry white men are coming together in a collective backlash against the benefits afforded blacks through civil rights over the last three decades.

The evidence frequently cited is that these men, who for years held an unfair advantage in the workplace and in society in general, now are attacking programs such as affirmative action, which were designed to give minorities the edge to compensate for the years they were not treated as equals.

The predominantly liberal media report that these white men make up   5
the core of the growing conservative audience of talk radio. As a nationally syndicated talk radio host who is on the air for three hours five days a week, I guess this means that I should be among the first to hear from these guys.

But in actuality, that misconception is shattered regularly on *The Ken Hamblin Show*. The most interesting evidence against the stereotype comes in call after call, day after day, from white men, white southern men in particular, whom I hear crying uncle in this tired debate about race.

They are not crying uncle in the sense that they are rolling over.

What they are saying is: "Look, I personally didn't do it. I've gone through the family Bible. I haven't found one instance where we owned slaves. But I'll admit that at one time in America an injustice was committed against people of color—against black people, African Americans, Negroes. And as a white person, I am willing to atone for that."

In January of 1994 my local Denver radio program was broadcast live on C-Span and then repeated several times over the following week. On that show I addressed this guilt factor among white Americans and, as a spoof, offered to send my listeners and my viewers a copy of my very own "Certificate of Absolution."

Some months earlier, a man had called me on the air, identified himself   10
as white, and told me with candor and some degree of desperation that he was tired of feeling guilty about "my people."

That prompted me to come up with an official pardon in the form of a certificate, which only a clear-thinking black American would be authorized to issue. Soon after that, a Denver printer named Rex Kniss, who listened to my show, called and said he would be willing to print the certificate.

Rex added some "certificate" language to my thoughts and we ended up with the following:

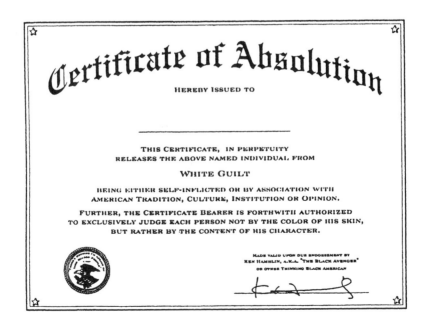

I signed the Certificate "The Black Avenger," a moniker that I use particularly with my radio listeners. The idea behind the name was that I wanted to avenge the lies and the disinformation that more than thirty years of liberalism have brought about in this country. More to the point, I wanted to present myself as living proof that America works for black people too. As the Black Avenger, I was a living, breathing challenge to the well-honed Myth of the Hobbled Black.[1]

"The Black Avenger" caught on among my fans in 1993 while I was on a local Denver radio station that also carried Rush Limbaugh. Limbaugh was hyping his newsletter by promoting an appearance in Colorado after one of his callers from Fort Collins, a man named Dan, said his wife wouldn't let him spend the money to buy a subscription. Limbaugh said he'd personally come out to Fort Collins if Dan would organize a bake sale to raise money for the subscription. The result was "Dan's Bake Sale," which drew Limbaugh fans from all over the country and raised money not only for Dan's newsletter but also for charity.

My local station got behind the event by lining up buses to take our   15
Limbaugh fans fifty miles north to Fort Collins.

Meanwhile, I had just gotten back into motorcycles—a couple of years late, I might add. As I tell my wife and all of my male friends circa fifty years of age, it's a male rite of passage to buy a motorcycle when you turn fifty. I was fifty-two, pushing fifty-three, and hadn't ridden one since I had a Honda 150 in the late 1960s.

A fellow motorcyclist called my show and said he didn't want to go to Dan's Bake Sale by bus, but that he and I should go on our scoots. That prompted a lot of on-air bravado, and I ended up leading a cavalcade of some forty bikes in front of that many more buses to Fort Collins. On the ride, I was dressed in black leather from head to toe and wearing a black helmet with a tinted face guard—exhibiting some resemblance to Darth Vader or—you got it—the Black Avenger. After that trip, the Black Avenger moniker stuck.

Over time, when asked why I called myself the Black Avenger, I must admit I started answering a bit flippantly, mocking the comic book characters of my youth: "Truth, justice, and the American way . . . honey."[2]

I added "honey" after a black caller, in all seriousness, challenged me, claiming that "truth, justice, and the American way" were not "black" values because these American principles weren't afforded to black people. He further insinuated that I was trying to "act white." Of course, I stood my ground.

I am an American first, I replied. Don't ask me to choose between this   20
Republic and the color of my skin. If you're a Pan-Africanist or a black nationalist, you won't like that answer.

---

[1]*Myth of the Hobbled Black:* Hamblin's name for the notions that African Americans are helplessly victimized by past and present racial discrimination, that few blacks are successful in America, that blacks can't make it without special assistance.

[2]*Truth, justice, and the American way:* The values that Superman stands for.

After thinking about the absurdity of this man trying to discount blacks as beneficiaries of the American Way, I decided to add "honey" with an ethnic ghetto drawl for the sole purpose of messing with self-righteous African Americans like him who still feed off the Myth of the Hobbled Black.

As a result of my appearance on C-Span, I received nearly 8,000 pieces of mail, more than 5,000 of them requesting the Certificate of Absolution. To this day I hear from people from all over America who remember the program, and my staff continues to fill orders for the certificate every week.

Needless to say, it warms my heart to know that so many white people are sleeping better at night, no longer writhing in pain brought about by their white guilt.

All joking aside, the extent of white guilt in this country is immense. It directly correlates with the endless depiction by the mass media of the profound pain that black people purportedly still suffer as a result of the years they were excluded from America's mainstream.

The constant reports of this pain and suffering that are broadcast   25 through the media, combined with the "blame whitey" syndrome that emanates from the black-trash[3] welfare culture, have caused some white Americans to suffer such a high degree of guilt that they have an almost fanatic desire to undo the injustices of slavery, perhaps beginning with guilt about not having delivered the forty acres and a mule promised to every Negro after the Civil War.

The greater majority of white Americans have passed on a nagging sense of social obligation from one generation to the next. After four or five generations, however, mass amnesia has set in. The people who are haunted by this guilt — the white majority, mainstream Americans obsessed with undoing this injustice — have forgotten exactly what their crime was. In fact, they have no idea what their particular crime was.

As is the case with my southern callers, most Americans can't trace their family tree back to the equivalent of Tara, the fictitious plantation in *Gone With the Wind,* or to the ownership of slaves. So the guilt no longer arises from having once personally owned slaves, be they black people or indentured Irishmen. The guilt now is imposed just because of a lack of melanin in their skin, just because they are white. Simply by virtue of the birth of a white child, another guilty American is created. It's as if we were talking about the burden of the national debt. That baby inherits the guilt of slavery, the guilt of an injustice of long, long ago.

Because of this guilt and the ongoing stories of black oppression, white people have been conditioned to accept just about any level of black rage and the illogical demands resulting from it.

All of which brings us back around to modern-day African-American revolutionaries like welfare queen Dorothy King.

---

[3]*black-trash*: Hamblin's counterpart to "white trash," these are black Americans who, in his words, are "unskilled and unemployed" and who "tend to be socially inept, possess limited education and few salable job skills."

Despite her crassness, in some ways King is very sophisticated. She   30
knowingly touches a little secret in white people who have been conditioned by years of hearing about black hardships—the little secret that
they are glad, they are relieved, to have been born white rather than a
disenfranchised minority. These white middle-class citizens—especially the
thirty- and forty-something crowd—have been inundated from the cradle
with news reports about the dreadful burden of being black in America—
reports of suffering the hardships of poverty, racism, and second-class citizenship.

While going through college, these white folks saw liberal administrators and professors excuse low test scores from black students because of
these inherent hardships. They felt sorry for affirmative action students who
obviously must have been scared, because they refused to compete. And
though clearly this discrimination was self-imposed by the blacks themselves, they watched black students segregate themselves at all levels of
campus life—from African-American studies to African-American student
unions to African-American graduations—in essence implementing a
post–civil rights version of "white only" and "colored" sections.

These white people graduated, got married, and began family life in
comfortable suburbs . . . and bingo! They see Dorothy King on the nightly
TV news, cataloging all the black hardships they have been conditioned to
believe exist.

So when King makes absurd demands, like "give me" a house, these
guilt-ridden white people shy away from standing up to her with what
should be the logical American response: "Heavens no, we won't give you a
house. Go out and work for it."

Nope. They stay out of it. Because they fear that X-ray vision might discern their little secret—the secret that they are eternally thankful they are
white, and just having that thought makes them racists.

I have heard white Americans express so much racial guilt that, being   35
the old Catholic that I am, on some days I feel as though my radio show has
become a confessional.

Because of the earnestness with which these people come to my show,
it has dawned on me that if we as minority people, as black Americans, can't
cut a deal with these average white Americans who are sitting at the table
apologizing for the past, then we are a flawed and a lost people.

Or we are a disingenuous people who demand to prolong the negotiation with no intention of ever ending the strife and the separation, with no
intention of ever doing our part to fill up the moat between the races or of
getting on with the business of continuing to build a strong America that
will benefit all of us.

I have a bigger, more selfish reason for wanting to avenge white guilt,
however, a reason that goes beyond relieving the strain on white America.
Guilt almost certainly inspires pity for the injured party—in this case black
Americans. I contend that we can never stand tall as a people and expect to

be treated as equals so long as we allow ourselves to be patronized in this fashion.

I also hear from white people across the country who call my radio show and say essentially, "Get over it."

They respond to the poverty pimps' demands for more and more repa-   40
rations for black people by asking what credit they get for all the taxes they have paid to support decades of Great Society programs that benefited black recipients. They want consideration for the years of affirmative action that gave black Americans a pass to automatically step to the front of the employment line.

Those kinds of queries undoubtedly contribute to the notion that there are angry white men. And I am certain there are, in fact, some white men who are angry, perhaps even racist. But the truth is that, as a black man, I ask some of the same questions, albeit from a different perspective.

When will black people recognize that we are able and willing to stand on our own? When will we acknowledge that we are able and willing to stand side by side with other Americans to compete for jobs and our piece of the American Dream? When will we get over that ugly and unjust period in our American history and evolve into healthy citizens of this great country?

I don't perceive that the majority of white Americans I talk to are saying "Get over it" sarcastically in order to dismiss the subject or to lobby for a return to the days of yore.

Rather, I think they are saying to black Americans: "Get over it, because even if we haven't paid the bill in full, we certainly have made enough of an effort to make amends that you should acknowledge some sincerity on our part."

I agree

Personally, I heartily second the call to get over it.   45

I am absolutely convinced that if we black Americans unequivocally throw in our lot with mainstream America today, we have much more to gain in the future than we have lost in the past. We have more to gain by putting our energies into the pursuit of the American Dream than we have to gain by continuing to whine about being compensated for having been kept out of the game in the past. We have an opportunity to realize all the benefits of being an American in the name of all of those who came before us, those Negroes who were kept unfairly from the full potential of this great country.

finally they realize

I would go so far as to say that we *owe* it to our forefathers to seize the opportunity that they helped to make available to us by their own stalwart faith in the American Dream. I know that all of my life I have felt I owed it to my mother and her sisters to make something of myself, to achieve the level of success that they only dreamed would be possible in their new homeland.

Today mainstream America has opened its full society and culture to us. The white majority has supported legislation that makes the American Dream truly accessible to all black citizens.

Oh, sure, there's still the old-guard club or the snooty neighborhood where the members or residents may look down their noses at black newcomers. But I would wager that those scenarios are few and far between.

And I am also willing to bet that in most cases the feelings of discrimination and exclusion are self-imposed by xenophobic quota blacks.   50

In fact, some of today's cries of racism have become downright ludicrous.

I wrote a column in the *Denver Post* in the summer of 1994 about a group of Denver area black women who claimed that a white shopkeeper in a Western Slope mountain town "stripped away our dignity, making us feel frustrated and powerless" by making an offhand remark when they walked into his store.

It seems one of the women was complaining about the heat, and the shopkeeper responded, "Hey! Watermelon's not served until one o'clock."

When he realized the ladies were seriously offended, he reportedly tried to make light of the situation, but alas, the oppressed travelers bustled out the door and followed up by writing a critical letter to the editor of the local newspaper.

I wrote that had I been presented with the watermelon-serving   55
schedule, I promptly would have inquired about the cantaloupe.

I don't doubt there are some angry white men. I'm still unconvinced that this shopkeeper was one of them, however.

More important is the fact that I am one black man who refuses to be shamed or made to feel powerless anymore by white bigots and racists. White folks can no longer intimidate me. I know better.

What I am constantly amazed at is how thin-skinned, how delicate, and how utterly afraid the beneficiaries of Dr. Martin Luther King's proud march for liberation have become.

Furthermore, as a black American, I am shamed by the Myth of the Hobbled Black. I am shamed that so many of my people have allowed themselves in one way or another to become part of the sham.

Someone must have the courage to kill this myth. Someone has to be   60
embarrassed that, with the opportunities available to us today, so many black Americans remain in a declining state of existence in Dark Town. Someone has to be embarrassed for the great number of middle-class black Americans who live in seclusion, apparently afraid to celebrate their success as educated and sophisticated Americans.

Someone must speak out to avenge the mythical disability of the Hobbled Black, and I think it's only logical that successful middle-class black Americans take the lead to meet this challenge.

White liberals won't do it because they continue to feed off the myth in order to further their own political and social agenda. White conservatives who speak out about ending the welfare culture have no credibility. They are summarily labeled racists.

And so I have lobbed a loud salvo by declaring myself the Black Avenger, standing tall to dispel the Myth of the Hobbled Black. I am standing up to put an end to the decades of liberal propaganda which deny that today opportunity exists for any American man or woman willing to pursue it.

I fully understand that it's not easy to be black and publicly refute the Myth of the Hobbled Black, because the quota blacks, the poverty pimps, the African Americans, will do all in their collective power to try to de-black you: "You ain't black no more. You don't understand the pain and suffering. You forgot your roots, boy."

But their admonishments have nothing to do with pain and suffering. 65 The real reason they are trying to de-black me and people like me is that we are telling the truth. And the truth is that being poor and black does not give you an excuse to gang-bang, to ruin a city, to make parks unsafe, to terrorize senior citizens, and to denounce the American Dream.

I am not a mean person. But I have run the gauntlet of ghetto life, and I have survived. I understand the value of life. And I understand that being poor is never an excuse to become a mugger or a killer.

Like a lot of black babies, I started out on the lowest social rung. I was raised by women. I grew up on welfare. I lived on the toughest streets of New York.

But I was not raised to be black trash or to be a victim. I never went through a drug rehab center. I have never been a guest of the government beyond my enlistment in the service. I have never believed—because I was never told—that because of the color of my skin I could never get the fullest measure of opportunity in America.

When you are poor, you may be so busy trying to survive that you miss the opportunity to smell the roses. You may miss the pure joy of watching your children grow up. But none of that gives you a valid reason to disregard what's right and what's wrong.

I am one American who is saying no to the myth that all people of color 70 are weak, illiterate, potentially violent, and substandard in their expectations for themselves and their children as contributors to the community.

Despite the attempted intimidation emanating from the black-trash welfare culture, every day I hear from more and more healthy black Americans—and guilt-free white Americans—who are joining the crusade to tell the truth about black people and their good fortune to be Americans.

My personal adventure in America is at its pinnacle today because I am able to talk every day on my radio show with so many people from coast to coast and from all walks of life. I hear personally from hundreds more Americans off the air every day through the Internet and via letters to the editors of newspapers that carry my column.

And every day I am reassured that the heartbeat of America remains strong. I am reassured that the great majority of Americans maintain the true American spirit, the spirit that ultimately will make it possible for us to prevail.

I draw my strength from that heartbeat of America; it gives me the power to be the Black Avenger.

ENGAGING THE TEXT

1. Working in groups, summarize the central claims Hamblin makes about the United States and the American Dream. To what extent do you agree or disagree with these assertions, and why?

2. Assess Hamblin's assertion that some white Americans "suffer such a high degree of guilt that they have an almost fanatic desire to undo the injustices of slavery" (para. 25). Have you seen evidence of such a compulsion in the media, in your education or reading, in your community? Discuss.

3. Hamblin often uses language that is rhetorically daring, to say the least — language that is pointedly *not* politically correct. What do you think he means by the terms listed below? What effect does such language have on you as a reader?

   welfare queen (para. 29)
   poverty pimp (para. 40)
   quota blacks (para. 50)
   Dark Town (para. 60)

4. Review Hamblin's account of how he assumed his alias, "The Black Avenger" (paras. 13–18); note the various components of this persona, including the motorcycle and motorcycle outfit, the Darth Vader connection, the Superman/comic books connection, and his ghetto pronunciation of "honey." What impression do you think Hamblin is trying to create? How well do you think he succeeds?

EXPLORING CONNECTIONS

5. Review Anne Witte Garland's "Good Noise: Cora Tucker" (p. 340). Compare and contrast her ideas about success with Hamblin's. Be sure to touch on Tucker's and Hamblin's views of poverty, welfare, and obstacles to success for African Americans.

6. Hamblin believes there are few barriers in the United States today for African Americans who are motivated to succeed. How do you think Gregory Mantsios might respond to this claim? Review "Class in America" (p. 318) for data or claims that challenge or complicate Hamblin's argument, and discuss how these two writers can come to such different conclusions about barriers to success.

7. Consider Cheryl Mitchell, the highly motivated African American woman that Gregory Mantsios profiles in "Class in America" (p. 318). Beginning

with the information Mantsios provides, write Mitchell's story so that she becomes a clear success. Share stories with classmates, and discuss the plausibility of each story. Do the results of this exercise tend to support or call into question Hamblin's claims about opportunity?

EXTENDING THE CRITICAL CONTEXT

8. In paragraph 31, Hamblin offers a brief description of black students segregating themselves on college campuses. How well would his description fit your campus today: to what extent are ethnic groups segregated or self-segregated?

9. Listen to one or more broadcasts of *The Ken Hamblin Show* and analyze what you hear. What issues are being discussed? What sort of persona does Hamblin project? How would you characterize his audience? To what extent does Hamblin echo themes found in the reading selection above?

Race at the End of History

RONALD TAKAKI

According to conventional wisdom, Asian Americans offer the best evidence that the American Dream is alive and well. Publications like Time *and* Newsweek *have celebrated Asian Americans as a "super minority" that has adopted the Puritan work ethic and outshone even the Anglo majority in terms of education and financial success. In this reading selection, Ronald Takaki challenges the idea of the model minority and provides an alternative interpretation of how myths of race and myths of success intertwine. The grandson of Japanese immigrant plantation workers in Hawaii, Takaki (b. 1939) is an award-winning historian whose mission, in his own words, has been "to write a more inclusive and hence more accurate history of Americans, Chicanos, Native Americans as well as certain European immigrant groups like the Irish and Jews." His most recent in a series of influential books is titled* Double Victory: A Multicultural History of America in World War II *(2000).*

Several years ago I was invited to deliver a keynote address at a national multicultural conference in Norfolk, Virginia. Once I arrived at the Norfolk airport I caught a cab, and soon was engaged in conversation with the driver. We looked at each other through the rearview mirror of the cab as we talked. At first, we discussed the weather and how this region was becoming a very important area for tourism. But it did not take long before the cab driver posed a more personal question: "How long have you been in this country?"

"All my life," I snapped; after a while, one gets impatient responding to that question. But then I calmed down and informed this white man in his forties, at whom I was looking in the rearview mirror, that my grandfather had come to the United States in 1886. I explained to him that we had been in this country as a family for more than one hundred years, and that I myself was born here. And then he looked at me in the rearview mirror and said, with a broad Southern drawl, "Well, I was wondering about you, because your English is excellent."

He did not see me as an American. I am not saying that he asked me this question because he was a Southerner, since Northerners have asked me the same question. Nor can I attribute his ignorance to economic class since, to be honest, Ph.D.s have also asked me this question. And it is not necessarily a matter of race, either, since African Americans have also questioned my nationality. I do not look American to a lot of people.

My experience in the cab mirrors a very common assumption that being "American" means being white or European in ancestry. But one need only look around the streets of just about any American city to realize how far from reality this perception is. Many of us came originally from Africa, others were already here, others came up from Latin America, and others, like my grandfather, came from a Pacific shore, and we're all Americans. Yet, despite that history, the prevailing debate about American citizenship revolves around identity: Who is an American and how does identity shape American society?

Racial and ethnic diversity is being promoted, and contested, of course, on university and college campuses across the country. In 1989, my colleagues at the University of California, Berkeley, voted favorably to establish a multicultural requirement for graduation. We call it the "American cultures requirement," and it applies to every student in the university. Even students in engineering, computer science, and business administration must take a course before graduation that is designed to deepen and broaden their understanding of American society in terms of race and ethnicity. The course is neither a cultural diversity requirement, nor a global studies requirement. It is a requirement that focuses on diversity in the United States of America. The curriculum is designed to study comparatively—and we underline "comparatively"—five groups, which we have identified as African American, Asian American, Latino, American Indian, and European immigrant groups, particularly those groups that arrived in the late nineteenth and early twentieth centuries from Italy, Greece, Poland, Hungary, and Russia. Berkeley today offers approximately 125 courses that fulfill this requirement, fielded by faculty in almost twenty different departments.

The Berkeley faculty instituted the American cultures requirement essentially for two reasons. The first motivation was intellectual, since we believed that it would bring our students to a more accurate understanding of American society. On a more urgent note, however, we believed that we were witnessing at the time the most serious racial crisis in America since the Civil War. Those fears were confirmed only three years later when, on 29 April 1992, we saw on our television screens terrifying images beamed out of Los Angeles: Korean stores burning out of control, black smoke rising to the skies above the city, and murderous melee in the streets. The most powerful image that came out of those events was the face of Rodney King. I still remember his trembling words, "Please, people, we're stuck here for a while; we can work it out, we can get along."

But many of us, educators and students alike, wondered, "How do we get along, how do we work it out, unless we learn more about one another?" The Berkeley faculty trusted that a comparative approach to multiculturalism would help our students understand the beauty and promise of a pluralistic America.

I am often asked by faculty, deans, and provosts across the country to describe what a multicultural approach to culture looks like. Offering a theoretical description is usually less effective than providing an actual demonstration. The remainder of this essay, then, serves as a demonstration of a comparative multicultural approach to history.

Francis Fukuyama, a fellow Asian American intellectual, proclaims in his book entitled *The End of History and the Last Man* that at the turn of the twentieth century the globe is witnessing the end of history. Liberal democracy, he declares, has triumphed over communism, and the capitalist economic system has emerged as the only coherent political and economic ideology. The overriding message Fukuyama offers is celebratory—the triumph of American liberal democracy and capitalism, the end of history.

But Fukuyama's conclusion that history has come to an end relies upon a   10
very specific view of history. If we define history as the conflict between liberal democracy and capitalism on the one hand, and feudalism, monarchy, and communism on the other hand, then perhaps we would have to agree with Fukuyama that history has ended. Alternatively, if one defines history as the expansion of Europe into Africa, the Americas, Asia, and the Pacific, if one defines history as the history of colonialism, if one defines history as a trail of racial and ethnic conflicts, then one would have to say that history has in no way ended.

Even Fukuyama would have to agree that U.S. history has not come to an end, for example, since racial inequality for Blacks is such an undeniable social fact. All the same, he does not accept any explanation that finds fault with liberal democracy for this state of affairs. He instead would frame racial inequality as a cultural problem for Blacks. In his analysis, Black poverty is a matter of cultural difference. Blacks lack middle-class values of thrift, hard work, self-reliance, and family values that they need in order to succeed, he argues. In other words, the Black problem is group specific and cultural. His remedy: the way for Blacks to make it into the mainstream is for the group to acquire the proper values.

Fukuyama's judgment of Black failure is juxtaposed with his estimation of economic success gained by other ethnic groups. In *The End of History,* for instance, he noted that Japan's economic miracle is based on the richness of its culture. He compares the Japanese cultural ethos favorably to the Protestant ethic: values rooted in hard work, thrift, industry, and family. Though Fukuyama did not develop this comparison any further in *The End of History,* in a subsequent book, entitled *Trust,* he expands this theory that links cultural values and material well-being. He confesses admiration for the gains of Asian Americans in the United States; more specifically, he lauds the broad achievements of Japanese Americans, Chinese Americans, and Korean Americans. He again attributes the success of Asian Americans to their strong family values and ethnic enterprise, and pointedly notes that Blacks are deficient in these values.

In making these comparisons and contrasts, Fukuyama continues the long and storied myth of the Asian American model minority. This myth rests on the claim that Asian Americans have made it economically, and is usually documented by statistics which show that Asian American families have incomes that even at times exceed those of white families. But statistics that measure family income make sense only in relation to the number of workers per family. A close look at these numbers reflects that Asian American families typically have more workers per family than white families, which serves to incline upward Asian American family incomes.

The myth of Asian American success also overlooks a second important reality. The majority of the Asian American population lives in three states: New York, California, and Hawaii, with the highest concentration situated in San Francisco, Los Angeles, New York City, and Honolulu. These cities annually report among the highest cost of living indexes in the entire country. So, of course, an inflated index will incline income upward. Those numbers do not necessarily suggest a higher standard of living, however.

And there is yet another problem with this myth. It lumps together all 15 Asian Americans, whether they be Chinese, Japanese, Koreans, Hmong, Vietnamese, Cambodians, or a host of other Asian immigrant groups. Such lumping together renders invisible those Asian American groups that have not yet made it economically in this country. Even within a group that seemingly is successful, say Chinese Americans, this myth overlooks the class heterogeneity within that community. In New York City, for example, wide class divisions divide the uptown Chinese from the downtown Chinese.

I am not trying to deny that there are many successful Asian Americans in the United States. But it is important to realize that many of them, probably the majority who are successful, are post-1965 immigrants. They often come from the professional and highly educated classes of South Korea, Taiwan, Hong Kong, and the Philippines. One study of Korean greengrocers in New York City, for example, revealed that nearly 78 percent of those interviewed had college degrees. Hence, many relatively recent immigrants

came here already middle-class and upper-middle-class. They did not pull themselves up by their bootstraps.

All the same, many of these professional Asian Americans complain that they experience a "glass ceiling." In other words, even though they may have degrees from elite universities, they find that they are not earning an income comparable to their skill level and their level of education.

But the point of this celebration of Asian Americans as a model minority, in reality, is not sociology. The debate between Fukuyama and me is not even about history. It is really about ideology, because embedded within that sociology, contained within that history, is an ideology. This message is this: The American dream still holds promise to all of us as Americans. Everyone, regardless of race, can make it into the mainstream through hard work and private effort.

The key word here is "private." Notice, these Asian Americans made it not through affirmative action, not through welfare, but through private activities—business, education, and individual effort. In other words, the way to make it into the mainstream, the way to advance oneself economically, is in the private domain, relying on family resources, not by means of government assistance.

As a historian, I have to raise the question whether this representation of Asian Americans as a model minority is a recent phenomenon. It certainly receives wide promotion from scholars such as Fukuyama, Thomas Sowell, Dinesh D'Souza, and Nathan Glazer. But it is not a recent idea.

20

Looking backward into the nineteenth century to just one year—1870—we find two fascinating examples of how Asian Americans were used as a model minority. The first series of events took place in the states of Mississippi and Louisiana. After the Civil War, following the emancipation of enslaved African Americans, planters in Mississippi, Louisiana, and other states in the South were confronted with a wage-earning class of Blacks. Often, the planters had labor conflicts with these newly freed Blacks. So in 1870, a coalition of planters transported into Mississippi and Louisiana more than five hundred Chinese immigrant laborers whom they pitted against Black wage-earners. A review of newspaper reports from the period as well as written correspondence among the planters themselves reveal the clear intent of this importation of Chinese labor. The planters blatantly admitted their plans to use these Chinese immigrant laborers as examples of obedient, hard-working laborers. A model minority for whom? For the newly freed Blacks.

In 1870, another significant event occurred, but this time in the North, in a small industrial town in Massachusetts. The largely immigrant Irish working class of North Adams had organized themselves into a union called the "Knights of St. Crispins." These Irish factory workers went out on strike against a factory owned by Charles Sampson in 1870. So Sampson transported across the country about seventy-five Chinese immigrant laborers, brought them to North Adams, Massachusetts, to break the strike. Again, the local newspapers went wild, proclaiming, here we have the solution to all of our labor problems; not only cheap labor but obedient labor, industrious labor. Their statistics in fact "proved"—and this was later hailed by the mainstream media beyond North Adams—that after four months the Chinese workers were out-producing the Irish workers. In short, the Chinese were touted as more efficient workers.

The Irish workers of North Adams initially tried to build class solidarity across racial lines, even attempting to organize a Chinese Lodge of the Knights of St. Crispins. But Sampson locked the Chinese within the compounds, separated them from the Irish strikers, and broke the strike. That was in 1870. In Mississippi, Alabama, and North Adams, Massachusetts, the Chinese were used as a model minority for Black workers and as a model minority for Irish immigrant workers.

But then nearly a decade later came a nativist backlash against Chinese immigrants that culminated in the 1882 Chinese Exclusion Act. The closing of the gates to Chinese immigration occurred within a larger context, however. American industrial development had become overheated by the 1880s and production was slowing down. America "discovered" unemployment for the first time in its history.

A young historian by the name of Frederick Jackson Turner[1] chose this 25
important cultural moment to deliver a seminal thesis at the meeting of the

---

[1]*Frederick Jackson Turner:* See pp. 683–90 to read an excerpt from Turner's famous paper announcing the end of America's frontier era.

American Historical Association in Chicago in 1893. The paper was entitled "The Significance of the Frontier in American History." Turner proposed that America's manifest destiny and national character were deeply shaped by the frontier experience. He hailed the westward migration of white settlers, and the expansion of what he called "the advance of civilization against savagery," a hard-fought victory won at the expense of the Native American Indians. Viewed from our present perspective, Turner's thesis could be very well retitled, "The Significance of the Frontier and Race in American History."

There stood Turner at the end of the nineteenth century, contemplating the social significance of the end of the frontier, and today we have Francis Fukuyama, contemplating the end of another century and the eclipse of that frontier he calls history. Turner idealized the triumphant advance of civilization across a continent, while Fukuyama trumpeted the advance of civilization across the entire world. In the 1870s Chinese immigrant laborers were used as a model minority against Blacks and Irish immigrant workers. The workplace—the plantation, the shoe factory—was a site of discipline, the site to create docile, obedient, efficient workers. Today, the site of discipline has shifted from the workplace to the cultural terrain. "Cultural terrain" refers to ideology and culture, to representations of minorities in the mass media, but also to representations in our scholarly and political discourse.

In the nineteenth century there was a need for Black labor. Today, we are witnessing a dramatic decline in the need for Black labor. We presently have what William Julius Wilson calls the formation and expansion of a "Black underclass" in our inner cities. Wilson identifies two very important factors behind this development in the U.S. economy. He highlights the deindustrialization of America and the emergence of a globalized economy. Now our factories can go overseas, our jobs can go to Mexico, to Indonesia, to Malaysia. This exportation of production is hollowing out the industrial inner cities.

Another development that Wilson underscores is the suburbanization of production, that is, the movement of sites of production away from our cities, that began in earnest in the early 1980s. Not just manufacturing production, but also information production thrives in suburban office parks. Downtowns are rapidly closing down, leaving the people who cannot move trapped in inner cities.

Jeremy Rifkin's study on the changing patterns of work in America adds a further perspective on the formation of an underclass that is largely Black. In his book, *The End of Work,* Rifkin shows very persuasively that while industrial and information production have both risen dramatically in the last two decades, the need for labor has remained level and in some cases even declined. Rifkin discovers these trends not only in manufacturing labor, but also in white-collar labor. In essence, our economy has less need for labor and so work is coming to an end. Rifkin claims that the creation of superfluous workers in American society will only increase in the twenty-first century, and this problem is having, and will continue to have, a disproportionate impact upon African Americans trapped in our inner cities.

In the nineteenth century the purpose of the model minority was to 30 control labor. The function of the model minority today is not to control Black or Irish immigrant labor, and not even to create obedient, hardworking laborers. The function today is social control, a reaffirmation of the American dream directed especially to those workers, many of them White and many of them Black, who are struggling simply to make ends meet. "Be like Asian Americans, emulate their family values."

But this message had a special targeting for African Americans who feel that their future is hopeless. It says to them, "Look at those Asian Americans. They were able to make it, they're shopkeepers, they're successful, they're getting their children into schools like Berkeley and Harvard and Princeton. And how did they do it? They did it through private activities, through emphasis on education, through family values."

"Family values" have become the code words for defining the problem of poverty in terms of the family and the individual rather than the structures of our economy and the structures of our society. Blacks are told to be like Asian Americans—be law-abiding, be civil members of society, don't depend on welfare, don't try to get ahead through affirmative action.

Many Asian Americans have inadvertently joined Fukuyama in touting Asian American success; in some cases even liberal Asian American organizations have done so. They actively promote Asian American family values, releasing sociological data showing that we have low welfare dependency rates. They also regularly provide information to the media about how we're contributing as Asian Americans to the economy through shopkeeping, through connections with businesses in South Korea, Taiwan, and Hong Kong. These liberal Asian Americans say they are performing these activities to resist racism, to combat the backlash against immigrants, to show that Asian Americans are good citizens, that we're good Americans. But like the conservative Fukuyama, these liberal Asian Americans overlook the social and economic structures that produce and reproduce racial inequality. In a complicated way, the Asian American model minority representation has become part of Michel Foucault's[2] concept of the panopticon—society controlled by an ideology dividing us into distinct groups, ever being watched and compared.

There are major differences that distinguish the economy and society at the end of the nineteenth century to that we are facing at the end of the twentieth century. But, as it turns out, there are also significant similarities.

---

[2]*Michel Foucault:* Philosopher, psychiatrist, and influential French intellectual (1926–1984). His book *Discipline and Punish*—a major work on the history, psychology, and architecture of imprisonment—discusses a prison called a panopticon whose key feature is that prisoners can always be seen by guards who can't be seen.

Both periods represent times of economic crisis and class tensions among Whites. Consider the labor turmoils and strikes in the late nineteenth century, the 1885 Haymarket Riot in Chicago, the Homestead Riot, and the Pullman Strike. These events were eruptions that shook American society, and it was within the context of white/white class conflicts that this young historian, Frederick Jackson Turner, gave his paper. He was in Chicago, only eight years after the bloody Haymarket Riot, presenting this paper on the significance of the frontier. He was worried about his country's future, and his interpretation of the end of the frontier was informed by that larger economic context of an industrial machine slowing down, rising unemployment, and the emergence of white/white class conflict.

Turner was not the only person contemplating the meaning of the end   35 of his century. At about the same time another American, Henry George, was calling for a radical redefinition of citizenship that would include shared ownership of the continent. In his book, *Progress and Poverty,* George argued that the advance of capitalism in American civilization would inevitably lead to more intense and violent class conflicts within white society. He proposed the idea of a tax on unearned income to reduce the conflict. Once land becomes valuable due to industrial production, then there should be a tax on the added value of that land. He argued, for instance, that Leland Stanford and the Central Pacific Railroad should not be the sole beneficiary of the increase in the value of the property due to the construction of that railroad. George believed that the income derived from that tax then should be used for the benefit of the society. But not for the entire society, for George argued that the funds should only be distributed to White Americans. Chinese immigrants were not real Americans in his estimation. So although he was a visionary of more economic equality, George scapegoated the Chinese as vehemently as other American intellectuals. He in fact was a leader in the movement calling for Chinese exclusion. He saw the Chinese as the lackeys of the monopolist capitalists. In the economic crises of the late nineteenth century, the Chinese were vilified by all sides.

The end of the nineteenth century was also a period of profound cultural crisis. The frontier had come to an end. Nineteenth-century America had drawn its energies, its buoyancy, from the seemingly endless potential offered by an open frontier. So Turner was pondering, as an historian looking backward, but also peering forward, what would happen to a frontierless America.

Today, a century later, we are also experiencing a cultural crisis. This crisis is actually more complicated than that of an earlier century. Our cultural crisis manifests itself most significantly within two arenas. The first arena is our expanding racial diversity. Some time in the twenty-first century Whites will become a minority of the total U.S. population. In other words, the faces of America are changing. Already you can see the changing faces in every major city in the United States—San Francisco, Cleveland, Chicago, New York, Philadelphia, Washington, San Antonio, Los Angeles.

And the question many people are asking is this: How will we define who is an American in the twenty-first century?

Fukuyama more dramatically addresses the second arena of our cultural crisis. Ever since the waning moments of World War II, the Cold War allowed us to discern our manifest destiny. America's manifest destiny was to contain communism. That would be the new frontier: the containment of communism—Vietnam, Cambodia, Laos, Cuba, Chile, Nicaragua, El Salvador, Guatemala. And now that the Soviet Union has collapsed and the Cold War is over, Francis Fukuyama encourages us to place our faith in liberal democracy and capitalism as guides to a brighter future. "History has ended."

Fukuyama's optimism is reflected in the way he ends his book, *The End of History.* He concludes with a story about a wagon train traveling west:

> Mankind will seem like a long wagon train, strung out along the road. Several wagons attacked by Indians will have been set aflame and abandoned along the way. There will be a few wagoneers who, stunned by the battle, will have lost their sense of direction and are temporarily heading in the wrong direction, but the great majority of wagons will be making the journey into town and most will eventually arrive there.

Here we have embedded in Fukuyama's final story a remarkable rendition of Turner's frontier thesis. Fukuyama intends his story about the wagon train moving west to illustrate his central thesis: All along "there had been only one journey and one destination."

Yet the very metaphor that Fukuyama has chosen raises more questions than it resolves: "Whose" journey, "whose" destination, and "who" are "we"? Certainly, a good citizen should be able to embrace the larger narrative of what America is, the collective memory of who we are as a nation. But a good citizen must also be able to look "in a different mirror" and see the diversity that Americans reflect, to accept that we come with different faces and different names, like Garcia and Takaki. We are all American, and we should not have to explain or defend our citizenship every time we jump into a taxicab. To draw from Walt Whitman's wonderful poetry, we must all become listeners—"to hear the varied carols of America," the songs and stories of our democratic diversity.

As we approach the coming multicultural millennium, we have to remind Fukuyama and his agreeing readers of William Faulkner's insight: "The past is not even past." Indeed, history has not ended. Rather it is sedimented into our present and our future. This powerful continuance of events and developments in our history requires us to know that history inclusively and accurately. This study of the past can enable us to confront the history of the enslavement of African Americans, the dispossession of Native Americans, the exploitation of Chinese immigrant workers, and the disciplining of Irish immigrant laborers. This understanding of our history can also guide us toward a future where we might be able to work it out and get along in our diversity. After all, how many nations in the world have been founded, "dedicated," to use Lincoln's language, to the "proposition" that "all men are created equal"?

ENGAGING THE TEXT

1. Central to this reading selection is the concept of the "model minority." Working in small groups, define the concept and discuss how you learned this myth. For example, have you seen evidence of the myth's operation in the media, in your reading, or in your own family, community, church, workplace, or school? Try to draw some conclusions about how this type of cultural "knowledge" is taught.

2. What is wrong with the myth of the model minority, in Takaki's view? In what specific ways does it misrepresent or distort reality? How can the myth, which on the surface seems to celebrate the success of Asian Americans, actually harm them?

3. Takaki critiques the myth of the model minority by analyzing particular events in the past that illustrate how the myth works. How persuasive do you find this historical critique, and why? What other types of evidence might he have used?

4. Review Takaki's summary of Francis Fukuyama's ideas in paragraphs 9–13. Paraphrase Takaki's critique of Fukuyama's book and explain why Takaki refers so extensively to a point of view with which he fundamentally disagrees.

5. If you have ever had an experience like Takaki's taxicab ride, relate your story in a brief essay or journal entry.

EXPLORING CONNECTIONS

6. When Stephen Cruz (p. 335) became successful, he was seen not as a member of a model minority group but rather as a model member of a minority group. In what ways was his situation as a successful young Chicano engineer comparable to that of Asian Americans today, and in what respects did it differ? To extend the assignment, answer the same question about Colin Powell (p. 305).

7. Compare the idea of the model minority with the idea of the "scholarship boy" as defined by Richard Rodriguez (p. 194). On what assumptions does each concept rest? What expectations does each create? Why is each of these labels dangerous?

EXTENDING THE CRITICAL CONTEXT

8. Although the news media have been quick to extol the virtues of Asian Americans as models of achievement, representations of Asians and Asian Americans are scarce in most forms of mass entertainment. Survey movies,

TV shows, music videos, song lyrics, and other forms of popular culture. How are Asian Americans represented, and how do these images compare with those implied by the myth of the model minority?

9. In paragraphs 5–7, Takaki outlines the multicultural requirement at the University of California, Berkeley. After reviewing his summary, research any multicultural requirements your school has adopted (for example, their origins, their stated purpose, the courses designed to meet them) and report your findings to the class. To extend this assignment, arrange for a teacher or administrator to visit your class to discuss the history of the requirement or to review any debates surrounding proposals of such a requirement.

The Lesson

Toni Cade Bambara

"The Lesson" looks at wealth through the eyes of a poor black girl whose education includes a field trip to one of the world's premier toy stores. The story speaks to serious social issues with a comic, energetic, and utterly engaging voice. Toni Cade Bambara (1939–1995) grew up in the Harlem and Bedford-Stuyvesant areas of New York City. Trained at Queens College and City College of New York in dance, drama, and literature, she is best known for her collections of stories, Gorilla, My Love *(1972) and* The Seabirds Are Still Alive and Other Stories *(1977), and for her novels,* If Blessing Comes *(1987) and* The Salt Eaters *(1980), winner of the American Book Award. Her novel* Those Bones Are Not My Child, *edited by Toni Morrison, was published posthumously in 1999. "The Lesson" is taken from* Gorilla, My Love.

Back in the days when everyone was old and stupid or young and foolish and me and Sugar were the only ones just right, this lady moved on our block with nappy hair and proper speech and no makeup. And quite naturally we laughed at her, laughed the way we did at the junk man who went about his business like he was some big-time president and his sorry-ass horse his secretary. And we kinda hated her too, hated the way we did the winos who cluttered up our parks and pissed on our handball walls and stank up our hallways and stairs so you couldn't halfway play hide-and-seek without a goddamn gas mask. Miss Moore was her name. The only woman on the block with no first name. And she was black as hell, cept for her feet, which were fish-white and spooky. And she was always planning these boring-ass things for us to do, us being my cousin, mostly, who lived on the block cause we all moved North the same time and to the same apartment then spread out gradual to breathe. And our parents would yank our heads into some kinda shape and crisp up our clothes so we'd be presentable for travel with Miss Moore, who always looked like she was going to church, though she never did. Which is just one of the things the grownups talked about when they talked behind her back like a dog. But when she came calling with some sachet[1] she'd sewed up or some gingerbread she'd made or some book, why then they'd all be too embarrassed to turn her down and we'd get handed out all spruced up. She'd been to college and said it only right that she should take responsibility for the young ones' education, and she not even related by marriage or blood. So they'd go for it. Specially Aunt Gretchen. She was the main gofer in the family. You got some ole dumb shit foolishness you want somebody to go for, you send for Aunt Gretchen. She been screwed into the go-along for so long, it's a blood-deep natural thing with her. Which is how she got saddled with me and Sugar and Junior in the first place while our mothers were in a la-de-da apartment up the block having a good ole time.

So this one day Miss Moore rounds us all up at the mailbox and it's puredee hot and she's knockin herself out about arithmetic. And school suppose to let up in summer I heard, but she don't never let up. And the starch in my pinafore scratching the shit outta me and I'm really hating this nappy-head bitch and her goddamn college degree. I'd much rather go to the pool or to the show where it's cool. So me and Sugar leaning on the mailbox being surly, which is a Miss Moore word. And Flyboy checking out what everybody brought for lunch. And Fat Butt already wasting his peanut-butter-and-jelly sandwich like the pig he is. And Junebug punchin on Q.T.'s arm for potato chips. And Rosie Giraffe shifting from one hip to the other waiting for somebody to step on her foot or ask her if she from Georgia so she can kick ass, preferably Mercedes'. And Miss Moore asking us do we know what money is, like we a bunch of retards. I mean real money, she say, like it's only poker chips or monopoly papers we lay on the grocer. So right away I'm tired of this and say so. And would much rather snatch Sugar and go to the Sunset and terrorize the West Indian kids and take their hair ribbons and their money too. And Miss Moore files that remark away for next week's lesson on brotherhood, I can tell. And finally I say we oughta get to the subway cause it's cooler and besides we might meet some cute boys. Sugar done swiped her mama's lipstick, so we ready.

So we heading down the street and she's boring us silly about what things cost and what our parents make and how much goes for rent and how money ain't divided up right in this country. And then she gets to the part

---

[1]*sachet:* A small bag filled with a sweet-smelling substance. Sachets are often placed in drawers to scent clothes.

about we all poor and live in the slums, which I don't feature. And I'm ready to speak on that, but she steps out in the street and hails two cabs just like that. Then she hustles half the crew in with her and hands me a five-dollar bill and tells me to calculate 10 percent tip for the driver. And we're off. Me and Sugar and Junebug and Flyboy hangin out the window and hollering to everybody, putting lipstick on each other cause Flyboy a faggot anyway, and making farts with our sweaty armpits. But I'm mostly trying to figure how to spend this money. But they all fascinated with the meter ticking and Junebug starts laying bets as to how much it'll read when Flyboy can't hold his breath no more. Then Sugar lays bets as to how much it'll be when we get there. So I'm stuck. Don't nobody want to go for my plan, which is to jump out at the next light and run off to the first bar-b-que we can find. Then the driver tells us to get the hell out cause we are there already. And the meter reads eighty-five cents. And I'm stalling to figure out the tip and Sugar say give him a dime. And I decide he don't need it bad as I do, so later for him. But then he tries to take off with Junebug foot still in the door so we talk about his mama something ferocious. Then we check out that we on Fifth Avenue[2] and everybody dressed up in stockings. One lady in a fur coat, hot as it is. White folks crazy.

"This is the place," Miss Moore say, presenting it to us in the voice she uses at the museum. "Let's look in the windows before we go in."

"Can we steal?" Sugar asks very serious like she's getting the ground   5
rules square away before she plays. "I beg your pardon," say Miss Moore, and we fall out. So she leads us around the windows of the toy store and me and Sugar screamin, "This is mine, that's mine, I gotta have that, that was made for me, I was born for that," till Big Butt drowns us out.

"Hey, I'm goin to buy that there."

"That there? You don't even know what it is, stupid."

"I do so," he say punchin on Rosie Giraffe. "It's a microscope."

"Whatcha gonna do with a microscope, fool?"

"Look at things."   10

"Like what, Ronald?" ask Miss Moore. And Big Butt ain't got the first notion. So here go Miss Moore gabbing about the thousands of bacteria in a drop of water and the somethinorother in a speck of blood and the million and one living things in the air around us is invisible to the naked eye. And what she say that for? Junebug go to town on that "naked" and we rolling. Then Miss Moore ask what it cost. So we all jam into the window smudgin it up and the price tag say $300. So then she ask how long'd take for Big Butt and Junebug to save up their allowances. "Too long," I say. "Yeh," adds Sugar, "outgrown it by that time." And Miss Moore say no, you never outgrow learning instruments. "Why, even medical students and interns and," blah, blah, blah. And we ready to choke Big Butt for bringing it up in the first damn place.

[2]*Fifth Avenue:* The street in New York most famous for its expensive stores.

"This here costs four hundred eighty dollars," say Rosie Giraffe. So we pile up all over her to see what she pointin out. My eyes tell me it's a chunk of glass cracked with something heavy, and different-color inks dripped into the splits, then the whole thing put into a oven or something. But for $480 it don't make sense.

"That's a paperweight made of semi-precious stones fused together under tremendous pressure," she explains slowly, with her hands doing the mining and all the factory work.

"So what's a paperweight?" asks Rosie Giraffe.

"To weigh paper with, dumbbell," say Flyboy, the wise man from the East.   15

"Not exactly," say Miss Moore, which is what she say when you warm or way off too. "It's to weigh paper down so it won't scatter and make your desk untidy." So right away me and Sugar curtsy to each other and then to Mercedes who is more the tidy type.

"We don't keep paper on top of the desk in my class," say Junebug, figuring Miss Moore crazy or lyin one.

"At home, then," she say. "Don't you have a calendar and a pencil case and a blotter and a letter-opener on your desk at home where you do your homework?" And she know damn well what our homes look like cause she nosys around in them every chance she gets.

"I don't even have a desk," say Junebug. "Do we?"

"No. And I don't get no homework neither," say Big Butt.   20

"And I don't even have a home," say Flyboy like he do at school to keep the white folks off his back and sorry for him. Send this poor kid to camp posters, is his speciality.

"I do," say Mercedes. "I have a box of stationery on my desk and a picture of my cat. My godmother bought the stationery and the desk. There's a big rose on each sheet and the envelopes smell like roses."

"Who want to know about your smelly-ass stationery," say Rosie Giraffe fore I can get my two cents in.

"It's important to have a work area all your own so that..."

"Will you look at this sailboat, please," say Flyboy, cuttin her off and   25
pointin to the thing like it was his. So once again we tumble all over each other to gaze at this magnificent thing in the toy store which is just big enough to maybe sail two kittens across the pond if you strap them to the posts tight. We all start reciting the price tag like we in assembly. "Handcrafted sailboat of fiberglass at one thousand one hundred ninety-five dollars."

"Unbelievable," I hear myself say and am really stunned. I read it again for myself just in case the group recitation put me in a trance. Same thing. For some reason this pisses me off. We look at Miss Moore and she lookin at us, waiting for I dunno what.

"Who'd pay all that when you can buy a sailboat set for a quarter at Pop's, a tube of glue for a dime, and a ball of string for eight cents? It must have a motor and a whole lot else besides," I say. "My sailboat cost me about fifty cents."

"But will it take water?" say Mercedes with her smart ass.

"Took mine to Alley Pond Park once," say Flyboy. "String broke. Lost it. Pity."

"Sailed mine in Central Park and it keeled over and sank. Had to ask   30
my father for another dollar."

"And you got the strap," laugh Big Butt. "The jerk didn't even have a string on it. My old man wailed on his behind."

Little Q.T. was staring hard at the sailboat and you could see he wanted it bad. But he too little and somebody'd just take it from him. So what the hell. "This boat for kids, Miss Moore?"

"Parents silly to buy something like that just to get all broke up," say Rosie Giraffe.

"That much money it should last forever," I figure.

"My father'd buy it for me if I wanted it."   35

"Your father, my ass," say Rosie Giraffe getting a chance to finally push Mercedes.

"Must be rich people shop here," say Q.T.

"You are a very bright boy," say Flyboy. "What was your first clue?" And he rap him on the head with the back of his knuckles, since Q.T. the only one he could get away with. Though Q.T. liable to come up behind you years later and get his licks in when you half expect it.

"What I want to know is," I says to Miss Moore though I never talk to her, I wouldn't give the bitch that satisfaction, "is how much a real boat costs? I figure a thousand'd get you a yacht any day."

"Why don't you check that out," she says, "and report back to the   40
group?" Which really pains my ass. If you gonna mess up a perfectly good swim day least you could do is have some answers. "Let's go in," she say like she got something up her sleeve. Only she don't lead the way. So me and Sugar turn the corner to where the entrance is, but when we get there I kinda hang back. Not that I'm scared, what's there to be afraid of, just a toy store. But I feel funny, shame. But what I got to be shamed about? Got as much right to go in as anybody. But somehow I can't seem to get hold on the door, so I step away for Sugar to lead. But she hangs back too. And I look at her and she looks at me and this is ridiculous. I mean, damn, I have never ever been shy about doing nothing or going nowhere. But then Mercedes steps up and then Rosie Giraffe and Big Butt crowd in behind and shove, and next thing we all stuffed into the doorway with only Mercedes squeezing past us, smoothing out her jumper and walking right down the aisle. Then the rest of us tumble in like a glued-together jigsaw done all wrong. And people lookin at us. And it's like the time me and Sugar crashed into the Catholic church on a dare. But once we got in there and everything so hushed and holy and the candles and the bowin and the hand-kerchiefs on all the drooping heads, I just couldn't go through with the plan. Which was for me to run up to the altar and do a tap dance while Sugar played the nose flute and messed around in the holy water. And Sugar kept

givin me the elbow. Then later teased me so bad I tied her up in the shower and turned it on and locked her in. And she'd be there till this day if Aunt Gretchen hadn't finally figured I was lying about the boarder takin a shower.

Same thing in the store. We all walkin on tiptoe and hardly touchin the games and puzzles and things. And I watched Miss Moore who is steady watchin us like she waitin for a sign. Like Mama Drewery watches the sky and sniffs the air and takes note of just how much slant is in the bird formation. Then me and Sugar bump smack into each other, so busy gazing at the toys, 'specially the sailboat. But we don't laugh and go into our fat-lady bump-stomach routine. We just stare at that price tag. Then Sugar run a finger over the whole boat. And I'm jealous and want to hit her. Maybe not her, but I sure want to punch somebody in the mouth.

"Watcha bring us here for, Miss Moore?"

"You sound angry, Sylvia. Are you mad about something?" Give me one of them grins like she tellin a grown-up joke that never turns out to be funny. And she's lookin very closely at me like maybe she plannin to do my portrait from memory. I'm mad, but I won't give her that satisfaction. So I slouch around the store bein very bored and say, "Let's go."

Me and Sugar at the back of the train watchin' the tracks whizzin by large then small then gettin gobbled up in the dark. I'm thinkin about this tricky toy I saw in the store. A clown that somersaults on a bar then does chin-ups just cause you yank lightly at his leg. Cost $35. I could see me askin my mother for a $35 birthday clown. "You wanna who that costs what?" she'd say, cockin her head to the side to get a better view of the hole in my head. Thirty-five dollars could buy new bunk beds for Junior and Gretchen's boy. Thirty-five dollars and the whole household could go visit Granddaddy Nelson in the country. Thirty-five dollars would pay for the rent and the piano bill too. Who are these people that spend that much for performing clowns and $1,000 for toy sailboats? What kinda work they do and how they live and how come we ain't in on it? Where we are is who we are, Miss Moore always pointin out. But it don't necessarily have to be that way, she always adds then waits for somebody to say that poor people have to wake up and demand their share of the pie and don't none of us know what kind of pie she talkin about in the first damn place. But she ain't so smart cause I still got her four dollars from the taxi and she sure ain't gettin it. Messin up my day with this shit. Sugar nudges me in my pocket and winks.

Miss Moore lines us up in front of the mailbox where we started from, 45
seem like years ago, and I got a headache for thinkin so hard. And we lean all over each other so we can hold up under the draggy-ass lecture she always finishes us off with at the end before we thank her for borin us to tears. But she just looks at us like she readin tea leaves. Finally she say, "Well, what did you think of F.A.O. Schwarz?"[3]

---

[3]*F.A.O. Schwarz:* The name and the toy store are real. The store, in fact, has become a tourist attraction.

Rosie Giraffe mumbles, "White folks crazy."

"I'd like to go in there again when I get my birthday money," says Mercedes, and we shove her out the pack so she has to lean on the mailbox by herself.

"I'd like a shower. Tiring day," say Flyboy.

Then Sugar surprises me by saying, "You know, Miss Moore, I don't think all of us here put together eat in a year what that sailboat costs." And Miss Moore lights up like somebody goosed her. "And?" she say, urging Sugar on. Only I'm standin on her foot so she don't continue.

"Imagine for a minute what kind of society it is in which some people 50 can spend on a toy what it would cost to feed a family of six or seven. What do you think?"

"I think," say Sugar pushing me off her feet like she never done before, cause I whip her ass in a minute, "that this is not much of a democracy if you ask me. Equal chance to pursue happiness means an equal crack at the dough, don't it?" Miss Moore is besides herself and I am disgusted with Sugar's treachery. So I stand on her foot one more time to see if she'll shove me. She shuts up, and Miss Moore looks at me, sorrowfully I'm thinkin. And somethin weird is going on, I can feel it in my chest.

"Anybody else learn anything today?" lookin dead at me. I walk away and Sugar has to run to catch up and don't even seem to notice when I shrug her arm off my shoulder.

"Well, we got four dollars anyway," she says.

"Uh hunh."

"We could go to Hascombs and get half a chocolate layer and then go 55 to the Sunset and still have plenty money for potato chips and ice-cream sodas."

"Uh hunh."

"Race you to Hascombs," she say.

We start down the block and she gets ahead which is O.K. by me cause I'm goin to the West End and then over to the Drive to think this day through. She can run if she want to and even run faster. But ain't nobody gonna beat me at nuthin.

ENGAGING THE TEXT

1. What is the lesson Miss Moore is trying to teach in this story? How well is it received by Mercedes, Sugar, and the narrator, Sylvia? Why does the narrator react differently from Sugar, and what is the meaning of her last line in the story, "But ain't nobody gonna beat me at nuthin"?

2. Why did Bambara write the story from Sylvia's point of view? How would the story change if told from Miss Moore's perspective? From Sugar's? How would it change if the story were set today as opposed to thirty years ago?

3. The story mentions several expensive items: a fur coat, a microscope, a paperweight, a sailboat, and a toy clown. Why do you think the author chose each of these details?

4. In paragraph 44 Sylvia says, "Where we are is who we are, Miss Moore always pointin out. But it don't necessarily have to be that way." What does Miss Moore mean by this? Do you agree? What does Miss Moore expect the children to do to change the situation?

EXPLORING CONNECTIONS

5. Write a dialogue between Miss Moore and Gregory Mantsios, author of "Class in America" (p. 318), in which they discuss Sylvia's future and her chances for success.

6. Compare Miss Moore with the matriarchs in "Envy" by Bebe Moore Campbell (p. 98). In particular, examine the goals they set, the behavior they expect, and their means of influencing the young women in their charge.

7. Compare Miss Moore with the "Seven-Lesson Schoolteacher" described by John Taylor Gatto (p. 152). To what extent does Miss Moore's approach to education avoid the pitfalls Gatto identifies with formal schooling? Does Miss Moore's "lesson" have a hidden curriculum?

8. Compare Sylvia and Sugar's relationship here with that of Teresa and the speaker of the poem in "Para Teresa" (p. 207). Which girls stand the better chance of achieving success? Why?

EXTENDING THE CRITICAL CONTEXT

9. For the next class meeting, find the most overpriced, unnecessary item you can in a store, catalog, TV ad, or newspaper. Spend a few minutes swapping examples, then discuss the information you've gathered: are there any lessons to be learned here about wealth, success, and status?

10. The opening lines of "The Lesson" suggest that Sylvia is now a mature woman looking back on her youth. Working in groups, write a brief biography explaining what has happened to Sylvia since the day of "The Lesson." What has she done? Who has she become? Read your profiles aloud to the class and explain your vision of Sylvia's development.

11. This chapter of *Rereading America* has been criticized by conservatives for undermining the work ethic of American college students. Rush Limbaugh, for example, claims that the chapter "presents America as a stacked deck," thus "robbing people of the ability to see the enormous opportunities directly in front of them." Do you agree? Write a journal entry in which you explain how these readings have influenced your attitudes toward work and success.

4

True Women and Real Men
Myths of Gender

Bree Scott-Hartland as Delphinia Blue, photo by Carolyn Jones. (From *Living Proof,* Abbeville Press, 1994.)

Common sense tells us that there are obvious differences between females and males: after all, biology, not culture, determines whether you're able to bear children. But culture and cultural myths do shape the roles men and women play in our public and private relationships: we may be born female and male, but we are made women and men. Sociologists distinguish between sex and gender—between one's biological identity and the conventional patterns of behavior we learn to associate with each sex. While biological sex remains relatively stable, the definition of "appropriate" gender behavior varies dramatically from one cultural group or historical period to the next. The variations show up markedly in the way we dress. For example, in Thailand, men who act and dress like women are not only socially accepted but encouraged to participate in popular, male-only beauty pageants; in contemporary Anglo-American culture, on the other hand, cross-dressers are usually seen as deviant or ridiculous. Male clothing in late-seventeenth- and early-eighteenth-century England would also have failed our current "masculinity" tests: in that period, elaborate laces, brocades, wigs, and even makeup signaled wealth, status, and sexual attractiveness for men and women alike.

History shows us how completely our gender derives from cultural myths about what is proper for men and women to think, enjoy, and do. And history is replete with examples of how the apparent "naturalness" of gender has been used to regulate political, economic, and personal relations between the sexes.

Many nineteenth-century scientists argued that it was "unnatural" for women to attend college; rigorous intellectual activity, they asserted, would draw vital energy away from a woman's reproductive organs and make her sterile. According to this line of reasoning, women who sought higher education threatened the natural order by jeopardizing their ability to bear children and perpetuate the species. Arguments based on nature were likewise used to justify women's exclusion from political life. In his classic 1832 treatise on American democracy, for instance, James Fenimore Cooper remarked that women's domestic role and "necessary" subordination to men made them unsuitable for participation in public affairs. Thus, he argued, denying women the right to vote was perfectly consistent with the principles of American democracy:

> In those countries where the suffrage is said to be universal, exceptions exist, that arise from the necessity of things.... The interests of women being thought to be so identified with those of their male relatives as to become, in a great degree, inseparable, females are, almost generally, excluded from the possession of political rights. There can be no doubt that society is greatly the gainer, by thus excluding one half its members, and the half that is best adapted to give a tone to its domestic happiness, from the strife of parties, and the fierce struggles of political controversies.... These exceptions, however, do not very materially affect the principle of political equality. (*The American Democrat*)

Resistance to gender equality has been remarkably persistent in the United States. It took over seventy years of hard political work by both black and white women's organizations to win the right to vote. But while feminists gained the vote for women in 1920 and the legal right to equal educational and employment opportunities in the 1970s, attitudes change even more slowly than laws. Contemporary antifeminist campaigns voice some of the same anxieties as their nineteenth-century counterparts over the "loss" of femininity and domesticity.

Women continue to suffer economic inequities based on cultural assumptions about gender. What's defined as "women's work"—nurturing, feeding, caring for family and home—is devalued and pays low wages or none at all. When women enter jobs traditionally held by men, they often encounter discrimination, harassment, or "glass ceilings" that limit their advancement. But men, too, pay a high price for their culturally imposed roles. Psychological research shows higher rates of depression among people of both sexes who adhere closely to traditional roles than among those who do not. Moreover, studies of men's mental and physical health suggest that social pressure to "be a man" (that is, to be emotionally controlled, powerful, and successful) can contribute to isolation, anxiety, stress, and illness, and may be partially responsible for men's shorter life spans. As sociologist Margaret Andersen observes, "traditional gender roles limit the psychological and social possibilities for human beings."

Even our assumption that there are "naturally" only two genders is a cultural invention that fails to accommodate the diversity of human experience. Some cultures have three or more gender categories. One of the best-known third genders is the American Indian *berdache,* a role that is found in as many as seventy North and South American tribes. The berdache is a biological male who takes the social role of a woman, does women's work (or in some cases both women's and men's work), and often enjoys high status in the society; the berdache has sex with men who are not themselves berdaches and in some cultures may also marry a man. Euro-American culture, by contrast, offers no socially acceptable alternative gender roles. As a result, gay men, lesbians, bisexuals, transsexuals, cross-dressers, and other gender rebels confront pervasive and often legally sanctioned discrimination similar to that once experienced by women. Just as many Americans in the past considered it "unnatural" and socially destructive for women to vote or go to college, many now consider it "unnatural" and socially destructive for gays and lesbians to marry, bear or adopt children, serve in the military, lead scout groups, or teach school.

This chapter focuses on cultural myths of gender and the influence they wield over human development and personal identity. The first three selections examine how dominant American culture defines female and male gender roles—and how those roles may define us. In "How the Americans Understand the Equality of the Sexes," Alexis de Tocqueville describes the status of American women in the early years of the Republic. Jamaica

Kincaid's "Girl," a story framed as a mother's advice to her daughter, presents a more contemporary take on what it means to be raised a woman. Holly Devor's "Becoming Members of Society" examines gender as a socially constructed category and discusses the psychological processes that underlie gender role acquisition.

Next, two personal narratives and a Visual Portfolio present strong rereadings of traditional gender roles. Judith Ortiz Cofer's personal reflection, "The Story of My Body," traces the shifting meanings of gender and identity for a woman of color who moves among different social and cultural contexts. In "Where I Come From Is Like This," Paula Gunn Allen counters dominant American myths of gender with an eloquent description of the powerful roles played by women in American Indian cultures. The portfolio presents both conventional and unconventional images of women and men that provide an opportunity to think about the ways that we "read" gender visually.

A cluster of pieces on popular culture examines the impact of gender stereotypes in advertising, movies, and children's toys. Jean Kilbourne's "'Two Ways a Woman Can Get Hurt': Advertising and Violence" argues that the objectification of women in ads constitutes a form of cultural abuse. In Kilbourne's view, ads that play with pornographic imagery and hint at sexual aggression contribute to an epidemic of real violence against women. Jackson Katz, in "Advertising and the Construction of Violent White Masculinity," interprets the popularity of violent masculine images in contemporary media as a sign of men's anxiety about losing power. "The Evolution of G.I. Joe" summarizes in visual form the results of a scholarly study that found potential connections between exaggerated, "pumped up" action figures, distorted body image, and eating disorders among boys.

Are we imprisoned by traditional gender roles, or has "liberation" itself become a prison? Christina Hoff Sommers, in "The Gender Wardens," warns that feminist attempts to eradicate traditional roles threaten our freedom of choice. Carmen Vázquez's "Appearances" deals with a different kind of threat to personal freedom: examining the connection between homophobic violence and "gender betrayal," Vázquez documents the penalties — from verbal harassment to murder — paid by both gay and straight people who dare to cross conventional gender boundaries. "The Bridge Builder" offers the story of Kathleen Boatwright, a devout Christian and a lesbian who refuses to be confined by gay stereotypes or rigid attitudes toward homosexuality.

The chapter ends with a pair of essays that probe the tensions between young men and women who struggle to define their roles in a culture where the old rules are rapidly changing. Susan Faludi's "Girls Have All the Power: What's Troubling Troubled Boys" represents a feminist reporter's effort to comprehend the motives and psychology of the Spur Posse, a group of teenage boys who gained notoriety in the early 1990s for competing with each other to see who could rack up the most "points" for having sex with the most girls, a number that included one ten-year-old. Finally, in "From Fly-Girls to Bitches and Hos," self-described "hip-hop feminist" Joan Morgan argues that it's necessary to look behind the violent misogyny of many rap lyrics in order to understand and heal the pain of the men who write and sing the words.

Sources

Margaret L. Andersen, *Thinking About Women: Sociological Perspectives on Gender,* 3rd ed. New York: Macmillan, 1993.

James Fenimore Cooper, *The American Democrat.* N.p.: Minerva Press, 1969.

Marilyn French, *Beyond Power: On Women, Men, and Morals.* New York: Ballantine Books, 1985.

Paula Giddings, *When and Where I Enter: The Impact of Black Women on Race and Sex in America.* New York: Bantam Books, 1984.

Ruth Hubbard, *The Politics of Women's Biology.* New Brunswick, NJ: Rutgers University Press, 1990.

Judith Lorber, *Paradoxes of Gender.* New Haven and London: Yale University Press, 1994.

James D. Weinrich and Walter L. Williams, "Strange Customs, Familiar Lives: Homosexualities in Other Cultures." *Homosexuality: Research Implications for Public Policy.* Ed. John C. Gonsiorek and James D. Weinrich. Newbury Park, CA: Sage, 1991.

BEFORE READING

- Imagine for a moment that you were born female (if you're a man) or male (of you're a woman). How would your life be different? Would any of your interests and activities change? How about your relationships with other people? Write a journal entry describing your past, present, and possible future in this alternate gender identity.

- Collect and bring to class images of girls and boys, women and men taken from popular magazines and newspapers. Working in groups, make a collage of either male or female gender images; then compare and discuss your results. What do these media images tell you about what it means to be a woman or a man in this culture?

- Do a brief freewrite focusing on the performer in the frontispiece to this chapter (p. 402). How would you describe this person's gender? In what ways does this image challenge traditional ideas about maleness and femaleness?

How the Americans Understand the Equality of the Sexes

ALEXIS DE TOCQUEVILLE

In 1831, Alexis de Tocqueville (1805–1859), a French aristocrat, left Europe to study the American penal system. The young democracy that he observed in the United States left a deep impression on Tocqueville, and in 1835 he published his reflections on this new way of life in Democracy in America—*a work that has since become the point of departure for many studies of American culture. In the following passage from* Democracy in America, *Tocqueville compares the social condition of American women to that of their European counterparts. Tocqueville's concept of equality and assumptions about women can seem foreign to modern readers, so it would be a good idea to take your time as you read this short passage.*

I have shown how democracy destroys or modifies the different inequalities which originate in society; but is that all? or does it not ultimately affect that great inequality of man and woman which has seemed, up to the present day, to be eternally based in human nature? I believe that the social changes which bring nearer to the same level the father and son, the master and servant, and, in general, superiors and inferiors, will raise woman, and make her more and more the equal of man. But here, more than ever, I feel the necessity of making myself clearly understood; for there is no subject on which the coarse and lawless fancies of our age have taken a freer range.

There are people in Europe who, confounding together the different characteristics of the sexes, would make man and woman into beings not only equal, but alike. They would give to both the same functions, impose on both the same duties, and grant to both the same rights; they would mix them in all things,—their occupations, their pleasures, their business. It may readily be conceived, that, by thus attempting to make one sex equal to the other, both are degraded; and from so preposterous a medley of the works of nature, nothing could ever result but weak men and disorderly women.

It is not thus that the Americans understand that species of democratic equality which may be established between the sexes. They admit that, as nature has appointed such wide differences between the physical and moral constitution of man and woman, her manifest design was to give a distinct employment to their various faculties; and they hold that improvement does not consist in making beings so dissimilar do pretty nearly the same things, but in causing each of them to fulfil their respective tasks in the best possible manner. The Americans have applied to the sexes the great principle of political economy which governs the manufactures of our age, by carefully dividing the duties of man from those of woman, in order that the great work of society may be the better carried on.

In no country has such constant care been taken as in America to trace two clearly distinct lines of action for the two sexes, and to make them keep pace one with the other, but in two pathways which are always different. American women never manage the outward concerns of the family, or conduct a business, or take a part in political life; nor are they, on the other hand, ever compelled to perform the rough labor of the fields, or to make any of those laborious exertions which demand the exertion of physical strength. No families are so poor as to form an exception to this rule. If, on the one hand, an American woman cannot escape from the quiet circle of domestic employments, she is never forced, on the other, to go beyond it. Hence it is, that the women of America, who often exhibit a masculine strength of understanding and a manly energy, generally preserve great delicacy of personal appearance, and always retain the manners of women, although they sometimes show that they have the hearts and minds of men.

Nor have the Americans ever supposed that one consequence of democratic principles is the subversion of marital power, or the confusion of the natural authorities in families. They hold that every association must have a head in order to accomplish its object, and that the natural head of the conjugal association is man. They do not therefore deny him the right of directing his partner; and they maintain that, in the smaller association of husband and wife, as well as in the great social community, the object of democracy is to regulate and legalize the powers which are necessary, and not to subvert all power.

This opinion is not peculiar to one sex, and contested by the other: I never observed that the women of America consider conjugal authority as a fortunate usurpation of their rights, nor that they thought themselves degraded by submitting to it. It appeared to me, on the contrary, that they attach a sort of pride to the voluntary surrender of their own will, and make it their boast to bend themselves to the yoke,—not to shake it off. Such, at least, is the feeling expressed by the most virtuous of their sex; the others are silent; and, in the United States, it is not the practice for a guilty wife to clamor for the rights of women, whilst she is trampling on her own holiest duties.[1]

It has often been remarked, that in Europe a certain degree of contempt lurks even in the flattery which men lavish upon women: although a European frequently affects to be the slave of woman, it may be seen that

[1]Allusion to Mary Wollstonecraft (1759–1797), English radical, political theorist, and author of *Vindication of the Rights of Woman*, who argued that women should enjoy complete political, economic, and sexual freedom; Wollstonecraft scandalized the "polite" society of her day by living according to her feminist principles.

he never sincerely thinks her his equal. In the United States, men seldom compliment women, but they daily show how much they esteem them. They constantly display an entire confidence in the understanding of a wife, and a profound respect for her freedom; they have decided that her mind is just as fitted as that of a man to discover the plain truth, and her heart as firm to embrace it; and they have never sought to place her virtue, any more than his, under the shelter of prejudice, ignorance, and fear.

It would seem that, in Europe, where man so easily submits to the despotic sway of women, they are nevertheless deprived of some of the greatest attributes of the human species, and considered as seductive but imperfect beings; and (what may well provoke astonishment) women ultimately look upon themselves in the same light, and almost consider it as a privilege that they are entitled to show themselves futile, feeble, and timid. The women of America claim no such privileges.

Again, it may be said that in our morals we have reserved strange immunities to man; so that there is, as it were, one virtue for his use, and another for the guidance of his partner; and that, according to the opinion of the public, the very same act may be punished alternately as a crime, or only as a fault. The Americans know not this iniquitous division of duties and rights; amongst them, the seducer is as much dishonored as his victim.

It is true that the Americans rarely lavish upon women those eager attentions which are commonly paid them in Europe; but their conduct to women always implies that they suppose them to be virtuous and refined; and such is the respect entertained for the moral freedom of the sex, that in the presence of a woman the most guarded language is used, lest her ear should be offended by an expression. In America, a young unmarried woman may, alone and without fear, undertake a long journey. 10

The legislators of the United States, who have mitigated almost all the penalties of criminal law, still make rape a capital offence, and no crime is visited with more inexorable severity by public opinion. This may be accounted for; as the Americans can conceive nothing more precious than a woman's honor, and nothing which ought so much to be respected as her independence, they hold that no punishment is too severe for the man who deprives her of them against her will. In France, where the same offence is visited with far milder penalties, it is frequently difficult to get a verdict from a jury against the prisoner. Is this a consequence of contempt of decency, or contempt of women? I cannot but believe that it is a contempt of both.

Thus, the Americans do not think that man and woman have either the duty or the right to perform the same offices, but they show an equal regard for both their respective parts; and though their lot is different, they consider both of them as beings of equal value. They do not give to the courage of woman the same form or the same direction as to that of man; but they never doubt her courage: and if they hold that man and his partner ought not always to exercise their intellect and understanding in the same manner, they at least believe the understanding of the one to be as sound as that of the other, and her intellect to be as clear. Thus, then, whilst they have allowed the social inferiority of woman to subsist, they have done all they could to raise her morally and intellectually to the level of man; and in this respect they appear to me to have excellently understood the true principle of democratic improvement.

As for myself, I do not hesitate to avow, that, although the women of the United States are confined within the narrow circle of domestic life, and their situation is, in some respects, one of extreme dependence, I have nowhere seen woman occupying a loftier position; and if I were asked, now that I am drawing to the close of this work, in which I have spoken of so many important things done by the Americans, to what the singular prosperity and growing strength of that people ought mainly to be attributed, I should reply, To the superiority of their women.

ENGAGING THE TEXT

1. What roles does Tocqueville assume are natural and appropriate for women? For men? Which of his assumptions, if any, seem contemporary? Which ones seem antiquated, and why?

2. How do American and European attitudes toward women differ, according to Tocqueville? In what ways, according to Tocqueville, is American democracy enabling women to become "more and more the equal of man" (para. 1)?

3. By the time Tocqueville wrote this selection, the first feminist manifesto, Wollstonecraft's *Vindication of the Rights of Woman* (1792), had been read and discussed in Europe for over forty years. Which parts of Tocqueville's essay seem to be intended as a response to feminist arguments for women's equality?

4. Tocqueville finds some forms of equality between women and men more desirable than others. Which forms does he approve, which does he disapprove, and why?

EXPLORING CONNECTIONS

5. Read the essay by Paula Gunn Allen (p. 433) for information on the various roles assigned to women and men in traditional tribal cultures. How are these roles similar to or different from the ones described by Tocqueville? Do they tend to support or challenge his observation that "the great inequality of man and woman" appears to be "eternally based in human nature" (para. 1)?

6. Both Tocqueville and Thomas Jefferson (p. 539) attempt to justify or rationalize a particular form of inequality. What strategies does each writer use to build his case for the subjection of women or for the enslavement of blacks? Which of their arguments appear least effective to you as a modern reader, and why?

EXTENDING THE CRITICAL CONTEXT

7. Work in groups to list the specific tasks involved in maintaining a household in the 1830s (keep in mind that electricity, indoor plumbing, ready-made clothing, and prepared foods were not available). How credible is Tocqueville's claim that no American woman is "ever compelled...to make any of those laborious exertions which demand the exertion of physical strength" (para. 4)? How do you explain his failure to acknowledge the hard physical labor routinely performed by many women during this time?

Girl

JAMAICA KINCAID

Although she now lives in New England, Jamaica Kincaid (b. 1949) retains strong ties, including citizenship, to her birthplace—the island of Antigua in the West Indies. After immigrating to the United States to attend college, she ended up educating herself instead, eventually becoming a staff writer for The New Yorker, *the author of several critically acclaimed books, and an instructor at Harvard University. About the influence of parents on children she says, "The magic is they carry so much you don't know about. They know you in a way you don't know yourself." Some of that magic is exercised in the story "Girl," which was first published in Kincaid's award-winning collection* At the Bottom of the River *(1983). She has written and edited several volumes of nonfiction on subjects ranging from colonialism to gardening and has published three novels,* Annie John *(1985),* Lucy *(1990), and* Autobiography of My Mother *(1996).*

Wash the white clothes on Monday and put them on the stone heap; wash the color clothes on Tuesday and put them on the clothesline to dry; don't walk barehead in the hot sun; cook pumpkin fritters[1] in very hot sweet oil; soak your little cloths right after you take them off; when buying cotton to make yourself a nice blouse, be sure that it doesn't have gum[2] on it, because that way it won't hold up well after a wash; soak salt fish overnight before you cook it; is it true that you sing benna[3] in Sunday school?; always eat

---

[1]*fritters:* Small fried cakes of batter, often containing vegetables, fruit, or other fillings.
[2]*gum:* Plant residue on cotton.
[3]*sing benna:* Sing popular music (not appropriate for Sunday school).

your food in such a way that it won't turn someone else's stomach; on Sundays try to walk like a lady and not like the slut you are so bent on becoming; don't sing benna in Sunday school; you mustn't speak to wharf-rat boys, not even to give directions; don't eat fruits on the street—flies will follow you; *but I don't sing benna on Sundays at all and never in Sunday school;* this is how to sew on a button; this is how to make a buttonhole for the button you have just sewed on; this is how to hem a dress when you see the hem coming down and so to prevent yourself from looking like the slut I know you are so bent on becoming; this is how you iron your father's khaki shirt so that it doesn't have a crease; this is how you iron your father's khaki pants so that they don't have a crease; this is how you grow okra[4]—far from the house, because okra tree harbors red ants; when you are growing dasheen,[5] make sure it gets plenty of water or else it makes your throat itch when you are eating it; this is how you sweep a corner; this is how you sweep a whole house; this is how you sweep a yard; this is how you smile to someone you don't like too much; this is how you smile to someone you don't like at all; this is how you smile to someone you like completely; this is how you set a table for tea; this is how you set a table for dinner; this is how you set a table for dinner with an important guest; this is how you set a table for lunch; this is how you set a table for breakfast; this is how to behave in the presence of men who don't know you very well, and this way they won't recognize immediately the slut I have warned you against becoming; be sure to wash every day, even if it is with your own spit; don't squat down to play marbles—you are not a boy, you know; don't pick people's flowers— you might catch something; don't throw stones at blackbirds, because it might not be a blackbird at all; this is how to make a bread pudding; this is how to make doukona;[6] this is how to make pepper pot;[7] this is how to make a good medicine for a cold; this is how to make a good medicine to throw away a child before it even becomes a child; this is how to catch a fish; this is how to throw back a fish you don't like, and that way something bad won't fall on you; this is how to bully a man; this is how a man bullies you; this is how to love a man, and if this doesn't work there are other ways, and if they don't work don't feel too bad about giving up; this is how to spit up in the air if you feel like it, and this is how to move quick so that it doesn't fall on you; this is how to make ends meet; always squeeze bread to make sure it's fresh; *but what if the baker won't let me feel the bread?;* you mean to say that after all you are really going to be the kind of woman who the baker won't let near the bread?

---

[4]*okra:* A shrub whose pods are used in soups, stews, and gumbo.

[5]*dasheen:* The taro plant, cultivated, like the potato, for its edible tuber.

[6]*doukona:* Plaintain pudding; the plantain fruit is similar to the banana.

[7]*pepper pot:* A spicy West Indian stew.

how to be a proper woman

ENGAGING THE TEXT

1. What are your best guesses as to the time and place of the story? Who is telling the story? What does this dialogue tell you about the relationship between the characters, their values and attitudes? What else can you surmise about these people (for instance, ages, occupation, social status)? On what evidence in the story do you base these conclusions?

2. Why does the story juxtapose advice on cooking and sewing, for example, with the repeated warning not to act like a slut?

3. Explain the meaning of the last line of the story: "you mean to say that after all you are really going to be the kind of woman who the baker won't let near the bread?"

4. What does the story tell us about male-female relationships? According to the speaker, what roles are women and men expected to play? What kinds of power, if any, does the speaker suggest that women may have?

EXPLORING CONNECTIONS

5. To what extent does Patricia Hill Collins's "Black Women and Motherhood" (p. 112) help explain the mother's attitude and advice in this story?

6. What does it mean to be a successful mother in "Girl"? How does this compare to being a good mother or parent in "Growing Pains" (p. 45), "Envy" (p. 98), "An Indian Story" (p. 89), or "Looking for Work" (p. 39)? Of all the parents in these narratives, which do you consider most successful, which least, and why?

EXTENDING THE CRITICAL CONTEXT

7. Write an imitation of the story. If you are a woman, record some of the advice or lessons your mother or another woman gave you; if you are a man, put down advice received from your father or from another male. Read what you have written aloud in class, alternating between male and female speakers, and discuss the results: How does parental guidance vary according to gender?

8. Write a page or two recording what the daughter might be thinking as she listens to her mother's advice; then compare notes with classmates.

Becoming Members of Society: Learning the Social Meanings of Gender

HOLLY DEVOR

*Gender is the most transparent of all social categories: we acquire gen-
der roles so early in life and so thoroughly that it's hard to see them as the
result of lessons taught and learned. Maleness and femaleness seem "natural," not the product of socialization. In this wide-ranging scholarly essay,
Holly Devor suggests that many of our notions of what it means to be female
or male are socially constructed. She also touches on the various ways that
different cultures define gender. A professor of sociology at the University of
Victoria in British Columbia, Devor (b. 1951) is a member of the International Academy of Sex Research and author of* FTM: Female-to-Male
Transsexuals in Society *(1997). This selection is taken from her ground-
breaking book,* Gender Blending: Confronting the Limits of Duality *(1989).*

The Gendered Self

The task of learning to be properly gendered members of society only
begins with the establishment of gender identity. Gender identities act as
cognitive filtering devices guiding people to attend to and learn gender role
behaviors appropriate to their statuses. Learning to behave in accordance
with one's gender identity is a lifelong process. As we move through our
lives, society demands different gender performances from us and rewards,
tolerates, or punishes us differently for conformity to, or digression from,
social norms. As children, and later adults, learn the rules of membership in
society, they come to see themselves in terms they have learned from the
people around them.

Children begin to settle into a gender identity between the age of eighteen months and two years.[1] By the age of two, children usually understand
that they are members of a gender grouping and can correctly identify other

[1]Much research has been devoted to determining when gender identity becomes solidi-
fied in the sense that a child knows itself to be unequivocally either male or female. John
Money and his colleagues have proposed eighteen months of age because it is difficult or impossible to change a child's gender identity once it has been established around the age of
eighteen months. Money and Ehrhardt, p. 243. [All notes are Devor's except 12, 20, and 21.]

members of their gender.[2] By age three they have a fairly firm and consistent concept of gender. Generally, it is not until children are five to seven years old that they become convinced that they are permanent members of their gender grouping.[3]

Researchers test the establishment, depth, and tenacity of gender identity through the use of language and the concepts mediated by language. The language systems used in populations studied by most researchers in this field conceptualize gender as binary and permanent. All persons are either male or female. All males are first boys and then men; all females are first girls and then women. People are believed to be unable to change genders without sex change surgery, and those who do change sex are considered to be both disturbed and exceedingly rare.

This is by no means the only way that gender is conceived in all cultures. Many aboriginal cultures have more than two gender categories and accept the idea that, under certain circumstances, gender may be changed without changes being made to biological sex characteristics. Many North and South American native peoples had a legitimate social category for persons who wished to live according to the gender role of another sex. Such people were sometimes revered, sometimes ignored, and occasionally scorned. Each culture had its own word to describe such persons, most commonly translated into English as "berdache." Similar institutions and linguistic concepts have also been recorded in early Siberian, Madagascan, and Polynesian societies, as well as in medieval Europe.[4]

Very young children learn their culture's social definitions of gender   5
and gender identity at the same time that they learn what gender behaviors are appropriate for them. But they only gradually come to understand the meaning of gender in the same way as the adults of their society do. Very young children may learn the words which describe their gender and be able to apply them to themselves appropriately, but their comprehension of their meaning is often different from that used by adults. Five-year-olds, for example, may be able to accurately recognize their own gender and the genders of the people around them, but they will often make such ascriptions on the basis of role information, such as hair style, rather than physical

[2]Mary Driver Leinbach and Beverly I. Fagot, "Acquisition of Gender Labels: A Test for Toddlers," *Sex Roles* 15 (1986), pp. 655–66.

[3]Maccoby, pp. 225–29; Kohlberg and Ullian, p. 211.

[4]See Susan Baker, "Biological Influences on Human Sex and Gender," in *Women: Sex and Sexuality,* ed. Catherine R. Stimpson and Ethel S. Person (Chicago: University of Chicago Press, 1980), p. 186; Evelyn Blackwood, "Sexuality and Gender in Certain Native American Tribes: The Case of Cross-Gender Females," *Signs* 10 (1984), pp. 27–42; Vern L. Bullough, "Transvestites in the Middle Ages," *American Journal of Sociology* 79 (1974), 1381–89; J. Cl. DuBois, "Transsexualisme et Anthropologie Culturelle," *Gynecologie Practique* 6 (1969), pp. 431–40; Donald C. Forgey, "The Institution of Berdache among the North American Plains Indians," *Journal of Sex Research* 11 (Feb. 1975), pp. 1–15; Walter L. Williams, *The Spirit and the Flesh: Sexual Diversity in American Indian Culture* (Boston: Beacon, 1986).

attributes, such as genitals, even when physical cues are clearly known to them. One result of this level of understanding of gender is that children in this age group often believe that people may change their gender with a change in clothing, hair style, or activity.[5]

The characteristics most salient to young minds are the more culturally specific qualities which grow out of gender role prescriptions. In one study, young school age children, who were given dolls and asked to identify their gender, overwhelmingly identified the gender of the dolls on the basis of attributes such as hair length or clothing style, in spite of the fact that the dolls were anatomically correct. Only 17 percent of the children identified the dolls on the basis of their primary or secondary sex characteristics.[6] Children five to seven years old understand gender as a function of role rather than as a function of anatomy. Their understanding is that gender (role) is supposed to be stable but that it is possible to alter it at will. This demonstrates that although the standard social definition of gender is based on genitalia, this is not the way that young children first learn to distinguish gender. The process of learning to think about gender in an adult fashion is one prerequisite to becoming a full member of society. Thus, as children grow older, they learn to think of themselves and others in terms more like those used by adults.

Children's developing concepts of themselves as individuals are necessarily bound up in their need to understand the expectations of the society of which they are a part. As they develop concepts of themselves as individuals, they do so while observing themselves as reflected in the eyes of others. Children start to understand themselves as individuals separate from others during the years that they first acquire gender identities and gender roles. As they do so, they begin to understand that others see them and respond to them as particular people. In this way they develop concepts of themselves as individuals, as an "I" (a proactive subject) simultaneously with self-images of themselves as individuals, as a "me" (a member of society, a subjective object). Children learn that they are both as they see themselves and as others see them.[7]

To some extent, children initially acquire the values of the society around them almost indiscriminately. To the degree that children absorb the generalized standards of society into their personal concept of what is correct behavior, they can be said to hold within themselves the attitude of the "generalized other."[8] This "generalized other" functions as a sort of monitoring or measuring device with which individuals may judge their own actions against those of their generalized conceptions of how members of

---

[5]Maccoby, p. 255.

[6]Ibid., p. 227.

[7]George Herbert Mead, "Self," in *The Social Psychology of George Herbert Mead,* ed. Anselm Strauss (Chicago: Phoenix Books, 1962, 1934), pp. 212–60.

[8]G. H. Mead.

society are expected to act. In this way members of society have available to them a guide, or an internalized observer, to turn the more private "I" into the object of public scrutiny, the "me." In this way, people can monitor their own behavioral impulses and censor actions which might earn them social disapproval or scorn. The tension created by the constant interplay of the personal "I" and the social "me" is the creature known as the "self."

But not all others are of equal significance in our lives, and therefore not all others are of equal impact on the development of the self. Any person is available to become part of one's "generalized other," but certain individuals, by virtue of the sheer volume of time spent in interaction with someone, or by virtue of the nature of particular interactions, become more significant in the shaping of people's values. These "significant others" become prominent in the formation of one's self-image and one's ideals and goals. As such they carry disproportionate weight in one's personal "generalized other."[9] Thus, children's individualistic impulses are shaped into a socially acceptable form both by particular individuals and by a more generalized pressure to conformity exerted by innumerable faceless members of society. Gender identity is one of the most central portions of that developing sense of self....

Gender Role Behaviors and Attitudes

The clusters of social definitions used to identify persons by gender are   10 collectively known as femininity and masculinity. Masculine characteristics are used to identify persons as males, while feminine ones are used as signifiers for femaleness. People use femininity or masculinity to claim and communicate their membership in their assigned, or chosen, sex or gender. Others recognize our sex or gender more on the basis of these characteristics than on the basis of sex characteristics, which are usually largely covered by clothing in daily life.

These two clusters of attributes are most commonly seen as mirror images of one another with masculinity usually characterized by dominance and aggression, and femininity by passivity and submission. A more even-handed description of the social qualities subsumed by femininity and masculinity might be to label masculinity as generally concerned with egoistic dominance and femininity as striving for cooperation or communion.[10] Characterizing femininity and masculinity in such a way does not portray the two clusters of characteristics as being in a hierarchical relationship to

[9]Hans Gerth and C. Wright Mills, *Character and Social Structure: The Psychology of Social Institutions* (New York: Harcourt, Brace and World, 1953), p. 96.

[10]Egoistic dominance is a striving for superior rewards for oneself or a competitive striving to reduce the rewards for one's competitors even if such action will not increase one's own rewards. Persons who are motivated by desires for egoistic dominance not only wish the best for themselves but also wish to diminish the advantages of others whom they may perceive as competing with them. See Maccoby, p. 217.

one another but rather as being two different approaches to the same question, that question being centrally concerned with the goals, means, and use of power. Such an alternative conception of gender roles captures the hierarchical and competitive masculine thirst for power, which can, but need not, lead to aggression, and the feminine quest for harmony and communal well-being, which can, but need not, result in passivity and dependence.

Many activities and modes of expression are recognized by most members of society as feminine. Any of these can be, and often are, displayed by persons of either gender. In some cases, cross gender behaviors are ignored by observers, and therefore do not compromise the integrity of a person's gender display. In other cases, they are labeled as inappropriate gender role behaviors. Although these behaviors are closely linked to sexual status in the minds and experiences of most people, research shows that dominant persons of either gender tend to use influence tactics and verbal styles usually associated with men and masculinity, while subordinate persons, of either gender, tend to use those considered to be the province of women.[11] Thus it seems likely that many aspects of masculinity and femininity are the result, rather than the cause, of status inequalities.

Popular conceptions of femininity and masculinity instead revolve around hierarchical appraisals of the "natural" roles of males and females. Members of both genders are believed to share many of the same human characteristics, although in different relative proportions; both males and females are popularly thought to be able to do many of the same things, but most activities are divided into suitable and unsuitable categories for each gender class. Persons who perform the activities considered appropriate for another gender will be expected to perform them poorly; if they succeed adequately, or even well, at their endeavors, they may be rewarded with ridicule or scorn for blurring the gender dividing line.

The patriarchal gender schema[12] currently in use in mainstream North American society reserves highly valued attributes for males and actively supports the high evaluation of any characteristics which might inadvertently become associated with maleness. The ideology which the schema grows out of postulates that the cultural superiority of males is a natural outgrowth of the innate predisposition of males toward aggression and dominance, which is assumed to flow inevitably from evolutionary and biological sources. Female attributes are likewise postulated to find their source in innate predispositions acquired in the evolution of the species. Feminine characteristics are thought to be intrinsic to the female facility for childbirth and breastfeeding. Hence, it is popularly believed that the social position of

---

[11]Judith Howard, Philip Blumstein, and Pepper Schwartz, "Sex, Power, and Influence Tactics in Intimate Relationships," *Journal of Personality and Social Psychology* 51 (1986), pp. 102–09; Peter Kollock, Philip Blumstein, and Pepper Schwartz, "Sex and Power in Interaction: Conversational Privileges and Duties," *American Sociological Review* 50 (1985), pp. 34–46.

[12]*schema:* A mental framework, scheme, or pattern that helps us make sense of experience.

females is biologically mandated to be intertwined with the care of children and a "natural" dependency on men for the maintenance of mother-child units. Thus the goals of femininity and, by implication, of all biological females are presumed to revolve around heterosexuality and maternity.[13]

Femininity, according to this traditional formulation, "would result in warm and continued relationships with men, a sense of maternity, interest in caring for children, and the capacity to work productively and continuously in female occupations."[14] This recipe translates into a vast number of proscriptions and prescriptions. Warm and continued relations with men and an interest in maternity require that females be heterosexually oriented. A heterosexual orientation requires women to dress, move, speak, and act in ways that men will find attractive. As patriarchy has reserved active expressions of power as a masculine attribute, femininity must be expressed through modes of dress, movement, speech, and action which communicate weakness, dependency, ineffectualness, availability for sexual or emotional service, and sensitivity to the needs of others.

Some, but not all, of these modes of interrelation also serve the demands of maternity and many female job ghettos. In many cases, though, femininity is not particularly useful in maternity or employment. Both mothers and workers often need to be strong, independent, and effectual in order to do their jobs well. Thus femininity, as a role, is best suited to satisfying a masculine vision of heterosexual attractiveness.

Body postures and demeanors which communicate subordinate status and vulnerability to trespass through a message of "no threat" make people appear to be feminine. They demonstrate subordination through a minimizing of spatial use: people appear feminine when they keep their arms closer to their bodies, their legs closer together, and their torsos and heads less vertical then do masculine-looking individuals. People also look feminine when they point their toes inward and use their hands in small or childlike gestures. Other people also tend to stand closer to people they see as feminine, often invading their personal space, while people who make frequent appeasement gestures, such as smiling, also give the appearance of femininity. Perhaps as an outgrowth of a subordinate status and the need to avoid conflict with more socially powerful people, women tend to excel over men at the ability to correctly interpret, and effectively display, nonverbal communication cues.[15]

---

[13]Chodorow, p. 134.

[14]Jon K. Meyer and John E. Hoopes, "The Gender Dysphoria Syndromes: A Position Statement on So-Called 'Transsexualism'," *Plastic and Reconstructive Surgery* 54 (Oct. 1974), pp. 444–51.

[15]Erving Goffman, *Gender Advertisements* (New York: Harper Colophon Books, 1976); Judith A. Hall, *Non-Verbal Sex Differences: Communication Accuracy and Expressive Style* (Baltimore: Johns Hopkins University Press, 1984); Nancy M. Henley, *Body Politics: Power, Sex and Non-Verbal Communication* (Englewood Cliffs, New Jersey: Prentice Hall, 1979); Marianne Wex, *"Let's Take Back Our Space": "Female" and "Male" Body Language as a Result of Patriarchal Structures* (Berlin: Frauenliteraturverlag Hermine Fees, 1979).

Speech characterized by inflections, intonations, and phrases that convey nonaggression and subordinate status also make a speaker appear more feminine. Subordinate speakers who use more polite expressions and ask more questions in conversation seem more feminine. Speech characterized by sounds of higher frequencies are often interpreted by listeners as feminine, childlike, and ineffectual.[16] Feminine styles of dress likewise display subordinate status through greater restriction of the free movement of the body, greater exposure of the bare skin, and an emphasis on sexual characteristics. The more gender distinct the dress, the more this is the case.

Masculinity, like femininity, can be demonstrated through a wide variety of cues. Pleck has argued that it is commonly expressed in North American society through the attainment of some level of proficiency at some, or all, of the following four main attitudes of masculinity. Persons who display success and high status in their social group, who exhibit "a manly air of toughness, confidence, and self-reliance" and "the aura of aggression, violence, and daring," and who conscientiously avoid anything associated with femininity are seen as exuding masculinity.[17] These requirements reflect the patriarchal ideology that masculinity results from an excess of testosterone, the assumption being that androgens supply a natural impetus toward aggression, which in turn impels males toward achievement and success. This vision of masculinity also reflects the ideological stance that ideal maleness (masculinity) must remain untainted by female (feminine) pollutants.

Masculinity, then, requires of its actors that they organize themselves and their society in a hierarchical manner so as to be able to explicitly quantify the achievement of success. The achievement of high status in one's social group requires competitive and aggressive behavior from those who wish to obtain it. Competition which is motivated by a goal of individual achievement, or egoistic dominance, also requires of its participants a degree of emotional insensitivity to feelings of hurt and loss in defeated others, and a measure of emotional insularity to protect oneself from becoming vulnerable to manipulation by others. Such values lead those who subscribe to them to view feminine persons as "born losers" and to strive to eliminate any similarities to feminine people from their own personalities. In patriarchally organized societies, masculine values become the ideological structure of the society as a whole. Masculinity thus becomes "innately" valuable and femininity serves a contrapuntal function to delineate and magnify the hierarchical dominance of masculinity.

Body postures, speech patterns, and styles of dress which demonstrate and support the assumption of dominance and authority convey an impression of masculinity. Typical masculine body postures tend to be <u>expansive</u>

20

---

[16]Karen L. Adams, "Sexism and the English Language: The Linguistic Implications of Being a Woman," in *Women: A Feminist Perspective,* 3rd edition, ed. Jo Freeman (Palo Alto, Calif.: Mayfield, 1984), pp. 478–91; Hall, pp. 37, 130–37.

[17]Elizabeth Hafkin Pleck, *Domestic Tyranny: The Making of Social Policy Against Family Violence from Colonial Times to the Present* (Cambridge: Oxford University Press, 1989), p. 139.

and aggressive. People who hold their arms and hands in positions away from their bodies, and who stand, sit, or lie with their legs apart—thus maximizing the amount of space that they physically occupy—appear most physically masculine. Persons who communicate an air of authority or a readiness for aggression by standing erect and moving forcefully also tend to appear more masculine. Movements that are abrupt and stiff, communicating force and threat rather than flexibility and cooperation, make an actor look masculine. Masculinity can also be conveyed by stern or serious facial expressions that suggest minimal receptivity to the influence of others, a characteristic which is an important element in the attainment and maintenance of egoistic dominance.[18]

Speech and dress which likewise demonstrate or claim superior status are also seen as characteristically masculine behavior patterns. Masculine speech patterns display a tendency toward expansiveness similar to that found in masculine body postures. People who attempt to control the direction of conversations seem more masculine.[19] Those who tend to speak more loudly, use less polite and more assertive forms, and tend to interrupt the conversations of others more often also communicate masculinity to others. Styles of dress which emphasize the size of upper body musculature, allow freedom of movement, and encourage an illusion of physical power and a look of easy physicality all suggest masculinity. Such appearances of strength and readiness to action serve to create or enhance an aura of aggressiveness and intimidation central to an appearance of masculinity. Expansive postures and gestures combine with these qualities to insinuate that a position of secure dominance is a masculine one.

Gender role characteristics reflect the ideological contentions underlying the dominant gender schema in North American society. That schema leads us to believe that female and male behaviors are the result of socially directed hormonal instructions which specify that females will want to have children and will therefore find themselves relatively helpless and dependent on males for support and protection. The schema claims that males are innately aggressive and competitive and therefore will dominate over females. The social hegemony[20] of this ideology ensures that we are all raised to practice gender roles which will confirm this vision of the nature of the sexes. Fortunately, our training to gender roles is neither complete nor uniform. As a result, it is possible to point to multitudinous exceptions to, and variations on, these themes. Biological evidence is equivocal about the source of gender roles; psychological androgyny[21] is a widely accepted concept. It seems most likely that gender roles are the result of systematic power imbalances based on gender discrimination.[22]

---

[18]Goffman, *Gender Advertisements;* Hall; Henley; Wex.

[19]Adams; Hall, pp. 37, 130–37.

[20]*hegemony:* System of preponderant influence, authority, or dominance.

[21]*androgyny:* The state of having both male and female characteristics.

[22]Howard, Blumstein, and Schwartz; Kollock, Blumstein, and Schwartz.

"We don't believe in pressuring the children. When the time is right, they'll choose the appropriate gender."

[handwritten annotations:]

myth

Gender is binary + permanent.
        2 parts   unchanging, lasting, forever
        2 divisions

ENGAGING THE TEXT

1. Devor charges that most languages present gender as "binary and perma-nent" (para. 3). Has this been your own view? How does Devor challenge this idea—that is, what's the alternative to gender being binary and perma-nent—and how persuasive do you find her evidence?

2. How, according to Devor, do children "acquire" gender roles? What are the functions of the "generalized other" and the "significant other" in this process?

3. Explain the distinction Devor makes between the "I" and the "me" (paras. 7 and 8). Write a journal entry describing some of the differences between your own "I" and "me."

4. Using examples from Devor and from other reading or observation, list some "activities and modes of expression" (para. 12) that society considers characteristically female and characteristically male. Which are acceptable crossgender behaviors, and which are not? Search for a "rule" that defines what types of crossgender behaviors are tolerated.

5. Do some aspects of the traditional gender roles described by Devor seem to be changing? If so, which ones, and how?

EXPLORING CONNECTIONS

6. Review Bebe Moore Campbell's "Envy" (p. 98); what evidence of gender role socialization do you find in the story? To what extent do Moore's childhood experiences complicate Devor's presentation of gender role acquisition?

7. To what extent do Tocqueville's views of women and men (p. 407) reflect the "patriarchal gender schema" as Devor defines it?

8. Drawing on Devor's discussion of gender role formation, analyze the difference between the "I" and the "me" of the girl in Jamaica Kincaid's story (p. 411).

9. How would Devor explain the humor of the cartoon on page 422? How do the details of the cartoon—the setting, the women's appearance, the three pictures on the coffee table—contribute to its effect?

EXTENDING THE CRITICAL CONTEXT

10. As a class, identify at least half a dozen men living today who are widely admired in American culture. To what extent do they embody the "four main attitudes of masculinity" outlined by Devor (para. 19)?

11. Write an essay or journal entry analyzing your own gender role socialization. To what extent have you been pressured to conform to conventional roles? To what extent have you resisted them? What roles have "generalized others" and "significant others" played in shaping your identity?

The Story of My Body

JUDITH ORTIZ COFER

Accepting the idea that gender roles are socially constructed might not be too difficult, but it may come as a shock to realize that even the way we see our bodies is filtered through the lens of social values and beliefs. In this personal essay, Judith Ortiz Cofer reflects on the different roles her own body has assumed in different contexts and cultures—the ways that different societies have "read" the meanings of her physical appearance. The story of her body becomes, to some extent, the story of her life, and woven into the tale are intriguing comments on gender and on cross-cultural perception. A native of Puerto Rico, Ortiz Cofer (b. 1952) is a professor of English and creative writing at the University of Georgia. Her publications include The Line of the Sun *(1989), a novel;* Silent Dancing *(1990), a collection of poetry and prose; and* The Latin Deli *(1993), in which "The Story of My*

Body" first appeared. Her most recent work is Woman in Front of the Sun: On Becoming a Writer *(2000)*.

> Migration is the story of my body.
> —VICTOR HERNÁNDEZ CRUZ

Skin

I was born a white girl in Puerto Rico but became a brown girl when I came to live in the United States. My Puerto Rican relatives called me tall; at the American school, some of my rougher classmates called me Skinny Bones, and the Shrimp because I was the smallest member of my classes all through grammar school until high school, when the midget Gladys was given the honorary post of front row center for class pictures and score-keeper, bench warmer, in P.E. I reached my full stature of five feet in sixth grade.

I started out life as a pretty baby and learned to be a pretty girl from a pretty mother. Then at ten years of age I suffered one of the worst cases of chicken pox I have ever heard of. My entire body, including the inside of my ears and in between my toes, was covered with pustules which in a fit of panic at my appearance I scratched off my face, leaving permanent scars. A cruel school nurse told me I would always have them—tiny cuts that looked as if a mad cat had plunged its claws deep into my skin. I grew my hair long and hid behind it for the first years of my adolescence. This was when I learned to be invisible.

Color

In the animal world it indicates danger: the most colorful creatures are often the most poisonous. Color is also a way to attract and seduce a mate. In the human world color triggers many more complex and often deadly re-actions. As a Puerto Rican girl born of "white" parents, I spent the first years of my life hearing people refer to me as *blanca*, white. My mother in-sisted that I protect myself from the intense island sun because I was more prone to sunburn than some of my darker, *trigueño*[1] playmates. People were always commenting within my hearing about how my black hair con-trasted so nicely with my "pale" skin. I did not think of the color of my skin consciously except when I heard the adults talking about complexion. It seems to me that the subject is much more common in the conversation of mixed-race peoples than in mainstream United States society, where it is a touchy and sometimes even embarrassing topic to discuss, except in a politi-cal context. In Puerto Rico I heard many conversations about skin color. A

---

[1]*trigueño:* Brown-skinned.

pregnant woman could say, "I hope my baby doesn't turn out *prieto*" (slang for "dark" or "black") "like my husband's grandmother, although she was a good-looking *negra*[2] in her time." I am a combination of both, being olive-skinned—lighter than my mother yet darker than my fair-skinned father. In America, I am a person of color, obviously a Latina. On the Island I have been called everything from a *paloma blanca*,[3] after the song (by a black suitor), to *la gringa*.[4]

My first experience of color prejudice occurred in a supermarket in Paterson, New Jersey. It was Christmastime, and I was eight or nine years old. There was a display of toys in the store where I went two or three times a day to buy things for my mother, who never made lists but sent for milk, cigarettes, a can of this or that, as she remembered from hour to hour. I enjoyed being trusted with money and walking half a city block to the new, modern grocery store. It was owned by three good-looking Italian brothers. I liked the younger one with the crew-cut blond hair. The two older ones watched me and the other Puerto Rican kids as if they thought we were going to steal something. The oldest one would sometimes even try to hurry me with my purchases, although part of my pleasure in these expeditions came from looking at everything in the well-stocked aisles. I was also teaching myself to read English by sounding out the labels on packages: L&M cigarettes, Borden's homogenized milk, Red Devil potted ham, Nestle's chocolate mix, Quaker oats, Bustelo coffee, Wonder bread, Colgate toothpaste, Ivory soap, and Goya (makers of products used in Puerto Rican dishes) everything—these are some of the brand names that taught me nouns. Several times this man had come up to me, wearing his blood-stained butcher's apron, and towering over me had asked in a harsh voice whether there was something he could help me find. On the way out I would glance at the younger brother who ran one of the registers and he would often smile and wink at me.

It was the mean brother who first referred to me as "colored." It was a few days before Christmas, and my parents had already told my brother and me that since we were in Los Estados[5] now, we would get our presents on December 25 instead of Los Reyes, Three Kings Day, when gifts are exchanged in Puerto Rico. We were to give them a wish list that they would take to Santa Claus, who apparently lived in the Macy's store downtown— at least that's where we had caught a glimpse of him when we went shopping. Since my parents were timid about entering the fancy store, we did not approach the huge man in the red suit. I was not interested in sitting on a stranger's lap anyway. But I did covet Susie, the talking schoolteacher doll that was displayed in the center aisle of the Italian brothers' supermarket.

5

[2]*negra:* Black.
[3]*paloma blanca:* White dove.
[4]*la gringa:* A white, non-Latina woman.
[5]*Los Estados:* "The States"—that is, the United States.

She talked when you pulled a string on her back. Susie had a limited reper-
toire of three sentences: I think she could say: "Hello, I'm Susie Schoolteacher," "Two plus two is four," and one other thing I cannot remember.
The day the older brother chased me away, I was reaching to touch Susie's
blond curls. I had been told many times, as most children have, not to touch
anything in the store that I was not buying. But I had been looking at Susie
for weeks. In my mind, she was my doll. After all, I had put her on my
Christmas wish list. The moment is frozen in my mind as if there were a
photograph of it on file. It was not a turning point, a disaster, or an earth-
shaking revelation. It was simply the first time I considered—if naively—
the meaning of skin color in human relations.

I reached to touch Susie's hair. It seems to me that I had to get on tiptoe, since the toys were stacked on a table and she sat like a princess on top
of the fancy box she came in. Then I heard the booming "Hey, kid, what do
you think you're doing!" spoken very loudly from the meat counter. I felt
caught, although I knew I was not doing anything criminal. I remember not
looking at the man, but standing there, feeling humiliated because I knew
everyone in the store must have heard him yell at me. I felt him approach,
and when I knew he was behind me, I turned around to face the bloody
butcher's apron. His large chest was at my eye level. He blocked my way. I
started to run out of the place, but even as I reached the door I heard him
shout after me: "Don't come in here unless you gonna buy something. You
PR kids put your dirty hands on stuff. You always look dirty. But maybe
dirty brown is your natural color." I heard him laugh and someone else too
in the back. Outside in the sunlight I looked at my hands. My nails needed a
little cleaning as they always did, since I liked to paint with watercolors, but
I took a bath every night. I thought the man was dirtier than I was in his
stained apron. He was also always sweaty—it showed in big yellow circles
under his shirt-sleeves. I sat on the front steps of the apartment building
where we lived and looked closely at my hands, which showed the only skin
I could see, since it was bitter cold and I was wearing my quilted play coat,
dungarees, and a knitted navy cap of my father's. I was not pink like my
friend Charlene and her sister Kathy, who had blue eyes and light brown
hair. My skin is the color of the coffee my grandmother made, which was
half milk, *leche con café* rather than *café con leche*.[6] My mother is the opposite mix. She has a lot of café in her color. I could not understand how my
skin looked like dirt to the supermarket man.

I went in and washed my hands thoroughly with soap and hot water,
and borrowing my mother's nail file, I cleaned the crusted watercolors from
underneath my nails. I was pleased with the results. My skin was the same
color as before, but I knew I was clean. Clean enough to run my fingers
through Susie's fine gold hair when she came home to me.

---

[6]*leche con café...café con leche:* Milk with coffee (light brown) ... coffee with milk (dark
brown).

Size

My mother is barely four feet eleven inches in height, which is average for women in her family. When I grew to five feet by age twelve, she was amazed and began to use the word tall to describe me, as in "Since you are tall, this dress will look good on you." As with the color of my skin, I didn't consciously think about my height or size until other people made an issue of it. It is around the preadolescent years that in America the games children play for fun become fierce competitions where everyone is out to "prove" they are better than others. It was in the playground and sports fields that my size-related problems began. No matter how familiar the story is, every child who is the last chosen for a team knows the torment of waiting to be called up. At the Paterson, New Jersey, public schools that I attended, the volleyball or softball game was the metaphor for the battle-field of life to the inner city kids—the black kids versus the Puerto Rican kids, the whites versus the blacks versus the Puerto Rican kids; and I was 4F,[7] skinny, short, bespectacled, and apparently impervious to the blood thirst that drove many of my classmates to play ball as if their lives depended on it. Perhaps they did. I would rather be reading a book than sweating, grunting, and running the risk of pain and injury. I simply did not see the point in competitive sports. My main form of exercise then was walking to the library, many city blocks away from my barrio.

Still, I wanted to be wanted. I wanted to be chosen for the team. Physical education was compulsory, a class where you were actually given a grade. On my mainly all A report card, the C for compassion I always received from the P.E. teachers shamed me the same as a bad grade in a real class. Invariably, my father would say: "How can you make a low grade for *playing games?*" He did not understand. Even if I had managed to make a hit (it never happened) or get the ball over that ridiculously high net, I already had a reputation as a "shrimp," a hopeless nonathlete. It was an area where the girls who didn't like me for one reason or another—mainly because I did better than they on academic subjects—could lord it over me; the playing field was the place where even the smallest girl could make me feel powerless and inferior. I instinctively understood the politics even then; how the *not* choosing me until the teacher forced one of the team captains to call my name was a coup of sorts—there, you little show-off, tomorrow you can beat us in spelling and geography, but this afternoon you are the loser. Or perhaps those were only my own bitter thoughts as I sat or stood in the sidelines while the big girls were grabbed like fish and I, the little brown tadpole, was ignored until Teacher looked over in my general direction and shouted, "Call Ortiz," or, worse, "Somebody's *got* to take her."

[7]*4F:* Draft-board classification meaning "unfit for military service;" hence, not physically fit.

No wonder I read Wonder Woman comics and had Legion of Super He-   10
roes daydreams. Although I wanted to think of myself as "intellectual," my
body was demanding that I notice it. I saw the little swelling around my
once-flat nipples, the fine hairs growing in secret places; but my knees were
still bigger than my thighs, and I always wore long- or half-sleeve blouses to
hide my bony upper arms. I wanted flesh on my bones—a thick layer of it. I
saw a new product advertised on TV, Wate-On. They showed skinny men and
women before and after taking the stuff, and it was a transformation like the
ninety-seven-pound-weakling-turned-into-Charles-Atlas ads that I saw on the
back covers of my comic books. The Wate-On was very expensive. I tried to explain my need for it in Spanish to my mother, but it didn't translate very well,
even to my ears—and she said with a tone of finality, eat more of my good food
and you'll get fat—anybody can get fat. Right. Except me. I was going to have
to join a circus someday as Skinny Bones, the woman without flesh.

Wonder Woman was stacked. She had a cleavage framed by the spread
wings of a golden eagle and a muscular body that has become fashionable
with women only recently. But since I wanted a body that would serve me
in P.E., hers was my ideal. The breasts were an indulgence I allowed
myself. Perhaps the daydreams of bigger girls were more glamorous, since
our ambitions are filtered through our needs, but I wanted first a powerful
body. I daydreamed of leaping up above the gray landscape of the city to
where the sky was clear and blue, and in anger and self-pity, I fantasized
about scooping my enemies up by their hair from the playing fields and
dumping them on a barren asteroid. I would put the P.E. teachers each on
their own rock in space too, where they would be the loneliest people in the
universe, since I knew they had no "inner resources," no imagination, and in
outer space, there would be no air for them to fill their deflated volleyballs
with. In my mind all P.E. teachers have blended into one large spiky-haired
woman with a whistle on a string around her neck and a volleyball under
one arm. My Wonder Woman fantasies of revenge were a source of comfort
to me in my early career as a shrimp.

I was saved from more years of P.E. torment by the fact that in my
sophomore year of high school I transferred to a school where the midget,
Gladys, was the focal point of interest for the people who must rank according to size. Because her height was considered a handicap, there was an unspoken rule about mentioning size around Gladys, but of course, there was
no need to say anything. Gladys knew her place: front row center in class
photographs. I gladly moved to the left or to the right of her, as far as I
could without leaving the picture completely.

Looks

Many photographs were taken of me as a baby by my mother to send to
my father, who was stationed overseas during the first two years of my life.
With the army in Panama when I was born, he later traveled often on tours

of duty with the navy. I was a healthy, pretty baby. Recently, I read that people are drawn to big-eyed round-faced creatures, like puppies, kittens, and certain other mammals and marsupials, koalas, for example, and, of course, infants. I was all eyes, since my head and body, even as I grew older, remained thin and small-boned. As a young child I got a lot of attention from my relatives and many other people we met in our barrio. My mother's beauty may have had something to do with how much attention we got from strangers in stores and on the street. I can imagine it. In the pictures I have seen of us together, she is a stunning young woman by Latino standards: long, curly black hair, and round curves in a compact frame. From her I learned how to move, smile, and talk like an attractive woman. I remember going into a bodega[8] for our groceries and being given candy by the proprietor as a reward for being *bonita*, pretty.

I can see in the photographs, and I also remember, that I was dressed in the pretty clothes, the stiff, frilly dresses, with layers of crinolines underneath, the glossy patent leather shoes, and, on special occasions, the skull-hugging little hats and the white gloves that were popular in the late fifties and early sixties. My mother was proud of my looks, although I was a bit too thin. She could dress me up like a doll and take me by the hand to visit relatives, or go to the Spanish mass at the Catholic church and show me off. How was I to know that she and the others who called me "pretty" were representatives of an aesthetic that would not apply when I went out into the mainstream world of school?

In my Paterson, New Jersey, public schools there were still quite a few   15
white children, although the demographics of the city were changing rapidly. The original waves of Italian and Irish immigrants, silk-mill workers, and laborers in the cloth industries had been "assimilated." Their children were now the middle-class parents of my peers. Many of them moved their children to the Catholic schools that proliferated enough to have leagues of basketball teams. The names I recall hearing still ring in my ears: Don Bosco High versus St. Mary's High, St. Joseph's versus St. John's. Later I too would be transferred to the safer environment of a Catholic school. But I started school at Public School Number 11. I came there from Puerto Rico, thinking myself a pretty girl, and found that the hierarchy for popularity was as follows: pretty white girl, pretty Jewish girl, pretty Puerto Rican girl, pretty black girl. Drop the last two categories; teachers were too busy to have more than one favorite per class, and it was simply understood that if there was a big part in the school play, or any competition where the main qualification was "presentability" (such as escorting a school visitor to or from the principal's office), the classroom's public address speaker would be requesting the pretty and/or nice-looking white boy or girl. By the time I was in the sixth grade, I was sometimes called by the principal to represent my class because I dressed neatly (I knew this from a progress report sent to

[8]*bodega:* Market.

my mother, which I translated for her) and because all the "presentable" white girls had moved to the Catholic schools (I later surmised this part). But I was still not one of the popular girls with the boys. I remember one incident where I stepped out into the playground in my baggy gym shorts and one Puerto Rican boy said to the other: "What do you think?" The other one answered: "Her face is OK, but look at the toothpick legs." The next best thing to a compliment I got was when my favorite male teacher, while handing out the class pictures, commented that with my long neck and delicate features I resembled the movie star Audrey Hepburn. But the Puerto Rican boys had learned to respond to a fuller figure: long necks and a perfect little nose were not what they looked for in a girl. That is when I decided I was a "brain." I did not settle into the role easily. I was nearly devastated by what the chicken pox episode had done to my self-image. But I looked into the mirror less often after I was told that I would always have scars on my face, and I hid behind my long black hair and my books.

After the problems at the public school got to the point where even nonconfrontational little me got beaten up several times, my parents enrolled me at St. Joseph's High School. I was then a minority of one among the Italian and Irish kids. But I found several good friends there—other girls who took their studies seriously. We did our homework together and talked about the Jackies. The Jackies were two popular girls, one blonde and the other red-haired, who had women's bodies. Their curves showed even in the blue jumper uniforms with straps that we all wore. The blonde Jackie would often let one of the straps fall off her shoulder, and although she, like all of us, wore a white blouse underneath, all the boys stared at her arm. My friends and I talked about this and practiced letting our straps fall off our shoulders. But it wasn't the same without breasts or hips.

My final two and a half years of high school were spent in Augusta, Georgia, where my parents moved our family in search of a more peaceful environment. Then we became part of a little community of our army-connected relatives and friends. School was yet another matter. I was enrolled in a huge school of nearly two thousand students that had just that year been forced to integrate. There were two black girls and there was me. I did extremely well academically. As to my social life, it was, for the most part, uneventful—yet it is in my memory blighted by one incident. In my junior year, I became wildly infatuated with a pretty white boy. I'll call him Ted. Oh, he was pretty: yellow hair that fell over his forehead, a smile to die for—and he was a great dancer. I watched him at Teen Town, the youth center at the base where all the military brats gathered on Saturday nights. My father had retired from the navy, and we had all our base privileges—one other reason we moved to Augusta. Ted looked like an angel to me. I worked on him for a year before he asked me out. This meant maneuvering to be within the periphery of his vision at every possible occasion. I took the long way to my classes in school just to pass by his locker, I went to football games, which I detested, and I danced (I too was a good dancer) in front of him at Teen Town—this took some fancy footwork, since it involved subtly moving my partner toward the right spot on the dance floor. When Ted finally approached me, "A Million to One" was playing on the jukebox, and when he took me into his arms, the odds suddenly turned in my favor. He asked me to go to a school dance the following Saturday. I said yes, breathlessly. I said yes, but there were obstacles to surmount at home. My father did not allow me to date casually. I was allowed to go to major events like a prom or a concert with a boy who had been properly screened. There was such a boy in my life, a neighbor who wanted to be a Baptist missionary and was practicing his anthropological skills on my family. If I was desperate to go somewhere and needed a date, I'd resort to Gary. This is the type of religious nut that Gary was: when the school bus did not show up one day, he put his hands over his face and prayed to Christ to get us a way to get to school. Within ten minutes a mother in a station wagon, on her way to town, stopped to ask why we weren't in school. Gary informed her that the Lord had sent her just in time to find us a way to get there in time for roll call. He assumed that I was impressed. Gary was even good-looking in a bland sort of way, but he kissed me with his lips tightly pressed together. I think Gary probably ended up marrying a native woman from wherever he may have gone to preach the Gospel according to Paul. She probably believes that all white men pray to God for transportation and kiss with their mouths closed. But it was Ted's mouth, his whole beautiful self, that concerned me in those days. I knew my father would say no to our date, but I planned to run away from home if necessary. I told my mother how important this date was. I cajoled and pleaded with her from Sunday to Wednesday. She listened to my arguments and must have heard the note of desperation in my voice. She said very gently to me: "You better be ready for disappointment." I did not ask what she meant. I did not want her fears for me to taint my happiness. I asked her to tell my father about my date. Thursday at breakfast my father looked at me across the table with his eyebrows together. My mother looked at him with her mouth set in a straight line. I looked down at my bowl of cereal. Nobody said anything. Friday I tried on every dress in my closet. Ted would be picking me up at six on Saturday: dinner and then the sock hop at school. Friday night I was in my room doing my nails or something else in preparation for Saturday (I know I groomed myself nonstop all week) when the telephone rang. I ran to get it. It was Ted. His voice sounded funny when he said my name, so funny that I felt compelled to ask: "Is something wrong?" Ted blurted it all out without a preamble. His father had asked who he was going out with. Ted had told him my name. "Ortiz? That's Spanish, isn't it?" the father had asked. Ted had told him yes, then shown him my picture in the yearbook. Ted's father had shaken his head. No. Ted would not be taking me out. Ted's father had known Puerto Ricans in the army. He had lived in New York City while studying architecture and had seen how the spics lived. Like rats. Ted repeated his father's words to me as if I should understand *his* predicament when I heard why he was breaking our date. I don't remember what I said before hanging up. I do re-call the darkness of my room that sleepless night and the heaviness of my blanket in which I wrapped myself like a shroud. And I remember my par-ents' respect for my pain and their gentleness toward me that weekend. My mother did not say "I warned you," and I was grateful for her understanding silence.

In college, I suddenly became an "exotic" woman to the men who had survived the popularity wars in high school, who were not practicing to be worldly: they had to act liberal in their politics, in their lifestyles, and in the women they went out with. I dated heavily for a while, then married young. I had discovered that I needed stability more than social life. I had brains for sure and some talent in writing. These facts were a constant in my life. My skin color, my size, and my appearance were variables—things that were judged according to my current self-image, the aesthetic values of the time, the places I was in, and the people I met. My studies, later my writing, the respect of people who saw me as an individual person they cared about, these were the criteria for my sense of self-worth that I would concentrate on in my adult life.

ENGAGING THE TEXT

1. Ortiz Cofer writes a good deal about how people perceived her and about how their perceptions changed according to time and place. Trace the stages Ortiz Cofer lived through, citing examples from the text, and discuss in each instance how her self-image was affected by people around her. What main point(s) do you think Ortiz Cofer may be trying to make with the narrative?

2. Which of the difficulties Ortiz Cofer faces are related specifically to gender (or made more serious by gender)? Do boys face comparable problems?

3. In your opinion, did Ortiz Cofer make the right decisions throughout her story? Is there anything she or her parents could have done to avoid or re-sist the various mistreatments she describes?

4. What role do media images play in Ortiz Cofer's story?

5. Does everyone have a story similar to Ortiz Cofer's, or not? Other people may be overweight, wear braces, mature very early or very late, have big noses or unusual voices, and so on. What, if anything, sets Ortiz Cofer's ex-perience apart from the usual "traumas" of childhood?

EXPLORING CONNECTIONS

6. Review Holly Devor's "Becoming Members of Society" (p. 414). How do Ortiz Cofer's experiences support and/or complicate Devor's explanation of gender role socialization?

7. Compare the childhood experiences of Ortiz Cofer and Gary Soto (p. 39). To what extent do their relationships, concerns, and behavior appear to be influenced by gender? What other social forces shape their lives?

8. Like Ortiz Cofer, Eric Liu (p. 611) and Veronica Chambers (p. 653) must find ways to define their identities within multiple cultures. What problems do they face, what strengths or advantages do they find within each culture, and what strategies do they adopt to negotiate the tensions that arise among conflicting cultural values?

EXTENDING THE CRITICAL CONTEXT

9. In her self-analysis, Ortiz Cofer discusses the "variables" in her physical appearance—the socially determined values that influence her perception of her body. She also reflects on personal "facts" or "constants"—more durable features, like her writing and her need for stability—that contribute to her identity. Write a series of journal entries that tell the story of your own body. What "variables" have influenced your perception of your appearance? What "facts" about yourself have become "constants"?

Where I Come From Is Like This

Paula Gunn Allen

Paula Gunn Allen was born in 1939 in Cubero, New Mexico, a Spanish-Mexican land grant village; where she comes from is life as a Laguna Pueblo–Sioux–Lebanese woman. In this essay she discusses some of the ways traditional images of women in American Indian cultures differ from images in mainstream American culture. Allen is a former professor of English and American Indian literature at the University of California, Los Angeles. In addition to her scholarship, Allen is widely recognized for her books of poetry and for her novel The Woman Who Owned the Shadows *(1983). Other works, including* Grandmothers of the Light *(1991) and* Women in American Indian Mythology *(1994), have focused on the female spiritual traditions of Native America. Her most recent book of essays,* Off the Reservation, *was published in 1998; this essay appeared in an earlier collection,* The Sacred Hoop: Recovering the Feminine in American Indian Traditions *(1986).*

I

Modern American Indian women, like their non-Indian sisters, are deeply engaged in the struggle to redefine themselves. In their struggle they must reconcile traditional tribal definitions of women with industrial and postindustrial non-Indian definitions. Yet while these definitions seem to be more or less mutually exclusive, Indian women must somehow harmonize and integrate both in their own lives.

An American Indian woman is primarily defined by her tribal identity. In her eyes, her destiny is necessarily that of her people, and her sense of herself as a woman is first and foremost prescribed by her tribe. The definitions of woman's roles are as diverse as tribal cultures in the Americas. In some she is devalued, in others she wields considerable power. In some she is a familial/clan adjunct, in some she is as close to autonomous as her economic circumstances and psychological traits permit. But in no tribal definitions is she perceived in the same way as are women in western industrial and postindustrial cultures.

In the west, few images of women form part of the cultural mythos, and these are largely sexually charged. Among Christians, the madonna is the female prototype, and she is portrayed as essentially passive: her contribution is simply that of birthing. Little else is attributed to her and she certainly possesses few of the characteristics that are attributed to mythic figures among Indian tribes. This image is countered (rather than balanced) by the witch-goddess/whore characteristics designed to reinforce cultural beliefs about women, as well as western adversarial and dualistic perceptions of reality.

The tribes see women variously, but they do not question the power of femininity. Sometimes they see women as fearful, sometimes peaceful, sometimes omnipotent and omniscient, but they never portray women as mindless, helpless, simple, or oppressed. And while the women in a given tribe, clan, or band may be all these things, the individual woman is provided with a variety of images of women from the interconnected supernatural, natural, and social worlds she lives in.

As a half-breed American Indian woman, I cast about in my mind for   5
negative images of Indian women, and I find none that are directed to Indian women alone. The negative images I do have are of Indians in general and in fact are more often of males than of females. All these images come to me from non-Indian sources, and they are always balanced by a positive image. My ideas of womanhood, passed on largely by my mother and grandmothers, Laguna Pueblo women, are about practicality, strength, reasonableness, intelligence, wit, and competence. I also remember vividly the women who came to my father's store, the women who held me and sang to me, the women at Feast Day, at Grab Days,[1] the women in the kitchen of my Cubero home, the women I grew up with; none of them appeared weak or helpless, none of them presented herself tentatively. I remember a certain reserve on those lovely brown faces; I remember the direct gaze of eyes framed by bright-colored shawls draped over their heads and cascading

---

[1]*Grab Days:* Laguna ritual in which women throw food and small items (like pieces of cloth) to those attending.

down their backs. I remember the clean cotton dresses and carefully pressed hand-embroidered aprons they always wore; I remember laughter and good food, especially the sweet bread and the oven bread they gave us. Nowhere in my mind is there a foolish woman, a dumb woman, a vain woman, or a plastic woman, though the Indian women I have known have shown a wide range of personal style and demeanor.

My memory includes the Navajo woman who was badly beaten by her Sioux husband; but I also remember that my grandmother abandoned her Sioux husband long ago. I recall the stories about the Laguna woman beaten regularly by her husband in the presence of her children so that the children would not believe in the strength and power of femininity. And I remember the women who drank, who got into fights with other women and with the men, and who often won those battles. I have memories of tired women, partying women, stubborn women, sullen women, amicable women, selfish women, shy women, and aggressive women. Most of all I remember the women who laugh and scold and sit uncomplaining in the long sun on feast days and who cook wonderful food on wood stoves, in beehive mud ovens, and over open fires outdoors.

Among the images of women that come to me from various tribes as well as my own are White Buffalo Woman, who came to the Lakota long ago and brought them the religion of the Sacred Pipe which they still practice; Tinotzin the goddess who came to Juan Diego to remind him that she still walked the hills of her people and sent him with her message, her demand, and her proof to the Catholic bishop in the city nearby. And from Laguna I take the images of Yellow Woman, Coyote Woman, Grandmother Spider (Spider Old Woman), who brought the light, who gave us weaving and medicine, who gave us life. Among the Keres she is known as Thought Woman who created us all and who keeps us in creation even now. I remember Iyatiku, Earth Woman, Corn Woman, who guides and counsels the people to peace and who welcomes us home when we cast off this coil of flesh as huskers cast off the leaves that wrap the corn. I remember Iyatiku's sister, Sun Woman, who held metals and cattle, pigs and sheep, highways and engines and so many things in her bundle, who went away to the east saying that one day she would return.

II

Since the coming of the Anglo-Europeans beginning in the fifteenth century, the fragile web of identity that long held tribal people secure has gradually been weakened and torn. But the oral tradition has prevented the complete destruction of the web, the ultimate disruption of tribal ways. The oral tradition is vital; it heals itself and the tribal web by adapting to the flow of the present while never relinquishing its connection to the past. Its adaptability has always been required, as many generations have experienced. Certainly the modern American Indian woman bears slight resemblance to her forebears—at least on superficial examination—but she is still a tribal woman in her deepest being. Her tribal sense of relationship to all that is continues to flourish. And though she is at times beset by her knowledge of the enormous gap between the life she lives and the life she was raised to live, and while she adapts her mind and being to the circumstances of her present life, she does so in tribal ways, mending the tears in the web of being from which she takes her existence as she goes.

My mother told me stories all the time, though I often did not recognize them as that. My mother told me stories about cooking and childbearing; she told me stories about menstruation and pregnancy; she told me stories about gods and heroes, about fairies and elves, about goddesses and spirits; she told me stories about the land and the sky, about cats and dogs, about snakes and spiders; she told me stories about climbing trees and exploring the mesas; she told me stories about going to dances and getting married; she told me stories about dressing and undressing, about sleeping and waking; she told me stories about herself, about her mother, about her grandmother. She told me stories about grieving and laughing, about thinking and doing; she told me stories about school and about people; about darning and mending; she told me stories about turquoise and about gold; she told me European stories and Laguna stories; she told me Catholic stories and Presbyterian stories; she told me city stories and country stories; she told me political stories and religious stories. She told me stories about living and stories about dying. And in all of those stories she told me who I was, who I was supposed to be, whom I came from, and who would follow me. In this way she taught me the meaning of the words she said, that all life is a circle and everything has a place within it. That's what she said and what she showed me in the things she did and the way she lives.

Of course, through my formal, white, Christian education, I discovered that other people had stories of their own—about women, about Indians, about fact, about reality—and I was amazed by a number of startling suppositions that others made about tribal customs and beliefs. According to the un-Indian, non-Indian view, for instance, Indians barred menstruating women from ceremonies and indeed segregated them from the rest of the people, consigning them to some space specially designed for them. This showed that Indians considered menstruating women unclean and not fit to enjoy the company of decent (nonmenstruating) people, that is, men. I was surprised and confused to hear this because my mother had taught me that white people had strange attitudes toward menstruation: they thought something was bad about it, that it meant you were sick, cursed, sinful, and weak and that you had to be very careful during that time. She taught me that menstruation was a normal occurrence, that I could go swimming or hiking or whatever else I wanted to do during my period. She actively scorned women who took to their beds, who were incapacitated by cramps, who "got the blues."

10

As I struggled to reconcile these very contradictory interpretations of American Indians' traditional beliefs concerning menstruation, I realized that the menstrual taboos were about power, not about sin or filth. My conclusion was later borne out by some tribes' own explanations, which, as you may well imagine, came as quite a relief to me.

The truth of the matter as many Indians see it is that women who are at the peak of their fecundity are believed to possess power that throws male power totally out of kilter. They emit such force that, in their presence, any male-owned or -dominated ritual or sacred object cannot do its usual task. For instance, the Lakota say that a menstruating woman anywhere near a yuwipi man, who is a special sort of psychic, spirit-empowered healer, for a day or so before he is to do his ceremony will effectively disempower him. Conversely, among many if not most tribes, important ceremonies cannot be held without the presence of women. Sometimes the ritual woman who empowers the ceremony must be unmarried and virginal so that the power she channels is unalloyed, unweakened by sexual arousal and penetration by a male. Other ceremonies require tumescent women, others the presence of mature women who have borne children, and still others depend for empowerment on postmenopausal women. Women may be segregated from the company of the whole band or village on certain occasions, but on certain occasions men are also segregated. In short, each ritual depends on a certain balance of power, and the positions of women within the phases of womanhood are used by tribal people to empower certain rites. This does not derive from a male-dominant view; it is not a ritual observance imposed on women by men. It derives from a tribal view of reality that distinguishes tribal people from feudal and industrial people.

Among the tribes, the occult power of women, inextricably bound to our hormonal life, is thought to be very great; many hold that we possess innately the blood-given power to kill—with a glance, with a step, or with a judicious mixing of menstrual blood into somebody's soup. Medicine women among the Pomo of California cannot practice until they are sufficiently mature; when they are immature, their power is diffuse and is likely to interfere with their practice until time and experience have it under control. So women of the tribes are not especially inclined to see themselves as poor helpless victims of male domination. Even in those tribes where something akin to male domination was present, women are perceived as powerful, socially, physically, and metaphysically. In times past, as in times present, women carried enormous burdens with aplomb. We were far indeed from the "weaker sex," the designation that white aristocratic sisters unhappily earned for us all.

I remember my mother moving furniture all over the house when she wanted it changed. She didn't wait for my father to come home and help— she just went ahead and moved the piano, a huge upright from the old days, the couch, the refrigerator. Nobody had told her she was too weak to do such things. In imitation of her, I would delight in loading trucks at my father's store with cases of pop or fifty-pound sacks of flour. Even when I was quite small I could do it, and it gave me a belief in my own physical strength that advancing middle age can't quite erase. My mother used to tell me about the Acoma Pueblo women she had seen as a child carrying huge ollas (water pots) on their heads as they wound their way up the tortuous stairwell carved into the face of the "Sky City" mesa, a feat I tried to imitate with books and tin buckets. ("Sky City" is the term used by the Chamber of Commerce for the mother village of Acoma, which is situated atop a high sandstone table mountain.) I was never very successful, but even the attempt reminded me that I was supposed to be strong and balanced to be a proper girl.

Of course, my mother's Laguna people are Keres Indian, reputed to be   15
the last extreme mother-right people on earth. So it is no wonder that I got notably nonwhite notions about the natural strength and prowess of women. Indeed, it is only when I am trying to get non-Indian approval, recognition, or acknowledgement that my "weak sister" emotional and intellectual ploys get the better of my tribal woman's good sense. At such times I forget that I just moved the piano or just wrote a competent paper or just completed a financial transaction satisfactorily or have supported myself and my children for most of my adult life.

Nor is my contradictory behavior atypical. Most Indian women I know are in the same bicultural bind: we vacillate between being dependent and strong, self-reliant and powerless, strongly motivated and hopelessly insecure. We resolve the dilemma in various ways: some of us party all the time; some of us drink to excess; some of us travel and move around a lot; some of us land good jobs and then quit them; some of us engage in violent exchanges; some of us blow our brains out. We act in these destructive ways because we suffer from the societal conflicts caused by having to identify with two hopelessly opposed cultural definitions of women. Through this destructive dissonance we are unhappy prey to the self-disparagement common to, indeed demanded of, Indians living in the United States today. Our situation is caused by the exigencies of a history of invasion, conquest, and colonization whose searing marks are probably ineradicable. A popular bumper sticker on many Indian cars proclaims: "If You're Indian You're In," to which I always find myself adding under my breath, "Trouble."

III

No Indian can grow to any age without being informed that her people were "savages" who interfered with the march of progress pursued by respectable, loving, civilized white people. We are the villains of the scenario when we are mentioned at all. We are absent from much of white history except when we are calmly, rationally, succinctly, and systematically dehumanized. On the few occasions we are noticed in any way other than as howling, bloodthirsty beings, we are acclaimed for our noble quaintness. In this definition, we are exotic curios. Our ancient arts and customs are used to draw tourist money to state coffers, into the pocketbooks and bank accounts of scholars, and into support of the American-in-Disneyland promoters' dream.

As a Roman Catholic child I was treated to bloody tales of how the savage Indians martyred the hapless priests and missionaries who went among them in an attempt to lead them to the one true path. By the time I was through high school I had the idea that Indians were people who had benefitted mightily from the advanced knowledge and superior morality of the Anglo-Europeans. At least I had, perforce, that idea to lay beside the other one that derived from my daily experience of Indian life, an idea less dehumanizing and more accurate because it came from my mother and the other Indian people who raised me. That idea was that Indians are a people who don't tell lies, who care for their children and their old people. You never see an Indian orphan, they said. You always know when you're old that someone will take care of you — one of your children will. Then they'd list the old folks who were being taken care of by this child or that. No child is ever considered illegitimate among the Indians, they said. If a girl gets pregnant, the baby is still part of the family, and the mother is too. That's what they said, and they showed me real people who lived according to those principles.

Of course the ravages of colonization have taken their toll; there are orphans in Indian country now, and abandoned, brutalized old folks; there are even illegitimate children, though the very concept still strikes me as absurd. There are battered children and neglected children, and there are battered wives and women who have been raped by Indian men. Proximity to the "civilizing" effects of white Christians has not improved the moral quality of life in Indian country, though each group, Indian and white, explains the situation differently. Nor is there much yet in the oral tradition that can enable us to adapt to these inhuman changes. But a force is growing in that direction, and it is helping Indian women reclaim their lives. Their power, their sense of direction and of self will soon be visible. It is the force of the women who speak and work and write, and it is formidable.

Through all the centuries of war and death and cultural and psychic destruction have endured the women who raise the children and tend the fires, who pass along the tales and the traditions, who weep and bury the dead, who are the dead, and who never forget. There are always the women, who make pots and weave baskets, who fashion clothes and cheer their children on at powwow, who make fry bread and piki bread, and corn soup and chili stew, who dance and sing and remember and hold within their hearts the dream of their ancient peoples — that one day the woman who thinks will speak to us again, and everywhere there will be peace. Meanwhile we tell the stories and write the books and trade tales of anger and woe and stories of fun and scandal and laugh over all manner of things that happen every day. We watch and we wait.

My great-grandmother told my mother: never forget you are Indian. And my mother told me the same thing. This, then, is how I have gone about remembering, so that my children will remember too.

ENGAGING THE TEXT

1. Outline how Allen's views of women differ from traditional Anglo-American views. Do you see any difference between Allen's perspective and "feminism" as you understand the term?

2. What does Allen mean by "bicultural bind" (para. 16)? How has it affected her, and how does she deal with it?

3. How does Allen represent relationships between American Indian women and men?

4. Why is remembering so important to Allen? What roles does it play in helping her live in a world dominated by an alien culture? How does it help her define herself as a woman?

5. Allen's essay includes much personal recollection. Try to "translate" some of this information into more abstract statements of theme or message. (For instance, you might write, "Women's roles in American Indian cultures are maintained through example, through oral tradition, and through ceremonial tribal practices.") What is gained, what lost in such "translations"?

6. Review how Allen uses the image of the web to explain tribal identity. In what ways is this an appropriate and effective metaphor?

EXPLORING CONNECTIONS

7. Review Holly Devor's discussion of gender role socialization (p. 414), and compare the influence of "generalized others" and "significant others" in the experiences of Allen and Judith Ortiz Cofer (p. 423). What tension does each woman feel between her "I" and her "me"? How does she resolve it?

8. Read or reread Roger Jack's "An Indian Story" (p. 89). What similarities do you find in Jack's and Allen's ideas about family and tribal identity?

9. According to Allen and to Patricia Hill Collins (p. 112), in what ways do many American Indian and African American women resist Anglo-European roles?

EXTENDING THE CRITICAL CONTEXT

10. Are you struggling to reconcile different definitions of what you should be? (For example, are family, friends, and school pushing you in different directions?) Write an essay or journal entry exploring this issue.

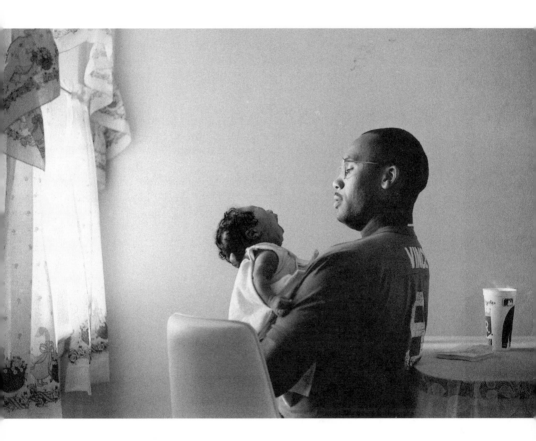

Visual Portfolio
READING IMAGES OF GENDER

1. Who is the intended audience for the Jim Beam ad? What implied difficulty does the text of the ad seek to address? How would you characterize the three young men in the photograph? How does the photo support or contradict the text of the ad? In what ways does the ad as a whole reflect or fail to reflect your own experience? How would Jackson Katz (p. 466) interpret this ad?

2. What does the photo of the victorious boxer suggest about her feelings at that moment? About her opponent's response to his loss? What other messages — about sports or gender or competition, for example — does the picture convey to you? Point to particular visual details that support your interpretations.

3. How would you describe the mood or feeling the photographer has captured in the picture of the father and child? How do the light, the setting, the stance, and the expression of each figure contribute to this impression?

4. Do you think that "Masculinity" would be an appropriate title for the picture of the man and child? Why or why not? Eli Reed, the photographer, titles the photo simply, "Mississippi, 1991"; why do you think he chose to identify it by place and time rather than by theme?

"Two Ways a Woman Can Get Hurt": Advertising and Violence

JEAN KILBOURNE

Most of us like to think of ourselves as immune to the power of ads — we know that advertisers use sex to get our attention and that they make exaggerated claims about a product's ability to make us attractive, popular, and successful. Because we can see through these subtle or not-so-subtle messages, we assume that we're too smart to be swayed by them. But Jean Kilbourne argues that ads affect us in far more profound and potentially damaging ways. The way that ads portray bodies — especially women's bodies — as objects conditions us to seeing each other in dehumanizing ways, thus "normalizing" attitudes that can lead to sexual aggression. Kilbourne (b. 1946) has spent most of her professional life teaching and lecturing about the world of advertising. She has produced award-winning documentaries on images of women in ads (Killing Us Softly, Slim Hopes) *and tobacco advertising* (Pack of Lies). *She has also been a member of the National Advisory Council on Alcohol Abuse and Alcoholism and has twice served as an advisor to the surgeon general of the United States. Currently she teaches at Wellesley College. This selection is taken from her 1999 book,* Can't Buy My Love: How Advertising Changes the Way We Think and Feel *(formerly titled* Deadly Persuasion*).*

Two Ways A Woman Can Get Hurt.

(Heartbreaker) (Soap and water shave)

Skintimate Shave Gel Ultra Protection formula contains 75% moisturizers, including vitamin E, to protect your legs from nicks, cuts and razor burn. So while guys may continue to be a pain, shaving most definitely won't.

SKINTIMATE SHAVE GEL
LOVE YOUR LEGS

© 1997 S.C. Johnson & Son, Inc. All rights reserved. www.skintimate.com

Sex in advertising is more about disconnection and distance than connection and closeness. It is also more often about power than passion, about violence than violins. The main goal, as in pornography, is usually power over another, either by the physical dominance or preferred status of men or what is seen as the exploitative power of female beauty and female sexuality. Men conquer and women ensnare, always with the essential aid of a product. The woman is rewarded for her sexuality by the man's wealth, as in an ad for Cigarette boats in which the woman says, while lying in a man's embrace clearly after sex, "Does this mean I get a ride in your Cigarette?"

Sex in advertising is pornographic because it dehumanizes and objectifies people, especially women, and because it fetishizes products, imbues them with an erotic charge—which dooms us to disappointment since products never can fulfill our sexual desires or meet our emotional needs. The poses and postures of advertising are often borrowed from pornography, as are many of the themes, such as bondage, sadomasochism, and the sexual exploitation of children. When a beer ad uses the image of a man

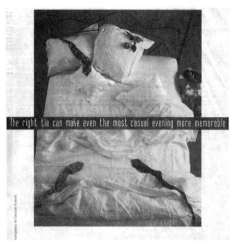

licking the high-heeled boot of a woman clad in leather, when bondage is used to sell neckties in the *New York Times,* perfume in *The New Yorker,* and watches on city buses, and when a college magazine promotes an S&M Ball, pornography can be considered mainstream.

Most of us know all this by now and I suppose some consider it kinky good fun. Pornography is more dangerously mainstream when its glorification of rape and violence shows up in mass media, in films and television shows, in comedy and music videos, and in advertising. Male violence is subtly encouraged by ads that encourage men to be forceful and dominant, and to value sexual intimacy more than emotional intimacy. "Do you want to be the one she tells her deep, dark secrets to?" asks a three-page ad for men's cologne. "Or do you want to be her deep, dark secret?" The last page advises men, "Don't be such a good boy." There are two identical women looking adoringly at the man in the ad, but he isn't looking at either one of them. Just what is the deep, dark secret? That he's sleeping with both of them? Clearly the way to get beautiful women is to ignore them, perhaps mistreat them.

"Two ways a woman can get hurt," says an ad for shaving gel, featuring a razor and a photo of a handsome man. My first thought is that the man is a batterer or date rapist, but the ad informs us that he is merely a "heartbreaker." The gel will protect the woman so that "while guys may continue to be a pain, shaving most definitely won't." Desirable men are painful—heartbreakers at best.

Wouldn't it be wonderful if, realizing the importance of relationships in all of our lives, we could seek to learn relational skills from women and to help men develop these strengths in themselves? In fact, we so often do the opposite. The popular culture usually trivializes these abilities in women, mocks men who have real intimacy with women (it is almost always married men in ads and cartoons who are jerks), and idealizes a template for relationships between men and women that is a recipe for disaster: a template that views sex as more important than anything else, that ridicules men who are not in control of their women (who are "pussy-whipped"), and that disparages fidelity and commitment (except, of course, to brand names).

Indeed the very worst kind of man for a woman to be in an intimate relationship with, often a truly dangerous man, is the one considered most sexy and desirable in the popular culture. And the men capable of real intimacy (the ones we tell our deep, dark secrets to) constantly have their very masculinity impugned. Advertising often encourages women to be attracted to hostile and indifferent men while encouraging boys to become these men. This is especially dangerous for those of us who have suffered from "condemned isolation" in childhood: like heat-seeking missiles, we rush inevitably to mutual destruction.

Men are also encouraged to never take no for an answer. Ad after ad implies that girls and

women don't really mean "no" when they say it, that women are only teasing when they resist men's advances. "NO" says an ad showing a man leaning over a woman against a wall. Is she screaming or laughing? Oh, it's an ad for deodorant and the second word, in very small print, is "sweat." Sometimes it's "all in good fun," as in the ad for Possession shirts and shorts featuring a man ripping the clothes off a woman who seems to be having a good time.

And sometimes it is more sinister. A perfume ad running in several teen magazines features a very young woman, with eyes blackened by makeup or perhaps something else, and the copy, "Apply generously to your neck so he can smell the scent as you shake your head 'no.'" In other words, he'll understand that you don't really mean it and he can respond to the scent like any other animal.

Sometimes there seems to be no question but that a man should force a woman to have sex. A chilling newspaper ad for a bar in Georgetown features a closeup of a cocktail and the headline, "If your date won't listen to reason, try a Velvet Hammer." A vodka ad pictures a wolf hiding in a flock of sheep, a hideous grin on its face. We all know what

IF YOUR DATE WON'T LISTEN TO REASON, TRY A VELVET HAMMER.

Sip exotic cocktails, dine and dance to Swing Era music at Georgetown's top nightspot. 1232 36th St., NW. Reservations, call 342-0009. Free valet parking. Jackets required.

F. SCOTT'S

wolves do to sheep. A campaign for Bacardi Black rum features shadowy figures almost obliterated by darkness and captions such as "Some people embrace the night because the rules of the day do not apply." What it doesn't say is that people who are above the rules do enormous harm to other people, as well as to themselves.

These ads are particularly troublesome, given that between one-third and three-quarters of all cases of sexual assault involve alcohol consumption by the perpetrator, the victim, or both.[1] "Make strangers your friends, and your friends a lot stranger," says one of the ads in a Cuervo campaign that uses colorful cartoon beasts and emphasizes heavy drinking. This ad is especially disturbing when we consider the role of alcohol in date rape, as is another ad in the series that says, "The night began with a bottle of Cuervo and ended with a vow of silence." Over half of all reported rapes on college campuses occur when either the victim or the assailant has been drinking.[2] Alcohol's role has different meaning for men and women, however. If a man is drunk when he commits a rape, he is considered less responsible. If a woman is drunk (or has had a drink or two or simply met the man in a bar), she is considered more responsible.

In general, females are still held responsible and hold each other responsible when sex goes wrong—when they become pregnant or are the victims of rape and sexual assault or cause a scandal. Constantly exhorted to be sexy and attractive, they discover when assaulted that that very sexiness is evidence of ~~their~~ guilt, ~~their lack~~ of "innocence." Sometimes the ads

PURE FANTASY.
SMIRNOFF

---

[1]Wilsnack, Plaud, Wilsnack, and Klassen, 1997, 262. [All notes are the author's, except 5, 9, 15, and 18.]

[2]Abbey, Ross, and McDuffie, 1991. Also Martin, 1992, 230–37.

play on this by "warning" women of what might happen if they use the product. "Wear it but beware it," says a perfume ad. Beware what exactly? Victoria's Secret tempts young women with blatantly sexual ads promising that their lingerie will make them irresistible. Yet when a young woman ac- ·cused William Kennedy Smith of raping her, the fact that she wore Victoria's Secret panties was used against her as an indication of her immorality. A jury acquitted Smith, whose alleged history of violence against women was not permitted to be introduced at trial.

It is sadly not surprising that the jury was composed mostly of women. Women are especially cruel judges of other women's sexual behavior, mostly because we are so desperate to believe we are in control of what happens to us. It is too frightening to face the fact that male violence against women is irrational and commonplace. It is reassuring to believe that we can avoid it by being good girls, avoiding dark places, staying out of bars, dressing "innocently." An ad featuring two young women talking intimately at a coffee shop says, "Carla and Rachel considered themselves open-minded and non-judgmental people. Although they did agree Brenda was a tramp." These terrible judgments from other women are an important part of what keeps all women in line.

If indifference in a man is sexy, then violence is sometimes downright erotic. Not surprisingly, this attitude too shows up in advertising. "Push my buttons," says a young woman, "I'm looking for a man who can totally floor me." Her vulnerability is underscored by the fact that she is in an elevator, often a dangerous place for women. She is young, she is submissive (her eyes are downcast), she is in a dangerous place, and she is dressed provocatively. And she is literally asking for it.

"Wear it out and make it scream," says a jeans ad portraying a man sliding his hands under a woman's transparent blouse. This could be a seduction, but it could as easily be an attack. Although the ad that ran in the

Czech version of *Elle* portraying three men attacking a woman seems unambiguous, the terrifying image is being used to sell jeans *to women*. So someone must think that women would find this image compelling or attractive. Why would we? Perhaps it is simply designed to get our attention, by shocking us and by arousing unconscious anxiety. Or perhaps the intent is more subtle and it is designed to play into the fantasies of domination and even rape that some women use in order to maintain an illusion of being in control (we are the ones having the fantasies, after all, we are the directors).

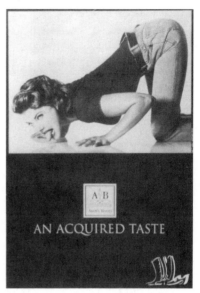

A camera ad features a woman's torso wrapped in plastic, her hands   15
tied behind her back. A smiling woman in a lipstick ad has a padlocked
chain around her neck. An ad for MTV shows a vulnerable young woman,
her breasts exposed, and the simple copy "Bitch." A perfume ad features a
man shadowboxing with what seems to be a woman.

Sometimes women are shown dead or in the process of being killed.
"Great hair never dies," says an ad featuring a female corpse lying on a bed,
her breasts exposed. An ad in the Italian version of *Vogue* shows a man aim-
ing a gun at a nude woman wrapped in plastic, a leather briefcase covering
her face. And an ad for Bitch skateboards, for
God's sake, shows a cartoon version of a similar
scene, this time clearly targeting young people.
We believe we are not affected by these images,
but most of us experience visceral shock when we
pay conscious attention to them. Could they be
any less shocking to us on an unconscious level?

Most of us become numb to these images,
just as we become numb to the daily litany in the
news of women being raped, battered, and killed.
According to former surgeon general Antonia
Novello, battery is the single greatest cause of injury to women in America, more common than
automobile accidents, muggings, and stranger
rapes combined, and more than one-third of

La Borsa è la Vita

women slain in this country die at the hands of husbands or boyfriends.[3] Throughout the world, the biggest problem for most women is simply surviving at home. The Global Report on Women's Human Rights concluded that "Domestic violence is a leading cause of female injury in almost every country in the world and is typically ignored by the state or only erratically punished."[4] Although usually numb to these facts on a conscious level, most women live in a state of subliminal terror, a state that, according to Mary Daly,[5] keeps

bitch skateboards

us divided both from each other and from our most passionate, powerful, and creative selves.[6]

Ads don't directly cause violence, of course. But the violent images contribute to the state of terror. And objectification and disconnection create a climate in which there is widespread and increasing violence. Turning a human being into a thing, an object, is almost always the first step toward justifying violence against that person. It is very difficult, perhaps impossible, to be violent to someone we think of as an equal, someone we have empathy with, but it is very easy to abuse a thing. We see this with racism,

[3]Novello, 1991. Also Blumenthal, 1995.
[4]Wright, 1995, A2.
[5]*Mary Daly:* Radical feminist scholar and author (b. 1928).
[6]Weil, 1999, 21.

with homophobia. The person becomes an object and violence is inevitable. This step is already taken with women. The violence, the abuse, is partly the chilling but logical result of the objectification.

An editorial in *Advertising Age* suggests that even some advertisers are concerned about this: "Clearly it's time to wipe out sexism in beer ads; for the brewers and their agencies to wake up and join the rest of America in realizing that sexism, sexual harassment, and the cultural portrayal of women in advertising are inextricably linked."[7] Alas, this editorial was written in 1991 and nothing has changed.

It is this link with violence that makes the objectification of women a 20 more serious issue than the objectification of men. Our economic system constantly requires the development of new markets. Not surprisingly, men's bodies are the latest territory to be exploited. Although we are growing more used to it, in the beginning the male sex object came as a surprise. In 1994 a "gender bender" television commercial in which a bevy of women office workers gather to watch a construction worker doff his shirt to quaff a Diet Coke led to so much hoopla that you'd have thought women were mugging men on Madison Avenue.[8]

There is no question that men are used as sex objects in ads now as never before. We often see nude women with fully clothed men in ads (as in art), but the reverse was unheard of, until recently. These days some ads do feature clothed and often aggressive women with nude men. And women sometimes blatantly objectify men, as in the Metroliner ad that says, "'She's reading Nietzsche,' Harris noted to himself as he walked towards the café car for a glass of cabernet. And as he passed her seat, Maureen looked up from her book and thought, 'Nice buns.'"

Although these ads are often funny, it is never a good thing for human beings to be objectified. However, there is a world of difference between the objectification of men and that of women. The most important difference is that there is no danger for most men, whereas objectified women are always at risk. In the Diet Coke ad, for instance, the women are physically separated from the shirtless man. He is the one in control. His body is powerful, not passive. Imagine a true role reversal of this ad: a group of businessmen gather to leer at a beautiful woman worker on her break, who removes her shirt before drinking her Diet Coke. This scene would be frightening, not funny, as the Diet Coke ad is. And why is the Diet Coke ad

[7]Brewers can help fight sexism, 1991, 28.
[8]Kilbourne, 1994, F13.

funny? Because we know it doesn't describe any truth. However, the ads featuring images of male violence against women do describe a truth, a truth we are all aware of, on one level or another.

When power is unequal, when one group is oppressed and discriminated against *as a group,* when there is a context of systemic and historical oppression, stereotypes and prejudice have different weight and meaning. As Anna Quindlen[9] said, writing about "reverse racism": "Hatred by the powerful, the majority, has a different weight—and often very different effects—than hatred by the powerless, the minority."[10] When men objectify women, they do so in a cultural context in which women are constantly objectified and in which there are consequences—from economic discrimination to violence—to that objectification.

For men, though, there are no such consequences. Men's bodies are not routinely judged and invaded. Men are not likely to be raped, harassed, or beaten (that is to say, men presumed to be heterosexual are not, and very few men are abused in these ways by women). How many men are frightened to be alone with a woman in an elevator? How many men cross the street when a group of women approaches? Jackson Katz, who writes and lectures on male violence, often begins his workshops by asking men to describe the things they do every day to protect themselves from sexual assault. The men are surprised, puzzled, sometimes amused by the question. The women understand the question easily and have no trouble at all coming up with a list of responses. We don't list our full names in the phone directory or on our mailboxes, we try not to be alone after dark, we carry our keys in our hands when we approach our cars, we always look in the back seat before we get in, we are wary of elevators and doorways and bushes, we carry pepper sprays, whistles, Mace.

Nonetheless, the rate of sexual assault in the United States is the highest of any industrialized nation in the world.[11] According to a 1998 study by the federal government, one in five of us has been the victim of rape or attempted rape, most often before our seventeenth birthday. And more than half of us have been physically assaulted, most often by the men we live with. In fact, three of four women in the study who responded that they had been raped or assaulted as adults said the perpetrator was a current or former husband, a cohabiting partner or a date.[12] The article reporting the results of this study was buried on page twenty-three of my local newspaper, while the front page dealt with a long story about the New England Patriots football team.

A few summers ago, a Diet Pepsi commercial featured Cindy Crawford being ogled by two boys (they seemed to be about twelve years old) as she

25

[9]*Anna Quindlen:* Novelist and Pulitzer Prize–winning journalist who often writes about women's issues (b. 1953).

[10]Quindlen, 1992, E17.

[11]Blumenthal, 1995, 2.

[12]Tjaden and Thoennes, 1998.

where women are women and men are roadkill.

harley-davidson motorclothes

got out of her car and bought a Pepsi from a machine. The boys made very suggestive comments, which in the end turned out to be about the Pepsi's can rather than Ms. Crawford's. There was no outcry: the boys' behavior was acceptable and ordinary enough for a soft-drink commercial.

Again, let us imagine the reverse: a sexy man gets out of a car in the countryside and two preteen girls make suggestive comments, seemingly about his body, especially his buns. We would fear for them and rightly so. But the boys already have the right to ogle, to view women's bodies as property to be looked at, commented on, touched, perhaps eventually hit and raped. The boys have also learned that men ogle primarily to impress other men (and to affirm their heterosexuality). If anyone is in potential danger in this ad, it is the woman (regardless of the age of the boys). Men are not seen as *property* in this way by women. Indeed if a woman does whistle at a man or touches his body or even makes direct eye contact, it is still *she* who is at risk and the man who has the power.

"I always lower my eyes to see if a man is worth following," says the woman in an ad for men's pants. Although the ad is offensive to everyone, the woman is endangering only herself.

"Where women are women and men are roadkill," says an ad for motorcycle clothing featuring an angry-looking African-American woman. Women are sometimes hostile and angry in ads these days, especially women of color who are often seen as angrier and more threatening than white women. But, regardless of color, we all know that women are far more likely than men to end up as roadkill—and, when it happens, they are blamed for being on the road in the first place.

Even little girls are sometimes held responsible for the violence against them. In 1990 a male Canadian judge accused a three-year-old girl of being "sexually aggressive" and suspended the sentence of her molester, who was then free to return to his job of baby-sitter.[13] The deeply held belief that all women, regardless of age, are really temptresses in disguise, nymphets, sexually insatiable and seductive, conveniently transfers all blame and responsibility onto women.

All women are vulnerable in a culture in which there is such widespread objectification of women's bodies, such glorification of disconnection, so much violence against women, and such blaming of the victim. When everything and

30

[13]Two men and a baby, 1990, 10.

everyone is sexualized, it is the powerless who are most at risk. Young girls, of course, are especially vulnerable. In the past twenty years or so, there have been several trends in fashion and advertising that could be seen as cultural reactions to the women's movement, as perhaps unconscious fear of female power. One has been the obsession with thinness. Another has been an increase in images of violence against women. Most disturbing has been the increasing sexualization of children, especially girls. Sometimes the little girl is made up and seductively posed. Sometimes the language is suggestive. "Very cherry," says the ad featuring a sexy little African-

American girl who is wearing a dress with cherries all over it. A shocking ad in a gun magazine features a smiling little girl, a toddler, in a bathing suit that is tugged up suggestively in the rear. The copy beneath the photo says, "short BUTTS from FLEMING FIREARMS."[14] Other times girls are juxtaposed with grown women, as in the ad for underpants that says "You already know the feeling."

This is not only an American phenomenon. A growing national obsession in Japan with schoolgirls dressed in uniforms is called "Loli-con," after Lolita.[15] In Tokyo hundreds of "image clubs" allow Japanese men to act out

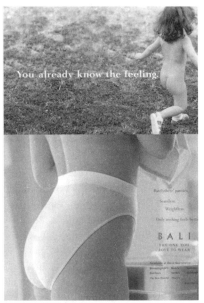

[14]Herbert, 1999, WK 17.
[15]*Lolita:* The title character of Vladimir Nabokov's 1955 novel, Lolita is a young girl who is sexually pursued by her stepfather.

their fantasies with make-believe schoolgirls. A magazine called *V-Club* featuring pictures of naked elementary-school girls competes with another called *Anatomical Illustrations of Junior High School Girls.*[16] Masao Miyamoto, a male psychiatrist, suggests that Japanese men are turning to girls because they feel threatened by the growing sophistication of older women.[17]

In recent years, this sexualization of little girls has become even more disturbing as hints of violence enter the picture. A three-page ad for Prada clothing features a girl or very young woman with a barely pubescent body, clothed in what seem to be cotton panties and perhaps a training bra, viewed through a partially opened door. She seems surprised, startled, worried, as if she's heard a strange sound or glimpsed someone watching her. I suppose this could be a woman awaiting her lover, but it could as easily be a girl being preyed upon.

The 1996 murder of six-year-old JonBenet Ramsey[18] was a gold mine for the media, combining as it did child pornography and violence. In November of 1997 *Advertising Age* reported in an article entitled "JonBenet keeps hold on magazines" that the child had been on five magazine covers in October, "Enough to capture the Cover Story lead for the month. The pre-adolescent beauty queen, found slain in her home last Christmas, garnered 6.5 points. The case earned a *triple play* [italics mine] in the *National Enquirer,* and one-time appearances on *People* and *Star.*"[19] Imagine describing a six-year-old child as "pre-adolescent."

Sometimes the models in ads are children, other times they just look like children. Kate Moss was twenty when she said of herself, "I look

35

---

[16]Schoolgirls as sex toys, 1997, 2E.

[17]Ibid.

[18]*JonBenet Ramsey:* Six-year-old beauty-pageant winner who was sexually molested and murdered in her Boulder, Colorado, home in 1996.

[19]Johnson, 1997, 42.

twelve."[20] She epitomized the vacant, hollow-cheeked look known as "heroin chic" that was popular in the mid-nineties. She also often looked vulnerable, abused, and exploited. In one ad she is nude in the corner of a huge sofa, cringing as if braced for an impending sexual assault. In another she is lying nude on her stomach, pliant, available, androgynous enough to appeal to all kinds of pedophiles. In a music video she is dead and bound to a chair while Johnny Cash sings "Delia's Gone."

It is not surprising that Kate Moss models for Calvin Klein, the fashion designer who specializes in breaking taboos and thereby getting himself public outrage, media coverage, and more bang for his buck. In 1995 he brought the federal government down on himself by running a campaign that may have crossed the line into child pornography.[21] Very young models (and others who just seemed young) were featured in lascivious print ads and in television commercials designed to mimic child porn. The models were awkward, self-conscious. In one commercial, a boy stands in what seems to be a finished basement. A male voiceover tells him he has a great body and asks him to take off his shirt. The boy seems embarrassed but he complies. There was a great deal of protest, which brought the issue into national consciousness but which also gave Klein the publicity and free media coverage he was looking for. He pulled the ads but, at the same time, projected that his jeans sales would almost double from $115 million to $220

[20]Leo, 1994, 27.
[21]Sloan, 1996, 27.

million that year, partly because of the free publicity but also because the controversy made his critics seem like prudes and thus positioned Klein as the daring rebel, a very appealing image to the majority of his customers.

Having learned from this, in 1999 Klein launched a very brief advertising campaign featuring very little children frolicking in their underpants, which included a controversial billboard in Times Square.[22] Although in some ways this campaign was less offensive than the earlier one and might have gone unnoticed had the ads come from a department store catalog rather than from Calvin Klein, there was the expected protest and Klein quickly withdrew the ads, again getting a windfall of media coverage. In my opinion, the real obscenity of this campaign is the whole idea of people buying designer underwear for their little ones, especially in a country in which at least one in five children doesn't have enough to eat.

Although boys are sometimes sexualized in an overt way, they are more often portrayed as sexually precocious, as in the Pepsi commercial featuring the young boys ogling Cindy Crawford or the jeans ad portraying a very little boy looking up a woman's skirt. It may seem that I am reading too much into this ad, but imagine if the genders were reversed. We would fear for a little girl who was unzipping a man's fly in an ad (and we would be shocked, I would hope). Boys are vulnerable to sexual abuse too, but cultural attitudes make it difficult to take this seriously. As a result, boys are less likely to report abuse and to get treatment.

[22]Associated Press, 1999, February 18, A7.

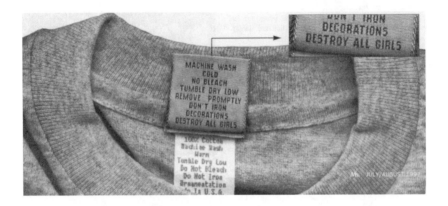

Many boys grow up feeling that they are unmanly if they are not always "ready for action," capable of and interested in sex with any woman who is available. Advertising doesn't cause this attitude, of course, but it contributes to it. A Levi Strauss commercial that ran in Asia features the shock of a schoolboy who discovers that the seductive young woman who has slipped a note into the jeans of an older student is his teacher. And an ad for BIC pens pictures a young boy wearing X-ray glasses while ogling the derriere of an older woman. Again, these ads would be unthinkable if the genders were reversed. It is increasingly difficult in such a toxic environment to see children, boys or girls, as *children.*

In the past few years there has been a proliferation of sexually 40 grotesque toys for boys, such as a Spider Man female action figure whose exaggerated breasts have antennae coming out of them and a female Spawn figure with carved skulls for breasts. Meantime even children have easy access to pornography in video games and on the World Wide Web, which includes explicit photographs of women having intercourse with groups of men, with dogs, donkeys, horses, and snakes; photographs of women being raped and tortured; some of these women made up to look like little girls.

It is hard for girls not to learn self-hatred in an environment in which there is such widespread and open contempt for women and girls. In 1997 a company called Senate distributed clothing with inside labels that included, in addition to the usual cleaning instructions, the line "Destroy all girls." A Senate staffer explained that he thought it was "kind of cool."[23] Given all this, it's not surprising that when boys and girls were asked in a recent study to write an essay on what it would be like to be the other gender, many boys wrote they would rather be dead. Girls had no trouble writing essays about activities, power, freedom, but boys were often stuck, could think of nothing.

[23]Wire and *Times* staff reports, 1997, D1.

It is also not surprising that, in such an environment, sexual harassment is considered normal and ordinary. According to an article in the journal *Eating Disorders:*

> In our work with young women, we have heard countless accounts of this contempt being expressed by their male peers: the girls who do not want to walk down a certain hallway in their high school because they are afraid of being publicly rated on a scale of one to ten; the girls who are subjected to barking, grunting and mooing calls and labels of "dogs, cows, or pigs" when they pass by groups of male students; those who are teased about not measuring up to buxom, bikini-clad [models]; and the girls who are grabbed, pinched, groped, and fondled as they try to make their way through the school corridors.
>
> Harassing words do not slide harmlessly away as the taunting sounds dissipate.... They are slowly absorbed into the child's identity and developing sense of self, becoming an essential part of who she sees herself to be. Harassment involves the use of words as weapons to inflict pain and assert power. Harassing words are meant to instill fear, heighten bodily discomfort, and diminish the sense of self.[24]

It is probably difficult for those of us who are older to understand how devastating and cruel and pervasive this harassment is, how different from the "teasing" some of us might remember from our own childhoods (not that that didn't hurt and do damage as well). A 1993 report by the American Association of University Women found that 76 percent of female students in grades eight to eleven and 56 percent of male students said they had been sexually harassed in school.[25] One high-school junior described a year of torment at her vocational school: "The boys call me slut, bitch. They call me a ten-timer, because they say I go with ten guys at the same time. I put up with it because I have no choice. The teachers say it's because the boys think I'm pretty."[26]

High school and junior high school have always been hell for those who were different in any way (gay teens have no doubt suffered the most, although "overweight" girls are a close second), but the harassment is more extreme and more physical these days. Many young men feel they have the right to judge and touch young women and the women often feel they have no choice but to submit. One young woman recalled that "the guys at school routinely swiped their hands across girls' legs to patrol their shaving prowess and then taunt them if they were slacking off. If I were running late, I'd protect myself by faux shaving—just doing the strip between the bottom of my jeans and the top of my cotton socks."[27]

[24]Larkin, Rice, and Russell, 1996, 5–26.
[25]Daley and Vigue, 1999, A12.
[26]Hart, 1998, A12.
[27]Mackler, 1998, 56.

Sexual battery, as well as inappropriate sexual gesturing, touching, and   45
fondling, is increasing not only in high schools but in elementary and
middle schools as well.[28] There are reports of sexual assaults by students on
other students as young as eight. A fifth-grade boy in Georgia repeatedly
touched the breasts and genitals of one of his fellow students while saying,
"I want to get in bed with you" and "I want to feel your boobs." Authorities
did nothing, although the girl complained and her grades fell. When her
parents found a suicide note she had written, they took the board of education to court.[29]

A high-school senior in an affluent suburban school in the Boston area
said she has been dragged by her arms so boys could look up her skirt and
that boys have rested their heads on her chest while making lewd comments. Another student in the same school was pinned down on a lunch
table while a boy simulated sex on top of her. Neither student reported any
of the incidents, for fear of being ostracized by their peers.[30] In another
school in the Boston area, a sixteen-year-old girl, who had been digitally
raped by a classmate, committed suicide.[31]

According to Nan Stein, a researcher at Wellesley College:

> Schools may in fact be training grounds for the insidious cycle of do-
> mestic violence.... The school's hidden curriculum teaches young
> women to suffer abuse privately, that resistance is futile. When they
> witness harassment of others and fail to respond, they absorb a differ-
> ent kind of powerlessness—that they are incapable of standing up to
> injustice or acting in solidarity with their peers. Similarly, in schools
> boys receive permission, even training, to become batterers through
> the practice of sexual harassment.[32]

This pervasive harassment of and contempt for girls and women constitute a kind of abuse. We know that addictions for women are rooted in
trauma, that girls who are sexually abused are far more likely to become addicted to one substance or another. I contend that all girls growing up in
this culture are sexually abused—abused by the pornographic images of female sexuality that surround them from birth, abused by all the violence
against women and girls, and abused by the constant harassment and threat
of violence. Abuse is a continuum, of course, and I am by no means implying that cultural abuse is as terrible as literally being raped and assaulted.
However, it hurts, it does damage, and it sets girls up for addictions and
self-destructive behavior. Many girls turn to food, alcohol, cigarettes, and
other drugs in a misguided attempt to cope.

[28]Daley and Vigue, 1999, A1, A12.
[29]Shin, 1999, 32.
[30]Daley and Vigue, 1999, A12.
[31]Daley and Abraham, 1999, B6.
[32]Stein, 1993, 316–17.

As Marian Sandmaier said in *The Invisible Alcoholics: Women and Alcohol Abuse in America,* "In a culture that cuts off women from many of their own possibilities before they barely have had a chance to sense them, that pain belongs to all women. Outlets for coping may vary widely, and may be more or less addictive, more or less self-destructive. But at some level, all women know what it is to lack access to their own power, to live with a piece of themselves unclaimed."[33]

Today, every girl is endangered, not just those who have been physically and sexually abused. If girls from supportive homes with positive role models are at risk, imagine then how vulnerable are the girls who have been violated. No wonder they so often go under for good—ending up in abusive marriages, in prison, on the streets. And those who do are almost always in the grip of one addiction or another. More than half of women in prison are addicts and most are there for crimes directly related to their addiction. Many who are there for murder killed men who had been battering them for years. Almost all of the women who are homeless or in prisons and mental institutions are the victims of male violence.[34]

Male violence exists within the same cultural and sociopolitical context that contributes to addiction. Both can be fully understood only within this context, way beyond individual psychology and family dynamics. It is a context of systemic violence and oppression, including racism, classism, heterosexism, weightism, and ageism, as well as sexism, all of which are traumatizing in and of themselves. Advertising is only one part of this cultural context, but it is an important part and thus is a part of what traumatizes.

Sources

Abbey, A., Ross, L., and McDuffie, D. (1991). Alcohol's role in sexual assault. In Watson, R., ed. *Addictive behaviors in women.* Towota, NJ: Humana Press.

Associated Press (1999, February 18). Calvin Klein retreats on ad. *Boston Globe,* A7.

Blumenthal, S. J. (1995, July). *Violence against women.* Washington, DC: Department of Health and Human Services.

Brewers can help fight sexism (1991, October 28). *Advertising Age,* 28.

Daley, B., and Vigue, D. I. (1999, February 4). Sex harassment increasing amid students, officials say. *Boston Globe,* A1, A12.

Hart, J. (1998, June 8). Northampton confronts a crime, cruelty. *Boston Globe,* A1, A12.

Herbert, B. (1999, May 2). America's littlest shooters. *New York Times,* WK 17.

Johnson, J. A. (1997, November 10). JonBenet keeps hold on magazines. *Advertising Age,* 42.

---

[33]Sandmaier, 1980, xviii.
[34]Snell, 1991.

Kilbourne, J. (1994, May 15). 'Gender bender' ads: Same old sexism. *New York Times,* F13.

Larkin, J., Rice, C., and Russell, V. (1996, Spring). Slipping through the cracks: Sexual harassment. *Eating Disorders: The Journal of Treatment and Prevention,* vol. 4, no. 1, 5–26.

Leo, J. (1994, June 13). Selling the woman-child. *U.S. News and World Report,* 27.

Mackler, C. (1998). Memoirs of a (sorta) ex-shaver. In Edut, O., ed. (1998). *Adios, Barbie.* Seattle, WA: Seal Press, 55–61.

Novello, A. (1991, October 18). Quoted by Associated Press, AMA to fight wife-beating. *St. Louis Post Dispatch,* 1, 15.

Quindlen, A. (1992, June 28). All of these you are. *New York Times,* E17.

Sandmaier, M. (1980). *The invisible alcoholics: Women and alcohol abuse in America.* New York: McGraw-Hill.

Schoolgirls as sex toys. *New York Times* (1997, April 16), 2E.

Shin, A. (1999, April/May). Testing Title IX. *Ms.* 32.

Sloan, P. (1996, July 8). Underwear ads caught in bind over sex appeal. *Advertising Age,* 27.

Snell, T. L. (1991). *Women in prison.* Washington, DC: U.S. Department of Justice.

Stein, N. (1993). No laughing matter: Sexual harassment in K–12 schools. In Buchwald, E., Fletcher, P. R., and Roth, M. (1993). *Transforming a rape culture.* Minneapolis, MN: Milkweed Editions, 311–31.

Tjaden, R., and Thoennes, N. (1998, November). *Prevalence, incidence, and consequences of violence against women: Findings from the National Violence Against Women Survey.* Washington, DC: U.S. Department of Justice.

Two men and a baby (1990, July/August). *Ms.* 10.

Vigue, D. J., and Abraham, Y. (1999, February 7). Harassment a daily course for students. *Boston Globe,* B1, B6.

Weil, L. (1999, March). Leaps of faith. *Women's Review of Books,* 21.

Wilsnack, S. C., Plaud, J. J., Wilsnack, R. W., and Klassen, A. D. (1997). Sexuality, gender, and alcohol use. In Wilsnack, R. W., and Wilsnack, S. C., eds. *Gender and alcohol: Individual and social perspectives.* New Brunswick, N.J.: Rutgers Center of Alcohol Studies, 262.

Wire and Times Staff Reports (1997, May 20). Orange County skate firm's 'destroy all girls' tags won't wash. *Los Angeles Times,* D1.

Wright, R. (1995, September 10). Brutality defines the lives of women around the world. *Boston Globe,* A2.

Engaging the Text

1. What parallels does Kilbourne see between advertising and pornography? How persuasive do you find the evidence she offers? Do the photos of the ads she describes strengthen her argument? Why or why not?

2. Why is it dangerous to depict women and men as sex objects, according to Kilbourne? Why is the objectification of women *more* troubling, in her view? Do you agree?

3. How does Kilbourne explain the appeal of ads that allude to bondage, sexual aggression, and rape—particularly for female consumers? How do you respond to the ads reproduced in her essay?

4. What does Kilbourne mean when she claims that the depiction of women in advertising constitutes "cultural abuse"? How does she go about drawing connections between advertising images and social problems like sexual violence, harassment, and addiction? Which portions of her analysis do you find most and least persuasive, and why?

EXPLORING CONNECTIONS

5. Media images constitute part of the "generalized other"—the internalized sense of what is socially acceptable and unacceptable—described by Holly Devor (p. 414). In addition to the violent and sexualized images Kilbourne examines, what other images or messages about gender do you encounter regularly in the media? Which ones have been most influential in the development of your "generalized other"?

6. Write an essay exploring the power of media to promote or curb violence, drawing on Kilbourne and on any or all of the selections by the following writers:

> Jackson Katz (p. 466)
> Carmen Vázquez (p. 492)
> Joan Morgan (p. 527)
> Henry Jenkins (p. 279)
> Stephanie Brail (p. 777)
> John Naisbitt et al. (p. 81)

EXTENDING THE CRITICAL CONTEXT

7. Kilbourne claims that popular culture idealizes dangerous, exploitative, or dysfunctional relationships between women and men. Working in small groups, discuss the romantic relationships depicted in movies you've seen recently. Does her critique seem applicable to those films? List the evidence you find for and against her argument and compare your results with those of other groups.

8. In her analysis of two ads (the Diet Pepsi commercial featuring Cindy Crawford and the Diet Coke ad with the shirtless construction worker), Kilbourne applies a gender reversal test in order to demonstrate the existence of a double standard. Try this test yourself on a commercial or ad that relies on sexual innuendo. Write a journal entry describing the ad and explaining the results of your test.

9. Working in pairs or small groups, survey the ads in two magazines—one designed to appeal to a predominantly female audience and one aimed at a largely male audience. What differences, if any, do you see in the kinds of images and appeals advertisers use in the two magazines? How often do you see the kinds of "pornographic" ads Kilbourne discusses? Do you find any ads depicting the "relational skills" that she suggests are rarely emphasized in popular culture?

Advertising and the Construction of Violent White Masculinity

JACKSON KATZ

Advertising offers us a glimpse of our cultural subconscious: designed to sell products by selling us desirable visions of ourselves, ads reflect our dreams and insecurities. According to Jackson Katz, recent advertising presents a disturbing image of American masculinity—an image that equates manhood with bulging muscles, aggression, and violence. Katz (b. 1960) co-founded the Mentors in Violence Prevention Program at Northeastern University's Center for the Study of Sport in Society; this program represented the first nationwide effort to enlist high school, collegiate, and professional athletes in combatting male violence against women. Katz also founded Real Men, an antisexist men's organization based in Boston, and lectures widely on images of violent masculinity in sports and media. Currently he directs worldwide implementation of the United States Marine Corps' gender violence prevention program. He recently created a video, "Tough Guise: Violence, Media, and the Crisis in Masculinity," available through his Web site, jacksonkatz.com. This essay appears in Gender, Race and Class in Media *(1995) edited by Gail Dines and Jean M. Humez.*

Violence is one of the most pervasive and serious problems we face in the United States. Increasingly, academics, community activists, and politicians have been paying attention to the role of the mass media in producing, reproducing, and legitimating this violence.[1]

Unfortunately, however, much of the mainstream debate about the effects of media violence on violence in the "real" world fails to include an analysis of gender. Although, according to the Federal Bureau of Investigation, approximately 90 percent of violent crime is committed by males, magazine headline writers talk about "youth" violence and "kids'" love affair with guns. It is unusual even to hear mention of "masculinity" or "manhood" in these discussions, much less a thorough deconstruction of the gender order and the way that cultural definitions of masculinity and femininity

---

[1]"Violence" refers to immediate or chronic situations that result in injury to the psychological, social, or physical well-being of individuals or groups. For the purpose of this chapter, I will use the American Psychological Association's (APA) more specific definition of interpersonal violence. Although acknowledging the multidimensional nature of violence, the APA Commission on Violence and Youth defines interpersonal violence as "behavior by persons against persons that threatens, attempts, or completes intentional infliction of physical or psychological harm" (APA, 1993, p. 1). [All notes are Katz's.]

might be implicated. Under these conditions, a class-conscious discussion of masculine gender construction is even less likely.

There is a glaring absence of a thorough body of research into the power of cultural images of masculinity. But this is not surprising. It is in fact consistent with the lack of attention paid to other dominant groups. Discussions about racial representation in media, for example, tend to focus on African Americans, Asians, or Hispanics, and not on Anglo Whites.[2] Writing about the representation of Whiteness as an ethnic category in mainstream film, Richard Dyer (cited in Hanke) argues that "white power secures its dominance by seeming not to be anything in particular"; "Whiteness" is constructed as the norm against which nondominant groups are defined as "other." Robert Hanke, in an article about hegemonic masculinity in transition, argues that masculinity, like Whiteness, "does not appear to be a cultural/historical category at all, thus rendering invisible the privileged position from which (white) men in general are able to articulate their interests to the exclusion of the interests of women, men and women of color, and children" (186).

There has been some discussion, since the mid-1970s, of the ways in which cultural definitions of White manhood have been shaped by stereotypical representations in advertising. One area of research has looked at the creation of modern masculine archetypes such as the Marlboro Man. But there has been little attention, in scholarship or antiviolence activism, paid to the relationship between the construction of violent masculinity in what Sut Jhally refers to as the "commodity image-system" of advertising and the pandemic of violence committed by boys and men in the homes and streets of the United States.

This chapter is an attempt to sketch out some of the ways in which   5 hegemonic constructions of masculinity in mainstream magazine advertising normalize male violence. Theorists and researchers in profeminist sociology and men's studies in recent years have developed the concept of *masculinities,* as opposed to *masculinity,* to more adequately describe the complexities of male social position, identity, and experience. At any given time, the class structure and gender order produce numerous masculinities stratified by socioeconomic class, racial and ethnic difference, and sexual orientation. The central delineation is between the hegemonic, or dominant, masculinity (generally, White and middle-class) and the subordinated masculinities.

But although there are significant differences between the various masculinities, in patriarchal culture, ~~violent behavior is typically gendered~~ male.

---

[2]Although hegemonic constructions of masculinity affect men of all races, there are important variables due to racial differences. Because it is not practical to do justice to these variables in a chapter of this length, and because the vast majority of images of men in mainstream magazine advertisements are of White men, for the purpose of this chapter, I will focus on the constructions of various White masculinities.

This doesn't mean that all men are violent but that violent behavior is considered masculine (as opposed to feminine) behavior. This masculine gendering of violence in part explains why the movie *Thelma and Louise* touched such a chord: Women had appropriated, however briefly, the male prerogative for, and identification with, violence.

One need not look very closely to see how pervasive is the cultural imagery linking various masculinities to the potential for violence. One key source of constructions of dominant masculinity is the movie industry, which has introduced into the culture a seemingly endless stream of violent male icons. Tens of millions of people, disproportionately male and young, flock to theaters and rent videocassettes of the "action-adventure" (a Hollywood euphemism for *violent*) films of Arnold Schwarzenegger, Sylvester Stallone, Bruce Willis, et al.

These cultural heroes rose to prominence in an era, the mid-to-late 1970s into the 1980s, in which working-class White males had to contend with increasing economic instability and dislocation, the perception of gains by people of color at the expense of the White working class, and a women's movement that overtly challenged male hegemony. In the face of these pressures, then, it is not surprising that White men (especially but not exclusively working-class) would latch onto big, muscular, violent men as cinematic heroes. For many males who were experiencing unsettling changes, one area of masculine power remained attainable: physical size and strength and the ability to use violence successfully.

Harry Brod and other theorists have argued that macro changes in postindustrial capitalism have created deep tensions in the various masculinities. For example, according to Brod,

> Persisting images of masculinity hold that "real men" are physically strong, aggressive, and in control of their work. Yet the structural dichotomy between manual and mental labor under capitalism means that no one's work fulfills all these conditions.
>
> Manual laborers work for others at the low end of the class spectrum, while management sits at a desk. Consequently, while the insecurities generated by these contradictions are personally dissatisfying to men, these insecurities also impel them to cling all the more tightly to sources of masculine identity validation offered by the system. (14)

One way that the system allows working-class men (of various races)   10
the opportunity for what Brod refers to as "masculine identity validation" is through the use of their body as an instrument of power, dominance, and control. For working-class males, who have less access to more abstract forms of masculinity-validating power (economic power, workplace authority), the physical body and its potential for violence provide a concrete means of achieving and asserting "manhood."

At any given time, individuals as well as groups of men are engaged in an ongoing process of creating and maintaining their own masculine identities.

Advertising, in a commodity-driven consumer culture, is an omnipresent and rich source of gender ideology. Contemporary ads are filled with images of "dangerous"-looking men. Men's magazines and mainstream newsweeklies are rife with ads featuring violent male icons, such as uniformed football players, big-fisted boxers, and leather-clad bikers. Sports magazines aimed at men, and televised sporting events, carry millions of dollars' worth of military ads. In the past decade, there have been hundreds of ads for products designed to help men develop muscular physiques, such as weight training machines and nutritional supplements.

Historically, use of gender in advertising has stressed difference, implicitly and even explicitly reaffirming the "natural" dissimilarity of males and females. In late-twentieth-century U.S. culture, advertising that targets young White males (with the exception of fashion advertising, which often features more of an androgynous male look) has the difficult task of stressing gender difference in an era characterized by a loosening of rigid gender distinctions. Stressing gender difference in this context means defining masculinity in opposition to femininity. This requires constantly reasserting what is masculine and what is feminine. One of the ways this is accomplished, in the image system, is to equate masculinity with violence (and femininity with passivity).

The need to differentiate from the feminine by asserting masculinity in the form of power and aggression might at least partially account for the high degree of male violence in contemporary advertising, as well as in video games, children's toys, cartoons, Hollywood film, and the sports culture.

By helping to differentiate masculinity from femininity, images of masculine aggression and violence—including violence against women—afford young males across class a degree of self-respect and security (however illusory) within the more socially valued masculine role.

Violent White Masculinity in Advertising

The appeal of violent behavior for men, including its rewards, is coded into mainstream advertising in numerous ways: from violent male icons (such as particularly aggressive athletes or superheroes) overtly threatening consumers to buy products, to ads that exploit men's feelings of not being big, strong, or violent enough by promising to provide them with products that will enhance those qualities. These codes are present in television and radio commercials as well, but this chapter focuses on mainstream American magazine ads (*Newsweek, People, Sports Illustrated,* etc.), from the early 1990s.

Several recurring themes in magazine advertising targeting men help support the equation of White masculinity and violence. Among them are violence as genetically programmed male behavior, the use of military and sports symbolism to enhance the masculine appeal and identification of

15

products, the association of muscularity with ideal masculinity, and the equation of heroic masculinity with violent masculinity. Let us now consider, briefly, each of these themes.

Violence as Genetically Programmed Male Behavior

One way that advertisers demonstrate the "masculinity" of a product or service is through the use of violent male icons or types from popular history. This helps to associate the product with manly needs and pursuits that presumably have existed from time immemorial. It also furthers the ideological premise, disguised as common sense, that men have always been aggressive and brutal, and that their dominance over women is biologically based. "Historical" proof for this is shown in a multitude of ways.

An ad for the Chicago Mercantile Exchange, an elite financial institution, depicts a medieval battlefield where muscle-bound toy figurines, accompanied by paradoxically muscular skeleton men, prepare to engage in a sword fight. They might wear formal suits and sit behind desks, the ad implies, but the men in high finance (and those whose money they manage) are actually rugged warriors. Beneath the veneer of wealth and class privilege, *all* men are really brutes. The text reads: "How the Masters of the Universe Overcame the Attack of the Deutschmarks."

An ad for Trojan condoms features a giant-sized Roman centurion, in full uniform, muscles rippling, holding a package of condoms as he towers over the buildings of a modern city. Condom manufacturers know that the purchase and use of condoms by men can be stressful, partially because penis size, in popular Western folklore, is supposedly linked to virility. One way to assuage the anxieties of male consumers is to link the product with a recognizably violent (read: masculine) male archetype. It is no coincidence that the two leading brands of condoms in the United States are named for ancient warriors and kings (Trojan and Ramses).

Sometimes products with no immediately apparent connection to gender or violence nonetheless make the leap. An ad for Dell computers, for example, shows a painting of a group of White cowboys on horseback shooting at mounted Indians who are chasing them. The copy reads: "Being Able to Run Faster Could Come in Real Handy." The cowboys are foregrounded and the viewers are positioned to identify with them against the Indian "other." The cowboys' violence is depicted as defensive, a construction that was historically used to justify genocide. The ad explains that "you never know when somebody (read: Indians, Japanese business competitors) is going to come around the corner and surprise you." It thus masculinizes the White middle-class world of the computer business by using the violent historical metaphor of cowboys versus Indians.

An even more sinister use of historical representations involves portraying violence that would not be acceptable if shown in contemporary settings. Norwegian Cruise Line, for example, in an ad that ran in major newsweekly magazines, depicted a colorful painting of a scene on a ship's

20

deck, set sometime in the pirate era, where men, swords drawn, appear simultaneously to be fighting each other while a couple of them are carrying off women. The headline informs us that Norwegian is the "first cruise line whose entertainment doesn't revolve around the bar."

It is highly doubtful that the cruise line could have set what is clearly a rape or gang rape scenario on a modern ship. It would no doubt have prompted feminist protests about the company's glorification of the rape of women. Controversy is avoided by depicting the scene as historical.[3] But Norwegian Cruise Line, which calls itself "The Pleasure Ships," in this ad reinforces the idea that rape is a desirable male pastime. Whether intentional or not, the underlying message is that real men (pirates, swashbucklers) have always enjoyed it.

The Use of Military and Sports Symbolism to Enhance the Masculine Identification and Appeal of Products

Advertisers who want to demonstrate the unquestioned manliness of their products can do so by using one of the two key subsets in the symbolic image system of violent masculinity: the military and sports. Uniformed soldiers and players, as well as their weapons and gear, appear frequently in ads of all sorts. Many of the Camel Smooth Character cartoon ads, for example, display submarines surfacing or fighter jets streaking by as Joe Camel stands confidently in the foreground. One ad features Joe Camel himself wearing an air force bomber pilot's jacket. The message to the young boys and adolescent males targeted by the campaign is obvious: Violence (as signified by the military vehicles) is cool and suave. The sexy blond woman gazing provocatively at the James Bond–like camel provides female ratification of Joe's masculinity.

Ads for the military itself also show the linkage between masculinity and force. The U.S. military spends more than $100 million annually on advertising. Not surprisingly, armed services advertisements appear disproportionately on televised sporting events and in sports and so-called men's magazines. Military ads are characterized by exciting outdoor action scenes with accompanying text replete with references to "leadership," "respect," and "pride." Although these ads sometimes promote the educational and financial benefits of military service, what they're really selling to young working-class males is a vision of masculinity—adventurous, aggressive, and violent—that provides men of all classes with a standard of "real manhood" against which to judge themselves.

Boxers and football players appear in ads regularly, promoting products   25
from underwear to deodorants. Sometimes the players are positioned simply to sanction the masculinity of a product. For example, an ad for Bugle

---

[3]Some feminist groups did protest the ad, such as the Cambridge, Massachusetts–based group Challenging Media Images of Women. But the protests never reached a wide audience and had no discernible effect.

Boy clothing depicts a clean-cut young White man, dressed in Bugle Boy jeans and posed in a crouching position, kneeling on a football. Standing behind him, inexplicably, is a large, uniformed football player flexing his muscles. The only copy says, in bold letters, "Bugle Boy Men." It seems reasonable to infer that the goal of this ad was to shore up the masculine image of a product whose name (Bugle Boy) subverts its macho image. The uniformed football player, a signifier of violent masculinity, achieves this task by visually transmitting the message: Real men wear Bugle Boy.

Advertisers know that using high-profile violent male athletes can help to sell products, such as yogurt and light beer, that have historically been gendered female. Because violence establishes masculinity, if these guys (athletes) use traditionally "female" products, they don't lose their masculinity. Rather, the masculinity of the product—and hence the size of the potential market—increases. Miller Brewing Company proved the efficacy of this approach in their long-running television ad campaign for Lite beer. The Miller Lite campaign, which first appeared in the early 1970s, helped bring Miller to the top of the burgeoning light beer market and is often referred to as the most successful TV ad campaign in history.

The Association of Muscularity with Ideal Masculinity

Men across socioeconomic class and race might feel insecure in their masculinity, relatively powerless or vulnerable in the economic sphere, and uncertain about how to respond to the challenges of women in many areas of social relations. But, in general, males continue to have an advantage over females in the area of physical size and strength. Because one function of the image system is to legitimate and reinforce existing power relations, representations that equate masculinity with the qualities of size, strength, and violence thus become more prevalent.

The anthropologist Alan Klein[4] has looked at how the rise in popularity of bodybuilding is linked to male insecurity. "Muscles," he argues, "are about more than just the functional ability of men to defend home and hearth or perform heavy labor. Muscles are markers that separate men from each other and, most important perhaps, from women. And while he may not realize it, every man—every accountant, science nerd, clergyman, or cop—is engaged in a dialogue with muscles" (16).

Advertising is one area of the popular culture that helps feed this "dialogue." Sports and other magazines with a large male readership are filled with ads offering men products and services to enhance their muscles. Often these ads explicitly equate muscles with violent power, as in an ad for a Marcy weight machine that tells men to "Arm Yourself" under a black and white photograph of a toned, muscular White man, biceps and forearms straining, in the middle of a weight-lifting workout. The military, too, offers

---

[4]The article cited here was excerpted from Klein's book *Little Big Men: Bodybuilding Subculture and Gender Construction* (Albany: State University of New York Press, 1993).

to help men enhance their bodily prowess. An ad for the Army National Guard shows three slender young men, Black and White, working out, over copy that reads "Get a Part-Time Job in Our Body Shop."

The discourse around muscles as signifiers of masculine power involves   30 not only working-class men but also middle- and upper-class males. This is apparent in the male sports subculture, where size and strength are valued by men across class and racial boundaries. But muscularity as masculinity is also a theme in advertisements aimed at upper-income males. Many advertisers use images of physically rugged or muscular male bodies to masculinize products and services geared to elite male consumers. An ad for the business insurance firm Brewer and Lord uses a powerful male body as a metaphor for the more abstract form of (financial) power. The ad shows the torso of a muscular man curling a barbell, accompanied by a headline that reads "the benefits of muscle defined." The text states that "the slow building of strength and definition is no small feat. In fact, that training has shaped the authority that others see in you, as well."

Saab, targeting an upscale, educated market, bills itself as "the most intelligent car ever built." But in one ad, they call their APC Turbo "the muscle car with a social conscience"—which signals to wealthy men that by driving a Saab they can appropriate the working-class tough guy image associated with the concept of a "muscle car" while making clear their more privileged class position.

The Equation of Heroic Masculinity with Violent Masculinity

The cultural power of Hollywood film in the construction of violent masculinity is not limited to the movies themselves. In fact, many more people see the advertising for a given film than see the film itself.

Advertising budgets for major Hollywood releases typically run in the millions of dollars. Larger-than-life billboards enhance the heroic stature of the icons. Movie ads appear frequently on prime time TV and daily in newspapers and magazines. Not surprisingly, these ads highlight the movies' most violent and sexually titillating scenes.

Violence on-screen, like that in real life, is perpetrated overwhelmingly by males. Males constitute the majority of the audience for violent films, as well as violent sports such as football and hockey. It is important to note, then, that what is being sold is not just "violence," but rather a glamorized form of violent masculinity.

Guns are an important signifier of virility and power and hence are an   35 important part of the way violent masculinity is constructed and then sold to audiences. In fact, the presence of guns in magazine and newspaper ads is crucial in communicating the extent of a movie's violent content. Because so many films contain explicit violence, images of gun-toting macho males (police detectives, old-west gunslingers, futuristic killing machines) pervade the visual landscape.

In an effort to reduce injuries, the Clodpell Valley Football Conference devised the two-hand tickle tackling rule.

Conclusion

Recent research in sociology, media, and cultural studies strongly suggests that we need to develop a much more sophisticated approach to understanding cultural constructions of masculinity. Feminists, who have been at the forefront in studying the social construction of gender, have, historically, focused on images and representations of women. Clearly we need a similarly intensive examination of the representation of men—particularly in light of the crisis of men's violence in our society.

This chapter focuses attention on constructions of violent White masculinity in mainstream magazine advertising. But we need also to examine critically a number of other areas where violent masculinities are produced and legitimated: comic books, toys, the sports culture, comedy, interactive video, music video, pornography. This will help us to understand more fully the links between the construction of gender and the prevalence of violence, which might then lead to effective antiviolence interventions.

References

American Psychological Association. (1993). *Violence and youth: Psychology's response.* Washington, DC: Author.

Brod, H. (Ed.). (1987). *The making of masculinities: The new men's studies.* Boston: Allen & Unwin.

Federal Bureau of Investigation. (1992). *Uniform crime reports.* Washington, DC: Author.

Hanke, R. (1992). Redesigning men: Hegemonic masculinity in transition. In S. Craig (Ed.), *Men, masculinity and the media* (pp. 185–198). Newbury Park, CA: Sage.

Jhally, S. (1990, July). Image-based culture: Advertising and popular culture. *The World and I,* pp. 508–519.

Klein, A. (1993, January). Little big men. *Northeastern University Magazine,* p. 14–19.

ENGAGING THE TEXT

1. What does Katz mean when he says that "violent behavior is typically gendered male" (para. 6) in American culture? What evidence do you see to support or challenge this assertion?

2. What role does Katz suggest that the media play in "producing, reproducing, and legitimating...violence" (para. 1)? Why does he believe that the issue of gender is typically ignored in discussions of media and violence?

3. How do images of male aggression, strength, and power appeal differently to working-class men and professional men, according to Katz? How does he explain the increasing popularity of such images—for example, in action-adventure movies—since the 1970s?

4. Katz describes and interprets several specific ads (for example, the rampaging pirates in the ad for Norwegian Cruise Lines in para. 21). Sketch out an alternate interpretation for one or more of these ads based on the details Katz provides. To what extent are the images and texts of the ads ambiguous?

EXPLORING CONNECTIONS

5. Play the role of Holly Devor (p. 414) and write a journal entry explaining how the advertising images described by Katz contribute to the "social hegemony" of the "patriarchal gender schema."

6. While Katz implies that our popular images of masculinity are overwhelmingly sexist and damaging, Judith Ortiz Cofer's (p. 423) account of her Wonder Woman fantasies suggests that images from popular media can influence us in complex and sometimes unexpected ways. Do you see superheroes, comic book characters, and action figures as sexist or liberating for children? Can they be both?

7. Both Katz and Jean Kilbourne (p. 444) suggest that violent media images at once reflect and help to perpetuate a culture of violence; however, they offer few suggestions about how this cycle of violence might be broken. Why do you think both writers focus more on analyzing the problem than on offering solutions? How would you begin to address the issue?

8. In the cartoon on page 474, how does the artist play with our assumptions about football players, football, and fans of the sport? Is he making fun of

football itself, of people who criticize violent sports, of masculine stereo-types, of bureaucratic solutions to complex problems, or something else?

EXTENDING THE CRITICAL CONTEXT

9. Katz maintains that "fashion advertising...often features more of an an-drogynous male look" (para. 12). Skim several magazines aimed at different audiences (for example, *Ebony, GQ, Rolling Stone, Sports Illustrated*) looking for ads that depict conventionally masculine images and others that present more androgynous images of men. What products are associated with each type of image? How are the images in the ads designed to appeal to the audience for each magazine?

10. Using Katz's analysis of "masculine" imagery as a model, survey several magazines designed primarily for women (for example, *Cosmopolitan, Essence, Vogue*) and develop a list of recurrent images that are associated with "femininity" in advertising. Compare your observations with those of classmates.

11. Working in pairs or groups, create an ad designed to appeal to women; the product may be real or imaginary but should be something anyone can use, such as a car, a soft drink, or a bar of soap. Then design another ad for the same product, this time aimed at men. Present the pair of ads to the class and discuss their effectiveness. What changes did you make in the "male" version of the ad, and why?

12. Although Katz concentrates on advertising, he suggests that the images of masculinity he describes also dominate other media like movies, video games, and television cartoons for children. As a class project, survey some of these media and test his claim. Pool your observations: Do they tend to support, challenge, or qualify Katz's argument?

The Evolution of G.I. Joe, 1964–1998
NEW YORK TIMES

War toys, including G.I. Joe, have long been criticized for encouraging kids to think of violence as a form of play. Now a new study suggests that Joe and similar action figures may also foster a dangerously unrealistic body image among impressionable boys. This short piece, summarizing research conducted by Harrison G. Pope Jr., M.D., appeared as a news item in the May 30, 1999, New York Times. A professor of psychiatry at Harvard Medical School, Pope specializes in studying the connection between psychiatry and physiology. He is coauthor of The Adonis Complex: The Secret Crisis of Male Body Obsession *(2000).*

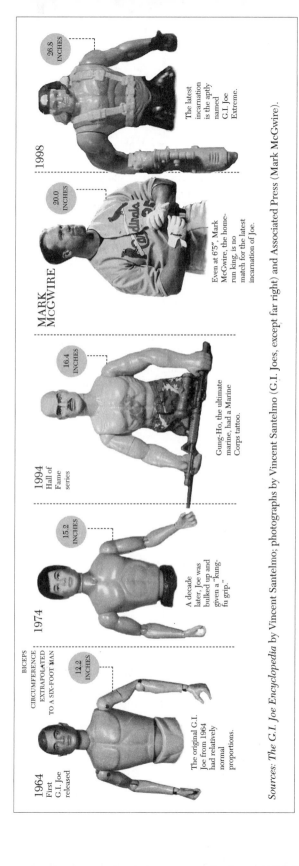

1964
First G.I. Joe released

BICEPS
CIRCUMFERENCE
EXTRAPOLATED
TO A SIX-FOOT MAN

12.2 INCHES

The original G.I. Joe from 1964 had relatively normal proportions.

1974

15.2 INCHES

A decade later, Joe was bulked up and given a "kung-fu grip."

1994
Hall of Fame series

16.4 INCHES

Gung-Ho, the ultimate marine, had a Marine Corps tattoo.

MARK MCGWIRE

20.0 INCHES

Even at 6'5", Mark McGwire, the home-run king, is no match for the latest incarnation of Joe.

1998

26.8 INCHES

The latest incarnation is the aptly named G.I. Joe Extreme.

Sources: *The G.I. Joe Encyclopedia* by Vincent Santelmo; photographs by Vincent Santelmo (G.I. Joes, except far right) and Associated Press (Mark McGwire).

Just as Barbie dolls have taunted little girls with an impossible ideal of the female body, G.I. Joes have morphed over the last three decades into muscle-bound hunks that can harm the self-esteem of boys, according to a new study.

Dr. Harrison Pope, a Harvard psychiatrist, studied the evolution of American action figures over the last thirty years to learn whether there was a connection between the toys and an increase in "body-image disturbances" among men. Dr. Pope and his researchers purchased G.I. Joes and other action figures manufactured since the 1960s, measured their waists, chests, and biceps, then calculated the figures for a six-foot man. The results were stark.

"Many modern figures display the physiques of advanced bodybuilders and some display levels of muscularity far exceeding the outer limits of actual human attainment," according to the study, published this month in the *International Journal of Eating Disorders.*

More research is needed to determine the effect on boys and, ultimately, adult men, the study warned, but added, "the impact of toys should not be underestimated." Male action toys accounted for $949 million in manufacturers' shipments in 1994, and action figures were $687 million of the total, the study said.

The study noted one exception to the bulking-up trend: Barbie's long-time boyfriend, Ken.

ENGAGING THE TEXT

1. Examine the pictures and graphics in this selection as a visual argument. What is the thesis? How persuasive is the evidence? How does the written text enhance or extend the argument?

2. What is the effect of including the picture of Mark McGwire? Why compare Joe to this particular athlete (why not a different baseball star or an equally famous athlete in another sport)? Why select this photo of McGwire?

3. Why do you think the designers of Ken have resisted "the bulking-up trend" that has transformed G.I. Joe?

EXPLORING CONNECTIONS

4. How would Jackson Katz (p. 466) explain the increasing muscularity of G.I. Joe? What other changes do you see in Joe's features? Can you think of alternate explanations for the evolution of this toy?

EXTENDING THE CRITICAL CONTEXT

5. Write a journal entry about a favorite toy you played with as a child. Looking back, what role, if any, do you think it played in shaping your attitudes, values, or self-image?

6. Look up the original study by Dr. Harrison G. Pope in the July 1999 *International Journal of Eating Disorders*. What differences do you note in the ways the two publications present the results of Pope's research? How do the audiences and purposes of the two articles explain these differences in presentation? What is gained and what is lost in the newspaper version?

7. Research how the design of the Barbie doll has changed over the years. How do Barbie's modifications differ from Joe's, and how do you explain the differences?

The Gender Wardens

CHRISTINA HOFF SOMMERS

In her controversial book, Who Stole Feminism? *(1994), Christina Hoff Sommers argues that the women's movement has been hijacked by "gender feminists," who, in her words, "believe that all our institutions, from the state to the family to the grade schools, perpetuate male dominance. Believing that women are virtually under siege, gender feminists naturally seek recruits to wage their side of the gender war." In the excerpt that follows, Sommers condemns "gender wardens" who try to impose feminist views on others and champions women—from religious conservatives to lipstick lesbians—whom she sees as resistance fighters in the "gender war." Sommers is an associate professor of philosophy at Clark University in Worcester, Massachusetts. She has edited two textbooks on ethics and published articles in the* Wall Street Journal, *the* New Republic, *the* New England Journal of Medicine, *and other periodicals. Her most recent book is titled* The War Against Boys: How Misguided Feminism Is Harming Our Young Men *(2000).*

> *Censorship is the strongest drive in human nature; sex is a weak second.*
> —PHIL KERBY, *Los Angeles Times*
> editorial writer, on a postcard to
> Nat Hentoff[1]

QUESTION: How many feminists does it take to screw in a light bulb?
FEMINIST ANSWER: That's not funny.

---

[1]Nat Hentoff, *Free Speech for Me—But Not for Thee* (New York: HarperCollins, 1992), p. 1. [All notes are Sommers's except 2 and 5.]

It is sometimes said that feminists don't have a sense of humor. Yet, there are some situations, not funny to most women, that gender feminists seem to find very amusing.

About a thousand feminists were present at Manhattan's 92nd Street Y on Mother's Day 1992 to hear a debate between Susan Faludi[2] and *Playboy* columnist Asa Baber. Baber opened his talk by observing that on Mother's Day, the phone lines throughout the United States are jammed because everyone is trying to call home to talk to their mothers. On Father's Day, the lines are free. "We have to ask why there is so much less interest in fathers," said Baber.[3]

The assembled women, most of them fans of Ms. Faludi, found this uproarious. "It brought down the house," said Baber. "At first, I didn't get it. I thought my fly was open." But then he caught on and said, "If you think that is funny, you are going to think this is a laugh riot: I think the fact that our fathers are so much out of the loop is a major tragedy in our culture."

Baber had taken another misstep, but this time he didn't tickle anyone's funny bone. An outraged audience hissed and booed him. Later, when he was asked whether this was because his hecklers believed that men were useless, irrelevant, and potentially dangerous, Baber answered, "You got it."[4] To them he appeared to be just another patriarch exacting homage.

The jeering, hooting atmosphere in which Baber found himself was familiar to me. I had encountered it in the "safe spaces" where gender feminists gather to tell one another put-down stories describing how a sister had routed some male who didn't have a clue at how offensive he was (recall the "Shut up, you fucker" with which one partisan had squelched an unsuspecting male student critic in a feminist classroom). I'd heard it in the appreciative laughter of the audience when feminist academics reported to them on how they had played on the liberal guilt of the faculty to get their projects approved. Baber was in the camp of the enemy, and anything he had to say was regarded as offensive or, if he were lucky, laughable.

The derision of the women who were hooting at Baber was safely directed at "men." One must wonder what Baber's audience would make of the millions of women who still observe the amenities of Father's Day. So intent are gender feminists on condemning the "patriarchy" that they rarely let on how they feel about women who "go along." Nevertheless, it is not hard to see that in jeering at Baber, they were also jeering at most American women.

That is the corrosive paradox of gender feminism's misandrist stance: no group of women can wage war on men without at the same time denigrating the women who respect those men. It is just not possible to incrimi-

5

---

[2]*Susan Faludi:* Faludi documents the rise of conservative resistance to feminism in *Backlash: The Undeclared War Against American Women* (1991).

[3]Jay Overocker, "Ozzie and Harriet in Hell," *Heterodoxy* 1, no. 6 (November 1992): 9.

[4]Ibid.

nate men without implying that large numbers of women are fools or worse. Other groups have had their official enemies—workers against capitalists, whites against blacks, Hindus against Muslims—and for a while such enmities may be stable. But when women set themselves against men, they simultaneously set themselves against other women in a group antagonism that is untenable from the outset. In the end, the gender feminist is always forced to show her disappointment and annoyance with the women who are to be found in the camp of the enemy. Misandry moves on to misogyny.

Betty Friedan once told Simone de Beauvoir[5] that she believed women should have the choice to stay home to raise their children if that is what they wish to do. Beauvoir answered: "No, we don't believe that any woman should have this choice. No woman should be authorized to stay at home to raise her children. Society should be totally different. Women should not have that choice, precisely because if there is such a choice, too many women will make that one."[6]

De Beauvoir thought this drastic policy was needed to prevent women from leading blighted conventional lives. Though she does not spell it out, she must have been aware that her "totally different" society would require a legion of Big Sisters endowed by the state with the power to prohibit any woman who wants to marry and stay home with children from carrying out her plans. She betrays the patronizing attitude typical of many gender feminists toward "uninitiated" women.

An illiberal authoritarianism is implicit in the doctrine that women are socialized to want the things the gender feminist believes they *should not want*. For those who believe that what women want and hope for is "constrained" or "coerced" by their upbringing in the patriarchy are led to dismiss the values and aspirations of most women. The next step may not be inevitable, but it is almost irresistible: to regard women as badly brought-up children whose harmful desires and immature choices must be discounted.

Gender feminists, such as Sandra Lee Bartky, argue for a "feminist reconstruction of self and society [that] must go far beyond anything now contemplated in the theory or politics of the mainstream women's movement."[7] Bartky, who writes on "the phenomenology of feminist consciousness," is

---

[5]*Friedan...Beauvoir:* Influential feminist writers and activists. Friedan (b. 1921) is best known for *The Feminine Mystique* (1963) and Beauvoir (1908–1986) for *The Second Sex* (1949).

[6]"Sex, Society, and the Female Dilemma" (a dialogue between Friedan and Beauvoir), *Saturday Review*, June 14, 1975, p. 18. As an equity feminist I find much to admire in de Beauvoir's works, but her bland tolerance for authoritarianism is not part of it. She was perhaps unduly influenced by Jean-Paul Sartre, joining him in his Maoist phase in the seventies. This may help to explain, although it would not excuse, her readiness to use state power to force people to live "correct" lives.

[7]Sandra Lee Bartky, *Femininity and Domination: Studies in the Phenomenology of Oppression* (New York: Routledge, 1990), p. 5.

concerned with what a proper feminist consciousness should be like. In her book *Femininity and Domination,* she says, "A thorough overhaul of desire is clearly on the feminist agenda: the fantasy that we are overwhelmed by Rhett Butler should be traded in for one in which we seize state power and reeducate him."[8] Bartky, however, does not advocate any authoritarian measures to protect women from incorrect values and preferences shaped by "the masters of patriarchal society." She points out that at present we do not know how to "decolonize the imagination."[9] She cautions that "overhauling" desires and "trading in" popular fantasies may have to wait for the day when feminist theorists develop an "adequate theory of sexuality." In her apocalyptic feminist vision, women as well as men may one day be radically reconstructed. We will have learned to *prefer* the "right" way to live.

Although they may disagree politically about what measures to take with women who make the wrong choices, Beauvoir and her latter-day descendants share a common posture: they condescend to, patronize, and pity the benighted females who, because they have been "socialized" in the sex/gender system, cannot help wanting the wrong things in life. Their disdain for the hapless victims of patriarchy is rarely acknowledged. When feminists talk of a new society and of how people must be changed, they invariably have in mind men who exploit and abuse women. But it is not difficult to see that they regard most women as men's dupes.

Consider how Naomi Wolf (in the *Beauty Myth*) regards the eight million American women members of Weight Watchers—as cultists in need of deprogramming. Most gender feminists may not be ready to advocate coercion of women of low feminist consciousness, but they are very much in favor of a massive and concerted effort to give the desires, aspirations, and values of American women a thorough makeover. As the feminist philosopher Alison Jaggar puts it, "If individual desires and interests are socially constituted..., the ultimate authority of individual judgment comes into question. Perhaps people may be mistaken about truth, morality, or even their own interests; perhaps they may be systematically self-deceived."[10] Note that Jaggar explicitly impugns the traditional liberal principle that the many individual judgments and preferences are the ultimate authority. I find that a chilling doctrine: when the people are systematically self-deceived, the ultimate authority is presumed to be vested in a vanguard that unmasks their self-deception. As Ms. Jaggar says, "Certain historical circumstances allow specific groups of women to transcend at least partially

---

[8]Ibid., p. 51.

[9]Ibid., pp. 56, 61. Ms. Bartky is also aware that her ideas about the radical reconstruction of self and society are not now popular. It does not worry her: "For it reveals the extent to which the established order of domination has taken root within our very identities." *Femininity and Domination,* p. 5.

[10]Alison Jaggar, *Feminist Politics and Human Nature* (Totowa, N.J.: Rowman and Littlefield, 1983), p. 44.

the perceptions and theoretical constructs of male dominance."[11] It is these women of high feminist consciousness who "inspire and guide women in a struggle for social change."

Respect for people's preferences is generally thought to be fundamental for democracy. But ideologues find ways of denying this principle. The gender feminist who claims to represent the true interests of women is convinced that she profoundly understands their situation and so is in an exceptional position to know their true interests. In practice, this means she is prepared to dismiss popular preferences in an illiberal way. To justify this, feminist philosopher Marilyn Friedman argues that popular preferences are often "inauthentic" and that even liberals are aware of this:

> Liberal feminists can easily join with other feminists in recognizing that political democracy by itself is insufficient to ensure that preferences are formed without coercion, constraint, undue restriction of options, and so forth. Social, cultural, and economic conditions are as important as political conditions, if not more so, in ensuring that preferences are, in some important sense, authentic.[12]

Friedman is quite wrong in her assumptions: anyone, liberal or conservative, who believes in democracy will sense danger in them. Who will "ensure" that preferences are "authentic"? What additions to political democracy does Friedman have in mind? A constitutional amendment to provide reeducation camps for men and women of false consciousness? Is she prepared to go the authoritarian route indicated by de Beauvoir?

The feminist who thinks that democracy is insufficient believes that seemingly free and enlightened American women have values and desires that, unbeknownst to them, are being manipulated by a system intent on keeping women subjugated to men. Romance, a major cause of defection from the gynocentric enclave, is ever a sticking point with gender feminists. Gloria Steinem, writing on the subject, engages in this kind of debunking "critique": "Romance itself serves a larger political purpose by offering at least a temporary reward for gender roles and threatening rebels with loneliness and rejection.... It privatizes our hopes and distracts us from making societal changes. The Roman 'bread and circuses' way of keeping the masses happy...might now be updated."[13] Jaggar, too, sees in romance a distraction from sexual politics: "The ideology of romantic love has now become so pervasive that most women in contemporary capitalism probably believe that they marry for love rather than for economic support."[14]

15

[handwritten margin note: "do not agree w/ reming"]

---

[11]Ibid., p. 150.

[12]Marilyn Friedman, "Does Sommers Like Women? More on Liberalism, Gender Hierarchy, and Scarlett O'Hara," *Journal of Social Philosophy* 21, no. 2 (Fall–Winter 1990): 83.

[13]Gloria Steinem, *Revolution from Within: A Book of Self-Esteem* (Boston: Little, Brown, 1992), p. 260.

[14]Jaggar, *Feminist Politics and Human Nature*, p. 219.

For her authoritarian disdain, de Beauvoir deserves our liberal censure. But the less authoritarian feminists also deserve it. No intelligent and liberal person—no one who has read and appreciated the limpid political prose of George Orwell or who has learned from the savage history of twentieth-century totalitarianism—can accept the idea of a social agenda to "overhaul" the desires of large numbers of people to make them more "authentic."

In her defense, the gender feminist replies that effective teachers or political leaders must always try to help others overcome benightedness. When women are caught in a system designed to perpetuate male domination, they must be enlightened. There is nothing intrinsically illiberal about seeking to make them conscious of their subjugation. It is the very essence of a liberal education to open minds and enlighten consciousness. If that entails "reeducating" them and overhauling their desires, so be it.

This argument could easily be made in an earlier era when classically liberal principles were being applied to men but not to women. In the nineteenth century, the proposition that all men are created equal was taken to mean "all males." Women did not have the rights that men had, and, what is more, they were being taught that their subordinate status was fitting and natural. Feminist philosophers like John Stuart Mill and Harriet Taylor rightly feared that such teaching was helping to perpetuate inequities. Under the circumstances, political democracy applied only minimally to women. Because they did not vote, their preferences were not in play, and the question of how authentic their preferences were was of importance inasmuch as it affected their ability to agitate for the rights that were being withheld from them.

But women are no longer disenfranchised, and their preferences are 20 being taken into account. Nor are they now taught that they are subordinate or that a subordinate role for them is fitting and proper. Have any women in history been better informed, more aware of their rights and options? Since women today can no longer be regarded as the victims of an undemocratic indoctrination, we must regard their preferences as "authentic." Any other attitude toward American women is unacceptably patronizing and profoundly illiberal.

Gender feminists are especially disapproving of the lives of traditionally religious women such as evangelical Christian women, Catholic women, or Orthodox Jewish women, whom they see as being conditioned for highly restricted roles. Surely, they say, it is evident that such women are subjugated, and the choices they make inauthentic. As Gloria Steinem explains it, the appeal of religious fundamentalism for women is that "the promise *is* safety in return for obedience, respectability in return for self-respect and freedom—a sad bargain."[15]

---

[15]Steinem, *Revolution from Within*, p. 309.

That is a harsh judgment to make about millions of American women. Ms. Steinem is of course free to disagree with conventionally religious women on any number of issues, but she is not morally free to cast aspersions on their autonomy and self-respect. The New Feminism is supposed to be about sisterhood. Why are its most prominent practitioners so condescending?

Steinem herself knows a thing or two about how to recruit adherents to a cause by promises of "safety" and "self-respect." The feminist orthodoxy she portrays promises safety in a sisterhood that will offer unhappy or insecure women a venue where they can build self-esteem and attain an authenticity enjoyed by no other group of women.[16]

The traditionally religious women of today, be they Protestant Christians, Orthodox Jews, or observant Catholics—emphatically do not think of themselves as subjugated, lacking in self-respect, or unfree. Indeed, they very properly resent being described that way. For they are perfectly aware that they have all the rights that men have. If they choose to lead the lives they do, that is their affair.

Of course there are feminists who disapprove of the way these women   25
live, and some may even think of them as pitiable. These feminists are perfectly at liberty to try to persuade them to change their way of life. For their part, traditional women might try to persuade the feminists of the merits of the religious way of life. Mostly, however, gender feminists are content to dismiss and even jeer at the religious women without engaging or confronting them in a respectful dialogue, and it is not surprising that the latter have grown increasingly impatient with their feminist critics.

Several years ago, Liz Harris wrote an extraordinary and much-talked-about article for the *New Yorker* on the ultraorthodox Hasidic women of Brooklyn, New York.[17] She had expected to find oppressed women—"self-effacing drudges" worn down by a family system that exalted men and denigrated women. Instead, she was impressed by their strong marriages, their large, thriving families, and their "remarkably energetic, mutually supportive community of women, an almost Amazonian society." "Most of the [Hasidic] women sped around like intergalactic missiles, and the greater majority of those I was to encounter seemed...to be as occupied with worthy projects as Eleanor Roosevelt, as hospitable as Welcome Wagoneers."[18]

My relatives on my husband's side are Jewish, and most are Orthodox. Ms. Harris's description fits them to a T. At family gatherings, I sometimes

---

[16]The theme of "safety" is central for gender feminism. Indeed, a favorite phrase for any place where feminists gather is "safe space." In this misogynist world, the "feminist classroom," for example, is advertised as a safe space where women can speak freely without fear of being humiliated by derisive or brutal males. On the other hand, as I tried to show in Chapter 6, the feminist classroom can be very *unsafe* for those who are not true believers in gender feminism.

[17]Later expanded and published in book form: Liz Harris, *Holy Days: The World of a Hasidic Family* (New York: Macmillan, 1985), p. 128.

[18]Ibid., p. 129.

tell my sister-in-law, my nieces, and their friends about the feminist theorists who pity them and would liberate them from their "gendered families." They are more amused than offended. It might surprise Gloria Steinem to hear they have a rather shrewd understanding of her kind of feminism. They simply want no part of it. They believe they have made an autonomous choice: they also believe their way of life offers them such basic advantages as community, grace, dignity, and spirituality. They see the patriarchal aspects of their tradition as generally benign. Some of them find aspects of Judaism insensitive to important concerns of women, but they are even more put off by the gender feminist's rejection of traditional religion.

But of course it is not only religious women who reject the gender feminist perspective. A clear majority of secular American women enjoy many aspects of "la différence." Many want things that gender feminists are trying to free them from, be it conventional marriages and families, or fashions and makeup that sometimes render them "sex objects." Such feminists are uncomfortably aware that they are not reaching these women; but instead of asking themselves where they may be going wrong, they fall back on the question-begging-theory of false consciousness to explain the mass indifference of the women they want to save.

For the gender feminists do want to save women—from themselves. False consciousness is said to be endemic in the patriarchy. And every feminist has her theory. Feminists who specialize in the theory of feminist consciousness talk about mechanisms by which "patriarchy invades the intimate recesses of personality where it may maim and cripple the spirit forever."[19] However, a growing number of women are questioning whether gender feminism, with its insistence that personal relationships be construed in terms of political power, has taken much of the joy out of male/female intimacy, maiming and crippling the spirit of some of its devotees forever.

A few years ago, an op-ed piece I wrote for the *Chronicle of Higher Education* aroused a storm of protest because it defended the "many women [who] continue to swoon at the sight of Rhett Butler carrying Scarlett O'Hara up the stairs to a fate undreamt of in feminist philosophy."[20] The Society for Women in Philosophy (SWIP), an organization within the American Philosophical Association, arranged for a public debate between Marilyn Friedman, a philosopher from the University of Washington, and me. Ms. Friedman informed the overflow audience that she was stunned by my flippant reaction to Rhett's rape of Scarlett—for rape she considered it to be. "The name of Richard Speck, to take one example, can remind us that real rape is not the pleasurable fantasy intimated in *Gone with the*

[19]Bartky, *Femininity and Domination,* p. 58.
[20]Christina Sommers, "Feminist Philosophers Are Oddly Unsympathetic to the Women They Claim to Represent," *Chronicle of Higher Education,* October 11, 1989, p. B3.

Wind. To put the point graphically: Would 'many women' still swoon over Butler's rape of O'Hara if they knew that he urinated on her?"[21] Lest readers wonder how they could have missed that lurid scene in *Gone with the Wind*, I hasten to say that Ms. Friedman made up this detail presumably to bolster her point. In my rejoinder, I told the audience about a recent poll taken by Harriet Taylor, the feminist author of *Scarlett's Women: "Gone with the Wind" and Its Female Fans*.[22] Ms. Taylor did not pretend that her survey was scientific, but what she found has the ring of truth. She asked GWTW fans what they thought had happened when Scarlett was carried up the stairs. The overwhelming majority of the four hundred respondents indicated that they did not think Rhett raped Scarlett, though there was some "mutually pleasurable rough sex."[23] Almost all reported that they found the scene "erotically exciting." As one respondent put it:

> Scarlett's story is that of a woman who has had lousy sex from two incompetent husbands (a "boy" and an "old man," as Rhett reminds her) [who] knew nothing about women. At last she finds out what *good* sex feels like, even if (or probably because) her first experience takes place in mutual inebriation and a spirit of vengeful anger.[24]

The idea of "mutually pleasurable rough sex" is not high on the gender feminist list of entertainments. All the same, if the New Feminist philosophers were honest about taking women seriously, they would be paying attention to what, in most women's minds, is a fundamental distinction: Scarlett was ravished, not raped. The next morning finds her relishing the memory. Ms. Friedman's insistence that Scarlett was raped was just another example of how gender feminists, estranged from the women they claim to represent, tend to view male/female relations as violent or humiliating to women.

Friedman, like Bartky, takes comfort in the idea that women's desires and aspirations will change in time. Younger women, she says, are already less inclined to be taken in by the Rhett Butler mystique, and his fascination should continue to diminish. That is, unless people like me give younger women the idea that there is nothing wrong with taking pleasure in Scarlett's enraptured submission.

"How sad it would be," she writes, "if Sommers's writings acted as an obstacle to change, bolstering those who interpret the sexual domination of women as pleasurable, and intimidating those who speak out against such domination."[25]

---

[21]Marilyn Friedman, "'They Lived Happily Ever After': Sommers on Women and Marriage," *Journal of Social Philosophy*, 21, nos. 2 and 3 (Fall–Winter 1990): 58.

[22]Helen Taylor, *Scarlett's Women: "Gone with the Wind" and Its Female Fans* (New Brunswick, N.J.: Rutgers University Press, 1989).

[23]Ibid., p. 130.

[24]Ibid., p. 133.

[25]Friedman, "Does Sommers Like Women?" p. 87.

Ms. Friedman considers Sandra Bartky to be one of her mentors and Bartky is, indeed, of the opinion that active measures should be taken to prevent the spread of "harmful" writings. In 1990 I was commissioned by the *Atlantic* to do a piece on campus feminism. When Sandra Bartky somehow learned of this, she wrote to the editors, pleading with them not to publish it. She told them that I was a disreputable philosopher and "a right-wing ideologue." The *Chronicle of Higher Education* found out about the flap, and called Ms. Bartky to ask her why she had written the letter. At first she denied having asked them to suppress my piece, claiming that she had only requested that my article be accompanied by another giving a different point of view. But when the *Chronicle* reporter pointed out that he had a copy of the letter and that it contained no such request, she defiantly admitted having tried to stop the piece: "I wouldn't want a nut case who thinks there wasn't a Holocaust to write about the Holocaust. Editors exercise discretion. By not asking someone to write a piece, that's not censorship, that's discretion."[26]

Inadvertently, Bartky got her way. By the time the whole matter was   35 sorted out, the *Atlantic* had gone on to other issues. Editor Michael Curtis told the *Chronicle* that he was embarrassed that the piece had not been published. The *Chronicle* reporter asked what he thought of Bartky's letter. "It seemed to confirm some of the darker aspects of Ms. Sommers's article, which pointed out the extraordinary lengths some of the women were prepared to go to shape all discussion in which they had an interest," he replied.[27]

Rhett Butler continues to pique the gender feminists. Naomi Wolf, at least in her earlier incarnation, was fond of explaining to the public how women cooperate in their own degradation. When asked why women enjoyed the "rape scene" in *Gone with the Wind,* Ms. Wolf answered that they had been "trained" to accept that kind of treatment and so grew to like it: "It's not surprising that, after decades of being exposed to a culture that consistently eroticizes violence against women, women, too, would often internalize their own training."[28]

I can't help being amused by how upset the New Feminists get over the vicarious pleasure women take in Scarlett's transports. All that incorrect swooning! How are we ever going to get women to see how wrong it is? Nevertheless, the gender feminists seem to believe that thirty years from now, with the academy transformed and the feminist consciousness of the population raised, there will be a new Zeitgeist. Women who interpret sexual domination as pleasurable will then be few and far between, and Scarlett, alas, will be out of style.

---

[26]*Chronicle of Higher Education,* January 15, 1992, p. A7.
[27]Ibid.
[28]"Men, Sex, and Rape," ABC News Forum, May 5, 1992, Transcript no. ABC-34, p. 9.

Is this scenario out of the question? I think it is. Sexuality has always been part of our natures, and there is no one right way. Men like Rhett Butler will continue to fascinate many women. Nor will the doctrine that this demeans them have much of an effect. How many women who like Rhett Butler types are in search of support groups to help them change? Such women are not grateful to the gender feminists for going to war against male lust. They may even be offended at the suggestion that they themselves are being degraded and humiliated; for that treats their enjoyment as pathological.

Defending women who enjoy the idea of ravishment is not the same as holding a brief for any specific kind of fantasy or sexual preference. Fantasies of female domination are also popular. Women are clearly capable of treating men as "sex objects" with an enthusiasm equal to, and in some cases exceeding, that of men for treating women as such. Male strip-shows seem to be as popular as Tupperware parties.

The dissident feminist Camille Paglia uses the term "pagan gazers" for 40 those who publicly watch males or females as sex objects. She has no quarrel with the male gazers, but she positively applauds the female ones. "Women are getting much more honest about looking at men, and about leering. Finally we're getting somewhere."[29]

If Paglia is right, sexual liberation may not be going in the direction of eliminating the Other as a sex object; it may instead be going in the direction of encouraging women to objectify the male as Other, too. Such a development would certainly be a far cry from the gender feminist utopia described by University of Massachusetts philosopher Ann Ferguson:

> With the elimination of sex roles, and the disappearance, in an over-populated world, of any biological need for sex to be associated with procreation, there would be no reason why such a society could not transcend sexual gender. It would no longer matter what biological sex individuals had. Love relationships, and the sexual relationships developing out of them, would be based on the individual meshing together of androgynous human beings.[30]

Ferguson's utopia conjures up visions of a world of gender-neutral characters like Pat on "Saturday Night Live." Although Pat-like people can be very nice (doubtless, never rough), their sexually correct meshings do not invite heated speculation. To put the matter bluntly: the androgynous society has always been a boring feminist fairy tale with no roots in psychological or social reality.

A group of gay women who call themselves "lipstick lesbians" are rebelling against the androgynous ideal that feminists like Ann Ferguson...

---

[29]*Boston Globe,* July 30, 1991, p. 54.

[30]Ann Ferguson, *Sexual Democracy: Women, Oppression, and Revolution* (Boulder, Colo.: Westview Press, 1991), p. 207.

celebrate. According to Lindsy van Gelder, a writer for *Allure* magazine, the lipstick lesbians are tired of Birkenstock and L. L. Bean couture, "womyn's" music festivals, potluck dinners, and all the "rigid dos and don'ts of feminist ideology."[31] She reports on several lesbian go-go bars in different parts of the country where lipstick lesbians congregate and treat each other in ways that are very much frowned upon in most gender feminist circles.

I believe that the Bartkys, the Friedmans, and the Fergusons are doomed to disappointment but that in any case no feminist should ever have an agenda of managing women's desires and fantasies. For suppose we could succeed in "trading in the fantasy of being overwhelmed by Rhett Butler for one in which we seize state power and reeducate him." Suppose, indeed, that we succeeded in getting most people to feel and to behave in ways that are sexually correct by gender feminist lights. Once the methods and institutions for overhauling desires are in place, what would prevent their deployment by new groups who have different conceptions of what is sexually correct and incorrect? Having seized state power, some zealous faction would find ready to hand the apparatus needed for reeducating people to *its* idea of what is "authentic," not only sexually but politically and culturally.

Engaging the Text

1. Who are the "gender wardens," according to Sommers? What are their goals and methods? What evidence of their influence does Sommers provide?

2. How do the views of "gender feminists" differ from those of traditionally religious women? How does Sommers's analysis of these differences contribute to her critique of feminism?

3. Sommers asserts that "women are no longer disenfranchised,...[n]or are they now taught that they are subordinate or that a subordinate role for them is fitting and proper" (para. 20). Do you agree? What evidence do you see that women today are or are not taught to play a subordinate role?

4. Throughout the essay Sommers evokes the idea of "gender wardens" who have the power to dictate "sexually correct" personal behavior and attitudes; however, she argues that those who endorse such repressive measures "are doomed to disappointment" (para. 44). If she does not believe that the "gender wardens" are likely to succeed, what is her purpose in raising the issue?

5. Sommers defends women who enjoy sexual domination in part by arguing that women are likewise "capable of treating men as 'sex objects'" (para. 39). Do you agree with her assumption that these two situations are equivalent? Why or why not? Is it liberating for women to objectify men?

---

[31]Lindsy van Gelder, "Lipstick Liberation," *Los Angeles Times Magazine,* March 15, 1992, p. 30.

"Some kids at school called you a feminist, Mom, but I punched them out."

EXPLORING CONNECTIONS

6. Like Tocqueville, Sommers warns that some feminists may be trying to eliminate all differences between men and women. What "differences" did Tocqueville wish to preserve? Have any of his fears been realized? How different are Sommers's concerns from Tocqueville's?

7. Sommers argues that contemporary women's choices must be considered "authentic" because they are no longer constrained by law as they were in the past. How might Holly Devor (p. 414), Jackson Katz (p. 466), Jean Kilbourne (p. 444), or Deborah Tannen (p. 233) respond to this argument? Besides legal constraints, what forces, if any, shape our values and desires?

8. What does the cartoon on this page suggest about generational attitudes toward feminism and about the effect of feminism on girls' lives? Why does the cartoonist depict mom at the stove and dad reading the paper?

EXTENDING THE CRITICAL CONTEXT

9. What evidence, if any, have you seen in your school, in your community, or in the media that "gender wardens" are enforcing conformity to feminist attitudes and behavior?

10. Sommers reports a heated debate that she has had with feminist scholars about whether Scarlett O'Hara, the heroine of *Gone with the Wind,* was ravished (that is, had "mutually pleasurable rough sex") or was raped by Rhett Butler. Find and read the passage in the novel that describes her ravishment or rape. Which interpretation seems more plausible to you, and why?

Appearances

CARMEN VÁZQUEZ

Have you ever gone for a walk in the evening, ridden a city bus, or gone out dancing? Did these activities make you fear for your life? In this essay, Vázquez writes about what can happen in such everyday situations when the pedestrian, commuter, or dancer is perceived as gay or lesbian. She also discusses some possible causes of homophobia, and she pleads for change. Vázquez (b. 1949) was born in Bayamon, Puerto Rico, and grew up in Harlem, New York. She has been active in the lesbian/gay movement for many years and currently serves as Director of Public Policy for the Lesbian and Gay Community Services Center in New York City; she also codirects Promote the Vote, a registration project sponsored by community centers across the nation. She has published essays and book reviews in a number of publications. "Appearances" comes from an anthology titled Homophobia: How We All Pay the Price *(1992).*

North of Market Street and east of Twin Peaks, where you can see the white fog mushroom above San Francisco's hills, is a place called the Castro. Gay men, lesbians, and bisexuals stroll leisurely up and down the bustling streets. They jaywalk with abandon. Night and day they fill the cafés and bars, and on weekends they line up for a double feature of vintage classics at their ornate and beloved Castro theater.

The 24 bus line brings people into and out of the Castro. People from all walks of life ride the electric-powered coaches. They come from the opulence of San Francisco's Marina and the squalor of Bayview projects. The very gay Castro is in the middle of its route. Every day, boys in pairs or gangs from either end of the city board the bus for a ride through the Castro and a bit of fun. Sometimes their fun is fulfilled with passionately obscene derision: "Fucking cocksucking faggots." "Dyke cunts." "Diseased butt fuckers." Sometimes, their fun is brutal.

Brian boarded the 24 Divisadero and handed his transfer to the driver one late June night. Epithets were fired at him the moment he turned for a seat. He slid his slight frame into an empty seat next to an old woman with silver blue hair who clutched her handbag and stared straight ahead. Brian stuffed his hands into the pockets of his worn brown bomber jacket and stared with her. He heard the flip of a skateboard in the back. The taunting shouts grew louder. "Faggot!" From the corner of his eye, he saw a beer bottle hurtling past the window and crash on the street. A man in his forties, wearing a Giants baseball cap and warmup jacket, yelled at the driver to stop the bus and get the hoodlums off. The bus driver ignored him and pulled out.

Brian dug his hands deeper into his pockets and clenched his jaw. It was just five stops to the top of the hill. When he got up to move toward the exit, the skateboard slammed into his gut and one kick followed another until every boy had got his kick in. Despite the plea of the passengers, the driver never called the police.

Brian spent a week in a hospital bed, afraid that he would never walk again. A lawsuit filed by Brian against the city states, "As claimant lay crumpled and bleeding on the floor of the bus, the bus driver tried to force claimant off the bus so that the driver could get off work and go home. Claimant was severely beaten by a gang of young men on the #24 Divisadero Bus who perceived that he was gay." 5

On the south side of Market Street, night brings a chill wind and rough trade. On a brisk November night, men with sculptured torsos and thighs wrapped in leather walked with precision. The clamor of steel on the heels of their boots echoed in the darkness. Young men and women walked by the men in leather, who smiled in silence. They admired the studded bracelets on Mickey's wrists, the shine of his flowing hair, and the rise of his laughter. They were, each of them, eager to be among the safety of like company where they could dance with abandon to the pulse of hard rock, the hypnotism of disco, or the measured steps of country soul. They looked forward to a few drinks, flirting with strangers, finding Mr. or Ms. Right or, maybe, someone to spend the night with.

At the end of the street, a lone black street lamp shone through the mist. The men in leather walked under the light and disappeared into the next street. As they reached the corner, Mickey and his friends could hear the raucous sounds of the Garden spill onto the street. They shimmied and rocked down the block and through the doors.

The Garden was packed with men and women in sweat-stained shirts. Blue smoke stung the eyes. The sour and sweet smell of beer hung in the air. Strobe lights pulsed over the dancers. Mickey pulled off his wash-faded black denim jacket and wrapped it around his waist. An iridescent blue tank top hung easy on his shoulders. Impatient with the wait for a drink, Mickey steered his girlfriend onto the crowded dance floor.

Reeling to the music and immersed in the pleasure of his rhythms, Mickey never saw the ice pick plunge into his neck. It was just a bump with a drunk yelling, "Lame-assed faggot." "Faggot. Faggot. Faggot. Punk faggot." Mickey thought it was a punch to the neck. He ran after the roaring drunk man for seven steps, then lurched and fell on the dance floor, blood gushing everywhere. His girlfriend screamed. The dance floor spun black.

Mickey was rushed to San Francisco General Hospital, where thirty-six   10 stitches were used by trauma staff to close the wound on his neck. Doctors said the pick used in the attack against him was millimeters away from his spinal cord. His assailant, charged with attempted murder, pleaded innocent.

Mickey and Brian were unfortunate stand-ins for any gay man. Mickey was thin and wiry, a great dancer clad in black denim, earrings dangling from his ear. Brian was slight of build, wore a leather jacket, and boarded a bus in the Castro. Dress like a homo, dance like a homo, must be a homo. The homophobic fury directed at lesbians, gay men, and bisexuals in America most often finds its target. Ironclad evidence of sexual orientation, however, is not necessary for someone to qualify as a potential victim of deadly fury. Appearances will do.

The incidents described above are based on actual events reported to the San Francisco Police and Community United Against Violence (CUAV), an agency serving victims of antilesbian and antigay violence where I worked for four years. The names of the victims have been changed. Both men assaulted were straight.

Incidents of antilesbian and antigay violence are not uncommon or limited to San Francisco. A *San Francisco Examiner* survey estimates that over one million hate-motivated physical assaults take place each year against lesbians, gays, and bisexuals. The National Gay and Lesbian Task Force conducted a survey in 1984 that found that 94 percent of all lesbians and gay men surveyed reported being physically assaulted, threatened, or harassed in an antigay incident at one time or another. The great majority of these incidents go unreported.

To my knowledge, no agency other than CUAV keeps track of incidents of antigay violence involving heterosexuals as victims. An average of 3 percent of the over three hundred victims seen by CUAV each year identify as heterosexuals. This may or may not be an accurate gauge of the actual prevalence of antigay violence directed at heterosexuals. Most law enforcement agencies, including those in San Francisco, have no way of documenting this form of assault other than under a generic "harassment" code. The actual incidence of violence directed at heterosexuals that is motivated by homophobia is probably much higher than CUAV's six to nine victims a year. Despite the official paucity of data, however, it is a fact that incidents of antigay and antilesbian violence in which straight men and women are victimized do occur. Shelters for battered women are filled with stories of lesbian baiting of staff and of women whose husbands and boyfriends repeatedly called them "dykes" or "whores" as they beat them.[1] I have personally experienced verbal abuse while in the company of a straight friend, who was assumed to be my lover.

Why does it happen? I have no definitive answers to that question. Understanding homophobic violence is no less complex than understanding racial violence. The institutional and ideological reinforcements of homophobia are myriad and deeply woven into our culture. I offer one perspective that I hope will contribute to a better understanding of how homophobia works and why it threatens all that we value as humane.

At the simplest level, looking or behaving like the stereotypical gay man or lesbian is reason enough to provoke a homophobic assault. Beneath the veneer of the effeminate gay male or the butch dyke, however, is a more basic trigger for homophobic violence. I call it *gender betrayal.*

The clearest expression I have heard of this sense of gender betrayal comes from Doug Barr, who was acquitted of murder in an incident of gay bashing in San Francisco that resulted in the death of John O'Connell, a gay man. Barr is currently serving a prison sentence for related assaults on the same night that O'Connell was killed. He was interviewed for a special report on homophobia produced by ABC's *20/20* (10 April 1986). When asked what he and his friends thought of gay men, he said, "We hate homosexuals. They degrade our manhood. We was brought up in a high school where guys are football players, mean and macho. Homosexuals are sissies who wear dresses. I'd rather be seen as a football player."

Doug Barr's perspective is one shared by many young men. I have made about three hundred presentations to high school students in San Francisco, to boards of directors and staff of nonprofit organizations, and at conferences and workshops on the topic of homophobia or "being lesbian or gay." Over and over again, I have asked, "Why do gay men and lesbians bother you?" The most popular response to the question is, "Because they act like girls," or, "Because they think they're men." I have even been told, quite explicitly, "I don't care what they do in bed, but they shouldn't act like that."

They shouldn't act like that. Women who are not identified by their relationship to a man, who value their female friendships, who like and are knowledgeable about sports, or work as blue-collar laborers and wear what they wish are very likely to be "lesbian baited" at some point in their lives. Men who are not pursuing sexual conquests of women at every available opportunity, who disdain sports, who choose to stay at home and be a househusband, who are employed as hairdressers, designers, or housecleaners, or

15

---

[1]See Suzanne Pharr, *Homophobia: A Weapon of Sexism* (Inverness, Calif.: Chardon, 1988). [All notes are Vázquez's.]

who dress in any way remotely resembling traditional female attire (an earring will do) are very likely to experience the taunts and sometimes the brutality of "fag bashing."

The straitjacket of gender roles suffocates many lesbians, gay men, and   20
bisexuals, forcing them into closets without an exit and threatening our very existence when we tear the closet open. It also, however, threatens all heterosexuals unwilling to be bound by their assigned gender identity. Why, then, does it persist?

Suzanne Pharr's examination of homophobia as a phenomenon based in sexism and misogyny offers a succinct and logical explanation for the virulence of homophobia in Western civilization:

> It is not by chance that when children approach puberty and increased sexual awareness they begin to taunt each other by calling these names: "queer," "faggot," "pervert." It is at puberty that the full force of society's pressure to conform to heterosexuality and prepare for marriage is brought to bear. Children know what we have taught them, and we have given clear messages that those who deviate from standard expectations are to be made to get back in line....
>
> To be named as lesbian threatens all women, not just lesbians, with great loss. And any woman who steps out of role risks being called a lesbian. To understand how this is a threat to all women, one must understand that any woman can be called a lesbian and there is no real way she can defend herself: there is no real way to credential one's sexuality. (*The Children's Hour,* a Lillian Hellman play, makes this point when a student asserts two teachers are lesbians and they have no way to disprove it.) She may be married or divorced, have children, dress in the most feminine manner, have sex with men, be celibate—but there are lesbians who do all these things. *Lesbians look like all women and all women look like lesbians.*[2]

I would add that gay men look like all men and all men look like gay men. There is no guaranteed method for identifying sexual orientation. Those small or outrageous deviations we sometimes take from the idealized mystique of "real men" and "real women" place all of us—lesbians, gay men, bisexuals, and heterosexuals alike—at risk of violence, derision, isolation, and hatred.

It is a frightening reality. Dorothy Ehrlich, executive director of the Northern California American Civil Liberties Union (ACLU), was the victim of a verbal assault in the Castro several years ago. Dorothy lives with her husband, Gary, and her two children, Jill and Paul, in one of those worn and comfortable Victorian homes that grace so many San Francisco neighborhoods. Their home is several blocks from the Castro, but Dorothy recalls the many times she and Gary could hear, from the safety of their bedroom, shouts of "faggot" and men running in the streets.

---

[2]Ibid., 17–19.

When Jill was an infant, Gary and Dorothy had occasion to experience for themselves how frightening even the threat of homophobic violence can be. One foggy, chilly night they decided to go for a walk in the Castro. Dorothy is a small woman whom some might call petite; she wore her hair short at the time and delights in the comfort of jeans and oversized wool jackets. Gary is very tall and lean, a bespectacled and bearded cross between a professor and a basketball player who wears jean jackets and tweed jackets with the exact same slouch. On this night they were crossing Castro Street, huddled close together with Jill in Dorothy's arms. As they reached the corner, their backs to the street, they heard a truck rev its engine and roar up Castro, the dreaded "faggot" spewing from young men they could not see in the fog. They looked around them for the intended victims, but there was no one else on the corner with them. They were the target that night: Dorothy and Gary and Jill. They were walking on "gay turf," and it was reason enough to make them a target. "It was so frightening," Dorothy said. "So frightening and unreal."

But it is real. The *20/20* report on homophobia ends with the story of Tom and Jan Matarrase, who are married, have a child, and lived in Brooklyn, New York, at the time of their encounter with homophobic violence. On camera, Tom and Jan are walking down a street in Brooklyn lined with brown townhouses and black wrought-iron gates. It is snowing, and, with hands entwined, they walk slowly down the street where they were assaulted. Tom is wearing a khaki trenchcoat, slacks, and loafers. Snowflakes melt into the tight dark curls on his head. Jan is almost his height, her short bobbed hair moving softly as she walks. She is wearing a black leather jacket, a red scarf, and burnt orange cords. The broadness of her hips and softness of her face belie the tomboy flavor of her carriage and clothes, and it is hard to believe that she was mistaken for a gay man. But she was.

They were walking home, holding hands and engrossed with each   25
other. On the other side of the street, Jan saw a group of boys moving toward them. As the gang approached, Jan heard a distinct taunt meant for her and Tom: "Aw, look at the cute gay couple." Tom and Jan quickened their step, but it was too late. Before they could say anything, Tom was being punched in the face and slammed against a car. Jan ran toward Tom and the car, screaming desperately that Tom was her husband. Fists pummeled her face as well. Outnumbered and in fear for their lives, Tom yelled at Jan to please open her jacket and show their assailants that she was a woman. The beating subsided only when Jan was able to show her breasts.

For the *20/20* interview, Jan and Tom sat in the warmth of their living room, their infant son in Jan's lap. The interviewer asked them how they felt when people said they looked like a gay couple. "We used to laugh," they said. "But now we realize how heavy the implications are. Now we know what the gay community goes through. We had no idea how widespread it was. It's on every level."

Sadly, it *is* on every level. Enforced heterosexism and the pressure to conform to aggressive masculine and passive feminine roles place fag bashers and lesbian baiters in the same psychic prison with their victims, gay or straight. Until all children are free to realize their full potential, until all women and men are free from the stigma, threats, alienation, or violence that come from stepping outside their roles, we are all at risk.

The economic and ideological underpinnings of enforced heterosexism and sexism or any other form of systematic oppression are formidable foes and far too complex for the scope of this essay. It is important to remember, however, that bigots are natural allies and that poverty or the fear of it has the power to seduce us all into conformity. In Castro graffiti, *faggot* appears right next to *nigger* and *kike.* Race betrayal or any threat to the sanctimony of light-skinned privilege engenders no less a rage than gender betrayal, most especially when we have a great stake in the elusive privilege of proper gender roles or the right skin color. *Queer lover* and *fag hag* are cut from the same mold that gave us *nigger lover,* a mold forged by fears of change and a loss of privilege.

Unfortunately, our sacrifices to conformity rarely guarantee the privilege or protection we were promised. Lesbians, gay men, and bisexuals who have tried to pass know that. Heterosexuals who have been perceived to be gay know that. Those of us with a vision of tomorrow that goes beyond tolerance to a genuine celebration of humanity's diversity have innumerable fronts to fight on. Homophobia is one of them.

But how will this front be won? With a lot of help, and not easily. Challenges to homophobia and the rigidity of gender roles must go beyond the visible lesbian and gay movement. Lesbians, gay men, and bisexuals alone cannot defuse the power of stigmatization and the license it gives to frighten, wound, or kill. Literally millions of us are needed on this front, straight and gay alike. We invite any heterosexual unwilling to live with the damage that "real men" or "real women" messages wreak on them, on their children, and on lesbians, gay men, and bisexuals to join us. We ask that you not let queer jokes go unchallenged at work, at home, in the media, or anywhere. We ask that you foster in your children a genuine respect for themselves and their right to be who and what they wish to be, regardless of their gender. We ask that you embrace your daughter's desire to swing a bat or be a carpenter, that you nurture your son's efforts to express affection and sentiment. We ask that you teach your children how painful and destructive words like *faggot* or *bulldyke* are. We ask that you invite your lesbian, gay, and bisexual friends and relatives into the routine of your lives without demanding silence or discretion from them. We invite you to study our history, read the literature written by our people, patronize our businesses, come into our homes and neighborhoods. We ask that you give us your vote when we need it to protect our privacy or to elect open lesbians, gay men, and bisexuals to office. We ask that you stand with us in public demonstra-

30

tions to demand our right to live as free people, without fear. We ask that you respect our dignity by acting to end the poison of homophobia.

Until individuals are free to choose their roles and be bound only by the limits of their own imagination, *faggot, dyke,* and *pervert* will continue to be playground words and adult weapons that hurt and limit far many more people than their intended victims. Whether we like it or not, the romance of virile men and dainty women, of Mother, Father, Dick, Jane, Sally, and Spot is doomed to extinction and dangerous in a world that can no longer meet the expectations conjured by history. There is much to be won and so little to lose in the realization of a world where the dignity of each person is worthy of celebration and protection. The struggle to end homophobia can and must be won, for all our sakes. Personhood is imminent.

ENGAGING THE TEXT

1. Do you think violent events like the ones described above are fairly common or quite rare? How aware of this problem are people in your community? How much attention have you seen paid to gay-bashing in the newspapers, on TV, in books or films, or in everyday conversation?

2. Vázquez waits a while to disclose that "Brian" and "Mickey" were actually straight men, but she *does* disclose this fact. Why does she wait? Why does she disclose it? Does the issue of antigay violence change in any way when we recognize that its victims are sometimes heterosexual?

3. Vázquez cites "gender betrayal" as a possible cause of antigay violence. Explain gender betrayal in your own words; discuss how it works and how well it explains the violence described in the narratives Vázquez recounts.

4. According to Vázquez, Suzanne Pharr links homophobia to misogyny, the hatred of women: the "lesbian" label, she says, can be used to threaten all women. Review and discuss this argument; then discuss how well it can be applied to men, as Vázquez suggests it might be.

5. Besides the threat of physical violence, how does homophobia place us *all* "at risk," according to Vázquez?

EXPLORING CONNECTIONS

6. To what extent does Vázquez's concept of "gender betrayal" (para. 16) explain the attitudes and behavior encountered by Anndee Hochman (p. 45), or Kathleen Boatwright (p. 500)?

7. Imagine that you are Vázquez and that you have just read the preceding essay by Christina Hoff Sommers (p. 479). In the role of Vázquez, write a letter to Sommers proposing an alternative definition of "gender wardens" and explaining how and why you see the issue differently than she does.

8. Vázquez suggests that we are imprisoned by "enforced heterosexism and the pressure to conform to aggressive masculine and passive feminine roles" (para. 27). How might advertising images contribute to this problem,

according to the analyses of Jean Kilbourne (p. 444) and Jackson Katz (p. 466)? What evidence, if any, do you find of ads working against conventional gender identities?

EXTENDING THE CRITICAL CONTEXT

9. Vázquez writes that "the institutional and ideological reinforcements of homophobia are myriad and deeply woven into our culture" (para. 15). Over a period of days, keep track of all references to gays, lesbians, or homosexuality in casual conversations, news reports, TV programs, and other media. To what extent do you agree with Vázquez that homophobia is deeply ingrained in our culture?

10. San Francisco, the city in which some of the incidents described took place, is known as one of the most tolerant in the United States. Research your own community's history of assaults on gay and lesbian people. You might begin by talking to gay and lesbian organizations; police or public health departments may also have pertinent information. Report to the class or write a formal paper presenting your findings.

11. Near the end of her essay, Vázquez lists a variety of ways that individuals can combat homophobia (para. 30). Write a journal entry assessing how easy or how difficult it would be for you to follow each of her suggestions, and why.

The Bridge Builder: Kathleen Boatwright

Eric Marcus

Conservative Christian, mother of four, lesbian activist—Kathleen Boatwright cheerfully defies categories and stereotypes. "The Bridge Builder" recounts the political and spiritual journey that begins for Boatwright when she discovers her sexual orientation and makes the courageous decision to be the person God created her to be. This selection originally appeared in Making History: The Struggle for Gay and Lesbian Equal Rights 1945–1990 *(1992), a collection of oral histories edited by Eric Marcus. A former associate producer for* CBS This Morning *and* Good Morning America, *Marcus (b. 1958) has written many books on gay and lesbian issues, including* Together Forever: Gay and Lesbian Marriage *(1998). He has also coauthored two autobiographies,* Breaking the Surface *(1995) with Olympic diving champion Greg Louganis, and* Ice Breaker *(1997) with figure skater Rudy Galindo.*

Invariably wearing a sensible Sears dress or skirt and jacket, Kathleen Boatwright doesn't look the part of a social activist, as she describes herself. But as vice president of the Western Region of Integrity, the gay and lesbian Episcopal ministry, Kathleen uses her conventional appearance, her status as a mother of four, her Christian roots, her knowledge of the scriptures, and her disarming personal warmth to wage a gentle battle for reform in the church she loves—and to change the hearts and minds of individuals within the church. According to Kathleen, "I see myself uniquely gifted to show people what we do to each other in ignorance."

Kathleen Boatwright's very difficult and painful journey from funda- mentalist Christian, director of the children's choir at her local church, and pillar of her community to Episcopal lesbian activist began one day in Au- gust, 1984, when Jean, a veterinary student at Oregon State University, walked through the door of Kathleen's church in Corvallis, Oregon.

The first time I met Jean, she was having a nice conversation with my fifteen-year-old daughter at our church. I was very impressed by the mature way in which she spoke to my daughter. Then, during the service, I sat in the front row and watched Jean sing. I was so enamored by her presence that she stuck in my mind. But then she left town and was gone until Janu- ary the following year.

Come January, I was sitting in church and I looked across the room, and there was Jean, carrying her guitar, walking down the aisle with such determination. I had this incredible lump in my throat, and I said to myself, *Jean's back.* After the service, and despite my difficulty talking to new people, I just had to ask Jean where she had been. I had to talk to her.

I found out that she was back in Corvallis for five months to finish her degree. She didn't have a place to live. So I said to her, "Don't worry, my parents have always wanted to take in a college student. You're redheaded like Dad. They'll love it!" I went and dragged my mother away from where she was talking and I said, "You remember Jean, she's looking for a place to stay. Why don't you and Dad take her in and board her?"

From early on my parents encouraged the friendship because they saw how much Jean meant to me. Meeting her brought me to life in a way they hadn't seen before. They knew that I used to cry for hours on end when I was a child because no girls liked me at school. My mother would come in and rub my leg or pat my hand. I was extremely intelligent and bright, but I had low self-esteem because I wasn't able to find friendship. So my parents encouraged Jean to invite me to lunch or to take me for a drive or go

5

horseback riding. They felt that her friendship was really wonderful for me. They were glad I was happy. For a while.

My husband didn't pay much attention—at first. He was a state policeman and had always been nonparticipatory, both as a parent and a spouse.

After four months of being friends, of having this wonderful platonic relationship, Jean had to go away for a month for her externship. While she was away she met a fundamentalist couple. Well, Jean sent me a postcard and said, "Something's going on. I'm playing with fire. I can't handle it. I've got to talk to you." My heart wrenched. What was going on?

When we were finally able to meet and talk, Jean explained to me how she and this fundamentalist woman started sharing in an intimate way. My response was to put my arm through hers and say, "Don't worry. We'll get it fixed." Jean couldn't be homosexual because it was wrong. Besides, if she was homosexual, then she would be leaving my life. And I think on a deeper level, I didn't want Jean exploring these things with anyone but me.

After her externship, Jean wanted to be more sensual with me. Her attitude was, "Now I'm going to show *you*." She said, "I'll give you a back rub some night." So one night—after Bible study, no less—she was over at my house and said, "Why don't you lay down on the blanket on the floor and take off your blouse and bra and I'll rub your back?" And I was like, "Okaaay!" My husband was working all night, and this just seemed like a great setup. So this nice little Christian lady rubbed my back, and I said to myself, *Gee, this is it!* 10

All the little pieces, all the little feelings came together. Even comments my mother made to me over the years began to make sense. She'd say things like, "don't cut your hair too short." "You can't wear tailored clothes." It was then that I also realized that the neighbors I had grown up with were a lesbian couple, even though I had never thought about that before. I recalled the feeling of walking through the Waldenbooks bookstore, looking at *The Joy of Lesbian Sex* and longing for that kind of intimacy. It all came upon me at that moment, and I felt a real willingness to release myself to this person in a way I had never done before. Then the phone rang. It was my son from Bible college. I thought, *Oh, God, saved by the bell! I don't know where this would have gone.*

By the end of the month, Jean was graduating, taking her national boards, and trying to figure out what to do about her feelings toward me and what to do about the fundamentalist woman. It was Pentecostal hysteria.

Now don't forget, at this time I still had a husband and four kids. I had a nineteen-year-old son at a conservative Bible college. I had a sixteen-year-old daughter in the evangelical Christian high school, of which I was a board member. Two children were in parochial day school. My father was the worship leader at church. And I was still very bound to my parents for emotional support. I was the favorite child. And my grandparents lived in town.

Well, shit, I was in way over my head. I was really painted into a corner because there wasn't a single place I could turn for even questioning. So I started looking to some Christian sources. Some of the advice was so incredible, like, "If you feel homosexual tendencies, you can't have the person you have those feelings for over to your house in the evening." "You can never let a member of the same sex sit on your bed while you're chatting." "Meet only in a public place." I thought this advice was ridiculous, but I also thought it was my only option because my spiritual nature was more important than my physical nature. Intellectually and emotionally, I was so hungry and so turned on that I didn't know what to do with my feelings.

At this point, people pull the trigger, turn to the bottle, take drugs, 15 leave town. But I didn't do any of those things because I was madly in love. If I had pulled the trigger, I wouldn't have been able to express the part of me I had discovered. I had found someone, someone who shared the same sort of values I had.

Everything reached a crisis point. I acknowledged to myself and to Jean that I was a lesbian and that I loved her. By this time we had already been sexually active. My husband began to get suspicious that something was going on, and he and I went into counseling. Jean was leaving for a job in Colorado and told me that I couldn't go with her because she was a responsible woman and didn't want to destroy my family. And I still hadn't yet found the spiritual guidance that I needed.

I had to get away and do some soul-searching. I needed to figure out if there was any Christian support somewhere that said I could reconcile my love for Jean and my love for my faith. I didn't feel I could build a life of love if I rejected my faith. So I packed my bags and told my parents that I was leaving to go to stay with my great-aunt in Los Angeles for ten days. I told my husband, "I am going to get away and I'm going to think about a bunch of issues, and then I'm coming back."

For the first time in my entire life, at the age of thirty-six, I was by myself with my own agenda. I had left my husband, my children, my parents, my support structures; got in a car; and started driving to West Hollywood, where I knew there was a lesbian mayor and a gay community. So surely, I thought, there had to be a spiritual gay community.

In West Hollywood I found Evangelicals Together. It's not a church, just a storefront ministry to the gay community for people coming out of an evangelical Christian background. It's led by a former American Baptist minister who talked my language. He said to me, "In order to deal with your dilemma, you have to take a step back from your relationship with Jean. Lay her aside and ask yourself, *Who did God create me to be?*"

Through our sharing, and by looking from a different perspective at the 20 gospel and what Jesus had to say, I could embrace the theology that said, "God knew me before I was born. He accepted me as I was made to be, uniquely and wholly." Ultimately, in an obedience to God, you answer that call to be all that He has created you to be. I felt firmly and wholly that what

I had experienced with Jean was no demonic possession, was not Satan tempting me with sins of lust, but an intimacy and a love that was beautiful and was God given. So now I had to figure out how to deal with it.

When you're my age, you're either going to go back to the way it's always been—go for the security you've always known—or take a chance. I felt that for the love I felt for Jean I was willing to risk all. Of course, having Jean there, I was hedging my bet a bit. I was jumping off a cliff, but I was holding somebody's hand.

Jean flew down a few days later to join me in Los Angeles. She agreed to commit to me and I to her. The first Sunday after we affirmed our relationship, we worshiped at All Saints' Episcopal Church in Pasadena because I was told that the Episcopals had the framework of faith I loved, as well as an ability to use reason in light of tradition and scripture.

It was God answering the cry of my heart to send me to that worshiping place. Jean and I had never been to an Episcopal church before. We went into this beautiful place with the largest Episcopal congregation west of the Mississippi River. We sat in the fourth row. It was just this incredible Gothic wonderful place. It was All Saints' Day at All Saints' Church. They played the Mozart Requiem with a full choir and a chamber ensemble, and a female celebrant sang the liturgy. We held hands and wept and wept. We could go forward because in the Anglican tradition, the Eucharist is open for everyone. God extends himself. There are no outcasts in the Episcopal church.

When I got back to town, I met with my husband at a counselor's office. I said, "Yes, you're right. I am gay and I'm going to ask for a divorce. I'm going to take this stand. I want to meet with my older children and my parents to talk about the decisions I've made." I felt at least I had a right to make my own decisions. I went to pick up my two youngest girls at my father's house. I went to open the door and I heard a flurry of activity, and the children saw me. "Oh, Mommy's home! Mommy's home!" And my dad stepped out on the front porch and pushed the children away and slammed the door. He took me forcibly by the arm and led me down the stairs and said, "You're never seeing your children again without a court order! Just go shack up with your girlfriend!" And he forced me down to the street.

It took going to court to see my two youngest children. They hadn't seen me for two weeks. They asked, "Mommy, Mommy, what's wrong?" I leaned over and whispered in their ears, "Mommy loves you." My husband wanted to know, "What are you telling the children?" I had only a minute with them, then went downstairs, and my husband told me that he wanted me to come back, that he would be my brother, not my husband.

I tell you, my whole world came down upon my ears. I wasn't allowed to see my children. I was denied access to my residence. The church had an open prayer meeting disclosing my relationship with Jean. They tried to get Jean fired from her job. And when that didn't work, they called Jean's parents, who then tried to have her committed or have me arrested. My family physically disinherited me and emotionally cut me off. My older daughter, upon the advice of her counselor-pastor, shook my hand and said, "Thank you for being my biological mother. I never want to have anything to do with you again." After that, whenever she saw me in town, she hid from me. I saw her lay flat on the asphalt in the grocery store parking lot so I wouldn't see her. People I'd known all my life avoided me like I had the plague. I was surprised that Jean didn't just say, "Hey, lady, I'm out of here!"

Fortunately, I wasn't entirely without support. I went to Parents and Friends of Lesbians and Gays and I met some wonderful loving, Christian, supportive parents and gay children who said, "You're not sick. You're not weird. Everybody's hysterical." They offered any kind of assistance possible. Through their emotional support, I felt like it was possible to survive the crush.

Living in a small rural county in Oregon, I didn't know anything about women's rights, let alone gay rights. So it's not surprising that I bought into the lie that children of lesbians or gays are better off living with the custodial heterosexual parent. I believed my husband could provide a sense of normality that I could not. So I signed away my custodial rights and became a secondary parent. After being the primary-care parent for twenty devoted years, the judge only let me see the children two days a week.

By then I'd had enough. So I packed one suitcase and a few things in grocery sacks and left my family and children behind. Jean and I just rode quietly out of town in the sunset to her job in Denver, Colorado.

As you drive into Denver, you go over this big hill about fifteen miles   30 from town. We stopped at a phone booth and called the local Parents FLAG president to ask if there was a supportive Episcopal parish in town. She said, "Yes, go to this place, look up this person." It was getting to be evening. It was clear, and we were going over the mountain. It was a whole new adventure. It was real closure to my past and a real opening toward my future. Still, the guiding force in my life was, "The church has the answers."

Jean and I called the church and found out when services were and asked if they had an Integrity chapter. Integrity is the Episcopal ministry to the gay and lesbian community. There was one, so two nights later we walked into our first Integrity meeting. There were twelve attractive men in their thirties and the rector. They were shocked to see two women because it's unusual for women to be in Integrity. The only thing dirtier than being a lesbian in a Christian community is being a Christian in the lesbian community because it brings in so many other issues besides sexual orientation, like women's issues and patriarchy and all that stuff.

Denver Integrity was an affirming congregation. We were out as a couple. We were healed of so many things through the unconditional love and acceptance of this parish of eighty people. The rector there encouraged me to become involved. Out of his own pocket he sent me to the first regional convention I went to, in 1987 in San Francisco. Now, I'm vice president of the Western Region for Integrity, and I'm on the national board of directors, I'm one of only maybe 125 women in Integrity's membership of about 1,500.

Integrity gives me a forum for the things I want to say, both as a lesbian woman and as a committed Christian. And because of my background and experience, I can speak to the church I love on a variety of issues that others cannot. I can say, "I call you into accountability. You are bastardizing children raised in nontraditional households. You're not affirming the people that love and guide them. You say you welcome us, but on the other hand you don't affirm us. You don't give us rites of passage and ritual and celebration like you do for heterosexual families."

The church needs to change. What we're asking for are equal *rites*. We're asking the church to bless same-sex unions. I'm asking for canonical changes that affirm my wholeness as a child of Christ who is at the same time in a loving committed relationship with a woman. We're also challenging the church to make statements asking the government to legitimize our relationships and give us the same sorts of tax breaks, pension benefits, et cetera. But most importantly, we need the church to get off the dime and start affirming gay and lesbian children's lives. I never want a girl to go through what I went through. I want to spare everybody right up front.

To get my point across when I go out and talk to groups as a representative of Integrity, I personalize the issue. I personalize my political activism by speaking to people as a person, as Kathleen Boatwright. People don't need to hear dogma or doctrine or facts or theology. They need to meet people.   35

Here's a great example. For the first time, the women of Integrity got seated at Triennial, which is this gigantic group of very traditional women who have a convention every three years. It used to be that while the men were making the decisions, the women held their own convention. With women's issues having changed so dramatically in the Episcopal church, that's no longer true. Now that women are allowed to serve in the House of Deputies and can be ordained into the priesthood, we've become full team members in the canonical process.

Triennial was made for me. Everybody wears their Sears Roebuck dress. Everybody is a mom. Everybody lived like I had lived for twenty years. I know how to network and how to deal with those women. But I also have a new truth to tell them that will have an impact on their lives in very special ways. Gays and lesbians are 10 percent of the population. Everybody is personally affected by that issue, including these women at Triennial.

During the convention, I attended a seminar given by conservative Episcopals who said gays and lesbians have confused gender identity. Later, we had an open meeting in which we talked about human sexuality. But no one talked about sexuality. Instead, we only talked about information on biological reproduction. After about forty minutes of hearing these women drone on, I stood up in my Sears Roebuck dress and said, "OK ladies, put on your seat belts because you're going to take a trip into reality. You won't want to hear it, but I need to say it because you need to know what people's lives are really like."

I talked to them about my journey. I talked to them about the misnomers, about "confused gender identity." I was wearing this circle skirt and I said, "As you can see from my appearance," and I curtsied, "I do not have a 'confused gender identity.'" Everybody who had been really stiff started laughing—and they started listening. The key is that I take risks. I risk being vulnerable. I risk sharing the secrets of my heart. We already know what the straight people feel in their hearts. But no one talks about how the lesbian or gay person feels in his or her heart.

For the next hour and a half, people talked about where they really live. They talked about their pregnant teenagers or the suicide attempts in their families. All those gut-level issues. But you have to have someone lead you to that. That's me—because I'm safe. I've also learned that instead of having all the answers, that God calls me to listen to people's pain, and not to judge it.

This one woman told me that she had been driving by her daughter's house for eight years and that her husband had never let her stop because her daughter was a lesbian. "But," she said, "I'm going to go home and I'm going to see her. My daughter's name is also Kathleen." Then she started to cry. She had never even told the women from her church about what had happened to her daughter. It's like the living dead for many Christian families. They just have a child who is lost prematurely in so many senses of the word.

Inevitably, everywhere I go I hear about parents who have made ultimatums. This one mother said, "I've never told anybody, but I said to my son, 'I wish you were dead.' And by forcing him into the closet, I fulfilled that prophecy. Three years later, he was dead." Then there was a woman who said to me, "Kathleen, I'm questioning my sexuality at seventy. Could you send me some information?"

I think in my heart that I represent the hidden majority of lesbian women because many, many are married or have been married, have children, and have too much to risk—like I've risked and lost—to come out. And those women who are out, who are much more political and aggressive, have seen enough successes happen, enough bridges built by my approach, that they're beginning to respect the fact that I can go through doors they never can.

The first time I spoke publicly to the leadership of the women of the church, I spoke along with another lesbian. She was politically correct and a strong feminist. *Feminist* was always a dirty word for me, so I've had to overcome a lot of my own bias. I said to her, "Please don't speak about politics. Don't browbeat these people. Stand up and say that you're a doctor,

40

that you've never been in a committed relationship, that you're a feminist. Because I want to stand up and say, 'I've been a Blue Bird leader.' What that will say is that we represent the gamut of human experience, just like the heterosexual community. It's just our ability to develop intimate relationships with the same sex that makes us different."

People don't have to identify with my ideology. They identify with my   45
person, and then the questions come from them. We don't have to tell them. They start asking us. People say to me, "What do you call your partner?" "You don't have any medical insurance?" To me that's the best sort of teaching process: answering questions rather than giving information.

My husband remarried; he married the baby-sitter. At Easter of 1987, I got a call informing me that he had removed my ten-year-old daughter from his house, accusing her of using "inappropriate touch" with his new stepsons. He wanted to unload the difficult child. Then he used that child as a weapon to try and deny me visitation for the younger one. The end result was that I had one child and he had one child. I filed suit against him without any hope or prayer of winning back custody of my other child.

I went to a lesbian minister to ask her about finding a lawyer to handle my case, and she said to me, "The best attorney in this town is Hal Harding,

but he's your husband's attorney. Maybe that will prove to be a blessing." So I had to find another attorney.

As part of the custody proceedings, Jean and I eventually met with my husband's attorney. He took depositions and asked Jean and me really heartfelt questions. Then he advised his client—my ex-husband—to go ahead and have a psychological evaluation. The court had not ordered it and, in fact, would not order it because there was no precedent in that county. But my former husband agreed to go to the psychologist of his choice. That psychologist, a woman, took the time and energy to interview every person involved and recommended to the court that Jean and I become custodial parents. We now have custody of both children, sole custody. It was indeed a blessing.

We just added Jean's ninety-one-year-old grandmother to our family. So we are all-American lesbians living here in Greenacres, Washington. We are Miss and Mrs. America living together. The thing that we need in our life now that our faith doesn't give us is a community of supportive women. We have yet to find that place.

Not long ago, I went to the National Organization for Women lesbian 50 rights agenda meeting and gave a workshop on spirituality for women, from the Christian perspective. And I took a deep breath in my Betty Crocker suit—if I ever write a book it's going to be *The Radicalization of Betty Crocker*—and thought, *I wonder what the Assemblies of God girls would say now? From their perspective, I'm walking into the total pit of hell, and I'm bringing the very gift that they should be giving.* Who would have believed it?

ENGAGING THE TEXT

1. What family, religious, and cultural bonds initially restrained Boatwright from acknowledging her sexuality? What were her options? How do you think she should have reacted when she realized that she was attracted to Jean? Why?

2. In what different ways does Boatwright's emerging lesbian identity change her and her life? What price does she pay?

3. How do Boatwright's attitudes toward the church develop during her story? How does her self-image change?

4. How do you interpret the title of this oral history? In what different senses is Boatwright a "bridge builder"?

5. From the information available about her past, write a brief character sketch of Boatwright, tracing the development of her personality from childhood through the occasion of this oral history.

EXPLORING CONNECTIONS

6. Write an imaginary conversation among Boatwright, Paula Gunn Allen (p. 433), and Christina Hoff Sommers (p. 479) about whether women continue to be oppressed in American society and about the role of religion in liberating or subordinating women.

7. To what extent does Boatwright's experience support Carmen Vázquez's (p. 492) assertion that "the straitjacket of gender roles suffocates many lesbians, gay men, and bisexuals, forcing them into closets without an exit and threatening our very existence when we tear the closet open" (para. 20)? What resources finally enable Boatwright to survive and thrive despite the open hostility of her family and community?

8. What flaws of logic does the cartoon on page 508 reveal in the speaker's antigay position? Why does the cartoonist depict both figures as relatively featureless?

EXTENDING THE CRITICAL CONTEXT

9. Browse the press releases and news postings about religion and lesbian/gay issues on one or more of the following Web sites:

> Parents and Friends of Lesbians and Gays (www.pflag.org)
>
> Integrity (www.integrityusa.org)
>
> Interfaith Working Group (www.iwgonline.org)
>
> Universal Fellowship of Metropolitan Community Churches (www.ufmcc.com)

Summarize your findings about how various religious groups are responding to questions about gay marriage, gay clergy, and violence against lesbians and gay men.

Girls Have All the Power: What's Troubling Troubled Boys

SUSAN FALUDI

Are American men in crisis? In a culture that equates manhood with power and dominance, men in the last fifty years have had to contend with cultural forces—war, recession, corporate restructuring, suburban isolation, new technology, consumerism, and media hype—that seem hell-bent on demonstrating that they aren't in control of their own lives. Described as "the story of a feminist's travels through a postwar male realm," Susan Faludi's Stiffed: The Betrayal of the American Man *(1999) traces the lives of these men as they struggle to come to terms with the limits of their power. In this passage from the book, Faludi reports from "ground zero of the American masculinity crisis," the suburban home of the Spur Posse, a group of high school boys whose competitive sex games briefly attracted the attention of the police and the media. Stiffed is in a sense a companion volume to her influential book* Backlash: The Undeclared War Against American Women *(1991). A Pulitzer Prize–winning journalist, Faludi (b. 1959) is a contributing editor for* Newsweek: *she has also written for the* Wall Street Journal, *the* New York Times, The Nation, Esquire, *and* The New Yorker.

We Could've Been Big

It was long past lunchtime on a weekday in early October, but Kris Belman had been awake for only a couple of hours. The nineteen-year-old with the dazed, shaggy surfer looks had risen, as was his custom, at noon. He had nowhere in particular to go. He had graduated from high school the previous spring—the spring of 1993—though he wouldn't get his diploma until he paid a $44 fine for ripping his football jersey. "I'm only paying it if I get my jersey back," he said. He hadn't been able to find a job, except for "picking up scraps for this guy who hangs dry wall," and that only lasted three days. In Lakewood, a bedroom community built to house tens of thousands of McDonnell Douglas workers, and later workers at aerospace firms like Rockwell (now closed) and nearby Northrop and Hughes (where thousands were being laid off), not to speak of all the companies that once supplied and serviced them, there was little work left to justify getting out of bed.[1]

He was home alone; his father, a salesman for an aerospace vendor whose prime contractor was McDonnell Douglas, was out and his mother had moved out after his parents' separation earlier that year. His older brother was off wandering, probably in search of gambling "action." Kris Belman stepped into a pair of baggy shorts and ventured forth into the flat grid of stucco-over-chicken-wire pillbox houses and browning lawns, looking for signs of life. The sidewalks were empty, shades drawn against the hard, biscuit sun that baked this suburb southeast of Los Angeles. The nearly identical houses, their foundations only a foot deep, dug by a bucket excavator in a mere fifteen minutes, had been thrown up in a hurry to create this virtually all-white town in the early 1950s—as many as a hundred a day, 17,500 homes in under three years, the biggest housing project American had ever seen. On the day the homes went on the market in April 1950, *Time* reported thirty thousand people "stampeded" to lay their claim. Only a few furnished models had been built, but that didn't stop more than six

---

[1]Patt Morrison, "Farewell to Arms," *Los Angeles Times,* Dec. 5, 1993, p. A1; James F. Peltz, "As Defense Cuts Deepen, Southern California's Aerospace Industry Is Down but Not Out," *Los Angeles Times,* Sept. 26, 1993, p. D1. [All notes are the author's, except 10 and 12.]

hundred customers that week from buying one of the eight- to nine-thousand-dollar units with automatic garbage disposals, stainless-steel kitchens, and picture windows. "The City as New as Tomorrow" was the development's motto. It was a slogan that the city's founders evidently approached with some uneasiness: as Lakewood author and city official D. J. Waldie observed in *Holy Land,* his poetic, ambivalent paean to his hometown, one of the town's first ordinances declared all forms of fortune-telling illegal.[2]

Kris Belman gravitated, as did much of Lakewood's young male populace, toward the parks. As a community, Lakewood had been designed to serve the aerospace sons. A network of small parks was built so that a baseball diamond and football field would be within reach of every boy—and they could walk to them on special service roads shielded from traffic. Park sports leagues were inaugurated in the late 1950s.[3]

The aerospace fathers were at a loss to explain to their sons what they did at work, much less to pass down a "mastery" of such bureaucratic duties. The park was where father-coaches transmitted their knowledge to son-players, and where the sons got the idea that such knowledge would be useful to them on the road past childhood. By the empty bleachers, Kris ran into Jimmy Rafkin and Shad Blackman, buddies from high school; Jimmy was aimlessly swinging a strip of discarded plywood as if at an invisible ball. Kris and Jimmy had played together on the football team. Shad had only made the badminton squad. Kris said he wasn't doing anything and they said they weren't doing anything either, and after a while they decided they might as well do nothing together at the Belman house. The three trooped down the service road and up the drive, all in identical plaid shorts with elastic waistbands — "for easy access," as Shad Blackman liked to say.

Kris headed like a homing pigeon for the television, which he liked to have tuned at all times to the white noise of MTV. Jimmy had a shoebox under his arm. He now placed it lovingly on the couch and opened the lid with a flourish. "Check this out, dude," Shad said to Kris in a rare state of enthusiasm. "Reeboks. Jimmy got 'em for thirty-eight bucks instead of forty-five, because the box was marked wrong." They were all pleased with this minor scam and the story of the mislabeled box had to be repeated several times before it was wrung dry of sweet triumph. Then they were ready for lunch. And lucky for them, since only Jimmy had any money from "working occasionally" at a ship-repair company where his dad was a supervisor, I was buying. Chili's, a fast-food Mexican franchise by the Lakewood mall, was their eatery of choice.

5

[2]D. J. Waldie, *Holy Land* (New York: W. W. Norton, 1996), pp. 7, 37, 41, 62, 158; "Birth of a City," *Time,* April 17, 1950, p. 99. See also Joan Didion, "Trouble in Lakewood," *The New Yorker,* July 26, 1993, p. 46.

[3]Waldie, *Holy Land,* pp. 49, 176.

They tumbled into the vinyl banquette, poking and elbowing each other and talking loudly about "whipping out our fake IDs," and how "I may be nineteen but this afternoon I'm twenty-three." An oblivious and chirpy-voiced waitress jotted down their drink orders without comment: three strawberry margaritas.

"She wants me, dude, I can tell," Shad said as the waitress disappeared to get their drinks. "I could hit on her, easy."

Kris leaned toward me. "See, that's what I mean. We can have any girl we want. Girls come daily to my friends; we don't have to *force* 'em. There's a gang of fish in the sea." He shot me a sly look. "There's one sitting right next to me."

"What I don't understand is why girls have so much say, you know?" Shad put in. "They can lie, you know, and just get anybody in trouble. Like you," he said, jabbing a butter knife in my direction. "Right now anything could happen and you could get us in trouble."

"How exactly?" I said.

"Well, this is just 'for instance,' right? Say, like we're driving and just fooling around or whatever, and say you hated the way we acted or whatever, say you totally despised us. You could go back and publish something like 'They tried to hit on me, blah, blah, blah.' Your say is bigger than ours. You know what I'm saying?"

Their burritos arrived and they dived in like they hadn't eaten in days. "Could we get some more of this cheese and salsa?" Shad asked plaintively. "Or do they charge you extra?" For all their swagger, the boys seemed a bit shaky on the basics of restaurant dining.

Jimmy picked up Shad's point. "Like Kris went out with this girl last night. She could say, 'Oh, he raped me,' or whatever, and no questions asked, automatically — "

"Automatically," Shad jumped in, "they'll throw you in jail just to find out if you did it. Girls can say whatever they want and it's believed. I just don't understand why they have so much pull, you know?"

Kris chimed in: "Girls have the power to have sex with somebody if they want to. They have the power. If you hear a girl scream, are you going to come running? Yep. But if you hear a guy scream, who comes running? Nobody."

Shad fished a maraschino cherry from Jimmy's drained glass. He chewed on the stem, still stewing about the unjust fate of his generation. "My dad did the same thing when he was young, a couple girls, one-night stands. It was no big deal. And now it's — after the Tyson thing, you know, it's been getting worse."

"Wait a second," Kris cut in. "What Tyson did, that's rape, dude. That's what I consider it. But a girl having sex with up to seven guys a night, daily, and then she turns around and — "

Was he talking about an actual girl? I ask.

10

15

"I'm talking about this girl who gave it up with seven people a night, I heard," Kris said. "And with her dad right there in the other room."

"I think they just were out to get us," Jimmy said.   20

"I'm glad to see girls get more authority in the world," Shad said magnanimously. "But it's like they already got enough authority when it comes to, you know ..." He made a thrusting motion with his butter knife. "Girls are like, I dunno, they're going to start getting up their courage in a couple years and going head to head with the guys. Fighting 'em and shit. And girls are going to have to get knocked out. That's how it's going to be, dude."

Jimmy giggled. Shad's remarks had jogged a memory. "It's funny. This girl, she got in a fight with her boyfriend. And this guy we know, he came by and started beating up her boyfriend. And then she came and started hitting *him* and everything. So he punched her."

"Punched her in the mouth," Shad interjected.

"So what happened?" I asked.

"Nothing for publication," Jimmy said.   25

Shad jumped back in. "See? There, right there, you can say, 'Oh, they hit girls.' That's your word over our word. And your word wins every time."

We drove back to the Belmans', my car radio blasting as loud as the boys could crank it. "Hey dude, did you taste how she put more alcohol in the second round of margaritas?" Shad said. "That girl definitely liked us. We shoulda hit on her." Kris jerked his thumb out the window at a passing young woman. "There's that girl who hates me."

From the backseat, Shad made obscene grunting noises.

"She called the cops on me and shit," Kris said.

"See," Shad said, leaning over the seat and tapping me insistently on   30
the shoulder. "See what I mean? Girls have all the power."

For several years in the mid-1990s the Belman boys and their teenage friends, a.k.a. the Spur Posse, had given form to America's suspicion that its male culture was misogynistic and violent, and that its boys were running amok. Their reign in the spotlight began on March 18, 1993, when the police showed up at Lakewood High School and arrested eight Spur Posse members (and one more boy over the weekend) on suspicion of nearly twenty counts of sexual crimes, ranging from rape to unlawful sexual intercourse to lewd conduct with a ten-year-old girl. In the end, the prosecutor's office concluded that the sex was consensual and all but one count were dropped. One boy spent less than a year in a juvenile rehabilitation center on the lewd conduct charge; the other eight Spurs were released after only a week.[4] The only serious jail time was served by Kris Belman's older brother, Dana, the founder of the Spurs, but that wasn't for sexual assault.

---

[4]David Ferrell, "One of 9 Students to Be Charged in Campus Sex Case," *Los Angeles Times*, March 23, 1993, p. A1; Robin Abcarian, "Spur Posse Case: The Same Old (Sad) Story," *Los Angeles Times*, April 7, 1993, p. E1.

He was sentenced to ten years in state prison on thirteen burglary and fraud convictions, most notably for stealing a young woman's credit card and racking up charges during a gambling binge in the Dunes Hotel in Las Vegas.[5] Nonetheless, the subsequent strutting and bragging of the boys, as they cut as comprehensive a swath through the TV talk shows as they had through their high-school yearbook, earned their hometown the moniker of "Rapewood."[6] They mugged on the front page of the *New York Times;* they posed everywhere from *Newsweek* to *Sassy* to *Penthouse;* and for a while in the spring of 1993, it was difficult to flip the channels without running into one Spur or another chatting up a television personality. The local paper, the *Long Beach Press-Telegram,* ran boxed announcements listing their upcoming television spots, under such headlines as POSSE PREMIERE and THE SPUR POSSE ON TV.[7] Most of the Spurs interviewed on the talk shows weren't the ones arrested, but it didn't seem to matter, as long as they were willing to elaborate on (or embellish) their sexual exploits. And they were.

Tirelessly they repeated the details of a Spur Posse "game" that had riveted the media. It was a sex-for-points intramural contest in which each time you had sex with a girl, which they called "hooking up," you racked up a point. You had to achieve penetration and you could only get one point per girl. "It doesn't count if you have, like, sex with a girl, like one hundred and fifty times, two hundred—that's only *one* point," as the Spurs' Kevin Howard took pains to clarify on *The Jenny Jones Show.*[8] When your points added up to the corresponding number on some sports star's jersey, you could then claim that player's name as your own, and the other Spurs would address you as, say, Dave Robinson of the San Antonio Spurs—the basketball player who had unwittingly inspired the posse's name. (Dana Belman was a Robinson fan, and when the Spurs signed Robinson, Belman and his buddies signed up too in the only way they knew how: they went to a sporting-goods store and bought Spurs caps.) This game had only one real winner, of course, the Spur with the most points. And for four years running that was Billy Shehan, with a final score of 67. . . . [9]

Their place in the national eye had transformed the Spurs into permanent celebrities, at least in their own minds. "You'll recognize me," Jeff

[5]Janet Wiscombe, "Visit to a Shattered Home," *Long Beach Press-Telegram,* Feb. 3, 1994, p. 8; "Alleged Founder of Spur Posse Sentenced in Burglary," *Los Angeles Times,* Jan. 7, 1994, p. B2; Andy Rose and G. M. Bush, "Founder of Spur Posse Already Facing Numerous Charges," *Long Beach Press-Telegram,* March 21, 1993, p. A1.

[6]Amy Cunningham, "Sex in High School," *Glamour,* Sept. 1993, p. 253.

[7]"Posse Premiere," *Long Beach Press-Telegram,* April 2, 1993, p. A8; "The Spur Posse on TV," *Long Beach Press-Telegram,* April 6, 1993, p. A6.

[8]*The Jenny Jones Show,* April 7, 1993.

[9]Amy Cunningham, "Sex in High School," p. 254; Jane Gross, "Where 'Boys Will Be Boys,' and Adults Are Bewildered," *New York Times,* March 29, 1993, p. A1; Jennifer Allen, "Boys: Hanging with the Spur Posse," *Rolling Stone,* July 8–22, 1993, p. 55; "Sex for Points Scandal," *The Jane Whitney Show,* April 1, 1993.

Howard said as we arranged by phone to meet just before Christmas 1993. "I was on *Maury Povich*."

When I arrived at Coco's, another of the Spurs' preferred dining establishments when someone else was picking up the bill, Howard had brought along a few of his Spur buddies—all twelve of them. The Spurs, as I was to learn, rarely traveled solo. The waitresses had to drag together four tables, and the Spurs took their places ceremonially as if attending a high-school varsity awards banquet. Only none of them were in high school anymore.

It was, in fact, almost a reunion, as Howard informed me when I first   35 walked in. He pointed out a slight boy, who at sixteen seemed barely pubescent, with scared, shadowy eyes that darted nervously around the room. He was the Spur who had been sent to the Kirby Juvenile Detention Center for lewd conduct with a ten-year-old girl. He had been released for a family visit, supposedly to the custody of relatives. But here he was, parentless in Coco's.

I passed a notebook around so the Spurs could write down their names. The nervous boy of honor perched next to me. I told him I wouldn't be identifying him because of his juvenile record, and he asked if he could go by a pseudonym of his choosing. "You could call me the Lost Boy," he said softly. I could see why. He lacked the brazen cockiness one would expect from the posse's lone decorated war hero, on leave from the juvy-hall front. "They called me 'pretty boy' at Kirby," he said in a low, flat voice. "They thought I was wimpish." He looked around furtively, then stared down at his place mat as I asked him questions. He answered passively but dutifully, in a dull monotone, describing one of his sexual encounters as if it were a story that belonged to someone else.

"She gave me oral copulation," he said bureaucratically. "Then I never saw her again." He stopped, waiting for further direction. Well, how did he happen to be in this girl's room? "I went there with two other guys," he went on in his mechanical tone, "and she sucked one of the guys' dicks and my dick."

"She's a whore," one of the boys shouted across the table.

"I heard she's been picked up for prostitution," the Lost Boy said, and then, as if that weren't outlandish enough, he added, "twice."

"She was seen at parties," Jeff Howard said, then delivered the coup de   40 grâce. "She was seen drinking beer."

The Lost Boy returned to his story. "The girl was giving me oral copulation for twenty minutes. Usually, it takes me only a couple of minutes, but it was—I guess I was feeling good, but—it wasn't..." He struggled to put a word to the particular state of mind he had found himself in that evening. "I was bored," he said finally. "I didn't want to sit there all night." He stopped.

So what finally happened? I asked.

"Ten minutes later, I pulled up my pants and left. I called my oldest brother to pick me up. Dana [Belman], I mean. I call Dana 'my oldest brother.' Another guy kept fucking her."

When I asked him about the incident with the ten-year-old girl that had landed him in jail, he said, "If I didn't admit it, maybe nothing would've happened to me either."

But something *did* happen, I said; he had a sexual encounter with a   45
ten-year-old.

"I didn't know how old she was. She had a body and everything. I just seen her at parties. I didn't even know her name."

"Points" king Billy Shehan, who was the unofficial philosopher of the Spurs, leaned across the table. "These girls are *no-names*. We've got a *name*." He gestured around the table. "That's why you're talking to us. It's all about brand names."

This seemed a strange segue from an appalling account of an appalling sexual episode, but once the subject of developing a "name" was introduced, there was no getting off it. "We could've been big," Kris Belman said. "If we had just got the right contacts."

"We're all into communication," Billy Shehan said.

"I want to be an actor, or a model," Jimmy Rafkin said. "I want fame   50
that way."

"I want to be a DJ at my own station," Kris Belman said. "Or a big-time comedian. When I was little, I wanted to play sports. That was my dream. Now, I want to move to Vegas, crack a joke at some casino and hopefully somebody will hear me. I've seen a lot of those guys on all the shows, like HBO—Eddie Murphy, [Andrew] Dice Clay. I just want to be up there with the big boys. Someday I think I might."

Billy Shehan summed up the exchange. "See, brand names are very important. It's like having Guess jeans on instead of some no-name pair."

The Lost Boy sat very still next to me, soaking up the swirl of voices. He didn't seem to mind their interrupting his story. I asked him why he'd been lewd with a ten-year-old. "There are only so many girls," he replied. "You had to have girls to hook up with. I had started keeping track of my points. So, if it's three girls and three guys, and say I had sex with one, after I finish, I'll say, 'Can we switch off?' and most of the time, the girls say yes. Sometimes they say no. And then you say, 'Can I have a phone number?' I never forced a girl. I looked at myself highly. I looked at it like they are passing up something great." These last remarks were delivered dully into the place mat, as if he were reading from a boilerplate script, auditioning for a character he didn't believe in.

"We tell a girl, we don't want to waste our time," he continued. "We don't want to waste time romancing."

Why have sex with girls you don't want to "waste time with" anyway,   55
girls who leave you "bored"?

He looked directly at me for the first time. "For the points," he said. "You *had* to have the points. I was developing my reputation. I was developing my *name*." It occurred to me that maybe Billy Shehan hadn't changed the subject after all.

The most fun they ever had, the Lost Boy told me, was when they would videotape themselves having sex with one of the girls. "Once, three of us were in the closet spying," he recalled. "We opened the door, and we took pictures and videos. It was funny. We could sell the video, but who would buy it?"

Billy Shehan began a story about the time he and another Spur had a porn movie playing while they took turns having sex with a girl and he began copying the moves he saw in the movie. "It felt like I was *in* the movie," he said, and that sensation was so gratifying that the next night he replayed it, this time with four Spurs in attendance. The night after that, he gathered ten Spurs—and a video camera. "We made a porn film of it," he said. "It was great."

But for all that, there was a strange affectlessness to the way he and other Spurs told their sex stories, a boredom that seemed to drop away only with the introduction of a video camera. Their sexual exploits evidently had less to do with the act itself than with being, themselves, an act.

That night, the boys would reconvene for a party at a Spur home, se- [60] lected because the parents were away. Spur parties were all the same: a blackjack game in one corner, a stereo blasting rap music (in this case, Public Enemy), and a circle of bodies collapsed around the television. But this party, like the Coco's luncheon, was a special event. They had gathered to watch themselves on *The Tonight Show*. Well, Billy Shehan conceded, they weren't really "on" the program. A few of them had managed to get passes to be in the audience for Howard Stern's appearance on the show. "We got this girl who works for KSLX to get us in.... We were yelling so hard, 'Spur Posse loves you, Howard!'" Shehan said. "I think he heard us. I know he did."

A Spur sporting a clash of logos—Spurs cap, Dodgers shirt, and Georgetown athletic shorts—sauntered up to Billy. "Hey dude, how'd you get on Jay Leno?" Billy explained. "And of course," he said, "there's the factor of our sales. It's good for marketability to have us in the audience." Advancing the Spurs "brand name" was the ultimate goal. "You gotta get your image out there. It's all about building that image on a worldwide basis."

Earlier, Kris Belman had filled me in on his fruitless efforts at Spur promotion in Hollywood. "You know Mickey Rourke, the actor? One of his roommates called us up, this guy Kizzy, I don't know his full name. And we went to visit his loft in Hollywood." (Rourke's publicist told me that while the actor does have a loft, he has no roommate named Kizzy.) "We didn't see Mickey Rourke, but I guess he told Kizzy to call us. Kizzy and some guys took us to pizza a couple of times. He took me and my two older brothers out to this club called Tatou. And he introduced us to some agents for movie deals.

"Then they decided to blow us over," Kris said of the agents and producers who had originally expressed interest in a TV movie about the Spurs. "They wanted to make us out as real bad guys, where we went to the parents' house and beat up the dad and took the daughter, that's what they wanted. We were like, no, that's not how we are." But Kris and his posse buddies quickly assented to the plotline anyway. "They were gonna pay out cash. But then all the shows, all the channels like Fox and them thought we were all *too* bad guys, rapists, and they said we don't want to make these guys rich." Kris suspected that the "female executives" were the ones who killed the project. After that, he said, Kizzy "moved out of that loft, and now we don't talk to him at all." For the first time, an emotion played across Kris Belman's face, and it was anger. "I'd like to get ahold of him, though," he said, slamming a fist on the table, "because he screwed us. He screwed us bad."

At the party that evening, I would witness several such bitter outbursts, always revolving around a media or entertainment personality who had helped advance their "name," but somehow hadn't done enough. "Maury Povich, he *lied* to us," Chris Albert shouted, kicking hard at the leg of the blackjack table. "He made it look like he was offering us a palace. Ten days in New York. Two limos. Povich is a cock-sucking bitch." Why he was so incensed he couldn't precisely say. He got his ten days, after all. In fact, eleven. He rode in a limo. But it had left him with the strong suspicion that he had been ripped off. There should have been something more, though he didn't know what.

With another hour before *The Tonight Show*, Billy Shehan went out back to smoke some dope. Lonnie Rodriguez was sitting on the stoop, idly poking a stick in the grass. They greeted each other like long-lost cellmates. Which they had been, in a way. "Lonnie and I did telemarketing together for, like, oh man, it felt like years," Billy said. They had sat in sterile cubicles in windowless rooms with nothing but a phone on a desk, dialing endless rows of numbers. "It was so stressful," said Lonnie, who had recently served six months in jail for violating probation. ("Assaults mostly," he told me when I asked why he'd been in jail, "that's what I'm known for.") He said he found incarceration at National Promotions more debilitating. 65

"It sucked," Billy agreed. "But you know, the first week, I was the second seller, at three hundred dollars. The second week, I was first. We'd just pitch to hook people, and we didn't care what happened after that. I would change my voice, like an act. I had ten different personalities. I was being fake with all these people. It was like, in telemarketing, even before the Spurs, we were hooking. We've been hooking for years."

Telemarketing was an important landmark in the Spurs' short history. "That's when we first started keeping track of points," Billy said. They had already been counting their rate of return on customer calls, and it seemed a natural progression to apply the same approach to their sex lives. "It's all about statistics," Billy added. As it was in the larger world they inhabited. Telemarketing and the "points system" were just two expressions of an economy in which ratings and rankings, marketing percentiles and slugging percentages, were what seemed to count most. The men who mattered were the ones who claimed the most points, whose number-one ranking in whatever category displayed a controlling dominance. As Billy Shehan told me that night, "I want to get control of the world. Well, not the world, but I want to get where they *see* me because I'm on top, where all heads turn when they say my name."

From the living room came howls of "It's on! It's on!" Billy and Lonnie leaped up and charged inside. On the carpet, the Spurs were jostling for a prime spot before the wide-screen TV, which took up much of the tiny living room. Billy and Lonnie settled in just as the show broke for commercials—Wal-Mart wishing America a very merry Christmas, followed by a promotion for an episode of a tabloid TV show on both the Menendez brothers[10] and Michael Jackson. The guys booed and moaned, barely able to contain themselves. "Get this shit off of there," one yelled. "This is our moment!"

And then, at last, Jay Leno was back, schmoozing with Howard Stern. The room went silent for the first time all evening, breaths held, eyes riveted, necks craned forward. The camera did a quick pan of the audience, nothing. Then another, and Chris Albert leaped up, thrusting his arms into the air, triumphant. "That's me! That's me! That's fucking me on the fucking *Tonight Show!*" Albert did a victory walk around the room, exchanging high fives with his compadres. Now the camera had returned to Howard Stern, and Billy Shehan nudged me. He swore he could see a glint of recognition in Stern's eyes. "See how he looked? Howard's acknowledging us."

The party dwindled after that. A few more rounds of blackjack and then   70
Spurs began streaming out the door into the darkened grid of right-angled streets. I walked out with Billy, Lonnie, and Chris, who was still glowing from his media moment.

"Spurs is how I gained my respect," Lonnie said. "But I'm going to have to get out of it soon." He had fathered an infant son and was about to start a job of sorts, behind the counter at Baskin-Robbins 31 Flavors. "The Spurs will never die down, though," he said. "My son will carry it on. We'll always exist."

"And we *do* exist," Billy said, as if someone had suggested otherwise. "I swear to God, we do exist!" Billy threw back his head and shouted to the impassive black firmament. "Howard Stern knows we exist. They all acknowledged us, all in one night."

I got in my car and headed toward Los Angeles. I would see Billy and Lonnie again, but not Chris Albert. A year and a half later, on the Fourth of July, he went to Huntington Beach to set off firecrackers, got into a street fight, and was shot to death. His passing would be noted in a small Associated Press item. "Albert," the brief obituary stated, citing his only achieve-

---

[10]*the Menendez brothers*: After two highly publicized trials in 1993 and 1995, Lyle and Erik Menendez were convicted of the brutal murder of their parents; Erik was eighteen and Lyle twenty-one at the time the crime was committed.

ment meriting mention, "appeared on several news and talk shows, including *Dateline NBC* and *The Jenny Jones Show.*"[11] His existence on *The Tonight Show* went unnoticed.

Visible and Not Ready to Be Visible

One day in the spring of 1994, I met Billy Shehan at a Lakewood park. He was sitting on a bench watching his old Pony League baseball team practice. The thirteen-year-old boys stood around thwacking their fists in their mitts and adjusting their caps, paying no attention to Billy, the lone observer.

He was brooding about his own truncated athletic career. He had been   75
cut a few weeks earlier from the Long Beach City College baseball team. Before Long Beach, he had played ball for Golden West College until he got into a fight in the outfield, and then at Rio Hondo College, where the team was lackluster and he had quit in disgust. His Spur celebrity had made him a standout at Long Beach (a celebrity based on media, not police, attention—Billy was never arrested). "People would call out from the stands, 'Hey, how many points did you score?'" But it also cost him a spot on the roster, or so he had convinced himself. "The coach told me, 'You didn't make the team because you were too much of a distraction. People aren't focused on the game.'" In a fury, Billy had "shredded" his Long Beach City College baseball cap.

It had all been so promising back in Pony League. "I had a good name through Pop Warner,[12] a good image," he said. "Lakewood Pop Warner never loses. My name was getting more recognized. But someone with a bigger brand name came along." That boy, whose batting stats weren't—so Billy told me—as good as his but whose father was a well-liked coach in town, got the slot on the All-Star team that Billy thought was meant for him. "I didn't get on All-Stars until later, and then it was too late. The guys who get drafted early get the brand name. It's like Pepsi."

Billy recognized the Pony League coaches from his own playing days and went over to say hello.

"Where is everybody?" Billy said, gesturing toward the empty bleachers. His question opened up a gusher.

"Oh, I don't know, it's just not as team oriented anymore the way it used to be," Coach Al Weiner said dispiritedly. He took off his cap and ran a hand through his thinning white hair.

"It's with the mothers never being home anymore and all," Coach Art   80
Tavizon commented.

"Naah, it's this thing with the kids," Weiner said. "In the old days, the kids who didn't get on, they would show up to watch. Now, if they're not playing, they won't watch."

[11]"Spur Posse Member Killed," Associated Press, July 6, 1995.

[12]*Pony League and Pop Warner*: Community-based youth sports organizations promoting baseball and football, respectively.

"And the girls don't watch anymore," Tavizon said.

Weiner nodded. "The girls aren't interested. They're more into girls' sports now."

Tavizon set his mouth in a thin line at the mention of girls' sports and looked grimly across the field as if he had just spotted a menacing thundercloud on the horizon. "Title Nine changed everything," he said, alluding to the 1972 federal law that prohibited sex discrimination at schools receiving federal money, thereby ushering girls into school athletics.... "All the big moneymakers—football, baseball—and we've got to give it all to girls' badminton! Coaches are getting out of the business because they have to spend all their time fund-raising because the money's been taken to give to girls' sports."

The coach paused, but only to take a breath. He was just getting started. "We had our weight room taken away because girls needed gymnastics. We had that weight room eleven years. We got pushed outside." His voice was getting louder, his face redder, and I suddenly realized that Billy had dropped out of the picture. The coach was directing his ire at me, the representative woman. "If the women would sit down and give a little bit, instead of insisting, 'Our half of the pie is fifty-fifty.' If they'd just back off and let the big sports be funded the way they used to be. Title Nine is going to be the destruction of high-school sports."

With that, he stormed back to his thirteen-year-old boy stars. Billy and I watched him go. "That's not the problem with baseball," Billy said, and offered his own more up-to-date diagnosis. "The problem with baseball is that it's a *dad's* game." And not a glamour game. "Baseball doesn't stand out because they don't have the cheerleaders, so there isn't as much of a star thing like you have with football." I wondered at the ranking of fathers under teenage girls in his version of the sports arena. When had the opinions of the older men who coached the game stopped mattering? Billy's father had devotedly coached Pop Warner for twelve years. So had Kris and Dana Belman's father, Don, who had also been a dedicated coach of Park League, Little League, Pony League, and Colt League.

What's so bad about a "dad's game"? I asked Billy.

"My dad, he was living through me with sports. When I got in trouble, he took it like *I* fucked *him* up. My dad provided anything that produced a championship. Sports is what our dads embedded in us. It was like a disease and it contaminated the whole town." Billy's father, doubtless, wanted only what every father wanted—to pass something along to his son, and in postwar suburbia, that patrimony was athletic achievement. Yet it turned out that the lines of inheritance ran upstream. In a generational reversal, the parents were getting their "name" through their children. As Dottie Belman, Kris and Dana's mother, told a reporter: "We became stars, too. We'd walk into Little League and we were hot stuff."[13] In his gut, Billy

85

---

[13]Janet Wiscombe, "An American Tragedy," *Los Angeles Times*, March 22, 1996, p. E1.

Shehan knew that the fathers had nothing to teach him about the way the world worked—but the girls did. The Spur Posse members, after all, prayed for what women had long commanded: the camera's attention. Far more than they ever courted women, they courted women's secret access to enshrinement in the public eye. As Billy Shehan told Jane Whitney on her show, he was trying to do from Lakewood what she was doing on the studio stage. "We probably have the same concept going here," he said.... [14]

The Pop Warner System

... The media misconceived the nature of the Spurs' "club," which was less like a gang or fraternity than a bunch of casual drinking buddies. "People kept calling us a gang," Kris Belman said to me. "We weren't anything like that. It was just some guys who wore hats.... And then, once we got famous, there were all these other guys claiming they were Spurs who we didn't even know." If the core group of Spurs all seemed to wear baggy plaid shorts and their caps turned backward, this was in obeisance more to consumer culture than to group bonding. "We weren't ever a real group," Billy Shehan told me one day. "We were just a few people who liked David Robinson. Once the media grouped us together, *that's* when we became more tight." And then it was for promotional, not emotional, reasons. The Spurs weren't looking for the intimacy of a close-knit group. They were looking for the celebrity that identification with a brand name like David Robinson might provide. Like their elders in aerospace, they had attached themselves not to one another but to a household label. Everybody knew the San Antonio Spurs, as everybody knew McDonnell Douglas—and by extension, they could be "known," too; Robinson's name would be theirs.

"Billy did not even really run with this group of kids," Billy's mother,   90
Joyce Shehan, observed to me. "He went to a different high school [from a lot of the other Spurs]. It was the lure of the media, which was overwhelming for all of these boys." She recalled how it all started, the day the eight Spurs were arrested: "I came home that afternoon and Billy said, 'Gotta go, Mom! *Current Affair* is at the Belmans'!' He felt like destiny was calling him." Joyce pleaded with her son, to no avail. When the door slammed shut, she sat down in her living room and wept. "I felt overtaken."

"Doing sports is up there with sexual activities," Billy Shehan explained to me, as he gave me a tour of his parents' home. The walls of the ten-by-ten-foot bedroom where he still lived then were decorated with posters of the scantily clad Bud Lite woman, Hooters women, and decals asserting BLOW ME, STAY HARD, BAD BOYS CLUB, and PUSSIES AREN'T HEROES. I was having trouble matching these sniggering mud-flap sentiments with Billy, who distinguished himself from the other Spurs by a certain capacity (albeit sometimes lost in a dope-induced fog) for self-analysis. He had been in the

---

[14]"Sex for Points Scandal," *The Jane Whitney Show*, April 1, 1993.

accelerated program for gifted students throughout school, had graduated with honors, and was one of the few Spurs in school, although his attendance at Long Beach City College was spotty. He was proud of his high SAT scores (1410 out of a possible 1600, he said). For all his weight lifting—he tried to work out every other day at the Family Fitness gym—Billy had a physical softness to him; he retained the loose-limbed downiness and padded gait of adolescence. Aside from the posters, his room could've been a kid's, with its sports pennants and discarded clumps of clothing on the floor.

The tour complete, we returned to the living room, where Billy's uncle Brian Shehan; Billy's new girlfriend, Holly Badger; and Spur Jeff Howard were watching a TV movie about baseball and eating corn chips out of a jumbo bag. "When I'm thinking of attraction to girls, I'm thinking I have to stand out," Billy said. "How else can it be done? Same thing with sports. You try for a hit. It's like a mirror." It was the first time I had heard someone equate playing sports to looking in a mirror, and I asked him what he meant.

"It's what Pop Warner is all about," Billy said, "and Lakewood was built around Pop Warner." Playing football in the Pop Warner league was one of the few continuities a Lakewood boy could count on. The city's fathers established the park sports leagues out of alarm over the vast and idle child population of the new suburb: by 1953, 45 percent of Lakewood was under the age of nineteen.[15] The leagues were supposed to keep the baby-boom progeny out of trouble; they needed something to do. But what the elaborate Lakewood regimen of Pop Warners and Pony Leagues and Colt Leagues and All-Stars became, Billy was saying, was not something to *do* but something to *be*. "Pop Warner is what made me like hooking."

His uncle leaned heavily against the wall, his lined face under a battered Pittsburgh Steelers cap, a beaten version of Billy's. He was visiting from Las Vegas, where one week before Christmas he had been laid off as head cook at a restaurant called Bubba's. He had once been a front-end-loader operator but wound up in the new economy slinging hash and ringing up purchases at Fedco's. "So," he said, almost wearily, "it's the Pop Warner Sex-Orgy System?"

"It *is* a system," Billy said. "In the Pop Warner system, you learn how to   95 stand out, you learn how to get people to recognize you. You wear your hat a certain way. Like I started wearing mine angled with the bangs showing, because it looks cute. And everybody else started doing it. I set a lot of fashion trends."

"Every guy is in Pop Warner to get attention," Holly Badger said, though from the exasperated set of her mouth it was clear she found this truth more pathetic than ennobling.

"Sports is not sports anymore," Billy told his uncle. "It's evolved to this whole other level. It's this gamble of are you going to hit it big."

[15]Waldie, *Holy Land,* p. 40.

"Why do you guys like to gamble?" Holly interrupted. "All you *do* is gamble." She turned to me. "Every weekend, these guys are off to Las Vegas."

"It's a rush, a fix," Billy said. "It's like Dana's fixation with stealing."

"Yeah, or like breaking and entering," Holly said pointedly. One of the Spurs arrested for sexual misconduct, she told me, had broken into her house four years earlier when she was in the ninth grade. "He forced himself down on top me and a girlfriend of mine. I kicked him and he called me a bitch. Then he took my ring off my finger and put it on his finger and ran out." Hers was not an isolated story. Some of the Spurs had been known to steal things from girls: credit cards and checkbooks and jewelry, and oddities like gym membership cards, which one of the Spurs even tried to use, in spite of the feminine face laminated on the square of plastic.

"Stealing *is* gambling," Billy said. "Gambling evolves into something else."

"Billy wastes his life pursuing baseball," his uncle told me later that day, as we stood on the front porch. He had as much chance making the pros as hitting the jackpot—and as a Las Vegas resident, Brian Shehan knew how good those chances were. As for himself, Brian said, he was considering becoming a nurse; at least society needed them. He crossed his arms and gazed out at the orderly row of houses across the street. "Baseball and celebrity. Billy promised his dad he wouldn't go on the talk shows, and a few days later, he's flying to New York City."

Holly appeared on the porch, her bag over her shoulder. She was on her way to class at a nearby junior college. Jeff and Billy, their baseball caps on backward—Jeff's said STÜSSY, Billy's said L.A.—kicked their designer sneakers at the concrete stoop and talked about job possibilities. Billy last found work as a box boy at Victoria's Secret, but it had only lasted through the Christmas rush. Holly apprised them coolly: "*I* go to school and *I* work," she said. Billy kept kicking at the stoop and said nothing. Holly leaned over to give him a distracted kiss good-bye and drove off.

We went back inside, and Billy booted up his computer to show me his "movie treatment," in which he starred as "Billy Sherwood," the one with "the most points" who "doesn't accept failure." He had quit writing after the cast list and had typed instead some notes to himself about his girlfriend troubles, in lyric form. Billy and a few Spurs formed a band a while back, and he was the songwriter.

> The girl I used to kiss used to only kiss me
> But she has changed and she is 'ho again.
> She's back to who she was.
> I thought I could make her mine ...

He had broken off there. Underneath, he had written, "But I realize by the answers to my questions, that I never needed her. What I needed was for her to need me."

The training grounds for the Spurs were supposed to be the playing 105
fields of Pony League and Pop Warner, and in a way, they were training
grounds for the celebrity age. The young men who flocked to Lakewood's
sports leagues certainly learned that they would be expected to climb the
star ladder, that fame based on your stats would be the determining factor
in modern masculinity. But they also learned how high the stakes were, how
few resources they had to win the stats war. Playing ball led to stardom for a
very few. For the rest, Pop Warner was ultimately a lesson in how impossible it was to be a masculine "player" today. As Spur Jimmy Rafkin told me:
"Growing up, everything revolved around Pop Warner. You try and do your
best in sports and try to be the best and try to become the best, but it's like
one out of a million make it, by far. So what was the point? What was it all
for?"

ENGAGING THE TEXT

1. How did the boys' experiences in telemarketing and amateur athletics (Pop
   Warner, Pony League) help shape their behavior and values as Spur Posse
   members?

2. Why is the idea of a "brand name" so important to Billy Shehan and his
   friends?

3. The Lakewood boys complain that "girls have all the power." What do they
   mean by this, and what is their perception based on? How realistic or unrealistic does their attitude seem to you, and why?

4. Faludi subtitled her book *The Betrayal of the American Man.* In what ways
   does she suggest that the Lakewood boys have been cheated or "betrayed"?
   How does her understanding of their betrayal differ from their own? Who
   or what is responsible for their problems according to each perspective?

5. Faludi treats Lakewood itself almost like a character in her narrative, including information about its origin, architecture, layout, economy, and social life. Why are these details important to the story of the "troubled boys"
   she profiles?

6. What does Faludi's language reveal about her attitude toward the Lost Boy
   and the other Spur Posse members she interviews? How does she seem to
   want readers to respond to them? How do you react to them, and why?

EXPLORING CONNECTIONS

7. Roleplay or write a script for a roundtable discussion among Jackson Katz
   (p. 466), Jean Kilbourne (p. 444), Carmen Vázquez (p. 492), Joan Morgan
   (p. 527), and Faludi about the influence of media in shaping attitudes toward masculinity, femininity, male-female relationships, and power.

8. Faludi highlights the stark disparity between the daily lives of the Lakewood boys and their dreams of fame and wealth. How do their dreams of
   success differ from those of Ragged Dick (p. 298), Colin Powell (p. 305), or

Stephen Cruz (p. 335)? Would you call them believers in the American Dream? Why or why not?

EXTENDING THE CRITICAL CONTEXT

9. Sensational daytime talk shows and other "reality-based" programs in which participants essentially live their lives on camera have gained tremendous popularity in recent years. What is the appeal of such shows for audiences? Why are participants willing or even eager to share intimate and sometimes humiliating details of their lives with a TV audience?

From Fly-Girls to Bitches and Hos

JOAN MORGAN

As a music writer and fan of hip-hop, Joan Morgan loves the power of rap. As a feminist, she is troubled by the pervasive sexism of its lyrics. The misogyny of rap, she argues, is a symptom of crisis in the black community; it must be confronted and understood, not simply condemned, as a step toward healing the pain that it both expresses and inflicts. This passage comes from her collection of essays, When Chickenheads Come Home to Roost ... My Life as a Hip-Hop Feminist *(1999). Morgan is editor-at-large at* Essence *magazine and lives in Brooklyn, New York. She has also written for* The Village Voice *and* Vibe.

> Feminist criticism, like many other forms of social analysis, is widely considered part of a hostile white culture. For a black feminist to chastise misogyny in rap publicly would be viewed as divisive and counterproductive. There is a widespread perception in the black community that public criticism of black men constitutes collaborating with a racist society....
>
> — MICHELE WALLACE, "When Black Feminism Faces the Music, and the Music Is Rap," *The New York Times*[1]

Lord knows our love jones for hip-hop is understandable. Props given to rap music's artistic merits, its irrefutable impact on pop culture, its ability

---

[1]Michele Wallace, "When Black Feminism Faces the Music, and the Music Is Rap," *The New York Times,* July 29, 1990. [All notes are Morgan's.]

to be alternately beautiful, poignant, powerful, strong, irreverent, visceral, and mesmerizing—homeboy's clearly got it like that. But in between the beats, booty shaking, and hedonistic abandon, I have to wonder if there isn't something inherently unfeminist in supporting a music that repeatedly reduces me to tits and ass and encourages pimping on the regular. While it's human to occasionally fall deep into the love thang with people or situations that simply aren't good for you, feminism alerted me long ago to the dangers of romancing a misogynist (and ridiculously fine, brilliant ones with gangsta leans are no exception). Perhaps the nonbelievers were right, maybe what I'd been mistaking for love and commitment for the last twenty years was really nothing but a self-destructive obsession that made a mockery of my feminism....

I guess it all depends on how you define the f-word. My feminism places the welfare of black women and the black community on its list of priorities. It also maintains that black-on-black love is essential to the survival of both.

We have come to a point in our history, however, when black-on-black love—a love that's survived slavery, lynching, segregation, poverty, and racism—is in serious danger. The stats usher in this reality like taps before the death march: According to the U.S. Census Bureau, the number of black two-parent households has decreased from 74 percent to 48 percent since 1960. The leading cause of death among black men ages fifteen to twenty-four is homicide. The majority of them will die at the hands of other black men.[2]

Women are the unsung victims of black-on-black crime. A while back, a friend of mine, a single mother of a newborn (her "babyfather"—a brother—abdicated responsibility before their child was born) was attacked by a pit bull while walking her dog in the park. The owner (a brother) trained the animal to prey on other dogs and the flesh of his fellow community members.

A few weeks later my moms called, upset, to tell me about the murder   5
of a family friend. She was a troubled young woman with a history of substance abuse, aggravated by her son's murder two years ago. She was found beaten and burned beyond recognition. Her murderers were not "skinheads," "The Man," or "the racist white power structure." More likely than not, they were brown men whose faces resembled her own.

Clearly, we are having a very difficult time loving one another.

Any feminism that fails to acknowledge that black folks in nineties America are living and trying to love in a war zone is useless to our struggle against sexism. Though it's often portrayed as part of the problem, rap music is essential to that struggle because it takes us straight to the battlefield.

---

[2]Joan Morgan, "Real Love," *Vibe*, April 1996, p. 38.

My decision to expose myself to the sexism of Dr. Dre, Ice Cube, Snoop Dogg, or the Nortorious B.I.G. is really my plea to my brothers to tell me who they are. I need to know why they are so angry at me. Why is disrespecting me one of the few things that make them feel like men? What's the haps, what are you going through on the daily that's got you acting so foul?

As a black woman and a feminist I listen to the music with a willingness to see past the machismo in order to be clear about what I'm *really* dealing with. What I hear frightens me. On booming track after booming track, I hear brothers talking about spending each day high as hell on malt liquor and Chronic. Don't sleep. What passes for "40 and a blunt" good times in most of hip-hop is really alcoholism, substance abuse, and chemical dependency. When brothers can talk so cavalierly about killing each other and then reveal that they have no expectation to see their twenty-first birthday, that is straight-up depression *masquerading* as machismo.

Anyone curious about the processes and pathologies that form the psy-   10
che of the young, black, and criminal-minded needs to revisit our dearly departed Notorious B.I.G.'s first album, *Ready to Die.* Chronicling the life and times of the urban "soldier," the album is a blues-laden soul train that took us on a hustler's life journey. We boarded with the story of his birth, strategically stopped to view his dysfunctional, warring family, his first robbery, his first stint in jail, murder, drug-dealing, getting paid, partying, sexin', rappin', mayhem, and death. Biggie's player persona might have momentarily convinced the listener that he was livin' phat without a care in the world but other moments divulged his inner hell. The chorus of "Everyday Struggle": *I don't wanna live no more / Sometimes I see death knockin' at my front door* revealed that "Big Poppa" was also plagued with guilt, regret, and depression. The album ultimately ended with his suicide.

The seemingly impenetrable wall of sexism in rap music is really the complex mask African-Americans often wear both to hide and express the pain. At the close of this millennium, hip-hop is still one of the few forums in which young black men, even surreptitiously, are allowed to express their pain.

When it comes to the struggle against sexism and our intimate relationships with black men, some of the most on-point feminist advice I've received comes from sistas like my mother, who wouldn't dream of using the term. During our battle to resolve our complicated relationships with my equally wonderful and errant father, my mother presented me with the following gems of wisdom, "One of the most important lessons you will ever learn in life and love, is that you've got to love people for what they are — not for who you would like them to be."

This is crystal clear to me when I'm listening to hip-hop. Yeah, sistas are hurt when we hear brothers calling us bitches and hos. But the real crime isn't the name-calling, it's their failure to love us — to be our brothers in the way that we commit ourselves to being their sistas. But recognize: Any man who doesn't truly love himself is incapable of loving us in the healthy way we need to be loved. It's extremely telling that men who can only see us as "bitches" and "hos" refer to themselves only as "niggas."

In the interest of our emotional health and overall sanity, black women have got to learn to love brothers realistically, and that means differentiating between who they are and who we'd like them to be. Black men are engaged in a war where the real enemies—racism and the white power structure—are masters of camouflage. They've conditioned our men to believe the enemy is brown. The effects of this have been as wicked as they've been debilitating. Being in battle with an enemy that looks just like you makes it hard to believe in the basics every human being needs. For too many black men there is no trust, no community, no family. Just self.

Since hip-hop is the mirror in which so many brothers see themselves, it's significant that one of the music's most prevalent mythologies is that black boys rarely grow into men. Instead, they remain perpetually postadolescent or die. For all the machismo and testosterone in the music, it's frighteningly clear that many brothers see themselves as powerless when it comes to facing the evils of the larger society, accepting responsibility for their lives, or the lives of their children.

So, sista friends, we gotta do what any rational, survivalist-minded person would do after finding herself in a relationship with someone whose pain makes him abusive. We've gotta continue to give up the love but *from a distance that's safe*. Emotional distance is a great enabler of unconditional love and support because it allows us to recognize that the attack, the "bitch, ho" bullshit—isn't personal but part of the illness.

And the focus of black feminists has got to change. We can't afford to keep expending energy on banal discussions of sexism in rap when sexism is only part of a huge set of problems. Continuing on our previous path is akin to demanding that a fiending, broke crackhead not rob you blind because it's *wrong* to do so.

If feminism intends to have any relevance in the lives of the majority of black women, if it intends to move past theory and become functional it has to rescue itself from the ivory towers of academia. Like it or not, hip-hop is not only the dominion of the young, black, and male, it is also the world in which young black women live and survive. A functional game plan for us, one that is going to be as helpful to Shequanna on 142nd as it is to Samantha at Sarah Lawrence, has to recognize hip-hop's ability to articulate the pain our *community* is in and use that knowledge to create a redemptive, healing space.

Notice the emphasis on "community." Hip-hop isn't only instrumental in exposing black men's pain, it brings the healing sistas need right to the surface. Sad as it may be, it's time to stop ignoring the fact that rappers meet "bitches" and "hos" daily—women who reaffirm their depiction of us on vinyl. Backstage, the road, and the 'hood are populated with women who would do anything to be with a rapper sexually for an hour if not a night. It's

15

time to stop fronting like we don't know who rapper Jeru the Damaja was talking about when he said:

> Now a queen's a queen but a stunt's a stunt
> You can tell who's who by the things they want

Sex has long been the bartering chip that women use to gain protection, [20] material wealth, and the vicarious benefits of power. In the black community, where women are given less access to all of the above, "trickin'" becomes a means of leveling the playing field. Denying the justifiable anger of rappers—men who couldn't get the time of day from these women before a few dollars and a record deal—isn't empowering and strategic. Turning a blind eye and scampering for moral high ground diverts our attention away from the young women who are being denied access to power and are suffering for it.

It might've been more convenient to direct our sistafied rage attention to "the sexist representation of women" in those now infamous Sir Mix-A-Lot videos, to fuss over *one* sexist rapper, but wouldn't it have been more productive to address the failing self-esteem of the 150 or so half-naked young women who were willing, unpaid participants? And what about how flip we are when it comes to using the b-word to describe each other? At some point we've all been the recipients of competitive, unsisterly, "bitchiness," particularly when vying for male attention.

Since being black and a woman makes me fluent in both isms, I sometimes use racism as an illuminating analogy. Black folks have finally gotten to the point where we recognize that we sometimes engage in oppressive behaviors that white folks have little to do with. Complexion prejudices and classism are illnesses which have their *roots* in white racism but the perpetrators are certainly black.

Similarly, sistas have to confront the ways we're complicit in our own oppression. Sad to say it, but many of the ways in which men exploit our images and sexuality in hip-hop is done with our permission and cooperation. We need to be as accountable to each other as we believe "race traitors" (i.e., one hundred or so brothers in blackface cooning in a skinhead's music video) should be to our community. To acknowledge this doesn't deny our victimization but it does raise the critical issue of whose responsibility it is to end our oppression. As a feminist, I believe it is too great a responsibility to leave to men.

A few years ago, on an airplane making its way to Montego Bay, I received another gem of girlfriend wisdom from a sixty-year-old self-declared nonfeminist. She was meeting her husband to celebrate her thirty-fifth wedding anniversary. After telling her I was twenty-seven and very much single, she looked at me and shook her head sadly. "I feel sorry for your generation. You don't know how to have relationships, especially the women." Curious, I asked her why she thought this was. "The women of your generation, you want to be right. The women of my generation, we didn't care about being right. We just wanted to win."

Too much of the discussion regarding sexism and the music focuses on being right. We feel we're *right* and the rappers are wrong. The rappers feel it's their *right* to describe their "reality" in any way they see fit. The store owners feel it's their *right* to sell whatever the consumer wants to buy. The consumer feels it's his *right* to be able to decide what he wants to listen to. We may be the "rightest" of the bunch but we sure as hell ain't doing the winning.

I believe hip-hop can help us win. Let's start by recognizing that its illuminating, informative narration and its incredible ability to articulate our collective pain is an invaluable tool when examining gender relations. The information we amass can help create a redemptive, healing space for brothers and sistas.

We're all winners when a space exists for brothers to honestly state and explore the roots of their pain and subsequently their misogyny, sans judgment. It is criminal that the only space our society provided for the late Tupac Shakur to examine the pain, confusion, drug addiction, and fear that led to his arrest and his eventual assassination was in a prison cell. How can we win if a prison cell is the only space an immensely talented but troubled young black man could dare utter these words: "Even though I'm not guilty of the charges they gave me, I'm not innocent in terms of the way I was acting. I'm just as guilty for not doing things. Not with this case but with my life. I had a job to do and I never showed up. I was so scared of this responsibility that I was running away from it."[3] We have to do better than this for our men.

And we have to do better for ourselves. We desperately need a space to lovingly address the uncomfortable issues of our failing self-esteem, the ways we sexualize and objectify ourselves, our confusion about sex and love and the unhealthy, unloving, unsisterly ways we treat each other. Commitment to developing these spaces gives our community the potential for remedies based on honest, clear diagnoses.

As I'm a black woman, I am aware that this doubles my workload — that I am definitely going to have to listen to a lot of shit I won't like — but without these candid discussions, there is little to no hope of exorcising the illness that hurts and sometimes kills us.

ENGAGING THE TEXT

1. What qualities of rap music and rap artists does Morgan admire or appreciate? What fears does she have for rap's female fans and for the artists themselves? To what extent do you agree with Morgan's assessment of the misogyny, anger, and despair expressed by rap?

---

[3]Kevin Powell, "The Vibe Q: Tupac Shakur, Ready to Live," *Vibe*, April 11, 1995, p. 52.

2. What evidence does Morgan offer that "black folks in nineties America are living and trying to love in a war zone"? How does she explain the causes of the violence she describes? How persuasive do you find her analysis, and why?

3. How do you interpret Morgan's call for establishing "a redemptive, healing space" for confronting the pain expressed by rap? What kind of "space" is she talking about, and how would you go about establishing it?

4. What audience is Morgan addressing and what persuasive strategies — of both argument and style — does she use to appeal to that audience? What do you find effective or ineffective about her approach?

EXPLORING CONNECTIONS

5. Compare Jean Kilbourne's analysis of sexism and violence in advertising (p. 444) to Morgan's discussion of the same themes in rap. What are the causes and consequences of "pornographic" depictions of women in popular culture according to each writer? Do you think Kilbourne would concur with Morgan about how we should respond to these images? Why or why not?

6. Although Morgan and Susan Faludi (p. 510) argue that we need to examine the lives of young men like Notorious B.I.G. and the members of the Spur Posse in order to understand the roots of their misogyny, critics might counter that these writers are simply making excuses for intolerable behavior. Do you agree with both Morgan and Faludi, with one of them, or with neither? Write an essay explaining and supporting your position.

EXTENDING THE CRITICAL CONTEXT

7. Survey the current issues of several magazines aimed at fans of rap music. What images do they present of women, men, and human relationships? How often do they reflect the themes that Morgan discusses? What other themes and patterns do you find, if any, and how do you explain their significance?

8. Examine the lyrics of several female rappers and compare them to those of the male rappers Morgan mentions. What similarities and differences do you find in the subjects they address and the feelings they express? If you're not a fan of rap, you may want to consult an online hip-hop dictionary for help in decoding some of the language (www.rapdict.org).

5

Created Equal

The Myth of the Melting Pot

Antiracism March, photo by Eli Reed.

The myth of the melting pot predates the drafting of the U.S. Constitution. In 1782, a year before the Peace of Paris formally ended the Revolutionary War, Hector St. Jean de Crèvecoeur envisioned the young American republic as a crucible that would forge its disparate immigrant population into a vigorous new society with a grand future:

> What, then, is the American, this new man? He is neither an European, or the descendant of an European....He is an American, who leaving behind him all his ancient prejudices and manners, receives new ones from the new mode of life he has embraced, the new government he obeys, and the new rank he holds....Here individuals of all nations are melted into a new race of men, whose labours and posterity will one day cause great changes in the world.

Crèvecoeur's metaphor has remained a powerful ideal for many generations of American scholars, politicians, artists, and ordinary citizens. Ralph Waldo Emerson, writing in his journal in 1845, celebrated the national vitality produced by the mingling of immigrant cultures: "In this continent—asylum of all nations,—the energy of...all the European tribes,—of the Africans, and of the Polynesians—will construct a new race, a new religion, a new state, a new literature." An English Jewish writer named Israel Zangwill, himself an immigrant, popularized the myth in his 1908 drama, *The Melting Pot*. In the play, the hero rhapsodizes, "Yes East and West, and North and South, the palm and the pine, the pole and the equator, the crescent and the cross—how the great Alchemist melts and fuses them with his purging flame! Here shall they all unite to build the Republic of Man and the Kingdom of God." The myth was perhaps most vividly dramatized, though, in a pageant staged by Henry Ford in the early 1920s. Decked out in the costumes of their native lands, Ford's immigrant workers sang traditional songs from their homelands as they danced their way into an enormous replica of a cast-iron pot. They then emerged from the other side wearing identical "American" business suits, waving miniature American flags, and singing "The Star-Spangled Banner."

The drama of becoming an American has deep roots: immigrants take on a new identity—and a new set of cultural myths—because they want to become members of the community, equal members with all the rights, responsibilities, and opportunities of their fellow citizens. The force of the melting pot myth lies in this implied promise that all Americans are indeed "created equal." However, the myth's promises of openness, harmony, unity, and equality were deceptive from the beginning. Crèvecoeur's exclusive concern with the mingling of *European* peoples (he lists the "English, Scotch, Irish, French, Dutch, Germans, and Swedes") utterly ignored the presence of some three-quarters of a million Africans and African Americans who then lived in this country, as well as the tribal peoples who had lived on the land for thousands of years before European contact. Crèvecoeur's vision of a country embracing "all nations" clearly applied only to northern European nations. Benjamin Franklin, in a 1751 essay, was more blunt: since Africa, Asia, and most of America were inhabited by dark-skinned people, he argued, the American colonies should consciously try to increase the white population and keep out the rest: "Why increase the Sons of Africa, by Planting them in America, where we have so fair an opportunity, by excluding Blacks and Tawneys, of increasing the lovely White...?" If later writers like Emerson and Zangwill saw a more inclusive cultural mix as a source of hope and renewal for the United States, others throughout this country's history have, even more than Franklin, feared that mix as a threat.

The fear of difference underlies another, equally powerful American myth—the myth of racial supremacy. This is the negative counterpart of the melting pot ideal: instead of the equal and harmonious blending of cultures, it proposes a racial and ethnic hierarchy based on the "natural superiority" of Anglo-Americans. Under the sway of this myth, differences become signs of inferiority, and "inferiors" are treated as childlike or even subhuman. This myth has given rise to some of the most shameful passages in our national life: slavery, segregation, and lynching; the near extermination of tribal peoples and cultures; the denial of citizenship and constitutional rights to African Americans, American Indians, Chinese and Japanese immigrants; the brutal exploitation of Mexican and Asian laborers. The catalog of injustices is long and painful. The melting pot ideal itself has often masked the myth of racial and ethnic superiority. "Inferiors" are expected to "melt" into conformity with Anglo-American behavior and values. Henry Ford's pageant conveys the message that ethnic identity is best left behind—exchanged for something "better," more uniform, less threatening.

This chapter explores the interaction between these two related cultural myths: the myth of unity and the myth of difference and hierarchy. It examines how the categories of race and ethnicity are defined and how they operate to divide us. These issues become crucial as the population of the United States grows increasingly diverse. The selections here challenge you to reconsider the fate of the melting pot myth as we enter the era of multi-ethnic, multicultural America. Can we learn to accept and honor our differences?

The first half of the chapter focuses on the problem of racism and the origins of prejudice. It opens with a selection by Thomas Jefferson that presents an unambiguous expression of the myth of racial superiority. Pondering the future of freed slaves, Jefferson concludes that because blacks "are inferior to whites in the endowments both of body and mind," they should be prevented from intermarrying and "staining the blood" of the superior race. Langston Hughes, writing 150 years later, offers a counterpoint to Jefferson; his poem, "Let America Be America Again," presents an impassioned appeal on behalf of the disenfranchised to make America a land that lives up to its finest myths—equality and freedom. Surveying the most common sociological and psychological theories of prejudice, Vincent N.

Parrillo provides a series of frameworks for understanding the roots of racial conflict. Studs Terkel's oral history "C. P. Ellis" at once reminds us of the persistence of racist beliefs and offers hope for change: this remarkable first-person account of Ellis's transformation from Klansman to union activist examines racism from the inside and shows how one man conquered his own bigotry.

Next, two essays examine some of the internal and external influences that can distort our perception of race in the United States. In "I'm Black, You're White, Who's Innocent?" Shelby Steele argues that the psychological need to feel innocent on the highly charged issue of race keeps us from honest dialogue; he proposes that African Americans take the initiative by ceasing to blame whites for the injustices of the past and by refusing to play the victim. Leonard Steinhorn and Barbara Diggs-Brown, on the other hand, contend that the media play a role in undermining racial progress. Television in particular—with its black superstars, multi-ethnic news teams, and diverse casting—shows us a harmoniously integrated virtual world, offering false reassurance that race is no longer a serious problem.

The second half of the chapter addresses the emerging myth of the "new melting pot." First, a group of selections explores the complexities of personal identity and human relationships in an increasingly multicultural America. George M. Fredrickson offers an overview of ethnic relations in American history, showing how concepts of ethnic hierarchy, assimilation, pluralism, and separatism have shaped group identities and interactions over time. "Notes of a Native Speaker" is Eric Liu's autobiographical meditation on his experience as an assimilated Chinese American—a man who has become "white by acclamation." In his pointedly funny short story, "Assimilation," Sherman Alexie introduces us to a Native American woman who begins to question the meaning of her marriage to a white man. A Visual Portfolio gives individual faces to abstractions like race, ethnicity, and assimilation; the photos also challenge us to rethink the ways we "read" identity.

The remainder of the chapter raises the idea of ethnic identity as a choice rather than a destiny. Mary C. Waters, in "Optional Ethnicities," delineates some of the ways that the development of ethnic identity is a very different process for whites than for people of color; her analysis of how these differences in perspective play out in the lives of students on campus is essential reading for entering college students. Veronica Chambers celebrates the "many tribes" of her Afro-Antilliano heritage in "Secret Latina at Large." Lynell George's essay, "Gray Boys, Funky Aztecs, and Honorary Homegirls," suggests that, even apart from genetic mixing, a new wave of cultural borrowing and blending—a "recombinant culture"—is already beginning to blur and redefine ethnic categories. Finally, in her poem "Child of the Americas," Aurora Levins Morales affirms both the value of her multicultural roots and the enduring power of the melting pot myth.

Sources

John Hope Franklin, *Race and History: Selected Essays,* 1938–1988. Baton Rouge: Louisiana State University Press, 1989, pp. 321–31.

Milton M. Gordon, *Assimilation in American Life: The Role of Race, Religion, and National Origins.* New York: Oxford University Press, 1964.

Itabari Njeri, "Beyond the Melting Pot." *Los Angeles Times,* January 13, 1991, pp. E1, E8–9.

Leonard Pitt, *We Americans,* vol. 2, 3rd ed. Dubuque: Kendall/Hunt, 1987.

Ronald Takaki, "Reflections on Racial Patterns in America." In *From Different Shores: Perspectives on Race and Ethnicity in America,* Ronald Takaki, ed. New York: Oxford University Press, 1987, pp. 26–37.

BEFORE READING

- Survey images in the popular media (newspapers, magazines, TV shows, movies, and pop music) for evidence of the myth of the melting pot. Do you find any figures in popular culture who seem to endorse the idea of a "new melting pot" in the United States? How closely do these images reflect your understanding of your own and other ethnic and racial groups? Explore these questions in a journal entry, then discuss in class.

- Alternatively, you might investigate the metaphors that are being used to describe racial and ethnic group relations or interactions between members of different groups on your campus and in your community. Consult local news sources and campus publications, and keep your ears open for conversations that touch on these issues. Do some freewriting about what you discover and compare notes with classmates.

- The frontispiece photo on page 534 was taken at an antiracism march. Why do you think that these people and this particular moment of the march caught the photographer's eye? What do the positions and expressions of the four main figures suggest about their feelings and concerns and about the cause they are marching for? Jot down your impressions and note the visual details that support your "reading" of the picture. Then compare your responses in small groups: How much consistency or variation do you find in your interpretations?

From *Notes on the State of Virginia*

THOMAS JEFFERSON

Thomas Jefferson is probably best known as the author of the Declaration of Independence. *As third president of the United States (1801–1809), Thomas Jefferson (1743–1826) promoted westward expansion in the form of the Louisiana Purchase and the Lewis and Clark Expedition. In addition to his political career he was a scientist, architect, city planner (Washington, D.C.), and founder of the University of Virginia. This passage from his* Notes on the State of Virginia *(1785) reveals a very different and, for many readers, shocking side of Jefferson's character—that of a slave owner and defender of white supremacy. Here he proposes that the new state of Virginia gradually phase out slavery rather than abolish it outright. He also recommends that all newly emancipated slaves be sent out of the state to form separate colonies, in part to prevent racial conflict and in part to prevent intermarriage with whites. Jefferson was not the first and was far from the last politician to advocate solving the nation's racial problems by removing African Americans from its boundaries. In 1862, the Great Emancipator himself, Abraham Lincoln, called a delegation of black leaders to the White House to enlist their support in establishing a colony for African Americans in Central America. Congress had appropriated money for this project, but it was abandoned after the governments of Honduras, Nicaragua, and Costa Rica protested the plan.*

Many of the laws which were in force during the monarchy being relative merely to that form of government, or inculcating principles inconsistent with republicanism, the first assembly which met after the establishment of the commonwealth appointed a committee to revise the whole code, to reduce it into proper form and volume, and report it to the assembly. This work has been executed by three gentlemen,[1] and reported.... The following are the most remarkable alterations proposed:

To change the rules of descent, so as that the lands of any person dying intestate shall be divisible equally among all his children, or other representatives, in equal degree.

To make slaves distributable among the next of kin, as other movables....

[1]*executed by three gentlemen:* Jefferson was one of the three men who wrote this set of proposed revisions to the legal code of Virginia.

To emancipate all slaves born after the passing [of] the act. The bill reported by the revisers does not itself contain this proposition; but an amendment containing it was prepared, to be offered to the legislature whenever the bill should be taken up, and farther directing, that they should continue with their parents to a certain age, then to be brought up, at the public expense, to tillage, arts, or sciences, according to their geniuses, till the females should be eighteen, and the males twenty-one years of age, when they should be colonized to such place as the circumstances of the time should render most proper, sending them out with arms, implements of household and of the handicraft arts, seeds, pairs of the useful domestic animals, &c., to declare them a free and independent people, and extend to them our alliance and protection, till they have acquired strength; and to send vessels at the same time to other parts of the world for an equal number of white inhabitants; to induce them to migrate hither, proper encouragements were to be proposed. It will probably be asked, Why not retain and incorporate the blacks into the State, and thus save the expense of supplying by importation of white settlers, the vacancies they will leave? Deep-rooted prejudices entertained by the whites; ten thousand recollections, by the blacks, of the injuries they have sustained; new provocations; the real distinctions which nature has made; and many other circumstances, will divide us into parties, and produce convulsions, which will probably never end but in the extermination of the one or the other race. To these objections, which are political, may be added others, which are physical and moral. The first difference which strikes us is that of color. Whether the black of the negro resides in the reticular membrane between the skin and scarf-skin, or in the scarf-skin itself; whether it proceeds from the color of the blood, the color of the bile, or from that of some other secretion, the difference is fixed in nature, and is as real as if its seat and cause were better known to us. And is this difference of no importance? Is it not the foundation of a greater or less share of beauty in the two races? Are not the fine mixtures of red and white, the expressions of every passion by greater or less suffusions of color in the one, preferable to that eternal monotony, which reigns in the countenances, that immovable veil of black which covers the emotions of the other race? Add to these, flowing hair, a more elegant symmetry of form, their own judgment in favor of the whites, declared by their preference of them, as uniformly as is the preference of the Oranootan[2] for the black woman over those of his own species. The circumstance of superior beauty, is thought worthy of attention in the propagation of our horses, dogs, and other domestic animals; why not in that of man? Besides those of color, figure, and hair, there are other physical distinctions proving a difference of race. They have less hair on the face and body. They secrete less by the kidneys, and more by the glands of the skin, which gives them a very strong and disagreeable odor. This greater degree of transpira-

---

[2]*Oranootan:* Orangutan.

tion, renders them more tolerant of heat, and less so of cold than the whites. Perhaps, too, a difference of structure in the pulminary apparatus, which a late ingenious experimentalist has discovered to be the principal regulator of animal heat, may have disabled them from extricating, in the act of inspiration, so much of that fluid from the outer air, or obliged them in expiration, to part with more of it. They seem to require less sleep. A black after hard labor through the day, will be induced by the slightest amusements to sit up till midnight, or later, though knowing he must be out with the first dawn of the morning. They are at least as brave, and more adventuresome. But this may perhaps proceed from a want of forethought, which prevents their seeing a danger till it be present. When present, they do not go through it with more coolness or steadiness than the whites. They are more ardent after their female; but love seems with them to be more an eager desire, than a tender delicate mixture of sentiment and sensation. Their griefs are transient. Those numberless afflictions, which render it doubtful whether heaven has given life to us in mercy or in wrath, are less felt, and sooner forgotten with them. In general, their existence appears to participate more of sensation than reflection. To this must be ascribed their disposition to sleep when abstracted from their diversions, and unemployed in labor. An animal whose body is at rest, and who does not reflect, must be disposed to sleep of course. Comparing them by their faculties of memory, reason, and imagination, it appears to me that in memory they are equal to the whites; in reason much inferior, as I think one could scarcely be found capable of tracing and comprehending the investigations of Euclid; and that in imagination they are dull, tasteless, and anomalous. It would be unfair to follow them to Africa for this investigation. We will consider them here, on the same stage with the whites, and where the facts are not apochryphal on which a judgment is to be formed. It will be right to make great allowances for the difference of condition, of education, of conversation, of the sphere in which they move. Many millions of them have been brought to, and born in America. Most of them, indeed, have been confined to tillage, to their own homes, and their own society; yet many have been so situated, that they might have availed themselves of the conversation of their masters; many have been brought up to the handicraft arts, and from that circumstance have always been associated with the whites. Some have been liberally educated, and all have lived in countries where the arts and sciences are cultivated to a considerable degree, and all have had before their eyes samples of the best works from abroad. The Indians, with no advantages of this kind, will often carve figures on their pipes not destitute of design and merit. They will crayon out an animal, a plant, or a country, so as to prove the existence of a germ in their minds which only wants cultivation. They astonish you with strokes of the most sublime oratory; such as prove their reason and sentiment strong, their imagination glowing and elevated. But never yet could I find that a black had uttered a thought above the level of plain narration; never saw even an elementary trait of painting or sculpture.

In music they are more generally gifted than the whites with accurate ears for tune and time, and they have been found capable of imagining a small catch.[3] Whether they will be equal to the composition of a more extensive run of melody, or of complicated harmony, is yet to be proved. Misery is often the parent of the most affecting touches in poetry. Among the blacks is misery enough, God knows, but no poetry. Love is the peculiar œstrum of the poet. Their love is ardent, but it kindles the senses only, not the imagination. Religion, indeed, has produced a Phyllis Whately [sic];[4] but it could not produce a poet. The compositions published under her name are below the dignity of criticism. The heroes of the Dunciad[5] are to her, as Hercules to the author of that poem. Ignatius Sancho[6] has approached nearer to merit in composition; yet his letters do more honor to the heart than the head. They breathe the purest effusions of friendship and general philanthropy, and show how great a degree of the latter may be compounded with strong religious zeal. He is often happy in the turn of his compliments, and his style is easy and familiar, except when he affects a Shandean[7] fabrication of words. But his imagination is wild and extravagant, escapes incessantly from every restraint of reason and taste, and, in the course of its vagaries, leaves a tract of thought as incoherent and eccentric, as is the course of a meteor through the sky. His subjects should often have led him to a process of sober reasoning; yet we find him always substituting sentiment for demonstration. Upon the whole, though we admit him to the first place among those of his own color who have presented themselves to the public judgment, yet when we compare him with the writers of the race among whom he lived and particularly with the epistolary class in which he has taken his own stand, we are compelled to enroll him at the bottom of the column. This criticism supposes the letters published under his name to be genuine, and to have received amendment from no other hand; points which would not be of easy investigation. The improvement of the blacks in body and mind, in the first instance of their mixture with the whites, has

[3]The instrument proper to them is the Banjar, which they brought hither from Africa, and which is the original of the guitar, its chords being precisely the four lower chords of the guitar. [Author's note]

[4]*Phyllis Whately:* Phillis Wheatley (175?–1784) was born in Africa but transported to the United States and sold as a slave when she was a young child. Her *Poems on Various Subjects, Religious and Moral* (1773) was the first book of poetry to be published by an African American.

[5]*the heroes of the Dunciad:* In the mock epic poem *The Dunciad* (1728), English satirist Alexander Pope (1688–1744) lampoons his literary rivals as fools and dunces.

[6]*Ignatius Sancho:* Born on a slave ship, Ignatius Sancho (1729–1780) became a servant in the homes of several English aristocrats, where he educated himself and became acquainted with some of the leading writers and artists of the period. He later became a grocer in London and devoted himself to writing. His letters were collected and published in 1782.

[7]*Shandean:* In the style of Laurence Sterne's comic novel, *The Life and Opinions of Tristram Shandy* (1758–1766). Sancho admired Sterne's writing and corresponded regularly with him.

been observed by every one, and proves that their inferiority is not the effect merely of their condition of life....

The opinion that they are inferior in the faculties of reason and imagi- 5
nation, must be hazarded with great diffidence. To justify a general conclusion, requires many observations, even where the subject may be submitted to the anatomical knife, to optical glasses, to analysis by fire or by solvents. How much more then where it is a faculty, not a substance, we are examining; where it eludes the research of all the senses; where the conditions of its existence are various and variously combined; where the effects of those which are present or absent bid defiance to calculation; let me add too, as a circumstance of great tenderness, where our conclusion would degrade a whole race of men from the rank in the scale of beings which their Creator may perhaps have given them. To our reproach it must be said, that though for a century and a half we have had under our eyes the races of black and of red men, they have never yet been viewed by us as subjects of natural history. I advance it, therefore, as a suspicion only, that the blacks, whether originally a distinct race, or made distinct by time and circumstances, are inferior to the whites in the endowments both of body and mind. It is not against experience to suppose that different species of the same genus, or varieties of the same species, may possess different qualifications. Will not a lover of natural history then, one who views the gradations in all the races of animals with the eye of philosophy, excuse an effort to keep those in the department of man as distinct as nature has formed them? This unfortunate difference of color, and perhaps of faculty, is a powerful obstacle to the emancipation of these people. Many of their advocates, while they wish to vindicate the liberty of human nature, are anxious also to preserve its dignity and beauty. Some of these, embarrassed by the question, "What further is to be done with them?" join themselves in opposition with those who are actuated by sordid avarice only. Among the Romans emancipation required but one effort. The slave, when made free, might mix with, without staining the blood of his master. But with us a second is necessary, unknown to history. When freed, he is to be removed beyond the reach of mixture.

ENGAGING THE TEXT

1. Jefferson proposes colonizing—that is, sending away—all newly emancipated slaves and declaring them "a free and independent people" (para. 4). In what ways would their freedom and independence continue to be limited according to this proposal?

2. Jefferson predicts that racial conflict in the United States "will probably never end but in the extermination of the one or the other race" (para. 4). Which of the divisive issues he mentions, if any, are still sources of conflict today? Given the history of race relations from Jefferson's time to our own, do you think his pessimism was justified? Why or why not?

3. Jefferson presents what seems on the surface to be a systematic and logical catalog of the differences he sees between blacks and whites; he then attempts to demonstrate the "natural" superiority of whites based on these differences. Working in pairs or small groups, look carefully at his observations and the conclusions he draws from them. What flaws do you find in his analysis?

EXPLORING CONNECTIONS

4. Consider the picture of Jefferson's descendants on page 78. Write a journal entry or essay comparing the image of Jefferson you received in American history classes to the impression you get from the photo and from the passage above. How do you account for the differences?

5. Working in groups, write scripts for an imaginary meeting between Jefferson and Malcolm X (p. 223) and present them to the class. After each group has acted out its scenario, compare the different versions of the meeting. What does each script assume about the motives and character of the two men?

EXTENDING THE CRITICAL CONTEXT

6. Read the Declaration of Independence and compare Jefferson's most famous document to the lesser-known passage reprinted here. How do the purposes of the two texts differ? What ideas and principles, if any, do they have in common, and where do they conflict? (The text of the Declaration is reprinted as an appendix in most unabridged dictionaries and is available online at http://lcweb2.loc.gov/const/declar.html.)

7. Write a letter to Jefferson responding to this selection and explaining your point of view. What would you tell him about how and why attitudes have changed between his time and ours?

8. Influenced by the heroic image of Jefferson as a champion of freedom and democracy, civic leaders have named libraries, schools, and other public institutions after him for the last two hundred years. Debate whether or not it is appropriate to honor Jefferson in this way given the opinions expressed in this passage.

Let America Be America Again

LANGSTON HUGHES

Written nine years into the Great Depression, "Let America Be America Again" (1938) offers a stinging indictment of the hypocrisy that Langston Hughes perceived everywhere in American life. Yet Hughes transcends his rage and dares to hope for America's future; in so doing he pays homage to ideals that retain their potency even today. (James) Langston Hughes (1902–1967) was a major figure in the Harlem Renaissance—a flowering of African American artists, musicians, and writers in New York City in the 1920s. His poems, often examining the experiences of urban African American life, use the rhythms of jazz, spirituals, and the blues. Among the most popular of his works today are The Ways of White Folks *(1934), a collection of short stories, and* Montage of a Dream Deferred *(1951), a selection of his poetry.*

Let America be America again.
Let it be the dream it used to be.
Let it be the pioneer on the plain
Seeking a home where he himself is free.

(America never was America to me.)   5

Let America be the dream the dreamers dreamed—
Let it be that great strong land of love
Where never kings connive nor tyrants scheme
That any man be crushed by one above.

(It never was America to me.)   10

O, let my land be a land where Liberty
Is crowned with no false patriotic wreath,
But opportunity is real, and life is free,
Equality is in the air we breathe.

(There's never been equality for me,   15
Nor freedom in this "homeland of the free.")

Say who are you that mumbles in the dark?
And who are you that draws your veil across the stars?

I am the poor white, fooled and pushed apart,
I am the red man driven from the land.   20
I am the refugee clutching the hope I seek—

But finding only the same old stupid plan
Of dog eat dog, of mighty crush the weak.
I am the Negro, "problem" to you all.
I am the people, humble, hungry, mean—   25
Hungry yet today despite the dream.
Beaten yet today—O, Pioneers!
I am the man who never got ahead.
The poorest worker bartered through the years.
Yet I'm the one who dreamt our basic dream   30
In that Old World while still a serf of kings,
Who dreamt a dream so strong, so brave, so true,
That even yet its mighty daring sings
In every brick and stone, in every furrow turned
That's made America the land it has become.   35
O, I'm the man who sailed those early seas
In search of what I meant to be my home—
For I'm the one who left dark Ireland's shore,
And Poland's plain, and England's grassy lea,
And torn from Black Africa's strand I came   40
To build a "homeland of the free."

The free?
Who said the free? Not me?
Surely not me? The millions on relief today?
The millions who have nothing for our pay   45
For all the dreams we've dreamed
And all the songs we sung
And all the hopes we've held
And all the flags we've hung,
The millions who have nothing for our pay—   50
Except the dream we keep alive today.

O, let America be America again—
The land that never has been yet—
And yet must be—the land where *every* man is free.
The land that's mine—the poor man's, Indian's, Negro's, ME—   55
Who made America,
Whose sweat and blood, whose faith and pain,
Whose hand at the foundry, whose plow in the rain,
Must bring back our mighty dream again.

O, yes,   60
I say it plain,
America never was America to me,
And yet I swear this oath—
America will be!

ENGAGING THE TEXT

1. Explain the two senses of the word "America" as Hughes uses it in the title and refrain of the poem.

2. According to Hughes, who must rebuild the dream, and why?

3. Why does Hughes reaffirm the dream of an ideal America in the face of so much evidence to the contrary?

4. Explain the irony of lines 40–41 ("And torn from Black Africa's strand I came / To build a 'homeland of the free'").

5. Examine the way Hughes uses line length, repetition, stanza breaks, typography, and indentation to call attention to particular lines of the poem. Why does he emphasize these passages?

EXPLORING CONNECTIONS

6. In the previous selection, Thomas Jefferson advocates sending former slaves to colonize the western wilderness as "a free and independent people." How does Hughes's understanding of freedom differ from Jefferson's? How do their historical circumstances shape their visions of freedom and the meaning of race?

7. Review some or all of the poems in *Rereading America:*

> Melvin Dixon, "Aunt Ida Pieces a Quilt" (p. 130)
> Wendy Rose, "Three Thousand Dollar Death Song" (p. 691)
> Sharon Olds, "From Seven Floors Up" (p. 371)
> Dana Gioia, "Money" (p. 372)
> Louise Erdrich, "Dear John Wayne" (p. 705)
> Aurora Levins Morales, "Child of the Americas" (p. 673)
> Inés Hernández-Ávila, "Para Teresa" (p. 207)
> Langston Hughes, "Let America Be America Again"

Then write an essay on poetry as a form of social action. What are the characteristics of this type of poetry? How does it differ from the poetry you have read before in school?

EXTENDING THE CRITICAL CONTEXT

8. Working in groups, "stage" a reading of the poem, using multiple speakers. Consider carefully how to divide up the lines for the most effective presentation. After the readings, discuss the choices made by the different groups in the class.

9. Working in pairs or in small groups, write prose descriptions of the two versions of America Hughes evokes. Read these aloud and discuss which description more closely matches your own view of the United States.

Causes of Prejudice

VINCENT N. PARRILLO

What motivates the creation of racial categories? In the following selection, Vincent Parrillo reviews several theories that seek to explain the motives for prejudiced behavior—from socialization theory to economic competition. As Parrillo indicates, prejudice cannot be linked to any single cause: a whole network of forces and frustrations underlies the reasons for this complex behavior. Parrillo (b. 1938) is chairperson of the Department of Sociology at William Paterson College in New Jersey. His books include Rethinking Today's Minorities *(1991) and* Diversity in America *(1996). He has also written and produced two award-winning documentaries for PBS television. This excerpt originally appeared in* Strangers to These Shores *(1999, 6th ed.).*

Prejudicial attitudes may be either positive or negative. Sociologists primarily study the latter, however, because only negative attitudes can lead to turbulent social relations between dominant and minority groups. Numerous writers, therefore, have defined *prejudice* as an attitudinal "system of negative beliefs, feelings, and action-orientations regarding a certain group or groups of people."[1] The status of the strangers is an important factor in the development of a negative attitude. Prejudicial attitudes exist among members of both dominant and minority groups. Thus, in the relations between dominant and minority groups, the antipathy felt by one group for another is quite often reciprocated.

Psychological perspectives on prejudice—whether behaviorist, cognitive, or psychoanalytic—focus on the subjective states of mind of individuals. In these perspectives, a person's prejudicial attitudes may result from imitation or conditioning (behaviorist), perceived similarity–dissimilarity of beliefs (cognitive), or specific personality characteristics (psychoanalytic). In contrast, sociological perspectives focus on the objective conditions of society as the social forces behind prejudicial attitudes and behind racial and ethnic relations. Individuals do not live in a vacuum; social reality affects their states of mind.

Both perspectives are necessary to understand prejudice. As psychologist Gordon Allport argued, besides needing a close study of habits, perceptions, motivation, and personality, we need an analysis of social settings, sit-

---

[1]Reported by Daniel Wilner, Rosabelle Price Walkley, and Stuart W. Cook, "Residential Proximity and Intergroup Relations in Public Housing Projects," *Journal of Social Issues* 8 (1) (1952): 45. See also James W. Vander Zanden, *American Minority Relations*, 3d ed. (New York: Ronald Press, 1972), p. 21. [All notes are the author's.]

uational forces, demographic and ecological variables, and legal and economic trends.[2] Psychological and sociological perspectives complement each other in providing a fuller explanation about intergroup relations.

The Psychology of Prejudice

We can understand more about prejudice among individuals by focusing on four areas of study: levels of prejudice, self-justification, personality, and frustration.

Levels of Prejudice.   Bernard Kramer suggests that prejudice exists on   5
three levels: cognitive, emotional, and action orientation.[3] The **cognitive level of prejudice** encompasses a person's beliefs and perceptions of a group as threatening or nonthreatening, inferior or equal (e.g., in terms of intellect, status, or biological composition), seclusive or intrusive, impulse-gratifying, acquisitive, or possessing other positive or negative characteristics. Mr. X's cognitive beliefs are that Jews are intrusive and acquisitive. Other illustrations of cognitive beliefs are that the Irish are heavy drinkers and fighters. African Americans are rhythmic and lazy, and the Poles are thick-headed and unintelligent. Generalizations shape both ethnocentric and prejudicial attitudes, but there is a difference. *Ethnocentrism* is a generalized rejection of all outgroups on the basis of an ingroup focus, whereas **prejudice** is a rejection of certain people solely on the basis of their membership in a particular group.

In many societies, members of the majority group may believe that a particular low-status minority group is dirty, immoral, violent, or lawbreaking. In the United States, the Irish, Italians, African Americans, Mexicans, Chinese, Puerto Ricans, and others have at one time or another been labeled with most, if not all, of these adjectives. In most European countries and in the United States, the group lowest on the socioeconomic ladder has often been depicted in caricature as also lowest on the evolutionary ladder. The Irish and African Americans in the United States and the peasants and various ethnic groups in Europe have all been depicted in the past as apelike:

> The Victorian images of the Irish as "white Negro" and simian Celt, or a combination of the two, derived much of its force and inspiration from physiognomical beliefs ... [but] every country in Europe had its equivalent of "white Negroes" and simianized men, whether or not they happened to be stereotypes of criminals, assassins, political radicals, revolutionaries, Slavs, gypsies, Jews, or peasants.[4]

[2]Gordon W. Allport, "Prejudice: Is It Societal or Personal?" *Journal of Social Issues* 18 (1962): 129–30.

[3]Bernard M. Kramer, "Dimensions of Prejudice," *Journal of Psychology* 27 (April 1949): 389–451.

[4]L. Perry Curtis, Jr., *Apes and Angels: The Irishman in Victorian Caricature* (Washington, D.C.: Smithsonian Press, 1971).

The **emotional level of prejudice** refers to the feelings that a minority group arouses in an individual. Although these feelings may be based on stereotypes from the cognitive level, they represent a more intense stage of personal involvement. The emotional attitudes may be negative or positive, such as fear/envy, distrust/trust, disgust/admiration, or contempt/empathy. These feelings, based on beliefs about the group, may be triggered by social interaction or by the possibility of interaction. For example, whites might react with fear or anger to the integration of their schools or neighborhoods, or Protestants might be jealous of the lifestyle of a highly successful Catholic business executive.

An **action-orientation level of prejudice** is the positive or negative predisposition to engage in discriminatory behavior. A person who harbors strong feelings about members of a certain racial or ethnic group may have a tendency to act for or against them—being aggressive or nonaggressive, offering assistance or withholding it. Such an individual would also be likely to want to exclude or include members of that group both in close, personal social relations and in peripheral social relations. For example, some people would want to exclude members of the disliked group from doing business with them or living in their neighborhood. Another manifestation of the action-orientation level of prejudice is the desire to change or maintain the status differential or inequality between the two groups, whether the area is economic, political, educational, social, or a combination. Note that an action orientation is a predisposition to act, not the action itself.

Self-Justification.   **Self-justification** involves denigrating a person or group to justify maltreatment of them. In this situation, self-justification leads to prejudice and discrimination against members of another group.

Some philosophers argue that we are not so much rational creatures as   10
we are rationalizing creatures. We require reassurance that the things we do and the lives we live are proper, that good reasons for our actions exist. If we can convince ourselves that another group is inferior, immoral, or dangerous, we may feel justified in discriminating against its members, enslaving them, or even killing them.

History is filled with examples of people who thought their maltreatment of others was just and necessary: As defenders of the "true faith," the Crusaders killed "Christ-killers" (Jews) and "infidels" (Moslems). Participants in the Spanish Inquisition imprisoned, tortured, and executed "heretics," "the disciples of the Devil." Similarly, the Puritans burned witches, whose refusal to confess "proved they were evil"; pioneers exploited or killed Native Americans who were "heathen savages"; and whites mistreated, enslaved, or killed African Americans, who were "an inferior species." According to U.S. Army officers, the civilians in the Vietnamese village of My Lai were "probably" aiding the Vietcong; so in 1968 U.S. soldiers fighting in the Vietnam War felt justified in slaughtering over 300 unarmed people there, including women, children, and the elderly.

Some sociologists believe that self-justification works the other way around. That is, instead of self-justification serving as a basis for subjugating others, the subjugation occurs first and the self-justification follows, resulting in prejudice and continued discrimination.[5] The evolution of racism as a concept after the establishment of the African slave trade would seem to support this idea. Philip Mason offers an insight into this view:

> A specialized society is likely to defeat a simpler society and provide a lower tier still of enslaved and conquered peoples. The rulers and organizers sought security for themselves and their children; to perpetuate the power, the esteem, and the comfort they had achieved, it was necessary not only that the artisans and labourers should work contentedly but that the rulers should sleep without bad dreams. No one can say with certainty how the myths originated, but it is surely relevant that when one of the founders of Western thought set himself to frame an ideal state that would embody social justice, he—like the earliest city dwellers—not only devised a society stratified in tiers but believed it would be necessary to persuade the traders and workpeople that, by divine decree, they were made from brass and iron, while the warriors were made of silver and the rulers of gold.[6]

Another example of self-justification serving as a source of prejudice is the dominant group's assumption of an attitude of superiority over other groups. In this respect, establishing a prestige hierarchy—ranking the status of various ethnic groups—results in differential association. To enhance or maintain self-esteem, a person may avoid social contact with groups deemed inferior and associate only with those identified as being of high status. Through such behavior, self-justification may come to intensify the social distance between groups.... *Social distance* refers to the degree to which ingroup members do not engage in social or primary relationships with members of various outgroups.

Personality.   In 1950, in *The Authoritarian Personality*, T. W. Adorno and his colleagues reported a correlation between individuals' early childhood experiences of harsh parental discipline and their development of an **authoritarian personality** as adults.[7] If parents assume an excessively domineering posture in their relations with a child, exercising stern measures and threatening to withdraw love if the child does not respond with weakness and submission, the child tends to be insecure and to nurture much latent hostility against the parents. When such children become adults, they may demonstrate **displaced aggression,** directing their hostil-

[5]See Marvin B. Scott and Stanford M. Lyman, "Accounts," *American Sociological Review* 33 (February 1968): 40–62.

[6]Philip Mason, *Patterns of Dominance* (New York: Oxford University Press, 1970), p. 7. See also Philip Mason, *Race Relations* (New York: Oxford University Press, 1970), pp. 17–29.

[7]T. W. Adorno, Else Frankel-Brunswik, Daniel J. Levinson, and R. Nevitt Sanford, *The Authoritarian Personality* (New York: Harper & Row, 1950).

ity against a powerless group to compensate for their feelings of insecurity and fear. Highly prejudiced individuals tend to come from families that emphasize obedience.

The authors identified authoritarianism by the use of a measuring instrument called an F scale (the *F* standing for potential fascism). Other tests included the A-S (anti-Semitism) and E (ethnocentrism) scales, the latter measuring attitudes toward various minorities. One of their major findings was that people who scored high on authoritarianism also consistently showed a high degree of prejudice against all minority groups. These highly prejudiced persons were characterized by rigidity of viewpoint, dislike for ambiguity, strict obedience to leaders, and intolerance of weakness in themselves and others. 15

No sooner did *The Authoritarian Personality* appear than controversy began. H. H. Hyman and P. B. Sheatsley challenged the methodology and analysis.[8] Solomon Asch questioned the assumptions that the F scale responses represented a belief system and that structural variables (such as ideologies, stratification, and mobility) do not play a role in shaping personality.[9] E. A. Shils argued that the authors were interested only in measuring authoritarianism of the political right while ignoring such tendencies in those at the other end of the political spectrum.[10] Other investigators sought alternative explanations for the authoritarian personality. D. Stewart and T. Hoult extended the framework beyond family childhood experiences to include other social factors.[11] H. C. Kelman and Janet Barclay pointed out that substantial evidence exists showing that lower intelligence and less education also correlate with high authoritarianism scores on the F scale.[12]

Despite the critical attacks, the underlying conceptions of *The Authoritarian Personality* were important, and research into personality as a factor in prejudice has continued. Subsequent investigators refined and modified the original study. Correcting scores for response bias, they conducted cross-cultural studies. Respondents in Germany and Near East countries, where more authoritarian social structures exist, scored higher on authoritarianism and social distance between groups. In Japan, Germany, and the United States, authoritarianism and social distance were moderately related. Other studies suggested that an inverse relationship exists between

[8]H. H. Hyman and P. B. Sheatsley, "The Authoritarian Personality: A Methodological Critique," in R. Christie and M. Jahoda (eds.), *Studies in the Scope and Method of "The Authoritarian Personality"* (Glencoe, Ill.: Free Press, 1954).

[9]Solomon E. Asch, *Social Psychology* (Englewood Cliffs, N.J.: Prentice-Hall, 1952), p. 545.

[10]E. A. Shils, "Authoritarianism: Right and Left," in *Studies in the Scope and Method of "The Authoritarian Personality."*

[11]D. Stewart and T. Hoult, "A Social-Psychological Theory of 'The Authoritarian Personality.'" *American Journal of Sociology* 65 (1959): 274.

[12]H. C. Kelman and Janet Barclay, "The F Scale as a Measure of Breadth of Perspective," *Journal of Abnormal and Social Psychology* 67 (1963): 608–15.

social class and F scale scores: the higher the social class, the lower the authoritarianism.[13]

Although studies of authoritarian personality have helped us understand some aspects of prejudice, they have not provided a causal explanation. Most of the findings in this area show a correlation, but the findings do not prove, for example, that harsh discipline of children causes them to become prejudiced adults. Perhaps the strict parents were themselves prejudiced, and the child learned those attitudes from them. Or as George Simpson and J. Milton Yinger say:

> One must be careful not to assume too quickly that a certain tendency —
> rigidity of mind, for example — that is correlated with prejudice necessarily causes that prejudice....The sequence may be the other way around....It is more likely that both are related to more basic factors.[14]

For some people, prejudice may indeed be rooted in subconscious childhood tensions, but we simply do not know whether these tensions directly cause a high degree of prejudice in the adult or whether other powerful social forces are the determinants. Whatever the explanation, authoritarianism is a significant phenomenon worthy of continued investigation. Recent research, however, has stressed social and situational factors, rather than personality, as primary causes of prejudice and discrimination.[15]

Yet another dimension of the personality component is that people with   20
low self-esteem are more prejudiced than those who feel good about themselves. Some researchers have argued that individuals with low self-esteem deprecate others to enhance their feelings about themselves.[16] One study asserts that "low self-esteem individuals seem to have a generally negative view of themselves, their ingroup, outgroups, and perhaps the world," and thus their tendency to be more prejudiced is not due to rating the outgroup negatively in comparison to their ingroup.[17]

Frustration.   Frustration is the result of relative deprivation in which expectations remain unsatisfied. **Relative deprivation** is a lack of resources, or rewards, in one's standard of living in comparison with those of

[13]For an excellent summary of authoritarian studies and literature, see John P. Kirscht and Ronald C. Dillehay, *Dimensions of Authoritarianism: A Review of Research and Theory* (Lexington: University of Kentucky Press, 1967).

[14]George E. Simpson and J. Milton Yinger, *Racial and Cultural Minorities: An Analysis of Prejudice and Discrimination* (New York: Harper & Row, 1953), p. 91.

[15]Ibid., pp. 62–79.

[16]Howard J. Ehrlich, *The Social Psychology of Prejudice* (New York: Wiley, 1974); G. Sherwood, "Self-Serving Biases in Person Perception," *Psychological Bulletin* 90 (1981): 445–59; T. A. Wills, "Downward Comparison Principles in Social Psychology," *Psychological Bulletin* 90 (1981): 245–71.

[17]Jennifer Crocker and Ian Schwartz, "Prejudice and Ingroup Favoritism in a Minimal Intergroup Situation: Effects of Self-Esteem," *Personality and Social Psychology Bulletin* 11 (4) (December 1985): 379–86.

others in the society. A number of investigators have suggested that frustrations tend to increase aggression toward others.[18] Frustrated people may easily strike out against the perceived cause of their frustration. However, this reaction may not be possible because the true source of the frustration is often too nebulous to be identified or too powerful to act against. In such instances, the result may be displaced aggression; in this situation, the frustrated individual or group usually redirects anger against a more visible, vulnerable, and socially sanctioned target, one unable to strike back. Minorities meet these criteria and are thus frequently the recipients of displaced aggression by the dominant group.

Blaming others for something that is not their fault is known as **scapegoating.** The term comes from the ancient Hebrew custom of using a goat during the Day of Atonement as a symbol of the sins of the people. In an annual ceremony, a priest placed his hands on the head of a goat and listed the people's sins in a symbolic transference of guilt; he then chased the goat out of the community, thereby freeing the people of sin.[19] Since those times, the powerful group has usually punished the scapegoat group rather than allowing it to escape.

There have been many instances throughout world history of minority groups serving as scapegoats, including the Christians in ancient Rome, the Huguenots in France, the Jews in Europe and Russia, and the Puritans and Quakers in England. Gordon Allport suggests that certain characteristics are necessary for a group to become a suitable scapegoat. The group must be (1) highly visible in physical appearance or observable customs and actions; (2) not strong enough to strike back; (3) situated within easy access of the dominant group and, ideally, concentrated in one area; (4) a past target of hostility for whom latent hostility still exists; and (5) the symbol of an unpopular concept.[20]

Some groups fit this typology better than others, but minority racial and ethnic groups have been a perennial choice. Irish, Italians, Catholics, Jews, Quakers, Mormons, Chinese, Japanese, Blacks, Puerto Ricans, Chicanos, and Koreans have all been treated, at one time or another, as the scapegoat in the United States. Especially in times of economic hardship, societies tend to blame some group for the general conditions, which often leads to

---

[18]John Dollard, Leonard W. Doob, Neal E. Miller, O. H. Mowrer, and Robert P. Sears, *Frustration and Aggression* (New Haven, Conn.: Yale University Press, 1939); A. F. Henry and J. F. Short, Jr., *Suicide and Homicide* (New York: Free Press, 1954); Neal Miller and Richard Bugelski, "Minor Studies in Aggression: The Influence of Frustration Imposed by the Ingroup on Attitudes Expressed Toward Out-Groups," *Journal of Psychology* 25 (1948): 437–42; Stuart Palmer, *The Psychology of Murder* (New York: T. Y. Crowell, 1960); Brenden C. Rule and Elizabeth Percival, "The Effects of Frustration and Attack on Physical Aggression," *Journal of Experimental Research on Personality* 5 (1971): 111–88.

[19]Leviticus 16:5–22.

[20]Gordon W. Allport, *The Nature of Prejudice* (Cambridge, Mass.: Addison-Wesley, 1954), pp. 13–14.

aggressive action against the group as an expression of frustration. For example, a study by Carl Hovland and Robert Sears found that, between 1882 and 1930, a definite correlation existed between a decline in the price of cotton and an increase in the number of lynchings of Blacks.[21]

In several controlled experiments, social scientists have attempted to measure the validity of the scapegoat theory. Neal Miller and Richard Bugelski tested a group of young men aged eighteen to twenty who were working in a government camp about their feelings toward various minority groups. The young men were reexamined about these feelings after experiencing frustration by being obliged to take a long, difficult test and being denied an opportunity to see a film at a local theater. This group showed some evidence of increased prejudicial feelings, whereas a control group, which did not experience any frustration, showed no change in prejudicial attitudes.[22]

Donald Weatherley conducted an experiment with a group of college students to measure the relationship between frustration and aggression against a specific disliked group.[23] After identifying students who were or were not highly anti-Semitic and subjecting them to a strongly frustrating experience, he asked the students to write stories about pictures shown to them. Some of the students were shown pictures of people who had been given Jewish names; other students were presented with pictures of unnamed people. When the pictures were unidentified, the stories of the anti-Semitic students did not differ from those of other students. When the pictures were identified, however, the anti-Semitic students wrote stories reflecting much more aggression against the Jews in the pictures than did the other students.

For over twenty years, Leonard Berkowitz and his associates studied and experimented with aggressive behavior. They concluded that, confronted with equally frustrating situations, highly prejudiced individuals are more likely to seek scapegoats than are nonprejudiced individuals. Another intervening variable is that personal frustrations (marital failure, injury, or mental illness) make people more likely to seek scapegoats than do shared frustrations (dangers of flood or hurricane).[24]

Some experiments have shown that aggression does not increase if the frustration is understandable.[25] Other experiments have found that people

[21]Carl I. Hovland and Robert R. Sears, "Minor Studies of Aggression: Correlation of Lynchings with Economic Indices," *Journal of Psychology* 9 (Winter 1940): 301–10.

[22]Miller and Bugelski, "Minor Studies in Aggression," pp. 437–42.

[23]Donald Weatherley, "Anti-Semitism and the Expression of Fantasy Aggression," *Journal of Abnormal and Social Psychology* 62 (1961): 454–57.

[24]See Leonard Berkowitz, "Whatever Happened to the Frustration-Aggression Hypothesis?" *American Behavioral Scientist* 21 (1978): 691–708; L. Berkowitz, *Aggression: A Social Psychological Analysis* (New York: McGraw-Hill, 1962).

[25]D. Zillman, *Hostility and Aggression* (Hillsdale, N.J.: Laurence Erlbaum, 1979); R. A. Baron, *Human Aggression* (New York: Plenum Press, 1977); N. Pastore, "The Role of Arbitrariness in the Frustration-Aggression Hypothesis," *Journal of Abnormal and Social Psychology* 47 (1952): 728–31.

become aggressive only if the aggression directly relieves their frustration.[26] Still other studies have shown that anger is a more likely result if the person responsible for the frustrating situation could have acted otherwise.[27] Clearly, the results are mixed, depending on the variables within a given social situation.

Frustration–aggression theory, although helpful, is not completely satisfactory. It ignores the role of culture and the reality of actual social conflict and fails to show any causal relationship. Most of the responses measured in these studies were of people already biased. Why did one group rather than another become the object of the aggression? Moreover, frustration does not necessarily precede aggression, and aggression does not necessarily flow from frustration.

The Sociology of Prejudice

Sociologist Talcott Parsons provided one bridge between psychology and sociology by introducing social forces as a variable in frustration–aggression theory. He suggested that both the family and the occupational structure may produce anxieties and insecurities that create frustration.[28] According to this view, the growing-up process (gaining parental affection and approval, identifying with and imitating sexual role models, and competing with others in adulthood) sometimes involves severe emotional strain. The result is an adult personality with a large reservoir of repressed aggression that becomes *free-floating*—susceptible to redirection against convenient scapegoats. Similarly, the occupational system is a source of frustration: its emphasis on competitiveness and individual achievement, its function of conferring status, its requirement that people inhibit their natural impulses at work, and its ties to the state of the economy are among the factors that generate emotional anxieties. Parsons pessimistically concluded that minorities fulfill a functional "need" as targets for displaced aggression and therefore will remain targets.[29]

Perhaps most influential in staking out the sociological position on prejudice was Herbert Blumer, who suggested that prejudice always involves the "sense of group position" in society. Agreeing with Kramer's delineation of three levels of prejudice, Blumer argued that prejudice can include beliefs, feelings, and a predisposition to action, thus motivating behavior that

[26]A. H. Buss, "Instrumentality of Aggression, Feedback, and Frustration as Determinants of Physical Aggression," *Journal of Personality and Social Psychology* 3 (1966): 153–62.

[27]J. R. Averill, "Studies on Anger and Aggression: Implications for Theories of Emotion," *American Psychologist* 38 (1983): 1145–60.

[28]Talcott Parsons, "Certain Primary Sources and Patterns of Aggression in the Social Structure of the Western World," in *Essays in Sociological Theory* (New York: Free Press, 1964), pp. 298–322.

[29]For an excellent review of Parsonian theory in this area, see Stanford M. Lyman, *The Black American in Sociological Thought: A Failure of Perspective* (New York: Putnam, 1972), pp. 145–69.

derives from the social hierarchy.[30] By emphasizing historically established group positions and relationships, Blumer shifted his focus away from the attitudes and personality compositions of individuals. As a social phenomenon, prejudice rises or falls according to issues that alter one group's position vis-à-vis that of another group.

Socialization. In the **socialization process,** individuals acquire the values, attitudes, beliefs, and perceptions of their culture or subculture, including religion, nationality, and social class. Generally, the child conforms to the parents' expectations in acquiring an understanding of the world and its people. Being impressionable and knowing of no alternative conceptions of the world, the child usually accepts these concepts without questioning. We thus learn the prejudices of our parents and others, which then become part of our values and beliefs. Even when based on false stereotypes, prejudices shape our perceptions of various peoples and influence our attitudes and actions toward particular groups. For example, if we develop negative attitudes about Jews because we are taught that they are shrewd, acquisitive, and clannish — all-too-familiar stereotypes — as adults we may refrain from business or social relationships with them. We may not even realize the reason for such avoidance, so subtle has been the prejudice instilled within us.

People may learn certain prejudices because of their pervasiveness. The cultural screen that we develop and through which we view the surrounding world is not always accurate, but it does permit transmission of shared values and attitudes, which are reinforced by others. Prejudice, like cultural values, is taught and learned through the socialization process. The prevailing prejudicial attitudes and actions may be deeply embedded in custom or law (e.g., the **Jim Crow laws** of the 1890s and the early twentieth century establishing segregated public facilities throughout the South, which subsequent generations accepted as proper, and maintained in their own adult lives).

Although socialization explains how prejudicial attitudes may be transmitted from one generation to the next, it does not explain their origin or why they intensify or diminish over the years. These aspects of prejudice must be explained in another way.

Economic Competition. People tend to be more hostile toward others 35
when they feel that their security is threatened; thus many social scientists conclude that economic competition and conflict breed prejudice. Certainly, considerable evidence shows that negative stereotyping, prejudice, and discrimination increase markedly whenever competition for available jobs increases.

An excellent illustration relates to the Chinese sojourners in the nineteenth-century United States. Prior to the 1870s, the transcontinental

[30]Herbert Blumer, "Race Prejudice as a Sense of Group Position," *Pacific Sociological Review* 1 (1958): 3–7.

railroad was being built, and the Chinese filled many of the jobs made available by this project in the sparsely populated West. Although they were expelled from the region's gold mines and schools and could obtain no redress of grievances in the courts, they managed to convey to some Whites the image of being a clean, hard-working, law-abiding people. The completion of the railroad, the flood of former Civil War soldiers into the job market, and the economic depression of 1873 worsened their situation. The Chinese became more frequent victims of open discrimination and hostility. Their positive stereotype among some Whites was widely displaced by a negative one: They were now "conniving," "crafty," "criminal," "the yellow menace." Only after they retreated into Chinatowns and entered specialty occupations that minimized their competition with Whites did the intense hostility abate.

One pioneer in the scientific study of prejudice, John Dollard, demonstrated how prejudice against the Germans, which had been virtually nonexistent, arose in a small U.S. industrial town when times got bad:

> Local Whites largely drawn from the surrounding farms manifested considerable direct aggression toward the newcomers. Scornful and derogatory opinions were expressed about the Germans, and the native Whites had a satisfying sense of superiority toward them.... The chief element in the permission to be aggressive against the Germans was rivalry for jobs and status in the local woodenware plants. The native Whites felt definitely crowded for their jobs by the entering German groups and in case of bad times had a chance to blame the Germans who by their presence provided more competitors for the scarcer jobs. There seemed to be no traditional pattern of prejudice against Germans unless the skeletal suspicion of all out-groupers (always present) be invoked in this place.[31]

Both experimental studies and historical analyses have added credence to the economic-competition theory. Muzafer Sherif directed several experiments showing how intergroup competition at a boys' camp led to conflict and escalating hostility.[32] Donald Young pointed out that, throughout U.S. history, in times of high unemployment and thus intense job competition, nativist movements against minorities have flourished.[33] This pattern has held true regionally—against Asians on the West Coast, Italians in Louisiana, and French Canadians in New England—and nationally, with the antiforeign movements always peaking during periods of depression. So

---

[31]John Dollard, "Hostility and Fear in Social Life," *Social Forces* 17 (1938): 15–26.

[32]Muzafer Sherif, O. J. Harvey, B. Jack White, William Hood, and Carolyn Sherif, *Intergroup Conflict and Cooperation: The Robbers Cave Experiment* (Norman: University of Oklahoma Institute of Intergroup Relations, 1961). See also M. Sherif, "Experiments in Group Conflict," *Scientific American* 195 (1956): 54–58.

[33]Donald Young, *Research Memorandum on Minority Peoples in the Depression* (New York: Social Science Research Council, 1937), pp. 133–41.

it was with the Native American Party in the 1830s, the Know-Nothing Party in the 1850s, the American Protective Association in the 1890s, and the Ku Klux Klan after World War I. Since the passage of civil rights laws on employment in the twentieth century, researchers have consistently detected the strongest antiblack prejudice among working-class and middle-class Whites who feel threatened by Blacks entering their socioeconomic group in noticeable numbers.[34] It seems that any group applying the pressure of job competition most directly on another group becomes a target of its prejudice.

Once again, a theory that offers some excellent insights into prejudice — in particular, that adverse economic conditions correlate with increased hostility toward minorities — also has some serious shortcomings. Not all groups that have been objects of hostility (e.g., Quakers and Mormons) have been economic competitors. Moreover, why is hostility against some groups greater than against others? Why do the negative feelings in some communities run against groups whose numbers are so small that they cannot possibly pose an economic threat? Evidently values besides economic ones cause people to be antagonistic to a group perceived as an actual or potential threat.

Social Norms.   Some sociologists have suggested that a relationship   40 exists between prejudice and a person's tendency to conform to societal expectations.[35] **Social norms** — the norms of one's culture — form the generally shared rules defining what is and is not proper behavior. By learning and automatically accepting the prevailing prejudices, an individual is simply conforming to those norms.

This theory holds that a direct relationship exists between degree of conformity and degree of prejudice. If so, people's prejudices should decrease or increase significantly when they move into areas where the prejudicial norm is lesser or greater. Evidence supports this view. Thomas Pettigrew found that Southerners in the 1950s became less prejudiced against Blacks when they interacted with them in the army, where the social norms were less prejudicial.[36] In another study, Jeanne Watson found that people moving into an anti-Semitic neighborhood in New York City became more anti-Semitic.[37]

---

[34]Andrew Greeley and Paul Sheatsley, "The Acceptance of Desegregation Continues to Advance," *Scientific American* 210 (1971): 13–19; T. F. Pettigrew, "Three Issues in Ethnicity: Boundaries, Deprivations, and Perceptions," in M. Yinger and S. J. Cutler (eds.), *Major Social Issues: A Multidisciplinary View* (New York: Free Press, 1978); R. D. Vanneman and T. F. Pettigrew, "Race and Relative Deprivation in the United States," *Race* 13 (1972): 461–86.

[35]See Harry H. L. Kitano, "Passive Discrimination in the Normal Person," *Journal of Social Psychology* 70 (1966): 23–31.

[36]Thomas Pettigrew, "Regional Differences in Anti-Negro Prejudice," *Journal of Abnormal and Social Psychology* 59 (1959): 28–36.

[37]Jeanne Watson, "Some Social and Psychological Situations Related to Change in Attitude," *Human Relations* 3 (1950): 15–56.

John Dollard's study, *Caste and Class in a Southern Town* (1937), provides an in-depth look at the emotional adjustment of Whites and Blacks to rigid social norms.[38] In his study of the processes, functions, and maintenance of accommodation, Dollard detailed the "carrot-and-stick" method social groups employed. Intimidation—sometimes even severe reprisals for going against social norms—ensured compliance. However, reprisals usually were unnecessary. The advantages Whites and Blacks gained in psychological, economic, or behavioral terms served to perpetuate the caste order. These gains in personal security and stability set in motion a vicious circle. They encouraged a way of life that reinforced the rationale of the social system in this community.

Two 1994 studies provided further evidence of the powerful influence of social norms. Joachim Krueger and Russell W. Clement found that consensus bias persisted despite the availability of statistical data and knowledge about such bias.[39] Michael R. Leippe and Donna Eisenstadt showed that induced compliance can change socially significant attitudes and that the change generalizes to broader beliefs.[40]

Although the social-norms theory explains prevailing attitudes, it does not explain either their origins or the reasons why new prejudices develop when other groups move into an area. In addition, the theory does not explain why prejudicial attitudes against a particular group rise and fall cyclically over the years.

Although many social scientists have attempted to identify the causes of prejudice, no single factor provides an adequate explanation. Prejudice is a complex phenomenon, and it is most likely the product of more than one causal agent. Sociologists today tend either to emphasize multiple-cause explanations or to stress social forces encountered in specific and similar situations—forces such as economic conditions, stratification, and hostility toward an outgroup.

45

ENGAGING THE TEXT

1. Review Parrillo's discussion of the cognitive, emotional, and action-oriented levels of prejudice. Do you think it's possible for an individual to hold prejudiced beliefs that do *not* affect her feelings and actions? Why or why not?

[38]John Dollard, *Caste and Class in a Southern Town,* 3d ed. (Garden City, N.Y.: Doubleday Anchor Books, 1957).

[39]Joachim Krueger and Russell W. Clement, "The Truly False Consensus Effect: An Ineradicable and Egocentric Bias in Social Perception," *Journal of Personality and Social Psychology* 67 (1994): 596–610.

[40]Michael R. Leippe and Donna Eisenstadt, "Generalization of Dissonance Reduction: Decreasing Prejudice through Induced Compliance," *Journal of Personality and Social Psychology* 67 (1994): 395–414.

2. How can prejudice arise from self-justification? Offer some examples of how a group can assume an attitude of superiority in order to justify ill-treatment of others.

3. How, according to Parrillo, might personal factors like authoritarian attitudes, low self-esteem, or frustration promote the growth of prejudice?

4. What is the "socialization process," according to Parrillo? In what different ways can socialization instill prejudice?

5. What is the relationship between economic competition and prejudice? Do you think prejudice would continue to exist if everyone had a good job with a comfortable income?

EXPLORING CONNECTIONS

6. Which of the theories Parrillo outlines, if any, might help to explain the attitudes toward blacks expressed by Thomas Jefferson (p. 539)? Which apply most clearly to the life story of C. P. Ellis (p. 562)?

7. Read or review Carmen Vázquez's "Appearances" (p. 492). How useful are the theories presented by Parrillo in analyzing prejudice against gays and lesbians? To what extent can concepts like levels of prejudice, self-justification, frustration, socialization, and economic competition help us understand antigay attitudes?

EXTENDING THE CRITICAL CONTEXT

8. List the various groups that you belong to (racial, economic, cultural, social, familial, and so forth) and arrange them in a status hierarchy. Which groups were you born into? Which groups did you join voluntarily? Which have had the greatest impact on your socialization? Which groups isolate you the most from contact with outsiders?

9. Working in small groups, research recent news stories for examples of incidents involving racism or prejudice. Which of the theories described by Parrillo seem most useful for analyzing the motives underlying these events?

C. P. Ellis

STUDS TERKEL

The following oral history brings us uncomfortably close to unambiguous, deadly prejudice: C. P. Ellis is a former Ku Klux Klan member who claims to have overcome his racist (and sexist) attitudes; he speaks here as a union leader who feels an alliance to other workers, including blacks and women. Studs Terkel (b. 1912) is probably the best-known practitioner of oral history in the United States. He has compiled several books by interviewing dozens of widely varying people—ordinary people for the most part—about important subjects like work, social class, race, and the Great Depression. The edited versions of these interviews are often surprisingly powerful crystallizations of American social history: Terkel's subjects give voice to the frustrations and hopes of whole generations of Americans. Terkel won a Pulitzer Prize in 1985 for "The Good War": An Oral History of World War II, and in 1997 he was awarded a National Humanities Medal by President Bill Clinton. "C. P. Ellis" first appeared in American Dreams: Lost and Found *(1980).*

We're in his office in Durham, North Carolina. He is the business manager of the International Union of Operating Engineers. On the wall is a plaque: "Certificate of Service, in recognition to C. P. Ellis, for your faithful service to the city in having served as a member of the Durham Human Relations Council. February 1977."

At one time, he had been president (exalted cyclops) of the Durham chapter of the Ku Klux Klan....

He is fifty-two years old.

My father worked in a textile mill in Durham. He died at forty-eight years old. It was probably from cotton dust. Back then, we never heard of brown lung. I was about seventeen years old and had a mother and sister depending on somebody to make a livin'. It was just barely enough insurance to cover his burial. I had to quit school and go to work. I was about eighth grade when I quit.

My father worked hard but never had enough money to buy decent   5
clothes. When I went to school, I never seemed to have adequate clothes to wear. I always left school late afternoon with a sense of inferiority. The other kids had nice clothes, and I just had what Daddy could buy. I still got some of those inferiority feelin's now that I have to overcome once in a while.

I loved my father. He would go with me to ball games. We'd go fishin' together. I was really ashamed of the way he'd dress. He would take this money and give it to me instead of putting it on himself. I always had the feeling about somebody looking at him and makin' fun of him and makin' fun of me. I think it had to do somethin' with my life.

My father and I were very close, but we didn't talk about too many intimate things. He did have a drinking problem. During the week, he would work every day, but weekends he was ready to get plastered. I can understand when a guy looks at his paycheck and looks at his bills, and he's worked hard all the week, and his bills are larger than his paycheck. He'd done the best he could the entire week, and there seemed to be no hope. It's an illness thing. Finally you just say: "The heck with it. I'll just get drunk and forget it."

My father was out of work during the depression, and I remember going with him to the finance company uptown, and he was turned down. That's something that's always stuck.

My father never seemed to be happy. It was a constant struggle with him just like it was for me. It's very seldom I'd see him laugh. He was just tryin' to figure out what he could do from one day to the next.

After several years pumping gas at a service station, I got married. We 10 had to have children. Four. One child was born blind and retarded, which was a real additional expense to us. He's never spoken a word. He doesn't know me when I go to see him. But I see him, I hug his neck. I talk to him, tell him I love him. I don't know whether he knows me or not, but I know he's well taken care of. All my life, I had work, never a day without work, worked all the overtime I could get and still could not survive financially. I began to say there's somethin' wrong with this country. I worked my butt off and just never seemed to break even.

I had some real great ideas about this great nation. (Laughs.) They say to abide by the law, go to church, do right and live for the Lord, and everything'll work out. But it didn't work out. It just kept gettin' worse and worse.

I was workin' a bread route. The highest I made one week was seventy-five dollars. The rent on our house was about twelve dollars a week. I will never forget: outside of this house was a 265-gallon oil drum, and I never did get enough money to fill up that oil drum. What I would do every night, I would run up to the store and buy five gallons of oil and climb up the ladder and pour it in that 265-gallon drum. I could hear that five gallons when it hits the bottom of that oil drum, splatters, and it sounds like it's nothin' in there. But it would keep the house warm for the night. Next day you'd have to do the same thing.

I left the bread route with fifty dollars in my pocket. I went to the bank and borrowed four thousand dollars to buy the service station. I worked seven days a week, open and close, and finally had a heart attack. Just about two months before the last payments of that loan. My wife had done the best she could to keep it runnin'. Tryin' to come out of that hole, I just couldn't do it.

I really began to get bitter. I didn't know who to blame. I tried to find somebody. I began to blame it on black people. I had to hate somebody. Hatin' America is hard to do because you can't see it to hate it. You gotta have somethin' to look at to hate. (Laughs.) The natural person for me to hate would be black people, because my father before me was a member of the Klan. As far as he was concerned, it was the savior of the white people. It was the only organization in the world that would take care of the white people. So I began to admire the Klan.

I got active in the Klan while I was at the service station. Every Monday night, a group of men would come by and buy a Coca-Cola, go back to the car, take a few drinks, and come back and stand around talkin'. I couldn't help but wonder: Why are these dudes comin' out every Monday? They said they were with the Klan and have meetings close-by. Would I be interested? Boy, that was an opportunity I really looked forward to! To be part of somethin'. I joined the Klan, went from member to chaplain, from chaplain to vice-president, from vice-president to president. The title is exalted cyclops.   15

The first night I went with the fellas, they knocked on the door and gave the signal. They sent some robed Klansmen to talk to me and give me some instructions. I was led into a large meeting room, and this was the time of my life! It was thrilling. Here's a guy who's worked all his life and struggled all his life to be something, and here's the moment to be something. I will never forget it. Four robed Klansmen led me into the hall. The lights were dim, and the only thing you could see was an illuminated cross. I knelt before the cross. I had to make certain vows and promises. We promised to uphold the purity of the white race, fight communism, and protect white womanhood.

After I had taken my oath, there was loud applause goin' throughout the building, musta been at least four hundred people. For this one little ol' person. It was a thrilling moment for C. P. Ellis.

It disturbs me when people who do not really know what it's all about are so very critical of individual Klansmen. The majority of 'em are low-income whites, people who really don't have a part in something. They have been shut out as well as the blacks. Some are not very well educated either. Just like myself. We had a lot of support from doctors and lawyers and police officers.

Maybe they've had bitter experiences in this life and they had to hate somebody. So the natural person to hate would be the black person. He's beginnin' to come up, he's beginnin' to learn to read and start votin' and run for political office. Here are white people who are supposed to be superior to them, and we're shut out.

I can understand why people join extreme right-wing or left-wing groups. They're in the same boat I was. Shut out. Deep down inside, we   20 want to be part of this great society. Nobody listens, so we join these groups.

At one time, I was state organizer of the National Rights party. I organized a youth group for the Klan. I felt we were getting old and our generation's gonna die. So I contacted certain kids in schools. They were havin' racial problems. On the first night, we had a hundred high school students. When they came in the door, we had "Dixie" playin'. These kids were just thrilled to death. I begin to hold weekly meetin's with 'em, teachin' the principles of the Klan. At that time, I believed Martin Luther King had Communist connections. I began to teach that Andy Young[1] was affiliated with the Communist party.

I had a call one night from one of our kids. He was about twelve. He said: "I just been robbed downtown by two niggers." I'd had a couple of drinks and that really teed me off. I go downtown and couldn't find the kid. I got worried. I saw two young black people. I had the .32 revolver with me. I said: "Nigger, you seen a little young white boy up here? I just got a call from him and was told that some niggers robbed him of fifteen cents." I pulled my pistol out and put it right at his head. I said: "I've always wanted to kill a nigger and I think I'll make you the first one." I nearly scared the kid to death, and he struck off.

This was the time when the civil rights movement was really beginnin' to peak. The blacks were beginnin' to demonstrate and picket downtown stores. I never will forget some black lady I hated with a purple passion. Ann Atwater. Every time I'd go downtown, she'd be leadin' a boycott. How I hated—pardon the expression, I don't use it much now—how I just hated the black nigger. (Laughs.) Big, fat, heavy woman. She'd pull about eight demonstrations, and first thing you know they had two, three blacks at the checkout counter. Her and I have had some pretty close confrontations.

I felt very big, yeah. (Laughs.) We're more or less a secret organization. We didn't want anybody to know who we were, and I began to do some thinkin'. What am I hidin' for? I've never been convicted of anything in my life. I don't have any court record. What am I, C. P. Ellis, as a citizen and a member of the United Klansmen of America? Why can't I go the city council meeting and say: "This is the way we feel about the matter? We don't want you to purchase mobile units to set in our schoolyards. We don't want niggers in our schools."

We began to come out in the open. We would go to the meetings, and   25 the blacks would be there and we'd be there. It was a confrontation every time. I didn't hold back anything. We began to make some inroads with the city councilmen and county commissioners. They began to call us friend.

---

[1]*Andy Young:* Andrew Jackson Young, Jr. (b. 1932), prominent black leader and politician. Young was a friend and adviser of Martin Luther King, Jr., and served as President Jimmy Carter's ambassador to the United Nations. In the 1980s, he was twice elected mayor of Atlanta.

Call us at night on the telephone: "C. P., glad you came to that meeting last night." They didn't want integration either, but they did it secretively, in order to get elected. They couldn't stand up openly and say it, but they were glad somebody was sayin' it. We visited some of the city leaders in their home and talk to 'em privately. It wasn't long before councilmen would call me up: "The blacks are comin' up tonight and makin' outrageous demands. How about some of you people showin' up and have a little balance?" I'd get on the telephone. "The niggers is comin' to the council meeting tonight. Persons in the city's called me and asked us to be there."

We'd load up our cars and we'd fill up half the council chambers, and the blacks the other half. During these times, I carried weapons to the meetings, outside my belt. We'd go there armed. We would wind up just hollerin' and fussin' at each other. What happened? As a result of our fightin' one another, the city council still had their way. They didn't want to give up control to the blacks nor the Klan. They were usin' us.

I began to realize this later down the road. One day I was walkin' downtown and a certain city council member saw me comin'. I expected him to shake my hand because he was talkin' to me at night on the telephone. I had been in his home and visited with him. He crossed the street. Oh shit, I began to think, somethin's wrong here. Most of 'em are merchants or maybe an attorney, an insurance agent, people like that. As long as they kept low-income whites and low-income blacks fightin', they're gonna maintain control.

I began to get that feeling after I was ignored in public. I thought: Bullshit, you're not gonna use me any more. That's when I began to do some real serious thinkin'.

The same thing is happening in this country today. People are being used by those in control, those who have all the wealth. I'm not espousing communism. We got the greatest system of government in the world. But those who have it simply don't want those who don't have it to have any part of it. Black and white. When it comes to money, the green, the other colors make no difference. (Laughs.)

I spent a lot of sleepless nights. I still didn't like blacks. I didn't want to associate with 'em. Blacks, Jews, or Catholics. My father said: "don't have anything to do with 'em." I didn't until I met a black person and talked with him, eyeball to eyeball, and met a Jewish person and talked to him, eyeball to eyeball. I found out they're people just like me. They cried, they cussed, they prayed, they had desires. Just like myself. Thank God, I got to the point where I can look past labels. But at that time, my mind was closed.

I remember one Monday night Klan meeting. I said something was wrong. Our city fathers were using us. And I didn't like to be used. The reactions of the others was not too pleasant: "Let's just keep fightin' them niggers."

I'd go home at night and I'd have to wrestle with myself. I'd look at a black person walkin' down the street, and the guy'd have ragged shoes or his clothes would be worn. That began to do somethin' to me inside. I went through this for about six months. I felt I just had to get out of the Klan. But I wouldn't get out.

Then something happened. The state AFL–CIO[2] received a grant from the Department of HEW,[3] a $78,000 grant: how to solve racial problems in the school system. I got a telephone call from the president of the state AFL–CIO. "We'd like to get some people together from all walks of life." I said: "All walks of life? Who you talkin' about?" He said: "Blacks, whites, liberals, conservatives, Klansmen, NAACP[4] people."

I said: "No way am I comin' with all those niggers. I'm not gonna be associated with those type of people." A White Citizens Council guy said: "Let's go up there and see what's goin' on. It's tax money bein' spent." I walk in the door, and there was a large number of blacks and white liberals. I knew most of 'em by face 'cause I seen 'em demonstratin' around town. Ann Atwater was there. (Laughs.) I just forced myself to go in and sit down.

The meeting was moderated by a great big black guy who was bushy-headed. (Laughs.) That turned me off. He acted very nice. He said: "I want you all to feel free to say anything you want to say." Some of the blacks stand up and say it's white racism. I took all I could take. I asked for the floor and cut loose. I said: "No, sir, it's black racism. If we didn't have niggers in the schools, we wouldn't have the problems we got today." 35

I will never forget. Howard Clements, a black guy, stood up. He said: "I'm certainly glad C. P. Ellis come because he's the most honest man here tonight." I said: "What's that nigger tryin' to do?" (Laughs.) At the end of that meeting, some blacks tried to come up shake my hand, but I wouldn't do it. I walked off.

Second night, same group was there. I felt a little more easy because I got some things off my chest. The third night, after they elected all the committees, they want to elect a chairman. Howard Clements stood up and said: "I suggest we elect two co-chairpersons." Joe Beckton, executive director of the Human Relations Commission, just as black as he can be, he nominated me. There was a reaction from some blacks. Nooo. And, of all things, they nominated Ann Atwater, that big old fat black gal that I had just hated with a purple passion, as co-chairman. I thought to myself: Hey, ain't no way I can work with that gal. Finally, I agreed to accept it, 'cause at this point, I was tired of fightin', either for survival or against black people or against Jews or against Catholics.

A Klansman and a militant black woman, co-chairmen of the school committee. It was impossible. How could I work with her? But after about

---

[2]*AFL–CIO:* American Federation of Labor and Congress of Industrial Organizations — a huge federation of independent labor unions in the United States, Canada, Mexico, Panama, and elsewhere.

[3]*HEW:* Health, Education, and Welfare — at the time, a department of the federal government.

[4]*NAACP:* National Association for the Advancement of Colored People.

two or three days, it was in our hands. We had to make it a success. This give me another sense of belongin', a sense of pride. This helped this inferiority feelin' I had. A man who has stood up publicly and said he despised black people, all of a sudden he was willin' to work with 'em. Here's a chance for a low-income white man to be somethin'. In spite of all my hatred for blacks and Jews and liberals, I accepted the job. Her and I began to reluctantly work together. (Laughs.) She had as many problems workin' with me as I had workin' with her.

One night, I called her: "Ann, you and I should have a lot of differences and we got 'em now. But there's somethin' laid out here before us, and if it's gonna be a success, you and I are gonna have to make it one. Can we lay aside some of these feelin's?" She said: "I'm willing if you are." I said: "Let's do it."

My old friends would call me at night: "C. P., what the hell is wrong 40 with you? You're sellin' out the white race." This begin to make me have guilt feelin's. Am I doin' right? Am I doin' wrong? Here I am all of a sudden makin' an about-face and tryin' to deal with my feelin's, my heart. My mind was beginnin' to open up. I was beginnin' to see what was right and what was wrong. I don't want the kids to fight forever.

We were gonna go ten nights. By this time, I had went to work at Duke University, in maintenance. Makin' very little money. Terry Sanford give me this ten days off with pay. He was president of Duke at the time. He knew I was a Klansman and realized the importance of blacks and whites getting along.

I said: "If we're gonna make this thing a success, I've got to get to my kind of people." The low-income whites. We walked the streets of Durham, and we knocked on doors and invited people. Ann was goin' into the black community. They just wasn't respondin' to us when we made these house calls. Some of 'em were cussin' us out. "You're sellin' us out, Ellis, get out of my door. I don't want to talk to you." Ann was gettin' the same response from blacks. "What are you doin' messin' with that Klansman?"

One day, Ann and I went back to the school and we sat down. We began to talk and just reflect. Ann said: "My daughter came home cryin' every day. She said her teacher was makin' fun of me in front of the other kids." I said: "Boy, the same thing happened to my kid. White liberal teacher was makin' fun of Tim Ellis's father, the Klansman. In front of other peoples. He came home cryin'." At this point—(he pauses, swallows hard, stifles a sob)—I begin to see, here we are, two people from the far ends of the fence, havin' identical problems, except hers bein' black and me bein' white. From that moment on, I tell ya, that gal and I worked together good. I begin to love the girl, really. (He weeps.)

The amazing thing about it, her and I, up to that point, had cussed each other, bawled each other, we hated each other. Up to that point, we didn't know each other. We didn't know we had things in common.

We worked at it, with the people who came to these meetings. They 45 talked about racism, sex education, about teachers not bein' qualified. After seven, eight nights of real intense discussion, these people, who'd never talked to each other before, all of a sudden came up with resolutions. It was really somethin', you had to be there to get the tone and feelin' of it.

At that point, I didn't like integration, but the law says you do this and I've got to do what the law says, okay? We said: "Let's take these resolutions to the school board." The most disheartening thing I've ever faced was the school system refused to implement any one of these resolutions. These were recommendations from the people who pay taxes and pay their salaries. (Laughs.)

I thought they were good answers. Some of 'em I didn't agree with, but I been in this thing from the beginning, and whatever comes of it, I'm gonna support it. Okay, since the school board refused, I decided I'd just run for the school board.

I spent eighty-five dollars on the campaign. The guy runnin' against me spent several thousand. I really had nobody on my side. The Klan turned against me. The low-income whites turned against me. The liberals didn't particularly like me. The blacks were suspicious of me. The blacks wanted to support me, but they couldn't muster up enough to support a Klansman on the school board. (Laughs.) But I made up my mind that what I was doin' was right, and I was gonna do it regardless what anybody said.

It bothered me when people would call and worry my wife. She's always supported me in anything I wanted to do. She was changing, and my boys were too. I got some of my youth corps kids involved. They still followed me.

I was invited to the Democratic women's social hour as a candidate. 50 Didn't have but one suit to my name. Had it six, seven, eight years. I had it cleaned, put on the best shirt I had and a tie. Here were all this high-class wealthy candidates shakin' hands. I walked up to the mayor and stuck out my hand. He give me that handshake with that rag type of hand. He said: "C. P., I'm glad to see you." But I could tell by his handshake he was lyin' to me. This was botherin' me. I know I'm a low-income person. I know I'm not wealthy. I know they were sayin': "What's this little ol' dude runnin' for school board?" Yet they had to smile and make like they're glad to see me. I begin to spot some black people in that room. I automatically went to 'em and that was a firm handshake. They said: "I'm glad to see you, C. P." I knew they meant it—you can tell about a handshake.

Every place I appeared, I said I will listen to the voice of the people. I will not make a major decision until I first contacted all the organizations in the city. I got 4,640 votes. The guy beat me by two thousand. Not bad for eighty-five bucks and no constituency.

The whole world was openin' up, and I was learnin' new truths that I had never learned before. I was beginnin' to look at a black person, shake hands with him, and see him as a human bein'. I hadn't got rid of all this stuff, I've still got a little bit of it. But somethin' was happenin' to me.

It was almost like bein' born again. It was a new life. I didn't have these sleepless nights I used to have when I was active in the Klan and slippin' around at night. I could sleep at night and feel good about it. I'd rather live now than at any other time in history. It's a challenge.

Back at Duke, doin' maintenance, I'd pick up my tools, fix the commode, unstop the drains. But this got in my blood. Things weren't right in this country, and what we done in Durham needs to be told. I was so miserable at Duke, I could hardly stand it. I'd go to work every morning just hatin' to go.

My whole life had changed. I got an eighth-grade education, and I wanted to complete high school. Went to high school in the afternoons on a program called PEP—Past Employment Progress. I was about the only white in class, and the oldest. I begin to read about biology. I'd take my books home at night, 'cause I was determined to get through. Sure enough, I graduated. I got the diploma at home. 55

I come to work one mornin' and some guy says: "We need a union." At this time I wasn't pro-union. My daddy was anti-labor, too. We're not gettin' paid much, we're havin' to work seven days in a row. We're all starvin' to death. The next day, I meet the international representative of the Operating Engineers. He give me authorization cards. "Get these cards out and we'll have an election." There was eighty-eight for the union and seventeen no's. I was elected chief steward for the union.

Shortly after, a union man come down from Charlotte and says we need a full-time rep. We've got only two hundred people at the two plants here. It's just barely enough money comin' in to pay your salary. You'll have to get out and organize more people. I didn't know nothin' about organizin' unions, but I knew how to organize people, stir people up. (Laughs.) That's how I got to be business agent for the union.

When I began to organize, I began to see far deeper. I began to see people again bein' used. Blacks against whites. I say this without any hesitancy: management is vicious. There's two things they want to keep: all the money and all the say-so. They don't want these poor workin' folks to have none of that. I begin to see management fightin' me with everything they had. Hire anti-union law firms, badmouth unions. The people were makin' a dollar ninety-five an hour, barely able to get through weekends. I worked as a business rep for five years and was seein' all this.

Last year, I ran for business manager of the union. He's elected by the workers. The guy that ran against me was black, and our membership is seventy-five percent black. I thought: Claiborne, there's no way you can beat that black guy. People know your background. Even though you've made tremendous strides, those black people are not gonna vote for you. You know how much I beat him? Four to one. (Laughs.)

The company used my past against me. They put out letters with a pic-   60
ture of a robe and a cap: would you vote for a Klansman? They wouldn't
deal with the issues. I immediately called for a mass meeting. I met with the
ladies at an electric component plant. I said: "Okay, this is Claiborne Ellis.
This is where I come from. I want you to know right now, you black ladies
here, I was at one time a member of the Klan. I want you to know, because
they'll tell you about it."

I invited some of my old black friends. I said: "Brother Joe, Brother
Howard, be honest now and tell these people how you feel about me." They
done it. (Laughs.) Howard Clements kidded me a little bit. He said: "I don't
know what I'm doin' here, supportin' an ex-Klansman." (Laughs.) He said:
"I know what C. P. Ellis come from. I knew him when he was. I knew him
as he grew, and growed with him. I'm tellin' you now: follow, follow this
Klansman." (He pauses, swallows hard.) "Any questions?" "No," the black
ladies said. "Let's get on with the meeting, we need Ellis." (He laughs and
weeps.) Boy, black people sayin' that about me. I won one thirty-four to
forty-one. Four to one.

It makes you feel good to go into a plant and butt heads with professional union busters. You see black people and white people join hands to
defeat the racist issues they use against people. They're tryin' the same
things with the Klan. It's still happenin' today. Can you imagine a guy who's
got an adult high school diploma runnin' into professional college graduates
who are union busters? I gotta compete with 'em. I work seven days a week,
nights and on Saturday and Sunday. The salary's not that great, and if I
didn't care, I'd quit. But I care and I can't quit. I got a taste of it. (Laughs.)

I tell people there's a tremendous possibility in this country to stop
wars, the battles, the struggles, the fights between people. People say:
"That's an impossible dream. You sound like Martin Luther King." An ex-
Klansman who sounds like Martin Luther King. (Laughs.) I don't think it's
an impossible dream. It's happened in my life. It's happened in other
people's lives in America.

I don't know what's ahead of me. I have no desire to be a big union official. I want to be right out here in the field with the workers. I want to walk
through their factory and shake hands with that man whose hands are dirty.
I'm gonna do all that one little ol' man can do. I'm fifty-two years old, and I
ain't got many years left, but I want to make the best of 'em.

When the news came over the radio that Martin Luther King was assas-   65
sinated, I got on the telephone and begin to call other Klansmen. We just
had a real party at the service station. Really rejoicin' 'cause that son of a
bitch was dead. Our troubles are over with. They say the older you get, the
harder it is for you to change. That's not necessarily true. Since I changed,
I've set down and listened to tapes of Martin Luther King. I listen to it and
tears come to my eyes 'cause I know what he's sayin' now. I know what's
happenin'.

POSTSCRIPT:

The phone rings. A conversation.

"This was a black guy who's director of Operation Breakthrough in Durham. I had called his office. I'm interested in employin' some young black person who's interested in learnin' the labor movement. I want somebody who's never had an opportunity, just like myself. Just so he can read and write, that's all."

ENGAGING THE TEXT

1. How does Ellis battle the racism he finds in himself? What gives him the motivation and strength to change? What specific changes does he undergo, and how successful is he in abandoning racist attitudes?

2. Would Ellis say that economic class is more important than race in determining job placement and occupational mobility? Find specific passages that reveal Ellis's beliefs about the connections between economic class, race, and success in American society. What do you believe?

3. How well does Ellis seem to understand himself, his feelings, his motives? Give evidence for your assertions.

4. What is Terkel's role in this selection? Is he unconsciously helping to rationalize or justify the actions of the Ku Klux Klan?

5. Does Ellis's story offer a credible way of overcoming misunderstanding and hatred between races? Do you think such a "solution" would be workable on a large scale? Why or why not?

EXPLORING CONNECTIONS

6. To what extent does Ellis's experience illustrate the theories of prejudice described by Vincent N. Parrillo in the previous selection (p. 548)? Which of these theories best account for Ellis's racism and for his eventual transformation?

7. Review the account of Malcolm X's self-education (p. 223). How does the dramatic self-transformation he experiences compare with C. P. Ellis's rebirth? What relationships can you find between the circumstances that led to their initial attitudes, the conditions or events that fostered their transformations, and the effects that these transformations had on their characters?

EXTENDING THE CRITICAL CONTEXT

8. Interview a friend, family member, or fellow student in another class to create your own oral history on the subject of racial attitudes. Ask your subject to describe a time when he or she was forced to re-evaluate his or her thoughts or feelings about someone from a different racial or ethnic group. Try to include as many relevant details as possible in your retelling of the story. Share and edit these oral histories in small groups, and then assemble them into a class anthology.

I'm Black, You're White, Who's Innocent?

SHELBY STEELE

This essay comes from one of the most controversial American books of the1980s — The Content of Our Character: A New Vision of Race in America. *Shelby Steele (b. 1946) believes that black Americans have failed to seize opportunities that would lead to social equality; he is also an outspoken critic of affirmative action, arguing that instead of promoting equality it locks its recipients into second-class status. Critics have accused him of underestimating the power of racism, of blaming victims for their predicament, of being a traitor to his race. In this selection, Steele offers his observations on why black and white Americans have not been able to sustain the kind of dialogue that would make mutual understanding possible. Steele's second book,* A Dream Deferred: The Second Betrayal of Black Freedom in America *(1998), elaborates the critique of innocence and guilt laid out in this essay. In his new work, Steele argues that programs —like affirmative action —that were devised to reduce racial inequality have actually harmed rather than helped most African Americans, and have benefitted only guilty white liberals and a black "grievance elite." Steele's essays have garnered a number of awards and have appeared in* Harper's, The American Scholar, The New Republic, *and many other journals and magazines. He is a research fellow at the Hoover Institution, Stanford University.*

It is a warm, windless California evening, and the dying light that covers the redbrick patio is tinted pale orange by the day's smog. Eight of us, not close friends, sit in lawn chairs sipping chardonnay. A black engineer and I (we had never met before) integrate the group. A psychologist is also among us, and her presence encourages a surprising openness. But not until well after the lovely twilight dinner has been served, when the sky has turned to deep black and the drinks have long since changed to scotch, does the subject of race spring awkwardly upon us. Out of nowhere the engineer announces, with a coloring of accusation in his voice, that it bothers him to send his daughter to a school where she is one of only three black children. "I didn't realize my ambition to get ahead would pull me into a world where my daughter would lose touch with her blackness," he says.

Over the course of the evening we have talked about money, past and present addictions, child abuse, even politics. Intimacies have been revealed, fears named. But this subject, race, sinks us into one of those shaming silences where eye contact terrorizes. Our host looks for something in the bottom of his glass. Two women stare into the black sky as if to locate the Big Dipper and point it out to us. Finally, the psychologist seems to gather herself for a challenge, but it is too late. "Oh, I'm sure she'll be just fine," says our hostess, rising from her chair. When she excuses herself to get the coffee, the psychologist and two sky gazers offer to help.

With four of us now gone, I am surprised to see the engineer still silently holding his ground. There is a willfulness in his eyes, an inner pride. He knows he has said something awkward, but he is determined not to give a damn. His unwavering eyes intimidate even me. At last the host's head snaps erect. He has an idea. "The hell with coffee," he says. "How about some of the smoothest brandy you've ever tasted?" An idea made exciting by the escape it offers. Gratefully, we follow him back into the house, quickly drink his brandy, and say our good-byes.

An autopsy of this party might read: death induced by an abrupt and lethal injection of the American race issue. An accurate if superficial assessment. Since it has been my fate to live a rather integrated life, I have often witnessed sudden deaths like this. The threat of them, if not the reality, is a part of the texture of integration. In the late 1960s, when I was just out of college, I took a delinquent's delight in playing the engineer's role, and actually developed a small reputation for playing it well. Those were the days of flagellatory white guilt: it was such great fun to pinion some professor or housewife or, best of all, a large group of remorseful whites, with the knowledge of both their racism and their denial of it. The adolescent impulse to sneer at convention, to startle the middle-aged with doubt, could be indulged under the guise of racial indignation. And how could I lose? My victims—earnest liberals for the most part—could no more crawl out from under my accusations than Joseph K. in Kafka's *Trial*[1] could escape the amorphous charges brought against him. At this odd moment in history the world was aligned to facilitate my immaturity.

About a year of this was enough: the guilt that follows most cheap thrills caught up to me, and I put myself in check. But the impulse to do it faded more slowly. It was one of those petty talents that is tied to vanity, and when there were ebbs in my self-esteem the impulse to use it would come alive again. In integrated situations I can still feel the faint itch. But then there are many youthful impulses that still itch and now, just inside the door of midlife, this one is least precious to me.

In the literature classes I teach I often see how the presence of whites all but seduces some black students into provocation. When we come to a novel by a black writer, say Toni Morrison, the white students can easily discuss the human motivations of the black characters. But, inevitably, a black student, as if by reflex, will begin to set in relief the various racial problems that are the background of these characters' lives. This student's tone will carry a reprimand: the class is afraid to confront the reality of racism.

5

---

[1]*Kafka's* Trial: Czech writer Franz Kafka (1883–1924) is famous for his dreamlike and ominous stories. In his novel *The Trial,* the character known only as Joseph K. battles an intricate legal and police system that never specifies his alleged crime.

Classes cannot be allowed to die like dinner parties, however. My latest strategy is to thank that student for his or her moral vigilance and then appoint the young man or woman as the class's official racism monitor. But even if I get a laugh—I usually do, but sometimes the student is particularly indignant, and it gets uncomfortable—the strategy never quite works. Our racial division is suddenly drawn in neon. Overcaution spreads like spilled paint. And, in fact, the black student who started it all does become a kind of monitor. The very presence of this student imposes a new accountability on the class.

I think those who provoke this sort of awkwardness are operating out of a black identity that obliges them to badger white people about race almost on principle. Content hardly matters. (For example, it made little sense for the engineer to expect white people to anguish terribly much over his decision to send his daughter to school with *white* children.) Race indeed remains a source of white shame; the goal of these provocations is to put whites, no matter how indirectly, in touch with this collective guilt. In other words, these provocations I speak of are *power* moves, little shows of power that try to freeze the "enemy" in self-consciousness. They gratify and inflate the provocateur. They are the underdog's bite. And whites, far more secure in their power, respond with self-contained and tolerant silence that is itself a show of power. What greater power than that of nonresponse, the power to let a small enemy sizzle in his own juices, to even feel a little sad at his frustration just as one is also complimented by it. Black anger always, in a way, flatters white power. In America, to know that one is not black is to feel an extra grace, a little boost of impunity.

I think the real trouble between the races in America is that the races are not just races but competing power groups—a fact that is easily minimized, perhaps because it is so obvious. What is not so obvious is that this is true quite apart from the issue of class. Even the well-situated middle-class (or wealthy) black is never completely immune to that peculiar contest of power that his skin color subjects him to. Race is a separate reality in American society, an entity that carries its own potential for power, a mark of fate that class can soften considerably but not eradicate.

The distinction of race has always been used in American life to sanction each race's pursuit of power in relation to the other. The allure of race as a human delineation is the very shallowness of the delineation it makes. Onto this shallowness—mere skin and hair—men can project a false depth, a system of dismal attributions, a series of malevolent or ignoble stereotypes that skin and hair lack the substance to contradict. These dark projections then rationalize the pursuit of power. Your difference from me makes you bad, and your badness justifies, even demands, my pursuit of power over you—the oldest formula for aggression known to man. Whenever much importance is given to race, power is the primary motive.

But the human animal almost never pursues power without first convincing himself that he is *entitled* to it. And this feeling of entitlement has

10

its own precondition: to be entitled one must first believe in one's innocence, at least in the area where one wishes to be entitled. By innocence I mean a feeling of essential goodness in relation to others and, therefore, superiority to others. Our innocence always inflates us and deflates those we seek power over. Once inflated we are entitled; we are in fact licensed to go after the power our innocence tells us we deserve. In this sense, *innocence is power.* Of course, innocence need not be genuine or real in any objective sense, as the Nazis demonstrated not long ago. Its only test is whether or not we can convince ourselves of it.

I think the racial struggle in America has always been primarily a struggle for innocence. White racism from the beginning has been a claim of white innocence and therefore of white entitlement to subjugate blacks. And in the sixties, as went innocence so went power. Blacks used the innocence that grew out of their long subjugation to seize more power, while whites lost some of their innocence and so lost a degree of power over blacks. Both races instinctively understand that to lose innocence is to lose power (in relation to each other). To be innocent someone else must be guilty, a natural law that leads the races to forge their innocence on each other's backs. The inferiority of the black always makes the white man superior; the evil might of whites makes blacks good. This pattern means that both races have a hidden investment in racism and racial disharmony despite their good intentions to the contrary. Power defines their relations, and power requires innocence, which, in turn, requires racism and racial division.

I believe it was his hidden investment that the engineer was protecting when he made his remark—the white "evil" he saw in a white school "depriving" his daughter of her black heritage confirmed his innocence. Only the logic of power explained his emphasis—he bent reality to show that he was once again a victim of the white world and, as a victim, innocent. His determined eyes insisted on this. And the whites, in their silence, no doubt protected their innocence by seeing him as an ungracious troublemaker, his bad behavior underscoring their goodness. What none of us saw was the underlying game of power and innocence we were trapped in, or how much we needed a racial impasse to play that game.

When I was a boy of about twelve, a white friend of mine told me one day that his uncle, who would be arriving the next day for a visit, was a racist. Excited by the prospect of seeing such a man, I spent the following afternoon hanging around the alley behind my friend's house, watching from a distance as this uncle worked on the engine of his Buick. Yes, here was evil and I was compelled to look upon it. And I saw evil in the sharp angle of his elbow as he pumped his wrench to tighten nuts. I saw it in the blade-sharp crease of his chinos, in the pack of Lucky Strikes that threatened to slip from his shirt pocket as he bent, and in the way his concentration seemed to shut out the human world. He worked neatly and efficiently, wiping his hands constantly, and I decided that evil worked like this.

I felt a compulsion to have this man look upon me so that I could see evil—so that I could see the face of it. But when he noticed me standing beside his toolbox, he said only, "If you're looking for Bobby, I think he went up to the school to play baseball." He smiled nicely and went back to work. I was stunned for a moment, but then I realized that evil could be sly as well, could smile when it wanted to trick you.

Need, especially hidden need, puts a strong pressure on perception, and my need to have this man embody white evil was stronger than any contravening evidence. As a black person you always hear about racists but rarely meet any who will let you know them as such. And I needed to incarnate this odious category of humanity, those people who hated Martin Luther King, Jr., and thought blacks should "go slow" or not at all. So, in my mental dictionary, behind the term "white racist," I inserted this man's likeness. I would think of him and say to myself, "There is no reason for him to hate black people. Only evil explains unmotivated hatred." And this thought soothed me; I felt innocent. If I hated white people, which I did not, at least I had a reason. His evil commanded me to assert in the world the goodness he made me confident of in myself.

In looking at this man I was *seeing for innocence*—a form of seeing that has more to do with one's hidden need for innocence (and power) than with the person or group one is looking at. It is quite possible, for example, that the man I saw that day was not a racist. He did absolutely nothing in my presence to indicate that he was. I invested an entire afternoon in seeing not the man but in seeing my innocence through the man. *Seeing for innocence* is, in this way, the essence of racism—the use of others as a means to our own goodness and superiority.

The loss of innocence has always to do with guilt, Kierkegaard[2] tells us, and it has never been easy for whites to avoid guilt where blacks are concerned. For whites, *seeing for innocence* means seeing themselves and blacks in ways that minimize white guilt. Often this amounts to a kind of white revisionism,[3] as when President Reagan declared himself "color-blind" in matters of race. The President, like many of us, may have aspired to racial color blindness, but few would grant that he ever reached this sublimely guiltless state. His statement clearly revised reality, moved it forward into some heretofore unknown America where all racial determinism would have vanished. I do not think that Ronald Reagan was a racist, as that term is commonly used, but neither do I think that he was capable of seeing color without making attributions, some of which may have been negative—nor am I, or anyone else I've ever met.

So why make such a statement? I think Reagan's claim of color blindness with regard to race was really a claim of racial innocence and guiltlessness—the preconditions for entitlement and power. This was the claim that

---

[2]*Kierkegaard:* Danish philosopher and religious thinker Søren Kierkegaard (1813–1855).

[3]*revisionism:* The reinterpretation or revising of reality to suit one's current purposes.

grounded Reagan's campaign against special entitlement programs—affirmative action, racial quotas, and so on—that black power had won in the sixties. Color blindness was a strategic assumption of innocence that licensed Reagan's use of government power against black power. . . .

Black Americans have had to find a way to handle white society's presumption of racial innocence whenever they have sought to enter the American mainstream. Louis Armstrong's[4] exaggerated smile honored the presumed innocence of white society—*I will not bring you your racial guilt if you will let me play my music.* Ralph Ellison[5] calls this "masking"; I call it bargaining. But whatever it's called, it points to the power of white society to enforce its innocence. I believe this power is greatly diminished today. Society has reformed and transformed—Miles Davis[6] never smiles. Nevertheless, this power has not faded altogether and blacks must still contend with it.

Historically, blacks have handled white society's presumption of innocence in two ways: they have bargained with it, granting white society its innocence in exchange for entry into the mainstream, or they have challenged it, holding that innocence hostage until their demand for entry (or other concessions) was met. A bargainer says, *I already believe you are innocent (good, fair-minded) and have faith that you will prove it.* A challenger says, *If you are innocent, then prove it.* Bargainers *give* in hope of receiving; challengers *withhold* until they receive. Of course, there is risk in both approaches, but in each case the black is negotiating his own self-interest against the presumed racial innocence of the larger society.   20

Clearly, the most visible black bargainer on the American scene today is Bill Cosby. His television show has been a perfect formula for black bargaining in the eighties. The remarkable Huxtable family—with its doctor/lawyer parent combination, its drug-free, college-bound children, and its wise yet youthful grandparents—is a blackface version of the American dream. Cosby is a subscriber to the American identity, and his subscription confirms his belief in its fair-mindedness. His vast audience knows this, knows that Cosby will never assault their innocence with racial guilt. Racial controversy is all but banished from the show. The Huxtable family never discusses affirmative action.

The bargain Cosby offers his white viewers—*I will confirm your racial innocence if you accept me*—is a good deal for all concerned. Not only does it allow whites to enjoy Cosby's humor with no loss of innocence, but it actually enhances their innocence by implying that race is not the serious problem for blacks that it once was. If anything, the success of this handsome, affluent black family points to the fair-mindedness of whites who, out

---

[4]*Louis Armstrong:* American jazz trumpet virtuoso and singer (1900–1971).

[5]*Ralph Ellison:* American novelist (1914–1994), best known for *Invisible Man,* the account of a nameless black youth coming of age in a hostile society.

[6]*Miles Davis:* Jazz musician and trumpeter (1926–1991).

of their essential goodness, changed society so that black families like the Huxtables could succeed. Whites can watch *The Cosby Show* and feel complimented on a job well done.

The power that black bargainers wield is the power of absolution. On Thursday nights, Cosby, like a priest, absolves his white viewers, forgives and forgets the sins of the past. And for this he is rewarded with an almost sacrosanct[7] status. Cosby benefits from what might be called the gratitude factor. His continued number-one rating may have something to do with the (white) public's gratitude at being offered a commodity so rare in our time; he tells his white viewers each week that they are okay, and that this black man is not going to challenge them.

When a black bargains, he may invoke the gratitude factor and find himself cherished beyond the measure of his achievement; when he challenges, he may draw the dark projections of whites and become a source of irritation to them. If he moves back and forth between these two options, as I think many blacks do today, he will likely baffle whites. It is difficult for whites either to accept or reject such blacks. It seems to me that Jesse Jackson is such a figure—many whites see Jackson as a challenger by instinct and a bargainer by political ambition. They are uneasy with him, more than a little suspicious. His powerful speech at the 1984 Democratic Convention was a masterpiece of bargaining. In it he offered a King-like[8] vision of what America could be, a vision that presupposed Americans had the fair-mindedness to achieve full equality—an offer in hope of a return. A few days after this speech, looking for rest and privacy at a lodge in Big Sur,[9] he and his wife were greeted with standing ovations three times a day when they entered the dining room for meals. So much about Jackson is deeply American—this underdog striving, his irrepressible faith in himself, the daring of his ambition, and even his stubbornness. These qualities point to his underlying faith that Americans can respond to him despite race, and this faith is a compliment to Americans, an offer of innocence.

But Jackson does not always stick to the terms of his bargain as Cosby does on TV. When he hugs Arafat,[10] smokes cigars with Castro,[11] refuses to repudiate Farrakhan,[12] threatens a boycott of major league baseball or, more recently, talks of "corporate barracudas," "pension-fund socialism," and "economic violence," he looks like a challenger in bargainer's clothing, and his positions on the issues look like familiar protests dressed in white-paper formality. At these times he appears to be revoking the innocence so

25

[7]*sacrosanct:* Sacred.
[8]*King-like:* Like that of Martin Luther King, Jr.
[9]*Big Sur:* Section of the California coast known for its natural beauty.
[10]*Arafat:* Yasir Arafat (b. 1929), leader of the Palestine Liberation Organization, or PLO.
[11]*Castro:* Fidel Castro (b. 1926), president of Cuba.
[12]*Farrakhan:* Louis Farrakhan (b. 1933), Nation of Islam leader, often accused of making anti-Semitic remarks. Many African American politicians carefully distance themselves from Farrakhan.

much else about him seems to offer. The old activist seems to come out of hiding once again to take white innocence hostage until whites prove they deserve to have it. In his candidacy there is a suggestion of protest, a fierce insistence on his *right* to run, that sends whites a message that he may secretly see them as a good bit less than innocent. His dilemma is to appear the bargainer while his campaign itself seems to be a challenge.

There are, of course, other problems that hamper Jackson's bid for the Democratic presidential nomination. He has held no elective office, he is thought too flamboyant and opportunistic by many, there are rather loud whispers of "character" problems. As an individual, he may not be the best test of a black man's chances for winning so high an office. Still, I believe it is the aura of challenge surrounding him that hurts him most. Whether it is right or wrong, fair or unfair, I think no black candidate will have a serious chance at his party's nomination, much less the presidency, until he can convince white Americans that he can be trusted to preserve their sense of racial innocence. Such a candidate will have to use his power of absolution; he will have to flatly forgive and forget. He will have to bargain with white innocence out of genuine belief that it really exists. There can be no faking it. He will have to offer a vision that is passionately raceless, a vision that strongly condemns any form of racial politics. This will require the most courageous kind of leadership, leadership that asks all the people to meet a new standard.

Now the other side of America's racial impasse: how do blacks lay claim to their racial innocence?

The most obvious and unarguable source of black innocence is the victimization that blacks endured for centuries at the hands of a race that insisted on black inferiority as a means to its own innocence and power. Like all victims, what blacks lost in power they gained in innocence—innocence that, in turn, entitled them to pursue power. This was the innocence that fueled the civil rights movement of the sixties and that gave blacks their first real power in American life—victimization metamorphosed into power via innocence. But this formula carries a drawback that I believe is virtually as devastating to blacks today as victimization once was. It is a formula that binds the victim to his victimization by linking his power to his status as a victim. And this, I'm convinced, is the tragedy of black power in America today. It is primarily a victim's power, grounded too deeply in the entitlement derived from past injustice and in the innocence that Western/Christian tradition has always associated with poverty.

Whatever gains this power brings in the short run through political action, it undermines in the long run. Social victims may be collectively entitled, but they are all too often individually demoralized. Since the social victim has been oppressed by society, he comes to feel that his individual life will be improved more by changes in society than by his own initiative. Without realizing it, he makes society rather than himself the agent of change. The power he finds in his victimization may lead him to collective action against society, but it also encourages passivity within the sphere of his personal life.

Not long ago, I saw a television documentary that examined life in De- 30
troit's inner city on the twentieth anniversary of the riots there in which forty-three people were killed. A comparison of the inner city then and now showed a decline in the quality of life. Residents feel less safe, drug trafficking is far worse, crimes by blacks against blacks are more frequent, housing remains substandard, and the teenage pregnancy rate has skyrocketed. Twenty years of decline and demoralization, even as opportunities for blacks to better themselves have increased. This paradox is not peculiar to Detroit. By many measures, the majority of blacks—those not yet in the middle class—are further behind whites today than before the victories of the civil rights movement. But there is a reluctance among blacks to examine this paradox, I think, because it suggests that racial victimization is not our real problem. If conditions have worsened for most of us as racism has receded, then much of the problem must be of our own making. To admit this fully would cause us to lose the innocence we derive from our victimization. And we would jeopardize the entitlement we've always had to challenge society. We are in the odd and self-defeating position in which taking responsibility for bettering ourselves feels like a surrender to white power.

So we have a hidden investment in victimization and poverty. These distressing conditions have been the source of our own real power, and there is an unconscious sort of gravitation toward them, a complaining celebration of them. One sees evidence of this in the near happiness with which certain black leaders recount the horror of Howard Beach,[13] Bensonhurst,[14] and other recent instances of racial tension. As one is saddened by these tragic events, one is also repelled at the way some black leaders—agitated to near hysteria by the scent of victim power inherent in them—leap forward to exploit them as evidence of black innocence and white guilt. It is as though they sense the decline of black victimization as a loss of standing and dive into the middle of these incidents as if they were reservoirs of pure black innocence swollen with potential power.

Seeing for innocence pressures blacks to focus on racism and to neglect the individual initiative that would deliver them from poverty—the only thing that finally delivers *anyone* from poverty. With our eyes on innocence we see racism everywhere and miss opportunity even as we stumble over it. About 70 percent of black students at my university[15] drop out before graduation—a flight from opportunity that racism cannot explain. It is an injustice that whites can see for innocence with more impunity than blacks can. The price whites pay is a certain blindness to themselves. Moreover, for

---

[13]*Howard Beach:* Scene in Queens, New York, of a December 1986 racial confrontation in which several young African American men were severely beaten and one died.

[14]*Bensonhurst:* Location in Brooklyn, New York, where the racially motivated murder of sixteen-year-old Yusuf Hawkins took place in August 1989.

[15]*my university:* Refers to San Jose State University where Steele was then teaching.

whites seeing for innocence continues to engender the bad faith of a long-disgruntled minority. But the price blacks pay is an ever-escalating poverty that threatens to make the worst off a permanent underclass. Not fair, but real.

Challenging works best for the collective, while bargaining is more the individual's suit. From this point on, the race's advancement will come from the efforts of its individuals. True, some challenging will be necessary for a long time to come. But bargaining is now—today—a way for the black individual to *join* the larger society, to make a place for himself or herself.

"Innocence is ignorance," Kierkegaard says, and if this is so, the claim of innocence amounts to an insistence on ignorance, a refusal to know. In their assertions of innocence both races carve out very functional areas of ignorance for themselves—territories of blindness that license a misguided pursuit of power. Whites gain superiority by not knowing blacks; blacks gain entitlement by not seeing their own responsibility for bettering themselves. The power each race seeks in relation to the other is grounded in a double-edged ignorance of the self as well as of the other.

The original sin that brought us to an impasse at the dinner party I   35
mentioned occurred centuries ago, when it was first decided to exploit racial difference as a means to power. It was a determinism that flowed karmically from this sin that dropped over us like a net that night. What bothered me most was our helplessness. Even the engineer did not know how to go forward. His challenge hadn't worked, and he'd lost the option to bargain. The marriage of race and power depersonalized us, changed us from eight people to six whites and two blacks. The easiest thing was to let silence blanket our situation, our impasse. . . .

What both black and white Americans fear are the sacrifices and risks that true racial harmony demands. This fear is the measure of our racial chasm. And though fear always seeks a thousand justifications, none is ever good enough, and the problems we run from only remain to haunt us. It would be right to suggest courage as an antidote to fear, but the glory of the word might only intimidate us into more fear. I prefer the word effort—relentless effort, moral effort. What I like most about this word are its connotations of everydayness, earnestness, and practical sacrifice. No matter how badly it might have gone for us that warm summer night, we should have talked. We should have made the effort.

ENGAGING THE TEXT

1. What does Steele mean by "innocence" and by "seeing for innocence"? How does he apply these terms to racial conflict and struggles for power in the United States? How do blacks and whites claim innocence through racial conflict? What does Steele mean when he says "innocence is power"?

2. According to Steele, what strategies have African Americans employed to handle "white society's presumption of racial innocence" (para. 19)? How

FEIFFER®

Feiffer © 1994 Jules Feiffer. Reprinted with permission of Universal Press Syndicate. All rights reserved.

does he account for public reactions to figures like Bill Cosby and Jesse Jackson in terms of these strategies? Are there other possible explanations of their appeal?

3. Steele believes that "bargaining is now—today—a way for the black individual to *join* the larger society" (para. 33). Do you agree? Is bargaining an available and acceptable alternative for all African Americans?

4. Steele writes that when the issue of race comes up in classes, "overcaution spreads like spilled paint" (para. 6). If you have observed this phenomenon in class or in other circumstances, write a journal entry describing one such incident and analyzing the behavior of the people involved.

EXPLORING CONNECTIONS

5. How might Ken Hamblin (p. 374), Vincent N. Parrillo (p. 548), George M. Fredrickson (p. 598), and Mary C. Waters (p. 642) evaluate Steele's assertion that racism grows out of the desire to claim "innocence"? Imagine that they are all participating in a panel discussion and role-play the conversation that would ensue.

6. Write an imaginary dialogue between C. P. Ellis (p. 562), Malcolm X (p. 223), and Steele on American racism. What might they each say about the causes of racist thinking and behavior? About the chances for curbing racism? How would they respond to each other's ideas and strategies for change?

7. What does Jules Feiffer's cartoon on this page suggest about the ways that black and white Americans see the world? How does Feiffer's view of the psychology of race compare to Steele's?

EXTENDING THE CRITICAL CONTEXT

8. At the end of this essay, Steele writes, "No matter how badly it might have gone for us...we should have talked. We should have made the effort." Working in groups, role-play the conversation that might have occurred that night. How might you initiate such conversations on your campus? Is talk the only or best solution to the kinds of tensions Steele describes?

Virtual Integration: How the Integration of Mass Media Undermines Integration

LEONARD STEINHORN AND BARBARA DIGGS-BROWN

According to their own description, the coauthors of this selection epitomize both the success and failure of integration in this country. Leonard Steinhorn, who is white, once worked for a black member of Congress; Barbara Diggs-Brown is the first black woman to win tenure in her department at American University in Washington, D.C. However, they grew up and continue to live in segregated neighborhoods and socialize almost exclusively with people of their own race. They maintain that this same disjunction—between the ideal of integration and the reality of continued segregation—is pervasive in the United States today. Television helps to perpetuate the divide by presenting us with a racially idealized world that makes us complacent about the real problems of race. Steinhorn and Diggs-Brown are colleagues at American University's School of Communication. This selection is taken from their book, By the Color of Our Skin: The Illusion of Integration and the Reality of Race *(1999).*

The *Time* magazine cover called it "a death in the family." The *New York Times* described the outpouring of grief "as if it were a death in the family. In a way it was." Americans black and white, from every region and social standing, grieved with Bill Cosby at the tragic loss of his son, Ennis, who was gunned down on the side of a freeway in January 1997. Few Americans knew much if anything about Ennis Cosby before his death, but we reacted almost as if we knew the family personally. And in a way we did. Seven months later we grieved again when Britain's Princess Diana lost her life in a sad and gruesome car accident. She was Diana to us, someone we felt we knew, a constant presence in our lives, a woman whose wedding we vicariously attended and whose intimacies seemed more familiar to us than those of our closest friends. For many of us the loss was profound and deeply personal. It reminded us of the shared national mourning for a dead president more than three decades earlier, when we felt the pain of a grieving widow and her two small children who were too young to comprehend the enormity of their loss. Since those poignant days in November 1963, the Kennedy family has become our own.

For half a century now people like Princess Diana and Bill Cosby have entered our lives and homes through the remarkable medium of television. Television has brought us national leaders and fictional characters, personalities and eccentrics, Kennedys and Seinfelds, Oprah Winfrey and Dan Rather, Beaver Cleaver and Mr. Whipple, Ronald Reagan and Michael Jordan, Barbara Walters and Bart Simpson—a list so long yet so personal that it is almost dazzling to think of the many names and faces, celebrities and entertainers who have become part of our conversations and lives. What they all have in common is the power of television to project them into our living rooms and turn them into neighbors, friends, extended family, into people we truly believe we have come to know. Television is an intimate medium that creates a bond between actor and viewer, between a character and the public. It offers what two communications scholars call a "synthetic experience," a substitute for reality that feels very real.[1] An actor who plays a doctor on television becomes a doctor; a television lawyer becomes our model for the real thing, and a fictional character—Murphy Brown[2]—engages a real vice president in a national debate. And so we ascribe personality traits to the images on the screen, we track every career move and romance of our favorite actors, and we discuss their lives and futures as if they were connected to our own. The name of the popular show *Friends* describes more than just the fictional friendship among the characters portrayed in the show—it is also a metaphor for the relationship we have with these and so many other actors on television, people who visit us weekly in our homes and whose lives are finely detailed in the mass media that wallpapers our lives.

Ours is an unsettled nation of people constantly on the move. The westward spirit of the nineteenth century remains alive today in a restlessness that constantly seeks new frontiers and challenges. These very dynamics of American society have weakened ties both to family and to the geographically defined communities of old. We reach out and touch someone not

---

[1]The "synthetic experience" of television is described in G. Funkhouser and F. Shaw, "How Synthetic Experience Shapes Reality," *Journal of Communication* vol. 42; no. 2 (1990), pp. 75–87. [All notes except 2 are Steinhorn and Diggs-Brown's.]

[2]*Murphy Brown:* In 1992, then–Vice President Dan Quayle attacked the TV sitcom character Murphy Brown as an affront to "family values" because of her decision to have a baby outside marriage. Writers for the show made the issue, and Quayle himself, an ongoing source of humor in subsequent episodes.

over a table breaking bread but over fiber-optic phone lines and in cyber-space. In the modern American era, we yearn for a sense of community that in reality has become more and more elusive. And so television has stepped in to fill the void. It has become our virtual community, a stable presence in the living room that packs our lives with characters that in an earlier age we might have met in the union hall or town square. Americans today spend more time watching television than doing any other activity besides sleeping. By the time the average American teenager graduates from high school, he or she will have logged more hours in front of the television than in front of the teacher. Television viewing has become a surrogate for civic activity, a chance to participate in the lives of others in what has become our electronic village.

Now think of the average American, whose daily life usually consists of clicking the garage door open in the morning, driving to work, putting in the eight hours, getting back in the car, stopping at the store, and driving back home for what will likely be a comfortable evening in front of the television set. On a typical evening in the late 1990s, close to half of all American households are watching TV, and one network alone—NBC—holds the attention of more than one in five households every Thursday night. Now think more specifically of the average white American family. They may not watch the same prime-time series as most blacks.... But even on the shows they do watch they see more blacks beamed into their living room on a typical evening than they have seen at any other time or place during the day. It could be Michael Jordan or James Earl Jones pitching a product, Bill Cosby or Della Reese starring in a show, Whoopi Goldberg or Denzel Washington doing the celebrity interview, Ed Bradley or Bryant Gumbel describing a news story, or any combination of black newscasters, reporters, athletes, entertainers, or actors who populate the airwaves hour after hour, day after day. Some of them we think we know, like Bill Cosby or Bryant Gumbel, while others simply pass through our lives, like the blacks featured in advertisements, but they are all there in our living rooms, joining us in the intimacy of our own homes, creating the impression that the world is more integrated than it truly is.

For whites generally unaccustomed to interacting with blacks, who walk out their front doors and see few black faces in the neighborhood, the mere presence of black images in their homes blurs the line between what is imagined and what is real about race relations in America. It also helps, as author Benjamin DeMott points out in his book *The Trouble with Friendship: Why Americans Can't Think Straight About Race*, that most of the blacks whom whites see on television either work with whites, have white friends, or operate in a predominantly white context. They have been tested, they are safe, and they fit in.[3] So what television has done is to give

5

---

[3]Benjamin DeMott, *The Trouble with Friendship: Why Americans Can't Think Straight About Race* (New York: Atlantic Monthly Press, 1995).

white Americans the sensation of having meaningful, repeated contact with blacks without actually having it. Black people have become part of white people's lives, virtually. We call this phenomenon "virtual integration," and it is a primary reason why the integration illusion—the belief that we are moving toward a color-blind nation—has such a powerful influence over race relations in America today.[4]

So powerful is this virtual integration that it seems to promote a color-blindness toward black celebrities almost unattainable for blacks in the real world. Columnist Clarence Page, a former television reporter in Chicago, describes how he used to be greeted warmly in the same white ethnic neighborhoods that once pelted Martin Luther King with rocks and bottles. "You're not black anymore, Clarence," a white producer explained. "You're on television now."[5] The rise of black media images over the last three decades has come at precisely the same time that celebrity has become the measure of individual success in America. And being on television automatically confers celebrity, whether to a Frank Perdue who hawks his own brand of chickens, or to a low-paid weathercaster stuck in a small-market television station who nonetheless becomes a local personality. So whites have made room in their lives for black celebrities, indeed for almost any black they see on television, and have embraced them as evidence of their own open-mindedness and as proof that the nation isn't so hard on blacks after all. Blacks like O. J. Simpson, before his fall, are welcomed not only into the virtual neighborhood but into the actual neighborhood as well, as if their celebrity erases any negatives that whites otherwise would associate with their color. "I'm not black, I'm famous," the black lead singer of the rock group Fine Young Cannibals once said. Or, as the redneck rapist tells the black sheriff in the film of John Grisham's book *A Time to Kill,* "I seen you play for the Rams. The way I figured a nigger sheriff's okay, been on TV and all. No offense."[6]

Television has certainly come a long way since the days when stations in the South were deluged with complaints because white singer Petula Clark innocently put her hand on Harry Belafonte's arm during a music special, and NBC couldn't find a sponsor for *The Nat "King" Cole Show* and had to cancel it after one year. Until Bill Cosby broke the color line in 1965 as costar of the secret-agent show *I Spy,* there had never been a black star of a dramatic series. Until Lever Brothers featured black and white children playing together in a 1963 commercial for the detergent *Wisk,* no black had

---

[4]We developed the phrase "virtual integration" in 1995 when discussing ideas for this book and did not know that another author, John Hoberman, was planning to use the same phrase in his 1997 book, *Darwin's Athletes.*

[5]Clarence Page, *Showing My Color: Impolite Essays on Race and Identity* (New York: HarperCollins, 1996), p. 252.

[6]The singer's quote is from Henry Louis Gates, Jr., "Thirteen Ways of Looking at a Black Man," *The New Yorker,* October 23, 1995, p. 63.

ever been on a nationwide television ad in a nonstereotypical role. At that time the only blacks who appeared regularly on television came via live sports telecasts. As recently as the early 1980s, advertisers approached by Michael Jordan's agent responded by saying "What on earth are we going to do with a black basketball player?"[7] So it would be difficult to argue that the change in television has been anything but deep and profound.

Yet there are some who claim that the medium has a much longer way to go than most of the viewing public might believe. They say there are no dramas on television built around a black family or protagonist, that most comedies are segregated, that too many black-oriented comedies reinforce clownish or sexual stereotypes, that the networks have few black programming executives with the power to green-light projects, and that there should be more ads featuring blacks other than athletes or entertainers. During the 1996–97 season, they point out, only three comedies on the top three networks featured more than one regular black character, and some high-profile shows — *Seinfeld, Friends, Ellen,* and *Cybill* — had none at all. Of the 245 made-for-TV movies on the four major networks in 1995 and 1996, only about twenty had blacks in leading roles.[8] These are serious, valid criticisms and must be addressed. But from the white perspective they may seem irrelevant or off base because the cumulative presence of blacks on television already provides such a contrast to their predominantly white lives that their virtual world seems thoroughly integrated as is. A black regular on *Seinfeld* or *Friends* probably wouldn't make much of a difference to whites, who believe, courtesy of television, that the world already is fully integrated.

Nothing better illustrates our virtually integrated world than the two prime-time specials aired by ABC on Sunday, November 2, 1997. More than one out of every four TV sets in use at the time was tuned into these shows. In the first, a Walt Disney update of Rodgers & Hammerstein's *Cinderella,* the future princess looks very different from the blond, blue-eyed Cinderella of the Disney animated version and the many storybooks that have followed. This Cinderella is played by the black actress Brandy, and the entire production is a bold and striking example of a new highbrow trend in the arts called color-blind casting. Cinderella's stepmother is white, one stepsister is white and the other black, the fairy godmother is black, the prince is of Filipino descent, his valet is white, the king is white, the queen is black, and the multi-ethnic cast of extras interact seamlessly in a fairy-tale kingdom of harmonious diversity broadcast right there in our own living rooms. Immediately following *Cinderella* that night was a well-publicized

---

[7]The Michael Jordan reference is found in Lynn Hirschberg, "The Big Man Can Deal," *New York Times Magazine,* November 17, 1996, p. 49.

[8]These and other facts can be found in Greg Braxton, "Roots Plus 20," *Los Angeles Times,* January 26, 1997, p. 8. See also Jacqueline Trescott, "'Roots,' Wrapped Around the American Psyche," *Washington Post,* February 16, 1997, p. G5.

made-for-TV movie starring Oprah Winfrey, *Before Women Had Wings.* Again, the audience welcomed a black into their homes as Winfrey, who also produced the film, played the role of friend and savior to two white children abused and neglected by their mother. Also note that these two shows aired after a full afternoon of televised football with its many black sportscasters and players. In short, much of white America spent the afternoon and evening in a virtually integrated environment. Although Monday morning at school or work might not come close to resembling the living room integration the night before, that might not matter in a virtually integrated America in which the image becomes the norm and the reality is made to feel like the exception. For whites whose lives are virtually integrated, the power of the image makes the racial reality all the more difficult to believe.

With the possible exception of the military, the television screen may   10 be the most integrated part of American life. We tracked three days of television programming in the fall of 1997 and found that black faces, personalities, newscasters, athletes, actors, and entertainers were intricately woven throughout the shows that most whites watch. To illustrate, we offer a snapshot of one evening, at this writing the highest rated on television, Thursday night on NBC.[9]

First up on October 2, 1997, was the local news at six, which featured one black anchor and four black reporters. We both live in the Washington metropolitan area, home to a large black population, so here one might expect a well-integrated local news team. In fact, though, throughout the country a racial mix on the news is fairly common. There are black men and women anchoring, reporting, forecasting the weather, and discussing sports on stations in every other market we checked: New York, Houston, Boston, Cincinnati, Kansas City, Omaha, Raleigh, and San Francisco. One scholar who viewed news programs on twenty-eight stations nationwide found that blacks made up 11 percent of the journalists he saw, a number almost equal to the percentage of blacks in America. As public opinion pollster Geoffrey Garin put it, there are so many black anchors and reporters on television that even Southern whites "never think twice about it" anymore.[10] In this respect, then, our Washington sample seems no different from the rest of the nation. Nor are the network news broadcasts any different. The *NBC Nightly News with Tom Brokaw,* the top-rated network news show during our viewing period, featured two black reporters doing major stories on the night we watched. A check of the other network news programs found a similar black presence.

---

[9]We also tracked ABC on Tuesday, September 30, 1997, and channel-surfed through all three networks on Monday, October 6, 1997.

[10]The 11 percent figure comes from Christopher P. Campbell, *Race, Myth and the News* (Thousand Oaks, Calif.: Sage Publications, 1995), p. 38; Geoffrey Garin is quoted in Ronald Brownstein, "4 Decades Later, Legacy of *Brown vs. Topeka* Is Cloudy," *Los Angeles Times,* May 15, 1994, p. A1.

The NBC prime-time schedule that Thursday night featured four sit-coms—*Friends, Union Square, Seinfeld,* and *Veronica's Closet*—and one dramatic series, *ER.* Although *Seinfeld* and *Friends* attract few black view-ers, they have for a number of years been among the most highly rated comedies on television, which means their audience is almost exclusively white. *Friends* began the evening at eight o'clock. Although set in ethnically diverse New York City, the show has no black regulars. In a previous season one of the characters on *Friends* had a pet chimpanzee, which led a critic to quip that monkeys had a better shot at getting on the show than blacks. But *Friends* may simply be more honest than many shows about the way we lead racially isolated lives, even in the big city. The token black cast mem-ber on the periphery of some other sitcoms can seem very contrived at times, leading one stand-up comedian to imagine network executives in a story meeting insisting that "three of the Klansmen in that sketch need to be black."[11] On the evening we watched, *Friends* was true to form, the only blacks being two extras sitting in a restaurant. But that doesn't mean the half hour was devoid of visible blacks. Commercials consume about 25 per-cent of all television time, and blacks played key roles in four ads during the show, including one for McDonald's showing a black male airline passenger and a black female car rental agent, and another for an NBC show that in-cluded a black female attorney. In other words, even during a show like *Friends,* the white audience welcomed a number of virtual blacks into their living rooms.

After *Friends* came a show called *Union Square,* whose six regulars in-clude a black West Indian man who runs a diner that has a racially mixed staff and clientele. Again, blacks played prominent roles in the commercials, this time in five of them. Next up was *Seinfeld,* like *Friends* a show set in New York with an exclusive cast of white regulars, although this particular episode included a scene with a black female university dean. Four com-mercials included blacks, most of them professionals. On the following show, *Veronica's Closet,* a black male plays a regular though somewhat mar-ginal part, and that night a few other blacks were visible as supporting cast and extras. Only one ad included blacks. Finally came the crown jewel of the evening, the number-one show in America, *ER.* The show features two prominent black members of the ensemble cast, a doctor and a physician's assistant, as well as seven blacks in recurring roles. That evening, as with most episodes of *ER,* there were a number of black extras serving as hospi-tal employees, patients, and visitors. Of the twenty-four commercials inter-spersed throughout the hour-long show, ten featured blacks, including a number that portrayed black executives.

Think about the cumulative number of blacks on television that Thurs-day evening. The black characters on *ER* alone exceeded the number of

[11]The comedian Patton Oswalt was quoted in the *New York Times,* March 4, 1997, p. C11.

blacks with whom many white Americans interact meaningfully each week. The other blacks on the commercials, the news, or the other shows further embroidered the integrated image they saw. Rarely did the typical viewer go for more than a few minutes without seeing a black face on the screen, even if one or two shows didn't include blacks. Over three or four hours of television that night, whites saw blacks on news shows, entertainment shows, promos, and commercials — as anchors, reporters, stars, supporting cast, walk-ons, extras, and product endorsers. Nor was there anything unusual about it. The presence of blacks in the living room has become a normal part of our virtual lives. Television represents reality, even if it doesn't represent mine, right?

Channel-surf through the rest of television and you'll find much the same thing. Whether in prime time or daytime, children's hour or late at night, the typical white American will have an integrated viewing experience. According to the Center for Media and Public Affairs, a research organization, blacks played 17 percent of all characters in prime-time entertainment shows in 1992, up from half a percent in the early 1960s.[12] Today you see blacks on the morning shows doing the news and the weather, blacks reporting stories for the newsmagazines, blacks playing and announcing sports, blacks interviewing or being interviewed, blacks on the cop shows investigating homicides, and blacks offering up opinions on the political talk-show circuit. Black TV surgeons treat white TV patients and black TV lawyers represent white TV clients in far greater proportion than they do in real life. Blacks are likewise well represented in commercials, constituting more than 12 percent of on-camera actors and more than 17 percent of all the extras in ads produced in 1995, according to the Screen Actors Guild. A 1989 study found that blacks appeared in 26 percent of all primetime ads, though they were less likely than whites to be the main focus of an ad and more likely to be part of a group, a sequence, or the background cast.[13] Ads feature high-profile black celebrities, entertainers, and athletes as well as black professionals, families, and blue-collar workers. The advertising images of blacks are so common they cascade one on top of another: clips of Will Smith and Tommy Lee Jones promoting their movie *Men in Black,* a black construction worker waiting for his white colleague in a spot for Tylenol Extra Strength, athletes Shaquille O'Neil and Deion Sanders drinking Pepsi while hanging out in a white kid's bedroom, a group of white guys and their one black buddy ogling women in a bar on behalf of Bud Lite, a black man playing one of the Three Musketeers in an ad for the candy bar, a group of black and white kids warming up the image of the

15

---

[12]The Center for Media and Public Affairs statistic is cited in Rick Du Brow, "Portrayals of Latinos on Television Regressing," *Los Angeles Times,* September 7, 1994, p. A5.

[13]We are grateful to the Screen Actors Guild for supplying these figures on advertising. For the 1989 study, see Robert E. Wilkes and Humberto Valencia, "Hispanics and Blacks in Television Commercials," *Journal of Advertising,* vol. 18, no. 1 (1989), pp. 19–25.

Chevy Astro van, a FedEx spot featuring a black business owner interacting with black and white employees. The list could consume this book.

On children's shows like *Wishbone, Barney,* and *Magic School Bus,* almost every group of cartoon characters or kids looks like the United Nations. A few teen and twenty-something shows are pushing the color line even further: MTV's dating game, *Singled Out,* is fully interracial, and Fox's *Party of Five* featured an ongoing interracial romantic relationship. Then there are the daytime soaps, faithfully watched by millions of college students and stay-at-home moms. Almost every soap opera features at least two regular black characters, including doctors, cops, musicians, lawyers, nurses, nannies, reporters, executives, models, photographers, and just plain people. Behind them are plenty of black extras who stroll the beach, shop at the malls, attend social events, and work at hospitals. Interracial friendships are common and a few soaps have shown interracial relationships and marriages. As with most (though not all) television shows targeted to a predominantly white audience, soaps take color-blindness to the absurd point that the black and white characters, even those in interracial relationships, rarely discuss race. The audience may want realistic portrayals, but not when it comes to black and white. In the virtually integrated world of our living rooms, the last thing we want is the discomfort of reality intruding on the illusion.

Let us not be mistaken: the rise of black images on television and throughout the visual media is an extraordinarily positive development. Television may not be truly color-blind, but if it can help increase interracial familiarity, shatter some stereotypes, fortify the comfort zone, and multiply the number of black role models for everyone in America, then it has served an important goal that most other institutions in society have not been willing or able to accomplish. To suggest, as we do, that television undermines real integration—that it enables whites to lead virtually integrated lives without having much real contact with blacks—is not meant to condemn the visibility of blacks on TV but rather to explain its impact. Indeed, the only academic study to look at the phenomenon we call "virtual integration" tested black viewers and found that they, like whites, "more frequently perceived that racial integration is more prevalent, that blacks and whites were more similar, and that blacks were middle-class."[14]

By its very nature television creates imaginary or virtual relationships among people. What makes its impact on race unique is that for most whites their television contact with blacks is the closest they will ever come to crossing the color line. More than half of all whites in one survey say that what they know about blacks they get from the media.[15] "You sure gotta

[14]P. W. Matabane, "Television and the Black Audience: Cultivating Moderate Perspectives on Racial Integration," *Journal of Communication,* vol. 38, no. 4 (1988), p. 26.

[15]For the survey showing that a majority of whites get their information about blacks from the media, see Matthew P. Smith, "Bridging the Gulf Between Blacks and Whites," *Pittsburgh Post-Gazette,* April 7, 1996, p. 1.

hand it to 'em," the Edith Bunker character said about blacks on the show *All in the Family,* "I mean, two years ago they was nothing but servants and janitors. Nowadays they're teachers and doctors and lawyers. They've come a long way on TV." Certainly it is ironic that one of the few visible institutions where black participation has advanced so far may also provide whites with an excuse not to move much beyond the status quo. If the world is so integrated, then my all-white neighborhood or social club just happens to be an exception, so it's not that big a deal. If the world is so integrated, if a black person can become famous, make so much money, and appear on television, then it is they who push us away through all their whining and self-righteous anger. How can I be part of the problem if my kids idolize Michael Jordan and Barry Sanders and if I watch Bill Cosby and Della Reese every week on TV?

In New York City there had never been a black female news director at a local television station until 1996, when Vassar College graduate Paula Walker took the job at the NBC affiliate. Almost immediately she grasped how local news perpetuates the fear of black crime. Typically, a reporter describing a crime will dutifully draw on the police report, which might list the suspect as a black male, five-eight, 160 pounds. On the surface there seems nothing wrong with this description. But, as Walker told us, there are thousands upon thousands of people in the viewing area who fit it. Given that the purpose of putting out a description is to help the public finger the criminal, Walker sees no point in broadcasting such useless information when the only tangible impact will be to increase suspicion of blacks. "What you're doing is making all those women who are walking down the street clutch their pocketbooks closer to them," she said. To her, there would be nothing wrong with including race if the description also mentioned specific clothing, hair style, identifying characteristics such as a scar or a limp, and the neighborhood in which the suspect was last seen. Skin color then becomes relevant and serves a purpose.[16]

If the televised image of black actors, athletes, and entertainers leads   20
whites to think the world is integrated, the portrayal of black crime on television news helps keep real integration from ever happening. There is no irony in this aspect of television. Whether by accident or unconscious design, the face of crime on TV, especially on local news, tends to be black. It is true that blacks commit a disproportionate share of violent crimes, especially in urban areas, but it is also true that blacks are identified with criminal acts on television all out of proportion to the number they commit. Advertisers have long known that repetition, not to mention saturation, sells on television. The relentless association between blacks and crime on the news has colored white perceptions of blacks and has seriously undermined any hope for racial integration in America.

[16]Personal interview with Paula Walker, March 10, 1997.

Years ago in the segregated South it was not uncommon for local newspapers to run all sex-crime accusations against blacks on page one, even if the incident took place on the other side of the country.[17] Today there are few if any in television news with such an intent to malign—yet in many ways the result is the same: crime in general is associated with blacks. Findings from a number of research studies clearly document the distortion.[18] Even though most violent crimes are committed by people the same race as their victims, one 1994 study of local TV newscasts in Chicago found that the majority of perpetrators portrayed in the news were black or persons of color, while the majority of victims shown were white. A study of Philadelphia newscasts found that nonwhites were almost twice as likely to be shown as perpetrators than as victims of crime, almost the reverse of the portrayal of whites. Another study found that the percentage of blacks shown as suspects on one Los Angeles station far exceeded the percentage of violent crimes committed by blacks in Los Angeles County. This distortion is also evident in reality-based television programs, such as *COPS* and *America's Most Wanted*. According to one study, half of all the blacks who appear in these shows are criminals, versus 10 percent of all whites, while another found that stories about white victims lasted 74 percent longer than stories about black victims. Furthermore, research shows that blacks accused of the same crime as whites tend to be portrayed as more threatening and intimidating on television news. Whites arrested for crimes might be shown next to their attorneys, if they are shown at all, whereas blacks tend to be shown in handcuffs, on police walks, or being physically restrained by the police. News reports also provide the names of black suspects less often than they do for white suspects, leading one scholar to conclude that the individual identity of black suspects is less important than their race.

[17]Ben H. Bagdikian, "Editorial Responsibility in Times of Urban Disorder," in *The Media and the Cities,* ed. Charles U. Daily (Chicago: University of Chicago Center for Policy Study, 1968), p. 15.

[18]We have drawn on the following research studies for our information: Robert M. Entman, "Modern Racism and the Images of Blacks in Local Television News," *Critical Studies in Mass Communication,* vol. 7 (1990), pp. 332–345; Robert M. Entman, "Blacks in the News: Television, Modern Racism, and Cultural Change," *Journalism Quarterly,* Summer 1992, pp. 341–361; Robert M. Entman, "Representation and Reality in the Portrayal of Blacks on Network Television News," *Journalism Quarterly,* Autumn 1994, pp. 509–520; Robert M. Entman, *Violence on Television: News and "Reality" Programming in Chicago* (Chicago: Chicago Council on Urban Affairs, 1994); George Gerbner, "Women and Minorities on Television: A Study of Casting and Fate," *Report to the Screen Actors Guild and the American Federation of Radio and Television Artists,* June 1993; Daniel Romer, Kathleen H. Jamieson, and Nicole DeCoteau, "Differential Standards of Newsworthiness and Ethnic Blame Discourse on Television News: A Study of Crime Reporting in Philadelphia," unpublished paper sent to us by its authors. Research on the Los Angeles station is described in Howard Kurtz, "A Guilty Verdict on Crime, Race Bias," *Washington Post,* April 28, 1997, pp. 1, 4, who cites the findings of University of California, Los Angeles, professors Shanto Iyengar and Franklin Gilliam, Jr. See also Du Brow, "Portrayals of Latinos on Television Regressing"; and Mark Lorando, "TV's 'Average' Reveals Double Standard," *New Orleans Times-Picayune,* September 13, 1993, p. A9.

Put all these studies together and the composite is clear: whites are vulnerable to crime, blacks are responsible for it. So powerful is this image that when Charles Stuart, a white, killed his wife in Boston and Susan Smith, white, killed her children in South Carolina, both were able to point a finger at an imaginary though vaguely described black killer, knowing full well that the public would almost reflexively believe them. According to research by two University of California–Los Angeles professors, Shanto Iyengar and Franklin Gilliam, Jr., even when news reports of a crime made no reference to a suspect, 42 percent of viewers later remembered seeing a perpetrator, and two thirds of these viewers recalled this phantom criminal as black. When the news report did show a perpetrator, viewers disproportionately recalled him as black. Nor were white viewers the only ones making this mistake. Black viewers did as well, though to a lesser extent, further attesting to the power of racial images in televised reports of crime.[19]

The black criminal image on the news is also part of a larger problem with the news media. Television news feeds on a dramatic structure in which every report must have a plot, an emotional story line, and a moral. Crime fits the mold perfectly: there's a villain, a victim, fear, and human interest. As the entertainment programmers have learned, it's simply good and gripping television. Although the emphasis on crime distorts the portrayal of daily life, this is incidental to the imperative of holding the audience and getting a good story—so much so that coverage of murders on network evening news increased 721 percent since 1993, even though the nationwide homicide rate declined by 20 percent.[20] Blacks are simply caught in this media vise, their image held hostage to the very nature of TV news and its focus on the seamy side of reality. When the *New Orleans Times-Picayune* surveyed local evening news broadcasts for one week in 1993, it found that more than 42.1 percent of the total black images were crime-related and only 18.5 percent involved political or community issues—this in a heavily black city with blacks in charge of city hall.[21] In part this may be due to television's overemphasis on black crime; it is also likely due to television's overall fixation on crime. Because television news plays up crime regardless of color, and because the white majority has little or no contact with blacks except for what they see on television, even an accurate portrayal of crime—one showing how whites victimize mostly whites and blacks victimize mostly blacks—will still likely magnify the role of the black criminal among whites. The fact that the information is frequently reported by a black reporter or anchor validates it further.

[19]Research by the University of California, Los Angeles, professors Shanto Iyengar and Franklin Gilliam, Jr., is reported in Kurtz, "A Guilty Verdict on Crime, Race Bias."

[20]The murder-coverage statistics are from the Center for Media and Public Affairs press release, "In 1990s TV News Turns to Violence and Show Biz," August 12, 1997; for the drop in the nationwide homicide rate, see Vincent Schiraldi, "The Latest Trend in Juvenile Crime," *Washington Post*, January 11, 1998, p. C5.

[21]Mark Lorando, "Mass Media Wields Power That Reinforces Prejudice," *New Orleans Times-Picayune*, September 13, 1993, p. A7.

Compounding the problem is that people take what they see on the news personally, as if the reality they see is the reality of their lives. By its very dependence on graphic images and compelling visuals, television news evokes emotions and creates impressions. People don't just think about the news—they feel it. That may be why surveys show that the public has more trust in the local TV news than the local newspaper. Surveys also show that up to two-thirds of Americans say their attitudes about crime are stirred by the media rather than their own experiences or those of friends.[22] Now add up all of these factors: the disproportionate portrayal of black crime, the emphasis on crime in the local news, the emotive power of the medium, the accumulation of images, the proximate reality of what's reported, the lack of real contact with blacks among the white audience, and the implicit validation provided by black journalists reporting the news. The result is a generalized fear of crime that translates to a generalized fear of blacks. It is a sad commentary to suggest that the only way to eliminate white fright is to eliminate the reporting of black crime altogether, not merely to make the reporting more accurate. But there may be no other way to change the defining image of crime that so profoundly shapes white Americans' view of their fellow black citizens.

For most white Americans, the only kind of integration they know is the virtual kind, and it may be the only kind they want. Virtual integration enables whites to live in a world with blacks without having to do so in fact. It provides a form of safe intimacy without any of the risks. It offers a clean and easy way for whites to establish and nourish what they see as their bona fide commitment to fairness, tolerance, and color-blindness. White Americans may genuinely feel they are open to blacks, as long as blacks—with their criminal tendencies—don't move into the neighborhood. So television giveth, in the form of the virtual community that transcends race, and it taketh away, by reinforcing an association between blacks and crime that makes real community building all but impossible. This curious television dynamic explains how, as Harvard Medical School psychiatrist Dr. Alvin Poussaint told us, "white kids who worship Michael Jordan will beat up black kids who come into their neighborhoods." It is another sad and tragic irony of race relations in America, brought to you in living color.

ENGAGING THE TEXT

1. What is "virtual integration," according to the authors? What evidence do they present to support their claim that television presents an integrated world? Think for a moment about the shows you watch regularly: Do you see any evidence that would contradict this view?

[22]The public's reliance on TV news for information on crime is described in Stephen Braun and Judy Pasternak, "With Terror on Its Mind," *Los Angeles Times,* February 13, 1994, p. A16.

THE BOONDOCKS   by **AARON MCGRUDER**

2. What potential benefits do Steinhorn and Diggs-Brown see in the increased visibility of blacks in mass media? What are its hazards? To what extent do you agree with their assessment?

3. How does news coverage misrepresent life in black communities? What are the effects of these distortions? What relationship do the authors see between the images of African Americans in the news and those in other forms of programming?

4. How has the representation of blacks changed since the early days of television? Do you see equally dramatic changes in the ways that other minorities are depicted?

EXPLORING CONNECTIONS

5. Compare Shelby Steele's analysis of black entertainers and white audiences (p. 573) to that of Steinhorn and Diggs-Brown. How do they explain the popularity of performers like Bill Cosby? What influence do they believe black celebrities have on race relations? Which view do you find more persuasive, and why?

6. What does the cartoon on this page suggest about the images of African Americans in film, about movie audiences, and about racial understanding? To what extent do you think the cartoonist would agree with Steinhorn and Diggs-Brown's contention that our virtual world is more integrated than our real lives?

EXTENDING THE CRITICAL CONTEXT

7. Steinhorn and Diggs-Brown offer a "snapshot" of an evening's worth of programming and advertising on one network to illustrate the idea of virtual integration. As a class, do a similar analysis: working in groups, assign one or two people to take notes on each hour of programming for one evening (6 P.M.–11 P.M.). How often and in what roles do actors, newscasters, and citizens of each race or ethnicity appear? Pool your results and discuss the extent to which your class's "snapshot" reflects a virtually integrated world.

8. Scan your local newspaper or watch local television news broadcasts for a week and keep a list of how people of different races or ethnicities are represented. Write a paper based on your observations. What portrait does this newspaper or TV station paint of various ethnic groups in your community?

9. Do an informal survey to investigate integration and segregation on your campus. How often do students talk to people of different ethnicities in their classes? How many of their close friends belong to their own ethnic group and how many to other groups? Do they live or work with people of different ethnicities? Do they participate in multi-ethnic clubs or service organizations? Do they belong to clubs or organizations focused on the interests of their own ethnic group? What are the ethnicities of their favorite musicians, actors, and athletes? To what extent do your survey results support the notion that we remain more segregated in our social lives than in our virtual lives?

Models of American Ethnic Relations: A Historical Perspective

GEORGE M. FREDRICKSON

Are Irish Americans white? The answer is so self-evident that the question seems absurd, but as historian George Fredrickson notes, the idea of "whiteness" has in the past excluded many Europeans, including the Irish. A survey of ethnic and racial categories in American history shows how much they change with the politics and prejudices of the time. Yet citizenship, civil rights, even human status have been granted or withheld on the basis of these shifting definitions. Fredrickson examines four models of ethnic relations—hierarchy, assimilation, pluralism, and separatism—that have defined how groups perceived as different from each other should interact. Fredrickson (b. 1934) has written extensively about race in the history of the United States and South Africa and is a past president of the Organization for American Historians. His books include The Black Image in the White Mind *(1987),* Black Liberation: A Comparative History of Black Ideologies in the United States and South Africa *(1995), and* The Comparative Imagination: On the History of Racism, Nationalism, and Social Movements *(1997). He is a professor of U.S. history at Stanford University and currently codirects the Stanford Research Institute for the Comparative Study of Race and Ethnicity.*

Throughout its history, the United States has been inhabited by a variety of interacting racial or ethnic groups. In addition to the obvious "color line" structuring relationships between dominant whites and lower-status blacks, Indians, and Asians, there have at times been important social distinctions among those of white or European ancestry. Today we think of the differences between white Anglo-Saxon Protestants and Irish, Italian, Polish, and Jewish Americans as purely cultural or religious, but in earlier times these groups were sometimes thought of as "races" or "subraces"—people possessing innate or inborn characteristics and capabilities that affected their fitness for American citizenship. Moreover, differences apparently defined as cultural have sometimes been so reified[1] as to serve as the functional equivalent of physical distinctions. Indians, for example, were viewed by most nineteenth-century missionaries and humanitarians as potentially equal and similar to whites. Their status as noncitizens was not attributed to skin color or physical appearance; it was only their obdurate adherence to "savage ways" that allegedly stood in the way of their possessing equal rights and being fully assimilated. Analogously, conservative opponents of affirmative action and other antiracist policies in the 1990s may provide a "rational" basis for prejudice and discrimination by attributing the disadvantages and alleged shortcomings of African Americans to persistent cultural "pathology" rather than to genetic deficiencies (D'Souza 1995).

It can therefore be misleading to make a sharp distinction between race and ethnicity when considering intergroup relations in American history. As I have argued extensively elsewhere, ethnicity is "racialized" whenever distinctive group characteristics, however defined or explained, are used as the basis for a status hierarchy of groups who are thought to differ in ancestry or descent (Fredrickson 1997, ch. 5).

Four basic conceptions of how ethnic or racial groups should relate to each other have been predominant in the history of American thought about group relations—ethnic hierarchy, one-way assimilation, cultural pluralism, and group separatism. This [essay] provides a broad outline of the historical career of each of these models of intergroup relations, noting some of the changes in how various groups have defined themselves or been defined by others.

Ethnic Hierarchy

Looking at the entire span of American history, we find that the most influential and durable conception of the relations among those American racial or ethnic groups viewed as significantly dissimilar has been hierarchical. A dominant group—conceiving of itself as society's charter membership—has claimed rights and privileges not to be fully shared with outsiders or "others," who have been characterized as unfit or unready for

---

[1]*reified:* Treated as if real, concrete, but actually abstract.

equal rights and full citizenship. The hierarchical model has its deepest roots and most enduring consequences in the conquest of Indians and the enslavement of blacks during the colonial period (Axtell 1981; Jordan 1968). But it was also applied in the nineteenth century to Asian immigrants and in a less severe and more open-ended way to European immigrants who differed in culture and religion from old-stock Americans of British origin (Higham 1968; Miller 1969). The sharpest and most consequential distinction was always between "white" and "nonwhite." The first immigration law passed by Congress in 1790 specified that only white immigrants were eligible for naturalization. This provision would create a crucial difference in the mid-nineteenth century between Chinese "sojourners," who could not become citizens and voters, and Irish immigrants, who could.

Nevertheless, the Irish who fled the potato famine of the 1840s by emi-   5
grating to the United States also encountered discrimination. Besides being Catholic and poor, the refugees from the Emerald Isle were Celts rather than Anglo-Saxons, and a racialized discourse,[2] drawing on British precedents, developed as an explanation for Irish inferiority to Americans of English ancestry (Knobel 1986). The dominant group during the nineteenth and early twentieth centuries was not simply white but also Protestant and Anglo-Saxon. Nevertheless, the Irish were able to use their right to vote and the patronage they received from the Democratic Party to improve their status, an option not open to the Chinese. Hence, they gradually gained the leverage and respectability necessary to win admission to the dominant caste, a process that culminated in Al Smith's nomination for the presidency in 1928 and John F. Kennedy's election in 1960.

The mass immigration of Europeans from eastern and southern Europe in the late nineteenth and early twentieth centuries inspired new concerns about the quality of the American stock. In an age of eugenics,[3] scientific racism,[4] and social Darwinism,[5] the notion that northwestern Europeans were innately superior to those from the southern and eastern parts of the continent—to say nothing of those light-skinned people of actual or presumed west Asian origin (such as Jews, Syrians, and Armenians)—gained wide currency. A determined group of nativists, encouraged by the latest racial "science," fought for restrictive immigration policies that discriminated against those who were not of "Nordic" or "Aryan" descent (Higham

---

[2]*racialized discourse:* Language that defines a group of people as a race and attributes distinctive "racial" characteristics to them.

[3]*eugenics:* Movement that advocated improving the human race by encouraging genetically "superior" people to reproduce and promoting the sterilization of "undesirables," including minorities, poor people, and those with mental and physical disorders.

[4]*scientific racism:* Refers to various efforts to find some scientific basis for white superiority, the results of which were inevitably bad science.

[5]*social Darwinism:* The belief that Darwin's theory of evolution and natural selection applies to society; thus the existence of extreme wealth and poverty (whether of individuals or nations) is rationalized as a "natural" result of competition and the survival of the fittest.

1968). In the 1920s the immigration laws were changed to reflect these prejudices. Low quotas were established for white people from nations or areas outside of those that had supplied the bulk of the American population before 1890. In the minds of many, true Americans were not merely white but also northern European. In fact, some harbored doubts about the full claim to "whiteness" of swarthy immigrants from southern Italy.

After immigration restriction had relieved ethnic and racial anxieties, the status of the new immigrants gradually improved as a result of their political involvement, their economic and professional achievement, and a decline in the respectability of the kind of scientific racism that had ranked some European groups below others. World War II brought revulsion against the genocidal anti-Semitism and eugenic experiments of the Nazis, dealing a coup de grâce to the de facto hierarchy that had placed Anglo-Saxons, Nordics, or Aryans at the apex of American society. All Americans of European origin were now unambiguously white and, for most purposes, ethnically equal to old-stock Americans of Anglo-Saxon, Celtic, and Germanic ancestry. Hierarchy was now based exclusively on color. Paradoxically, it might be argued, the removal of the burden of "otherness" from virtually all whites made more striking and salient than ever the otherness of people of color, especially African Americans.

The civil rights movement of the 1960s was directed primarily at the legalized racial hierarchy of the southern states. The Civil Rights Acts of 1964 and 1965 brought an end to government-enforced racial segregation and the denial of voting rights to blacks in that region. But the legacy of four centuries of white supremacy survives in the disadvantaged social and economic position of blacks and other people of color in the United States. The impoverished, socially deprived, and physically unsafe ghettos, barrios, and Indian reservations of this nation are evidence that ethnic hierarchy in a clearly racialized form persists in practice if not in law.

One-Way Assimilation

Policies aimed at the assimilation of ethnic groups have usually assumed that there is a single and stable American culture of European, and especially English, origin to which minorities are expected to conform as the price of admission to full and equal participation in the society and polity of the United States (Gordon 1964, ch. 4). Assimilationist thinking is not racist in the classic sense: it does not deem the outgroups in question to be innately or biologically inferior to the ingroup. The professed goal is equality — but on terms that presume the superiority, purity, and unchanging character of the dominant culture. Little or nothing in the cultures of the groups being invited to join the American mainstream is presumed worthy of preserving. When carried to its logical conclusion, the assimilationist project demands what its critics have described — especially in reference to the coercive efforts to "civilize" Native Americans — as "cultural genocide."

Estimates of group potential and the resulting decisions as to which   10
groups are eligible for assimilation have varied in response to changing definitions of race. If an ethnic group is definitely racialized, the door is closed
because its members are thought to possess ineradicable traits (biologically
or culturally determined) that make them unfit for inclusion. At times there
have been serious disagreements within the dominant group about the eligi-
bility of particular minorities for initiation into the American club.

Although one-way assimilationism was mainly a twentieth-century ideology, it was anticipated in strains of nineteenth-century thinking about
Irish immigrants, Native Americans, and even blacks. Radical white aboli-
tionists and even some black antislavery activists argued that prejudice
against African Americans was purely and simply a result of their peculiarly
degraded and disadvantaged circumstances and that emancipation from
slavery would make skin color irrelevant and open the way to their full
equality and social acceptability (Fredrickson 1987, ch. 1). These abolition-
ists had little or no conception that there was a rich and distinctive black
culture that could become the source of a positive group identity, and that
African modes of thought and behavior had been adapted to the challenge
of surviving under slavery.

If the hope of fully assimilating blacks into a color-blind society was
held by only a small minority of whites, a majority probably supposed that
the Irish immigrants of the 1840s and 1850s could become full-fledged
Americans, if they chose to do so, simply by changing their behavior and beliefs. The doctrine of the innate inferiority of Celts to Anglo-Saxons was not
even shared by all of the nativists who sought to slow down the process of
Irish naturalization (Knobel 1986). A more serious problem for many of
them was the fervent Catholicism of the Irish; Anglo-Protestant missionaries hoped to convert them en masse. The defenders of unrestricted Irish
immigration came mostly from the ranks of the Democratic Party, which relied heavily on Irish votes. Among them were strong believers in religious
toleration and a high wall of separation between church and state. They saw
religious diversity as no obstacle to the full and rapid Americanization of all
white-skinned immigrants.

The most sustained and serious nineteenth-century effort to assimilate
people who differed both culturally and phenotypically[6] from the majority
was aimed at American Indians. Frontier settlers, military men who fought
Indians, and many other whites had no doubts that Indians were members
of an inherently inferior race that was probably doomed to total extinction
as a result of the conquest of the West. Their views were graphically expressed by General Philip Sheridan when he opined that "the only good Indian is a dead Indian." But an influential group of eastern philanthropists,
humanitarian reformers, and government officials thought of the Indians as
having been "noble savages" whose innate capacities were not inferior to

[6]*phenotypically:* Physically.

those of whites. Thomas Jefferson, who had a much dimmer view of black potentialities, was one of the first to voice this opinion (Koch and Peden 1944, 210–11). For these ethnocentric humanitarians, the "Indian problem" was primarily cultural rather than racial, and its solution lay in civilizing the "savages" rather than exterminating them. Late in the century, the assimilationists adopted policies designed to force Indians to conform to Euro-American cultural norms; these included breaking up communally held reservations into privately owned family farms and sending Indian children to boarding schools where they were forbidden to speak their own languages and made to dress, cut their hair, and in every possible way act and look like white people. The policy was a colossal failure; most Native Americans refused to abandon key aspects of their traditional cultures, and venal whites took advantage of the land reforms to strip Indians of much of their remaining patrimony[7] (Berkhofer 1978; Hoxie 1984; Mardock 1971).

In the early twentieth century, the one-way assimilation model was applied to the southern and eastern European immigrants who had arrived in massive numbers before the discriminatory quota system of the 1920s was implemented. While some nativists called for their exclusion on the grounds of their innate deficiencies, other champions of Anglo-American cultural homogeneity hoped to assimilate those who had already arrived through education and indoctrination. The massive "Americanization" campaigns of the period just prior to World War I produced the concept of America as a "melting pot" in which cultural differences would be obliterated. The metaphor might have suggested that a new mixture would result—and occasionally it did have this meaning—but a more prevalent interpretation was that non-Anglo-American cultural traits and inclinations would simply disappear, making the final brew identical to the original one (Gordon 1964, ch. 5).

Before the 1940s, people of color, and especially African Americans, were generally deemed ineligible for assimilation because of their innate inferiority to white ethnics, who were now thought capable of being culturally reborn as Anglo-Americans. Such factors as the war-inspired reaction against scientific racism and the gain in black political power resulting from mass migration from the South (where blacks could not vote) to the urban North (where the franchise was again open to them) led to a significant reconsideration of the social position of African Americans and threw a spotlight on the flagrant denial in the southern states of the basic constitutional rights of African Americans. The struggle for black civil rights that emerged in the 1950s and came to fruition in the early 1960s was premised on a conviction that white supremacist laws and policies violated an egalitarian "American Creed"—as Gunnar Myrdal had argued in his influential wartime study *An American Dilemma* (1944). The war against Jim Crow[8]

15

---

[7]*patrimony:* Inheritance.
[8]*Jim Crow:* Collective term for southern segregation laws.

was fought under the banner of "integration," which, in the minds of white liberals at least, generally meant one-way assimilation. Blacks, deemed by Myrdal and others as having no culture worth saving, would achieve equal status by becoming just like white Americans in every respect except pigmentation.

When it became clear that the civil rights legislation of the 1960s had failed to improve significantly the social and economic position of blacks in the urban ghettos of the North, large numbers of African Americans rejected the integrationist ideal on the grounds that it had been not only a false promise but an insult to the culture of African Americans for ignoring or devaluing their distinctive experience as a people. The new emphasis on "black power" and "black consciousness" conveyed to those whites who were listening that integration had to mean something other than one-way assimilation to white middle-class norms if it was to be a solution to the problem of racial inequality in America (Marable 1991; Van Deburg 1992).

It should be obvious by now that the one-way assimilation model has not proved to be a viable or generally acceptable way of adjusting group differences in American society. It is based on an ethnocentric ideal of cultural homogeneity that has been rejected by Indians, blacks, Asians, Mexican Americans, and even many white ethnics. It reifies and privileges one cultural strain in what is in fact a multicultural society. It should be possible to advocate the incorporation of all ethnic or racial groups into a common civic society without requiring the sacrifice of cultural distinctiveness and diversity.

Cultural Pluralism

Unlike assimilationists, cultural pluralists celebrate differences among groups rather than seek to obliterate them. They argue that cultural diversity is a healthy and normal condition that does not preclude equal rights and the mutual understandings about civic responsibilities needed to sustain a democratic nation-state. This model for American ethnic relations is a twentieth-century invention that would have been virtually inconceivable at an earlier time. The eighteenth and nineteenth centuries lacked the essential concept of the relativity of cultures. The model of cultural development during this period was evolutionary, progressive, and universalistic. People were either civilized or they were not. Mankind was seen as evolving from a state of "savagery" or "barbarism" to "civilization," and all cultures at a particular level were similar in every way that mattered. What differentiated nations and ethnic groups was their ranking on the scale of social evolution. Modern Western civilization stood at the apex of this universal historical process. Even nineteenth-century black nationalists accepted the notion that there were universal standards of civilization to which people of African descent should aspire. They differed from white supremacists in believing that blacks had the natural capability to reach the same heights as Caucasians if they were given a chance (Moses 1978).

The concept of cultural pluralism drew on the new cultural anthropology of the early twentieth century, as pioneered by Franz Boas. Boas and his disciples attempted to look at each culture they studied on its own terms and as an integrated whole. They rejected theories of social evolution that ranked cultures in relation to a universalist conception of "civilization." But relativistic cultural anthropologists were not necessarily cultural pluralists in their attitude toward group relations within American society. Since they generally believed that a given society or community functioned best with a single, integrated culture, they could favor greater autonomy for Indians on reservations but also call for the full assimilation of new immigrants or even African Americans. Boas himself was an early supporter of the National Association for the Advancement of Colored People (NAACP) and a pioneering advocate of what would later be called racial integration.

An effort to use the new concept of culture to validate ethnic diversity   20 within the United States arose from the negative reaction of some intellectuals to the campaign to "Americanize" the new immigrants from eastern and southern Europe in the period just before and after World War I. The inventors of cultural pluralism were cosmopolitan critics of American provincialism or representatives of immigrant communities, especially Jews, who valued their cultural distinctiveness and did not want to be melted down in an Americanizing crucible. The Greenwich Village intellectual Randolph Bourne described his ideal as a "transnational America" in which various ethnic cultures would interact in a tolerant atmosphere to create an enriching variety of ideas, values, and lifestyles (Bourne 1964, ch. 8). The Jewish philosopher Horace Kallen, who coined the phrase "cultural pluralism," compared the result to a symphony, with each immigrant group represented as a section of the orchestra (Higham 1984, ch. 9; Kallen 1924). From a different perspective, W. E. B. DuBois celebrated a distinctive black culture rooted in the African and slave experiences and heralded its unacknowledged contributions to American culture in general (Lewis 1993). But the dominant version advocated by Kallen and Bourne stopped, for all practical purposes, at the color line. Its focus was on making America safe for a variety of European cultures. As a Zionist, Kallen was especially concerned with the preservation of Jewish distinctiveness and identity.

Since it was mainly the viewpoint of ethnic intellectuals who resisted the assimilationism of the melting pot, cultural pluralism was a minority persuasion in the twenties, thirties, and forties. A modified version reemerged in the 1950s in Will Herberg's (1960) conception of a "triple melting pot" of Protestants, Catholics, and Jews. The revulsion against Nazi anti-Semitism and the upward mobility of American Jews and Catholics inspired a synthesis of cultural pluralism and assimilationism that made religious persuasion the only significant source of diversity among white Americans. Herberg conceded, however, that black Protestants constituted a separate group that was not likely to be included in the Protestant melting pot. He therefore sharpened the distinction between race or color and ethnicity that was central to postwar thinking about group differences. Nevertheless, Herberg's view that significant differences between, say, Irish and Italian Catholics were disappearing was challenged in the 1960s and later, especially in the "ethnic revival" of the 1970s, which proclaimed that differing national origins among Euro-Americans remained significant and a valuable source of cultural variations.

The "multiculturalism" of the 1980s operated on assumptions that were similar to those of the cultural pluralist tradition, except that the color line was breached and the focus was shifted from the cultures and contributions of diverse European ethnic groups to those of African Americans, Mexican Americans, Asian Americans, and Native Americans. Abandonment of the earlier term "multiracialism" signified a desire to escape from the legacy of biological or genetic determinism and to affirm that the differences among people who happened to differ in skin color or phenotype were the result of their varying cultural and historical experiences. Under attack was the doctrine, shared by assimilationists and most earlier proponents of cultural pluralism, that the cultural norm in the United States was inevitably European in origin and character. Parity was now sought for groups of Asian, African, and American Indian ancestry. This ideal of cultural diversity and democracy was viewed by some of its critics as an invitation to national disunity and ethnic conflict (Schlesinger 1992). But its most thoughtful proponents argued that it was simply a consistent application of American democratic values and did not preclude the interaction and cooperation of groups within a common civic society (Hollinger 1995). Nevertheless, the mutual understandings upon which national unity and cohesion could be based needed to be negotiated rather than simply imposed by a Euro-American majority.

Group Separatism

Sometimes confused with the broadened cultural pluralism described here is the advocacy of group separatism. It originates in the desire of a culturally distinctive or racialized group to withdraw as much as possible from American society and interaction with other groups. Its logical outcome, autonomy in a separate, self-governing community, might conceivably be achieved either in an ethnic confederation like Switzerland or in the dissolution of the United States into several ethnic nations. But such a general theory is a logical construction rather than a program that has been explicitly advocated. Group separatism emanates from ethnocentric concerns about the status and destiny of particular groups, and its advocates rarely if ever theorize about what is going to happen to other groups. Precedents for group separatism based on cultural differences can be found in American history in the toleration of virtually autonomous religious communities like the Amish and the Hutterites[9] and in the modicum of self-government and immunity from general laws accorded to Indian tribes and reservations since the 1930s.

The most significant and persistent assertion of group separatism in American history has come from African Americans disillusioned with the prospects for equality within American society. In the nineteenth century, several black leaders and intellectuals called on African Americans to emigrate from the United States in order to establish an independent black republic elsewhere; Africa was the most favored destination. In the 1920s, Marcus Garvey created a mass movement based on the presumption that blacks had no future in the United States and should identify with the independence and future greatness of Africa, ultimately by emigrating there. More recently, the Nation of Islam has proposed that several American states be set aside for an autonomous black nation (Fredrickson 1995, chs. 2, 4, 7). At the height of the black power movement of the 1960s and early 1970s, a few black nationalists even called for the establishment of a noncontiguous federation of black urban ghettos—a nation of islands like Indonesia or the Philippines, but surrounded by white populations rather than the Pacific Ocean.

The current version of black separatism—"Afrocentrism"[10]—has not as yet produced a plan for political separation. Its aim is a cultural and spiritual secession from American society rather than the literal establishment of a black nation. Advocates of total separation could be found among other disadvantaged groups. In the late 1960s and 1970s Mexican American militants called for the establishment of the independent Chicano nation of Aztlán[11] in the American Southwest (Gutierrez 1995, 184–85) and some Native American radicals sought the reestablishment of truly independent tribal nations.

25

Group separatism might be viewed as a utopian vision or rhetorical device expressing the depths of alienation felt by the most disadvantaged racial or ethnic groups in American society. The extreme unlikelihood of realizing such visions has made their promulgation more cathartic than politically efficacious. Most members of groups exposed to such separatist appeals have recognized their impracticality, and the clash between the fixed and essentialist[12] view of identity that such projects entail and the fluid and hybrid quality of group cultures in the United States has become increasingly evident to many people of color, as shown most dramatically by the

---

[9]*the Amish and the Hutterites:* Religious groups that reject the values and technology of contemporary society, living in relatively isolated, self-sufficient farming communities.

[10]*Afrocentrism:* An academic movement intended to counter the dominant European bias of Western scholarship; Afrocentric scholars seek to show the influence of African cultures, languages, and history on human civilization.

[11]*Aztlán:* Includes those parts of the United States once governed by Mexico.

[12]*essentialist:* Refers to the idea that group characteristics are innate, or "essential," rather than cultural.

recent movement among those of mixed parentage to affirm a biracial identity. Few African Americans want to celebrate the greater or lesser degree of white ancestry most of them possess, but many have acknowledged not only their ancestral ties to Africa but their debt to Euro-American culture (and its debt to them). Most Mexican Americans value their cultural heritage but do not have the expectation or even the desire to establish an independent Chicano nation in the Southwest. Native Americans have authentic historical and legal claims to a high degree of autonomy but generally recognize that total independence on their current land base is impossible and would worsen rather than improve their circumstances. Asian Americans are proud of their various cultures and seek to preserve some of their traditions but have shown little or no inclination to separate themselves from other Americans in the civic, professional, and economic life of the nation. Afrocentrism raises troubling issues for American educational and cultural life but hardly represents a serious threat to national unity.

Ethnic separatism, in conclusion, is a symptom of racial injustice and a call to action against it, but there is little reason to believe that it portends "the disuniting of America." It is currently a source of great anxiety to many Euro-Americans primarily because covert defenders of ethnic hierarchy or one-way assimilation have tried to confuse the broad-based ideal of democratic multiculturalism with the demands of a relatively few militant ethnocentrists for thoroughgoing self-segregation and isolation from the rest of American society.

Of the four models of American ethnic relations, the one that I believe offers the best hope for a just and cohesive society is a cultural pluralism that is fully inclusive and based on the free choices of individuals to construct or reconstruct their own ethnic identities. We are still far from achieving the degree of racial and ethnic tolerance that realization of such an ideal requires. But with the demographic shift that is transforming the overwhelmingly Euro-American population of thirty or forty years ago into one that is much more culturally and phenotypically heterogeneous, a more democratic form of intergroup relations is a likely prospect, unless there is a desperate reversion to overt ethnic hierarchicalism by the shrinking Euro-American majority. It that were to happen, national unity and cohesion would indeed be hard to maintain. If current trends continue, minorities of non-European ancestry will constitute a new majority sometime in the next century. Well before that point is reached, they will have the numbers and the provocation to make the country virtually ungovernable if a resurgent racism brings serious efforts to revive the blatantly hierarchical policies that have prevailed in the past.

References

Axtell, James. (1981). *The European and the Indian: Essays in the Ethnohistory of Colonial North America.* New York: Oxford University Press.

Berkhofer, Robert F., Jr. (1978). *The White Man's Indian: Image of the American Indian from Columbus to the Present*. New York: Alfred A. Knopf.

Bourne, Randolph S. (1964). *War and the Intellectuals: Collected Essays, 1915–1919*. New York: Harper Torch.

D'Souza, Dinesh. (1995). *The End of Racism: Principles for a Multiracial Society*. New York: Free Press.

Fredrickson, George M. (1987). *The Black Image in the White Mind: The Debate on Afro-American Character and Destiny, 1817–1914*. Middletown, Conn.: Wesleyan University Press.

———. (1995). *Black Liberation: A Comparative History of Black Ideologies in the United States and South Africa*. New York: Oxford University Press.

———. (1997). *The Comparative Imagination: On the History of Racism, Nationalism, and Social Movements*. Berkeley: University of California Press.

Gordon, Milton M. (1964). *Assimilation in American Life: The Role of Race, Religion, and National Origins*. New York: Oxford University Press.

Gutierrez, David. (1995). *Walls and Mirrors: Mexican Americans, Mexican Immigrants, and the Politics of Ethnicity*. Berkeley: University of California Press.

Herberg, Will. (1960). *Protestant-Catholic-Jew: An Essay in American Religious Sociology*. Garden City, N.Y.: Anchor Books.

Higham, John. (1968). *Strangers in the Land: Patterns of American Nativism, 1860–1925*. New York: Atheneum.

———. (1984). *Send These to Me: Jews and Other Immigrants in Urban America*. Baltimore: Johns Hopkins University Press.

Hollinger, David. (1995). *Postethnic America: Beyond Multiculturalism*. New York: Basic Books.

Hoxie, Frederick E. (1984). *A Final Promise: The Campaign to Assimilate the Indians, 1880–1920*. Lincoln: University of Nebraska Press.

Jordan, Winthrop D. (1968). *White Over Black: American Attitudes Toward the Negro, 1550–1812*. New York: University of North Carolina Press.

Kallen, Horace. (1924). *Culture and Democracy in the United States: Studies in the Group Psychology of American Peoples*. New York: Boni & Liveright.

Koch, Adrienne, and Peden, William. (Eds.). (1944). *The Life and Selected Writings of Thomas Jefferson*. New York: Modern Library.

Knobel, Dale T. (1986). *Paddy and the Republic: Ethnicity and Nationality in Antebellum America*. Middletown, Conn.: Wesleyan University Press.

Lewis, David Levering. (1993). *W. E. B. DuBois: Biography of a Race, 1868–1919*. New York: Henry Holt.

Marable, Manning. (1991). *Race, Reform, and Rebellion: The Second Reconstruction in Black America*. Jackson, Miss.: University of Mississippi Press.

Mardock, Robert W. (1971). *The Reformers and the American Indian.* Columbia: University of Missouri Press.

Miller, Stuart Creighton. (1969). *The Unwelcome Immigrant: The American Image of the Chinese, 1785–1882.* Berkeley: University of California Press.

Moses, Wilson Jeremiah. (1978). *The Golden Age of Black Nationalism, 1850–1925.* Hamden, Conn.: Archon Books.

Myrdal, Gunnar. (1944). *An American Dilemma.* New York: Harper and Row.

Schlesinger, Arthur M., Jr. (1992). *The Disuniting of America.* New York: Norton.

Van Deburg, William L. (1992). *New Day in Babylon: The Black Power Movement and American Culture, 1965–1975.* Chicago: University of Chicago Press.

ENGAGING THE TEXT

1. How does Fredrickson distinguish between race and ethnicity? How and under what circumstances can ethnicity become "racialized" (para. 2)?

2. What does Fredrickson mean by "the burden of 'otherness'"? Summarize the ways in which racial categories and definitions of "whiteness" have changed during the course of American history.

3. What are some of the ways that ethnic hierarchy has been eliminated? In what ways does it persist, according to Fredrickson? What evidence can you think of that would support or challenge this contention?

4. Fredrickson writes that "assimilationist thinking is not racist in the classic sense" (para. 9)—thereby implying that such thinking may be racist in some other sense. What does he mean by this? Do you agree?

5. How does Fredrickson distinguish cultural pluralism from assimilation? How did earlier forms of pluralism differ from the current concept of multiculturalism?

6. Why does Fredrickson reject the claim that an emphasis on ethnic identity threatens the unity and stability of American society? Why does a Euro-American backlash against ethnic diversity pose a greater risk in his view? Have you observed any recent examples of either divisiveness or backlash? Compare your observations with those of classmates.

EXPLORING CONNECTIONS

7. Write an essay examining the ways in which various models of ethnic relations can be seen operating in one or more of the following selections:

> Richard Rodriguez, "The Achievement of Desire" (p. 194)
>
> Malcolm X, "Learning to Read" (p. 223)
>
> Studs Terkel, "Stephen Cruz" (p. 335)
>
> Judith Ortiz Cofer, "The Story of My Body" (p. 423)

8. In the cartoon on page 623, what model of ethnic relations is reflected in the white executive's comment that Worthington is "not turning out to be as black as we had hoped"? Which model has Worthington apparently been following?

9. Look ahead to the Visual Portfolio on pages 639–41. Identify the model of ethnic relations you see embodied in each image and explain your reasoning.

EXTENDING THE CRITICAL CONTEXT

10. If your campus or community is involved in a debate concerning affirmative action, immigration, bilingual education, multiculturalism, or ethnic studies, analyze several opinion pieces or position papers on the issue. What models of ethnic relations are expressed or assumed by each side of the debate?

Notes of a Native Speaker
ERIC LIU

The son of Chinese immigrant parents, Eric Liu is an unrepentant as-similationist. As he details in this essay, he has worked hard to master the codes of the dominant culture. By any measure, he has succeeded, having graduated from an Ivy League university and worked in the U.S. Senate, the State Department, and the White House, where he served as a speech writer for President Clinton. He concedes that he has neglected or lost some measure of Chinese culture along the way, but rejects the idea that this makes him a "traitor" to his heritage. Instead, he suggests that his experience represents a much larger process that is transforming the face of America as a new, multi-ethnic generation comes into its own. "America is white no longer," he concludes, "and it will never be white again." Liu (b. 1968) founded the political journal The Next Progressive *and has edited an anthology titled* Next: Young American Writers on the New Generation *(1994). Currently he is a fellow at the New American Foundation and writes*

for MSNBC. This selection is taken from his collection of personal essays,
The Accidental Asian *(1998).*

1

Here are some of the ways you could say I am "white":

I listen to National Public Radio.
I wear khaki Dockers.
I own brown suede bucks.
I eat gourmet greens.
I have few close friends "of color."
I married a white woman.
I am a child of the suburbs.
I furnish my condo à la Crate & Barrel.
I vacation in charming bed-and-breakfasts.
I have never once been the victim of blatant discrimination.
I am a member of several exclusive institutions.
I have been in the inner sanctums of political power.
I have been there as something other than an attendant.
I have the ambition to return.
I am a producer of the culture.
I expect my voice to be heard.
I speak flawless, unaccented English.
I subscribe to *Foreign Affairs.*
I do not mind when editorialists write in the first person plural.
I do not mind how white television casts are.
I am not too ethnic.
I am wary of minority militants.
I consider myself neither in exile nor in opposition.
I am considered "a credit to my race."

I never asked to be white. I am not literally white. That is, I do not have
white skin or white ancestors. I have yellow skin and yellow ancestors, hundreds of generations of them. But like so many other Asian Americans of
the second generation, I find myself now the bearer of a strange new status:
white, by acclamation. Thus it is that I have been described as an "honorary
white," by other whites, and as a "banana,"[1] by other Asians. Both the hon-
orific and the epithet take as a given this idea: to the extent that I have
moved away from the periphery and toward the center of American life, I
have become white inside. *Some are born white, others achieve whiteness,*

---

[1]*"banana":* Derogatory term for an assimilated Asian American who is seen as a sellout,
"yellow on the outside and white on the inside."

still others have whiteness thrust upon them. This, supposedly, is what it means to assimilate.

There was a time when assimilation did quite strictly mean whitening. In fact, well into the first half of this century, mimicry of the stylized standards of the WASP[2] gentry was the proper, dominant, perhaps even sole method of ensuring that your origins would not be held against you. You "made it" in society not only by putting on airs of anglitude, but also by assiduously bleaching out the marks of a darker, dirtier past. And this bargain, stifling as it was, was open to European immigrants almost exclusively; to blacks, only on the passing occasion; to Asians, hardly at all.

Times have changed, and I suppose you could call it progress that a Chinaman, too, may now aspire to whiteness. But precisely because the times have changed, that aspiration—and the *imputation* of the aspiration—now seems astonishingly outmoded. The meaning of "American" has undergone a revolution in the twenty-nine years I have been alive, a revolution of color, class, and culture. Yet the vocabulary of "assimilation" has remained fixed all this time: fixed in whiteness, which is still our metonym for power; and fixed in shame, which is what the colored are expected to feel for embracing the power.

I have assimilated. I am of the mainstream. In many ways I fit the psychological profile of the so-called banana: imitative, impressionable, rootless, eager to please. As I will admit in this essay, I have at times gone to great lengths to downplay my difference, the better to penetrate the "establishment" of the moment. Yet I'm not sure that what I did was so cut-and-dried as "becoming white." I plead guilty to the charges above: achieving, learning the ways of the upper middle class, distancing myself from radicals of any hue. But having confessed, I still do not know my crime.

To be an accused banana is to stand at the ill-fated intersection of class   5 and race. And because class is the only thing Americans have more trouble talking about than race, a minority's climb up the social ladder is often willfully misnamed and wrongly portrayed. There is usually, in the portrayal, a strong whiff of betrayal: the assimilist is a traitor to his kind, to his class, to his own family. He cannot gain the world without losing his soul. To be sure, something *is* lost in any migration, whether from place to place or from class to class. But something is gained as well. And the result is always more complicated than the monochrome language of "whiteness" and "authenticity" would suggest.

My own assimilation began long before I was born. It began with my parents, who came here with an appetite for Western ways already whetted by films and books and music and, in my mother's case, by a father who'd been to the West. My parents, who traded Chinese formality for the more laissez-faire stance of this country. Who made their way by hard work and quiet adaptation. Who fashioned a comfortable life in a quiet development

[2]*WASP:* Acronym for "White Anglo-Saxon Protestant."

in a second-tier suburb. Who, unlike your "typical" Chinese parents, were not pushy, status-obsessed, rigid, disciplined, or prepared. Who were haphazard about passing down ancestral traditions and "lessons" to their children. Who did pass down, however, the sense that their children were entitled to mix and match, as they saw fit, whatever aspects of whatever cultures they encountered.

I was raised, in short, to assimilate, to claim this place as mine. I don't mean that my parents told me to act like an American. That's partly the point: they didn't tell me to do anything except to be a good boy. They trusted I would find my way, and I did, following their example and navigating by the lights of the culture that encircled me like a dome. As a function of my parents' own half-conscious, half-finished acculturation, I grew up feeling that my life was Book II of an ongoing saga. Or that I was running the second leg of a relay race. *Slap!* I was out of the womb and sprinting, baton in hand. Gradually more sure of my stride, my breathing, the feel of the track beneath me. Eyes forward, never backward.

Today, nearly seven years after my father's death and two years after my marriage into a large white family, it is as if I have come round a bend and realized that I am no longer sure where I am running or why. My sprint slows to a trot. I scan the unfamiliar vista that is opening up. I am somewhere else now, somewhere far from the China that yielded my mother and father; far, as well, from the modest horizons I knew as a boy. I look at my limbs and realize I am no longer that boy; my gait and grasp exceed his by an order of magnitude. Now I want desperately to see my face, to see what time has marked and what it has erased. But I can find no mirror except the people who surround me. And they are mainly pale, powerful.

How did I end up here, standing in what seems the very seat of whiteness, gazing from the promontory of social privilege? How did I cover so much ground so quickly? What was it, in my blind journey, that I felt I should leave behind? And what *did* I leave behind? This, the jettisoning of one mode of life to send another aloft, is not only the immigrant's tale; it is the son's tale, too. By coming to America, my parents made themselves into citizens of a new country. By traveling the trajectory of an assimilist, so did I.

2

As a child, I lived in a state of "amoebic bliss," to borrow the felicitous   10 phrase of the author of *Nisei Daughter*, Monica Sone. The world was a gossamer web of wonder that began with life at home, extended to my friendships, and made the imaginary realm of daydream seem as immediate as the real. If something or someone was in my personal web of meaning, then color or station was irrelevant. I made no distinctions in fourth grade between my best friend, a black boy named Kimathi, and my next-best friend, a white boy named Charlie—other than the fact that one was number one, the other number two. I did not feel, or feel for, a seam that separated the textures of my Chinese life from those of my American life. I was not "bicultural" but omnicultural, and omnivorous, too. To my mind, I differed from others in only two ways that counted: I was a faster runner than most, and a better student. Thus did work blend happily with play, school with home, Western culture with Eastern: it was all the same to a self-confident boy who believed he'd always be at the center of his own universe.

As I approached adolescence, though, things shifted. Suddenly, I could no longer subsume the public world under my private concept of self. Suddenly, the public world was more complicated than just a parade of smiling teachers and a few affirming friends. Now I had to contend with the unstated, inchoate, but inescapable standards of *cool*. The essence of cool was the ability to conform. The essence of conformity was the ability to anticipate what was cool. And I wasn't so good at that. For the first time, I had found something that did not come effortlessly to me. No one had warned me about this transition from happy amoeboid to social animal; no one had prepared me for the great labors of fitting in.

And so in three adjoining arenas — my looks, my loves, my manners — I suffered a bruising adolescent education. I don't mean to overdramatize: there was, in these teenage banalities, usually something humorous and nothing particularly tragic. But in each of these realms, I came to feel I was not normal. And obtusely, I ascribed the difficulties of that age not to my age but to my color. I came to suspect that there was an order to things, an order that I, as someone Chinese, could perceive but not quite crack. I responded not by exploding in rebellion but by dedicating myself, quietly and sometimes angrily, to learning the order as best I could. I was never ashamed of being Chinese; I was, in fact, rather proud to be linked to a great civilization. But I was mad that my difference should matter now. And if it had to matter, I did not want it to defeat me.

Consider, if you will, my hair. For the first eleven years of my life, I sported what was essentially the same hairstyle: a tapered bowl cut, the handiwork of my mother. For those eleven joyful years, this low-maintenance do was entirely satisfactory. But in my twelfth year, as sixth grade got under way, I became aware — gradually at first, then urgently — that bangs were no longer the look for boys. This was the year when certain early bloomers first made the height-weight-physique distribution in our class seem startlingly wide — and when I first realized that I was lingering near the bottom. It was essential that I compensate for my childlike mien by cultivating at least a patina of teenage style.

This is where my hair betrayed me. For some readers the words "Chinese hair" should suffice as explanation. For the rest, particularly those who have spent all your lives with the ability to comb back, style, and part your hair *at will*, what follows should make you count your blessings. As you may recall, 1980 was a vintage year for hair that was parted straight down the middle, then feathered on each side, feathered so immaculately that the ends would meet in the back like the closed wings of angels. I dreamed of such hair. I imagined tossing my head back casually, to ease into place the one or two strands that had drifted from their positions. I dreamed of wearing the fluffy, tailored locks of the blessed.

Instead, I was cursed. My hair was straight, rigid, and wiry. Not only did it fail to feather back; it would not even bend. Worse still, it grew the wrong way. That is, it all emanated from a single swirl near the rear edge of my scalp. Parting my hair in any direction except back to front, the way certain balding men stage their final retreat, was a physical impossibility. It should go without saying that this was a disaster. For the next three years, I experimented with a variety of hairstyles that ranged from the ridiculous to the sublimely bad. There was the stringy pothead look. The mushroom do. Helmet head. Bangs folded back like curtains. I enlisted a blow-dryer, a Conair set on high heat, to force my hair into stiff postures of submission. The results, though sometimes innovative, fell always far short of cool.

I feigned nonchalance, and no one ever said anything about it. But make no mistake: this was one of the most consuming crises of my inner life as a young teen. Though neither of my parents had ever had such troubles, I blamed this predicament squarely on my Chinese genes. And I could not abide my fate. At a time when homogeneity was the highest virtue, I felt I stood out like a pigtailed Manchu.

My salvation didn't come until the end of junior high, when one of my buddies, in an epiphany as we walked past the Palace of Hair Design, dared me to get my head shaved. Without hesitation, I did it — to the tearful laughter of my friends and, soon afterward, the tearful horror of my mother. Of course, I had moments of doubt the next few days as I rubbed my peach-fuzzed skull. But what I liked was this: I had managed, without losing face, to rid myself of my greatest social burden. What's more, in the eyes of some classmates, I was now a bold (if bald) iconoclast. I've worn a crew cut ever since.

Well-styled hair was only one part of a much larger preoccupation during the ensuing years: wooing girls. In this realm I experienced a most frustrating kind of success. I was the boy that girls always found "sweet" and "funny" and "smart" and "nice." Which, to my highly sensitive ear, sounded like "leprous." Time and again, I would charm a girl into deep friendship. Time and again, as the possibility of romance came within reach, I would smash into what I took to be a glass ceiling.

The girls were white, you see; such were the demographics of my school. I was Chinese. And I was convinced that this was the sole obstacle to my advancement. It made sense, did it not? I was, after all, sweet and funny and smart and nice. Hair notwithstanding, I was not unattractive, at least compared with some of the beasts who had started "going out" with girls. There was simply no other explanation. Yet I could never say this out loud: it would have been the whining of a loser. My response, then, was to secretly scorn the girls I coveted. It was *they* who were subpar, whose small-mindedness and veiled prejudice made them unworthy.

My response, too, was to take refuge in my talents. I made myself into a   20
Renaissance boy, playing in the orchestra but also joining the wrestling
team, winning science prizes but also editing the school paper. I thought I
was defying the stereotype of the Asian American male as a one-
dimensional nerd. But in the eyes of some, I suppose, I was simply another
"Asian overachiever."

In hindsight, it's hard to know exactly how great a romantic penalty I
paid for being Chinese. There may have been girls who would have had
nothing to do with me on account of my race, but I never knew them. There
were probably girls who, race aside, simply didn't like me. And then there
were girls who liked me well enough but who also shied from the prospect
of being part of an interracial couple. With so many boys out there, they
probably reasoned, why take the path of greater resistance? Why risk so
many status points? Why not be "just friends" with this Chinese boy?

Maybe this stigma was more imagined than real. But being an ABC
("American-born Chinese," as our parents called us) certainly affected me
another way. It made me feel like something of a greenhorn, a social immigrant. I wanted so greatly to be liked. And my earnestness, though endear-
ing, was not the sort of demeanor that won girls' hearts. Though I was observant enough to notice how people talked when flirting, astute enough to
mimic the forms, I was oblivious to the subterranean levels of courtship,
blind to the more subtle rituals of "getting chicks" by spurning them. I held
the view that if you were manifestly a good person, eventually someone of
the opposite sex would do the rational thing and be smitten with you. I was
clueless. Many years would pass before I'd wise up.

It wasn't just dating rituals that befuddled me as a youth. It was ritual of
all kinds. Ceremony, protocol, etiquette—all these made me feel like an
awkward stranger. Things that came as second nature to many white kids
were utterly exotic to me. American-style manners, for instance. Chinese
families often have their own elaborate etiquette, but "please" and "may I"
weren't the sort of words ever heard around my house. That kind of formality seemed so beside the point. I was never taught by my parents to write
thank-you notes. I didn't even have the breeding to *say* "Thank you" after
sleeping over at a friend's house. I can recall the awful, sour feeling in my
stomach when this friend told me his mother had been offended by my im-
politeness. (At that point, I expressed my thanks.)

Eating dinner at the home of a *yangren* could be especially trying. The
oaken furniture seemed scaled-up, chairs like thrones. The meal would
begin with someone, usually the father, mumbling grace. Furtively, I'd steal
a glance at the heads bowed in prayer. What if they asked me to say something? I looked back down and kept my mouth shut. Next was the question
of silverware: which pieces to use, in which order, and so forth. I'd realize
then that at home I ate by using chopsticks to shove rice and meat straight
from bowl to slurping mouth. Then the whole thing about passing platters

of food around the table, instead of just reaching over and getting what you wanted. I would hear myself ask, in too-high tones, "Would you please pass the carrots, please?" It was usually at that point that I would notice that my napkin was the only one still folded neatly on the table.

All this, of course, was in the context of being with my friends and hav-   25 ing a nice time. But something made me feel vaguely sad while I sat there, swallowing huge servings of gravy-drenched food with this other family. These were the moments when I realized I was becoming something other than my parents. I wanted so badly then just to be home, in my own kitchen, taking in the aroma of stir-fry on the wok and the chattery sounds of Chinglish. And yet, like an amphibian that has just breached the shore, I could not stop inhaling this wondrous new atmosphere. My moist, blinking eyes opened wide, observing and recording the customs and predilections of these "regular" Americans. The more time I spent in their midst, the more I learned to be like them. To make their everyday idioms and idiosyncrasies familiar. To possess them.

This, the mundane, would be the locus of my conversion. It was through the small things that I made myself over. I wish, if only for storytelling purposes, that I could offer a more dramatic tale, a searing incident of racism that sent me into deep, self-abnegating alienation. The truth is, I can't. I was sometimes uncomfortable, but never really alienated. There were one or two occasions in seventh grade when the toughs in the back of the bus taunted me, called me *chink,* shot spitballs at me. I didn't like it. But each time, one of my friends—one of my white friends, in whose house I'd later eat dinner—would stand with me and fire back both spitballs and insults. Our insults were mean, too: scornful references to the trailer parks where these kids lived or the grubby clothes they wore or the crummy jobs their parents had. These skirmishes weren't just about race; they were also about mobility.

The same could be said, ultimately, about my own assimilation. To say simply that I became a banana, that I became white-identified, is somewhat simplistic. As an impressionable teen, I came to identify not with white people in general but with that subset of people, most of them white, who were educated, affluent: *going places.* It was their cues that I picked up, their judgments that I cared about. It was in their presence that old patterns of thought began to fall away like so much scaffolding around my psyche. It was in their presence that I began to imagine myself beyond race.

3

I recently dug up a photograph of myself from freshman year of college that made me smile. I have on the wrong shoes, the wrong socks, the wrong checkered shirt tucked the wrong way into the wrong slacks. I look like what I was: a boy sprung from a middlebrow burg who affected a secondhand preppiness. I look nervous. Compare that image to one from my senior-class dinner: now I am attired in a gray tweed jacket with a green plaid bow tie and a sensible button-down shirt, all purchased at the Yale Co-op. I look confident, and more than a bit contrived.

What happened in between those two photographs is that I experienced, then overcame, what the poet Meena Alexander has called "the shock of arrival." When I was deposited at the wrought-iron gates of my residential college as a freshman, I felt more like an outsider than I'd thought possible. It wasn't just that I was a small Chinese boy standing at a grand WASP temple; nor simply that I was a hayseed neophyte puzzled by the refinements of college style. It was *both:* color and class were all twisted together in a double helix of felt inadequacy.

For a while I coped with the shock by retreating to a group of my own   30
kind—not fellow Asians, but fellow marginal public-school grads who resented the rah-rah Yalies to whom everything came so effortlessly. Aligning myself this way was bearable—I was hiding, but at least I could place myself in a long tradition of underdog exiles at Yale. Aligning myself by race, on the other hand, would have seemed too inhibiting.

I know this doesn't make much sense. I know also that college, in the multicultural era, is supposed to be where the deracinated minority youth discovers the "person of color" inside. To a point, I did. I studied Chinese, took an Asian American history course, a seminar on race politics. But ultimately, college was where the unconscious habits of my adolescent assimilation hardened into self-conscious strategy.

I still remember the moment, in the first week of school, when I came upon a table in Yale Station set up by the Asian American Student Association. The upperclassman staffing the table was pleasant enough. He certainly did not strike me as a fanatic. Yet, for some reason, I flashed immediately to a scene I'd witnessed days earlier, on the corner outside. Several Lubavitcher Jews, dressed in black, their faces bracketed by dangling side curls, were looking for fellow travelers at this busy crossroads. Their method was crude but memorable. As any vaguely Jewish-looking male walked past, the zealots would quickly approach, extend a pamphlet, and ask, "Excuse me, sir, are you Jewish?" Since most were not, and since those who weren't about to stop, the result was a frantic, nervous, almost comical buzz all about the corner: Excuse me, are you Jewish? Are you Jewish? Excuse me. Are you Jewish?

I looked now at the clean-cut Korean boy at the AASA table (I think I can distinguish among Asian ethnicities as readily as those Hasidim thought they could tell Gentile from Jew), and though he had merely offered an introductory hello and was now smiling mutely at me, in the back of my mind I heard only this: *Excuse me, are you Asian? Are you Asian? Excuse me. Are you Asian?* I took one of the flyers on the table, even put my name on a mailing list, so as not to appear impolite. But I had already resolved not to be active in any Asians-only group. I thought then: I would never *choose* to be so pigeonholed.

This allergic sensitivity to "pigeonholing" is one of the unhappy hall-marks of the banana mentality. What does the banana fear? That is, what did *I* fear? The possibility of being mistaken for someone more Chinese. The possibility of being known only, or even primarily, for being Asian. The possibility of being written off by whites as a self-segregating ethnic clumper. These were the threats—unseen and, frankly, unsubstantiated—that I felt I should keep at bay.

I didn't avoid making Asian friends in college or working with Asian classmates; I simply never went out of my way to do so. This distinction seemed important—it marked, to my mind, the difference between self-hate and self-respect. That the two should have been so proximate in the first place never struck me as odd, or telling. Nor did it ever occur to me that the reasons I gave myself for dissociating from Asians as a group—that I didn't want to be part of a clique, that I didn't want to get absorbed and lose my individuality—were the very developments that marked my own assimilation. I simply hewed to my ideology of race neutrality and self-reliance. I didn't need that crutch, I told myself nervously, that crutch of racial affinity. What's more, I was vaguely insulted by the presumption that I might.

But again: Who was making the presumption? Who more than I was taking the mere existence of Korean volleyball leagues or Taiwanese social sets or pan-Asian student clubs to mean that *all* people of Asian descent, myself, included, needed such quasi-kinship groups? And who more than I interpreted this need as infirmity, as a failure to fit in? I resented the faintly sneering way that some whites regarded Asians as an undifferentiated mass. But whose sneer, really, did I resent more than my own?

I was keenly aware of the unflattering mythologies that attach to Asian Americans: that we are indelibly foreign, exotic, math and science geeks, numbers people rather than people people, followers and not leaders, phys-ically frail but devious and sneaky, unknowable and potentially treacherous. These stereotypes of Asian otherness and inferiority were like immense blocks of ice sitting before me, challenging me to chip away at them. And I did, tirelessly. All the while, though, I was oblivious to rumors of my *own* otherness and inferiority, rumors that rose off those blocks like a fog, waft-ing into my consciousness and chilling my sense of self.

As I had done in high school, I combated the stereotypes in part by try-ing to disprove them. If Asians were reputed to be math and science geeks, I would be a student of history and politics. If Asians were supposed to be feeble subalterns, I'd lift weights and go to Marine officer candidate school. If Asians were alien, I'd be ardently patriotic. If Asians were shy and retir-ing, I'd try to be exuberant and jocular. If they were narrow-minded special-ists, I'd be a well-rounded generalist. If they were perpetual outsiders, I'd join every establishment outfit I could and show that I, too, could run with the swift.

35

I overstate, of course. It wasn't that I chose to do all these things with no other purpose than to cut against a supposed convention. I was neither so Pavlovian nor so calculating that I would simply remake myself into the opposite of what people expected. I actually *liked* history, and wasn't especially good at math. As the grandson of a military officer, I *wanted* to see what officer candidates school would be like, and I enjoyed it, at least once I'd finished. I am *by nature* enthusiastic and allegiant, a joiner, and a bit of a jingo.

At the same time, I was often aware, sometimes even hopeful, that oth-   40
ers might think me "exceptional" for my race. I derived satisfaction from being the "atypical" Asian, the only Chinese face at OCS or in this club or that.

The irony is that in working so duteously to defy stereotype, I became a slave to it. For to act self-consciously against Asian "tendencies" is not to break loose from the cage of myth and legend; it is to turn the very key that locks you inside. What spontaneity is there when the value of every act is measured, at least in part, by its power to refute a presumption about why you act? The *typical Asian* I imagined, and the *atypical Asian* I imagined myself to be, were identical in this sense: neither was as much a creature of free will as a human being ought to be.

Let me say it plainly, then: I am not proud to have had this mentality. I believe I have outgrown it. And I expose it now not to justify it but to detoxify it, to prevent its further spread.

Yet it would be misleading, I think, to suggest that my education centered solely on the discomfort caused by race. The fact is, when I first got to college I felt deficient compared with people of *every* color. Part of why I believed it so necessary to achieve was that I lacked the connections, the wealth, the experience, the sophistication that so many of my classmates seemed to have. I didn't get the jokes or the intellectual references. I didn't have the canny attitude. So in addition to all my coursework, I began to puzzle over this, the culture of the influential class.

Over time, I suppose, I learned the culture. My interests and vocabulary became ever more worldly. I made my way onto what Calvin Trillin once described as the "magic escalator" of a Yale education. Extracurriculars opened the door to an alumni internship, which brought me to Capitol Hill, which led to a job and a life in Washington after commencement. Gradually, very gradually, I found that I was not so much of an outsider anymore. I found that by almost any standard, but particularly by the standards of my younger self, I was actually beginning to "make it."

It has taken me until now, however, to appraise the thoughts and acts   45
of that younger self. I can see now that the straitening path I took was not the only or even the best path. For while it may be possible to transcend race, *it is not always necessary to try.* And while racial identity is sometimes a shackle, it is not *only* a shackle. I could have spared myself a great deal of

heartache had I understood this earlier, that the choice of race is not simply "embrace or efface."

I wonder sometimes how I would have turned out had I been, from the start, more comfortable in my own skin. What did I miss by distancing myself from race? What friendships did I forgo, what self-knowledge did I defer? Had certain accidents of privilege been accidents of privation or exclusion, I might well have developed a different view of the world. But I do not know just how my view would have differed.

What I know is that through all those years of shadow-dancing with my identity, something happened, something that had only partially to do with color. By the time I left Yale I was no longer the scared boy of that freshman photo. I had become more sure of myself and of my place—sure enough, indeed, to perceive the folly of my fears. And in the years since, I have assumed a sense of expectation, of access and *belonging*, that my younger self could scarcely have imagined. All this happened incrementally. There was no clear tipping point, no obvious moment of mutation. The shock of arrival, it would seem, is simply that I arrived.

4

"The world is white no longer, and it will never be white again." So wrote James Baldwin after having lived in a tiny Swiss village where, to his knowledge, no black man had ever set foot. It was there, in the icy heart of whiteness, that the young expatriate began to comprehend the desire of so many of his countrymen to return to some state of nature where only white people existed. It was there too that he recognized just how impossible that was, just how intertwined were the fates and identities of the races in America. "No road whatever will lead Americans back to the simplicity of this European village where white men still have the luxury of looking on me as a stranger," he wrote. "I am not, really, a stranger any longer for any American alive."

That is precisely how I feel when I consider my own journey, my own family's travels. For here I am now, standing in a new country. Not as an expatriate or a resident alien, but as a citizen. And as I survey this realm—this Republic of Privilege—I realize certain things, things that my mother and father might also have realized about *their* new country a generation ago. I realize that my entry has yielded me great opportunities. I realize, as well, that my route of entry has taken a certain toll. I have neglected my ancestral heritage. I have lost something. Yes, I can speak some Mandarin and stir-fry a few easy dishes. I have been to China and know something of its history. Still, I could never claim to be Chinese at the core.

Yet neither would I claim, as if by default, to be merely "white inside." I 50 do not want to be white. I only want to be integrated. When I identify with white people who wield economic and political power, it is not for their whiteness but for their power. When I imagine myself among white people

*"Gosh, it kills me to do this to you, Worthington, but you're
not turning out to be as black as we had hoped."*

who influence the currents of our culture, it is not for their whiteness but
for their influence. When I emulate white people who are at ease with the
world, it is not for their whiteness but for their ease. I don't like it that the
people I should learn from tend so often to be white, for it says something
damning about how opportunity is still distributed. But it helps not at all to
call me white for learning from them. It is cruel enough that the least privileged Americans today have colored skin, the most privileged fair. It is cru-
eler still that by our very language we should help convert this fact into rule.
The time has come to describe assimilation as something other than the
White Way of Being.

The time has also come, I think, to conceive of assimilation as more
than a series of losses—and to recognize that what is lost is not necessarily
sacred. I have, as I say, allowed my Chinese ethnicity to become diluted.
And I often resolve to do more to preserve, to conserve, my inheritance.
But have my acts of neglect thus far, my many omissions, been inherently
wrong? G. K. Chesterton once wrote that "conservatism is based upon the
idea that if you leave things alone, you leave them as they are. But you do
not. If you leave a thing alone, you leave it to a torrent of change." I may
have been born a Chinese baby, but it would have taken unremitting

reinforcement, by my parents and by myself, for me to have remained Chinese. Instead, we left things alone. And a torrent of change washed over me.

This, we must remember, has been an act of creation as much as destruction. Something new is emerging from the torrent, in my case and the many millions like it. Something undeveloped, speaking the unformed tongue of an unformed nation. Something not white, and probably more Chinese than I know. Whatever it is that I am becoming, is it any less authentic for being an amalgam? Is it intrinsically less meaningful than what I might otherwise have been? In every assimilation, there is a mutiny against history—but there is also a destiny, which is to redefine history. What it means to be American—in spirit, in blood—is something far more borrowed and commingled than anything previous generations ever knew. Alongside the pain of migration, then, and the possibility, there is this truth: America is white no longer, and it will never be white again.

ENGAGING THE TEXT

1. Liu opens his essay with a list of the ways in which he could be seen as "white." What does each item on his list suggest about the characteristics of "whiteness"? Do you share these assumptions about what it means to be white? Why or why not?

2. What is Liu's reaction to being called a "banana"? What does he mean when he comments that the process of assimilation is "more complicated than the monochrome language of 'whiteness' and 'authenticity' would suggest" (para. 5)?

3. How do Liu's motives for conforming as a teenager differ from his motives as a college student? What efforts does he make to fit in, and to what extent does he succeed in each of these phases of his life?

4. How do you explain Liu's comment that he became a slave to stereotype even as he conscientiously worked to disprove stereotypical beliefs about Asians? What does he mean by saying that he wants to expose his former mentality in order to "detoxify it" (para. 42)?

5. What does Liu believe he has lost and gained by assimilating? How and why does he believe the idea of assimilation is changing in the United States?

6. In the final paragraph of the essay, Liu observes that a new "borrowed and commingled" American identity is emerging. What indications of this trend, if any, have you observed?

EXPLORING CONNECTIONS

7. Compare Liu's experience of assimilation to that of Richard Rodriguez (p. 194). What similarities and differences do you see in the process of change each man goes through? How does each assess his gains and losses? How do you explain the differences in their perspectives?

8. What role does education play for Liu, Rodriguez (p. 194), Malcolm X (p. 223), and Judith Ortiz Cofer (p. 423) as they struggle to define their identities within a context of racial or cultural conflict?

9. How would Liu respond to George Fredrickson's (p. 598) assertion that "when carried to its logical conclusion, the assimilationist project demands what its critics have described...as 'cultural genocide'"? Write an imaginary conversation in which these two writers discuss the meaning of assimilation.

EXTENDING THE CRITICAL CONTEXT

10. If you have ever consciously attempted to disprove a stereotype or stereotypes about a group that you're a part of, write a journal entry describing that experience. Why did you feel the need to refute the stereotype, how did you go about combatting it, and what was the result of your efforts, if any?

11. Liu writes that in college he deliberately avoided joining any groups associated with Asian identity but that he now sees this behavior as foolish and immature. As a group or class project, interview students of various ethnic backgrounds about why they have chosen to join or not to join campus organizations based on ethnicity. What are the benefits and drawbacks of such groups, according to your survey?

Assimilation

SHERMAN ALEXIE

Sherman Alexie won the 1999 World Heavyweight Championship Poetry Bout by improvising, in thirty seconds, a poetic riff on the word "dumbass." The poem, according to one reporter, was both humorous and poignant. Alexie's performance captures his sense of humor, his inventiveness, and his ability to wring insight from unlikely material. True to form, this story—about a Coeur d'Alene Indian woman who decides to cheat on her white husband—is a comedy that poses serious questions about race, class, culture, deception, and love. Alexie (b. 1966) grew up on the Spokane Indian Reservation in Washington State, but attended a high school where, in his words, he was "the only Indian ... except the school mascot." He claims not to believe in writer's block, and has the publications to prove it: two novels, Reservation Blues *(1995) and* Indian Killer *(1996); eleven volumes of poems and short stories; many essays and reviews. He also coauthored the script for the award-winning film* Smoke Signals *(1998), which was based on one of his short stories, and is working on a movie adaptation of* Reservation Blues. *"Assimilation" comes from Alexie's most recent short story collection,* The Toughest Indian in the World *(2000).*

Regarding love, marriage, and sex, both Shakespeare and Sitting Bull knew the only truth: treaties get broken. Therefore, Mary Lynn wanted to have sex with any man other than her husband. For the first time in her life, she wanted to go to bed with an Indian man only because he was Indian. She was a Coeur d'Alene Indian married to a white man; she was a wife who wanted to have sex with an indigenous stranger. She didn't care about the stranger's job or his hobbies, or whether he was due for a Cost of Living raise, or owned ten thousand miles of model railroad track. She didn't care if he was handsome or ugly, mostly because she wasn't sure exactly what those terms meant anymore and how much relevance they truly had when it came to choosing sexual partners. Oh, she'd married a very handsome man, there was no doubt about that, and she was still attracted to her husband, to his long, graceful fingers, to his arrogance and utter lack of fear in social situations — he'd say anything to anybody — but lately, she'd been forced to concentrate too hard when making love to him. If she didn't focus completely on him, on the smallest details of his body, then she would drift away from the bed and float around the room like a bored angel. Of course, all this made her feel like a failure, especially since it seemed that her husband had yet to notice her growing disinterest. She wanted to be a good lover, wife, and partner, but she'd obviously developed some form of sexual dyslexia or had picked up a mutant, contagious, and erotic strain of Attention Deficit Disorder. She felt baffled by the complications of sex. She haunted the aisles of bookstores and desperately paged through every book in the self-help section and studied every diagram and chart in the human sensuality encyclopedias. She wanted answers. She wanted to feel it again, whatever *it* was.

A few summers ago, during Crow Fair, Mary Lynn had been standing in a Montana supermarket, in the produce aisle, when a homely white woman, her spiky blond hair still wet from a trailer-house shower, walked by in a white t-shirt and blue jeans, and though Mary Lynn was straight — having politely declined all three lesbian overtures thrown at her in her life — she'd felt a warm breeze pass through her DNA in that ugly woman's wake, and had briefly wanted to knock her to the linoleum and do beautiful things to her. Mary Lynn had never before felt such lust — in Montana, of all places, for a white woman who was functionally illiterate and underemployed! — and had not since felt that sensually about any other woman or man.

Who could explain such things, these vagaries of love? There were many people who would blame Mary Lynn's unhappiness, her dissatisfaction, on her ethnicity. God, she thought, how simple and earnest was that particular bit of psychotherapy! Yes, she was most certainly a Coeur d'Alene—she'd grown up on the rez, had been very happy during her time there, and had left without serious regrets or full-time enemies—but that wasn't the only way to define her. She wished that she could be called Coeur d'Alene as a description, rather than as an excuse, reason, prescription, placebo, prediction, or diminutive. She only wanted to be understood as eccentric and complicated!

Her most cherished eccentricity: when she was feeling her most lonely, she'd put one of the Big Mom Singers' powwow CDs on the stereo (*I'm not afraid of death, hey, ya, hey, death is my cousin, hey, ya, ha, ha*) and read from Emily Dickinson's poetry (*Because I could not stop for Death— / He kindly stopped for me—*).

Her most important complication: she was a woman in a turbulent mar-   5
riage that was threatening to go bad, or had gone bad and might get worse.

Yes, she was a Coeur d'Alene woman, passionately and dispassionately, who wanted to cheat on her white husband because he was white. She wanted to find an anonymous lover, an Indian man who would fade away into the crowd when she was done with him, a man whose face could appear on the back of her milk carton. She didn't care if he was the kind of man who knew the punch lines to everybody's dirty jokes, or if he was the kind of man who read Zane Grey before he went to sleep, or if he was both of those men simultaneously. She simply wanted to find the darkest Indian in Seattle—the man with the greatest amount of melanin—and get naked with him in a cheap motel room. Therefore, she walked up to a flabby Lummi Indian man in a coffee shop and asked him to make love to her.

"Now," she said. "Before I change my mind."

He hesitated for a brief moment, wondering why he was the chosen one, and then took her by the hand. He decided to believe he was a handsome man.

"Don't you want to know my name?" he asked before she put her hand over his mouth.

"Don't talk to me," she said. "Don't say one word. Just take me to the   10
closest motel and fuck me."

The obscenity bothered her. It felt staged, forced, as if she were an actress in a three-in-the-morning cable-television movie. But she was acting, wasn't she? She was not an adulteress, was she?

Why exactly did she want to have sex with an Indian stranger? She told herself it was because of pessimism, existentialism, even nihilism, but those reasons—*those words*—were a function of her vocabulary and not of her motivations. If forced to admit the truth, or some version of the truth, she'd testify she was about to go to bed with an Indian stranger because she wanted to know how it would feel. After all, she'd slept with a white stranger in her life, so why not include a Native American? Why not practice a carnal form of affirmative action? By God, her infidelity was a political act! Rebellion, resistance, revolution!

In the motel room, Mary Lynn made the Indian take off his clothes first. Thirty pounds overweight, with purple scars crisscrossing his pale chest and belly, he trembled as he undressed. He wore a wedding ring on his right hand. She knew that some Europeans wore their wedding bands on the right hand—so maybe this Indian was married to a French woman—but Mary Lynn also knew that some divorced Americans wore rings on their right hands as symbols of pain, of mourning. Mary Lynn didn't care if he was married or not, or whether he shared custody of the sons and daughters, or whether he had any children at all. She was grateful that he was plain and desperate and lonely.

Mary Lynn stepped close to him, took his hand, and slid his thumb into her mouth. She sucked on it and felt ridiculous. His skin was salty and oily, the taste of a working man. She closed her eyes and thought about her husband, a professional who had his shirts laundered. In one hour, he was going to meet her at a new downtown restaurant.

She walked a slow, tight circle around the Indian. She stood behind him, reached around his thick waist, and held his erect penis. He moaned and she decided that she hated him. She decided to hate all men. Hate, hate, hate, she thought, and then let her hate go. 15

She was lovely and intelligent, and had grown up with Indian women who were more lovely and more intelligent, but who also had far less ambition and mendacity. She'd once read in a book, perhaps by Primo Levi or Elie Wiesel, that the survivors of the Nazi death camps were the Jews who lied, cheated, murdered, stole, and subverted. You must remember, said Levi or Wiesel, that the best of us did not survive the camps. Mary Lynn felt the same way about the reservation. Before she'd turned ten, she'd attended the funerals of seventeen good women—the best of the Coeur d'Alenes—and had read about the deaths of eighteen more good women since she'd left the rez. But what about the Coeur d'Alene men—those liars, cheats, and thieves—who'd survived, even thrived? Mary Lynn wanted nothing to do with them, then or now. As a teenager, she'd dated only white boys. As an adult, she'd only dated white men. God, she hated to admit it, but white men—her teachers, coaches, bosses, and lovers—had always been more dependable than the Indian men in her life. White men had rarely disappointed her, but they'd never surprised her either. White men were neutral, she thought, just like Belgium! And when has Belgium ever been sexy? When has Belgium caused a grown woman to shake with fear and guilt? She didn't want to feel Belgian; she wanted to feel dangerous.

In the cheap motel room, Mary Lynn breathed deeply. The Indian smelled of old sweat and a shirt worn twice before washing. She ran her finger along the ugly scars on his belly and chest. She wanted to know the scars' creation story—she hoped this Indian man was a warrior with a history of knife fighting—but she feared he was only carrying the transplanted heart and lungs of another man. She pushed him onto the bed, onto the scratchy comforter. She'd once read that scientists had examined a hotel-room comforter and discovered four hundred and thirty-two different samples of sperm. God, she thought, those scientists obviously had too much time on their hands and, in the end, had failed to ask the most important questions: Who left the samples? Spouses, strangers? Were these exchanges of money, tenderness, disease? Was there love?

"This has to be quick," she said to the stranger beside her.

Jeremiah, her husband, was already angry when Mary Lynn arrived thirty minutes late at the restaurant and he nearly lost all of his self-control when they were asked to wait for the next available table. He often raged at strangers, though he was incredibly patient and kind with their four children. Mary Lynn had seen that kind of rage in other white men when their wishes and desires were ignored. At ball games, in parking lots, and especially in airports, white men demanded to receive the privileges whose very existence they denied. White men could be so predictable, thought Mary Lynn. She thought: O, Jeremiah! O, season ticket holder! O, monthly parker! O, frequent flyer! She dreamed of him out there, sitting in the airplane with eighty-seven other white men wearing their second-best suits, all of them traveling toward small rooms in the Ramadas, Radissons, and sometimes the Hyatts, where they all separately watched the same pay-per-view porno that showed everything except penetration. What's the point of porno without graphic penetration? Mary Lynn knew it only made these lonely men feel all that more lonely. And didn't they deserve better, these white salesmen and middle managers, these twenty-first-century Willy Lomans,[1] who only wanted to be better men than their fathers had been? Of course, thought Mary Lynn, these sons definitely deserved better — they were smarter and more tender and generous than all previous generations of white American men — but they'd never receive their just rewards, and thus their anger was justified and banal.

"Calm down," Mary Lynn said to her husband as he continued to rage   20
at the restaurant hostess.

Mary Lynn said those two words to him more often in their marriage than any other combination of words.

"It could be twenty, thirty minutes," said the hostess. "Maybe longer."

"We'll wait outside," said Jeremiah. He breathed deeply, remembering some mantra that his therapist had taught him.

Mary Lynn's mantra: I cheated on my husband, I cheated on my husband.

"We'll call your name," said the hostess, a white woman who was tired   25
of men no matter what their color. "When."

---

[1]*Willy Lomans:* Willy Loman, the protagonist of Arthur Miller's play *Death of a Salesman,* is an ordinary but driven man struggling to find meaning in his work and family life; he becomes a symbol of the problems and despair faced by the "little guy" in an increasingly impersonal world.

Their backs pressed against the brick wall, their feet crossed on the sidewalk, on a warm Seattle evening, Mary Lynn and Jeremiah smoked faux cigarettes filled with some foul-tasting, overwhelmingly organic herb substance. For years they had smoked unfiltered Camels, but had quit after all four of their parents had simultaneously suffered through at least one form of cancer. Mary Lynn had called them the Mormon Tabernacle Goddamn Cancer Choir, though none of them was Mormon and all of them were altos. With and without grace, they had all survived the radiation, chemotherapy, and in-hospital cable-television bingo games, with their bodies reasonably intact, only to resume their previously self-destructive habits. After so many nights spent in hospital corridors, waiting rooms, and armchairs, Mary Lynn and Jeremiah hated doctors, all doctors, even the ones on television, especially the ones on television. United in their obsessive hatred, Mary Lynn and Jeremiah resorted to taking vitamins, eating free-range chicken, and smoking cigarettes rolled together and marketed by six odoriferous white liberals in Northern California.

As they waited for a table, Mary Lynn and Jeremiah watched dozens of people arrive and get seated immediately.

"I bet they don't have reservations," he said.

"I hate these cigarettes," she said.

"Why do you keep buying them?" 30

"Because the cashier at the health-food store is cute."

"You're shallow."

"Like a mud puddle."

Mary Lynn hated going out on weeknights. She hated driving into the city. She hated waiting for a table. Standing outside the downtown restaurant, desperate to hear their names, she decided to hate Jeremiah for a few seconds. Hate, hate, hate, she thought, and then she let her hate go. She wondered if she smelled like sex, like indigenous sex, and if a white man could recognize the scent of an enemy. She'd showered, but the water pressure had been weak and the soap bar too small.

"Let's go someplace else," she said. 35

"No. Five seconds after we leave, they'll call our names."

"But we won't know they called our names."

"But I'll feel it."

"It must be difficult to be psychic and insecure."

"I knew you were going to say that." 40

Clad in leather jackets and black jeans, standing inches apart but never quite touching, both handsome to the point of distraction, smoking crappy cigarettes that appeared to be real cigarettes, they could have been the subjects of a Schultz photograph or a Runnette poem.

The title of the photograph: "Infidelity."

The title of the poem: "More Infidelity."

Jeremiah's virtue was reasonably intact, though he'd recently been involved in a flirtatious near-affair with a coworker. At the crucial moment, when the last button was about to be unbuttoned, when consummation was just a fingertip away, Jeremiah had pushed his potential lover away and said I can't, I just can't, I love my marriage. He didn't admit to love for his spouse, partner, wife. No, he confessed his love for marriage, for the blessed union, for the legal document, for the shared mortgage payments, and for their four children.

Mary Lynn wondered what would happen if she grew pregnant with the Lummi's baby. Would this full-blood baby look more Indian than her half-blood sons and daughters?   45

"Don't they know who I am?" she asked her husband as they waited outside the downtown restaurant. She wasn't pregnant; there would be no paternity tests, no revealing of great secrets. His secret: he was still in love with a white woman from high school he hadn't seen in decades. What Mary Lynn knew: he was truly in love with the idea of a white woman from a mythical high school, with a prom queen named *If Only* or a homecoming princess named *My Life Could Have Been Different*.

"I'm sure they know who you are," he said. "That's why we're on the wait list. Otherwise, we'd be heading for McDonald's or Denny's."

"Your kinds of places."

"Dependable. The Big Mac you eat in Hong Kong or Des Moines tastes just like the Big Mac in Seattle."

"Sounds like colonialism to me."   50

"Colonialism ain't all bad."

"Put that on a bumper sticker."

This place was called Tan Tan, though it would soon be trendy enough to go by a nickname: Tan's. Maybe Tan's would become T's, and then T's would be identified only by a slight turn of the head or a certain widening of the eyes. After that, the downhill slide in reputation would be inevitable, whether or not the culinary content and quality of the restaurant remained exactly the same or improved. As it was, Tan Tan was a pan-Asian restaurant whose ownership and chefs—head, sauce, and line—were white, though most of the wait staff appeared to be one form of Asian or another.

"Don't you hate it?" Jeremiah asked. "When they have Chinese waiters in sushi joints? Or Korean dishwashers in a Thai noodle house?"

"I hadn't really thought about it," she said.   55

"No, think about it, these restaurants, these Asian restaurants, they hire Asians indiscriminately because they think white people won't be able to tell the difference."

"White people can't tell the difference."

"I can."

"Hey, Geronimo, you've been hanging around Indians too long to be white."

"Fucking an Indian doesn't make me Indian."   60

"So, that's what we're doing now? Fucking?"

"You have a problem with fucking?"

"No, not with the act itself, but I do have a problem with your sexual thesaurus."

Mary Lynn and Jeremiah had met in college, when they were still called Mary and Jerry. After sleeping together for the first time, after her first orgasm and his third, Mary had turned to Jerry and said, with absolute seriousness: If this thing is going to last, we have to stop the end rhyme. She had majored in Milton and Blake. He'd been a chemical engineer since the age of seven, with the degree being only a matter of formality, so he'd had plenty of time to wonder how an Indian from the reservation could be so smart. He still wondered how it had happened, though he'd never had the courage to ask her.

Now, a little more than two decades after graduating with a useless de- 65
gree, Mary Lynn worked at Microsoft for a man named Dickinson. Jeremiah didn't know his first name, though he hoped it wasn't Emery, and had never met the guy, and didn't care if he ever did. Mary Lynn's job title and responsibilities were vague, so vague that Jeremiah had never asked her to elaborate. She often worked sixty-hour weeks and he didn't want to reward that behavior by expressing an interest in what specific tasks she performed for Bill Gates.

Waiting outside Tan Tan, he and she could smell ginger, burned rice, beer.

"Are they ever going to seat us?" she asked.

"Yeah, don't they know who you are?"

"I hear this place discriminates against white people."

"Really?" 70

"Yeah, I heard once, these lawyers, bunch of white guys in Nordstrom's suits, had to wait, like, two hours for a table."

"Were those billable hours?"

"It's getting hard for a white guy to find a place to eat."

"Damn affirmative action is what it is."

Their first child had been an accident, the result of a broken condom 75
and a missed birth control pill. They named her Antonya, Toni for short. The second and third children, Robert and Michael, had been on purpose, and the fourth, Ariel, came after Mary Lynn thought she could no longer get pregnant.

Toni was fourteen, immature for her age, quite beautiful and narcissistic, with her translucent skin, her long blond hair, and eight-ball eyes. Botticelli eyes, she bragged after taking an Introduction to Art class. She never bothered to tell anybody she was Indian, mostly because nobody asked.

Jeremiah was quite sure that his daughter, his Antonya, had lost her virginity to the pimply quarterback of the junior varsity football team. He found the thought of his daughter's adolescent sexuality both curious and disturbing. Above all else, he believed that she was far too special to sleep with a cliché, let alone a junior varsity cliché.

Three months out of every year, Robert and Michael were the same age. Currently, they were both eleven. Dark-skinned, with their mother's black hair, strong jawline, and endless nose, they looked Indian, very Indian. Robert, who had refused to be called anything other than Robert, was the smart boy, a math prodigy, while Mikey was the basketball player.

When Mary Lynn's parents called from the reservation, they always asked after the boys, always invited the boys out for the weekend, the holidays, and the summer, and always sent the boys more elaborate gifts than they sent the two girls.

When Jeremiah had pointed out this discrepancy to Mary Lynn, she   80
had readily agreed, but had made it clear that his parents also paid more attention to the boys. Jeremiah never mentioned it again, but had silently vowed to love the girls a little more than he loved the boys.

As if love were a thing that could be quantified, he thought.

He asked himself: What if I love the girls more because they look more like me, because they look more white than the boys?

Towheaded Ariel was two, and the clay of her personality was just beginning to harden, but she was certainly petulant and funny as hell, with the ability to sleep in sixteen-hour marathons that made her parents very nervous. She seemed to exist in her own world, enough so that she was periodically monitored for incipient autism. She treated her siblings as if they somehow bored her, and was the kind of kid who could stay alone in her crib for hours, amusing herself with all sorts of personal games and imaginary friends.

Mary Lynn insisted that her youngest daughter was going to be an artist, but Jeremiah didn't understand the child, and despite the fact that he was her father and forty-three years older, he felt inferior to Ariel.

He wondered if his wife was ever going to leave him because he was   85
white.

When Tan Tan's doors swung open, laughter and smoke rolled out together.

"You got another cigarette?" he asked.

"Quit calling them cigarettes. They're not cigarettes. They're more like rose bushes. Hell, they're more like the shit that rose bushes grow in."

"You think we're going to get a table?"

"By the time we get a table, this place is going to be very unpopular."   90

"Do you want to leave?"

"Do you?"

"If you do."

"We told the baby-sitter we'd be home by ten."

They both wished that Toni were responsible enough to baby-sit her   95
siblings, rather than needing to be sat along with them.

"What time is it?" she asked.

"Nine."

"Let's go home."

Last Christmas, when the kids had been splayed out all over the living room, buried to their shoulders in wrapping paper and expensive toys, Mary Lynn had studied her children's features, had recognized most of her face in her sons' faces and very little of it in her daughters', and had decided, quite facetiously, that the genetic score was tied.

We should have another kid, she'd said to Jeremiah, so we'll know if   100 this is a white family or an Indian family.

It's a family family, he'd said, without a trace of humor.

Only a white guy would say that, she'd said.

Well, he'd said, you married a white guy.

The space between them had grown very cold at that moment, in that silence, and perhaps one or both of them might have said something truly destructive, but Ariel had started crying then, for no obvious reason, relieving both parents of the responsibility of finishing that particular conversation. During the course of their relationship, Mary Lynn and Jeremiah had often discussed race as a concept, as a foreign country they occasionally visited, or as an enemy that existed outside their house, as a destructive force they could fight against as a couple, as a family. But race was also a constant presence, a houseguest and permanent tenant who crept around all the rooms in their shared lives, opening drawers, stealing utensils and small articles of clothing, changing the temperature.

Before he'd married Mary Lynn, Jeremiah had always believed there   105 was too much talk of race, that white people were all too willing to be racist and that brown people were just as willing and just as racist. As a rational scientist, he'd known that race was primarily a social construct, illusionary, but as the husband of an Indian woman and the father of Indian children, he'd since learned that race, whatever its construction, was real. Now, there were plenty of white people who wanted to eliminate the idea of race, to cast it aside as an unwanted invention, but it was far too late for that. If white people are the mad scientists who created race, thought Jeremiah, then we created race so we could enslave black people and kill Indians, and now race has become the Frankenstein monster that has grown beyond our control. Though he'd once been willfully blind, Jeremiah had learned how to recognize that monster in the faces of whites and Indians and in their eyes.

Long ago, Jeremiah and Mary Lynn had both decided to challenge those who stared by staring back, by flinging each other against walls and tongue-kissing with pornographic élan.

Long ago, they'd both decided to respond to any questions of why, how, what, who, or when by simply stating: Love is Love. They knew it was romantic bullshit, a simpleminded answer only satisfying for simpleminded people, but it was the best available defense.

Listen, Mary Lynn had once said to Jeremiah, asking somebody why they fall in love is like asking somebody why they believe in God.

You start asking questions like that, she had added, and you're either going to start a war or you're going to hear folk music.

You think too much, Jeremiah had said, rolling over and falling asleep.   110

Then, in the dark, as Jeremiah slept, Mary Lynn had masturbated while fantasizing about an Indian man with sundance scars on his chest.

After they left Tan Tan, they drove a sensible and indigenous Ford Taurus over the 520 bridge, back toward their house in Kirkland, a five-bedroom rancher only ten blocks away from the Microsoft campus. Mary Lynn walked to work. That made her feel privileged. She estimated there were twenty-two American Indians who had ever felt even a moment of privilege.

"We still have to eat," she said as she drove across the bridge. She felt strange. She wondered if she was ever going to feel normal again.

"How about Taco Bell drive-thru?" he asked.

"You devil, you're trying to get into my pants, aren't you?"   115

Impulsively, he dropped his head into her lap and pressed his lips against her black-jeaned crotch. She yelped and pushed him away. She wondered if he could smell her, if he could smell the Lummi Indian. Maybe he could, but he seemed to interpret it as something different, as something meant for him, as he pushed his head into her lap again. What was she supposed to do? She decided to laugh, so she did laugh as she pushed his face against her pubic bone. She loved the man for reasons she could not always explain. She closed her eyes, drove in that darkness, and felt dangerous.

Halfway across the bridge, Mary Lynn slammed on the brakes, not because she'd seen anything—her eyes were still closed—but because she'd felt something. The car skidded to a stop just inches from the bumper of a truck that had just missed sliding into the row of cars stopped ahead of it.

"What the hell is going on?" Jeremiah asked as he lifted his head from her lap.

"Traffic jam."

"Jesus, we'll never make it home by ten. We better call."   120

"The cell phone is in the glove."

Jeremiah dialed the home number but received only a busy signal.

"Toni must be talking to her boyfriend," she said.

"I don't like him."

"He doesn't like you."   125

"What the hell is going on? Why aren't we moving?"

"I don't know. Why don't you go check?"

Jeremiah climbed out of the car.

"I was kidding," she said as he closed the door behind him.

He walked up to the window of the truck ahead of him.   130

"You know what's going on?" Jeremiah asked the truck driver.

"Nope."

Jeremiah walked farther down the bridge. He wondered if there was a disabled car ahead, what the radio liked to call a "blocking accident." There was also the more serious "injury accident" and the deadly "accident with fatality involved." He had to drive this bridge ten times a week. The commute. White men had invented the commute, had deepened its meaning, had diversified its complications, and now spent most of the time trying to shorten it, reduce it, lessen it.

In the car, Mary Lynn wondered why Jeremiah always found it necessary to insert himself into every situation. He continually moved from the passive to the active. The man was kinetic. She wondered if it was a white thing. Possibly. But more likely, it was a Jeremiah thing. She remembered Mikey's third-grade-class's school play, an edited version of *Hamlet*. Jeremiah had walked onto the stage to help his son drag the unconscious Polonius, who had merely been clubbed over the head rather than stabbed to death, from the stage. Mortally embarrassed, Mikey had cried himself to sleep that night, positive that he was going to be an elementary-school pariah, while Jeremiah vainly tried to explain to the rest of the family why he had acted so impulsively.

I was just trying to be a good father, he had said.   135

Mary Lynn watched Jeremiah walk farther down the bridge. He was just a shadow, a silhouette. She was slapped by the brief, irrational fear that he would never return.

Husband, come back to me, she thought, and I will confess.

Impatient drivers honked their horns. Mary Lynn joined them. She hoped Jeremiah would recognize the specific sound of their horn and return to the car.

Listen to me, listen to me, listen to me, she thought as she pounded the steering wheel.

Jeremiah heard their car horn, but only as one note in the symphony of   140
noise playing on the bridge. He walked through that noise, through an ever-increasing amount of noise, until he pushed through a sudden crowd of people and found himself witnessing a suicide.

Illuminated by headlights, the jumper was a white woman, pretty, wearing a sundress and good shoes. Jeremiah could see that much as she stood on the bridge railing, forty feet above the cold water.

He could hear sirens approaching from both sides of the bridge, but they would never make it through the traffic in time to save this woman.

The jumper was screaming somebody's name.

Jeremiah stepped closer, wanting to hear the name, wanting to have that information so that he could use it later. To what use, he didn't know, but he knew that name had value, importance. That name, the owner of that name, was the reason why the jumper stood on the bridge.

"Aaron," she said. The jumper screamed, "Aaron."   145

In the car, Mary Lynn could not see either Jeremiah or the jumper, but she could see dozens of drivers leaving their cars and running ahead.

She was suddenly and impossibly sure that her husband was the reason for this commotion, this emergency. He's dying, thought Mary Lynn, he's dead. This is not what I wanted, she thought, this is not why I cheated on him, this is not what was supposed to happen.

As more drivers left their cars and ran ahead, Mary Lynn dialed 911 on the cell phone and received only a busy signal.

She opened her door and stepped out, placed one foot on the pavement, and stopped.

The jumper did not stop. She turned to look at the crowd watching her. 150 She looked into the anonymous faces, into the maw, and then looked back down at the black water.

Then she jumped.

Jeremiah rushed forward, along with a few others, and peered over the edge of the bridge. One brave man leapt off the bridge in a vain rescue attempt. Jeremiah stopped a redheaded young man from jumping.

"No," said Jeremiah. "It's too cold. You'll die too."

Jeremiah stared down into the black water, looking for the woman who'd jumped and the man who'd jumped after her.

In the car, or rather with one foot still in the car and one foot placed on 155 the pavement outside of the car, Mary Lynn wept. Oh, God, she loved him, sometimes because he was white and often despite his whiteness. In her fear, she found the one truth Sitting Bull never knew: there was at least one white man who could be trusted.

The black water was silent.

Jeremiah stared down into that silence.

"Jesus, Jesus," said a lovely woman next to him. "Who was she? Who was she?"

"I'm never leaving," Jeremiah said.

"What?" asked the lovely woman, quite confused. 160

"My wife," said Jeremiah, strangely joyous. "I'm never leaving her." Ever the scientist and mathematician, Jeremiah knew that his wife was a constant. In his relief, he found the one truth Shakespeare never knew: gravity is overrated.

Jeremiah looked up through the crossbeams above him, as he stared at the black sky, at the clouds that he could not see but knew were there, the invisible clouds that covered the stars. He shouted out his wife's name, shouted it so loud that he could not speak in the morning.

In the car, Mary Lynn pounded the steering wheel. With one foot in the car and one foot out, she honked and honked the horn. She wondered if this was how the world was supposed to end, with everybody trapped on a bridge, with the black water pushing against their foundations.

Out on the bridge, four paramedics arrived far too late. Out of breath, exhausted from running across the bridge with medical gear and stretchers, the paramedics could only join the onlookers at the railing.

A boat, a small boat, a miracle, floated through the black water. They 165 found the man, the would-be rescuer, who had jumped into the water after the young woman, but they could not find her.

Jeremiah pushed through the crowd, as he ran away from the place where the woman had jumped. Jeremiah ran across the bridge until he could see Mary Lynn. She and he loved each other across the distance.

ENGAGING THE TEXT

1. What is the significance of the title "Assimilation" in the context of this story? How do you interpret the "truths" that Mary Lynn and Jeremiah discover at the end of the story? Do you think that Alexie is endorsing assimilation in this story? Why or why not?

2. What is the purpose and effect of the paired cultural references—to Shakespeare and Sitting Bull, the Big Mom Singers and Emily Dickinson—that Alexie includes in the story?

3. What glimpses does Alexie give us of reservation life and of Indians less privileged than Mary Lynn? What do these allusions tell us about her character and motives? What do they suggest about the nature of the "white" culture she is immersed in?

4. Mary Lynn and the narrator make a number of observations about white men—that they are dependable but "neutral … like Belgium," that they invented the commute, and so forth. What overall portrait of white men emerges from these comments and from the character of Jeremiah? Explain why you think that Alexie is being fair or unfair in his characterization of white men.

5. What attitudes, behavior, and cultural phenomena does Alexie make fun of, and why? What values and ideas does he appear to take seriously? Are these categories mutually exclusive? Why or why not?

EXPLORING CONNECTIONS

6. Review the passages in the story that speak specifically about race. To what extent would Alexie endorse George Fredrickson's (p. 598) assertion that "ethnic hierarchy in a clearly racialized form persists in practice if not in law" in the United States?

7. If Mary Lynn were to list some of the ways that she could be seen as "white," as Eric Liu does at the beginning of the previous essay (p. 611), what characteristics and details of her life could be included in the list? To what extent is she, like Liu, a citizen of the "Republic of Privilege"? How does Alexie's treatment of the issues of assimilation and class privilege compare to Liu's?

8. Write an imaginary dialogue between Mary Lynn and Linda Hogan (p. 826). How might Hogan explain Mary Lynn's desire to have sex with an indigenous stranger? How do you think she would respond to Mary Lynn's conclusion that "there was at least one white man who could be trusted" (para. 155)?

EXTENDING THE CRITICAL CONTEXT

9. *Smoke Signals* was the first feature-length film written, directed, produced, and acted by American Indians. Watch the movie on videotape and compare it to any recent film that portrays, but was not made by, Indians (e.g., *Pocahontas, Last of the Mohicans*). What differences, if any, do you see in the way the films depict Indian/white cultures and relationships?

Visual Portfolio

READING IMAGES OF THE MELTING POT

1. What is the significance of making the ad for the American Civil Liberties Union look like a "Wanted" poster from the wild West? What is the purpose of pairing the photos of Dr. Martin Luther King Jr. and Charles Manson? What values does the ad associate with the ACLU, and how does it communicate those values? Do you find the ad effective? Why or why not?

2. The second image in the portfolio shows construction workers erecting a segment of the fence that marks the border between the U.S. and Mexico. Freewrite for ten minutes about what you think the wall means to the people on each side. What sense does the picture give you of the photographer's perspective on the fence? What details of the picture itself—angle, lighting, proportion—suggest that perspective?

3. How many different ways could you describe the ethnic or cultural identity of each of the four friends on page 641 based on the visual cues provided by the photo? What knowledge or assumptions about race, ethnicity, and culture underlie your interpretations?

Optional Ethnicities: For Whites Only?

MARY C. WATERS

"Ethnic options" may sound like something you'd find in a futuristic genetic shopping mall, but as Mary C. Waters argues, many white Americans do have some choices about their ethnic identities. If you are descended from Swedes or Italians or Russians, or all three, you can choose to be "just American" or to embrace one or more of these ethnic heritages. Waters also points out that the experience of ethnicity differs significantly for white and nonwhite Americans. If your ancestors came from Europe, you're not likely to be asked "Where are you from?" or complimented on your English or quizzed about your hair. On the other hand, if your ancestors came from Latin America, Asia, or Africa, you've probably encountered these questions and comments more than once. In this essay, Waters presents a thought-provoking discussion of how such disparities in the lived experience of ethnicity can affect individual and group relations on college campuses. A professor of sociology at Harvard University, Waters is the author of Ethnic

Options: Choosing Ethnic Identities in America *(1990) and* Black Identities: West Indian Immigrant Dreams and American Realities *(2000).*

What does it mean to talk about ethnicity as an option for an individual? To argue that an individual has some degree of choice in their ethnic identity flies in the face of the commonsense notion of ethnicity many of us believe in—that one's ethnic identity is a fixed characteristic, reflective of blood ties and given at birth. However, social scientists who study ethnicity have long concluded that while ethnicity is based on a *belief* in a common ancestry, ethnicity is primarily a *social* phenomenon, not a biological one (Alba 1985, 1990; Barth 1969; Weber [1921] 1968, p. 389). The belief that members of an ethnic group have that they share a common ancestry may not be a fact. There is a great deal of change in ethnic identities across generations through intermarriage, changing allegiances, and changing social categories. There is also a much larger amount of change in the identities of individuals over their lives than is commonly believed. While most people are aware of the phenomenon known as "passing"—people raised as one race who change at some point and claim a different race as their identity—there are similar life-course changes in ethnicity that happen all the time and are not given the same degree of attention as racial passing.

White Americans of European ancestry can be described as having a great deal of choice in terms of their ethnic identities. The two major types of options White Americans can exercise are (1) the option of whether to claim any specific ancestry, or to just be "White" or American (Lieberson [1985] called these people "unhyphenated Whites") and (2) the choice of which of their European ancestries to choose to include in their description of their own identities. In both cases, the option of choosing how to present yourself on surveys and in everyday social interactions exists for Whites because of social changes and societal conditions that have created a great deal of social mobility, immigrant assimilation, and political and economic power for Whites in the United States. Specifically, the option of being able to not claim any ethnic identity exists for Whites of European background in the United States because they are the majority group—in terms of holding political and social power, as well as being a numerical majority. The option of choosing among different ethnicities in their family backgrounds exists because the degree of discrimination and social distance attached to specific European backgrounds has diminished over time....

Symbolic Ethnicities for White Americans

What do these ethnic identities mean to people and why do they cling to them rather than just abandoning the tie and calling themselves American? My own field research with suburban Whites in California and

Pennsylvania found that later-generation descendants of European origin maintain what are called "symbolic ethnicities." Symbolic ethnicity is a term coined by Herbert Gans (1979) to refer to ethnicity that is individualistic in nature and without real social cost for the individual. These symbolic identifications are essentially leisure-time activities, rooted in nuclear family traditions and reinforced by the voluntary enjoyable aspects of being ethnic (Waters 1990). Richard Alba (1990) also found later-generation Whites in Albany, New York, who chose to keep a tie with an ethnic identity because of the enjoyable and voluntary aspects to those identities, along with the feelings of specialness they entailed. An example of symbolic ethnicity is individuals who identify as Irish, for example, on occasions such as Saint Patrick's Day, on family holidays, or for vacations. They do not usually belong to Irish American organizations, live in Irish neighborhoods, work in Irish jobs, or marry other Irish people. The symbolic meaning of being Irish American can be constructed by individuals from mass media images, family traditions, or other intermittent social activities. In other words, for later-generation White ethnics, ethnicity is not something that influences their lives unless they want it to. In the world of work and school and neighborhood, individuals do not have to admit to being ethnic unless they choose to. And for an increasing number of European-origin individuals whose parents and grandparents have intermarried, the ethnicity they claim is largely a matter of personal choice as they sort through all of the possible combinations of groups in their genealogies. . . .

Race Relations and Symbolic Ethnicity

However much symbolic ethnicity is without cost for the individual, there is a cost associated with symbolic ethnicity for the society. That is because symbolic ethnicities of the type described here are confined to White Americans of European origin. Black Americans, Hispanic Americans, Asian Americans, and American Indians do not have the option of a symbolic ethnicity at present in the United States. For all of the ways in which ethnicity does not matter for White Americans, it does matter for non-Whites. Who your ancestors are does affect your choice of spouse, where you live, what job you have, who your friends are, and what your chances are for success in American society, if those ancestors happen not to be from Europe. The reality is that White ethnics have a lot more choice and room for maneuver than they themselves think they do. The situation is very different for members of racial minorities, whose lives are strongly influenced by their race or national origin regardless of how much they may choose not to identify themselves in terms of their ancestries.

When White Americans learn the stories of how their grandparents and great-grandparents triumphed in the United States over adversity, they are usually told in terms of their individual efforts and triumphs. The important role of labor unions and other organized political and economic actors in

5

their social and economic successes are left out of the story in favor of a generational story of individual Americans rising up against communitarian, Old World intolerance, and New World resistance. As a result, the "individualized" voluntary, cultural view of ethnicity for Whites is what is remembered.

One important implication of these identities is that they tend to be very individualistic. There is a tendency to view valuing diversity in a pluralist environment as equating all groups. The symbolic ethnic tends to think that all groups are equal; everyone has a background that is their right to celebrate and pass on to their children. This leads to the conclusion that all identities are equal and all identities in some sense are interchangeable— "I'm Italian American, you're Polish American. I'm Irish American, you're African American." The important thing is to treat people as individuals and all equally. However, this assumption ignores the very big difference between an individualistic symbolic ethnic identity and a socially enforced and imposed racial identity.

My favorite example of how this type of thinking can lead to some severe misunderstandings between people of different backgrounds is from the *Dear Abby* advice column. A few years back a person wrote in who had asked an acquaintance of Asian background where his family was from. His acquaintance answered that this was a rude question and he would not reply. The bewildered White asked Abby why it was rude, since he thought it was a sign of respect to wonder where people were from, and he certainly would not mind anyone asking HIM about where his family was from. Abby asked her readers to write in to say whether it was rude to ask about a person's ethnic background. She reported that she got a large response, that most non-Whites thought it was a sign of disrespect, and Whites thought it was flattering:

> Dear Abby,
> I am 100 percent American and because I am of Asian ancestry I am often asked "What are you?" It's not the personal nature of this question that bothers me, it's the question itself. This query seems to question my very humanity. "What am I? Why I am a person like everyone else!"
> Signed, A REAL AMERICAN

> Dear Abby,
> Why do people resent being asked what they are? The Irish are so proud of being Irish, they tell you before you even ask. Tip O'Neill has never tried to hide his Irish ancestry.
> Signed, JIMMY

In this exchange Jimmy cannot understand why Asians are not as happy to be asked about their ethnicity as he is, because he understands his ethnicity and theirs to be separate but equal. Everyone has to come from somewhere—his family from Ireland, another's family from Asia—each has a history and each should be proud of it. But the reason he cannot understand the perspective of the Asian American is that all ethnicities are not equal; all are not symbolic, costless, and voluntary. When White Americans equate their own symbolic ethnicities with the socially enforced identities of non-White Americans, they obscure the fact that the experiences of Whites and non-Whites have been qualitatively different in the United States and that the current identities of individuals partly reflect that unequal history.

In the next section I describe how relations between Black and White students on college campuses reflect some of these asymmetries in the understanding of what a racial or ethnic identity means. While I focus on Black and White students in the following discussion, you should be aware that the myriad other groups in the United States—Mexican Americans, American Indians, Japanese Americans—all have some degree of social and individual influences on their identities, which reflect the group's social and economic history and present circumstance.

Relations on College Campuses

Both Black and White students face the task of developing their race 10 and ethnic identities. Sociologists and psychologists note that at the time people leave home and begin to live independently from their parents, often ages eighteen to twenty-two, they report a heightened sense of racial and ethnic identity as they sort through how much of their beliefs and behaviors are idiosyncratic to their families and how much are shared with other people. It is not until one comes in close contact with many people who are different from oneself that individuals realize the ways in which their backgrounds may influence their individual personality. This involves coming into contact with people who are different in terms of their ethnicity, class, religion, region, and race. For White students, the ethnicity they claim is more often than not a symbolic one—with all of the voluntary, enjoyable, and intermittent characteristics I have described above.

Black students at the university are also developing identities through interactions with others who are different from them. Their identity development is more complicated than that of Whites because of the added element of racial discrimination and racism, along with the "ethnic" developments of finding others who share their background. Thus Black students have the positive attraction of being around other Black students who share some cultural elements, as well as the need to band together with other students in a reactive and oppositional way in the face of racist incidents on campus.

Colleges and universities across the country have been increasing diversity among their student bodies in the last few decades. This has led in many cases to strained relations among students from different racial and ethnic backgrounds. The 1980s and 1990s produced a great number of racial incidents and high racial tensions on campuses. While there were a number of racial incidents that were due to bigotry, unlawful behavior, and violent or vicious attacks, much of what happens among students on campuses involves a low level of tension and awkwardness in social interactions.

Many Black students experience racism personally for the first time on campus. The upper-middle-class students from White suburbs were often isolated enough that their presence was not threatening to racists in their high schools. Also, their class background was known by their residence and this may have prevented attacks being directed at them. Often Black students at the university who begin talking with other students and recognizing racial slights will remember incidents that happened to them earlier that they might not have thought were related to race.

Black college students across the country experience a sizeable number of incidents that are clearly the result of racism. Many of the most blatant ones that occur between students are the result of drinking. Sometimes late at night, drunken groups of White students coming home from parties will yell slurs at single Black students on the street. The other types of incidents that happen include being singled out for special treatment by employees, such as being followed when shopping at the campus bookstore, or going to the art museum with your class and the guard stops you and asks for your I.D. Others involve impersonal encounters on the street—being called a nigger by a truck driver while crossing the street, or seeing old ladies clutch their pocketbooks and shake in terror as you pass them on the street. For the most part these incidents are not specific to the university environment, they are the types of incidents middle-class Blacks face every day throughout American society, and they have been documented by sociologists (Feagin 1991).

In such a climate, however, with students experiencing these types of incidents and talking with each other about them, Black students do experience a tension and a feeling of being singled out. It is unfair that this is part of their college experience and not that of White students. Dealing with incidents like this, or the ever-present threat of such incidents, is an ongoing developmental task for Black students that takes energy, attention, and strength of character. It should be clearly understood that this is an asymmetry in the "college experience" for Black and White students. It is one of the unfair aspects of life that results from living in a society with ongoing racial prejudice and discrimination. It is also very understandable that it makes some students angry at the unfairness of it all, even if there is no one to blame specifically. It is also very troubling because, while most Whites do not create these incidents, some do, and it is never clear until you know someone well whether they are the type of person who could do something like this. So one of the reactions of Black students to these incidents is to band together.

In some sense then, as Blauner (1992) has argued, you can see Black students coming together on campus as both an "ethnic" pull of wanting to be together to share common experiences and community, and a "racial"

15

push of banding together defensively because of perceived rejection and tension from Whites. In this way the ethnic identities of Black students are in some sense similar to, say, Korean students wanting to be together to share experiences. And it is an ethnicity that is generally much stronger than, say, Italian Americans. But for Koreans who come together there is generally a definition of themselves as "different from" Whites. For Blacks reacting to exclusion, there is a tendency for the coming together to involve both being "different from" but also "opposed to" Whites.

The anthropologist John Ogbu (1990) has documented the tendency of minorities in a variety of societies around the world, who have experienced severe blocked mobility for long periods of time, to develop such oppositional identities. An important component of having such an identity is to describe others of your group who do not join in the group solidarity as devaluing and denying their very core identity. This is why it is not common for successful Asians to be accused by others of "acting White" in the United States, but it is quite common for such a term to be used by Blacks and Latinos. The oppositional component of a Black identity also explains how Black people can question whether others are acting "Black enough." On campus, it explains some of the intense pressures felt by Black students who do not make their racial identity central and who choose to hang out primarily with non-Blacks. This pressure from the group, which is partly defining itself by not being White, is exacerbated by the fact that race is a physical marker in American society. No one immediately notices the Jewish students sitting together in the dining hall, or the one Jewish student sitting surrounded by non-Jews, or the Texan sitting with the Californians, but everyone notices the Black student who is or is not at the "Black table" in the cafeteria.

An example of the kinds of misunderstandings that can arise because of different understandings of the meanings and implications of symbolic versus oppositional identities concerns questions students ask one another in the dorms about personal appearances and customs. A very common type of interaction in the dorm concerns questions Whites ask Blacks about their hair. Because Whites tend to know little about Blacks, and Blacks know a lot about Whites, there is a general asymmetry in the level of curiosity people have about one another. Whites, as the numerical majority, have had little contact with Black culture; Blacks, especially those who are in college, have had to develop bicultural skills — knowledge about the social worlds of both Whites and Blacks. Miscommunication and hurt feelings about White students' questions about Black students' hair illustrate this point. One of the things that happens freshman year is that White students are around Black students as they fix their hair. White students are generally quite curious about Black students' hair — they have basic questions such as how often Blacks wash their hair, how they get it straightened or curled, what products they use on their hair, how they comb it, etc. Whites often wonder to themselves whether they should ask these questions. One thought experiment

Whites perform is to ask themselves whether a particular question would upset them. Adopting the "do unto others" rule, they ask themselves, "If a Black person was curious about my hair would I get upset?" The answer usually is "No, I would be happy to tell them." Another example is an Italian American student wondering to herself, "Would I be upset if someone asked me about calamari?" The answer is no, so she asks her Black roommate about collard greens, and the roommate explodes with an angry response such as, "Do you think all Black people eat watermelon too?" Note that if this Italian American knew her friend was Trinidadian American and asked about peas and rice the situation would be more similar and would not necessarily ignite underlying tensions.

Like the debate in *Dear Abby,* these innocent questions are likely to lead to resentment. The issue of stereotypes about Black Americans and the assumption that all Blacks are alike and have the same stereotypical cultural traits has more power to hurt or offend a Black person than vice versa. The innocent questions about Black hair also bring up a number of asymmetries between the Black and White experience. Because Blacks tend to have more knowledge about Whites than vice versa, there is not an even exchange going on; the Black freshman is likely to have fewer basic questions about his White roommate than his White roommate has about him. Because of the differences historically in the group experiences of Blacks and Whites there are some connotations to Black hair that don't exist about White hair. (For instance, is straightening your hair a form of assimilation, do some people distinguish between women having "good hair" and "bad hair" in terms of beauty and how is that related to looking "White"?) Finally, even a Black freshman who cheerfully disregards or is unaware that there are these asymmetries will soon slam into another asymmetry if she willingly answers every innocent question asked of her. In a situation where Blacks make up only 10 percent of the student body, if every non-Black needs to be educated about hair, she will have to explain it to nine other students. As one Black student explained to me, after you've been asked a couple of times about something so personal you begin to feel like you are an attraction in a zoo, that you are at the university for the education of the White students.

Institutional Responses

Our society asks a lot of young people. We ask young people to do   20
something that no one else does as successfully on such a wide scale—that is to live together with people from very different backgrounds, to respect one another, to appreciate one another, and to enjoy and learn from one another. The successes that occur every day in this endeavor are many, and they are too often overlooked. However, the problems and tensions are also real, and they will not vanish on their own. We tend to see pluralism working in the United States in much the same way some people expect capitalism to work. If you put together people with various interests and abilities

and resources, the "invisible hand" of capitalism[1] is supposed to make all the parts work together in an economy for the common good.

There is much to be said for such a model—the invisible hand of the market can solve complicated problems of production and distribution better than any "visible hand" of a state plan. However, we have learned that unequal power relations among the actors in the capitalist marketplace, as well as "externalities" that the market cannot account for, such as long-term pollution, or collusion between corporations, or the exploitation of child labor, means that state regulation is often needed. Pluralism and the relations between groups are very similar. There is a lot to be said for the idea that bringing people who belong to different ethnic or racial groups together in institutions with no interference will have good consequences. Students from different backgrounds will make friends if they share a dorm room or corridor, and there is no need for the institution to do any more than provide the locale. But like capitalism, the invisible hand of pluralism does not do well when power relations and externalities are ignored. When you bring together individuals from groups that are differentially valued in the wider society and provide no guidance, there will be problems. In these cases the "invisible hand" of pluralist relations does not work, and tensions and disagreements can arise without any particular individual or group of individuals being "to blame." On college campuses in the 1990s some of the tensions between students are of this sort. They arise from honest misunderstandings, lack of a common background, and very different experiences of what race and ethnicity mean to the individual.

The implications of symbolic ethnicities for thinking about race relations are subtle but consequential. If your understanding of your own ethnicity and its relationship to society and politics is one of individual choice, it becomes harder to understand the need for programs like affirmative action, which recognize the ongoing need for group struggle and group recognition, in order to bring about social change. It also is hard for a White college student to understand the need that minority students feel to band together against discrimination. It also is easy, on the individual level, to expect everyone else to be able to turn their ethnicity on and off at will, the way you are able to, without understanding that ongoing discrimination and societal attention to minority status makes that impossible for individuals from minority groups to do. The paradox of symbolic ethnicity is that it depends upon the ultimate goal of a pluralist society, and at the same time makes it more difficult to achieve that ultimate goal. It is dependent upon the concept that all ethnicities mean the same thing, that enjoying the traditions of one's heritage is an option available to a group or an individual, but that such a heritage should not have any social costs associated with it.

[1]*the "invisible hand" of capitalism:* Scottish economist Adam Smith (1723–1790) theorized that, left unregulated, the forces of the marketplace would "naturally" guide the economy to productivity and prosperity, like a benevolent invisible hand.

As the Asian Americans who wrote to *Dear Abby* make clear, there are many societal issues and involuntary ascriptions associated with non-White identities. The developments necessary for this to change are not individual but societal in nature. Social mobility and declining racial and ethnic sensitivity are closely associated. The legacy and the present reality of discrimination on the basis of race or ethnicity must be overcome before the ideal of a pluralist society, where all heritages are treated equally and are equally available for individuals to choose or discard at will, is realized.

References

Alba, Richard D. 1985. *Italian Americans: Into the Twilight of Ethnicity.* Englewood Cliffs, NJ: Prentice-Hall.

————. 1990. *Ethnic Identity: The Transformation of White America.* New Haven: Yale University Press.

Barth, Frederick. 1969. *Ethnic Groups and Boundaries.* Boston: Little, Brown.

Blauner, Robert. 1992. "Talking Past Each Other: Black and White Languages of Race." *American Prospect* (Summer): 55–64.

"Before I became a black conservative, I was a white liberal."

Feagin, Joe R. 1991. "The Continuing Significance of Race: Anti-Black Discrimination in Public Places." *American Sociological Review* 56: 101–17.

Gans, Herbert. 1979. "Symbolic Ethnicity: The Future of Ethnic Groups and Cultures in America." *Ethnic and Racial Studies* 2: 1–20.

Ogbu, John. 1990. "Minority Status and Literacy in Comparative Perspective." *Daedalus* 119: 141–69.

Waters, Mary C. 1990. *Ethnic Options: Choosing Identities in America.* Berkeley: University of California Press.

Weber, Max. [1921] 1968. *Economy and Society: An Outline of Interpretive Sociology*, Eds. Guenther Roth and Claus Wittich, trans. Ephraim Fischoff. New York: Bedminister Press.

ENGAGING THE TEXT

1. What reasons does Waters give for considering ethnicity a social construct rather than a biological fact? In what ways is ethnicity optional for white European Americans today? How is "symbolic ethnicity" learned and expressed?

2. Waters argues that while symbolic ethnicity can be beneficial for the individual, it can pose a problem for society as a whole. What is the reasoning behind this claim, how persuasive do you find it, and why?

3. Waters observes that the college experience—when students leave home for the first time and come into close contact with people very different from themselves—can be a critical juncture in an individual's developing sense of personal and ethnic identity. In what ways, if any, has your own experience of college challenged your sense of identity, values, or beliefs about others?

4. Why do some black students develop "oppositional identities," according to Waters? What influences or experiences "push" and "pull" them toward that stance? How do "asymmetries" between black and white students' experiences lead to racial tension?

5. Examine the analogy Waters draws between the workings of pluralism and capitalism and list the parallels she sees between them. What is the purpose of this extended comparison? How do you respond to it?

EXPLORING CONNECTIONS

6. How might Eric Liu (p. 611) respond to Waters's assertion that "for all the ways in which ethnicity does not matter for White Americans, it does matter for non-Whites" (para. 4)?

7. Given the asymmetries in black and white students' experiences that Waters describes, what would be the personal costs to black students of letting whites "have their innocence," as Shelby Steele (p. 573) advocates?

8. Like George Fredrickson (p. 598), Waters sees pluralism as an ideal, but one that is far from being realized. What obstacles must be overcome to

achieve a truly pluralistic society, according to each writer? What signs of hope do they offer for reaching this ideal? What is your own assessment?

9. What do you think the cartoon on page 651 is saying about politics, ethnicity, and the politics of identity? What does the appearance of the two men suggest about their similarities and differences?

EXTENDING THE CRITICAL CONTEXT

10. If you have witnessed a racial conflict or experienced a moment of awkwardness or tension due to ethnicity, write a journal entry describing the incident and your reaction to it. After reading Waters's essay, do you understand any aspect of the incident differently than you did before? If so, how?

11. What, if anything, is being done on your campus to help students from different ethnic backgrounds better understand each other's perspectives? What can or should colleges do to minimize misunderstandings that arise from the asymmetries of ethnic experience Waters discusses?

Secret Latina at Large

VERONICA CHAMBERS

As a black Panamanian American, Veronica Chambers extends and complicates the idea of ethnic options. Although she speaks Spanish and identifies strongly with her Latin heritage, her appearance doesn't immediately reveal her cultural identity; as a result, she says, "I find myself making judgment calls—do I come out of the closet and when?" In this essay, she opens the closet door to share with readers the confusions, joys, and rich culture that define her life as a "secret Latina at large." Chambers (b. 1970) has been a contributor to Kirkus Reviews *and a contributing editor at* Glamour; *at present she writes about cultural issues for* Newsweek. *She has published several books for young adults, including an autobiography,* Mama's Girl *(1996), and the novel that she mentions in this essay,* Marisol and Magdalena: The Sound of Our Sisterhood *(1998).*

She's a *platanos*-frying,[1] Malta Dukesa–drinking,[2] salsa-dancing *mamacita*—my dark-skinned Panamanian mother. She came to this country

[1] *platanos:* Plantains.
[2] *Malta Dukesa:* Brand of beer.

when she was twenty-one—her sense of culture intact, her Spanish flaw-less. Today, more than twenty years since she left her home country and be-came an American citizen, my mother still considers herself a Panamanian, checks "Hispanic" on the census form.

As a black woman in America, my Latina identity is murkier than my mother's. Without a Spanish last name or my mother's fluent Spanish at my disposal, I've often felt isolated from the Latin community. Latinos can be as racist as anybody else: there are pecking orders and hierarchies that favor blue-eyed blonde *rubios* over *negritas* like me. Sometimes, I feel that I put up with enough racism from white Americans, why should I turn to white Latinos for a second share? In much the same way that you can meet a per-son and not know if they are gay or straight, you could meet me and not know whether I was of Latin heritage. So I find myself making judgment calls—do I come out of the closet and when?

I was born in Panama to black Panamanian parents. My father's parents came from Costa Rica and Jamaica. My mother's family came from Mar-tinique. I left Panama when I was two years old, we lived in England for three years, and I came to the U.S. when I was five. Having dark skin and growing up in Brooklyn in the '70s meant that I was black—period. I spent my childhood on Brooklyn streets that morphed, quickly, into worlds away. A stroll down Utica Avenue and the music or the smell of somebody's grandmother's cooking could transform a New York City corner into Santo Domingo, Kingston, Port-au-Prince. Long before I ever set out in search of the world, it found me. My friends, their families, and the histories they car-ried on their backs, kept me glued to the globe. I traced nations with my fin-gertips and knew that America was neither the beginning nor the end, just the crazy mixed-up right now that we all lived in. I also knew that we were only the latest wave of immigrants to make a home in our East Flatbush neighborhood. Every day after school, I rubbed my fingers across the Jew-ish mezuzah[3] that ornamented our door frame. The super had painted over the mezuzahs, an ugly brown, but I never saw anyone ripping one off. I un-derstood it to be out of respect, and I wondered how we would leave our mark.

Still, despite the international flavor of our neighborhood, I found it al-most impossible to explain to my elementary school friends why my mother would speak Spanish at home. They asked me if I was Puerto Rican and I would tell them I was not. But Panama was a kind of nowhere to my young Brooklyn friends. They understood Puerto Ricans because there were so many of them and because of movies like *West Side Story* and groups like Menudo. Everybody knew where Jamaicans were from because of famous singers like Bob Marley. Panamanians had Ruben Blades and we loved him like royalty. But even if my friends knew who he was, because he sang in

---

[3]*mezuzah:* A small box or tube containing a brief biblical text in Hebrew that is mounted on the doorframes of observant Jewish homes.

Spanish, they probably thought he was Puerto Rican too. So in my neighborhood, my brother and I were a sort of fish with feathers. We weren't so much Panamanians as much as we were assumed to be Jamaicans who spoke Spanish. An analogy that isn't without historical basis—Panama's black community was largely drawn to the country from all over the Caribbean as cheap labor for the Panama Canal.

My father didn't mind us considering ourselves black as opposed to   5
Latino. He named my brother Malcolm X. If my mother hadn't put her foot down, I would've been called Angela Davis[4] Chambers. It's not that my mother didn't admire Angela Davis, but you only have to hear how "Veronica Victoria" flows off of her Spanish lips to know that she was homesick for Panama and names that sang like *timbales*[5] on carnival day. So between my mother and my father, there was a black/Latin divide. Because of my father, we discussed and read books about black history and civil rights. Because of my mother, we ate Panamanian food, listened to salsa music, and heard Spanish around the house.

I learned Spanish at home like a dog learns English, and understood mostly commands: *"Callate la boca!"* ("Shut your mouth!") when I dared to interrupt grown-folk's talk. Or *"Baja la cabeza!"* ("Drop your head!") when my mother was braiding my hair and I kept looking up to see my favorite show on TV. My father was also Panamanian, but his mentality was simple. "You're in America," he ordered. "Speak English." It wasn't until my parents were divorced, when I was ten, that my mother tried to teach Malcolm and me to speak Spanish.

My mother was a terrible language teacher. She had no sense of how to explain the structure when we asked questions such as why we were supposed to say *"Toma café"*—literally, "He takes coffee"—instead of "He drinks coffee." Her answer to everything was "That's just the way it is." A few short weeks after our Spanish lessons began, my mother gave up and we were all relieved. I remained intent on learning my mother's language. Nosiness, mostly. What was she saying to her friends on the phone? But there was more to it than that. When my mother spoke Spanish, it was a fast current of words, a stream of language that was colorful, passionate, fiery. I wanted to speak Spanish because I wanted to swim in the river of her words, her history, my history, too.

At Ditmas Junior High School, I had to petition the principal so I could take Spanish. All the other kids in the gifted and talented program were taking French. Apparently, to the powers that were, French was more cultural, more intellectual. The principal approved my request to take Spanish and for two years, I dove into the language, matching what little I knew from home with all that I learned at school. I never asked my mother for help

---

[4]*Angela Davis:* African American professor and activist who stirred controversy with her outspoken political views in the 1960s.
[5]*timbales:* Kettledrums.

with my Spanish homework; she never asked me about my lessons. But one day when I was in the ninth grade, I felt confident enough to start speaking Spanish with my mother and it's been that way ever since.

My brother, who was born in England, never learned Spanish and still doesn't speak it. When I was younger, my Spanish became a point of pride, a typical case of sibling rivalry. Now, I know that my Spanish was also an important bond that I shared with my mother. When I was little, she used to watch astrologer Walter Mercado and *telenovelas* on the Spanish-language TV station. I would sit impatiently as she translated Mercado's horoscope for me or tried to explain what was going on in the latest installment of *La Tragedia de Lisette*. After I learned Spanish, I watched these programs with my mother—not needing translations, poking fun at the campiness of Spanish-language TV. My mother and I would talk to each other in Spanish at our jobs or anywhere we needed some semblance of privacy.

When I spoke only English, I was the daughter, the little girl. As I   10
began to learn Spanish, I became something more—an *hermanita*, a sister-friend, a Panamanian homegirl who could hang with the rest of them. I kissed *boricua*[6] boys on my grandmother's porch and wondered when they whispered *prieta*[7] whether that meant they loved me more or loved me less. When Puerto Rican girls talked about me in front of my face, looking at my dark skin and assuming that I couldn't understand, I would playfully throw out, *"Oye, sabes que yo entiendo?"*[8] Being *Latinegra*—black and Latin— has become a sort of a hidden weapon, something that you can't see at first glance. I know that many people look at my dark skin and don't expect me to be fluent in anything but homegirl.

After college, I put Panama on the back burner for seven years, travel-ing instead to Spain, Morocco, London, Paris, even China. Then last year, at the age of twenty-seven, I wrote my first young adult novel, *Marisol and Magdalena,* about a black Panamanian girl growing up in Brooklyn who goes to live with her grandmother in Panama. In many ways, the novel was a way for me to live a dream that never came true. When I was a young girl, my *abuela* Flora came to live with us in New York. She was old, eighty-four, and sick, but we became fast friends. She told me stories about Panama, promising me that she and I would go together. My grandmother told me that she would make me a festive *pollera*[9] dress and I could dance in the carnival. She died when I was eleven, but writing *Marisol and Magdalena* I imagined what all of those things would be like. Then I decided that it was finally time. With or without my grandmother, with or without my mother, I would have to make my way home. The first thing I did was enlist my cousin, Digna. She was thrilled. *"Ay prima!"* she exclaimed, calling me as

[6]*boricua:* Slang term for a Puerto Rican.
[7]*prieta:* Dark-skinned.
[8]*"Oye, sabes que yo entiendo?":* "Hey, do you know that I can understand you?"
[9]*pollera:* The traditional costume of Panama.

she always does by the Spanish word for cousin. "To visit our *patria* (homeland) together. We'll have so much fun." We planned our trip for the last week in February and made arrangements to stay with my godparents, whom I had never met.

Like Mardi Gras in New Orleans and the big carnivals in Brazil, carnival in Panama is the year's biggest event. We had no problem finding cheap fares. I flew from New York to Miami, where most of the flights to Panama depart from. Arriving in the Miami airport was like stepping into a huge family reunion. The waiting room was filled with hundreds of black Panamanians, speaking in Spanish and calling out the familiar greeting, *"Wappin'!"* (It's short for "What's happening?") On the plane, I found myself seated nest to a family friend from New York.

It's a narrow slither of a country. Panamanians like to say that is the only place in the world where you can swim in the Atlantic in the morning and backstroke across the Pacific in the afternoon. In Panama, the oceans are close—suburbs of each other. But for most of my life, the ocean has been a divide—separating me from my homeland. There were days, weeks, even years, when I could turn my back on the Atlantic, turn American and no one would know or care that there was another country that I called home. Other times, when I danced in dark Brooklyn basements to the rhythms of Celia Cruz and Tito Puente or sat at my aunt's kitchen table listening to the round rhythms of her Panamanian-accented English roll across the table like lucky dice, Panama seemed impossibly close.

When I was little and I told my friends that I was from Panama, they would invariably ask, "Were you born in the Canal?" And I would close my eyes for a second, and I would picture myself, a chocolate-colored little girl, swaddled in pink, floating like the baby Moses down the Panama Canal. Then I would solemnly answer, "Yes, I was." I am not much of a swimmer. I am not even a water sign. But water is significant to me. There are days when I find myself longing to be near a river or a lake, to put my hand into water that stops with my touch then keeps on moving. Other days, in the midst of a crisis or a full-scale panic attack, I will sit in a bathtub full of warm water to clear my mind. As human beings, we are drawn to the water. But I think with me, there is another layer. If you could lift my soul, like a piece of parchment paper, and hold it to the light, you would see an S-like watermark in the shape of Panama. It is brown and green and blue along the edges. Even landlocked in New York City, there are days that my spirit awakens in the Atlantic and falls to sleep, dreaming in the Pacific. And on those days, I feel whole and secure. When the airplane touched down in Panama, bringing me home for the first time since I was two years old, I felt the same way.

My cousin Digna likes to say that women in Panama know how to be 15 *mujeres de cache.*[10] I grew up in a world of Panamanian women who used

---

[10]*mujeres de cache:* Slang for "classy women."

cocoa butter to make their skin smooth and coconut oil to keep their hair soft, women who never went out without nail polish and immaculately pressed clothes. Even poor Panamanian women wear gold with the lavish indulgence that some women wear perfume: dripping from their arms and their ears, fourteen-karat trinkets glistening between their breasts. The first thing my godmother Olga did was book appointments for me and my cousin to get our eyebrows plucked and our nails and feet done with Panamanian-style manicures and pedicures with names like *Medialuna* and *La Secretaria*. "It's carnival," she said. "And you girls have to look your best." We just laughed. It was already feeling like home.

I know that I belong to many tribes. Sometimes, I see a dreadlocked girl on the subway reading a book or carrying a canvas and a bag from Lee's Art Supplies and I identify her as part of my artsy boho black girl tribe. Or I'll be out with a multi-culti group of friends and we'll see another group as wildly diverse as our own and identify them as fellow members of the Rainbow Tribe. In Panama, I went from being a lone black girl with a curious Latin heritage to being part of the *Latinegro* tribe or the *Afro-Antillianos*, as we are officially called. On my first day in Panama, my godfather took me to a party for SAMAAP (Society of Afro-Antilliano People). I was thrilled to learn that there was actually a society for people like me; my only disappointment was that there was no secret handshake. Everyone was black, everyone spoke Spanish, and it could have been a fiesta on Flatbush Avenue because everyone danced the way they danced in Brooklyn, stopping only to chow down on the same smorgasbord of souse, rice with black-eyed peas, beef patties, empanadas, and codfish fritters. I immediately started to call my cousin Digna "Pipa" because the whole trip she kept guzzling *agua de pipa*, which is coconut water drunk straight from a ripe coconut.

In the Afro-Antilliano museum, I took a quiet moment to explore my history. I was struck by the faces of the men who worked and died building the Panama Canal. I thought of the feminist anthology that had changed my life in college, editors Cherrie Moraga and Gloria Anzaldua's *This Bridge Called My Back,* and the phrase took on new meaning. The famous Panama Canal which so efficiently linked the East and the West was built on the backs of my ancestors. The locks of the canal were made strong with the gristle from their bones. My ancestors' tears filled two oceans. I had been taught to be proud of my heritage, but there is a difference between head knowledge and heart knowledge. Standing in the Afro-Antilliano museum, I stood a little taller, knowing in my heart what my people had done. I looked at the pictures and I could feel the family connection in each of their eyes—they resembled my uncles, my grandfathers, the young men who were doing the *salsa con sabor* right outside the museum door. So many of the objects in the museum, like the beautiful *molas* (Matisse-like prints made by Panamanian Indians) reminded me of things that I had grown up with in my mother's home. It was remarkable how comfortable I felt in Panama. There was none of the culture shock that I'd expected. I had my mother and my aunts to thank for that. Although we came to the U.S. with so little material possessions, somehow my family had managed to carry whole bushels of Panamanian culture in their bones and in their hearts.

The actual carnival was the all-night bacchanal that you might expect: elaborate floats, brilliantly colored costumes, live musicians, and dancing. The black Panamanian community had a formal dance which felt like a real debutante ball for a long-lost native daughter like myself. My godmother took my cousin and me to a photo studio where we had our pictures taken in the traditional costume of Panama, the *pollera*. Suffice it to say, it was a real trip. After an hour of makeup, hair, and a rented costume, I looked like a Latin version of Scarlett in *Gone With the Wind*. But when I gave the photo to my mother, she almost cried. She says she was so moved to see me in a *pollera* because it was "such a patriotic thing to do." I had become so Americanized over the years, but when I reached out to Panama, it reached right back to me. On the flight back home, I felt a quiet sense of completeness. To paraphrase the Jamaican tourist ads, I had come back to Panama, my old island home.

A friend left a voice-mail message for me once, calling me a "secret Latina-at-large." The message made me ridiculously happy. I saved it and played it again and again. He had hit on a perfect description for me. Ever since I was a little girl, I have wanted to be like my mother—a Latina with a proud sense of self. In one of my most vivid memories, I am seven or eight and my parents are having a party. Salsa music is blaring and the refrain, "*Wappin'* Colon? *Hola*, Panama," is bouncing off the walls. My mother is dancing and laughing. She sees me standing off in a corner, so she pulls me into the circle of grown-ups and tries to teach me how to dance to the music. Her hips are electric. She puts her hands on my sides and she says, "Move these," and I start shaking my hip bones like my life depends on it. Now I'm a grown woman, and I have hips and booty to spare. I can salsa. My Spanglish is flawless, and my Spanish isn't shabby. You may not look at me and know that I am Panamanian, that I am an immigrant, that I am both black and Latin. But like my homeland, I am a narrow being flanked by two oceans of heritage. I'm a secret Latina-at-large and that is more than enough for me.

ENGAGING THE TEXT

1. Why does Chambers sometimes feel estranged from other Latinos in the United States? Why does she have a hard time explaining her heritage to her non-Latino friends in Brooklyn?

2. What aspects of her "two oceans of heritage" does Chambers identify with?

3. What roles do Chambers's mother and grandmother play in helping her to understand and appreciate her Panamanian roots? Why is her trip to Panama so important to her?

EXPLORING CONNECTIONS

4. Unlike Eric Liu (p. 611), Chambers devotes very little attention to analyzing her relationship to the dominant culture in the United States. How do you account for this difference?

5. Playing the role of Mary C. Waters (p. 642), write an analysis of Chambers's "identity development." To what extent are her "ethnic options" free or circumscribed? In what ways, if any, does her experience show that ethnic categories are socially defined or that ethnic identifications can change?

6. Compare the experiences of Chambers and Judith Ortiz Cofer (p. 423) in their "home" countries of Panama and Puerto Rico and as immigrant Latinas in the United States. What parallels do you see in their lives and in their relationships to each country? What differences do you note, and how do you explain them?

EXTENDING THE CRITICAL CONTEXT

7. Research the history of U.S. involvement in Panama. Why and how was the canal built, and what role did the United States play?

Gray Boys, Funky Aztecs, and Honorary Homegirls

LYNELL GEORGE

Over a quarter of a century after the civil rights movement, some Americans, like Shelby Steele (p. 573), worry about the future of race relations in the United States, while others, like the students Lynell George describes in this essay, feel ready to leave old definitions of race behind. According to George, teens in cities like Los Angeles are living on the edge of a new way of looking at race and ethnicity: they're part of a new melting pot that's merging their varied backgrounds into a new, composite culture. Although George expresses reservations about this cultural ideal, she clearly sees hope that a new generation of Americans has already begun learning how to bridge racial divides. George (b. 1962) was born and raised in Los Angeles, where she works as a staff writer for the Los Angeles Times, *the source of this essay. In addition to her work in journalism, she has published* No Crystal Stair: African Americans in the City of Angels *(1992).*

Let's call him "Perry."

If you grew up in Los Angeles (back when it was still hip to dub the mix "melting pot") and sat through a homeroom roll call sandwiching you some-

where between a Martinez, Masjedi, Matsuda, and Meizel, you knew one—
but more than likely two. This Culver City "Perry," a classmate of mine, had
Farrah Fawcett–feathered blond hair, moist blue-gray eyes, and a *Tiger
Beat* dimple in his chin. Tall and gregarious, at first glimpse he seemed destined for the surfers' corner in the cafeteria—that tight tangle of dreamy
adolescents who, in wet suits under their hooded Bajas, made their way
down to Zuma Beach on slate-gray February mornings. Blaring Led Zep-
pelin, Boston, or Aerosmith, they trailed westward, away from the sun.

In broad-lapel Qianna shirts and denim flares, Perry, who looked less
like Peter Frampton than Barry Gibb, embraced the electronic trickery of
Parliament-Funkadelic, the East Coast soul of the Isley Brothers, or some
Ohio Players midnight jam swelling from the boombox. He certainly never
surfed. He shadowed the intricate steps of the Soul Train dancers, sat with
the black basketball players in the back of the bus, and attempted to chat up
their little sisters in a sonorous baritone carefully fashioned after (who else
but) Barry White.

"Oh, man, he's like K.C., you know, in the Sunshine Band," those who
knew him would tease. But new faces would take a second look, then bristle
and inevitably inquire: "Hasn't anybody told him he ain't black?"

"Chill out," Perry's best partner, the tallest, most imposing BMOC   5
would always defend. "He's OK. He's gray...."

After a while, most everyone forgot what Perry wasn't—even forgot
that he was "gray": the hard-won badge worn by those white kids who
seemed much more comfortable hovering in the space between.

It often worked other ways, too. White kids, honorary homeboys and
homegirls who dressed like *cholos* and talked the grand talk about *mi vida
loca*. Blue-blood black kids who surfed and played mean, tireless sets of
country club tennis. Japanese kids who saved their lunch money to buy
forum floor seats for Earth, Wind and Fire spectaculars and were slipping
everyone hallway high-fives during passing period long before it became
proball decorum.

Over the years, L.A.'s mix has only evolved into a much more complex
jumble as immigration patterns shift and swell, as blurred neighborhood
boundaries subdivide or change hands. However, Los Angeles (as shown by
the chaos last spring[1]) is still a segregated city, despite such "border towns"
as Culver City, Echo Park, or Carson and the disparate bodies that inhabit
them, blending and sharing their cultural trappings and identifiers. These
contiguous neighborhoods inspire intercultural dialogue. And those living at
the fringes have (not without incident) found it necessary to learn something about adaptation. Dealing not in dualities but in pluralities, survival in
this city requires a cultural dexterity heretofore unimagined.

L.A. has metamorphosed into a crazy incubator, and the children who
live on these streets and submit to their rhythm rise up as exquisite

---

[1]*the chaos last spring:* The L.A. uprising of 1992 following the acquittal of four police officers in the Rodney King beating case.

hothouse flowers. They beget their own language, style, codes—a short-hand mode of communication and identification. It's more than learning a handy salutation in Tagalog, being conversant in street slang or sporting hip-hop-inspired styles. This sort of cultural exchange requires active partic-ipation and demands that one press past the superficial toward a more meaningful discourse and understanding.

By no means a full-blown movement, these young people, a small co- 10
terie, exhibit large-scale possibilities. Unaware and without fanfare, they are compelling examples of how effortless and yet edifying reaching out can be.

Their free-form amalgamation billows up in street style (like the "Gangsta"/*cholo*-style baggy chinos and Pendletons that hit the mainstream fashion pages a few months back) as well as in street music. Latino rapper Kid Frost shook it up with his icy, tough-as-nails Public Enemy delivery, then sharpened the edges with staccato snatches in Spanish. For raw power, post-punk badboys the Red Hot Chili Peppers don't have a thing on their counterparts, the Badbrains.

Recently, the Funky Aztecs have taken the baton. Their new recording, "Chicano Blues," offers samples from soul crooner Bill Withers while vamp-ing on traditional twelve-bar delta blues. When not dipping into reggae dub-style or funk, Merciless, Indio, and Loco pay homage to the rich Cali-fornia melange with the raucous single, "Salsa *con* Soul Food."

For Merciless, who's nineteen, the mixing was almost inevitable. His family moved to an all-black neighborhood in Vallejo when he was nine, and before he shaved his head a year ago, "I had real curly hair," he says. "Just, I guess, by the way I dress, a lot of people mix me up with either being black or mixed with black." And the rhythms of hip-hop were a break from the street. "My Chicano partners they were all into their little gangs, you know, their little Notre XIV. Everyone was talking about gangster stuff: 'I'ma kill you,' 'I gotta gun,' 'this bitch is my "ho."' But I wasn't into that, I was more like expressing myself politically. It was mainly my black friends who were into rapping and deejaying and stuff like that.

"It's a trip because my own race trips off me. I even got chased out of my own barrio. But the brothers are real cool with me. It's not that I side on them or whatever because my race always puts me down. It's not like that, but if you're cool to me, I don't care what color you are—I'm going to give you that love right back."

Lives and attitudes like that wreak havoc with stubborn stereotypes and 15
archaic notions about what it is to be African-American, Latino, Asian-American, or Anglo in a quickly transfiguring metropolitan center. In a re-cent Village Voice Literary Supplement, L.A. expatriate Paul Beatty elo-quently shared a vision of home: "Growing up in Los Angeles," writes Beatty, "I couldn't help noticing that language was closely tied to skin color" but not exclusively. "Black folks was either 'fittin' or 'fixin' to go to Taco Bell.... The four Asian kids I knew talked black.... When I started writing, I realized that me and my friends had difficulty processing the language. We

felt like foreigners because no one understood us. We were a gang of verbal mulattoes. Black kids with black brains but white mouths—inbred with some cognitively dissonant Mexicans who didn't speak Spanish and looked crazy at anyone who thought they did."

Some argue that this sort of mixing dilutes culture and creates innumerable lost souls; but many of those who live it see this sharing as realistically inclusive and ultimately enriching—so long as one holds on to integral bits and pieces of one's own. Those more optimistic hear rumblings in and of this New Age patois as harbingers; these young people are well-equipped bellwethers of the new cultural hybrids of Los Angeles.

The mixing starts earlier and earlier, as Jai Lee Wong of the L.A. County Human Relations Commission points out: "My child is four and a half and is fluent in Spanish because his baby-sitter teaches it to him." He tends, she explains, to identify people by the language they speak, not by their racial or ethnic designations. "If they speak English, they are English or American. If they speak Korean, they're Korean," Wong says. "And even though his father is Chinese and speaks only English, my son thinks he's American. For him it's not based on race or ethnicity. He hears me and his father sitting around identifying people by race and it confuses him. Then one day he started talking about that 'green kid over there.' Turns out that he was talking about a white kid wearing a green shirt." Race is a concept not beyond but perhaps already behind him, Wong realizes; a clumsy piece of baggage that already weighs him down.

The new world view? "It's a people thing," Merciless says. "It's not a black or brown or white or red or orange thing. It's a people thing. We all just need to grow up."

On a recent postcard-bright Saturday afternoon, performance artist Danny Tisdale, assuming his flashy alter ego, Tracey Goodman, sets up a folding table with a matte-black cassette deck and a small P.A. system. Microphone in hand, he begins "hawking" a few specialty products for people of color: skin bleach, rainbow-hued hair extensions, and the "new" Contours Sculpting System ("used for refining the nose, lips and buttocks") to inquisitive Santa Barbara Paseo Nuevo mall denizens. Eyes concealed behind inky black shades, Tisdale/Goodman shouts out carnival-barker style: "Transitions, Incorporated!" just above Frank Sinatra's live, over-the-top rendition of "New York, New York." He promises "the ticket to success" as he displays photos of Michael Jackson, the smiling and yet-unaltered preteen juxtaposed with the blanched and angular post-"Thriller" visage.

Taking the proceedings as the real thing, an African-American woman 20 in a pin-striped suit and patent-leather sling-back heels breaks free from the circle, approaching the display at a quick clip. Interrupting the pitch, she requests a card, asks if surgery is at all involved. For a moment, most everyone gathered around the table incorrectly assumes she's a clever plant, a perfect foil. But as the woman becomes more insistent, arms flailing, voice ascending several octaves, Tisdale's manner appears less certain. He's fresh out of snappy retorts; smiles vanish slowly from the surrounding faces. "But will this really work for me?" She wants to know. "Will it truly help?" She's tried so many others.

The piece makes some people angry and renders others silent and bewildered. On a basic level it forces participants to confront, on the spot, the scope and texture of that uncomfortable quandary: What should one give up to achieve success in contemporary American society? The varied responses of those critiquing from the sidelines mirror the real-life incertitude of people enmeshed in this cultural gamble. A prime place in the mainstream isn't won without a price, or without compromise.

What happens when what was carried over from the Old Country becomes cumbersome, archaic, better to be swept under the rug lest anyone see? It is that loss of organic culture that sits at the heart of many debates about cultural accommodation. Most frequently, we see the conflict in terms of whitewash assimilation versus the "who stole the soul"–style wholesale cultural appropriation. Shelby Steele and Clarence Thomas[2] are trotted around (depending on the camp) as products or "victims" of the former. And rappers the Beastie Boys, Vanilla Ice, or Young Black Teenagers (an all-white rap crew) are seen as the latter: opportunists who pilfer the million-dollar beats and mimic the belligerent stance of this black urban art form without having the cultural understanding or sensitivity to carry it off effectively.

But even the most seemingly clear-cut examples of cultural compromise—like the mainstream-bound black woman tugging at Danny Tisdale's coat—are shaded or haunted by a wide array of weighty ramifications based on that choice, the consequences of turning one's back on one's culture. "...Blacks who imitate whites continue to regard whiteness with suspicion, fear, and even hatred," says professor and culture critic bell hooks in her latest book, *Black Looks,* revealing just one nuance in the many hues of assimilation—this one with a conditional cultural safety net woven in. And hooks suggests that what appears to be, at face, an embrace, is something much more complex, even duplicitous: an ingenious, sophisticated tool fashioned especially for urban survival.

L.A., after all, is not at all the Shangri-La it often presents itself as being, especially when it comes to ethnic/cultural relations. Hate crimes, crosscultural gang violence, ethnic "nationalists" such as skinheads, randomly hurled racial epithets along city byways are all a part of the city's fiber, woven in among flashes of accord and affinity. Xenophobia fueled by ignorance, rigid class stratification, and skewed and outmoded media representations have all played a part in stoking interracial tensions in this city as well as across the nation.

---

[2]*Shelby Steele and Clarence Thomas:* African American author (see p. 573) and Supreme Court justice who have been criticized by some as cultural sellouts.

That has helped make assimilation, for people of color, a weighty cul-   25
tural gamble, a risky compromise in the journey toward success within the
American status quo. Nowadays, asking one to assume bits and pieces of another's culture at the expense of one's own is viewed as an exercise out of
the question, especially when attacks from without are so pointed and re-
gaining what was lost in the past has been so painful.

But alternative forms of assimilation — for example, that of slipping in
and out of multiple cultural identities — don't demand that people reject
their own identifiers. They stress inclusion. In light of L.A.'s rapidly meta-
morphosing demographics, this drift is likely to become not the exception
but the rule.

The mere fact of L.A.'s diversity makes the contentious concept of assimilation far less cut-and-dried than it was in the past, when widespread use of
the term *melting pot* suggested that a soul branded with "minority" status in
the United States had to "melt down" his or her cultural trappings — language,
dress, religious ritual, or even body type — to aspire to the American ideal.

Here, where Central and South America meet the Pacific Rim and
West Indies, the definitions of what it means to be black, white, brown, or
yellow blur, and fitting in requires an entirely different set of tools and techniques. Paule Cruz Takash, a UC San Diego anthropologist and ethnic studies professor, notes that "assimilation is not a one-way street," with everyone
striving to adopt Anglo culture. As the phrase "Ellis Island West" spices
news reports about the growing lines winding around the city's Immigration
and Naturalization Service office, the question of assimilation becomes
broader, takes on new definitions.

Ironically enough, in the past two decades, the media and other information arteries, traditional tools for stratifying cultures with the uncomplicated, and erroneous, shorthand of stereotypes, have been invaluable tools
for breaking down stereotypes and reworking prevailing theories about
cultural identity. New mixes take shape at monster movie-plexes, super-
bookstores, and the alternative glitz of underground clubs (and the easy
access to them). The ears and eyes take it all in — and the brain then reas-
sembles it, gives it new form.

And an increasing number of L.A. newcomers embody and advance the   30
recombinant culture. Nahom Tassew, a seventeen-year-old Ethiopian who's
a junior at Belmont High, came to the United States knowing "just what I
saw on movies and TV" about African-Americans. "I thought if I came here,
I'd have to become a thief," he says, "or that was what people would think I
was." After two and a half years, he has a new attitude ("I saw that [African-
Americans at Belmont] were people . . . that there were good people and bad
people, that every race has good people") as well as friends from Mexico,
Guatemala, El Salvador, Japan, and China. And he's studying Spanish. "I
need some Spanish words," he says. Just what will emerge from these ad-
mixtures is difficult to say. Tassew, at least, will acquire an early-age sophistication, learning classroom English along with the street Spanish of his

neighborhood, finding astonishing cultural parallels (from salutation rituals to food) with his Chinese friends. In that environment, he and others have found, there is no room for xenophobia.

Principals and their support staffs at high schools around the city have been looking closely at their campuses' rapidly altering idiosyncratic mixes and the way students like Tassew work within them. At Carson's Banning High, principal Augustine Herrera has watched the numbers shift dramatically over the past six years. Upon his arrival, the school was 57 percent Latino. That ratio has changed drastically: Banning's population is now 72 percent Latino, 20 percent African-American, and 8 percent Asian/Pacific Islander. "For the most part they get along but I don't want to sugarcoat it." Herrera says: "We have the same problems that the city faces. We have kids who don't get along. What goes on in the city goes on on campus...a mindless name-calling that sometimes degenerates into a fight."

Race riots on L.A. high school campuses last fall were physical manifestations of city frictions at the boiling point. Students battling over abstracts or what, at face, seems frivolous—like the kind of music played at a Friday night dance.

"For many, it is the first time they have to mix," Herrera says, and conflicts and more positive exchanges are inevitable. "One feeder junior high is predominantly Latino, one is predominantly black—they must interact. At first there is a sense of distrust, so being in this environment is a good experience for them."

Assistant principal Bea Lamothe has noticed that the hip-hop-inspired cross colors, usually associated with black students, have caught on with the Samoans and Latinos this year, and she's carefully observed what is a quieter form of cultural exchange and communication as well. "There are a few African-Americans who live on the Eastside in Wilmington who wear white T-shirts and khakis and speak Spanish." Students are often unaware that they are mixing codes or modes, she says. They're living their lives, just trying to fit in.

At this age, these adolescents—native-born or immigrant—are not   35
looking for, or relying on, words to describe or define their lives. They prefer action over theory. For many of them, it's working. And like the music that fuels them and serves as an anthem: It's all in the mix.

The students have unfurled a cloth banner and hung it high above the stage of Belmont High School's cavernous auditorium. In electric, wild-style lettering it proclaims: La Raza Unida (The United Race). As the SRO crowd mills around her, principal Martha Bin stands on the sidelines, blond hair folded into an elegant updo, her walkie-talkie poised in a freshly manicured hand. This year, voting to pass on the usual Columbus Day assembly, the student body, Bin explains, chose instead to pay homage to the campus's Latin cultural mix—spanning several countries and continents.

In what looks like an elaborate show-and-tell, students bring bits and pieces of their culture to Belmont's stage. Since the auditorium won't accommodate the 4,000-plus student body at one seating, there are two assemblies—one morning, another in the afternoon. The second performance begins with several girls in frothy turquoise dresses, their partners in dark, pressed suits, displaying *rancheras*. Later come the *cumbias*, a mambo and an elaborate dance performed with lit candles that originated in Peru. Capping the show is a trio in below-the-knee, extra-large baggy shorts, who rap and joke in English, Spanish, and French.

"We are a school of immigrants," says Bin, sitting down for a moment in a quiet classroom next to the auditorium, her walkie-talkie close by. "Many of the black kids are Hispanic. We have Chinese-Cubans. We have Koreans who speak Portuguese." Belmont, one of the largest high schools in the nation, with 4,500 students on campus, buses out another 3,000 to accommodate the crush of the Temple/Beaudry/Echo Park district youth population from which it draws. Bin says 78 percent of the student body is Latino; the rest is a mix that includes citizens of Romania, Colombia, Armenia, Ethiopia, and Biafra. "You sit them together," Bin says, "they just have to get along— *conjunto*—together."

William Han, an eighteen-year-old Belmont senior, thinks he knows why. "Students who attend Belmont," he says, "are first-generation American students, whereas at other schools they are second or third. We are immigrants. This is our first experience." Han knows the struggle to adjust. It was just four years ago that he and his Korean parents moved here from their home in Brazil. A bright and talkative "American" teen, he wears an oversized jersey with "William" embroidered in green, green-gray pressed slacks, and black sneakers. His black hair is close-cropped and sticks up like the bristles of a stiff brush. Like many of the kids around him, he's something of a citizen of the world—he speaks Portuguese, Spanish, English, and Korean. "Things at Belmont are honest," he says. In the common fight to cope with a new culture, "people accept you for who you are."

Because of the intricate cultural mix surrounding the school, there are 40 concerns and needs that are unique to Belmont. "Our ESL students tend to be Spanish speaking, but a lot of Asians speak Spanish before English on our campus because they hear it in their neighborhood," says assistant principal Rosa Morley, herself an embodiment of ethnic and cultural blending. (She has Chinese parents but grew up in Cuba. Fluent in Spanish, she feels most connected to Cuban culture.)

"The kids feel that the whole world is like this," Bin says, and that can be a problem later on. "They have some difficulty when they move out of this environment and are no longer the majority."

"We don't tell them this isn't the real world," Morley says. "They will find out sooner or later. We are sheltering them in a sense but cannot control what life will bring for them."

By college, one doesn't see as many "Culver City Perrys." The university, for those who make it, is often the startling baptism, a reawakening or first-awakening of self. Students moving out of ethnically/racially diverse environments and into the austere university setting come face to face with cultural stratification. It is, for many, the first time that they are called upon to choose sides or feel a need to become politically active.

The Institute for the Study of Social Change, based at UC Berkeley, reported on diversity at the university level a year ago in a study called the Diversity Project. The study's goal was to address "a vital and constantly unfolding development emerging in American social life," focusing primarily on demographic changes in the country and how they affect interpersonal communication on college campuses. There would be no solution to the problems of diversity, the report stressed, as long as we think in polar terms. The extremes of "assimilation to a single dominant culture where differences merge and disappear vs. a situation where isolated and self-segregated groups [retreat] into...enclaves" don't work, researchers concluded. The report was based on sixty-nine focus-group interviews with 291 UC Berkeley students.

The report advises a "third and more viable" option: "the simultaneous 45 possibility of strong ethnic and racial identities (including ethnically homogeneous affiliations and friendships) *alongside* a public participation of multiracial and multiethnic contacts that enriches the public and social sphere of life."

In testimonials in the Diversity Project, students spoke frankly about the problems of bridging two worlds and the inexorable pressure to fit in. An Asian-American male was traumatized when presented with a completely alien environment: "I was totally unaccustomed to being in [a] social situation where only Asians were there. So I was completely lost....I got so frustrated, I rejected...my Asian-American identity and had a lot of Hispanic friends."

In this period of self-searching, what will help these students realize this "third experience"—recognizing diversity while maintaining their own distinctive cultural identity—is to develop the cultural equivalent of achieving bilingual or multilingual proficiency, to be sensitive enough to adapt to one's surroundings without losing sight of self.

This concept of cultural pluralism—where each group makes an influential and duly recognized contribution to American society—may seem naive or merely whimsical, but in light of the tremendous cultural shift, it is tenable. "Racial and ethnic identities are always formed in dialogue with one another," says George Lipsitz, professor of ethnic studies at UC San Diego and author of *Time Passages,* a collection of essays on diversity and contemporary pop culture. "So to be Chicano in L.A. means to have a long engagement with black culture. What kind of Anglo you are depends on what group of color you're in dialogue with."

Lipsitz has noted that this mixing once was a more class-based phenomenon, but that drift has altered dramatically in recent years. "When I see desegregated groups of graffiti writers, one of the things that strikes me is that they're also mixed by class," he says. "Style leaders are working-class kids who present themselves as poorer than they are but they have a suburban following. One writer told me: 'Y'know, I go down to the Belmont Tunnel, I go out to the motor yard in Santa Monica, I meet a guy who lives in Beverly Hills, I meet someone who went to Europe last summer.' It's the way they expand what's open to them."

Lipsitz doesn't see this mixing as a grievous threat or as diluting culture, as some nationalists do. People find allies wherever they find them, he believes. "For example, there is a group of graffiti writers who call themselves 'ALZA'—which stands for African, Latino, Zulu, and Anglo. ALZA, Lipsitz says, is Chicano slang for *rise up*. They found each other. Nobody set this up. Nobody put an ad in the paper. They look for spaces that are what we call 'multicultural.' I don't think that they ever think to look at it in those ways. But there's a sense of interest and excitement and delight in difference that makes them look for more complexity."

But painting this phenomena as some sort of "we are the world" harmonious culture fest would be erroneous. Like those in the Diversity Project, Lipsitz has witnessed some of the more painful outcomes of "fitting nowhere," what isolation and alienation can do to a young person's spirit and soul. "I've talked to many students who are either from racially mixed backgrounds or who have what they consider to be an odd history—maybe they were the only black student in a white high school or something like that," he explains. "Then at the university it seems that there is an inside that they are not part of, and there is no obvious subgroup that they can join.

"They don't feel comfortable maybe with African-American culture. Or there are Chicanos who come in but they don't speak Spanish well enough for MEChA [a college-level Latino political organization]; or there are Asian-Americans who are Korean or Vietnamese, and the campus is dominated by Japanese- or Chinese-Americans." It is their love of difference, danger, and heterogeneity that brings them together. When a singer like George Clinton comes along—who's too black for the whites, too white for the blacks—"in a way he's talking to people whose lives are like that."

Susan Straight titled her first short-story collection after one of her favorite herky-jerky, George Clinton–sired Parliament-Funkadelic jams, "Aqua Boogie." Maybe it was something about the rhythm. But probably it was the music's quicksilver spirit—arrogantly individual and all over the map. When Straight's *Aquaboogie* hit the stores, book reviews, and small journals almost two years ago, she inspired quite a few double takes. In her stark, sober portrait, her blond hair framed a steely face out of which light

50

eyes stared boldly into the camera. A novel in short stories, *Aquaboogie* finds its center in a depressed Southern California locale called Rio Seco and its characters among the working-class blacks who live and die there.

The writing—eloquent, sensitive, and honest—wouldn't have riled so many except for the fact that Susan Straight is white, one of the few white artists giving voice to what's considered to be a black experience. "If I was a lousy writer and I was trying to write about a neighborhood like the one I'm writing about and had all these details wrong…then I don't think I deserve to be published," Straight says. "I know my little corner of the world and that's what I write about. And I think I do a good job. I don't fit into a box," she adds with that same tough, unblinking stare, "and see this is a big problem for people. It's like everywhere I go, which box do I fit into? I don't. Sorry."

Straight, who balances a UC Riverside lecturing position with writing, leading various local writing workshops and household duties, was born in Riverside. She still makes her home there with her husband (her high school sweetheart, who is black) and two daughters in a sunny, rambling California Craftsman on a wide, tree-lined street. For Straight, fitting in was more of an issue once she left her Riverside friends and environs.   55

"I went to USC straight from high school. I got a scholarship—my Dad was unemployed at the time. I loved going to USC—once I found some friends," she recalls with a laugh. "When I first got there it was like I talked funny, I came from a bad neighborhood, I had a T-shirt that said 'Itsy-Bit' on the back in that Gothic writing. USC was a really scary place for me coming from Riverside, where everything was country."

She ended up hanging out with athletes—mostly black football players from places like Pomona and Inglewood. "Those were my friends," she says. The problem didn't end at USC's boundaries. It shadowed her crosscountry, shot up at the University of Massachusetts, Amherst, where she was constantly embroiled in fiction workshop debates, then later took shape and form in the publishing world when she sent stories to *The New Yorker* and *The Atlantic*. "Of course everybody thought I was black, which I didn't know, but I understand," says Straight. "They just didn't want to read about that kind of stuff. They had problems with the dialect, they had problems with the subject. It was a little bit 'harsh.' One person wrote back: 'Your world view is very bleak….' I thought, 'Man, I'm sorry. Fix the world, and then my view won't be so bleak.'"

What Straight was attempting to do with her body of work made some blacks angry, some whites a shade of uncomfortable that some found difficult to articulate—people like her first agent, who took it upon herself to chastise her client soundly. "She said: 'I didn't know you were white.' And then she said: 'I think you're deceiving people.' She sent all my stories back and wrote me a big, old long letter about '…the American public isn't ready for something like me….' She really thought that I should be writing about something different," she says with a shrug, palms upturned. "So what am I supposed to do? Go back and get born again? Have different parents? Grow up in a different place? Marry a different man? Then I'll be writing about different things, right? That's a big order." Confronting her "bleak world view," Straight started writing mostly out of a sense of frustration and a need to take some sort of definitive action.

"Look at me," she says. "I weigh ninety-nine pounds. I mean what can I do? I can't bring my friends back from the dead. I can't stop people from doing what they're doing. Drugs have been a big problem. I've so many friends who have no brains left, and that's not from rock, that's from angel dust. I thought: 'Well I can go home and just write these little stories.'" Her "little" stories deal with enormous and grave issues—death, drug addiction, poverty, abandonment—but they also speak to nurturing aspects, the strength of black family structure, about love, about relationships between fathers and sons, mothers and daughters, community resilience. Not *the* black experience, Straight stresses, but a "particular" black experience.

What rests at the core of understanding, Straight believes, is reaching out and treating others with respect. "People have always said that black people know white people much better than white people know black people, because it's a matter of survival. And that's what I grew up hearing," says Straight. "Now being black is in vogue as far as the movies and stuff. Maybe it should be a matter of survival for white people to know how black people live now." As UC San Diego's Lipsitz notes, "You look around to see who has something to teach you," a new Golden Rule that can be looked 60

upon as an informal paradigm for Twenty-first–Century survival. Kids on the borders of several cultures are "trying to be honest in a dishonest world," he says. "I think if something good were to happen, it would come from them. I think that they're trying to live a life that's not a lie."

Those who might be viewed by some as having "odd histories" because they've spent their lives juggling codes or responding to the various influences within them are breaking down walls and erecting sturdy bridges through the mere act of living their lives. Granted, this vision appears mere chimera, almost utopian. But it is, for them, proving to be an integral component of psychic survival. In this period of uneasy transition, complicated by overwhelmingly rapid change, young people ride the periphery, and their lives do impressive battle with notions of a now-archaic "norm." But their quiet revolution is fueled by much more than simply the adolescent ache to belong. It is a more honest, eyes-wide-open way to reach out and greet a world as confounding as they are.

ENGAGING THE TEXT

1. What, according to George, does it mean to be "gray"? How does someone become a "gray boy," a "funky Aztec," or an "honorary homegirl"?

2. Review several examples of the kind of "recombinant culture" that George describes. Can you think of examples of this new cultural style you have observed in your neighborhood, on campus, or in the media?

3. Working in small groups, discuss whether it is possible to adopt multiple cultural styles, as George suggests, without losing your own cultural identity.

4. How does George explain the increase in racially motivated conflict within the new urban melting pot? Can you offer any additional explanations for the increase of racial tension within the new "recombinant culture"?

5. What, according to George, is the impact of college on the complex cultural identities of many entering students?

EXPLORING CONNECTIONS

6. Review the discussions of prejudice and ethnic relations offered by Vincent N. Parrillo (p. 548), George M. Fredrickson (p. 598), and Mary C. Waters (p. 642). How might they respond to George's assertion that the "concept of race" is already "behind" some young Americans—already a "clumsy piece of baggage" from the past that weighs them down?

7. Write a dialogue between Shelby Steele (p. 573) and George on the future of race relations in the United States.

8. George, Eric Liu (p. 611), and Mary C. Waters (p. 642) all speak of college as a crucial period in shaping students' perceptions of and attitudes toward ethnic identity. To what extent do they agree or disagree about the *kind* of

impact college has on ethnic relations and self-definitions? How consistent with your own college experience are each writer's observations?

9. Brainstorm several possible interpretations for the cartoon on page 671. Which interpretation do you prefer, and why? Do you think that the cartoonist would support George's vision of a "recombinant culture" emerging in the United States?

EXTENDING THE CRITICAL CONTEXT

10. Collect as many media images as you can (from films, TV shows, ads, music videos and lyrics, and so forth) that reflect the "recombinant culture" George discusses. Are these images evidence of a genuine cultural shift occurring in the United States, or is all this talk of a "new melting pot" just a marketing ploy, a matter of fashion? What evidence do you find, if any, that America's "racial categories" are actually changing?

11. Write a journal entry describing your personal experience of moving from the culture(s) of your neighborhood to the culture of college. To what extent does your experience confirm George's claims that students in college often must deal with "cultural stratification" for the first time in their lives and that they are often forced to "choose sides"? Share your experiences in small groups and discuss whether you feel college works to polarize the racial, cultural, and economic differences between students.

12. Is it possible or appropriate to speak with authority about the experience of a group whose sexual, racial, economic, and cultural background differs from one's own? In this selection, George presents the case of Susan Straight, a white writer who has published a collection of stories featuring the experiences of African American characters. Do you agree that Straight represents a "quiet revolution" in American society? Why or why not?

Child of the Americas

AURORA LEVINS MORALES

This poem concentrates on the positive aspects of a multicultural heritage, as Morales celebrates her uniqueness, her diversity, and her wholeness. It's an up-to-date and sophisticated reinterpretation of the melting pot myth. As this autobiographical poem states, Aurora Levins Morales (b. 1954) was the child of a Puerto Rican mother and a Jewish father. She moved to the United States when she was thirteen and now writes, performs, and teaches in the San Francisco Bay Area. "Child of the Americas" is from the collection Getting Home Alive *(1986), which she coauthored with her mother, Rosario Morales. Her mother has written that the book "began in long, budget-breaking telephone calls stretched across the width of this country... the phone line strung between us like a 3,000-mile umbilical cord from navel to navel, mine to hers, hers to mine, each of us mother and daughter by turns, feeding each other the substance of our dreams."* Morales has taught Jewish studies and women's studies at Berkeley and is a history educator and program historian for the Latino History Project at the Oakland Museum of California. *She is the author of* Remedios: Stories of Earth and Iron from the History of Puertorriqueñas *(1998) and* Medicine Stories: History, Culture, and the Politics of Integrity *(1998)*.

I am a child of the Americas,
a light-skinned mestiza of the Caribbean,
a child of many diaspora,[1] born into this continent at a crossroads.

I am a U.S. Puerto Rican Jew,
a product of the ghettos of New York I have never known.   5
An immigrant and the daughter and granddaughter of immigrants.
I speak English with passion: it's the tongue of my consciousness,
a flashing knife blade of crystal, my tool, my craft.

I am Caribeña,[2] island grown. Spanish is in my flesh,
ripples from my tongue, lodges in my hips: 10
the language of garlic and mangoes,
the singing in my poetry, the flying gestures of my hands.
I am of Latinoamerica, rooted in the history of my continent:
I speak from that body.

I am not african. Africa is in me, but I cannot return.   15
I am not taína.[3] Taíno is in me, but there is no way back.
I am not european. Europe lives in me, but I have no home there.

I am new. History made me. My first language was spanglish.[4]
I was born at the crossroads
and I am whole.   20

ENGAGING THE TEXT

1. Does this poem do more to challenge or to promote the myth of the melting pot? Explain.

[1]*diaspora:* Scattered colonies. The word originally referred to Jews scattered outside Palestine after the Babylonian exile; it is now used to refer to African and other peoples scattered around the world.

[2]*Caribeña:* Caribbean woman.

[3]*taína:* Describing the Taíno, an aboriginal people of the Greater Antilles and Bahamas.

[4]*spanglish:* Spanish and English combined.

2. Why does the poet list elements of her background that she scarcely knows ("the ghettos of New York" and Taíno)? How can they be part of her?

3. How do you interpret the last stanza? Rephrase its messages in more complete, more explicit statements.

EXPLORING CONNECTIONS

4. What similarities and differences do you see between Morales's celebration of her diverse heritage and the "recombinant culture" embraced by the young people Lynell George describes (p. 660)?

5. Many of the writers in this book express a sense of internal fragmentation or cultural conflict. How does the speaker of this poem avoid the feeling of cultural schizophrenia? How does her response compare to those of Richard Rodriguez (p. 194), Judith Ortiz Cofer (p. 423), Paula Gunn Allen (p. 433), Eric Liu (p. 611), and Veronica Chambers (p. 653)? Which responses do you find most appealing or most realistic, and why?

EXTENDING THE CRITICAL CONTEXT

6. Write your own version of "Child of the Americas," following Morales's structure but substituting ideas and images from your own heritage. Read it to the class.

6

Westward Ho!
The Myth of Frontier Freedom

Buffalo Bill's Wild West Show

On a summer evening in 1947, Mac Brazel looked up to see the sky illuminated with the flash of an explosion. The next day he discovered what seemed to be the wreckage of an unearthly vehicle some miles from his New Mexico ranch house. Initial reports indicated the craft was a "flying disk," but the Air Force eventually revised its story and claimed that the debris was from an experimental weather balloon. Despite the best efforts of the U.S. government over the next fifty years, the story of the infamous Roswell incident simply wouldn't die. Rumors about flying saucers, little green men with enormous eyes, and alien autopsies at top-secret military facilities in "Area 51" outside Coyote Peak, Nevada, have worked their way into the fabric of contemporary American popular culture and folklore. And with good reason, for the American West has always been fertile ground for mythmaking; the western frontier has always offered a free space where the American imagination can express its deepest hopes and fears, its most compelling fantasies.

The first mythologists of the American West were the Native Americans who were its original inhabitants. Native American tales enact the relationship between tribal societies and the natural world in which they live. Tribal myths explain the origin of the universe and specify the proper place of human and animal societies within it. One well-known legend of the Crow Indians, for example, tells the story of how "Old Man Coyote"—the Crow god of creation—enlists the aid of a pair of red-eyed ducks to shape mountains, valleys, lakes, and streams from mud left behind by the waters that once covered the world. Then, in collaboration with another, wilier coyote, he gives life to the first animals and the first humans and equips them with everything that makes life worth living—music, dance, song, weapons, warfare, and sex. Native American myths like this one celebrate the close association of humanity and the natural world. Animals in American Indian legends talk and interact with their counterparts on equal terms. The land itself comes alive to play a part in the imaginative ecology of Native American storytelling.

Europeans began fantasizing about the New World even before Columbus sailed westward for India in 1492. Classical Greeks and Romans envisioned a dreamland inhabited by "fabulous races" unlike any other people in the known world. Trying to capture in words the promise of this uncharted West, the Classical poet and orator Horace encouraged his fellow Romans to

See, see before us the distant glow,
Through the thin dawn-mists of the West,
Rich sunlit plains and hilltops gemmed with snow,
The islands of the Blest!

To European minds, straining to imagine what eyes could not see beyond the curve of the Atlantic, the West was an enchanted place. It was Atlantis, Avalon, the Garden of the Hesperides, the Seven Cities of Antillia, the New

Eden, the promised land of Canaan. It was Elysium, the "happy land," where the weather was always gentle and people lived forever "untouched by sorrow." It was Eldorado, the mythic lost city where streets were paved in gold and precious jewels littered the earth like common stones. It was home to the Fountain of Youth, whose fabled waters lured adventurers like Ponce de Leon to destruction. It was the island of Calipha, Queen of the Amazons, who lent her name to America's west coast when Spanish explorers, greeted by bands of indigenous women while cruising the Pacific, assumed they had arrived in the realm of female warriors.

Indeed, Europeans were so mastered by their own fantasies of the West that they often had trouble sorting out fact from fiction. By the end of his third voyage to "Hispaniola" in 1498, Columbus was so deeply impressed by the lush beauty of the land he explored and by the similarities it bore to the biblical story of Adam and Eve, he came to the conclusion that he had found not merely an island but Eden itself. Amerigo Vespucci reached the same conclusion after assessing all he had seen in the Americas:

> The inhabitants of the New World do not have goods of their own, but all things are held in common. They live together without king, without government, and each is his own master.... There is a great abundance of gold, and by them it is in no respect esteemed or valued.... Surely if the terrestrial paradise be in any part of this earth, I esteem that it is not far distant from these parts.

Before Columbus, the West was an imagined land of promise that held out the hope of something better, something that represented progress beyond the centuries of warfare, famine, and plague associated with the Middle Ages. From the moment the first European set foot on American soil, the West became the future, and Europe became the past.

To the Puritans who founded Plymouth Plantation in 1620 and the Massachusetts Bay Colony in 1630, the West was much more than an earthly paradise gaudily crusted with gold. Puritan fantasies of America were shaped by the stories that dominated the Puritan imagination—the legends of suffering and redemption related in the Bible. Persecuted by what they saw as a corrupt and authoritarian church, the Pilgrims viewed America through Old Testament stories of exile, enslavement, and salvation. They came to see themselves as the new "children of Israel," "the chosen people" destined to embark on an "errand in the wilderness" in search of the New Jerusalem, the new Promised Land. Journeying westward, from the Puritan point of view, was more than simply a quest for riches or the promise of eternal youth; it was a pilgrimage undertaken for self-transformation and the spiritual rebirth of the human race. Colonial poets Philip Freneau and Hugh Brackenridge celebrated this biblical vision of America's destiny in their "Poem on the Rising Glory of America":

> A new Jerusalem, sent down from heaven
> Shall grace our happy earth....

Paradise anew
Shall flourish, by no second Adam lost....
Another Canaan shall excell the old....

In the space of two generations, the Puritan fantasy of America as the cradle of the world's spiritual rebirth would collapse into the mass hysteria of the Salem witch trials and genocidal warfare against the same Native Americans who helped the Pilgrims survive their first winter. But the Puritan legacy to the myth of the West would live on. From the founding of the Massachusetts Bay Colony to the present day, America has seen itself as a place apart, a nation with a special role to play on the stage of world history. The New World has long dreamed itself the home of the "New Adam," a new kind of man, capable of rising above the sins and weaknesses of the old, "fallen" world of Europe. Growing directly from the Puritan religious vision of the New World as a place of spiritual progress and personal rebirth, this belief in America's "exceptionalism" would become a central tenet in the mythology of the American West.

As settlers fanned out from the eastern seaboard in the eighteenth century, Puritan spiritualism was replaced by secular fantasies inspired by the prospect of free land. According to the myth of the frontier, the vastness of the American West offered newly arrived immigrants the chance to cast off the social, economic, and cultural restraints of European civilization and to reinvent themselves as independent Americans in a land of unlimited opportunity. The wide-open spaces of the West guaranteed that newly arrived Americans would live free from the pernicious influences of overcrowded cities and governmental control; the West's apparently limitless natural resources promised that every American could be his own master and make the most of his own best efforts. Within a generation, a new kind of American hero embodying the virtues of the West rose up in the popular imagination: tales of American frontiersmen like Daniel Boone and Davey Crockett filled the "dime novels" of America's fast-growing publishing industry with examples of how life in the wilderness bred toughness and rugged self-reliance. By the end of the century, the American cowboy had emerged as the ideal of frontier freedom. Better with a rope than with words and more at home on the prairie than in town, the cowboy set a standard for virtue that has shaped the values of generations of Americans from the era of Teddy Roosevelt and his "Rough Riders" to the rancher presidency of Ronald Reagan.

But the myth of the West, like most mythologies, is full of tensions and contradictions. The frontier offered Americans the chance to liberate themselves through contact with wilderness, yet it also reaffirmed the nation's deep belief in technological progress. Many saw westward movement (including the appropriation of Native American lands and the conquest of Mexican territories) as the fulfillment of America's "Manifest Destiny." Western expansion was seen as part of a divine plan whose central purpose was to "civilize" the land by making it fruitful and productive—supplying food for growing cities, coal and oil for burgeoning factories, iron ore for railroads and bridges. The 1845 *Emigrants' guide to Oregon and California* epitomizes this faith in progress through the subjugation of nature:

> ... the time is not distant when those wild forests, trackless plains, untrodden valleys, and the unbounded ocean, will present one grand scene, of continuous improvements, universal enterprise, and unparalleled commerce: when those vast forests, shall have disappeared, before the hardy pioneer; those extensive plains, shall abound with innumerable herds, of domestic animals; those fertile valleys, shall groan under the immense weight of their abundant products; when those numerous rivers, shall team with countless steam-boats, steam-ships, ships, bargues, and brigs; when the entire country, will be everywhere intersected with turnpike roads, rail-roads, and canals; and when, all the vastly numerous, and rich resources, of that now almost unknown region, will be fully and advantageously developed.
>
> ... And in fine, we are also led to contemplate the time, as fast approaching, when the supreme darkness of ignorance, superstition, and despotism, which now, so entirely pervade many portions of those remote regions, will have fled forever, before the march of civilization, and the blazing light, of civil and religious liberty; when genuine *republicanism,* and unsophisticated *democracy,* shall be reared up, and tower aloft, even upon the now wild shores, of the great Pacific; where they shall forever stand forth, as enduring monuments, to the increasing wisdom of *man,* and the infinite kindness and protection, of an all-wise, and overruling *Providence.*

The myth of progress, divinely sanctioned, gave the United States the justification it needed to seize the land and its resources. The stories America told itself about Manifest Destiny and free land made it possible to interpret the invasion of Native American homelands as a divinely inspired act of providence. The myth of frontier freedom loomed so large in the mind of America that it was possible to forget that there were and still are "many Wests," many different versions of the frontier experience. The heroic exploits of free-thinking cowboys have served to silence other stories of the West, like those of the Native Americans displaced by land speculation, or those of Mexican citizens who became Americans overnight after the signing of the treaty of Guadalupe Hidalgo, or those of the Chinese immigrants who crossed the Pacific to build the first transcontinental railroad, or those of the African American slaves who staked out new lives as freemen on the plains, or those of the thousands of indigenous and immigrant women who found freedom or struggled to survive in this male-dominated "paradise."

This chapter invites you to reflect on the meanings associated with the American frontier and to explore the legacy of the myth of frontier freedom in contemporary American culture. It opens with a suite of readings that introduces the history and heroes associated with the frontier experience. Frederick Jackson Turner's classic 1883 essay, "The Significance of the Frontier in American History," begins the chapter by assessing the impact of western settlement on the nation's institutions and national character. Wallace Stegner's "The Twilight of Self-Reliance" builds on Turner's essay by offering a twentieth-century celebration of the "Indian virtues" of America's frontier heroes. Next, cultural historians Robert V. Hine and John Mack Faragher trace the coevolution of America's growing mass-media industry and the legend of the frontier hero—from Daniel Boone through the Wild West shows of Buffalo Bill Cody to the rough-and-ready westerns of early Hollywood. N. Scott Momaday's "The American West and the Burden of Belief," Wendy Rose's "Three Thousand Dollar Death Song," and Louise Erdrich's "Dear John Wayne" complete this overview by offering Native American perspectives on the myth of the frontier and the burdens it has imposed on the indigenous peoples of the West.

Always a colorful place, the West has long exerted a strong attraction for American artists and photographers; as a result, the visual history of frontier experience is particularly compelling. Among the selections included in this chapter's Visual Portfolio, you'll find a classic representation of the cowboy by Frederick Remington, a portrait of the spirit of Manifest Destiny making her way across the plains, early photographic documentation of the West's ecological excesses, and a father-and-child portrait that raises questions about America's frontier gun culture.

After this visual interlude, the second half of the chapter explores the impact of frontier thinking in contemporary America. The section opens with "The Adventures of the Frontier in the Twentieth Century," Patricia Nelson Limerick's assessment of frontier mythology in modern America. Next come two selections that focus more narrowly on the limits of freedom in modern America. In "The Price of Admission: Harassment and Free Speech in the Wild Wild West," Stephanie Brail examines the high cost of liberty on the new frontier of electronic technology. In his essay on the rise of America's gun culture, Michael A. Bellesiles offers a critical reappraisal of the history of gun ownership in the early Republic and, through it, challenges conventional wisdom about the meaning of the Second Amendment.

The chapter's last three selections center on the role of nature in the mythic West. In "Freedom and Want: The Western Paradox," Donald Worster argues that American attitudes toward nature are deeply divided as a result of its frontier mythology: wilderness from the perspective of the frontiersman is both a liberating force and a constant source of threat that must be controlled. Linda Hogan presents an indigenous view of nature and an example of Native American spirituality in her aptly titled "Department of the Interior." The chapter closes with "Looking for Nature at the Mall," journalist Jennifer Price's exploration of the commercialization of wilderness and public space in contemporary America.

Sources

Paula Gunn Allen, "Magic and Realism in the Southwest Borderlands," in David M. Wrobel and Michael C. Steiner, eds., *Many Wests: Place, Culture, and Regional Identity*. Lawrence: University of Kansas Press, 1997.

Loren Baritz, "The Idea of the West," in *The American Historical Review*, vol. 66, no. 3, April 1961.

Frank Bergon and Zeese Papanikolas, eds., *Looking Far West: The Search for the American West in History, Myth, and Literature*. New York: Meridian/New American Library, 1978.

Robert V. Hine and John Mack Faragher, *The American West: A New Interpretive History*. New Haven: Yale University Press, 2000.

Krishan Kumar, *Utopia and Anti-Utopia in Modern Times*. Oxford: Basil Blackwell, 1987.

Clyde A. Milner II, Carol A. O'Connor, and Martha A. Sandweiss, eds., *The Oxford History of the American West*. New York: Oxford University Press, 1994.

"Old Man Coyote Makes the World," in Richard Erdoes and Alfonso Ortiz, eds., *American Indian Myths and Legends*. New York: Pantheon Books, 1984.

BEFORE READING

- Write a journal entry in which you describe your own experience with the myth of the frontier. What books, movies, television shows—or personal encounters—have helped to shape your understanding of what the frontier means in American culture?

- Analyze the ad for Buffalo Bill Cody's Wild West show that serves as the frontispiece to this chapter (p. 676). How would you characterize the figure of Cody in this ad? What is conveyed by his facial features and expression? By his posture, the way he holds his rifle, and his dress? What do you make of the other elements of the image—the tepees, western landscape, and Cody's horse? Overall, what does this poster tell its audience about the myth of the West?

From *"The Significance of the Frontier in American History"*

FREDERICK JACKSON TURNER

When Frederick Jackson Turner arrived in Chicago to participate in the World's Columbian Exposition in 1893, the United States was little more than a century old and already on the way to becoming a leader in global business and political affairs. Dubbed "White City" by its promoters, the exposition offered visitors from around the world an unstinting celebration of progress, with exhibits touting America's expansive natural resources and recent technological innovations. The scholarly paper Turner came to deliver echoed this spirit of national pride and progressivism. In "The Significance of the Frontier in American History," Turner announced the "closing" of the American frontier and the end of the frontier era. In doing so, he argued that the experience of the frontier — and not the influence of Europe — had been the primary force in shaping American history and national character. The "primitive" conditions of western settlement had, in Turner's view, "Americanized" European immigrants and created a new kind of person to inhabit the New World. Although it stirred little reaction when it was first delivered, Turner's "frontier thesis" had a lasting impact on American historical studies and popular folklore. Accepted as unassailable fact for more than a quarter of a century, his optimistic vision of the American West as a liberating force reassured generations that America was always the "land of the free and the home of the brave." Until his death in 1932, Turner published widely and taught at the University of Wisconsin and at Harvard University.

In a recent bulletin of the superintendent of the census for 1890 appear these significant words: "Up to and including 1880 the country had a frontier of settlement, but at present the unsettled area has been so broken into by isolated bodies of settlement that there can hardly be said to be a frontier line. In the discussion of its extent, its westward movement, etc., it cannot, therefore, any longer have a place in the census reports." This brief official statement marks the closing of a great historic movement. Up to our own day American history has been in a large degree the history of the colonization of the Great West. The existence of an area of free land, its continuous recession, and the advance of American settlement westward explain American development.

Behind institutions, behind constitutional forms and modifications, lie the vital forces that call these organs into life and shape them to meet changing conditions. The peculiarity of American institutions is the fact that they have been compelled to adapt themselves to the changes of an expanding people—to the changes involved in crossing a continent, in winning a wilderness, and in developing at each area of this progress, out of the primitive economic and political conditions of the frontier, the complexity of city life. Said Calhoun[1] in 1817, "We are great, and rapidly—I was about to say fearfully—growing!" So saying, he touched the distinguishing feature of American life. All peoples show development.... In the case of most nations, however, the development has occurred in a limited area; and if the nation has expanded, it has met other growing peoples whom it has conquered. But in the case of the United States we have a different phenomenon. Limiting our attention to the Atlantic coast, we have the familiar phenomenon of the evolution of institutions in a limited area, such as the rise of representative government; the differentiation of simple colonial governments into complex organs; the progress from primitive industrial society, without division of labor, up to manufacturing civilization. But we have in addition to this *a recurrence of the process of evolution in each Western area reached in the process of expansion.* Thus American development has exhibited not merely advance along a single line but a return to primitive conditions on a continually advancing frontier line, and a new development for that area. American social development has been continually beginning over again on the frontier. This perennial rebirth, this fluidity of American life, this expansion westward with its new opportunities, its continuous touch with the simplicity of primitive society, furnish the forces dominating American character. The true point of view in the history of this nation is not the Atlantic coast, it is the Great West. Even the slavery struggle, which is made so exclusive an object of attention by writers like Professor von Holst, occupies its important place in American history because of its relation to westward expansion.

In this advance the frontier is the outer edge of the wave—the meeting point between savagery and civilization. Much has been written about the frontier from the point of view of border warfare and the chase, but as a field for the serious study of the economist and the historian it has been neglected.

What is the [American] frontier? It is not the European frontier—a fortified boundary line running through dense populations. The most significant thing about it is that it lies at the hither edge of free land. In the census reports it is treated as the margin of that settlement which has a density of two or more to the square mile. The term is an elastic one, and for our purpose does not need sharp definition. We shall consider the whole frontier belt, including the Indian country and the outer margin of the "settled area" of the census reports. This paper will make no attempt to treat the

[1]*Calhoun:* John Caldwell Calhoun (1782–1850), American statesman and vice president from 1825 to 1832.

subject exhaustively; its aim is simply to call attention to the frontier as a fertile field for investigation, and to suggest some of the problems which arise in connection with it.

...The frontier is the line of most rapid and effective Americanization. The wilderness masters the colonist. It finds him a European in dress, industries, tools, modes of travel, and thought. It takes him from the railroad car and puts him in the birch canoe. It strips off the garments of civilization, and arrays him in the hunting shirt and the moccasin. It puts him in the log cabin of the Cherokee and the Iroquois, and runs an Indian palisade around him. Before long he has gone to planting Indian corn and plowing with a sharp stick; he shouts the war cry and takes the scalp in orthodox Indian fashion. In short, at the frontier the environment is at first too strong for the man. He must accept the conditions which it furnishes, or perish, and so he fits himself into the Indian clearings and follows the Indian trails. Little by little he transforms the wilderness, but the outcome is not the old Europe.... The fact is that here is a new product that is American. At first the frontier was the Atlantic coast. It was the frontier of Europe in a very real sense. Moving westward, the frontier became more and more American. *As successive terminal moraines result from successive glaciations, so each frontier leaves its traces behind it, and when it becomes a settled area the region still partakes of the frontier characteristics.* Thus the advance of the frontier has meant a steady movement away from the influence of Europe, a steady growth of independence on American lines. And to study this advance, the men who grew up under these conditions, and the political, economic, and social results of it, is to study the really American part of our history....

The Indian Trader's Frontier

... The effect of the Indian frontier as a consolidating agent in our history is important. From the close of the seventeenth century various intercolonial congresses have been called to treat with the Indians and establish common measures of defense. Particularism was strongest in colonies with no Indian frontier. This frontier stretched along the western border like a cord of union. The Indian was a common danger, demanding united action. Most celebrated of these conferences was the Albany Congress of 1754, called to treat with the Six Nations, and to consider plans of union. Even a cursory reading of the plan proposed by the Congress reveals the importance of the frontier. The powers of the general council and the officers were, chiefly, the determination of peace and war with the Indians, the regulation of Indian trade, the purchase of Indian lands, and the creation and government of new settlements as a security against the Indians. It is evident that the unifying tendencies of the Revolutionary period were facilitated by the previous co-operation in the regulation of the frontier. In this connection may be mentioned the importance of the frontier, from that day to this, as a military training school, keeping alive the power of resistance to aggression, and developing the stalwart and rugged qualities of the frontiersman....

Land

The exploitation of the beasts took hunter and trader to the West, the exploitation of the grasses took the rancher West, the exploitation of the virgin soil of the river valleys and prairies attracted the farmer. Good soils have been the most continuous attraction to the farmer's frontier. The land hunger of the Virginians drew them down the rivers into Carolina, in early colonial days; the search for soils took the Massachusetts men to Pennsylvania and to New York. As the Eastern lands were taken up, migration flowed across them to the West. Daniel Boone, the great backwoodsman, who combined the occupations of hunter, trader, cattle-raiser, farmer, and surveyor—learning, probably from the traders, of the fertility of the lands on the upper Yadkin, where the traders were wont to rest as they took their way to the Indians—left his Pennsylvania home with his father, and passed down the Great Valley road to that stream. Learning from a trader of its game and the rich pastures of Kentucky, he pioneered the way for the farmers to that region. Thence he passed to the frontier of Missouri, where his settlement was long a landmark on the frontier. Here again he helped to open the way for civilization, finding salt licks, and trails, and land. His son was among the earliest trappers in the passes of the Rocky Mountains, and his party are said to have been the first to camp on the present site of Denver. His grandson, Colonel A. J. Boone of Colorado, was a power among the Indians of the Rocky Mountains, and was appointed an agent by the government. Kit Carson's mother was a Boone. Thus this family epitomizes the backwoodsman's advance across the continent.

The farmer's advance came in a distinct series of waves. In Peck's *New Guide to the West,* published in Cincinnati in 1837, occurs this suggestive passage:

> Generally, in all the western settlements, three classes, like the waves of the ocean, have rolled one after the other. First, comes the pioneer, who depends for the subsistence of his family chiefly upon the natural growth of vegetation, called the "range," and the proceeds of hunting. His implements of agriculture are rude, chiefly of his own make, and his efforts directed mainly to a crop of corn and a "truck patch." The last is a rude garden for growing cabbage, beans, corn for roasting ears, cucumbers and potatoes. A log cabin and, occasionally, a stable and corn-crib, and a field of a dozen acres, the timber girdled or "deadened," and fenced, are enough for his occupancy. It is quite immaterial whether he ever becomes the owner of the soil. He is the occupant for the time being, pays no rent, and feels as independent as the "lord of the manor." With a horse, cow, and one or two breeders of swine, he strikes into the woods with his family, and becomes the founder of a

new county, or perhaps state. He builds his cabin, gathers around him a few other families of similar tastes and habits, and occupies till the range is somewhat subdued, and hunting a little precarious, or, which is more frequently the case, till neighbors crowd around, roads, bridges, and fields annoy him, and he lacks elbow room. The pre-emption law enables him to dispose of his cabin and corn-field to the next class of emigrants, and, to employ his own figures, he "breaks for the high timber," "clears out for the New Purchase," or migrates to Arkansas, or Texas, to work the same process over.

The new class of emigrants purchase the lands, add field to field, clear out the roads, throw rough bridges over the streams, put up hewn log houses, with glass windows, and brick or stone chim-neys, occasionally plant orchards, build mills, school-houses, court-houses, etc., and exhibit the picture and forms of plain, frugal, civilized life.

Another wave rolls on. The men of capital and enterprise come. The "settler" is ready to sell out, and take the advantage of the rise of property—push farther into the interior, and become, himself, a man of capital and enterprise in turn. The small village rises to a spacious town or city; substantial edifices of brick, extensive fields, orchards, gardens, colleges and churches are seen. Broadcloths, silks, leghorns, crapes, and all the refinements, luxuries, elegancies, frivolities and fashions are in vogue. Thus wave after wave is rolling westward:—the real *Eldorado* is still farther on.

A portion of the two first classes remain stationary amidst the gen-eral movement, improve their habits and condition and rise in the scale of society.

The writer has traveled much amongst the first class—the real pi-oneers. He has lived many years in connection with the second grade; and now the third wave is sweeping over large districts of Indiana, Illi-nois and Missouri. Migration has become almost a habit in the West. Hundreds of men can be found, not over fifty years of age, who have settled for the fourth, fifth or sixth time on a new spot. To sell out, and remove only a few hundred miles, makes up a portion of the variety of backwoods life and manners.

Omitting those of the pioneer farmers who move from the love of ad-venture, the advance of the more steady farmer is easy to understand. Obvi-ously the immigrant was attracted by the cheap lands of the frontier, and even the native farmer felt their influence strongly. Year by year the farmers who lived on soil, whose returns were diminished by unrotated crops, were offered the virgin soil of the frontier at nominal prices. Their growing fami-lies demanded more lands, and these were dear. The competition of the un-exhausted, cheap, and easily tilled prairie lands compelled the farmer either to go West and continue the exhaustion of the soil on a new frontier or to adopt intensive culture. Thus the census of 1890 shows, in the Northwest, many counties in which there is an absolute, or a relative, decrease of popu-lation. These states have been sending farmers to advance the frontier on the plains, and have themselves begun to turn to intensive farming and to manufacture. A decade before this, Ohio had shown the same transition stage. Thus the demand for land and the love of wilderness freedom drew the frontier ever onward.

Having now roughly outlined the various kinds of frontiers, and their 10 modes of advance, chiefly from the point of view of the frontier itself, we may next inquire what were the influences on the East and on the Old World. A rapid enumeration of some of the more noteworthy effects is all that I have time for.

Composite Nationality

First, we note that the frontier promoted the formation of a composite nationality for the American people. The coast was preponderantly English, but the later tides of continental immigration flowed across to the free lands. This was the case from the early colonial days. The Scotch-Irish and the Palatine Germans, or "Pennsylvania Dutch," furnished dominant elements in the stock of the colonial frontier. With these peoples were also the freed indented servants, or redemptioners,[2] who at the expiration of their time of service passed to the frontier. Governor Alexander Spotswood of Virginia writes in 1717, "The Inhabitants of our frontiers are composed generally of such as have been transported hither as Servants, and being out of their time, and settle themselves where Land is to be taken up and that will produce the necessarys of Life with little Labour." Very generally these redemptioners were of non-English stock. In the crucible of the frontier the immigrants were Americanized, liberated, and fused into a mixed race, English in neither nationality nor characteristics. The process has gone on from the early days to our own. Burke and other writers in the middle of the eighteenth century believed that Pennsylvania was threatened with the "danger of being wholly foreign in language, manners, and perhaps even inclinations." The German and Scotch-Irish elements in the frontier of the South were only less great. In the middle of the present century the German element in Wisconsin was already so considerable that leading publicists looked to the creation of a German state out of the commonwealth by concentrating their colonization. Such examples teach us to beware of misinterpreting the fact that there is a common English speech in America into a belief that the stock is also English....

Growth of Democracy

But the most important effect of the frontier has been in the promotion of democracy here and in Europe. As has been pointed out, the frontier is productive of individualism. Complex society is precipitated by the wilder-

---

[2]*indented servants, or redemptioners:* Immigrants who had sold themselves for a set period of time in order to secure their passage to America.

ness into a kind of primitive organization based on the family. The tendency is anti-social. It produces antipathy to control, and particularly to any direct control. The tax-gatherer is viewed as a representative of oppression. Professor Osgood, in an able article, has pointed out that the frontier conditions prevalent in the colonies are important factors in the explanation of the American Revolution, where individual liberty was sometimes confused with absence of all effective government. The same conditions aid in explaining the difficulty of instituting a strong government in the period of the confederacy. The frontier individualism has from the beginning promoted democracy.

The frontier states that came into the Union in the first quarter of a century of its existence came in with democratic suffrage provisions,[3] and had reactive effects of the highest importance upon the older states whose peoples were being attracted there. It was *western* New York that forced an extension of suffrage in the constitutional convention of that state in 1821; and it was *western* Virginia that compelled the tidewater region to put a more liberal suffrage provision in the constitution framed in 1830, and to give to the frontier region a more nearly proportionate representation with the tidewater aristocracy. The rise of democracy as an effective force in the nation came in with Western preponderance under Jackson and William Henry Harrison, and it meant the triumph of the frontier—with all of its good and with all of its evil elements.

An interesting illustration of the tone of frontier democracy in 1830 comes from the debates in the Virginia convention already referred to. A representative from western Virginia declared: "But, sir, it is not the increase of population in the West which this gentleman ought to fear. It is the energy which the mountain breeze and western habits impart to those emigrants. They are regenerated, politically I mean, sir. They soon become *working politicians;* and the difference, sir, between a *talking* and a *working* politician is immense. The Old Dominion has long been celebrated for producing great orators; the ablest metaphysicians in policy; men that can split hairs in all abstruse questions of political economy. But at home, or when they return from congress, they have negroes to fan them asleep. But a Pennsylvania, a New York, an Ohio, or a western Virginia statesman, though far inferior in logic, metaphysics and rhetoric to an old Virginia statesman, has this advantage, that when he returns home he takes off his coat and takes hold of the plough. This gives him bone and muscle, sir, and preserves his republican principles pure and uncontaminated." ...

Intellectual Traits

From the conditions of frontier life came intellectual traits of profound   15
importance. The works of travelers along each frontier from colonial days onward describe for each certain traits, and these traits have, while soften-

---

[3]*democratic suffrage provisions:* Amendments allowing white males to vote.

ing down, still persisted as survivals in the place of their origin, even when a higher social organization succeeded. The result is that to the frontier the American intellect owes its striking characteristics. That coarseness and strength combined with acuteness and inquisitiveness, that practical, inventive turn of mind, quick to find expedients, that masterful grasp of material things, lacking in the artistic but powerful to effect great ends, that restless, nervous energy, that dominant individualism, working for good and for evil, and withal that buoyancy and exuberance which comes with freedom, these are traits of the frontier, or traits called out elsewhere because of the existence of the frontier. Since the days when the fleet of Columbus sailed into the waters of the New World, America has been another name for opportunity, and the people of the United States have taken their tone from the incessant expansion which has not only been open but has even been forced upon them. He would be a rash prophet who should assert that the expansive character of American life has now entirely ceased. Movement has been its dominant fact, and, unless this training has no effect upon a people, the American intellect will continually demand a wider field for its exercise. But never again will such gifts of free land offer themselves. For a moment at the frontier the bonds of custom are broken, and unrestraint is triumphant. There is not *tabula rasa*.[4] The stubborn American environment is there with its imperious summons to accept its conditions; the inherited ways of doing things are also there; and yet, in spite of environment, and in spite of custom, each frontier did indeed furnish a new field of opportunity, a gate of escape from the bondage of the past; and freshness, and confidence, and scorn of older society, impatience of its restraints and its ideas, and indifference to its lessons, have accompanied the frontier. What the Mediterranean Sea was to the Greeks, breaking the bond of custom, offering new experiences, calling out new institutions and activities, that, and more, the ever retreating frontier has been to the United States directly, and to the nations of Europe more remotely. And now, four centuries from the discovery of America, at the end of a hundred years of life under the Constitution, the frontier has gone, and with its going has closed the first period of American history.

ENGAGING THE TEXT

1. How does Turner define the concept of the frontier? What, in his view, distinguishes the frontier from the eastern seaboard of the United States? What role, according to Turner, did the frontier play in the process of "Americanization"? Why?

2. What effect did the "Indian Frontier" have on the development of the United States? What motivations drove settlers westward, according to Turner?

---

[4]*tabula rasa:* Latin for "blank slate," meaning a mind without prior knowledge.

3. How did the frontier shape American character and culture, according to Turner? Overall, what does Turner see as the meaning of the frontier for America?

EXPLORING CONNECTIONS

4. Review "Race at the End of History" by Ronald Takaki (p. 383), paying close attention to his discussion of Turner and the economic and social context surrounding the conception of his "frontier thesis." According to Takaki, what motive did Turner have for propounding this vision of the American frontier? How might Turner account for social conditions in the United States at the end of the nineteenth century?

5. Compare Turner's view of "composite nationality" with the models of assimilation offered by George M. Fredrickson in "Models of American Ethnic Relations: A Historical Perspective" (p. 598). Which one of Fredrickson's models does Turner's view of assimilation most nearly resemble? Which ethnic or racial groups does Turner exclude from his discussion of cultural amalgamation along the frontier?

EXTENDING THE CRITICAL CONTEXT

6. Working in groups, research the frontier history of any of the ethnic or racial groups that Turner omits in his portrayal of American settlement and report your findings to class. What role did these groups play in the settlement of the American West?

7. What evidence do you find in contemporary American society for the continued influence of the more radical, antigovernment attitudes that Turner believed to be associated with frontier life?

Three Thousand Dollar Death Song

WENDY ROSE

This poem is a proud song of protest against the assumption that the lands of the West were free for the taking. It is also a chilling inventory of how costly the European invasion of the New World was for its original inhabitants. Wendy Rose (b. 1948) is a Hopi-Miwok poet, visual artist, editor, and anthropologist. She currently serves as coordinator of American Indian studies at Fresno City College. Twice nominated for the Pulitzer Prize in poetry, Rose is the author of eight volumes of poetry, including Going to War with All My Relations: New and Selected Poems *(1993) and* Bone Dance:

New and Selected Poems 1965–1993 *(1995). This poem is from the most acclaimed collection of her poetry,* Lost Copper *(1980), which was nominated for an American Book Award.*

> Nineteen American Indian Skeletons from Nevada
> . . . valued at $3000 . . .
> — MUSEUM INVOICE, 1975

Is it in cold hard cash? the kind
that dusts the insides of men's pockets
lying silver-polished surface along the cloth.
Or in bills? papering the wallets of they
who thread the night with dark words. Or   5
checks? paper promises weighing the same
as words spoken once on the other side
of the grown grass and damned rivers
of history. However it goes, it goes
Through my body it goes   10
assessing each nerve, running its edges
along my arteries, planning ahead
for whose hands will rip me
into pieces of dusty red paper,
whose hands will smooth or smatter me   15
into traces of rubble. Invoiced now,
it's official how our bones are valued
that stretch out pointing to sunrise
or are flexed into one last foetal bend,[1]
that are removed and tossed about,   20
catalogued, numbered with black ink
on newly-white foreheads.
As we were formed to the white soldier's voice,
so we explode under white students' hands.
Death is a long trail of days   25
in our fleshless prison.

From this distant point we watch our bones
auctioned with our careful beadwork,
our quilled medicine bundles, even the bridles
of our shot-down horses. You: who have   30
priced us, you who have removed us: at what cost?

---

[1]*foetal bend:* Throughout history, many cultures have buried their dead in a curled position resembling that of a fetus.

What price the pits where our bones share
a single bit of memory, how one century
turns our dead into specimens, our history
into dust, our survivors into clowns.   35
Our memory might be catching, you know;
picture the mortars,[2] the arrowheads, the labrets[3]
shaking off their labels like bears
suddenly awake to find the seasons have ended
while they slept. Watch them touch each other,   40
measure reality, march out the museum door!
Watch as they lift their faces
and smell about for us; watch our bones rise
to meet them and mount the horses once again!
The cost, then, will be paid   45
for our sweetgrass-smelling having-been
in clam shell beads and steatite,[4]
dentalia[5] and woodpecker scalp, turquoise
and copper, blood and oil, coal
and uranium, children, a universe   50
of stolen things.

ENGAGING THE TEXT

1. What do the Indian skeletons mentioned in the epigraph represent?

2. What is the "distant point" Rose mentions in the second stanza?

3. What item seems unusual or out of place in the catalog of "stolen things" that ends the poem? Why does Rose include it in the list? In what ways were all these things stolen from the Indians?

4. How do time, place, and point of view shift in the poem? How do these shifts contribute to the poem's meaning?

5. A cynical reader might dismiss lines 36–51 as an empty threat: after all, the bones of slain warriors will not literally rise again and remount their horses. What symbolic or rhetorical purposes might these lines serve?

EXPLORING CONNECTIONS

6. How does Rose's poem call into question the concept of "free land" as it is presented in Frederick Jackson Turner's view of the frontier (p. 683)? What alternative view of western settlement does she offer in this poem?

---

[2]*mortars:* Bowl-shaped vessels.
[3]*labrets:* Ornaments of wood or bone worn in holes pierced through the lip.
[4]*steatite:* A soft, easily carved stone; soapstone.
[5]*dentalia:* A type of mollusk shell resembling a tooth.

EXTENDING THE CRITICAL CONTEXT

7. Play the role of museum director. Write a letter to the *Reno Times* explaining and defending your museum's purchase of the skeletons. Make up any circumstances you think plausible. Then evaluate the effectiveness of your defense.

8. Investigate a museum in your area with an American Indian collection. What is displayed for public view, and how? What further materials are reserved for research or special exhibits? Has there been any controversy over rightful ownership of skeletons or artifacts? Report your findings to the class.

The Twilight of Self-Reliance: Frontier Values and Contemporary America

WALLACE STEGNER

Wallace Stegner was by his own admission a "wild man from the West." Born in Iowa in 1905, Stegner spent the first half of his childhood on a hardscrabble homestead in Saskatchewan and the second half wandering with his family from town to town across some eighteen western American states. In a 1950 essay called "Why I Like the West," Stegner summed himself up like this:

> *I have been breezy, frank, healthy, relaxed, with a drawling soul and an open heart and a friendly smile. I have obediently liked my beef well done and my r's hard and have let it be known that I eat fried potatoes with my scrambled eggs for breakfast.... I have served as a self-appointed evangelist to rescue unfortunate eastern heathens from the climate, topography, theology, prejudices, literature, railroads, traditions, narrowness, and geographical ignorance that are their heritage. I have not always been thanked, but I have been earnest.*

Stegner's love of all things western expressed itself most eloquently in more than fifteen novels, twelve works of nonfiction, and literally hundreds of short stories and essays during a writing career that spanned fifty-five years. A historian, biographer, professor of American literature, founder of the Stanford Writing Program, and recipient of the Pulitzer Prize and the National Book Award, Stegner was perhaps the most prolific spokesman for traditional western values in the twentieth century. In this selection, originally delivered as a Tanner Lecture on Human Values at the University of Utah in 1980, Stegner provides a historical context for understanding the emergence of the self-reliant frontiersman, the forerunner of the cowboy and the model of the American hero to this day.

1

Henry David Thoreau was a philosopher not unwilling to criticize his country and his countrymen, but when he wrote the essay entitled "Walking" in 1862, at a time when his country was engaged in a desperate civil war, he wrote with what Mark Twain would have called the calm confidence of a Christian with four aces. He spoke America's stoutest self-confidence and most optimistic expectations. Eastward, he said, he walked only by force, but westward he walked free: he must walk toward Oregon and not toward Europe, and his trust in the future was total.

> If the moon looks larger here than in Europe, probably the sun looks larger also. If the heavens of America appear infinitely higher, and the stars brighter, I trust that these facts are symbolical of the height to which the philosophy and poetry and religion of her inhabitants may one day soar.... I trust that we shall be more imaginative, that our thoughts will be clearer, fresher, and more ethereal, as our sky— our understanding more comprehensive and broader, like our plains— our intellect generally on a grander scale, like our thunder and lightning, our rivers and mountains and forests—and our hearts shall even correspond in breadth and depth and grandeur to our inland seas. Perchance there will appear to the traveler something, he knows not what, of *laeta* and *glabra,* of joyous and serene, in our very faces. Else to what end does the world go on, and why was America discovered?

The question was rhetorical; he knew the answer. To an American of his generation it was unthinkable that the greatest story in the history of civilized man—the finding and peopling of the New World—and the greatest opportunity since the Creation—the chance to remake men and their society into something cleansed of past mistakes, and closer to the heart's desire—should end as one more betrayal of human credulity and hope.

Some moderns find that idea perfectly thinkable....Popular books which attempt to come to grips with American values in these times walk neither toward Oregon nor toward Europe, but toward dead ends and jumping-off places. They bear such titles as *The Lonely Crowd, The Organization Man, Future Shock, The Culture of Narcissism.* This last, subtitled "American Life in an Age of Diminishing Expectations," reports "a way of life that is dying—the culture of competitive individualism, which in its decadence has carried the logic of individualism to the extreme of a war of all against all, the pursuit of happiness to the dead end of a narcissistic preoccupation with the self." It describes "a political system in which public lying has become endemic and routine," and a typical citizen who is haunted by anxiety and spends his time trying to find a meaning in his life. "His sexual attitudes are permissive rather than puritanical, even though his emancipation from ancient taboos brings him no sexual peace....Acquisitive in the sense that his cravings have no limits, he does not accumulate goods and provisions against the future, in the manner of the acquisitive individualist of the nineteenth-century political economy, but demands immediate gratification and lives in a state of restless, perpetually unsatisfied desire."

Assuming that Thoreau spoke for his time, as he surely did, and that Chistopher Lasch[1] speaks for at least elements and aspects of his, how did we get from there to here in little more than a century? Have the sturdiness of the American character and the faith in America's destiny that Thoreau took for granted been eroded entirely away? What happened to confidence, what happened to initiative and strenuousness and sobriety and responsibility, what happened to high purpose, what happened to hope? Are they gone, along with the Puritans' fear of pleasure? Was the American future, so clear in Thoreau's day, no more than a reflection of apparently unlimited resources, and does democracy dwindle along with the resources that begot it? Were we never really free, but only rich? In any event, if America was discovered only so that its citizens could pursue pleasure or grope for a meaning in their lives, then Thoreau and Lasch would be in agreement: Columbus should have stood at home.

Even if I knew answers, I could not detail them in an hour's lecture, or   5
in a book. But since I believe that one of our most damaging American traits is our contempt for all history, including our own, I might spend an hour looking backward at what we were and how America changed us. A certain kind of modern American in the throes of an identity crisis is likely to ask, or bleat, "Who am I?" It might help him to find out who he started out to be, and having found that out, to ask himself if what he started out to be is still valid. And if most of what I touch on in this summary is sixth-grade American history, I do not apologize for that. History is not the proper midden for digging up novelties. Perhaps that is one reason why a nation bent on novelty ignores it. The obvious, especially the ignored obvious, is worth more than a Fourth of July or Bicentennial look.

2

Under many names—Atlantis, the Hesperides, Groenland, Brazillia, the Fortunate Isles—America was Europe's oldest dream. Found by Norsemen about the year 1000, it was lost again for half a millennium, and only emerged into reality at the beginning of the modern era, which we customarily date from the year 1500. There is even a theory, propounded by the historian Walter Webb in *The Great Frontier*, that the new world cre-

---

[1]*Christopher Lasch:* American sociologist (1932–1994).

ated the modern era—stimulated its birth, funded it, fueled it, fed it, gave it its impetus and direction and state of mind, formed its expectations and institutions, and provided it with a prosperity unexampled in history, a boom that lasted fully four hundred years. If Professor Webb pushes his thesis a little hard, and if it has in it traces of the logical fallacy known as *post hoc, ergo propter hoc*,[2] it still seems to me provocative and in some ways inescapable, and Webb seems entirely justified in beginning his discussion of America in medieval Europe. I shall do the same.

Pre-Columbian Europe, then. For one hundred and fifty years it has been living close to the limit of its resources. It is always short of money, which means gold and silver, flat money being still in the future. Its land is frozen in the structures of feudalism, owned by the crown, the church, and an aristocracy whose domains are shielded by laws of primogeniture[3] and entail[4] from sale or subdivision—from everything except the royal whim which gave, and can take away. Its food supply comes from sources that cannot be expanded, and its population, periodically reduced by the Black Death, is static or in decline. Peasants are bound to the soil, and both they and their masters are tied by feudal loyalties and obligations. Except among the powerful, individual freedom is not even a dream. Merchants, the guilds, and the middle class generally, struggle against the arrogance of the crown and an aristocracy dedicated to the anachronistic code of chivalry, which is often indistinguishable from brigandage. Faith is invested in a politicized, corrupt, but universal church just breaking up in the Reformation that will drown Europe in blood. Politics are a nest of snakes: ambitious nobles against ambitious kings, kings against pretenders and against each other, all of them trying to fill, by means of wars and strategic marriages, the periodic power vacuums created by the cracking of the Holy Roman Empire. The late Middle Ages still look on earthly life as a testing and preparation for the Hereafter. Fed on this opium, the little individual comes to expect his reward in heaven, or in the neck. Learning is just beginning to open out from scholastic rationalism[5] into the empiricism of the Renaissance. Science, with all it will mean to men's lives and ways of thinking, has barely pipped its shell.

Out of this closed world Columbus sails in 1492 looking for a new route to Asia, whose jewels and silks are coveted by Europe's elite, and whose spices are indispensable to nations with no means of preserving food except smoking and salting, and whose meat is often eaten high.[6] The voyage of the

---

[2]*post hoc, ergo propter hoc:* Latin for "after this, therefore because of this," denoting the logical fallacy of assuming that one event causes another simply because it precedes it in time.

[3]*primogeniture:* Traditional European system in which the elder son inherits all of a family's estate.

[4]*entail:* To be limited by the type of person who can inherit land.

[5]*scholastic rationalism:* The educational approach that dominated Catholic universities during the late Middle Ages and early Renaissance.

[6]*eaten high:* Eaten when slightly spoiled.

three tiny ships is full of anxiety and hardship, but the end is miracle, one of those luminous moments in history: an after-midnight cry from the lookout on the *Pinta,* Columbus and his sailors crowding to the decks, and in the soft tropical night, by the light of a moon just past full, staring at a dark ambiguous shore and sniffing the perfumed breeze off an utterly new world.

Not Asia. Vasco da Gama will find one way to that, Magellan another. What Columbus has found is puzzling, of unknown size and unknown relation to anything. The imagination has difficulty taking it in. Though within ten years of Columbus' first voyage Vespucci will demonstrate that the Americas are clearly not Asia, Europe is a long time accepting the newness of the new world. Pedro de Castañeda, crossing the plains of New Mexico, Oklahoma, and Kansas with Coronado in 1541, is confident that they make one continuous land mass with China and Peru; and when Champlain sends Jean Nicolet to explore among the Nipissings on the way to Georgian Bay and the great interior lakes in 1635—133 years after Vespucci—Nicolet will take along in his bark canoe an embroidered mandarin robe, just in case, out on those wild rivers among those wide forests, he should come to the palace of the Great Khan and need ceremonial dress.

Understanding is a slow dawning, each exploration bringing a little   10
more light. But when the dawn arrives, it is a blazing one. It finds its way through every door and illuminates every cellar and dungeon in Europe. Though the discovery of America is itself part of Europe's awakening, and results from purely European advances—foreshadowings of Copernican astronomy,[7] a method for determining latitude, the development of the caravel[8] and the lateen sail[9]—the new world responds by accelerating every stir of curiosity, science, adventure, individualism, and hope in the old.

Because Europe has always dreamed westward, America, once realized, touches men's minds like fulfilled prophecy. It has lain out there in the gray wastes of the Atlantic, not only a continent waiting to be discovered, but a fable waiting to be agreed upon. It is not unrelated to the Hereafter. Beyond question, before it is half known, it will breed utopias and noble savages, fantasies of Perfection, New Jerusalems.[10]

Professor Webb believes that to closed and limited Europe America came as a pure windfall, a once-in-the-history-of-the-world opportunity. Consider only one instance: the gold that Sir Francis Drake looted from Spanish galleons was the merest fragment of a tithe of what the Spaniards had looted from Mexico and Peru; and yet Queen Elizabeth out of her one-fifth royal share of the *Golden Hind's* plunder was able to pay off the entire

[7]*Copernican astronomy:* The heliocentric theory of the solar system formulated by Nicholas Copernicus (1473–1543), as opposed to the older, earth-centered Ptolemaic system.

[8]*caravel:* A small fifteenth- or sixteenth-century sailing vessel with a broad bow and a high, narrow stern.

[9]*lateen sail:* A triangular, as opposed to a square, sail.

[10]*New Jerusalems:* Refers to the Puritan view of the New World as the site of a future holy land.

national debt of England and have enough left to help found the East India Company.

Perhaps, as Milton Friedman[11] would insist, increasing the money supply only raised prices. Certainly American gold didn't help Europe's poor. It made the rich richer and kings more powerful and wars more implacable. Nevertheless, trickling outward from Spain as gift or expenditure, or taken from its ships by piracy, that gold affected all of Europe, stimulating trade and discovery, science, invention, everything that we associate with the unfolding of the Renaissance. It surely helped take European eyes off the Hereafter, and it did a good deal toward legitimizing the profit motive. And as the French and English, and to a lesser extent the Dutch and Swedes, began raiding America, other and more substantial riches than gold flooded back: new food plants, especially Indian corn and the potato, which revolutionized eating habits and brought on a steep rise in population that lasted more than a century; furs; fish from the swarming Newfoundland banks, especially important to countries still largely Catholic; tobacco for the indulgence of a fashionable new habit; timber for ships and masts; sugar and rum from the West Indies.

Those spoils alone might have rejuvenated Europe. But there was something else, at first not valued or exploited, that eventually would lure Europeans across the Atlantic and transform them. The most revolutionary gift of the new world was land itself, and the independence and aggressiveness that land ownership meant. Land, unoccupied and unused except by savages who in European eyes did not count, land available to anyone with the initiative to take it, made America, Opportunity, and Freedom synonymous terms.

But only later. The early comers were raiders, not settlers. The first Spanish towns were beachheads from which to scour the country for treasure, the first French settlements on the St. Lawrence were beachheads of the fur trade. Even the English on Roanoke Island, and later at Jamestown, though authentic settlers, were hardly pioneers seeking the promised land. Many were bond servants and the scourings of debtors' prisons. They did not come, they were sent. Their hope of working off their bondage and starting new in a new country was not always rewarded, either. Bruce and William Catton[12] estimate that eight out of ten indentured servants freed to make new lives in America failed—returned to pauperism, or became the founders of a poor-white class, or died of fevers trying to compete with black slaves on tobacco or sugar plantations, or turned outlaw.

Nevertheless, for the English who at Jamestown and Plymouth and the Massachusetts Bay Colony began to take ownership of American land in the early seventeenth century, land was the transfiguring gift. The historian who

[11]*Milton Friedman:* Twentieth-century American economist (b. 1912).

[12]*Bruce and William Catton:* Bruce (1899–1978) and William (b. 1926), father-and-son American historians.

remarked that the entire history of the United States could be read in terms of real estate was not simply making words.

Here was an entire continent which, by the quaint assumptions of the raiders, was owned by certain absentee crowned heads whose subjects had made the first symbolic gesture of claiming it. They had rowed a boat into a rivermouth, sighted and named a cape, raised a cross on a beach, buried a brass plate, or harangued a crowd of bewildered Indians. Therefore Ferdinand and Isabella, or Elizabeth, or Louis[13] owned from that point to the farthest boundary in every direction. But land without people was valueless. The Spaniards imported the *encomienda* system — that is, transplanted feudalism — and used the Indians as peons. The French built only forts at which to collect the wilderness wealth of furs. But the English were another kind, and they were the ones who created the American pattern.

"Are you ignorant of the difference between the king of England and the king of France?" Duquesne asked the Iroquois in the 1750s. "Go see the forts that our king has established and you will see that you can still hunt under their very walls.... The English, on the contrary, are no sooner in possession of a place than the game is driven away. The forest falls before them as they advance, and the soil is laid bare so that you can scarce find the wherewithal to erect a shelter for the night."

To be made valuable, land must be sold cheap or given away to people who would work it, and out of that necessity was born a persistent American expectation. The very word "claim" that we came to use for a parcel of land reflected our feeling that free or cheap land was a right, and that the land itself was a commodity. The Virginia Company and Lord Calvert both tried to encourage landed estates on the English pattern, and both failed because in America men would not work land unless they owned it, and would not be tied to a proprietor's acres when they could go off into the woods and have any land they wanted, simply for the taking. Their claim might not be strictly legal, but it often held: hence the development of what came to be known as squatters' rights. As Jefferson would later write in *Notes on Virginia*, Europe had an abundance of labor and a dearth of land, America an abundance of land and a dearth of labor. That made all the difference. The opportunity to own land not only freed men, it made labor honorable and opened up the future to hope and the possibility of independence, perhaps of a fortune.

The consequences inform every notion we have of ourselves. Admittedly there were all kinds of people in early America, as there are all kinds in our time — saints and criminals, dreamers and drudges, pushers and con men. But the new world did something similar to all of them. Of the most energetic ones it made ground-floor capitalists; out of nearly everyone it leached the last traces of servility. Cut off from control, ungoverned and vir- 20

---

[13]*Ferdinand and Isabella, or Elizabeth, or Louis:* Monarchs, respectively, of fifteenth-century Spain, England, and France.

tually untaxed, people learned to resent the imposition of authority, even that which they had created for themselves. Dependent on their own strength and ingenuity in a strange land, they learned to dismiss tradition and old habit, or rather, simply forgot them. Up in Massachusetts the idea of the equality of souls before God probably helped promote the idea of earthly equality; the notion of a personal covenant with God made the way easier for social and political agreements such as the Plymouth Compact and eventually the Constitution of the United States. In the observed freedom of the Indian from formal government there may have been a dangerous example for people who had lived under governments notably unjust and oppressive. Freedom itself forced the creation not only of a capitalist economy based on land, but of new forms of social contract. When thirteen loosely allied colonies made common cause against the mother country, the League of the Iroquois may well have provided one model of confederation.

"The rich stay in Europe," wrote Hector St. John de Crèvecoeur[14] before the Revolution. "It is only the middling and poor that emigrate." Middle-class values emigrated with them, and middle-class ambitions. Resentment of aristocrats and class distinctions accompanied the elevation of the work ethic. Hardship, equal opportunity to rise, the need for common defense against the Indians, and the necessity for all to postpone the rewards of labor brought the English colonists to nearly the same level and imbued all but the retarded and the most ne'er-do-well with the impulse of upward mobility. And if the practical need to hew a foothold out of the continent left many of them unlettered and ignorant, that deficiency, combined with pride, often led to the disparagement of cultivation and the cultivated as effete and European. Like work, barbarism and boorishness tended to acquire status, and in some parts of America still retain it.

Land was the base, freedom the consequence. Not even the little parochial tyranny of the Puritans in Massachusetts could be made to stick indefinitely. In fact, the Puritans' chief objection to Roger Williams,[15] when they expelled him, was not his unorthodoxy but his declaration that the Colonists had no right to their lands, the king not having had the right to grant them in the first place. Williams also expressed an early pessimistic view of the American experiment that clashed with prevailing assumptions and forecast future disillusion. "The common trinity of the world—Profit, Preferment, and Pleasure—will be here the tria omnia, as in all the world besides…and God Land will be as great a God with us English as God Gold was with the Spaniard." A sour prophet indeed—altogether too American in his dissenting opinions and his challenging of authority. And right besides. No wonder they chased him off to Rhode Island.

[14]*Hector St. John de Crèvecoeur:* Pen name of Michel-Guillaume-Jean de Crèvecoeur (1731–1813), French essayist famous for his evaluation of colonial American culture in his *Letters from an American Farmer.*

[15]*Roger Williams:* Puritan dissident and founder of the Rhode Island Colony (1603?–1683).

Students of the Revolution have wondered whether it was really British tyranny that lit rebellion, or simply American outrage at the imposition of even the mildest imperial control after decades of benign neglect. Certainly one of George III's worst blunders was his 1763 decree forbidding settlement beyond the crest of the Alleghenies. That was worse than the Stamp Act or the Navigation Acts, for land speculators were already sniffing the western wind. When Daniel Boone took settlers over the Cumberland Gap in 1775 he was working for speculators. George Washington and Benjamin Franklin, who had a good deal to do with the Revolution, both had interests in western land. Only a very revisionist historian would call our Revolution a real-estate rebellion, a revolt of the subdividers, but it did have that aspect.

And very surely, as surely as the endless American forests put a curve in the helves of the axes that chopped them down, the continent worked on those who settled it. From the first frontiers in Virginia and Massachusetts through all the successive frontiers that, as Jefferson said, required Americans to start fresh every generation, America was in the process of creating a democratic, energetic, practical, profit-motivated society that resembled Europe less and less as it worked westward. At the same time, it was creating the complicated creature we spent our first century as a nation learning to recognize and trying to define: the American.

3

who is the real American?

"Who then is the American, this new man?" asked Crèvecoeur, and answered his own question in a book published in 1782 as *Letters from an American Farmer*. We were, he said, a nation of cultivators; and it was the small farmer, the independent, frugal, hard-working, self-respecting freeholder, that he idealized—the same yeoman farmer that only a little later Jefferson would call the foundation of the republic. But out on the fringes of settlement Crèvecoeur recognized another type. Restless, migratory, they lived as much by hunting as by farming, for protecting their crops and stock against wild animals put the gun in their hands, and "once hunters, farewell to the plough. The chase renders them ferocious, gloomy, and unsocial"; they exhibit "a strange sort of lawless profligacy"; and their children, having no models except their parents, "grow up a mongrel breed, half civilized, half savage." …

virtues of frontiersmen

The virtues of the frontiersman, real or literary, are Indian virtues, warrior qualities of bravery, endurance, stoical indifference to pain and hardship, recklessness, contempt for law, a hawk-like need of freedom. Often in practice an outlaw, the frontiersman in literature is likely to display a certain noble savagery, a degree of natural goodness that has a more sophisticated parallel in the common American delusion, shared even by Jefferson, who should have known better, that untutored genius is more to be admired than genius schooled. In the variants of the frontiersman that Henry Nash Smith traces in *Virgin Land*—in flatboatman, logger, cowboy, miner, in lit-

25

erary and mythic figures from the Virginian[16] to the Lone Ranger and Superman—the Indian qualities persist, no matter how overlaid with comedy or occupational detail. Malcolm Cowley[17] has shown how they emerge in a quite different sort of literature in the stiff-upper-lip code hero of Ernest Hemingway.

We need not admire them wholeheartedly in order to recognize them in their modern forms. They put the Winchesters on the gunracks of pickups and the fury into the arguments of the gun lobby. They dictate the leather of Hell's Angels and the whanged buckskin of drugstore Carsons.[18] Our most ruthless industrial, financial, and military buccaneers have displayed them. The Sagebrush Rebellion[19] and those who would open Alaska to a final stage of American continent-busting adopt them as a platform. Without them there would have been no John Wayne movies. At least as much as the sobriety and self-reliant industry of the pioneer farmer, it is the restlessness and intractability of the frontiersman that drives our modern atavists away from civilization into the woods and deserts, there to build their yurts and geodesic domes and live self-reliant lives with no help except from trust funds, unemployment insurance, and food stamps.

This mythic figure lasts. He is a model of conduct of many kinds. He directs our fantasies. Curiously, in almost all his historic forms he is both landless and destructive, his kiss is the kiss of death. The hunter roams the wilderness but owns none of it. As Daniel Boone, he served the interests of speculators and capitalists; even as Henry David Thoreau he ended his life as a surveyor of town lots. As mountain man he was virtually a bond servant to the company, and his indefatigable labors all but eliminated the beaver and undid all the conservation work of beaver engineering. The logger achieved his roughhouse liberty within the constraints of a brutally punishing job whose result was the enrichment of great capitalist families such as the Weyerhausers and the destruction of most of the magnificent American forests. The cowboy, so mythically free in books and movies, was a hired man on horseback, a slave to cows and the deadliest enemy of the range he used to ride....

The romantic figure of the frontiersman was doomed to pass with the wilderness that made him. He was essentially over by the 1840s, though in parts of the West he lingered on as an anachronism. His epitaph was read, as Frederick Jackson Turner[20] noted in a famous historical essay, by the census of 1890, which found no continuous line of frontier existing anywhere in the United States. He was not the only one who died of that

---

[16]*the Virginian:* Frontiersman-hero of the 1902 novel of the same name by Owen Wister.

[17]*Malcolm Cowley:* American literary critic (1889–1989).

[18]*drugstore Carsons:* Christopher "Kit" Carson was an early-nineteenth-century American frontiersman; hence, "urban cowboys."

[19]*Sagebrush Rebellion:* Movement by several western states from 1979 through 1981 to reclaim federally controlled land for private use.

[20]*Frederick Jackson Turner:* See headnote on page 683.

census report. The pioneer farmer died too, for without a frontier there was no more free land. But whether the qualities that the frontier had built into both frontiersman and farmer died when the line of settlement withered at the edge of the shortgrass plains—that is not so clear.

Engaging the Text

1. What was life like in pre-Columbian Europe, according to the brief historical sketch provided by Stegner? What did the New World offer Europeans by contrast?

2. What role did "free land" play in the formation of Europe's view of the Americas, according to Stegner?

3. In Stegner's view, what is an "American" and how has the frontier experience shaped the American character? What specific characteristics or virtues does he associate with this mythic national character? What is his attitude toward this "heroic" American type?

"If I may say so, sir, that chapeau makes you
look like one tough hombre!"

Exploring Connections

4. Compare Stegner's view of the American character with that of Frederick Jackson Turner (p. 683). To what extent does Stegner's view of the impact of the frontier on what it means to be an American agree with that of Turner?

5. Compare Stegner's description of the heroically self-reliant American with the images of General Colin Powell (p. 305) and Malcolm X (p. 223). Which of these men better fits Stegner's depiction of a distinctly self-reliant form of American heroism? Why?

6. In light of their analyses of gender roles, how might Jackson Katz (p. 466) and Jean Kilbourne (p. 444) interpret the features of the American hero as depicted by Stegner?

7. What does the Gahan Wilson cartoon on page 704 suggest about the current status of the cowboy hero in American culture?

Extending the Critical Context

8. Working in groups, identify an obviously "heroic" figure in a recent American film and discuss to what extent this person projects the qualities Stegner associates with the self-reliant American hero. Do you agree that the "Indian virtues" Stegner associates with the frontiersman still define what it means to be a hero in American popular culture today?

9. Working in groups, discuss Stegner's depiction of European civilization and its relation to American values. How have American attitudes toward Europe changed over the past hundred years? What evidence do you see that "barbarism and boorishness" still have status in American culture?

Dear John Wayne

Louise Erdrich

Most stories of the American frontier neglect the perspective of the peoples who were displaced by the westward expansion of the United States. This contemporary poem, about a group of Native Americans watching a John Wayne movie at a drive-in, questions some of the assumptions about frontier history and heroism found in earlier readings. Louise Erdrich (b. 1954) is one of America's premier contemporary novelists. The author of four best-sellers, Love Medicine *(1984),* The Beet Queen *(1986),* Tracks *(1988), and* The Crown of Columbus *(1992), she has also written several collections of poetry, including* Jacklight *(1984) and* Baptism of Desire *(1990). Her latest works are* The Birchbark House *(1999) and* The Last

Report on the Miracles at Little No Horse *(2000). This poem originally appeared in an earlier version in* Jacklight.

August and the drive-in picture is packed.
We lounge on the hood of the Pontiac
surrounded by the slow-burning spirals they sell
at the window, to vanquish the hordes of mosquitoes.
Nothing works. They break through the smoke-screen for blood.   5

Always the look-out spots the Indians first,
spread north to south, barring progress.
The Sioux, or Cheyenne, or some bunch
in spectacular columns, arranged like SAC[1] missiles,
their feathers bristling in the meaningful sunset.   10

The drum breaks. There will be no parlance.
Only the arrows whining, a death-cloud of nerves
swarming down on the settlers
who die beautifully, tumbling like dust weeds
into the history that brought us all here   15
together: this wide screen beneath the sign of the bear.

The sky fills, acres of blue squint and eye
that the crowd cheers. His face moves over us,
a thick cloud of vengeance, pitted
like the land that was once flesh. Each rut,   20
each scar makes a promise: *It is
not over, this fight, not as long as you resist.*

Everything we see belongs to us.
A few laughing Indians fall over the hood
slipping in the hot spilled butter.   25
The eye sees a lot, John, but the heart is so blind.
How will you know what you own?
He smiles, a horizon of teeth
the credits reel over, and then the white fields
again blowing in the true-to-life dark.   30
The dark films over everything.
We get into the car
scratching our mosquito bites, speechless and small

[1]*SAC:* Strategic Air Command.

as people are when the movie is done.
We are back in ourselves.   35

How can we help but keep hearing his voice,
the flip side of the sound-track, still playing:
Come on, boys, we've got them
where we want them, drunk, running.
They will give us what we want, what we need: 40
The heart is a strange wood inside of everything
we see, burning, doubling, splitting out of its skin.

ENGAGING THE TEXT

1. Identify which lines refer to actions and characters in the movie and which
   lines describe what's going on at the drive-in. What parallels or contrasts
   does Erdrich draw between the movie and the people watching it?

2. Does the speaker of the poem change? If so, where do the changes occur
   and how can you tell?

3. This poem is filled with details that suggest meanings beyond the simple
   denotations of the things themselves. What do you make of the way
   Erdrich emphasizes the mosquitoes that attack for blood, the "SAC missiles," the "meaningful sunset," the "sign of the bear," the "land that was
   once flesh"? What do these details say about the history of American Indians?

4. Whose point of view does the line "The Sioux, or Cheyenne, or some
   bunch" reflect? What unspoken assumptions does it reveal?

5. Why do the Indians laugh in stanza 5? Why, at the end of the stanza, does
   the speaker say, "We are back in ourselves"?

6. What do you make of the poem's enigmatic concluding metaphor? How
   does the poem as a whole illustrate the heart "burning, doubling, splitting"?

EXPLORING CONNECTIONS

7. How does Erdrich's poem call into question the idea of the frontier and the
   image of the frontier hero as presented by Frederick Jackson Turner
   (p. 683) and Wallace Stegner (p. 694)?

EXTENDING THE CRITICAL CONTEXT

8. Watch a John Wayne western on videotape and write an analysis of the
   myths and messages it conveys about cowboys, Indians, women, nature,
   and life in frontier America.

9. Read Joan Didion's 1965 essay "John Wayne: A Love Story," collected in
   Didion's *Slouching Towards Bethlehem.* Compare Didion's perspective to
   Erdrich's.

The Myth of the West

ROBERT V. HINE AND JOHN MACK FARAGHER

"Space...the final frontier"—Long before Captain James Kirk intoned these words at the beginning of the each weekly segment of the original Star Trek *television series, leaders of America's media industry well understood their dependence on the mythology of the Old West. As Robert V. Hine and John Mack Faragher observe in this selection from* The American West: A New Interpretive History *(2000), the myth of the frontier fueled the development of the modern publishing industry in the United States during the nineteenth century, just as the western has shaped attitudes toward masculinity, heroism, and popular entertainment through its dominance of American cinema since* The Great Train Robbery *in 1903. Robert V. Hine is professor emeritus at the University of California at Riverside and Irvine. John Mack Faragher is a professor of American history at Yale University and the author of* Women and Men on the Overland Trail *(1979) and* Sugar Creek: Life on the Illinois Prairie *(1986).*

In the year or two preceding Daniel Boone's death in 1820 at the age of nearly eighty-six, a steady stream of visitors beat a path to the door of his home on Femme Osage Creek in Missouri. When the old man saw strangers approaching, one of his sons later recalled, he would "take his cane and walk off to avoid them," but if cornered he would sit and talk with them. "Though at first reserved and barely answering questions," one visitor remembered, Boone soon "warmed up and became animated in narrating his early adventures in the West." Frequently visitors brought personal copies of *The Adventures of Col. Daniel Boon* (1782), the account written by Kentucky promoter John Filson that had made Boone famous. Filson claimed to have used the authentic first-person voice of Boone himself, although comparing the text with surviving Boone letters suggests that few of the words were actually his. It never seemed to bother him. Although never shy about complaining of those whom he thought misrepresented his life or deeds, for Filson's account Boone had nothing but praise. "All true! Every word true!" the old man exclaimed after one of his visitors read a portion aloud. "Not a lie in it."[1]

Filson's text had made Boone into a household name. Appearing in at least a dozen American editions before Boone's death, it has rarely been out of print in the more than two centuries since its publication. In English,

---

[1] John Mack Faragher, *Daniel Boone: The Life and Legend of an American Pioneer* (New York, 1992), 7, 298. [All notes are Hine and Faragher's except 11, 20, 24, 31, and 32.]

Daniel Boone in Missouri, eighty-five years old. Engraving by James Otto Lewis, 1820, based on a lost portrait by Chester Harding. Missouri Historical Society.

Irish, German, and French editions it created a minor sensation among Europaean intellectuals, who celebrated Boone as an American original, a "natural man" of the wilderness. Filson's Boone was the archetypal frontier hero, the leading man in a unique narrative tradition that would come to be known as the "western." He is a man most at home in the wilderness, a world he understands and loves as the Indians do. And Boone's intimate knowledge of the Indians enables him to confront and defeat them.

This was the story old Boone's admirers had imbibed from childhood, and the old man delighted in the honor it brought to the family name. Yet he did not hesitate to confront his visitors with the fact that in the years since the Revolution his life had taken some disappointing turns. He had taken up surveying, opened a general store, and planned to settle his children and grandchildren on nearby plots of land. "But alas!" he lamented, "it was then my misery began." As recompense for patriotic service to the country "I thought I was entitled to a home for my family," but "another man bought the land over my head." Boone became involved in legal squabbles over title, was forced to defend himself in court, and eventually lost both his lands and his business. Disappointed and downhearted, "I determined to quit my native land," moving the family to Spanish Missouri, where authorities granted them a generous estate. But "my misfortune did not end," he continued, for when the United States acquired the territory with the Louisiana Purchase, in came the lawyers and the speculators, and eventually his Spanish grants also were declared null and void. "I have lived to learn," Boone concluded with a world-weary sigh, "that your boasted civilization is nothing more than improved ways to overreach your neighbor."[2]

And through all his trials, Boone asked, who do you suppose turned out to be my most constant friends? Why, the Indians, the very people I helped to dispossess. Boone had never been an Indian hater, maintaining that he always "fought the Indians fairly" and "respected the rights of the preemptor of the soil." He disliked recounting war stories and refused to count scalps. Legend portrayed him as "a wonderful man who had killed a host of Indians," and, he allowed, "many was the fair fire I have had at them." But "I am very sorry to say that I ever killed any," Boone avowed, to the shock of his visitors, "for they have always been kinder to me than the whites." In fact, during his last years in Missouri, Boone frequently hunted with old Indian friends. A descendant told of watching old Boone and his Indian friends rehearsing their former adventures around a campfire. If forced to choose, Boone concluded, he would "certainly prefer a state of nature to a state of civilization." This admission was embarrassing to partisans of the "Indian-hating school" of frontier history. Perhaps senility had contributed to such sentimental and "weak" feelings toward the Indians, one critic sug-

real man / sorry for action [handwritten marginalia]

[2]Faragher, *Daniel Boone*, 277, 299–300.

gested, and hoped that Boone's controversial statements be allowed to "quietly sleep in the newspaper where it was printed."[3]

Boone's life story, appearing as it did during the formative years of the early Republic, was one of the foundation stones for what Richard Slotkin calls "the myth of the frontier." In our debunking age the word *myth* has become a synonym for erroneous belief. Slotkin, however, employs the term in an anthropological way to mean the body of tales, fables, and fantasies that help a people make sense of their history. The myth of the frontier has always promised authenticity—"Every word true!"—and it is right to be skeptical of such claims. But a myth is not necessarily false; some legends, in fact, may be accurate in most details.

Myth, like history, interprets and attempts to find meaning in past events. But when transformed into myth, history is reduced to its ideological essence. The western—the characteristic story form of the frontier myth—is essentially a tale of progress, a justification of violent conquest and untrammeled development. Boone's story—as the frontier pathfinder for American civilization—was a prominent piece of that triumphal tale. Yet the stories Boone told in his last years raised troubling questions. If the western country had been wrested from the Indians by men like him, why had the rewards been swept up by the merchants and lawyers? Why were poor backwoodsmen dispossessed of their lands, just as the Indians had been? Was that the real meaning of the term *civilization?* Because myth is composed in the figurative language of metaphor and symbol rather than the logical language of analysis, it may incorporate such doubts without confronting them. As Slotkin writes, "The most potent recurring hero-figures in our mythologies are men in whom contradictory identities find expression." Thus the progressive narrative of the western is consistently subverted by the presence of pathfinders who are also critics of civilization, outlaws who are Robin Hoods, and whores who have hearts of gold. Americans are drawn to characters of paradoxical impulse, to "good-badmen," or army scouts who identify with the Indian enemy. Things are simple in the western, but not always as simple as they seem. It is an example of what the critic Stuart Hall calls the "double-stake in popular culture, the double movement of containment and resistance."[4]

During the generation following Boone's death the character of the frontiersman became a ubiquitous presence in American culture. Of primary significance was the work of American novelist James Fenimore

---

[3]Faragher, *Daniel Boone*, 300–301; Faragher, "They May Say What They Please: Daniel Boone and the Evidence," *Register of the Kentucky Historical Society* 88 (Autumn 1990): 391.

[4]Richard Slotkin, "Myth and the Production of History," in Sacvan Bercovitch and Myra Jehlen, eds., *Ideology and Classic American Literature* (Cambridge, Mass., 1986), 70, 86; Ralph Samuel, ed., *People's History and Socialist Theory* (London, 1981), 228.

Cooper, who created an enduring literary version of the Boone character—variously identified as Leatherstocking, Hawkeye, or Deerslayer—in a series of five novels known as "The Leatherstocking Tales." An early review of Cooper's first western, *The Pioneers* (1823), noted that Leatherstocking was "modeled from the effigies of old Daniel Boone." The association was strengthened when, in the opening pages of his third tale, *The Prairie* (1827), Cooper explicitly linked his character with "Colonel Boone, the patriarch of Kentucky,...hardy pioneer of civilization." From its beginnings the western has insisted on the authenticity of its presentation as a story drawn from life.[5]

Cooper did not, however, intend Leatherstocking as the hero. According to the literary conventions of the day, heroes had to be men of genteel birth. Thus Cooper's plots feature well-bred officers romancing pale ladies, the kind likely to swoon when the going gets rough. Most readers have little interest in the leading characters of *The Last of the Mohicans* (1826). It is the supporting cast that fascinates: strong and resourceful Cora, condemned by her heritage of mixed blood; noble Indian warrior Uncas, instinctively understanding Cora's worth and loving her for it; brave and honest Hawkeye, nature's aristocrat.

The two groupings of characters, however, allowed Cooper to stage a conflict between civilized restraint and natural freedom. On the surface, his novels offer a progressive reading of America's frontier history and make a case for "the march of our nation across the continent." Judge Temple in *The Pioneers* is a visionary, patterned on Cooper's own father, the founder of Cooperstown, New York. "Where others saw nothing but a wilderness," the judge sees "towns, manufactories, bridges, canals, mines, and all the other resources of an old country." Nonetheless Cooper allows Leatherstocking to make a powerful argument against civilization. "The garden of the Lord was the forest," declares the old hunter, and was not patterned "after the miserable fashions of our times, thereby giving the lie to what the world calls its civilizing"—a paraphrase of one of old Boone's lines. Cooper's sentimental attachments lie with "forest freedom," compelling his readers to dwell on the price of progress. Francis Parkman, the great nineteenth-century romantic historian, proposed this summary of Cooper's message: "Civilization has a destroying as well as a creating power" and "must eventually sweep before it a class of men, its own precursors and pioneers, so remarkable both in their virtues and their faults that few will see their extinction without regret. Of these men Leatherstocking is the representative." Cooper's ambivalence about progress resonated with a deeply felt American regret about the loss of the wilderness as an imagined place of unbound freedom.[6]

---

[5]Faragher, *Daniel Boone,* 331; James Fenimore Cooper, *The Leatherstocking Tales,* 2 vols. (New York, 1985), 1:888.

[6]*Leatherstocking Tales,* 1:250, 324.

Dime novel hero Seth Jones. From Edward S. Ellis, *Seth Jones; or, The Captives of the Frontier* (New York, 1860). Beinecke.

The frontiersman entered the broader realms of American popular cul-   10
ture in the 1830s. In his popular play *The Lion of the West* (1830), James
Kirk Paulding featured the character of Nimrod Wildfire, a bragging,
buckskin-clad frontiersman who had come to Washington, D.C., as a congressman. Obviously based on real-life David Crockett of Tennessee, Wildfire's apotheosis came the evening Congressman Crockett attended a performance and the audience called him to the stage to take a bow with the
company, an early example of the indiscriminate mixing of fact and fancy in
the western. Knowing a good thing, Crockett published his own story, *A
Narrative of the Life of David Crockett of the State of Tennessee* (1834), the
first autobiography of a western American. Although the book considerably
stretched the truth, it was written in Crockett's authentic voice and introduced frontier tall tales to a wide popular audience.

Soon there were many imitations, including a long-running series of the
Davy Crockett Almanac, supposedly recounting his ongoing feats in his own
words, although Crockett himself had no connection with the publications,
which saw their heyday long after their protagonist had been killed at the
Alamo. "I can outlook a panther and outstare a flash of lightening; tote a
steamboat on my back and play at rough and tumble with a lion," thunders
the Davy of the almanacs. "I can walk like an ox, run like a fox, swim like an
eel, yell like an Indian, fight like a devil, and spout like an earthquake, make
love like a mad bull, and swallow a nigger whole without choking if you

butter his head and pin his ears back." This ribald character violates all the standards of polite society, observes Carroll Smith-Rosenberg. "Crockett denied the naturalness, the desirability, and the inevitability of bourgeois values and class distinctions." Crockett's over-the-top shenanigans, she argues, offered a subversive alternative to Victorian convention.[7]

Crockett was also a character in the first of the "dime novels," cheap paperbacks with sensational themes, that began appearing with the invention of the steam-powered printing press in the 1840s. It was the publishing house of Beadle and Adams, however, that first began issuing them in large numbers. In 1860 Erastus and Irwin Beadle, with their partner Robert Adams, set out to apply the techniques of mass production to publishing. Their first great success came almost immediately. *Seth Jones; or, The Captives of the Frontier* (1860), by Edward S. Ellis, tells the story of a white girl captured by Mohawks on the frontier of late-eighteenth-century New York—a locale familiar to Cooper's readers. In a stirring finale, she is rescued by Seth Jones, a lovable scout in buckskin, who knows the wilderness and its native inhabitants as he knows the back of his hand. Ellis reveals Seth to be a gentleman in disguise, thus neatly combining the roles of frontier scout with well-born hero, suggesting the gradual democratization of American cultural forms. The book sold four hundred and fifty thousand copies in just six months and established Beadle and Adams as a publishing powerhouse. Although the frontier was not the only setting for their stories, it was by far the most popular, with more than two-thirds of the 3,158 titles they published between 1860 and 1898 set in the West. Hunter-scouts like Seth Jones gradually gave way to outlaw, ranger, and cowboy heroes, and the requirement of genteel parentage was eventually dropped.

Novel followed novel, with Beadle's corps of writers churning out copy at the astounding rate of a thousand words per hour, a complete story every three days. Prentiss Ingraham, champion of the dime writers, was said to have delivered a thirty-five-thousand-word story to his publisher after a single marathon writing session lasting a day and a night. Literary historian Henry Nash Smith calls this "automatic writing." Forced to suspend any pretense of literary creativity, Smith suggests that dime novelists met their deadlines by identifying with the preoccupations of their readers, producing works he characterizes as "an objectified mass dream." It is an intriguing idea, if a difficult one to prove. But assuming that dime novels did map the fixations of their readers, it was a terrain both familiar and exotic. In the standard plot, savage redskins, vicious greasers, or heathen Chinee were laid low by conventional white heroes. By this point the relatively genteel Boone and even the more lascivious Crockett had given way to excessively violent characters—Indian-fighting Kit Carson, or big Jim Bowie, with a chip on his shoulder to match the massive knife in his belt. The stories also

---

[7]Carroll Smith-Rosenberg, *Disorderly Conduct: Visions of Gender in Victorian America* (New York, 1985), 97, 103.

Calamity Jane, the first dime novel heroine. From Edward L. Wheeler, *Deadwood Dick in Leadville; or, A Strange Stroke for Liberty* (Cleveland, 1908). Beinecke.

took subversive turns. In the early 1880s the James gang, then terrorizing banks and railroads on the Missouri border, became a favorite subject. Week after week Jesse and Frank defied the law and got away with it in the dimes—until respectable outrage finally forced the postmaster general to ban the series from the mails.[8]

Female characters were central to many recurring dime-novel fantasies. The first Beadle and Adams novel, *Malaeska: The Indian Wife of the White Hunter* (1860), by Ann Sophia Stephens, retold America's oldest frontier legend—the Pocahontas story. Stephens's tear-jerker recounts the tragic tale of an Indian maiden who, against the wishes of her own people, rescues a white frontiersman, marries him, and bears his child, is exiled from her own land, and suffers a lonely death in an urban slum. As Folklorist Rayna Green notes, "The Indian woman finds herself burdened with an image that can only be understood as dysfunctional." True enough. On the other hand, there is no way that this could be characterized as a triumphal narrative of progress. Yet *Malaeska* sold three hundred thousand copies, and Stephens followed her success by writing three more romances with native women as protagonists. Another persistent dime-novel fantasy was the "woman with the whip"—the western gal who acts a man's part but is all the more alluring for it. Frederick Whittaker's *The Mustang-Hunters; or, The Beautiful Amazon of the Hidden Valley* (1871) features a crossdressing heroine, "a marvelous mixture of feminine gentleness and masculine firmness."[9]

Dozens of similar dime-novel "she-males" followed, most famously Calamity Jane, introduced in Edward L. Wheeler's *Deadwood Dick on Deck; or, Calamity Jane, the Heroine of Whoop-Up* (1878), based on the life of a real western woman, Martha Jane Canary. Beadle's writers loved using real westerners as subjects. Edward Ellis could write about Seth Jones one week, Daniel Boone, Davy Crockett, or Kit Carson the next. In dime novels the fact and the fancy came indiscriminately mixed. But Beadle warned his authors to avoid "repetition of any experience which, though true, is yet better untold." It remained "better untold," for example, that Martha Jane Canary had turned tricks in the end-of-track helldorados of the plains or that she had ridden with General Crook's troops and was banished from camp for swimming nude with the enlisted men. Dime novelist Wheeler turned whoring Canary into kindhearted Calamity. Yet unlike Cooper's swooning ladies, Calamity Jane was a woman who knew how to get things moving. In an age when women's freedom was inhibited by genteel conventions, she captured the public imagination by demanding and receiving equal rights in a man's world. And although readers surely had little trouble

15

[8]Henry Nash Smith, *Virgin Land: The American West as Symbol and Myth* (1950; Cambridge, Mass., 1970), 91–92.

[9]Rayna Green, "The Pocahontas Perplex," *Massachusetts Review* 16 (Autumn 1976): 704; Smith, *Virgin Land,* 113.

recognizing the dime novels as fictions, the intermixture of authentic details encouraged a suspension of their disbelief. All true! Just think of it!...[10]

During the long cycle of economic hard times and farmer-worker protest that began with the Panic of 1873 and lasted until the late 1890s, many Americans became concerned about the "close of the frontier"—a catch phrase of the day that included fears of the end of "free land" as well as the exhaustion of the West's natural resources, component parts of the "safety valve," believed to have moderated the country's class tensions. In his influential *Progress and Poverty* (1879), Henry George[11] argued that the nation's economic progress had depended on western expansion. "But our advance has reached the Pacific," he warned. "Further west we cannot go." In 1889 fifty thousand people participated in a frenzied rush to stake claims to two million acres of "unoccupied" land in Indian Territory, almost overnight creating the territory of Oklahoma. That year and the next, six new western states entered the union (North and South Dakota, Montana, Washington, Idaho, and Wyoming), and over the next twenty years the admission of the final four—Utah, Oklahoma, Arizona, and New Mexico—completed the process of statemaking in the nation's contiguous territory that Thomas Jefferson had inaugurated with his Land Ordinance of 1784. Worry over the closing frontier echoed in government reports, scholarly treatises, and ministers' sermons but was not confined to the nation's intellectuals. Humorist and western newspaper editor Bill Nye expressed the fears of ordinary folks: "There ain't no frontier any more."[12]

These apprehensions seemed confirmed by the conclusions of statisticians and cartographers who examined the returns of the federal census of 1890. "Up to and including 1880 the country had a frontier of settlement," they reported. "But at present the unsettled area has been so broken into by isolated bodies of settlement that there can hardly be said to be a frontier line.... It can not, therefore, any longer have a place in the census reports." These words fired the imagination of young Wisconsin historian Frederick Jackson Turner. In his essay "The Significance of the Frontier in American History"—delivered in 1893 at a meeting of historians at the World's Columbian Exhibition in Chicago, a celebration of the four-hundredth anniversary of Columbus's first voyage to America—Turner made this famous declaration: "Up to our own day American history has been in large degree the history of the colonization of the Great West. The existence of an area of free land, its continuous recession, and the advance of settlement westward, explain American development." But now, Turner concluded, "four

---

[10]Albert Johannsen, *The House of Beadle and Adams and Its Dime and Nickel Novels: The Story of a Vanished Literature*, 3 vols. (Norman, Okla., 1950–62), 1:4.

[11]*Henry George:* American economist (1839–1897).

[12]Alan Bogue, *Frederick Jackson Turner: Strange Roads Going Down* (Norman, Okla., 1998), 104, 106.

centuries from the discovery of America, at the end of a hundred years of life under the Constitution, the frontier has gone, and with its going has closed the first period of American history."[13]

There were some serious problems with the notion of a closed frontier. Far more land in the trans-Mississippi West, both public and private, was taken up in the years after 1890 than in the years before. And tens of thousands of Americans crossed the northern border to pioneer what the Canadians promoted as the "last best West." Western settlements continued to expand in the years after 1890, yet on the census maps of 1900 and 1910 the "frontier line" made a mysterious reappearance. Geographer Frank Popper, reporting on "the strange case of the contemporary American frontier," points out that using Turner's own definition of "unsettled," there are in the late twentieth century 149 "frontier" counties in the West and that many areas of the western Great Plains are steadily losing population. The cartography that so inspired Turner, it turns out, was less a work of science than one of the imagination. A century later, the West has yet to fill up.[14]

The "closing of the frontier" became part of the myth. If expansion was the key to understanding the American past for Turner, for others it seemed also to offer the solution to contemporary problems. After reading Turner's frontier essay Woodrow Wilson wrote that with the continent occupied "and reduced to the uses of civilization," the nation must inevitably turn to "new frontiers in the Indies and in the Far Pacific." Theodore Roosevelt agreed, arguing that American colonies in the Caribbean and the Pacific were the logical and necessary extension of continental westering. He likened Filipinos to Apaches and condemned anti-imperialists as "Indian lovers." If the United States was "morally bound to abandon the Philippines," he blustered during the debate on annexation after the Spanish-American War, "we were also morally bound to abandon Arizona to the Apaches."[15]

Just as expansionists of the 1840s had marshaled public enthusiasm for   20
westering to justify a war against Mexico, so imperialists of the 1890s exploited fears of the end of frontier opportunity in order to build support for the creation of an American overseas empire. As historian William Appleman Williams observed, it offers "a classic illustration of the transformation of an idea into an ideology." But even as Roosevelt was urging his countrymen into battle for imperial possessions, Turner was lamenting the "wreckage of the Spanish War." Rather than overseas expansion, Turner placed his hopes for the American future in the expansion of higher educa-

[13]John Mack Faragher, ed., *Rereading Frederick Jackson Turner: "The Significance of the Frontier in American History" and Other Essays* (New Haven, 1999), 31, 60.

[14]Paul F. Sharp, "When Our West Moved North," *American Historical Review* 55 (1949): 289; Frank Popper, "The Strange Case of the Contemporary American Frontier," *Yale Review* 76 (Autumn 1986): 101–21.

[15]William Appleman Williams, *History as a Way of Learning* (New York, 1973), 148; Fred Hoxie, ed., *Indians in American History: An Introduction* (Arlington Heights, Ill., 1988), 244.

Theodore Roosevelt in his hunter's costume. From Theodore Roosevelt, *Hunting Trips of a Ranchman...* (New York, 1886). Beinecke.

tion. "The test tube and the microscope are needed rather than ax and rifle," he wrote. "In place of old frontiers of wilderness, there are new frontiers of unwon fields of science." He made a case for what amounted to a moral equivalent to westering.[16]

Simultaneous with Turner's promotion of the frontier thesis, three prominent easterners were doing their part to bring the myth of the frontier to popular attention: politician Theodore Roosevelt, artist Frederic Remington, and writer Owen Wister. Born into prominent families in the era of the Civil War, educated at Harvard or Yale, each of these men went west seeking personal regeneration at a critical point in their early twenties. Historian G. Edward White persuasively argues that these sojourns convinced each man that only by coming to grips with the experience of westering— with the myth of the frontier—could Americans preserve important aspects of their culture being swept away by the rush of industrialization. Most important, they sought to encourage a rugged version of American manhood. Their heroes were all "men with the bark on."

[16]Williams, *History as a Way of Learning,* 145; Faragher, ed., *Rereading Frederick Jackson Turner,* 144, 149.

Roosevelt's encounter with the West followed the devastating death of his young wife (in childbirth) and his mother (from disease) on the same dark day in 1884. Leaving his baby daughter in the care of his extended family, the young man abandoned New York and for three years lived on a Dakota cattle ranch, "far off from mankind." For Roosevelt this western sojourn became a critical test of manhood. At first the cowboys ridiculed him as an effete easterner, but things turned around for him once he stood up to a bully and floored him with a lucky punch. Roosevelt learned to hunt, graduating from killing deer to stalking panthers. He joined a posse and participated in the capture of a gang of desperadoes. "We knew toil and hardship and hunger and thirst," he wrote, "but we felt the beat of hearty life in our being, and ours was the glory of work and the joy of living." He returned to New York in 1886, a rough-and-tumble westerner. This experience would inform all his subsequent work—as author of hunting memoirs, including the best-selling *Ranch Life and the Hunting Trail* (1887), his multivolume history *The Winning of the West* (1889–96), and a dozen other popular books with similar themes; as president of the Boone and Crockett Club, conservationist, sports hunter, and advocate of "the strenuous life"; as Rough Rider during the Spanish-American War; and as America's first "cowboy president." What was good for the American male was good for the country. An appreciation of the West and its traditions, Roosevelt believed, would help to cultivate "that vigorous manliness for the lack of which in a nation, as in an individual, the possession of no other qualities can possibly atone."[17]

Frederic Remington went West in 1883 to escape a domineering mother who ridiculed his ambition to be an artist and insisted that he "take a real man's job." Writing that he wished to "cut women out of his life altogether," Remington used a small inheritance to purchase a Kansas ranch. Although he failed to make the operation pay and eventually lost it to creditors, he considered his three years in the West the happiest of his life. Western men "have all the rude virtues," he wrote. They were "untainted by the enfeebling influences of luxury and modern life." His admiration was mixed with a heavy dose of nostalgia. "I saw the living, breathing end of three centuries of smoke and dust and sweat," he later mused. Simultaneously Remington rediscovered his talent and joy for art and, like Catlin and Bingham before him, resolved to capture on paper the last days of the frontier. In 1885 he accompanied troopers through New Mexico during the campaign against Geronimo and placed his sketches in *Harper's Monthly* and *Outing,* one of the new men's sporting magazines. Returning East in the wake of this success, Remington struck his friends as a man transformed. "He had turned himself into a cowboy," wrote a former Yale classmate. Captivated by Remington's work, Roosevelt asked him to illustrate the forthcoming

---

[17]G. Edward White, *The Eastern Establishment and the Western Experience: The West of Frederic Remington, Theodore Roosevelt, and Owen Wister* (New Haven, 1968), 80, 85, 91.

Ranch Life and the Hunting Trail. It was the beginning of a lucrative career as fin-de-siècle America's most successful commercial illustrator. Soon oils and bronzes were also pouring from his studio, all commanding top dollar. "It is a fact that admits of no question," wrote an art critic in 1892, "that Eastern people have formed their conceptions of what the Far-Western life is like, more from what they have seen in Mr. Remington's pictures than from any other source."[18]

In his devotion to the cult of masculinity, Remington rivaled his friend Roosevelt. He was always uncomfortable and discontented with women, claiming to have "never drawn a woman — except once, and then had washed her out." This was an exaggeration, but not by much, for amid the thousands of men in his many works women appear only four times. True manliness, he believed, developed in the struggle with raw nature, the individual pitted against drought and wind. His works include dozens of images of men against a barren landscape. In *Friend or Foe* (1895) a lone rider strains his eyes to identify a barely visible speck on the bleak horizon. The Indians were part of hostile nature, dangerous yet useful as an abrasion against which the white man could prove his mettle. *Downing the Nigh Leader* (1907), one of his most celebrated paintings, features a group of mounted Indians attacking a speeding stagecoach. The lead horse on the left pitches violently to the ground, felled by a spear from a galloping warrior, while the drivers struggle stoically against their impending destruction. In *The Last Stand* (1890), Remington's depiction of the Custer myth, a group of cavalry troopers converge in heroic formation against an unseen enemy. Indians were only one of the enemies threatening the country. In a letter to a friend written at about the same time he painted that image, Remington lumped Indians together with immigrants. "Jews, Injuns, Chinamen, Italians, Huns — the rubbish of the earth I hate — I've got some Winchesters and when the massacring begins, I can get my share of 'em, and what's more, I will." In his art, Remington proclaimed the American male triumphant over nature and the Anglo-Saxon dominant over "the rubbish of the earth."[19]

Owen Wister, the third of this influential trio and a classmate of   25
Roosevelt's at Harvard, went West on a doctor's orders in 1885 when he was twenty-five. According to his daughter, he "freed himself from what to him was a deadly life," a career as a Boston businessman, exchanging it for a position as manager of a large Wyoming cattle ranch. Like Roosevelt and Remington, Wister self-consciously conceived of his western experience as a test of his manhood. He slept outdoors with the cowboys, bathed in an icy creek, drank his steaming coffee from a tin cup, and joined in the roundup. "The slumbering Saxon[20] awoke in him," Wister wrote in a story with

---

[18]White, *Eastern Establishment and Western Experience,* 58, 59, 100, 106, 107, 121; Prown et al., *Discovered Lands, Invented Pasts,* 106.

[19]White, *Eastern Establishment and Western Experience,* 57, 109.

[20]*Saxon:* One of the Germanic tribes that invaded Britain in the fifth century.

autobiographical implications, and he reinvented himself as "kin with the drifting vagabonds who swore and galloped by his side."[21]

He soon returned east, but over the next fifteen years Wister spent his summers in Wyoming. He began writing about cattle country, publishing short stories, essays, and novels in the 1890s. Ultimate triumph came with *The Virginian* (1902), a runaway best-seller and the most influential and widely read of all western novels. But curiously, although Wister continued writing, he never again wrote about the West. Indeed, after the publication of *The Virginian* he refused to travel West, fearful, perhaps, that the development of the region would destroy the ghost of his past. The mythical country of the open range, the classic setting of the western story, was entirely masculine, the playground of young men, Wister called it. But it was far more than play. It restored health, as it had for Wister himself, and it offered to re-create American men as self-reliant individuals. Underscoring self-reliance is the namelessness of the hero in *The Virginian*. His given name is used but once, in an offhanded manner, and the reader learns precious little of his background, except that he comes from the South. Wister asks that he be judged solely in the present, by what he accomplishes. Moreover, this vagueness contributes to his mystery and power. "It was by design he continued nameless," Wister later wrote, "because I desired to draw a sort of heroic circle about him, almost a legendary circle and thus if possible create an illusion of remoteness."[22]

He staged *The Virginian* as a series of tests of manhood. The hero rides at the head of a posse that captures and lynches a group of cattle rustlers, including his best friend. They once rode together as wild and woolly comrades, but the Virginian has the foresight to see that the frontier days are passing. He confronts the threatening outlaw Trampas—"When you call me that, smile!"—and in the prototype of the western duel shoots him dead in the dusty main street of Medicine Bow. By dint of intelligence and industry he rises from cowboy to foreman, eventually becoming "an important man, with a strong grip on many various enterprises." But the central test is the Virginian's courtship of Molly Wood, the eastern schoolmarm. In a series of arguments the cowboy convinces the lady to abandon sentimental attachments and accept his moral code, the rule of honor. "Can't you see how it is about a man?" he implores as he rejects her pleas to leave town and avoid the final confrontation with Trampas. She cannot see—but in the end she accepts. After all, Molly had come West because she "wanted a man who was a man." Old South is united with Old East in the New West.[23]

[21]Richard Slotkin, *Gunfighter Nation: The Myth of the Frontier in Twentieth-Century America* (New York, 1992), 171.

[22]Lee Clark Mitchell, *Westerns: Making the Man in Fiction and Film* (Chicago, 1996), 287.

[23]Owen Wister, *The Virginian: A Horseman of the Plains* (New York, 1903), 29, 474, 503.

Sitting Bull and William "Buffalo Bill" Cody. Photograph by W. R. Cross, c. 1885. Kansas State Historical Society, Topeka.

Annie Oakley. Photograph by J. Wood, c. 1885. Beinecke.

If Turner, Roosevelt, Remington, and Wister brought intellectual respectability to their version of the frontier myth, "Buffalo Bill" Cody was the man who turned that myth into America's most bankable commercial entertainment. Born in Iowa in 1846, William Frederick Cody grew up on the frontier. As a teenage boy he tramped to the Colorado gold rush and rode for the Pony Express. He fought with an irregular force of border Jayhawkers during the Civil War, scouted for the frontier army in campaigns against the Comanches, Sioux, and Kiowas, and earned his nickname hunting buffalo to feed railroad construction gangs. In 1869 dime novelist Ned Buntline (real name Edward Z. C. Judson) met Cody and wrote him up in the fanciful *Buffalo Bill, King of the Bordermen* (1869). Buntline's character was "the greatest scout of the West," skilled in the techniques of wilderness survival, Indian fighting, and vigilante justice. Honor motivated all his actions, whether protecting public virtue by vows of high purpose or rescuing white women from dastardly attacks by Indians or banditti. Before Cody's death in 1917 he had been the subject of no fewer than fifteen hundred dime novels, a score written by Buntline, at least two hundred by Prentiss Ingraham.

Cody was such a showman, such a ham actor, that he tried his best to live the role in which Buntline had cast him. Capitalizing on his moment of dime-novel fame, he went on the stage, touring eastern cities in *Scouts of the Plains,* a melodrama written by Buntline. In 1873 he organized the "Buffalo Bill Combination," a troupe of cowboy and Indian actors who dramatized adventures from dime novels and reenacted actual events in western history. This curious alchemy of the spurious and the authentic produced gold for Cody in the spring of 1876, when from the stage he dramatically announced the suspension of his tour so he could join cavalry units fighting the Sioux and Cheyennes. In a minor engagement a few days after Custer's defeat, Cody shot, killed, and scalped a Cheyenne warrior. Within days he was back on stage, reenacting his triumph and displaying the actual dried scalp before droves of sensation seekers. In Cody's hands, dime-novel illusions were embodied in flesh and blood, and western history was converted into living melodrama.

In 1882 Cody organized the greatest of his shows, "Buffalo Bill's Wild   30 West," which toured America and the world for the next three decades. The performance began with an overture played by thirty-six "cowboy" musicians wearing flannel shirts and slouch hats. Laced throughout were exhibitions of shooting and riding. Annie Oakley, the sweetheart of the show, entered trippingly throwing kisses. Then her rifle would begin to crack as she dispatched glass balls, clay pigeons, and little three-by-five-inch cards embossed with her picture, thrown high, sliced by her bullets, then thrown to the delighted audience. Buck Taylor, King of the Cowboys, clung to bucking broncos and led a troop in square dances and Virginia reels on horseback.

There was always a large contingent of Indians, mostly Sioux, performing their dances and displaying life as it had been lived on the plains before the coming of men like Buffalo Bill. Sitting Bull[24] joined the tour for the 1885 season, partly because he had met Annie Oakley the year before and had taken a liking to her. He named her "Little Sure Shot," and their relationship appears to have been genuinely warm. But it was difficult for the audience to accept the great Sioux chief into the show. After all, he was Custer's enemy, the embodiment of Buffalo Bill's troubles when he had scouted for the boys in blue. When Sitting Bull came on in his great ceremonial feathers, he was hissed, and in spite of his respect for Annie, he refused to tour for another season. Most of his salary of fifty dollars a week he gave away to bootblacks and street urchins. He was unable to understand why wealthy white men allowed such poverty to exist.

Historian L. G. Moses comments on the ambiguous legacy Cody's Wild West bequeathed to American Indians. On one hand it encouraged Americans to believe that all "real Indians" slept in tepees, wore feathered bonnets, hunted buffalo, and spoke using sign language. The Wild West was the source of many of the negative stereotypes later featured in motion pictures and on television. On the other hand the Indian performances also were critical to the development of the "powwow," an important twentieth-century pan-Indian institution, "a means by which people could retain, restore, or, in certain instances, create through adaptation a modern Indian identity." Reformers complained that Cody exploited his Indian performers, but most of the historical evidence suggests that Indians enjoyed the work and considered themselves well treated. Black Elk, a young Oglala dancer who later became a famous spiritual leader, came down with a bad case of homesickness during a tour of England in the early 1890s. "He would fix that," Black Elk remembered Cody telling him. "He gave me a ticket [home] and ninety dollars. Then he gave me a big dinner. Pahuska [Long Hair] had a strong heart."[25]

Authenticity through historic reenactment was the highlight of the Wild West. "Its distinctive feature lies in its realism," read Cody's promotional copy. "The participants repeat the heroic parts they have played in actual life upon the plains." Hunters chased buffalo, Indians attacked the Deadwood stage, and the Pony Express once again delivered the mail to isolated frontier outposts. The climax was a staging of "Custer's Last Fight," with Buffalo Bill arriving just after Custer's demise, the words "Too Late" projected by lantern slide on a background screen. That was the dark before the dawn. In the grand finale, Cody led a galloping victory lap of all the company's players—"The Congress of Rough Riders of the World"—with the American flag proudly flying in the van. The whole spectacle, in the

[24]*Sitting Bull:* Sioux leader (1831–1890) and victor over General George Armstrong Custer at the battle of Little Bighorn.

[25]L. G. Moses, *Wild West Shows and the Images of American Indians, 1883–1933* (Albuquerque, N.Mex., 1996), 272; John G. Neihardt, *Black Elk Speaks: Being the Life Story of a Holy Man of the Oglala Sioux* (1932; New York, 1972), 193.

words of the souvenir program sold during the performance, was designed to illustrate "the inevitable law of the survival of the fittest."[26]

Cody consistently updated these reenactments. In 1899, after the Spanish-American War, he featured Roosevelt's Rough Rider charge up San Juan Hill, then a few years later replaced it with a staging of the American occupation of Beijing during the Boxer Rebellion, the roles of the Chinese played by the company's Sioux contingent. In 1908 he introduced "The Great Train Hold-Up." It was an attempt to compete with *The Great Train Robbery* (1903), the first motion picture to tell a complete story, the first movie western.

Director Edwin S. Porter based his one-reel film on the holdup in 1901   35 of the eastbound Union Pacific by an outlaw gang known as the Wild Bunch, led by "Butch" Cassidy and the "Sundance Kid." Porter shot the

George Barnes aims at the audience. Frame from *The Great Train Robbery* (1903). The Museum of Modern Art, Film Stills Archive.

[26]Slotkin, *Gunfighter Nation*, 81–82.

picture, however, on the tracks of the Delaware and Lackawanna Railroad in New Jersey. The plot built on the Wild West formula pioneered by Cody—a dastardly attack, a dramatic chase, and a violent climactic shoot-out. In the film's final image, one of the outlaws points his gun directly at the audience and fires. People were thrilled. They flocked to nickelodeons to see the picture, and theaters throughout the country installed projectors and screens simply to exhibit it. *The Great Train Robbery* marked the birth of the American motion picture industry, which from its beginnings was preoccupied with western stories. Over the next sixty years at least a third of all the films made in the United States were westerns. "Rather than the cinema inventing the western," suggests film historian Tag Gallagher, exaggerating only a little, "it was the western, already long existent in popular culture, that invented the cinema."[27]

Motion pictures exploited the western with as much gusto as had the dime novel. Film companies churned out short westerns by the hundreds. The first identifiable movie actor to assume the mantle of the western hero was Max Aronson, a traveling salesman from Arkansas whose first screen role was playing one of the outlaws in *The Great Train Robbery*. When Aronson auditioned, Porter told him the role demanded expert riding. Although he was a complete tenderfoot, Aronson claimed he could "ride as well as a Texas Ranger." When the outlaws make their escape in the film, he is the one attempting to mount his horse from the wrong side! Despite subsequent lessons, Aronson never became comfortable on a horse, but under the stage name of Bronco Billy Anderson he starred in some four hundred astoundingly popular western two-reelers, all with essentially the same plot—Bronco Billy as a "good-badman" redeemed by the love of a virtuous woman or the disarming cuteness of a helpless child. The public eventually tired of Aronson but fell for a new hero of dime-novel proportions, Tom Mix, a veteran of wild west shows who was a master of trick riding and fancy shooting. In his snow-white ten-gallon Stetson, hand-tooled boots, and dandified cowboy clothes, Mix cut a fantastic figure, and by the 1920s, in addition to dozens of cheap films, he was being featured in a regular weekly radio program and his own series of comic books.[28]

Bronco Billy and Tom Mix were comic book characters, but other film-makers went to lengths to emphasize the authenticity of their westerns. In 1912 director Thomas Ince, one of the founders of the southern California film industry, arranged to use the equipment and personnel of the Miller Brothers' 101 Ranch Wild West Show, which kept winter quarters in the Santa Monica mountains near Hollywood. Ince's *Custer's Last Fight* (1912) featured a cast of more than a hundred Sioux that the Miller Brothers had brought to Hollywood from the Pine Ridge Reservation in South Dakota. "The history—the true history—of the Wildest West is being written on

---

[27]Barry Keith Grant, ed., *Film Genre Reader* (Austin, Tex., 1986), 204.
[28]John Tuska, *The Filming of the West* (Garden City, New Jersey, 1976), 11.

film," wrote an enthusiastic critic after seeing an Ince production. Here was "the great West as it really was and is." Ince was soon joined by actor William S. Hart, who made a name for himself playing Trampas in the Broadway adaptation of *The Virginian.* Together they made a series of pictures celebrated for their authentic portrayal of the West. Who cared if the plot of Hart's *Hell's Hinges* (1916) was contrived and maudlin, the acting stilted and melodramatic? The picture's appeal and lasting influence was Hart's good-badman character and the verisimilitude of its mise-en-scène—the wonderfully mangy prairie town populated by authentic-looking western types. Many of the extras in the westerns made during the silent era actually *were* authentic—rodeo cowboys or ranch hands picking up a few extra dollars by wrangling horses on the set, performing stunts, or filling out the ranks of cinematic outlaw gangs and vigilante posses. Until the 1920s there were plenty of places within a few hours of Hollywood that retained the look and feel of the late-nineteenth-century West—favorite shooting locations included the old gold rush town of Sonora in the Sierra Nevadas or the arid Owens Valley, frozen in time by the construction of the Los Angeles aqueduct. Viewing these films today, says Kevin Brownlow, "it is possible to stumble across unique glimpses of western history."[29]

The concern for authenticity inspired the production of a number of "epic" westerns during the 1920s. Hart directed and starred in *Tumbleweeds* (1924), an ambitious and gritty depiction of the Oklahoma land rush of 1889. *The Iron Horse* (1924), directed by John Ford, who had been making hard-edged cowboy pictures since 1917, told the story of the construction of the transcontinental railroad. The *New York Times* described it as "an instructive and inspiring film, one which should make every American proud of the manner of men who were responsible for great achievements in the face of danger, sickness, and fatigue." Ford's film was a celebration of the country's epic western adventure, seen as a founding myth that distinguished the United States from all other nations. Perhaps the most impressive of this set of nationalistic westerns from the 1920s was *The Covered Wagon* (1923), a depiction of an overland migration shot on location in Wyoming that included several hundred Indians from nearby reservations as well as dozens of men, women, and children from local ranches, who also supplied the wagons and oxen, lending the film a documentary look that remains startling today. "There is one adjective that one thinks of first" after seeing the picture, wrote the film critic of the *New York Herald.* "That adjective is 'honest.'"[30]

Authenticity thus continued as one of the most powerful attractions of western image-making. There was, however, more artifice than honesty in western films. Most were adaptations of the patterned western stories being

---

[29]Kevin Brownlow, *The War, the West, and the Wilderness* (New York, 1979), 223.

[30]Ralph E. Friar and Natasha A. Friar, *The Only Good Indian... The Hollywood Gospel* (New York, 1972), 123–24, 160; Brownlow, *War, West, and Wilderness*, 381.

William S. Hart (center). Production still from *The Gunfighter* (1917). The Museum of Modern Art, Film Stills Archive.

published in the "pulps," weekly or monthly magazines printed on cheap paper made of wood pulp, the twentieth-century successors of the dime novels. Growing up on a ranch in Colorado, Carey McWilliams[31] watched as his father's cowboys spent long hours in the bunkhouse "devouring cheap romances," from which they took instruction on how to dress and act in the manner of their western heroes. The most successful writer of western pulp fiction was Zane Grey, a midwestern dentist who wrote serials before hitting the big time with his novel *Riders of the Purple Sage* (1912), in which the lightning-fast gunman Lassiter rescues his lover from Mormon perfidy. Filled with violence, intrigue, cross-dressing, hard-riding women, and plenty of sex, the novel was a blockbuster, eventually selling nearly two million copies. Over the next twenty years Grey published a total of fifty-six westerns, sold at least seventeen million books, and his name was rarely absent from the best-seller list. His were tales of violent action set in spectacular Bierstadtian landscapes[32] of towering peaks and hidden valleys — making them perfect for adaptation to the screen. Between the world wars more

[31]*Carey McWilliams:* American cultural historian (1905–1980).
[32]*Bierstadtian landscapes:* Albert Bierstadt (1830–1902) was famed for his dramatic western nature paintings.

than a hundred Hollywood

cessful pulp writers of Hollywo..

Frederick Faust) and Ernest Hay based on Grey's novels. Other suc-
provided by a character in Haycock's included Max Brand (real name
East is settled, it is orderly, it is govern..a of the tone of their work is
but the West "is still a man's country." He g..n, *Free Grass* (1928). "The
on the imperatives of western manhood: "..n's ideas," he declares,
never reveal it to a living creature.... This is a ro..ise his young friend
to hear about your feelings." The most notable the..w you are hurt,
films is their obsessive attention to hardshell masculin..Nobody wants

Indeed, taking the cues provided by Roosevelt, Rem..stories and
western movies became a primary source for twentieth-ce..
American manhood. For sheer masculinity, probably no movi..
World War II was more powerful than Gary Cooper, who appe..ster,   40
least a dozen westerns by 1940, including a number of Zane Grey a..
tions. In the role that made him a star, Cooper played the greatest wes..
hero of them all in *The Virginian* (1929). The book had already appeared in
three screen adaptations by the time Cooper was pitted against Walter
Huston's Trampas. But this time their classic confrontation and shoot-out
could be heard as well as seen, for the film was the first western to feature
sound. In spite of the audio track, however, the picture is most notable for
the way Cooper and the other male characters hold their tongues, following
Haycock's classic proscription about excessive talking. It was in western
films that Cooper developed his screen persona as the laconic all-American
male, an object lesson in manhood.

Part of the appeal of westerns undoubtedly lies in the psychological
realm. Feminist film critics argue persuasively that Hollywood pictures impose a male-oriented perspective—"the male gaze"—which encourages
women as well as men to view women on the screen as the objects of male
pleasure. But surely an actor like Cooper—lithe and sexually smoldering—
was equally the object of an admiring "female gaze." The strong man with a
gun certainly has sexual connotations, and as the roles of women changed
and broadened in the twentieth century there may have been women as
well as men who looked on images of male dominance with a shiver of nostalgia. But there seems little doubt that the primary audience for westerns
was male. The masculine world of the cowboy was especially attractive to
boys feeling constrained by the authoritarian controls of childhood....

...Director John Ford's *Stagecoach* (1939) was the most impressive and
influential western of the late 1930s. A dangerous stagecoach journey
through Apache country during Geronimo's uprising throws together a colorful cast of characters drawn directly from dime novels and pulp fiction: a

[33]Robert G. Athearn, *The Mythic West in Twentieth-Century America* (Lawrence, Kans., 1986), 267; Ernest Haycock, *Free Grass* (Garden City, N.J., 1928), 9, 14.

Gary Cooper. Production still from *I Take This Woman* (1931). The Museum of Modern Art, Film Stills Archive.

good-badman seeking revenge (John Wayne, in the role that made him a star), a whore with a heart of gold, a traveling salesman, an alcoholic doctor, a respectable army wife, an aristocratic southerner, and a venal banker. The film was mostly shot on a Hollywood sound stage but included location work in spectacular Monument Valley on the Navajo Reservation, with its fantastic buttes towering above the desert—a site fully worthy of Bierstadt's art. There is wonderful B-western action and a stunt sequence in which renegade Apaches (played by local Navajos) chase the stagecoach through the desert until the day is saved by the last-minute arrival of the cavalry, flags flying and bugles blowing. But Ford manipulates and recombines these conventional elements into a film that amounts to considerably more than the sum of its parts. He skillfully reveals the "civilized" members of the party as snobs, hypocrites, or crooks and recruits audience sympathy for the outcasts, who become the heroes of the melodrama. The film celebrates westering while it simultaneously debunks the civilization brought to the West by the East. In the end the good-badman and the whore ride off to spend their lives together on a ranch in Mexico, "saved from the blessings of civilization," as one of the characters puts it. *Stagecoach* is able to have it both ways, which is the way the western has always wanted to tell the story of America.

ENGAGING THE TEXT

1. How do Hine and Faragher define the notion of myth? What, in their view, does a myth do within a culture? What do they believe is the mythic meaning of the American western?

2. What "contradictions" appear in the characters of early frontier or western heroes like Daniel Boone, Davy Crockett, and Cooper's Leatherstocking? What strikes you as appealing about these historical and fictional characters? What aspects of their personalities strike you as negative or repellent?

3. Why did Americans fear the closing of the frontier in the 1890s, according to the authors? What happened to the myth of the West when the historical frontier line disappeared from maps of the United States?

4. How has the myth of the frontiersman/western hero shaped American attitudes about men and masculinity? What role did the personal histories of transplanted easterners like Teddy Roosevelt, Frederic Remington, and Owen Wister play in the development of America's masculine ideal? Do you agree that the myth of the heroic frontiersman continues to shape American attitudes about masculinity?

5. According to Hine and Faragher, the myth of the frontier has always promised "authenticity" in its depiction of the history of the American West. From the information presented in this selection, what is your opinion of the authenticity of the stories that make up the myth of the Old West? To what extent do they reflect the real or the imagined history of the American West?

6. How would you characterize the relationship between the myth of the West and the development of the mass media and entertainment industries in the United States? What contradictions might you find between the messages conveyed by the myth of the West and the means used for its distribution?

EXPLORING CONNECTIONS

7. In what ways does the history of the western hero presented by Hine and Faragher complicate Frederick Jackson Turner's (p. 683) and Wallace Stegner's (p. 694) view of the impact of the frontier on American character?

8. What connections can you find between the figure of the western hero and the prevalence of gender-linked violence in modern advertising as described by Jean Kilbourne (p. 444) and Jackson Katz (p. 466)?

EXTENDING THE CRITICAL CONTEXT

9. Hine and Faragher note that the western has often transformed itself to adapt to changes in modern society and culture. Working in groups, discuss the extent to which the spirit of the western lives on today in other contexts, such as in contemporary science fiction or action adventure films like *Space Cowboys*, *The Matrix*, or *Armageddon*. Why, in your view, does the western seem to have had greater impact on American cinema than on contemporary television programming?

10. Analyze one of the classic western films that Hine and Faragher mention in this selection and discuss the way it portrays masculinity, femininity, nature, Native Americans, and members of other ethnic minority groups. What messages do such films convey about what it means to be an American?

The American West and the Burden of Belief
N. SCOTT MOMADAY

As recent critics of frontier ideology have noted, the story of western settlement looks heroic only if you view it from the perspective of the settlers. From the perspective of the indigenous Americans, the frontier was not the birthplace of American freedoms but the site of an unprecedented human and ecological tragedy. As N. Scott Momaday (b. 1934) reminds us in this essay, the West was not "won," it was invaded. The stories Momaday tells here about intercultural conflict and misunderstanding in the West challenge the tales of freedom and heroism that are commonly associated with the myth of the American frontier. Momaday is a Kiowa poet, play-wright, painter, Pulitzer Prize–winning novelist, and professor of English at the University of Arizona. His publications include House Made of Dawn *(1968),* The Way to Rainy Mountain *(1969), and* Circle of Wonder *(1994). He is currently working on a study of nineteenth-century American poetry. This selection originally appeared as part of the Public Broadcasting System's television series* The West *in 1996.*

I

West of Jemez Pueblo there is a great red mesa, and in the folds of the earth at its base there is a canyon, the dark red walls of which are sheer and shadow stained; they rise vertically to a remarkable height. You do not suspect that the canyon is there, but you turn a corner and the walls contain you; you look into a corridor of geologic time. When I went into that place I left my horse outside, for there was a strange light and quiet upon the walls, and the shadows closed upon me. I looked up, straight up, to the serpentine strip of the sky. It was clear and deep, like a river running across the top of the world. The sand in which I stood was deep, and I could feel the cold of it through the soles of my shoes. And when I walked out, the light and heat of the day struck me so hard that I nearly fell. On the side of a hill in the plain of the Hissar I saw my horse grazing among sheep. The land inclined into the distance, to the Pamirs, to the Fedchenko Glacier. The river which I had seen near the sun had run out into the endless ether above the Karakoram range and the Plateau of Tibet.

—*The Names*

When I wrote this passage, some years ago, it did not seem strange to me that two such landscapes as that of northern New Mexico and that of central Asia should become one in the mind's eye and in the confluence of image and imagination. Nor does it seem strange to me now. Even as we look back, the partitions of our experience open and close upon each other; disparate realities coalesce into a single, integrated appearance.

This transformation is perhaps the essence of art and literature. Certainly it is the soul of drama, and historically it is how we have seen the American West. Our human tendency is to concentrate the world upon a stage. We construct proscenium arches and frames in order to contain the thing that is larger than our comprehension, the plane of boundless possibility, that which reaches almost beyond wonder. Sometimes the process of concentration results in something like a burden of belief, a kind of ambiguous exaggeration, as in the paintings of Albert Bierstadt,[1] say, or in the

---

[1]*Albert Bierstadt:* German-born American painter (1830–1902), famed for his dramatic western landscapes.

photographs of Ansel Adams,[2] in which an artful grandeur seems superimposed upon a grandeur that is innate. Or music comes to mind, a music that seems to pervade the vast landscape and emanate from it, not the music of wind and rain and birds and beasts, but Virgil Thomson's "The Plow That Broke the Plains," or Aaron Copland's "Rodeo," or perhaps the sound track from *The Alamo* or *She Wore a Yellow Ribbon*. We are speaking of overlays, impositions, a kind of narcissism that locates us within our own field of vision. But if this is a distorted view of the West, it is nonetheless a view that fascinates us.

And more often than not the fascination consists in peril. In *My Life on the Plains*, George Armstrong Custer describes a strange sight:

> I have seen a train of government wagons with white canvas covers moving through a mirage which, by elevating the wagons to treble their height and magnifying the size of the covers, presented the appearance of a line of large sailing vessels under full sail, while the usual appearance of the mirage gave a correct likeness of an immense lake or sea. Sometimes the mirage has been the cause of frightful suffering and death by its deceptive appearance.

He goes on to tell of emigrants to California and Oregon who, suffering terrible thirst, were deflected from their route by a mirage, "like an *ignis fatuus*,"[3] and so perished. Their graves are strewn far and wide over the prairie.

This equation of wonder and peril is for Custer a kind of exhilaration, as indeed it is for most of those adventurers who journeyed westward, and even for those who did not, who escaped into the Wild West show or the dime novel.

For the European who came from a community of congestion and confinement, the West was beyond dreaming; it must have inspired him to formulate an idea of the infinite. There he could walk through geologic time; he could see into eternity. He was surely bewildered, wary, afraid. The landscape was anomalously beautiful and hostile. It was desolate and unforgiving, and yet it was a world of paradisal possibility. Above all, it was wild, definitively wild. And it was inhabited by a people who were to him altogether alien and inscrutable, who were essentially dangerous and deceptive, often invisible, who were savage and unholy—and who were perfectly at home. 5

This is a crucial point, then: the West was occupied. It was the home of peoples who had come upon the North American continent many thousands of years before, who had in the course of their habitation become the spirit and intelligence of the earth, who had died into the ground again and again and so made it sacred. Those Europeans who ventured into the West must have seen themselves in some wise as latecomers and intruders. In

---

[2]*Ansel Adams:* Twentieth-century American photographer renowned for his images of Yosemite National Park and western landscapes.

[3]*ignis fatuus:* Strange, floating balls of light said to lure travelers astray.

spite of their narcissism, some aspect of their intrusion must have occurred to them as sacrilege, for they were in the unfortunate position of robbing the native peoples of their homeland and the land of its spiritual resources. By virtue of their culture and history—a culture of acquisition and a history of conquest—they were peculiarly prepared to commit sacrilege, the theft of the sacred.

Even the Indians succumbed to the kind of narcissism the Europeans brought to bear on the primeval landscape, the imposition of a belief—essentially alien to both the land and the peoples who inhabited it—that would locate them once again within their own field of vision. For the Indian, the mirage of the ghost dance—to which the concepts of a messiah and immortality, both foreign, European imports, were central—was surely an *ignis fatuus*, and the cause of frightful suffering and death.

II

George Armstrong Custer had an eye to the country of the Great Plains, and especially to those of its features that constituted a "deceptive appearance." As he stealthily approached Black Kettle's camp on the Washita River, where he was to win his principal acclaim as an Indian fighter, he and his men caught sight of a strange thing. At the first sign of dawn there appeared a bright light ascending slowly from the skyline. Custer describes it sharply, even eloquently:

> Slowly and majestically it continued to rise above the crest of the hill, first appearing as a small brilliant flaming globe of bright golden hue. As it ascended still higher it seemed to increase in size, to move more slowly, while its colors rapidly changed from one to the other, exhibiting in turn the most beautiful combinations of prismatic tints.

Custer and his men took it to be a rocket, some sort of signal, and they assumed that their presence had been detected by the Indians. Here again is the equation of fascination and peril. But at last the reality is discovered:

> Rising above the mystifying influences of the atmosphere, that which had appeared so suddenly before us and excited our greatest apprehensions developed into the brightest and most beautiful of morning stars.

In the ensuing raid upon Black Kettle's camp, Custer and his troopers, charging to the strains of "Garry Owen," killed 103 Cheyenne, including Black Kettle and his wife. Ninety-two of the slain Cheyenne were women, children, and old men. Fifty-three women and children were captured. Custer's casualties totaled one officer killed, one officer severely and two more slightly wounded, and eleven cavalrymen wounded. After the fighting, Custer ordered the herd of Indian ponies slain; the herd numbered 875 animals. "We did not need the ponies, while the Indians did," he wrote.

In the matter of killing women and children, Custer's exculpatory rhetoric   10
seems lame, far beneath his poetic descriptions of mirages and the break of day:

> Before engaging in the fight orders had been given to prevent the
> killing of any but the fighting strength of the village; but in a struggle
> of this character it is impossible at all times to discriminate, particu-
> larly when, in a hand-to-hand conflict such as the one the troops were
> then engaged in the squaws are as dangerous adversaries as the war-
> riors, while Indian boys between ten and fifteen years of age were
> found as expert and determined in the use of the pistol and bow and
> arrow as the older warriors.

After the fighting, too, Black Kettle's sister, Mah-wis-sa, implored
Custer to leave the Cheyenne in peace. Custer reports that she approached
him with a young woman, perhaps seventeen years old, and placed the girl's
hand in his. Then she proceeded to speak solemnly in her own language,
words that Custer took to be a kind of benediction, with appropriate manners and gestures. When the formalities seemed to come to a close, Mah-
wis-sa looked reverently to the skies and at the same time drew her hands
slowly down over the faces of Custer and the girl. At this point Custer was
moved to ask Romeo, his interpreter, what was going on. Romeo replied
that Custer and the young woman had just been married to each other.

In one version of the story it is said that Mah-wis-sa told Custer that if
he ever again made war on the Cheyenne, he would die. When he was
killed at the Little Bighorn, Cheyenne women pierced his eardrums with
awls, so that he might hear in the afterlife; he had failed to hear the warning
given him at the Washita.

In the final paragraph of *My Life on the Plains,* Custer bids farewell to
his readers and announces his intention "to visit a region of country as yet
unseen by human eyes, except those of the Indian—a country described by
the latter as abounding in game of all varieties, rich in scientific interest, and
of surpassing beauty in natural scenery." After rumors of gold had made the
Black Hills a name known throughout the country, General (then Lieutenant Colonel) George Armstrong Custer led an expedition from Fort
Abraham Lincoln into the Black Hills in July and August, 1874. The Custer
expedition traveled six hundred miles in sixty days. Custer reported proof of
gold, but he had an eye to other things as well. He wrote in his diary:

> Every step of our march that day was amid flowers of the most exquisite
> colors and perfume. So luxuriant in growth were they that men plucked
> them without dismounting from the saddle.... It was a strange sight to
> glance back at the advancing columns of cavalry and behold the men
> with beautiful bouquets in their hands, while the headgear of the horses
> was decorated with wreaths of flowers fit to crown a queen of May.
> Deeming it a most fitting appellation, I named this Floral Valley.

In the evening of that same day, sitting at mess in a meadow, the officers
competed to see how many different flowers could be picked by each man

without leaving his seat. Seven varieties were gathered so. Some fifty different flowers were blooming in Floral Valley.

Imagine that Custer dreamed that night. In his dream he saw a man approaching on horseback, approaching slowly across a meadow full of wildflowers. The man drew very close and stopped, sitting straight up on the horse, holding Custer fast in his gaze. There could be no doubt that he was a warrior, and fearless, though he flourished no scalps and made no signs of fighting. His unbound hair hung below his waist. His body was painted with hail spots, and a white bolt of lightning ran down one of his cheeks, and on his head he wore the feathers of a redbacked hawk. Except for moccasins and breechcloth he was naked.

"I am George Armstrong Custer," Custer said, "called Yellowhair, 15 called Son of the Morning Star."

"I am Curly," the man said, "called Crazy Horse."[4]

And Custer wept for the nobility and dignity and greatness of the man facing him. And through his tears he perceived the brilliance of the meadow. The wildflowers were innumerable and more beautiful than anything he had even seen or imagined. And when he thought his heart could bear no more, a thousand butterflies rose up, glancing and darting and floating around him, to spangle the sky, to become prisms of the sun. And he awoke serene and refreshed in his soul.

George Armstrong Custer sees the light upon the meadows of the Plains, but he does not see disaster lurking at the Little Bighorn. He hears the bugles and the band, but he does not hear or heed the warning of the Cheyenne women. All about there is deception; the West is other than it seems.

III

In 1872, William Frederick Cody was awarded the Medal of Honor for his valor in fighting Indians. In 1913, U.S. Army regulations specified that only enlisted men and officers were eligible to receive the Medal of Honor, and Cody's medal was therefore withdrawn and his name removed from the records. In 1916, after deliberation, the army decided to return the medal, having declared that Cody's service to his country was "above and beyond the call of duty."

Ambivalence and ambiguity, like deception, bear upon all definitions of 20 the American West. The real issue of Cody's skill and accomplishment as an Indian fighter is not brought into question in this matter of the Medal of Honor, but it might be. Beyond the countless Indians he "killed" in the arena of the Wild West show, Cody's achievements as an Indian fighter are suspect. Indeed, much of Cody's life is clouded in ambiguity. He claimed that in 1859 he became a pony express rider, but the pony express did not

[4]*Crazy Horse:* Sioux Indian chief (1842–1877).

come into being until 1860. Even the sobriquet "Buffalo Bill" belonged to William Mathewson before it belonged to William Frederick Cody.

Buffalo Bill Cody was an icon and an enigma, and he was in some sense his own invention. One of his biographers wrote that he was "a man who was so much more than a western myth." One must doubt it, for the mythic dimension of the American West is an equation much greater than the sum of its parts. It would be more accurate, in this case, to say that the one dissolved into the other, that the man and myth became indivisible. The great fascination and peril of Cody's life was the riddle of who he was. The thing that opposed him, and perhaps betrayed him, was above all else the mirage of his own identity.

If we are to understand the central irony of Buffalo Bill and the Wild West show, we must first understand that William Frederick Cody was an authentic western hero. As a scout, a guide, a marksman, and a buffalo hunter, he was second to none. At a time when horsemanship was at its highest level in America, he was a horseman nearly without peer. He defined the plainsman. The authority of his life on the Plains far surpassed Custer's.

But let us imagine that we are at Omaha, Nebraska, on May 17, 1883, in a crowd of 8,000 people. The spectacle of the "Wild West" unfolds before us. The opening parade is led by a twenty-piece band playing "Garry Owen," perhaps, or "The Girl I Left Behind Me." Then there comes an Indian in full regalia on a paint pony. Next are buffalo, three adults and a calf. Then there is Buffalo Bill, mounted on a fine white horse and resplendent in a great white hat, fringed buckskin coat, and glossy thigh boots. He stands out in a company of cowboys, Indians, more buffalo, and the Deadwood Stage, drawn by six handsome mules, and the end is brought up by another band, playing "Annie Laurie" or "When Johnny Comes Marching Home." Then we see the acts—the racing of the pony express, exhibitions of shooting, the attack on the Deadwood Stagecoach, and the finale of the great buffalo chase. Buffalo Bill makes a stirring speech, and we are enthralled; the applause is thunderous. But this is only a modest beginning, a mere glimpse of things to come.

What we have in this explosion of color and fanfare is an epic transformation of the American West into a traveling circus and of an American hero into an imitation of himself. Here is a theme with which we have become more than familiar. We have seen the transformation take place numberless times on the stage, on television and movie screens, and on the pages of comic books, dime novels, and literary masterpieces. One function of the American imagination is to reduce the American landscape to size, to fit that great expanse to the confinement of the immigrant mind. It is a way to persist in our cultural being. We photograph ourselves on the rim of Monument Valley or against the wall of the Tetons, and we become our own frame of reference. As long as we can transform the landscape to accommodate our fragile presence, we can be saved. As long as we can see ourselves on the picture plane, we cannot be lost.

Arthur Kopit's play *Indians* is a remarkable treatise on this very subject   25
of transformation. It can and ought to be seen as a tragedy, for its central
story is that of Buffalo Bill's fatal passage into myth. He is constrained to
translate his real heroism into a false and concentrated reflection of itself.
The presence of the Indians is pervasive, but he cannot see them until they
are called to his attention.

> BUFFALO BILL: Thank you, thank you! A great show lined up tonight!
>   With all-time favorite Johnny Baker, Texas Jack and his twelve-
>   string guitar, the Dancin' Cavanaughs, Sheriff Brad and the
>   Deadwood Mail Coach, Harry Philamee's Trained Prairie Dogs,
>   the Abilene County Girls' Trick Roping and Lasso Society, Pecos
>   Pete and the—
> VOICE: Bill.
> BUFFALO BILL: (Startled.) Hm?
> VOICE: Bring on the Indians.
> BUFFALO BILL: What?
> VOICE: The *Indians.*
> BUFFALO BILL: Ah . . .

Solemnly the Indians appear. In effect they shame Buffalo Bill; they
tread upon his conscience. They fascinate and imperil him. By degrees his
desperation to justify himself—and by extension the white man's treatment
of the Indians in general—grows and becomes a burden too great to bear.
In the end he sits trembling while the stage goes completely black. Then all
lights up, rodeo music, the glaring and blaring; enter the Rough Riders of
the World![5] Buffalo Bill enters on his white stallion and tours the ring, doff-
ing his hat to the invisible crowd. The Rough Riders exit, the Indians approach, and the lights fade to black again.

At five minutes past noon on January 10, 1917, Buffalo Bill died. Western Union ordered all lines cleared, and, in a state of war, the world was
given the news at once. The old scout had passed by. Tributes and condo-
lences came from every quarter, from children, from old soldiers, from
heads of state.

In ambivalence and ambiguity, Cody died as he had lived. A week before his death, it was reported that Buffalo Bill had been baptized into the
Roman Catholic Church. His wife, Louisa, was, however, said to be an
Episcopalian, and his sister Julia, to whom he declared, "Your church suits
me," was a Presbyterian. Following his death there was a controversy as to
where Cody should be buried. He had often expressed the wish to be
buried on Cedar Mountain, Wyoming. Notwithstanding, his final resting
place is atop Mount Lookout, above Denver, Colorado, overlooking the
urban sprawl.

---

[5]*Rough Riders:* Cavalry group led by Teddy Roosevelt (1858–1919) during the Spanish-
American War.

IV

DECEMBER 29, 1890

Wounded Knee Creek

*In the shrine of photographs
are the slain, frozen and black*

*on a simple field of snow.
They image ceremony:*

*women and children dancing,
old men prancing, making fun.*

*In autumn there were songs, long
since muted in the blizzard.*

*In summer the wild buckwheat
shone like fox fur and quillwork,*

*and dusk guttered on the creek.
Now in serene attitudes*

*of dance, the dead in glossy
death are drawn in ancient light.*

On December 15, 1890, the great Hunkpapa leader Sitting Bull, who had opposed Custer at the Little Bighorn and who had toured for a time with Buffalo Bill and the Wild West show, was killed on the Standing Rock reservation. In a dream he had foreseen his death at the hands of his own people.

Just two weeks later, on the morning of December 29, 1890, on Wounded Knee Creek near the Pine Ridge agency, the Seventh Cavalry of the U.S. Army opened fire on an encampment of Big Foot's band of Miniconjou Sioux. When the shooting ended, Big Foot and most of his people were dead or dying. It has been estimated that nearly 300 of the original 350 men, women, and children in the camp were slain. Twenty-five soldiers were killed and thirty-nine wounded.

Sitting Bull is reported to have said, "I am the last Indian." In some sense he was right. During his lifetime the world of the Plains Indians had changed forever. The old roving life of the buffalo hunters was over. A terrible disintegration and demoralization had set in. If the death of Sitting Bull marked the end of an age, Wounded Knee marked the end of a culture.

I did not know then how much was ended. When I look back now from the high hill of my old age, I can still see the butchered women and children lying heaped and scattered all along the crooked gulch as plain as when I saw them with eyes still young. And I can see that something else died there in the bloody mud, and was buried in the blizzard. A people's dream died there. It was a beautiful dream....

—Black Elk

In the following days there were further developments. On January 7, 1891, nine days after the massacre at Wounded Knee, a young Sioux warrior named Plenty Horses shot and killed a popular army officer, Lieutenant Edward W. Casey, who wanted to enter the Sioux village at No Water for the purpose of talking peace. The killing appeared to be unprovoked. Plenty Horses shot Casey in the back at close quarters.

On January 11, two Sioux families, returning to Pine Ridge from hunting near Bear Butte, were ambushed by white ranchers, three brothers named Culbertson. Few Tails, the head of one of the families, was killed, and his wife was severely wounded. Somehow she made her way in the freezing cold a hundred miles to Pine Ridge. The other family—a man, his wife, and two children, one an infant—managed to reach the Rosebud agency two weeks later. This wife, too, was wounded and weak from the loss of blood. She survived, but the infant child had died of starvation on the way.

On January 15 the Sioux leaders surrendered and established themselves at Pine Ridge. The peace for which General Nelson A. Miles had worked so hard was achieved. The Indians assumed that Plenty Horses would go free, and indeed General Miles was reluctant to disturb the peace. But there were strong feelings among the soldiers. Casey had been shot in cold blood while acting in the interest of peace. On February 19, Plenty Horses was quietly arrested and removed from the reservation to Fort Meade, near Sturgis, South Dakota.

On March 27, General Miles ordered Plenty Horses released to stand trial in the federal district court at Sioux Falls. Interest ran high, and the courtroom was filled with onlookers of every description. The Plenty Horses trial was one of the most interesting and unlikely in the history of the West. Eventually the outcome turned upon a question of perception, of whether or not a state of war existed between the Sioux and the United States. If Plenty Horses and Casey were belligerents in a state of war, the defense argued, then the killing could not be considered a criminal offense, subject to trial in the civil courts.

General Nelson A. Miles was sensitive to this question for two reasons in particular. First, his rationale for bringing troops upon the scene—and he had amassed the largest concentration of troops in one place since the Civil War—was predicated upon the existence of a state of war. When the question was put to him directly, he replied, "It was a war. You do not suppose that I am going to reduce my campaign to a dress-parade affair?" Second, Miles had to confront the logically related corollary to the defense argument, that, if no state of war existed, all the soldiers who took part in the Wounded Knee affair were guilty of murder under the law.

Miles sent a staff officer, Captain Frank D. Baldwin, to testify on behalf of Plenty Horses' defense. This testimony proved critical, and decisive. It is a notable irony that Baldwin and the slain Casey were close friends. Surely one of the principal ironies of American history is that Plenty Horses was very likely to have been the only Indian to benefit in any way from the

35

slaughter at Wounded Knee. Plenty Horses was acquitted. So too—a final irony—were the Culbertson brothers; with Plenty Horses' acquittal, there was neither a logical basis for nor a practical possibility of holding them accountable for the ambush of Few Tails and his party.

We might ponder Plenty Horses at trial, a young man sitting silent under the scrutiny of curious onlookers, braving his fate with apparent indifference. Behind the mask of a warrior was a lost and agonized soul.

As a boy Plenty Horses had been sent to Carlisle Indian School in Pennsylvania, the boarding school founded by Richard Henry Pratt, whose obsession was to "kill the Indian and save the man." Carlisle was the model upon which an extensive system of boarding schools for Indians was based. The boarding schools were prisons in effect, where Indian children were exposed to brutalities, sometimes subtle, sometimes not, in the interest of converting them to the white man's way of life. It was a grand experiment in ethnic cleansing and psychological warfare, and it failed. But it exacted a terrible cost upon the mental, physical, and spiritual health of Indian children.

Plenty Horses was for five years a pupil at Carlisle. Of his experience there he said: 40

> I found that the education I had received was of no benefit to me. There was no chance to get employment, nothing for me to do whereby I could earn my board and clothes, no opportunity to learn more and remain with the whites. It disheartened me and I went back to live as I had before going to school.

But when Plenty Horses returned to his own people, they did not fully accept him. He had lost touch with the old ways; he had lived among whites, and the association had diminished him. He rejected the white world, but he had been exposed to it, and it had left its mark upon him. And in the process he had been dislodged, uprooted from the Indian world. He could not quite get back to it. His very being had become tentative; he lived in a kind of limbo, a state of confusion, depression, and desperation.

At the trial Plenty Horses was remarkably passive. He said nothing, nor did he give any sign of his feelings. It was as if he were not there. It came later to light that he was convinced beyond any question that he would be hanged. He could not understand what was happening around him. But in a strange way he could appreciate it. Indeed he must have been fascinated. Beneath his inscrutable expression, his heart must have been racing. He was the center of a ritual, a sacrificial victim; the white man must dispose of him according to some design in the white man's universe. This was perhaps a ritual of atonement. The whites would take his life, but in the proper way, according to their notion of propriety and the appropriate. Perhaps they were involving him in their very notion of the sacred. He could only accept what was happening, and only in their terms. With silence, patience, and respect he must await the inevitable.

Plenty Horses said later:

> I am an Indian. Five years I attended Carlisle and was educated in the
> ways of the white man.... I was lonely. I shot the lieutenant so I might
> make a place for myself among my people. Now I am one of them. I
> shall be hung and the Indians will bury me as a warrior. They will be
> proud of me. I am satisfied.

But Plenty Horses was not hanged, nor did he make an acceptable place for
himself among his people. He was acquitted. Plenty Horses lived out his life
between two worlds, without a place in either.

Perhaps the most tragic aspect of Plenty Horses' plight was his silence,
the theft of his language and the theft of meaning itself from his ordeal. At
Carlisle he had been made to speak English, and his native Lakota was forbidden, thrown away, to use a term that indicates particular misfortune in the
Plains oral tradition, where to be "thrown away" is to be negated, excluded,
eliminated. After five years Plenty Horses had not only failed to master the
English language, he had lost some critical possession of his native tongue as
well. He was therefore crippled in his speech, wounded in his intelligence. In
him was a terrible urgency to express himself—his anger and hurt, his sorrow
and loneliness. But his voice was broken. In terms of his culture and all it held
most sacred, Plenty Horses himself was thrown away.

In order to understand the true nature of Plenty Horses' ordeal—and a   45
central reality in the cultural conflict that has defined the way we historically
see the American West—we must first understand something about the nature of words, about the way we live our daily lives in the element of language. For in a profound sense our language determines us; it shapes our
most fundamental selves; it establishes our identity and confirms our existence, our human being. Without language we are lost, "thrown away."
Without names—language is essentially a system of naming—we cannot
truly claim to be.

To think is to talk to oneself. That is to say, language and thought are
practically indivisible. But there is complexity in language, and there are
many languages. Indeed, there are hundreds of Native American languages
on the North American continent alone, many of them in the American West.
As there are different languages, there are different ways of thinking. In
terms of what we call "worldview," there are common denominators of experience that unify language communities to some extent. Although the Pueblo
peoples of the Rio Grande valley speak different languages, their experience
of the land in which they live, and have lived for thousands of years, is by and
large the same. And their worldview is the same. There are common denominators that unify all Native Americans in certain ways. This much may be said
of other peoples, Europeans, for example. But the difference between Native
American and European worldviews is vast. And that difference is crucial to
the story of the American West. We are talking about different ways of thinking, deeply different ways of looking at the world.

The oral tradition of the American Indian is a highly developed realization of language. In certain ways it is superior to the written tradition. In the oral tradition words are sacred; they are intrinsically powerful and beautiful. By means of words, by the exertion of language upon the unknown, the best of the possible—and indeed the seemingly impossible—is accomplished. Nothing exists beyond the influence of words. Words are the names of Creation. To give one's word is to give oneself, wholly, to place a name, than which nothing is more sacred, in the balance. One stands for his word; his word stands for him. The oral tradition demands the greatest clarity of speech and hearing, the whole strength of memory, and an absolute faith in the efficacy of language. Every word spoken, every word heard, is the utterance of prayer.

Thus, in the oral tradition, language bears the burden of the sacred, the burden of belief. In a written tradition, the place of language is not so certain.

Those European immigrants who ventured into the Wild West were of a written tradition, even the many who were illiterate. Their way of seeing and thinking was determined by the invention of an alphabet, the advent of the printed word, and the manufacture of books. These were great landmarks of civilization, to be sure, but they were also a radical departure from the oral tradition and an understanding of language that was inestimably older and closer to the origin of words. Although the first Europeans venturing into the continent took with them and held dear the Bible, Bunyan,[6] and Shakespeare, their children ultimately could take words for granted, throw them away. Words, multiplied and diluted to inflation, would be preserved on shelves forever. But in this departure was also the dilution of the sacred, and the loss of a crucial connection with the real, that plane of possibility that is always larger than our comprehension. What follows such loss is overlay, imposition, the distorted view of the West of which we have been speaking.

V

> My children, when at first I liked the whites,
> My children, when at first I liked the whites,
> I gave them fruits,
> I gave them fruits.
>
> —Arapaho
>
> Restore my voice for me.
>
> —Navajo

The landscape of the American West has to be seen to be believed. And perhaps, conversely, it has to be believed in order to be seen. Here is the confluence of image and imagination. I am a writer and a painter. I am   50

[6]*Bunyan:* John Bunyan (1628–1688), English writer and preacher whose allegorical novel *Pilgrim's Progress* was a staple of Puritan American households.

therefore interested in what it is to see, how seeing is accomplished, how the physical eye and the mind's eye are related, how the act of seeing is or can be expressed in art and in language, and how these things are sacred in nature, as I believe them to be.

Belief is the burden of seeing. And language bears the burden of belief rightly. To see into the heart of something is to believe in it. In order to see to this extent, to see and to accomplish belief in the seeing, one must be prepared. The preparation is a spiritual exercise.

In order to be perceived in its true character, the landscape of the American West must be seen in terms of its sacred dimension. "Sacred" and "sacrifice" are related. Something is made sacred by means of sacrifice; that which is sacred is earned. I have a friend who wears on a string around his neck a little leather pouch. In the pouch is a pebble from the creek bed at Wounded Knee. Wounded Knee is sacred ground, for it was purchased with blood. It is the site of a terrible human sacrifice. It is appropriate that my friend should keep the pebble close to the center of his being, that he should see the pebble and beyond the pebble to the battlefield and beyond the battlefield to the living earth.

The history of the West, that is, the written story that begins with the record of European intervention, is informed by tensions that arise from a failure to see the West in terms of the sacred. The oral history, the oral tradition that came before the written chronicles, is all too often left out of the equation. Yet one of the essential realities of the West is centered in this still living past. When Europeans came into the West they encountered a people who had been there for untold millennia, for whom the landscape was a kind of cathedral of their spiritual life, the home of their deepest being. It had been earned by sacrifice forever. But the encounter was determined by a distortion of image and imagination and language, by a failure to see and believe.

George Armstrong Custer could see and articulate the beauty of the Plains, but he could not see the people who inhabited them. Or he could see them only as enemies, impediments to the glory for which he hungered. He could not understand the sacred ceremony, the significance of the marriage he was offered, and he could not hear the words of warning, nor comprehend their meaning.

Buffalo Bill was a plainsman, but the place he might have held on the picture plane of the West was severely compromised and ultimately lost to the theatrical pretensions of the Wild West show. Neither did he see the Indians. What he saw at last was a self-fabricated reflection of himself and of the landscape in which he had lived a former life.

The vision of Plenty Horses was that of reunion with his traditional world. He could not realize his vision, for his old way of seeing was stolen from him in the white man's school. Ironically, just like the European emigrants, Plenty Horses attempted by his wordless act of violence to persist in his cultural being, to transform the landscape to accommodate his presence once more, to save himself. He could not do so. I believe that he wanted more than anything to pray, to make a prayer in the old way to the old deities of the world to which he was born. But I believe too that he had lost the words, that without language he could no longer bear the burden of belief.

> *The sun's beams are running out*
> *The sun's beams are running out*
> *The sun's yellow rays are running out*
> *The sun's yellow rays are running out*
>
> *We shall live again*
> *We shall live again*
>
> *—Comanche*

> *They will appear—may you behold them!*
> *They will appear—may you behold them!*
> *A horse nation will appear.*
> *A thunder-being nation will appear.*
> *They will appear, behold!*
> *They will appear, behold!*
>
> *—Kiowa*

Engaging the Text

1. What does Momaday mean when he says that when confronted with the enormity of the American West we superimpose upon it "overlays, impositions, a kind of narcissism" (para. 2)? What role do such impositions or "mirages" play in the stories Momaday tells of George Armstrong Custer and Buffalo Bill Cody? In what sense were their visions and transformations of the West dangerous mirages?

2. What is the point of the story Momaday tells about the killing of Edward Casey and the trial of Plenty Horses? How does this anecdote complement the stories of Custer and Cody? What does the experience of Plenty Horses say about the impact of the frontier experience on Native Americans?

3. What, according to Momaday, is the difference between language use and meaning in an oral and a written tradition? How do these different orientations to language and meaning influence our ability to "see" and believe in an idea as complex as the American West?

4. What is the significance of the quotation from the novel *The Names* that introduces this selection? How does this introductory "vision" relate to the themes of sacredness, belief, and transformation that Momaday develops throughout the essay? To what extent might this vision also be considered a mirage?

Exploring Connections

5. How does Momaday's portrayal of Custer and Cody complicate the image of the self-reliant frontiersman presented by Frederick Jackson Turner

(p. 683) and Wallace Stegner (p. 694)? From Momaday's perspective, in what ways might Turner's and Stegner's views of the West be seen as deceptive or limited?

6. Drawing on information presented by Momaday and by Robert V. Hine and John Mack Faragher in "The Myth of the West" (p. 708), write an analysis of the role that fantasy has played in the creation of the idea of frontier freedom.

EXTENDING THE CRITICAL CONTEXT

7. Working in small groups, assemble a series of images or ads from popular magazines that evoke the spirit of the American West. What does each image attempt to tell us about the West? What limitations are built into each of these potentially deceptive interpretations?

8. View *Dances with Wolves, Last of the Mohicans,* or any film that focuses on the interrelationships of Native Americans and whites along the frontier. How are white/Native American relations portrayed in these films? In what ways might they also distort our view of the American West and its original inhabitants?

9. View *Smoke Signals* or any other recent film made by a Native American director. How are Native Americans depicted in this "indigenous" movie? How do portrayals of Native Americans in this film compare with most common contemporary images of Native Americans in popular media?

Visual Portfolio

Reading Images of the West, Wildness, and the Myth of American Freedom

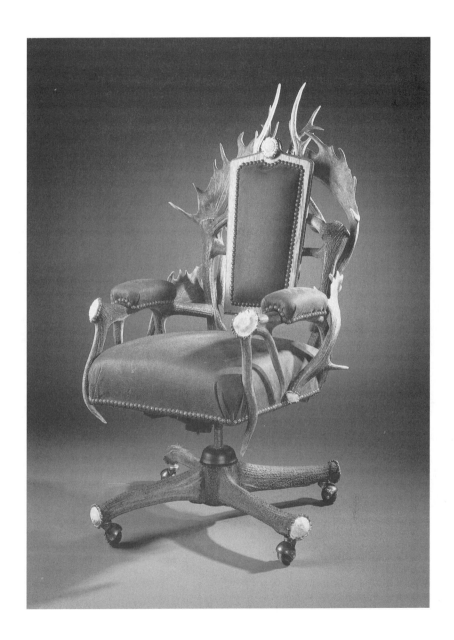

Visual Portfolio

READING IMAGES OF THE WEST, WILDNESS, AND THE MYTH OF AMERICAN FREEDOM

1. What is the representation of the cowboy by Remington meant to tell us about life in the Old West? How does it confirm or differ from commonplace stereotypes of the western hero?

2. In what ways does the image of the five-year-old Navajo boy challenge traditional views of cowboys and Indians in the American West? What responses might it evoke from N. Scott Momaday (p. 734) and Linda Hogan (p. 826)?

3. After reading the introductory essay provided at the beginning of this chapter, comment on the symbolism of the painting *Manifest Destiny*. What do its elements say about the meaning of westward expansion, white America's view of its role in the process of settlement, and the importance of technology to the frontier?

4. Who do you think might use the antler chair? Where would the person work or live? What does this chair tell us about the person who might use it? What does it tell us about the relationship of business, power, and nature in American culture?

5. What does the photo of the man holding a baby and a handgun suggest about American attitudes toward guns? To what extent does it affirm values and beliefs associated with the myth of the frontier? How does the historical information presented in Michael A. Bellesiles's historical analysis of gun culture in early America (p. 792) complicate this image?

The Adventures of the Frontier in the Twentieth Century

PATRICIA NELSON LIMERICK

Ever since Frederick Jackson Turner announced the closing of the frontier and the end of America's westward expansion in 1893, historians have debated the future of the frontier in American culture. Some, indeed, have argued that even today literally hundreds of counties in the West would qualify as "unsettled" because they meet the population density limit of less than two persons per square mile that Turner himself used at the turn of the century. Whether or not the frontier continues to exist as a demographic reality, there can be no doubt about its survival as a cultural touchstone. Patricia Nelson Limerick has dedicated her career to challenging traditional understandings of the myth of the American West. In this selection, she traces some of the ways that the specter of the frontier has haunted America's cultural consciousness. Limerick has authored a number of books and scholarly articles on the frontier in American history, including Legacy of Conquest: The Unbroken Past of the American West *(1988) and* Something in the Soil: Field-Testing the New Western History *(2000). She currently teaches at the University of Colorado at Boulder.*

Travels in Frontierland

The year 1988 signified the fortieth anniversary of humanity's escape from zippers and buttons. In May of that year a journal of science and technology called *Discover* published an article commemorating this occasion. "Velcro," the headline read: "The Final Frontier."

To the specialist in Western American history, this is a title to ponder. In what sense might Velcro constitute a frontier? In his 1893 essay "The Significance of the Frontier in American History," Frederick Jackson Turner left his central term curiously befogged: The word "frontier," he said, "is an elastic one, and for our purposes does not need sharp definition."[1] But Turner did join the director of the United States census in offering one clear and concrete definition: the frontier was a place occupied by fewer than two people per square mile. Thus, if the headline writer were a strict follower of Turner's quantitative definition, then the Velcro Frontier would be a place where fewer than two people per square mile used Velcro. The writer, on the other hand, might have been following one of the more poetic and less precise Turnerian definitions, finding in a society's choice of fasteners a symbolic line of division between wilderness and human culture, backwardness and progress, savagery and civilization. The habit-bound users of zippers would now represent the primitive and backward people of North America, with the hardy, adventurous users of Velcro living on the cutting edge of progress.

Historians of the American West might puzzle over the shifting definitions of the world "frontier," but few readers experience any confusion when they see this headline. To them, the frontier analogy says simply that makers, marketers, and users of Velcro stand on the edge of exciting possibilities. Velcro is a frontier because Velcro has thousands of still-to-be-imagined uses. No normal reader, if one defines "normal reader" as a per-

---

[1]In Frederick Jackson Turner, *The Frontier in American History* (1920; rpt. Tucson: University of Arizona Press, 1986), 2. [All notes are Limerick's except 17, 38–41, and 43.]

son who is not a Western American historian, would even notice the peculiar implications of the analogy. For most Americans in the twentieth century, the term "frontier" is perfectly clear, reliable, and simple in its meanings.

"Frontier," the historian David Wrobel writes, "has become a metaphor for promise, progress, and ingenuity."[2] And yet, despite the accuracy of this summation, the relation between the frontier and the American mind is not a simple one. Clear and predictable on most occasions, the idea of the frontier is still capable of sudden twists and shifts of meaning, meanings considerably more interesting than the conventional and familiar definition of the frontier as a zone of open opportunity.

Conventional thinking is at its most powerful, however, in twentieth- 5 century reconstructions of the nineteenth-century experience of westward expansion, reconstructions quite explicitly designed for sale. To see this commercialized vision of the Old Frontier in concrete, three-dimensional form, the best place to go is Disneyland in Anaheim, California. When they enter Frontierland, visitors might ask Disneyland employees for directions, but they do not have to ask for a definition of the frontier. The frontier, every tourist knows, was the edge of Anglo-American settlement, the place where white Americans struggled to master the continent. This frontier, as everything in Frontierland confirms, was populated by a colorful and romantic cast of characters—mountain men, cowboys, prospectors, pioneer wives, saloon girls, sheriffs, and outlaws. Tepees, log cabins, and false-front stores were the preferred architecture of the frontier; coonskin caps, cowboy hats, bandannas, buckskin shirts and leggings, moccasins, boots, and an occasional sunbonnet or calico dress constituted frontier fashion; canoes, keelboats, steamboats, saddle horses, covered wagons, and stagecoaches gave Americans the means to conquer the rivers, mountains, deserts, plains, and other wide-open spaces of the frontier; firearms, whether long rifles or sixshooters, were everywhere and in frequent use. These images are very well understood. Tourists do not need any assistance in defining Frontierland.

And yet, even in the tightly controlled world of Disneyland, the idea of the frontier has encountered complications. At the Golden Horseshoe, Frontierland's saloon, every show once had a "spontaneous" gunfight in which Black Bart and Sheriff Lucky blazed away at each other. In 1958, as a reporter for the *Saturday Evening Post* watched, the gunfight underwent some slippage at the joint that connects fantasy to reality: "As the sheriff advanced toward the wounded bandit," the writer said, "a tow-headed fiveyear-old, wearing a cowboy suit and holding a cap pistol, came running from the crowd," asking earnestly, "'Can I finish him off, sheriff, can I?'" The sheriff consented, and everyone fired.

---

[2]David M. Wrobel, *The End of American Exceptionalism: Frontier Anxiety from the Old West to the New Deal* (Lawrence: University Press of Kansas, 1993), 145.

Black Bart shuddered, then lay deathly still.

The lad took one look, dropped his gun and fled, screaming, "Mommy, mommy! I didn't mean to! I didn't mean to!"

Scholars with a penchant for interpreting signs, symbols, and signifiers could go to town with this incident, pondering the way in which the appeal to "mommy" follows hard and fast on the attempted initiation into the manly sport of gunplay. But my own attention fixes on the line, "I didn't mean to!" Since the child wanted to kill Black Bart, and, with an impressive deference to authority, asked the sheriff for permission to kill him, why would he then make the claim, "I didn't mean to"? His worries of intention and outcome were, in any case, soon ended: "His tears stopped a moment later, however, when he turned and saw Black Bart and Sheriff Lucky walking into the Golden Horseshoe to get ready for their next performance."[3] Rather than feeling soothed, another sort of child might at that moment have conceived a long-range ambition to kill *both* Black Bart and Sheriff Lucky for their complicity in tricking him.

In the twentieth century, as this boy learned, the image of the frontier balances precariously between too much reality and too little. Properly screened and edited, the doings of the Old Frontier are quite a bit of fun. But when encounters with death, or injury, or conflict, or loss become unexpectedly convincing and compelling, then fun can make an abrupt departure, while emotions considerably more troubling take its place.

The outlaw-killing lad was not the only child encountering the limits of Frontierland's fun, not the only one to stumble in the uncertain turf along the border between the imagined and the actual. As the *Saturday Evening Post* writer described it, one "seven-year-old boy was certain he could tell the real from the unreal."

As they jogged along on the burro side, the leathery mule-skinner warned, "Look out for them thar cactus plants. Them needles is mighty sharp."

The skeptical boy leaned over and took a swipe at the cactus. On the way to the first-aid station, he decided all was not fantasy at Disneyland. The management has since moved the cactus out of reach.[4]

Moving the cactus—finding the place where its thorns could *look* sharp and scary but not *be* sharp and scary—can serve as a fine representation of the whole process of getting authenticity into the proper adjustment at Frontierland. When too many surprised innocents made visits to the first-aid stand, the frontier was clearly out of alignment, and a repositioning was in order.

And yet, in other parts of Frontierland's turf, wounds and injuries were a taken-for-granted dimension of frontier life. At Tom Sawyer's Island, as

---

[3]Robert Cahn, "The Intrepid Kids of Disneyland," *Saturday Evening Post*, June 18, 1958, 22–23.

[4]Ibid., 120.

the *Saturday Evening Post* writer put it, kids "can fire air-operated, bullet-less rifles at the plastic Indians."[5] A writer for the *Reader's Digest* described the same opportunity in 1960: "From the top of a log fort you can sight in with guns on a forest in which Indians lurk. The guns don't fire bullets—they're hydraulically operated—but the recoil is so realistic that you'd never guess they aren't the genuine article."[6]

The Indians of this frontier were not, however, the sort to hold a   10 grudge. Visitors could fire away at the Indians and then move on to a voyage in "Indian canoes paddled by real Indians."[7] "Realness" was not, in this case, an easy matter to arrange. "Wanting authentic Native Americans to paddle canoes full of guests around the rivers of the theme area, Disneyland recruited employees from southwestern tribes," the historian John Findlay writes in his book *Magic Lands*. "These Indians, of course, came from the desert rather than a riverine or lakes environment, so they had to be taught how to paddle canoes by white employees of the park who had learned the skill at summer camp."[8]

Over the decades, life at Frontierland has become, if anything, more confusing for those rare individuals who stop and think about what they are seeing. There is, for instance, the question of the frontier's geographical location. On one side of a path, a roller coaster rushes through a southwestern mesa, carved into a mine. On the other side of the path, the great river, with its stately steamboat, rolls by. Where is the frontier? Evidently where New Mexico borders on the Mississippi River, where western gold and silver miners load their ore directly onto steamboats heading to New Orleans.

In recent times, even the ritualized violence between whites and Indians has become a matter of some awkwardness. On the various rides along the Rivers of America, one passes a settler's cabin, wildly in flames. In my childhood, the guides announced that the cabin was on fire because Indians had attacked it. In current times, the cabin is just on fire, usually without commentary or blame. At the further reaches of cultural change lies the recent experience of an acquaintance: the guide told his group that the cabin was on fire because the settler had been ecologically and environmentally careless.[9]

Consider, as well, the curious politics of the shooting gallery encountered at the entrance to Frontierland. Visitors can take firearm in hand and

---

[5]Ibid., 119.

[6]Ira Wolfert, "Walt Disney's Magic Kingdom," *Reader's Digest,* April 1960, 147.

[7]Ibid., 147.

[8]John M. Findlay, *Magic Lands: Western Cityscapes and American Culture after 1940* (Berkeley: University of California Press, 1992), 93–94.

[9]Change seems to have been equally dramatic in Disney thinking about Indians. In 1993, the Walt Disney Company announced plans for a new American history theme park in Virginia. The section called "Native America," one company representative said, would now display "the sophisticated, intelligent societies that existed here before European settlers came, and in fact wiped out their societies" (Michael Wines, "Disney Will 'Recreate' U.S. History Next to a Place Where It Was Made," *New York Times,* November 12, 1993).

shoot at a variety of targets—including a railroad train, winding its way through a sculpted landscape. But if you are shooting at a railroad train, then *who*—in this frontier role-play—*are you*? Which side are you on? If you are firing on the train, then you seem to be either a hostile Indian or a murderous and larcenous outlaw. What is going on here? Is the visitor receiving an invitation to play with point of view, to reconsider the whole question of the identity and interests of good guys and bad guys, champions of progress and opponents of progress? Or is this casting of the railroad as target simply the product of Disneyland's designers working under the mandate to create a scene chock-full of the shapes and forms that will say "frontier," with the assumption that any visitor so stimulated visually will fall into step with the mythic patterns of frontier life, pick up a gun, and blast away at whatever is in sight?

If professional Western American historians find themselves conceptually without anchor when they visit Frontierland, the reason is clear: with the possible exception of the suggestion that environmental carelessness produced the settler's cabin fire, the work of academic historians has had virtually no impact either on Disneyland's vision of the frontier or on the thinking of Disneyland's visitors. That cheerful and complete indifference to the work of frontier historians may, in truth, be the secret of the place's success.

The Fight for the Frontier in the History Department

In recent years, academic historians have given the idea of the frontier a pretty rough overhauling. Nicknamed the "f-word" and pummeled for its ethnocentrism and vagueness, the term has from time to time landed on the ropes, perilously close to conceding the match. But a determined group of trainers and handlers has always trooped out to the rescue, braced up the frontier, and gotten it back on its feet for the next round.

The academic boxing match centers on this question: how well does the concept of the frontier perform the task of describing, explaining, and encapsulating the story of the colonization of North America? "Miserably," answers one group of historians, of which I happen to be a member.[10] "Pretty well," responds a different set of historians, "if you make a few adjustments and realignments in its definition."

The case for the frailty of the "f-word" is an easy one to make. First, built into the idea is an inflexible point of view. For the term to have clear meaning, historians have had to hand their point of view over to the custody of English-speaking white people. In its clearest and most concrete meaning, as Richard White has said, the frontier was where white people got scarce—or, with a friendly amendment, the frontier was where white

15

---

[10]See Patricia Nelson Limerick, Clyde A. Milner II, and Charles E. Rankin, eds., *Trails: Toward a New Western History* (Lawrence: University Press of Kansas, 1991).

people got *scared* because they were scarce. This perspective has certainly been an important psychological reality in American history, and it is a psychological reality well worth study. But using the frontier as an analytic concept puts the historian at risk of adopting the point of view of only one of the contesting groups. Moreover, the frontier came with two sides, the Anglo-American side and the one labeled "the other side of the frontier." Jammed into the second category were Indians of all tribes (often tribes that fought against each other as well as against Anglo Americans), long-term Hispano settlers, and more recent Mexican immigrants. In lived reality, the people on this "other side of the frontier" did not form anything remotely resembling a united team or a homogeneous society. Conceptually, neither "side" of the frontier offered much in the way of accommodations for Asian Americans, who came from the "wrong" direction, or for African Americans, participants in the westward movement who encountered a full measure of restrictions and exclusions. Trying to grasp the enormous human complexity of the American West is not easy under any circumstances, and the effort to reduce a tangle of many-sided encounters to a world defined by a frontier line only makes a tough task even tougher.

Second, the idea of the frontier runs almost entirely on an east-to-west track. Indeed, to most of its users, the term "frontier" has been a synonym for the American nation's westward movement. Can such a term do justice to the prior presence of Indian people, to the northward movement of Spanish-speaking people, or the eastward movement of Asians? The east-to-west movement of Anglo Americans and African Americans is enormously important, but so are these movements of other people. Try to wrap the term "frontier" around all these movements, and the poor idea stretches to the point of snapping.

Third, it is nearly impossible to define either the beginning or the ending of a frontier. If one cannot define the beginning or ending of a condition, it is not going to be easy to say when that condition is present and when it is *not* present. Return, for instance, to Frederick Jackson Turner's definition of a frontier, borrowed from the Census Department, as a place where the population numbers fewer than two people per square mile. Then think of a mining rush—where, as soon as the news of the gold or silver gets out, the population instantly exceeds two people per square mile, with enough people to form a camp or a town. By Turner's definition, then, one would have to declare the mining frontier closed virtually the moment it opened.

Other scholars have offered more enterprising, and certainly more colorful, definitions of the closing of the frontier. One of the best comes from the historian Paula Petrik, who studied prostitutes in Helena, Montana. In the early years of Helena, Petrik reports, the prostitutes tended to be their own employers. They were able to hold on to the rewards of their labors, and some of them saved significant amounts of money, owned real estate, and lent money at interest. But then, as the frontier phase passed, men took

20

control of the prostitutes and their earnings. This, I thought when I first heard Petrik's evidence and argument, is the most interesting marker of the end of the frontier I am ever going to hear: the frontier ends when the pimps come to town.[11]

My own entry in the "closing" competition rests on the popularization of tourism and the quaintness of the folk. When Indian war dances became tourist spectacles, when the formerly scorned customs of the Chinese drew tourists to Chinatown, when former out-groups found that characteristics that once earned them disapproval could now earn them a living, when fearful, life-threatening deserts became charming patterns of color and light, the war was over and the frontier could be considered closed, even museumized. But this nomination comes with its own fatal flaw. Let the car break down in the desert, or let the Indians file a lawsuit to reassert an old land claim, and the quaint appeal of nature and native can abruptly vanish. The frontier is suddenly reopened, and the whole question of beginnings and endings becomes unsettled again.

Fourth, a presumption of innocence and exceptionalism is interwoven with the roots of frontier history, as Americans have understood it. The contrast becomes clearest when one thinks of a nation like South Africa. Europeans forcibly took South Africa from the natives, everyone understands, and the residents still struggle with the consequences. But the idea of the frontier permits the United States to make an appeal to innocence and exceptionalism: while South Africa underwent an invasion and a conquest, the United States had an expanding frontier of democracy, opportunity, and equality.

The term "frontier" blurs the fact of conquest and throws a veil over the similarities between the story of American westward expansion and the planetary story of the expansion of European empires. Whatever meanings historians give the term, in popular culture it carries a persistently happy affect, a tone of adventure, heroism, and even fun very much in contrast with the tough, complicated, and sometimes bloody and brutal realities of conquest. Under these conditions, the word "frontier" uses historians before historians can use it.

Fifth, an unthinking reliance on the idea of the frontier almost ruined Western American history. For too many years, Western historians let Frederick Jackson Turner do most of their thinking for them. By accepting many of Turner's boundaries, Western historians drastically narrowed the scope of their field. Consider, for instance, the number of important economic activities ignored by conventional frontier historians. Scholars wrote voluminously about the mining frontier and the cattle frontier, but the logging frontier, the fishing frontier, the tourism-promoting frontier, the investing-in-real-estate-and-mortgages frontier, and the labor-contracting frontier remained very much understudied. Grain-based agriculture domi-

[11]Paula Petrik, *No Step Backward* (Helena: Montana Historical Society Press, 1987), chapter 2, "Capitalists with Rooms: Prostitution in Helena, 1865–1900," 25–58.

nated the category of the farming-frontier; no book appeared under the title *The Vegetable Frontier* or *The Fruit Frontier*. Few of the important economic enterprises resting on women's labor registered in the occupational frontier model: *The Poultry Frontier, The Laundry Frontier, The Sewing Frontier, The Boardinghouse Frontier,* and *The Sexual Services Frontier* all await their authors.[12] Similarly, since conventional frontier historians rigorously observed the 1890 Turnerian deadline for the closing, enterprises that started late—the copper, coal, petroleum, moviemaking, skiing, atomic-weapons-developing, and defense-spending frontiers—could not qualify for study.

The field of Western American history could never achieve its full vitality and range of subjects unless the crucial term "frontier" underwent critical reexamination. To some scholars, critical reexamination could lead to rehabilitation, with a more carefully thought-out, more inclusive, less ethnocentric definition of the term. In 1962 the historian Jack Forbes began a campaign to define the frontier "as an *intergroup contact situation*," "an instance of dynamic interaction between human beings," involving "such processes as acculturation, assimilation, miscegenation, race prejudice, conquest, imperialism, and colonialism."[13]

In a collection of essays comparing colonization in North America and southern Africa, published in 1981, the historians Howard Lamar and Leonard Thompson joined the campaign for a transformed definition of the frontier, "not as a boundary or line, but a territory or zone of interpenetration between two previously distinct societies." What marked the beginning or the ending of such a condition of interpenetration? "The frontier 'opens' in a given zone when the first representatives of the intrusive society arrive," Lamar and Thompson explained; "it 'closes' when a single political authority has established hegemony over the zone."[14]

In the most recent campaigns to brace up the idea of the frontier, the historians William Cronon, George Miles, and Jay Gitlin offer a six-part definition of the frontier process: species shifting, market making, land taking, boundary setting, state forming, and self shaping.[15] Stephen Aron argues for what he calls "the Greater Western History," a reconceived model of the westward movement with more recognition of cultural and moral complexity.[16] ...

25

---

[12]Historians have, of course, written on these topics, but they have sensibly avoided trying to package any of them as kinds of frontiers, parallel to the "mining frontier" or the "cattle frontier."

[13]Jack D. Forbes, "Frontiers in American History," *Journal of the West* 1, nos. 1 and 2 (1962): 63–74, and "Frontiers in American History and the Role of the Frontier Historian," *Ethnohistory* 15 (Spring 1968): 203–35. I am quoting from the second, 207 and 205.

[14]Howard Lamar and Leonard Thompson, eds., *The Frontier in History: North America and Southern Africa Compared* (New Haven, Conn.: Yale University Press, 1981), 7.

[15]William Cronon, George Miles, and Jay Gitlin, "Becoming West: Toward a New Meaning for Western History," in *Under an Open Sky: Rethinking America's Western Past,* ed. Cronon, Miles, and Gitlin (New York: Norton, 1992), 3–27.

[16]Stephen Aron, "Lessons in Conquest: Towards a Greater Western History," *Pacific Historical Review* 63 (May 1994).

Presidential Politics on the Frontier

Presidents and presidential candidates are a distinct minority in the American population. And yet their circumstances render them useful as case studies in popular attitudes. In the last half of the twentieth century, electoral politics makes a presidential candidate into the navigational equivalent of a bat, sending off signals, reading the signals as they bounce back, and attempting to set a course based on what these signals reveal. When presidential candidates and presidents put the frontier analogy to use, there is a broader lesson available on the persuasive powers given to that analogy by particular styles of presentation at particular times.

On July 15, 1960, in Los Angeles, California, John F. Kennedy faced "west on what was once the last frontier" and accepted the Democratic presidential nomination. In mid-speech he retold the familiar Turnerian story of westward expansion:

> From the lands that stretch three thousand miles behind me, the pioneers of old gave up their safety, their comfort, and sometimes their lives to build a new world here in the West.... They were determined to make that new world strong and free, to overcome its hazards and its hardships, to conquer the enemies that threatened from within and without.

These "enemies" were, presumably, a combination of natural forces, natives, and cautious naysayers who resisted the currents of Manifest Destiny.[17] The success of John F. Kennedy's rhetoric rested not only on oratorical skill but also on historical timing: he gave this speech before the rise of environmentalism, the resurgence of Indian activism, and the onset of widespread queasiness over American overseas imperialism shifted the terrain of national opinion regarding those "enemies that threatened from within and without."[18] Kennedy was free to offer an image of the New Frontier, premised on the assumption that the campaigns of the Old Frontier had been successful and morally justified.

Like Turner, most Americans in Kennedy's audience assumed that the   30
frontier had closed in the nineteenth century.[19] "Today," Kennedy proclaimed, "some would say that those struggles are all over—that all the horizons have been explored, that all the battles have been won, that there is no longer an American frontier." That notion, however, could no longer stand: "For the problems are not all solved and the battles are not all won—and we stand today on the edge of a New Frontier—the frontier of the

[17]*Manifest Destiny:* The nationalistic belief that the United States was preordained to expand westward to the Pacific Ocean, articulated in the 1840s during debate over the annexation of Texas and Oregon.

[18]*"Let the Word Go Forth": The Speeches, Statements, and Writings of John F. Kennedy,* selected and with an introduction by Theodore C. Sorensen (New York: Delacorte Press, 1988), 100–102.

[19]For a wide-ranging discussion of this assumption, see Wrobel, *The End of American Exceptionalism.*

1960s—a frontier of unknown opportunities and perils—a frontier of un-fulfilled hopes and threats." Here was an image of the frontier that seemed composed of equal parts of Buffalo Bill Cody and Frederick Jackson Turner: half a frontier of violence and inverted conquest, in which innocent Ameri-cans defended themselves against the attacks of savages, and half a frontier of peaceful, pastoral Americans seeking a better world. "I tell you," Kennedy declared, "the New Frontier is here, whether we seek it or not."

> Beyond that frontier are the uncharted areas of science and space, un-solved problems of peace and war, unconquered pockets of ignorance and prejudice, unanswered questions of poverty and surplus. It would be easier to shrink back from that frontier.... But I believe the times demand invention, innovation, imagination, decision. I am asking you to be new pioneers on that New Frontier.

And then, with the topic of foreign affairs, the analogy made a clear shift to-ward the violent frontier of Cody:

> For the harsh facts of the matter are that we stand on this frontier at a turning point in history. We must prove all over again whether this na-tion—or any nation so conceived—can long endure; whether our so-ciety...can compete with the single-minded advance of the Commu-nist system.

On this "race for mastery of the sky and the rain, the ocean and the tides, the far side of space and the inside of men's minds" hinged the prospects of the New Frontier.[20] Drawn from both Cody and Turner, the 1890s vision of the frontier as the triumphant but demanding crusade of the American people made a nearly perfect match with the 1960s search for language to direct and motivate the American public in the midst of the Cold War.

Twenty years later, one might expect a few things to have changed in the usefulness of the frontier analogy. Indian people were active in pressing their rights; the environmental price of conquest was visible and publicized; the imposition of American will by force had stumbled in Vietnam. But none of this discouraged President Ronald Reagan. The imagery of pioneers and frontiers echoed through his speeches and through his "life-style," as he vacationed on the "ranch" in Southern California, with horse and cowboy hat in conspicuous display. In a memorable conflation of Washington, D.C., and the West, the Secret Service named the riding trails after streets in Washington, D.C., and code-named the president "Rawhide." Thus, the phrase "Rawhide entering Pennsylvania Avenue" meant that the president was "entering the main trail" at his ranch. "Rawhide" rode down "Pennsyl-vania Avenue" with some frequency. "There is nothing better for the inside of a man," Reagan was fond of saying, "than the outside of a horse."[21]

---

[20]"*Let the Word Go Forth*," 100–102.

[21]"President Very Much at Home on Ranch," *Denver Post,* August 23, 1986 (originally *Washington Post*).

On the Fourth of July, 1982, greeting the return of the space shuttle to Edwards Air Force Base, Reagan gave his fullest tribute to Turnerian frontier history. "The conquest of new frontiers for the betterment of our homes and families," he said, "is a crucial part of our national character." Like Kennedy, Reagan parted from Turner to affirm the openness of America's frontiers: "There are those who thought the closing of the Western frontier marked an end to America's greatest period of vitality. Yet we're crossing new frontiers every day." With the specter of a closed frontier disposed of, Reagan returned to the Turnerian terms of basic American character; the space shuttle's astronauts "reaffirm to all of us that as long as there are frontiers to be explored and conquered, Americans will lead the way."[22]

In his second inaugural address, Reagan pitched into a celebration of westward expansion:

> [T]he men of the Alamo call out encouragement to each other; a settler pushes west and sings his song, and the song echoes out forever and fills the unknowing air.
>
> It is the American sound: It is hopeful, bighearted, idealistic— daring, decent and fair. That's our heritage, that's our song. We sing it still. For all our problems, we are together as of old.[23]

Twenty-five years after Kennedy's New Frontier, could such rhetoric still work? The columnist William Safire felt that it certainly did. The song of the settler, Safire thought, was "a lovely metaphor, and enabled [the President] to use the half-dozen adjectives that describe his vision of America: 'hopeful, bighearted, idealistic—daring, decent and fair.' "[24] In his State of the Union speech two weeks later, Reagan stuck with the frontier, celebrating "a revolution carrying us to new heights of progress by pushing back frontiers of space and knowledge."[25] ...

The Headline Frontier

...Headline writers are, predictably, heavy users of the words "frontier" and "pioneer." They trust those words, and the words repay that trust. They are words that carry the master key to the reader's mind; with that key, they can slip into the mind and deposit their meanings before anyone quite knows they are there.

To assemble a set of artifacts demonstrating the persistent and widespread power of these words, I looked at roughly four thousand headlines, from 1988 through the first half of 1993, that made use of "frontier" and "pi-

35

[22]United Press International, "Complete text of President Reagan's remarks," July 5, 1982.

[23]"Transcript of Second Inaugural Address by Reagan," *New York Times*, January 22, 1985.

[24]William Safire, "Grading the Speech," *New York Times*, January 24, 1985.

[25]"Text of the President's State of the Union Address to Congress," *New York Times*, February 7, 1985.

oneer." The first time through, I made a strategic error, and simply looked to see how silly these references were. This was an easy exercise, because many of the usages are indeed goofy. But at the end of the exercise, I had to realize that simply chuckling over these phrases was not accomplishing much for the cause of understanding.

The next time, then, I tried to find the patterns in the usage of these words. What seems to be going on in people's minds in the late twentieth century when they call someone a pioneer or refer to an activity or an enterprise as a frontier? Answering this question can illuminate even the sillier usages, showing just how far from historical reality this historical reference has strayed. This exercise works best if the reader picks a nineteenth-century pioneer and then imagines how that pioneer might respond to his or her twentieth-century descendants. Or one might think only of Frederick Jackson Turner and imagine his response to what the twentieth century has done to his favorite term and his favorite people.

Let us begin on the comparatively neutral frontier of food. "Eating to Heal: The New Frontiers," the *New York Times* announced in 1990. Apparently fighting on the wrong side of this frontier was the "Cookie Pioneer," "creator of the fortune cookie folding machine and a line of risqué fortune cookies." The Cookie Pioneer may have held only a superficial kinship to the Cinnamon Roll Pioneers, but all of these pioneers could have joined forces with the Fast Food Pioneer and the Pioneer of the Snack Food Industry to defend their turf against the insinuations of the Natural Foods Pioneer, the Vegetarian Pioneer, and the Pioneer of the Edible Landscape. Occupying less contested territory were the Pasta Pioneers, the Potato Pioneer, and the Microwave Popcorn Pioneer, and surely the most memorable of the food pioneers—the Pioneer of the South Philadelphia Hoagie.[26]

As striking as the food pioneers are the "lifestyle pioneers": the Passionate Pioneer of Fitness Franchising (the woman who founded Jazzercise Inc.); the Surfing Pioneer ("he pioneered a whole way of surfing for thousands"); the Psychedelic Pioneer; the New Age Pioneer; the Sex-Change

[26]Molly O'Neill, "Eating to Heal: The New Frontiers," *New York Times,* February 7, 1990; "Edward Louie Is Dead, Cookie Pioneer Was 69," Associated Press, May 31, 1990; "Two Cinnamon Roll Pioneers Are Spicing Up Product Line," *Nation's Restaurant News,* June 6, 1988; Cecilia Deck, "Fast-Food Pioneer A&W Survives to Map Comeback," *Chicago Tribune,* November 19, 1989; Berkley Hudson, "Laura Scudder Was More than a Name; Monterey Park Will Honor 'Pioneer, Instigator, Doer' Who Helped Create Snack-Food Industry," *Los Angeles Times,* April 9, 1989; Marcia Dunn, "Pioneer in Natural Foods; Organic Farm Founder Had 50-Year Head Start," *Los Angeles Times,* January 15, 1989; Felicia Gressette, "Pioneer Vegetarian Fests Get '90s Update," *Miami Herald,* February 18, 1993; Judith Sims, "A Walk in the Garden with Pioneer of Edible Landscape," *Los Angeles Times,* February 25, 1989; Andrew Gumbel, "Pasta Pioneers," *Chicago Tribune,* December 15, 1988; "Potato Pioneer Dead at 73," United Press International, June 20, 1989; Russell Mitchell, "Golden Valley Needs a Side of Fries: A Pioneer in Microwave Popcorn," *Business Week,* November 7, 1988; Andy Wallace, "Antoinette Iannelli, Restaurateur and Pioneer of the South Philadelphia Hoagie," *Philadelphia Inquirer,* April 8, 1992.

Pioneer; the Porn Pioneer; the Pioneer in the Crack Business; and the Peekaboo Pioneer, the founder of Frederick's of Hollywood. Frederick's pioneering work did not exhaust the possibilities of the underwear frontier: "Underwear Pioneers Targeting Men," one headline reads, and the story opens with this promising line: "The two designing women who revolutionized the bra industry in the 1970s with the invention of the first jogging bra have turned their talents to men's underwear." On the subject of fabrics and new materials, there is the memorable Polyester Pioneer as well as a Pioneer of Plastics and a Stainless Steel Cookware Pioneer.[27]

Forced into the discomfort and disorientation of time travel, Frederick Jackson Turner, or any of his contemporaries, would have to experience astonishment at the applications of the word "pioneer" in the late twentieth century, at this implied kinship between overland travelers and marketers of underwear, stainless steel, and hoagies. Of all these contestants, the award for the most unsettling pioneer would have to go to Dr. Louis Irwin Grossman, Pioneer in Root Canal Dentistry. And if there were an award for the twentieth-century pioneer of the product that nineteenth-century pioneers would have had the most occasions to appreciate, then that prize would go to Bernard Castro, described as the Pioneer of the Sleeper-Sofa.[28]

Beneath and beyond the silliness of these references lies a clear set of patterns. The pioneers and frontiers cluster in particular areas and enterprises. Art, music, sports, fashion, commerce, law, and labor activism get their full share of the analogy. Technology holds the biggest cluster: technology of transportation (bicycles, automobiles, helicopters, airplanes, rockets, and spacecraft); technology of communications and information (radio, television, talk shows, CD players, laser discs, computers, software, programming); technology of medicine (heart transplants, plastic surgery, 40

---

[27]Mary Rowland, "The Passionate Pioneer of Fitness Franchising," *Working Woman,* November 1988; Joe Ditler, "Surfing Pioneer Donald Takayama Is Chairman of the Board Again," *Los Angeles Times,* May 3, 1990; Steve Morse, "A Psychedelic Pioneer Remembered," *Boston Globe,* June 16, 1989; Marianne Meyer, "New Age Pioneers," *Marketing and Media Decisions,* February 1988; Eric Lichtblau, "Sex-Change Pioneer Sues a Mission Viejo Hospital for Damages," *Los Angeles Times,* December 2, 1988, and "Sex-Change Pioneer Jorgensen," Associated Press, May 4, 1989; John Johnson and Michael Connelly, "A Porn Pioneer Still Baffles Police, Peers," *Los Angeles Times,* August 20, 1989; Pete Bowles, "A Drug 'Pioneer' Gets Life—Pioneer in the City's Crack Business," *Newsday,* December 2, 1989; Michael Kilian, "Frederick's: Peekaboo Pioneer," *Chicago Tribune,* June 6, 1990; "Underwear Pioneers Targeting Men," *Chicago Tribune,* December 24, 1989; Michael Arndt, "Amoco Spins a Reward for Polyester Pioneer," *Chicago Tribune,* May 4, 1989; "Inventor of Lexan®, Resin and Plastics Pioneer Dies," PR Newswire, February 17, 1989; Lisa Ann Casey, "Stainless Steel Cookware Pioneer," *Weekly Home Furnishings Newspaper,* April 17, 1989.

[28]"Pioneer in Root Canal Dentistry," *Los Angeles Times,* March 29, 1988; David Hancock, "Sleeper-Sofa Pioneer Bernard Castro Dies," *Miami Herald,* August 25, 1991.

headache treatment, weight reduction, gene therapy); technology of weaponry (rocketry, atomic bombs). Indeed, it is impossible to read all these references to the frontiers of technology without recognizing that the American public has genuinely and completely accepted, ratified, and bought the notion that the American frontiering spirit, sometime in the last century, picked itself up and made a definitive relocation—from territorial expansion to technological and commercial expansion.

In November 1944, as the end of World War II neared, President Franklin Roosevelt asked Vannevar Bush, director of the Office of Scientific Research and Development, to report on the prospects for American science after the war. "New frontiers of the mind," Roosevelt said, "are before us, and if they are pioneered with the same vision, boldness, and drive with which we have waged this war we can create a fuller and more fruitful employment and a fuller and more fruitful life."[29] Called *Science—The Endless Frontier*, Bush's response to Roosevelt's request set the agenda for federally funded science. "It is in keeping with basic United States policy," Bush wrote, "that the Government should foster the opening of new frontiers," and federal investment in science "is the modern way to do it."[30] Casting science as the nation's new frontier, a frontier maintained by hearty federal funding, Vannevar Bush captured and promoted the popular understanding of the frontier's relocation after Turner.

Certainly the space program has provided the best example of this pattern. The promoters of space exploration and development may well qualify as the nation's most committed and persistent users of the frontier analogy. *Pioneering the Space Frontier,* the 1986 Paine commission report on the future of the space program, shows the analogy at its most fervent. The story of the American nation, as imagined by the Paine commissioners, was a triumphant and glorious story of success, with the complex stories of Indian conquest and African American slavery simply ignored and eliminated. "The promise of virgin lands and the opportunity to live in freedom," the commissioners declared, "brought our ancestors to the shores of North America." The frontiers have not closed, and Manifest Destiny has just taken a turn skyward: "Now space technology has freed humankind to move outward from Earth as a species destined to expand to other worlds." The best that the Paine commissioners could offer in recognizing that frontiers might not always be vacant was this memorable line: "As we move outward into the Solar System, we must remain true to our values as Americans: To go forward peacefully and to respect the integrity of planetary bodies and

---

[29]Roosevelt letter to Vannevar Bush, reprinted in Bush's *Science—the Endless Frontier: A Report to the President on a Program for Postwar Scientific Research* (Washington, D.C.: National Science Foundation, 1945; rpt. 1960), 3–4.
    [30]Ibid., 8.

alien life forms, with equality of opportunity for all."[31] If one thinks of the devastation of Indians by disease, alcohol, war, loss of territory, and coercive assimilation, and then places that reality next to the Paine commissioners' pious intentions, one feels some obligation to take up the mission of warning the "alien life forms," to suggest that they keep their many eyes on their wallets when they hear these intentions invoked, especially the line about "equality of opportunity for all."

However this frontier experience plays out for alien life forms, the mental act of equating the frontier of westward expansion with the development of space proved to be an enterprise that ran itself. In the selling of space as "the final frontier," the aerospace industry, the National Aeronautics and Space Administration, presidents, the news media, and the entertainment business collaborated with perfect harmony, with no need for centralized direction or planning, with a seamless match in their methods and goals. The split infinitive was regrettable, but the writers of *Star Trek* came up with the phrase to capture the essential idea brought to mind at the mention of the words "frontier" and "pioneer": "to boldly go where no man has gone before."

Meanwhile, *La Frontera*

Anglo Americans have fixed their attention on the definition of the frontier drawn from the imaginative reconstruction of the story of the United States and its westward expansion. But North America has, in fact, had two strong traditions in the use of the term. There is the much more familiar, English, usage of the frontier as the place where white settlers entered a zone of "free" land and opportunity. But there is the much less familiar, but much more realistic, usage of *la frontera*, the borderlands between Mexico and the United States. This is not simply a place where two groups meet; Indian people have been influential players in the complicated pattern of human relations in the area. In the nineteenth century, trade, violence, conquest, and cultural exchange punctuated and shaped life in the borderlands. In the twentieth century, with conflicts over the restriction of immigration, with disputes over water flow and environmental pollution, and with a surge of industrial development and population growth from

---

[31]*Pioneering the Space Frontier: The Report of the National Commission on Space* (New York: Bantam Books, 1986), 3–4. See also Gerard K. O'Neill, *The High Frontier: Human Colonies in Space* (Princeton, N.J.: Space Studies Institute Press, 1989); and Harry L. Shipman, *Humans in Space: Twenty-first Century Frontiers* (New York: Plenum Press, 1989). Shipman's remark—"Americans, in particular, value exploration in and of itself because of the importance of the frontier in our history" (27)—typifies the space boosters' understanding of the history of westward expansion. For a more extensive discussion of the cultural psychology of the space program, see Patricia Nelson Limerick, "Imagined Frontiers: Westward Expansion and the Future of the Space Program," in *Space Policy Alternatives*, ed. Radford Byerly, Jr. (Boulder, Colo.: Westview, 1992).

American-owned businesses (*maquiladoras*) operating in northern Mexico, conditions along the border remain far from tranquil.[32]

In the idea of *la frontera,* there is no illusion of vacancy, of triumphal conclusions, or of simplicity. As the writer Gloria Anzaldúa puts it, the United States–Mexican border is "where the Third World grates up against the first and bleeds."[33] It is a unique place on the planet's surface, a zone where an industrialized nation shares a long land border with a nation much troubled by poverty. "Ambivalence and unrest," Anzaldúa says, "reside there and death is no stranger."[34] Any temptation to romanticize *la frontera*—as a place of cultural syncretism, a place where the Spanish and English languages have learned to cohabit and even merge—runs aground on the bare misery of poverty in the border towns.[35]

The idea of the frontier is extremely well established as cultural common property. If the idea of *la frontera* had anywhere near the standing of the idea of the frontier, we would be well launched toward self-understanding, directed toward a realistic view of this nation's position in the hemisphere and in the world. "The struggle of borders is our reality still," Anzaldúa writes.[36] One can tinker a bit with that line to draw the crucial contrast: "The adventure of frontiers is our fantasy still; the struggle of borders is our reality still."

In truth, this idea of the frontier as border has made some inroads in popular thinking. If you are reading a headline for a news story set outside the United States, there is a chance that the word "frontier" will carry a meaning completely different from its usual one. References to "the Romania-Bulgaria frontier" or to "the Lebanese-Israeli frontier" are quite a different matter from references to the frontier where the pioneer stands on the edge of vacancy and opportunity. These are frontiers in the old, concrete, down-to-earth sense, much closer in meaning to *la frontera:* borders between countries, between peoples, between authorities, sometimes between armies. When "Algeria and Morocco reopen their frontier," or when the nation of Turkey decides it "will close its frontier with Bulgaria," these are references to borders that are full of possibilities for both cooperation and friction, places where the meaning of "opening" and "closing" differs

---

[32]See Oscar J. Martínez, *Troublesome Border* (Tucson: University of Arizona Press, 1986); Mario T. García, "La Frontera: The Border as Symbol and Reality in Mexican-American Thought," *Mexican Studies,* Summer 1985, 195–225; Alan Weisman and Jay Dusard, *La Frontera: The United States Border with Mexico* (Tucson: University of Arizona Press, 1986); Tom Miller, *On the Border: Portraits of America's Southwestern Frontier* (New York: Harper and Row, 1981).

[33]Gloria Anzaldúa, *Borderlands/La Frontera: The New Mestiza* (San Francisco: Aunt Lute Books, 1987), 3.

[34]Ibid., 4.

[35]See Luis Alberto Urrea, *Across the Wire: Life and Hard Times on the Mexican Border* (New York: Doubleday, 1993).

[36]Anzaldúa, *Borderlands/La Frontera,* 63.

dramatically from what Frederick Jackson Turner and the director of the census meant in the 1890s.[37]

In these references to international borders and boundaries, the word "frontier" takes a firmer hold on reality. In my collection of headlines, the frequent appearance of this definition of frontier caught me by surprise. Perhaps, it began to seem, there is more hope for this word than seemed possible at first; perhaps popular thinking has already dug a sizable channel for thinking about the frontier in a manner quite different from the *Star Trek* mode.

One other pattern of usage, however, struck me as equally surprising: the omnipresence in headlines of African American pioneers. Here, the usage was again closer to the *Star Trek* definition, with pioneers boldly going where no one like them had gone before. Pioneers in civil rights— "Desegregation's Pioneers"—were everywhere, from A. Philip Randolph[38] to Rosa Parks,[39] from Julian Bond[40] to Charlayne Hunter-Gault.[41] The range of African American pioneers covers a great deal of turf: a Pioneer Black Professional Golfer; a Pioneer of Black Pride; the National Football League's Pioneer Black Coach; a Pioneer Black (Theatrical) Producer; a Pioneer Black Announcer; Negro League Pioneers; a Pioneer Black Ivy League Teacher; a Black Radio Pioneer; a Black Foreign Service Pioneer; a Pioneer Black Los Angeles Judge; a Pioneer Black Journalist; a Pioneer in Black Film; and Sidney Poitier, the winner of the "coveted Pioneer Award," bestowed at the Black Oscar Nominees dinner in 1989. As all these headlines suggest, the idea of calling African American people pioneers, as an appropriately complimentary way to refer to their dignity, courage, and determination in traveling where no black person had gone before, has established itself as part of the American cultural vocabulary. When in 1989 Secretary of Health and Human Services Louis Sullivan "told the graduating class of A. Philip Randolph Campus High School in Manhattan that they will become 'pioneers' if they meet the challenges of fighting inequality, racism, and poverty in the 21st century," Sullivan was employing the term in its standard usage.[42]

---

[37]"Thousands Form Human Chain across Romania-Bulgaria Frontier," Reuters, June 8, 1990; "Palestinian Guerrilla is Killed at Lebanese-Israeli Frontier," *New York Times,* September 6, 1989; "Algeria and Morocco Reopen their Frontier," Reuters, June 5, 1988; Jim Bodgener, "Turkey Will Close its Frontier with Bulgaria Today," *Financial Times,* August 22, 1989.

[38]*A. Philip Randolph:* Asa Philip Randolph (1889–1979), African American labor leader.

[39]*Rosa Parks:* Rosa Lee Parks (b.1913), American civil rights activist famous for refusing to give up her seat to a white rider on a segregated bus in 1955.

[40]*Julian Bond:* African American politician and civil rights leader (b. 1940).

[41]*Charlayne Hunter-Gault:* African American journalist and author.

[42]David Maraniss, "Memories in Black and White; Desegregation's Pioneers," *Washington Post,* June 6, 1990; "Genevieve Stuttaford Reviews *A. Philip Randolph: Pioneer of the Civil Rights Movement,*" *Publishers Weekly,* May 11, 1990; "Rights Pioneer Parks Hospitalized," *Los*

This usage was so well understood that it gave rise to one of the few cases   50
where a person interviewed in a newspaper article actually engaged and questioned the meaning of the term "pioneer," and its application to him. "National League President Plays Down 'Pioneer' Talk," the headline read. The opening sentence explained, "National League President Bill White says he's getting tired of people referring to him as a black pioneer.... 'I'm not a pioneer,' White said. 'Jackie [Robinson][43] was the pioneer.'"[44] To Bill White, "pioneer" was the term reserved for the unusually courageous person who went first, and the one who faced the worst and the most intense opposition and resistance.

The African American applications of the pioneer analogy caught me completely by surprise. They took the ground out from under any remaining inclination I might have had simply to mock the analogy. The lesson of these references is this: the whole package of frontier and pioneer imagery has ended up as widely dispersed intellectual property. One could argue, as I probably at other times *would* have argued, that African Americans would be well advised to keep their distance from the metaphors and analogies of conquest and colonialism, that there are other, and better, ways to say that someone was a person of principle, innovation, and determination without calling him or her a pioneer. Even though they have been significant participants in the westward movement and in the life of the American West in

---

Angeles Times, February 2, 1989; "City in Ohio Honors Civil Rights Pioneer," *Chicago Tribune,* May 11, 1990; Tanya Barrientos, "Civil Rights Pioneer Julian Bond Perplexed by Persistence of Racism," *Philadelphia Inquirer,* May 9, 1992; David Treadwell, "She is the First Black to Give Commencement Address: Integration Pioneer Returns to Speak at U. of Georgia," *Los Angeles Times,* June 12, 1988; "Thelma Cowans, Pioneer Black Professional Golfer, Dies," United Press International, February 7, 1990; Rosemary L. Bray, "Renaissance for a Pioneer of Black Pride," *New York Times,* February 4, 1990; G. D. Clay, "First, There Was Fritz; Long before Art Shell, Pollard was NFL's Pioneer Black Coach," *Newsday,* December 20, 1989; "Didi Daniels Peter; Pioneer Black Producer," *Los Angeles Times,* March 2, 1989; "Joseph W. Bostic: Pioneer Black Announcer," *Los Angeles Times,* June 2, 1988; Charles Fountain, "A Baseball Historian Goes to Bat for Some Negro League Greats: Blackball Stars: Negro League Pioneers," *Christian Science Monitor,* April 15, 1988; C. Gerald Fraser, "J. Saunders Redding, 81, Is Dead; Pioneer Black Ivy League Teacher," *New York Times,* March 5, 1988; David Mills, "Tuned In to Jockey Jack; Tribute to a Black Radio Pioneer," *Washington Post,* June 23, 1990; "Clifton R. Wharton Sr. Dies; Foreign Service Pioneer," *Jet,* May 14, 1990; "Pioneer Black L.A. Judge Edwin Jefferson Dies at 84," *Jet,* September 18, 1989; "Pioneer Black Journalist Albert J. Dunsmore, 73, Praised at Detroit Rites," *Jet,* February 20, 1989; Tia Swanson, "A Pioneer in World of Black Film," *Philadelphia Inquirer,* June 4, 1992; "Black Oscar Nominees Gala Celebrates Movie Talents (Sidney Poitier Wins Pioneer Award)," *Jet,* April 17, 1989; Gene Siskel, "Poitier the Pioneer: He's Back on Screen—and Taking a Second Look at a Life Full of Firsts," *Chicago Tribune,* January 31, 1988; Nick Jesdanun, "'Pioneer' Futures," *Newsday,* June 24, 1989.

[43]*Jackie Robinson:* First African American baseball player (1919–1972) to cross the "color line" and join a major-league team in 1947.

[44]"NL President Plays Down 'Pioneer' Talk," *Chicago Tribune,* May 16, 1989. See also "NL Boss Won't Wear Pioneer Tag," *USA Today,* May 16, 1989.

the twentieth century, African Americans barely figured in the traditional tellings of frontier history; the history of pioneering Americans was for far too long a segregated, "whites-only" subject matter.[45] The image of the heroic pioneer was in many ways a vehicle of racial subordination, exalting the triumph of whites over Indians. Jackie Robinson, A. Philip Randolph, and Rosa Parks were people of great courage and spirit, and getting them entangled in the whole inherited myth of Manifest Destiny, nationalistic cheerleading, and justifications for conquest does not seem to be the best way to honor them.

But it is a bit too late to avoid that entangling. Greatly troubled by the problem of violence inflicted by blacks against blacks, Rev. Jesse Jackson pled with people to "Stop the violence!" The campaign to end the violence, he said, is "the new frontier of the civil rights movement."[46] Logic and history say that the frontier was, in fact, a place where violence served the causes of racial subordination, but a more powerful emotional understanding says that the frontier is where people of courage have gone to take a stand for the right and the good. For people of a wide range of ethnicities, when it comes to the idea of the frontier, logic and history yield to the much greater power of inherited image.

This is the curious conclusion that these headlines forced upon me: a positive image of the frontier and the pioneer is now implanted in nearly everyone's mind. It would not surprise me to see headlines referring to an American Indian lawyer as "a pioneer in the assertion of Indian legal rights," "pushing forward the frontier of tribal sovereignty"—even though it was the historical pioneers who assaulted those rights, even though it was

---

[45]The first efforts at including African Americans within Western American history left the framework of traditional frontier history unchallenged. In the introduction to the first edition of *The Black West* (1971; rpt. Seattle, Wash.: Open Hand Publishing, 1987), William Loren Katz remarked, "When historian Frederick Jackson Turner told how the frontier shaped American democracy, he ignored the black experience—not because it challenged his central thesis, but because he wrote in a tradition that had denied the existence of black people" (xii). By the time of a later edition, Katz was developing a more critical approach; consider this remark from the 1987 introduction:

> A U.S. Army that treated its Buffalo Soldiers [African American men enlisted in the post–Civil War western army] shabbily and cynically buried their military record, has accepted an image rehabilitation and trumpeted black heroism the better to recruit despairing, unemployed black youths. Will it, in the name of troopers who battled Apaches, Sioux, and Commanches, train dark young men to stem Third World liberation forces? This would be a tragic misuse of the past. (xi)

See also William Leckie, *The Buffalo Soldiers* (Norman: University of Oklahoma Press, 1967). The recent issuing of a United States Post Office stamp commemorating the Buffalo Soldiers puts an unintended spotlight on the question of the African American role in conquest; see "Part of America's Past Becomes a Stamp of Tomorrow," *New York Times*, December 8, 1993.

[46]Don Terry, "A Graver Jackson's Cry: Overcome the Violence!" *New York Times*, November 11, 1993.

the pioneers' historical frontier that charged head-on into tribal sovereignty. And yet Indian people have adopted any number of items introduced by whites. They wear cowboy hats, drive pickup trucks and automobiles, shop in supermarkets, study constitutional law in law schools, and remain Indian. In all sorts of ways, Indian people put Anglo-American artifacts, mental and physical, to use for Indian purposes. There is no very convincing argument for saying they must put a stop to their adopting and incorporating when it comes to the idea of the frontier and the image of the pioneer.

The historian Arthur Schlesinger, Jr., and many others have recently lamented "the disuniting of America" through the expansion of multicultural history.[47] We hear frequent expressions of nostalgia for an imagined era of unity, before an emphasis on race, class, and gender divided Americans into contesting units and interests. Reading several thousand headlines about pioneers and frontiers, however, convinced me that matters are by no means as disunited as the lamenters think. When African Americans turn comfortably to the image of the pioneer, then the idea of the frontier and the pioneer have clearly become a kind of multicultural common property, a joint-stock company of the imagination. As encounters with scholars from other countries usually demonstrate, this is not just multicultural, this is international. People from the Philippines, people from Senegal, people from Thailand, people with plenty of reasons to resent the frontier and cowboy diplomacy inflicted on their nations by our nation: many of them nonetheless grew up watching western movies and yearning for life on the Old Frontier and the open range.[48]

As a mental artifact, the frontier has demonstrated an astonishing stick-   55
iness and persistence. It is virtually the flypaper of our mental world; it attaches itself to everything—healthful diets, space shuttles, civil rights campaigns, heart transplants, industrial product development, musical innovations. Packed full of nonsense and goofiness, jammed with nationalistic self-congratulation and toxic ethnocentrism, the image of the frontier is nonetheless universally recognized, and laden with positive associations. Whether or not it suits my preference, the concept works as a cultural glue—a mental and emotional fastener that, in some very curious and unexpected ways, works to hold us together.

The frontier of an expanding and confident nation; the frontier of cultural interpenetration; the frontier of contracting rural settlement; the frontier of science, technology, and space; the frontier of civil rights where black pioneers ventured and persevered; the frontiers between nations in Europe, Asia, and Africa; *la frontera* of the Rio Grande and the deserts of the

---

[47]Arthur Schlesinger, Jr., *The Disuniting of America: Reflections on a Multicultural Society* (New York: Whittle Books, 1991).

[48]These impressions come from a number of speaking engagements with United States Information Agency tour groups, where international scholars have told me about their early encounters with the American frontier myth.

southwestern United States and northern Mexico: somewhere in this weird hodgepodge of frontier and pioneer imagery lie important lessons about the American identity, sense of history, and direction for the future. Standing in the way of a full reckoning with those lessons, however, is this fact: in the late *twentieth* century, the scholarly understanding formed in the late *nineteenth* century still governs most of the public rhetorical uses of the word "frontier"; the vision of Frederick Jackson Turner still governs the common and conventional understandings of the term. If the movement of ideas from frontier historians to popular culture maintains its velocity, sometime in the next century we might expect the popular usage of the word to begin to reckon with the complexity of the westward movement and its consequences. Somewhere in the mid-2000s the term might make a crucial shift, toward the reality of *la frontera* and away from the fantasy of the frontier. And that shift in meaning, *if* it occurs, will mark a great change in this nation's understanding of its own origins.

ENGAGING THE TEXT

1. What questions emerge from Limerick's exploration of Disneyland's Frontierland? How do the contradictions of Frontierland illustrate the complexity of the frontier as a historical concept?

2. What, according to Limerick, has the idea of the frontier come to mean in contemporary American culture? What areas of cultural and economic activity are most commonly associated with the frontier today? Why, in Limerick's view, has the concept of the frontier maintained its grasp on the American imagination? Do you agree that the idea of the frontier still maintains a central place in contemporary America—or is it giving way to new cultural myths?

3. What problems does Limerick see associated with the concept of the frontier? What does she mean when she says that the idea of the frontier bears the assumption of American "innocence" and that it "uses historians before historians can use it" (para. 23)?

4. What is involved in the notion of "*la frontera*," according to Limerick, and why does she believe that this concept offers a positive alternative to the traditional idea of the frontier? Do you agree that this understanding of the frontier offers a better model for understanding American history and culture?

5. Why does the use of terms like "frontier" and "pioneer" by African Americans make Limerick uneasy? How does she reconcile herself to this use? Do you think she is right to do so? Why or why not?

EXPLORING CONNECTIONS

6. How might Frederick Jackson Turner (p. 683) explain the fact that, as Limerick notes, African Americans have enthusiastically appropriated the language of the frontier and that Native Americans have adopted the lan-

guage and personal style of the cowboy? To what extent do these cross-cultural borrowings support or challenge the concept of the frontier as a site of cultural struggle?

7. To what extent might the three stories in N. Scott Momaday's "The American West and the Burden of Belief" (p. 734) be seen as offering examples of the frontier as defined "as an intergroup contact situation" or "*la frontera*"? What cultural or moral complexity do you find in this approach to frontier history?

EXTENDING THE CRITICAL CONTEXT

8. Working in groups and with the aid of maps of the United States and your local area, discuss where you would draw the boundaries of "*la frontera*" as described by Limerick in this selection. Would the frontier defined in this way run along both the northern and southern borders of the United States? Would it extend to the western and eastern borders as well? Would you locate other, more circumscribed "frontiers" within your state, county, or city? Why or why not?

9. Conduct an informal survey in which you ask informants to tell you where they think the frontier is today—or to "free associate" a list of five or more words with the concept of the frontier. Summarize your results and compare them with those of your classmates. What conclusions can you draw about the status of the idea of the frontier in the contemporary American imagination?

10. Replicate Limerick's newspaper-headline research project to test the durability of the myth of the frontier in contemporary American discourse. What issues are most commonly associated with frontier imagery, according to your findings? What meanings seem to be conveyed by contemporary uses of the frontier/pioneer story?

The Price of Admission: Harassment and Free Speech in the Wild Wild West

STEPHANIE BRAIL

The wild wild West of range wars, shootouts at high noon, and vigilante justice may seem like a thing of the past, but according to Stephanie Brail (b. 1970), it's alive and well on the World Wide Web. In Brail's view, instead of withering away in the 1890s, the frontier, with all of the freedoms and rough justice associated with it, simply morphed from the world of geographical boundaries and interracial warfare to the ostensibly more civilized world of the Internet. As Brail reminds us in this essay, however, frontier freedoms are often associated with significant dangers for women — even in the twenty-first century. How to cope with violence on the new electronic frontier while maintaining the freedoms it offers is the focus of this selection. An Internet resident since 1988, Brail discovered the price of freedom when she became involved in the first case of sexual harassment on the Net to attract national attention. Brail created the Spiderwoman mailing list for women Web designers and is also cofounder of Digital Amazon, an Internet company dedicated to promoting the interests of women online. This essay was anthologized in Wired Women: Gender and New Realities in Cyberspace *(1996), Lynn Cherny and Elizabeth R. Weire, editors.*

Online harassment has became a media headliner in the last few years. I should know: I was the target of one of the more sensationalized cases of "sexual harassment" on the Internet. When I wrote about my and others' experiences with online harassment, I found myself inundated by requests for interviews with other reporters writing the same story. I've been quoted in *USA Today,* interviewed by *Glamour,* pursued by the local ABC news affiliate and pounced on by editors at *Mademoiselle,* who wanted, I assume, a juicy tale of cyberspace stalking to sell more issues of their magazine.

Online harassment is a tough issue. Finding the fine line between censorship and safety and creating a better environment for women in cyberspace are complex tasks. As I've wrestled with these issues, one of the sharpest areas of concern for me has become the effect harassment has on our most precious online commodity: Free speech.

Wanna Fuck?

Just what is online harassment? If someone sends you a request for sex in email, is that harassment? What if someone calls you a name online? A woman is called a "curmudgeon" and complains that the poster is harassing and slandering her. Is he? Many might define online harassment as unwanted, threatening, or offensive email, "instant messages" ("sends" or "chats" on some systems) or other personal communication that persists in spite of requests that it stop. But this is a poor definition, because what is unwanted, threatening, or offensive to one person may not be to another. Sometimes it seems as if the definition boils down to a personal one of "I know it when I see it."

There is a huge gap between legal definitions of harassment and what we describe as online harassment in common parlance. The legal aspects will come later; for now, let's look at the nonlegal definition.

Much of what is termed "online harassment" is "wanna fuck" email. A   5
"wanna fuck" is simply an email request for a date or sex. An email asking
for a date is not in and of itself harassment, but what bothers many women
on the Internet and on online services is the frequency and persistence of
these kinds of messages. America Online's (AOL) chat rooms, for example,
are notorious for having a barlike atmosphere...should you enter a chat
room using a woman's login name, you're likely to find yourself the target of
a wanna fuck "instant message" from some man you've never even heard of.
Though AOL has strict rules of conduct, called their Terms of Service,
which explicitly ban harassment, as well as obscenity, chain letters, and
other "offensive" types of online communication, the staff at AOL is hard-
pressed to be at all places at once, so the Terms of Service do not guarantee
a "safe environment," however hard AOL tries.

I would guess that wanna fuck email generates the bulk of online harassment complaints, and that repeated, targeted harassment of the kind I
experienced is actually quite rare. So I'm not sure if online harassment has
become a media hot-button because it is a matter of concern or because it
creates another sensational headline, or both. So much hype and angst has
been whipped up over this issue, it's hard to look at it objectively anymore.
Many users get really riled up about having a safe environment online, but
equal numbers, many of them women, are so sick of this subject they don't
ever want to see another article about it as long as they live.

Enter the Online Harassment Poster Queen

That I had a harrowing online experience in 1993 was one thing. That it
brought me my fifteen minutes of fame was more disappointing, to say the
least. When I first spoke out about online harassment, I meant it as a call to
arms, a message to women that it was time to take hold of the keyboard and
carve out some female space in the online world. I was apparently riding a
wave of media interest, set in motion by some genuine activism on the part
of many dedicated women activists and computer mavens, but the bigger
force was, of course, the American lust for a new victim.

My experience of harassment coincided with an article I was writing on
sexism online for *On the Issues,* a small feminist quarterly out of New York.
When my editor found out I was being harassed, she thought it would be
great to add that personal touch to my story, which turned into an article
about online harassment called "Take Back the Net."

When I began writing the article I noticed that what seemed like every
other reporter and freelance writer in the business was working on the same
story I was. Next thing I knew, I was being interviewed about my experience instead of writing about it. That was 1993, when the Internet was still
just a blip on the national media scene. If the number of interviews I did is
any indication, harassment took up an inordinate amount of ink that year.
Two years later I was still getting calls from reporters.

I believe these stories of online harassment are told and retold partially   10
because of the "car wreck fascination" factor, but more importantly because
we all keenly feel our vulnerability in the new medium of computer-
mediated communication. Women, especially, need to discuss and understand the implications of online harassment because it affects our ability to
use the medium and, thereby, to take part in something that will only become more important to our freedom. How many women would have voted
had polling places been in dark alleys?

The Online Car Wreck

Here's my story. It has become, even in my mind, more of a sound bite
than something real. The gory details have been swept away in the interest
of something quotable; the actual event a faint memory while the intellectu-
alizations I created around it abound.

What happened is less interesting than why it happened. I was harassed
not because I was an innocent bystander, or another female using the Internet, but because I had a mouth. I dared to speak out in the common space
of the Internet, Usenet.

Usenet is a collection of online discussion conferences or forums available to almost all Internet users. My boyfriend and I had been reading the
Usenet newsgroup *alt.zines* to discuss underground, homemade publications, because we were in the process of creating our own zine.

I don't remember exactly how the flame war/argument started, but a
young woman had posted to the group a request to talk about Riot Grrls
zines. Riot Grrls is a political and social movement of young punk postfemi-
nists, inspired by girl bands like Bikini Kill and the Breeders, and a hallmark
of the movement is the numerous fanzines created to support these bands.
At the mention of Riot Grrls, some of the men on the group started posting
vehemently in protest. They didn't want to talk about those stupid girl
bands; the girls couldn't play anyway. Someone suggested that the young
woman start her own newsgroup called "alt.grrl.dumbcunts."

In spite of having been online for years, I had never really participated   15
in Usenet before and had no idea how much anti-female sentiment was running, seemingly unchecked, on many Usenet forums. When I saw the treatment this woman was getting in response to her request to discuss Riot
Grrls, I was not only appalled, but also incredibly angry.

The woman who wrote the original note fought back, posting angry,
curt responses to the one or two men who were leading the charge against
the "stupid" Riot Grrls. My blood pressure increasing, my heart pounding
and my body aching for justice, I joined the fray. I'm a natural writer —
wordy, passionate — and, in a world where you are your words, I am loud. I
bellow, I scream, I prognosticate. I was writing what I thought at the time
were noble words, defending the honor of all women.

That was my first flame war. Probably my best. What an ego-driven experience! I had fans of both sexes emailing me letters of encouragement. Most of my detractors responded with a lot of sexist drivel, and several people, who identified themselves as Internet old-timers, tried to explain (to my deaf ears) that I obviously must be a newbie or I wouldn't be getting so upset. (Looking back, they were right; being online for a while makes you increasingly blasé about online slights.) To a certain extent, the whole thing embarrasses me now, but at the time, I didn't think I was doing anything wrong. I felt I had to speak up, largely because a few men were telling us women to sit down, shut up, and go away.

It's hard to explain the kind of high you can get while participating in a flame war; in some ways it's like being on a roller coaster—your stomach may be churning, but it is a delicious kind of sickening feeling, steeped with adrenaline. I had never participated so much online. I came home from work dying to see what the responses were to my posts. Then the harassment started.

I was not the first target. One of the women sticking up for Riot Grrls, perhaps the one who originally started the topic, received obscene email from a guy named "Mike." The email was anonymous—sent with no real name and with a fake return email address. She posted the letter to the group to show how the flame war had degraded. Others received similar emails. Then my boyfriend, who had been one of the guys sticking up for women, received a few nasty ones, asking him why he supported Riot Grrls—"fuck 'em, their daddies did," one anonymous email said. Another one said: "Heh heh—I'd love to see a porno with a father doing his Riot Grrl daughter—she has a bad haircut and is wearing boots with a pink mini. He says, this will give you something to rant about! As he sodomizes her little riot ass."

"What should I do with this?" my boyfriend asked. 20

"Just ignore it," I responded. "What a jerk."

Easier said than done. My boyfriend posted one of the notes back to the group anyway, with a sarcastic message of disapproval. Even though "Mike" had no idea my boyfriend and I knew each other, soon after that I became the target.

When I received email with the word "cunt" splashed across the screen, I became sick to my stomach. The harassment was a shock; in spite of the mess on the newsgroup, I hadn't expected it. But I was shaking, less from fear than from anger. I tried to email a response to the guy, but the message automatically bounced back to my mailbox, compounding the insult. So, as everyone else had done, I posted the note back to the group, coupled with some very nasty comments.

In response, I found more email messages in my box the next day, and the next day, and the next. Reams of pornographic text detailing gang rapes. Strange, poorly formatted messages full of long ramblings about how the poster was a writer and how he found all this so interesting. There were details about a girlfriend, Valerie, who purportedly worked at some great book publisher in New York. He was harassing me because he was going to write a story about it, he told me.

Each message was from a different fake email address, with a different name on it. I had no way of telling which messages were from friends and which were from my foe. It made me sick to read much of the stuff he sent me, but I went through most of it, trying to find a clue as to who this person was.

At this same time, a man on the group sympathetic to our side, Ron, was receiving several emails a day from the same person, although his were less frequent and much tamer. Ron had taken up my cause like the proverbial knight in shining armor. I didn't know him but was relieved to have an ally. We were now battling detractors on the newsgroup, who were sick of the flame wars and totally unsympathetic when we posted public notes telling Mike to stop. Some even told us that by complaining about Mike we were censoring him!

Mike wreaked havoc with my email inbox for several weeks. He wrote a story about the incident, which he posted to the group, but in his warped version of events, I was supposedly turned on by the whole thing. He also faked some posts to another Usenet group, to make it look as if I had posted something he had written. It was only when I got a strange message from someone from *alt.sex.bondage* that I found out Mike had been emailing people there and putting my name and return address on the messages.

Ron and I tried to get help from the system administrators at the university from which the posts originated, but to no avail. The sysadmins told us the only way they could catch him was "in the act." We considered calling the police and the FBI, and only after we made the threat "in public" on the newsgroup did Mike's email slow down to a trickle, though I continued to receive occasional pornographic email from him. Months later I received an email from him at one of my other email addresses. I have no idea how he found the address, but the message he chose to send was chilling: "I know you're in Los Angeles," he wrote. "Maybe I can come for a date and fix your 'plumbing.'"

By this time I was incredibly paranoid. I made sure the doors to our bungalow were always locked; I practiced self-defense. When a male friend called us and left a prank message, I thought Mike had found our number, and I panicked.

But finally, Mike goofed. He sent a message to my boyfriend that left some tracks. My months of dealing with the inner workings of Internet mail paid off, and I was able to track him down. I forwarded the message to his real email box without comment, and I haven't heard from him since.

Although the experience was horrific, it was a tempering kind of fire. It forced me to learn UNIX, the computer language much of the Internet is based on. In response to similar types of harassment, other women created their own spaces to be free of attacks of this kind. In response to the events on *alt.zines,* one young woman began a private female-only mailing list called Riot Grrls, which is still going strong. The support and advice I received on that mailing list during that time were invaluable in keeping me sane and active on the net.

The whole incident has taken its toll, though. I don't trust that this is the last I'll ever hear from Mike, or anyone else, for that matter. I'm careful what kind of information I give out online now—never my home phone number and certainly not my home address. I certainly know how easy it is to make an enemy on the Internet, and I stopped participating in *alt.zines* long ago. I'll probably never post there again. And that's the true fallout: I've censored myself out of fear.

The Big C-word: Censorship

I've censored myself. My choice, right? I'm not so sure. Do I or do I not have the right to speak my mind in public without being harassed, stalked, and threatened because of what I say?

The Internet is the Wild Wild West—as far from the civilized, or at least patrolled, corridors of the commercial online services such as Prodigy as the West was from the streets of Boston. And just as it's easy to romanticize the Wild West, forgetting the abuses that took place during that savage time, it's easy to romanticize these pioneer days of the Internet as well. I myself have loved this time of openness on the net, when relative freedom and a lack of government control made it one of the coolest places to be. It saddens me that some people abuse the freedoms many have taken for granted on the Internet, and that these freedoms are now threatened thanks to such immaturity.

It seems that a truly free space for public discourse is too threatening to the American public and we've only begun to see the start of what's likely to be a long and drawn-out fight to keep alive the delicious anarchy that's been such a fertile ground. Without free speech, the Internet will be as lifeless as, well, corporate broadcasting. 35

At the same time, I believe that online harassment is, to some extent, already killing free speech on the Internet, in particular the free speech of women, although women aren't the only targets of these vigilante censors.

Shut Up or Put Up

Unfortunately, because of rightful fear of government control, many people see this harassment issue as one that shouldn't be mentioned. And many don't believe it should matter anyway. Just fight back, they tell you. This is easy advice for a loud-mouthed, college-aged know-it-all who has all the time in the world, but does it apply to real, working women, who don't have the time and luxury to "fight back" against online jerks? And should we have to, as the price of admission? Men don't usually have to jump through a hoop of sexual innuendo and anti-feminist backlash simply to participate. They use their energy for posting, while we often use ours wondering if we'll be punished for opening our mouths. And with all our training to be "nice," are most women even prepared to do such battle?

This is not to say that supportive people aren't out there to help. When I was being harassed, new Internet friends from all over the world offered me technical assistance.[1] Many gave freely of their time and knowledge, and some offered to help me construct mail filters to keep out the offensive messages. Some offered to track the harasser down. Many friends offered to email bomb the perpetrator in return, but I declined.

For years a laissez-faire attitude has governed behavior on the Internet. Users didn't turn to lawsuits to solve their problems; they dealt with them using the technical tools available. Any talk of regulation scares users. When I first started talking about online harassment, people criticized me for trying to bring the regulators down on our heads. They should have been yelling at the jerks who abuse the system. For speaking out against online harassment I was likened to an Andrea Dworkin[2] disciple, or worse, Phyllis Schlafly,[3] out to wipe the Internet clean of smut.

Pornography Is Not Harassment

Despite those who believe that certain types of sexual content are   40
harmful to women, there is a difference between pornography available on-line and harassment. If someone wants to post nude pictures to a news-group, I don't have to see them. Not only would I have to decide to go to the newsgroup myself to see the pictures, I would have to download them *and* decode them *and* have the proper configuration on my computer to see them. If I accidentally went to one of these newsgroups, all I would see on my screen is a bunch of garbled text: the encoded version of the smut. (And maybe some lewd words, but that's about it.)

Unwanted erotica and pornography do become more of an issue with the World Wide Web, where the availability of embedded graphics makes it harder to avoid the online equivalent of *Hustler*. A friend looking for do-mestic violence resources on the net checked out an address and within two "clicks" was looking at pornography. A page linked to another page linked to another page, and she'd gone from an informational Web site to a porno-graphic one. It can be disconcerting.

---

[1]Thanks to such help, I now know exactly how "Mike" faked his email messages to me, through a loophole in the UNIX mail system that anyone could exploit. (Mike's not a hacker, but a hack.) Remember: There is no guarantee on the Internet that you are talking to whom you think you are. [Brail's note]

[2]*Andrea Dworkin:* Feminist theorist best known for "radical" theories like her belief that all acts of intercourse amount to rape.

[3]*Phyllis Schlafly:* Conservative activist and former president of the Eagle Forum who gained fame by championing antifeminist positions on social issues.

Fortunately, new software is making it easy to avoid explicit material on the Internet and World Wide Web. All you have to do is screen it out. But when someone starts sending detailed descriptions of gang rape to my email box as a veiled threat or starts to post pornographic stories with me as a main character, the issue has gone far beyond pornography. I am concerned that harassment and pornography have somehow become confused in the minds of our lawmakers: The harassment issue has been co-opted to create an excuse for banning so-called indecent material. The two are not the same at all.

So What About the Law?

From my discussions with many women online, I have found that most forms of online harassment are mere annoyances, desperate men looking for sex in the electronic ether and hitting on anything vaguely female. To give them the benefit of the doubt, many do stop when asked; many don't mean to hurt people. Many (and I've heard from some of them) are really not trying to scare anyone and are simply trying to make new friends. They may be kind of awkward and clueless, but they're mostly harmless.

Women are often annoyed and put out by this behavior, but as many of the strong women online will tell you, they can handle it. The problem is when the date requests (or "wanna fucks") continue after you've said no twice, or when you're sent repeated email messages calling you a "bitch" for stating something on *alt.feminism*. The question then becomes, how does this atmosphere affect the culture, and does it discourage women from being online in the first place? Is this behavior against the law? And can women speak in this atmosphere?

When I was harassed, I thought a lot about going to the police, but I didn't relish being the start of a high-profile online harassment case, and at the time I thought it would be incredibly difficult to prosecute. 45

According to Mike Godwin, staff counsel for the Electronic Frontier Foundation, the legal definition of harassment does not apply to most online harassment cases, since harassment is something that technically occurs in a school or work environment. However, civil and criminal laws that deal with issues of online harassment do exist. For example, on the civil side, you might sue for "intentional infliction of emotional distress." It is also against the law to misappropriate someone's name or license, that is, to send mail under another person's name. And Godwin points out that laws of defamation and libel also apply to the online world. In addition, federal laws exist that outlaw threats "through a means of interstate commerce."

Unfortunately, these legal remedies are often either unknown or misunderstood. And, while the good news is that someone can't threaten you in email legally, not every wanna fuck email is legally a "threat" (which is probably for the better in the long run, what with lawsuits running rampant in this country). As Godwin says: "It's not whether you feel threatened. It's whether an objective person looking at it would say it was a threat."

It's also perfectly legal to insult someone in public or by email. While sometimes I believe the laissez-faire attitude regarding net behavior goes overboard, those who call for banning words that hurt are way off base. When I see women call for strict email conduct rules (as I've seen on the women's online service, Women's Wire), or when women call it sexist and harassment when their Web pages are linked to the "Babes of the Web" site, I'm concerned that their fear is constricting free speech as much as real and perceived harassment might be.

Dealing with the Current Atmosphere

Because not everyone is going to file a lawsuit, and not everything is prosecutable, women have come up with many different ways to battle the bombardment online. Many women I've talked to have resorted to using male or gender-neutral names to avoid getting hit on online.

One young woman I spoke with, a college senior majoring in English, 50 decided to put "MRS!" next to her name on all her electronic correspondence because of the constant requests for dates. Her comments on sexism online included:

> I think (the Internet) is the last bastion of real ugly sexism because it's unmoderated and faceless. I've received more 'wanna fucks' ... and 'shut up bitch' mail than I care to count. I've posted to *alt.feminism* and had men posting me back screamingly hateful email calling me everything from a lesbian to a whore. One man told me that as a woman "you have so little to complain about in real life that you stay on the net all day whining about how bad things are."

I've talked with system administrators who've dealt with harassment on the Internet Relay Chat (IRC) simply by shutting down the service altogether. The IRC is a CB-like collection of the live chat "channels," much like the notorious chat rooms on America Online. Like those on America Online, many IRC channels are harmless, fun places to hang out, but many others are places where certain men apparently like to "camp out," waiting for an unsuspecting female to log on. It is unfortunate that shutting down the system has been one of the only ways to deal with annoying people online.

While it can be said that "wanna fuck" email is "only words" and "not real," I can't help but wonder how many women are discouraged from speaking up online for fear of being targeted for some sort of sexual advance or another. I wonder how many women have stopped posting their words because they were sick of constantly being attacked for their opinions. I'll be the first person to stand up for good old-fashioned disagreement and even flaming, but I have a problem with women being silenced through sexist attacks and vague physical threats. It is the threat of the physical behind the virtual that makes online harassment a very scary thing.

Sandy's Story

Sandy,[4] a polite and friendly forty-year-old woman with a soft Southern accent, loves cats and frequented the newsgroup *rec.pets.cats.*

In 1993 a gang of people from several newsgroups, *alt.tasteless,* *alt.syntax.tactical,* and *alt.bigfoot,* "invaded" the *rec.pets.cats* newsgroup. By the time the invasion had ended, Sandy had received death threats, hate mail, and harassing phone calls; was having her email monitored at work; and had almost lost her job.

The incident began when one of the invaders who joined her news- 55 group posted a message asking if he could get help destroying his girlfriend's cat. He said the cat was bothering him, but he didn't want the girlfriend to find out if he killed it. When he began discussing poison and drowning as options, Sandy spoke up.

First she sent email urging him not to kill the cat, but if he insisted, to have it "put to sleep" humanely. When the email didn't help, Sandy became concerned, then terrified for the cat. She had nightmares. Eventually she wrote a letter to the police that was subsequently distributed on the Internet.

The flame war exploded. The request for help in killing the cat was actually a fake. The poster and his friends had purposefully chosen a quiet little newsgroup to start a flame war of mythic proportions. Their stated goal was to inflame the members of the group with their posts. And it worked. But when Sandy contacted the police, the invaders became ugly and turned their attention to her.

Soon Sandy found herself on the member list of a *Net.Invaderz* FAQ (Frequently Asked Questions document) that was being passed around Usenet and even several computer conventions. Rather than being a victim, Sandy was singled out as one of the victimizers. "Those of us that opposed the group coming in and invading us (were added to the list)," she said. "It was spammed all over the network as a true document with our names on it."

Sandy was disturbed but tried to ignore the problems as much as possible until she found herself under investigation by her own company. An irate "U.S. taxpayer" had written her employer complaining that he didn't want the Internet used for actions such as those described in the *Net.Invaderz* document. "I'm a twenty-two year employee with this company, with a good reputation which is now in the pooper because of this," she said.

Sandy hasn't prosecuted but the incident exhausted her and made her 60 fearful. She no longer participates in or even reads *rec.pets.cats;* concerned friends email her posts of interest privately. She cannot afford her own home computer, so she can only access the Internet through work, where her supervisor now watches her every move.

---

[4]Sandy is a fictitious name. The woman described prefers to remain anonymous. [Brail's note]

Because she acted (in this case alerting the authorities to what she believed to be cruelty to animals), Sandy became the target of a vicious attack launched by a group of people she had never even met.

In part, the wars going on in cyberspace are cultural wars. Who is to decide what is polite and acceptable? Some time ago, I talked with one of the founders of *alt.syntax.tactical,* who calls himself Antebi. His response to those who suggest his tactics are uncivilized? "Learn to use killfiles," he says. "Grow up, welcome to reality."

After talking with him, I understood his group to be somewhat like an Internet fraternity, a bunch of young men who like to do virtual "panty raids" on unsuspecting newsgroups. They per se aren't the problem (I do not think *alt.syntax.tactical* was responsible for the death threats to Sandy), but that kind of mischievous mentality, coupled with a lot of free time, means that certain people can abuse their power in the virtual world.

But should the virtual world be one where war is the only metaphor? An invading army swept through Sandy's village, and when she reached out to protect someone else, they turned their sights on her. She was attacked, accused, harassed, and threatened—with no possible recourse. The army captain merely says she should have armed herself. But perhaps there are other ways to live than by the rule of the strongest? Isn't that what civilization is supposed to be about?

Tools, Not Rules

A popular phrase you'll hear on the venerable California-based online 65 service, the WELL, is "Tools, Not Rules." In other words, don't regulate the Internet, train people how to use it and let them decide for themselves what they want to read and see.

I'm all for it, since I believe that overregulation would stifle the Internet. Women can and should learn more about their online environment so they can exert more control over their corner of cyberspace. The move of many women to create mailing lists and online services is a positive one. Rather than playing the victim, we can take charge and fight back with the same tools being used against us.

But the Tools, Not Rules philosophy has its limits. On the WELL, a small cybercommunity of 12,000 where such issues of free speech and community are cherished and routinely thrashed about, user Preston Stern wrote:

> Like any other good thing, though, embraced wholly with no conditional moderation [Tools, Not Rules] can easily be turned over and create effects opposite to those intended.... We can insure that everyone has equal access to the tools, but we cannot guarantee that everyone will have equal proficiency. This means that some people, by virtue of having more expertise, more time and/or more experience with the tools, are able to become more powerful, to bend the public discourse and agenda toward their own ends.

Stern wasn't writing this in response to a topic about online harassment, but the concern is the same. Tools can empower, but they can also be a barrier. Women, especially, have a greater problem using Internet "tools"—the typical barriers being lack of time and knowledge and the male domination of all things technical in our society.

Whose Responsibility?

Harassment isn't just a women's issue. In this kind of free-for-all climate, the only people who will have free speech are those who have the gall to stand up to threats or frequent requests for sex, and those who have been lucky enough not to step on the wrong person's toes yet. And while women bear the brunt of this climate, men can also be affected. The man who spoke up in my case, Ron, was harassed and at one point challenged to meet his attacker "face-to-face"—for what, we can only imagine.

Is this the atmosphere that encourages enlightened discourse and free   70
speech? Sandy compares the current atmosphere online to the dark science fiction movie *Blade Runner*:

> It's like another world, it's like another planet. It's like a totally unregulated dirty nasty little underworld. It's got some really nice, great, shining pockets of humanity and education and conversation, and then it's got this horrible seamy gutter-ridden filth ... they're spreading like a cancer. As far as how to eradicate that without cutting out the good, I don't know what's going to happen to it. I really sincerely do not think censorship and government regulation is the way to go, I just wish people were a little nicer to each other.

So what can be done? Most women will continue to receive wanna fucks, and many will not even prosecute when they do receive a legitimate threat.

I don't think a legal remedy is the real answer anyway. Like Sandy, most women I know online are opposed to censorship. I would rather put up with the harassment than have Uncle Sam reading all my email. But I don't think that living with harassment should be necessary to enjoy the Internet, nor do I think the current "everything goes" environment is healthy. I think we can take steps to make the online world a little more safe. Part of what I would consider to be healthy would be an environment where community responsibility, not rampant individualism, was more the emphasis.

Unfortunately, whenever you so much as mention that you want something done about harassment, you are accused of being procensorship. Certainly, the strict rules you can find on online services such as Prodigy and America Online are double-edged swords. Perhaps these services are a little "safer," but is that truly free speech? Maybe the price of freedom is tolerance. Tolerance of jerks who want to put up a "rate the Babes Home Page," tolerance of a few unwanted emails, tolerance of women online. But sometimes it feels as if the price of freedom also means I must be willing to risk my personal safety for free speech.

In real life, harassment isn't confused with free speech. If I get death threats through regular mail and I reported that to the police, am I "censoring" the person who sent the threat? Threats are not free speech. Extortion is not free speech. Defamation is not free speech. Shouldn't the question be: Do we really have free speech on the Internet in its present form? Isn't the tyranny of vigilante bullies, however rare and arbitrary, the same as tyranny by an officially sanctioned body like a government or corporation? When people tell me the Internet is just words I can't help but remember checking the locks on my house, looking for a young man who might have decided that words weren't enough.

Easy answers are hard to come by, and extreme positions on either side   75
will do more harm than good. An Internet police state, for example, would undoubtedly not have the freedom of women as its first concern.

Although I would hope that our vigilante friends would take responsibility for their actions and realize that each abuse bodes ill for their and our future enjoyment of the Internet, the burden of action lies with ourselves. Women must take action. The more of us that speak up, the more of us that exist online, the harder it will be to silence us. Perhaps there are places that we won't want to go to—if a place offends us, perhaps we should just stay away—but instead of withdrawing totally from the online world, with all its riches and opportunities, we can form our own networks, online support groups, and places to speak. We can support each other in existing online forums. Women cannot be left behind, and we cannot afford to be intimidated.

ENGAGING THE TEXT

1. What are some of the complex, contrasting feelings Brail expresses about the "flame war" she became involved in? Why didn't she simply withdraw from her usergroup? Should she have? Why or why not?

2. Do you agree with Brail's claim that an antifemale culture dominates life online? Do you believe that "wanna fucks" constitute a serious form of sexual harassment? In what ways do "electronic" propositions resemble or differ from the kind of sexual harassment that occurs on a college campus or in a workplace?

3. What is Brail's attitude toward the Internet and the freedoms it offers? What response does she suggest to the problems associated with this freedom—the problems of sexual harassment and pornography? Do you think her response to these problems is adequate? Why or why not?

4. In what ways is the Internet similar to the "Wild Wild West" for Brail? What other similarities can you find between the idea of the frontier and life on line? In your estimation, does the Internet represent a genuinely new frontier or is the Net/frontier comparison simply a metaphor used for dramatic purposes?

EXPLORING CONNECTIONS

5. How might Wallace Stegner (p. 694) react to the notion that the Internet represents the latest incarnation of the frontier in American culture? How do the values of the Internet users described by Brail compare with the "Indian values" Stegner associates with the frontiersman?

6. To what extent would the Wild Wild West of Brail's Internet fulfill the definition of the frontier as a place of cultural struggle as forwarded by Patricia Nelson Limerick (p. 755)? Would Limerick be likely to see the Internet as a true cultural frontier or dismiss it as simply another example of *Star Trek* thinking?

7. What does the *This Modern World* cartoon on this page suggest about contemporary uses of the myth of the frontier in American culture? To what extent do you agree with this view of contemporary American frontiers?

EXTENDING THE CRITICAL CONTEXT

8. Investigate the issue of freedom of speech on the Internet at your college. Has your campus instituted any rules or restrictions concerning the types of

information that may be communicated using college facilities? If so, what topics or types of speech are restricted, and why? How effective and fair are these rules?

The Origins of Gun Culture in the United States, 1760–1865

MICHAEL A. BELLESILES

What could be more patriotic than the image of minutemen steadying their rifles against a troop of approaching redcoats at Concord Bridge? What could be more authentically American than the image of a western sheriff squaring off with his Colt .45 against a gun fighter on a dusty street at high noon? Actually, as historian Michael A. Bellesiles suggests, neither of these cultural memories accurately reflects the real status of guns and gun owner-ship in the early United States. Basing his interpretation of America's gun cul-ture on careful analysis of probate records and other forms of documentation, Bellesiles argues that, contrary to the myth of the frontier, guns were rela-tively rare possessions in the early republic and that gun ownership was often seen as an affectation of the leisure class. Bellesiles teaches history at Emory University and is the author of Revolutionary Outlaws: Ethan Allen and the Struggle for Independence on the Early American Frontier *(1993).*

An astoundingly high level of personal violence separates the United States from every other industrial nation. In 1993, when the number of murders in Canada reached a high of 630, the United States (with nearly ten times the population) experienced 24,526 murders, out of a total of nearly 2 million violent crimes. The weapon of choice in 69.6 percent of those murders was a gun, and thousands more are killed by firearms every year in accidents and suicides.[1] More people are killed with guns in the

---

[1] In 1990 there were 36,866 deaths involving firearms in the United States. The high point for American murders so far was 24,703 in 1991. In 1993 there were 22,526 murders and 1,932,270 violent crimes reported; in 1994, 1,924,188 violent crimes. U.S. Department of Jus-tice, *Uniform Crime Reports for the United States, 1993* (Washington, 1994), 10, 13; *The World Almanac, 1994* (Mahwah, 1994), 936–64, 967; *Statistics Canada, 1995* (Ottawa, 1995). [All notes are Bellesiles's except 4, 6, 44, and 46.]

United States in a typical week than in all of western Europe in a year. It is now thought normal and appropriate for American urban elementary schools to use metal detectors to check students for firearms.

We are familiar with the manifestations of American gun culture; the sincere love and affection with which our society views its weapons pours forth daily from the television and movie screens. Every form of the media reinforces the notion that the solution to your problems can be held in your hand and provide immediate gratification. Since the United States does not register guns, we have no idea how many there are or who actually buys them. The FBI (Federal Bureau of Investigation) estimates that there are 250 million firearms in private hands; an additional 5 million are purchased every year. The National Sporting Goods Association estimates that 92 percent of all rifles are bought by men (94 percent of the shotguns). Most of those men fall into the 25-to-34-year-old age group, make between $35,000 and $50,000 annually, and do not need to kill animals for their survival.[2]

The consequence of this culture is also very familiar. To select just a few more statistics as indicators: the chief of police and mayor of New York City were nearly euphoric that the number of murders in the city dropped below two thousand (to 1,995) in 1993; it reached a contemporary low of 1,581 in 1994. Yet the total number of murders in New York City in those two years exceeds by over 500 the 3,000 killed in Northern Ireland since the beginning of the "Troubles" in 1969.[3]

It is assumed that the nation's love affair with the gun is impervious to change, since its roots are so deep in our national history and psyche. The origin of this culture of violence is routinely understood to lie in our frontier heritage. With guns in their hands and bullets on their belts, the American frontiersmen conquered the wilderness and created modern America. In the imagined past, "the requirements for self-defense and food-gathering," as Daniel Boorstin[4] has said, "had put firearms in the hands of nearly everyone."[5] The almost universal ownership of guns in the eighteenth century was enshrined in the Second Amendment to the Constitution, and its continuation is defended with ferocity by the National Rifle Association today. That frontiers elsewhere did not replicate our violent culture is thought irrelevant. The frontier experience simply required that every westward migrant carry a gun. The result was a deep inward faith that, as Richard

[2]*Atlanta Constitution,* June 18, 1992.

[3]*New York Times,* Jan. 3, 1994. Jan. 2, 1995.

[4]*Daniel Boorstin:* Twentieth-century American historian (b. 1914).

[5]Daniel J. Boorstin, *The Americans: The Colonial Experience* (New York, 1958), 353; see also, for instance, Richard Maxwell Brown, *Strain of Violence: Historical Studies of American Violence and Vigilantism* (New York, 1975); Robert Elman, *Fired in Anger* (Garden City, 1968); and John Hope Franklin, *The Militant South, 1800–1861* (Cambridge, Mass., 1956), 10–25.

Slotkin[6] so eloquently put it, regeneration came through violence. In short, we have always been killers.[7]

Such statements are often presented as logically obvious. An examina- 5 tion of the social practices and cultural customs prevalent in the United States in the late eighteenth and early nineteenth centuries, however, will show that we have it all backwards. Before we accept an individual right to gun ownership in the Second Amendment, we must establish who were "the people" who were allowed to "keep and bear arms." Did they in fact own guns? What was the popular attitude toward firearms? Did such perceptions change over time? We will find that gun ownership was exceptional in the eighteenth and early nineteenth centuries, even on the frontier, and that guns became a common commodity only with industrialization, with ownership concentrated in urban areas. The gun culture grew with the gun industry. The firearms industry, like so many others, relied on the government not just for capital development but for the support and enhancement of its markets. From its inception, the United States government worked to arm its citizens; it scrambled to find sources of weapons to fulfill the mandate of the Second Amendment. From 1775 until the 1840s the government largely failed in this task, but the industrialization of the arms industry from 1820 to 1850 allowed the government to move toward its goal with ever-increasing speed, though against residual public indifference and resistance.

Probate Records

The evidence for this contrary thesis began with the dog that did not bark. In Sir Arthur Conan Doyle's "Silver Blaze," the Scotland Yard inspector asked Sherlock Holmes, was there "any other point to which you would wish to draw my attention?" Holmes responded, "To the curious incident of the dog in the night-time." "The dog did nothing in the night-time." "That was the curious incident."[8]

While studying county probate records (inventories of property after a death) for a project on the legal and economic evolution of the early American frontier, I was puzzled by the absence of what I assumed would be found in every record: guns. An examination of more than a thousand probate records, which listed everything from acreage to broken cups, from the frontiers of northern New England and western Pennsylvania for the years 1765–1790 revealed that only 14 percent of the inventories included firearms; over half of those guns (53 percent) were listed as broken or

---

[6]*Richard Slotkin:* Contemporary American historian (b. 1942) and specialist in the ideology of firearms and violence.

[7]Richard Slotkin, *Regeneration through Violence: The Mythology of the American Frontier, 1600–1860* (Middletown, 1973).

[8]Arthur Conan Doyle, *Memoirs of Sherlock Holmes* (1893; Garden City, 1990), 23.

otherwise dysfunctional. A musket or rifle in good condition often drew special notice in the probate inventories and earned a very high valuation. Obviously guns could have been passed on to heirs before the death of the original owner. Yet wills generally mention previous bequests, even of minor items, and they list only a handful of firearms.

Integrating Alice Hanson Jones's valuable probate compilation into this general study and examining counties in sample periods during the eighty-five years from 1765 to 1850 reveals a startling distribution of guns in early America. Probate records are not a perfect source for information, and there has been a long, instructive debate on their reliability as historical sources.[9] Nonetheless, they do provide much information on common household objects and can be used as a starting point for determining the level of gun ownership. Stated briefly, the probate inventories reveal that gun ownership was more common in the South and in urban centers than in the countryside or on the frontier, and that it rose slowly up to the 1830s; it increased to half again as much over the next twenty years. By 1849–1850, guns appeared in nearly one-third of all probate inventories.[10]

Almost all of the probate inventories studied are for white males. Most states had laws forbidding blacks to own guns, and no woman's inventory lists a gun. The inventories, therefore, are from the people most likely to own guns. The figures indicate that few people actually had guns in their possession, at least at the time of death. White males older than fifteen made up just under a quarter (23.8 percent) of the population in 1820; if we dare to include women and blacks in our definition of Americans, it would appear that at no time prior to 1850 did more than a tenth of the people own guns.

Militia Records

Looking at militia records can also provide some sense of gun ownership in early America. Militia units were based in their home communities or counties, but they existed under state authority. "All adults" (white, Protestant, non-immigrant, property-owning males) were expected to serve, with exceptions for those with specific jobs; in time, the list of those

10

---

[9]Alice Hanson Jones, *American Colonial Wealth: Documents and Methods* (3 vols., New York, 1977), I, 13–24, III, 1847–59. On the value of probate records, see Gloria L. Main, "Probate Records as a Source for Early American History," *William and Mary Quarterly,* 32 (Jan. 1975), 89–99; Daniel S. Smith, "Underregistration and Bias in Probate Records: An Analysis of Data from Eighteenth-Century Hingham, Massachusetts," ibid., 100–110; Lois Green Carr and Lorena S. Walsh, "Inventories and the Analysis of Wealth and Consumption Patterns in St. Mary's County, Maryland, 1658–1777," *Historical Methods,* 13 (Spring 1980), 81–104; Peter Benes, ed., *Early American Probate Inventories* (Boston, 1989); and Carole Shammas, *The Pre-Industrial Consumer in England and America* (Oxford, 1990), 18–46, 95–112.
[10]No differentiation is made between functioning and dysfunctional firearms.

Percentage of Probate Inventories Listing Firearms

	1765–1790	1808–1811	1819–1821	1830–1832	1849–1850
Frontier[a]	14.2	15.8	16.9	20.4	32.9
Northern coast, urban	16.1	16.6	17.3	20.8	27.3
Northern coast, rural	14.9	13.1	13.8	14.3	18.7
Southern	18.3	17.6	20.2	21.6	39.3
National average	14.7	16.1	17.0	20.7	30.8

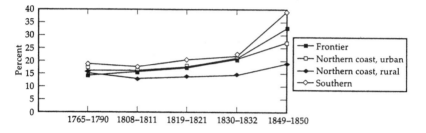

Source: Probate records for the following thirty-eight counties (modern names): Bennington, Rutland, Windham, and Windsor, Vermont; Luzerne, Northampton, Philadelphia, Washington, and Westmoreland, Pennsylvania; Litchfield and New Haven, Connecticut; Essex, Hampshire, Plymouth, Suffolk, and Worcester, Massachusetts; Burlington, New Jersey; Kent, Delaware; Anne Arundel and Queen Anne, Maryland; Fairfax, Spotsylvania, Chesterfield, Charlotte, Halifax, Mecklenburg, Brunswick, and Southampton, Virginia; Orange and Halifax, North Carolina; Charleston, South Carolina; Baldwin, Chatham, and Glynn, Georgia; Jefferson and Knox, Indiana; Adams and Washington, Ohio.
[a]Frontier counties moved into other categories with each new time period.

expected to serve expanded, as did the list of exceptions. Age and other requirements varied widely with time and place.

In the colonial period, the militias drew their authority from colonial legislatures operating in the name of the king. After the ratification of the Constitution, the authority was in the state governments as authorized and regulated by Congress (Article I, Section 8). On several occasions states and communities ordered censuses of the firearms in the possession of their citizens. Militia records also sometimes include accurate counts of the total number of guns in the possession of those eligible for militia service. Such records are scattered, but they do provide a sampling of the number of firearms and a reflection of the public attitude toward them.

The old myth of the military effectiveness of the militia has taken a battering over the last twenty years as historians have studied its performance more carefully. Military historians have debated the utility and commitment of the militia, and they generally doubt both. Those scholars have noted the absence of a well-armed and efficient militia in the period from the French and Indian War through the War of 1812.[11] Those findings are strongly supported by extant military records, though the period of militia ineffectiveness should be extended into the 1850s. Right up to the beginning of the Civil War, nearly every militia officer's report, even from the frontier, complained of the shortage and poor quality of the weapons available and the routine failure of their rank and file to care for the weapons they did possess. Regular army officers noted this same paucity and inferiority of firearms and commented often on the recruits' unfamiliarity with guns. Such comments ran right up the chain of command. For instance, Capt. Charles Johnston reported to the New Hampshire Provincial Congress in June 1775 that his company was "in difficult circumstances; we are in want of both arms and ammunition. There is but very little, or none worth mentioning—perhaps one pound of powder to twenty men, and not one-half our men have arms." On the top of the military hierarchy, Gen. George Washington complained incessantly about his lack of arms. Every volume of *The Papers of George Washington: Revolutionary War Series* has dozens of letters with such complaints as "Being in the greatest distress here for Arms without the most distant prospect of obtaining a Supply." The shortage of guns and ammunition even led Washington to dismiss troops he could not arm. He concluded that he and his officers were but "amusing ourselves with the appearance of strength, when at the same time we want the reality."[12]

A quarter century later, the situation remained unaltered. In 1801, Gov. William Claiborne of Mississippi Territory informed James Madison that the settlers did not have guns, nor could they acquire any. Six years later, as governor of Orleans Territory, Claiborne reported that he had 126 muskets for 4,971 members of the militia. That same year, three of Delaware's five regiments had no serviceable firearms at all; Gov. Nathaniel Mitchell told the legislature that the militia was effectively unarmed and

---

[11]Don Higginbotham, *War and Society in Revolutionary America: The Wider Dimensions of Conflict* (Columbia, S.C., 1988), 106–31; George D. Moller, *Massachusetts Military Shoulder Arms, 1784–1877* (Lincoln, 1988), xi; Donald R. Hickey, *The War of 1812: A Forgotten Conflict* (Chicago, 1989), 33–34, 221–23; Kenneth O. McCreedy, "Palladium of Liberty: The American Militia System, 1815–1861" (Ph.D. diss., University of California, Berkeley, 1991). The entire militia system has been blamed for the debacle of the War of 1812: Emory Upton, *The Military Policy of the United States* (Washington, 1907), 91–106; and Harry L. Coles, *The War of 1812* (Chicago, 1965), 265.

[12]Frederic P. Wells, *History of Newbury, Vermont* (St. Johnsbury, 1902), 71–73; George Washington to Artemus Ward, June 26, 1776, in *The Papers of George Washington: Revolutionary War Series*, ed. Philander D. Chase (5 vols., Charlottesville, 1993–), V, 111; Washington to James Clinton, July 7, 1776, ibid, V, 232. For a later period, see, for instance, Worcester County Regiment of Cavalry, Records, 1786–1804, Local Records (American Antiquarian Society, Worcester, Mass.); Oxford, Mass., Militia Muster Records, ibid.; and Records and Orderly Book of the Boston Rifle Corps, ibid. All three companies found that the majority of their members did not own guns.

that it was ridiculous to expect the people to arm themselves.[13] During the interminable Seminole wars of the 1830s, Gen. Winfield Scott discovered that the Florida militia was essentially unarmed, and he frantically sought firearms from Washington for those frontier militia companies.[14]

Quantitative evidence supports the views of those officials. In the first official inventory of American arms in 1793, Secretary of War Henry Knox found that 37 percent of the 44,442 muskets owned by the government were unusable, and an additional 25 percent were either archaic or in serious need of repair and cleaning. The following year Knox estimated that there were 450,000 militia members in the United States, of whom no more than 100,000 either owned or had been supplied with guns.[15] A decade later Secretary of War Henry Dearborn conducted a more precise census of the militia and its arms. Counting weapons both privately and publicly owned, Dearborn discovered that 45 percent of the militia bore arms. His census of weapons, which was certainly incomplete, indicated that just 4.9 percent of the nation's population was armed, or 23.7 percent of its white adult males. In 1810 Secretary of War William Eustis, in what was probably the most thorough and exact of all the studies, found that almost nothing had changed: 45.4 percent of the militia bore arms; the total number of guns recorded was sufficient for 4.3 percent of the American population, or 20.9 percent of the white adult males. Ten years later, John C. Calhoun found some slight improvement, with 47.8 percent of the militia bearing arms, and enough guns for 4.7 percent of the American population, or 19.9 percent of the white adult males (down a point). But Calhoun found it rather disturbing that several states had simply ceased bothering to issue militia returns; their governments just no longer cared if their militia carried guns or not. In

---

[13]Mark Pitcavage, "Ropes of Sand: Territorial Militias, 1801–1812, *"Journal of the Early Republic,* 13 (Winter 1993), 485, 494; *Delaware Archives, Military Records* (5 vols., Wilmington, 1911–1919), IV, 155–56, 271–76, 307–9.

[14]Winfield Scott's inspection of the militia was validated by numerous observers, including Gov. John Eaton. U.S. Congress, *House Document 78,* 25 Cong., 2 sess., 1839, 52, 145, 334, 420; U.S. Congress, *Senate Document 278,* 26 Cong., 1 sess., 1840, 126, 179; *Niles' Weekly Register,* July 2, 1836, pp. 309–10; *Florida Herald* (St. Augustine), March 14, 1839; Clarence E. Carter, ed., *The Territorial Papers of the United States* (28 vols., Washington, 1934–), XXV, 199. The citizens of Key West bought guns for their militia from the Spanish in Havana: *Key West Inquirer,* Feb. 3, 1836. For nearly identical concerns about the Michigan militia during the Black Hawk war, see Gen. John R. Williams to Lewis Cass, May 27, 1832, in "The Black Hawk War, Papers of Gen. John R. Williams," ed. Burton, in *Collections and Researches Made by the Michigan Pioneer and Historical Society,* XXXI, 388–89; and Williams to Stevens T. Mason, May 31, 1832, ibid, 397–98.

[15]Henry Knox, "Return of Ordnance, Arms, and Military Stores," Dec. 16, 1793, in *American State Papers: Documents, Legislative and Executive, of the Congress of the United States,* class V: *Military Affairs* (7 vols., Washington, 1832–1861), I, 44–60, 70. Censuses of firearms for the militia generally ignored fowling pieces, which were not considered to have any military value.

Census of American Militia Members and Firearms, 1803–1830

	1803[a]	1810[b]	1820[c]	1830
Militia members	524,086	677,681	837,498	1,128,594
Muskets	183,070	203,517	315,459	251,019
Rifles	39,648	55,632	84,816	108,036
Other[d]	13,113	49,105	0	0
Total arms	235,831	308,254	400,275	359,055

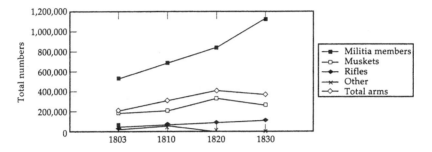

Sources: Frederick Bernays Wiener, "The Militia Clause of the Constitution," *Harvard Law Review,* 54 (Dec. 1960), 181–219.

[a]In 1803 Tennessee, Delaware, and Maryland did not respond to Secretary of War Henry Dearborn's request for information. Population is based on the 1800 census, producing an overstatement in percentages since the population had grown in the intervening three years. On the other hand, Dearborn's study would not have indicated those instances in which an individual owned several firearms, nor the arms of those avoiding the militia officers who conducted this survey (though there is no evidence of anyone doing so).

[b]The 1810 returns from Michigan, Orleans, and Illinois territories were incomplete and are therefore not included.

[c]By 1820 statistics were becoming significantly less reliable. The adjutant general noted that Delaware last made a return in 1814, Maryland in 1811, South Carolina in 1815, Mississippi in 1812, Arkansas never, Alabama's return left out sixteen regiments, and the District of Columbia's returns vanished. Most surveys were actually conducted in 1821. The 1820 census was used for population figures, leading to a slight overstatement in percentages.

[d]*Other* includes pistols, fowling pieces, blunderbusses, and other curiosities. From 1820 on, such pieces are included with *muskets.*

1830, Secretary of War J. H. Eaton found that just 31 percent of America's militia bore arms. With only enough arms for 3 percent of the population (12.5 percent of the adult white males), the militia was obviously no longer able to defend the United States—if it ever was.

By comparison, the current figures, based on FBI estimates, indicate enough firearms for 102.5 percent of the total population, 334.9 percent of the adult white male population, and 49,765.8 percent of the militia (the current National Guard, which has 512,400 members, or 0.2 percent of the population)....   15

Statistics alone give no indication of the condition of these firearms nor of the ability of the citizenry to employ them. Practically every adjutant general and militia commander in the United States in the antebellum period

Total Firearms as a Percentage of Selected Populations, 1803–1830

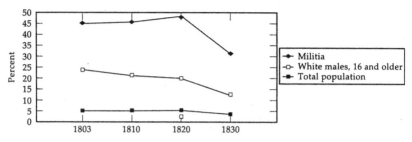

Sources: See previous table.

complained of the indifference with which Americans treated their weapons, and many state governments discovered that their armories were full of useless firearms.[16] Unlike today's glistening beauties, firearms in the eighteenth and nineteenth centuries were made mostly of iron and, as a consequence, required constant attention to keep them from rusting. Most people who owned guns brought them forth but once a year, on muster day; it is little wonder that those who did not have servants tended to let their weapons rot. In 1817 Virginia's adjutant general, G. W. Gooch, warned that the state's militia companies did not keep their arms "in good order—indeed, I might say, [not even] to preserve them from ruin." Gooch tried issuing orders demanding greater attention to the care and maintenance of the militia's weapons, but he found such efforts worthless; he finally ordered that all public arms be collected and stored in a single location. An awareness of this lack of enthusiasm for firearms by the public led a House special committee on the militia, chaired by William Henry Harrison, to propose in 1818 that the government keep its arms in armories under federal control and maintenance rather than giving them directly to the people. The committee felt that the nation's guns, so grossly abused by the public, should be left in the care of experts who could keep them operational. Their recom-

---

[16]For instance, in 1843 Massachusetts determined that 6,649 (47.5%) of the 13,994 muskets in the Cambridge Armory were useless and sold them over the next several years for less than $3 each: Annual Report of the Massachusetts Adjutant General, 1840, p. 30, Commonwealth of Massachusetts Military Division, Military Records: Annual Report of the Massachusetts Adjutant General, 1849, p. 32, ibid; Quartermaster General's Letter Book 3, p. 76, ibid. See also Adjutant General to Gov. Pierce M. Butler, Nov. 27, 1837, Military Affairs Committee Files, Legislative Group (South Carolina Department of Archives and History, Columbia); Frederick Townsend, "Annual Report of the Adjutant General of the State of New York, Transmitted to the Legislature March 20, 1857," *Assembly Document #15* (Albany, 1857), 9; Doc. 36, *Documents Accompanying the Journal of the Senate of the State of Michigan, at the Annual Session of 1841* (2 vols., Detroit, 1841), II, 83–86; *Annual Report of the Adjutant General of the State of Michigan for the Year of 1856* (Lansing, 1857), 3–5, 21; *Annual Report of the Adjutant and Quarter Master General of the State of Michigan for the Year 1858* (Lansing, 1859), 15–16.

Private Gun Ownership in Massachusetts

| | Number of Privately Owned Muskets or Rifles | Population | % of Population with Guns | |
			Total Population (%)	White Males 16 or Older (%)
1789	27,619	475,327	5.81	23.00
1795	34,000	524,946	6.48	25.60
1808	50,000	675,509	7.40	28.70
1812	49,000	482,289	10.16	27.80
1815	50,000	497,664	10.05	29.80
1824	32,128	557,978	5.76	19.40
1839	21,760	724,931	3.00	9.50

Sources: Adjutant General, annual Return of the Militia for Massachusetts, Commonwealth of Massachusetts Military Division, Military Records (National Guard Armory, Natick, Mass.); Quartermaster General's Letter Book 6, p. 9, ibid.
Note: Population estimates are based on per year increase during the decade. The adjutant general tended to round up the number of muskets in the state.

mendation was ignored, only to be repeated time and again over the next twenty years. In 1838, Secretary of War Joel R. Poinsett complained to Congress that military expenses were nearly four times what they should be, largely because the militia did not seem capable of caring for their arms. The following year he reported that "when mustered, a majority of [the militia] are armed with walking canes, fowling pieces, or unserviceable muskets."[17] Nothing had changed.

Even those with arms lacked experience in their use. Musters were, after all, usually held but once a year; parading, drinking, and partying clearly took priority over target practice; and uniforms evoked far more passion and interest than musket fire.[18] For example, the militia records of Ox-

[17]G. W. Gooch to Commanding Officer, 3d Regt., Orange, Sept. 20, 1817, Barbour Family Papers, p. 919 (Virginia Historical Society, Richmond); Gooch to Regimental Commanders, March 7, 1818, sect. 58, ibid., p. 923; *American State Papers,* class V: *Military Affairs,* I, 675; *Army and Navy Chronicle,* 6 (1838), 263–64; U.S. Congress, Senate, "Report of the Secretary of War," Nov. 30, 1839, *Senate Journal,* Serial Set 354, 26 Cong., 1 sess., 1839, 44. See also *American State Papers,* class V: *Military Affairs,* I, 318; Thomas H. McKee, comp., *Reports of the Committee on the Militia, House of Representatives* (Washington, 1887), Report 584, 26 Cong., 1 sess. Calls for reform came from the states as well: see, for instance, H. A. S. Dearborn, Annual Report of the Adjutant General for 1839, Commonwealth of Massachusetts Military Division, Military Records.

[18]*Militia Laws of the United States and Massachusetts* (Boston, 1836), viii–ix, 33–37; Jerome B. Lucke, *History of the New Haven Grays* (New Haven, 1876), 29–30; D.A. Winslow, "The Old Vermont June Training," *Vermonter,* 6 (1901), 250; J. Trasker Plumer, "The Old Times Muster," *Manchester Historical Association Collections,* 3 (1902–1903), 176; John L. Sibley, *History of the Town of Union* (Boston, 1851), 350–86; E. G. Austin, "Memorandum of the Boston Light Infantry from Its Foundation in 1798 to 1838," Military Records (Massachusetts Historical Society, Boston).

ford, Massachusetts, which begin in 1755, devote more space to uniforms than to any other subject. The company argued over the color of their pantaloons (white or blue) from just after the Revolution until 1823, and of their plumes (white or black) until 1824. They spent a year debating whether to require each member to powder his beard when appearing at muster, voting in May 1821 to so require, repealing that act in October. There were instances of companies disbanding because of a change in uniform. In 1819 Charles K. Gardner wrote an instruction manual for use by militia companies after discovering during the War of 1812 that "so many militiamen ... are not skilled in the use of the Rifle or Musket." Drills in muster books involved marching, not shooting. The Oxford, Massachusetts, militia voted for the first time in May 1819 to meet once a year "for the purpose of fireing at a mark." In 1823 they voted thirty-five to five to stop this annual target practice in order to avoid public humiliation.[19]

Target-shooting contests, which began in the 1820s, were often major embarrassments. When the Second Company of New York's Seventh Regiment held their first target-shooting contest in 1825, it was a miserable show. As the company's official historian admitted, it was "not a very brilliant exhibition of sharp shooting"; but then very few members had ever fired a musket before. When the prestigious New Haven Grays held its first target-shooting contest in 1822, forty-three men fired 172 shots at a target six feet high by twenty inches wide at one hundred yards. Only twenty shots (11 percent) hit any part of the target. The winner, Frederick T. Stanley, admitted that he had "but little experience in the use of firearms, and have neither before or since owned a pistol, rifle, musket, or fowling piece." His gun was on loan from the state arsenal. In 1826 the Grays shortened the distance to one hundred feet, which improved their ratio to 65 hits out of 198 shots fired (33 percent). Shortening the distance again over the next several years raised their percentage of successful shots as high as 48 percent in 1827. As a Pennsylvania newspaper unkindly said of one company's effort at target shooting: "The size of the target is known accurately having been

---

[19]Members of the New Haven Grays each fired four shots at the annual muster: Lucke, *History of the New Haven Grays*, 15–17, 26, 29–31, 44, 47, 107. Charles K. Gardner, *Compend of the United States System of Infantry Exercise and Maneuvers* (New York, 1819), 247; Oxford, Massachusetts, Militia Muster Records, Local Records (American Antiquarian Society); Regimental Orders, 75th Regt., New York State Infantry, 1815–1820, June 22, 1816, Military Records (New-York Historical Society, New York); Minutes of the Charleston Washington Light Infantry, April 21, 1841, Caroliniana Collection; *American State Papers*, class V: *Military Affairs*, I, 20–21, 26, II, 314–19, 329–37, 389–95, 527–29; Gayle Thornbrough, *Outpost on the Wabash* (Indianapolis, 1957), 125, 155; Arthur St. Clair, *A Narrative of the Manner in Which the Campaign against the Indians, in the Year 1791, was Conducted* (Philadelphia, 1812), 199; William Guthman, *March to Massacre: A History of the First Seven Years of the United States Army, 1784–1791* (New York, 1975), 93, 105–6; Ebenezer Denny, *Military Journal of Major Ebenezer Denny* (Philadelphia, 1860), 344.

carefully measured. It was precisely the size and shape of a barn door." The prize went to the man "who came nearest to hitting the target."[20]

Several historians have suggested that proficiency with a gun carried a necessary definitive power for manliness.[21] If so, we must wonder what it means that American men were generally such terrible shots. There are instances of militia units shooting their officers, bystanders, and one another during target practice. Even that man's man, Robert E. Lee, could bag but four birds in a pigeon shoot (a captured pigeon is placed in a black box, shaken, and released, whereupon the shooter raises his gun and hopes to blow the bird away) that lasted all afternoon and was outshot by his British opponent.[22] . . .

Militia companies reflected this public sentiment; many made a deliber-ate mockery of the whole enterprise. Officers were often elected specifically on their promise that they would not call musters. Jean Baptiste Beaubien was elected colonel of Chicago's militia every year from 1834 to 1847, calling only one muster during that entire period. The ever-pained William H. Sum-ner, adjutant general of Massachusetts, complained in 1834 that "The records of my office are disgraced with returns of persons of infamous character to honorable places—of town paupers, idlers, vagrants, foreigners, itinerants, drunkards and the outcasts of society" elected militia officers. Most militia companies died from inattention or hostility by the early 1830s.[23]

When the members of a militia did not mock themselves, the crowds would. Locals, including many who should have been taking part in the

20

---

[20]William H. Zierdt, *Narrative History of the 109th Field Artillery: Pennsylvania National Guard, 1775–1930* (Wilkes-Barre, 1932), 67; Emmons Clark, *History of the Second Company, Seventh Regiment, New York State Militia* (New York, 1864), 62; Lucke, *History of the New Haven Grays,* 30–31, 50–51. By 1833, with the target back at 100 feet, one-third of the company was hitting the target: ibid, 79–80.

[21]Edmund S. Morgan, *American Freedom, American Slavery: The Ordeal of Colonial Virginia* (New York, 1975), 239–40, 377–79; Bertram Wyatt-Brown, *Southern Honor: Ethics and Behavior in the Old South* (New York, 1982), 357–60; Franklin, *Militant South,* 14–62.

[22]Fred Anderson, *A People's Army: Massachusetts Soldiers and Society in the Seven Years' War* (Chapel Hill, 1984), 75–76; Anthony Marro, "Vermont's Local Militia Units, 1815–1860," *Vermont History,* 40 (Winter 1972), 28, 31; *American Turf Register and Sporting Magazine,* 1 (1829–1830), 338–39, 359. Outside the pages of fiction, hunters miss more often than they find their targets. See also *Western Monthly Magazine,* 3 (1835), 65–66; *Brother Jonathan,* 6 (1843), 43.

[23]A.T. Andreas, *History of Cook County, Illinois* (Chicago, 1884), 206–7; *Report of the Adjutant General and Acting Quartermaster General Accompanying the Annual Returns of the Militia of Massachusetts,* Senate Document #27 (1834), p. 91, Commonwealth of Massachu-setts Military Division, Military Records. See also Joseph J. Holmes, "The Decline of the Penn-sylvania Militia, 1815–1870," *Western Pennsylvania Historical Magazine,* 57 (April 1974), 108; Charles W. Burpee and Charles F. Chapin, "Military Life Since the Revolution," in *The Town and City of Waterbury, Connecticut,* ed. Joseph Anderson (3 vols., New Haven, 1896), III, 1186; Randall Parrish, *Historic Illinois: The Romance of the Earlier Days* (Chicago, 1905), 368; Oxford, Massachusetts, Militia Muster Records, Local Records (American Antiquarian Soci-ety); *American State Papers,* class V: *Military Affairs,* II, 320.

exercises, often gathered to make fun of the militia. The crowd's favorite target was the poor marksmanship of the militia. Some state legislatures attempted to outlaw heckling the militia; for instance, in 1835 South Carolina passed a law fining any person who heckled or disrupted a militia muster $50. In 1841 the legislature added to the fine a five-day jail sentence. Both efforts apparently proved ineffective.[24] ...

Hunting

This widespread rejection of the militia was paralleled in public attitudes toward hunting. From the time of the earliest colonial settlements, frontier families had relied on Indians or professional hunters for wild game, and the colonial assemblies regulated all forms of hunting, as did Britain's Parliament.[25] Also as in England, most hunters were actually trappers, finding the use of traps more efficient and less expensive than the time-consuming process of tracking animals with guns. Most Americans in the seventeenth and eighteenth centuries got nearly all their meat from domesticated animals, and it was rather unusual to use a musket to slaughter a cow or pig. From the start, hunting was an inessential luxury. In the first decades of the nineteenth century, hunting was held up to ever-increasing ridicule as a waste of time, money, and resources and mocked as the play of insufficiently grown-up boys. In the popular press, hunting had become both exotic and foolish. Hunters themselves were often portrayed as little more than tedious bores looking for any opportunity to tell the same tired story of the glorious hunt.[26] An 1825 article in the *Atheneum* described the incredible number of animals killed by various aristocratic hunters, the thousands of deer, ducks, and rabbits, and expressed amazement at the pride that those aristocrats took in totting up such statistics: "A magnificent list of animal slaughter carefully and systematically recorded as achievements." Another article warned that citizens of Philadelphia interested in a walk in the country should "go a consider-

[24]Turpie, "Pioneer Militia," 48; Richard W. Musgrove, *History of the Town of Bristol, Grafton County, New Hampshire* (2 vols., Bristol, 1904), I, 187; David J. McCord, ed., *The Statutes at Large of South Carolina* (10 vols., Columbia, 1836–1841), VIII, 2650, XI, 2856.

[25]To take just one example, see Bernard Bush, ed., *Laws of the Royal Colony of New Jersey* (5 vols., Treton, 1980), II, 294–95, III, 181, 189–90, 253, 489–90, 580, IV, 52–53, 237, 326–27, 582–85, V, 52–53, 69–72, 162–63. In general, see Paul C. Phillips, *The Fur Trade* (2 vols., Norman, 1961), I, 377–430; Thomas E. Norton, *The Fur Trade in Colonial New York, 1686–1776* (Madison, 1974), 60–82.

[26]See, for instance, *Atheneum*, 2d ser., 7 (Boston, 1827), 29–34, 53–59, 167–68, 276–77, 408, 426–27; ibid, 3d ser., 1 (1828), 207–8; *Godey's Lady's Book*, 2 (1831), 150; *Army and Navy Chronicle*, 5 (1837), 59–60; *Anglo-American*, 5 (1845), 200–201, 390–91; *Brother Jonathan*, 6 (1843), 43; *Eclectic Magazine*, 33 (1854), 563; Norton, *Fur Trade in Colonial New York*, 83–99; Patrick Malone, *The Skulking Way of War: Technology and Tactics among the New England Indians* (Lanham, 1991), 60–66; Sarah F. McMahon, "A Comfortable Subsistence: The Changing Composition of Diet in Rural New England, 1620–1840," *William and Mary Quarterly*, 42 (Jan. 1985), 26–65; Henry M. Miller, "An Archaeological Perspective on the Evolution of Diet in the Colonial Chesapeake, 1620–1745," in *Colonial Chesapeake Society*, ed. Lois Green Carr, Philip D. Morgan, and Jean B. Russo (Chapel Hill, 1988), 176–99.

able distance from the city, to avoid the showers of shot" sent skyward by a few overenthusiastic bird hunters.[27]

Judging from the popular literature of the day, the public seemed completely uninterested in firearms. In 1843, the first book to lavish attention on the details of gun production, part of the Marco Paul's Adventures series for children, closes with a long condemnation of the gun. Carrying weapons makes men "fierce in spirit, boastful, and revengeful." Men with guns are like little boys with sticks, bound to hit each other with them.[28]

Even western magazines showed a decided coolness toward hunting and militarism, with occasional opposition to both. For instance, the *Western Monthly Magazine* of Cincinnati stated, "We aspire to be useful"; yet it found no need to publish anything on guns, hunting, or the military or militia, being much more concerned with education. In its first three years, 1833–1835, it published thirty-six issues and 356 articles; there was one article on hunting, one on a shooting match, and four on Indian wars—and not a single other article on any gun-related themes. Likewise, the *Western Miscellany* published 300 articles in its first year, 1849, but only two were hunting articles. An article "On Western Character" in *Western Miscellany* describes westerners as marked primarily by autodidacticism and ingenuity, insisting that respect for the law and the avoidance of violence were far more notable in the West than in the East. While these magazines were, in part, promoting the West, their observations that eastern and European cities were more violent are valid. In those few instances when guns appeared in articles, it is surprising how often firearms prove useless in combat. Again and again in these and other magazines, hunters and soldiers fire and miss. After the first errant shots, battle descends to tomahawks and knives, the real weapons of frontier combat. Sometimes the descriptions border on the comic, as in one historical account of the siege of Ft. McIntosh, Ohio, in 1782. Volley after volley is exchanged without anyone getting injured. Finally a relief column appears, the Indians run away, and the "battle" is over.[29] ...

[27]"Sporting," *Atheneum*, 2d ser., 2 (1825), 444; *Ariel*, 3 (1829), 94.

[28]Jacob Abbott, *Marco Paul's Adventures in Pursuit of Knowledge* (Boston, 1843), 111–12. Some children's books and magazines questioned the necessity for violence at all, even in the American Revolution: Increase N. Tarbox, *Winnie and Walter's Evening Talks with Their Father About Old Times* (Boston, 1861); Joseph Alden, *The Old Revolutionary Soldier* (New York, 1849); *Evils of the Revolutionary War* (Boston, 1846); *Parley's Magazine*, 3 (1835), 17, 81; Henry C. Wright, *A Kiss for a Blow: or, A Collection of Stories for Children* (Boston, 1842).

[29]*Western Monthly Magazine*, 1 (1833), 2–3, 49–55, 238–39, 318; ibid, 2 (1834), 268; *Western Miscellany*, 1 (1849); Robert S. Dykstra, *The Cattle Towns* (New York, 1965), 112–48; Luc Sante, *Low Life: Lures and Snares of Old New York* (New York, 1991), 197–235; Elliot J. Gorn, "'Good-Bye Boys, I Die a True American': Homicide, Nativism, and Working-Class Culture in Antebellum New York City," *Journal of American History*, 74 (Sept. 1987), 388–410; Paul A. Gilje, *The Road to Mobocracy: Popular Disorder in New York City, 1763–1834* (Chapel Hill, 1987), 235–64; Carl E. Prince, "The Great 'Riot Year': Jacksonian Democracy and Patterns of Violence in 1834," *Journal of the Early Republic*, 5 (Spring 1985), 1–19; David Grimsted, "Rioting in Its Jacksonian Setting," *American Historical Review*, 77 (April 1972), 361–97.

Gun Promotion

Increased production fed a gradual expansion of interest in and appreci-   25
ation for guns. Hunting became increasingly popular with an urban middle
class seemingly desperate for the instant status granted by possession of a
gun. Largely through the efforts of John Stuart Skinner's *American Turf Register and Sporting Magazine,* which began publication in 1829, and William
T. Porter's *Spirit of the Times,* first published in 1831, hunting became an appropriate enterprise for would-be gentlemen.[30] It is extremely difficult to find
an article published in either of those journals or a gun advertisement in any
newspaper that did not use the word "gentleman" in describing a hunter. Amateur hunters looked for legitimacy to the British aristocracy, modeling their
notions of sportsmanship, hunting styles, clothing, appropriate game, and
even patterns of speech after the British elite. The very portraits of hunters
the magazines published mimic the style of those available in British sporting
journals. Porter and his colleagues sought to rescue hunting from public disdain and to translate it into "the very corinthian columns of the community,"
the mark of the true gentleman and of a real man. The magazines pushed for
the acceptance of the idea that "our rifles and our liberties are synonymous."
Owning and using a firearm is therefore "a moral decision."[31]

There is much in mid-nineteenth-century hunting literature that we
would recognize. The male bonding and the deep romantic affection for a
favorite gun stand out. In the 1830s the first loving descriptions of every detail of firearms appear in print. No longer is it sufficient simply to say "He
held a musket in his arms." From this date the dedicated author of hunting
articles must have the precise name and maker of the piece noted, with sensual descriptions of the well-oiled stock and the long, gleaming barrel, as
well as the delicate intricacies of the lock. The gun is no longer held; it is
now "cradled," "caressed," "hugged," and ultimately "grasped with firmness" in order to fulfill its "deadly purpose." Real men hunt, while "the effeminate young man may die at home, or languish in a dead calm for the
want of some external impulse to give circulation to the blood."[32]

On the other hand, the magazines sought to separate the participants in
their luxurious sport from hoi polloi. Thus there are constant references to
servants almost as necessities of the hunt. Close attention is paid to the
quality of the dogs, horses, food, and spirits appropriate for a fruitful hunt.

---

[30]The first issue of the nation's first hunting magazine states that hunting as a sport is just
beginning to attract the attention of American men: *American Turf Register and Sporting
Magazine,* 1 (1829), 1.

[31]*Spirit of the Times,* 7 (1837), 4; Bosworth, *Treatise on the Rifle, Musket, Pistol, and
Fowling Piece,* 64, 97; see also *Spirit of the Times,* 5 (1935), 1; ibid., 9 (1839), 1; *American
Turf Register and Sporting Magazine,* 1 (1829–1830), 240, 441; ibid., 5 (1834), 371–73,
474–75, 615.

[32]*Army and Navy Chronicle,* 6 (1838), 209–11; *American Turf Register and Sporting
Magazine,* 1 (1829–1830), 79, 338–39.

The decadence of this elite romanticism is favored by connoisseurs, those with the education and intelligence to appreciate the deeper meanings of this close contact with nature.[33] The mixture of nature, sociability, and killing comes together perfectly in one of the many hunting songs popular at the time:

> The cordial takes its merry round,
>   The laugh and joke prevail,
> The huntsman blows a jovial sound,
>   The dogs snuff up the gale;
> The upland hills they sweep along,
>   O'er fields, through breaks they fly,
> The game is roused; too true the song,
>   This day a stag must die.[34]

Samuel Colt initially appealed to these gentleman hunters with his elegant revolvers; but his ambitions demanded a broader market. Colt had hit on the perfect weapon for a gun culture: his revolvers were relatively inexpensive; fired several rounds quickly, negating the need for skill; were perfect for urban life, being easy to conceal; had no function other than "self-defense," being useful in neither hunting nor militia service; and, in short, were clearly intended for personal use in violent situations. Unable to discover a large demand for such weaponry, Colt tried to create one through the cleverest advertising yet seen in America. He engraved his guns with heroic scenes, such as a man protecting his wife and child against a pack of savage Indians, armed only with a Colt revolver. He filled eastern newspapers with advertisements identifying his revolver with the romance of the West, commissioning Currier & Ives to craft beautiful portraits of Colt hunting buffalo with a revolver. His most ingenious move was to include instructions, carefully printed on the cleaning rag that came with every Colt firearm; he realized that most Americans did not actually know how to use a gun.[35] . . .

. . . The same people who revived hunting in the 1830s breathed new life into the militia in the 1840s. But just as they sought to separate hunting from its plebeian American roots, so urban militia companies rejected the traditional republican ideal of universal citizen service and embraced the notion of elite volunteer companies, creating for the first time a gun subculture.[36]

---

[33]See, for instance, *American Turf Register and Sporting Magazine,* 1 (1829–1830), 88, 238, 400, 443–45; ibid., 5 (1834), 298–99; *American Penny Magazine,* 1 (1845), 387; *Ariel,* 3 (1829), 117; *Army and Navy Chronicle,* 6 (1838), 209–11.

[34]*American Turf Register and Sporting Magazine,* 1 (1829–1830), 352. See also ibid., 447–50, 595–96; *Ariel,* 5 (1832), 308–9; *American Penny Magazine,* 1 (1845), 388.

[35]James E. Serven, *Colt Firearms, 1836–1958* (Santa Ana, 1954), 99–159.

[36]One sign of that new subculture was the creation of urban pistol galleries: Bosworth, *Treatise on the Rifle, Musket, Pistol, and Fowling Piece,* 82, 101.

The volunteer movement got off the ground in Massachusetts. The   30
state legislature finally got tired of trying to make its tradition-bound but
nearly invisible militia system work, so in 1840 it created a volunteer militia.
A new "active militia" of no more than ten thousand soldiers would form the
core of this reorganized structure; all other adult males were theoretically in
the inactive "enrolled militia."[37] The state also acknowledged its other key
problem of arming its soldiers by no longer requiring each soldier to supply
his own musket; the new volunteer militia companies were to apply to the
Adjutant General's Office for arms, which they were required to maintain.
The volunteers were thus not only better armed than the old militia but
they kept their arms in good repair—a drastic innovation. Volunteer companies attracted those who valued guns and enjoyed the military style, and
the state rewarded them with all the arms they needed. Within four years
the state had issued more than 10,000 of its 17,000 muskets to the active
militia.[38]

There were dangers in these better-armed volunteer militia units. The
companies included a small minority of their communities, were usually organized along ethnic and class lines, and demonstrated a disturbing willingness to use their guns. The Philadelphia riots of 1844 devolved into a battle
between nativist, Irish, and state militias that ended with twelve deaths. In
1849, the Astor Place riot in New York City culminated with the Seventh
Regiment firing on a crowd and killing twenty people. For the first time,
American militia opened fire on unarmed fellow citizens.[39] . . .

The Civil War

The Civil War dramatically accelerated the slow cultural shift that had
been instigated by the increase in arms production in the 1840s. By 1865 it
would seem that most Americans believed that the ability to use a gun made
one a better man as well as a patriot more able to defend the nation's liber-

[37]This proposal replicated the suggestions of Henry Knox and George Washington back
in the 1790s. There had been a few such "select militia" units in the colonial period, but they
had died out in the years after the War of 1812. *American State Papers,* class V: *Military Affairs,* I, 7–8; McCreedy, "Palladium of Liberty," 16–46; Lyle D. Brundage, "The Organization,
Administration, and Training of the United States Ordinary and Volunteer Militia, 1792–1861"
(Ph.D. diss., University of Michigan, 1958), 52–55, 142–47.

[38]See, for example, "Report of Committee on Volunteer Companies," Sept. 18, 1856, Military Affairs (South Carolina Department of Archives and History, Columbia); "Petition of Volunteer Companies of St. Philip's and St. Michael's" [1849], ibid. Committee Files, Legislative
Group; Annual Report of the Massachusetts Adjutant General, 1840–1844, Commonwealth of
Massachusetts Military Division, Military Records.

[39]McCreedy, "Palladium of Liberty," 267–324; Michael Feldberg, *The Philadelphia Riots
of 1844: A Study of Ethnic Conflict* (Westport, 1975); Richard Moody, *The Astor Place Riot*
(Bloomington, 1958).

ties—they certainly showed a willingness to act on that assumption. Technological innovation coupled with government support had powerfully altered the national character and sensibilities within a single generation. The Civil War established these attitudes permanently by demonstrating the need for one American to be able to kill another. In 1865 the army allowed Union soldiers to take their firearms home with them. The government had finally succeeded in arming America.[40]

The initial consequence of all those guns is easy to guess: a rising murder rate. It was not simply that the number of murders increased; the very nature of the crime shifted dramatically. The rare prewar murders had been seen in the public imagination as outbursts of madness or acts of demons. After the war, murder took on an air of calculation or anonymity. The gun itself changed the workings of murder. The face-to-face fury of strangling or the ax attack gave way to the bullet in the back of the head.[41] Prior to the war, the emerging middle class viewed with disdain the ugliness of personal confrontation and violence, though workers tended to find some defining manliness in the ability to fight well. Yet resorting to violence in antebellum America rarely involved the use of firearms. That attitude changed considerably after the war, most especially in the cities, with revolvers now small enough to fit in a coat pocket. Inexpensive and readily available guns changed many social equations, as the Ku Klux Klan demonstrated in their terror campaigns in the South, most notoriously in Louisiana's Colfax Massacre of 1873.[42]

Despite the war's end, firearms production levels remained high, while prices fell. Coupled with the expansion of advertising that built on Samuel Colt's antebellum equation of firearms possession and manly security, high

---

[40]Officially, Union soldiers had to purchase their firearms before taking them home. But the army did not make a concerted effort to collect this money. Even most Confederate soldiers took guns home with them when the war ended. See Noah Andre Trudeau, *Out of the Storm: The End of the Civil War, April–June, 1865* (New York, 1994), 379; Edith Abbott, "The Civil War and the Crime Wave of 1865–70," *Social Service Review*, 1 (1929), 212–34.

[41]Abbott, "Civil War and the Crime Wave of 1865–70"; Sante, *Low Life;* Waldo L. Cook, "Murders in Massachusetts," *Journal of the American Statistical Association*, 3 (Sept. 1893), 357–78; Harry G. Nutt, "Homicide in New Hampshire," ibid., 9 (1905), 220–30.

[42]Michael Kaplan, "New York City Tavern Violence and the Creation of a Working-Class Male Identity," *Journal of the Early Republic*, 15 (Fall 1995), 591–617; Eliot J. Gorn, *The Manly Art: Bare-Knuckle Prize Fighting in America* (Ithaca, 1986), 129–47; Elizabeth Pleck, *Domestic Tyranny: The Making of American Social Policy against Family Violence from Colonial Times to the Present* (New York, 1987), 49–66; Jerome Nadelhaft, "Wife Torture: A Known Phenomenon in Nineteenth-Century America," *Journal of American Culture*, 10 (Fall 1987), 39–59; Ted Tunnell, *Crucible of Reconstruction: War, Radicalism, and Race in Louisiana, 1862–1877* (Baton Rouge, 1984), 185–202; *United States v. Cruikshank*, 92 U.S. 542 (1876); Ralph L. Peek, "Lawlessness in Florida, 1868–1871," *Florida Historical Quarterly*, 40 (Oct. 1961), 164–85.

levels of production led to the wide distribution of guns, both geographically and socially. It was now possible for anyone to own a gun. But the production of firearms is not in itself sufficient to create a gun culture; otherwise Britain would have developed such a culture sooner than did the United States. There needed to be a conviction, supported by the government, that the individual ownership of guns served some larger social purpose; for instance, that they preserved the nation's freedom or the security of the family. The advertising campaigns of all the gun manufacturers played up those two angles, with the added incentive of low prices. Having finally succeeded in arming its citizens, the government generally maintained a benign neutrality in the further promotion of the gun culture, with one exception: subsidies to the National Rifle Association (NRA).

The very existence of the National Rifle Association is a testament to   35
the absence of a widespread gun culture in the antebellum period. Many former Union officers recalled their soldiers' lack of familiarity with firearms and hoped to avoid that situation in the future. The NRA's founders, the veterans William Conant Church and George Wood Wingate, sought to maintain widespread familiarity with firearms in times of peace. Doing so required teaching a new generation of American men to shoot. Church and Wingate understood that accuracy was irrelevant with the traditional muzzle-loading musket, while the new mass-produced breech-loading rifle offered the opportunity to develop sharpshooting skills. But American men had to own guns and use them regularly to develop these skills. With support from the state of New York—monetary backing that would later be taken over by the federal government—the NRA opened its first target-shooting range at Creedmore in 1872. The NRA's influence, along with its emphasis on individual gun ownership, spread west from Long Island.[43]

These developments may appear, and have generally been treated as, arcane historical details. But recently, the arguments of scholars have spilled over into more public forums. In looking back over the nation's obsession with firearms, historians, political scientists, and politicians usually come to rest at the Second Amendment. Those who adhere to the self-described "standard model" of the Second Amendment insist on their un-

---

[43]There is surprisingly little historical study of the National Rifle Association (NRA): one dissertation, Russell S. Gilmore, "Crackshots and Patriots: The National Rifle Association and America's Military-Sporting Tradition" (Ph.D. diss., University of Wisconsin, 1974); an official history, James Trefethen and James Serven, *Americans and Their Guns: The National Rifle Association's Story through Nearly a Century of Service to the Nation* (Harrisburg, 1967); and a biography, Donald N. Bigelow, *William Conant Church and* The Army and Navy Journal (New York, 1952). On the modern NRA, see Osha Gray Davidson, *Under Fire: The NRA and the Battle for Gun Control* (New York, 1993).

derstanding of the original intent of the Framers. Looking to the second half of the amendment—"the right of the people to keep and bear Arms, shall not be infringed"—adherents of the standard model argue for an individualist reading of the amendment. The Framers intended free access to firearms for every American. The historical roots of this right lie deep in the British heritage and drew intellectual validation from Niccolò Machiavelli[44] and the British commonwealth writers. Good republican citizens did not bear arms simply for the protection of the state; there was also the presumption of a right to self-protection and even armed insurrection—despite the Constitution's treason clause in Article III, Section 3.[45] But as Garry Wills[46] and others have pointed out, the second is the only amendment with a preamble establishing its purpose, clearly stated to be "a well-regulated Militia" preserving national security and civic order. The context for the amendment was the antifederalist fear that the Constitution diminished state power, particularly in granting Congress authority to "provide for organizing, arming, and disciplining the Militia" (Article I, Section 8). The debates addressing the Second Amendment demonstrate that no one cared about an individual right to bear arms; they were concerned with the fate of the militia. James Madison formulated this amendment as a political response to the antifederalists, guaranteeing state control of the militia yet promising federal support.[47]

The point this article seeks to make is that Madison attempted to deliver on that promise. Since the passage of the Second Amendment, the

---

[44]*Machiavelli:* Niccolò Machiavelli (1469–1527), Italian courtier and political philosopher famous for the harshly pragmatic advice contained in his handbook for rulers, *The Prince.*

[45]Glenn Harlan Reynolds, "A Critical Guide to the Second Amendment," *Tennessee Law Review,* 62 (Spring 1995), 461–512. This entire issue of the *Tennessee Law Review* is an uncritical celebration of the "standard model." See also Robert J. Cottrol, ed., *Gun Control and the Constitution: Sources and Explorations on the Second Amendment* (New York, 1994), ix–xlviii; Joyce Lee Malcolm, *To Keep and Bear Arms: The Origins of an Anglo-American Right* (Cambridge, Mass., 1994); Don B. Kates, "Handgun Prohibition and the Original Meaning of the Second Amendment," *Michigan Law Review,* 82 (Nov. 1983), 204–73; Stephen Halbrook, *That Every Man Be Armed* (San Francisco, 1984); Robert E. Shalhope, "The Ideological Origins of the Second Amendment," *Journal of American History,* 69 (Dec. 1982), 599–614.

[46]*Garry Wills:* Scholar and Pulitzer Prize–winning author (b. 1934) of books on American history, politics, and culture.

[47]The finest critique of the "standard model" is Garry Wills, "To Keep and Bear Arms," *New York Review of Books,* Sept. 21, 1995, pp. 62–72. See also Lawrence D. Cress, "An Armed Community: The Origins and Meaning of the Right to Bear Arms," *Journal of American History,* 71 (June 1984), 22–42; Roy G. Weathrup, "Standing Armies and Armed Citizens: An Historical Analysis of the Second Amendment," *Hastings Constitutional Law Quarterly,* 2 (Fall 1975), 961–1001; and Dennis A. Henigan, "Arms, Anarchy, and the Second Amendment," *Valparaiso University Law Review,* 26 (Fall 1991), 107–29.

federal government has worked to arm and regulate the militia. The first and most persistent problem was that there just were not enough guns available for the militia to arm itself, or even for the government to provide free to the militia. The government also ran into resistance—not from adherents of states' rights, for the southern states actually took greater advantage of federal largess than did the northern and western states—but from the people at large. It took seventy years of government and industrial efforts to produce sufficient firearms for the American market and twenty years of promotion to convince even a proportion of the public that private gun ownership was a necessity. The Civil War finally presented the federal government with the opportunity to fashion a well-regulated militia. The war brought home the idea that firearms were necessary for social control and order: guns preserved the Union and, in the Reconstruction years, helped to reestablish white supremacy in the South. And, perhaps most important, the war's end brought guns into the home, making them part of the domestic environment and an unquestioned member of the American family.

Engaging the Text

1. What, according to Bellesiles, is the traditional story about the relation of gun ownership and violence and the American frontier? To what extent does your own understanding of life on the frontier support this view of frontier violence?

2. What specific myths of frontier and Revolutionary War–era gun ownership does Bellesiles question in this selection? What alternative image does he offer of attitudes toward firearms and hunting in pre–Civil War America? What evidence does he present in support of his position? How persuasive do you find his argument?

3. What factors were involved in the rise of "the gun culture" in the United States after the Civil War? What myths had to be created about gun ownership, according to Bellesiles, in order to make this culture effective?

4. In Bellesiles's view, what was the original intent of the Second Amendment of the Bill of Rights? Why is this point so critical in his assessment of early American attitudes toward firearms? What do Bellesiles's conclusions about early American attitudes toward gun ownership and the Second Amendment suggest about the right to bear arms?

Exploring Connections

5. Review the selections by Frederick Jackson Turner (p. 683) and Wallace Stegner (p. 694), paying attention to the role ascribed in each to guns in frontier America. To what extent do they support or contradict Bellesiles's

analysis of the role of firearms in early American history? How might you account for differences in their treatment of firearms on the frontier?

6. Selections earlier in this chapter by N. Scott Momaday (p. 734) and Patricia Nelson Limerick (p. 755) both suggest that the frontier was, in fact, the site of significant violence against Native Americans and others. How might you explain the apparent discrepancy between Bellesiles's view of gun culture in early American history and the violence Momaday and Limerick associate with the frontier?

7. How might Bellesiles respond to the "NRA hotline" advice given in the *Boondocks* cartoon on this page?

EXTENDING THE CRITICAL CONTEXT

8. Research current publications of firearm advocacy groups like the National Rifle Association to determine how they present the role of guns in the early history of the United States. How closely do they agree with Bellesiles's story of firearms in the early republic? To what extent does Bellesiles's interpretation of the origin of gun culture in the United States weaken the case for individual gun ownership?

9. Hold a class debate on the issue of gun ownership and gun control. How should Americans balance their right to "life, liberty, and the pursuit of happiness" with the right to bear arms? To what extent has the right to bear arms been based on a misreading of the Constitution encouraged by the myth of the American frontier?

THE BOONDOCKS   **by AARON MCGRUDER**

Freedom and Want:
The Western Paradox

DONALD WORSTER

The West in the mind of America is an open, wind-swept plain or a vast, desert expanse, punctuated by a few lonely buttes and presided over by a clear blue sky. It is a place of sunsets and vistas that go on forever, a place where you can drink straight from a mountain stream or sleep outside under the stars. According to Donald Worster, the pristine wilderness of the American West is what freed the frontiersman from the prejudices of Europe. But, as Worster notes, Americans have long been of two minds about frontier nature: the vast expanses of the western wilderness may set you free, but they also can threaten your very survival. Since the first American settlers ventured into the lands of the West, they have gloried in its wild beauty and also tried their best to bring it under their control. In this selection, Worster suggests that a paradoxical combination of love and fear has underscored America's relationship with nature since the beginning of westward migration. The Hall Distinguished Professor of American History at the University of Kansas, Worster is the author of Dust Bowl *(1979),* Rivers of Empire *(1985), and, the source of this selection,* Under Western Skies: Nature and History in the American West *(1992).*

We Americans are supposed to be a practical, level-headed people with a firm grip on reality, but it is not quite true. We are also a nation of dreamers. Our imaginations are easily captured by a whiff of myth or romance, our feelings are quick to rush after a promise, and some of our dreams are more extravagant than those of any hallucinating jungle tribe. It takes all the disciplined effort we can muster simply to bring our tangled yearnings to the surface of discussion, never mind being able to identify their ambiguities and confront their contradictions.

Nowhere is this tendency more pronounced than when we talk about one of our favorite dreams, the American West. Say the word "West" and, immediately, vistas of mustangs galloping across wide-open spaces under immense, unclouded skies fill our imaginations, and sober reason has to come panting after. Say the word and we are off living in a dream, experiencing its old powerful emotions but as ever finding it difficult to say how the dream ends. As a people, we are quick to invent fantasies but slower to find plausible, realistic endings for them.

The most famous novel ever written about the Old West, the cowboy West, illustrates the tendency well. I mean, of course, *The Virginian*, published in 1902 by the Philadelphia socialite and Harvard graduate Owen Wister. It is a book that has stirred the imaginations of millions, but it does not succeed in giving those imaginations a rational course to follow. In the end the book is plagued by a serious paradox, of which the author seems unaware. To the extent that it expresses what we as a people have felt about the West, it reveals that we have been chasing after conflicting ends, which we have not carefully sorted out or reconciled, and therefore we stand naively divided against ourselves.

Wister's story is about the discovery of a new kind of man the West is supposed to have produced. One day, it goes, the narrator, getting off a train in Medicine Bow, Wyoming, is met by a paragon of manly youth and goodness. The paragon is called simply "the Virginian," though at the age of fourteen he abruptly abandoned his native home, parents, and siblings—lit out for the territories, like a taller, cleaner Huck Finn—and ever since has supported himself by his own abilities. Apparently he has eaten well, for he has grown up to physical perfection. None of the privations or the hard knocks or the bad companions along the way has managed to leave a blemish on either his physique or character. Though working as a mere hired hand on the Sunk Creek Ranch, he stands tall besides his companions: a twenty-four-year-old demigod, free-spirited and independent, uncompromising in his integrity, exhibiting an utter confidence in himself, ranking as a true gentleman in all but outward circumstances. And, withal, he is completely unassuming. Wister portrays him as a natural nobleman, formed not by civilization and its institutions but by the spontaneous influence of the land working on an innate goodness. Here in the West, Wister believes, he has discovered a finer type of American growing up than can be found back east in Pennsylvania or Massachusetts.

Then comes the difficulty of knowing what to do with a man so nicely   5
formed outside civilization: How is he to find a living, make a marriage, take a hand in the running of society? For the marriage part, Wister manages, after a tediously long mating dance, to hitch his Virginian to a blue-blooded New England schoolmarm, Molly Stark Wood, and they go for their honeymoon to a high mountain meadow, skinny-dipping together and broiling trout. But solving the career part gives Wister a little more trouble. Part way through the book he tells us that the hero has for years been carefully saving his wages, indicating that he does not intend to remain a cowhand all his life; however, Wister is far too enthralled by this cowboy's simple ways to want to see him actually put those savings to work. Not until page 502 in my edition does the author throw together a hasty sketch of the Virginian's eventual worldly success. This hired man at last rises to become a partner with his boss, the distinguished Judge Henry. With all those savings, he buys a spread of his own and lays out modern improvements, fencing the range and stocking it with improved breeds of cattle. And that is not all: "When I took up my land," the Virginian explains, "I chose a place where there is coal. It will not be long before the new railroad needs that." Sure

enough, the railroad soon lays tracks to his door and carries away fuel for its locomotives. Eventually, we are told in the last paragraph, the simple man of the saddle becomes "an important man, with a strong grip on many various enterprises, and able to give his wife all and more than she asked or desired." So ends the saga of a man of nature, now elevated wonderfully to the rank of industrial capitalist, his adoring wife becoming in the end an indulged child of the consumer culture.[1]

By holding it off so long and then leaving it so sketchy, Wister appears not to have had his whole heart in that ending. He intended to recreate nostalgically a frontier world that was passing away, and all the while he was worrying whether in the future we would be able to find such men again. Probably most readers have shared Wister's nostalgia — and liked the Virginian less the more he rises. Not one in ten who knows the story remembers or cares much about that ending. The vision we hold of the West, the vision we most want to hold onto, lies in some shadowy, receding realm of nature, as it did for Wister, and we would rather not think too hard about endings.

Yet to put matters thus is too simple. We *do* care, or say we care, as Wister cared and said he cared, about the future West too. And many among us believe, as he did, that building railroads, digging coal, and bringing the industrial revolution to this region is a noble act; many still believe that such a technological future is one worth saving and working for. And come to that, we too (most of us anyway) want to loll around with Mrs. Virginian in a cornucopia of purchased things — furniture, clothing, and everything else that we could ask for or desire. There can be no denying that the ending, short and flat as it may be, has behind it as powerful a dream as any that has animated America or the West.

Two dreams then are tugging at our feelings: one of a life in nature, the other with machines; one of a life in the past, the other in the future. Nature makes us what we are, we still like to think, makes us good and decent; but it is technology that makes us better. If the West has any spiritual claim to uniqueness, I believe it lies in its intensity of devotion to those opposing dreams. Call it then, without too much risk of distortion, the "Western Paradox." Without quite being able to acknowledge the fact consciously or intellectually, we know that our hopes for this region do not quite hang together, that there is no easy, smooth progression from one dream to another, as Wister's novel pretends, that at some point we may even have to choose between them.

The western paradox exists in large part because the landscape has encouraged it. Here nature wears a face that is at once powerfully attractive and powerfully repellant, leading westerners both to embrace and repudiate it. The West is, by national standards, terribly dry. Its average precipitation is less than twenty inches a year, less than half that of the East Coast or Eu-

---

[1]Owen Wister, *The Virginian* (New York: Grosset & Dunlap, 1904), 502–3. [All notes are Worster's.]

rope. The most obvious effect of so low a rainfall is the kind of vegetation that naturally grows here: the sporadic, bunchy grasses and forbs, the scattering of greasewood and sagebrush, the relative paucity of forests. A second effect is that the West can count only a very few rivers, all well distanced from one another and many of them drying up by summer's end. For all its scenic grandeur, for all its abundance of rock and minerals, this region's landscape says, at least in biological terms, that this is a place of scarcity. Sometimes it says the word scarcity in a whisper, hinting faintly and uncertainly of droughts to come; then again it says it in a hard, dry rasp that only the deafest can fail to hear. Water, or rather its absence, is at the very heart of the western paradox.

John Wesley Powell was the first person to define the West as the "arid   10 region" of the country. That was in 1878, and a number of historians have since pondered the implications of his concept. What impact, they have wondered, has scarcity in a vital natural resource like water had on the habits, institutions, modes of producing a living, values and identities of the people who have taken possession of this land? Have they accommodated themselves to that scarcity? Has it set them free? Or have they sought to overcome it? Have they sought even to the point of forging a new kind of servitude for themselves? Have they sought to the point of regret?

One side of the western paradox, I have suggested, is the dream of growing up happily in a state of nature. It is basically a dream of achieving unlimited personal freedom. An ancient dream, it was active long before there was an America and was brought to this continent in the heads of millions of immigrants. But the eastern part of the United States was not the ideal landscape, at least not to the degree the West was, for stirring up such hopes of a free life in nature. The East astonished immigrants with its spontaneous abundance, but not with its openness or ease of movement. While still at sea and approaching the land, the first European travelers marveled at the aromatic, organic smell of plenty wafting out to them. Once ashore, they could not talk enough about the wild grapes festooning the trees, for all the grapes they had seen back home had been carefully cultivated, pruned, and staked in vineyards. They were impressed by the richness of the land, the wealth of wood for building and fuel; here in the New World they could have bigger farms, bigger farmhouses, bigger fires in those farmhouses than they had had in the Old World, and the poor could have them as readily as the well-to-do. But this easy abundance of the eastern American environment could be an obstacle as much as a blessing. Men still had to hack their way through it, chop it down, bring it under control. Only when they had done all that could they at last talk about how free they were. And the places they could not penetrate and clear—the Great Dismal Swamp of Virginia, the dark, twisty bayous of Louisiana, teeming with bird life, crawfish, cypresses, and tattered draperies of gray-green Spanish moss—never came to be associated in the American mind with liberation, unless it was in the mind of a runaway slave.

Come into the western country, however, and the reactions of travelers were unanimous: here at last was the true promise of American freedom. Here in a landscape generally free of trees, where no forests crowded in and impinged on the view, all physical restraint seemed to be removed. Among the earliest white men to experience that openness were the two explorers whom President Thomas Jefferson sent out in the summer of 1804, Captains Meriwether Lewis and William Clark. As they were pushing their pirogues up the Platte River, they decided one morning to scramble up the bank and walk for a short distance into the interior. Clark wrote in his journal this description of what they saw:

> This Prarie is Covered with Grass of 10 or 12 inches in hight, Soil of good quality & at the Distance of about a mile still further back the Countrey rises about 80 or 90 feet higher, and is one Continued Plain as fur as Can be seen, from the Bluff on the 2nd rise imediately above our Camp, the most butifull prospect of the River up & Down and the Countrey Opsd. prosented it Self which I ever beheld.[2]

Clark gives no indication that any deeper thoughts occupied his mind at this moment; but if he did not feel a sense of utter release, of total liberation from duty, authority, responsibility, and work, then he should have stayed on the boat and washed the skillet. Many of us who have read the Lewis and Clark journals have no doubt what *we* would have felt had *we* been fortunate enough to have been there at that historic moment, and the feeling would have been freedom — freedom not available to people living in the East, freedom made possible only by the dry air, the short grass, and the horizon running off to infinity.

Similar versions of encountering the pristine West occur again and again in the literature of both fact and fiction. For an example from fiction we could turn to that marvelous evocation of the Rocky Mountain fur trade, A. B. Guthrie, Jr.'s *The Big Sky*. In an early scene Uncle Zeb Caloway, a trapper of many years, returns from the mountains to visit his Kentucky kin and, with his tales of mountains and plains, lights up the eyes of a young boy named Boone Caudill: "He spoke in a big voice and waved his arms and talked about being free like it was something you could heft."[3] It is not long after that Boone himself leaves Kentucky to find his future in the West.

For an example from nonfiction we could turn to the autobiographical sketch of a twentieth-century man, Richard Erdoes, author of *Lame Deer, Seeker of Visions*. In the epilogue of that book Erdoes explains that he grew up in Vienna in a mixed Jewish-Catholic-Protestant family, and when faced with Nazi repression, he felt compelled to flee to America. He entered the region in 1940:

---

[2]*The Journals of Lewis and Clark,* Bernard DeVoto, ed. (Boston: Houghton Mifflin, 1953), 14.

[3]A. B. Guthrie, Jr., *The Big Sky* (New York: Time-Life, 1947), 8.

My first encounter with the American West was a strangely emotional experience. Naturally, it took place in South Dakota. We had been driving all day through corn country, flat and rather monotonous—widely spaced farms with white picket fences, each house surrounded by enormous cornfields. We crossed the Missouri and the old highway began to undulate, dip and rise, dip and rise, roller-coaster fashion. We drove over one dip and suddenly found ourselves in a different world. Except for the road there was no sign of man. Before me stretched an endless ocean of hills, covered with sage and prairie grass in shades of silver, subtle browns and ochers, pale yellows and oranges. Above all this stretched the most enormous sky I had ever seen. Nothing in my previous life had prepared me for this scene of utter emptiness which had come upon me without warning. I stopped the car and we all got out. There was emptiness of sound, too. The calls of a few unseen birds only accentuated it. I found myself overwhelmed by a tremendous, surging sensation of freedom, of liberation from space. I experienced a moment of complete happiness.[4]

Erdoes was writing about South Dakota, but he might just as well have   15
been encountering Nevada, Wyoming, eastern Oregon, or Alberta. All those places have their open spaces too, and all of them have had the effect of setting people free. Even a stay-at-home like Henry David Thoreau, who never saw any of those spaces, who got no farther west than the Sioux Agency in Redwood, Minnesota, could easily imagine and put into enduring words the experience so many others would have: "Eastward I go only by force," he wrote, "but westward I go free."[5]

Free of what, we might ask? For many, the bondage has been the expectations of others, their importunings and demands, their dependency, their entrapments, emotional and economic. Men have gone west to get away from women, women to get away from men. Children have left the confinement or authority of their parents, and parents have left their children behind. The novelist Owen Wister came to escape the pressures of an imperious, snobbish mother and her social class in Philadelphia. Another famous refugee, Theodore Roosevelt, came to North Dakota in 1885 to forget the painful and near-simultaneous loss of his wife and mother and, after a string of career failures, to get a new start for himself.[6] Others have fled bills or mortgage holders or jobs. Or pollen. Or bureaucracy. Or noise. Or, in the case of Erdoes, the threat of being placed in a concentration camp. Praiseworthy or ignoble, trivial or profound, the reasons for seeking freedom are

[4]John (Fire) Lame Deer and Richard Erdoes, *Lame Deer, Seeker of Visions* (New York: Washington Square Press, 1972), 265.

[5]Henry David Thoreau, "Walking" [1862], *Excursions*, Leo Marx, ed. (New York: Corinth, 1962), 176.

[6]The experiences of both men are recounted in G. Edward White, *The Eastern Establishment and the Western Experience: The West of Frederic Remington, Theodore Roosevelt, and Owen Wister* (New Haven: Yale Univ. Press, 1968), chaps. 3, 4, 6.

less important to us here than the fact the West has served them all. Its dessicated, unobstructed land has cleaned out many consciences, given many people comfort, and renewed much self-confidence.

Not only have Americans of European ancestry been served by the West in this way. For thousands of years the native people also came and went, celebrating *their* freedom on the land. The peculiarity of the European newcomers lay in their tendency to attach an intensely private meaning to freedom. They came with a strongly developed sense of selfhood, of individuality, conceiving of themselves as more solitary than collective. They assumed, along with the French philosopher Jean-Jacques Rousseau, that before there was a "society" there was a "me," and that "me" was, on the whole and more often than not, a "good me." The white freedom-seekers came repeating to themselves, "I need more space than I am getting. Give me enough room, give me the whole wide West, and I will put myself right."

So individual following individual, family following family, we white Americans have come into this land of scarcity, of natural deprivation, and gloried in it. We dispossessed the native race that was holding and using it, and ever since we have been taking great gulps of free air. We have found a vast space in which to be natural again, to be unencumbered except by the encumbrances we freely choose and then only as long as we choose them. But here is the rub: If this vision of liberation is to endure, this western space must *stay open,* which is to say, it must *stay dry.* Freedom in our western vision requires aridity. It depends on a brilliance of light, an openness of terrain, a clean spaciousness that gives us plenty of room to spread out and look around, to get some distance from the crowd, to deal with our private selves, to renew hope. It requires the West as it naturally was and is. A little more water might spoil it all.

That has been one of our western dreams then. But there is the other and opposing one, the dream of putting technology to work making the West over into something else. The arid West may offer a kind of freedom to the individual spirit, but it may also suggest the deadly specter of poverty. You cannot eat freedom, the cynic says. What will you do for food in such a land? How will you grow crops without water? Can you get along without property and fences, and if not, where will you get wood for those fences? Where is your fuel? Where are your housing materials? Where are your grapes garlanding the trees, ready to be plucked? Will you have to buy all those things from people in the East, and if so, where will you get enough cash to pay for them? Can you get much of a living here without bringing in more water?

Like Owen Wister's novel, this western region has had some difficulty 20 figuring out how it can achieve material success and yet maintain the landscape of freedom. And that is where it gets snared in the coils of paradox.

For a long time now scarcity has not been an appealing prospect in the white American, or in the white European, mind. We have reorganized our whole way of life, our institutions and laws, to triumph over it. I maintain, in fact, that the drive to overcome the fear of scarcity has been one of the greatest forces pushing us toward the modern world. That fear orginated in early modern Europe. As their populations began to press against the land and their resource base to decline, the European people heaved themselves up to make a mighty cultural revolution. They determined they would never again be denied anything. A dream began to take form of endless plenty delivered through the benevolent agency of science and technology.

Among the first to express that dream of unlimited abundance were the early capitalistic entrepreneurs of England, France, Germany, and Italy. Everything with them came to be regarded as potential merchandise, everything existed to be made to yield greater and greater quantities of wealth. Save your capital, they urged their fellows, and invest it in technology. Learn to grow two blades of grass where one grew before. Search the globe over for unexploited raw materials to feed into your industrial apparatus. Work twice as hard as the man next to you to get those raw materials and the apparatus into your possession. Let everyone drive himself exactly in this way, accumulating as much private wealth as he can, and eventually we will all be as rich as kings and never have to suffer privation again.

This fear of scarcity and this determination to escape its hold once and for all animated not only early merchants and entrepreneurs, not only those innovating capitalists who gave the world modern industrialism with all its factories and wage slaves, but it also animated the socialists. In the view of Karl Marx, for instance, humankind will never achieve its full measure of self-realization until there is an abundance of goods provided for every man, woman, and child on earth. For the socialists as well as for the capitalists, technology has been the only true source of that abundance; such wealth does not come spontaneously from nature. The two groups of ideologues may argue endlessly over who can do a better job of producing and distributing that contrived abundance, but they do not disagree on one fundamental belief—on the necessity of banishing all material scarcity from the earth. They are both devoted to the maximum production of commodities.

This profound cultural revolution has drastically changed our species' relationship to the rest of nature. It has made man the measure of all things, elevated him to be the end and goal of history, set him up as the master of the planet. It could hardly be otherwise. To banish all conceivable scarcity requires our total domination of nature. With the rise of bourgeois society, Karl Marx wrote approvingly in his book, *The Grundrisse,*

> nature becomes purely an object for humankind, purely a matter of utility; ceases to be recognized as a power for itself; and the theoretical discovery of its autonomous laws appears merely as a ruse so as to subjugate it under human needs, whether as an object of consumption or as a means of production.[7]

What this social observer did not go on to say is just as important as what he said. When nature becomes purely a matter of utility, a thing inviting its

[7]Karl Marx, *The Grundrisse,* ed. and trans. by David McLellan (New York: Harper Torchbooks, 1971), 94.

domination by technology, it dies for us. It ceases to be significant in our lives, except as we can turn it to use. Henceforth we live alienated from it.

I have made this short digression into abstract and general ideas, the ideological underpinnings of modern technological civilization, because I believe there is no understanding of life in the American West in isolation from the broader currents of history. This West has never been a wholly self-defining society. It has taken its leading ideas from larger circles of thought, including the intellectual history of capitalism and socialism, of Adam Smith and Karl Marx, and has participated in what is now the world-wide dream of controlling nature. Here as elsewhere, that dream has been the most powerful force for change around. It has carried all of us along, as it has the earth, in its train. The dream has come into our heads, into all our heads to some degree, simply as a function of being alive at this time, and any future that will be invented here in the West must come to terms with it.

More than that, the people who have settled this western region of the United States have shown themselves to be especially receptive to the vision of a technologically dominated environment. If the fear of scarcity drove Europeans, living in one of the most moderate climates, to undertake a cultural revolution, consider what such a fear must do to those coming into a desert or near-desert. Then the fear would tend to concentrate the mind even more. It would still the voices of critics and doubters. We must find more water, settlers would say to themselves; we must use every possible technology to extract as much of it as we can out of this place. We must not rest until we have achieved control over every molecule of moisture. Each river we come to must be turned into a commodity and consumed entirely. The West must be redeemed everywhere by hard work and unflagging dedication until it has lost all semblance of naturalness, until it is a luxuriant oasis of ease and delight.

An early expression of that spirit of conquest appears in a 1906 issue of the *North American Review*, which grandly predicted that one day irrigation would redeem one hundred million acres of the West and put them to productive use. As that happened, the West of emigrant trains and free-roaming cowboys would disappear forever. Already, the article continues,

> The old cabins and dugouts are [being] replaced by modern dwellings. The great ranges are fast passing into orderly farms, where cultivated crops take the place of wild grasses. Steadily is man's rational selection directing the selection of nature. Even the cowboy, the essential creation of Western conditions, is rapidly passing away. Like the buffalo, he has had his place in the drama of civilization. The Indian of the plain must yield to civilization or pass away. Custer, Cody, Bridger, and Carson did their work and passed on. Pioneers of the old school are giving place to a young and vigorous group of men of intellect, will and ceaseless activity, who are turning the light of scientific discovery on plain and mountain.... [A] nation of two hundred millions of

25

freemen, living under American Common and Statute law, stretching from the Atlantic to the Pacific, fifty millions of whom occupy the arid region of the continent, where the word "desert" is unknown, will soon be a mighty reality.[8]

Such confidence would prove, over the ensuing years, to be a little too grandiose. But all the same much of the prediction would come true.

But the drive for technological control does not involve simply commanding every river to flow where we want it to go. In dry farming, ranching, mining, and manufacturing, there have been manifestations of the same drive to conquer. And once again, the West is not alone in its quest for unlimited abundance; it is merely striving to stay abreast of a competitive world intent everywhere on intensifying production and consumption, with no end in sight.

To be sure, the dream of abolishing scarcity through technology has not yet been fully achieved, not when half a billion of the world's people are still living on the edge of starvation and the world's population is set to double in the next four decades. Not when thousands in every western American state want, but have no access to, a middle-class standard of living. Not when the wealthiest classes still maintain that they do not yet have enough—do not yet "have it all." After several centuries of technological wizardry, including all the damming and siphoning and diverting of water that has been done here in the West, the old pinch of scarcity is felt as sharply as ever. Will we ever have enough water to slake our thirst? Will we ever have enough to sell? Will we ever be in paradise?

The elusiveness of success is not the only problem becoming apparent in this drive to control nature. Another is that the control we achieve, as it is pushed to higher and higher levels of intensity, turns out to be self-defeating. The water we command becomes increasingly degraded in quality. Instead of becoming more useful to more people, it becomes less so. The silt carried in the dammed-up rivers coagulates behind the dams, until finally it forms great brown tubs of mud drying in the sun and the days of water control are finished. Western towns and industries that have built their fortunes on hydraulic engineering may, if present trends continue, someday end in collapse. What we once thought was so permanent comes to seem increasingly a passing and even self-destructive relationship with the place.

There is also the consequence that a nature intensely controlled is no longer a nature capable of offering a sense of freedom. Increasingly, we find ourselves trapped in the very technology we have devised to master the world around us. For example, the irrigating farmer learns, as he rushes about from headgate to headgate, turning so many acre feet a day into his beans or alfalfa, just how demanding his life has become. He has to regi-

30

[8]Frank W. Blackmar, "The Mastery of the Desert," *North American Review* 182 (May 1906): 688.

ment himself in order to regiment the river. And that may be only the first loss of freedom the individual experiences in such a situation. To get more water from farther away, he or she may be compelled to join a formal irrigation district, hire technical experts, and submit to the leadership of a privileged local elite. The tables of organization governing the irrigating rancher or farmer get more and more complicated year by year. He or she may have to consult regularly with a state authority or with a federal reclamation bureaucracy, strung out all the way to Denver or Washington, holding the vital capital and knowledge that the man on the land needs. Government officials, engineers, bankers, water lawyers, labor organizers, equipment manufacturers, all enter into the individual water user's life, all of them demanding, clamoring, legislating, all of them furnishing something the irrigator can no longer furnish for himself. It is a plain fact that only the simplest kinds of scarcity can be overcome without some loss of personal freedom. You cannot maximize technological abundance without setting up powerful government agencies, corporations, and other chains of command, other hierarchies of authority, and these endanger democracy and independence as they grow. You cannot have it both ways. And thus we are once more in the realm of paradox....

Engaging the Text

1. What is the "paradox" alluded to in Worster's title? In what ways does it grow out of the natural conditions of life in the West?

2. Why, according to Worster, do the natural features of the western landscape promote the growth of freedom more effectively than do the natural features of the East? Would you agree that a particular type of natural landscape can stimulate a sense of freedom among its inhabitants more than another?

3. In Worster's view, what role has the "fear of scarcity" played in westward expansion? How has it revolutionized humanity's view of itself and its relationship to nature? To what extent would you agree with Worster that the fear of scarcity jeopardizes the American Dream of the West?

Exploring Connections

4. Compare Worster's analysis of the meaning of nature in the American West with the views of nature presented by Frederick Jackson Turner (p. 683) and Wallace Stegner (p. 694) to determine whether these classic texts reflect the notion that nature has set Americans free.

5. How might N. Scott Momaday (p. 734) respond to Worster's analysis of American attitudes toward nature in the West?

6. How do the cowboys in Charles Barsotti's cartoon on page 825 reflect the complex attitudes that Worster claims Americans have toward the West?

Extending the Critical Context

7. Working in groups, assemble a collection of advertising images that feature western or wilderness landscapes and analyze these images in terms of what they are suggesting, overtly or indirectly, about freedom and technological domination.

8. Research one of the major technological interventions that has left its mark on the American West over the past seventy-five years, including, but not limited to, water reclamation projects, military bases, nuclear-test and materials-disposal sites, mining and oil operations, and city building. Report your findings to your class and discuss the extent to which you agree with Worster's suggestion that technological control threatens to undermine the ability of the West to provide us with a sense of freedom.

Department of the Interior
LINDA HOGAN

Fear, not love, governs the white world's relation to nature and the West. At least that is how Native American writer Linda Hogan sees it. In this essay, Hogan assesses the state of the white world's soul and reflects on how religious beliefs imported with settlers from their European homelands predisposed them to view the western wilderness as a place of terror. Hogan's account of a sweat-lodge ceremony on her Colorado reservation offers a living counterexample of the relation of culture and nature in Native American societies. Hogan (b. 1947) is a renowned poet and novelist. Her books include Dwellings: A Spiritual History of the Living World *(1995),* Solar Storms *(1995), and* Power *(1998). She is associate professor of American Indian studies at the University of Minnesota.*

> *The mud mother shaped her little ones, the humans, and held them in her lap. She rocked them, those red clay children with their tiny fingers, their smooth faces. She rocked them and swayed. And the wind came to breathe life into them. That first aliveness, that first gust of air inside the clay people and they came to life and the mud mother loved her children and she sang to them, O bodies, O infants, our future, my children, flesh of the earth.*

1. Disembodying America

A few miles from where I live is the buffalo herd. Dark and massive, they are a remnant of a more whole world, of a mighty tribe of animals. Near their fenced refuge is the grave of Buffalo Bill Cody, one of America's killer heroes, whose fame grew out of the horrifying slaughter of the powerful creatures contained in such diminished numbers nearby, and the starvation and near destruction of many tribes of people.

On a recent holiday, a cluster of white Americans stood at the fence gazing at the buffalo, trying to get their attention. It was late spring and the light-brown calves were sitting in tall grasses while their elders grazed around them. Looking at them, I wondered if they felt anger and despair being watched that way by the descendants of their killers. Do their cells, like mine, remember the terror, the changed world and destroyed land?

The people of science would say this question is a projection. It is anthropomorphism, one of those words that change compassion and empathy into pathologies. During the fire in Yellowstone, a park ranger told the people not to feed starving elk. "There is no scientific proof that animals feel pain," he said, over National Public Radio.

This was not an alien form of thinking to me. I've heard it said to cover various forms of suffering. It's only been in the last few years, after all, that newborn babies were determined to feel pain. Before this, surgery was performed on them without anesthesia. The denial of the nervous systems of animals and infants has a historical precedent in the denial of intelligence and soul in Indians and other peoples. In the late 1800s a trial involving Ponca leader Standing Bear was held to determine if he and his band of people were human beings.

As American Indian people in the political body of the U.S. we are   5
overseen by and located under the governmental offices of the Department of the Interior, along with the rest of wilderness, forest, animals, fish. Like them, we are held in low regard.

Tribal people, animals, wilderness, life itself has been powerless against the force of weapons forged first by a violence-loving Europe and then by the American legal system. And I think now that the reason so many of us yet identify with animals is the shared helplessness we've experienced against a death-loving culture and the extreme powers it uses against us and others. It is a culture that fears and destroys what it perceives as wild, including its own innerness and physicality.

The wilderness, mentioned in the Bible nearly three hundred times, is almost always referred to as the place of evil, as the devil's place. It is seen as a dangerous realm, the untouched place of demons. It lives at the edge of the civilized world, and in the human mapping, it is the place inside humans that behaves according to instinct and inner drive that cannot be controlled by will. Wilderness is what the dominating have tried to push away from themselves, both in the outside world and inside their own bodies. Because of human denial of their own predation and human fears, wolves came to a near end for insisting on their own wildness, as did bears and mountain lions. It is the domestic and submissive, those who can be controlled and contained in a human-determined territory, who have most easily survived.

Of course, there were some who preferred the wilds of America. In the nineteenth century, there were those few mountain men who entered the wild willingly and were changed by it. There were also the white women who found their ways into tribal communities and did not wish to return to the white world. Although fictions of the frontier included captivity narratives that claimed white women were abducted, tortured, and raped by tribal men, the truth was that most simply did not wish to return. They had stepped out of a world surrounded by emptiness, by inanimate matter, and they had entered the living body of land, self, people, the soul of matter in a world where everything was alive and depended on all the rest.

For white Americans in the present time, Indians have come to represent spirit, heart, an earth-based way of living, all things they have felt missing from their lives that have been split off from a larger living. In this way, we fill a need for them. But we do not fit easily into their system of symbols and what that system, even now, wants us to be. This need of theirs goes back to earlier times, to when we were on the receiving end of federal policies of extermination. At this time of hunger and killing, while the true stories of Indian lives were missing, images of Indians were manipulated to present what the image-makers knew white America wanted. While the living bodies of tribal people were destroyed, photographs and paintings romanticized Indian lives. There were the photographs of dying leaders, the posed depictions of people living traditional lives they no longer, in reality, were allowed to live. What comes to my mind first, however, is a portrait photograph of Charles Eastman. Dressed in traditional clothing, he appears to be a chief. What isn't supplied in the portrait is that Eastman, author and medical doctor, a Santee Sioux survivor, was the attending physician at the massacre of Indian people, primarily women and children, at Wounded Knee. The grief inside him must have been enormous. And yet he was portrayed as the brave warrior, the precise image of what the Americans had tried to kill.

And there was Four Bears, a Mandan leader who wanted peace. Four   10
Bears was painted by Catlin[1] in his traditional clothing at the same time that he and his people were dying of the smallpox the painters and photographers helped to spread. Catlin, by the way, was also invited to Osceola's[2] death in order to paint him as he was dying.

As America has become increasingly disembodied, what is killed has appeared as part of their symbol system—in the abstract. Human lives were traded for the image of that life; embodied matter exchanged for an idea of spirit. For settlers and missionaries, this originated with a belief in transcendence and an afterlife in heaven. They wanted to escape the body, to rid the continent of heathens, to civilize and cultivate the land. They wanted a world of spirit that was apart from, and better than, the body. They wanted to rise above bodily needs, desires, and all forms of human pain and being.

In the north, as the fur trade nearly extincted the beaver, the Northwest Company produced currency that carried the images of a beaver and an Indian. One of these bills was the value of a beaver hide. The money became the sign for the value of the living thing, and its worth was not in its life but in its death, carried out in the name of European high fashion.

This was the case for later currency as well, the Indian head, the buffalo nickel, replacements for what was being slaughtered. This disembodiment continues today in various shapes and forms; in a recent commercial a jeep is superimposed over a herd of running buffalo, teddy bears that have taken the place of the real bears, cars—Cherokee, Mustang—named for the very tribes and wild animals that were violated. In the safety of our

---

[1]*Catlin:* George Catlin (1796–1872), American artist famed for his portraits of Native Americans.

[2]*Osceola:* A Creek Indian (1804?–1838) who led the Seminole Indians during the Second Seminole War. He died in Fort Moultrie Prison in South Carolina.

homes, we can listen to tapes of the disappearing rain forest, whales, and wolves, or watch videos of wilderness, all safely contained inside an appliance, inside our walls.

Ironically, for those who have forgotten to listen to the earth's voice, there is admiration for all the things and places they have tried to disappear. In a country where spirit has been so pitted against body, it's a form of crude mythmaking, of story without meaning, without truth, without understanding. As wilderness and Indians have been seen as a part of the mythic past of white America, the destruction to them has been immense and ongoing; a recent issue of *LIFE*,[3] with a focus on the American West, carried a photograph of Buffalo Bill and several native men from his Wild West show on its final page. In the photograph they are traveling by gondola through Venice. The caption reads: *No, it's not a scene from a spaghetti western. It's 1890, and those guys in warbonnets aren't just typical featherheads from central casting. They're real Indians in a Siouxreal situation—touring Europe with Buffalo Bill's Wild West show. They stopped off to see Venice on their way—and to introduce the Italians to buffalo mozzarella.*

Such ridicule of native people is the same kind of thinking that allowed   15 for genocide, then carved faces of presidents into Sioux holy land, a thinking that has no imagination, no place for respect, empathy, or compassion, no love. What does it say that women and men who had intelligence, grace, and bearing, who were powerful leaders, who led strong resistance movements, were forced to be showmen, to be on display, who in order to survive became bodies owned by Buffalo Bill, the very man who had carried out starvation policies against them and was famous for his efficient slaughtering of buffalo?

It's evident that we are still containers for the needs and desires of white America, and yet our bodies themselves still suffer. Even those of us who walked out of that genocide by some cast of fortune struggle with the brokenness of our bodies and hearts, with hungers never fulfilled, with self-destruction in the forms of suicide, alcoholism, and child abuse that is a hatred of what comes from the body. The terror, even now, remains inside us. History is present in our cells that came from ancestral cells, from bodies hated, starved, and killed. It is clear to us that the destruction of the body and the destruction of the land have coincided in our joined American history. And it is our task, and the work of others, to return to and hold dear the beautiful, flawed, embodied spirit alive in its imperfect matter.

2. Reanimation of the World

Culture evolves out of the experience of living with a land. For traditional Indian people, this habitation with land has developed over centuries, in some cases longer than 10,000 years. Deep knowledge of the land has

[3]*LIFE:* Popular American photography magazine.

meant survival, in terms of both sustenance and healing. Native people recognize that disease of the body is often caused by imbalance, sometimes originating within the human body and spirit, sometimes in the outside world. Either way, relationship with all the rest of creation is central to healing. Cure begins, and ends, with relationship. The purpose of ceremony is to restore the individual to their place within all the rest. If medicinal herbs are used, the effectiveness of the cure depends on an intimate knowing of the plant, the land around it, the mineral content of the soil, whether there has been lightning in the region, rainfall, and even which animals have passed through the territory of the plant. The healing capacity of plants is strengthened inside human knowledge; the stories of the plant, both mythic and historical, are essential, adding the human dimension to the world of nonhuman nature. It's an intricate science, reconnecting and restoring the human body with earth, cosmos.

There has been a growing understanding among non-Indians of the need for such relationship and connectedness. In the young science of ecology, it is known that every piece of the puzzle of life is necessary. This is a time of what I call the reanimation of the natural world by white men, as they are newly discovering an old understanding, that everything on earth is alive and that the relationship between all these lives makes for the whole living planet. While native people have been ridiculed for these views, James Lovelock has been hailed as a genius for his return to old Indian ways of thinking and knowing, for originating what he has called the Gaia hypothesis.[4]

This is not an entirely new concept to Western culture; Paracelsus,[5] like traditional Indian people, knew that harmony with the land and universe was the goal of healing, that body and land, such as in the tribal ceremonial sense, are intricately connected.

But by and large, the Western way of knowing has lost track of this understanding of the world, and the body is still associated with a kind of wilderness; there are dangers inside us, it is believed. And the body truly speaks its own tongue. When we go inside ourselves, there is fear, sometimes, and sorrow, a language of pain and need that we wish to avoid. What dancer Martha Graham[6] meant when she spoke of the house of pelvic truth is that the body is a landscape of truth-telling. Our animal selves are more than nails and teeth that remain from before evolution, and that have torn their way through the world. The experience of the wild is inside us, beyond our mental control, and it lies alongside the deep memory of wilderness, and it has rules and laws that do not obey our human will.

20

---

[4]*James Lovelock...Gaia hypothesis:* The Gaia hypothesis, first put forward by atmospheric geoscientist James Lovelock, is an ecological theory that holds that the entire earth is a single living entity.

[5]*Paracelsus:* Pseudonym of Philippus Aureolus Theophrastus Bombast von Hohenheim (1493–1541), Swiss-born alchemist and physician.

[6]*Martha Graham:* American choreographer and dancer (1893–1991).

More than symbol, more than the bread and wine of Christ, the body is a knowing connection, it is the telling thing, the medium of experience, expression, being, and knowing. Just as the earth is one of the bodies of the universe, we are the bodies of earth, accidental atoms given this form. An ancient and undivided world lies curled inside us with an ancestral memory that remembers our lives in the wilderness. What the body knows and where it takes us is navigated from an inner map not always carried in daily consciousness.

There are other dangers to these inner truths. Psychologist C. A. Meier said that as the wilderness decreases outside us the wilderness inside us will grow. While the word "wilderness" is still used by him in its most negative connotation, in many ways his statement has proved accurate. There was a recent case in New York where boys went "wilding," attacked a woman, raping and beating her, and left her for dead. In their own term, "wilding" is a truth distorted but carried down through American history with its aggression against tribes, its loss of species, its body hatred and fear of the true, untouched by humans wild.

For some, the only connection to this inner world has been violence. It is why so many men have described times of war as times when they felt the most alive. It is through events of war that they are thrown into the powerful world of bodily feeling. This is one of the unfortunate results of our broken connection with self and with land. And it seems, with the ever-increasing violence of our contemporary world, that we are losing the ability to be genuinely touched, both physically and emotionally, and that our lack of connection is destroying our capacity for deep love.

We are in need of an integrity of being that recognizes this disregarded inner world. I mean integrity in the true sense of this word, the sense that addresses a human wholeness and completeness, an entirety of living, with body, land, and the human self in relationship with all the rest, and with a love that remembers itself.

There are sacred dimensions to such love and they allow for viewing the world in all its beauty with gratitude, depth, and the thread of connection. For as we breathe, we are air. We are water. We are earth. We are what is missing from the equation of wholeness. 25

The body, made of earth's mud and breathed into, is the temple, and we need to learn to worship it as such, to move slowly within it, respecting it, loving it, treating ourselves and all our loved ones with tenderness. And the love for the body and for the earth are the same love.

Crazy Horse, one of the brilliant and compassionate leaders of the Sioux nation who witnessed the death of the animals and loved ones, wore a stone beneath his arm that was given him by an old medicine man named Chips. The stone was his ally. For Indian people, even now, the earth and its inhabitants all have spirit, matter is alive, and the world is an ally. This is necessary to remember as we go about a relearning of the sacred flesh, that we are energized by the stars, by the very fire of life burning within all the containers and kinds of skin, even the skin of water, of stone.

3. All My Relations

It is a sunny, clear day outside, almost hot, and a slight breeze comes through the room from the front door. We sit at the table and talk. As is usual in an Indian household, food preparation began as soon as we arrived and now there is the snap of potatoes frying in the black skillet, the sweet smell of white bread overwhelming even the grease, and the welcome black coffee. A ringer washer stands against the wall of the kitchen, and the counter space is taken up with dishes, pans, and boxes of food.

I am asked if I still read books and I admit that I do. Reading is not "traditional" and education has long been suspect in communities that were broken, in part, by that system, but we laugh at my confession because a television set plays in the next room.

In the living room there are two single beds. People from reservations, 30 travelers needing help, are frequent guests here. The man who will put together the ceremony I have come to request sits on one, dozing. A girl takes him a plate of food. He eats. He is a man I have respected for many years, for his commitment to the people, for his intelligence, for his spiritual and political involvement in concerns vital to Indian people and nations. Next to him sits a girl eating potato chips, and from this room we hear the sounds of the freeway.

After eating and sitting, it is time for me to talk to him, to tell him why we have come here. I have brought him tobacco and he nods and listens as I tell him about the help we need.

I know this telling is the first part of the ceremony, my part in it. It is a story, really, that finds its way into language, and story is at the very crux of healing, at the heart of every ceremony and ritual in the older America.

The ceremony itself includes not just our own prayers and stories of what brought us to it, but includes the unspoken records of history, the mythic past, and all the other lives connected to ours, our family, nations, and all other creatures.

I am sent home to prepare. I tie fifty tobacco ties, green. This I do with Bull Durham tobacco, squares of cotton that are tied with twine and left strung together. These are called prayer ties. I spend the time preparing in silence and alone. Each tie has a prayer in it. I will also need wood for the fire, meat and bread for food.

On the day of the ceremony, we meet in the next town and leave my car 35 in public parking. My daughters and I climb into the backseat of my friend's car. The man who will help us is drumming and singing in front of us. His wife drives and chats. He doesn't speak. He is moving between the worlds, beginning already to step over the boundaries of what we think, in daily and ordinary terms, is real and present. He is already feeling, hearing, knowing what else is there, that which is around us daily but too often unacknowledged, a larger life than our own small ones. We pass billboards and little towns and gas stations. An eagle flies overhead. It is "a good sign," we all agree. We stop to watch it.

We stop again, later, at a convenience store to fill the gas tank and to buy soda. The leader still drums and is silent. He is going into the drum, going into the center, even here as we drive west on the highway, even with our conversations about other people, family.

It is a hot balmy day, and by the time we reach the site where the ceremony is to take place, we are slow and sleepy with the brightness and warmth of the sun. In some tribes, men and women participate in separate sweat lodge ceremonies, but here, men, women, and children all come together to sweat. The children are cooling off in the creek. A woman stirs the fire that lives inside a circle of black rocks, pots beside her, a jar of oil, a kettle, a can of coffee. The leaves of the trees are thick and green.

In the background, the sweat lodge structure strands. Birds are on it. It is still skeletal. A woman and man are beginning to place old rugs and blankets over the bent cottonwood frame. A great fire is already burning and the lava stones that will be the source of heat for the sweat are being fired in it.

A few people sit outside on lawn chairs and cast-off couches that have the stuffing coming out. We sip coffee and talk about the food, about recent events. A man tells us that a friend gave him money for a new car. The creek sounds restful. Another man falls asleep. My young daughter splashes in the water. Heat waves rise up behind us from the fire that is preparing the stones. My tobacco ties are placed inside, on the framework of the lodge.

By late afternoon we are ready, one at a time, to enter the enclosure.   40 The hot lava stones are placed inside. They remind us of earth's red and fiery core, and of the spark inside all life. After the flap, which serves as a door, is closed, water is poured over the stones and the hot steam rises around us. In a sweat lodge ceremony, the entire world is brought inside the enclosure. The soft odor of smoking cedar accompanies this arrival of everything. It is all called in. The animals come from the warm and sunny distances. Water from dark lakes is there. Wind. Young, lithe willow branches bent overhead remember their lives rooted in ground, the sun their leaves took in. They remember that minerals and water rose up their trunks, and that birds nested in their leaves, and that planets turned above their brief, slender lives. The thunder clouds travel in from far regions of earth. Wind arrives from the four directions. It has moved through caves and breathed through our bodies. It is the same air elk have inhaled, air that passed through the lungs of a grizzly bear. The sky is there, with all the stars whose lights we see long after the stars themselves have gone back to nothing. It is a place grown intense and holy. It is a place of immense community and of humbled solitude; we sit together in our aloneness and speak, one at a time, our deepest language of need, hope, loss, and survival. We remember that all things are connected.

Remembering this is the purpose of the ceremony. It is part of a healing and restoration. It is the mending of a broken connection between us and the rest. The participants in a ceremony say the words "All my relations" before and after we pray; those words create a relationship with other people, with animals, with the land. To have health it is necessary to keep all these relations in mind.

The intention of a ceremony is to put a person back together by restructuring the human mind. This reorganization is accomplished by a kind of inner map, a geography of the human spirit and the rest of the world. We make whole our broken-off pieces of self and world. Within ourselves, we bring together the fragments of our lives in a sacred act of renewal, and we reestablish our connections with others. The ceremony is a point of return. It takes us toward the place of balance, our place in the community of all things. It is an event that sets us back upright. But it is not a finished thing. The real ceremony begins where the formal one ends, when we take up a new way, our minds and hearts filled with the vision of earth that holds us within it, in compassionate relationship to and with our world.

We speak. We sing. We swallow water and breathe smoke. By the end of the ceremony, it is as if skin contains land and birds. The places within us have become filled. As inside the enclosure of the lodge, the animals and ancestors move into the human body, into skin and blood. The land merges with us. The stones come to dwell inside the person. Gold rolling hills take up residence, their tall grasses blowing. The red light of canyons is there. The black skies of night that wheel above our heads come to live inside the skull. We who easily grow apart from the world are returned to the great store of life all around us and there is the deepest sense of being at home here in this intimate kinship. There is no real aloneness. There is solitude and the nurturing silence that is relationship with ourselves, but even then we are part of something larger.

After a sweat lodge ceremony, the enclosure is abandoned. Quieter now, we prepare to drive home. We pack up the kettles, the coffeepot. The prayer ties are placed in nearby trees. Some of the other people prepare to go to work, go home, or cook a dinner. We drive home. Everything returns to ordinary use. A spider weaves a web from one of the cottonwood poles to another. Crows sit inside the framework. It's evening. The crickets are singing. All my relations.

ENGAGING THE TEXT

1. How does Hogan portray Anglo-American culture and dominant American cultural attitudes toward nature? Toward Native Americans?

2. What does Hogan mean when she says that "America has become…disembodied" (para. 11)? Why, according to Hogan, has this happened? To what extent do you agree that American culture is disembodied, as Hogan claims?

3. How does disease arise and how is it cured in the context of Native American beliefs? What is the function of ceremony in this process? What is the alternative?

4. What happens during the sweat-lodge ceremony that Hogan participates in? What is the ceremony's purpose? How does this purpose relate to the title of Hogan's essay?

5. How would you describe the structure of Hogan's essay? In what ways does it differ from the kind of writing that is typically taught in composition classes? How effective do you find Hogan's approach?

EXPLORING CONNECTIONS

6. Compare Hogan's depiction of American attitudes toward nature with that offered by Donald Worster (p. 814). How would you expect Hogan to explain the "paradox" that Worster perceives at the heart of American views of wilderness?

7. To what extent do the nature images presented in the Visual Portfolio earlier in the chapter (p. 750) support Hogan's depiction of American attitudes toward nature?

EXTENDING THE CRITICAL CONTEXT

8. In a journal entry or a brief paper, describe a ceremony you have participated in related to your own home culture or family traditions. To what extent did this experience focus on the establishment or celebration of relationships or connections?

9. View *Dances with Wolves, Last of the Mohicans,* or any other recent western film to evaluate its presentation of indigenous peoples. Based on your analysis, would you agree with Hogan that Native Americans "have come to represent spirit, heart, an earth-based way of living, all things they [white Americans] have felt missing from their lives..." (para. 9)? Do recent film depictions of Native Americans suggest that progress is being made in Native/white American relations—or do such depictions represent a new form of cultural exploitation?

Looking for Nature at the Mall

JENNIFER PRICE

Have you ever wondered what twenty-first-century Americans are thinking when they climb aboard their SUVs made with parts from six different countries and burn up two gallons of gas imported from Bahrain driving to a fully enclosed air-conditioned shopping mall that simulates a Parisian street scene to buy an "authentic" whale-song CD at the environmental retail outlet? Jennifer Price (b. 1961) did the very first time she entered a Nature Company store. In "Looking for Nature at the Mall," Price theorizes about contemporary American attitudes toward wilderness and retailing, and wonders if our contemporary nostalgia for all things natural isn't a marketing ploy meant to obscure the workings of corporate capitalism. Price is an essayist whose work has been featured in several nature anthologies. This selection is included in her most recent work of nonfiction, Flight Maps: Adventures with Nature in Modern America *(1999).*

Entry

I don't recall the exact mall where I first encountered The Nature Company. It was around 1989, in the St. Louis Union Station, or perhaps the Bridgewater Commons in central New Jersey. Say it was a Saturday afternoon, and I was searching for the exit after three hours of shopping. I do remember that I stopped in my tracks, after which I slowly toured the entire store and bought something—but I do not remember what it was. "Customers often exclaim, 'Wow!'" The Nature Company's press release begins, and that accurately describes my reaction.[1] ...

The Nature Company itself was founded in Berkeley in 1973 by a young couple, Tom and Priscilla Wrubel, who had met in the late 1960s in the Peace Corps. They gambled that a store "devoted to the observation, understanding, and appreciation of the natural world" might fill a useful niche for a "population taking to the wilderness in record numbers," and for a generation of new parents, like themselves, who wanted to introduce children to the joys of nature. By 1983, they had four stores in the Bay Area. Seeking expansion capital, they sold their enterprise to the parent CML Group, which specialized in companies that might track the baby boomers' wealth into the 1990s, and which also has owned NordicTrack[2] and Smith & Hawken[3]—or in the not-so-sensitive words of *Business Week,* "a

---

[1]The Nature Company press kit (Berkeley, CA, 1994). See also Pete Dunne, "In the Natural State," *New York Times,* 7 May 1989. [All notes are Price's except 2, 3, 7, 10, 11, and 17.]

[2]*NordicTrack:* An exercise machine that simulates crosscountry skiing.

[3]*Smith & Hawken:* An upscale gardening store.

package of yuppie goodies unlike anybody else's." By 1994, The Nature Company ran 124 stores in the United States, three in Canada, twelve in Japan, and seven in Australia. At the end of 1993, they posted net sales of $162 million. The baby boomers who set out hiking and backpacking in a generational drove in the 1960s clearly had taken to the malls as well.[4]

. . . Not without skepticism, however. "People come in and say, 'Ahhh!'" the Company's marketing director has said. But "wow" better describes my own reaction. It's subtler, more ambivalent. In 1989, a *New York Times* columnist wrote a glowing report after a first visit, to the Bridgewater Commons store, yet asked what is perhaps *the* nagging question: "Why, on earth, weren't the people in the store outside experiencing [nature] instead of . . . indoors buying it?"[5] The Nature *Company?* In the Mall of America? The very name and habitat can provoke a post-1960s nature lover's deepest anti-materialist suspicions. I, too, have marveled at the wondrous array of bird feeders, kites, telescopes, fossils, and jewelry, and at the trademark bins of wind-up dinosaurs, rubber animal noses, and cow-moo noise boxes. As a birder and hiker, I have lingered by the shelves of videos and natural history books. "I bought a beautiful pair of gardening shears there," a friend explained, "but I feel somehow manipulated. It feels inauthentic"—but she loves the wildlife ties her brother gives her husband for Christmas. "It feels fake," another friend says—but she had just bought a spectacular geode there. If The Nature Company beckons irresistibly, to more than a few of its patrons it also feels vaguely troubling. And the real revelations of eighties nature stores, I'm convinced, and the persistent troubles with our definitions of Nature, rest squarely in that contradiction. . . .

Natural Selection

What has The Nature Company been selling? Images of nature, pieces of nature, and tools for going out into nature. By 1994, the company was marketing over twelve thousand products. They have sold bird T-shirts, wind chimes, paperweights, bird feeders, wildflower seeds, field guides, videos, note cards, CDs, herb teas, bat shelters, rain gauges, field hats, Swiss army knives, Rainforest Crunch, plastic periscopes, amethyst geodes, stuffed tigers, Zuni fetishes, petrified wood, rock polishers, dinosaur everything, star charts, and galaxy boxer shorts. At first glance, it seems that anything that has to do with the natural world must be here. But The Nature

[4]Wrubel quotes: informational handout for employees (current March 1994), 1–3 (hereafter cited as handout). *Business Week:* Bock, "CML Group," 75. Stores: "The Nature Company Profile," press kit; CML Group, *Annual Report* (Acton, MA: 1993), 2.

[5]"Ahhh!": Kathryn Jackson Fallon, "Wet Seals and Whale Songs," *Time* 137 (3 June 1991), 45. "Why, on earth": Dunne, "Natural State." A harsher, less ambivalent critique of The Nature Company is Neil Smith, "The Production of Nature," in *FutureNatural: Nature, Science, Culture,* ed. George Robertson et al. (London: Routledge, 1996), 35–54.

Company is not a biome. It is on average 2,900 square feet of retail space—a very small space for all of nature—and what lives here must sell. The company has, from the start, hewed to strict principles of natural selection.[6] ...

To see the definition clearly, it is easier to begin with what the company will *not* sell. What has it classified as not-Nature? The Nature Company refuses to market "trophy" items, which require the killing of animals: no butterflies, seashells, or furs. No mounted heads. Under the Wrubels' regime, the company avoided products that anthropomorphize animals. The popular children's book *Goodnight Moon* is still non grata, since the bunny wears pajamas and sleeps in a bed. Anthropomorphizers, as a species, were also unwelcome: you could discover almost no human images on the posters, and (until the Discovery takeover) very few human voices on the CDs. And no Enya,[7] though often requested. Domestic animals have been in short supply. The company has selected nonhuman, wilder, and unused forms of nature. When asked to sum up their inventory, Nature Company personnel have used the terms "authenticity," "uniqueness," and "quality." Also "whimsy"—but only authentic whimsy. The toy animals here do not smile or wag their tails. The dolphins and cicadas on the keychains have been accurate replicas. The bat puppets look like real bats, the piggy banks like real pigs, and the angelfish bathtub toys like real angelfish. The wind-up dinosaurs in the stores' "ning-ning" bins (the Wrubels' children coined the term) still come in bright colors "in line with new scientific thought," and the inflatable emperor penguins are anatomically correct. Nature Company products have been humorous, but not kitschy, cliché, or sentimental. They are inexpensive, but not cheap. You see real rocks, plastic grasshoppers, dolphin keychains, and stone bird sculptures—but no I ♥ dolphins bumperstickers, plastic pink flamingos, real grasshoppers, or plastic rocks.[8]

Among all the items, the products that limn the definitions of Nature here most visibly are the ones that do not, if you think about it, look like nature as a separate place, or summon it to you or send you out into it. For example, The Nature Company has marketed handmade paper lamps and Amish oak-hickory rockers. And why Zuni fetishes? The company has enjoyed a brisk business in Native American crafts, and, until the CML sale, the few human voices on the CDs were ethnic or indigenous. "Each product," says the company's press kit, "... introduces customers to an aspect of

5

[6]Twelve thousand: handout, 3. All products mentioned here were marketed February 1993–August 1994. Store size: CML Group, "Annual Report," 5.

[7]*Enya:* An Irish "New Age" singer (b. 1961).

[8]Items the company will *not* sell: handout, 2; store entrance plaques; Maureen O'Brien, "The Nature Company Jumps into Japan," *Publishers Weekly* 238 (17 May 1991), 37. Terms: e.g., handout, 1–3; "What Is The Nature Company?"; CML Group, *Annual Report*, 10; interview with store manager, 23 June 1994 (hereafter cited as interview). Real items: Liz Lufkin, "Natural History Gets Hip," *San Francisco Chronicle,* 18 December 1986; *The Nature Company,* catalog (Holiday 1993), 14, 48, 32 (hereafter, catalogs cited as *TNC*). "in line with": *TNC* (Fall 1994), sale section, A–B.

the natural world"—so how do the Australian wool throw blankets connect you to nature? They don't, at least not directly. Zulu baskets satisfy the entrance criteria not because they are nature, but because like the brightly colored wind-up dinosaurs, they are "authentic" or "unique": many of us tend to invest rocks and Zulu handcrafts with the same meanings. Each item here, the company states more accurately in a handout for employees, "[relates] in some magical way to…natural phenomena." *Viento de los Andes,* a CD of Andean folk music, got in by meaningful association, since to so many baby boomers, both nature and indigenous cultures connote authenticity and simplicity in a modern era. And why ask for Enya, a New Age Irish singer, in a nature store? The piggy bank has to look like a real pig, but more important, it comes with "layers and layers of associations," including "French farmyards," "childhood dreams," and "the good old days." The Nature Company has billed itself as your direct connection to the natural world. But the stores connect us not so much to what nature is as to what Nature *means:* they tap the powerful, meaningful routes by which we use Nature to define who we are, and with which we have navigated late-twentieth-century American life.[9]

At The Nature Company, you can really put Nature to work. If the stores have sold over twelve thousand products, they have hawked a small and well-chosen set of outsized meanings. The *Glacier Bay* CD invites shoppers to "escape" to one of the "Last Great Places"; and in 1994 you could buy a trip to "Alaska: the Last Great Adventure," as advertised in the catalog:

> People in towns … dream of serene sanctuaries far away from fax machines…. This is where you pull out of the fast lane and change the course of your revved-up life…. Please see the order form.

You can buy walking sticks, vests, and backpacks here, too, to enjoy nonhuman Nature as Wilderness—a distant and untamed realm, a solitary refuge from the modern city, which is ideally as unpeopled (and as devoid of cows and cats) as The Nature Company's poster collection. Nature as Adventure is vivified in the subgenre of books (the book section has anchored the stores as a kind of philosophy section) that the head book buyer in 1987 classified as "tales of personal adventure in a wild land." *Wolf: Spirit of the Wild. Forgotten Edens: Experiencing the Earth's Wild Places.* A canvas hat from the Sierra Club John Muir[10] collection will "give me the Simple Life." The Zuni fetishes, Zulu baskets, and African jewelry associate Nature nearly interchangeably with indigenous peoples. The throw blankets "might have come from the cedar chest of your great-grandmother." And the whole inventory constitutes a monument to an understanding of Nature as a place

---

[9]"Each product": "What Is The Nature Company?" "relates": handout, 3. "layers": *TNC* (Holiday 1992), 43.

[10]*John Muir:* American naturalist (1838–1914).

for Leisure: the Nature Company Cap is "for days off...afoot and light-hearted down an open road." Leisure, Adventure, Simplicity, Uniqueness, Authenticity, the Primitive, the Past, the Autochthonous,[11] Tranquility, Exoticism, Wildness, Freedom. Here you can use the definition of Nature as a Place Apart to define, critique, or counteract the urbanism, anonymity, commercialism, technological control, complexity, white-collar work, artifice, and alienations of the postwar era. What is for sale here is exactly the established definition of Nature that well-to-do baby boomers adapted for themselves in the 1960s and marshaled as a chief weapon to critique what troubled them about American society. On the first page of *Walden*, Thoreau opposed Nature to "civilized life"—and you can buy the essay here in a pocket size edition for hikers.[12]

Nature is available for purchase above all as what is Real: what is enduring, nonreplicated, non–mass culture, Authentic, non-Artificial, and absolute. The amethyst pieces "vary according to natural structure." The Polish folk-art candles are "one-of-a-kind handmade." The Get Real generation have always used Nature to combat their postwar anxieties about mass culture and high-tech society.

> Jet has been fashioned into beads and amulets for 5,000 years and Native Americans have fashioned turquoise into ... jewelry for centuries. Now Chilean artists combine the gems to create a ... handmade necklace, bracelet and pair of earrings which follow the natural curve of the throat, wrist and ear.... Bracelet $95.00

> Our Dakota Earth Mailbox is a piece of history, made of reclaimed barnwood ... to look like a rustic, wind-weathered birdhouse. Each one-of-a-kind piece ... recalls a way of life amid hard Great Plains winters $49.95

The fossils, "sculpted by nature...more than 350 million years ago," and "quarried and polished by Morocan craftspeople," are "handfinished." "Our Nature Company Recordings" in the Last Great Places series, the company assured us in a 1994 catalog, "blend the elemental harmonies of music and the earth." Nature Company products, Priscilla Wrubel stated in the Fall 1994 catalog, are "tools"—and "human hands have guided tools since the Ice Age."[13]

---

[11]*autochthonous:* Indigenous; native.

[12]*Glacier Bay* CD: *TNC* (Summer 1994), 27, 5. "tales": Allene Symons, "Marketing Nature Tie-ins at Nature Company," *Publishers Weekly* 231 (1 May 1987), 37. "give me the": *TNC* (Summer 1994), 15 (uppercase mine). "might have come": *TNC* (Holiday 1994), 48. "for days off": *TNC* (Summer 1994), 7. Henry David Thoreau, *The Selected Works of Thoreau*, rev. and with a new introd. by Water Harding (Cambridge: Houghton Mifflin, 1975), 43. Countermodern meanings of Nature: I've benefited from William Cronon, ed., *Uncommon Ground: Toward Reinventing Nature* (New York: W.W. Norton, 1995), and have drawn especially on the essays by Cronon, Candace Slater, Richard White, Susan G. Davis, and Giovanna Di Chiro.

[13]"vary according": *TNC* (Fall 1994), 21. "one-of-a-kind": *TNC* (Holiday 1994), 53. "Jet": ibid. 28. "Our Dakota" : *TNC* (Holiday 1994), 51. "sculpted by": *TNC* (Fall 1994), 21. "Our Nature Company": *TNC* (Summer 1994), 26–27. "tools": *TNC* (Fall 1994), 2.

Of course, while baby boomers in the 1960s adapted the idea of Nature as a Place Apart to combat artifice, conformity, and anonymity, in the 1980s—as we became affluent professionals and consumers—we began to use Nature less as a tool for battling the System than to get some temporary relief from it. CML's stated mission was to "enhance people's health, understanding of the natural world, and sense of well-being." Or in the slightly different words of an investment-analysis firm, CML marketed "products for stress relief." At The Nature Company, the "yuppie leisure market," in *Business Week's* words, could enjoy Nature as a key therapeutic resource for what has become a virtual obsession with stress relief:

> Pachelbel Canon in D Blended with the Eternal Sound of the Sea— Creates a tranquil atmosphere for quiet meditation.... CD $16.98.

The *Cloud Forest* CD, in the 1994 catalog, "weave[s] a spell of peace." If you sited the birdbath fountain indoors, "the sound of running water [had] a calming, beautiful effect." And *Tranquility,* a video "moodtape" of sunrises, clouds, and "peaceful ocean waves," "perfect for relaxing, entertaining, love-making" and designed to create a "soothing and harmonious atmosphere," was an especially safe bet to sell well. Of course, the yuppies have searched for stress relief, and harvested Nature for a psychic yield, not just to escape the system but to act more effectively within it. "Clearly," the investment-analysis firm remarked with enthusiasm, "anything which reduces stress increases time and energy, which are always valuable commodities."[14]

Reality, stress relief, self-improvement, and emotional healing: these had   10 more generally emerged in force as chief New Age goals in the 1980s. The explosive New Age movement is multifaceted, but on average the pursuits have tended to exalt a search for a more Authentic self and more Authentic experience in a modern society that seems to fail to offer it. The well-off baby boomers had always advertised themselves as the Real generation. But New Age philosophies have tended to reorient the quest for Reality away from society and the self—that is, from changing both one's head and the system— toward the Self *in* Society. And New Age adherents have recruited the countermodern definition of Nature as an essential and authoritative tool. The Nature Company's mission statement says: "Authenticity and knowledge are balanced with sufficient humor to give our customers an experience which makes them *feel good* about themselves and the world in which they live." At The Nature Company, you can construct an authentic, Real Self in an unReal society. The whale and eagle calls on the *Glacier Bay* CD "create moods

---

[14]"enhance people's": CML Group, *Annual Report,* cover. "products": "CML Group (20½)," report on company by Adams, Harkness & Hill, 22 March 1994, 4. *Business Week:* Bock, "CML Group," 75. "Pachelbel," "weaves": *TNC* (Summer 1994), 27. "moodtape": *TNC* (Holiday 1993), 3. "perfect for": box notes for Ron Roy, producer and director, *Tranquility* (Studio City, CA: Ron Roy Productions, 1986). "Clearly": "CML Group (20½)," 4.

and emotions within us." Environmental Sounds CDs "will open your mind and awaken your heart." Nature is the source of Real emotion, Real thinking, Real feeling. To appreciate Nature here is to be a more Real person. It is to be a *better* person and the right *sort* of person.[15]

Who can use Nature as a route to the Real? The use of Nature to define a certain kind of person recalls the fifties suburban lawn owners, and the English landowners who lounged in Natural postures in their own vast and Natural landscapes. The Nature Company brand of Nature appreciation can work best if you have the means to shop here, and to travel to Glacier Bay and other far wildernesses on your vacation. Like others before us, affluent baby boomers have tended to invest a lot of human social authority in our encounters with nature. We graft meanings onto nature to make sense out of modern middle-class life, but also define ourselves by what we think nature means. What better resource, then, to use to educate the baby boomers' children? Nature is also the source of Real values. The company's large, highly publicized kids' section usefully teaches children about the nonhuman natural world—but you can also use it to teach them how to be the right sort of person, and how to join the human company of the Real. As the company's Summer 1994 catalog assures us, "Kids are the original naturalists."

If The Nature Company's trademark sense of humor, or "whimsy," caters to the baby boomers' evolving parental desires, it also appeals directly to a consumer generation who once vowed notoriously, in an enduring gesture of self-identity, to remain forever young. "Pretend it's for the kids," the company advertised its butterfly raise-and-release kit. Spy Scope: "if the kid in you isn't quite a serious grown-up yet." Rubber noses, wild-animal cookies, *Scaly & Slimy, Everyone Poops*, gecko ties, bird-droppings T-shirts, UnpredictaBalls! Whimsy is a tricky meaning here. Laughter in the American tradition of Nature has been notably scarce.... Not too many jokes in Thoreau: Nature and Reality must not be trivialized, so The Nature Company walks a fine line here. But the 1960s children of Nature have also always been the ironic lovers of Artifice.... Whether partial to Nature or Artifice, we've committed to a boundary between the two. As a source of laughs, the angelfish bathtub toys that look like real angelfish encourage the children of baby boomers to be at once Real children and initiates into Artifice. Kites, bubble kits, bat puppets, and paint-a-snakes encourage the par-

[15]New Age: I've found helpful Paul Heelas, *The New Age Movement: The Celebration of the Self and the Sacralization of Modernity* (Oxford: Blackwell, 1996); Susan Love Brown, "Baby Boomers, American Character, and the New Age: A Synthesis," in *Perspectives on the New Age*, ed. James R. Lewis and J. Gordon Melton (Albany: State Univ. of New York Press, 1992), 87–96. "Authenticity": front cover of The Nature Company folder, 1994. "create moods": Leighton Taylor, *Glacier Bay: Last Great Places on Earth*, pamphlet (Berkeley: The Nature Company, 1991), 3, accompanies Dennis Hysom, CD of same title (vol. 2, The Nature Company Audio Library). "will open": *TNC* (Summer 1994), 26–27.

ents to remain ironic, young, and playful, and to stay trustworthy past the age of thirty.[16] ...

Habitat

Yet in the 1980s, backed by CML capital, The Nature Company set out to expand into shopping malls, of all places—and their competitors followed suit. Why sell Nature or anti-Artifice at a site that is famous as a black hole for Artifice? Why hawk Authenticity at a locale whose reputation for genericness is so notorious that we call every mall on the continent "the mall"? And why the glitziest sites and the megamalls? It is not difficult to predict where to find a Nature Company. In Denver, the Cherry Creek Mall. In St. Louis, the Galleria and Union Station. In Los Angeles, the Century City Shopping Center and the Beverly Center in Beverly Hills. In Orange County, South Coast Plaza. The Mall of America has one.

The logic lies surely in how malls work, and in the intricacies of the *mall's* particular worlds of meaning—and how these worlds have intertwined with the meanings of Nature. Shopping malls: Americans have called them "gardens of delight," "worlds of artifice," and "palaces of consumption." And since the 1950s, when the first enclosed centers began to dot the suburban landscape, they've been targets of derision, or at least ambivalence. Between 1957 and the mid-1970s, developers built fourteen thousand shopping malls to cater to the postwar affluence and the expanding suburban populations. With large open spaces and deliberately modern in design, most of these malls looked essentially like broad indoor avenues, with a few plants, that connected the "magnet" department stores at either end. In 1979, Joan Didion branded them "toy garden cities in which no one lives but everyone consumes." Malls have been accused, before and since, of being identityless, unReal, devoid of character, and, along with TV, a major culprit in the postwar homogenization of American culture. With interstate highways, they have homogenized the American landscape. Lost along the corridors of chain-outlet shoe stores, you could be anywhere. The mall, as Frank Lloyd Wright[17] has said about the postwar sprawl generally, is every place and no place.[18]

---

[16]"Kids are": *TNC* (Summer 1994), 36. Nature and a Real Self: I've drawn heavily on Susan G. Davis's comments and work—see "'Touch the Magic,'" in Cronon, *Uncommon Ground*, 204–17; *Spectacular Nature: Corporate Culture and the Sea World Experience* (Berkeley: Univ. of California Press, 1997). "Pretend," "if the kid": *TNC* (Summer 1994), 18, 14.

[17]*Frank Lloyd Wright:* American architect (1867–1959).

[18]Stores: in The Nature Company catalogs. Joan Didion, *The White Album* (New York: Simon and Schuster, 1979), 180. Wright: in Thomas Hine, *Populuxe* (New York: Alfred A. Knopf, 1986), 9. Shopping-center design: I've drawn on Barry Maitland, *Shopping Malls: Planning and Design* (New York: Nichols, 1985); Margaret Crawford, "The World in a Shopping Mall," in *Variations on a Theme Park: The New American City and the End of Public Space,* ed. Michael Sorkin (New York: Hill and Wang, 1992), 3–30.

In the 1980s, mall developers hired architects crosscountry to outfit   15
these installations with more individuality. The new designers gave face-lifts
to most of the larger malls built in the sixties and seventies, injected the new
eighties megamalls with more character, and designed the malls to be more
upscale on average—and these are exactly the malls The Nature Company
moved into. Many malls now look like European villages or Mexican hacien-
das. The corridor spaces are more mazelike, irregular, and niched. The designers favored tropical settings, especially—in no small part because
plants such as figs and rhododendrons grow well in climate-controlled indoor spaces. In other words, the ungeneric malls of the 1980s, like the Foot
Locker stores, are essentially replicants. They simulate and connote other
places. (The Los Angeles malls tend to simulate Los Angeles, a city notorious as both a simulation of place and an outsize shopping mall.) The Italian
piazza and Caribbean courtyard are places out of place. Architects have
gathered together the *meanings* of more Real-seeming places than suburbs
and malls, mixing and matching as if the globe were a giant salad bar. And
the replicants say less about the real places than about what consumers
want them to mean. The 1992 Mall of America, Minneapolis's mall for the
twenty-first century, contains within its ninety-six acres an "East Broadway"
avenue, a mock European railway station, a seven-acre theme park with a
Minnesota woodland motif, and the Rainforest Cafe, with live animals, wa-
terfalls, fog, and a "star-filled" sky.[19]

The Nature Company has been a one-store global assemblage itself: it
sells posters, videos, and calendars of Alaska, Tanzania, and the Galapagos.
And most of the nature here is simulated: the plastic whales and sculpted
giraffes, the inflatable penguins, the spiders on the T-shirts. The Nature
Company markets nature out of place. You can buy African malachite earrings patterned on Indonesian designs. Here you can connect to the world's
wild things close to home, because the company has installed similar assem-
blages in malls in thirty-four states and two Canadian provinces, in Australia, and in the giant malls in Japan's underground railway stations. The
stores at South Coast Plaza (store no. 7), the St. Louis Galleria (no. 60), and
the Century City Shopping Center (no. 21) stock the same *Virtual Nature*
videos and inflatable globes. On a 1994 visit to the store at the breezy Century City center in Los Angeles, where The Nature Company faces Rand-
McNally, a "map and travel store," I could choose to eat at the Market food

---

[19]1980s malls: e.g., Barry Maitland, *The New Architecture of the Retail Mall* (New York:
Van Nostrand Reinhold, 1990); Robert Davis Rathbun, *Shopping Centers and Malls,* orig.,
Book 2, and Number 4 (New York: Retail Reporting Corporation, 1986, 1988, 1992). On mall
logic, I've drawn especially on Jon Goss, "The 'Magic of the Mall': An Analysis of Form, Function, and Meaning in the Contemporary Retail Built Environment," *Annals Association American Geographers* 83 (March 1993), 18–47; idem, "Disquiet on the Waterfront: Reflections on
Nostalgia and Utopia in the Urban Archetypes of Festival Marketplaces," *Urban Geography* 17
(1996), 221–47; Crawford, "World in a Shopping Mall." "star-filled": "Restaurants, Nightclubs
& Food," Mall of America press kit (Bloomington, MN, 1994).

court next door, at Bueno Bueno, Gulen's Mediterranean Cuisine, DeMartino's Pizzeria, Raja, La Crepe, or Kisho An. On the store's other flank sat El Portal Luggage, two doors down from Toys International and within sight of the United Colors of Benetton. The "now playing" CD combined Western instrumental forms with Baka Pygmy music from the border of Congo and Cameroon. I sifted through the zebra- and panda-footprint stamps, but bought the polar bear.[20]

The Nature Company makes sense here. If I harbor doubts about the mall as a suitable habitat, The Nature Company feels intuitively well sited. Why? Since the late-nineteenth-century adventures (and misadventures) with bird hats and wild pigeons, Americans' encounters with wild nature have become as thoroughly disconnected from place, but also as intensively simulated, as malls themselves. Economic globalization, and explosive postwar advances in manufacturing and communications technologies, have made my generation's adventures more consistently long distance, and far more mediated. Even postwar nature lovers—who hike and camp, and make vacation pilgrimages to wild places—encounter wild nature more often in the everyday urban and suburban haunts of living rooms, shopping malls, magazines, and TVs. Most of our daily encounters with nature transpire quite separately from real pieces of nature rooted in specific places. We have become globe coasters all. *Where* have we been looking for nature most often since the 1980s? Not in the "where" where we generally think of nature as being. It is not surprising that one of the more successful Nature Company stores, while not in a mall, has been in the Pittsburgh Airport.[21]

...We've used Nature Company totems to tell meaningful stories about where we live and who we are—as all humans do in their encounters with nature—but these totems often tell us markedly little about the pieces of nature. And yet, The Nature Company's stated mission is to connect us to nature—not disconnect us. And to be sure, postmodern globe coasting works both ways. The products teach their owners potentially a great deal about distant places and animals. The toy plastic whale in the Ocean Authentics Collection, for example, can convey information about the blue whale, and about the circumpolar oceans the species inhabits. What it basically does, however, is to bring a miniature, essentially accurate image of a whale into one's life. What one does with it is up to its new owner. To a child in suburban Chicago, the palm-size whale might look like an endangered blue whale, the largest animal that ever lived. And it might look like Jonah, Shamu, Monstro, the hero in *Free Willy*, or a friend or enemy of a Mighty Morphin Power Ranger. The distance from the Pacific makes the whale unusually open to interpretation.

And if The Nature Company connects us less to nature itself than to what Nature *means*, the modern unmoored-ness of meanings has not been

---

[20]Stores: "The Nature Company Stores," press kit.
[21]Pittsburgh Airport: interview.

flatly undesirable. As always, modern complexities of geography and economics conveniently encourage a consumer's desire to make a piece of nature—or Nature itself—mean whatever one wants it to. Far from the ocean, the plastic whale reduces more readily to a motif, a feeling, an association, a meaning. The company's best-selling *Glacier Bay* CD comes with a booklet that reads: "ALASKA—...a superlative for...unbounded wilderness"—or as the catalog blurb reads, "Escape to Glacier Bay's arctic cathedrals." The CD is "for relaxation," one sales clerk told me—so I bought it. The music has a New Age dreamlike quality. It's a quiet, flowing mélange of flute, cello, whales, eagles, and waves, that sounds not unlike the flute, cello, frogs, wrens, and flowing water on the Costa Rica *Cloud Forest* CD. It's self-advertised mood music, in which the humpback whale makes a cameo appearance. From a boat in the bay itself, would Alaska be relaxing? Isn't the far North notorious as mosquito country? I've been to a rain forest: in Peru, at least, the jungle is not relaxing. It requires alertness; it has mildew. In suburban somewhere, however, after a stressful day at work, in counterpoint to noise, enclosure, and schedules—even if one reads the notes on natural history in the booklets—Glacier Bay and a Central American rain forest easily reduce to meaningful abstractions such as Wilderness, Relaxation, and Tranquility: the call of the humpback whale promotes human peace of mind. Distant landscapes and wild animals become ever more shadowy realities. And what better place to sell these abstractions of Nature and the Last Places than in the placeless vacuum of the mall?[22] ...

Ecology

If a run-in with The Nature Company sets one's consumer instincts into motion, the store can also trigger a nature lover's anticonsumer instincts. Many of us use Nature, too, to define who we are and to navigate the world. Nature means a countermodern Force, an antidote to modern life—and critics and enthusiasts alike have so often pegged consumerism as the economic and cultural lifeblood of modern American society. Simple, primitive, and Natural, Nature is a palliative for modern materialism. Like the *Times* columnist, many Nature Company patrons define Nature as something we should experience rather than consume, and the whole store flashes NATURE like a neon warning sign. "Thoreau was right," the company has advertised their Survival Tool, which has twelve tools in one: "Simplify, simplify." Doesn't that feel contradictory? If I define myself using the things I buy, I define myself also by what I think Nature means. At The Nature Company, I am an anticonsumer consumer.[23]

Again, "wow," in all its ambivalent glory. The definition of Nature that The Nature Company sells tells me Nature is separate from consumerism.

20

[22]"ALASKA": *TNC* (Summer 1994), 27. "Escape to": Taylor, *Glacier Bay,* 6. Best-selling: interview.

[23]"Thoreau": *TNC* (Summer 1994), 22.

And the store telegraphs that an essential way I connect to nature, and make it meaningful, is via consumerism. The Nature Company is nothing if not self-contradictory and ironic. And no ironies get more complicated here than those swirling around consumerism. The company has countered anti-consumer instincts — "It looks so mercantile," Tom Wrubel said during the 1986 interview, as he took down a "cash only" sign in the San Jose store — in ways that are both well-intentioned and very strategic. Essentially, The Nature Company has positioned the store as a site for *better* consumerism. To begin with, it emphasizes "quality" consumer products — lifelike bronze frogs for $995, for example, rather than plastic lawn creatures — with a rhetoric that echoes Taste, and urges consumers to exercise restraint on quality, if not on quantity. The company makes concerted efforts, too — and publicizes them avidly — to sell recycled products, such as luminaria, "waste not" stationery, and flying-animals wrapping paper. Riding the crest of Green Consumerism in the 1980s, The Nature Company has divided acts of consumption into good and bad. A customer can put a quarter in the Rainforest Meter and send her money off to a worthy cause. You can buy home recycling kits and books about tropical deforestation. A percentage of profits goes to the Nature Conservancy. Here, you can consume to preserve nature.[24]

At the same time, in the Mall of America or South Coast Plaza — a monument to overconsumption — it can be hard not to conceive of shopping as a quantity more than a quality experience. If there are hundreds of ways to shop for a better world, do we shop too much? And this, I'll venture, points to the most stubborn irony, and to the most troubling and deeply buried source for "wow." Every "nature-oriented" product — recycled, nonrecycled, "quality," nature-preserving, Nature Conservancy-supporting — has literally been manufactured *from* nature. An inflatable plastic penguin constitutes approximately the same natural resources and energy as the utterly non-grata plastic pink flamingo. Who thinks about that? Looking for the meanings of Glacier Bay from my living room, I so readily lose track of real facts about the actual Arctic landscape — yet doubly ironic, its oil might be in my stereo system, or in the CD itself. Who thinks of the whale calls on the *Glacier Bay* CD as Petroleum more than Freedom? Has The Nature Company connected people to nature? Absolutely: perhaps too much. And it would be impossible not to find nature at the mall: Nature provides the raw materials the malls are made from. Here, the definition of Nature as a Place Apart — as separate from modern consumerism — not only tells us little about what nature is and where we

[24]Wrubel: Lufkin, "Natural History Gets Hip." "Green marketing": e.g., Jacquelyn A. Ottman, *Green Marketing* (Lincolnwood, IL: NTC Business Books, 1993); "Selling Green," *Consumer Reports* 56 (October 1991), 687–92; and for an excellent critique, Robert Goldman and Stephen Papson, *Sign Wars: The Cluttered Landscape of Advertising* (New York: Guilford Press, 1996), 187–215.

actually connect to it. It also actively *hides* our connections, as the definition always has done. And can I really be a better consumer if I fail to identify my connections to nature?[25]

The mall itself historically has been designed to disguise all these connections, natural and economic, to the world outside. Architects and managers deliberately sequester all traces of producing, sending, and receiving: for example, they relegate business offices to the basement, and truck in goods in the early morning hours before the invitees arrive to shop. They have actively set out to erase connections — to encourage us to focus on the meanings we make, but not on our complicity in the economic networks through which people convert nature and human labor into the stuff and sustenance of everyday lives. As Leah Hager Cohen has written about our modern brand of fetishism: "The notion of connections seems charming, but not quite real." Retail stores, too, set out to create slices of magic that bear few traces of where products came from, other than "made in China," of how they got to suburban Chicago, or where your money will go after you trade it for a shirt. "Gardens of delight," "palaces of consumption." The Nature Company calls its stores a "magical space." The back rooms, however, are windowless spaces of steel and concrete stacked with boxes floor to ceiling. And while the nature store may be Oz, like the mall it is also a flow chart.[26]

As the company has detailed its own workings in an informational sheet for the sales staff: "Although the public would hardly be aware of it, there is, in fact, an order to the magic in the form of eight professionally managed buying departments." The Nature Company has sold products from Brazil, China, Zaire, Portugal, Chile, and the Philippines, among other countries. All the products are shipped to a distribution center in Kentucky, which in 1994 was reshipping them to 146 stores in four countries. Profits from these products have gone far too many places to map, but among other places: the eight buying departments; 850 sales employees (in 1994); a vice president of real-estate development; a director of public relations, image, and special events; a company naturalist; mall managers and leasing agents; advertising agencies; the CEO and the president of CML, who earned $1.38 million and $1.37 million, respectively, in fiscal year 1993; and among CML's stock-

---

[25]My analysis here is informed both by Agnew's insistence that, while celebrating consumerism as an imaginative act, we not forget economic power and the social relations of production, and by William Cronon's insistence that we not forget that commodities are products not only of human labor but of nature: Agnew, "Coming Up for Air"; Cronon, *Nature's Metropolis: Chicago and the Great West* (New York: W. W. Norton, 1991). A wonderfully readable work on alienation and fetishism is Leah Hager Cohen, *Glass, Paper, Beans: Revelations on the Nature and Value of Ordinary Things* (New York: Doubleday, 1997).

[26]Strategies: David Guterson, "Enclosed. Encyclopedic. Endured: One Week at the Mall of America," *Harper's* 287 (August 1993), 54. Cohen, *Glass, Paper, Beans*, 13. "magical space": handout, 3.

holders, Reader's Digest, the Ford Foundation, my former phone company US West, and the Bank of Tokyo, IBM, and GE.[27]

"Commodity consumption," the historian Jean-Christophe Agnew has   25
written, has not "enhanced our appreciation of the remote consequences of our acts or ... clarified our responsibilities for them." During my research visits, I spent $180.18 at The Nature Company—mostly on gifts. The *Glacier Bay* CD (recorded in San Francisco, with notes printed in Canada), a polar bear stamp (made in China), and other items connect me to the working conditions and everyday lives of people worldwide who mine, plant, assemble, and transport the company's materials and products. A hummingbird feeder on my back porch connects me to the CML Group chairman, who in the 1980s delved into his $1 million–plus salary to contribute to his friend George Bush's political campaigns. These items also connect me to nature—to the abundant pieces of nature worldwide that The Nature Company's operations touch on, and that stockholder companies mine with the profits. To shop at The Nature Company has been to plug into the flows of energy and resources, economic power and influence that have defined the American capitalist economy in the 1980s and 1990s. And one of the touchstones of this economy has been the ravenous global consumption of natural resources. Like any successful company, The Nature Company has expanded as rapidly as possible. In 1992, *Fortune* named CML one of the best hundred growth stocks—one of seven to make the list two years in a row—and *Money* named it one of the seven best growth buys. Perhaps the perfect metaphor for The Nature Company is a famous outdoor sculpture by Isamu Noguchi at South Coast Plaza, called "California Scenario"—a strikingly serene landscape of rock and cactus and water. If you turn around, you see its perfect reflection in the thirty-story glass walls of the Great Western Bank.[28]

And who controls the bulk of this economic activity? The class of shoppers the stores have drawn—*whose* meaningful Nature the company has marketed—are exactly the affluent baby boomers who, coming into their economic power in the 1980s, now own and invest substantial capital and reap the material benefits. CML's target consumers, in the words of

---

[27]"Although": handout, 3. Countries: E. J. Muller, "Global Strategies for Small Shippers," *Distribution* 90 (October 1991), 29; Byron Greer, "Nature Company Expansion in High Gear," *San Francisco Chronicle,* 13 July 1987. Distribution: CML Group, "Annual Report," 7. Where the money goes: handout, 4; O'Brien, "Nature Company Jumps into Japan," 37, 38. Salaries, stockholders: CML Group, company records, *Disclosure* database, April 1994.

[28]Agnew, "Coming Up for Air," 33. Bush: Jack Anderson and Michael Binstein, "Cuff Links and Trade Deal Come Undone," *Washington Post,* 3 February 1992. Susan E. Kuhn, "The Best & Worst Stocks of 1992," *Fortune* 127 (25 January 1993), 20–23; Gary Belsky, "Seven Growth Stocks to Spice Up Your Blue-chip Portfolio," *Money,* iss. 13 (Forecast 1993), 79. CML began to lose money in 1994, had its revenues peak in 1995, and posted its worst year in 1996: CML Shareholder Direct, www.shareholder.com/cml; Stock Reports on America Online.

Business Week, are the "folks [with] lots of money to spend and a seemingly irrepressible urge to spend it": we have come to control, according to a 1988 *Forbes* profile of CML, "a great deal of the economy's discretionary income." If Americans in the late twentieth century are globe coasters all, the globe has increasingly belonged to my generation of higher-income baby boomers not only figuratively but literally. The *Glacier Bay* CD channels serenity into my leisure hours, and channels profits from Alaskan oil mining into my portfolio. As Susan Davis has concluded, of her own visits to Sea World, the kind of person who has appreciated Nature is likely to be the kind of person who has consumed more nature than most.[29]

The very people who have used an idea of a Nature Out There to define who we are, and to navigate the hallmarks and confusions of postwar American life, are also the people who use nature the most. And evasions are themselves a way of navigating. We've used Nature to circumvent our own complicity in the serious modern problems we critique. And here, at last, are the ur-ironies that lie at the heart both of the new nature stores and of the affluent baby boomers' encounters with nature since the 1980s. The Nature Company has marketed twelve thousand products that, on one hand, have sustained an American middle- to upper-class definition of Nature that mitigates the materialism and artifice of modern capitalist society—and at the same time, have sustained, through the creation of artifice, the capitalist overconsumption of resources that underpins American middle- to upper-class life. The Nature Company constitutes a store-size contradiction between how we want to connect to nature and how we actually do, and between what we want Nature to be and what nature actually is. It is also a store-size monument to the convenience, however willful or half-conscious, of these contradictions....

ENGAGING THE TEXT

1. What, according to Price, is The Nature Company selling? How is nature defined at The Nature Company? What is included as "natural"? What is excluded? Why?

2. In Price's view, what meanings are conveyed by the objects available for purchase at environmental retail outlets? What do they tell us about ourselves and contemporary American culture? To what extent do you agree with Price's analysis?

3. How does Price view the modern American mall? What is its relation to nature? To other places and environments?

4. In what ways, according to Price, do environmental retailers embody "the flows of energy and resources, economic power and influence that have defined the American capitalist economy in the 1980s and 1990s" (para. 25)?

[29]"folks with": Bock, "CML Group," 75. "a great deal": Angrist, "Earn-Out," 52. Davis, *Spectacular Nature*.

What contradictions of values and intentions does she perceive in the mass marketing of nature in contemporary America?

EXPLORING CONNECTIONS

5. Compare the view of nature that is for sale at The Nature Company, according to Price, with the attitudes toward nature and wilderness expressed in the visions of frontier life of Frederick Jackson Turner (p. 683), Wallace Stegner (p. 694), and N. Scott Momaday (p. 734). How does Price account for changes in the dominant culture's attitudes toward nature? What other reasons might explain why many Americans see nature differently today than our predecessors did a century ago?

6. How might Worster (p. 814) interpret the success of The Nature Company—and the concept of the mall—in terms of what he calls the paradox of the American West? Do you see any way in which the "fear of scarcity" that Worster describes might be involved in the marketing strategies of environmental retailers?

7. Compare the experience of nature that is marketed at The Nature Company and other eco-retailers with Linda Hogan's sweat-lodge experience in "Department of the Interior" (p. 826). What might Hogan say to Price in response to the ambivalence Price feels shopping at nature stores?

EXTENDING THE CRITICAL CONTEXT

8. Write a journal entry about your most prolonged or intense experience with real, physical nature. Share these experiences in small groups and discuss how they compare with the "nature" that is for sale at the environmental retail store.

9. Conduct an informal survey of local environmentally oriented retailers to see how nature is currently being defined by corporate America. Has the commercial identity of nature or wilderness changed since Price wrote this essay?

10. Go on a field trip to the nearest mall and analyze the environment—or environments—it offers consumers. What other place or places does your mall simulate? To what extent would you agree with Price's assertion that a shopping mall is a "placeless vacuum" (para. 19)?

Text Acknowledgments

Sherman Alexie, "Assimilation." From *The Toughest Indian in the World* by Sherman Alexie. Copyright © 2000 by Sherman Alexie. Used by permission of Grove/Atlantic, Inc.

Horatio Alger, from *Ragged Dick*. Reprinted with the permission of Simon & Schuster, Inc., from *Ragged Dick and Mark the Match Boy* by Horatio Alger. Copyright © 1962 Macmillan Publishing Company.

Paula Gunn Allen, "Where I Come From Is Like This." From *The Sacred Hoop* by Paula Gunn Allen. Copyright © 1986, 1992 by Paula Gunn Allen. Reprinted by permission of Beacon Press, Boston.

Jean Anyon, from "Social Class and the Hidden Curriculum of Work," edited. Reprinted from *Journal of Education*, Boston University School of Education (1980), vol. 162, no. 1, with permission from The Trustees of Boston University and the author.

Toni Cade Bambara, "The Lesson." From *Gorilla, My Love* by Toni Cade Bambara. Copyright © 1972 by Toni Cade Bambara. Reprinted by permission of Random House, Inc.

Michael A. Bellesiles, "The Origins of Gun Culture in the United States, 1760–1865." Reprinted with permission from *The Journal of American History* 83 (2) (September 1996), 425–55. Copyright © 1996 by the Organization of American Historians.

Rose Blue and Corinne J. Naden, from *Colin Powell: Straight to the Top*. Copyright © 1991 by Rose Blue and Corinne J. Naden. Reprinted by permission of The Millbrook Press, Inc., Brookfield, Connecticut.

Stephanie Brail, "The Price of Admission: Harassment and Free Speech in the Wild Wild West." Copyright © 1996 by Stephanie Brail from *Wired Women: Gender and New Realities in Cyberspace,* edited by Lynn Cherny and Elizabeth Reba Wise. Reprinted by permission of Seal Press.

Bebe Moore Campbell, "Envy." Chapter 5 from *Sweet Summer* by Bebe Moore Campbell. Copyright © 1989 by Bebe Moore Campbell. Used by permission of G. P. Putnam's Sons, a division of Penguin Putnam, Inc.

Veronica Chambers, "Secret Latina at Large." From *Becoming American: Personal Essays by First-Generation Immigrant Women,* edited by Meri Nana-Ama Danquah. Copyright © 2000 Meri Nana-Ama Danquah. Reprinted by permission of Hyperion.

Lynne V. Cheney, "Politics in the Schoolroom." Reprinted with the permission of Simon & Schuster, Inc., from *Telling the Truth* by Lynne V. Cheney. Copyright © 1995 by Lynne V. Cheney.

Patricia Hill Collins, "Black Women and Motherhood." Copyright © 1990, 2000. From *Black Feminist Thought* by Patricia Hill Collins. Reproduced by permission of Taylor & Francis, Inc./Routledge, Inc., http://www.routledge-ny.com.

Stephanie Coontz, "What We Really Miss About the 1950s." From *The Way We Really Are* by Stephanie Coontz. Copyright © 1997 by Basic Books, a division of HarperCollins Publishers, Inc. Reprinted by permission of Basic Books, a member of Perseus Books, LLC.

Danielle Crittenden, "About Marriage." From *What Our Mothers Didn't Tell Us* by Danielle Crittenden. Copyright © 1999 by Danielle Crittenden. Reprinted by permission of Simon & Schuster, Inc.

Harlon L. Dalton, "Horatio Alger." From *Racial Healing* by Harlon L. Dalton. Copyright © 1995 by Harlon L. Dalton. Used by permission of Doubleday, a division of Random House, Inc.

Holly Devor, "Becoming Members of Society: Learning the Social Meanings of Gender." From *Gender Blending: Confronting the Limits of Duality* by Holly Devor. Copyright © 1989 by Indiana University Press, Bloomington, IN. Reprinted by permission of Indiana University Press and the author.

Melvin Dixon, "Aunt Ida Pieces a Quilt." From *Love's Instruments* (Tia Chucha Press, 1995). Reprinted with the permission of the Estate of Melvin Dixon.

Louise Erdrich, "Dear John Wayne." From *Jacklight: Poems* by Louise Erdrich. Copyright © 1984 by Louise Erdrich. Reprinted by permission.

James Fallows, "The Invisible Poor." From *The New York Times Magazine*, March 19, 2000. Copyright © 2000 by James Fallows. Reprinted by permission.

Susan Faludi, "Girls Have All the Power: What's Troubling Troubled Boys." Originally published in *Stiffed: The Betrayal of the American Man* by Susan Faludi. Copyright © 1999 by Susan Faludi. Reprinted by permission of HarperCollins Publishers, Inc.

George M. Fredrickson, "Models of American Ethnic Relations: A Historical Perspective." From *Cultural Divides: Understanding and Overcoming Group Conflict*, edited by Deborah A. Prentice and Dale T. Miller. Copyright © 1999 Russell Sage Foundation. Reprinted by permission of the Russell Sage Foundation.

Anne Witte Garland, "Good Noise: Cora Tucker." From *Women Activists: Challenging the Abuse of Power* by Anne Witte Garland. Foreword by Ralph Nader. Introduction by Frances T. Farenthold. Published by The Feminist Press at The City University of New York. Copyright © 1988 by the Center for the Study of Responsive Law. Reprinted by permission of The Feminist Press at The City University of New York.

John Taylor Gatto, "The Seven-Lesson Schoolteacher." From *Dumbing Us Down: The Hidden Curriculum of Compulsory Schooling* by John Taylor Gatto, 1992, New Society Publishers, http://www.newsociety.com, 1(800)567-6772. Reprinted by permission.

Lynell George, "Gray Boys, Funky Aztecs, and Honorary Homegirls." From the January 17, 1993, issue of *The Los Angeles Times Magazine*. Copyright © 1993 by Lynell George. Reprinted by permission of the author.

Dana Gioia, "Money." From *Forbes* magazine, May 17, 1999. Copyright © 1999 by Dana Gioia. Reprinted by permission.

E. J. Graff, "What Is Marriage For?" From *What Is Marriage For?* by E. J. Graff. Copyright © 1999 by E. J. Graff. Reprinted by permission of Beacon Press, Boston.

Ken Hamblin, "The Black Avenger." Reprinted with permission of Simon & Schuster, Inc., from *Pick a Better Country* by Ken Hamblin. Copyright © 1996 by Ken Hamblin.

Inés Hernández-Ávila, "Para Teresa." From *Con Rázon, Corazón* by Inés Hernández-Ávila. Copyright © 1987 by Inés Hernández-Ávila. Reprinted by permission.

Robert V. Hine and John Mack Faragher, "The Myth of the West." From *The American West* by Robert V. Hine and John Mack Faragher. Copyright © 2000 by Robert V. Hine and John Mack Faragher. Reprinted by permission of Yale University Press.

Anndee Hochman, "Growing Pains: Beyond 'One Big Happy Family.'" From *Everyday Acts and Small Subversions* by Anndee Hochman (Portland, OR: The Eight Mountain Press, 1994). Copyright © 1994 by Anndee Hochman. Reprinted by permission of the publisher.

Linda Hogan, "Department of the Interior." From *Minding the Body*, edited by Patricia Foster. Copyright © 1994 by Linda Hogan. Reprinted by permission of Linda Hogan.

Langston Hughes, "Let America Be America Again." From *Collected Poems* by Langston Hughes. Copyright © 1994 by the Estate of Langston Hughes. Reprinted by permission of Alfred A. Knopf, a division of Random House, Inc.

Roger Jack, "An Indian Story." From *Dancing on the Rim of the World*, edited by Andrea Lerner (University of Arizona Press). Reprinted by permission.

Henry Jenkins, "Empowering Children in the Digital Age: Towards a Radical Media Pedagogy." From *Radical Teacher*, no. 50, pp. 30–35. Copyright © Radical Teacher, Spring 1997. All rights reserved. Reprinted by permission.

Jackson Katz, "Advertising and the Construction of Violent White Masculinity." From *Gender, Race, and Class in Media: A Critical Text-Reader* by Gail Dines et al. Copyright © 1994 by Gail Dines et al. Reprinted by permission of Sage Publications, Inc.

Jean Kilbourne, "'Two Ways a Woman Can Get Hurt': Advertising and Violence." From *Can't Buy My Love: How Advertising Changes the Way We Feel and Think* (formerly titled *Deadly Persuasions*) by Jean Kilbourne. Copyright © 1999 by Jean Kilbourne. Reprinted by permission of The Free Press, a division of Simon & Schuster, Inc.

Jamaica Kincaid, "Girl." From *At the Bottom of the River* by Jamaica Kincaid. Copyright © 1983 by Jamaica Kincaid. Reprinted by permission of Farrar, Straus and Giroux, LLC.

Patricia Nelson Limerick, "The Adventures of the Frontier in the Twentieth Century." From *The Frontier of American Culture: An Exhibition at the Newberry Library, August 26, 1994–January 7, 1995*, edited by James Grossman, pp. 67–102. Copyright © 1995 by the Regents of the University of California. Reprinted by permission of the University of California Press and the author.

Eric Liu, "Notes of a Native Speaker." From *The Accidental Asian* by Eric Liu. Copyright © 1998 by Eric Liu. Reprinted by permission of Random House, Inc.

Malcolm X, "Learning to Read." From *The Autobiography of Malcolm X* by Malcolm X with the assistance of Alex Haley. Copyright © 1964 by Alex Haley and Malcolm X. Copyright © 1965 by Alex Haley and Betty Shabazz. Reprinted by permission of Random House, Inc.

Gregory Mantsios, "Class in America: Myths and Realities." From *Race, Class, and Gender in the United States: An Integrated Study*, 4th edition, Paula Rothenberg, editor (New York: St. Martin's Press, 1998). Reprinted by permission of the author.

Eric Marcus, "The Bridge Builder: Kathleen Boatwright." From *Making History: The Struggle for Gay and Lesbian Rights 1945–1990* by Eric Marcus. Copyright © 1992 by Eric Marcus. Reprinted by permission.

N. Scott Momaday, "The American West and the Burden of Belief." From *The West* by Geoffrey Ward. Copyright © 1997 by The West Company. Reprinted by permission of Little, Brown and Company, Inc.

Aurora Levins Morales, "Child of the Americas." From *Getting Home Alive* by Aurora Levins Morales and Rosario Morales. Copyright © 1986 by Aurora Levins Morales and Rosario Morales. Reprinted by permission of Firebrand Books, Ithaca, NY.

Kyoko Mori, "School." From *Polite Lies: On Being a Woman Caught Between Cultures* by Kyoko Mori. Copyright © 1997 by Kyoko Mori. Reprinted by permission of Henry Holt and Company, LLC.

Joan Morgan, "From Fly-Girls to Bitches and Hos." From *Vibe* magazine. Copyright © 1999 by Joan Morgan. Reprinted by permission.

John Naisbitt with Nana Naisbitt and Douglas Phillips, "The Military-Nintendo Complex." From *High Tech–High Touch* by John Naisbitt with Nana Naisbitt and Douglas Phillips. Copyright © 1999 by High Tech–High Touch, Inc. Used by permission of Broadway Books, a division of Random House, Inc.

New York Times, "The Evolution of G.I. Joe, 1964–1998." From the *New York Times*, May 30, 1999. Copyright © 1999 by the New York Times Company. Reprinted by permission.

Sharon Olds, "From Seven Floors Up." From *The Nation*, July 12, 1999. Copyright © 1999 by Sharon Olds. Reprinted by permission.

Judith Ortiz Cofer, "The Story of My Body." From *The Latin Deli: Prose and Poetry* by Judith Ortiz Cofer. Copyright © 1993 by Judith Ortiz Cofer. Reprinted by permission of The University of Georgia Press.

Vincent N. Parrillo, "Causes of Prejudice." From *Strangers to These Shores: Race and Ethnic Relations in the United States*, 3rd edition, by Vincent N. Parrillo. Copyright © 1990 by Allyn & Bacon. Reprinted by permission.

Jennifer Price, "Looking for Nature at the Mall." From *Flight Maps: Adventures with Nature in Modern America* by Jennifer Price. Copyright © 1999 by Jennifer Price. Reprinted by permission of Perseus Books, LLC.

Richard Rodriguez, "The Achievement of Desire." From *Hunger of Memory*. Copyright © 1982 by Richard Rodriguez. Reprinted by permission of David R. Godine, Publisher, Inc.

Theodore Roethke, "My Papa's Waltz." From *The Collected Poems of Theodore Roethke* by Theodore Roethke. Copyright © 1950 by Theodore Roethke. Used by permission of Doubleday, a division of Bantam Doubleday Dell Publishing Group, Inc.

Mike Rose, "'I Just Wanna Be Average.'" Reprinted with the permission of The Free Press, a Division of Simon & Schuster, Inc., from *Lives on the Boundary: The Struggles and Achievements of America's Underprepared* by Mike Rose. Copyright © 1989 by Mike Rose.

Wendy Rose, "Three Thousand Dollar Death Song." From *Lost Copper* by Wendy Rose. Copyright © 1980 by Wendy Rose. Reprinted by permission of the author.

Christina Hoff Sommers, "The Gender Wardens." Reprinted with the permission of Simon & Schuster, Inc., from *Who Stole Feminism? How Women Have Betrayed Women* by Christina Hoff Sommers. Copyright © 1994 by Christina Hoff Sommers.

Gary Soto, "Looking for Work" from *Living up the Street: Narrative Recollections* by Gary Soto. Copyright © 1985 by Gary Soto. Used by permission of the author.

Claude M. Steele, "Thin Ice: 'Stereotype Threat' and Black College Students." First published as "Race and the Schooling of Black Americans" in *The Atlantic Monthly*. Copyright © 1992 by Claude M. Steele. Reprinted by permission of the author.

Shelby Steele, "I'm Black, You're White, Who's Innocent?" From *The Content of Our Character* by Shelby Steele. Copyright © 1990 by Shelby Steele. Reprinted by permission of St. Martin's Press, LLC.

Wallace Stegner, "The Twilight of Self-Reliance: Frontier Values and Contemporary America." From *Marking the Sparrow's Fall: The Making of the American West*, edited by Page Stegner. Copyright © 1980. Reprinted by permission of Henry Holt and Company, LLC.

Leonard Steinhorn and Barbara Diggs-Brown, "Virtual Integration: How the Integration of Mass Media Undermines Integration." From *By the Color of Our Skin* by Leonard Steinhorn and Barbara Diggs-Brown. Copyright © 1999 by Leonard Steinhorn and Barbara Diggs-Brown. Used by permission of Dutton, a division of Penguin Putnam, Inc.

Deborah Tannen, "The Roots of Debate in Education and the Hope of Dialogue." From *The Argument Culture* by Deborah Tannen. Copyright © 1997 by Deborah Tannen. Reprinted by permission of Random House, Inc.

Ronald Takaki, "Race at the End of History." From *The Good Citizen* by Ronald Takaki. Copyright © 1999 by Ronald Takaki. Reprinted by permission of Little, Brown and Company, Inc.

Studs Terkel, "C. P. Ellis" and "Stephen Cruz." From *American Dreams: Lost and Found* by Studs Terkel. Copyright © 1980 by Studs Terkel. Reprinted by permission of Donadio & Ashworth, Inc.

Frederick Jackson Turner, from "The Significance of the Frontier in American History." Editor's Introduction and Comments to Turner in *An American Primer*, edited by Daniel Boorstin. Copyright © 1986 by The University of Chicago Press. Reprinted by permission of the University of Chicago Press.

Carmen Vázquez, "Appearances." From *Homophobia* by Warren J. Blumenfeld. Copyright © 1992 by Warren J. Blumenfeld. Reprinted by permission of Beacon Press, Boston.

Mary C. Waters, "Optional Ethnicities: For Whites Only?" From *Origins and Destinies: Immigration, Race, and Ethnicity in America*, 1st edition, by S. Pedraza and R. Rumbaut. Copyright © 1996. Reprinted with permission of Wadsworth, a division of Thomson Learning, fax: 800-730-2215.

Donald Worster, "Freedom and Want: The Western Paradox." From *Under Western Skies: Nature and History in the American West* by Donald Worster. Copyright © 1992 by Donald Worster. Used by permission of Oxford University Press, Inc.

Art Acknowledgments

CHAPTER 1: HARMONY AT HOME

"The Donna Reed Show" (p. 17) photo. Courtesy of Archive Photos.

A Family Tree (p. 22), *Freedom from Want* (p. 23), and *Freedom from Fear* (p. 24) by Norman Rockwell. Photos courtesy of The Norman Rockwell Museum at Stockbridge. Printed by permission of the Norman Rockwell Family Trust. Copyright 1997 the Norman Rockwell Family Trust.

"Roger realizes . . ." (p. 55) cartoon by Andrew Struthers. Copyright © 1988, Andrew Struthers. Used with permission.

"So, are you still with the same parents?" (p. 71) cartoon by Bruce E. Kaplan. Copyright Bruce E. Kaplan, *The New Yorker* from cartoonbank.com. All rights reserved. Used with permission.

"HDTV. It's A Joy" (p. 76) ad. Used by permission of Samsung Electronics.

"Mother bathing child in tub in kitchen" (p. 77) photo by Tony O'Brien/LIFE Magazine. Copyright © Time Inc. Used with permission.

"Jefferson's family in front of monument" (p. 78) photo by Erica Berger/LIFE Magazine. Copyright © Time Inc. Used with permission.

"Domestic partnership ceremony" (p. 79) photo by Nicole Bengiveno. Copyright © 1996 Matrix. Used with permission.

"In ancient times, our primitive . . ." (p. 84) *This Modern World* cartoon by © Tom Tomorrow. Used with permission.

"In this modern world, friends . . ." (p. 111) *This Modern World* cartoon by © Tom Tomorrow. Used with permission.

"More Nontraditional Family Units" (p. 126) cartoon by Roz Chast. Copyright © 1992 The New Yorker Magazine, Inc. Used with permission.

CHAPTER 2: LEARNING POWER

"Skeptical student" (p. 134) photo by Charles Agel. Copyright © Charles Agel. Used with permission.

"If all the 'education reforms' . . ." (p. 151) cartoon by Lloyd Dangle/Troubletown. Used with permission.

"Lesson 4: Wake Up! You'll Be Late for Your First Day of School" (p. 160) cartoon by Matt Groening. From *School Is Hell*. Copyright © 1987 Matt Groening. All rights reserved. Reprinted by permission of Pantheon Books, a division of Random House, Inc., NY.

"Life in School (Devious Little Weasels)" (p. 161) cartoon by Matt Groening. From *Love Is Hell*. Copyright © 1987 Matt Groening. All rights reserved. Reprinted by permission of Pantheon Books, a division of Random House, Inc., NY.

The Spirit of Education (p. 191) and *The Graduate* (p. 192) by Norman Rockwell. Photos courtesy of The Curtis Publishing Company. Printed by permission of the Norman Rockwell Family Trust. Copyright 1997 the Norman Rockwell Family Trust.

The Problem We All Live With (p. 193) by Norman Rockwell. Photo courtesy of The Norman Rockwell Museum at Stockbridge. Printed by permission of the Norman Rockwell Family Trust. Copyright 1997 the Norman Rockwell Family Trust.

"Pssst—Huey what time is it?" (p. 232) cartoon by Aaron McGruder. *Boondocks* © 2000 Aaron McGruder. Reprinted with permission of Universal Press Syndicate. All rights reserved.

"Don't we have a parents' open . . ." (p. 252) *Doonesbury* cartoon by Garry Trudeau. Copyright © 1992 G. B. Trudeau. Reprinted with permission of Universal Press Syndicate. All rights reserved.

"Please don't give him any ideas" (p. 279) cartoon by William Haefeli. Copyright © 2000 William Haefeli from cartoonbank.com. All rights reserved.

CHAPTER 3: MONEY AND SUCCESS

"Affluence: Man in Cap by Rolls Royce" (p. 294) Copyright © Steven Weinrebe/The Picture Cube. Used with permission.

"And just how do you plan . . ." (p. 315) *Boondocks* © Aaron McGruder. Dist. by Universal Press Syndicate. Reprinted with permission. All rights reserved.

"In today's cater to your every . . ." (p. 332) cartoon by Lloyd Dangle. Copyright © Lloyd Dangle/Troubletown. Used with permission.

"The only thing better than waking . . ." (p. 352) ad. Courtesy of Simmons.

"Commercial bank, Duluth, Minnesota, 1995" (p. 353) photo. Used with permission.

"Eye on L.A." (p. 354) photo by James Jeffrey. 1992 © by Jeffrey. From *Life in a Day of Black L.A.: The Way We See It.* Used by permission.

"Man Repairing Novelty Item, Chicago 1996" (p. 355) photo by Paul D'Amato. Copyright © Paul D'Amato. Used by permission.

"In the Shadow of Wealth. Brooklyn: Angelica Rosete with her one-year-old daughter, Angie" (p. 358) and "Manhattan: Julio Santiago, next to FDR Drive" (p. 359) photos by Taryn Simon. Copyright © Taryn Simon/Art + Commerce. Used with permission.

"$165 Billion . . . huge amount of money . . ." (p. 367) cartoon by Roz Chast. Copyright © The New Yorker Collection 2000 Roz Chast from cartoonbank.com. All rights reserved. Used by permission.

Search and Destroy: "If Present Trends Continue" (p. 387) cartoon by Ted Rall. Copyright 1999 © Ted Rall. Used with permission. All rights reserved.

CHAPTER 4: TRUE WOMEN AND REAL MEN

"Bree Scott-Hartland as Delphinia Blue" (p. 402) photo by Carolyn Jones. Copyright © 1992 by Carolyn Jones. From *Living Proof: Courage in the Face of AIDS,* published by Abbeville Press, 1994. Used by permission.

"We don't believe in pressuring the children . . ." (p. 422) cartoon by Robert Mankoff. Copyright © The New Yorker Collection 1995 Robert Mankoff from cartoonbank.com. All rights reserved. Used by permission.

"Real Friends" (p. 441) ad. Used by permission of Jim Beam Brands, Inc. All rights reserved.

"Female boxer, Margaret MacGregor " (p. 442) photo by Patrick Hagerty. Copyright © Patrick Hagerty/Corbis Sygma. Used by permission.

"Mississippi, 1991" (p. 443) photo by Eli Reed. Copyright © 1978 Eli Reed/Magnum Photos Inc. Used by permission.

Ads (pp. 445–460) in "'Two Ways a Woman Can Get Hurt': Advertising and Violence" from Jean Kilbourne, *Can't Buy My Love: How Advertising Changes the Way We Think and Feel,* New York: The Free Press, 1999. Used by permission.

"In an effort to reduce injuries . . ." (p. 474) from *High School Isn't Pretty.* Copyright © 1993 John McPherson, reprinted by permission of Andrews and McMeel, A Universal Press Syndicate Company.

"G.I. Joe" (p. 477). G.I. Joe photos by Vincent Santelmo from *The Complete Encyclopedia to G.I. Joe,* Krause Publications, 1997. Mark McGwire photo by Rusty Kennedy/AP/Wide World Photos. Used by permission.

"Some kids at school called you a feminist" (p. 491) cartoon by Liza Donnelly. Copyright © 1996 Liza Donnelly, *The New Yorker* from cartoonbank.com. All rights reserved. Used by permission.

"The trouble with you gays . . ." (p. 508) *Toles* © 2000 The Buffalo News. Reprinted with permission of Universal Press Syndicate. All rights reserved.

CHAPTER 5: CREATED EQUAL

"Forsyth County, GA, 1987, Antiracism March" (p. 534) photo by Eli Reed. Copyright © 1987 Eli Reed/Magnum Photos Inc. Used by permission.

"Why You Wearin' a Mask?" (p. 583) cartoon by Jules Feiffer. Copyright © 1994 Jules Feiffer. Reprinted with permisssion of Universal Press Syndicate. All rights reserved.

"Do you think a movie named *Booty Call* . . ." (p. 597) cartoon by Aaron McGruder. *Boondocks* © Aaron McGruder. Distributed by Universal Press Syndicate. Reprinted with permission. All rights reserved.

"Gosh it kills me to do this to you . . ." (p. 623) cartoon by Robb Armstrong. Copyright © The New Yorker Collection 1996 Robb Armstrong from cartoonbank.com. All rights reserved. Used by permission.

"The Man on the Left Is 75 Times More . . ." (p. 639) ad reproduced with permission of the American Civil Liberties Union/Devito/Verde.

"Fence on the Border of Mexico" (p. 640) photo by Alon Reininger. Copyright © Alon Reininger/Contact Press Images. Used by permission.

"Four young men in L.A." (p. 641) photo by Roland Charles. Copyright © Roland Charles Fine Art Collection & Black Photographers of California. Used by permission.

"Before I became a black conservative . . ." (p. 651) cartoon by Peter Steiner. Copyright © The New Yorker Collection 1997 Peter Steiner from cartoonbank.com. All rights reserved. Used by permission.

"US/THEM" (p. 671) cartoon by Jeff MacNelly. Copyright © Jeff MacNelly, Tribune Media Services. All rights reserved. Reprinted with permission.

CHAPTER 6: WESTWARD HO!

"Buffalo Bill's Wild West Show: 'The Farewell Shot'" (p. 676). Used by permission of the Buffalo Bill Historical Center.

"If I may say so, sir, that chapeau . . ." (p. 704) cartoon by Gahan Wilson. Copyright © The New Yorker Collection 1990 Gahan Wilson from cartoonbank .com. All rights reserved. Used by permission.

"Colonel Daniel Boone" (p. 709). Used by permission of the Missouri Historical Society, St. Louis.

"Dime novel hero, Seth Jones" (p. 713). Used by permission of the Beinecke Rare Book and Manuscript Library.

"Calamity Jane from Edward Wheeler's *Deadwood Dick*" (p. 715) Used by permission of the Yale Collection of Western Americana, Beinecke Rare Book and Manuscript Library.

"Theodore Roosevelt from *Hunting Trips of a Ranchman*" (p. 719). Used by permission of the Yale Collection of Western Americana, Beinecke Rare Book and Manuscript Library.

"Sitting Bull and William 'Buffalo Bill' Cody" (p. 723). Used by permission of the Kansas State Historical Society, Topeka, KS.

"Annie Oakley" (p. 724). Used by permission of the Yale Collection of Western Americana, Beinecke Rare Book and Manuscript Library.

"George Barnes in *The Great Train Robbery*" (p. 727). Used by permission of the Museum of Modern Art, Film Stills Archive.

"William S. Hart in *The Gunfighter*" (p. 730). Used by permission of the Museum of Modern Art, Film Stills Archive.

"Gary Cooper in *I Take This Woman*" (p. 732). Used by permission of the Museum of Modern Art, Film Stills Archive.

The Cowboy (p. 750) by Frederic S. Remington, 1902. Oil on canvas 40¼ × 27⅛ in. 1961.382. Used by permission of Amon Carter Museum, Fort Worth, TX.

"Five-year-old Navajo Cowboy" (p. 751). Used by permission of Gene Peach Photography, Santa Fe, NM.

Manifest Destiny (p. 752) by John Gast, 1972. Library of Congress (LCU5ZC4-668). Used by permission.

"Antler Chair" (p. 753). Used by permission of Nesbit Graphics/Crystal Farm.

"USA 'Gun Nation'" (p. 754), © 2000. Used by permission of Zed Nelson/IPG/Matrix.

"Hey Kids!" (p. 791), © Tom Tomorrow. All rights reserved. Used with permission.

"NRA Freedom hotline . . ." (p. 813) cartoon by Aaron McGruder. *Boondocks* © Aaron McGruder. Distributed by Universal Press Syndicate. Reprinted with permission. All rights reserved.

"Let's name it Indian Hills Estates . . ." (p. 825) cartoon by Charles Barsotti. Copyright © The New Yorker Collection 1989 Charles Barsotti from cartoonbank .com. All rights reserved. Used by permission.

Index of Authors and Titles

Research and Writing Online

Whether you want to investigate the ideas behind a thought-provoking essay or conduct in-depth research for a paper, the Web resources for *Rereading America* can help you find what you need on the Web — and then use it once you find it.

The English Research Room for Navigating the Web

www.bedfordstmartins.com/english_research

The Web brings a flood of information to your screen, but it still takes skill to track down the best sources. Not only does *The English Research Room* point you to some reliable starting places for Web investigations, it also lets you tune up your skills with interactive tutorials.

- Want to improve your skill at searching electronic databases, online catalogs, and the Web? Try the *Interactive Tutorials* for some hands-on practice.

- Need quick access to online search engines, reference sources, and research sites? Explore *Research Links* for some good starting places.

- Have questions on evaluating the sources you find, navigating the Web, or conducting research in general? Consult one of our *Reference Units* for authoritative advice.

Research and Documentation Online for Including Sources in Your Writing

www.bedfordstmartins.com/resdoc

Including sources correctly in a paper is often a challenge, and the Web has made it even more complex. This online version of the popular booklet *Research and Documentation in the Electronic Age,* by Diana Hacker, provides clear advice for the humanities, social sciences, history, and the sciences on —

- Which Web and library sources are relevant to your topic (with links to Web sources)

- How to integrate outside material into your paper

- How to cite sources correctly, using the appropriate documentation style

- What the format for the final paper should be